America in the World, 1776 to the Present

America in the World, 1776 to the Present

A Supplement to the Dictionary of American History

VOLUME I

A–L

Edward J. Blum
EDITOR IN CHIEF

CHARLES SCRIBNER'S SONS
A part of Gale, Cengage Learning

GALE
CENGAGE Learning

Farmington Hills, Mich • San Francisco • New York • Waterville, Maine
Meriden, Conn • Mason, Ohio • Chicago

America in the World, 1776 to the Present: A Supplement to the Dictionary of American History
Edward J. Blum, *Editor in Chief*

Associate Publisher: Hélène G. Potter

Project Editor: Alan Hedblad

Manuscript Editors: Judith Culligan, Jessica Hornik Evans, Michael J. O'Neal

Proofreaders: Deborah J. Baker, Judith Clinebell, Amy L. Unterburger

Editorial Assistant: Dolores Perales

Rights Acquisition and Management: Moriam Aigoro, Ashley M. Maynard

Composition: Evi Abou-El-Seoud

Manufacturing: Rita R. Wimberley

Imaging: John Watkins

Product Design: Kristine Julien

Indexing: Andriot Indexing LLC

LIBRARY OF CONGRESS CATALOGING-IN-PUBLICATION DATA

America in the world, 1776 to the present : a supplement to the Dictionary of American history / Edward J. Blum, Editor in Chief.
pages cm
Includes bibliographical references and index.
ISBN 978-0-684-32502-6 (set : alk. paper) — ISBN 978-0-684-32503-3 (vol. 1 : alk. paper) — ISBN 978-0-684-32504-0 (vol. 2 : alk. paper)
1. United States—Foreign relations. I. Blum, Edward J., editor.

E183.7.A53 2016
327.73—dc23 2015029101

Gale, a part of Cengage Learning
27500 Drake Rd.
Farmington Hills, MI 48331-3535

ISBN-13: 978-0-684-32502-6 (set)
ISBN-13: 978-0-684-32503-3 (vol. 1)
ISBN-13: 978-0-684-32504-0 (vol. 2)

This title is also available as an e-book.
ISBN-13: 978-0-684-32505-7
Contact your Gale, a part of Cengage Learning, sales representative for ordering information.

Printed in Mexico
1 2 3 4 5 6 7 20 19 18 17 16

Editorial Board

Contents

Introduction

There was no "America" before Christopher Columbus determined to sail westward to get to the East in 1492. In fact, it was not until the opening years of the sixteenth century that "America" came into being. The land masses we now call North and South America existed; people and animals populated them; rivers flowed there, trees fell there, and fires burned there. But only in 1507 did these land masses receive the name America, after a German mapmaker labeled them with a Latinized version of the name Amerigo, for Amerigo Vespucci, an Italian explorer. Moreover, there was no "world" before America. The globe existed before then of course. The planet rotated as it revolved around the sun between Venus and Mars. But only after the peoples of North and South America, Europe, Africa, Asia, and the Middle East came to know that other places and people existed did the concept of "the world" emerge. The birth of "America" and that of "the world" were contingent upon one another, and they occurred only five hundred years ago.

The United States is even younger. Established as a separate nation in the late eighteenth century, the most powerful country of the late twentieth and early twenty-first centuries has existed for less than three hundred years. During that time, the nation scrapped one founding government for another, survived a horrific Civil War, and found means to split atoms and send women and men beyond Earth's gravitational field. The United States, too, was and is a creation of these new entities "America" and "the world." From its people to its government, from its imports to its exports, from its inventions to its conventions, the United States was made by and has remade both America and the world.

America in the World, 1776 to the Present is a two-volume dictionary. In its entirety and through its individual entries, this work recasts our views of US history and world history. The essential argument of this work is that neither the United States nor the world can be understood without sufficient attention to the other. In fact, the separation of "America" and "the world" is a false dichotomy that hides far more than it reveals.

The entries herein begin with two key assumptions: (1) that global events, peoples, ideas, creations, and the like profoundly shaped and reshaped the United States; and (2) that events, peoples, ideas, and creations emanating from the United States profoundly shaped and reshaped the world. From this perspective, the entirety of American history and world history must be rethought. We hope these entries will help scholars and students alike in the process of that reevaluation.

A NEW APPROACH

These two volumes continue, expand, and redirect the ten-volume third edition of the *Dictionary of American History (DAH)*, edited by Stanley I. Kutler and published in 2003. Kutler's epic work built on earlier editions of the *DAH*, which was originally edited by James Truslow Adams and first published in 1940. At its most expansive, the *DAH* contained more than seven thousand entries that encompassed everything from the highest political offices and the most important military decisions to particular works of art and individual entrepreneurs tinkering away in small laboratories. The *DAH* is, was, and remains an incredible achievement that became a historical treasure as its authors described and detailed historical treasures.

The *DAH*'s main emphasis on the United States and its national existence, however, limits what it can offer to contemporary readers in this global age. Now, in the twenty-first century, Americans have access to global events and peoples in "real time," while groups throughout the world engage American products and concepts from sneakers to dreams of freedom and home ownership. Americans run through the so-called global community. They speak to it and with it; they embrace it and fight with it. And, just as much, the global community attunes to the United States every step of the way.

These realities have compelled a new approach to the *DAH*. Rather than re-create the *DAH* with a global approach, we decided to demonstrate what American history can look like from the starting point of its intricate, unbreakable ties with the world. *America in the World, 1776 to the Present* offers more than five hundred entries that feature particular people, events, ideas, organizations, and geographical spaces. At the end of each entry, there are cross-references and bibliographies so that readers can learn more about each subject. We have also included a thematic outline of contents as another point of access. The thematic outline, which groups articles into related ideas and topics, serves as a kind of map. Finally, a thorough subject index guides the reader to additional details, including references to more than one hundred images that were chosen to provide further context.

ACKNOWLEDGMENTS

America in the World, 1776 to the Present features many of the finest historians writing in the field. The nature of this enterprise demanded that many of the entries be written by junior scholars, those who have been trained since the 1990s with an eye and ear toward the globe.

To create the list of entries and general outlines for the major points that needed to be covered, and to locate the best scholar for each entry, I called upon three of the finest young historians currently working in the field of America in the world. Emily Conroy-Krutz of Michigan State University, an expert on international missionary work during the early republic, tackled the period from 1776 to 1898. The University of Northern Iowa's Cara Burnidge focused on the period from the end of the nineteenth century to the middle of the twentieth century. As a scholar of Woodrow Wilson, religion, and foreign diplomacy, she crafted the entries that explore the emergence of the United States as a major player in world affairs. Finally, David Kinkela of SUNY Fredonia, a scholar of global environmentalism, covered the period from World War II to the present day. Together, and with the immeasurable help of associate publisher Hélène Potter and project editor Alan Hedblad, we compiled a list of almost one thousand entries, whittled it down to the roughly 550 included here, and provided authors the vision for how to approach their individual topics. After our review process for each submitted entry was completed, the approved manuscript was entrusted to capable copyeditors Judith Culligan, Michael J. O'Neal, and Jessica Hornik Evans, who helped to ensure factual accuracy and consistency of style while editing the prose.

CONCLUSION

Many of the entries herein are not found in previous editions of the *DAH*. We have included entries on areas throughout the globe, such as Africa, Asia, and the Middle East, in an effort to examine how the United States has interacted with and considered these places. In addition, many people and events from around the world are included because they helped shape the direction of the United States, such as the 1955 Bandung Conference and the nineteenth-century Italian patriot Giuseppe Garibaldi.

While the new entries provide exciting additions to *DAH*'s coverage of US history and world history, the entries that recast familiar faces, events, and organizations are just as fascinating. Take, for instance, the entry on Martin Luther King Jr. In this volume, King's childhood and labor in the US South are discussed as background for his global thinking, his efforts in other countries, and his worldwide appeal. The author shows how King long cast an eye beyond the United States, that his efforts to help African Americans were premised on his broader view of economic injustice around the globe, and that throughout the world public monuments have been erected in his honor. An interesting assignment would be to compare and contrast the entries in this dictionary with those in the original *DAH*. How does a global approach provide a new sense of American influence in the world and a new understanding of how global inspirations have propelled the United States itself?

The two volumes of *America in the World, 1776 to the Present* are not intended to be an endpoint. They are meant to be a launching pad. We hope scholars and students will consult these entries with new research projects in mind. What, for example, would a history of video gaming look like from this vantage point? How about health care or particular songs or musical expressions? We hope readers will bring their interests and passions to these volumes, learn how to ask new questions by considering the interplay of the local with the global, and create for themselves new ways of rendering the histories of the United States, America, and the world.

Edward J. Blum

Editor in Chief

October 7, 2015

List of Articles

List of Contributors

Donald Abelson
Professor, Department of Political Science
The University of Western Ontario
THINK TANKS

Jessica L. Adler
Assistant Professor, Departments of History and Health Policy and Management
Florida International University
DEPARTMENT OF VETERANS AFFAIRS

Kristin L. Ahlberg
Office of the Historian
US Department of State
BUNDY, MCGEORGE

Michael Altman
Assistant Professor of Religious Studies
University of Alabama
HINDUISM
INDIA

Matthew J. Ambrose
Independent Scholar
IRAQ

Anna Amundson
Adjunct Instructor of History
Tallahassee Community College
IMMIGRATION

Carol Anderson
Associate Professor, African American Studies and History
Emory University
AN APPEAL TO THE WORLD! (NAACP, 1947)

Ryan Anningson
Doctoral Candidate
Wilfrid Laurier University–University of Waterloo, Joint PhD Program in Religious Diversity in North America
BUDDHISM

Allan W. Austin
Professor of History
Misericordia University
SUPERMAN

Anni Baker
Associate Professor, Department of History
Wheaton College, Norton, Massachusetts
MARINE CORPS, US
WEAPONRY

Randall Balmer
John Phillips Professor in Religion
Dartmouth College
PROTESTANTISM

R. M. Barlow
PhD Candidate
University of Virginia
ADAMS, JOHN

Matthew Basilico
Department of Economics, Harvard University
Harvard Medical School
WORLD HEALTH ORGANIZATION

Nicholas Bayne
Fellow, International Trade Policy Unit
The London School of Economics and Political Science
GROUP OF FIVE AND ITS SUCCESSORS (G5, G7, G8, G20)

Laura Belmonte
Professor of History
Oklahoma State University
SMITH-MUNDT ACT (US INFORMATION AND EDUCATIONAL EXCHANGE ACT OF 1948)
STONEWALL RIOTS

John M. Belohlavek
Professor of History

University of South Florida
DEPARTMENT OF FOREIGN AFFAIRS
JACKSON, ANDREW
"LYNCOYA" *(SIDEBAR TO JACKSON, ANDREW)*

Adam P. Berg
Doctoral Candidate, History and Philosophy of Sport, Department of Kinesiology
Pennsylvania State University, University Park
OLYMPICS

Mark T. Berger
Adjunct Professor, Department of Defense Analysis
Naval Postgraduate School
LEAGUE OF NATIONS
UNITED NATIONS

William H. Bergmann
Assistant Professor, Department of History
Slippery Rock University
SIMCOE, JOHN GRAVES

Michael Bertrand
Associate Professor of History
Tennessee State University
PRESLEY, ELVIS AARON
ROCK 'N' ROLL

Kiran F. Bhai
Partners In Health
WORLD HEALTH ORGANIZATION

Denise Bielby
Professor of Sociology
University of California–Santa Barbara
TELEVISION

Carmen Birkle
Professor, Institute of English and American Studies
Philipps-Universität Marburg
THE MIKADO (ARTHUR SULLIVAN AND W. S. GILBERT, 1885)

Michael J. Birkner
Professor of History
Gettysburg College
BUCHANAN, JAMES

Ryan Bishop
Professor of Global Art and Politics
Winchester School of Art, University of Southampton
MARX BROTHERS

Edward J. Blum
Professor of History
San Diego State University
ALCOHOLICS ANONYMOUS

Elizabeth D. Blum
Professor, Department of History
Troy University
GLOBAL WARMING

Dirk Bönker
Associate Professor of History
Duke University
PREPAREDNESS

Kathryn Boodry
Instructor of History
University of Oregon
ECONOMICS

Megan Perle Bowman
Visiting Lecturer
Georgia State University
COMMUNITARIAN SOCIALISM

Rebecca Brannon
Assistant Professor
James Madison University
LOYALISTS

Ramune Braziunaite
Lecturer, School of Media and Communication
Bowling Green State University
ABU GHRAIB

Richard Breitman
Distinguished Professor of History, Emeritus
American University
ROOSEVELT, FRANKLIN D.

Robert K. Brigham
Shirley Ecker Boskey Professor of History and International Relations
Vassar College
SEPTEMBER 11, 2001

Nancy K. Bristow
Professor of History
University of Puget Sound
FLU EPIDEMIC, 1918–1919

John A. Britton
Professor Emeritus
Francis Marion University
TELEGRAPH

Christopher T. Brooks
Associate Professor, Department of History
East Stroudsburg University
EUROPE

Claudia Franziska Brühwiler
Lecturer and Post-Doc in American Studies
University of St. Gallen, Switzerland
RAND, AYN

Denver Brunsman
Associate Professor of History
George Washington University
NAPOLEON BONAPARTE
NATURALIZATION ACT OF 1790
WASHINGTON, GEORGE

Kevin Bruyneel
Professor of Politics
Babson College
INDIAN CITIZENSHIP ACT (1924)

Malcolm Byrne
Director of Research
The National Security Archive at The George Washington University
IRAN
IRAN-CONTRA SCANDAL

Michael Cairo
Professor of Political Science
Transylvania University
"AL-QAEDA" *(SIDEBAR TO WAR ON TERROR)*
BUSH, GEORGE W.
WAR ON TERROR

Vincent Cannato
Associate Professor of History
University of Massachusetts Boston
ELLIS ISLAND
THE PASSING OF THE GREAT RACE (MADISON GRANT, 1916)

Chris Capozzola
Associate Professor of History
Massachusetts Institute of Technology
HAGUE CONFERENCES (1899, 1907)
LUCE, HENRY
MACARTHUR, DOUGLAS

Céline Carayon
Assistant Professor of History
Salisbury University
INDIAN REMOVAL ACT (1830)

Curt Cardwell
Associate Professor, Department of History
Drake University
NSC-68

Jessica Carr
Assistant Professor in Religious Studies
Lafayette College
BALFOUR DECLARATION (1917)
HOLOCAUST
JUDAISM
PALESTINE
ZIONISM

Francis M. Carroll
Professor Emeritus
St. John's College, University of Manitoba
NORTH AMERICA

Mina Carson
Associate Professor, College of Liberal Arts
Oregon State University
SETTLEMENT HOUSE MOVEMENT

Heath Carter
Assistant Professor of History
Valparaiso University
OUR COUNTRY (JOSIAH STRONG, 1885)

Emily Clare Casey
Department of Art History
University of Delaware
COPLEY, JOHN SINGLETON

Andrew Cayton
University Distinguished Professor of History
Miami University
WOLLSTONECRAFT, MARY

Jessica M. Chapman
Associate Professor, Department of History
Williams College
DOMINO THEORY
GULF OF TONKIN RESOLUTION

Dennis Choi
Madison, Wisconsin
SOUTH KOREA

Emily Suzanne Clark
Assistant Professor, Department of Religious Studies
Gonzaga University
MOORISH SCIENCE TEMPLE

Thomas Clark
Visiting Associate Professor of American Studies
University of Tübingen, Germany
DEMOCRACY IN AMERICA (ALEXIS DE TOCQUEVILLE, 1835–1840)

Linda Clemmons
Associate Professor of History
Illinois State University
RESERVATION

John Cloud
Historian
NOAA Central Library
NATIONAL OCEANIC AND ATMOSPHERIC ADMINISTRATION (NOAA)

Elizabeth A. Cobbs
Melbern G. Glasscock Professor
Texas A&M University
PEACE CORPS

Michael David Cohen
Research Assistant Professor of History
University of Tennessee, Knoxville
POLK, JAMES K.

Warren I. Cohen
University Distinguished Professor Emeritus, Michigan State University, and Distinguished University Professor Emeritus, University of Maryland, Baltimore County
Senior Scholar, Woodrow Wilson Center
CHINA

Aaron Nathan Coleman
Associate Professor of History and Higher Education
University of the Cumberlands
ALIEN ACT (1798)

David Coleman
Senior Research Fellow
National Security Archive
DETERRENCE

Douglas Comer
Distinguished Professor of Computer Science
Purdue University
INTERNET

Richard S. Conley
Associate Professor of Political Science
University of Florida
BUSH, GEORGE H. W.

Stephen Connor
Assistant Professor of History
Nipissing University
GENEVA CONVENTIONS

Tanner R. Cooke
PhD Candidate
The Pennsylvania State University
ADVERTISING AND MARKETING

James E. Crisp
Professor of History
North Carolina State University
TEXAS REPUBLIC

Michael Patrick Cullinane
Senior Lecturer in US History
Northumbria University
ANTI-IMPERIALIST LEAGUE
FORD FOUNDATION

Finbarr Curtis
Assistant Professor of Religious Studies
Georgia Southern University
RELIGIONS

Kati Curts
PhD Candidate
Yale University
FORD, HENRY
FORDLÂNDIA

H. Louise Davis
Associate Professor of American Studies
Miami University
USA FOR AFRICA ("WE ARE THE WORLD")

John Davis
Emiliana Pasca Noether Chair in Modern Italian History
University of Connecticut
GARIBALDI, GIUSEPPE

Robert Julio Decker
Lecturer in North American History
University of Bristol
IMMIGRATION RESTRICTION LEAGUE

Sarah Dees
Lecturer
University of Tennessee
WHITENESS

Jonathan Den Hartog
Associate Professor of History
University of Northwestern–St. Paul, Minnesota
JAY, JOHN
JAY TREATY (1795)
XYZ AFFAIR

Christopher Dietrich
Assistant Professor of History
Fordham University
NEOLIBERALISM

Hasia Diner
Professor
New York University
POGROM

Jason Dittmer
Reader in Human Geography
University College London
CAPTAIN AMERICA

Charles M. Dobbs
Professor Emeritus
Iowa State University
"THE AMERICAN CENTURY" (HENRY LUCE, 1941)
JOINT CHIEFS OF STAFF
MANCHURIA
ROBBER BARONS
YALTA CONFERENCE (1945)

Alan P. Dobson
Professor (honorary)
Swansea University
REAGAN, RONALD WILSON

Justus D. Doenecke
Emeritus Professor of History
New College of Florida
CASH AND CARRY
ISOLATIONISM

Michael E. Donoghue
Associate Professor of History
Marquette University
PANAMA CANAL

Seth Dowland
Assistant Professor of Religion
Pacific Lutheran University
GRAHAM, WILLIAM (BILLY) FRANKLIN, JR.

Janine Giordano Drake
Assistant Professor of History
University of Great Falls
HAYMARKET BOMBING

Ellen DuBois
Distinguished Professor of History and Gender Studies
University of California, Los Angeles
SUFFRAGE

Lucia Ducci
Lecturer
University of Massachusetts, Amherst
MARSH, GEORGE PERKINS

John Dumbrell
Professor of Government
Durham University, United Kingdom
CLINTON, WILLIAM JEFFERSON

Brandon Dupont
Associate Professor of Economics
Western Washington University
STEAMSHIP

Mark S. Dyreson
Professor of Kinesiology and Affiliate Professor of History
Pennsylvania State University, University Park
OLYMPICS

David J. Dzurec III
Associate Professor of History
University of Scranton
CAPTIVITY NARRATIVES

Charles Edel
Assistant Professor
Naval War College
ADAMS, JOHN QUINCY

Mark Thomas Edwards
Associate Professor, History
Spring Arbor University
FEDERAL COUNCIL OF CHURCHES

Bartow J. Elmore
Assistant Professor of History
University of Alabama
COCA-COLA

David Eltis
Robert W. Woodruff Emeritus Professor of History
Emory University
ATLANTIC SLAVE TRADE

John R. Eperjesi
Associate Professor, School of English

Kyung Hee University, Seoul, South Korea
AMERICAN ASIATIC ASSOCIATION

Paul Erickson
History Department
Wesleyan University
RAND CORPORATION

Dario A. Euraque
Professor of History and International Studies
Trinity College, Hartford, Connecticut
BANANA REPUBLICS

Sterling Evans
Department of History
University of Oklahoma
PHILIPPINES

Bronwen Everill
Department of History
King's College London
LIBERIA

Adam Ewing
Assistant Professor
Virginia Commonwealth University
BACK-TO-AFRICA MOVEMENT
UNIVERSAL NEGRO IMPROVEMENT ASSOCIATION (UNIA)

Ogechukwu C. Ezekwem
PhD Candidate
University of Texas at Austin
AFRICA

Michael Ezra
Professor of American Multicultural Studies
Sonoma State University
ALI, MUHAMMAD

Andrew J. B. Fagal
The Papers of Thomas Jefferson
Princeton University
FRENCH REVOLUTION
JEFFERSON, THOMAS
MODEL TREATY OF 1776

Toyin Falola
Jacob and Frances Sanger Mossiker Chair in the Humanities and University Distinguished Teaching Professor
University of Texas at Austin
AFRICA

Thomas Field
Assistant Professor, College of Security and Intelligence
Embry-Riddle Aeronautical University
ROSTOW, WALT W.

David P. Fields
PhD Candidate, US Diplomatic History
University of Wisconsin–Madison
NORTH KOREA

Richard M. Filipink
Associate Professor
Western Illinois University
ATLANTIC CHARTER (1941)
CARTER, JAMES EARL, JR.
LODGE, HENRY CABOT
TRIPLE ENTENTE

Paul Finkelman
Senior Fellow, Penn Program on Democracy, Citizenship, and Constitutionalism, University of Pennsylvania
Scholar-in-Residence, National Constitution Center, Philadelphia, Pennsylvania
NORTHWEST ORDINANCE (1787)

Andrew Finstuen
Dean, Honors College
Boise State University
NIEBUHR, (KARL PAUL) REINHOLD

Marilyn Fischer
Professor of Philosophy
University of Dayton
ADDAMS, JANE

Jennifer Fish Kashay
Associate Professor of History
Colorado State University
HAWAI'I

Andre M. Fleche
Associate Professor of History
Castleton College
THE CIVIL WAR

M. Ryan Floyd, Sr.
Assistant Professor of History, Social Science Secondary Education Coordinator
Department of History and Philosophy, Lander University
NEUTRALITY

Robert Forrant
Professor of History
University of Massachusetts Lowell
DEINDUSTRIALIZATION

Andrew K. Frank
Allen Morris Associate Professor of History
Florida State University
CIVILIZATION FUND

Christos D. Frentzos
Associate Professor, Department of History
Austin Peay State University
AIR FORCE, US

Jonathan Z. Friedman
Adjunct Professor
New York University
UNIVERSITIES

Stefan Fritsch
Assistant Professor of International Relations and Comparative Government
Bowling Green State University
INTERNATIONAL BUSINESS MACHINES CORPORATION (IBM)
MULTINATIONAL CORPORATIONS

Peter Fritzsche
Professor of History
University of Illinois
NAZISM

Julia Gaffield
Assistant Professor

Georgia State University
HAITIAN REVOLUTION

Christopher Gainor
Historian
Foresight Science and Technology
INTERCONTINENTAL BALLISTIC MISSILES

Abdullahi Gallab
Associate Professor, African and African American Studies, Religious Studies
Arizona State University
QUTB, SAYYID

Carlos Gallego
Associate Professor, English Department
St. Olaf College
CHICANO MOVEMENT

Shreena N. Gandhi
Assistant Professor of Religion
Kalamazoo College
MELTING POT
ORIENT

Daniel Geary
Mark Pigott Assistant Professor of US History
Trinity College Dublin
STUDENTS FOR A DEMOCRATIC SOCIETY (SDS)

Noah L. Gelfand
Adjunct Assistant Professor
University of Connecticut at Stamford
DYLAN, BOB

Paola Gemme
Professor of English
Arkansas Tech University
RISORGIMENTO

Nathaniel George
PhD Candidate, Department of History
Rice University
MIDDLE EAST

David Gibbs
Professor of History
University of Arizona
YUGOSLAV WARS

Paul A. Gilje
George Lynn Cross Research Professor, Department of History
University of Oklahoma
IMPRESSMENT
NON-INTERCOURSE ACT (1809)

Lesley Gill
Professor
Vanderbilt University
US ARMY SCHOOL OF THE AMERICAS (WESTERN HEMISPHERE INSTITUTE FOR SECURITY COOPERATION)

Philippe Girard
Professor of Caribbean History
McNeese State University
CARIBBEAN

Seth Givens
PhD Candidate
Ohio University
BERLIN WALL

Elena Glasberg
Lecturer, Program in Expository Writing
New York University
ANTARCTICA/ARCTIC

Piero Gleijeses
Professor of American Foreign Policy, School of Advanced International Studies
Johns Hopkins University
COVERT WARS

Brendan Goff
Assistant Professor, American History
New College of Florida
ROTARY CLUB

David Howard Goldberg
Middle East Scholar
Toronto, Ontario, Canada
ISRAEL

Joel K. Goldstein
Vincent C. Immel Professor of Law
Saint Louis University School of Law
CHENEY, DICK

Michael Goodrum
Senior Lecturer, Department of History & American Studies
Canterbury Christ Church University
SANTA ANNA, ANTONIO LÓPEZ DE
SPANISH-AMERICAN WAR

Bertram M. Gordon
Professor of History
Mills College
FRANCE

James L. Gormly
Professor of History
Washington and Jefferson College
IRON CURTAIN

Van E. Gosse
Associate Professor
Franklin and Marshall College
NEW LEFT

Jeffrey D. Gottlieb
PhD Candidate in Religion, Ethics and Philosophy
Florida State University
ETHNIC CLEANSING
UNIVERSAL DECLARATION OF HUMAN RIGHTS

Eliga H. Gould
Professor and Chair, Department of History
University of New Hampshire
AMERICAN REVOLUTION

Lewis L. Gould
Professor Emeritus
University of Texas
TAFT, WILLIAM HOWARD

Richard Gowan
Adjunct Associate Professor
Columbia School of International and Public Affairs
SECURITY COUNCIL, UN

Michael Graziano
PhD Candidate
Florida State University
DEPARTMENT OF HOMELAND SECURITY
NATIONAL SECURITY AGENCY (NSA)

David Greenberg
Professor of History
Rutgers University
THE NEW REPUBLIC (MAGAZINE)

Kerri Greenidge
Lecturer, Department of American Studies
University of Massachussetts, Boston
AN APPEAL TO THE COLOURED CITIZENS OF THE WORLD (DAVID WALKER, 1829)
NATIONAL ASSOCIATION FOR THE ADVANCEMENT OF COLORED PEOPLE (NAACP)

Sarah M. Griffith
Assistant Professor of History
Queens University of Charlotte
FOREIGN MISSION MOVEMENT

T. Jeremy Gunn
Professor of Political Science and Law
International University of Rabat, Morocco
DEPARTMENT OF DEFENSE, US

Nichola D. Gutgold
Associate Dean for Academics, Schreyer Honors College
The Pennsylvania State University
ROSIE THE RIVETER

Patrick Hagopian
Senior Lecturer in History and American Studies
Lancaster University, England
NGUYỄN NGỌC LOAN EXECUTING NGUYỄN VĂN LÉM (EDDIE ADAMS, 1968)

Barbara Hahn
Associate Professor, Department of History
Texas Tech University
COTTON

Eric Allen Hall
Assistant Professor of History and Africana Studies
Georgia Southern University
ASHE, ARTHUR

Michael R. Hall
Professor of History
Armstrong State University
ORIENT EXPRESS
ROUGH RIDERS
VODOU

Fiona Deans Halloran
Rowland Hall-St. Mark's School
NAST, THOMAS

David J. Hancock
Professor of History
University of Michigan
MADEIRA

Jussi M. Hanhimäki
Professor of International History
Graduate Institute of International and Development Studies, Geneva, Switzerland
DÉTENTE

David Hanlon
Professor and Chair, Department of History
University of Hawai'i at Mānoa
PACIFIC ISLANDS

Victoria A. Harden
Founding Director, Emerita, Office of NIH History
US National Institutes of Health
ACQUIRED IMMUNODEFICIENCY SYNDROME (AIDS)

C. Lee Harrington
Professor of Sociology
Miami University
TELEVISION

Jennifer Harris
Associate Professor
University of Waterloo
WINFREY, OPRAH

Paul William Harris
Professor of History
Minnesota State University Moorhead
AMERICAN BOARD OF COMMISSIONERS FOR FOREIGN MISSIONS

Susan Kumin Harris
Hall Distinguished Professor of American Literature and Culture
University of Kansas
TWAIN, MARK

Aaron Hatley
PhD Candidate, History of American Civilization
Harvard University
AUTOMOBILES

John B. Hattendorf
Ernest J. King Professor of Maritime History
US Naval War College
THE INFLUENCE OF SEA POWER UPON HISTORY (ALFRED THAYER MAHAN, 1890)
NAVY, US

Lawrence B. A. Hatter
Assistant Professor of History
Washington State University
EMPIRE OF LIBERTY

Sam W. Haynes
Director, Center for Greater Southwestern Studies
University of Texas at Arlington
ANGLOPHOBIA
MEXICAN-AMERICAN WAR

Michael J. Heale
Emeritus Professor of American History, Lancaster University
Supernumerary Fellow, Rothermere American Institute, Oxford
RED SCARE

Matthew S. Hedstrom
Associate Professor of Religious Studies and American Studies
University of Virginia
SECULARIZATION

Eric Heinze
Associate Professor of Political Science and International Studies
University of Oklahoma
CONTEMPORARY GENOCIDES AND US POLICY

Amanda Hendrix-Komoto
Assistant Professor
Montana State University
MISCEGENATION
PACIFIC OCEAN

Beth Shalom Hessel
Executive Director, Presbyterian Historical Society, Philadelphia
INTERNMENT CAMPS

Hannah Nicole Higgin
History Faculty
Blair Academy
AMERICAN COMMISSION TO NEGOTIATE PEACE
FIRESTONE TIRE AND RUBBER COMPANY
JAZZ
"THE REAL AMBASSADORS" *(SIDEBAR TO JAZZ)*

Frederick Hitz
Senior Lecturer in Public Policy, Frank Batten School of Leadership and Public Affairs
University of Virginia
SPIES AND ESPIONAGE

Walter L. Hixson
Distinguished Professor
University of Akron
ARAB-ISRAELI CONFLICT
CAMP DAVID ACCORDS (1978)
COLONIALISM

Karen S. Hoffman
Visiting Assistant Professor and Director of Undergraduate Studies
Marquette University
CLEVELAND, GROVER

Mischa Honeck
Research Fellow
German Historical Institute, Washington, DC
AMERICANIZATION

David Hostetter
Independent Scholar
La Crescenta, CA
PAUL, ALICE STOKES

Joshua P. Howe
Assistant Professor of History and Environmental Studies
Reed College
GORE, ALBERT, JR.

Justine Howe
Assistant Professor
Case Western Reserve University
ISLAM

Charles M. Hubbard
Professor of History and Lincoln Historian
Lincoln Memorial University, Harrogate, Tennessee
CONFEDERATE STATES OF AMERICA

John Huffman
Assistant Editor, The Papers of Benjamin Franklin
Yale University
FRANKLIN, BENJAMIN
PASSPORT

Patrick W. Hughes
University of Pittsburgh
PAINE, THOMAS

Daniel J. Hulsebosch
The Charles Seligson Professor of Law
New York University School of Law
DECLARATION OF INDEPENDENCE

Andrew Hund
Assistant Professor of Sociology
The United Arab Emirates University
LEND-LEASE ACT (1941)
MISSIONARY DIPLOMACY

R. Douglas Hurt
Professor and Department Head
Department of History, Purdue University
BORLAUG, NORMAN
GREEN REVOLUTION

Chloe Ireton
Doctoral Candidate
The University of Texas at Austin
BLACK ATLANTIC

Ryan Irwin
Assistant Professor of History
University at Albany–SUNY
DECOLONIZATION
FRIEDMAN, MILTON
NONGOVERNMENTAL ORGANIZATIONS (NGOs)

Piki Ish-Shalom
Associate Professor, Department of International Relations
The Hebrew University of Jerusalem
MODERNIZATION THEORY

Robert Jacobs
Associate Professor, Hiroshima Peace Institute
Hiroshima City University
BIKINI ATOLL

Steven Leonard Jacobs
Aaron Aronov Endowed Chair of Judaic Studies
University of Alabama, Tuscaloosa
GENOCIDE

Sheyda F. A. Jahanbani
Associate Professor of History
University of Kansas
THIRD WORLD

Zubeda Jalalzai
Department of English
Rhode Island College
AFGHANISTAN

Maartje Janse
Lecturer
Institute of History, Leiden University, The Netherlands
TRANSATLANTIC REFORM

Sue Curry Jansen
Professor, Media & Communication
Muhlenberg College
LIPPMANN, WALTER

Glen Jeansonne
Professor of History
University of Wisconsin–Milwaukee
BOLSHEVISM
EINSTEIN, ALBERT
MARX, KARL
OTTOMAN EMPIRE

Ronald Angelo Johnson
Assistant Professor of History
Texas State University
TOUSSAINT LOUVERTURE

Sylvester A. Johnson
Associate Professor of African American Studies and Religious Studies
Northwestern University
EMPIRE, US

Andrew Johnstone
Senior Lecturer in American History
University of Leicester
CARNEGIE ENDOWMENT FOR INTERNATIONAL PEACE
INTERNATIONALISM

Jeannette Eileen Jones
Associate Professor of History and Ethnic Studies
University of Nebraska–Lincoln
BERLIN CONFERENCE (1884–1885)

Marian Moser Jones
Assistant Professor
University of Maryland College Park
RED CROSS

Peter J. Kastor
Professor of History and American Culture Studies
Washington University in St. Louis
LOUISIANA PURCHASE

Mary C. Kelly
Professor of History
Franklin Pierce University
GREAT FAMINE

Patrick William Kelly
A. W. Mellon Postdoctoral Fellow in the Humanities and Humanistic Sciences
University of Wisconsin–Madison
"AMNESTY INTERNATIONAL"
(SIDEBAR TO HUMAN RIGHTS)

David M. Kennedy
Donald J. McLachlan Professor of History Emeritus
Stanford University
FOUR FREEDOMS

Daniel Kilbride
Professor of History
John Carroll University
GRAND TOUR

Amy Kittelstrom
Associate Professor of History
Sonoma State University
WORLD'S PARLIAMENT OF RELIGIONS (1893)

Dean J. Kotlowski
Professor of History
Salisbury University
WOUNDED KNEE (1890 AND 1973)

Stephanie Kowalczyk
Instructor
Kent State University
EXPATRIATE ARTISTS

Lloyd S. Kramer
Professor of History
University of North Carolina, Chapel Hill
LAFAYETTE, MARQUIS DE

Michael L. Krenn
Professor of History
Appalachian State University
RACE

Charles Laderman
Research Fellow, Peterhouse
University of Cambridge
ROOSEVELT, THEODORE
ROOSEVELT COROLLARY (1904)

Fiona Lander
Harvard T. H. Chan School of Public Health
WORLD HEALTH ORGANIZATION

Lester D. Langley
Professor Emeritus of History
University of Georgia
BOLÍVAR, SIMÓN

Kyle M. Lascurettes
Assistant Professor of International Affairs
Lewis & Clark College
REALISM (INTERNATIONAL RELATIONS)

Nicholas Lawrence
Assistant Professor of English
University of South Carolina Lancaster
MELVILLE, HERMAN

Eugene E. Leach
Professor of History and American Studies, Emeritus
Trinity College
MULTICULTURALISM

John Patrick Leary
Assistant Professor, Department of English
Wayne State University
CUBA

Leslie Lenkowsky
Professor of Practice in Public Affairs and Philanthropic Studies
Indiana University
GATES FOUNDATION

Sharon Leon
Associate Professor, Department of History and Art History
George Mason University
KNIGHTS OF COLUMBUS

Mark Levene
Reader in Comparative History, and member of Parkes Centre for Jewish/non-Jewish Relations
University of Southampton
ARMENIAN GENOCIDE

Sanford V. Levinson
W. St. John Garwood and W. St. John Garwood Jr. Centennial Chair in Law, University of Texas Law School

Professor of Government, University of Texas at Austin
INSULAR POSSESSIONS

Allan J. Lichtman
Distinguished Professor of History
American University
ROOSEVELT, FRANKLIN D.

Robert Lifset
Donald Keith Jones Associate Professor of Honors and History
University of Oklahoma
ORGANIZATION OF THE PETROLEUM EXPORTING COUNTRIES (OPEC)

Michael Limberg
PhD Candidate, Department of History
University of Connecticut
KELLOGG-BRIAND PACT

John M. Logsdon
Professor Emeritus, Space Policy Institute
Elliott School of International Affairs, The George Washington University, Washington, DC
APOLLO PROGRAM
NATIONAL AERONAUTICS AND SPACE ADMINISTRATION (NASA)
SPUTNIK

Bonnie Lucero
Department of History and Philosophy
University of Texas–Pan American
CASTRO, FIDEL

Matthew Luckett
Dean's Lecturer on Social Research, Department of History
University of California Los Angeles (UCLA)
FRONTIER WARS

Jeff Ludwig
Director of Education
William Seward House Museum
TURNER, FREDERICK JACKSON

David Luhrssen
Editor
Shepherd Express
BOLSHEVISM
EINSTEIN, ALBERT
MARX, KARL
OTTOMAN EMPIRE

Jonathan Lurie
Professor of History, Emeritus
Rutgers University
WORLD WAR I

Jean Marie Lutes
Associate Professor, Department of English
Villanova University
BLY, NELLIE

Jeffrey Lyon
Department of Religion
University of Hawai'i at Mānoa
"OBOOKIAH" *(SIDEBAR TO HAWAI'I)*

Felicia W. Mack
Part-time Faculty
Eastern Kentucky University
POWELL, ADAM CLAYTON, JR.

Stuart MacKay
PhD candidate, Department of History
Carleton University
MINSTRELSY

Grant Madsen
Assistant Professor
Brigham Young University
EISENHOWER, DWIGHT D.

Malcolm Magee
Associate Professor, Department of History
Michigan State University
WILSON, WOODROW

Edward Marolda
Adjunct Instructor
Georgetown University
McNAMARA, ROBERT S.

Michelle Mart
Associate Professor of History
Penn State University, Berks Campus
SILENT SPRING (RACHEL CARSON, 1962)

Scott C. Martin
Professor of History and American Culture Studies
Bowling Green State University
TEMPERANCE MOVEMENT

Edwin Martini
Professor of History
Western Michigan University
AGENT ORANGE

Hajimu Masuda
Department of History
National University of Singapore
JAPAN

James I. Matray
Professor of History
California State University, Chico
KOREAN WAR

Anne F. Mattina
Professor and Chair, Department of Communication
Stonehill College
CLINTON, HILLARY RODHAM

Doreen J. Mattingly
Associate Professor, Department of Women's Studies
San Diego State University
THE FEMININE MYSTIQUE (BETTY FRIEDAN, 1963)

Robert E. May
Professor of History
Purdue University
FILIBUSTER

David Mayers
Professor, History Department, Political Science Department
Boston University
KENNAN, GEORGE F.

B. Theo Mazumdar
Annenberg School for Communication

University of Southern California
VOICE OF AMERICA

Matthew P. McAllister
Professor of Communications
The Pennsylvania State University
ADVERTISING AND MARKETING

William B. McAllister
Special Projects Division Chief, Office of the Historian, United States Department of State
Adjunct Associate Professor, Graduate School of Foreign Service, Georgetown University
DRUGS

Conor D. McCarthy
Department of English
Maynooth University, Ireland
SAID, EDWARD

Charles J. McClain
Vice Chair (emeritus), Jurisprudence and Social Policy Program, Lecturer in Residence, School of Law
University of California Berkeley
CHINESE EXCLUSION ACT (1882)

Peter A. McCord
Professor of History
State University of New York, Fredonia
CLASH OF CIVILIZATIONS (SAMUEL HUNTINGTON)
KEYNESIAN ECONOMICS
MOSSADEGH, MOHAMMAD
NEW WORLD ORDER
POSTMODERNISM
WORLD BANK

Maurie D. McInnis
Professor of Art History
University of Virginia
CROWE, EYRE

Asa McKercher
Assistant Professor, Department of History
McMaster University
ORGANIZATION OF AMERICAN STATES (OAS)

Elizabeth McKillen
Professor of History
University of Maine
INTERNATIONAL LABOR ORGANIZATION

John McNay
Professor of History
University of Cincinnati
POTSDAM CONFERENCE (1945)

Robert McParland
Professor of English
Felician College
DICKENS, CHARLES

Alan McPherson
Professor of International and Area Studies
University of Oklahoma
HAITI

Amanda Kay McVety
Associate Professor of History
Miami University
POINT FOUR

James McWilliams
Ingram Professor of History
Texas State University, San Marcos
DEPARTMENT OF AGRICULTURE, US

Willliam C. Meadows
Department of Sociology-Anthropology
Missouri State University
CODE TALKERS

Ted Merwin
Associate Professor of Religion & Judaic Studies; Director of the Milton B. Asbell Center for Jewish Life
Dickinson College, Carlisle, PA
THE JAZZ SINGER
JEWISH WELFARE BOARD

Yanek Mieczkowski
Professor
Dowling College
FORD, GERALD R.

Edward G. Miller
Associate Professor of History
Dartmouth College
VIETNAM WAR

James Edward Miller
Independent Scholar
Washington, DC
ITALY

Brandon Mills
Lecturer, Department of History
University of Colorado Denver
AMERICAN COLONIZATION SOCIETY
COLONIZATION MOVEMENT

Nicolaus Mills
Professor of American Studies
Sarah Lawrence College
MARSHALL PLAN

Margot Minardi
Associate Professor of History and Humanities
Reed College
AMERICAN PEACE SOCIETY

Heena Mistry
PhD candidate, Department of History
Queen's University
INDIAN OCEAN

Kaeten Mistry
Lecturer in American History
University of East Anglia
INTERVENTIONISM

Ashley Moreshead Pilkington
Visiting Assistant Professor, Department of History
University of Central Florida
FOREIGN MISSION SCHOOL (CORNWALL, CT)

Maribel Morey
Assistant Professor of History
Clemson University
AN AMERICAN DILEMMA: THE NEGRO PROBLEM AND MODERN DEMOCRACY (GUNNAR MYRDAL, 1944)

Eric J. Morgan
Assistant Professor, Department of Democracy and Justice Studies
University of Wisconsin–Green Bay
APARTHEID

Nancy Morgan
Instructor, School of Historical, Philosophical & Religious Studies
Arizona State University
CHEROKEE NATION V. GEORGIA (1831)
WORCESTER V. GEORGIA (1832)

Erik Mortenson
Assistant Professor
Koç University
BEAT GENERATION

Gretchen Murphy
Professor of English
University of Texas–Austin
"THE WHITE MAN'S BURDEN" (RUDYARD KIPLING, 1899)

Jason R. Musteen
United States Military Academy
WAR OF 1812

Brian K. Muzas
Assistant Professor, School of Diplomacy and International Relations
Seton Hall University
TRUMAN DOCTRINE

Jörg Nagler
Professor of North American History
Friedrich-Schiller-Universität, Historisches Institut
LINCOLN, ABRAHAM

Susan Nance
Associate Professor of US History
University of Guelph
ARABIAN NIGHTS

Philip Nash
Associate Professor of History
Penn State University, Shenango Campus
CUBAN MISSILE CRISIS

Daniel A. Nathan
Professor of American Studies
Skidmore College
NATIONAL BASKETBALL ASSOCIATION (NBA)

Thomas Nichols
Professor of National Security Affairs
US Naval War College
MUTUAL ASSURED DESTRUCTION (MAD)

Luke Nichter
Associate Professor of History
Texas A&M University–Central Texas
NIXON, RICHARD MILHOUS

Jocelyn Olcott
Associate Professor of History
Duke University
FEMINISM, WOMEN'S RIGHTS
INTERNATIONAL WOMEN'S YEAR (IWY), 1975

Ranen Omer-Sherman
Jewish Heritage Fund for Excellence Endowed Chair of Judaic Studies
University of Louisville
"THE NEW COLOSSUS" (EMMA LAZARUS, 1883)

Katherine Osburn
Associate Professor of History
Arizona State University
GENERAL ALLOTMENT ACT (DAWES SEVERALTY ACT, 1877)

Christopher O'Sullivan
Lecturer in History
University of San Francisco
POWELL, COLIN

Meredith Oyen
Assistant Professor
University of Maryland, Baltimore County
IMMIGRATION AND NATIONALITY ACT OF 1965

Daniel Ozarow
Lecturer and Deputy Head, Latin American Studies Research Group
Middlesex University, London
NORTH AMERICAN FREE TRADE AGREEMENT (NAFTA)

Chester Pach
Associate Professor, Department of History
Ohio University
FREEDOM FIGHTERS
JOHNSON, LYNDON BAINES

Joseph Palermo
Professor of History
California State University, Sacramento
KENNEDY, ROBERT

Michael Parker
Professor of Church History and Director of Graduate Studies
Evangelical Theological Seminary in Cairo
STUDENT VOLUNTEER MOVEMENT FOR FOREIGN MISSIONS

Israel Pastrana
PhD Candidate, History
University of California, San Diego
BRACERO PROGRAM

Columba Peoples
Senior Lecturer in International Relations, School of Sociology, Politics, and International Studies
University of Bristol
STRATEGIC DEFENSE INITIATIVE (STAR WARS)

Sean T. Perrone
Professor of History
Saint Anselm College
NEUTRALITY ACT OF 1794

Tony Perucci
Associate Professor
The University of North Carolina at Chapel Hill
ROBESON, PAUL LEROY

Lawrence A. Peskin
Professor of History

Morgan State University
BARBARY WARS
MACON'S BILL NO. 2 (1810)

Jason Peterson
Assistant Professor of Communication
Charleston Southern University
JOHN CARLOS AND TOMMIE SMITH, MEXICO CITY OLYMPICS (JOHN DOMINIS, 1968)

Nicole Phelps
Associate Professor of History
University of Vermont
EMBASSIES, CONSULATES, AND DIPLOMATIC MISSIONS
FOREIGN SERVICE, US

Karen E. Phoenix
Instructor
Washington State University
GENDER
WORLD'S YWCA/YMCA

G. Kurt Piehler
Director and Associate Professor of History, Institute on World War II and the Human Experience
Florida State University
ARMY, US

John Pinheiro
Professor of History
Aquinas College
ST. PATRICK BATTALION

Anna Pochmara
Assistant Professor, Institute of English Studies
The University of Warsaw
HARLEM RENAISSANCE/NEW NEGRO MOVEMENT

Reiner Pommerin
Professor for Modern and Contemporary History
University of Dresden, Germany
GERMANY

Robert Poole
Guild Research Fellow, History
University of Central Lancashire, United Kingdom
EARTHRISE (BILL ANDERS, 1968)

Jeremy W. Pope
Assistant Professor of History
The College of William and Mary
WASHINGTON, BOOKER T.

Brook Poston
Assistant Professor of History
Stephen F. Austin State University
MONROE, JAMES

Margaret Power
Professor of History
Illinois Institute of Technology
FUERZAS ARMADAS DE LIBERACIÓN NACIONAL (FALN, ARMED FORCES OF PUERTO RICAN NATIONAL LIBERATION)

Naima Prevots
Professor Emerita
American University
MUSICALS

Ronald Pruessen
Professor of History
University of Toronto
DULLES, ALLEN W.
DULLES, JOHN FOSTER

Sophie Quinn-Judge
Associate Professor of History, Associate Director of Center for Vietnamese Philosophy, Culture and Society
Temple University
HO CHI MINH

Donald Rakestraw
University College Professor of American Studies
Winthrop University
BRITAIN

Robert Rakove
Lecturer
Stanford University
NON-ALIGNED MOVEMENT

Fabio Rambelli
Professor of Japanese Religions and Cultural History and ISF Endowed Chair of Shinto Studies
Department of East Asian Languages and Cultural Studies and Department of Religious Studies, University of California, Santa Barbara
SHINTO

Stephen J. Randall
Faculty Professor, Emeritus Professor of History
University of Calgary
CANADA

James Read
Professor of Political Science
College of St. Benedict and St. John's University
WAR HAWKS

Monica Cook Reed
Instructor of Religious Studies
Louisiana State University
NATION OF ISLAM
RASTAFARI

Bob H. Reinhardt
Executive Director
Willamette Heritage Center
SMALLPOX ERADICATION

David S. Reynolds
Distinguished Professor
The Graduate Center of the City University of New York
UNCLE TOM'S CABIN (HARRIET BEECHER STOWE, 1852)

Steven A. Riess
Bernard Brommel Research Professor, Emeritus
Northeastern Illinois University
BASEBALL

Natalie J. Ring
Associate Professor of History
University of Texas at Dallas
GLOBAL SOUTH

George Ritzer
Distinguished University Professor, Department of Sociology
University of Maryland
McDONALD'S

Efrén Rivera Ramos
Professor of Law
University of Puerto Rico
PUERTO RICO

Priscilla Roberts
Associate Professor of History
University of Hong Kong
COUNCIL ON FOREIGN RELATIONS
FOREIGN AFFAIRS (MAGAZINE)

Timothy M. Roberts
Associate Professor, Department of History
Western Illinois University
1848 REVOLUTIONS
EXCEPTIONALISM
KOSSUTH, LOUIS

Thomas Robertson
Associate Professor of History
Worcester Polytechnic Institute
UNITED STATES AGENCY FOR INTERNATIONAL DEVELOPMENT (USAID)

Valleri J. Robinson
Associate Professor, Department of Theatre
University of Illinois at Urbana-Champaign
FOREIGN PERFORMING ARTISTS

Ian Rocksborough-Smith
Visiting Assistant Professor of History
Saint Francis Xavier University
BLACK POWER MOVEMENT
PAN-AFRICANISM

Karen S. Roggenkamp
Professor of English
Texas A&M University–Commerce
NEW WOMAN

Renee Romano
Professor of History, Africana Studies and Comparative American Studies
Oberlin College
KING, MARTIN LUTHER, JR.

Thomas Rorke
Doctoral Candidate, History and Philosophy of Sport, Department of Kinesiology
Pennsylvania State University, University Park
OLYMPICS

Steve Rosenthal
Professor of Middle Eastern History
University of Hartford
AMERICAN ISRAEL PUBLIC AFFAIRS COMMITTEE (AIPAC)

Tamar Y. Rothenberg
Associate Professor
Bronx Community College–City University of New York
NATIONAL GEOGRAPHIC MAGAZINE

Dietmar Rothermund
Emeritus Professor
University of Heidelberg
GREAT DEPRESSION

Brian Rouleau
Assistant Professor of History
Texas A&M University
EXTRATERRITORIALITY
MANIFEST DESTINY

Jacqueline Jones Royster
Dean, Ivan Allen College of Liberal Arts
Georgia Institute of Technology
WELLS-BARNETT, IDA B.

Paul Rubinson
Assistant Professor
Bridgewater State University
NUCLEAR WEAPONS

Robert W. Rydell
Professor of History
Montana State University
BARNUM, P. T.
WORLD'S FAIRS

David Sachsman
George R. West, Jr. Chair of Excellence in Communication and Public Affairs and Professor of Communication
University of Tennessee at Chattanooga
YELLOW JOURNALISM

Nick Salvatore
Maurice and Hinda Neufeld Founders Professor of Industrial and Labor Relations
Cornell University
DEBS, EUGENE V.
SOCIALISM

Eric J. Sandeen
Professor of American Studies and Founding Director, Wyoming Institute for Humanities Research
University of Wyoming
KITCHEN DEBATE

Victoria Sanford
Professor and Chair, Department of Anthropology & Director, Center for Human Rights and Peace Studies
Lehman College, City University of New York
GUATEMALA

Maureen Connors Santelli
Assistant Professor
North Virginia Community College
GREEK REVOLUTION

Jennifer R. Scanlon
William R. Kenan Jr. Professor of Gender and Women's Studies
Bowdoin College
LIFE (MAGAZINE)

Lindsay Schakenbach Regele
Assistant Professor
Miami University
ATLANTIC OCEAN
IMMIGRATION QUOTAS
INDUSTRIALIZATION
LEVI STRAUSS & CO.
MEXICO
MORGAN, J. P.
SINGER MANUFACTURING COMPANY
SOUTH AMERICA
TARIFF

Anja Schüler
Research Associate
Heidelberg Center for American Studies at the University of Heidelberg
ROOSEVELT, ELEANOR
V-J DAY IN TIMES SQUARE (ALFRED EISENSTAEDT, 1945)

Frank Schumacher
Associate Professor of History
University of Western Ontario
ANTI-IMPERIALISM
IMPERIALISM

Stephen Irving Max Schwab
Assistant Professor of History
University of Alabama
GUANTÁNAMO BAY

Thomas A. Schwartz
Professor of History and Political Science
Vanderbilt University
KISSINGER, HENRY

Christina Schwenkel
Associate Professor of Anthropology
University of California, Riverside
PHAN THỊ KIM PHÚC (NICK UT, 1972)

Kim Scipes
Associate Professor of Sociology
Purdue University North Central, Westville, Indiana
AFL-CIO: LABOR'S FOREIGN POLICY

Katherine A. Scott
Assistant Historian
US Senate Historical Office
SENATE FOREIGN RELATIONS COMMITTEE

Giles Scott-Smith
Professor of Diplomatic History
Leiden University
CONGRESS FOR CULTURAL FREEDOM

Christine Sears
Associate Professor of History
University of Alabama in Huntsville
SLAVE REGIMES

Douglas Seefeldt
Assistant Professor, Department of History, Ball State University
Senior Digital Editor, The Papers of William F. Cody
BUFFALO BILL'S WILD WEST

Matthew Shannon
Department of History
Emory and Henry College
IRAN HOSTAGE CRISIS

Alan Sharp
Emeritus Professor of International History
University of Ulster
TREATY OF VERSAILLES

David M. K. Sheinin
Professor of History
Trent University
PAN-AMERICANISM

Brooke Sherrard
Instructor
Louisiana State University
HOLY LAND

Shawn Shimpach
Associate Professor, Department of Communication and Interdepartmental Program in Film Studies
University of Massachusetts, Amherst
DISNEY
HOLLYWOOD

James F. Siekmeier
Associate Professor of History
West Virginia University
OPEN DOOR POLICY

David Sim
Lecturer in US History
University College London
FENIAN BROTHERHOOD
SEWARD, WILLIAM H.

Bradley Simpson
Associate Professor of History and Asian Studies
University of Connecticut
HUMAN RIGHTS
SELF-DETERMINATION

Joseph Siracusa
Professor of Human Security and International Diplomacy
Royal Melbourne Institute of Technology
BAY OF PIGS
COLD WAR
KENNEDY, JOHN FITZGERALD
LAOS
LIMITED TEST BAN TREATY
McCARTHYISM

William E. Skidmore, II
PhD Candidate
Rice University
ANTISLAVERY

Nico Slate
Associate Professor of History
Carnegie Mellon University
OBAMA, BARACK HUSSEIN

Rebecca Slayton
Assistant Professor
Cornell University
MILITARY-INDUSTRIAL COMPLEX

Stanley Sloan
Visiting Scholar in Political Science
Middlebury College
NORTH ATLANTIC TREATY ORGANIZATION (NATO)

Roy C. Smith
Kenneth Langone Professor of Finance and Entrepreneurship
Stern School of Business, New York University
THE WEALTH OF NATIONS (ADAM SMITH, 1776)

John Soluri
Associate Professor
Carnegie Mellon University
UNITED FRUIT COMPANY

Bartholomew Sparrow
Professor of Government

The University of Texas at Austin
NATIONAL SECURITY COUNCIL (NSC)

Ronit Stahl
Postdoctoral Research Associate
Washington University in St. Louis
PROTESTANT-CATHOLIC-JEW (WILL HERBERG, 1955)

Maren Stange
Professor of American Studies, Faculty of Humanities and Social Sciences
The Cooper Union, New York
HOW THE OTHER HALF LIVES (JACOB RIIS, 1890)

Susan Gaunt Stearns
Visiting Assistant Professor
Northwestern University
PINCKNEY'S TREATY (1795)

Paul Steege
Associate Professor, Department of History
Villanova University
BERLIN AIRLIFT

Benn Steil
Director of International Economics
Council on Foreign Relations
BRETTON WOODS

Kenneth Stevens
Professor of History
Texas Christian University
WEBSTER, DANIEL

Mark Storey
Assistant Professor of English
University of Warwick
THE QUIET AMERICAN (GRAHAM GREENE, 1955)

Tyler Stovall
Professor of History
University of California, Berkeley
PARIS PEACE CONFERENCE (1919)

Charles Strauss
Assistant Professor
Mount St. Mary's University
CATHOLICISM

Fionnghuala Sweeney
Senior Lecturer in American Literature
School of English Literature, Language and Linguistics, Newcastle University
DOUGLASS, FREDERICK

Jeffrey F. Taffet
Professor of History
United States Merchant Marine Academy
ALLIANCE FOR PROGRESS

David Tal
Yossi Harel Chair in Israel Studies, Department of History
University of Sussex
STRATEGIC ARMS LIMITATION TALKS (SALT I AND SALT II)

Adam Tate
Professor of History
Clayton State University
MADISON, JAMES

Jon E. Taylor
Associate Professor of History
University of Central Missouri
TRUMAN, HARRY S.

Steven L. Taylor
Professor and Chair, Department of Political Science
Troy University
COLOMBIA

Aileen Teague
PhD Candidate, History
Vanderbilt University
WAR ON DRUGS

Paul Teed
Professor of History
Saginaw Valley State University
VIVEKANANDA, SWAMI

Robbie J. Totten
Chair and Assistant Professor, Political Science Department
American Jewish University
IMMIGRATION AND NATURALIZATION SERVICE

Luca Trenta
Department of Political and Cultural Studies
Swansea University
ALBRIGHT, MADELEINE

William Tsutsui
President and Professor of History
Hendrix College
GODZILLA

Stephen Tuffnell
British Academy Postdoctoral Fellow
University of Oxford
MONROE DOCTRINE (1823)

Thomas Tunstall Allcock
Lecturer in American History
The University of Manchester
GOOD NEIGHBOR POLICY

Frank Uekötter
Reader in Environmental Humanities
University of Birmingham
EARTH DAY

Corrina Unger
Associate Professor of Modern European History
Jacobs University Bremen
ROCKEFELLER FOUNDATION

Andrew T. Urban
Assistant Professor, American Studies and History
Rutgers University, New Brunswick
ALIEN CONTRACT LABOR LAW/ FORAN ACT (1885)

Rachel Tamar Van
Assistant Professor of History
Cal Poly Pomona
OPIUM WAR

F. Robert van der Linden
Curator of Air Transportation

Smithsonian National Air and Space Museum
AIRPLANES
BOEING COMPANY

Eugene Van Sickle
Associate Professor of History
University of North Georgia
AFRICA SQUADRON

Jennifer Van Vleck
Assistant Professor of History
Yale University
PAN AMERICAN WORLD AIRWAYS

Cyrus Veeser
Professor of History
Bentley University
DOLLAR DIPLOMACY

Timothy Verhoeven
Senior Lecturer, School of Philosophical, Historical, and International Studies
Monash University, Australia
AMERICAN PROTECTIVE ASSOCIATION
KNOW-NOTHINGS
NATIVISM

Joseph Vogel
Instructor
University of Rochester
JACKSON, MICHAEL

Steven Volk
Professor of History
Oberlin College
ALLENDE, SALVADOR

Michael Wala
Professor of North American History
Ruhr-Universität Bochum
RUSSIA

Dustin Walcher
Associate Professor and Chair, Department of History and Political Science
Southern Oregon University
INTERNATIONAL MONETARY FUND

Jeffrey Wasserstrom
Professor of History
University of California, Irvine
BOXER REBELLION

Kaylin Haverstock Weber
Assistant Curator, American Painting and Sculpture
The Museum of Fine Arts, Houston
WEST, BENJAMIN

William E. Weeks
Lecturer in History
San Diego State University
ADAMS-ONÍS TREATY (1819)

Gerhard L. Weinberg
William Rand Kenan, Jr., Professor of History Emeritus
University of North Carolina at Chapel Hill
WORLD WAR II

Mark Whalan
Robert D. and Eve E. Horn Professor of English
University of Oregon
LOST GENERATION

Cameron White
Researcher
University of Technology, Sydney
MARLBORO

George White, Jr.
Associate Professor of History and Chair, Department of History & Philosophy
York College, CUNY
COLD WAR: RACE AND THE COLD WAR

F. Hugh Wilford
Professor of History
California State University, Long Beach
CENTRAL INTELLIGENCE AGENCY (CIA)

Fanon Che Wilkins
Associate Professor of African American History and Culture
Graduate School of Global Studies, Doshisha University
BANDUNG CONFERENCE (1955)
STUDENT NONVIOLENT COORDINATING COMMITTEE (SNCC)

Jamie J. Wilson
Professor, African American and Modern United States History
Salem State University
MALCOLM X

Diane Winston
Knight Chair in Media and Religion, Annenberg School for Communication and Journalism
University of Southern California
SALVATION ARMY

Audra J. Wolfe
Philadelphia, Pennsylvania
ATOMIC BOMB
MANHATTAN PROJECT
"J. ROBERT OPPENHEIMER" *(SIDEBAR TO MANHATTAN PROJECT)*

Robert S. Wolff
Professor of History
Central Connecticut State University
AMISTAD

Christian Wolmar
London, United Kingdom
TRAINS
TRANS-SIBERIAN RAILWAY

Wendy H. Wong
Research Associate
McNeil Center for Early American Studies
EMBARGO ACT (1807)

Amy Wood
Associate Professor of History
Illinois State University
LYNCHING

Molly Wood
Professor of History
Wittenberg University
DEPARTMENT OF STATE

Nicholas P. Wood
Cassius Marcellus Clay Postdoctoral Associate
Yale University
ACT PROHIBITING IMPORTATION OF SLAVES (1807)

Randall B. Woods
Distinguished Professor, John A. Cooper Professor of History
University of Arkansas
FULBRIGHT, J. WILLIAM

David R. Woodward
Emeritus Professor
Marshall University
PERSHING, JOHN JOSEPH

Ben Wright
Assistant Professor of History
University of Texas at Dallas
EMANCIPATION DAY

Yujin Yaguchi
Professor
The University of Tokyo
PEARL HARBOR

Grace I. Yeh
Associate Professor of Ethnic Studies
California Polytechnic State University, San Luis Obispo
ANGEL ISLAND

Kariann Akemi Yokota
Associate Professor
University of Colorado Denver
ASIA
CANTON

Mari Yoshihara
Professor of American Studies
University of Hawai'i
ORIENTALISM

Elliott Young
Professor of History
Lewis & Clark College
BORDERLANDS
COOLIES

G. Pascal Zachary
Professor of Practice
Arizona State University
BUSH, VANNEVAR

Rosemarie Zagarri
University Professor and Professor of History
George Mason University
LAW, THOMAS

Thomas W. Zeiler
Professor of History
University of Colorado Boulder
EXPORTS, EXPORTATION
GLOBALIZATION
RUSK, DEAN
THE WORLD IS FLAT (THOMAS L. FRIEDMAN, 2005)
WORLD TRADE ORGANIZATION

Frank Zelko
Associate Professor, History and Environmental Studies
University of Vermont
GREENPEACE

David B. Zierler
Office of the Historian
US Department of State
OZONE DEPLETION

Kenyon Zimmer
Assistant Professor of History
University of Texas at Arlington
ANARCHISM

Topical and Thematic Outline of Contents

The following classification of articles, arranged thematically and by topic, offers an overview of the wide variety of subjects treated in this set. Ideally, this feature will facilitate a kind of browsing that invites the reader to discover additional articles, related perhaps tangentially to those originally sought. (Please see also the specific lists of related entries that appear with each article, as well as the comprehensive subject index in volume 2.) Because the rubrics used here as section headings are not mutually exclusive, many entries are listed in more than one section below.

ATLANTIC WORLD

BIOGRAPHY

CIVIL RIGHTS

COLD WAR

COLONIALISM

DIPLOMACY AND INTERNATIONAL RELATIONS

ECONOMICS: BUSINESS, INDUSTRY, LABOR

ENVIRONMENT AND HEALTH

EXCEPTIONALISM

GENDER

GLOBALIZATION

HUMAN RIGHTS

IDEOLOGIES

IMMIGRATION

IMPERIALISM

LAW, LEGISLATION

MEDIA

MILITARY, DEFENSE, AND WARFARE

NATIVE AMERICANS

ORGANIZATIONS

PACIFIC WORLD

POLITICS AND POLITICAL THOUGHT: ORGANIZATIONS, EVENTS, AND IDEAS

PRESIDENTS

RACE

REGIONS

Africa

Asia

Caribbean

US GOVERNMENT AGENCIES

A

ABU GHRAIB

As early as March 2003, human rights activists raised questions about cruel and humiliating treatment of war captives by coalition forces, including US and British troops, operating in Iraq and Afghanistan (Umansky 2006). Such treatment of prisoners violates the Geneva Conventions as well as US and British official policies on combat and occupation. The accusations gained little attention until April 28, 2004, when CBS News aired a story on *60 Minutes II* that broke the news of prisoner torture by US troops at Baghdad's Abu Ghraib prison. The CBS report included graphic photographs showing naked prisoners in humiliating positions, some piled on top of each other, some hooded and wired with electrodes, with American soldiers posing in many of the scenes. That report was followed in two days by a *New Yorker* article written by Seymour Hersh (2004) with more details about torture and ill treatment at Abu Ghraib. Both CBS and Hersh relied on information generated by an investigation undertaken for the Pentagon by Major General Antonio Taguba (2004). That Pentagon report documented abuse and included accusations against individual soldiers, as well as a more broadly based indictment of military organizational and leadership failures that made the Abu Ghraib abuses possible.

In the wake of the *60 Minutes II* and *New Yorker* reports, the Abu Ghraib abuses became a scandal that dominated the news media around the world. By April 30, 2004, the image of a hooded figure balancing on a box with electrical wires running from the prisoner's hands and many others had been broadcast worldwide, including on the Arab satellite TV channels Al Jazeera and Al Arabiya. The papers in Baghdad chose not to publish these images as they were considered too offensive for the Muslim culture (Rajiva 2005).

International debate surrounding Abu Ghraib expanded beyond questions of alleged torture. Journalists, politicians, and activists speculated whether the abuse would heighten animosity against the United States among people in Muslim nations. Many also questioned whether the United States would lose its reputation as the defender of universal human rights. The United Kingdom's journalist for the *Guardian* newspaper, Luke Harding, reported that victims' family members suggested that the abuse would serve the interests of resistance against the occupation (Harding 2004). Other reporters for the *Guardian* observed that in the Middle East the scandal was portrayed as symbolic of American intentions towards the region (Whitaker, Goldenberg, and McCarthy 2004). The *Times* of London reporters quoted an Iraqi scientist generalizing Abu Ghraib abuse as "the American way of handling other humans" where standards of decency and morality were lacking (Watson and Loyd 2004). The newspaper also published testimony by Mr. Melik, a Sunni Muslim from Fallujah who was detained at Abu Ghraib, stating that the post-9/11 measures of the US government were based on the "rules of collective punishment" of all Muslims for the actions of a few who attacked the Twin Towers (Loyd and Hoyle 2004). Iran's state-run *Tehran Times* claimed that "the pictures of torture, brutality and sexual sadism are representative of the entire criminal operation being conducted in Iraq" (*Tehran Times* 2004).

The US government was aware of how damaging the Abu Ghraib scandal was to the reputation of the United States and its military. To minimize the effects of the scandal, the US government employed the rhetoric of investigation and transparency, proclaiming that torture and democracy cannot coexist. President George W. Bush stated that prisoner treatment at Abu Ghraib "does not reflect the nature of the American people" (Milbank 2004). However, US Department of Defense investigations (Independent Panel 2004; Jones and Fay 2004) revealed that the abuses were not limited to the actions of just a few low-ranking soldiers but were sanctioned from the highest ranks (Amann 2005).

Some scholars, such as Darius Rejali (2007), have pointed to a long history of torture carried out by democracies, including the history of American slavery. Military operations in French and British colonies made use of various physical torture techniques that induce pain without leaving visible signs, known as "clean techniques." Many of the torture techniques that came to light in Afghanistan and Iraq such as waterboarding, forced standing, sleep deprivation, or exposure to loud noise were used by modern democracies well before World War II; Rejali has argued that the use of clean techniques goes hand in hand with democracies because of public monitoring. That is, democracies are interested in hiding torture and making torture allegations less credible by avoiding leaving visible wounds (Kerrigan 2007).

As more incidents came to light, Abu Ghraib became the measuring stick by which later instances of abuse and torture would be evaluated. For example, when the media reported on members of the 3rd Battalion 1st Marine Regiment carrying out an alleged massacre in the town of Haditha in November 2005, the Abu Ghraib incident was used as evidentiary proof that the war on terror was producing human rights abuses and violations of international law (Schorr 2007). Some observers suggested that the Abu Ghraib scandal was indicative of prejudice against people from Middle Eastern and Muslim backgrounds, which increased after the September 11, 2001, attacks.

SEE ALSO *Bush, George W.; Cheney, Dick; War on Terror*

BIBLIOGRAPHY

Amann, Diane M. "Abu Ghraib." *University of Pennsylvania Law Review* 153, 6 (2005): 2083–141.

CBS News. "Abuse of Iraqi POWs by GIs Probed." *60 Minutes II*. April 28, 2004. http://www.cbsnews.com/news/abuse-of-iraqi-pows-by-gis-probed/

Harding, Luke. "Torture Commonplace, Say Inmates' Families." *Guardian*, May 2, 2004. http://www.theguardian.com/world/2004/may/03/iraq.usa2

Hersh, Seymour. "Torture at Abu Ghraib." *New Yorker*. Online version, April 30, 2004; print edition, May 10, 2004. http://www.newyorker.com/magazine/2004/05/10/torture-at-abu-ghraib

Jones, Anthony R., and George R. Fay. *Investigation of Intelligence Activities at Abu Ghraib*. (Fay Report.) US Army. August 23, 2004. http://www.au.af.mil/au/awc/awcgate/army/abu_ghraib_fay.pdf

Kerrigan, Michael. *The Instruments of Torture*. Rev. ed. Guilford, CT: Lyons Press, 2007.

Loyd, Anthony, and Ben Hoyle. "Search for Adventure that Ended in Death." *Times*, May 12, 2004.

Milbank, Dana. "U.S. Tries to Calm Furor Caused by Photos; Bush Vows Punishment for Abuse of Prisoners." *Washington Post*, May 1, 2004.

Rajiva, Lila. *The Language of Empire: Abu Ghraib and the American Media*. New York: Monthly Review Press, 2005.

Rejali, Darius M. *Torture and Democracy*. Princeton, NJ: Princeton University Press, 2007.

Schorr, Daniel. "War Crimes in Iraq: Haditha and Abu Ghraib." National Public Radio. September 2, 2007. http://www.npr.org/templates/story/story.php?storyId=14124158

Taguba, Antonio, Maj. Gen. "Article 15-6 Investigation of the 800th Military Police Brigade." (Taguba Report.) US Army. May 27, 2004. Available from Federation of American Scientists, www.fas.org/irp/agency/dod/taguba.pdf.

Umansky, Eric. "Failures of Imagination." *Columbia Journalism Review* 45, 3 (2006): 16–31.

US Department of Defense. *Final Report of the Independent Panel to Review DoD Detention Operations*. James R. Schlesinger, Chairman. August 2004. http://www.defense.gov/news/Aug2004/d20040824finalreport.pdf

"U.S. War Crimes: Torture of Iraqi Prisoners Exposed." *Tehran Times*, May 1, 2004.

Watson, Roland, and Anthony Loyd. "Bush Orders Punishment for Soldiers over Abuse." *Times*, May 4, 2004.

Whitaker, Brian, Suzanne Goldenberg, and Rory McCarthy. "Arab World Scorns Bush's TV 'Apology': Pressure Mounts in US over Iraq Torture Scandal." *Guardian*, May 3, 2004.

Ramune Braziunaite
Lecturer
School of Media and Communication
Bowling Green State University

ACQUIRED IMMUNODEFICIENCY SYNDROME (AIDS)

Acquired immunodeficiency syndrome (AIDS) is the cluster of end-stage disease symptoms caused by infection, often many years earlier, by the human immunodeficiency virus (HIV). The disease is now often called HIV/AIDS. The causative virus was traced by molecular biologists to have originated in equatorial Africa about 1910, when a virus that infected chimpanzees and monkeys gained the ability to infect human beings.

THE HISTORY OF THE DISEASE

In 1981, the first medical publications about the disease described unusual infections and cancer previously seen only in severely immunosuppressed patients, such as those undergoing organ transplants. By mid-1982, epidemiological evidence indicated that the disease was caused by a virus transmissible via sexual intercourse, transfusion of contaminated blood or blood products, and intravenous drug injections. Later, it was also determined that AIDS could be passed from mother to baby during delivery or in breast milk. In 1983 and 1984, groups of medical researchers in France and the United States identified a virus and demonstrated that it was the cause of this disease. They developed a blood test to identify those infected.

In 1987, a drug called AZT (azidothymidine) was approved as the first therapy that extended the lives of infected people somewhat. AZT and a few other drugs of similar chemical composition caused toxic side effects but were the only available therapies until 1996, when a cocktail of several drugs, now called ART for antiretroviral therapy, was introduced. ART proved highly effective in enabling those infected with HIV to resume normal lives, although they need to take ART daily for the rest of their lives. In the larger history of disease, medicine moved stunningly fast—in only fifteen years—to recognize a new disease, find its cause, and develop an effective therapy to permit those infected to return to normal lives.

THE NATIONAL RESPONSE TO THE EPIDEMIC

AIDS was first recognized in the gay communities of Los Angeles, San Francisco, and New York City in the United States, although it was soon identified in other countries and as an infection of both men and women. The initial link to male homosexuals, however, led to political and social discrimination against homosexuals. Some religious leaders alleged that AIDS was sent by God to punish homosexuals and the society that tolerated them. In contrast, other religious leaders established programs to care for AIDS patients.

In the political realm, the 1980s was a time of conservative economic and social ideas, and talk about a sexually transmitted disease was abhorrent to politicians. President Ronald Reagan (1911–2004) did not mention AIDS in public until September 1985, after his fellow actor Rock Hudson (1925–1985) had revealed in July that he was dying of AIDS. Hudson's death in October 1985 was the event that triggered the Reagan administration to support greater funding for research on AIDS. Reagan's surgeon general, C. Everett Koop (1916–2013), soon moved quickly to prepare a report, released in 1986, that informed the public about AIDS and how people could protect themselves from contracting it. In 1988, the US Congress funded a mailing to every household in the United States, *Understanding AIDS*. This mailing marked the first time the US government had attempted to contact every citizen with regard to a public health problem.

From the beginning of the epidemic, members of gay communities in the United States organized to care for those who became ill. In 1982, the Gay Men's Health Crisis (GMHC) was founded in New York, and shortly thereafter similar groups appeared in other cities. In 1983, AIDS activists met in Denver, Colorado, and issued the Denver Principles, which demanded that people suffering from AIDS not be called "victims" but rather "People with AIDS" (PWAs) and that PWAs be appointed to government and medical committees at every level when policy decisions about AIDS were being made. Never before had those with a disease self-identified as an interest group, but their example led many other disease-focused groups, such as those for breast cancer and spinal cord injury, to take similar action. Throughout the 1980s, AIDS activists also staged public protests demanding more money for research and care. They also launched the Names Project, which encouraged individuals to make quilt squares memorializing someone who died from AIDS. The squares were assembled into what became known as the AIDS Quilt.

Discrimination against hemophiliacs who had become infected with HIV from blood products used to control bleeding peaked in the late 1980s, when some parents and some school districts refused to let them attend school with uninfected students. The home of a Florida family was burned down after the county school board ruled in favor of permitting three infected hemophiliac brothers to attend school. The family had to leave the area. In 1985, the family of Ryan White (1971–1990) battled with Indiana school officials for permission for him to attend public school. Over the next five years, White and many celebrities joined forces to make public appearances to educate people about AIDS. In 1990, when White died, a number of AIDS charities were organized in his name, and the US Congress passed the Ryan White Comprehensive AIDS Resources Emergency (CARE) Act to provide better care for poor or uninsured AIDS patients.

African Americans suffered disproportionate HIV infection rates in the United States, largely for two reasons. First was the specter of the Tuskegee experiment, which made them suspicious of government health messages. Between 1932 and 1972, researchers in the US Public Health Service studied African American men infected with syphilis in Tuskegee, Alabama, but left them untreated in order to learn more about the disease's natural history. When penicillin was discovered as a cure for syphilis, these men were not treated, while white syphilitic patients received the new drug. The second reason was that the African American Christian church, which served as the authoritative vehicle for transmitting messages to the black community, strongly opposed homosexuality, and since AIDS was associated with homosexuality in the 1980s, it was simply not on the agendas of most churches. Denial of the need for safe-sex instruction sadly paved the way for HIV to become established in African American men and, since a sizable proportion of men who had sex with men also had sex with women, in their female partners.

THE INTERNATIONAL RESPONSE

Some governments worldwide took steps early in the epidemic to provide harm-reduction programs, such as needle exchanges to reduce HIV infection among injecting drug users, another population through which HIV infection spread rapidly. Other governments, including the United States, were slow to adopt needle exchanges, with the United States banning them until 2009. In 1996, the United Nations established UNAIDS (the Joint United Nations Programme on HIV/AIDS). UNAIDS, along with private philanthropic organizations, particularly the Bill and Melinda Gates Foundation and the US President's Emergency Plan for AIDS Relief (PEPFAR), launched in 2003 and expanded in 2008, provides major funding for AIDS prevention and treatment activities around the world. The challenge remains daunting, however. In 2013, thirty-five million people around the world were living with HIV infection, of whom 3.2 million were children under fifteen years old.

SEE ALSO *Clinton, William Jefferson; Reagan, Ronald Wilson*

BIBLIOGRAPHY

Harden, Victoria A. *AIDS at 30: A History.* Washington, DC: Potomac, 2012.

Joint United Nations Programme on HIV/AIDS (UNAIDS). *Global Report: UNAIDS Report on the Global AIDS Epidemic 2013.* Geneva, Switzerland: UNAIDS, 2013. http://www.unaids.org/en/resources/documents/2013/20130923_UNAIDS_Global_Report_2013

Piot, Peter. *No Time to Lose: A Life in Pursuit of Deadly Viruses.* New York: Norton, 2012.

Reverby, Susan M. *Examining Tuskegee: The Infamous Syphilis Study and Its Legacy.* Chapel Hill: University of North Carolina Press, 2009.

Victoria A. Harden
Founding Director, Emerita, Office of NIH History
US National Institutes of Health

ACT PROHIBITING IMPORTATION OF SLAVES (1807)

On March 2, 1807, President Thomas Jefferson (1743–1826) signed an Act to Prohibit the Importation of Slaves, banning the importation of enslaved Africans after January 1, 1808. Three weeks later, King George III (1738–1820) signed similar legislation, phasing out Britain's Atlantic slave trade between May 1, 1807, and March 1, 1808. These laws were relatively effective at ending slave importations into their respective dominions, but had much less effect on the scale of the slave trade in the rest of the Atlantic. Moreover, the failure to establish effective policies for mutually enforcing the laws hindered efforts to suppress the contraband slave trade to foreign nations.

EARLIER LAWS CURTAILING THE SLAVE TRADE

By 1807, most American participation in the Atlantic slave trade had already been outlawed through a combination of state and federal laws. Under the US Constitution, Congress could not prohibit the importation of enslaved Africans before 1808, but every state voluntarily prohibited the importation of slaves from abroad, at least temporarily. The state legislatures acted from a variety of motives. Pressure from abolitionists was often a decisive factor in northern states, where slavery was of relatively little economic importance (although New Englanders were prominent in the slave trade to other regions). States in the Upper South already had large enslaved populations that grew through natural reproduction; they banned slave imports while selling some of their slaves further south. Between 1787 and 1794, Georgia and South Carolina passed laws temporarily prohibiting slave imports out of fear of slave insurrection and in order to improve trade imbalances and facilitate the collection of taxes and other debts.

In 1794 and 1800, the federal government responded to antislavery lobbying by passing laws prohibiting American involvement in the foreign slave trade. These laws forbade Americans from having any involvement in transporting slaves to foreign places, such as the Caribbean. Therefore, after 1794, Americans were prohibited by state laws from importing slaves and by federal law from transporting slaves to foreign places. However, in December 1803, South Carolinians repealed their ban on slave imports. During the next four years, slave traders brought at least fifty thousand enslaved Africans into the state, many of whom they then sold into the newly acquired Louisiana Territory.

BRITISH EFFORTS TO END THE SLAVE TRADE

Britain, meanwhile, was the world's largest transporter of enslaved Africans, both to its own colonies and for sale to foreign territories. British abolitionists were more numerous than those in the United States, although they also faced more political opposition because of the British slave trade's greater economic importance. In 1792, the House of Commons passed a resolution calling for the abolition of the slave trade by 1796, but the House of Lords refused to support the measure. British abolitionists renewed their campaign in 1804, but the news that the Americans had resumed slave importations undermined such efforts. The slave trade's defenders argued that if the British withdrew from the trade, the United States and other nations would simply take over Britain's market share. Yet it was clear that public opinion in the United States opposed the slave trade and that Congress would abolish the trade once the US Constitution allowed it. British abolitionists pointed to the expectation of an American ban in 1808 and encouraged a "race of glory" between the nations to end the trade. This sense of national competition, and a massive antislavery petition campaign, encouraged Parliament to conform to the US Constitution's time frame for ending the Atlantic slave trade.

In the fall of 1806, British and American diplomats negotiated the Monroe-Pinkney Treaty, which included a provision laying a foundation for mutually enforcing each nation's future laws regarding the Atlantic slave trade. However, President Jefferson refused to submit the treaty for ratification because it did not satisfy his concerns about neutral shipping rights or the British Navy's practice of impressing sailors from American ships into service. In December 1806, Jefferson called on Congress to pass a slave-trade abolition law during its next session.

PROVISIONS AND ENFORCEMENT

In Congress, there was near consensus in favor of banning the importation of slaves, but sharp disagreements over specific provisions of the bill. Some northern congressmen advocated executing slave smugglers, but the final law limited punishments to forfeiture of the ship, fines of up to $20,000, and imprisonment for up to ten years. A few congressmen argued that African victims of slave smuggling should be sent back to Africa, and many northerners wanted the federal government to grant them their freedom within the United States. The final law conformed to the desires of southern politicians, allowing individual states to determine how to treat such Africans. In practice, this meant that southern states could confiscate the smuggled Africans as contraband and sell them as slaves. The domestic slave trade remained legal, but the law required that coastal vessels transporting slaves be forty tons or larger and keep a manifest identifying every slave on board, in order to prevent slave smuggling from Spanish Florida. Incentives to promote enforcement included granting informants and prosecutors a moiety of the fines collected from slave smugglers. The British law differed from the American one most significantly in its treatment of "recaptured" Africans confiscated from smugglers. The British law expressly forbade the government from treating them as slaves, but empowered the king to enlist them in the military or "apprentice" them as laborers for up to fourteen years. In contrast to the US Navy, the Royal Navy actively searched for slave smugglers in the Caribbean and along the African coast.

IMPLICATIONS FOR THE FUTURE OF SLAVERY

The American and British laws had diverging implications for the future of slavery based on demographic and political differences between the two nations. North America had generally been a minor market within the Atlantic slave trade, accounting for less than 500,000 of the more than ten million enslaved Africans whom slave traders brought to the Americas between 1500 and 1888 (when Brazil outlawed slavery). In sharp contrast to most Caribbean slave societies, the enslaved population of North America grew rapidly through natural increase. After 1808, American domestic slave traders facilitated slavery's expansion by transferring between one and three million enslaved African Americans from the Upper South to the Lower South and Southwest. Moreover, the 1807 act's provision allowing state governments to sell African victims of slave smuggling reinforced the legal legitimacy of slavery, while the federal nature of the American Union ensured that southern congressmen could block future efforts to end the domestic slave trade or slavery. The British Act of 1807, on the other hand, had greater antislavery implications. It significantly curbed the expansion of slavery in the British Caribbean and lent further popularity and political legitimacy to the abolitionist movement.

The 1807 laws proved quite effective at ending slave importations into the United States and the British Empire; however, the US law was much less effective at preventing involvement in the contraband trade to foreign territories, such as Cuba and Brazil. In such cases, the majority of illegal activity occurred on the coast of Africa or in the Caribbean, areas where the US Navy did not typically patrol. Congress passed revisions to the slave trade law in 1818, 1819, and 1820, transporting recaptured Africans back to Africa and declaring slave smuggling a form of piracy punishable by death, but the contraband foreign slave trade continued. The British sought to establish treaties with the United States allowing mutual enforcement of their respective laws, permitting the British Navy to board ships they suspected of smuggling slaves if they were flying an American flag. The United States resisted such proposals but agreed to establish its own Africa Squadron in 1842. Americans' opposition to a policy of mutual enforcement resulted mostly from their traditional hostility to British naval impressment and attacks on neutral trade. Nonetheless, the lack of international cooperation protected not only American slave smugglers but also foreigners who falsely flew American colors.

The two largest importers of slaves, the Portuguese and Spanish, began phasing out the slave trade in the 1820s in response to diplomatic pressure from Britain, but slave smuggling remained rampant, often under the American flag. Between 1808 and 1888, legal and illegal slave traders transported nearly three million enslaved Africans to the Americas, mostly to Cuba and Brazil. The American and British laws of 1807 began the international suppression of the Atlantic slave trade, but had little immediate effect on its scale.

SEE ALSO *Africa; Africa Squadron; American Colonization Society; Antislavery; Atlantic Slave Trade; Colonization Movement; Liberia*

BIBLIOGRAPHY

Eltis, David. "Was Abolition of the U.S. and British Slave Trade Significant in the Broader Context?" *William and Mary Quarterly* 66, 4 (2009): 717–736.

Mason, Matthew. "Keeping Up Appearances: The International Politics of Slave Trade Abolition in the Nineteenth-Century Atlantic World." *William and Mary Quarterly* 66, 4 (2009): 809–832.

Morgan, Kenneth. "Proscription by Degrees: The Ending of the African Slave Trade to the United States." In *An Ambiguous Anniversary: The Bicentennial of the International Slave Trade Bans,* edited by David T. Gleeson and Simon Lewis, 1–34. Columbia: University of South Carolina Press, 2012.

Nicholas P. Wood
Cassius Marcellus Clay Postdoctoral Associate
Yale University

ADAMS, JOHN

1735–1826

John Adams played a central role in early American foreign policy. He was the author of the Model Treaty (1776), represented the United States in Europe (1778–1788), secured a loan and commercial treaty with the United Netherlands (1782), and helped to negotiate the Definitive Treaty of Peace in which Great Britain acknowledged American independence (1783). Adams was the first American minister at the Court of St. James (1785–1788), and served as the Republic's first vice president (1789–1797) and second president (1797–1801). His term as president was almost wholly occupied with the Quasi-War with France. His loss in the presidential election of 1800 ended his public career but did not end his interest in foreign policy.

Adams served in the Continental Congress as a delegate from Massachusetts. In 1776 he penned the Model Treaty, or "Plan of Treaties," a blueprint for American foreign policy that called for a commercial treaty with France—but no military alliance—and obligated France to recognize the United States as the heir to all British and French territory in North America. In later years he would point to the Model Treaty as evidence that he had long envisioned "a system of neutrality" in which, ideally, the United States would form no military alliances with either Great Britain or France. For Adams, opposition to entangling alliances was not a timeless, idealistic principle based on Enlightenment philosophy but a measured response to the current rivalry between Great Britain and France. It would not be in American interests for either France or Britain to be destroyed, and so Adams understood that the United States might have to become involved. In the event that the United States would need to make such alliances, however, he did not treat these powers as interchangeable options. He believed that France was the "natural ally" and argued that, though the United States should be slow to make an alliance with France, it should be even more hesitant to ally with Great Britain. If France became "the Aggressor," however, the United States would need to resist her.

Adams had preferred that the United States avoid a military alliance with France, but American commissioners Benjamin Franklin, Arthur Lee (1740–1792), and Silas Deane (1737–1789) were unable to convince the French to sign a commercial treaty unless the United States also agreed to an alliance. When Adams arrived in France in 1778, the commissioners had already signed treaties with France. Adams returned to America in 1779 but soon set sail again for France, arriving in 1780. Adams quarreled with Charles Gravier, comte de Vergennes (1717–1787), over French conduct of the war, and in July he went to Holland, where he successfully negotiated both a loan and a commercial treaty in 1782. Adams then returned to France and joined the other commissioners in negotiating a peace treaty with Great Britain that was signed in 1783.

Adams signed commercial treaties with Prussia in 1785 and Morocco in 1787. While in London, Adams also met with Sidi Haji Abdrahaman, the ambassador of Tripoli. He would later, as president, sign the first American treaty with Tripoli in 1797. He was, however, unable to persuade Great Britain to sign a commercial treaty and eventually understood that a stronger central government was needed before the United States could form a unified trade policy. Adams asked for permission to retire and returned to the United States in 1788.

During his eight years as vice president, Adams had little direct impact on foreign policy. He did, however, think that he and Washington shared a similar view of the importance of neutrality. In his old age, Adams would claim that Washington's Farewell Address was based on the principles of neutrality he had learned from Adams.

When Adams became president he inherited strained relations with both France and Great Britain. The French Revolution had alienated many Americans, including Alexander Hamilton. The Jay Treaty, which Adams had supported, had eased tensions between the United States and Britain, but many Americans, including Thomas Jefferson, remained suspicious of Britain. The French used the Jay Treaty as an excuse to unleash attacks on American merchantmen. Adams had to face this crisis in foreign policy while dealing with a divided nation and a mediocre secretary of war, James McHenry (1753–1816), and secretary of state, Timothy Pickering (1745–1829). He did, however, have other advisors who were competent and trustworthy, such as his secretary of the navy, Benjamin Stoddert (1744–1813), and his son, minister to Berlin, John Quincy Adams.

Adams sent commissioners to negotiate with the French in 1797, but Charles Maurice de Talleyrand (1754–1838), the French minister, had his agents demand a bribe and a loan before talks could begin. This incident, known as the XYZ Affair, provoked outrage in the United States. Adams asked Congress to support measures such as improving coastal defenses, permitting merchant ships to arm, readying 80,000 militiamen, and continuing to build frigates. America's new frigate navy successfully countered the French privateers and insurance rates fell, permitting the profitable operation of the merchant marine.

Adams considered asking Congress for a declaration of war but decided against it, perhaps because he did not want his options to be constrained if Congress refused. As part of his struggle with the French, Adams cooperated with the British and with the Haitian revolutionary Toussaint Louverture (1743–1803), but he did not make formal treaties with them. Adams was not interested in a British offer to form a military alliance and seize Spanish possessions, and instead he authorized a second diplomatic mission to France. Talks eventually led to the Treaty of Mortefontaine in 1800.

In his retirement Adams continued to be interested in foreign policy. In a letter to Thomas Jefferson in 1812, Adams argued that without an American navy, "our Union will be a brittle China Vase, a house of Ice or a Palace of Glass." He blamed the War of 1812 on Republican neglect of the navy.

Adams's approach to foreign affairs can be summarized as a rejection of isolationism in favor of an independent foreign policy that rested on a small frigate navy, neutrality in European wars, and a prudent awareness of the balance of power in Europe.

SEE ALSO *Adams, John Quincy; Alien Act (1798); American Revolution; Franklin, Benjamin; Jay, John; Jefferson, Thomas; Naturalization Act of 1790; Washington, George; XYZ Affair*

BIBLIOGRAPHY

Adams, John, et al. *Microfilms of the Adams Papers.* Boston: Massachusetts Historical Society, 1954–1959.

DeConde, Alexander. *The Quasi-War: The Politics and Diplomacy of the Undeclared War with France 1797–1801.* New York: Scribner, 1966.

Elkins, Stanley M., and Eric L. McKitrick. *The Age of Federalism.* New York: Oxford University Press, 1993.

Ferling, John E. *John Adams: A Life.* Knoxville: University of Tennessee Press, 1992; New York: Oxford University Press, 2010.

Hutson, James H. *John Adams and the Diplomacy of the American Revolution.* Lexington: University Press of Kentucky, 1980.

Johnson, Ronald Angelo. *Diplomacy in Black and White: John Adams, Toussaint Louverture, and Their Atlantic World Alliance.* Athens: University of Georgia Press, 2014.

Stinchcombe, William C. *The XYZ Affair.* Westport, CT: Greenwood Press, 1980.

R. M. Barlow
PhD Candidate
University of Virginia

ADAMS, JOHN QUINCY

1767–1848

The life of John Quincy Adams, the leading American diplomat of the nineteenth century, spanned most of antebellum America. The eldest son of John and Abigail Adams, John Quincy was born in Braintree, Massachusetts. Brought to Europe in the midst of the American Revolution as his father's personal secretary, Adams was exposed to international politics and American policy making from an early age. When he returned to America for college, he was perhaps the most well-traveled American of the era. Entering the political fray with a series of newspaper articles defending the Washington administration, Adams was shortly thereafter appointed as the American minister to Holland at the age of twenty-seven. He worked in the foreign service under Presidents Washington, Adams, and Madison in a variety of diplomatic postings in Europe, before serving as secretary of state for eight years under James Monroe. Elected president in the controversial 1824 election, Adams served one term before being defeated by Andrew Jackson in

1828. After a brief retirement, he returned to Washington as a Massachusetts congressman, remaining in that post for the final seventeen years of his life. He suffered a cerebral hemorrhage and died on the floor of the House of Representatives. His career was so broad, and his influence so great, that Adams touched nearly every major event in early American history, and knew nearly every important individual.

THE LAUNCH OF A PUBLIC CAREER

Adams spent much of his adolescence overseas. When John Adams was appointed by the Continental Congress as American envoy to France and the Netherlands, John Quincy accompanied him. As a fourteen-year-old residing in Europe and fluent in French, he traveled to St. Petersburg for nearly three years as part of an American attempt to open official diplomatic relations with Russia. Returning to America, Adams attended Harvard, began a legal career, and took his first steps into the political arena. His early writings highlight his belief in the value of a strong navy, robust commerce, and reliable servicing of the national debt. They also contain the foundation of Adams's belief that America's republicanism stood in distinct opposition to the monarchies of the old world, and that America's mission extended far beyond the country's shores. He left unanswered whether that mission was intended to serve as a call to export America's revolution or just its republican principles of opposition to unjust and tyrannical regimes.

While practicing law in Boston, Adams formally launched his public career with a series of essays defending the Washington administration and laying out his developing approach to the country's foreign affairs. These essays, penned under the pseudonyms Publicola and Columbus, were written in response to the French Revolution and the resulting divide it caused in American politics. Adams focused on the value of neutrality in foreign affairs and defended President Washington's recall of the French minister Citizen Genêt in 1793. He asserted that European meddling in the internal affairs of the United States posed a great danger to America's independence. In an argument that would grow more robust as his diplomatic career advanced, Adams warned that America should take pains to avoid becoming overly involved in the internal politics or wars of Europe. He claimed that doing so would risk bringing America into regional conflicts, which could then justify European intervention in North America.

Shortly after these essays were published, and in large part because of them, George Washington appointed John Quincy Adams American minister to The Hague. Posted abroad from 1794 to 1801 in the Netherlands and Prussia, Adams served as America's eyes and ears on the European continent through the early phases of the Napoleonic Wars. There, Adams strengthened his desire to insulate America from the violent churn of European wars. He worried that America's republican form of government would not succeed if the North American continent became like the multipolar world of warring Europe, where vast armies were required and civil liberties suffered. In this context, isolation from European affairs meant further strengthening the United States' deterrent capabilities. Adams believed this would prevent further European encroachment in North America, and eventually allow the United States to replace the European powers as the hegemonic power on the North American continent.

John Quincy Adams. *Before serving as sixth president of the United States (1825–1829), Adams was an influential statesman who held a variety of diplomatic posts during the administrations of Washington, John Adams, and Madison. He was also Secretary of State during both terms of Monroe's presidency.*

STATE AND NATIONAL POLITICS

Recalled to America at the end of his father's presidency, John Quincy Adams resumed his legal career in Boston before entering first state and then national politics. Elected to the United States Senate in 1803, and arriving in Washington shortly after the vote was cast on the Louisiana Purchase, Adams publicly supported Jefferson's executive action. This upset Massachusetts politicians, who saw the acquisition of western territories as likely to undercut their political influence. He further angered his Federalist supporters by publicly siding with Jefferson after the British warship HMS *Leopard* attacked the USS *Chesapeake* in the summer of 1807 near Norfolk, Virginia. Considering this an affront to American honor and an attack on America's policy of neutral commerce, Adams helped draft an embargo against the British. This hit the New England shipping industry especially hard and infuriated his party. Resigning his senatorial seat as the Federalist-dominated Massachusetts legislature recalled him, Adams suffered in the short term but soon was rewarded by a newly elected James Madison, who appointed him American minister to Russia.

It was at this stage that Adams's diplomatic career began to shift into high gear. In Russia, during the final stages of the Napoleonic Wars, Adams promoted commercial trade between the nations and forged a close relationship with Czar Alexander I. When war broke out between the United States and Great Britain in 1812, Adams was appointed chairman of the American delegation to Ghent tasked with negotiating an end to hostilities with the British. After successfully concluding a peace treaty on Christmas Eve that helped preserve the prewar boundaries, Adams was named minister to Great Britain. Under Adams's guidance, the two nations pursued a rapprochement that was cemented with the Rush-Bagot Treaty of 1817, authorizing the demilitarization of the Great Lakes and Lake Champlain, and the Commercial Convention the following year.

When James Monroe was elected president in 1816, he named John Quincy Adams secretary of state. In this role Adams worked to push Spanish, Russian, and British interests out of, or nearly out of, North America and to project American power all the way to the Pacific. He concluded treaties with Great Britain, Spain, France, and Russia, managed relations with the new South American republics, and secured American borders in Florida. Responding to those who advocated armed intervention on behalf of Greek and South American independence, Adams cautioned restraint. Although he believed that the American Revolution, embodied in the principles of the Declaration of Independence, was the first ideology destined "to cover the surface of the globe," he also held that such interventions would accomplish little and might even hold back the cause of republicanism. In his most famous speech, Adams proclaimed on July 4, 1821, that "America goes not abroad in search of monsters to destroy." In his final year as secretary of state, Adams drafted the Monroe Doctrine, which asserted that henceforth the Western hemisphere was off-limits to European colonization efforts and affirmed America's commitment to refrain from interference in European affairs.

Adams was elected president in 1824 in a disputed election. He focused on promoting closer commercial relations with the South American republics. He supported Simon Bolívar's Pan-American Congress of Republics in Panama with the hopes of creating a prosperous hemisphere aligned in trade, defense, and ideological sympathy. An increasingly vocal and organized political opposition defeated this initiative, along with most of the Adams administration's other foreign and domestic policies. Although Adams had some diplomatic successes, they were largely overshadowed by his failure to acquire Texas, settle a boundary dispute between Maine and the British colony of New Brunswick, and gain most-favored-nation status in the British West Indies.

Defeated in his reelection bid of 1828, Adams was elected to the House of Representatives from Massachusetts in 1830 and held this post until his death in 1848. Adams was noted for his increasingly harsh attacks on slavery. Morally and strategically opposed to what he perceived as an expansionist foreign policy driven by the South's desire for acquiring new territories open to slavery, Adams fought against the annexation of Texas, the Mexican War, and the abandonment of claims to Oregon north of the 49th parallel.

Adams had one of the most broad-ranging careers of any American politician. In the 1790s he advocated neutrality in foreign policy. During the first two decades of the 1800s he pushed for continental and commercial expansion. During his presidency, he promoted an energetic and activist government. And in the 1830s and 1840s, he fiercely opposed slavery and its extension. But it is in foreign policy that Adams is best remembered. Although Adams was not successful in all stages of his career, historians generally agree that he was one of the greatest statesmen in American history and that his strategy for continental and hemispheric dominance shaped the official policy of the country for more than a century.

SEE ALSO *Adams-Onís Treaty (1819); Amistad; Antislavery; Monroe Doctrine (1823); Monroe, James*

BIBLIOGRAPHY

Bemis, Samuel Flagg. *John Quincy Adams and the Foundations of American Foreign Policy*. New York: Knopf, 1949; repr., Westport, CT: Greenwood, 1981.

Bemis, Samuel Flagg. *John Quincy Adams and the Union*. New York: Knopf, 1956; repr., Westport, CT: Greenwood, 1980.

Edel, Charles N. *Nation Builder: John Quincy Adams and the Grand Strategy of the Republic.* Cambridge, MA: Harvard University Press, 2014.

Hargreaves, Mary W. M. *The Presidency of John Quincy Adams.* Lawrence: University Press of Kansas, 1985.

Howe, Daniel Walker. *The Political Culture of the American Whigs.* Chicago: University of Chicago Press, 1979.

Lewis, James E., Jr. *John Quincy Adams: Policymaker for the Union.* Wilmington, DE: SR Books, 2001.

Nagel, Paul C. *John Quincy Adams: A Public Life, a Private Life.* New York: Knopf, 1997.

Parsons, Lynn Hudson. *John Quincy Adams.* Lanham, MD: Rowman and Littlefield, 2001.

Remini, Robert V. *John Quincy Adams.* New York: Times Books, 2002.

Richard, Leonard L. *The Life and Times of Congressman John Quincy Adams.* New York: Oxford University Press, 1986.

Sexton, Jay. *The Monroe Doctrine: Empire and Nation in Nineteenth-Century America.* New York: Hill and Wang, 2011.

Waldstreicher, David, ed. *A Companion to John Adams and John Quincy Adams.* Malden, MA: Wiley-Blackwell, 2013.

Weeks, William Earl. *John Quincy Adams and American Global Empire.* Lexington: University Press of Kentucky, 1992.

Charles Edel
Assistant Professor
Naval War College

ADAMS-ONÍS TREATY (1819)

The Adams-Onís Treaty of 1819, also known as the Transcontinental Treaty and the Florida Treaty, is one of the major territorial acquisition treaties in US history. The chief terms of the treaty, named for its principal negotiators, US secretary of state John Quincy Adams (1767–1848) and the Spanish minister to the United States, Don Luis de Onís (1762–1827), were the transfer of the Spanish provinces of East and West Florida to the United States and the demarcation of a transcontinental boundary between Spanish and US possessions. It finalized unresolved claims related to the Louisiana Purchase of 1803 and established the foundations of the controversies that led to the Mexican Cession, the region in the American Southwest that Mexico ceded to the United States in 1848.

The agreement arose out of a long-standing controversy between Spain and the United States over the legitimacy and dimensions of the Louisiana Purchase from France. The Spanish government first contested the legality of that agreement in 1804, claiming that under the terms of the retrocession of Louisiana to France in 1800, Louisiana could not be transferred. That position was eventually replaced by grudging recognition of the legality of the sale, but Spain aimed to restrict the Louisiana territory to an area bounded by the Mississippi River and to exclude the Floridas, effectively reducing the territory to a small area in the vicinity of New Orleans. Meanwhile, US leaders, led by Thomas Jefferson and James Madison, expanded the vague boundaries of Louisiana to include the province of Texas. Early talks to resolve these differences went nowhere; Napoleon's invasion of Spain in 1808 and US involvement in the War of 1812 delayed further negotiations until 1817.

Spain, with the expectation of British support, refused to alter its tough negotiating position, prompting President James Monroe (at Adams's urging) to act unilaterally. In December 1817, US forces seized Amelia Island in East Florida, just south of the Georgia border, using the pretext that the island had become a haven for pirates and runaway slaves outside of Spain's control. That same month, Andrew Jackson launched a punitive mission into East Florida. Officially justified as a mission to punish the Seminole Indians for cross-border forays into Georgia, it evolved into a full-scale invasion of East Florida that resulted in the seizure of the province from Spain and the execution of two British subjects in the province charged with instigating the Indians. Known as the First Seminole War, Jackson's campaign has been cited by John Lewis Gaddis (Gaddis 2004) as an early example of a preemptive strike against a rogue state.

Jackson's conquest of East Florida, done without explicit congressional or presidential authorization, proved controversial domestically but achieved the desired effect of forcing Spain to make concessions when the expected British support for Spain's position did not materialize. At this crucial moment in the talks, Monroe, concerned that Texas would be fertile ground for the expansion of slavery, directed Adams to sacrifice the long-standing US claim to the province of Texas in exchange for a transcontinental boundary line extending to the Pacific Ocean. The United States also agreed to assume $5 million in claims of its citizens against the Spanish government. The treaty was signed on February 22, 1819, but its final US ratification was delayed until 1821 because of a controversy over the legitimacy of Spanish land grants in Florida. Although the treaty was initially well received by Americans, the abandonment of the Texas claim would later lead proslavery expansionists to call for the "reannexation" of Texas.

SEE ALSO *Adams, John Quincy; Jackson, Andrew; Louisiana Purchase; North America*

BIBLIOGRAPHY

Gaddis, John Lewis. *Surprise, Security, and the American Experience.* Cambridge, MA: Harvard University Press, 2004.

Stagg, J. C. A. *Borderlines in Borderlands: James Madison and the Spanish-American Frontier, 1776-1821.* New Haven, CT: Yale University Press, 2009.

Weeks, William Earl. *John Quincy Adams and American Global Empire.* Lexington: University of Kentucky Press, 1992.

Wright, J. Leitch, Jr. *Creeks and Seminoles: The Destruction and Regeneration of the Muscogulge People.* Lincoln: University of Nebraska Press, 1990.

William E. Weeks
Lecturer in History
San Diego State University

ADDAMS, JANE
1860–1935

Jane Addams was an American social reformer, author, and peace activist. In 1931, she received the Nobel Peace Prize for her work toward international peace. This honor resulted from more than forty years of engagement with international and transnational humanitarian efforts.

Addams was immersed in international contexts from the beginning of her adult life. In the 1880s, she took two European tours, studying languages, history, and culture. In 1888, she visited Toynbee Hall and the People's Palace in London. After founding Hull House in Chicago in 1889, Addams quickly became a pivotal figure in international social reform movements. Traveling to Europe in 1896, 1900, and 1913, she exchanged ideas on social reforms in labor, education, and housing with leading British social reformers, including Henrietta and Samuel Barnett, Beatrice and Sidney Webb, Margaret and J. Ramsay MacDonald, Kier Hardie, and John Burns. She also visited the writer Leo Tolstoy in Russia. Addams lectured at and served as a juror for the Social Economy exhibit at the 1900 Paris Exposition and attended the 1913 International Woman Suffrage Alliance Congress in Budapest.

Hull House was a site of continuous cross-cultural and cross-national exchange. International visitors included British social reformers, as well as Austrian pacifist and author Bertha von Suttner, Russian scientist and anarchist Peter Kropotkin, Czech philosopher and statesman Tomáš Masaryk, and Indian poet and political activist Sarojini Naidu. Addams was fascinated by the mix of cultures in her Chicago neighborhood, made up primarily of immigrants from southern and eastern Europe. Her ideas on how to work toward international understanding were derived from working with her multiethnic neighbors on labor issues, municipal reforms, and child and immigrant protection measures. Addams's underlying question for proposed social reforms was whether they would lead to increased tolerance and appreciation for differences and provide opportunities for cross-class, cross-cultural, and cross-national cooperation. Living in Hull House's immigrant community led her to envision the United States as a cosmopolitan nation whose citizens were intimately linked with other nations throughout the world.

With the beginning of World War I in 1914, Addams's primary focus turned toward international peace. She presided over the April 1915 International Congress of Women at The Hague, attended by women from the Central Powers, the Triple Entente, and neutral nations. She formed enduring friendships with feminists, pacifists, and reformers from across Europe, including Lida Heymann, Anita Augsburg, Rosika Schwimmer, and Aletta Jacobs. Immediately following the conference, Addams brought the congress's proposal for continuous mediation to heads of state and foreign ministers on both sides of the belligerency and neutral nations. The congress, renamed the Women's International League for Peace and Freedom (WILPF), met in Zurich during the time of the Paris Peace Conference in 1919. WILPF's criticisms of the Paris Peace Treaties were the first of what became standard critiques. Following the war, Addams worked with many relief organizations, including the International Red Cross, the American Relief Administration, and the Society of Friends, to bring food and provisions to people across Europe, the Near East, and Russia. She also served on the American Commission on Conditions in Ireland.

Addams served as international president of WILPF until 1929. The organization quickly expanded to include chapters around the globe, and by functioning within networks of international organizations, helped create a global community of social justice activists. Addams traveled to Europe frequently during the 1920s and embarked on a world tour in 1923, meeting with WILPF chapters, women's organizations, and government officials in countries throughout southern and eastern Asia. She presided over many international conferences, including WILPF biennial congresses, the Conference for a New Peace at The Hague in 1922, and the Pan-Pacific Women's Conference in Hawaii in 1928.

Addams's international connections are reflected in her vast international correspondence. Her proposals for social reform frequently drew examples from Germany, France, Great Britain, New Zealand, and countries in the Far East. With fellow pragmatists William James and John Dewey, Addams shared commitments to testing ideas in concrete experience and to stepwise reform based on widespread, democratic participation. Hers can be called a transnational pragmatism, as its scope was explicitly international and cross-cultural. Her concept of social democracy was based on a vision of universal humanitarianism, drawn in part from Giuseppe

Mazzini's concept of expanding circles of affiliation from family, to nation, and out to all of humanity, and from evolutionary versions by philosopher Edward Caird, psychologist Wilhelm Wundt, and sociologist L. T. Hobhouse. Addams's pacifism was based on her observation that violence increased hatred, set back humanitarian social reform efforts, and made universal comity more difficult to achieve. She reinforced her pacifist stance with the claims of evolutionary biologists such as Georg Friedrich Nicolai and Peter Kropotkin that cooperation had a stronger historical lineage than strife. Addams's ten books, hundreds of articles, and thousands of speeches reflect her many international contacts, extensive reading, and deep engagement with global issues.

SEE ALSO *Feminism, Women's Rights; Great Depression; Immigration; Settlement House Movement; Suffrage; World War I*

BIBLIOGRAPHY

Addams, Jane. *Newer Ideals of Peace.* Urbana: University of Illinois Press, 2007. First published 1907.

Addams, Jane. *Peace and Bread in Time of War.* Urbana: University of Illinois Press, 2002. First published 1922.

Knight, Louise W. *Jane Addams: Spirit in Action.* New York: Norton, 2010.

Patterson, David S. *The Search for Negotiated Peace: Women's Activism and Citizen Diplomacy in World War I.* New York: Routledge, 2008.

Marilyn Fischer
Professor of Philosophy
University of Dayton

ADVANCED RESEARCH PROJECTS AGENCY NETWORK (ARPANET)

SEE *Internet.*

ADVERTISING AND MARKETING

Advertising and marketing have influenced both how US consumers view the rest of the world and how those outside of the United States view Americans. Stereotyped brand symbols, war propaganda, tourism advertising, nation branding, commercial gender norms, and trends in globalization all play roles in affecting how people may understand other cultures.

EARLY BRAND ADVERTISING

Early brand advertising in US magazines and newspapers of the late 1800s used stereotypical images of other cultures to exoticize their products, using, for example, orientalist icons of the Middle East such as colorfully adorned sheiks and harems to sell cigarettes. The cigarette brand Camel has its roots in such Eastern iconography. On World War I war propaganda posters, the Committee on Public Information, staffed by personnel from the advertising industry, created jingoistic images of Germans as sexually violent murderers and beasts. Similar tactics were used in World War II, adding racist images of the Japanese. Later, other advertising personifications including the Frito Bandito (a stereotype of a Mexican bandit) and the Swedish Bikini Team (for Old Milwaukee beer) featured crude national stereotypes as a way to sell US brands.

Similarly, early US brands that used racialized images from the post–Civil War South—such as Cream of Wheat and Aunt Jemima—were prominently featured at the World's Columbian Exposition in Chicago in 1893. The linkage of these brands to such racialized characterizations may have influenced not just how US consumers saw African Americans but also how people abroad saw Americans, since these brands were sold in other nations.

Advertising for tourism products and services also regularly presented Americans with a world full of unusual others. Relying on tropes of exotic spaces and natives, advertising agencies presented the rest of the world as inherently different from Americans and the US. Ads for products such as cameras, cruise lines, and later airlines appearing in travel or international-themed magazines such as *National Geographic* and *Holiday* framed Americans' relationship to indigenous people in such tourism-based places as Singapore, Aruba, and Polynesia as subservient and inferior. Tourism advertising later became a central element in the public-diplomacy practice of "nation branding": a construction and management of a nation's image, often using marketing and promotional techniques. Nation-branding practices allow national governments to present themselves as desirable tourist destinations featuring imagined histories and as worthy of investment from transnational corporations. At the same time they reconstruct national identities based on the conceptions of social and political elites.

THE POST–WORLD WAR II ERA

After World War II, as US companies expanded their markets and visually oriented television became globally pervasive, international and eventually global advertising strategies spread images of the United States throughout

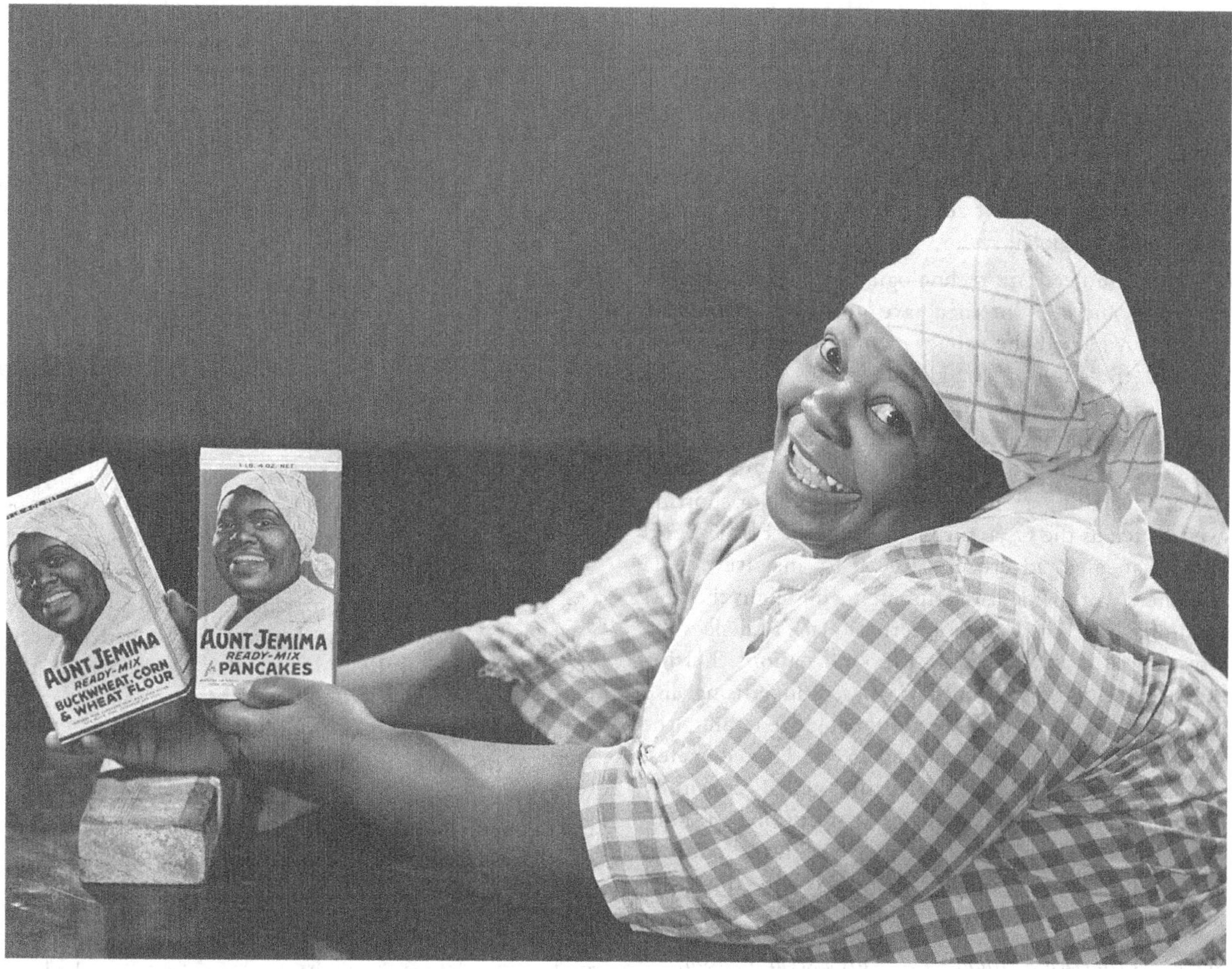

Anna Robinson, portrayer of the Aunt Jemima brand image. *Early US brands that used images of African Americans, such as Aunt Jemima, may have influenced not just how US consumers saw African Americans but also how people abroad, who purchased these products, saw Americans.* BETTMANN/CORBIS

the world. Arguably the most consistent message that global advertising conveyed was one of US consumer abundance and choice, seen in endless television commercials and magazine ads for such products as Coca-Cola, Kellogg's cereals, Procter & Gamble soaps, and US car brands such as GM. Collectively, advertising offered a world of endless consumer goods, a powerful symbolic force for the West during the Cold War. Coke's "Buy the World a Coke" television commercial in the 1970s (featuring the song "I'd Like to Teach the World to Sing") offered the brand as a global unifier. McDonald's linked its fast-food restaurant with fun and family solidarity and may have influenced how different cultures approached meals and other sociocultural practices.

The portrayal of Americans in modern advertising shown throughout the world has signaled rugged individualism and masculinity (such as the linkage of the United States with cowboys via the Marlboro Man), or youth culture, trendiness, and modernity. The visibility of Hollywood stars in global brand campaigns, and the marketing of movies featuring stars, has also constructed an image of the United States as glamorous and attractive. Beauty products and the use of white American models in many global advertising campaigns have perpetuated Westernized standards of beauty. These campaigns have led to a preponderance of light-skinned indigenous models for ads in regions such as Asia and to the popularity of skin-lightening products or other commodities promising the fulfillment of American beauty norms.

Conversely, in advertising in the United States, postwar international brands such as Volkswagen, Sony, or Foster's beer reinforced such nation-defining concepts as German engineering precision, Japanese inventiveness, or Australian unconventionality. Another major source of international images came through campaigns designed to encourage charitable giving for impoverished countries or regions, such as television commercials for the Christian Children's Fund. Such ads presented images of emaciated children in South America and Africa while often offering white Americans as saviors. US military recruitment advertising also created images of the US as a global savior.

Communication technologies such as satellite television and the Internet have greatly increased the flow and widened the venues of international advertising and the exposure of global brands. Social media encourage consumers to spread commercials virally across national borders by "sharing" or "liking" such commercials. Large-scale communication systems and global advertising agencies also facilitate major sporting events such as the Olympic Games and the FIFA World Cup that give advertisers access to massive media audiences worldwide. Advertisements highlight the host locations for local and international audiences in attempts to brand the host cities and nations. During the telecast of these events, US-based advertising also features images of non-Western people enjoying the same goods and services enjoyed in the United States, such as Coke and Visa. As this global consumer phenomenon shapes Americans' perceptions of non-Western peoples, it also influences Americans' conception of the United States and the role of US companies in the world.

SEE ALSO *Americanization; Cold War; Exceptionalism; Exports, Exportation; Industrialization; Internationalism; Isolationism; Navy, US; Orientalism; Vietnam War; War on Terror; World War I; World War II; World's Fairs*

BIBLIOGRAPHY

Aronczyk, Melissa. *Branding the Nation: The Global Business of National Identity.* New York: Oxford University Press, 2013.

Frith, Katherine T., and Barbara Mueller. *Advertising and Societies: Global Issues,* 2nd ed. New York: Peter Lang, 2010.

Jowett, Garth S., and Victoria O'Donnell. *Propaganda and Persuasion.* 5th ed. Thousand Oaks, CA: Sage, 2012.

Kern-Foxworth, Marilyn. *Aunt Jemima, Uncle Ben, and Rastus: Blacks in Advertising, Yesterday, Today, and Tomorrow.* Westport, CT: Greenwood, 1994.

McAllister, Matthew P. "Sponsorship, Globalization, and the Summer Olympics." In *Undressing the Ad: Reading Culture in Advertising,* edited by Katherine T. Frith, 35–63. New York: Peter Lang, 1997.

O'Barr, William M. *Culture and the Ad: Exploring Otherness in the World of Advertising.* Boulder, CO: Westview Press, 1994.

Popp, Richard K. *The Holiday Makers: Magazines, Advertising, and Mass Tourism in Postwar America.* Baton Rouge: Louisiana State University Press, 2012.

Swiger, Molly. "Sally Struthers, Christian Children's Fund, and the Construction of Whiteness." *Journal of American and Comparative Cultures* 25, 1–2 (March 2002): 199–208.

Matthew P. McAllister
Professor of Communications
The Pennsylvania State University

Tanner R. Cooke
PhD Candidate
The Pennsylvania State University

AFGHANISTAN

In *Moby Dick* (1851) Herman Melville makes a nineteenth-century connection between America and Afghanistan when he lays out the context for Ishmael's voyage: In the "grand programme of Providence" the "Whaling Voyage by One Ishmael" is wedged between "Grand Contested Election for the Presidency of the United States" (the 1840 defeat of Martin Van Buren by William Henry Harrison) and "BLOODY BATTLE IN AFFGANISTAN," referring to the First Anglo-Afghan War, from 1838 to 1842. Melville's bloody battle refers to the dramatic outbreak of the war and retreat from Kabul that left thousands of British citizens and soldiers dead.

EARLY PERCEPTIONS OF AFGHANISTAN

Early US perceptions of Afghanistan initially relied on accounts derived from such experiences of the British Empire in Hindustan and areas west. Some of the most famous British depictions of their defeat include the 1879 oil painting by Elizabeth Thompson (1846–1933), *Remnant of an Army,* and the 1843 memoir by Florentia Sale (1790–1853), *A Journal of the Disasters in Affghanistan.* Prior to the 1919 signing of the Anglo-Afghan Treaty of Rawalpindi under the Barakzai emir Amanullah Khan (1892–1960) that officially established the nation of Afghanistan, the region was more broadly known as Khorasan and came under the rule of a regional dynasty or ruler. The Treaty of Rawalpindi established Afghan independence and ended British subsidies, but British involvement reverted to patterns of commerce and currency that ultimately left Afghanistan economically marginalized. One of the few direct American-Afghan contacts from the nineteenth century involved Josiah Harlan (1799–1871), a Quaker from Chester County, Pennsylvania, who fought as a mercenary soldier for various Indian and Afghan rulers, including Ranjit Singh (1780–1839) and Dost Mohammed Khan (1793–1863).

The earliest contracts between Afghans and Americans were issued from the early twentieth century and at first involved US companies, experts, or educators. For example, from 1911 to 1919, under the direction of an American, A. C. Jewett, a former General Electric engineer, the emir Habibullah (1872–1919) built the nation's first hydroelectric power plant south of Kabul, and in 1936 the short-lived Inland Exploration Company was given a seventy-five-year right to explore Afghan oil fields. While Afghanistan did seek US recognition and economic collaboration, there was little active political interest in Afghanistan until it joined the League of Nations in 1934. At that point the United States and other nations officially recognized Afghanistan, and the first nonresident US minister to Afghanistan was assigned in 1935. The next year a US diplomatic visit to Afghanistan resulted in the first formal relationship between the two countries and a "treaty of friendship" in 1936. After World War II Afghans continued to see the United States favorably in part because of its anti-imperialist reputation, which seemed more amenable to Afghan self-determination. In 1943 Afghanistan established its first US embassy in New York and joined the United Nations in 1946, with a visit to the United States by the Afghan prime minister, Shah Mahmud Khan (1890–1959), following in August 1947. Americans came to live and work in Afghanistan after 1946 when the Afghan regime began the costly Helmand Valley Project, which was undertaken by the Idaho company Morrison Knudson. This initiated efforts to collaborate on economic, development, and education projects, although many of these ran into logistical trouble. In 1949 the Afghan minister for the economy went to Washington with an aid and development plan, but the project ultimately ran aground due to inadequate financing, manpower, and infrastructure.

COLD WAR DEVELOPMENTS

In the mid-twentieth century, Afghanistan's relationship with the United States was situated uncertainly between its own territorial conflict with the newly formed Pakistan (over the British Durand Line, which determined the border between the two countries) and the escalation of the Cold War between the United States and the Soviet Union. At the same time that Afghanistan became increasingly important in the region for the United States, it also resonated culturally for travelers as a stop on the so-called Hippie Trail, an overland route from Europe to Nepal—a popular tour in the 1960s and 1970s for those identifying with a counterculture informed by freedom of movement and thought and by recreational drugs (especially those specific to the region).

The Cold War set the stage for all contemporary interactions between the United States and Afghanistan. With mounting tensions, the United States and the Soviet Union provided Afghanistan with increasing levels of support. In 1965, for example, the United States and the Soviets provided millions of dollars in loans for Afghan development and infrastructure projects—the United States for the Herat-to-Islam Qala highway and both the Kunduz and Mazar-i-Sharif airports and the Soviets for the importation of consumer goods and food production technology. In 1979, an important year in Afghan history, US relations, and the Cold War, American ambassador Adolph Dubs (1920–1979) was killed in a rescue attempt by Afghan forces after he was taken hostage in Kabul, and American hostages were taken from the embassy in Tehran, Iran. Late in 1979 the Soviets invaded Afghanistan following the success of the Afghan communist party, the People's Democratic Party of Afghanistan (PDPA). The Soviet-Afghan War continued for a little over nine years (ending in 1989). The war was waged between the Soviet-backed PDPA and the Afghan mujahideen (Arabic for "those engaged in struggle"), who were heavily supported by the United States and Saudi Arabia as well as other nations such as Pakistan, although M. Hasan Kakar (2005) suggests that somewhere between one third and one half of the aid was rerouted as it came through Pakistan.

At first the mujahideen were united ideologically against the Soviet Union on the basis of Afghan self-determination and also their common resistance to the perceived atheism inherent in communism. The war resulted in millions of Afghans being killed, injured, and displaced and the infusion of foreign capital and weapons, including billions in US dollars to arm the resistance. President Ronald Reagan (1911–2004) met with representatives of the mujahideen in the White House in 1986 and famously identified them as "freedom fighters" (Coll 2005, 70). Supplying Stinger missiles to the mujahideen significantly impacted the course of the Soviet-Afghan War. According to Larry Goodson (2001), this shift in 1986, "provided the Mujahideen with credible air defense for the first time [and] … induced the Soviets to change their hitherto successful air war strategy" (68). At the end of the war US aid scaled down, though the fight for Kabul persisted even after withdrawal of the Soviets, who continued to aid Najibullah (1947–1996), the president of Afghanistan, in Kabul. The PDPA was defeated only when the United States and the Soviet Union agreed to end their covert funding.

During the war, places like Peshawar in Pakistan became a hub for international players concerned with the Afghan struggle—and for a growing international Islamist interest that also contributed to the rise of Osama bin Laden (1957–2011), who would later lead al-Qaeda's fight against the West. Following the decline of Western involvement in Afghanistan, the former mujahideen failed to agree on a power-sharing arrangement in constructing a new government. As a result, mujahideen factions fought each other in a civil war that involved numerous parties, including Ahmad Shah Massoud's (1953–2001) Shura-i Nazar, Burhanuddin Rabbani's (1940–2011) Jamiat-i Islami, and Gulbuddin Hekmatyar's (b. 1947) Hezb-i Islami. In an attempt to quell the violence and destruction that resulted in over 1.5 million Afghan casualities from decades of war, a group of Islamic students, issuing originally from Pakistani refugee camps, would come to form the Taliban, who took control in 1994 first of Kandahar and then of Kabul. The connections forged between the Taliban and international fighters would put Afghanistan at the center of the US war on terror following the September 11, 2001, attacks involving Pennsylvania, New York, and Washington, DC.

THE TWENTY-FIRST CENTURY WAR ON TERROR

In October 2001, George W. Bush (b. 1946) declared the start of Operation Enduring Freedom and identified the United States as engaged in an international "war on terror," centered on the Afghan Taliban and al-Qaeda but expanding in 2003 to include Iraq under Saddam Hussein (1937–2006). The US-led NATO forces began the offensive through a bombing campaign against Afghanistan on October 7, 2001, after the Taliban refused to hand over bin Laden, the primary suspect in the 9/11 attacks. The deployment of thousands of international troops followed, as did implementation of the Guantánamo Bay prison for terrorism suspects. The operation would last thirteen more years. As the Taliban were pushed back, NATO, the United States, and numerous international nongovernmental organizations (NGOs) engaged in active nation building and reconstruction projects with the Western-backed government of President Hamid Karzai (b. 1957). Overall casualties of Operation Enduring Freedom as of 2014 included over two thousand US soldiers (of the thirty-five hundred or so coalition deaths); twenty thousand Afghan civilians; over thirty thousand Afghan soldiers, security forces, and police officers; and between twenty thousand and thirty-five thousand Taliban soldiers.

Under the leadership of President Barack Obama (b. 1961), US policy in Afghanistan shifted. In 2009 Obama pronounced his effort to include Pakistan and the tribal areas in the Afghan theater as well as an initial surge of over thirty-four thousand troops, whose goal was to defeat the Taliban and transfer the security mission to the Afghan National Army. The inclusion of Pakistani tribal regions was coordinated with drone strikes on both sides of the Afghan border and other international areas of interest such as Yemen. During his first campaign Obama promised to close the Guantánamo Bay detention camp, but the transfer of prisoners proved difficult to effect. Obama renewed this stance during his second term, and from 2009 to 2014 the population of the camp decreased by over six hundred prisoners. The killing of bin Laden in 2011 by US forces in Abbottabad, Pakistan, further justified the subsequent troop drawdown, as did the election of Ashraf Ghani (b. 1949) in 2014.

The end of Operation Enduring Freedom was declared on December 28, 2014, by officials in Kabul and Washington. Obama and Secretary of Defense Chuck Hagel (b. 1946) issued statements ending the combat mission, ushering in a new phase in US-Afghan relations, Operation Freedom's Sentinel or OFS (the American component of NATO's Operation Resolute Support). This revised operation promised a smaller but continued international presence in Afghanistan to, in Hagel's words, "help secure and build upon the hard-fought gains of the last 13 years" (U.S. Department of Defense 2014). Approximately ninety-eight hundred troops and staff would remain in Afghanistan to carry out "training, advising and assisting Afghan security forces" and participate in counterterrorist missions (U.S. Department of Defense 2014).

In 2015 the intersection of other international forces and events such as the Arab revolutions, war in Syria, and threats from the group assuming the name Islamic State of Iraq and the Levant (ISIL), especially against the Iraqi army, have made complete withdrawal more tenuous. The controversies involving civilian deaths, prison abuses, enhanced interrogation and torture, and drone strikes have hurt the standing of the United States in many Muslim majority nations. Furthermore, the stability, economic autonomy, and overall security of Afghanistan have not been widely or definitively acknowledged, with some claims by the Taliban that it will once again gain control. Despite Afghan army troop declines—a decrease of 11 percent in 2014, according to Matthew Rosenberg and Azam Ahmed—John F. Campbell (b. 1957), OFS commander, asserted in 2015 that Afghan security forces could still overpower any Taliban gains, but the continued influence of al-Qaeda or possible rebranding of some Taliban under ISIL required a smaller troop withdrawal than originally planned. In addition to such immediate concerns are broader questions regarding the world's involvement in Afghanistan. As Shah Mahmoud Hanifi (2008) suggests, contemporary economic activities in Afghanistan have replicated British colonial patterns in the numerous development and NGO projects (such as the Kabul–Kandahar highway). Likewise, the infusion of international experts and foreign capital in the Afghan state budget have maintained Afghan dependence. Like the British in the nineteenth century, current international players have sustained Kabul as the center point of activity to the exclusion of other locations in Afghanistan. The war has also taken a toll on US servicemen and women, many of whom have returned with physical and mental wounds and who show well-documented increases in suicide rates. US-Afghan relations promise to continue their complicated course as tensions in the region shift and envelop earlier understandings of the combat and reconstruction missions.

SEE ALSO *Cold War; Self-Determination; United Nations; War on Terror; World War II*

BIBLIOGRAPHY

Adamec, Ludwig W. *Historical Dictionary of Afghanistan.* 4th ed. Lanham, MD: Scarecrow Press, 2012.

AP News Research Center Web Services. Afghanistan Causalities, January 15, 2015. http://nrcdata.ap.org/afghancasualties/default.aspx?username=casualty&password=2005battle

Aslam, Wali. "Drones and the Issue of Continuity in America's Pakistan Policy under Obama." In *Obama's Foreign Policy: Ending the War on Terror,* edited by Michelle Bentley and Jack Holland, 139–161. New York: Routledge, 2014.

BBC News Asia. "Afghanistan Taliban 'Confident of Victory' over NATO." Interview with John Simpson, January 16, 2014. http://www.bbc.com/news/world-asia-25765603

Clements, Frank. *Conflict in Afghanistan: A Historical Encyclopedia.* Santa Barbara, CA: ABC-CLIO, 2003.

Coll, Steve. *Ghost Wars: The Secret History of the CIA, Afghanistan, and Bin Laden, from the Soviet Invasion to September 10, 2001.* New York: Penguin, 2005.

Costs of War. "Afghanistan: At Least 21,000 Civilians Killed." Brown University's Watson Institute for International Studies, updated May 2014. http://costsofwar.org/article/afghan-civilians

Goodson, Larry P. *Afghanistan's Endless War: State Failure, Regional Politics, and the Rise of the Taliban.* Seattle: University of Washington Press, 2001.

Hanifi, Shah Mahmoud. *Connecting Histories in Afghanistan: Market Relations and State Formation on a Colonial Frontier.* New York: Columbia University Press, 2008.

Isani, Mukhtar Ali. "Melville and the 'Bloody Battle in Affghanistan.'" *American Quarterly* 20, 3 (Autumn 1968): 645–649.

Jewett, A. C., and Marjorie Jewett Bell. *An American Engineer in Afghanistan.* Minneapolis: University of Minnesota, 1948.

Kakar, M. Hasan. *Afghanistan: The Soviet Invasion and the Afghan Response, 1979–1982.* Berkeley: University of California Press, 1997.

Kepel, Gilles. *Jihad: The Trail of Political Islam.* 4th ed. London: I. B. Tauris, 2006.

Nordland, Rod. "War Deaths Top 13,000 in Afghan Security Forces." *New York Times,* March 3, 2014. http://www.nytimes.com/2014/03/04/world/asia/afghan-cabinet-releases-data-on-deaths-of-security-personnel.html

Pew Research Center: Global Attitudes and Trends. http://www.pewglobal.org/2014/07/14/chapter-1-the-american-brand/

Rashid, Ahmed. *Taliban: Militant Islam, Oil and Fundamentalism in Central Asia.* New Haven, CT: Yale University Press, 2001.

Roberts, Jeffery J. *The Origins of Conflict in Afghanistan.* Westport, CT: Praeger, 2003.

Rosenberg, Matthew, and Azam Ahmed. "Figures from U.S.-Led Coalition Show Heavy 2014 Losses for Afghan Army." *New York Times,* March 3, 2015. http://www.nytimes.com/2015/03/03/world/figures-from-us-led-coalition-show-heavy-2014-losses-for-afghan-army.html?_r=0

Sale, Lady Florentia. *A Journal of the Disasters in Affghanistan.* Franklin, TN: Tantallon Press, 2002.

U.S. Department of Defense. "Obama, Hagel Mark End of Operation Enduring Freedom." *DoD News,* December 28, 2014. http://www.defense.gov/news/newsarticle.aspx?id=123887

Zubeda Jalalzai
Department of English
Rhode Island College

AFL-CIO: LABOR'S FOREIGN POLICY

The American Federation of Labor (AFL), which has dominated the US labor movement since its founding in 1886, has had its own foreign policy since 1898. This continued after its merger in 1955 with the Congress of Industrial Organizations (CIO), creating the AFL-CIO, and it continues into the twenty-first century.

This foreign policy emerged as the United States began projecting its military power on other countries around the world, beginning in 1898 with the Spanish-American War in the Caribbean (Cuba and Puerto Rico) and the Pacific (Guam and the Philippines). American labor began operations in Mexico in 1915 during the Mexican Revolution (1910–1920).

Labor's foreign policy has always been determined by a very small number of highly placed labor leaders, beginning with Samuel Gompers (1850–1924), first president of the AFL. Accepting and projecting American nationalism, these leaders have supported the United States' efforts to dominate other countries, an undertaking collectively known as the US empire. These labor leaders have long thought that the United States *should* rule the world. Beginning foreign operations before the Bolshevik Revolution in October 1917, they used the threat of "communism" to justify their activities around the world, but these operations have continued beyond the fall of the Soviet Union and its empire.

This foreign policy is unknown to all but a few union members, and even most national labor leaders are unaware, so the policy is carried out behind their backs but in their names. Although previously thought to be driven by the US government or the Central Intelligence

Agency (CIA), American labor's foreign policy is now understood to have emerged from within the labor movement. And these leaders have strongly resisted any discussion of their foreign policy, even when approached through the formal procedures of the AFL-CIO.

The foreign policy leaders of the AFL and AFL-CIO have been directly involved in helping to overthrow democratically elected governments in such countries as Guatemala (1954), Brazil (1964), and Chile (1973), and indirectly involved in the attempted coup in Venezuela (2002). American labor leaders have also backed labor movements that supported dictatorships in the Philippines, South Korea, Indonesia, Zaire, South Africa, and, after their respective coups, Guatemala, Brazil, and Chile.

While those efforts have affected workers in those countries—each for the worse—it was when the AFL-CIO supported the US government in its war in Vietnam and elsewhere in Southeast Asia that it also specifically hurt Americans. Despite protest across US society and, over time, within some AFL-CIO unions, the AFL-CIO leadership steadfastly stood behind Presidents Lyndon Johnson (1908–1973) and Richard Nixon (1913–1994) in their brutal war against the Vietnamese, as they sent American working-class men into the maelstrom.

The AFL-CIO leadership, especially in the person of its president, Lane Kirkland (1922–1999), later worked with the Ronald Reagan (1911–2004) administration to create what is known as the National Endowment for Democracy (NED), a project of the US government, despite the repeated claim that it is independent. NED has worked vigorously since 1983 to impose top-down or "polyarchal" democracy on countries around the world whose governments or peoples refuse to passively accept US domination. Key components of NED include the National Democratic Institute (headed by former US secretary of state Madeleine Albright), the International Republican Institute (headed by US senator John McCain), the international wing of the US Chamber of Commerce, and the American Center for International Labor Solidarity (the Solidarity Center) of the AFL-CIO. The Solidarity Center, which has never given an honest accounting of its overseas activities, currently operates in over sixty countries.

American labor activists have discovered and have sought to end labor's foreign policy operations. Efforts to reform the AFL-CIO foreign policy program have had some successes. Most notable was the successful effort to keep the AFL-CIO leadership from endorsing the Reagan administration's apparent plan to invade Nicaragua in the mid-1980s. More recently, US Labor Against the War (USLAW) has mobilized about a quarter of the AFL-CIO's unions to oppose the organization's foreign policy in regard to Iraq and Afghanistan and its support of US militarism.

The leaders of the AFL-CIO have continued to support the US empire while governmental leaders within the United States have stood by and accepted, if not led, the attack against the union movement. This contradiction confronts the AFL-CIO foreign policy leadership, and will become more severe as escalating weaknesses in the US labor movement force it to seek global labor solidarity.

SEE ALSO *Cold War; Deindustrialization*

BIBLIOGRAPHY

Armstrong, Gregg. *Shoulder to Shoulder? The American Federation of Labor, the United States, and the Mexican Revolution, 1910–1924.* Berkeley: University of California Press, 1991.

Bass, G. Nelson. 2012. "Organized Labor and US Foreign Policy: The Solidarity Center in Historical Context." PhD diss., Department of Political Science, Florida International University, Miami. http://digitalcommons.fiu.edu/etd/752

Battista, Andrew. "Unions and Cold War Foreign Policy in the 1980s: The National Labor Committee, the AFL-CIO, and Central America." *Diplomatic History* 26, 3 (2002): 419–451.

Buhle, Paul. *Taking Care of Business: Samuel Gompers, George Meany, Lane Kirkland, and the Tragedy of American Labor.* New York: Monthly Review Press, 1999.

Carew, Anthony. "The American Labor Movement in Fizzland: The Free Trade Union Committee and the CIA." *Labor History* 39, 1 (1998): 25–42.

Cox, Ronald W., and G. Nelson Bass. "The Foreign Policy of Organized Labor in the Context of Globalization." In *Corporate Power and Globalization in US Foreign Policy*, edited by Ronald W. Cox, 69–78. New York: Routledge, 2012.

Filipelli, Ronald L. *American Labor and Postwar Italy, 1943–1953.* Stanford, CA: Stanford University Press, 1989.

Hirsch, Fred. *An Analysis of Our AFL-CIO Role in Latin America, or, Under the Covers with the CIA.* San Jose, CA: Self-published, 1974.

Lewis, Penny. *Hardhats, Hippies, and Hawks: The Vietnam Antiwar Movement in Myth and Memory.* Ithaca, NY: ILR Press, 2013.

Murolo, Priscilla, and A. B. Chitty. *From the Folks Who Brought You the Weekend: A Short, Illustrated History of Labor in the United States.* New York: New Press, 2001.

Scipes, Kim. "Labor's Foreign Policy: Its Origins with Samuel Gompers and the AFL." *Newsletter of International Labour Studies* 40–41 (1989): 4–20.

Scipes, Kim. *The AFL-CIO's Secret War against Developing Country Workers: Solidarity or Sabotage?* Lanham, MD: Lexington: 2010.

Scipes, Kim. "Why Labor Imperialism? AFL-CIO's Foreign Policy Leaders and the Developing World." *Working USA* 13, 4 (2010): 465–479.

Scipes, Kim. "Globalization from Below: Labor Activists Challenging the AFL-CIO Foreign Policy Program." *Critical Sociology* 38, 2 (2012): 303–323.

Scipes, Kim. "The Stealth Destabilizer: The National Endowment for Democracy in Venezuela." *Counterpunch,* February 28–March 2, 2014. www.counterpunch.org/2014/02/28/the-national-endowment-for-democracy-in-venezuela/

Shorrock, Tim. "Labor's Cold War: Freshly Unearthed Documents May Force the AFL-CIO to Face up to Past Betrayals." *The Nation,* May 19, 2002. www.thenation.com/article/labors-cold-war

Sims, Beth. *Workers of the World Undermined: American Labor's Role in US Foreign Policy.* Boston: South End Press, 1992.

Zweig, Michael. "Iraq and the Labor Movement: The Remarkable Story of USLAW." *New Labor Forum* 14, 3 (2005): 61–67.

Kim Scipes
Associate Professor of Sociology
Purdue University North Central, Westville, Indiana

AFRICA

Africa has always been conceptualized by Americans as a homogenous entity. This notion is traceable to media images and discussions of the continent as a monolithic big-game reserve rather than a plethora of cultures, ethnicities, and nationalities. The variety of national designations encompasses even larger diversities: for instance, Nigerians comprise groups like the Hausa, Igbo, Yoruba, Efik, and Ibibio just as Ghana is made up of Akan, Fante, Ewe, and other ethnic compositions that subscribe to different cultures and speak different languages. The composition of the African continent is as complex as its relations with the United States and the world.

Africa's relationship with the United States began with the establishment of British settlements in North America and the forceful transporting of Africans to these colonies through the Atlantic slave trade. In the aftermath of the international slave trade, the United States maintained a tangible connection with the African continent through the formation of Liberia, a colony created by the American Colonization Society in 1822 for the resettlement of free blacks from the United States. Another significant event that affected the American relationship with Africa was the Cold War between the United States and the Soviet Union, with each country seeking to spread its influence to various parts of the world to the other's exclusion. Since the dissolution of the Soviet entity in 1991 and the end of the Cold War, the United States has adopted several economic, political, diplomatic, and cultural policies toward Africa. In the face of the September 11, 2001, attacks on the United States and terrorist threats in Africa, the United States pursued a policy of militarization and intervention in the African continent. Africa, meanwhile, has left enduring social, cultural, and economic impressions on America through the presence of the old and new African diaspora in the United States.

EIGHTEENTH AND NINETEENTH CENTURIES

Following European conquest of the Americas in the sixteenth century, European powers, in search of labor supply for their colonial plantations, initiated the Atlantic slave trade. The first Africans to be imported into British North America arrived in Virginia Colony in 1619, launching the traffic that created the African diaspora in the Americas. This initial group of Africans were not considered slaves but indentured servants who eventually became free to acquire properties following the fulfillment of their contracts. By the 1640s, however, the use of blacks as indentured servants declined, and they were viewed instead as chattel, subject to perpetual servitude. Scholars have attributed this transition to slavery to mostly economic concerns. Freed indentured servants who acquired lands represented competition for resources, whereas enslaved persons were bound to their slave status and considered personal property. As a source of unpaid labor, they further allowed their owners to drop their obligations to indentured servants. Such economic rationalizations gave rise to various racial and scientific claims to justify the supposed inferiority of Africans and their enslavement. In 1641 Massachusetts became the first of the original thirteen colonies to make perpetual bondage of Africans legal, and the practice then spread to the other colonies.

From the mid-seventeenth century up to the abolition of the international slave trade in 1807, an estimated 472,000 Africans were forcefully transported across the Atlantic to the United States. Many captives died en route. The majority of these Africans came from regions in West and Central Africa, such as present-day Liberia, Sierra Leone, Nigeria, Cameroon, Ghana, Gabon, Togo, Benin, Ivory Coast, Burkina Faso, Senegal, Gambia, Republic of the Congo, and Angola. Although these various African peoples came from different cultures, their alienation from their ethnicities caused them to unite to forge new identities and cultural practices revolving around their belief systems, music, dance, arts, and other cultural elements. These cultural elements became part of American life.

By 1816, the foundations for US relations with Africa for most of the nineteenth century were taking shape. The American Colonization Society (ACS), founded by whites in 1816, established a new colony in Liberia with the aim of relocating freed African slaves to Africa. Some members of the ACS hoped that emancipated slaves would resettle in Africa rather than proliferate in American cities, seeking rights and resources, and some members did not regard the integration of free blacks into the American society as feasible. In 1822 the first group of free blacks was relocated to the colony of Liberia. Within the next five years, slave states' increasing interest in getting rid of their free black population led to the emergence of several other colonization societies, such as in Maryland, Virginia, and Mississippi, that were independent of the ACS and founded their own settlements in Liberia. By 1838, the settlers numbered about 20,000. During this period and until the First World War (1914–1918), US relations with Africa focused chiefly on Liberia.

During the nineteenth century missionary movements arose in the United States whose aim was to spread the Christian gospel to foreign lands, including Africa. Founded in 1810, the American Board of Commissioners for Foreign Missions (ABCFM) sent missionaries primarily to West and Southern Africa. By 1900, missionary organizations in the United States had multiplied and extended their evangelism into different parts of Africa, continuing through the twentieth century. Major denominations in the United States formed their own missionary groups. These individual missions accumulated large resource bases that enabled them to fund foreign missionary activities such as building programs for churches, hospitals, and orphanages. This rise in missionary expeditions to Africa was born partly out of the view that the United States owed some obligations to Africa for the slave trade, and that this liability could be fulfilled only through the sponsorship of missions and spread of Christianity and "civilization" in the continent.

FIRST AND SECOND WORLD WARS

During the First World War (1914–1918), US relations with Africa remained restricted to Liberia. Events during the interwar years and the onset of the Second World War (1939–1945) compelled a wider focus of US attention. The invasion of Ethiopia by Italy in October 1935 forced the US government to review its neutrality policies in international conflicts. Ethiopia, then the only independent African country besides Liberia, had a cultural significance for African Americans, some of whom joined in its defense. Notable among them was Hubert Julian (1897–1983), who helped train the Ethiopian air force and served as its commander. He was replaced in this capacity by another African American, John Robinson (1903–1954). Despite African Americans' agitations over the Italian invasion of Ethiopia, they failed to pressure Congress to enact neutrality legislation that favored Ethiopia. Thus Ethiopia remained isolated and its military surrendered to Italy in May 1936.

Upon its entry into World War II, the United States considered more seriously the strategic importance of Africa as a location for military bases, a sphere of influence, and a source of raw material. Realizing Liberia's strategic value as a center for military operations, it rebuilt Liberian infrastructure and signed a mutual defense agreement. The United States also recognized Ethiopia's bid to reassert its independence and in 1943 signed a Mutual Aid Agreement with Emperor Haile Selassie (1892–1975). In the same year, the United States set up a radio communication center in Eritrea, a territory whose status was still under negotiations among Ethiopia, Britain, and the United States. Tactical needs, rather than a desire for African independence, drove US policy in Africa as the United States fought to defeat Germany and its allies. With the commencement of the Cold War, successive US administrations took positions against several liberation struggles in Africa because of their concerns over communist influences on these movements.

THE CASE OF SOUTH AFRICA

President Harry Truman (in office 1945–1953) forged close ties with South Africa's apartheid regime. Despite anticipated criticism in the United Nations, the United States established an embassy in South Africa and desisted from voting on anti-apartheid measures. The two nations negotiated a Mutual Defense Assistance Pact, and the United States supplied South Africa with weapons estimated at over $100 million. In return, the United States received shipments of uranium worth more than $1 billion.

During the 1950s, however, following the headway made by the American civil rights movement against segregation and other state-sanctioned discrimination against African Americans, the US government changed its policy toward South Africa and voted in the United Nations against apartheid. Beginning in 1981, under the presidency of Ronald Reagan (1981–1989), the United States worked continuously to dismantle the apartheid regime. It also provided economic aid to Zimbabwe and Mozambique in order to maintain stability in the Southern African region. The Comprehensive Anti-Apartheid Act was passed in 1986, imposing tough sanctions on South Africa. In 1994 apartheid collapsed and the African National Congress, under the leadership of Nelson Mandela (1918–2013), assumed power.

THE COLD WAR

During the first term of President Dwight D. Eisenhower (in office 1953–1961), emerging African nations received no palpable support from the United States. The 2 percent of US aid that went to Africa was given to governments in North Africa or white-ruled African nations. During

Eisenhower's second term, US policy shifted following the realization of Africa's importance in the Cold War. In 1958 the State Department opened a Bureau of African Affairs and funded trips to Africa by African American athletes and musicians as a kind of cultural diplomacy.

The Cold War also drew US attention to events in the Congo. After Belgium's rapid evacuation of its colony in 1960, Patrice Lumumba (1925–1961) became Congo's first democratically elected leader. Faced with the outbreak of a rebellion in the mineral-rich Katanga, he appealed to the Soviets for help when the United Nations failed to provide him with resources to quell the rebellion. The United States, in an effort to block Soviet influence in Third World countries, made plans to dispose of Lumumba and support a pro-American, Colonel Joseph Mobutu (1930–1997). Lumumba was murdered by troops loyal to Mobutu on January 17, 1961.

US policy toward the Congo changed during the presidency of John F. Kennedy (1961–1963), who supported a United Nations campaign to end the Katanga rebellion. US policy changed again during the administration of Lyndon B. Johnson (1963–1969). In another Congo uprising led by former Lumumba supporters in 1964, the Johnson administration decided it could not risk the overthrow of the Congo government and the rise of a new government that it considered anti-American. Therefore it offered extensive military assistance to the government of Moise Tshombe (1919–1969).

As part of the effort to improve US-Africa relations, Kennedy created the Peace Corps on March 1, 1961, to help foster understanding of American culture among Third World nations and dismantle emerging nations' views of Americans as racists. The first groups of Peace Corps volunteers were sent to Ghana and Tanzania. The volunteers not only contributed to education but influenced lives outside the classroom through efforts geared toward social and economic development. Preceding the Peace Corps was Operation Crossroads Africa, a nongovernmental organization created in 1958 by a Presbyterian clergyman, James Herman Robinson (1907–1972).

With passage of the Fulbright-Hays Act of 1961 the US Congress reinforced the aims of the Fulbright program, instituted in 1946 by Senator J. William Fulbright (1905–1995) to promote mutual understanding between the United States and the rest of the world through educational and cultural exchange. Under the program, African professionals taught and conducted research in the United States for a specific period. The program also provided funds for US students, faculty, and professionals to study, teach, or conduct research abroad. US participants were empowered to partner with African host countries in building nonprofit organizations that promoted the program's core objectives.

On November 3, 1961, the United States Agency for International Development (USAID) was created to extend disaster and poverty relief, socioeconomic aid, and technical assistance to developing countries. In 1973 USAID objectives were adjusted to emphasize food and nutrition, population planning and health, education, and human resources development. In the early twenty-first century, the organization had forty-two stations in Africa. Its programs across the continent included the Feed the Future Initiative, geared toward agricultural productivity, and the Global Health Initiative, with emphasis on strengthening healthcare systems. It also offered assistance to African governments in their struggle for democracy, human rights, and good governance and promoted quick responses to humanitarian crises.

During the 1960s, in the scramble to gain spheres of influence in Africa, the United States became increasingly entangled in postindependence African conflicts. In 1966 the United States imposed an oil embargo on Southern Rhodesia; the British colony's white government, led by Ian Smith (1919–2007), had declared unilateral independence from Britain in the midst of deteriorating race relations between the white minority and the African majority. In 1971, however, the Defense Procurement Bill created an opportunity for the United States to violate sanctions against Smith's government and resume importation of Southern Rhodesian chrome, a product that the United States historically imported from the country.

A major conflict in Africa that the United States became involved in was the Nigerian Civil War of 1967 to 1970, a war between the Nigerian government and secessionist Biafra. Both Johnson and his successor, President Richard M. Nixon (1969–1974), desisted from any major involvement in the war. Instead, Johnson's administration implemented an arms embargo on the two warring camps. In 1968, however, media reports of widespread starvation in the Biafra camp forced Johnson to authorize official US support for relief efforts by the Red Cross and other organizations. The American public mobilized and sent significant donations and food supplies in aid of Biafra. Nixon continued Johnson's policy of noninterference but sought to play a more significant role in the conflict so as to maintain a good relationship with Nigeria and retain access to the country's huge oil reserves.

In 1975 Portuguese withdrawal from Angola sparked another civil war. Three groups—the Popular Movement for the Liberation of Angola (MPLA), the National Front for the Liberation of Angola (FNLA), and the National Union for the Total Independence of Angola (UNITA)—that had been engaged in the struggle for independence commenced a vicious struggle for power. Each group had foreign support—the MPLA from Cuba and the Soviet

Union, UNITA from South Africa, and the FNLA from the United States. Henry Kissinger, secretary of state under President Gerald R. Ford (1974–1977), considered this war a test of America's resolve to halt the spread of communism. When the US press reported in December 1975 that the government was spending about $36 million in Angola, an angry post-Vietnam Congress barred any further funding for the FNLA. By February 1976 the MPLA emerged victorious and declared the People's Republic of Angola.

To forestall other Soviet victories in Africa, the US government turned to Southern Rhodesia, where conflict was brewing between the white minority government and the African population. Secretary of State Kissinger anticipated that a settlement orchestrated by the United States would prevent any Soviet intervention, but he was not immediately successful, as the conflict raged on for another three years. In 1980 the government of President Jimmy Carter (1977–1981), in collaboration with Britain, achieved a settlement in Rhodesia that resulted in the creation of an independent Zimbabwe.

Carter also altered the US relationship with South Africa by terminating its nuclear collaboration with the Pretoria government and encouraging multilateral diplomacy for the resolution of the Namibia issue (Namibia was then under South Africa's control). US relations with Nigeria and Tanzania also improved tremendously during the Carter administration. Nonetheless, like most presidents during the Cold War, Carter could not escape the US-Soviet rivalry and was drawn into events in the Horn of Africa. In July 1977 Somalia, formerly supported by the Soviet Union, invaded Ethiopia in an attempt to establish control over Ogden. Historically, Ethiopia had been a major US ally, but after Selassie was dethroned in 1974 the country gravitated toward the Soviets. Carter, in attempts to maintain leverage in the Horn, assured Somalia of US support. However, because Somalia was the clear aggressor, the United States remained neutral while also warning Ethiopia to desist from invading Somalia. With Soviet and Cuban military assistance, Ethiopia defeated Somalia in January 1978.

POST–COLD WAR

In the post–Cold War era, the United States commenced a policy that granted assistance to democratic governments in Africa while withholding assistance from countries, even former allies, resisting democracy. The United States also led a United Nations–sanctioned intervention in Somalia in 1992–1993, deploying more than 25,000 troops to secure humanitarian assistance. In October 1993 a confrontation between US forces and Somali militia forces resulted in the deaths of eighteen US soldiers and US withdrawal from the country.

The Somalia incident had major ramifications for the US response to the Rwandan genocide of 1994. President Bill Clinton (1993–2001) issued a directive limiting future US interventions, including any significant involvement in Rwanda. The Department of Defense issued a position paper that reinforced Clinton's position and asserted that Africa was of minimal strategic importance to the United States. During the Liberian civil war, from 1989 to 1997, the US government refused any direct involvement in peacekeeping efforts. It also in some instances favored political stability even when counter to democracy, as in Burundi, where it supported the military regime of Pierre Buyoya, who seized power in 1996.

In line with a policy that favored regional resolution of conflicts, the United States proposed a bilateral training program that would groom African military forces and improve their capacity in peacekeeping and humanitarian assistance. This idea resulted in the formation of the African Crisis Response Initiative (ACRI) in 1996, later transformed into African Contingency Operations Training and Assistance (ACOTA) in 2004 with emphasis on offensive training.

TWENTY-FIRST CENTURY

The bombings of the US embassies in Kenya and Tanzania in August 1998 had sparked increasing concern about terrorism in Africa. But it was the September 11, 2001, terrorist attacks that led to massive military investments in the continent. ACOTA became a part of the United States' Global Peace Operations Initiative (GPOI) program. In 2007 the United Combatant Command for Africa (AFRICOM) and the African Coastal and Border Security Program were created to strengthen the global war on terror. The US Central Command (CENTCOM) created a joint task force in the Horn of Africa, targeting the extermination of terrorist activities in the volatile region. In North Africa the US Department of State launched the Pan-Sahel Initiative (PSI) and the Trans-Saharan Counter-Terrorism Initiative (TSCTI) to increase counterterrorism capacities in the region and neighboring areas.

US economic policies in Africa, and aid programs, have been varied. The African Growth and Opportunity Act (AGOA) was created toward the end of the Clinton administration to facilitate US trade and investment in Africa. The trade relations mostly involved US export of high-technology goods and machinery and import of oil, minerals, and other important natural resources required by US industries. In 2004, President Bush created the President's Emergency Plan for AIDS Relief (PEPFAR), a program that provided antiretroviral treatments for HIV/AIDs patients in Africa. PEPFAR partnered with various African countries to provide care, financial assistance, and policy reforms related to HIV/AIDS. It formed a core component of the Obama administration's Global Health Initiative (GHI). In 2011 USAID launched the Famine, War, and Drought (FWD) campaign, which raised awareness on that year's drought across East Africa. The Obama administration achieved a milestone in US-Africa relations by organizing a US-Africa Leaders Summit on August 4–6, 2014, the first time a US president invited all leaders of African nations, with the exception of Zimbabwe, Western Sahara, Central African Republic, and Eritrea, to a single event.

US relations with Africa also involved programs that encouraged the immigration of Africans to the United States, creating a new African diaspora. One of these is the Diversity Visa Lottery, implemented in 1995 and aimed at providing a certain number of permanent resident visas annually to countries with low immigration rates to the United States. Economic, social, and political conditions in Africa as well as wealth- and skill-selective US immigration policies generated the migration of skilled African labor to the United States. Thus the African diaspora has contributed to the economic development of the host country as well as to the countries of origin through remittances to the latter. The African diaspora in the United States has added to American cultural diversity.

The United Sates remains a strong actor in Africa through various educational, political, diplomatic, and cultural programs. US missionary organizations also remain active in various parts of the continent, such as Uganda and South Sudan. The US encounter with Africa, beginning with the era of the slave trade, continues to shape American culture and society.

SEE ALSO *Act Prohibiting Importation of Slaves (1807); American Colonization Society; Americanization; An Appeal to the Coloured Citizens of the World (David Walker, 1829); Antislavery; Atlantic Slave Trade; Back-to-Africa Movement; Berlin Conference (1884-1885); Colonization Movement; Ethnic Cleansing; Foreign Mission Movement; Genocide; Liberia; Moorish Science Temple; Nation of Islam; Race; Singer Manufacturing Company; Universal Negro Improvement Association (UNIA)*

BIBLIOGRAPHY

Berlin, Ira. *The Making of African America: The Four Great Migrations.* New York: Viking, 2010.

Conniff, Michael L., and Thomas J. Davis. *Africans in the Americas: A History of the Black Diaspora.* Caldwell, NJ: Blackburn Press, 2002.

DeRoche, Andrew. "Relations with Africa since 1900." In *A Companion to American Foreign Relations,* edited by Robert D. Schulzinger, 103–120. Malden, MA: Blackwell, 2003.

Falola, Toyin. *The African Diaspora: Slavery, Modernity, and Globalization.* Rochester, NY: University of Rochester Press, 2013.

Falola, Toyin, and Charles Thomas. *Securing Africa: Local Crises and Foreign Interventions.* New York: Routledge, 2014.

Fink, Carole. *Cold War: An International History.* Boulder, CO: Westview, 2014.

Jalloh, Alusine, and Toyin Falola, eds. *The United States and West Africa: Interactions and Relations.* Rochester, NY: University of Rochester Press, 2008.

Kikaya, David Kenda Adaka. "A Vulnerable Continent: Africa." In *Global Responses to Terrorism: 9/11, Afghanistan, and Beyond,* edited by Mary Buckley and Rick Fawn, 165–175. London and New York: Routledge, 2003.

Killingray, David. "The Black Atlantic Missionary Movement and Africa, 1780s–1920s." *Journal of Religion in Africa* 33, 1 (2003): 3–31.

Krenn, Michael L., ed. *Race and U.S. Foreign Policy during the Cold War.* New York: Garland, 1998.

Laqueur, Walter, and Brad Roberts, eds. *America in the World 1962–1987: A Strategic Political Reader.* New York: St. Martin's, 1987.

Lansing, Marion F., W. Linwood Chase, and Allan Nevins. *America in the World.* Boston: D.C. Heath, 1949.

Liang-Fenton, Debra, ed. *Implementing US Human Rights Policy.* Washington, DC: United States Institute of Peace Press, 2004.

Nwaubani, Ebere. *The United States and Decolonization in West Africa, 1950–1960.* Rochester, NY: University of Rochester Press, 2001.

Schraeder, Peter J. *United States Foreign Policy toward Africa: Incrementalism, Crisis, and Change.* Cambridge and New York: Cambridge University Press, 1994.

Skinner, Elliott P. *African Americans and U.S. Policy toward Africa, 1850–1924: In Defense of Black Nationality.* Washington, DC: Howard University Press, 1992.

Southall, Roger, and Henning Melber, eds. *A New Scramble for Africa? Imperialism, Investment, and Development.* Scottsville, South Africa: University of KwaZulu-Natal Press, 2009.

Toyin Falola

Jacob and Frances Sanger Mossiker Chair in the Humanities and University Distinguished Teaching Professor

University of Texas at Austin

Ogechukwu Ezekwem

PhD Candidate

University of Texas at Austin

AFRICA SQUADRON

The Africa Squadron of the United States Navy came into existence in 1842 as a result of the Webster-Ashburton Treaty, an agreement aimed at setting the northern boundary between the United States and British Canada. The treaty also formed the basis of an

Anglo-American effort to eliminate the illegal Atlantic slave trade. Articles eight and nine of the treaty specified that each nation establish a naval force to fight the slave trade. The squadron had a colorful but short lifespan existing from 1842 to 1861. The creation of the squadron was significant because the United States finally agreed to the cooperative patrolling of the Atlantic to stop the African slave trade, something Britain had been trying to get the United States to do for more than twenty years. The United States rejected previous efforts to build a bilateral cruising force because of concerns about national sovereignty. Even with the 1842 treaty, the United States continued to reject the right of search at sea that Britain sought as a tool in fighting the slave trade.

Article eight of the treaty, which created the squadron, stipulated that each nation deploy a force with no fewer than eighty guns. The actual unit dispatched by the United States in 1842 barely met the eighty-gun "rule"; only four ships—the frigate *Macedonian*, the brig *Porpoise*, and two sloops of war, the *Saratoga* and *Decatur*—made up the squadron. Though the primary purpose of the squadron was to work in "consultation and cooperation" with the British navy to eliminate the illegal slave trade, the squadron fulfilled a much larger role for the United States. Secretary of the Navy Abel P. Upshur (1791–1844) instructed the first commodore of the squadron, Matthew Calbraith Perry (1794–1858), to patrol for slavers as required by the agreement. Upshur also instructed Perry on a secondary but arguably more important mission to protect American commerce along the African coast. Commodore Perry's interpretation of his orders set important precedents for the squadron, for American relations in West Africa, particularly near the American colonies comprising Liberia, and for Perry's actions in Japan in 1853.

Commodore Perry was an appropriate choice for command of the Africa Squadron, having served as a junior officer on a Navy vessel assigned to escort the first colonists to Liberia in 1819. Liberia was also well situated to serve as a base for the squadron in patrolling for slave ships. Unfortunately, the squadron was generally unsuccessful as a brake on the slave trade during Commodore Perry's tenure. Perry plied Atlantic waters with a trusting eye, ignoring ships of other nations and looking only for slavers flying American colors. His interpretation of Upshur's orders, combined with the more common American attitude regarding sovereignty at sea, artificially annulled the potential effectiveness of the squadron in checking the slave trade. In comparison to its British counterpart, the Africa Squadron had virtually no impact on slave trading along the West African coast. The British squadron pursued slavers with significantly more vigor, indirectly providing the incentive for Liberian colonists to accelerate their move for independence in 1847. In contrast, the US Africa Squadron did not intercept its first slaver until March of 1844, the one and only slave ship taken while Perry commanded the fleet.

The Africa Squadron made its real mark in upholding Secretary Upshur's secondary directive by engaging in what is now described as *gunboat* diplomacy. While the squadron was en route to its station on the African coast, a number of attacks were carried out on American vessels; attackers plundered cargoes and murdered crew members from multiple vessels. Perry followed his directives in supporting American interests—in this case, commerce in the region. Perry specifically noted his intention to teach Africans a proper respect and "awe" for the American flag. He extracted treaties from African villages near the southeastern border of Maryland County, Liberia, and even leveled one village where he suspected the inhabitants had murdered American sailors from a trading vessel. By the time operations came to an end, Perry's squadron, along with its marines, had destroyed five towns and killed at least fifty Africans in the name of protecting commerce.

The Africa Squadron proved significantly more effective at combating slavery under later commodores. When compared to the other American squadrons patrolling the Atlantic Ocean, the Africa Squadron apprehended the most slave ships, nabbing thirty-six slavers between 1844 and June 14, 1861, when the squadron disbanded. Even so, the effect of the squadron in slowing the illegal slave trade was marginal at best.

SEE ALSO *Act Prohibiting Importation of Slaves (1807); American Colonization Society; Antislavery; Atlantic Ocean; Britain; Colonization Movement; Liberia*

BIBLIOGRAPHY

Barrow, Clayton R., Jr., ed. *America Spreads Her Sails: U.S. Seapower in the 19th Century*. Annapolis, MD: Naval Institute Press, 1973.

Canney, Donald L. *Africa Squadron: The U.S. Navy and the Slave Trade, 1842–1861*. Washington, DC: Potomac, 2006.

de Kay, James Tertius. *Chronicles of the Frigate Macedonian, 1809–1922*. New York: Norton, 1995.

Hall, Richard L. *On Afric's Shore: A History of Maryland in Liberia, 1834–1857*. Baltimore, MD: Maryland Historical Society, 2003.

Morison, Samuel Eliot. *"Old Bruin": Commodore Matthew C. Perry, 1794–1858: The American Naval Officer Who Helped Found Liberia*. Boston: Little, Brown, 1967.

Schroeder, John H. *Matthew Calbraith Perry: Antebellum Sailor and Diplomat*. Annapolis, MD: Naval Institute Press, 2001.

Van Sickle, Eugene S. "Reluctant Imperialists: The U.S. Navy and Liberia, 1819–1845." *Journal of the Early Republic* 31, 1 (2011): 107–134.

Webster-Ashburton Treaty. 1842. Office of the Historian, US Department of State. https://history.state.gov/milestones/1830-1860/webster-treaty

Eugene S. Van Sickle
Associate Professor of History
University of North Georgia

AGENT ORANGE

From 1961 to 1971, the United States and its allies sprayed nearly seventy-three million liters of chemical agents over 2.5 million acres of southern and central Vietnam to defoliate the landscape and limit the access of the National Liberation Front to local food supplies. About 62 percent—over 45 million liters—of the chemicals deployed consisted of Agent Orange, a 1:1 mixture of the herbicides 2,4-Dichlorophenoxyacetic acid (2,4-D) and 2,4,5-Trichlorophenoxyacetic acid (2,4,5-T). By the late 1960s, 2,4,5-T was known to contain often dangerous levels of dioxin, specifically 2,3,7,8-tetrachlorodibenzo-p-dioxin (TCDD), one of the most deadly toxins ever created. Agent Orange was one of several "rainbow herbicides" used by US forces during the Vietnam War. Along with Agents Blue, Pink, Purple, Green, and White, Agent Orange was named for the color-coded bands on the drums in which it was shipped.

Herbicidal warfare was first authorized by President John F. Kennedy (1917–1963) in November 1961 and expanded into Operation Ranch Hand in 1962. Although Kennedy intended the use of tactical herbicides as a substitute for US troops, the use of herbicides escalated proportionately after President Lyndon Johnson (1908–1973) introduced US ground forces in March 1965. Agent Orange was not introduced in Vietnam until 1965, but several other herbicides used in Vietnam prior to 1965 also contained 2,4,5-T and TCDD.

While intermittent reports of health concerns among civilians exposed to herbicides surfaced across southern Vietnam in the early 1960s, widespread concern about the potentially harmful effects of Agent Orange did not emerge until later in the decade. In 1966 and 1967, a series of studies documented the dangers of TCDD and 2,4,5-T, leading many scientists to call for an end to Operation Ranch Hand. The White House and Pentagon rejected the claims, but the Richard Nixon (1913–1994) administration eventually suspended the use of Agent Orange in April 1970, and ended Operation Ranch Hand in early 1971.

Several years after the Vietnam War ended, veterans in the United States and elsewhere began to raise concerns about the effects of exposure to Agent Orange. A class-action lawsuit filed against the manufacturers of Agent Orange in 1978 claimed that the herbicide was responsible for a variety of conditions, ranging from cancer to birth defects. The suit was settled in 1982, but neither the chemical companies nor the US government admitted that Agent Orange was responsible for the veterans' conditions. Long-term studies of veterans from multiple countries have also produced mixed results. Despite the lack of certainty about the effects of Agent Orange on veterans' health, the United States has greatly expanded service-related benefits since the 1980s. Veterans who served in Vietnam can receive benefits for fourteen different conditions without having to demonstrate that they were directly exposed to Agent Orange.

Investigations and lawsuits over Agent Orange have continued in New Zealand, South Korea, Canada, and elsewhere well into the twenty-first century, but the clearest demonstration of the long-term effects of 2,4,5-T and TCDD is in Vietnam. In the 1990s, scientists identified dozens of dioxin "hotspots" throughout the country, primarily at former US military sites. The dioxin levels at these sites remain at dangerous levels, leading to multigenerational effects on those born long after the war ended.

SEE ALSO *Johnson, Lyndon Baines; McNamara, Robert S.; Military-Industrial Complex; Vietnam War*

BIBLIOGRAPHY

Buckingham, William A., Jr. *Operation Ranch Hand: The Air Force and Herbicides in Southeast Asia, 1961–1971.* Washington, DC: US Air Force, Office of Air Force History, 1982.

Fox, Diane Niblack. "Agent Orange: Coming to Terms with a Transnational Legacy." In *Four Decades On: Vietnam, the United States, and the Legacies of the Second Indochina War*, edited by Scott Laderman and Edwin A. Martini, 207–241. Durham, NC: Duke University Press, 2013.

Martini, Edwin A. *Agent Orange: History, Science, and the Politics of Uncertainty.* Amherst: University of Massachusetts Press, 2012.

Scott, Wilbur J. *Vietnam Veterans since the War: The Politics of PTSD, Agent Orange, and the National Memorial.* Norman: University of Oklahoma Press, 2004.

Wilcox, Fred. *Scorched Earth: Legacies of Chemical Warfare in Vietnam.* New York: Seven Stories Press, 2011.

Young, Alvin L. *The History, Use, Disposition, and Environmental Fate of Agent Orange.* New York: Springer, 2009.

Zierler, David. *The Invention of Ecocide: Agent Orange, Vietnam, and the Scientists Who Changed the Way We Think about the Environment.* Athens: University of Georgia Press, 2012.

Edwin A. Martini
Professor of History
Western Michigan University

AIR FORCE, US

The United States Air Force is one of the three military branches of the armed forces of the United States and an organization within the US Department of Defense. Although officially created on September 18, 1947, as part of the National Security Act, the US Air Force traces its lineage back to August 1, 1907, when it was known as the Aeronautical Division of the US Army Signal Corps. The organization has grown tremendously over the last one hundred years, and its inventory and equipment have evolved from simple hot-air balloons to a fleet of the most sophisticated fighter and bomber aircraft in the world (Yenne 1984, 6).

EARLY YEARS

The US military first began venturing into the air during the American Civil War (1861–1865), when hot-air balloons were used by the Signal Corps for observation and directing artillery fire. Following the success of the first heavier-than-air flying machine invented by Orville Wright (1871–1948) and Wilbur Wright (1867–1912) in 1903, the Signal Corps established the Aeronautical Division on August 1, 1907, and tasked it with developing all forms of flying (Anderton 1981, 9–14). Shortly thereafter, the Signal Corps purchased a number of dirigible balloons and contracted with the Wright brothers for an airplane. The US Army became the world's first military organization to acquire an airplane when the Wrights delivered the plane, which officially entered service in August 1909 as Aeroplane Number 1 (Yenne 1984, 21–22; Budiansky 2004, 31).

On July 18, 1914, Congress awarded the US Army's air force official status by creating the Aviation Section of the Signal Corps. With America's entry into World War I (1914–1918) in April 1917, the United States began its first attempts to formulate an official doctrine of air warfare. Commanders, such as Brigadier General William "Billy" Mitchell (1879–1936), advocated both "strategic" operations deep inside Germany targeting industry and "tactical" operations designed to support Allied ground forces on the front lines. By the war's end, the United States had approximately 750 American aircraft in France and had developed the twelve-cylinder, 400-horsepower Liberty engine, which proved to be the most efficient aircraft engine of the conflict and America's most important technological contribution to the war effort. Although the airplane's primary role was reconnaissance and observation over enemy trenches, by the end of the war both sides were using planes to harass troops and drop bombs (Daso 2006, 52; McFarland 1997, 5–11).

WORLD WAR II

In the early 1930s, the recently renamed US Army Air Corps begin to put its resources into developing America's first strategic bombers. The long-range B-17 officially entered service in 1938 and was the most important American bomber in World War II (1939–1945). The aircraft was capable of flying at nearly 300 miles (483 kilometers) per hour with a range of approximately 800 miles (1,288 kilometers) and a payload of more than two tons of bombs. The B-17 reflected the strategic airpower doctrine that emerged in the 1930s, which emphasized the use of heavily armed long-range aircraft against enemy industrial targets (Anderton 1981, 40–42; McFarland 1997, 14).

US air power finally came into its own with the nation's entry into World War II. In June 1941, President Franklin D. Roosevelt (1882–1945) issued an executive order that changed the Air Corps to the US Army Air Forces (USAAF), thereby giving the United States an autonomous, if not fully independent, air arm (Yenne 1984, 26). In Europe, the United States worked very closely with the British Royal Air Force (RAF) on a strategic bombing offensive against Germany, primarily utilizing the B-17. In addition, USAAF fighters and tactical bombers targeted German planes and supported Allied ground operations in the European and Mediterranean theaters. In the Pacific, US bombers attacked Japanese cities using the new B-29 Superfortress—the largest airplane deployed in World War II. The B-29 could fly at over 350 miles (563 kilometers) per hour, had a range of 1,600 miles (2,575 kilometers) and could carry 15,000 pounds (6,804 kilograms) of bombs (Boot 2006, 282).

American air power grew tremendously during World War II. At the beginning of the conflict, the United States had about three thousand planes; by 1944, USAAF strength peaked at almost seventy-nine thousand aircraft, making it the largest air force in the world. The National Security Act of 1947 officially created the Department of the Air Force and gave the branch equal status with the Army and Navy (Yenne 1984, 7, 39–40). With the emergence of the Cold War, the new US Air Force (USAF) began to focus on a strategy of nuclear deterrence, and the development of a long-range bombing force was given top priority. The newly organized USAF established three major commands: the Strategic Air Command (SAC), the Air Defense Command (ADC), and the Tactical Air Command (TAC) (McFarland 1997, 40).

THE COLD WAR TO THE TWENTY-FIRST CENTURY

Upon entering the Oval Office in 1953, President Dwight D. Eisenhower (1890–1969) instituted the "New Look" defensive posture, which aimed at deterring a Soviet attack by targeting Russian cities with nuclear annihilation.

Toward this end, during the 1950s, the Eisenhower administration cut spending for conventional forces and increased America's nuclear deterrent. America's nuclear arsenal came to rely on the so-called "triad," which included new long-range strategic bombers, such as the B-52, along with intercontinental ballistic missiles (ICBMs) and submarine-launched ballistic missiles (SLBMs) (McFarland 1997, 50–57).

The United States' involvement in the Vietnam War from the 1960s through the early 1970s saw a big increase in the Air Forces' conventional capabilities, but nevertheless demonstrated its limitations when combating an insurgency. Although the United States would drop three times as many bombs over Southeast Asia as it had during the entire Second World War, victory remained elusive. As in the Korean conflict (1950–1953), US strategy was to wage a limited war aimed at punishing the enemy in an attempt to force them to the negotiating table (McFarland 1997, 59–60).

In the post–Cold War period, the USAF has had to adapt to a rapidly changing world. While the emphasis on strategic nuclear power has declined, conventional air power in support of ground operations has remained vitally important as demonstrated during conflicts in the Persian Gulf and the Balkans, and more recently in Iraq and Afghanistan. In the years to come, USAF technology will remain on the cutting edge through the development of better precision-guided bombs and munitions, along with increased use of unmanned drone aircraft for reconnaissance and direct-action strikes.

SEE ALSO *Cold War; Department of Defense, US; Nuclear Weapons; Rand Corporation*

BIBLIOGRAPHY

Anderton, David A. *The History of the U.S. Air Force.* New York: Crescent, 1981.

Boot, Max. *War Made New: Technology, Warfare, and the Course of History, 1500 to Today.* New York: Gotham, 2006.

Boyne, Walter J. *Beyond the Wild Blue: A History of the U.S. Air Force, 1947–1997.* New York: St. Martin's Press, 1998.

Budiansky, Stephen. *Air Power: The Men, Machines, and Ideas That Revolutionized War, from Kitty Hawk to Gulf War II.* New York: Penguin, 2004.

Daso, Dik Alan, and the Air Force Historical Foundation. *U.S. Air Force: A Complete History.* Westport, CT: Hugh Lauter Levin, 2006.

McFarland, Stephen L. *A Concise History of the United States Air Force.* Washington, DC: US Air Force, History and Museums Program, 1997.

Olsen, John Andreas. *A History of Air Warfare.* Washington, DC: Potomac, 2010.

US Air Force, Air Force Historical Studies Office. *Evolution of the Department of the Air Force.* US Air Force Fact Sheet, 2011. http://www.afhso.af.mil/afhistory/factsheets/factsheet.asp?id=15236

Yenne, Bill. *The History of the U.S. Air Force.* New York: Exeter, 1984.

Christos G. Frentzos
Associate Professor, Department of History
Austin Peay State University

AIRPLANES

On December 17, 1903, Orville (1871–1948) and Wilbur (1867–1912) Wright, two enterprising brothers from Dayton, Ohio, achieved the first sustained, controlled, heavier-than-air powered flight. This achievement, which culminated in four remarkable flights on the sand dunes of Kill Devil Hills, near Kitty Hawk, North Carolina, was the result of years of intense research, using knowledge from the brothers' predecessors in Europe and the United States and their own thorough experimentation. The Wrights solved the problem of controlled powered flight, which had vexed humankind for centuries, and invented a technology that would quickly revolutionize the world. Since that time, aviation has united the world, breaking down the barriers of travel and communications while providing new weapons of unprecedented destructiveness, a conundrum that deeply concerned the Wrights.

EARLY DEVELOPMENTS IN FLIGHT

Once the genie of flight escaped from the proverbial bottle, it grew with remarkable speed. Ironically, although the airplane was invented in the United States, its initial development came from inventive minds in Europe. Safely protected from international conflict by two oceans, the United States was slow to invest in this new technology. This problem was compounded by the Wrights' litigiousness in protecting their patent for the airplane, which hindered development at home. European countries, often on the brink of war with their neighbors, quickly recognized the significance of the airplane. France, in particular, assumed the leadership in aviation following the dramatic flight of Louis Blériot (1872–1936) across the English Channel in 1909, which made it clear that geography was no longer a barrier. The airplane was quickly defined into a form recognizable for decades to come, based in large part on French efforts; it is no accident that most aircraft parts carry French names. This point was made clearly during World War I when, after America entered the war in 1917, most of its combat aircraft were provided by France as well as Great Britain. The war ended in 1918 before America's prodigious economy could produce its own aircraft, but the leadership in aircraft design was soon to cross back across the Atlantic.

During the First World War, German aircraft designers sought ingenious ways to overcome that nation's lack of natural resources, which made conventional aircraft construction difficult. The results were a series of practical and theoretical breakthroughs that would change the shape of the airplane and a highly creative aeronautical industry that produced innovative aircraft along with the science and engineering to support it. Because Germany lost the war, however, it was forbidden to develop aircraft much further. Although the United States was slow off the mark after inventing the airplane, it made huge strides in catching up, particularly after the establishment of the National Advisory Committee for Aeronautics (NACA), a government agency dedicated to the development of the science and engineering of aviation. The NACA quickly created research establishments and publications that disseminated not only American research but that of all nations. Through these mechanisms, American designers learned of monocoque (hollow, shell-like) fuselages, cantilevered (internally braced) wings, and all-metal construction. US propulsion work resulted in a series of new and powerful engines, particularly reliable air-cooled power plants developed for the US Navy. By the late 1920s and early 1930s, these technological breakthroughs had led to a design revolution that produced reliable, efficient, high-performance aircraft. The first of these was the Boeing 247 airliner of 1933, which was as fast as a military fighter and 60 percent faster than any other airliner in the sky. This all-metal monoplane set the pattern for all modern aircraft that followed, including the milestone Douglas DC-3 of 1936—the first airliner capable of making money without a subsidy. From this point on, America assumed a leadership position in aircraft development, which, although often challenged, has yet to be ceded.

EARLY MILITARY AIRCRAFT

These ground-breaking technologies also resulted in a new generation of high-performance military aircraft, highlighted by the incomparable Boeing B-17 Flying Fortress bomber of 1935. American breakthroughs did not go unnoticed and, by the mid- to late 1930s, just as the Second World War was looming, modern all-metal monoplane designs were appearing in Europe, the Soviet Union, and Japan. The two decades between the wars saw unprecedented development of aircraft and the organizations and systems to make aviation work. Aviation went from slow, wood and fabric biplanes to fast, all-metal civilian and military aircraft, including the first jet and the first practical helicopter.

From 1939 to 1945, aircraft design underwent a steady and rapid refinement under the pressures of the Second World War. It is important to note that the vast majority of these aircraft were designed before the war. This conflict validated the many theories of airpower first demonstrated two decades before in World War I. By the 1940s, military airpower came of age and became a war-winning weapon, whether in the direct support of ground troops, in airlifting troops and supplies, or in the destruction of an enemy's means of production through strategic bombardment. While not capable of achieving victory by itself, massive airpower enabled the Allies to decisively strike the Axis, as demonstrated most dramatically by the atomic bombing of Hiroshima and Nagasaki, Japan, by two Martin-built Boeing B-29s, bringing an end to the conflict.

POSTWAR DEVELOPMENTS

The end of World War II left the United States in a dominant international position and with a solid economy. As the so-called Arsenal of Democracy, the United States supplied the Allies with mountains of arms and supplies while building an international network of airports. Because of the size of its economy and the fact that the nation's infrastructure had been largely untouched by the war, the United States was able to dominate aviation for several decades. Soon after the war, advanced American airliners, such as the Lockheed Constellation and the Douglas DC-6, became the aircraft of choice for most of the world's major airlines. Featuring four powerful piston engines and pressurized fuselages, these aircraft set the mark for comfort and efficiency.

Britain sought to challenge America's dominance with the introduction of the revolutionary de Havilland DH 106 Comet—the world's first jet-powered airliner—in 1952. Turbojet engines, developed by the Germans and the British during World War II, promised much greater speed, reliability, and efficiency. Unforeseen fatal problems with metal fatigue cost the Comet its lead. By the time it returned to service in 1958, it was superseded by newer and faster American designs, particularly the Boeing 707.

THE JET REVOLUTION

The 707 was originally intended as a jet-powered aerial tanker to refuel America's fleet of strategic bombers, especially the Boeing B-47 and B-52. These bombers incorporated significant features of German swept-wing innovations as well as jet engines based on axial flow technology, both pioneered by Germany during the war. The 707, and the Douglas DC-8 that immediately followed, led the world into the "Jet

Age" of air travel. Reaching speeds of well over five hundred miles per hour, these jetliners and the designs they inspired radically changed society, for now virtually anywhere on the planet was accessible within twenty-four to forty-eight hours—an unprecedented accomplishment. Despite the abortive attempt at commercial supersonic flight with the graceful Anglo-French Concorde, airliners traveling today fly no faster than the classic 707.

In 1970 air travel was revolutionized once again with the introduction of the massive Boeing 747. Carrying two-and-a-half times the passenger load of a 707, the massive "Jumbo Jet" set marks for range and efficiency as seat-mile costs dropped dramatically, allowing lower fares and consequently more passengers. The 747 spurred a wide-body revolution led by the McDonnell Douglas DC-10, the Lockheed L-1011, and the Airbus A300, which all made air travel affordable to millions more people. Later, several new generations of wide bodies, particularly the Boeing 777 and 787 and the European Airbus A330, A350, and massive A380—the world's largest airliner—vied for the world's air traffic. These aircraft feature ever more powerful and efficient turbofan engines first used on the Boeing 747 and the Lockheed C-5A military transport. Smaller versions of these engines, when they are installed on the hugely popular single-aisle, narrow-bodied Boeing 737 and Airbus A320, the two most popular airliners in the world, have allowed the spread of jet travel to virtually every city around the globe. The advent of composite construction, first pioneered by the military, is bringing even greater efficiencies because of its strength and lightness. Combined, these innovations keep air travel safe and affordable.

The jet revolution reached the military earlier in World War II with the introduction of the German Messerschmitt Me 262 fighter and Arado Ar 234 bomber and the British Gloster Meteor fighter. These stunning designs quickly made propeller-driven military aircraft obsolete. The race was on to build faster and more powerful combat aircraft. Locked in a titanic struggle with the Soviet Union during the Cold War, the US Air Force and Navy embarked on programs to build ever more effective aircraft. US North American F-86 Sabres locked horns with the superlative Soviet MiG-15 over the skies of Korea from 1950 to 1953; both featured German swept-wing technologies. Fifteen years later over Vietnam, McDonnell Douglas F-4 Phantom IIs, Republic F-105 Thunderchiefs, and Vought F-8 Crusaders again engaged Soviet MiG-17 and MiG-21 fighters. Jet engines also provided the power necessary to make helicopters effective, led by the classic Bell UH-1 Huey and subsequent designs.

Supersonic flight was pioneered in the United States by NACA and the US Air Force when, on October 14, 1947, the rocket-powered Bell X-1, with Captain Charles "Chuck" Yeager (b. 1923) at the controls, became the first aircraft to fly faster than the speed of sound. The lessons learned from these and other experimental aircraft, particularly from the National Aeronautics and Space Administration—NASA, the successor to NACA—helped to keep the United States in the forefront of military and civil aircraft design.

Today modern military aircraft such as the Boeing F-15 Eagle and F-18 Hornet and the Lockheed F-16 Fighting Falcon feature supersonic speeds coupled with unprecedented maneuverability made possible by advanced computer-driven controls, as demonstrated in several conflicts in the Middle East. Incorporating the latest construction materials, such as composites and radar-absorbing and -deflecting technologies, aircraft such as the Lockheed F-22 bring unprecedented accuracy and effectiveness to the fight and will continue to do so well into the future.

SEE ALSO *Americanization; Automobiles; Berlin Airlift; Cold War; Exceptionalism; Exports, Exportation; Industrialization; Internationalism; Isolationism; Navy, US; Pan American World Airways; Trains; World War I; World War II; World's Fairs*

BIBLIOGRAPHY

Bilstein, Roger E. *Flight in America: From the Wrights to the Astronauts,* 3rd ed. Baltimore, MD: Johns Hopkins University Press, 2001.

Crouch, Tom D. *Wings: A History of Aviation from Kites to the Space Age.* New York: Norton, 2003.

Emme, Eugene M., ed. *Two Hundred Years of Flight in America: A Bicentennial Survey.* San Diego, CA: American Astronautical Society, 1977.

Gibbs-Smith, Charles H. *Aviation: An Historical Survey from Its Origins to the End of World War II.* London: Her Majesty's Stationery Office, 1970.

Grant, R. G. *Flight: The Complete History.* London: DK Publishing, 2007.

Kinney, Jeremy R. *Airplanes: The Life Story of a Technology.* Baltimore, MD: Johns Hopkins University Press, 2008.

Spenser, Jay P. *The Airplane: How Ideas Gave Us Wings.* New York: Smithsonian Books, 2008.

F. Robert van der Linden
Curator of Air Transportation
Smithsonian National Air and Space Museum

ALAMO

SEE *Texas Republic.*

ALBRIGHT, MADELEINE

1937–

Madeleine Jana Korbel was born in 1937, near Prague. Her father, Josef Korbel (1909–1977), was a diplomat. Josef's links with Czech president Edvard Beneš (1884–1948) meant that the family had to abandon the country soon after the Munich agreement (1938) and that it could return only for a brief spell at the end of the war, before the Communist takeover. The lessons of Munich would strongly impact Josef and, as an extension, Albright's outlook on international politics. The Korbel family finally settled in the United States in 1948. Madeleine attended Wellesley College, whose alumni also include Hillary Clinton. While on an internship at the *Denver Post*, Madeleine met her future husband, Joseph Medill Patterson Albright. When Albright's new family, including two daughters, moved to Washington, DC, she continued her studies at Columbia University, where she earned a PhD in public law and government in 1976 and attended a graduate course led by Zbigniew Brzezinski.

Having found a passion for (and an ability in) fundraising, Albright was invited to work for Senator Edmund Muskie, a Democrat from Maine. After the election of Jimmy Carter in 1976, Brzezinski asked Albright to work for the National Security Council as liaison with Congress. Albright makes clear both her admiration for Brzezinski, and the rivalries between the NSC staff and the State Department. With Ronald Reagan's victory in 1980, Albright went back to her academic career at Georgetown University. She maintained a strong interest in Eastern Europe, traveling to Poland to interview dissidents. In spite of going through the trauma of a divorce in the early 1980s, she remained an important figure in the Democratic Party, with roles in both the 1984 and 1988 presidential campaigns. Ironically, she was not involved in the 1992 Clinton campaign.

After Bill Clinton's election, Albright led the transition team. A momentous decision was the granting of cabinet-level status to the US ambassador to the United Nations. Upon becoming UN ambassador, Albright had to confront problematic situations both abroad and in Washington. Abroad, the end of the Cold War had brought about a "new world disorder," but for Albright, the end of the superpower rivalry did not mean the end of America's responsibilities. Initially, the Clinton administration faced several major crises, largely inherited from the Bush years, including conflicts in Somalia, Haiti, and Bosnia. The Clinton campaign had expressed a strong position on the Balkans, and Albright had supported it. Once in office, however, the administration was cautious—a frustrating experience for Albright.

At the United Nations, Albright, one of the few women with a high-ranking position in the organization, had strong disagreements with Secretary-General Boutros Boutros-Ghali. In Washington, the decision-making process in the first months of the Clinton administration was disorganized. Albright struggled with her position shuttling between Washington and New York. Furthermore, both Colin Powell, the chairman of the Joint Chiefs of Staff, and National Security Advisor Anthony Lake seemed to look down on Albright and to resent her assertiveness. In her 2003 memoir, Albright describes the shock of the 1994 Rwandan genocide, the difficulties in grasping the gravity of the situation, and the president's political predicament after the 1993 debacle in Somalia. Albright's assertive views eventually prevailed in the administration's decisions regarding the crisis in Bosnia, but only after a spike in violence in the summer of 1995.

In 1997, Albright became the United States' first woman secretary of state. As secretary, she confronted five main issues: Kosovo and what was soon called "Madeleine's war," terrorism and the rise of al-Qaeda, the containment of Iraq, the Middle East peace process, and the fine balance between expansion of NATO and preservation of relations with Russia. On Kosovo, after the failure of the 1999 Rambouillet conference, the United States and NATO gambled that the threat of force would compel Slobodan Milošević (1941–2006) to surrender. This only occurred at the end of a strong bombing campaign. On terrorism, Albright identified the dangerousness of this "new kind of evil" and supported Clinton's missile strikes in Afghanistan and Sudan following al-Qaeda's bombing of US embassies in Africa in 1998. On Iraq, Albright hints in her memoir that although containment had proven successful during the Clinton years, regime change was perhaps inevitable. The success of the Russia-NATO partnership was obscured by the rise of Vladimir Putin and by the inconclusive Camp David summit on the Middle East.

Throughout her career, Albright coupled sensitivity for her position as a woman and for women's issues with an assertive and sometimes aggressive posture. Albright's definition of Clinton's foreign policy as "assertive multilateralism" was heavily criticized, but it encapsulated her understanding of the United States in the post–Cold War world, where, in her view, the United States needed to do the right thing but in a tough-minded way.

SEE ALSO *Clinton, William Jefferson; Contemporary Genocides and US Policy; North American Free Trade Agreement (NAFTA); Yugoslav Wars*

BIBLIOGRAPHY

Albright, Madeleine. *Madam Secretary: A Memoir.* New York: Miramax, 2003.

Albright, Madeleine. "Interview with Madeleine K. Albright." William J. Clinton Oral History. Miller Center, University of Virginia. 2014. http://millercenter.org/president/clinton/oralhistory/madeleine-k-albright

Dobbs, Michael. *Madeleine Albright: A Twentieth-Century Odyssey.* New York: Holt, 1999.

Luca Trenta
Department of Political and Cultural Studies
Swansea University

ALCOHOLICS ANONYMOUS

Alcoholics Anonymous (AA) traces its origins to the middle of the 1930s when two heavy drinkers of alcoholic beverages, Bill W. (William Griffith Wilson, 1895–1971) and Dr. Bob (Robert Holbrook Smith, 1879–1950), met in Akron, Ohio. They created a new program to help people stop drinking alcohol and, more importantly, refrain from beginning to drink alcohol. The group developed slowly, and in 1939 published what has become its core text, *Alcoholics Anonymous*. The hallmarks of AA became its "Twelve Step" approach to recovery from addiction, its regular meetings of alcoholics, and its commitment to serving people who suffer from alcoholism. From then until the present, AA has grown to become an international organization with millions of members throughout the world. Moreover, it has spawned numerous other Twelve Step organizations, including Overeaters Anonymous, Narcotics Anonymous, and Sexaholics Anonymous, which also have global reach in the twenty-first century.

Although AA's origins were extraordinarily local (two men in a small American city), its roots were international. Before AA, the most noteworthy organization to help alcoholics was the Oxford Group. Founded by an American clergyman who had experienced a Christian conversion in England, the Oxford Group had gained a strong following in Britain and in British colonies. In fact, the group got its name because its largest membership was at the University of Oxford in England.

Moreover, AA's philosophy developed through the interplay of scholarly insights of Americans and Europeans. Writings by American philosopher William James (1842–1910) and the psychological insights of Swiss psychotherapist Carl Jung (1875–1961) were instrumental in forming the AA approach to the religious experiences and psychic transformations needed to become and remain sober. From its very beginning, AA was tied to international religious and scholarly communities.

In its earliest years, AA had most of its success in the United States and in urban areas. Originating during the Great Depression, AA found countless men and women out of work and unable to stop drinking. For several decades, the group grew slowly but steadily. By 1950, AA had almost one hundred thousand members in the United States and Canada. By 1970, it had almost two hundred thousand.

By 1990, the organization had more than one million members in the United States and Canada, plus another one million members globally. Additionally, the book *Alcoholics Anonymous* has traveled the globe. By the end of the twentieth century, it had been translated into more than forty languages. By 2013, it had been translated into seventy languages.

AA grew slowly beyond the United States and Canada during its first decades. In 1950, Bill W. traveled to Europe and visited the few AA groups that had started in Sweden, France, and Great Britain. Other AA members carried the program during their business and social trips, and in the 1940s, the message of AA reached Brazil, El Salvador, Japan, and Romania. It was not until the end of the 1960s that AA formed its World Service Meeting, an every-other-year convention in which members from around the world had the opportunity to meet. At these meetings, and other "zonal meetings" among members from neighboring countries and regions, AA members and leaders created ties across national boundaries and borders. During the next decades, AA grew by leaps and bounds from country to country. As of 2013, AA estimated that it had functioning meetings and memberships in 170 countries.

AA's global reach, its conventions, and the large numbers of immigrants entering the United States after 1965 helped transform the organization in profound ways. While AA began with a strong Christian and biblical emphasis, it came to incorporate other religious traditions and values as well. Books on practicing the Twelve Steps as a Buddhist or as Jewish can be located easily, while Twelve Step groups incorporate quotations and sayings from Native American traditions, the Qur'an, Rastafarian music, and various other spiritual approaches to life.

Another reason for AA's growth has been its detachment from political and national matters. From its beginning, AA's leaders made it clear that they wished to have no opinion on issues of war, politics, economics, and broader society. The radical individualism of the group and its focus on one alcoholic helping another alcoholic allowed AA to grow and expand even as nations warred, empires rose and fell, and international conflicts threatened the safety of the globe.

With the expansion of digital technologies and the World Wide Web in the twenty-first century, AA and other Twelve Step addiction programs expanded. Meetings held on the phone and online make it possible for alcoholics and addicts from different countries to interact. In addition, the new technology has created new sets of addictions and subsequently new Twelve Step fellowships, such as Internet & Tech Addiction Anonymous and Facebook Addicts Anonymous. What began as the meeting of two alcoholics in Akron, Ohio, now spans the globe, circulates throughout the Internet, and helps individuals to contend with a number of human maladies beyond those mentioned above.

BIBLIOGRAPHY

Alcoholics Anonymous: The Story of How Many Thousands of Men and Women Have Recovered from Alcoholism. 4th ed. New York: Alcoholics Anonymous World Services, 2001.

Kurtz, Ernest. *A.A.: The Story.* San Francisco: Harper and Row, 1988.

Edward J. Blum
Professor of History
San Diego State University

ALI, MUHAMMAD

1942–

After taking a gold medal at the 1960 Olympics, Muhammad Ali (born January 17, 1942, and given the name Cassius Clay) began his professional boxing career. When he won the world heavyweight championship in 1964, he announced to the press that he had joined the Nation of Islam, a religious organization that, in contrast to mainstream civil rights groups, urged its followers to separate from white society and organize themselves as part of a black collective. In the months following Ali's title victory, he visited the United Nations with his friend Malcolm X (1925–1965), and then embarked on a tour of West Africa, where hundreds of thousands of people paid their respects to the new titleholder. Ali had emerged as a powerful international symbol at the age of twenty-two, with special importance to the world Islamic community.

When Ali was drafted into the US military during the Vietnam War two years later, he made clear that he would not cooperate. Politicians targeted his draft resistance, and boxing's main American operators colluded to ban him from the sport. Ali foiled the boycott by fighting in Canada, England, and Germany—places where there had not been world heavyweight championship fights in decades. Ali claimed conscientious objector status, but the federal government filed suit against him. In 1967, a court found Ali guilty of draft evasion and sentenced him to the maximum five years in prison. Ali remained out of prison on appeal, and the US Supreme Court vindicated him in 1971, but major damage had been done. As a convicted felon, he could not leave the country, and no state would license him to fight. As his case dragged through the courts, Ali lost three and a half years of his career, when his boxing skills were at their peak.

When Ali returned to the ring he gravitated toward the international stage, capitalizing on his enormous worldwide popularity not only as an entertainer and boxer nonpareil, but even more importantly as the man who stood up to US imperialism and lived to tell the tale, which could not be said about his contemporaries Malcolm X and Martin Luther King Jr. (1929–1968). Simultaneously the most beloved and hated man in America, Ali consistently enjoyed strong international support. From 1971 to 1976, he fought in Switzerland, Japan, Canada, Ireland, Indonesia, Zaire, Malaysia, the Philippines, Puerto Rico, and West Germany. Two of these bouts, victories in Kinshasa against George Foreman and in Manila against Joe Frazier, are Ali's most celebrated. These great fights, in addition to the Supreme Court decision in his favor and the growing consensus at home that Ali had been right about the Vietnam War, warmed American attitudes toward him. President Gerald Ford (1913–2006) invited Ali to the White House in 1974, as every president has since and none had prior, a sign of greater acceptance of the fighter by those who had once opposed him.

Late in his career and after his 1981 retirement, Ali served as a humanitarian and maintained an extensive international travel schedule that reached parts of the world few Americans had visited. In 1978, he toured the Soviet Union and spoke to Soviet premier Leonid Brezhnev (1906–1982); an ABC television crew filmed the trip for a *Wide World of Sports* episode. The television newsmagazine *60 Minutes* featured a story about Ali's 1996 trip to Cuba, where he met with President Fidel Castro. The media documentation of Ali's life showed Americans footage of places they could not visit, and Ali's amicable meetings with so-called enemies of the United States provided living examples of world peace that highlighted his potency as a unifying force. For many years, until his health finally prevented him from taking long trips, Ali spanned the globe promoting important causes.

Although he largely removed himself from the spotlight by 1990, refusing almost all interview requests, Ali remains a relevant figure who continues to make public appearances and allows people to be photographed with him. Most of his story is now told by his family, particularly his wife Yolanda, who was the driving force behind the creation of the Muhammad Ali Center, a museum in Louisville, Kentucky, dedicated to chronicling Ali's life, accomplishments, and philosophies. The center is a successful tourist destination, rests on a parcel of donated government land, and institutionalizes permanently the recognition of his contributions. Controversy has not touched Ali in decades, and he now stands as one of the most beloved men in the world, with the licensing of his name and image generating millions of dollars of income per year for him and his family.

SEE ALSO *Malcolm X; Nation of Islam; Olympics; Vietnam War*

BIBLIOGRAPHY

Ezra, Michael. *Muhammad Ali: The Making of an Icon.* Philadelphia: Temple University Press, 2009.

Hauser, Thomas. *Muhammad Ali: His Life and Times.* New York: Touchstone, 1991.

Marqusee, Mike. *Redemption Song: Muhammad Ali and the Spirit of the Sixties.* London: Verso, 1999.

Olsen, Jack. *Black Is Best: The Riddle of Cassius Clay.* New York: Putnam, 1967.

Remnick, David. *King of the World: Muhammad Ali and the Rise of an American Hero.* New York: Random House, 1998.

Michael Ezra
Professor of American Multicultural Studies
Sonoma State University

ALIEN ACT (1798)

In the summer of 1798, as the United States inched closer to war with France, Congress passed a series of sweeping legislative measures aimed at curbing foreign immigration. Known collectively as the Alien Act, the legislation was actually three separate laws: the Naturalization Act, the Alien Friends Act, and the Alien Enemies Act.

The Naturalization Act of 1798 repealed the more liberal Naturalization Acts of 1790 and 1795. It mandated that before an alien resident could become a naturalized citizen, the person had to have lived in the United States for at least fourteen years and was required to declare his intention for citizenship at least five years before being granted an application. The measure applied only to new immigrants who arrived from nations with which the United States was not at war.

The Alien Friends Act empowered President John Adams to deport any alien resident he deemed a threat to the United States. Should the suspected alien refuse deportation, that individual could face three years in prison. At the president's discretion, alien residents could receive a license to remain in the United States. The measure also required any ship entering American ports to declare any on-board aliens.

The Alien Enemies Act applied only when the United States was in an actual declared war with another nation. It designated all nonnaturalized males over the age of fourteen who originated from the belligerent country as "enemy aliens" and forced them to leave the United States. Although Congress eventually modified or outright repealed the Naturalization and Alien Friends Acts, the Alien Enemies Act remains an active statute.

The stringency these laws placed on naturalization was a reaction to the international crisis the United States faced in the late 1790s. As the French Revolutionary Wars continued to engulf Europe, American relations with France deteriorated. France had reluctantly accepted American neutrality in 1793, but it considered the 1795 Jay Treaty between England and the United States as an Anglo-American alliance. France's hostility led it to interfere in the 1796 presidential election, seize and torture American maritime merchants, and refuse to meet an American peace delegation unless the Americans first paid a bribe. Each of these actions exacerbated American anger with France.

By 1798 the United States was engaged in small naval skirmishes with France, and full-scale war seemed inevitable. At the same time, many Americans feared a French invasion. Although the measures technically applied to immigrants from all nations, the clear targets of the Alien Acts were French immigrants. These measures corresponded with the largest military buildup in American history to that point. The Federalist-controlled Congress justified the Alien Acts on the grounds that they were proactive measures aimed at preventing possible domestic intrigue and sabotage by French and pro-French Irish immigrants, sympathizers, or spies.

SEE ALSO *Adams, John*

BIBLIOGRAPHY

Coleman, Aaron N. "'A Second Bounaparty'?: A Reexamination of Alexander Hamilton during the Franco-American Crisis, 1796–1801." *Journal of the Early Republic* 28, 2 (2008): 183–214.

DeConde, Alexander. *The Quasi-War: The Politics and Diplomacy of the Undeclared War with France 1797–1801.* New York: Scribner, 1966.

Smith, James Morton. *Freedom's Fetters: The Alien and Sedition Laws and American Civil Liberties.* Ithaca, NY: Cornell University Press, 1956.

Wood, Gordon. *Empire of Liberty: A History of the Early Republic, 1789–1815.* Oxford, UK, and New York: Oxford University Press, 2009.

Aaron Nathan Coleman
Associate Professor of History and Higher Education
University of the Cumberlands

ALIEN CONTRACT LABOR LAW/ FORAN ACT (1885)

The Alien Contract Labor Law of February 26, 1885, also known as the Foran Act after its sponsor, Martin Foran, a Democratic congressman from Ohio, barred American employers from paying for the transportation costs of alien laborers entering the United States, and from importing workers under contract. Building on the success and logic of the Chinese exclusion movement, the law's main advocates, the Federation of Organized Trades and Labor Unions and Knights of Labor, argued that the statute would further strengthen the position of American workers by depriving manufacturers, mining corporations, railroads, and other capital interests of a supply of cheap laborers who could be mobilized to undermine the interests of organized labor.

The legal historian Kitty Calavita (1984) describes the Foran Act as a "symbolic law" enforced with largely "symbolic action." Employers and the brokers who functioned as middlemen recruited strikebreakers from the labor exchanges clustered around the Castle Garden Labor Bureau and at other ports of entry, a practice that was more effective than contracting workers from abroad and waiting for their arrival. It took Congress until February 1887 to amend the original act to even allow for the deportation of violators. In 1901 the Congressional Industrial Commission discovered that, out of nearly six million immigrants, only eight thousand immigrants had been barred from landing by the law and that immigration officials rarely investigated contract status unless this information was volunteered. Immigrants who were unable to demonstrate employment prospects were far more likely to be denied entry on the grounds of being likely to become a public charge. In Europe, where industrial, agricultural, and land agents had actively recruited and in some cases provided credit to emigrants in years past, the Foran Act did mean that efforts to drum up migration business passed to steamship company agents instead.

The Foran Act included a number of exemptions that also contributed to its nebulous enforcement. Domestic and personal servants, for instance, could be contracted abroad, on the assumption that formal job arrangements protected white women from sexual and economic exploitation during the migration process. Artists and performers did not fall under the purview of the legislation. New industries in the United States were allowed to import skilled labor in cases where it was determined that American expertise did not exist. Finally, because an importer could be held liable for violating the law only if an employment contract was completed, prosecution of employers was exceedingly rare. The most prominent case tried under the Foran Act, *Church of the Holy Trinity v. United States*, 143 U.S. 457 (1892), involved an English minister who had been hired to work in an Episcopal church in Manhattan while living abroad. Even though the law in its original wording ostensibly applied to all imported workers, the Supreme Court ruled unanimously that it had not been legislators' intent to target occupations that did not involve manual labor.

Despite its limited application, the Foran Act signaled an important shift in American racial attitudes. In 1862 Congress had prohibited American vessels from participating in the Chinese "coolie trade." In 1875 the Page Act required Chinese emigrants to prove to consular officials that they were departing for the United States of their own volition, and voided all contracts made prior to arrival. With the Foran Act, nativists' fears came to encompass the alleged threats posed by "new" immigrants from southern and eastern Europe, who, like the Chinese, were depicted as "coolies" and slaves incapable of controlling the sale of their labor power. As Republican senator John Sherman of Ohio argued during debate on the bill that would become the Foran Act,

> if there is in any country of Europe a class of people who are in such a condition of life that they can be classed as … the coolies of Asia, people who do not own themselves, who work only for others, who have never conceived of the idea of independent manhood, we should prohibit their importation into this country.

The cultural standard of free labor that Sherman and others touted bore little resemblance to the way in which global labor markets actually operated. Migrants entered into contracts due to economic necessity, and not because they intrinsically lacked a desire for independence.

Injunctions against imported foreign labor remained part of immigration law until the 1952 Immigration and Nationality Act, despite suspensions during both the First and Second World Wars, when labor shortages made the contract of guest workers from the Caribbean and Mexico imperative. Present-day immigration policy, with special visas emphasizing the targeted and selective absorption of skilled labor and workers in industries in which supply is deemed insufficient, such as nursing, often makes employment contracts a prerequisite of eligibility for migration.

SEE ALSO *Asia; Coolies; Economics; Immigration; Nativism*

BIBLIOGRAPHY

Alien Contract Labor Act of 1885. HR 2550. 48th Cong., 2nd sess., Congressional Record 16, pt. 2: 1621–1636.

Calavita, Kitty C. *U.S. Immigration Law and the Control of Labor, 1820–1924.* London and Orlando, FL: Academic Press, 1984.

Erickson, Charlotte. *American Industry and the European Immigrant, 1860–1885*. Cambridge, MA: Harvard University Press, 1957.

Gabaccia, Donna. "The 'Yellow Peril' and the 'Chinese of Europe': Global Perspectives on Race and Labor, 1815–1930." In *Migrations, Migration History, History: Old Paradigms and New Perspectives*, edited by Jan Lucassen and Leo Lucassen, 177–196. Bern, Switzerland, and New York: Peter Lang, 1997.

Hutchinson, Edward P. *Legislative History of American Immigration Policy, 1798–1965*. Philadelphia: University of Pennsylvania Press, 1981.

Jung, Moon-Ho. *Coolies and Cane: Race, Labor, and Sugar in the Age of Emancipation*. Baltimore: Johns Hopkins University Press, 2006.

Peck, Gunther. *Reinventing Free Labor: Padrones and Immigrant Workers in the North American West, 1880–1930*. Cambridge and New York: Cambridge University Press, 2000.

United States House of Representatives, Industrial Commission. *Reports of the Industrial Commission on Immigration: Including Testimony, with Review and Digest, and Special Reports... Volume XV of the Commission's Reports*. 57th Cong., 1st sess., 1901. H. Doc. 184. Washington, DC: US Government Printing Office, 1901.

Zolberg, Aristide R. *A Nation by Design: Immigration Policy in the Fashioning of America*. Cambridge, MA: Russell Sage Foundation Books at Harvard University Press, 2008.

Andrew Urban
Assistant Professor, American Studies and History
Rutgers University

ALLENDE, SALVADOR
1908–1973

Salvador Allende was democratically elected as Chile's president in 1970, pledging to move Chile to socialism while respecting the country's constitutional framework. Allende trained as a medical doctor but soon entered politics. He helped found Chile's Socialist Party in 1933, won a seat in the Chamber of Deputies at twenty-eight, and became minister of health the following year. In 1945 he was elected to the Senate, serving until his election as president.

Allende ran for that office four times, narrowly losing in 1958. In 1964 he ran against Eduardo Frei Montalva (1911–1982), a Christian Democrat. The Central Intelligence Agency (CIA) provided an estimated $4 million in covert assistance to Frei's winning campaign while pressuring conservative parties to remove their own candidates. However, conservatives refused to withdraw in 1970. With the vote divided, Allende and his Popular Unity (UP) coalition of Socialists, Communists, and smaller parties won a tight vote that required congressional confirmation. The administration of President Richard Nixon (1913–1994), fearing the impact that a democratic transition to socialism might have on other countries, concluded "that Allende [should] be overthrown by a coup" (Kornbluh 2003, 64) and set in motion a plan to kidnap army chief General René Schneider (1913–1970). The plot failed (Schneider was killed) and Allende was confirmed as president. Yet he would continue to face the intransigent opposition of Washington as well as the archconservative National Party. The Christian Democrats' initial distrust soon became open hostility.

Allende's program centered on nationalizing US-owned copper companies, extending state control of critical industrial and banking firms, expanding social services, returning land to peasant farmers, promoting worker control of workplaces, and shifting income toward Chile's workers, peasants, and poor. For the first year, these policies worked well, and in April 1971 municipal elections, the first following Allende's victory, the combined UP parties gained substantial ground.

Yet the economy soon began to buckle as Allende's programs were undercut by conflicts within his governing coalition, an upsurge of revolutionary grassroots activism, and an opposition-controlled Congress that blocked his legislative agenda and impeached his cabinet ministers. His adversaries found willing partners in Washington. Nixon and Henry Kissinger (b. 1923), his national security adviser, never altered in their determination to remove Allende. They implemented a multifaceted program of economic warfare, intervened concertedly in Chile's domestic politics, cultivated contacts within Chile's officer corps, enforced an embargo of Chilean copper sales abroad, and deprived Chile of most US and international aid.

In late August 1973, the congressional opposition, accusing Allende of "unconstitutional acts," called on the military to "put an end" to his presidency. With loyalists generals removed from leadership positions, the military launched a coup on September 11, 1973. Allende refused to resign, remaining in La Moneda, Chile's presidential palace, as air force jets bombed the building. Allende took to the airwaves four times while under attack. In his last broadcast, he told his supporters not to sacrifice themselves and promised that one day Chile's great avenues (*grandes alamedas*) would again be open to them. He took his own life. In 2008, a Chilean poll named him the most important figure in the nation's history.

The role played by Washington in Allende's downfall remains hotly debated. The Nixon administration's attempts to overthrow Allende's democratically elected government in 1970, now fully documented, proved highly embarrassing to Washington. Nixon administration officials have always maintained that the government observed a cool but correct posture toward Allende and his Popular Unity government. Yet scores of declassified government documents, telephone conversations, and other evidence provide strong support for the case that while the United States may not have directly intervened on the day of the coup, it coordinated and funded opposition activities, particularly those of the opposition *El Mercurio* newspaper, trained and communicated with Chilean military officials, acted to isolate Allende's government from aid and external markets, and broadly signaled that a military coup would be received favorably in Washington, as it quickly was.

SEE ALSO *Central Intelligence Agency (CIA); Cold War; Covert Wars; Kissinger, Henry; Nixon, Richard Milhous*

BIBLIOGRAPHY

Amorós, Mario. *Allende. La biografía.* Barcelona: Grupo Zeta, 2013.

Bitar, Sergio. *Chile: Experiment in Democracy.* Philadelphia, PA: Institute for the Study of Human Issues, 1986.

Clark, Victor Figueroa. *Salvador Allende: Revolutionary Democrat.* London: Pluto Press, 2013.

Davis, Nathaniel. *The Last Two Years of Salvador Allende.* Ithaca, NY: Cornell University Press, 1985.

Harmer, Tanya. *Allende's Chile and the Inter-American Cold War.* Chapel Hill: University of North Carolina Press, 2011.

Kornbluh, Peter. *The Pinochet Files: A Declassified Dossier on Atrocity and Accountability.* New York: New Press, 2003.

Roxborough, Ian, Philip J. O'Brien, and Jackie Roddick. *Chile: The State and Revolution.* New York: Holmes & Meier, 1977.

U.S. Senate, Staff Report of the Select Committee to Study Government Operations with Respect to Intelligence Activities. *Covert Action in Chile, 1963–73.* Washington, DC: Government Printing Office, 1975.

Steven S. Volk
Professor of History
Oberlin College

ALLIANCE FOR PROGRESS

In March 1961, President John F. Kennedy (1917–1963) proposed constructing the Alliance for Progress as a ten-year program that would promote economic development, political and social reform, and mutual understanding throughout Latin America. Later that year, in August, representatives of the United States and Latin American governments met in Uruguay to develop a framework for the program and lay out its goals. At the conclusion of this meeting, they signed the Charter of Punta del Este. Most importantly, they agreed that the Alliance for Progress would focus on ensuring that the rate of economic growth in every Latin American country should be no less than 2.5 percent per year through the 1960s.

Kennedy introduced the program for a series of reasons. Most pressingly, he was concerned that Fidel Castro's (b. 1926) successes in Cuba might be replicated elsewhere in the region. His advisors believed that systematic corruption in Fulgencio Batista's (1901–1973) regime and a general lack of economic development on the island had prompted the Cuban Revolution and subsequently guaranteed its success. As they scanned the rest of Latin America, they saw these conditions almost everywhere, and they worried that many more Castros might emerge. The Alliance for Progress became the solution to this problem because of a set of ideas that Kennedy had about the utility of foreign aid. In the 1950s, he had become interested in the theories of a set of economists, most notably Walt Rostow (1916–2003), who argued that foreign aid could spur growth and help economies become more dynamic. This belief, usually called *modernization theory*, appealed to Kennedy because he assumed that while poor people might find communism attractive, people experiencing economic development would reject it.

The Alliance for Progress faced a series of hurdles immediately. Kennedy believed it was important that the program appear to be a cooperative hemispheric effort; if it was entirely US directed, it might look like a new form of US imperialism. However, Latin American and US goals and priorities were not the same. Most Latin American states wanted money for their own internal development, but they did not want to pursue structural and political reforms. The Charter of Punta del Este did have a mechanism to handle this issue. Latin American states were to submit development and reform proposals to a nine-member panel of experts, known as the "Wise Men" (and they were all men). This panel would then approve and pass on to the United States and other institutions only well-constructed plans to be funded. This rarely happened, as all parties generally ignored the procedure. Latin American leaders went straight to the US government to ask for loans, and the United States offered loans without vetting them with the panel.

At the beginning, Kennedy insisted that evidence of reform precede the granting of loans, but fairly quickly he abandoned that idea. Because he wanted to show that the program was working immediately, it was not possible to wait for Latin American states to implement broad reforms that they were not enthusiastic about. The United States instead offered loans and hoped that they would spur growth and reform. More importantly, by 1962, the Kennedy administration began to use loans to achieve short-term political goals, rather than promote long-term growth. For example, in Chile, the United States offered loans (as much as $150 million) designed to ensure that the Marxist candidate in their 1964 presidential election, Salvador Allende (1908–1973), would not win. In Chile, and throughout Latin America, short-term political considerations trumped long-term economic development goals and the push for structural reforms.

It is important to note that the Alliance for Progress did promote a great deal of economic development in Latin America. US grants and loans in the 1960s, amounting to upwards of six billion dollars, helped construct schools, roads, hospitals, housing developments, airports, hydroelectric dams, rural irrigation systems, and urban sewage plants. While the program did not achieve the lofty goals outlined in the Charter of Punta del Este, it did improve the quality of life for millions of Latin Americans.

The Alliance for Progress lost momentum in the mid-1960s. No Cuba-like revolutions actually happened, and the region started to look stable. For President Lyndon Johnson (1908–1973), spending on the Great Society, and eventually on the Vietnam War, was far more important. President Richard Nixon (1913–1994) was even less interested. In Latin America, as elsewhere, he believed that right-wing dictatorship was a cheap and effective means of fighting the Cold War. He did not imagine that grandiose development aid programs could create lasting stability, and thus, the Alliance for Progress, as a formal program, ended during his first years as president.

SEE ALSO *Castro, Fidel; Kennedy, John Fitzgerald; Modernization Theory; Organization of American States (OAS); Rostow, Walt W.*

BIBLIOGRAPHY

Field, Thomas C. *From Development to Dictatorship: Bolivia and the Alliance for Progress in the Kennedy Era.* Ithaca, NY: Cornell University Press, 2014.

Levinson, Jerome, and Juan de Onís. *The Alliance That Lost Its Way: A Critical Report on the Alliance for Progress.* Chicago: Quadrangle, 1970.

Martin, Edwin M. *Kennedy and Latin America.* Lanham, MD: University Press of America, 1994.

Rabe, Stephen G. *The Most Dangerous Area in the World: John F. Kennedy Confronts Communist Revolution in Latin America.* Chapel Hill: University of North Carolina Press, 1999.

Taffet, Jeffrey F. *Foreign Aid as Foreign Policy: The Alliance for Progress in Latin America.* New York: Routledge, 2007.

Jeffrey F. Taffet
Professor of History
United States Merchant Marine Academy

AL-QAEDA

SEE *War on Terror.*

AMERICAN ASIATIC ASSOCIATION

In 1897, Germany seized Jiaozhou and Qingdao in the Shandong Province of China. That same year, Russia, France, Japan, and Britain also acquired "spheres of influence" or "spheres of interest" in China. This situation created a panic among New York merchants who, on January 6, 1898, responded by forming a Committee on American Interests in China. The committee directed the New York Chamber of Commerce to push the Department of State to act against the potential partitioning of China. Following success in this effort, the committee, renamed the American Asiatic Association, looked to maintain regular contact with Washington. When organized in 1898, the American Asiatic Association was the only interest group concerned exclusively with Far East policy. Through close contact with John Hay (1838–1905), secretary of state during the William McKinley (1843–1901) and Theodore Roosevelt (1858–1919) administrations, the association became an influential organization whose goal, as stated in its constitution, was: "To foster and safeguard the trade and commercial interests of the citizens of the United States, and others associated therewith, in the Empires of China, Japan, and Korea, and in the Philippine Islands, and elsewhere in Asia or Oceania" (Eperjesi 2005, 87).

The mouthpiece of the organization was the *Journal of the American Asiatic Association.* The editor of the journal and secretary of the association was John Foord (1842–1922). Before organizing the association, Foord was a member of the editorial staff of the New York *Journal of Commerce*, a specialist in economic and foreign policy, and the most vocal public exponent of the China market. In his editorial for the first issue of the journal, Foord wrote:

> In order to facilitate the interchange of views among the members of the Association and to provide a medium for the diffusion of information bearing on the development of commercial enterprise in the Far East, it is proposed to issue, as occasion may require, a record to be known as the "Journal of the American Asiatic Association." As the influence of the Association expands, and its touch with affairs in Eastern Asia and Oceania becomes more intimate, the value of this Journal will necessarily increase. (Eperjesi 2005, 88)

The American Asiatic Association initially provided a meeting place for the interests of northeastern industrial and merchant capital, yet gradually grew to include southern cotton interests and Pacific Coast states within its ranks. Beginning with a membership of forty-five prominent eastern firms in 1898, by 1904 that number had jumped to 250, five of which were from the Pacific Coast. Members included most of the large firms of New York engaged in the import-export business with Asia, as well as manufacturers of iron and steel, machinery, and locomotives from Philadelphia, Bethlehem, and Pittsburgh. By 1911, of the association's six vice-presidents, one was from New York, one was from Portland, Oregon, one was from Washington, DC, one was from Chicago, and two were from South Carolina.

The first issue of the journal appeared on July 25, 1898. Subsequent issues came out sporadically, usually every other month, until April 1902, when the format of the journal was standardized in order to increase circulation. New issues then appeared monthly, contained a table of contents and subscription rates, featured an editorial summary by Foord, regularly listed figures for exports to China and Hong Kong, and began to include advertising. The web of trade comparisons anchoring each issue included import/export figures between the United States and China, Japan, Korea, and the Philippines, as well as figures comparing the United States to Great Britain, France, Germany, Japan, India, and Spain. The journal also featured intensive descriptions of economically important locations in Asia and Oceania, detailing size, climate, population, imports, exports, politics, currency, and labor. The journal's catalogue of Asia included Ceylon, China, British India and the British East Indies, the Dutch East Indies, the French East Indies, Hong Kong, Japan, Korea, Persia, Asiatic Russia, Siam, and the Straits Settlements. As for Oceania, it included the Philippine Islands, the Commonwealth of Australia, New Zealand, Mauritius, and the Hawaiian Islands.

Articles included excerpts from the writings of imperialist state intellectuals, such as Brooks Adams (1848–1927), Charles Conant (1861–1915), and Alfred Thayer Mahan, (1840–1914), as well as passages from Senate and congressional debates, political speeches, and laws related to foreign trade. The discursive terrain of the journal reflected events both in Washington—such as debates over Asian immigration, the administration of the Philippines, and the funding of the transpacific cable and Panama Canal—and in the region, including the Boxer Rebellion (1900), the Russo-Japanese War (1904–1905), and Chinese nationalism.

During the 1890s, the United States seized colonies in the Pacific as business and political leaders struggled to find a way out of the postbellum economic crises of overproduction, economic depression, and financial panic that were resulting in high unemployment and intensified class conflict. Between 1881 and 1905, there were more than thirty-seven thousand labor strikes in the United States. The American Asiatic Association worked to stabilize this explosive period by putting together a political will amongst a group of political and economic leaders that would have otherwise remained dispersed. Through its promotion of increased trade with Asia as a solution to economic crisis, the association played a fundamental role in the formation of the Pacific as an American lake.

SEE ALSO *Asia; Economics*

BIBLIOGRAPHY

Conant, Charles A. "The Economic Basis of 'Imperialism.'" *North American Review* 167, 502 (1898): 326–340.

Connery, Chris L. "Pacific Rim Discourse: The U.S. Global Imaginary in the Late Cold War Years." *boundary 2* 21, 1 (1994): 30–56.

Dirlik, Arif. "The Asia-Pacific Idea: Reality and Representation in the Invention of a Regional Structure." *Journal of World History* 3, 1 (1992): 55–79.

Eperjesi, John R. *The Imperialist Imaginary: Visions of Asia and the Pacific in American Culture.* Hanover, NH: University Press of New England, 2005.

Hobson, J. A. *Imperialism: A Study.* Ann Arbor: University of Michigan Press, 1965. First published 1902.

Hunt, Michael H. *The Making of a Special Relationship: The United States and China to 1914.* New York: Columbia University Press, 1983.

Kaplan, Amy, and Donald Pease, eds. *Cultures of United States Imperialism.* Durham, NC: Duke University Press, 1993.

Lorence, James J. "The American Asiatic Association, 1898–1925: Organized Business and the Myth of the China Market." PhD diss., University of Wisconsin, 1970.

McCormick, Thomas J. *China Market: America's Quest for Informal Empire, 1893–1901.* Chicago: Quadrangle, 1967.

Wilson, Rob. *Reimagining the American Pacific: From* South Pacific *to Bamboo Ridge and Beyond.* Durham, NC: Duke University Press, 2000.

John R. Eperjesi
Associate Professor, School of English
Kyung Hee University, Seoul, South Korea

AMERICAN BOARD OF COMMISSIONERS FOR FOREIGN MISSIONS

The American Board of Commissioners for Foreign Missions (ABCFM) was the first and for a long time the largest sending agency in the American missionary enterprise. The instigation for its founding in 1810 came from a group of students in Massachusetts who had committed themselves to the work. Despite skepticism, the push benefited from the outpouring of organizing energy generated by the evangelical revivals of the Second Great Awakening. Like other large voluntary associations of the day, such as the American Bible Society, the ABCFM sought to unite evangelical denominations in common cause, and the New England Congregationalists who spearheaded the effort were joined by the Presbyterian, Dutch Reformed, and German Reformed churches. Those denominations gradually broke off to go their own way, and after 1871 the ABCFM became a Congregationalist body.

THE ABCFM MISSION

The stated goal of the ABCFM from its founding was the conversion of the whole world. Accordingly, ABCFM missions were soon established across the globe. By the mid-nineteenth century, there were ABCFM missions in Africa, Asia, the Middle East, and the Pacific. Missionaries began their work by establishing schools, translating scriptures and religious pamphlets, and preaching. Missionaries also offered medical services to varying degrees, though this was not a main priority of ABCFM missions until later in the century. In addition to sending missionaries out into the world, the ABCFM published missionary writings for the consumption of American audiences. This missionary literature provided supporters of the ABCFM with information about foreign lands and peoples.

The ABCFM was involved in missions to American Indians, as well as to foreign lands. The organization became famously embroiled in the Cherokee removal crisis, and one of its missionaries was the principal figure in the Supreme Court case of *Worcester v. Georgia* (1832), a victory for native rights that unfortunately failed to prevent the infamous Trail of Tears, during which it is estimated over four thousand Cherokees perished. That experience convinced the leadership of the ABCFM that avoiding direct involvement in politics better served their interests. Nonetheless, operating in the foreign field involved unavoidable entanglements with the expanding reach of the global North. ABCFM expansion into new fields was essentially opportunistic, meaning that missionaries rarely operated in places that had not already experienced significant contact. Although they were not the "vanguard of empire" as sometimes alleged, missions and empire interacted in various ways.

ENTANGLEMENTS IN COMMERCE AND POLITICS

Relations between missions and commerce could be particularly complex. When the ABCFM's very first company of missionaries landed in India, they were rebuffed by the British East India Company, and merchants often, though not always, feared that missionaries would jeopardize friendly trade by antagonizing the locals. In the Hawaiian Islands, by contrast, that tension was rooted in the unusually close ties that the missionaries developed with Hawaii's rulers. In one of their earliest and most successful missions, ABCFM missionaries promoted reforms in hopes of building up Hawaiian resistance to foreign domination, although in their own way they too undermined native control of their own affairs. In 1848, the ABCFM decided to end its Hawaiian mission and offer the missionaries the opportunity to become settled pastors, the ultimate result of which was that their children helped to engineer the coup that overthrew Queen Liliuokalani's government in 1893.

Surprisingly perhaps, tension between missionaries and merchants did not necessarily extend to the opium trade. In Izmir (Smyrna), American merchants involved in the export of Turkish opium enjoyed cordial relations with ABCFM missionaries, but in China, where missionaries witnessed the consequences of opium trafficking, the issue was more fraught. Although some missionaries condemned the trade, they did not hesitate to seize on the Opium Wars as a providential opening, and ABCFM missionaries Samuel Wells Williams (1812–1884) and Peter Parker (1804–1888) became diplomats through their involvement in postwar treaty negotiations.

EDUCATIONAL ENDEAVORS

Rufus Anderson (1796–1880), a major figure in the history of Protestant missions, is often seen as leading foreign missions away from imperialist entanglements. As the foreign secretary of the ABCFM in the mid-nineteenth century, he became convinced that the organization needed to concentrate on raising up native pastors for native churches that would be self-governing, self-supporting, and self-propagating—what became known as the "Three-Self policy." The new policy had major implications for educational work, as Anderson concluded that the ABCFM should only support vernacular education for training ministers. When he implemented that policy during his 1854 Deputation to India, he generated enormous controversy. Although the Three-Self policy retained appeal for its vision of developing an indigenous Christianity, his educational directives would be largely disavowed.

Indeed, mission schools had many consequences beyond making converts and training native workers. Because the ABCFM made a practice of educating girls as well as boys, its schools often challenged gender norms. As schools once again proliferated in ABCFM missions during the late nineteenth and early twentieth centuries, single females became a large part of the mission force. Missions thus helped to open new opportunities and give women a new voice both at home and overseas.

Perhaps the greatest unintended consequence of mission schools was the impact they had on the rise of nationalism in the global South. Along with the effect of translation work in fostering vernacular literatures, mission schools could be breeding grounds for new expressions of cultural nationalism. Nor were nationalistic influences limited to culture. John Dube (1871–1946), who was raised in the ABCFM's Zulu Mission, became the founding president of the South African Native National Congress, the forerunner of the African National Congress. Nationalistic ideas also led a group of Japanese converts to challenge the missionaries on theological grounds and over control of Dôshisha University in Kyoto.

ABCFM ACTIVITY IN THE CRUMBLING OTTOMAN EMPIRE

The ABCFM was deeply caught up in the nationalist struggles that ended in the dissolution of the Ottoman Empire. In one of its earliest ventures, the ABCFM had sought to establish a mission in the Holy Land. That effort eventually led to the founding of Syrian Protestant College, now the American University of Beirut, which was home to several important Arab nationalists. However, the missionaries found their most receptive audience among the Armenians, and beginning in the 1830s, they developed an extensive operation centered in Constantinople (modern Istanbul). Educational influences there centered around Bebek Seminary, later Robert College. The reach of the mission ultimately extended into Bulgaria and provided a stimulus to nationalism there as well. As the Ottoman Empire crumbled under the weight of all this, it reacted with brutal repression against the Armenians, culminating in the genocide during and after World War I (1914–1918). ABCFM missionaries were in the forefront of efforts to draw international attention to the plight of the Armenians and organize relief.

SHIFT TOWARD HUMANITARIAN ASSISTANCE

Involvement in Near East Relief pointed toward a shift in the twentieth century away from preaching for conversions and toward humanitarian assistance. That change was abetted by the growing influence of theological liberalism among Congregationalists, a trend to which ABCFM missionaries also contributed. Because the ABCFM was dependent on voluntary contributions from thousands of church members, its publications had from the beginning served as an important source of information about other peoples. Such depictions typically dwelled on the moral abominations of heathenism, but long familiarity over time had a tendency to make missionaries more appreciative of foreign cultures and more aware of commonalities within the human family. Such sympathies were often particularly marked among missionary children. An excellent example is the Hume family of the Ahmednagar Mission in India. Broad sympathies for indigenous aspirations led three generations of Hume men to butt heads with the missionary establishment and seek ways of shaping American opinion, notably through contributions to the study of comparative religions.

During the twentieth century, both the ABCFM and its parent denomination went into decline. Since the merger of Congregationalists into the United Church of Christ in 1957, the ABCFM has been absorbed into a series of successor organizations.

SEE ALSO *Africa; Asia; Cherokee Nation v. Georgia (1831); Foreign Mission Movement; Indian Removal Act (1830); North America; Student Volunteer Movement for Foreign Missions*

BIBLIOGRAPHY

Conroy-Krutz, Emily. *Christian Imperialism: Converting the World in the Early American Republic.* Ithaca, NY: Cornell University Press, 2015.

Harris, Paul William. *Nothing but Christ: Rufus Anderson and the Ideology of Protestant Foreign Missions.* New York: Oxford University Press, 1999.

Hutchison, William R. *Errand to the World: American Protestant Thought and Foreign Missions.* Chicago: University of Chicago Press, 1987.

Phillips, Clifton Jackson. *Protestant America and the Pagan World: The First Half Century of the American Board of Commissioners for Foreign Missions, 1810–1860.* Cambridge, MA: Harvard University Press for the East Asian Research Center, 1969.

Putney, Clifford, and Paul T. Burlin, eds. *The Role of the American Board in the World: Bicentennial Reflections on the Organization's Missionary Work, 1810–2010.* Eugene, OR: Wipf and Stock, 2012.

Paul W. Harris
Professor of History
Minnesota State University Moorhead

"THE AMERICAN CENTURY" (HENRY LUCE, 1941)

On February 17, 1941, the founder and publisher of *Time, Life,* and *Fortune* magazines, Henry Luce (1898–1967), published an editorial on "The American Century." Luce, the son of missionary parents in China, believed in the idea of American exceptionalism and the superiority of a Christian-driven American culture and economy. Ten months before the Japanese attack on Pearl Harbor, he sought to rouse the American people to take the leading role in the defense of Western values against the onslaught of Nazi conquest in Europe and Japanese barbarism in China.

Many American elites held a similar view. It began with the Puritan ideal of "the city on a hill," in which a new America would set an example for England and the rest of the European world to follow. It continued with the notion of an American manifest destiny, a term coined in 1845 by the columnist John L. O'Sullivan (1813–1895), which came to identify a mission to remake the North American continent and eventually the larger world. As Luce wrote, this

> must be a sharing with all people of our Bill of Rights, our Declaration of Independence, our Constitution, our magnificent industrial products, our technical skills.... [W]e have that indefinable, unmistakable sign of leadership: prestige. And unlike the prestige of Rome or Genghis Khan or 19th century England, American prestige throughout the world is [the result of] faith in the good intentions as well as in the ultimate intelligence and strength of the whole of the American people. (1941)

Luce's idea held for half a century. It helped explain Americans' embrace of the Cold War as a battle against Godless communism in the guise of the Soviet Union and its client states. It helped explain the National Security Council Paper NSC-68 of December 1950, which provided the rationale for a massive military buildup to deter Soviet aggression; that rationale was reinforced by Soviet dominance over the Iron Curtain countries in Central Europe, by the Chinese intervention in Korea, and by the spread of communism in the so-called Bamboo Curtain countries in eastern Asia.

With the Vietnam War, support for Luce's view of an expansive America leading the world began to crumble. The idea of an America spreading its values faded in the 1970s as the military efforts in Vietnam became enveloped by failure and controversy. In 1972 President Richard Nixon's opening of relations with the People's Republic of China, which Washington had tried to isolate for the previous twenty-five years, further altered America's view of its relationship to the rest of the world.

During his presidency (1981–1989), Ronald Reagan again invoked the image of America as "the city on a hill," and the 1991 collapse of the Soviet Union, which made America the world's only superpower, perhaps helped revive the idea of exceptionalism. In the late twentieth and early twenty-first centuries, Presidents Bill Clinton (in office 1993–2001), George W. Bush (2001–2009), and Barack Obama (2009–), endeavored to create new senses of an American century, with Obama even calling for "a new American century."

SEE ALSO *Exceptionalism; LIFE (magazine); Luce, Henry*

BIBLIOGRAPHY

Bacevich, Andrew. "Farewell to the American Century." *Salon*. April 30, 2009. http://www.salon.com/2009/04/30/bacevich_2/

Hogan, Michael J., ed. *The Ambiguous Legacy: U.S. Foreign Relations in the "American Century."* Cambridge, UK, and New York: Cambridge University Press, 1999.

Luce, Henry. "The American Century," *Life*, February 17, 1941.

White, Donald W. *The American Century: The Rise and Decline of the United States as a World Power.* New Haven, CT: Yale University Press, 1996.

Charles M. Dobbs
Professor Emeritus
Iowa State University

AMERICAN COLONIZATION SOCIETY

The American Colonization Society (ACS) was an organization, supported mainly by white political leaders and evangelical Christian ministers, that advocated for creating a colony of African Americans in West Africa. One of the most influential and controversial reform societies in the antebellum United States, the ACS went on to help found the nation of Liberia.

In the decades around the turn of the nineteenth century, white politicians and antislavery writers proposed several plans to create colonies for African Americans outside of the United States. While many of these proposals were focused on sites within North America, some were also inspired by British efforts to create a colony of freed slaves in Sierra Leone during the late 1780s. In the 1810s a black shipping merchant, Paul Cuffee (1759–1817), attempted to foster commercial ties with Sierra Leone that would also facilitate the emigration of African Americans from the United States to the colony. Although Cuffee's efforts were largely frustrated, they prompted two white Protestant ministers, Robert Finley (1772–1817) and Samuel J. Mills (1783–1818), to enlist a substantial number of prominent white men to sponsor plans for a similar colony that would be created by the United States. As a result, some of the most renowned public figures in the early republic lent their initial support to the movement, including Chief Justice John Marshall (1755–1835), General Andrew Jackson, and Speaker of the House Henry Clay (1777–1852).

With an impressive roster of names attached to it, the ACS convened its first meeting in the chambers of the United States Congress in December 1816. The example of Sierra Leone influenced the group's early goals of establishing Christianity, commerce, and civilization in Africa. In particular, the ACS emulated the British antecedent by claiming that the proposed colony could establish itself as a site of "legitimate trade," thus counteracting the widespread influence of the slave trade in West Africa. However, the colonization movement in the United States would also seek to distinguish itself from the British effort, in part by claiming that the settlement would eventually become an independent republic, modeled on US political institutions, rather than a formal colony of the United States.

The new movement used its numerous connections to prominent political figures to lobby for a national colonization policy. Although the ACS failed to garner direct federal support for African colonization, it did persuade President James Monroe to support a broad interpretation of the Slave Trade Act of 1819, thus enabling the US government to provide limited financial and military support to an ACS colony. Monroe justified this stance by emphasizing the colony's potential to help combat the international slave trade. Specifically, he argued that the colony could provide a settlement for slaves recaptured by the US naval unit that would be stationed in West Africa for this purpose, eventually to be known as the "Africa Squadron." Although the United States offered limited support for African colonization, it played a crucial role in establishing the colony, particularly after the ACS had failed in its initial attempt to found a colony on Sherbro Island off the coast of Sierra Leone. In late 1821 Robert Stockton (1795–1866), a US naval officer, accompanied by Eli Ayers (1778–1822), an ACS agent, helped secure title to land in Cape Mesurado by threatening the use of force against a group known as the Dey people who lived in the region. The area would provide the basis for an expanding Liberian settlement, and its eventual capital of Monrovia, despite the fact that many of the indigenous peoples in the region did not recognize the settlers' right to claim this land in perpetuity.

During the 1820s this initial establishment of Liberia helped the ACS to build support for African colonization in the United States even though native groups consistently challenged the colony and the settlers suffered devastating rates of fatality from malaria and other illnesses. The ACS downplayed the colony's harsh conditions in order to expand its support among elite whites, yet it was largely unsuccessful in assuaging the concerns of African Americans, who had remained deeply skeptical of the movement since its inception. During this period the organization established a large number of auxiliary organizations, a substantial base of donors, and further endorsements from prominent political figures. Reform-minded evangelical Christian leaders, for whom the missionary language of the movement resonated, helped build much of this early support. However, by the early 1830s the movement was increasingly criticized by slaveholders who feared that the ACS was merely a clandestine vehicle for ending slavery. At the same time it also faced an insurgent abolitionist movement, which branded the ACS as racist, ineffectual, and pro-slavery. As a result, colonizationists were unable to successfully lobby for expanded federal support, donations to the ACS began to drop steeply, and by the end of the 1830s the organization faced dwindling membership and financial ruin.

Despite these setbacks on the national level, many local colonization efforts persisted, sometimes when auxiliaries broke from the national organization, as in Maryland, Pennsylvania, and New York. However, the weakened state of the ACS, as well as the colony's inadequate realization of settler governance, helped inspire a movement among black colonists to reestablish the colony as the Republic of Liberia in 1847. Though initially resisted by the ACS, ultimately this action helped revive the organization by reducing its financial burden and rebranding its efforts as an emigration society that supported a burgeoning, and now independent, black republic. This shift helped enable a relative surge in African American emigration to Liberia from the late 1840s through the mid-1850s, even though the total number of African Americans sent to Liberia had not surpassed 15,000 by the late 1860s. Although the renewed ACS helped inspire a brief revival of colonizationism during the Civil War, Liberia was no longer the focus of these efforts, and after emancipation at the war's end the organization became increasingly irrelevant. Although the organization continued to transport dwindling numbers of African Americans to Liberia through the early twentieth century, it increasingly functioned as a philanthropic aid society and by 1963 ceased operations altogether.

SEE ALSO *Act Prohibiting Importation of Slaves (1807); Africa; Africa Squadron; Antislavery; Atlantic Ocean; Atlantic Slave Trade; Colonization Movement; Liberia*

BIBLIOGRAPHY

Burin, Eric. *Slavery and the Peculiar Solution: A History of the American Colonization Society.* Gainesville: University Press of Florida, 2005.

Clegg, Claude A., III. *The Price of Liberty: African Americans and the Making of Liberia.* Chapel Hill: University of North Carolina Press, 2004.

Everill, Bronwen. *Abolition and Empire in Sierra Leone and Liberia.* Houndmills, Basingstoke, Hampshire, UK: Palgrave Macmillan, 2013.

Fredrickson, George M. *The Black Image in the White Mind: The Debate on Afro-American Character and Destiny, 1817–1914.* New York: Harper and Row, 1971.

Melish, Joanne Pope. *Disowning Slavery: Gradual Emancipation and "Race" in New England, 1780–1860.* Ithaca, NY: Cornell University Press, 1998.

Newman, Richard S. *The Transformation of American Abolitionism.* Chapel Hill: University of North Carolina Press, 2002.

Staudenraus, P. J. *The African Colonization Movement, 1816–1865.* New York: Columbia University Press, 1961.

Tomek, Beverly. *Colonization and Its Discontents: Emancipation, Emigration, and Antislavery in Antebellum Pennsylvania.* New York: New York University Press, 2011.

Tyler-McGraw, Marie. *An African Republic: Black & White Virginians in the Making of Liberia.* Chapel Hill: University of North Carolina Press, 2007.

Brandon Mills
Lecturer, Department of History
University of Colorado Denver

AMERICAN COMMISSION TO NEGOTIATE PEACE

The American Commission to Negotiate Peace represented the United States and served as its negotiating team at the 1919 Paris Peace Conference at the close of World War I. Created and led by President Woodrow Wilson (in office 1913–1921) upon the signing of the armistice on November 11, 1918, the body negotiated formal treaties to end the war and shape the ensuing peace. Wilson's primary preoccupation was the creation of the League of Nations and its covenant, and this focus affected all other aspects of the commission's work and its reception by the American government, press, and public, as well as their foreign counterparts.

Determined to shape the peace and enact his new world order, Wilson headed the commission, becoming the first American president to go to Europe while in office. Wilson built on earlier notions of American exceptionalism and envisioned a new world order that eschewed European balance-of-power politics, imperialism, and militarism, which he saw as the root causes of war, in favor of the progressive ideals contained in his Fourteen Points, which he had put forth in a 1918 speech to Congress. Wilson sought lasting peace based on arms reduction, self-determination, and collective security, to which, in his view, the League of Nations was central. The commission had the task of making those aims a reality.

Wilson created the American Commission for the sole purpose of serving at the peace conference, where its five commissioners plenipotentiary wielded the diplomatic authority to represent and make decisions on behalf of the United States government. Despite the decision-making power of the commission overseas and its ability to make treaties on behalf of the executive branch, as outlined in the Constitution the US Senate still had to ratify those treaties. Though Wilson achieved his goal of pushing the covenant and the League of Nations through at the conference, numerous senators objected to various sections of the Treaty of Versailles, and it did not win approval in the Senate.

The United States had begun preparing for a postwar settlement soon after its April 1917 entry into the First World War. That autumn, President Wilson instructed his advisor and personal confidant Edward M. House (1858–1938), known as "Colonel," to organize and oversee the efforts of some 150 experts, selected mostly from academia. The body, known as the Inquiry, examined the historical, territorial, ethnic, economic, and political problems of Europe, Eurasia, the Middle East, and Africa to prepare for the anticipated peace negotiations following the end of the conflict. Drawing their information primarily from the Library of Congress and the Columbia University library, groups of specialists of differing ideological orientations created papers and reports to guide policy makers.

Members of the American Commission to Negotiate Peace, which replaced the Inquiry after the end of the war, left for Paris on the USS *George Washington* on December 4, 1918. Wilson, who arrived along with the rest of the commission on December 14, received much public adulation in Europe. Jubilant receptions in Paris, London, Rome, and Milan strengthened Wilson's hand early on at the conference and paved the way for acceptance of the League of Nations Covenant in the peace treaty.

Placing himself in charge, the president selected fellow Democrats Colonel House, Secretary of State Robert Lansing, and Gen. Tasker H. Bliss (already in France as the American military representative on the Supreme War Council), and Republican and retired career diplomat Henry White as his fellow commissioners plenipotentiary. Of these five, only House and Bliss had been directly involved with European affairs during the war. Many congressional Republicans saw the selection of a lone, not particularly prominent Republican as a serious partisan slight on the part of the president. During the nearly six months that Wilson spent overseas, Republican leadership undermined the president's vision for the League of Nations and a new world order.

AN UNWIELDY UNDERTAKING

The American Commission proved unwieldy. Wilson, housed by the French government at Murat Palace, the former residence of Napoléon's marshal, was preoccupied by peace conference meetings and devoted little time to strictly American meetings. Even Lansing, Bliss, and White, who took up residence, along with House, at the American Commission's headquarters at the ornate Hôtel Crillon, could reach the president only through House. Wilson provided few explicit instructions to his fellow commissioners, and on many matters of major concern he did not inform or consult with them nor clarify his opinions. The commission lacked unity and direction, and Wilson made no effort to encourage or coordinate its workings. Preferring to act on his own, in many instances the president would call the plenipotentiaries to meet in House's office only when he needed their signatures.

A large administrative and advisory staff including technical advisors, security officers, clerks, orderlies, and service personnel drawn from regular and wartime government bureaucracies supported the five commissioners plenipotentiary. Though a number of American delegates had little to no experience in diplomacy, many served as negotiators on the conference's fifty-eight committees. The group numbered over a thousand, reaching thirteen hundred at its height. The staff included twenty-three former members of the Inquiry, who were no longer providing briefing papers but focused instead on practical solutions. A certain unease arose between them and personnel from the State Department, who saw the former Inquiry personnel, despite their academic expertise, as diplomatic amateurs. Notable members of the commission staff included Bernard M. Baruch, Archibald Cary Coolidge, Allen W. Dulles, John Foster Dulles, Samuel Gompers, Ulysses Grant III, Joseph C. Grew, Herbert C. Hoover, Edward M. Hurley, Vance McCormick, Gen. Frank R. McCoy, Henry Morgenthau, Gen. John Pershing, Nicholas Roosevelt, and Robert A. Taft. Though Wilson did not give much attention to champions of the press, labor, and women's rights, some of the American peace delegates did. Wilson and the delegates alike were less responsive to stands taken by representatives of American minority groups, including W. E. B. Du Bois (1868–1963), who called for support of racial minorities at home and abroad.

With both President Wilson and his secretary of state overseas for the majority of the proceedings, Under Secretary of State Frank L. Polk (1871–1943) served not only as acting secretary of state but also as liaison between the commission and Congress. As acting secretary he received little direct communication from the commission, and the information that he did receive was often conflicting, unclear, and overwhelming in volume. Polk was thus handicapped in fulfilling his task of advising Congress on the conference. He was similarly hindered in advising the commission about the political situation at home—particularly the increasingly hostile climate in Congress.

With his health failing (a stroke was imminent), Wilson departed the conference permanently in June 1919, at which point Polk took over as head of the commission. Despite representing America on the Supreme Council, as at home Polk had limited influence, often deferring to those who had been in Paris longer, were more expert, or had closer ties to the president, who continued serving as the primary figurehead even though he no longer ran the commission. Active American participation in the conference ended when the commission returned home on December 9, 1919.

Though the Wilsonian ideals of the American Commission to Negotiate Peace fell out of favor until the end of World War II and the creation of the United Nations in 1945, a persistent undercurrent of American internationalism persisted. During the interwar period, even those who participated in the American Commission largely disavowed its work after ratification of the Treaty of Versailles failed in the Senate. Nevertheless the Council on Foreign Relations, a nonpartisan think tank that has been in continuous operation since 1921 and is a direct heir of the Inquiry, continued to champion the commission's internationalist ideals during the interwar period and after. Following the Second World War, a number of the major debates raised by the commission over international borders, race, women's rights, and human rights reasserted themselves. The Charter of the United Nations perhaps most significantly articulated many of the conversations begun in Paris and championed by Wilson and the commission.

SEE ALSO *Department of State; Empire, US; Exceptionalism; Internationalism; Interventionism; Isolationism; League of Nations; Missionary Diplomacy; Paris Peace Conference (1919); Self-Determination; Treaty of Versailles; United Nations; Wilson, Woodrow; World War I; World War II*

BIBLIOGRAPHY

Boemeke, Manfred F., Gerald D. Feldman, and Elisabeth Glaser, eds. *The Treaty of Versailles: A Reassessment after 75 Years.* Cambridge and New York: Cambridge University Press, 2006.

Gelfand, Lawrence E. *The Inquiry: American Preparations for Peace, 1917–1919.* New Haven, CT: Yale University Press, 1963.

Graebner, Norman A., and Edward M. Bennett. *The Versailles Treaty and Its Legacy: The Failure of the Wilsonian Vision.* New York: Cambridge University Press, 2011.

Grose, Peter. *Continuing the Inquiry: The Council on Foreign Relations from 1921 to 1996.* New York: Council on Foreign Relations Press, 1996.

Lansing, Robert. *The Peace Negotiations: A Personal Narrative.* Boston and New York: Houghton Mifflin, 1921; Westport, CT: Greenwood, 1971.

MacMillan, Margaret. *Paris 1919: Six Months that Changed the World.* New York: Random House, 2002.

Mitchell, Kell Freeman, Jr. *Frank L. Polk and the Paris Peace Conference, 1919.* PhD diss., University of Georgia, 1966.

Walworth, Arthur. *Wilson and His Peacemakers: American Diplomacy at the Paris Peace Conference, 1919.* New York: Norton, 1986.

Hannah Higgin
History Faculty
Blair Academy

AMERICAN ENTERPRISE INSTITUTE

SEE *Think Tanks.*

AMERICAN ISRAEL PUBLIC AFFAIRS COMMITTEE (AIPAC)

AIPAC, the American Israel Public Affairs Committee, is one of the most powerful lobbies in America. Its self-declared mission, "to strengthen, protect and promote the U.S.-Israel relationship in ways that enhance the security of Israel and the United States," is supported by a budget of $70 million, hundreds of Washington staffers, and over 100,000 members across America (AIPAC website). AIPAC's influence derives from its brilliant grass-roots organization. In every congressional district local members communicate Israel's needs to congressional representatives and senators, track their voting record, and dispense often massive campaign funds through informally affiliated political action committees. AIPAC also identifies and cultivates future pro-Israel leaders and provides free trips to Israel for politicians and opinion makers.

AIPAC's most significant achievement has been to assure massive military and financial aid to Israel, currently over $3 billion per year. In the 1950s and 1960s this task was relatively straightforward. But Israel's victory in the 1967 War transformed her image from underdog to occupier and provided new potential peace options, resulting in an increasingly divided American and American Jewish public. With the victory of the conservative Likud Party in 1979, Israeli politics similarly fractured. Exclusively concerned with lobbying for Israel and eschewing the liberal agenda of most American Jews, AIPAC increasingly served as an intermediary between the expansionist Likud and the conservative anticommunism of the administration of President Ronald Reagan (1911–2004). When Reagan's successor, George H. W. Bush (b. 1924), opposed Israeli settlement expansion on the West Bank, AIPAC, in defiance of American Jewish public opinion, fought with such ferocity as to earn rebukes from both Bush and from Yitzhak Rabin (1922–1995) when he later became the Labor Party prime minister.

AIPAC's support of Labor's 1993 Oslo Accord with the Palestinians was lukewarm at best. Against the wishes of the Labor government, it supported a bill to transfer the capital of Israel to Jerusalem, a move that would have scuttled the peace process. With the advent of the anti-Oslo Likud government of Benjamin Netanyahu (b. 1949), AIPAC mobilized Congress to prevent President Bill Clinton (b. 1946) from pressuring Israel to freeze settlements on the West Bank and make concessions to the Palestinians. This caused a split with an increasingly dovish American Jewish public, which, however, did little to diminish the lobby's influence.

In recent years AIPAC has come under increasing scrutiny. In 2005 two AIPAC staffers were accused of receiving classified documents, although charges against them were later dropped. Two years later, in 2007, John Mearsheimer (b. 1947) and Steven Walt (b. 1955) published *The Israel Lobby and U.S. Foreign Policy,* which accused AIPAC of having "an almost unchallenged hold on Congress" and of promoting the Iraq War (162). While it was a best seller, critics contended that its thesis was inaccurate or exaggerated (Foxman 2007, 53–55). The emergence in 2008 of J Street, a liberal Jewish lobby that saw Israel's West Bank policies as inimical to liberal Jewish values, provided a small but increasingly visible dovish alternative on Capitol Hill.

During the administration of President Barack Obama (b. 1961), AIPAC aligned itself with Likud. It has consistently fought Obama's desire to freeze settlements and extend rights to the Palestinians. In 2009 it induced the US House of Representatives overwhelmingly to condemn a United Nations report accusing Israel of committing human rights violations in Gaza. It was, however, unable to prevail in its strong desire for tougher sanctions against Iran, which Obama contended would end negotiations over its nuclear program. Despite a less supportive American Jewry, AIPAC retains its status and power.

SEE ALSO *Arab-Israeli Conflict; Israel*

BIBLIOGRAPHY

American Israel Public Affairs Committee (AIPAC) website. www.AIPAC.org.

Foxman, Abraham H. *The Deadliest Lies: The Israeli Lobby and the Myth of Jewish Control.* New York: Palgrave Macmillan, 2007.

Goldberg, J. J. *Jewish Power: Inside the American Jewish Establishment.* Reading, MA: Basic Books, 1996.

J Street: The Political Home for Pro-Israel, Pro-peace Americans. http://jstreet.org

Mearsheimer, John J., and Stephen M. Walt. *The Israel Lobby and U.S. Foreign Policy.* New York: Farrar, Straus and Giroux, 2007.

Rosenthal, Steven T. *Irreconcilable Differences?: The Waning of the American Jewish Love Affair with Israel.* Hanover, NH: Brandeis University Press/University Press of New England, 2001.

Urofsky, Melvin I. *American Zionism from Herzl to the Holocaust.* Garden City, NY: Anchor Press, 1975.

Steven Rosenthal
Professor of Middle Eastern History
University of Hartford

AMERICAN MISSIONARY SOCIETY

SEE *Foreign Mission Movement.*

AMERICAN PEACE SOCIETY

The earliest peace societies were organized on both sides of the Atlantic in the wake of the War of 1812 and the Napoleonic Wars (1803–1815). In 1828, some of these organizations in the United States, with Captain William Ladd (1778–1841) as prime mover, joined together to create the American Peace Society (APS). In its early years, the APS membership consisted primarily of elite, Christian men, including ministers, statesmen, businessmen, and even military veterans. Its methods centered on moral appeals and established political mechanisms, including circulating pamphlets and periodicals, forming alliances with churches and religious organizations, and mounting lecture tours and petition drives. From its beginnings, the APS corresponded with foreign peace groups, especially the London Peace Society, and members attended several international peace conferences held in Europe in the 1840s and 1850s. The APS promulgated its ideas through a long-standing journal, known for much of its history as the *Advocate of Peace.*

DEFINING PEACE

In the 1830s, 1840s, and 1850s, the APS promoted alternatives to resolving international conflicts through war, including diplomatic negotiation and "stipulated arbitration" (the advance agreement in treaties to send future disputes to an arbiter). The APS also consistently advocated the formation of a congress of nations, an international governing body with both legislative and judicial functions. A major issue of debate during the organization's early years was whether to limit its opposition to offensive war or to oppose all war categorically. Though some members and affiliated organizations continued to hold that defensive war was justifiable, the society voted in 1837 to repudiate all war as anti-Christian. The tensions did not end there, however. The APS framed peace solely as the resolution of international conflict, rather than the cessation of all kinds of violence. By the 1840s, many peace advocates, including some with leadership roles in the APS, were pushing for a more expansive definition of peace that embraced nonviolence in all aspects of interpersonal relations and placed the sanctity of human life at the center of ethical and political debates. This tension over the legitimate object of peace reform led to a schism within the APS in 1846, with those who preferred the broader definition of peace departing. This schism confirmed the APS as the most conservative of the major American peace groups of the nineteenth century.

THE APS RESPONSE TO AMERICAN WARS

In wartime, the APS favored nonconfrontational approaches that balanced patriotism and peace principles. At a time when antiwar sentiment ran high, especially in the Northern states, the *Advocate of Peace* regularly criticized the Mexican-American War (1846–1848) and called on citizens to petition Congress against it. The Civil War (1861–1865) proved a more difficult test. As sectional tensions heated, the APS reiterated that its priority was to eliminate violence between nations, not between individuals or within nations. Ultimately, the APS interpreted the secession of the Southern states as an internal rebellion that threatened legitimate governmental authority. Accepting force as justified when putting down a rebellion *within* a state, the APS endorsed the Union war effort.

Financial difficulties and declining membership troubled the society in the wake of the war, but it rebuilt in the 1870s and 1880s. Its membership still consisted primarily of elite, well-educated, professional men, with an increasing number of women among them. The society renewed its advocacy of international governance and arbitration agreements. In collaboration with other peace organizations, the APS made gaining support for arbitration as an alternative to war its major goal. Beginning in 1889, international peace congresses were revived on an annual basis. Most of these conferences were held in Europe and included the participation of APS members. The society played a key role in organizing the two congresses held in the United States: in Chicago in 1893 (coincident with the World's Columbian Exposition) and in the APS's headquarters city of Boston in 1904. Around the turn of the twentieth century, leaders and members of the APS—most notably, its charismatic longtime secretary, Benjamin Franklin Trueblood (1847–1916)—participated in a number of other conferences oriented around international governance and international law, including the Pan-American Conferences of 1889 to 1890 and the Hague Conferences of 1899 and 1907.

Even as the society pushed hard to promote alternatives to war, its responses to the outbreak of new wars were complex. The APS opposed the Spanish-American War of 1898 and favored independence for the Philippines. The organization also expressed regret at the outbreak of World War I (1914–1918) and supported Woodrow Wilson's early efforts to maintain American neutrality and mediate the European crisis. However, when US entry into the war appeared imminent, the APS again privileged patriotism over pacifism, just as it had done during the Civil War. The society contended that the war was indeed a tragedy, but a predictable one for a world lacking in robust forms of international governance. For the APS, the Great War highlighted the need to create international institutions to stave off war in the future, but in the present the best way to ensure peace and progress was for the United States and its allies to win the war and contain German aggression.

SHIFT IN FOCUS TO WORLD AFFAIRS

After World War I, the society continued to advocate international organization, but it deplored the League of Nations covenant for permitting the use of force to enforce the decisions of international governing bodies. In 1932, the society changed its journal's title to *World Affairs* and focused its reportage on nonpartisan analysis of international affairs. Publishing the journal became the APS's main activity for the remainder of the twentieth century. During World War II (1939–1945), *World Affairs* focused on plans for the postwar order, and after the war, it endorsed the formation of the United Nations. What had in its original nineteenth-century guise been a publication devoting much of its attention to the Christian teachings of peace was now focused on examining the major international issues underpinning US foreign policy. In this evolution of its flagship publication, the APS reflected the diversity of those who have called themselves peace advocates, whose commitments have ranged from utopian ideals to practical politics. For most of its history, the APS tended toward the latter end of that spectrum.

SEE ALSO *Transatlantic Reform*

BIBLIOGRAPHY

Brock, Peter. *Pacifism in the United States from the Colonial Era to the First World War.* Princeton, NJ: Princeton University Press, 1968.

Davis, Harold Eugene. "One Hundred and Fifty Years of the American Peace Society." *World Affairs* 141, 2 (1978): 92–103.

DeBenedetti, Charles. *The Peace Reform in American History.* Bloomington: Indiana University Press, 1980.

Patterson, David S. *Toward a Warless World: The Travail of the American Peace Movement, 1887–1914.* Bloomington: Indiana University Press, 1976.

Rosenberger, Homer T. "The American Peace Society's Reaction to the Covenant of the League of Nations." *World Affairs* 141, 2 (1972): 139–152.

Whitney, Edson L. *The American Peace Society: A Centennial History.* Washington, DC: American Peace Society, 1928.

Ziegler, Valarie H. *The Advocates of Peace in Antebellum America.* Bloomington: Indiana University Press, 1992.

Margot Minardi
Associate Professor of History and Humanities
Reed College

AMERICAN PROTECTIVE ASSOCIATION

Founded in 1887 by Henry Bowers (1837–1911), a lawyer from Clinton, Iowa, the American Protective Association (APA) became the most popular anti-Catholic organization in the United States in the last decade of the nineteenth century. Drawing heavily on the themes and rhetoric that had animated the Know-Nothings in the antebellum era, the APA mobilized widespread fears of an international Catholic plot to undermine the liberties of the United States.

A number of developments in the 1880s set the stage for the APA's rise. The recurring suspicion that the Vatican sought political as well as spiritual domination was reignited by the mass immigration of Catholics from southern and eastern Europe after the Civil War (1861–1865). Nativists viewed these arrivals as an army of uneducated and pliable voters under the command of the Catholic hierarchy, and pointed to election results as proof of a looming Catholic takeover. In 1880, William Russell Grace (1832–1904) was elected as the first Irish-born Catholic mayor of New York City, followed four years later by the first Irish mayor of Boston, Hugh O'Brien (1827–1895). The growth of the Catholic school network also fed nativist anxieties. In 1884, the American bishops decreed at the Third Plenary Council that all parishes should provide Catholic education, a move which, combined with the church's long-running campaign for state funding of its parochial schools, provoked fears of a Vatican-directed assault on the public education system.

Despite this, the growth of the APA was steady rather than spectacular until 1893, when Bowers was replaced as supreme president by William J. H. Traynor (1845–c. 1915), a Detroit publisher and committed nativist. Traynor brought a new zeal and vigor to the leadership at a moment when a severe economic crisis was fostering a climate of anxiety and resentment. For the APA, the depression that began in 1893 was part of a Vatican-led plot to weaken the United States and to prepare the ground for the domination of Rome. In magazine articles and popular lectures, the APA hammered home the message that the Jesuits and other Catholic agents were responsible for the bank runs, layoffs, and bitter strikes that were devastating the nation. The APA even published a fake encyclical in which Pope Leo XIII (1810–1903) called on Catholics to massacre American heretics. The APA also revived the old nativist theme of sexual corruption at the heart of Catholicism. The convent was a favorite target; across the nation, the APA warned, young women were held captive in these dark institutions, where they were exposed to a hellish regime of violence, torture, and sexual abuse.

To thwart the political aspirations of the Vatican, the APA called for a series of safeguards. Members pledged never to employ a Catholic or to vote for a Catholic office-seeker. In order to prevent a Catholic political takeover, the APA demanded that all supporters of what it termed the "ecclesiastical power" be barred from elected office. Institutions where people were held under restraint, a sly reference to convents, were to be subject to state inspection. Finally, to counter the Catholic plot to weaken the public school system, all state funding of sectarian schools was to be forbidden. This platform, combined with Traynor's active leadership, found a receptive audience. By 1895, the APA had a membership that numbered in the hundreds of thousands, and had spread from its base in the Midwest to both the Northeast and the West Coast.

This was the peak of the APA's strength. By then, a number of influential figures had come out in opposition. The Republican Theodore Roosevelt (1858–1919) publicly denounced the movement as intolerant and "utterly un-American." Another prominent figure to repudiate the APA and its brand of anti-Catholicism was the Protestant minister Washington Gladden (1836–1918), who went as far as praising Pope Leo XIII for his progressive and enlightened policies. Angered by the refusal of the Republican Party to bring into law any of his proposals, Traynor chose to not endorse William McKinley (1843–1901) for president in 1896. His subsequent proposal to form a third political party raised significant opposition within the APA, leading to his removal from the leadership. With the election of McKinley, and the intense national focus on Cuba and Spain, the issue of anti-Catholicism lost much of its mobilizing power. Wracked by disagreement and dissension, the APA quickly subsided as a political force, and disbanded in 1911.

SEE ALSO *Immigration Quotas; Know-Nothings; Nativism*

BIBLIOGRAPHY

Kinzer, Donald L. *An Episode in Anti-Catholicism: The American Protective Association.* Seattle: University of Washington, 1964.

Wallace, Les. *The Rhetoric of Anti-Catholicism: The American Protective Association, 1887–1911.* New York: Garland, 1990.

Timothy Verhoeven
Senior Lecturer
School of Philosophical, Historical, and International Studies
Monash University, Australia

AMERICAN REVOLUTION

The American Revolution (1775–1783) was a global transformation of the first importance. Not only did it produce a new union of independent states in a region where Europeans had only been present as colonists, but the revolution unsettled politics across Europe, both through the Republic's quest for diplomatic recognition and through its democratic example. Americans also struck the first blow against the ascendancy of Europe's colonial powers in their own hemisphere. In Haiti and Spanish America, the American Revolution set a precedent for later colonial revolts. No less important, Americans remained active in the African slave trade, and they became aggressive participants in Western efforts to open markets in China, India, and eventually Japan. In their attempt to join "the powers of the earth," as Thomas Jefferson (1743–1826) wrote in the Declaration of Independence, Americans changed the world.

THE DEMOCRATIC EXAMPLE

The first, and in many ways most important, of the American Revolution's global consequences was the democratic example that Americans set for other people. During the 1760s and 1770s, American objections to being taxed by Parliament, a legislature in which British colonists were not represented, resonated with ordinary men and women in England, Scotland, and Wales, many of whom also paid taxes without having a vote. For Britain's emerging working and middle classes, and for religious minorities of all faiths, the American endorsement of popular sovereignty was an important counterpoint to a Parliament controlled by landed gentlemen and aristocrats. There was also widespread sympathy for the American Revolution in Ireland, which had its own parliament but was controlled by the British government. During the Revolutionary War, Irish patriots demanded broader legislative representation for themselves and greater autonomy from Britain. In 1780, the discontent in Ireland and England brought the British government to the verge of collapse, with political protests, industrial unrest, a threatened rebellion in the British House of Commons, and London's Gordon riots, the most destructive urban disturbance in Europe before the French Revolution (Butterfield 1968).

The radicalism of the former colonies' British and Irish friends echoed with American sympathizers elsewhere in Europe. In Paris, Benjamin Franklin (1706–1790), Congress's ambassador to France, was memorialized in popular songs and poetry, feted with banquets, parties, and balls, and depicted on plates, teacups, walking sticks, and snuff boxes (Palmer 1959–1964, Vol. 1). Admirers in Europe and the Americas also sought to imitate the American experiment in self-government.

"Bostonians in Distress," illustration published in a London newspaper soon after the Boston Tea Party. *The grievances of the American colonists resonated with ordinary men and women in Britain, as suggested by this image of captive Bostonians hanging from the Liberty Tree while surrounded by British cannons and warships.* INTERIM ARCHIVES/ARCHIVE PHOTOS/GETTY IMAGES

The Declaration of Independence and the new state constitutions were all widely reprinted and played a role in the coming of the French Revolution. Although the Haitian Revolution terrified slaveholders like Jefferson, the French island colony of Saint-Domingue was among the places that the American Revolution affected in the Union's own neighborhood. In 1804, liberated slaves on the island declared independence and took the name Haiti with a document based partly on Jefferson's original. By the time of Jefferson's death on July 4, 1826, the list of countries with declarations based on the one that Congress had adopted fifty years before included Belgium, Venezuela, Bolivia, Argentina, and Mexico (Armitage 2007).

THE QUEST FOR INTERNATIONAL RECOGNITION

At the same time that they set a democratic example for others, Americans' quest for international recognition had a major impact on the structure of government within the United States. As Americans knew, declaring independence from Britain was only a beginning. To claim a place among the world's independent powers, they would need the consent of other nations. With this wider context in mind, George Washington (1732–1799) insisted during the Revolutionary War that soldiers under his command treat British prisoners of war with the humanity that the European rules of war required. In so doing, Americans hoped to convince foreign powers of their determination to be good international citizens. Similar calculations helped strengthen the American movement to abolish slavery, including in slaveholding states like Virginia, which took the lead in outlawing the slave trade in 1776. Speaking of the clause in the Constitution of 1787 that authorized Congress to abolish the slave trade after a waiting period of two decades, James Wilson (1742–1798) of Pennsylvania claimed that there was no more "lovely part" of the new document, nor one more likely to appeal to "a benevolent and philanthropic European" (Gould 2012).

In their quest for recognition in Europe, Americans eventually also had to strengthen the loose-knit union that Congress initially envisioned for the new union of states. Under the Articles of Confederation, which the last of the thirteen states ratified in 1781, the United States was not a nation but an alliance or system of states, each with its own sovereign government and people. Although we do not usually think of the US Constitution in this way, the diplomatic consequences of this loose-knit alliance dominated the thinking of the delegates who met in Philadelphia to revise the Articles in 1787. Most believed that the Union would need a stronger central government if it was to gain the recognition of nations beyond its borders. With that goal in mind, the Constitution's framers gave the federal government most of the powers that Congress had lacked. These included the power to levy taxes for revenue, the power to negotiate and enforce treaties, and the power to regulate and (eventually) abolish slavery. According to John Adams (1735–1826), the Articles of Confederation had cast Congress in the role of a "diplomatic assembly," not a national legislature. Under the new Constitution, it was possible for "the United States … to unite their wills and forces as a single nation" (Adams 1787–1788, 1:362–364, 3:505–506). The change allowed Americans to take an important step toward becoming the responsible international actors that Congress had promised the world in 1776 they would be.

GLOBAL DISRUPTIONS

Along with America's democratic example and the internal reforms that the United States undertook to win international recognition, the American Revolution was a disruption of truly global proportions, with aftershocks that were felt around the world. The sixty thousand (and possibly more) Loyalists who left the territory of the United States during and after the Revolutionary War were by far the most visible manifestation of this upheaval. Despite a tendency to think of the Loyalists as a wealthy, privileged group, most were neither, and quite a few were from the humblest ranks of American society. During the Revolutionary War, thousands of Indians and escaped slaves fought for the Crown, as did substantial numbers of poor whites. In the war's aftermath, the largest group of exiles went to four of Britain's remaining colonies: Nova Scotia, the Bahamas, New Brunswick, and Upper Canada (Ontario), the last two of which were founded as Loyalist sanctuaries after the war. Loyalists also moved to points as distant as India, Australia, and Africa, where African Americans who had served in the Revolutionary War founded the colony of Sierra Leone in 1787. Among their number was a Virginian named Harry Washington (c. 1740–c. 1801), who left New York in 1783 and built a plantation near Freetown that he called Mount Vernon in honor of his former master.

Because it disrupted trading relationships that had once bound Americans to the rest of the British Empire, the American Revolution also had far-reaching economic consequences. For American merchants who had carried goods to and from the British West Indies before 1776 and for West Indians who had depended on them, the revolution was an especially heavy blow. In 1783, Britain refused to allow ships from the now-independent United States to resume trading with its island colonies, forcing people on both sides to adapt. In the Pacific and Indian Oceans, New Englanders responded by seeking new Asian markets in porcelain, tea, and opium, and many turned to whaling. At the same time, Americans discovered new ways to access the Caribbean. Sometimes, they formed partnerships with British and Loyalist firms. On other occasions, they disguised their cargo's true destination by stopping at the islands of other European powers. As a result of such schemes, Saint-Domingue became for a time the United States' largest trading partner, a status that the Adams administration recognized in 1798 by signing a commercial treaty with Toussaint Louverture (1743–1803), the former slave who was the French colony's de facto leader. By the early nineteenth century, the United States had the second-largest merchant marine (after Britain) in the world.

The American Revolution's biggest disruption of all was the creation of an aggressive new imperial power—an "empire of liberty," as Jefferson called it—in a part of the world where Europeans had only lived as colonists (Wood 2009). For the vast majority of African Americans and Indians, the creation of this empire was an unmitigated disaster. At the end of the Revolutionary War, the United States acquired millions of acres of Indian land, doing so without so much as mentioning the rights of the native proprietors. Meanwhile, the Constitution left most decisions about slavery's fate in the hands of the states. Until 1861 and the start of the American Civil War, the right to own slaves was far more secure in Jefferson's Virginia than it was in Britain's remaining West Indian colonies, where Parliament abolished chattel servitude in 1834. Yet if the liberty that the United States had to offer was less than perfect, it was a liberty that people elsewhere admired and wanted for themselves, and that fact was also disruptive. In the decades following the revolution, tens of thousands of men, women, and children from Britain, Ireland, and northern Europe flocked to North America, helping turn the fledgling union of 1776 into a nation that could claim to be "among the first nations of the world," as Henry Clay (1777–1852) boasted in 1819. The Unites States' "very existence is an attack upon the monarchies of Europe," wrote the *North American Review* in 1823: "its policy condemns their ambition, their unnecessary wars, and their whole political system" (Gould 2012). If the immigrants who came in growing numbers to the United States' shores were any indication, people in Europe and beyond agreed.

SUMMARY

Whether through the democratic example that the new American Republic set to other nations, or through its character as a nation seeking the recognition of other nations, or through the disruption that its growing power caused in nearly every corner of the world, the American Revolution had consequences that defy easy answers and simple categories of analysis. While proclaiming the "self-evident" truth that "all men are created equal," Americans founded a nation that forced thousands of Loyal Americans into exile, that continued to dispossess Indians, and that was one of the world's leading slaveholding powers. Writers elsewhere celebrated the revolution, but they feared it as well. In other words, to convey what the American Revolution meant to people at the time is to convey a story full of contradictions and complexity. In that regard, at least, America's relationship to the world of 1776 was not so different from the place that America occupies in the world today.

SEE ALSO *Adams, John; Franklin, Benjamin; French Revolution; Haitian Revolution; Jay, John; Jefferson, Thomas; Lafayette, Marquis de; Washington, George*

BIBLIOGRAPHY

Adams, John. *A Defence of the Constitutions of Government of the United States of America*. 3 vols. London, 1787–1788.

Armitage, David. *The Declaration of Independence: A Global History*. Cambridge, MA: Harvard University Press, 2007.

Butterfield, Herbert. *George III, Lord North, and the People, 1779–80*. New York: Russell and Russell, 1968. First published in 1949.

Gould, Eliga H. *Among the Powers of the Earth: The American Revolution and the Making of a New World Empire*. Cambridge, MA: Harvard University Press, 2012.

Jasanoff, Maya. *Liberty's Exiles: American Loyalists in the Revolutionary World*. New York: Knopf, 2011.

Palmer, R. R. *The Age of the Democratic Revolution: A Political History of Europe and America, 1760–1800*. 2 vols. Princeton, NJ: Princeton University Press, 1959–1964.

Pybus, Cassandra. *Epic Journeys of Freedom: Runaway Slaves of the American Revolution and Their Global Quest for Liberty*. Boston: Beacon Press, 2006.

Wood, Gordon S. *Empire of Liberty: A History of the Early Republic, 1789–1815*. Oxford: Oxford University Press, 2009.

Eliga H. Gould
Professor and Chair, Department of History
University of New Hampshire

AMERICANIZATION

Few words have been as central to describing the rising world-historical significance of the United States and yet so amorphous and hard to define as the term *Americanization*. It has enjoyed a mercurial career among historians, social scientists, policy makers, pundits, and ordinary citizens. Although Americanization is now widely considered to be of limited analytical value because it has been thoroughly politicized and incorporates multiple if not divergent meanings, the term continues to trigger positive and negative emotions the world over, from reverent invocation and jubilant acceptance to skeptical evaluation and angry rejection. To embed Americanization in these various social, cultural, and territorial contexts, therefore, is to reflect on the nation's dynamic and ambiguous relationship with population groups both inside and outside its recognized boundaries.

AMERICANIZATION VIEWED DOMESTICALLY

While attempting to find a single, all-encompassing definition of Americanization is bound to fail, the concept owes its longevity mainly to two globally intertwined processes—one of an incoming, the other of an outgoing nature. Domestically, notions of Americanization have been intrinsically tied up with the assimilation of immigrants within the borders of the United States. The country's Anglo-Saxon elites have been concerned about the political loyalties and cultural tastes of immigrants since the founding of the Republic, but it was not until the early twentieth century that the contours of a self-described "Americanization Movement" became visible. Americanization was conceived so broadly that it encompassed people and institutions alike—organizations with foreign roots such as the Red Cross and the Boy Scouts were thoroughly nationalized, that is, Americanized, by Progressive Era Americans. Female middle-class reformers such as Jane Addams (1860–1935) in Chicago and Frances Kellor (1873–1952) in New York sought to bind old and new Americans together into a homogeneous citizenry by encouraging immigrants to use the English language, change their names, dress styles, and work habits, and adopt "American" ways of housekeeping and child rearing. Meanwhile, the proponents of an aggressively masculine, racially charged, and overtly nationalistic Americanization policy found their hero in Theodore Roosevelt (1858–1919), whose denunciation of the "hyphenated American" during World War I (1914–1918) set the tone for the restrictive immigration legislation of the 1920s.

Expecting that foreign-born Americans and their children accept and internalize Anglo-American norms of citizenship, the supporters of Roosevelt's brand of Americanization distanced themselves from the cultural pluralism associated with the melting-pot ideal and moved toward the rigidly conformist ideology of Americanism. Although whiteness remained a prerequisite for full inclusion into the body politic, the advocates of a moderate, gradual Americanization occupied a middle ground between an exclusionary nativism and the multicultural ideal of a "Trans-National America," as introduced by the progressive intellectual Randolph Bourne (1886–1918) in 1916. It was only after World War II (1939–1945), particularly in the wake of the civil rights movement and the countercultures of the 1960s, that 100 percent Americanism and the melting-pot theory of Americanization came under increasing attack. Critics pointed to the term's ideological blind spots, such as its tendency to mitigate the violent legacies of slavery, racism, and settler colonialism, rallying instead around the "salad bowl" metaphor to express their appreciation of cultural diversity.

AMERICANIZATION VIEWED INTERNATIONALLY

At the same time that Americanization was entering the political lexicon as a term to describe the nation's influence on immigrants, contemporaries also began to use it to gauge the influence of the United States on the world. This second application puts Americanization in close proximity to notions of globalization, Westernization, and modernization while ascribing a leading role to the United States in the transnational spread of goods, technologies, and ideas. Among the first Europeans to prominently articulate the correlation between American power and a sprawling mass culture were the British aristocrat Sir Christopher Furness (1852–1912), author of *The American Invasion* (1902), and English newspaperman William T. Stead (1849–1912). Although criticized by Stead's peers as a vast exaggeration of American influence, Stead's book *The Americanization of the World* (1902) painted a prophetic picture of US global hegemony. Americanization, Stead argued, and as reflected in the book's subtitle, was "the trend of the twentieth century," and every British gentleman could find proof of that trend in the products laid out on his breakfast table. Stead anticipated some of the anti-American resentments coming from Europe's conservative elites, who were denouncing American-style modernity as vulgar and superficial. At the same time, Stead hoped that Americanization would usher in an age of Anglo-Saxon supremacy if American ingenuity and British imperialism could be conjoined in a special relationship.

The linkage of modernization, consumerism, and empire described by Stead became a staple of positive and negative images about "America" on both sides of the Atlantic after World War I. Both discourses grew in size and stature during the boom years of the 1920s as European exposure to economic, cultural, and political innovations associated with the United States increased markedly. The European infatuation with American models of business organization and mass production revolved around two philosophies in particular: Taylorism, which introduced scientific forms of managerial leadership, and Fordism, which stood for a system of producing affordable, standardized goods involving assembly lines and semiskilled labor. The advance of what historian Victoria de Grazia, in *Irresistible Empire* (2005), termed America's "market empire" through postwar Europe also included the proliferation of new social and professional networks. Business-oriented service clubs such as Rotary International, whose members propagated a capitalist ethic of philanthropy based on border-crossing male camaraderie and entrepreneurial expertise, found imitators across the continent, although Rotary's popularity differed from country to country.

AMERICANIZATION AND THE ENTERTAINMENT INDUSTRIES

Coinciding with the expansion of American big business was the rise of a modern entertainment industry that stretched from Hollywood and Harlem to Paris and Berlin. Some historians date the beginnings of Europe's encounter with American forms of showmanship to Buffalo Bill's internationally successful Wild West spectacles, yet the social and technological transformations of the early twentieth century widened the scope of this encounter considerably. Reduced working hours and rising wages, which gave people more money to spend on fashion, music, sports, and other recreational activities, led to a democratization of leisure on both sides of the Atlantic and made innovations such as radio and film part of a thriving machinery of mass consumption. The demand for US-made movies was particularly high in the postwar period, which turned that medium into a battleground between supporters and opponents of Americanization. For young consumers, Hollywood represented the allure of modern technology and the promise of stardom, whereas older cultural elites saw in the American film industry a symbol of declining artistic standards and moral decadence. Still, Hollywood was able to conquer foreign markets thanks to a superior distribution system, a wealth of incoming domestic and international talent, and greater financial power that allowed American filmmakers to make longer films and experiment with new technologies. At the onset of the Great Depression, Hollywood was producing more than 90 percent of the feature films shown worldwide.

Jazz was another cultural export from the United States that received a mixed reception overseas. Again it was mostly young people with purchasing power who embraced modern music as a liberating form of cultural expression and incorporated it into the rebellion against what they perceived as the stifling social conventions of their elders. Jazz and the Charleston became the soundtrack of a young generation represented by the female "flapper," who wore makeup, loved fast cars, enjoyed cigarettes and a good drink, and rejected Victorian sexual norms. The flapper and her male companions were mimicked by progressive artists and young bohemians in Europe who praised traveling jazz musicians for successfully blending high and popular culture and opening a window onto America's "Roaring Twenties." Emancipation and barbarism were the key themes that accompanied African American dancer Josephine Baker (1906–1975) and her *La Revue Nègre* ensemble as they were performing to sellout crowds in London, Paris, and Berlin. Conservative white critics responded with outrage to Baker's acrobatics on stage, which they associated with primitivism and promiscuity. Condemning jazz as vulgar "negro music" that was beneath the dignity of the white bourgeoisie betrayed more than a small share of racism on the part of European audiences. Yet the fact that black artists managed to turn jazz into an object of desire, not derision, suggests that African Americanization, rather than Americanization, is the more fitting term for describing much of the global dissemination of popular music with historical roots in the United States during the interwar years.

AMERICANIZATION AND POLITICAL IDEOLOGY

A third thread that ran through the debate about US global influence apart from economic innovation and cultural practice was political ideology. Woodrow Wilson (1856–1924) and the US architects of a liberal internationalism linked Americanization to promoting national self-determination, democratic self-rule, and free markets as the pillars of a future world order, although they had little to say on their country's imperial interests and the nationalist movements of colonized peoples. Exceptionalism colored the judgment of these liberal internationalists. The sociologist Emory S. Bogardus (1882–1973) claimed in *Essentials of Americanization* that Wilson "had made the United States a world factor in the struggle for democracy instead of a world force for imperial dominion" (1920, 73). With the rise of communism and fascism, proponents of an internationally engaged America struck a more defensive tone. Bolshevik revolutionaries lambasted the US government as a counterrevolutionary force and branded its policies as inimical to working-class solidarity. Nazi agitators, on the other hand, gladly exploited fears about the influx of "alien" values into German society, denouncing American "showbiz" and communist propaganda as extended arms of corrupt Jewish elites who had conspired to pollute the bodies of healthy nations. In the fascist imagination, American capitalism, ethnic pluralism, and liberal democracy ran counter to the vision of a society based on racial purity and national homogeneity. Working against isolationist sentiments, US statesmen and public commentators recast America as a global force for good and tied Americanization to the defense and expansion of democratic principles. As Franklin Delano

Roosevelt (1882–1945) declared in December 1940, the United States should accept its role as the "arsenal of democracy" whose industrial might could turn the tide in the worldwide conflict between freedom and tyranny. Two months later, journalist Henry Luce urged his countrymen to take up the mantle of global leadership to ensure that the twentieth century would become an "American century." Paraphrasing Abraham Lincoln, Luce wanted Americans to redeem the world with "our Bill of Rights, our Declaration of Independence" and spearhead "an internationalism of the people, by the people, and for the people" (Luce 1941, 64). That the inviting language of American democracy was more than matched by the country's hard military power became evident after the Japanese attack on Pearl Harbor in December 1941.

THE ALLIED VICTORY

The Allied victory in World War II marked the transition of the United States from world power to a superpower whose military dominance and political clout had no rival except the Soviet Union. Postwar politics opened up new channels of Americanization, especially through novel institutions such as the International Monetary Fund (IMF), founded in 1945, the North Atlantic Treaty Organization (NATO), established in 1949, and regimes of military occupation in Germany, Austria, Italy, and Japan. For Western Europe, the Marshall Plan of 1947–48 provided the political and monetary stimulus for the adoption of American managerial expertise, business methods, and technology, which promised to expedite the continent's economic recovery. The Marshall Plan helped reignite transatlantic trade and reconciled Western European leaders with US hegemony as long as their war-torn societies returned on the path to prosperity. Meanwhile, direct investment of US corporations in non-US firms quickly surpassed prewar heights, cementing America's status as the world's economic superpower.

In the military sphere, after a brief ban on fraternizing with the enemy, US soldiers and their families were expected to act as ambassadors of democracy. Military communities were enlisted in the effort to remake former adversaries; their activities ranged from supervising the liberalization of the press and the decartelization of domestic industries to launching massive reeducation programs designed to democratize and, in the case of Germany, denazify local populations. Regarded as malleable and less encumbered by the past, youth became a preferred target of official Americanization policies carried out in the former Axis powers. Exchange programs such as the one initiated by Senator J. William Fulbright (1905–1995) created transatlantic and transpacific networks for young students and their teachers, and the newly founded "America Houses" in West Germany projected the image of a young and culturally vibrant United States. In Japan, as historian Hiroshi Kitamura has shown in *Screening Enlightenment*, US military authorities joined forces with Hollywood producers to screen more than six hundred films in Japanese theaters in order to present the "American way of life" (2010, 12) as a cultural and political model to local moviegoers. This Americanization "from above," however, produced limited and uneven results, in part because the hierarchical structures of military occupation stood in an uneasy relationship with the ideals of participatory democracy.

AMERICANIZATION "FROM BELOW"

Just as the postwar advocates of the Americanization "from above" approach underestimated the agency of local populations, theories of Americanization that simply rely on models of unilateral imposition are insufficient to explain the presumed relationship between Americanizers and Americanized. Because of this, historians informed by the methodologies of cultural and postcolonial studies have begun to emphasize the ability of subjugated groups to contest and subvert the hegemonic or imperial aspirations of a superior political power. In their accounts, the one-sided focus on patterns of ideological and cultural expansion has been superseded by narratives stressing modes of negotiation and cooperation that enabled local people to selectively appropriate and reject ideas, goods, and institutions disseminated by the agents of Americanization. While these transnational exchanges may have started on unequal terms, there are good reasons to conceive of the global sites of Americanization as examples of transculturation, that is, the gradual convergence of different cultures, instead of manifestations of cultural imperialism.

This is not to say that processes of transculturation occurred without conflict. Much to the chagrin of older elites, young people were at the forefront of the voluntary adoption of American cultural artifacts, which historians have termed Americanization "from below." Similar to the adolescent consumers of the 1920s, postwar youths in foreign countries with sufficient buying power mimicked the fashion styles, movie icons, and musical tastes popular among their American peers. The dress habits of young consumers, which were traced back to the ascendancy of Madison Avenue–style advertisements, clashed with traditional norms of sexuality and female respectability. For these youths, wearing leather jackets, tight pants, and short skirts, reading comics, drinking Coca-Cola, and listening to rock and roll music were less about producing offshore Americas than staking out their own identities in societies emerging from the rubbles of war and living under the threat of nuclear annihilation. Traditional narratives tend to focus on West Germany, Italy, France, Britain, and to some extent Japan as the main sites of this Americanization "from below," yet newer research has shown that cultural exports identifiable as "American" bridged the Cold War divide and also penetrated Eastern Europe, despite the efforts of communist officials to disrupt such transfers. The image of America as the birthplace of a modern teen culture revived many of the fears of civilizational decline shared by the self-anointed guardians of middle-class taste and morality. Curiously, generational conflict about the virtues and vices of popular culture led to new transnational alliances. While the intertwined concerns about the rise of juvenile delinquency and the "coca-colonization" of the world aided the rapprochement of conservative elites across geographical boundaries, young men and women saw in the increasing availability of American-made consumer goods and local offshoots the possibility of a more liberal, autonomous way of life. Only by the late 1970s did the attitudes of older people in Western Europe toward the supposedly "Americanized" consumption habits of their sons and daughters become more relaxed, perhaps because the former had themselves been active cultural transmitters in their youth.

The youthful counterculture of the 1960s, which was intimately tied to the student activism that emerged on both sides of the Atlantic primarily in response to the Vietnam War, made civil disobedience and protest the watchwords of an Americanization of a different sort. As globally informed histories of the New Left have shown, young dissenters in Western Europe and other parts of the world found common ground in criticizing US foreign policy, which they denounced as neocolonial and imperialistic. Forging personal and ideological bonds with protesters in the United States, they imagined themselves as part of what historian Martin Klimke has called "The Other Alliance" (2010) a transnational counterforce to the official Western Cold War alliance. Student leader Karl Diedrich Wolff (b. 1943), who was chairman of the German *Sozialistischer Deutschen Studentenbund* (SDS), traveled to the United States to meet student protesters and civil rights workers, eager to learn from their tactics. The African American activist Angela Davis (b. 1944), on the other hand, was revered and instrumentalized as an icon of the global struggle for black and female emancipation by leftists in the West and communist governments in the East. Declaring solidarity with the American civil rights and antiwar movements and opposing the discrimination against African American GIs stationed in Europe, European students adopted protest techniques from the United States such as "sit-ins" and "teach-ins" and imported African American symbols of resistance, most prominently the logo of the Black Panther Party, which inspired the formation of the German Red Army Faction. Americanization, in this context, thus meant the selective borrowing of presumably "American" methods and symbols of antiestablishment politics that entered the lexicon of an international protest culture. The formula "with America against America," introduced by the historian Philipp Gassert in 2004 to avoid referring to such processes as manifestations of a crude anti-Americanism, gained additional contours in the 1980s with the antinuclear peace movements, in the 1990s with the antiglobalization campaigns, and in the 2000s with protests against the Iraq War.

CONTEMPORARY VIEWS

The changing meanings and shifting parameters of debates about US influence in the world, as they became manifest in the second half of the twentieth century, once again point to the ambivalences and limitations of Americanization as an analytical term. Most scholars who defend the concept—and even those who do not—agree that Americanization is a dynamic and dialogic process that can mean different things at different times and in different places. They further agree that Americanization can never imply a unidirectional transfer of people, goods, ideas, and practices that make non-American societies more like the original. Because nations are not holistic entities or impermeable monoliths, their relationship to other nations has to be multilayered, internally contested, even paradoxical. If this is true, and if it is at times impossible in an interconnected world to tell whether something really originated in the United States, how does one justify speaking of Americanization? This quandary has led some historians to jettison the term and graft different categories on their discussions of American political, economic, and cultural power. Westernization is one such category embraced by historians focusing on transatlantic (less so, transpacific) interdependencies, although this concept, too, comes with significant normative baggage. Westernization scholarship is usually not limited to the study of post-1945 elite military-political networks such as NATO and liberal intellectual forums such as the Bilderberg Group or the Cultural Congress for Freedom (CCF), which functioned as anticommunist discussion groups for journalists, business leaders, and policy makers from Western Europe and the United States. Westernization also privileges traditional aspects of "Western" community building over simultaneous projects of transnational networking that transcended the bipolarity of the Cold War and connected Western actors to movements in Asia, Latin America, and Africa. Because of this, historians increasingly favor replacing questions about the scope and substance of Americanization with broader transcultural perspectives that emphasize the multiplicity of global flows in which "America" is one among many contested signs.

Still, it would be premature to ring the death knell for Americanization. As the twenty-first century progresses, the term may reclaim some of its lost allure. The idea of Americanization continues to enjoy high currency in media outlets and diplomatic circles, where one regularly encounters it, explicitly or implicitly, in discussions about balancing hard and soft power in US foreign relations. From journalist Thomas Friedman, who famously stated in his article "Foreign Affairs" (1998) that "globalization wears Mickey Mouse ears, it drinks Pepsi and Coke, eats Big Macs, does its computing on an IBM laptop" to Benjamin Barber's problematic juxtaposition in *Jihad vs. McWorld* (1995) of a "McWorld" global capitalism facing off against an Islamic tribalism, the intellectual hubris that US democratic culture might offer a template for remaking the Middle East in America's image was widespread at the turn of the millennium. Political scientist Joseph Nye, who popularized the concept of soft power, made a similar point, arguing in *Soft Power* (2004) that Americanization and globalization share important characteristics by virtue of the fact that, historically, the United States has met several key requirements that make it an exemplary global society: continuous immigration, multiculturalism, religious diversity, the incorporation of foreign ideas, and the formation of a huge marketplace that both attracts and exports products to places around the world. Of course, it remains to be seen how long Americans can justifiably claim privileged ownership of these features at a time when China and India are well positioned to challenge the exceptionalist notion that globalization begins and ends with the United States.

SEE ALSO *Empire, US; Exceptionalism; Internationalism; Isolationism; Nativism; Whiteness*

BIBLIOGRAPHY

Barber, Benjamin R. *Jihad vs. McWorld: Terrorism's Challenge to Democracy.* New York: Crown, 1995.

Bogardus, Emory S. *Essentials of Americanization.* Los Angeles: University of Southern California Press, 1920.

Bourne, Randolph. "Trans-National America." *Atlantic Monthly,* July 1916, 86–97.

de Grazia, Victoria. *Irresistible Empire: America's Advance through 20th-Century Europe.* Cambridge, MA: Belknap Press, 2005.

D'Innocenzo, Michael, and Josef P. Sirefman, eds. *Immigration and Ethnicity: American Society—"Melting Pot" or "Salad Bowl"?* Westport, CT: Greenwood Press, 1992.

Friedman, Thomas L. "Foreign Affairs: Angry, Wired, and Deadly." *New York Times,* August 22, 1998.

Furness, Christopher. *The American Invasion.* London: Simpkin, Marshall, Hamilton, Kent & Co., 1902.

Gassert, Philipp. "With America Against America: Anti-Americanism in West Germany." In *The United States and Germany in the Era of the Cold War, 1945–1990; A Handbook, Volume 2, 1968–1990,* edited by Detlef Junker et al., 502–509. New York: Cambridge University Press, 2004.

Gassert, Philipp. "The Spectre of Americanization: Western Europe in the American Century." In *The Oxford Handbook of Postwar European History,* edited by Dan Stone, 182–200. Oxford: Oxford University Press, 2012.

Kitamura, Hiroshi. *Screening Enlightenment: Hollywood and the Cultural Reconstruction of Defeated Japan.* Ithaca, NY: Cornell University Press, 2010.

Klimke, Martin. *The Other Alliance: Student Protest in West Germany and the United States in the Global Sixties.* Princeton, NJ: Princeton University Press, 2010.

Luce, Henry R. "The American Century." *Life,* February 17, 1941, 61–65.

Nye, Joseph S., Jr. *Soft Power: The Means to Success in World Politics.* New York: Public Affairs, 2004.

Pickus, Noah. *True Faith and Allegiance: Immigration and American Civic Nationalism.* Princeton, NJ: Princeton University Press, 2007.

Rydell, Robert W., and Rob Kroes. *Buffalo Bill in Bologna: The Americanization of the World, 1869–1922.* Chicago: University of Chicago Press, 2005.

Stead, William T. *The Americanization of the World, or, the Trend of the Twentieth Century.* New York: H. Markley, 1902.

van Elteren, Mel. *Americanism and Americanization: A Critical History of Domestic and Global Influence.* Jefferson, NC: McFarland & Co., 2006.

Wynn, Neil A., ed. *Cross the Water Blues: African American Music in Europe.* Jackson: University Press of Mississippi, 2010.

Mischa Honeck
Research Fellow
German Historical Institute, Washington, DC

AMISTAD

In August 1839, an American naval vessel seized *La Amistad* off the coast of Long Island, igniting a political, legal, and diplomatic controversy that pitted the presidential administration of Martin Van Buren (1782–1862) and its southern Democratic political allies against the rising tide of northern antislavery sentiments. The *Amistad,* a coastal schooner, had been commissioned by two slave owners to carry fifty-three recently enslaved Africans from the slave markets of Havana to Puerto Príncipe (now Camagüey), Cuba. On a rainy night, the Africans, many of them Mende speakers from what is today Sierra Leone, rose up, killed the ship's captain and cook, and then took command of the vessel, ordering the slave owners to pilot the vessel back across the Atlantic. The slave owners secretly altered course each night, however, steering the vessel north so that it zigzagged along the American coast for nearly two months. After capturing the *Amistad,* American naval officers towed it to

New London, Connecticut, where they freed the slave owners, turned the Africans over to the custody of a federal marshal, and filed a salvage claim for the ship and its human cargo with the district court. The slave owners, supported by the Spanish consul and the district attorney, demanded the return of the ship and the Africans under the terms of Pinckney's Treaty of 1795.

For American abolitionists like Lewis Tappan (1788–1873), the arrival of the *Amistad* captives was nothing less than providential. They knew that despite the illegality of the transatlantic slave trade under British, American, and Spanish law, slave ships flying false flags and carrying bogus papers continued to transport enslaved Africans across the Atlantic. Abolitionists had also identified the American consul in Havana, Nicholas Trist (1800–1874), as an important ally of slave-trading interests. By championing the cause of the *Amistad* Africans, they could highlight American complicity in the trade and by extension criticize slaveholding throughout the South.

Tappan and his allies provided lawyers to defend the Africans as free persons in federal court. This set the stage for a legal confrontation between abolitionists and President Van Buren. Anxious to maintain southern support in the 1840 presidential election, the Van Buren administration acted aggressively to ensure that both the vessel and the Africans would be returned to their putative owners. Presuming a favorable outcome in the federal district court, the secretary of state, John Forsyth (1780–1841), arranged to have an American naval vessel on hand to whisk the Africans back to Cuba before abolitionists could lodge an appeal. Yet Van Buren and his allies failed to grasp growing antislavery sentiments in northern states, believing wrongly that support for the *Amistad* captives would be limited to abolitionists. The Africans themselves, led by the charismatic Joseph Cinqué, played an instrumental role in their own deliverance from the American legal system, embracing the opportunity to learn English and the fundamentals of the abolitionists' Christian faith so they could better plead their case for freedom. The plight of "the Mendi people" rapidly transcended the abolitionist movement as many northerners came to see their incarceration as unjust and the possibility of their forced return to Cuba as unconscionable.

In January 1840, Judge Andrew Judson (1784–1853) of Connecticut's district court heard the arguments of the various parties. Abolitionists knew Judson as the person who had hounded Prudence Crandall (1803–1890) when she opened a school for African American girls in the state. Judson dismissed the salvage claim on the value of the Africans as slaves that had been pressed by the American naval officers. He further rejected the argument made by the Cuban slave owners and the district attorney that the court had no right to question the documents provided by Havana officials that described the Africans as Cuban-born. The Africans, Judson ruled, could not have been legally enslaved and were therefore free. When the Van Buren administration appealed, the circuit court upheld Judson's ruling, staging a showdown in the US Supreme Court. In February 1841, after Van Buren's defeat in the 1840 presidential election, Roger Sherman Baldwin (1793–1863) and former president John Quincy Adams (1767–1848) successfully argued the Africans' case before the Court, and the Africans were released from custody. Nine months later, after the Africans and abolitionists had raised funds for their return, "the Mendi people" sailed back to Sierra Leone in the company of Christian missionaries.

The dramatic events of the *Amistad* affair captured the popular imagination in the North, but the legal argument that secured the Africans' freedom turned on the narrow question of whether American officials could impugn documents signed by a Spanish official in Havana. Even though many southerners were appalled at the outcome, the Supreme Court's decision did not threaten the institution of slavery in the United States. In 1857, the Court ruled in the *Dred Scott* case that persons of African descent could not be citizens, adding that they "had no rights which the white man was bound to respect." Yet in the final analysis, the polarization of political opinion surrounding the *Amistad* case provided a harbinger of the American Civil War.

SEE ALSO *Adams, John Quincy; Antislavery; Atlantic Slave Trade; Colonization Movement*

BIBLIOGRAPHY

Dred Scott v. John F. A. Sandford, 60 U.S. 393 (1857).

Jones, Howard. *Mutiny on the Amistad: The Saga of a Slave Revolt and Its Impact on American Abolition, Law, and Diplomacy.* Rev. ed. New York: Oxford University Press, 1987.

Rediker, Marcus. *The Amistad Rebellion: An Atlantic Odyssey of Slavery and Freedom.* New York: Viking, 2012.

United States v. Libellants and Claimants of the Schooner Amistad, 40 U.S. 518 (1841).

Robert S. Wolff
Professor of History
Central Connecticut State University

AN AMERICAN DILEMMA: THE NEGRO PROBLEM AND MODERN DEMOCRACY (GUNNAR MYRDAL, 1944)

Running to a length of 1,483 pages, Gunnar Myrdal's *An American Dilemma: The Negro Problem and Modern*

Democracy presented to an American public an unprecedented collection of empirical data on African Americans that had been amassed by a team of more than seventy social scientists throughout the United States from 1938 to 1941. Myrdal noted that he and his team had arrived at the general conclusion that any differences between black and white Americans were caused largely by the latter's discrimination against the former, not by any innate biological or cultural differences. Going into detail into the ways that white Americans forced a system of disadvantages upon black Americans, the two volumes included chapters covering topics such as racial beliefs, population, migration, economic inequality, and political practices.

ORIGINS OF THE STUDY

The author, however, did not simply want to provide his readers with a catalogue of white Americans' discriminatory practices against black Americans and of black Americans' lived experience as a group targeted by discrimination. After all, the Carnegie Corporation of New York had appointed Myrdal director of this study and had tasked him with providing an outsider's dispassionate analysis of the so-called Negro problem that national policy makers could then use as a vehicle for achieving a solution to the problem.

In the 1910s and well into the 1930s, many white Americans had perceived that southern black Americans had begun to move to the North in droves, and they began to associate black Americans with some of the ills of urban life such as crime, poverty, unemployment, and illness. Echoing this perspective, Carnegie Corporation board member and former secretary of war Newton D. Baker (1871–1937) argued to his fellow trustees in 1935 that the Hampton-Tuskegee model was an outdated panacea to white-black relations in the United States: No longer a southern issue worthy of a southern-based solution, white-black relations were becoming a national problem demanding a national remedy.

Inspired by the foundation's social scientific studies of white-black relations in British Africa such as the Carnegie Commission's *Poor White Problem in South Africa* (1932) and the ongoing survey of colonial policies in Africa by British civil servant Lord Hailey (William Malcolm Hailey, 1872–1969), Carnegie Corporation president Frederick P. Keppel (1875–1943) proposed an American study comparable to Hailey's. He expected that someone such as Hailey, who had no exposure to American race relations but who had experience translating social scientific research into public policies on subordinate groups, could serve as an objective and productive observer of American race relations. In consultation with American social scientists, though, Keppel reconsidered his definition of what it meant to be objective and narrowed his search to European men originating from countries free of majority-minority group relations. In the fall of 1937, Keppel reached out to Swedish economist and member of the Swedish Parliament, Gunnar Myrdal.

PURPOSE OF THE STUDY

In line with the study's purpose, *An American Dilemma* provided a sociological theory that could guide northern whites and particularly New Dealers in Washington, DC, in mobilizing themselves to eradicate discrimination against black Americans throughout the country. Writing primarily to this white audience, Myrdal acknowledged that they discriminated against black Americans. However, he further observed that during the Second World War, white northerners were waking up to the discrepancy between this discriminatory behavior and their shared national ethos, the American creed. He explained that, rooted in the country's early struggle for independence, these were the ideals "of the essential dignity of the individual human being, of the fundamental equality of all men, and of certain inalienable rights to freedom, justice, and a fair opportunity" (4). Once they were cognizant of the gulf between their democratic ideals and behavior toward black Americans, Myrdal expected that leading white Americans would work toward bridging this gulf. They not only would shift their behavior and policies to meet these ideals but also mobilize the national state apparatus to achieve these goals.

With this national policy recommendation, Myrdal applied some of his and his wife Alva Myrdal's own experience drafting a policy prescription addressing decreased fertility rates in 1930s Sweden. Echoing the findings of American cultural anthropologists such as Franz Boas (1858–1942) and his students, the couple had proposed in *Kris i befolkningsfrågan* (1934) that Swedes of lower classes were not biologically predisposed to producing children of inferior stock. Rather, these Swedes' inferior living standards caused the visible differences between poorer and more affluent children. The couple proposed that if the state improved these Swedes' environment, all Swedes could be encouraged to play their part in increasing fertility rates without any fear of decreasing the quality of the national *folk*. Much as in Sweden in 1934, Myrdal suggested in *An American Dilemma* that black Americans faced no biological impediments to becoming part of the national social body. Rather, the differences between their conditions and those of white America were caused largely by environmental factors, and the state could play an important role in facilitating this group's assimilation and integration into the national body.

DEVELOPMENTS DURING THE 1940s

During a hiatus from the American study and while they awaited a likely Third Reich invasion of Sweden, the Myrdals coauthored a pro–United States propaganda book in Sweden, *Kontakt med Amerika* (1941). Here, they explained that Americans were morally superior to Germans and thus deserved the allegiance of Swedes during the war. The following year, the couple returned to the United States and Myrdal completed the manuscript for *An American Dilemma.* Much as in this 1941 book, Myrdal explained in *An American Dilemma* that leading white Americans harbored national egalitarian ideals that distinguished their treatment of black Americans from Germans' treatment of Jews: Once awakened to the discrepancies between their ideals and behavior toward black Americans, leading white Americans would mobilize to alter this behavior to meet their ideals.

After the publication of *An American Dilemma* in 1944 and during the 1940s, US social scientists and journalists peppered the pages of newspapers, magazines, and academic journals with criticisms of Myrdal's means for achieving racial equality and the speed with which that goal could be accomplished. To put this criticism in perspective, however, more than sixty-five glowing reviews of *An American Dilemma* were published in American newspapers and magazines within a year of the book's publication. Across the Atlantic, too, reviewers such as Lord Hailey celebrated *An American Dilemma* for its objective lens and for illustrating the gulf between American ideals and practice toward black Americans.

IMPACT OF *AN AMERICAN DILEMMA*

Aside from receiving these public accolades, the study also made an impact in the nation's capital. The Office of Education and the Public Affairs Committee, which had been collaborating since the mid-1930s in distributing pamphlets for the American public dealing with pressing economic and social problems, published a thirty-two-page summary of *An American Dilemma.* With Americans' engagement in the Second World War, the target audience of these pamphlets had become not only the American public in general but also those Americans serving in the armed forces. For example, another pamphlet published the same year alongside this summary of *An American Dilemma* was titled "Facts and Tips for Service Men and Women." Far from ignoring these pamphlets, Americans eagerly consumed them. By 1945, over nine million public affairs pamphlets had been distributed throughout the US and presumably, too, among servicemen abroad.

In 1947, the President's Committee on Civil Rights, commissioned by Harry Truman (1884–1972), prepared a report that relied heavily on Myrdal's description of race in the United States as a moral problem and of the federal government's role in facilitating black Americans' assimilation into white American life. In 1954, the US Supreme Court cited the study in its decision in the groundbreaking school desegregation case, *Brown v. Board of Education.*

After the Second World War and during the Cold War, many Americans would remember Gunnar Myrdal's *An American Dilemma* as a founding text of modern civil rights discourse. A staunch ally of the United States, Myrdal had hoped in 1942 that he had given white liberals the blueprints for solving their "race problem," and in the process, for distinguishing themselves from Germans on the global stage. In the 1940s and 1950s, leading white Americans embraced and applied Myrdal's blueprints in the United States. In the process, they might have thought that they were distinguishing themselves as a morally exceptional people and differentiating American race relations on a global stage. However, *An American Dilemma* grounded them in a global history. Even if Americans reading and applying *An American Dilemma* were not cognizant of it, they were not so unlike British colonial administrators and white settlers in Africa who, in their efforts to shape public policies on race, had leaned on social scientific studies of white-black relations funded by the Carnegie Corporation. Even more, they were not too unlike Swedes who had heeded the Myrdals' advice on how to use the national state apparatus in order to shape a cohesive national *folk.* Though perhaps more than Swedes, Americans seemed to have taken to heart Gunnar Myrdal's wartime message that they were an exceptional people whose "race problem" had no global parallels.

SEE ALSO *Carnegie Endowment for International Peace; Cold War: Race and the Cold War; Human Rights*

BIBLIOGRAPHY

Alva and Gunnar Myrdal. Papers. Labor Movement Archives and Library. Stockholm, Sweden.

Carnegie Commission. *The Poor White Problem in South Africa: Report of the Carnegie Commission.* Stellenbosch, South Africa: Pro ecclesia-drukkery, 1932.

Carnegie Corporation of New York. Records. Columbia University Rare Book & Manuscript Library. New York: Columbia University Libraries, Archival Collections. http://library.columbia.edu/locations/rbml/units/carnegie/ccny.html

Hailey, William Malcolm, Baron Hailey. *An African Survey: A Study of Problems Arising in Africa South of the Sahara.* London: Oxford University Press, 1938.

Johnson, Dallas. "Facts and Tips for Service Men and Women." *Public Affairs Pamphlet No. 92.* New York: Public Affairs Committee, 1944.

Keppel, Frederick P. Papers [ca. 1880]–1943. Columbia University Rare Book & Manuscript Library. New York: Columbia University Libraries, Archival Collections.

http://www.columbia.edu/cu/lweb/archival/collections/ldpd_4078981/

Mills, Phyllis D, comp. *Public Affairs Pamphlets: An Index to Inexpensive Pamphlets on Social, Economic, Political, and International Affairs, Supplement No. 1.* Bulletin 1937, no. 3. Office of Education, United States Department of the Interior. Washington DC: Government Printing Office, 1937. http://0-eric.ed.gov.opac.msmc.edu/?q=%22%22&ff1=subPamphlets&ff2=eduAdult+Education&id=ED542532

Myrdal, Gunnar. *An American Dilemma: The Negro Problem and Modern Democracy.* New York: Harper & Brothers Publishers, 1944.

Myrdal, Gunnar, and Alva Myrdal. *Kris i befolkningsfrågan* [*Crisis in the population question*]. Stockholm, Sweden: Bonnier, 1934.

Myrdal, Gunnar, and Alva Myrdal. *Kontakt med Amerika* [*Contact with America*]. Stockholm, Sweden: Bonnier, 1941.

President's Committee on Civil Rights. *To Secure These Rights: The Report of the President's Committee on Civil Rights.* New York: Simon and Schuster, 1947.

Public Affairs Pamphlets: An Index to Inexpensive Pamphlets on Social, Economic, Political, and International Affairs. Bulletin 1937, no. 3, rev. Office of Education, United States Department of the Interior. Washington DC: Government Printing Office, 1937. http://0-eric.ed.gov.opac.msmc.edu/?q=%22%22&ff1=subPamphlets&ff2=eduAdult+Education&id=ED542531

"Public Affairs Pamphlets Are Best Sellers." *The News Digest: The Journal of Education* 128, 6 (1945).

Social Science Research Council. Papers [1924–1990]. Rockefeller Archive Center. Tarrytown, New York. http://dimes.rockarch.org/FA021/collection

Steward, Maxwell S. "The Negro in America." *Public Affairs Pamphlet No. 95.* New York: Public Affairs Committee, 1944.

Maribel Morey
Assistant Professor of History
Clemson University

AN APPEAL TO THE COLOURED CITIZENS OF THE WORLD (DAVID WALKER, 1829)

David Walker's *Appeal to the Coloured Citizens of the World* was published in Boston, Massachusetts, in September 1829 in the aftermath of independence movements in Latin America and at a time when United States hegemony in the Americas was asserted through the 1825 Monroe Doctrine. Thus, in addition to articulating the radical rebellion against slavery of Denmark Vesey (1767–1822) and the liberation theology of the African Methodist Episcopal Church, the *Appeal* also indicted the contradiction of a supposed "Empire of Liberty" built upon southern slavery and white supremacy.

Walker (1796–1830), a free black who settled in Boston and there became active in the abolitionist movement, divides the *Appeal* into a preamble and four articles. In the preamble and article I, he places American slavery in the context of slave systems throughout world history, arguing that, unlike enslavement in ancient Egypt and Rome, American slavery is "more wicked." It occurs in a "Republican land of liberty" in which human equality is supposed to be paramount. According to the *Appeal*, this wickedness allows white republican leaders like Thomas Jefferson to deny that black people are "members of the human family." By excluding black people from republicanism, slavery is able to spread across America rather than gradually die out, and therefore republicanism itself is predicated on white supremacy.

In 1823 President James Monroe's announcement of the Monroe Doctrine, drafted by Secretary of State John Quincy Adams, stated that "the American continents, by the free and independent condition which they have assumed and maintain," could not be colonized by European powers. According to Walker, this freedom and independence was an additional reason why American slavery was so "wretched": white American leaders claimed republican ideals as the basis of their government and their foreign policy while expanding slavery and continuing to deny black humanity. And because "God [was] just," the entire American system was destined to fail, including its opposition to European recolonization of the Americas, unless and until slavery and racial inequality were eradicated.

Articles II and III continue to challenge America's identification as a bulwark for "freedom and independence" in the Western hemisphere by denying a strand of European intellectualism used to justify white supremacy. In his 1817 work *The Animal Kingdom (Le Règne Animal)*, the French naturalist Georges Cuvier had popularized the belief that there were three distinct human races, Caucasian (white), Mongolian (yellow), and Ethiopian (black). According to Cuvier, within this hierarchy blacks had always "remained in a complete state of barbarism." This classification was eventually adopted by white physicians and anthropologists like Josiah Clark Nott (1804–1873) and Samuel George Morton (1799–1851) to justify southern slavery and northern racism. After the Civil War this "American anthropology" was used to racialize Cubans and Filipinos as the Monroe Doctrine evolved into "big stick" imperialism. During Walker's time, slaveholding politicians like Henry Clay (1777–1852) used Cuvier's "science" to promote the institution's spread into the newly acquired territories of the Southwest, particularly during the war with Mexico during the 1840s.

According to the *Appeal*, however, Cuvier's theory of racial hierarchy was a lie. In article II, Walker points out that "the arts and sciences—the wise legislators—the Pyramids, and other magnificent buildings" were founded by "the sons of Africa, or of Ham," and carried into Greece to create the entire basis for Western civilization. Europeans denied this fact, and according to Walker they perverted the word of God in order to convince African people across the world of the notion that white supremacy and black enslavement were ordained by the Bible. Until the United States freed its slaves, and acknowledged the true meaning of freedom and independence in the Western Hemisphere, the country was destined to "ruin," and slavery, not liberty, would become the prevailing ideology in the Western world.

Finally, in article IV Walker dismantles the entire basis for the role of the American Colonization Society (ACS) in Africa. In the 1810s the black sea captain Paul Cuffee (1759–1817) had captained a fleet of ships out of New England to explore the possibility of settling free blacks in the British colony of Sierra Leone. Whites had then co-opted the idea of the colonization of the western African coast by African Americans as a means for slaveholding politicians to "solve" the problem of free people of African descent in a republic that denied their right to exist. The ACS, founded in 1817, attracted an all-white committee that included Henry Clay, Supreme Court Justice Bushrod Washington (1762–1829), and the lawyer and author of the lyrics to "The Star-Spangled Banner," Francis Scott Key (1779–1843). By 1825 the ACS had settled free African Americans on land, for which they had negotiated with local tribal leaders at gunpoint, just north of the British colony of Sierra Leone.

Although some free African Americans, including the future abolitionists John B. Russwurm (1799–1851) and Martin R. Delany (1812–1885), supported black resettlement outside of the United States, most northern black people understood the frustrations of Cuffee, who in the last year of his life despaired that his plan for black economic independence and political autonomy had been overtaken by white slaveholders who refused to allow black men to lead their organization. The ACS, and the independent colonization societies that it inspired across the South, led directly to American economic and political exploitation in Liberia, which was founded as a commonwealth in 1838.

Although Walker died in 1831, before Liberia's official creation, his warnings against African American colonization were prescient. The *Appeal* insisted that, through their participation in the Revolution and the War of 1812, and in their constant toil in southern economies that were fast becoming the basis for the entire American socioeconomic system, African Americans were as entitled to American citizenship "as the whites." And, by transporting free blacks out of the country, America would further descend into a false republic in which all black people were enslaved. White colonizers would use their supremacy over black settlements in Africa to further spread their antirepublicanism across the Atlantic. As Walker concluded, slaveholders like ACS leader Henry Clay "want [African descended people], the property of the Holy Ghost, to serve them," a commitment to human inequality that violated Revolutionary principles of liberty and self-government.

As a denunciation of American slavery and white supremacy that indicted the entire premise of Thomas Jefferson's proposed "Empire of Liberty," the *Appeal* provided an important legacy for future African American critics of American foreign policy. Less than a decade after publication, the *Appeal*'s rhetoric of black political independence was adopted by a short-lived, yet significant, Haitian emigration movement among free blacks in New York and Philadelphia. By the 1850s Delany, a father of black nationalism, used similar rhetoric to raise funds for a black settlement in Abeokuta, West Africa. And despite American support for Liberia for the remainder of the nineteenth century, the white supremacist ideology behind the colony's founding left a legacy of civil war and economic dependency that, as some scholars argue, have characterized America's relationship to Africa since before the Civil War.

SEE ALSO *Africa; American Colonization Society; Back-to-Africa Movement; Colonization Movement; Liberia; Monroe Doctrine (1823)*

BIBLIOGRAPHY

Hinks, Peter P., ed. *David Walker's* Appeal to the Coloured Citizens of the World. University Park: Pennsylvania State University Press, 2000.

Jarrett, Gene A. *Representing the Race: A New Political History of African American Literature.* New York: New York University Press, 2011.

Wood, Gordon S. *Empire of Liberty: A History of the Early Republic, 1789–1815.* Oxford and New York: Oxford University Press, 2009.

Kerri Greenidge
Lecturer, Department of American Studies
University of Massachusetts Boston

AN APPEAL TO THE WORLD! (NAACP, 1947)

Stung by the local, state, and federal governments' refusal to end a wave of lynchings that had terrorized African Americans after World War II (1939–1945), and fed up with the ongoing effects of legalized racial discrimination in housing, health care, education, and employment, the National Association for the Advancement of Colored People (NAACP) took its concerns directly to the United Nations. The association's leadership of Walter White (1893–1955), secretary, and W. E. B. Du Bois (1868–1963), director of special research, believed that a well-crafted petition outlining the deplorable human rights conditions African Americans endured would lay bare the chasm between the nation's profession of democracy and its actual practice and compel the US government to act. In October 1947, the NAACP, therefore, submitted its petition, *An Appeal to the World! A Statement on the Denial of Human Rights to Minorities in the Case of Citizens of Negro Descent in the United States of America and an Appeal to the United Nations for Redress,* to the United Nations.

The initial idea came from a 1946 attempt by a small, fledgling black communist group, the National Negro Congress (NNC), which sent a thirteen-page document to the UN Secretary General's office charging the United States with violating African Americans' human rights. The US government easily quashed that petition and, eventually, the organization as well.

Du Bois and White, however, believed that the NNC had stumbled upon a great idea—to take the fight for black equality beyond the Mason-Dixon, even beyond the nation's borders, and demonstrate that the conditions that had led to horrific life expectancy rates, staggering unemployment and wage discrimination, uninhabitable urban slums and rural shacks, and mass illiteracy were not just national issues but were worthy of international scrutiny.

Du Bois assembled a team of scholars from the University of Chicago, Howard University, and Cornell University to write a comprehensive treatise detailing the systematic violation of human rights that African Americans had endured since the founding of the United States, the impact of those violations on the quality of life for fourteen million blacks, and, equally important, the statutory authority the United Nations had to intervene. This last point was the trickiest. Historian Rayford Logan (1897–1982), to whom Du Bois had assigned that section, knew he had a daunting task. Article 2(7) of the UN Charter made clear that the United Nations had no authority "to intervene in matters which are essentially within the domestic jurisdiction of the state concerned."

The United States had insisted on that clause at the founding conference of the United Nations in 1945 to ensure that the UN would not be able to even scrutinize Jim Crow legislation or its effects. The NAACP argued, however, that the human rights crisis that had engulfed black Americans was not a mere domestic issue. The power and might of the United States meant that Jim Crow held enormous ramifications for the rest of the world, most of whom were not white. The evidence was clear: Nazi Germany had proven that a major industrial power, steeped in white supremacy was a threat to peace because that operating governing principle was too dangerous to be contained within a nation's borders.

Walter White believed that Eleanor Roosevelt (1884–1962), an NAACP board member and chair of the UN's Commission on Human Rights, would be an ally in this struggle. He was wrong. The Cold War had transformed the association's cry for help into a weapon ready to be wielded by the Americans' arch nemesis, the Soviet Union. The Kremlin relished the opportunity to use a credible, noncommunist source to verify that the purported leader of the free world was really not so free after all. The United States, afraid that it would be "exposed as a nation of hypocrites," used virtually every Roberts Rules of Order maneuver and barely veiled threats to keep the USSR from putting *An Appeal to the World* on the UN agenda for discussion.

It worked. But now, despite its strong anticommunist credentials, the NAACP was dangling close to the same Red Scare abyss that had consumed the National Negro Congress. The association's efforts to define the crisis in black America as a human rights, not a civil rights, issue, and the organization's willingness to work beyond the broken judicial and political systems in the United States and take the fight into the international realm, led Eleanor Roosevelt to blast the NAACP's leadership as Soviet dupes. She resigned from the board of directors. Walter White, duly chastised, believed the association could not absorb her loss. In exchange for her continued presence on the board, the NAACP abandoned *An Appeal to the World* and retreated to a civil rights remedy to deal with America's human rights ills.

SEE ALSO *Cold War; Human Rights; United Nations*

BIBLIOGRAPHY

Anderson, Carol. *Eyes off the Prize: The United Nations and the African American Struggle for Human Rights, 1944–1955.* New York: Cambridge University Press, 2003.

National Association for the Advancement of Colored People (NAACP). *An Appeal to the World! A Statement on the Denial of Human Rights to Minorities in the Case of Citizens of Negro Descent in the United States of America and an Appeal to the United Nations for Redress.* New York: NAACP, 1947.

National Negro Congress (NNC). *A Petition to the United Nations on Behalf of 13 Million Oppressed Negro Citizens of the United States of America.* New York: NNC, 1946.

Carol Anderson

Associate Professor, African American Studies and History

Emory University

ANARCHISM

Anarchism is an antiauthoritarian form of socialism that first emerged in mid-nineteenth-century Europe. Rather than chaos, anarchists advocate the abolition of both capitalism and the state, and the creation of a radically decentralized, directly democratic, egalitarian society. The American anarchist movement peaked between the 1880s and 1910s, though it has survived to the present and has experienced a resurgence in recent decades. Throughout, it has been closely linked to anarchist movements abroad.

THE ORIGINS AND GROWTH OF AMERICAN ANARCHISM

In the 1860s and 1870s, anarchism's strongholds were the French, Italian, Spanish, and Swiss sections of the socialist International Workingmen's Association, but government repression then dispersed anarchists throughout the Mediterranean and Atlantic. In 1881, anarchist delegates—including five representing US groups—met in London to form a new international organization. This motivated the 1883 creation of the International Working People's Association in the United States, intended to be the American affiliate of the largely ephemeral new Anarchist International. This organization grew to more than five thousand members—mostly German and Czech immigrants—but was repressed in 1886 after eight of its leaders were convicted of conspiracy in connection with a bomb thrown at police in Chicago's Haymarket Square during a nationwide campaign for the eight-hour workday. The executions of four of the Haymarket martyrs (and the suicide of a fifth) sparked an international outcry, and led to the commemoration of May First as International Workers' Day, or May Day, still celebrated worldwide by radicals and workers (Avrich 1984).

American anarchism continued to grow until World War I (1914–1918), with Italian, Eastern European Jewish, Spanish, and Mexican immigrants predominating. Formal and informal networks and internationally distributed publications closely linked these anarchists with others throughout the globe, and America was home to many internationally renowned activists, including Johann Most (1846–1906), Emma Goldman (1869–1940), and Luigi Galleani (1861–1931). Several American newspapers, including Most's *Freiheit*, the Yiddish *Fraye Arbeter Shtime*, and Italian papers like *La Questione Sociale* and *L'Adunata dei Refrattari*, served as global anarchist organs. American-produced publications and return migrants also helped launch anarchist movements in countries such as Russia, Bohemia, Denmark, and Japan.

PROPAGANDA BY DEED AND OTHER ANARCHIST ACTIVITIES

The United States was further an epicenter of "propaganda by deed," or violent acts targeting elites to avenge popular wrongs and spread anarchist ideas. The Haymarket bombing was likely inspired by similar attacks in Europe, and in 1892 Russian-Jewish immigrant Alexander Berkman (1870–1936) attempted to assassinate steel baron Henry Clay Frick (1849–1919). In 1900, immigrant Gaetano Bresci (1869–1901) returned to Italy and killed King Umberto I (b. 1844), and the following year anarchist Leon Czolgosz (1873–1901), the child of Polish immigrants, assassinated President William McKinley (b. 1843). In 1912, Spanish anarchist Manuel Pardiñas (b. 1886), who until a few months earlier had resided in Tampa, Florida, killed the Spanish premier and then himself, and in 1923 German-born Kurt Wilckens (1886–1923), who became an anarchist while living in the United States, killed the Argentinean colonel responsible for the bloody suppression of an anarchist-led uprising in Patagonia the previous year. Twice in the 1930s, return migrants from the United States were arrested in Italy while plotting to assassinate Dictator Benito Mussolini (1883–1945). Anarchists were responsible for dozens more deaths in the United States, Europe, and Latin America in these decades (Jensen 2014). Such acts, however, rarely met with popular approval, and tainted public perceptions of both anarchism and European immigrants.

But anarchist strategies extended far beyond bombings and assassinations. At one extreme, hundreds of anarchists left the United States to fight in the Cuban War of Independence (1895–1898), the Mexican Revolution (1910–1920), the Russian Revolutions of 1905 and 1917, and the Spanish Civil War (1936–1939). At the other, most anarchists campaigned against state-sponsored conflicts, including the Spanish-American (1898) and Philippine-American (1899–1902) wars and World War I. World War II (1939–1945), however, split anarchist ranks between those who offered qualified support to the struggle against fascism and those who refused to support militarism, including a growing number of anarchist pacifists.

Anarchists were also instrumental in disseminating syndicalism and experimental education methods in America. First developed in France in the 1890s, syndicalism viewed labor unions as the primary vehicle of revolution—through sabotage and the general strike—as well as the foundations of a postrevolutionary political and economic order. Anarchists comprised an influential faction within the syndicalist Industrial Workers of the World (IWW), founded in the United States in 1905, and dominated some of its locals. Following international outcry over the 1909 execution of anarchist educator Francisco Ferrer y Guardia (b. 1859) by Spanish authorities, anarchists in the United States, like their counterparts elsewhere, founded more than twenty "Modern Schools" for children and adults based on Ferrer y Guardia's libertarian pedagogy (Avrich 1980).

GOVERNMENT EFFORTS TO SUPPRESS ANARCHISM

In the late nineteenth century, the United States was a haven for anarchist exiles, some of whom, like Most, remained in the country permanently. European leaders claimed McKinley's assassination was the result of America's excessive freedoms and tolerance of anarchism, and convened a 1904 international antianarchist meeting in St. Petersburg, Russia, where ten governments signed an agreement that laid the foundations of what would become Interpol, but the United States did not participate. The US Congress did, however, pass the Anarchist Exclusion Act of 1903, which barred entry to anarchist immigrants, and in 1918 Congress empowered authorities to deport any foreign-born anarchist. Hundreds of anarchists and other radicals were expelled under these provisions during the post–World War I Red Scare.

Further legislation in 1921 and 1924 cut off virtually all immigration from southern and eastern Europe. Nevertheless, a number of anarchist refugees from fascist Italy, Nazi Germany, and the Soviet Union arrived in the United States in the 1920s and 1930s, through both legal and illegal means. The dubious murder trial and 1927 executions of Italian-born anarchists Nicola Sacco (b. 1891) and Bartolomeo Vanzetti (b. 1888) ignited global protests and stoked anti-American sentiments abroad; even Mussolini secretly attempted to intervene on their behalf (McGirr 2007; Cannistraro 1996).

REVIVAL

The crises of the Spanish Civil War and World War II demoralized anarchists worldwide, and the diminished movement was further marginalized by the new Cold War. But anarchism enjoyed a modest revival within the New Left of the 1960s, strongly influenced by contemporaneous European movements, including surrealism, situationism, and autonomous Marxism. Anarchist intellectuals and activists also played prominent roles in protests against the Vietnam War. The ideas of American ecological anarchist Murray Bookchin (1921–2006) influenced the early green movement in Europe, and in 1999, the Kurdistan Workers' Party abandoned Marxism for Bookchin's "libertarian municipalism" (Jongerden and Akkaya 2013).

In the 1970s and 1980s, punk rock bands like England's Crass introduced anarchism to a new generation of discontented youth, and the collapse of the USSR and rise of the Internet contributed to the further growth of anarchism both in the United States and abroad. Small North American anarchist federations formed between the 1970s and the 2000s included chapters in Canada and, in some cases, Mexico. American anarchists were also active supporters of the 1994 Zapatista uprising in Chiapas, heavily influenced both the anti–corporate globalization movement of the 1990s to 2000s and the Occupy Wall Street movement of the 2010s, and used their informal networks to link these struggles to protest movements in Europe, Latin America, and the Middle East.

SEE ALSO *AFL-CIO: Labor's Foreign Policy; Americanization; Exceptionalism; Immigration; Immigration Quotas; Industrialization; International Labor Organization; Socialism*

BIBLIOGRAPHY

Avrich, Paul. *The Modern School Movement: Anarchism and Education in the United States.* Princeton, NJ: Princeton University Press, 1980.

Avrich, Paul. *The Haymarket Tragedy.* Princeton, NJ: Princeton University Press, 1984.

Avrich, Paul. *Anarchist Voices: An Oral History of Anarchism in America.* Princeton, NJ: Princeton University Press, 1995.

Cannistraro, Philip V. "Mussolini, Sacco-Vanzetti, and the Anarchists: The Transatlantic Context." *Journal of Modern History* 68, 1 (1996): 31–62.

Cornell, Andrew. "'For a World without Oppressors': U.S. Anarchism from the Palmer Raids to the Sixties." PhD diss., New York University, 2011.

Goyens, Tom. *Beer and Revolution: The German Anarchist Movement in New York City, 1880–1914.* Urbana: University of Illinois Press, 2007.

Hargis, Mike. *Notes on Anarchism in North America, 1940–1996.* Chicago: Autonomous Zone, 1998.

Higham, John. *Strangers in the Land: Patterns of American Nativism, 1860–1925.* New Brunswick, NJ: Rutgers University Press, 1955.

Jensen, Richard Bach. *The Battle against Anarchist Terrorism: An International History, 1878–1934.* New York: Cambridge University Press, 2014.

Jongerden, Joost, and Ahmet Hamdi Akkaya. "Democratic Confederalism as a Kurdish Spring: The PKK and the Quest for Radical Democracy." In *The Kurdish Spring: Geopolitical Changes and the Kurds,* edited by Mohammed M. A. Ahmed and Michael M. Gunter, 163–186. Costa Mesa, CA: Mazda, 2013.

Marshall, Peter. *Demanding the Impossible: A History of Anarchism.* Oakland, CA: PM Press, 2010.

McGirr, Lisa. "The Passion of Sacco and Vanzetti: A Global History." *Journal of American History* 93, 4 (2007): 1085–1115.

Salerno, Salvatore. *Red November, Black November: Culture and Community in the Industrial Workers of the World.* Albany, NY: State University of New York Press, 1989.

Sitrin, Marina, and Dario Azzellini. *They Can't Represent Us! Reinventing Democracy from Greece to Occupy.* New York: Verso, 2014.

Turcato, Davide. "Italian Anarchism as a Transnational Movement, 1885–1915." *International Review of Social History* 52 (2007): 407–445.

Zimmer, Kenyon. *Immigrants against the State: Yiddish and Italian Anarchism in America.* Chicago: University of Illinois Press, 2015.

Kenyon Zimmer
Assistant Professor of History
University of Texas at Arlington

ANDERSON, RUFUS

SEE *Foreign Mission Movement.*

ANGEL ISLAND

Angel Island's history parallels the history of uneven and selective migrations, settlements, and displacements that created the United States. Encompassing just over one square mile and situated in San Francisco Bay where it opens to the Pacific Ocean, the island was a site where the boundaries of the New World were contested and defined, and where the Americas engaged with other parts of the world even before the establishment of an immigration station in 1910.

THE ISLAND BEFORE 1910

The Hookooeko tribe of the Coast Miwok American Indians used the island for at least a thousand years before the arrival of the Spanish. The Miwok, who traveled to the island by boat, set up temporary camps for hunting and fishing (Angel Island State Park 2012, 8). The European presence beginning in the eighteenth century displaced indigenous communities like the Miwok. In 1775, Juan Manuel de Ayala (b. 1745) led a Spanish expedition to chart San Francisco Bay and laid claim to the island, naming it "Isla de Los Angeles," or "Angel Island." The island's location made it central to the Spanish settlement of San Francisco. While Ayala had taken to the sea to find a route to San Francisco, Juan Bautista de Anza (1735–1788) found an overland route, colonizing San Francisco in 1776. With the rise of European traders, hunters, explorers, and naval forces in the region during the Spanish colonial era, the island also served as a way station.

After Mexico gained independence from Spain in 1821, the Mexican government issued land grants to individuals like Antonio Osio, who thus acquired Angel Island in 1839 and used the land for ranching. In 1850, after Mexico lost California to the United States, the US federal government established the island as a military reserve, and through a protracted legal process, evicted Osio. Angel Island later served as a Civil War army post, a prison for enemy aliens and federal prisoners, the launching point for troops sent or received from Hawai'i and the Philippines, and a quarantine station (Angel Island State Park 2012, 9).

INSPECTION AND EXCLUSION

Control over land represents one way that nation-states draw boundaries and constitute empire. With the establishment of the immigration station in 1910, the island became a theater for deciding which individuals could become incorporated into such national spaces. Since the colonial period, immigration to the United States had been relatively unrestricted. With the 1875 Page Law and the 1882 Chinese Exclusion Act barring entry of Chinese laborers, the need arose for a federal immigration inspection site on the West Coast. The primary and original purpose of the Angel Island Immigration Station was to determine which Chinese arrivals were to be excluded (Lee and Yung 2010, 6).

Subsequent immigration laws excluded more categories of people, thus directing more arrivals to the immigration station. The First World War (1914–1918) also brought immigrants and refugees from Russia, Mexico, Australia, New Zealand, and Central and South America (US Senate 2005). In all, about half a million people from eighty countries arrived or departed through the island, with the largest groups originating from China, Japan, Korea, India, Russia, Mexico, and the Philippines (Lee and Yung 2010, 4, 328–329). The Chinese, however, were by far the largest group processed through Angel Island.

Between 1910 and 1940, when a passenger ship arrived in San Francisco Bay, passengers went through "primary inspection" and were separated into two groups: those that could land and those that were sent to the Angel Island Immigration Station for further determination of their eligibility to enter the United States. Passengers who appeared to be ill were sent to the hospital on Angel Island (Lee and Yung 2010, 32–33). Besides nationality and race, other categories of persons subjected to exclusion or deportation included those charged with prostitution, criminal offenses, or radical politics and those deemed likely to become a public charge. Certain contagious diseases or conditions affecting one's ability to work were also reasons for denying entry (Shah 2001, 186).

Perceptions of who was diseased were intimately connected to perceptions of race. At the hospital, Asian and white detainees were segregated. Asians, in particular, were subjected to thorough, even humiliating, medical inspections. Eyes, nose, throat, the stripped body, blood, and stool were examined for parasites and bacteria (Shah 2001, 185). The immigration station facilities themselves were inadequate: living quarters for Asian detainees raised criticism, and even at the hospital, unsanitary conditions led to infection among those sent for treatment (Lee and Yung, 2010, 38). After arrivals were examined, they were assigned to a dormitory and bunk: "Occidentals" resided on the second floor of the Administration Building; "Orientals" were assigned to less comfortable detention barracks (Lee and Yung 2010, 56). There, applicants awaited interrogation by the Board of Special Inquiry.

At the Board of Special Inquiry hearings, detainees were asked a battery of questions to decide whether they had a legal basis to enter the country. Witnesses, such as family or acquaintances in the United States, could be called to corroborate the applicant's testimony. Chinese applicants faced the most rigorous questioning by the board. As historian and former president of the Chinese Historical Society Him Mark Lai noted, the Chinese protested "that many questions asked by the immigration officials were unreasonable, impossible to answer correctly, and intended to entrap rather than to elucidate information. They alleged that some officials even questioned female applicants on intimate details of their marital lives and embarrassed them into silence" (Lai 1978, 89).

Three inspectors composed the board, assisted by an interpreter (if necessary) and a stenographer. After an applicant's hearing, the board members would vote to exclude, admit, or admit with conditions or bonds (a paid sum of money that would be returned to the admitted individual when he or she exited the country). If one board member cast a dissenting vote, that board member could appeal. If the board decided to deny an applicant admission, the applicant could appeal the decision to either the San Francisco commissioner of immigration or to the commissioner-general of immigration in Washington, DC (Lee and Yung 2010, 46–48).

The length of time in detention depended on how many applicants were awaiting a hearing, the length of the hearing, the appeals process (if applicable), and, starting in 1921, whether monthly and yearly per-nation quotas for admission had been reached. While most non-Asians arriving in San Francisco avoided Angel Island or stayed only a few days, 76 percent of Chinese arrivals were sent to Angel Island, where they faced the longest rates of detention and the most intense interrogations. The Board of Special Inquiry interrogation could last three to four days; the appeals process added weeks, sometimes months, to their detainment. With three appeals attempting to prove that she was the wife of a Chinese merchant, a young woman named Quok Shee held the record for the longest-known detention at Angel Island; she waited twenty-three months, from September 1916 to August 1918, before she was finally admitted to the United States (Lee and Yung 2010, 57).

NATIONAL HISTORIC LANDMARK

In 1940, a fire destroyed the administration building, leading to the abandonment of the immigration station. Classical-style Chinese poetry carved by detainees on the walls of the barracks survived the fire (Lai, Lim, and Yung 2014). The characters had been plastered over, suppressing the Chinese detainees' sentiments, but over time, the plaster fell away, and the poetry was rediscovered by a park ranger in 1970. In 1963, the island became a California state park, and, in 1997, the Angel Island Immigration Station was designated a National Historic Landmark (US Senate 2005). Today, Angel Island primarily draws local residents for recreational and educational activities (Angel Island State Park 2012, 21).

SEE ALSO *Alien Contract Labor Law/Foran Act (1885); Chinese Exclusion Act (1882); Ellis Island; Immigration and Naturalization Service; Immigration Quotas; Nativism*

BIBLIOGRAPHY

Angel Island State Park. *Interpretation Master Plan.* September 2012. http://www.parks.ca.gov

Lai, Him Mark. "Island of Immortals: Chinese Immigrants and the Angel Island Immigration Station." *California History* 57, 1 (1978): 88–103.

Lai, Him Mark, Genny Lim, and Judy Yung, eds. *Island: Poetry and History of Chinese Immigrants on Angel Island, 1910–1940.* 2nd ed. Seattle: University of Washington Press, 2014.

Lee, Erika. *At America's Gates: Chinese Immigration during the Exclusion Era, 1882–1943.* Chapel Hill: University of North Carolina Press, 2003.

Lee, Erika, and Judy Yung. *Angel Island: Immigrant Gateway to America.* Oxford: Oxford University Press, 2010.

Shah, Nayan. *Contagious Divides: Epidemics and Race in San Francisco's Chinatown.* Berkeley: University of California Press, 2001.

US Senate. *U.S. Senate Report 109–157: Angel Island Immigration Station Restoration and Preservation Act.* Washington, DC: GPO, 2005. http://www.gpo.gov/fdsys/pkg/CRPT-109srpt157/html/CRPT-109srpt157.htm

Grace I. Yeh
Associate Professor of Ethnic Studies
California Polytechnic State University, San Luis Obispo

ANGLOPHOBIA

The American relationship with Great Britain during the nineteenth century was a complex one. American citizens of English descent often expressed a fondness for British life and the cultural connections that bound the two countries together. Great Britain served as the United States' most important trading partner and source of capital investment. At the same time, however, a growing non-English population felt little affinity for Britain, while many citizens of the Republic regarded British influences as detrimental to the growth of an independent American identity. In addition, Great Britain continued to exercise a dominant presence in the Western Hemisphere, with interests that frequently collided with those of the United States. As a result, Anglophilia and Anglophobia—an affection for England and a fear of it—coexisted in American society throughout the nineteenth century.

SUSPICION OF GREAT BRITAIN IN THE EARLY REPUBLIC

For the most part, the two countries maintained amicable diplomatic relations after the War of 1812. By the terms of the 1817 Rush-Bagot Treaty, both sides agreed to a disarmament of the Great Lakes, while the Convention of 1818 fixed the US-Canadian border at the forty-ninth parallel and stipulated that the two countries would, for the time being, jointly hold the Oregon Territory. Nonetheless, Americans continued to harbor suspicions of the British Empire, which not only held sway over Canada and much of the Caribbean, but was extending its commercial reach into the new Latin America republics, which had recently won their independence from Spain.

Meanwhile, many Americans believed Great Britain remained committed to a policy of destabilizing the Republic using surrogates within its borders. British military leaders had sponsored Native American resistance in the War of 1812. At the end of the war, they had invaded Louisiana with one thousand Afro-Caribbean troops, encouraging the region's slaves to join them. Such fears played a major role in prompting General Andrew Jackson (1767–1845) to invade Spanish Florida in 1819, creating an international incident when he executed two Britons whom he suspected of supplying Seminole Indians and runaway slaves who were raiding American settlements in the Southeast.

THE POLITICAL EXPLOITATION OF ANTI-BRITISH SENTIMENT

With the rise of a more democratic political system, anti-British sentiment was manipulated and exploited by leaders of both parties. Fear-mongering became a staple of political campaigns, as candidates charged their opponents with having fallen victim to "British influence." Such warnings played a particularly prominent role in the debates over the young Republic's economic development. With regard to the tariff question, free trade advocates and protectionists articulated very different visions for the United States—the former sought to repudiate the British industrial model, the latter sought to imitate it—even as they emphasized a similar goal: a healthy economic system free of British interference. Similarly, the Bank of the United States was regarded as an instrument by which British financiers could gain control of the American economy, fears that weighed heavily on Andrew Jackson's decision to destroy the Second Bank of the United States. While "hard money" Democrats feared the corrupting effects of British capital, the bank's supporters insisted that only a strong national bank could allow the United States to remain independent of the British financial system.

Great Britain's opposition to slavery and the slave trade represented to many southerners still another aspect of a campaign to undermine the institutions of the United States. Parliament's decision in 1833 to emancipate slaves in the British West Indies galvanized the cause of the American antislavery movement, leading to the founding of the American Anti-Slavery Society that same year. When New England abolitionists urged the nation to follow the British example, slaveholders saw evidence of northern involvement in a conspiracy to overthrow the so-called "peculiar institution."

TRANSATLANTIC CULTURAL RIVALRIES

Transatlantic cultural rivalries also fueled American hostility toward Britain. American writers such as James Fenimore Cooper (1789–1851) resented British influence over American arts and letters and called for an independent "national" literature. Meanwhile, the travel writings of such British authors as Frances Trollope (1779–1863), Charles Dickens (1812–1870), and many others, which were often critical of the United States, contributed to anti-British feeling among the public at large. These tensions sometimes manifested themselves in the realm of commercial entertainment, with British-owned theater companies serving as targets of public anger. New York City would experience half a dozen major riots directed against British actors, the most serious being the Astor Place riot in 1849, which claimed twenty-two lives.

US TERRITORIAL AMBITIONS AND THE CIVIL WAR

A fear of Great Britain was also a major factor in fostering US territorial ambitions. Although the term *Manifest Destiny* has generally been viewed as an expression of national self-confidence, expansionist rhetoric often masked geopolitical anxieties. Once again, US policy makers managed to resolve specific diplomatic issues with Great Britain peacefully, ending disputes over the US-Canada boundary in the 1842 Webster-Ashburton Treaty and reaching a permanent agreement over ownership of the Oregon Territory in 1846. Yet Washington remained concerned by Britain's apparent interest in Texas, an emerging producer of cotton, and in California, with its deep-water ports on the Pacific. Acting on the fear that British leaders were seeking to "encircle" the United States, US policy makers annexed the Texas Republic in 1845 and seized California in a war with Mexico that began the following year.

Anglophobia lost much of its urgency as tensions between North and South came to dominate American political life, although Great Britain continued to be an important factor during the sectional crisis. While Her Majesty's government remained neutral in the Civil War (1861–1865), British textile manufacturers favored the cotton-producing Confederacy, a position that strained relations between London and Washington. In 1861, a US naval commander seized two Confederate diplomats from a British steamship, the RMS *Trent*, sparking a diplomatic incident and threats of war. Fearing Britain might enter the war on the side of the Confederacy, President Abraham Lincoln (1809–1865) issued the Emancipation Proclamation in 1862. By making abolition a Union goal, Lincoln aimed to influence British public opinion, which favored the antislavery position.

As the United States emerged as the dominant nation in the Western Hemisphere, it began to take steps to block Britain's long-held influence over the region. By midcentury, the Monroe Doctrine had become a bold declaration of American hemispheric power. US policy makers used the doctrine to challenge British power in Central America in the Clayton-Bulwer Treaty of 1850, and in South America in the Venezuela boundary dispute in 1895.

SEE ALSO *Britain; War of 1812*

BIBLIOGRAPHY

Crapol, Edward P. *America for Americans: Economic Nationalism and Anglophobia in the Late Nineteenth Century.* Westport, CT: Greenwood Press, 1973.

Haynes, Sam W. *Unfinished Revolution: The Early American Republic in a British World.* Charlottesville: University of Virginia Press, 2010.

Sexton, Jay. *The Monroe Doctrine: Empire and Nation in Nineteenth-Century America.* New York: Hill and Wang, 2011.

Sam W. Haynes
Director, Center for Greater Southwestern Studies
University of Texas at Arlington

ANTARCTICA/ARCTIC

The cultures of exploration, heroism, and science entwined to first construct and then to exploit polar territories. For any useful account of US involvement at the poles, it is first necessary to consider the polar regions as a geographic construct conditioned by a global imaginary. A globe, as opposed to the practical mappings of navigators and explorers, depicts a whole earth that, once projected, can—and must be—made complete (Cosgrove 2001). Even to designate polar regions misleadingly suggests their similitude beyond their position beyond 66 degrees latitude north and south. Despite their persistent cultural conflation, the polar regions, in fact, ring truth to the cliché of "polar opposites": the north is an open polar sea and the south an ice-covered continent; the north has long been populated by both sovereign and incorporated indigenous groups, as well as later Indo-European settlers, while the south lacks any natives and is separated from its nearest neighbor by the convergence of the Atlantic, Indian, and Pacific Oceans. Shaped in response to distinct hemispheric geopolitics, as well as to domestic concerns, US polar involvement has been "a safer form of conquest, offering many of the advantages of war without the messy commitments of empire" (Robinson 2006, 22).

THE ARCTIC

US involvement in the Arctic began in 1850 with an expedition funded by textile magnate Henry Grinnell (1799–1874) in search of an earlier British expedition led by Royal Navy officer John Franklin (b. 1786) that had disappeared in 1845. Franklin's expedition was one of many voyages launched in the hope of discovering the Northwest Passage, a geographical fantasy fueled in great part by Lieutenant Matthew Fontaine Maury (1806–1873) of the US Navy, whose charting of the ocean tides and temperatures seemed to provide evidence of shorter trade routes through high latitudes. Grinnell funded several more expeditions, even as the Civil War, wars of extermination against the native population, and controversies over extending slavery to western territories made Arctic exploration seem both redundant and ancillary.

Amid the western land appropriation and the gold rush of the 1880s, however, the Arctic again drew attention. The quest for practical scientific knowledge for extractive industries also drove exploration. Yet despite his expedition's serious commitment to science, army officer Adolphus Greely's (1844–1935) disastrous 1882–1883 expedition ended government funding for north polar pursuits. Among many who used Arctic endeavor as a proving ground for personal ambition, Greely nevertheless went on to thrive in the colonial military service in the Philippines, Puerto Rico, and Alaska, as well as to cofound the National Geographic Society. In the mode of the British Royal Geographic Society—which in 1895 declared the South Pole the ultimate geographic goal—the National Geographic Society set the agenda for funding of expeditions and for the gathering and coordinating and dissemination of knowledge of the polar territories.

By the twentieth century, the polar regions were yoked within a global imaginary. The competition to reach the North Pole peaked in 1909 with the race between Robert E. Peary (1856–1920) and Frederick A. Cook (1865–1940), who had served as Peary's ship surgeon in 1891. The sensationalist press's reporting of their personal rivalry suggests how Arctic competition echoed other territorial contests, both domestic and global. Due to the nature of polar travel and terrain, both Peary's and Cook's claims to being the first to reach the North Pole have proven unverifiable and the practical and cultural significance of their geographic feats remains open to interpretation.

Even to the present, accounts of survival amid exotic icy landscapes and encounters with native cultures underscore a broader history of Anglo-American invasion of what seemed to be territory available for occupation and annexation. Arctic exploits extended a frontier romanticism that reinforced white masculinity against perceived "threats to manly character and racial purity" (Robinson 2006, 3). The myth of the lone explorer (Riffenburgh 1993) obscured the crucial contributions of (white) crewmen and especially of the native men and women, whose deep knowledge of their homelands was both appropriated and depended upon by explorers. Recognition of the "social relations of discovery" (Bloom 1993, 96)—or the complex interdependence of cultures and people subtending contact—continues to challenge simplistic accounts of heroic conquest.

The career of Matthew Henson (1866–1955), an African American employed as Peary's valet but in actuality as much a trained and tested professional as Peary, illustrates the distorting lens of race. After twenty-two years of exploring alongside and even ahead of Peary, Henson was never acknowledged as codiscoverer. One indication of a broadening of the cultural frame for understanding the lasting effects of polar exploration, however, is the role *National Geographic Magazine* played in finding and connecting the descendants of the children that Henson and Peary each fathered with native women (Counter 1991).

THE ANTARCTIC

Early nineteenth-century US involvement in the Antarctic took shape through the economically motivated voyages of sealers and whalers who collectively, despite European reports of temperate ocean currents beyond the ice, helped to establish the existence of an ice-covered continent. One such sealer, Nathaniel Palmer (1799–1877), has been credited with first sighting, in 1820, an Antarctic continent. Often building on navigators' reports, US writers, including Edgar Allan Poe (*The Narrative of Arthur Gordon Pym* [1838]) and James Fenimore Cooper (*The Monikins* [1835] and *The Sea Lions* [1849]), projected a lost race and hidden worlds onto the still-unknown southern territories, often reflecting and even amplifying the racism of natural science.

Antarctic imagining was further fueled by the "hollow earth" theory of Captain John Cleves Symmes (1780–1829), an Ohio veteran of the War of 1812. In 1826, Jeremiah N. Reynolds (1799–1858) deployed Symmes's theory of an inhabited and richly stocked interior earth attainable through "holes at the poles" in an address to the US Congress, setting in motion the government-funded 1828–1832 Wilkes Exploration Expedition, led by naval officer Charles Wilkes (1798–1877). Despite its lavish scale and real accomplishments, by the time the expedition returned, both Wilkes and the Antarctic were forgotten (Stanton 1975) until after World War I (1914–1918), when Reynolds's vision of US global supremacy seemed to materialize through US Navy pilot Richard E. Byrd's (1888–1957) overflights of the North Pole in 1926 and the South Pole in 1929.

Despite Byrd's great popularity and his establishment of a series of "Little America" military settlements on the shifting Ross Ice Shelf (1926–1938), the Hughes Doctrine, a policy set out in 1924 by Secretary of State Charles Evans Hughes (1862–1948), considered discovery to be insufficient for claims of sovereignty unless accompanied by actual settlement. This US-led shift from an "imperial tactic of spatial discovery by occupation to one of territorial ubiquity through technology and representation" (Michie and Thomas 2002, 17) would characterize the beginnings of modern Antarctic governance. The massive scale of the US Navy's Operation Highjump (1946) established another research base in the Antarctic while complementing Arctic cold-weather training by providing year-round opportunity and greater freedom and security. By the 1958 International Geophysical Year, advances in nuclear power and satellite communications heightened the geopolitical salience of the Antarctic in the Cold War era and opened the way for a practical consensus to create an international zone for science. The Antarctic Treaty System, entered into force in 1961 and originally signed by twelve countries, had grown to include fifty-two states by 2015. Parties to the treaty agree to defer claims and industrial development in favor of scientific internationalism until 2048. While the treaty has proven extraordinarily effective, one by-product of the treaty has been the domination of Antarctic governance by national science programs (Elzinga 1993) that in their nature open the door to the private corporations that the treaty specifically forbids (Belanger 2006, 16; Glasberg 2012).

In the renewed "scramble for the Arctic," the United States continues to vie for advantage with other nations, native populations and environmental groups, transportation and energy corporations, and militaries (Craciun 2009, 107). The "melting of the Arctic ice has uncovered a newly vulnerable sea" open to new territorial claims by Russia and Norway; it has enriched private owners of newly passable shipping lanes; and has created a new energy frontier within the unfolding global environmental crisis. In 2015, the United States had the greatest presence in the Antarctic, with six research stations, including McMurdo Station, the largest installation on the continent, and Amundsen-Scott South Pole Station, where having a foothold in each degree of latitude powerfully positions the US for the possibility of future claims.

SEE ALSO *Atlantic Ocean; Indian Ocean; Pacific Ocean*

BIBLIOGRAPHY

Belanger, Dian Olsen. *Deep Freeze: The United States, the International Geophysical Year, and the Origins of Antarctica's Age of Science.* Boulder: University of Colorado Press, 2006.

Bloom, Lisa. *Gender on Ice: American Ideologies of Polar Expeditions.* Minneapolis: University of Minnesota Press, 1993.

Cosgrove, Denis. *Apollo's Eye: A Cartographic Genealogy of the Earth in the Western Imagination.* Baltimore, MD: Johns Hopkins University Press, 2001.

Counter, S. Allen. *North Pole Legacy: Black, White, and Eskimo.* Amherst: University of Massachusetts Press, 1991.

Craciun, Adriana. "The Scramble for the Arctic." *Interventions: International Journal of Postcolonial Studies* 11, 1 (2009): 103–114.

Elzinga, Aant. "Antarctica: The Construction of a Continent by and for Science." In *Denationalizing Science: The Contexts of International Scientific Practice*, edited by Elisabeth Crawford, Terry Shinn, and Sverker Sörlin, 73–106. Dordrecht, Netherlands: Kluwer Academic, 1993.

Glasberg, Elena. *Antarctica as Cultural Critique: The Gendered Politics of Scientific Exploration and Climate Change.* New York: Palgrave, 2012.

Kramer, Andrew E. "Russia Stakes New Claim to Expanse in the Arctic." *The New York Times* (August 4, 2015). http://www.nytimes.com/2015/08/05/world/europe/kremlin-stakes-claim-to-arctic-expanse-and-its-resources.html

Michie, Helena, and Ronald Thomas, eds. "Introduction." In *Nineteenth-Century Geographies: The Transformation of Space from the Victorian Age to the American Century.* Rutgers, NJ: Rutgers University Press, 2002.

Riffenburgh, Beau. *The Myth of the Explorer: The Press, Sensationalism, and Geographical Discovery.* London: Belhaven Press, 1993.

Robinson, Michael. *The Coldest Crucible: Arctic Exploration and American Culture.* Chicago: University of Chicago Press, 2006.

Stanton, William. *The Great United States Exploring Expedition of 1828–1832.* Berkeley: University of California Press, 1975.

Elena Glasberg
Lecturer, Program in Expository Writing
New York University

ANTI-IMPERIALISM

Throughout history, empire-building was a matter of dispute. As modern imperialism swept the globe, so did anti-imperial opposition, particularly after the Enlightenment. Just as the advocates and practitioners of imperialism in the United States were connected in myriad ways through networks and circuits of imperial exchange, so were the opponents of empire. American anti-imperialism was thus always deeply embedded in transnational discourses on empire.

THE DIVERSITY OF OPPOSITION TO IMPERIALISM

Since the eighteenth century, anti-imperialism has encompassed a wide range of criticisms against the American way of empire. While originally directed at British colonial policies in North America, it evolved into a multifaceted intellectual catch basin for opposition against US expansion. Throughout the last two and a half centuries, anti-imperialism has served as a platform for critique of continental expansion, overseas colonial empire, military interventions, economic and cultural hegemony, and globalization.

Because their movements encompassed a wide range of geographies, professions, and political outlooks, anti-imperialists never shared much political, socioeconomic, and ethno-cultural homogeneity. Anti-imperial dissent was broad enough to accommodate New England abolitionists, southern expansionists, midwestern progressives, and western peace activists. It included writers; political, religious, and social reformers; and civil, labor, and environmental rights advocates; as well as opposition from those living under US imperial rule within the nation and in its colonies and protectorates in the Caribbean basin and the Pacific Ocean.

The dissenters' diverse backgrounds and motives were also reflected by the variety of their criticisms. While those living under imperial rule objected to its exploitative and violent nature and pursued coherent demands for decolonization, anti-imperialism in the metropole rarely constituted a fundamental, all-encompassing opposition to empire. More often it highlighted disagreement with specific cases of empire-building or forms and techniques of imperial rule. As time went on, many critics became less concerned with the specific imperial trajectories of the United States but challenged the negative consequences of globalized capitalism. The evolution of such critique, along a broad band of anti-imperial dissent, was not uniquely American but a reflection and integral part of a global discourse on empire.

These discourses developed cyclically in the United States. At certain times, galvanized by national and international developments, the critique was stronger and more pronounced than during other periods of national history. The upswing of opposition and its ability to capture a wider audience often accompanied the nation's wars, including the Mexican-American War (1846–1848), the Philippine-American Wars (1899–1913), the Vietnam War (1954–1975), and the Iraq War (2003–2011).

The exclusive domain of neither a liberal nor conservative critique of the nation's role in world affairs, anti-imperialism developed in the United States through four overlapping, discursively interconnected, and mutually reinforcing phases highlighted by revolution and continental expansion, turn-of-the-century debates over colonial empire, interwar opposition to economic and cultural expansion, and opposition to the nation's quest for global hegemony since 1945.

REVOLUTION AND SETTLER EMPIRE

Although the terms *imperialism* and *anti-imperialism* would not be commonly used until the late nineteenth century, American opposition to empire dates back to the days of the Revolution and the struggle for independence. This late eighteenth-century dissent was characterized by two perspectives, both of which drew on Enlightenment thought but arrived at radically different visions for the new Republic. While the first perspective outlined a general and fundamental critique of empire, the second view formulated specific grievances against the practice of British rule.

While those who objected to empire on fundamental grounds viewed a republican polity and empire as incompatible and advocated the perfection of a model republic for international emulation, the critics of British rule hoped to replace a corrupt and dysfunctional empire with an expansive "empire of liberty" that would not only displace its European rivals but enjoy global spread. Both sides viewed the United States as an exceptional national experiment. Those who subscribed to the fundamental incompatibility of republic and empire argued that the new polity could not expand by conquest and hope to successfully reproduce its constitutional system. The process of expansion would advance special interests, militarism, and the centralization of political power and thus undermine the democratic foundations of the United States. The advocates of expansion, on the other hand, claimed that continuous expansion would not only ensure the survival of the new Republic against its European competitors but safeguard the polity against the preeminence of special interests.

The debates between these two perspectives have not only shaped the political, economic, social, and legal organization of the new Republic but have had a powerful and enduring grip on the American political imagination. They have laid the conceptual foundations for much of the anti-imperial critique of successive generations. They have also contributed to the obfuscation of US expansion and empire-building and transcribed and enshrined the thirteen colonies' successful independence struggle in the pantheon of national mythology as evidence and affirmation for the new Republic's enduring anti-imperial orientation.

Although the proponents of empire carried the day and set the nation on a trajectory of continuous expansion with continental, hemispheric, and global ambitions, America's empire-building efforts remained controversial. Key battlegrounds during the antebellum period were the debates between Federalists and Anti-Federalists during the ratification of the Constitution in the late 1780s, the Louisiana Purchase of 1803, the Indian removals of the 1830s, the annexation of Texas in 1845, the Mexican-American War of 1846 to 1848, and the Gadsden Purchase of 1854. The dissenters in the imperial metropole constituted a highly heterogeneous group with a wide range of backgrounds and political motives. They encompassed Anti-Federalists, Federalists, northern Whigs, abolitionists, missionaries, social reformers, and pacifists. Native American anti-imperial opposition consisted of military resistance, legal challenges, multiethnic millenarian movements, and efforts at cultural preservation.

While the destructive impact of transcontinental conquest on Native Americans was an important issue of contention to some anti-imperialists like Lydia Maria Child (1802–1880), opposition to expansion among metropolitan critics was mostly concerned with the institution of slavery and the balance of power between free and slaveholding states. This sectional issue, with its potentially corrosive and destructive effects on the United States, shaped the arguments against expansion every step of the way.

Such concerns also affected the opposition to the annexation of Hawai'i and islands in the Caribbean basin. More importantly, the anti-imperialists' introspective concern with the American polity and their widespread racist preconceptions fueled their opposition to the complete annexation of Mexico in 1848 and informed their dissent from post–Civil War annexation plans in the Pacific and the Caribbean. The specific objections advanced by such anti-expansionists such as Carl Schurz (1829–1906), James A. Garfield (1831–1881), and John Tyler Morgan (1824–1907) were based on the assumption that the inclusion of ethno-culturally diverse populations perceived to be unfit for self-government would erode the Anglo-Saxon foundations of the American polity. While racism could serve as a driving force for expansion and empire-building, it could equally function on occasion as an inhibitor to the acquisition of new territories.

DEBATING COLONIAL EMPIRE

While eighteenth and nineteenth century anti-imperial dissent had a mixed record in containing the steady expansion of US settler imperialism, its conceptual and discursive foundations proved highly relevant to the American debate over colonial empire after 1898 during the second phase of American anti-imperialism. After victory in the Spanish-American War of 1898, the Peace of Paris (1899) transferred the Philippines, Guam, Puerto Rico, and Cuba to US control. The United States also annexed Hawai'i and later added Wake Island (1899), parts of Samoa (1900), the Panama Canal Zone (1904), and the Virgin Islands (1917) to its colonial empire.

The anti-imperialist arguments against colonialism tapped into longstanding notions of democracy, civilization, race, and international affairs. Despite their emphasis on democratic universalism, anti-imperialists shared many of the imperialists' notions of Anglo-Saxon racial and civilizational superiority. They claimed that the admission of territories with a heterogeneous ethno-cultural makeup would threaten the fabric of the American polity.

They also suggested that colonial empires would neither advance peace nor international stability but deepen friction and competition among empires, which would result in future wars. The constant preparedness for such wars would further militarism, undermine the "virility" of American society, and drain the nation's resources away from reform projects at home.

Finally, anti-imperialists objected to the imperialists' ultranationalism, which celebrated US membership in the club of colonial powers as a natural step on the way to great-power status. Instead, the dissenters argued that the United States had lost much of its international credibility through its colonialism and urged the nation to give priority to the perfection of democracy at home before engagement with the global arena.

In this "great debate," the anti-imperialists in the imperial metropole mustered an impressive array of activists, including writers, scholars, labor leaders, social reformers, politicians, religious leaders, and industrialists. Prominent Americans like Mark Twain (1835–1910), Jane Addams (1860–1935), John Dewey (1859–1952), Samuel Gompers (1850–1924), Moorfield Storey (1845–1929), W. E. B. Du Bois (1868–1963), Carl Schurz, Edward Atkinson (1827–1905), Henry James (1843–1916), and Andrew Carnegie (1835–1919) joined the anti-imperialist cause.

The Anti-Imperialist League, founded in November 1899, became the organizational platform for much of the anti-imperial opposition. Despite the league's steady growth across the nation and its influential membership, however, the dissenters were neither able to prevent Senate ratification of the Treaty of Paris in 1899 nor decisively influence the presidential elections of 1900 in favor of William Jennings Bryan (1860–1925), whose Democratic Party platform had embraced the anti-imperialist cause.

The anti-imperialist cause gained momentum again when reports about torture and abuse of Filipinos by US troops received widespread attention in the United States in 1901. The Anti-Imperialist League intensified its collaboration with Filipino witnesses and independence activists in collecting evidence for the systematic use of torture during the US Army's colonial war in the distant archipelago. The anti-imperialists published reports and documentary evidence while their congressional supporters held hearings on the matter. Although the torture allegations against US military personnel captured the public's attention for much of 1901 and 1902, the advocates of colonial empire were ultimately able to contain the public outrage. Unable to affect a fundamental change of political direction, the anti-imperialist opposition fractured and declined.

OPPOSITION TO DOLLAR DIPLOMACY

During its third phase, between 1914 and the 1930s, anti-imperialism was characterized by organizational, thematic, and strategic transformations. Although the Anti-Imperialist League steadily lost influence and dissolved by late 1920, anti-imperialist dissent flourished. Many league activists now took on influential roles in a myriad of new anti-imperial organizations, such as the Haiti–Santo Domingo Independence Committee (1921), the American Fund for Public Service Committee on American Imperialism (1924), the All-American Anti-Imperialist League (1925), and the American Civil Liberties Union's Puerto Rico Committee (1933).

Simultaneously, the anti-imperial opposition steadily broadened its critique away from the Anti-Imperialist League's sole focus on colonial empire. Conceptually inspired by British economist John A. Hobson (1858–1940), whose work *Imperialism* (1902) had emphasized the economic driving forces of imperial expansion, many American anti-imperialists increasingly focused on the economics of imperial domination.

Much anti-imperialist hope had initially rested with Woodrow Wilson's (1856–1924) election to the presidency in 1912, but the dissenters soon found themselves disappointed. Although anti-imperialism had been incorporated into the platform of the Democratic Party as early as 1900, Wilson expressed no interest in relinquishing control over US colonies, nor in abandoning America's fledging commercial and economic empire in Latin America. On the contrary, the Wilson administration tightened control over US colonies, expanded the US colonial empire through the purchase of the Virgin Islands in 1917, and embarked on a string of military interventions, invasions, and occupations, such as in Mexico (1914), Nicaragua (1914), and Haiti (1915).

For the anti-imperial opposition, this interventionist outlook belied some of the central paradigms of Wilsonian liberal-democratic internationalism, with its concern for openness, democracy, and self-determination. In particular, Wilson's Fourteen Points statement of 1919, with its emphasis on self-determination and attention to the interests of the colonized, had raised worldwide expectations for decolonization. This seemingly anti-imperial trajectory, however, was undercut by the affirmation given to imperialism at the Versailles Peace Conference.

During the interwar years, American anti-imperialists and their international allies focused their opposition on the practice of "dollar diplomacy." Under this policy, private American banks extended controlled loans to a variety of nations in Latin America, West Africa, and the Middle East. Adherence to the terms of the loan agreement was controlled and enforced by the US government. This private-public partnership afforded the United States a near colonial degree of control over nominally sovereign nations without much public scrutiny.

Anti-imperialist critics concentrated their attacks on these state-private networks of economic imperialism. Among the most prominent critics were members of Congress, such as William Borah (1865–1940), Robert La Follette (1855–1925), William H. King (1863–1949), George W. Norris (1861–1944), and Edwin F. Ladd (1859–1925); women activists, such as Jane Addams (1860–1935) and Emily Greene Balch (1867–1961), the cofounders of the Women's League for Peace and Progress; the NAACP and W. E. B. Du Bois, who organized four Pan-African congresses during the 1920s; journalists and commentators, many associated with the magazine *The Nation*, such as Ernest Gruening (1887–1974), William Hard (1878–1962), and Oswald Garrison Villard (1872–1949); activists and political and economic commentators, such as Samuel Guy Inman (1877–1965) and Scott Nearing (1883–1983); and international supporters, such as Costa Rican foreign minister Alejandro Alvarado Quirós (1876–1945).

ANTI-IMPERIALISM SINCE 1945

The impact of such opposition was mixed. While the Franklin D. Roosevelt (1882–1945) administration's Good Neighbor Policy engaged many of the criticisms, doubts about the extent of America's commitment to decolonization persisted. Contradictions between anticolonial rhetoric and imperial practice in US foreign relations also persisted and became a main battleground after 1945 during the fourth phase of American anti-imperialism.

During the Cold War, anti-imperialist rhetoric became an important propagandistic asset in the struggle for world opinion. The success of opinion management, however, hinged decidedly on the credibility of message and messenger. In this context, government attempts to appropriate anticolonial traditions were often contradicted by the imperial projection of preponderant US power in international affairs.

As the containment of the Soviet Union overrode other strategic concerns, the United States limited its commitment to decolonization and engaged in military interventions abroad, most prominently in Southeast Asia. The Vietnam War in particular galvanized the critique against the American way of empire, led Americans to question the Cold War consensus, and gave rise to mass antiwar movements. As with anti-imperial critique before, the dissenters encompassed a wide range of political positions and social backgrounds, exemplified by linguist and political commentator Noam Chomsky (b. 1928), civil rights activist Martin Luther King Jr. (1929–1968), and Senator J. William Fulbright (1905–1995).

While earlier manifestations of anti-imperialism had also been embedded in a transnational critique of empire, the protests of the 1960s and 1970s were of a new quality. The near instantaneous international dissemination of the war's media coverage produced a truly global phenomenon of protest from Port Huron to Paris, Toronto to Tokyo, and Buenos Aires to Berlin. This development also affected the coherence of the anti-imperial dissent, which now included discussions of the nuclear arms race, environmental degradation, globalization, women's rights, civil liberties, and abuses of political power.

After the Vietnam-era protests, anti-imperial dissent in the United States lost much of its focus. The terms *empire* and *imperialism* increasingly assumed the quality of political invectives in public discourses and were no longer able to semantically unite a highly heterogeneous social and political movement.

Since the terrorist attacks on the United States in 2001 and the start of the nation's "war on terror," the concept of empire has experienced a dramatic renaissance in debates about the benefits and pitfalls of a *Pax Americana*. This recent anti-imperial opposition has been characterized by a wide range of political orientations from libertarianism to ultraconservatism. It has utilized diverse protest modalities at home and abroad, and has been galvanized by war, imperial abuses of power, and the crisis of the global economic order. While it has expanded the concerns of earlier generations about the structural foundations of imperial power, it has also been deeply embedded in a more-than-two-centuries-old tradition of anti-imperial opposition, which remains a powerful corrective and integral element of the American political discourse.

SEE ALSO *Empire, US; Internationalism; Isolationism; League of Nations; Paris Peace Conference (1919); Realism (International Relations); Roosevelt, Theodore; Spanish-American War; Twain, Mark; Wilson, Woodrow; World War I*

BIBLIOGRAPHY

Ballantyne, Tony, and Antoinette Burton. *Empires and the Reach of the Global, 1870–1945*. Cambridge, MA: Harvard University Press, 2014.

Beisner, Robert L. *Twelve against Empire: The Anti-Imperialists, 1898–1900*. New York: McGraw-Hill, 1968.

Butler, Leslie. *Critical Americans: Victorian Intellectuals and Transatlantic Liberal Reform*. Chapel Hill, NC: University of North Carolina Press, 2007.

Buzzanco, Robert. "Anti-Imperialism" In *Encyclopedia of American Foreign Policy*, edited by Alexander DeConde, Richard Dean Burns, and Frederik Logevall, 49–60. 2nd ed. New York: Scribner's, 2002.

Cullinane, Michael Patrick. "Transatlantic Dimensions of the American Anti-Imperialist Movement, 1899–1909."*Journal of Transatlantic Studies* 8, 4 (2010): 301–314.

Cullinane, Michael Patrick. *Liberty and American Anti-Imperialism, 1898–1909*. New York: Palgrave Macmillan, 2012.

Foner, Philip S., ed. *The Anti-Imperialist Reader: A Documentary History of Anti-Imperialism in the United States*, Vol. 2: *The Literary Anti-Imperialists*. New York: Holmes and Meier, 1986.

Foner, Philip S., and Richard C. Winchester, eds. *The Anti-Imperialist Reader: A Documentary History of Anti-Imperialism in the United States*, Vol. 1: *From the Mexican War to the Election of 1900*. New York: Holmes and Meier, 1984.

Greenberg, Amy S. *Manifest Manhood and the Antebellum American Empire*. Cambridge: Cambridge University Press, 2005.

Hendrickson, David C. *Union, Nation, or Empire: The American Debate over International Relations, 1789–1941*. Lawrence: University Press of Kansas, 2009.

Hilfrich, Fabian. *Debating American Exceptionalism: Empire and Democracy in the Wake of the Spanish-American War*. New York: Palgrave Macmillan, 2012.

Hoganson, Kristin L. *Fighting for American Manhood: How Gender Politics Provoked the Spanish-American and Philippine-American Wars*. New Haven, CT: Yale University Press, 1998.

Hunt, Michael. *Ideology and U.S. Foreign Policy*. New Haven, CT: Yale University Press, 1987.

Johnson, Robert David. *The Peace Progressives and American Foreign Relations*. Cambridge, MA: Harvard University Press, 1995.

Love, Eric T. *Race over Empire: Racism and U.S. Imperialism, 1865–1900*. Chapel Hill: University of North Carolina Press, 2004.

Manela, Erez. *The Wilsonian Moment: Self-Determination and the International Origins of Anti-Colonial Nationalism*. New York: Oxford University Press, 2007.

Mayers, David. *Dissenting Voices in America's Rise to Power*. Cambridge: Cambridge University Press, 2007.

Montgomery, David. "'Workers' Movements in the United States Confront Imperialism: The Progressive Era Experience." *Journal of the Gilded Age and Progressive Era* 7, 1 (2008): 7–42.

Murphy, Erin. "Women's Anti-Imperialism: The 'White Man's Burden,' and the Philippine-American War." *Gender and Society* 23, 2 (2009): 244–270.

Nichols, Christopher M. *Promise and Peril: America at the Dawn of a Global Age*. Cambridge, MA: Harvard University Press, 2011.

Ninkovich, Frank. *The United States and Imperialism*. Malden, MA: Blackwell, 2001.

Ninkovich, Frank. "Anti-Imperialism in U.S. Foreign Relations." In *Vietnam and the American Political Tradition: The Politics of Dissent*, edited by Randall B. Woods, 12–41. Cambridge: Cambridge University Press, 2003.

Raucher, Alan. "American Anti-Imperialists and the Pro-India Movement, 1900–1932." *Pacific Historical Review* 43, 1 (1974): 83–110.

Rosenberg, Emily S. *Financial Missionaries to the World: The Politics and Culture of Dollar Diplomacy, 1900–1930*. Cambridge, MA: Harvard University Press, 1999.

Rosenberg, Emily S. "World War I, Wilsonianism, and the Challenges to U.S. Empire." *Diplomatic History* 38, 4 (2014): 852–863.

Schroeder, John H. *Mr. Polk's War: American Opposition and Dissent, 1846–1848*. Madison: University of Wisconsin Press, 1973.

Sexton, Jay. *The Monroe Doctrine: Empire and Nation in Nineteenth-Century America*. New York: Hill and Wang, 2011.

Seymour, Richard. *American Insurgents: A Brief History of American Anti-Imperialism*. Chicago: Haymarket, 2012.

Tompkins, E. Berkeley. *Anti-Imperialism in the United States: The Great Debate, 1890–1920*. Philadelphia: University of Pennsylvania Press, 1970.

Tyrell, Ian, and Jay Sexton, eds. *Empire's Twin: U.S. Anti-Imperialism from the Founding Era to the Age of Terrorism*. Ithaca, NY: Cornell University Press, 2015.

Von Eschen, Penny M. *Race against Empire: Black Americans and Anticolonialism, 1937–1957.* Ithaca, NY: Cornell University Press, 1997.

Welch, Richard E. *Response to Imperialism: The United States and the Philippine-American War, 1899–1902.* Chapel Hill: University of North Carolina Press, 1979.

Zwick, Jim. "The Anti-Imperialist Movement, 1898–1921." In *Whose America? The War of 1898 and the Battles to Define the Nation,* edited by Virginia M. Bouvier, 171–192. Westport, CT: Praeger, 2001.

Zwick, Jim. *Confronting Imperialism: Essays on Mark Twain and the Anti-Imperialist League.* West Conshohocken, PA: Infinity, 2007.

Frank Schumacher
Associate Professor of History
University of Western Ontario

ANTI-IMPERIALIST LEAGUE

While traveling through Europe on a lecture tour in 1898, Mark Twain (1835–1910) observed a prevailing anti-American sentiment among Europeans critical of his country's intervention in Cuba. For decades, the Spanish attempted to subjugate Cuba's popular anticolonial insurgency while the United States watched idly. The humanitarian crisis eventually generated enough public outrage to warrant US intervention, and Twain felt compelled to defend that decision. In his estimation, the war against Spain in Cuba was "the worthiest one that was ever fought," even more so than the American Revolution or Civil War. "It is a worthy thing to fight for one's freedom," he commended, but "it is another sight finer to fight for another man's. And I think this is the first time it has been done" (Mark Twain to Joseph Twichell, June 17, 1898, in Twain 1917, vol. 2, 663).

ORIGINS IN THE WAR AGAINST SPAIN

American military operations in what is traditionally called the Spanish-American War began in Cuba in April 1898, but soon extended to Spanish colonies in the Pacific and elsewhere in the Caribbean. When the war ended in an American victory later that year, US forces occupied most of Spain's overseas empire, including Puerto Rico, Guam, and the Philippines. President William McKinley (1843–1901) determined to acquire and govern these territories, a decision that led hundreds of thousands of Americans to organize in protest. A meeting of four hundred self-proclaimed "anti-imperialists" met in Boston on June 15, 1898, and quickly spawned nationwide correspondence and propaganda campaigns. In less than a year, more than a dozen cities hosted anti-imperialist leagues. A national office opened in Chicago and a lobbying office in Washington, DC. To encourage membership, the leagues conscripted famous Americans, including former presidents Benjamin Harrison (1833–1901) and Grover Cleveland (1837–1908) and a bipartisan assortment of senators and congressmen. Newspaper editors like E. L. Godkin (1831–1902), labor leaders like Samuel Gompers (1850–1924), businessmen like Andrew Carnegie (1835–1919), and celebrities like Mark Twain joined the movement. After returning from Europe, Twain declared himself committed to the New York league. When asked about joining, he said, "A year ago I … thought it would be a great thing to give a whole lot of freedom to the Filipinos, but I guess now it's better to let them give it to themselves" ("Mark Twain in America Again," *Chicago Tribune,* October 16, 1900).

An anti-imperial tradition developed alongside arguments for American expansion long before 1898. Federalists questioned the constitutionality of expansion when Thomas Jefferson (1743–1826) purchased Louisiana; Whigs protested James Polk's (1795–1849) annexation of Mexico in 1848; and, with greater success, anti-imperialists opposed Ulysses S. Grant's (1822–1885) acquisition of Santo Domingo after the Civil War. Despite this tradition, the anti-imperialist movement that followed the liberation of Spanish territory set itself apart by insisting that the United States planned, for the first time in its history, to govern distant possessions as colonies. Unlike previous episodes of territorial expansion, the United States made no effort to extend representation to ten million Filipinos, and although two million Puerto Ricans were granted a small measure of representation, the United States would not extend statehood to the island. This conflicted with past precedents that put territories on a path to equal status in the Union and inspired the first anti-imperialist meeting in Boston. The membership drive increased when President McKinley insisted, in overt racial rhetoric, that indigenous populations untrained in democratic government could not successfully rule the islands. The anti-imperialist leagues condemned McKinley's policy as despotic and anti-American.

The acquisition of the Philippines instigated the movement, but what propelled it was the subjugation of Filipino nationalists who had once fought alongside Americans in toppling the Spanish regime. In 1899, while US senators debated McKinley's foreign policy, Filipino and American forces in Manila, suspicious of each others' intentions, clashed violently. The conflict prompted McKinley to order the absolute pacification of the archipelago before any further discussion concerning governance of the islands could take place. Anti-imperialists condemned McKinley as a militarist bent on securing an overseas empire by conquest. The Philippine-American War continued until 1902 and inspired an anti-imperialist protest against the means, as well as the merits, of expansion.

A DIVERSE CHORUS OF ANTI-IMPERIALIST RESISTANCE

Although constitutional interpretations and antiwar sentiment formed the bedrock of anti-imperialist opposition, a diverse chorus of resistance arose in reaction to American expansion, with a multitude of voices that included unlikely bedfellows. Racial intolerance led many Americans to join the leagues to prevent the United States from acquiring territories with people of different racial backgrounds. Class anxieties stirred speculation that Filipinos would steal American jobs and led labor leaders to support the crusade. Preachers like William Jennings Bryan (1860–1925) declared overseas expansion a sinful policy capable of destroying the republic and blamed the lust for economic markets. Even so, businessmen joined to oppose military spending that might detract from international commerce and trade.

Initially, the leagues coordinated attacks on political opponents. They challenged the legitimacy of territorial acquisition and colonial government as arbitrary in a democratic system. They opposed the Treaty of Paris, the peace agreement that formally ceded Spain's colonies, and campaigned against imperial candidates during the 1900 presidential election. They even challenged the constitutional basis for American imperialism in the US Supreme Court. Each instance failed to reverse the policy. In 1899, the Senate ratified the Treaty of Paris. In 1900, President McKinley won reelection by a resounding majority. In 1901, the Supreme Court ruled in a series of cases—the most important of which were *De Lima v. Bidwell* and *Downes v. Bidwell*—that the president's imperial policy was entirely legal.

THE RESPONSE TO MILITARY ATROCITIES IN THE PHILIPPINES

The movement's fortunes changed when news of military atrocities in the Philippines came to light. Filipino revolutionaries dedicated to fighting Spanish rule turned on their new occupiers and began a guerrilla war designed to cripple the political will of the United States. It prompted President McKinley to adopt a counterinsurgency strategy that employed a variety of unethical tactics, including torture, starvation, looting, burning of villages, and mass murder to suppress the revolution. Anti-imperialists publicized news of these military atrocities, whose grim nature required no added editorializing for the American public to understand that they were antithetical to national values. Although weakened by the political failures that preceded this, anti-imperialists gained new supporters and helped bring US soldiers to trial for the atrocities. That fortunate turn ended on July 4, 1902, when McKinley's successor, President Theodore Roosevelt (1858–1919), declared the Philippine-American War over. Although resistance to American occupation continued until 1915, Roosevelt announced the end of large-scale combat operations and the arrest of the uprising's most important leaders. It also ended the widespread use of heinous counterinsurgency tactics.

DECLINE IN MEMBERSHIP AND INFLUENCE

From 1903, many anti-imperialist leagues closed, including the national offices in Chicago, and membership declined. Internal differences hardened after years of activism, and members splintered into new associations. The New England League was reconstituted as the national office and dedicated its operations to eradicating imperialism in all forms. These protesters considered American capital as equally exploitative as territorial colonization. Other groups, like the Filipino Independence Society, focused solely on withdrawal from the Philippines. As the United States granted the Philippines more independence, these groups dwindled too, and the New England branch stood alone. It continued to operate until 1920, but never wielded the same degree of influence that it had during the war against Spain or when atrocities committed against Filipinos came to light.

American anti-imperialism existed in a global context. League members boasted a cosmopolitan view of empire and defended subjugated people worldwide. They worked closely with Filipinos to establish a sustainable campaign against American imperialism while supporting South African Boers against Britain, and they opposed King Leopold's rule in the Congo. The late nineteenth-century surge of imperial abuses spawned an abundance of anti-imperial activity. Members of the American anti-imperialist leagues worked with like-minded activists in India, Egypt, Korea, Indochina, and Africa. Although unsuccessful in reversing American foreign policy, the anti-imperialist leagues dulled the once optimistic impression of an American empire.

SEE ALSO *Spanish-American War; Twain, Mark*

BIBLIOGRAPHY

Beisner, Robert L. *Twelve against Empire: The Anti-imperialists, 1898–1900.* New York: McGraw-Hill, 1968.

Cullinane, Michael Patrick. *Liberty and American Anti-imperialism, 1898–1909.* New York: Palgrave, 2012.

De Lima v. Bidwell, 182 U.S. 1 (1901).

Downes v. Bidwell, 182 U.S. 244 (1901).

Go, Julian. *American Empire and the Politics of Meaning: Elite Political Cultures in the Philippines and Puerto Rico during U.S. Colonialism.* Durham, NC: Duke University Press, 2008.

Harrington, Fred Harvey. "The Anti-imperialist Movement in the United States, 1898–1900." *Mississippi Valley Historical Review* 22, 2 (1935): 211–230.

Harrington, Fred Harvey. "The Literary Aspects of Anti-imperialism, 1898–1902." *New England Quarterly* 10, 4 (1937): 650–667.

Hilfrich, Fabian. "Anti-imperialist Fears in the Debate on the Philippine-American War, 1899–1902." In *Emotions in American History*, edited by Jessica Gienow-Hecht. New York: Berghahn, 2010.

Hoganson, Kristin L. *Fighting for American Manhood: How Gender Politics Provoked the Spanish-American and Philippine-American War.* New Haven, CT: Yale University Press, 1998.

Kaplan, Amy. *The Anarchy of Empire in the Making of U.S. Culture.* Cambridge, MA: Harvard University Press, 2002.

Kramer, Paul A. *The Blood of Government: Race, Empire, the United States, and the Philippines.* Chapel Hill: University of North Carolina Press, 2006.

"Mark Twain in America Again," *Chicago Tribune*, October 16, 1900.

May, Ernest R. *American Imperialism: A Speculative Essay.* Chicago: Imprint, 1967.

Miller, Stuart Creighton. *Benevolent Assimilation: The American Conquest of the Philippines, 1899–1903.* New Haven, CT: Yale University Press, 1982.

Murphy, Erin. "Women's Anti-Imperialism: 'The White Man's Burden,' and the Philippine-American War." *Gender and Society* 23, 2 (2009): 244–270.

Nichols, John, ed. *Against the Beast: A Documentary History of American Opposition to Empire.* New York: Nation, 2003.

Ninkovich, Frank A. *The United States and Imperialism.* Malden, MA: Blackwell, 2001.

Schirmer, Daniel B. *Republic or Empire: American Resistance to the Philippine War.* Cambridge, MA: Schenkman, 1972.

Tompkins, E. Berkeley. *Anti-imperialism in the United States: The Great Debate, 1890–1920.* Philadelphia: University of Pennsylvania Press, 1970.

Twain, Mark. *Mark Twain's Weapons of Satire: Anti-imperialist Writings on the Philippine-American War.* Edited by Jim Zwick. Syracuse, NY: Syracuse University Press, 1992.

Twain, Mark. *Mark Twain's Letters.* Edited by Albert Bigelow Paine. Vol. 2. New York: Harper Brothers, 1917.

Welch, Richard E., Jr. *Response to Imperialism: The United States and the Philippine American War, 1899–1902.* Chapel Hill: University of North Carolina Press, 1979.

Zwick, Jim. *Confronting Imperialism: Essays on Mark Twain and the Anti-imperialist League.* West Conshohocken, PA: Infinity, 2007.

Michael Patrick Cullinane
Senior Lecturer, US History
Northumbria University

ANTISEMITISM

SEE *Judaism.*

ANTISLAVERY

Since the late eighteenth century, American abolitionism has been both a domestic and a transnational crusade. Early American abolitionists such as Anthony Benezet (1713–1784), James Pemberton (1723–1808), and Benjamin Franklin (1706–1790) worked closely with leading European abolitionists such as Thomas Clarkson (1760–1846) and Granville Sharp (1735–1813) of England and Jacques-Pierre Brissot (1754–1793) of France to fight slavery by abolishing the trans-Atlantic slave trade. These transnational networks were established and maintained through meticulous exchanges of information by way of personal letters, petitions, memorials, pamphlets, books, and other printed texts. Such exchanges planted the seeds for what would grow, by the mid-nineteenth century, into an extensive and effective network of abolitionists dedicated to the universal eradication of slavery, the slave trade, and forced labor.

By 1808, the United States and Great Britain had abolished the Atlantic slave trade, leading many abolitionists to turn their attention toward West Africa. During this period, organized Anglo-Atlantic abolitionism focused on gradual change through legislative action. The growing number of free blacks in the United States and England, however, led many white abolitionists to consider colonizing West Africa through the repatriation of blacks. American and British abolitionists argued that settling free blacks in West Africa would provide them with the best opportunities for success, while also offering a peaceful way to Christianize and "civilize" Africa. Under the auspices of Granville Sharp, in 1787 the British had made the first attempt at colonization by establishing the Province of Freedom on the coastline of present-day Sierra Leone. For the next several decades, this colony provided a depot for the British to resettle Africans living in England, Nova Scotia, and Jamaica, and those captured and liberated from slave ships.

Drawing inspiration from the British, American abolitionists formed the American Colonization Society (ACS) in 1816 and established the colony of Liberia in 1822 for similar purposes. The ACS garnered support from a mixed group of factions. Northern abolitionists and evangelicals felt that colonization would further gradual abolition, while American slaveholders viewed colonization as an opportunity to remove free blacks from the United States. By 1830, the ACS had established more than 200 auxiliary societies across the nation, but support for this organization started to wane as northern free blacks started resisting colonization and a new generation of American abolitionists arose, led by William Lloyd Garrison (1805–1879).

ABOLITIONISM AT A TIME OF SOCIAL CHANGE

During the 1830s, American abolitionism underwent significant changes as a result of what historians have termed the Market Revolution and the Second Great Awakening. The dramatic social and economic changes created by the Market Revolution sent a tidal wave of religious revivalism coursing across America. Premised on Protestant spiritualism and a commitment to social purification, the Second Great Awakening led to a number of reform movements centered on eradicating social ills and moral vices. These reform movements were not unique to the United States but also occurred in Western European countries that faced similar problems associated with industrialization, urbanization, and class struggle. Reformers on both sides of the Atlantic collaborated with each other in seeking change on a variety of social issues—education, alcoholism, commerce, labor, politics, and slavery.

Major transformations in transportation and communication during this period deepened the ties between US and European reformers. The emergence of the steamboat, the canal system, and railroads connected people across vast distances, while the penny press led to a significant reduction in printing costs that allowed reformers to reach audiences across the world. American abolitionists capitalized on these new inventions and reform sensibilities to revolutionize the antislavery movement. Unlike their predecessors, this second generation of abolitionists called for immediate emancipation without compensation or colonization while also incorporating African Americans into the antislavery fold. One result of this new approach was the formation of the American Anti-Slavery Society (AASS) by Garrison, Lewis Tappan (1788–1873), and Frederick Douglass (1818–1895).

American abolitionists were always aware of the developments of slavery and antislavery in foreign lands, but this new generation showed a much more pronounced international sensitivity to such issues. For example, the motto on the masthead of Garrison's famous antislavery newspaper, the *Liberator*—"Our Country Is the World, Our Countrymen Are All Mankind"—attested to the shared sense of kinship and struggle among American and foreign abolitionists. The newspaper's name also happened to be the moniker of the Latin American revolutionary Simón Bolívar (1783–1830) and the Irish reformer Daniel O'Connell (1775–1847), who were themselves abolitionists and friends of Garrison.

INTERNATIONAL COOPERATION

As transnational antislavery strengthened, American and European abolitionists also started crossing the Atlantic to visit their foreign allies in greater numbers. Garrison traveled to England where he met and commiserated with British abolitionists in 1833, the same year that Great Britain passed an act abolishing slavery in the West Indies. During his journey, Garrison met the British abolitionist George Thompson (1804–1878), who became his lifelong friend and ally. Before returning home, Garrison persuaded Thompson to travel to the United States and lecture on British slavery and emancipation. Although Garrison felt British emancipation was fundamentally flawed because the British Parliament compensated slaveholders and forced freed slaves to work for six years under their former masters, he accomplished his overarching goal: to establish a strong relationship with British abolitionists and to unite their efforts in abolishing slavery around the world.

Thompson arrived in the United States in 1834 and immediately started lecturing up and down the New England coast. Thompson's aggressive approach created a contentious atmosphere, especially as he pointedly called out those who benefited from the horrors of slavery. Under the threat of mob violence, Thompson was forced to end his trip early and return to the safety of Great Britain. Garrison's and Thompson's voyages across the Atlantic encouraged a number of other abolitionists, including Douglass, William Wells Brown (1814–1884), Parker Pillsbury (1809–1898), Wendell Phillips (1811–1884), Lucretia Mott (1793–1880), and Joseph Sturge (1793–1859), to make similar trips.

As abolitionists were building their networks, American slaves used their own networks to escape slavery. Using what has been termed the Underground Railroad, fugitive slaves made their way toward Mexico, the Caribbean, and Canada. The Underground Railroad became an important tool for American abolitionists, especially after the passage of the Fugitive Slave Act of 1850, which forced federal agents and American citizens, under the threat of hefty fines and imprisonment, to assist fugitive slave catchers in their pursuit of runaway slaves. Although few documents relating to the Underground Railroad exist, historians have estimated that around fifteen hundred slaves per year used this network to escape bondage.

ANTISLAVERY CONVENTIONS

American abolitionists also strengthened their transnational networks by attending and organizing international antislavery gatherings, starting with the General Anti-Slavery Convention of 1840. In many ways these meetings were joint efforts by British and American abolitionists interested in encouraging international collaboration between abolitionist factions. In March 1839 Joshua Leavitt (1794–1873) of the AASS published a call in his New York newspaper for an international abolitionist gathering.

He envisioned a convention that would harmonize national antislavery forces into a single enterprise committed to the universal eradication of slavery and the slave trade. Leavitt's interest in such a convention developed shortly after the formation of the British and Foreign Anti-Slavery Society (BFASS), which became the first organization dedicated to the universal abolition of slavery, the slave trade, and human bondage. Leavitt wanted the BFASS to host this international meeting in London, which he believed would unite abolitionists and philanthropists from around the world.

The BFASS answered Leavitt's call and hosted the General Anti-Slavery Convention of 1840 at Exeter Hall in London. This meeting came at a time of intense disagreement within the American antislavery ranks. Tappan and his followers separated from Garrison and the AASS, citing irreconcilable differences over issues such as religion, political agitation, and the role of female abolitionists. At the convention, this American antislavery schism widened, especially when the question of women's involvement at the conference came to the fore. Although the BFASS negotiated a truce at the conference between the Garrison and Tappan antislavery wings, other issues also threatened to divide this international delegation such as questions over free trade, free labor, the success of West Indian emancipation, and the use of coolie indentured labor.

Despite these contentious issues, more than five hundred abolitionists gathered at Exeter Hall, primarily coming from North America and Great Britain, in an effort to unite their antislavery efforts into a unified movement. The delegation heard dozens of lectures presented on topics ranging from Russian serfdom and Egyptian "slave hunts" to slavery and indentured labor in the United States and the West Indies. Collectively, these reports formed the most comprehensive examination of slavery to date, and demonstrated that abolitionists were thinking about slavery and abolition in global terms. More important, the information gathered at this meeting provided the foundation for the global antislavery movement, which continued to fight slavery around the world for the rest of the nineteenth century. Although Garrisonian abolitionists felt dissatisfied with the 1840 convention, and subsequently boycotted the Second General Anti-Slavery Convention of 1843, American abolitionists continued to play active roles in the global antislavery movement. Garrison and his followers continued their relationships with many European antislavery organizations, and Garrison himself eventually put aside his objections and took on a leadership role at the Paris Anti-Slavery Conference of 1867, also hosted by the BFASS.

Although the American Civil War brought an end to American slavery, it did not end American abolitionists' crusade. In fact, many abolitionists redoubled their efforts against slavery in Cuba, Puerto Rico, and East Africa. During the Paris Anti-Slavery Conference, British, American, Spanish, and French abolitionists recommitted themselves to the universal eradication of slavery, while also vowing to protect the rights and liberties of the emancipated. These efforts helped abolish slavery in various parts of the world while maintaining the networks of communication and activism needed to fight such a dynamic and unrelenting institution. From the late eighteenth century, American abolitionism was both a domestic and transnational crusade, and the actions of American abolitionists during the nineteenth century laid the foundation for the fight that continues today against modern slavery and human trafficking.

SEE ALSO *Act Prohibiting Importation of Slaves (1807); Africa; Africa Squadron; American Colonization Society; Atlantic Slave Trade; Colonization Movement; Race; Transatlantic Reform*

BIBLIOGRAPHY

Davis, David Brion. *Inhuman Bondage: The Rise and Fall of Slavery in the New World.* Oxford and New York: Oxford University Press, 2006.

Drescher, Seymour. *Abolition: A History of Slavery and Antislavery.* Cambridge and New York: Cambridge University Press, 2009.

Huzzey, Richard. *Freedom Burning: Anti-Slavery and Empire in Victorian Britain.* Ithaca, NY: Cornell University Press, 2012.

McDaniel, W. Caleb. *The Problem of Democracy in the Age of Slavery: Garrisonian Abolitionists and Transatlantic Reform.* Baton Rouge: Louisiana State University Press, 2013.

Mulligan, William, and Maurice Bric, eds. *A Global History of Anti-Slavery Politics in the Nineteenth Century.* Houndmills, Basingstoke, Hampshire, UK, and New York: Palgrave Macmillan, 2013.

Oldfield, J. R. *Transatlantic Abolitionism in the Age of Revolution: An International History of Anti-Slavery, c. 1787–1820.* Cambridge and New York: Cambridge University Press, 2013.

W. E. Skidmore
PhD Candidate
Rice University

APARTHEID

Although the origins of apartheid in South Africa reach far back into the nation's past, it was the National Party's victory in the 1948 election that initiated a systematic process of codifying a strict racial hierarchy, control of the black labor force, and a policy of separate development—the numerous laws known collectively as apartheid. The National Party's ascent coincided with the early years of the Cold War struggle between the United States and the Soviet Union. As staunch anticommunists and capitalists, the South African government received both moral and tangible support from Western nations, particularly the United States, as well as from corporations and financial institutions. Yet grassroots opposition to apartheid in the United States emerged as an alternative to official US foreign policy, forcing Americans to confront both racial supremacy abroad as well as the United States' complicated relationship with decolonization and global human rights. Activists created numerous organizations, such as the American Committee on Africa, founded in 1953, to offer support to the burgeoning liberation struggles across the African continent, raising consciousness and exposing the divide between US foreign policy and the widespread decolonization of the developing world.

The United States' tacit support of apartheid revealed inherent hypocrisies within several of the nation's most basic underlying ideals, including the support of democracy, self-determination, and human rights. Apartheid's rise also coincided with the nascent civil rights movement in the United States, and many prominent leaders, such as Martin Luther King Jr., Malcolm X, and Stokely Carmichael (1941–1998), drew parallels between the struggles of African Americans and nonwhites in South Africa.

The Sharpeville Massacre of 1960, in which South African police killed sixty-nine nonwhite protesters, briefly shocked the world and brought attention to the viciousness of apartheid. As a result, nearly $200 million in Western capital fled the country, and in 1962 the United Nations General Assembly passed a nonbinding resolution advocating economic and cultural sanctions against South Africa. The Western powers, including the United States, refused to join the campaign, and within a few years outside investment returned and rapidly increased throughout the rest of the decade. The various presidential administrations of the 1960s and early 1970s maintained rhetorical condemnation of apartheid but refused to act further, and in the case of the Nixon administration actually embraced a closer relationship with the South African government.

By the 1970s, divestment—the selling of stocks in corporations with a physical presence in or financial dealings with South Africa—emerged as one of the major strategies of anti-apartheid forces in the United States, buoyed by student populations at colleges and universities across the country. Divestment also occurred throughout numerous other institutions, from churches to corporations to local and state governments. Other efforts, such as the Sullivan Principles, a corporate code of conduct developed by an African American Baptist minister, urged US corporations to treat their South African employees equally regardless of apartheid's discriminatory laws. Early prominent and successful divestment campaigns on college campuses occurred at Michigan State University, the University of Wisconsin-Madison, and Columbia University. By the end of 1986, at least 125 colleges and universities had divested a combined total of nearly $4 billion. Also that year Congress passed the Comprehensive Anti-Apartheid Act over President Ronald Reagan's veto, enacting limited economic sanctions against South Africa. The ultimate effectiveness of the various divestment and sanctions campaigns has been contested, though the widespread movements across the United States were critical in educating the public about apartheid and forcing various institutions to both confront apartheid from afar and uphold the nation's deep democratic virtues.

Following apartheid's demise and the birth of a multiracial democracy in 1994, relations between the United States and South Africa improved. With the ending of sanctions and boycotts, the United States emerged as South Africa's largest trade partner. South Africa has fallen short of the lofty ambitions set forth by Nelson Mandela (1918–2013), the anti-apartheid leader who was imprisoned for nearly three decades and in 1994 was elected South Africa's first black president. Despite the promise of reconciliation, a process of restorative justice, crime, economic inequality, HIV/AIDS, political corruption, and the dominance of the African National Congress persist as real challenges. But the history of apartheid and its end has remained of interest to Americans, particularly as embodied by Mandela. Movies such as *Catch a Fire* (2006), *Invictus* (2009), and *Mandela: Long Walk to Freedom* (2013) have gained both popular and critical acclaim in the United States, and Mandela's death and legacy have been widely discussed in the US media.

SEE ALSO *Human Rights*

BIBLIOGRAPHY

Borstelmann, Thomas. *Apartheid's Reluctant Uncle: The United States and Southern Africa in the Early Cold War.* New York: Oxford University Press, 1993.

Borstelmann, Thomas. *The Cold War and the Color Line: American Race Relations in the Global Arena.* Cambridge, MA: Harvard University Press, 2001.

Coker, Christopher. *The United States and South Africa, 1968–1985: Constructive Engagement and Its Critics.* Durham, NC: Duke University Press, 1986.

Culverson, Donald R. *Contesting Apartheid: U.S. Activism, 1960–1987.* Boulder, CO: Westview, 1999.

De Villiers, Les. *In Sight of Surrender: The U.S. Sanctions Campaign against South Africa, 1946–1993.* Westport, CT: Praeger, 1995.

Dudziak, Mary L. *Cold War Civil Rights: Race and the Image of American Democracy*. Princeton, NJ: Princeton University Press, 2000.

Hostetter, David L. *Movement Matters: American Antiapartheid Activism and the Rise of Multicultural Politics*. New York: Routledge, 2005.

Irwin, Ryan M. *Gordian Knot: Apartheid and the Unmaking of the Liberal World Order*. Oxford and New York: Oxford University Press, 2012.

Love, Janice. *The U.S. Anti-Apartheid Movement: Local Activism in Global Politics*. New York: Praeger, 1985.

Massie, Robert Kinloch. *Loosing the Bonds: The United States and South Africa in the Apartheid Years*. New York: Nan A. Talese/Doubleday, 1997.

Nesbitt, Francis Njubi. *Race for Sanctions: African Americans against Apartheid*. Bloomington: Indiana University Press, 2004.

Noer, Thomas J. *Cold War and Black Liberation: The United States and White Rule in Africa, 1948–1968*. Columbia: University of Missouri Press, 1985.

Skinner, Rob. *The Foundations of Anti-Apartheid: Liberal Humanitarians and Transnational Activists in Britain and the United States, c. 1916–64*. Houndmills, Basingstoke, Hampshire, UK, and New York: Palgrave Macmillan, 2010.

Westad, Odd Arne. *The Global Cold War: Third World Interventions and the Making of Our Times*. Cambridge and New York: Cambridge University Press, 2005.

Eric J. Morgan
Assistant Professor, Department of Democracy and Justice Studies
University of Wisconsin–Green Bay

APOLLO PROGRAM

Historian Arthur Schlesinger Jr. (1917–2007) once suggested that "the one thing for which this century will be remembered 500 years from now was: This was the century when we began the exploration of space" (Orloff 2000, v). That beginning was the result of the Apollo program, which, between December 1968 and December 1972, sent twenty-seven US astronauts to the vicinity of the Earth's moon. Twelve of those voyagers walked on the lunar surface, beginning with the July 20, 1969, landing of *Apollo 11* crew members Neil Armstrong (1930–2012) and Buzz Aldrin (b. 1930).

BEGINNINGS OF THE APOLLO PROGRAM

The Apollo program had its origins as the National Aeronautics and Space Administration (NASA), soon after it began operation in October 1958, planned its program of human spaceflight for the next decade. As a result of science fiction writings, early television programs, and the popularization of the idea by individuals like Walt Disney (1901–1966) and German émigré Wernher von Braun (1912–1977), the possibility that travel to the moon, Mars, and other space destinations was just around the corner had become part of American popular culture. By mid-1959, NASA had decided that sending humans to the moon should be its goal for the 1970s, and that during the 1960s it should prepare for achieving that goal. In mid-1960, the program to take those first steps toward the moon was named Apollo.

THE DECISION TO GO TO THE MOON

The schedule for a lunar landing program was accelerated soon after John F. Kennedy (1917–1963) was sworn in as president on January 20, 1961. Less than three months later, the Soviet Union, the Cold War rival to the United States for global leadership, became the first country to launch a human, Yuri Gagarin (1934–1968), into orbit and successfully return him to Earth. This April 12, 1961, feat, like the Soviet launch of *Sputnik-1* in October 1957, was an international propaganda coup for the USSR and produced a tidal wave of US domestic demands for an adequate response. In the days following the Gagarin launch, as Kennedy also dealt with the aftermath of the Bay of Pigs failure, the president decided that the United States could not allow the Soviet Union to dominate this new sphere of human activity, with its uncertain impact on international relations and national security. On April 20, Kennedy asked his vice president, Lyndon B. Johnson (1908–1973), to lead a rapid review to identify a "space program which promises dramatic results in which we could win" (Logsdon 2010, 80). Because both the United States and the Soviet Union would have to develop a new, large rocket to send people to the moon, a lunar landing effort became the response to Kennedy's request. Johnson's response reached Kennedy on May 8; it suggested setting a lunar landing as a national goal, commenting that the prestige to be gained from such an achievement was "part of the battle along the fluid front of the Cold War" (Logsdon 2010, 105).

Kennedy accepted this recommendation, and on May 25, 1961, in a nationally televised speech to a joint session of Congress, he asked the country to make a commitment to the goal of, "before this decade is out, landing a man on the moon and returning him safely to earth." Kennedy noted that "no single space project … will be more impressive to mankind" (Logsdon 2010, 114). With this proposal, Apollo became an undertaking of high geopolitical significance. In his most famous space speech, delivered at Rice University in Houston, Texas, on September 12, 1962, Kennedy justified the lunar landing effort, saying "we choose to go to the moon in this decade and do the other things, not because they are easy, but because they are hard" (Logsdon 2010, 150).

Kennedy's May 1961 speech was followed by an unprecedented, warlike but peaceful, mobilization of the financial and human resources required to meet the "end of the decade" goal. NASA's budget was increased by 89 percent after Kennedy's speech and by another 101 percent the following year. At its peak in 1965, the NASA budget was more than 4 percent of federal spending; by 1967, over 400,000 government and industry workers were engaged in the Apollo program. NASA's astronauts had become well-known and highly respected celebrities.

By 1963, however, the Apollo program also had become the target of criticism from both the liberal and conservative ends of the political spectrum. Liberals saw the program as an example of misplaced priorities, arguing that funds for Apollo would be better spent on social programs and education. Conservatives suggested that priority in space should be given to military efforts to counter the Soviet space threat. Reacting to these criticisms, and judging that an expensive space race with the Soviet Union was no longer needed, given the outcome of the 1962 Cuban missile crisis and his desire to pursue a new "strategy of peace," President Kennedy, in a little-remembered initiative, proposed in September 1963 that Apollo should become a US-Soviet cooperative undertaking. But when Kennedy was assassinated two months later, the lunar landing effort became a memorial to a fallen young president, and the cooperative initiative was stillborn.

THE APOLLO MISSIONS

It took NASA several years after Kennedy's 1961 charge to get its plans for Apollo fully in order. The space agency decided in late 1961 to develop a large rocket, christened Saturn V, for the lunar landing missions, and in 1962 chose a controversial approach to carrying out the voyage itself, one that required a rendezvous between two spacecraft in lunar orbit for its success. Running behind schedule in 1963, NASA adopted an ambitious test schedule in order to maximize the chances of achieving the first landing by the end of 1969. The program suffered a major setback in January 1967 when the crew preparing for the first mission of the Apollo spacecraft died during a launchpad test. But NASA had the public and political support needed to press forward. The first test flight of the Saturn V booster took place in November 1967, and the first crewed flight of a redesigned Apollo spacecraft, *Apollo 7*, took place in October 1967. This flight cleared the way for a bold step. In December 1968, *Apollo 8*, the first mission with an Apollo spacecraft launched on the Saturn V, took its three-person crew all the way to lunar orbit. On Christmas Eve, as a global audience watched and listened, the *Apollo 8* crew sent back close-up television images of the forbidding lunar surface as they read from the first verses of the Bible. They brought back to Earth the iconic "Earthrise" photograph, an image that had an immediate and lasting impact on environmental awareness.

Two more test missions quickly followed. *Apollo 9* in March 1969 was an Earth-orbit test of the lunar landing spacecraft and *Apollo 10* in May 1969 was a dress rehearsal, flying the whole mission profile except for the actual lunar landing and ascent. Then, on July 16, 1969, the historic *Apollo 11* mission was launched, carrying Armstrong and Aldrin on July 20, 1969, to "one small step" but "one giant leap" onto the surface of another celestial body. As he greeted the *Apollo 11* crew on their return to Earth, President Richard Nixon (1913–1994), with substantial hyperbole, declared their mission "the greatest week in the history of the world since the Creation" (Logsdon 2015, 24).

AFTERMATH AND IMPACT

While Nixon may have overstated the significance of the first lunar landing, the achievement was greeted with banner headlines and a global outpouring of praise for the country that had first reached the moon. The landing and moonwalk were the first events televised live worldwide; the satellite network needed for global communication had just begun operation. Immediately after greeting the astronauts, Nixon embarked on an around-the-world tour, citing at every stop the "spirit of Apollo," as he suggested "if man can reach the moon … we can bring peace to the earth" (Logsdon 2015, 25). The *Apollo 11* crew was heralded by ticker-tape parades in New York and Chicago, then undertook a world tour labeled "Giant Step," in which the three astronauts visited twenty-seven cities in twenty-four countries. The tour was a success in public diplomacy as millions of people caught sight of the astronauts as they communicated the message of US leadership to presidents, prime ministers, and kings and queens in the countries they visited.

While the success of the *Apollo 11* mission created a long-lasting image of US power and exceptionalism, the subsequent missions in the Apollo program had far less political impact. Public interest in lunar flights rapidly declined. In addition, the near-tragic mission of *Apollo 13*, as a spacecraft explosion on the way to the moon threatened the crew's survival, underlined the risks of continued landing attempts. In 1970, due to a combination of perceived risks and funding constraints, NASA canceled two of the remaining six planned missions, and President Nixon throughout 1971 urged his associates to cancel the final two of the remaining four flights. He was persuaded that the scientific payoffs from those missions were worth having and that the missions could be rescheduled so that, if they were to fail, they would not have a negative impact on his openings to China and the Soviet Union and his 1972 reelection prospects. Already in 1970, Nixon had rejected an ambitious post-Apollo proposal to continue lunar exploration and to prepare for initial human missions to Mars in the 1980s.

The Apollo program thus stands as a singular effort in human spaceflight beyond Earth orbit. In terms of John F. Kennedy's fundamentally political motivations in approving a fast-paced effort to win the US-Soviet space race by being first to the moon, Apollo was a substantial success. It had both short-term and lasting influence on US international prestige and national morale. Investment in the technologies needed to carry out the program accelerated the pace of innovation in many sectors, such as miniaturization of electronic components, computer software, and new materials. For some, Apollo represented the first step in humanity's migration off the surface of its home planet.

In other ways, however, Apollo was a dead-end program. Much of the program's more than $150 billion cost (in 2014 dollars) went to develop equipment, particularly the Saturn V rocket and Apollo spacecraft, that found no other use. Despite several presidential attempts since 1961 to set a new exploratory goal for the US space program, no human has traveled beyond Earth orbit since December 1972. Nixon's decision, announced in 1970, that the space program would become "a normal and regular part of our national life" has limited government space budgets, and the kind of political imperatives and public excitement that helped propel Apollo to the moon have not reappeared (Logsdon 2015, 115). Arthur Schlesinger's forecast that space exploration would be the historical highlight of the twentieth century thus seems ill-conceived.

SEE ALSO *Cold War; Earthrise (Bill Anders, 1968); Kennedy, John Fitzgerald; National Aeronautics and Space Administration (NASA); Sputnik; Television*

BIBLIOGRAPHY

Chaikin, Andrew. *A Man on the Moon: The Voyages of the Apollo Astronauts.* New York: Viking, 1994.

Collins, Michael. *Carrying the Fire: An Astronaut's Journeys.* New York: Coupler Square, 2001. Originally published by Farrar, Straus, and Giroux in 1974.

Compton, W. David. *Where No Man Has Gone Before: A History of Apollo Lunar Exploration Missions.* NASA SP-4214. Washington, DC: GPO, 1989.

Hansen, James R. *First Man: The Life of Neil A. Armstrong.* New York: Simon and Schuster, 2005.

Lambright, W. Henry. *Powering Apollo: James E. Webb of NASA.* Baltimore, MD: Johns Hopkins University Press, 1995.

Launius, Roger. "Interpreting the Moon Landings: Project Apollo and the Historians." *History and Technology* 22, 3 (2006): 225–255.

Logsdon, John M. *John F. Kennedy and the Race to the Moon.* New York: Palgrave Macmillan, 2010.

Logsdon, John M. *After Apollo? Richard Nixon and the American Space Program.* New York: Palgrave Macmillan, 2015.

Logsdon, John M., and Roger D. Launius, eds. *Exploring the Unknown: Selected Documents in the History of the U.S. Civil Space Program,* Vol. 7: *Human Spaceflight.* NASA SP-2008-4407. Washington, DC: NASA, 2008.

Mailer, Norman. *Of a Fire on the Moon.* Boston: Little, Brown, 1969.

McDougall, Walter A. *The Heavens and the Earth: A Political History of the Space Age.* New York: Basic Books, 1985.

Murray, Charles, and Catherine Bly Cox. *Apollo: Race to the Moon.* New York: Simon and Schuster, 1989.

Orloff, Richard W. *Apollo by the Numbers.* Washington, DC: NASA SP-4209, 2000.

Scott, David Meerman, and Richard Jurek. *Marketing the Moon: The Selling of the Apollo Lunar Program.* Cambridge, MA: MIR Press, 2014.

Tribbe, Matthew D. *No Requiem for the Space Age: The Apollo Moon Landings and American Culture.* New York: Oxford University Press, 2014.

John M. Logsdon
Professor Emeritus, Space Policy Institute
Elliott School of International Affairs, The George Washington University

ARABIAN NIGHTS

The *Arabian Nights* is a name commonly given to Western adaptations of the tales of the *One Thousand and One Nights*, although in common usage the two have often been interchangeable. The stories, originating in Asia centuries ago and transmitted to the Arab world, came to the United States as English translations from Europe. Compilations of the stories have been among the most popular books in the United States (along with the Bible). Many early editions were bootlegged and included the famous frame tale, in which a Persian woman named Scheherezade each night recounts to her husband, King Shahriyar, a gripping story but withholds its resolution until the next evening to prevent the king from killing her the following morning. Particular stories within the frame, like "Aladdin and the Magic Lamp," "Ali Baba and the Forty Thieves," the "Seven Voyages of Sindbad the Sailor," and tales of the venerable Haroun al-Raschid, powerful but generous "governor of Old Baghdad," became favorites.

POPULARITY IN THE UNITED STATES

Americans recognized the stories as a global masterpiece of imagination that many believed rivaled William Shakespeare in literary importance. American writers, performers, and graphic artists found great inspiration in the complex, clever, and varied tales. Most professional writers, as well as countless amateur authors, created homegrown imitations called "Oriental tales" and "Tales of the East" in books, literary magazines, or newspapers. Many readers were not always certain when they were reading translated adaptations of the *1001 Nights*, a heavily reworked adaptation, or a completely domestic imitation because all reproduced, exaggerated, or even caricatured the flowery, metaphorical language found in Edward W. Lane's particularly influential English translation, *The Thousand and One Nights, Commonly Called, in England, The Arabian Nights' Entertainments* (1839–1841).

For Americans, the *Arabian Nights* were first and foremost children's literature, often richly illustrated—like New York publisher McLoughlin Brothers' *Arabian Nights' Entertainments* (1885)—and edited "for family reading" in a nation with extremely high literacy rates and many nostalgic parents. American adults remembered that as children the stories' descriptions of incredible riches, "houses of gold and streets paved with diamonds," for instance, made them compelling because the mind-boggling luxuries described in the *Nights* contrasted sharply with readers' modest, hardworking lives.

A growing middle class drove an 1880s fad for Oriental-style men's studies or "Oriental cozy corners" in middle-class parlors featuring generously stuff upholstered furniture, draped fabric wall decoration, and much "bric-a-brac" like scimitars, oriental carpets, and other imported consumer items that reflected the scenes of luxury and contentment people saw in the richly illustrated editions. At the same moment, reform groups headed by Anthony Comstock challenged sales of John Payne's *Tales from the Arabic* (1882–1884) as "obscene" literature. Most Americans still saw the *Nights* as a trusted classic, even though some of the stories did explore female sexual desire and infidelity. Because women's sexuality was becoming more publicly acceptable, many Americans now focused on the stories' sexually powerful harem women, dancing girls, or *houris*. For a generation thereafter, sexually suggestive shows of dancing women came framed as "Arabian Nights" dances, with Eastern-style belly dancers advertised as "Houris of the East!"

INSPIRATION FOR DESIGN AND PERFORMANCE

The *Nights* as an artistic source and style of performance proliferated in every venue of creative expression, including live theater, graphic design, circus show productions, parade decoration, advertising, retail space design, and common colloquialism. Americans often described something beautiful or amazing as "more incredible than the *Arabian Nights*." Parades and amateur theater were some of the most ubiquitous venues for live performance of the stories, or loose adaptations of it. In particular, after their founding in the 1880s, the fraternal order known as the Ancient Arabic Order, Nobles of the Mystic Shrine, or Shriners, employed a subculture that combined Masonic iconography and regalia with costuming and storytelling drawn from the *Arabian Nights*. Hundreds of thousands of men joined the order, and in the twentieth century Shriners often staged *Arabian Nights*–themed banquets and decorated their newsletters, invitations, menus, and other ephemera with imagery and language drawn from the stories. Nonmembers knew the Shriners' ubiquitous street parades featuring characters and vignettes from the stories mixed with other elements of the order's subculture, which continue to the present.

Through the twentieth century, the *Arabian Nights* as literature continued to be popular while Americans adapted the stories to new entertainment media. In cinema, individual stories from the *Nights* were heavily reworked and, like circus, theater, and parade productions in the style of the *Nights*, offered an opportunity for lavish, glittering sets and costumes. However, cinema was costly to produce and hence in practice offered audiences more conservative, even xenophobic representations of nonwhites than modern literature or vaudeville theater had, and often gave short shrift to Americans' love for the complex characters, humor, and sophistication of the stories. *The Thief of Baghdad* (1924, 1940, 1961), originally featuring top Hollywood actor Douglas Fairbanks, employed cinematic tricks that made story elements—such as a flying carpet—come to life for audiences for the first time, and was followed by many other films of varying quality. Hollywood also produced satirical reinterpretations, such as *Ali Baba Goes to Town* (1937) and, famously, *The Road to Morocco* (1942), featuring lucrative box-office stars Dorothy Lamour, Bob Hope, and Bing Crosby. Many of these films ridiculed famous characters from the stories with simplistic, two-dimensional portrayals for supporting characters, or through hackneyed jokes about their ostensible decadence, violence, arrogance, or stupidity.

The *Arabian Nights* receded from adult entertainment by the 1970s, but persisted for children in television and film adaptations, including animated shorts featuring Popeye and Olive Oyl, *Aladdin and His Magic Lamp* (1939), or Bugs Bunny's *A-Lad-In His Lamp* (1948). Disney's *Aladdin* (1992) was a groundbreaking animated film that demonstrated how perhaps Americans were becoming more critical of the racism in motion picture *Arabian Nights* renditions. No doubt due in part to increased immigration to the United States from West Asia and heightened public concern for US relations with the Muslim world, Disney agreed to make minor edits to a notorious song in the film, sung by Robin Williams, that discussed the Arab world as a "barbaric" place. The long and varied history of American engagement with the *Arabian Nights* reveals that as much as artists and audiences employed versions or copies of the stories to express racism, American exceptionalism, or other political tensions, they also sincerely admired the stories as great art. As such, the line dividing sinister American appropriation of the *Nights* from well-meaning integration of the *Nights* into American culture (with all its political complexity) is often difficult to discern.

SEE ALSO *Americanization; Exceptionalism; Immigration; Islam; Middle East; Orientalism; Ottoman Empire*

BIBLIOGRAPHY

Irwin, Robert. *Visions of the Jinn: Illustrators of the Arabian Nights.* Oxford: Oxford University Press, 2010.

Nance, Susan. *How the Arabian Nights Inspired the American Dream, 1790–1935.* Chapel Hill: University of North Carolina Press, 2009.

Schacker-Mill, Jennifer. "Otherness and Otherworldliness: Edward W. Lane's Ethnographic Treatment of the Arabian Nights." *Journal of American Folklore* 113, 448 (2000): 164–184.

Shaheen, Jack G. *Reel Bad Arabs: How Hollywood Vilifies a People.* 3rd ed. Northampton, MA: Olive Branch Press, 2014.

Susan Nance
Associate Professor of US History
University of Guelph

ARAB-ISRAELI CONFLICT

The Arab-Israeli conflict, which would become a central focus of global instability and US foreign policy for decades, had deep roots. Following British authorization under the Balfour Declaration in 1917, Jewish settlers flocked to the biblical Holy Land in hopes of establishing a Jewish homeland. Under the World War I (1914–1918) mandate system, Britain administered Palestine, a colony overwhelmingly inhabited by Muslim Arabs. Jews, Arabs, and the British occupiers clashed even before the Nazi Holocaust fueled the pace of Zionist emigration to Palestine. The Jewish influx sparked continuing conflict, as Britain lost control of the situation in Palestine by the end of World War II (1939–1945).

AMERICAN SUPPORT FOR ISRAEL AND ZIONISM

Americans proved strong supporters of Zionism, which resonated powerfully with US religious and cultural mores. Theodore Roosevelt (1858–1919) declared that it would be "entirely proper to start a Zionist State around Jerusalem." President Woodrow Wilson (1856–1924) endorsed the Balfour Declaration during the Great War. Although a longtime Zionist, President Franklin Roosevelt (1882–1945) observed prophetically during World War II that as European Jews poured into the region "the millions of surrounding Arabs might easily proclaim a Holy War and then there would be no end of trouble" (Little 2002, 22). Roosevelt's death left the matter in the hands of Harry Truman (1884–1972) and the newly established United Nations, neither of which succeeded in forging a peaceful settlement of the burgeoning conflict.

In 1947, a UN special committee called for termination of the British Mandate and partition of Palestine into an Arab and a Jewish state. The Arabs, including neighboring Egypt, opposed the creation of the new Zionist state but lacked powerful allies, whereas both the United States and the Soviet Union endorsed partition. In 1948, Truman rejected the advice of Secretary of State George Marshall (1880–1959) and the State Department by formally recognizing the new Jewish state of Israel. The diplomats warned of perpetual turmoil and threats to Middle East oil supplies, opportunities they feared the Soviets might exploit, but Truman embraced the Zionist cause. Motivated by his own biblical fundamentalism, sympathy for Jews in the wake of the Holocaust, and domestic political considerations, Truman overruled his advisers. "America could not stand by while the victims of Hitler's racial madness were denied the opportunities to build new lives," Truman declared (1956, 140).

Truman's decision was popular in the United States, which had the largest Jewish population in the world at the time, but Jews were not alone in embracing Zionism. Many fundamentalist Protestants supported the establishment of a Jewish homeland, and other Americans perceived parallels between Israeli settler colonialism and the US history of frontier expansion. The Arabs fought back against the partition of Palestine. In 1948, in the first Arab-Israeli War, Israel crushed the Palestinian opposition and repulsed regional Arab armies. The Jewish settlers perpetrated massacres while driving some 750,000 Palestinian Arabs from their homes in hundreds of towns and villages. By the time of the ceasefire in January 1949, Israel had increased in size from the 55 percent of the former British Mandate under the UN partition plan to 77 percent. In September 1948, Jewish extremists assassinated a Swedish diplomat appointed by the United

Nations, which had condemned Israel's aggression and called for repatriation of Palestinian refugees, as well as international status for Jerusalem.

THE 1956 SUEZ CRISIS

Israel's refusal to give up land beyond the boundaries of the UN partition conjoined with Arab vows to destroy the Jewish state to ensure that the conflict would continue. Raids, border clashes, and lethal Israeli reprisals prevailed between the 1949 armistice agreements and the Suez crisis in 1956. The canal crisis erupted when Gamal Abdel Nasser (1918–1970) ousted the Egyptian monarch and quickly emerged as a charismatic leader of the Arab world and a critic of Israel and Zionism. The British and French decided to intervene over Nasser's nationalization of the Suez Canal, though he had pledged to keep it open and pay compensation. Nasser had also angered President Dwight D. Eisenhower (1890–1969) by proclaiming neutralism in the Cold War and offering diplomatic recognition of "Red" China. At the same time, however, the Eisenhower administration sought to improve American standing with the Arab states as part of the Cold War policy of containing communism by limiting Soviet influence in the region. Thus Eisenhower was incensed when the nation's closest allies—Britain, France, and Israel—launched the surprise invasion of Egypt, which also diverted international attention from the Soviet repression in Hungary. Under intense US and UN pressure, Britain and France withdrew from Suez, but Israel initially defied the Americans. Israel grudgingly withdrew only after vowing to reintervene if the maritime access was cut off or if cross-border attacks on the Jewish state continued.

THE 1967 SIX-DAY WAR

In large measure because of the Arab-Israeli conflict, the Middle East was a perennial tinderbox, one that exploded anew in 1967. Palestinians and other Arabs had continued to oppose Israel, as *fedayeen* ("redeemers") launched episodic attacks on Israeli border settlements, to which the Israelis responded aggressively. The Palestine Liberation Organization (PLO), proclaimed in 1964, condemned Zionism and agitated worldwide for the creation of a Palestinian state. Democratic presidents John F. Kennedy (1917–1963) and especially Lyndon Johnson (1908–1973) strengthened the US alliance with Israel, increasingly viewed as an outpost of democracy and a bulwark of anticommunism in the Middle East. They urged Israel to compromise with the Arabs, but refrained from pressuring Tel Aviv on the matter. The United States began to send more military aid to Israel than it provided to any other country in the world, including tanks, missiles, and fighter aircraft. US leaders accepted Israel's oft-repeated but ultimately mendacious pledge that it would refrain from developing a nuclear weapons program.

By the time of the 1967 war, or the Six-Day War, Israel had developed an aggressive military strategy emphasizing preemptive strikes and rapid deployments to quickly subdue its enemies. On June 5, as tensions boiled over into war, Israel implemented the strategy with a massive assault on Egyptian airfields, taking Cairo out of the war from the outset. The Israelis then crushed Syria and Jordan. The United States, the Soviet Union, and the United Nations called for an immediate ceasefire, but the Israelis pushed ahead. On June 8, Israeli fighter aircraft and torpedo boats carried out successive assaults on the *Liberty*, a US intelligence vessel monitoring the conflict from its anchorage in international waters and flying a large American flag. Thirty-four sailors were killed and 174 injured in the attacks, which the United States sharply condemned. Israel claimed the attacks were accidental and eventually paid a $3.3 million indemnity, but the CIA and most US officials concluded the attacks had been deliberate and were apparently intended to preclude any US effort to head off the Israeli assault on Syria. The brief but decisive six-day conflict ended in complete victory for the Israelis, who celebrated while the Arabs suffered another devastating defeat.

The United States backed UN Security Council Resolution 242, a "land for peace" formula under which Israel would withdraw from the newly seized territories—the West Bank, the Sinai and Gaza Strip, and the Golan or Syrian Heights—in return for Arab recognition. Egypt, Jordan, and Israel endorsed Resolution 242, but the Israelis soon claimed the resolution's reference to "the inadmissibility of the acquisition of territory by war" did not mean specifically "the" territories it had just seized. Overwhelming public support for Israel precluded US officials from pressuring Tel Aviv to pursue a "land for peace" agreement encompassing withdrawal from the territories occupied in the 1967 war. By this time, the American Israel Public Affairs Committee (AIPAC), founded in 1951, emerged as one of the most powerful lobbies in Congress.

THE 1973 ARAB-ISRAELI WAR

The Six-Day War shattered the leadership of Nasser, who died in 1970, but the Arabs remained determined to strike back against Israel. In October 1973, Egypt, now led by Anwar Sadat (1918–1981), allied with Syria and attacked Israel on Yom Kippur, the holiest day under Judaism, which also fell during the Muslim holy month of Ramadan. The Egyptians drove back the Israelis in the surprise assault at the outset of the 1973 Arab-Israeli War, but the Israeli forces quickly regrouped and went on the offensive. As in 1967, Israel dispatched the Syrians in short order and—aided by a resupply of US arms—prepared for a punishing assault on Egypt. At this point, the Soviet Union, which had clashed with the Israelis at sea, threatened to intervene on behalf of its Arab allies. When this threat arrived in Washington, and in the midst of the Watergate crisis, the Richard Nixon (1913–1994) administration went to DEFCON 3, or defense condition three, a state of readiness for all-out war.

On October 25, all the parties agreed to a ceasefire, bringing an end to the war after nearly three weeks of intense conflict. The Egyptians claimed some measure of restored pride for their early success in the war, but the Israelis remained fully ensconced in the occupied territories and embittered by the surprise attack. The Arab members of the Organization of the Petroleum Exporting Countries (OPEC) punished the United States for its support for Israel early in the war by embargoing oil supplies. Oil prices skyrocketed as a result of the 1973 OPEC oil embargo, leading to long lines at US gas pumps and an economic downturn, and underscoring US and Western European oil dependence.

PURSUIT OF A PEACE AGREEMENT AMID CONTINUING VIOLENCE

The impetus for achievement of the Camp David Accords, over which President Jimmy Carter presided in 1978, came from Sadat. The talks at the US presidential compound in Maryland led to an Israeli-Egyptian peace agreement the following year. Israeli prime minister Menachem Begin (1913–1992) agreed to vacate the Sinai in return for Egyptian recognition and normalization of diplomatic relations between the two states. The proposed comprehensive Middle East peace, including the creation of a viable Palestinian state, never materialized. Moreover, the pace of Israeli settlements accelerated in the occupied territories. Following his landslide victory, President Ronald Reagan (1911–2004) stepped up aid to Israel and initially backed an effort by Tel Aviv to destroy the PLO infrastructure through an attack on neighboring Lebanon. In October 1983, Islamic militants responded with a massive suicide bombing on the US marine compound in Beirut, killing 241 US marines, as well as scores of French soldiers.

In 1987, as Israel continued to establish "facts on the ground" by constructing new settlements in the occupied territories, the Palestinians launched a mostly nonviolent resistance known as the Intifada, or "shaking off" of the occupation. The Israelis responded to public demonstrations and stone throwing with mass arrests, snipers, and destruction of Palestinian homes and villages. By the end of 1989, the Palestinian death toll in the Intifada reached 626, as compared with 43 Israeli dead. Some 38,000 Arabs were wounded and as many as 40,000 had been arrested. In February and again in April 1988, the United States vetoed UN Security Council resolutions condemning violations of Palestinian human rights and calling on Israel to pursue a two-state solution under UN auspices. On both occasions, the vote was fourteen to one, with only the US vote preventing passage of the resolutions.

While Israel and the United States branded the PLO a terrorist organization, more militant groups had arisen in the wake of the 1979 Iranian Revolution and amidst the Israeli occupation. Hezbollah, Islamic Jihad, the Muslim Brotherhood, and Hamas ("Enthusiasm"), all took a more militant stance than the PLO. Indeed, in 1988, Yasser Arafat (1929–2004) made a historic offer to accept the 1947 UN borders and to recognize the state of Israel. The Israeli government refused to recognize or negotiate with the PLO and continued to authorize new settlements in the occupied territories.

The George H. W. Bush administration avowed that victory in the Persian Gulf War (1990–1991) created a climate conducive to the pursuit of a general Middle East peace accord as part of the "new world order." US public opinion remained solidly behind Israel, which kept its pledge to stay out of the Persian Gulf War despite Iraqi Scud missile attacks targeting Israel. Bush, however, emphasized that the proliferation of Israeli settlements in the occupied territories impeded the creation of a Palestinian state and thus stymied the quest to forge a general Mideast peace accord. The US president pressured Israel to halt settlements and, in an unprecedented move, withheld a $10-billion loan guarantee promised to Tel Aviv for its cooperation in Persian Gulf War strategy.

From 1991 to 1993, the Bush administration sponsored the Madrid Conference in Spain, but the peace talks between the Arabs and Israelis failed. Israeli prime minister Yitzhak Shamir (1915–2012) pursued a rejectionist path and continued to authorize new settlements in defiance of the US president. Shamir later acknowledged that Tel Aviv's strategy over the years had been to "drag out talks on Palestinian self-rule … while attempting to settle hundreds of thousands of Jews in the occupied territories" (Smith 2010, 419). Despite the failure to achieve a peace settlement, the Madrid talks had at least brought the Arabs and Israelis together, leading to a broader agreement in the Oslo Accords. In 1993, with Washington uninvolved in the negotiations in Norway, Arafat and the PLO affirmed "the right of the state of Israel to exist in peace and security" and pledged to end resistance in return for Palestinian statehood. Israel officially recognized the PLO as the representative of the Palestinian people and pledged to begin negotiating a settlement. Tel Aviv did not, however, recognize a Palestinian state, nor did Israel agree to withdraw from the occupied territories. President Bill Clinton, meanwhile, did not pressure Israel on new settlements and defied the United Nations and the vast majority of governments and world opinion by refusing to condemn the ongoing Israeli occupation of territory beyond its recognized international borders.

The Oslo agreements thus allowed the occupation and settlements to continue alongside the establishment of a weak new Palestinian Authority—a quasi government and police force with a headquarters but no state. In 1994, Israel and Jordan came to peace terms, but Israeli-Syrian talks over the occupation of the Golan Heights broke down. Oslo produced no agreement on the right of Palestinian refugees to return or on the status of Jerusalem. Palestinians continued to suffer from increasingly high unemployment and deprivations, including lack of reliable access to basic services, such as water and power. The conditions were especially dire in the refugee camps and in the densely populated Gaza Strip. Terror assaults by both Arabs and Jews continued. In 1994, Hamas killed twenty-two Israelis in a suicide bombing in Tel Aviv. That same year, a Jewish immigrant from New York killed twenty-nine Arabs in an assault on a Muslim holy site in the occupied West bank city of Hebron.

Arab suicide bombing attacks traumatized Israelis and fueled the right-wing Likud Party. The militant Ariel Sharon (1928–2014) and rising Likud politicians, such as the US-educated Benjamin Netanyahu, condemned the Labor Party for recognizing the PLO. On November 4, 1995, an Israeli fanatic assassinated Prime Minister Yitzhak Rabin, the Labor Party leader who had signed the Oslo Accords and famously shook hands with Arafat. The Oslo process broke down under Netanyahu, elected prime minister the following year, as the occupation became increasingly permanent. Israel divided the occupied territories with new bypass roads, roadblocks, and checkpoints cutting off and isolating the Arab population. Arab terror attacks accelerated in 1996 and brought swift and brutal Israeli reprisals, including a sixteen-day bombardment of southern Lebanon in which a UN compound at Qana was deliberately targeted, killing 106 civilians.

A FALTERING PEACE PROCESS

In July 2000, Clinton sponsored a last-gasp effort to save the Oslo "peace process" in the Camp David summit at the presidential retreat. Israeli prime minister Ehud Barak refused to negotiate directly with Arafat, thus requiring Clinton to act as a go-between. While Clinton and Barak later blamed Arafat for rejecting Israel's "generous offer," the terms would have required a rump and disjointed Palestinian state to attempt to function amid the rapidly proliferating roadblocks and checkpoints. The number of Jewish settlements in the West Bank had doubled since the Oslo talks began in 1993, undermining the prospects of a viable Palestinian state connecting the West Bank, East Jerusalem, and Gaza.

Following the failure of the Camp David summit in 2000, the Arab-Israeli conflict became increasingly violent, with the Arabs paying by far the heaviest price. In October 2000, the right-wing Likud Party leader, Sharon, sabotaged plans for the resumption of peace talks with a carefully orchestrated visit to the al-Aqsa Mosque, a Muslim holy site in Jerusalem. The provocative visit, underscoring Israeli claims to control over all of the holy spaces in Jerusalem, triggered the Second Intifada, mass demonstrations that became much more violent than the original Intifada. Over the next two years, Arabs carried out suicide bombings, while Israel carried out disproportionate military reprisals. A total of 325 Palestinians died, along with thirty-six Israelis and four others. More than 10,600 Palestinians were injured compared to 362 Israelis.

The Palestinian uprising paved Sharon's path to power, as he won election as prime minister in 2001 and became a close ally of President George W. Bush amid the global war on terror. Bush fully backed Sharon, who was hostile to the so-called peace process, which thus broke down completely. Traumatized by Arab suicide bombings of civilian targets, Israel attacked Palestinian communities with lethal force, expanded settlements in the occupied territories, and constructed a new "security wall," as well as new roads and checkpoints, deepening the isolation of Arab communities and neighborhoods. In August 2002, a UN General Assembly resolution demanding an immediate end to new settlements and to the violence passed by a vote of 114 to 4, with only Israel, the United States, and the US Pacific outposts of Micronesia and the Marshall Islands opposed.

Under international pressure, Bush announced a "road map" for peace and the creation of a Palestinian state, but the road came to a familiar dead end. In 2004, Sharon uprooted settlements and withdrew Israel from the Gaza Strip, a 140-square-mile (363-square-kilometer) territory packed with a population of nearly two million people, including hundreds of thousands of refugees from the previous wars. Bush lauded the Israeli withdrawal from Gaza, which paved the way, however, for an expansion of Jewish settlements aimed at permanent occupation of the West Bank and Arab East Jerusalem. Bush, backed by the powerful Israel lobby, both political parties, and fundamentalist Christians, among others, declared that the recognized international boundaries should no longer constrain Israel. In 2006, Washington backed another Israeli military assault into Lebanon, including massive bombing of civilian targets, but Hezbollah held fast, forcing a UN-brokered Israeli withdrawal.

In 2006, the people of Gaza elected the more radical group Hamas over Fatah, the only Palestinian entity recognized by Israel and the United States. Viewing Hamas purely as a terrorist organization, the United States and Israel refused to recognize the outcome of the democratic election and closed off the borders of Gaza, undermining its ability to function economically. In 2008 to 2009 and again in 2014, Israel reduced the vulnerable strip of land to rubble, killing thousands of civilians while also carrying out targeted assassinations. The action came in response to the sporadic lobbing of rockets from Gaza across the border, which spread fear within nearby Israeli communities but did comparatively little damage. Amid the attacks on Gaza, the United States called for a ceasefire while fully backing Israel amid a chorus of international condemnation of Tel Aviv's often-indiscriminate use of force.

NETANYAHU, OBAMA, AND THE STRAINED US-ISRAELI RELATIONSHIP

Upon entering office, President Barack Obama called for an end to Israeli settlements in the occupied territories and urged a viable two-state solution, but these proposals fell on deaf ears. Netanyahu disliked Obama, ignored his call for a two-state solution, and won support from the majority of the US and Israeli publics. By the time of the second assault on Gaza in 2014, the peace process was dead and the Israelis continued to build settlements aimed at absorbing the West Bank and East Jerusalem while relegating Palestinians to enclaves enclosed by roadblocks, checkpoints, and the separation wall. In 2004, the wall isolating the Palestinian enclaves had been ruled illegal by an advisory opinion of the International Court of Justice.

Republicans shared Netanyahu's dislike of Obama, and they thus invited the Israeli leader to address the US Congress in March 2015 to decry ongoing negotiations over Iran's nuclear development, which Netanyahu condemned as appeasement. On the eve of the Israeli elections in March 2015, Netanyahu appealed to right-wing voters by declaring there would be no Palestinian state under his leadership, a statement he retracted following his successful reelection. Obama condemned Israeli intransigence and denial of Palestinian human rights, but as his second term wound down, the Arab-Israeli conflict continued with no end in sight.

SEE ALSO *Camp David Accords (1978); Carter, James Earl, Jr.; Israel; Organization of the Petroleum Exporting Countries (OPEC); Palestine*

BIBLIOGRAPHY

Anderson, Irvine H. *Biblical Interpretation and Middle East Policy: The Promised Land, America, and Israel, 1917–2002.* Gainesville: University Press of Florida, 2005.

Khalidi, Rashid. *The Iron Cage: The Story of the Palestinian Struggle for Statehood.* Boston: Beacon Press, 2006.

Krämer, Gudrun. *A History of Palestine: From the Ottoman Conquest to the Founding of the State of Israel.* Translated by Graham Harman and Gudrun Krämer. Princeton, NJ: Princeton University Press, 2008.

Little, Douglas. *American Orientalism: The United States and the Middle East since 1945.* Chapel Hill: University of North Carolina Press, 2002.

Morris, Benny. *Israel's Border Wars, 1949–1956: Arab Infiltration, Israeli Retaliation, and the Countdown to the Suez War.* New York: Oxford University Press, 1993.

Quandt, William B. *Camp David: Peacemaking and Politics.* Washington, DC: Brookings Institution, 1986.

Raz, Avi. *The Bride and the Dowry: Israel, Jordan, and the Palestinians in the Aftermath of the June 1967 War.* New Haven, CT: Yale University Press, 2012.

Rogan, Eugene L., and Avi Shlaim, eds. *The War for Palestine: Rewriting the History of 1948.* 2nd ed. Cambridge: Cambridge University Press, 2007.

Shlaim, Avi. *The Iron Wall: Israel and the Arab World.* Updated ed. New York: Norton, 2014.

Smith, Charles D. *Palestine and the Arab-Israeli Conflict: A History with Documents.* 7th ed. New York: Bedford/St. Martin's, 2010.

Truman, Harry S. *Memoirs,* Vol. 2: *Years of Trial and Hope.* Garden City, NY: Doubleday, 1956.

Walter L. Hixson
Distinguished Professor
University of Akron

ARMENIAN GENOCIDE

The Armenian genocide (known by Armenians as the *Medz Yeghern,*"the great crime," or *Aghet,* "catastrophe") was the attempted extermination of nearly all Armenians living in the Ottoman Empire by the Committee of Union and Progress (CUP), the empire's governing regime. Most of the mass killing was perpetrated in a sustained, near-continuous sequence from mid-1915 through the autumn of 1916.

ORIGINS

The origins of the genocide are complex. During the late nineteenth and early twentieth centuries a total Ottoman collapse seemed quite possible. The revolutionary overthrow of the sultan's imperial government by the CUP in 1908 was a direct response to this crisis. The CUP solution to the crisis was to radically transform a traditional Islamic-based but multiethnic polity into a modern national state centered on its majority Turkish population. This solution included a plan on paper to break up and move the diverse non-Turkish (usually but not always non-Muslim) elements, such as the Armenians, to places where they would be absorbed into the Turkish majority. By entering the First World War on the side of Germany, the CUP also sought to conquer Turkic-speaking regions in Russian Central Asia to compensate in part for territories already lost in Europe. The intended bridgehead for this advance was across eastern Anatolia, the historic Armenian heartlands.

These goals, however, did not determine the Armenian fate. The Armenian Christian community (*millet*) had traditionally been viewed as a loyal if subordinate element of the Ottoman population. But by 1914 calls from the Christian community's own radicalized communal leadership for some form of national autonomy collided with the CUP's domestic and foreign policy objectives, which took a turn for the worse with a major military defeat in the Russian Caucasus in the first winter of World War I (1914–1918). Turncoat Armenians were particularly blamed for this disaster. The charge that Armenians were collectively acting as a Trojan horse on behalf of the Allies redoubled at the moment when it looked as though an Anglo-French naval force might break through the Dardanelles to the capital, Constantinople, in late April 1915. At the center of government, key CUP leaders, notably Mehmed Talaat Pasha (1874–1921), the minister of the interior, and Ismail Enver Pasha (1881–1922), the minister of war, backed by an inner core of political and military chiefs, began looking toward mass Armenian deportations, initially from the eastern provinces and then from across the entire Ottoman Empire.

These deportations began in late spring of 1915. Whether the deportations got out of hand or rather, as many historians believe, were only a pretext for mass murder, the situation rapidly turned into one of full-blown extermination. In some eastern provinces there were no deportations at all, only the direct slaughter of all men, women, and children. Armenian men in the army were also disarmed and usually killed. As for the deportations, these quickly turned into death marches either by direct murder, often by Kurdish tribesmen mobilized by the state for this purpose, or from ill treatment, exposure, starvation, or sickness. In 1916 those who survived were often killed in further mass exterminations in or close to the holding areas in the Syrian desert to which the CUP had deported them. Modern-day scholarship suggests that of an estimated 1.7 to 2.1 million Ottoman Armenians, at least half a million and possibly twice or even nearly three times that number perished. Other groups, especially Christian Syriac-speaking communities and, later, Ottoman Greeks, were also sucked into this vortex. Nevertheless, the scope and scale of the Armenian fate was monumental, leading most genocide scholars to put it in the same tier as the Holocaust of World War II and the 1994 Rwandan genocide.

THE AMERICAN RESPONSE

Armenia was very far away, but for significant sections of American society consciousness of the 1915–16 events and their aftermath loomed large, and the repercussions on American life carry through to the present day. All the major European powers were troubled by the geopolitical ramifications of a wartime Ottoman collapse. What made America different was that it was not a direct party to these calculations, and even after 1917, when the United States declared war on the Central Powers, it did not do so against the Ottomans. However, American attention was gripped by reports of the Armenian massacres, and early on the US public was well informed about them, largely because in previous decades American Protestant missionaries had set up many missionary schools, colleges, and clinics throughout the core Armenian regions. Further, like many British evangelists, American Protestants embraced Armenians as fellow Christians, seeing them on the one hand as like-minded, forward looking, and "Western" (many Armenians converted from their traditional faith to Protestantism, and many also sought US citizenship) and, on the other, as victims of Muslim persecution. Often these perceptions involved distorted or confused views of what was actually occurring in the Ottoman Empire. For instance, until 1913 the main victims of the vast upheavals in and adjacent to the empire were ethnically cleansed Muslims who ended up as impoverished and brutalized refugees, often in areas inhabited by Armenians. Similarly, positive representations of a modern Armenian national identity, disseminated by a growing Armenian immigrant (often refugee) community that settled in the United States in the late nineteenth and early twentieth centuries, regularly failed to address the complexity of emerging and competing nationalisms in a multiethnic eastern Anatolian arena where no single ethno-religious group formed a majority.

These considerations aside, American anxieties for the fate of Armenians were heightened by stories such as that of Mary Louise Graffam (1871–1921), the schoolteacher-turned-nurse from Washington, DC, who insisted on accompanying her Armenian flock as they were deported from the town of Sivas and who sent coded messages to her mission board back home telling of the Armenians' horrendous suffering. At a diplomatic level, events were confirmed in reports transmitted to the US State Department by Henry Morgenthau Sr. (1856–1946), the US ambassador in Constantinople. These reports emanated from consular bureaus in places such as Harput, at the center of the deportations, or Aleppo, close to their terminus.

THE POSTWAR RESPONSE

Morgenthau came to an early conclusion that what was at stake was not only the wholesale extermination of Armenians but a seizure of all their assets in the Turkish state interest, observations reinforced by open if self-justifying comments made to him by both Enver and Talaat. His reportage helped precipitate the Allied Powers' declaration of May 24, 1915, promising to hold Ottoman leaders and officials accountable for the atrocities. America, as a neutral power, was not a party to this declaration, but at the Paris Peace Conference in 1919 US secretary of state Robert Lansing (1864–1928), as chair of the newly established Commission on the Responsibility of the Authors of the War and on Enforcement of Penalties, played a key role in drawing up indictments against CUP leaders. The commitment to prosecute the then acting heads of state was incorporated into the projected Treaty of Sèvres (1920), which would have concluded the Allied peace settlement with a defeated Ottoman Empire the following year. Today that commitment is seen as a key staging-post on the road to the international recognition of genocide as a crime against humanity, as defined in the 1948 United Nations Convention on the Prevention and Punishment of the Crime of Genocide. In addition to convening such an international tribunal, President Woodrow Wilson (1856–1924) demonstrated a particular commitment to the Armenian plight. Building on his 1917 Fourteen Points, which included the goal of autonomous development for subject Ottoman peoples, he sent a fact-finding mission led by Major General James G. Harbord (1866–1947) to the Armenian region. The mission recommended that the region be placed under an American mandate. Meanwhile a much wider American humanitarian effort to support starving, displaced, and orphaned survivors of the genocide led to the creation in 1919 of Near East Relief (NER), which saved hundreds of thousands of Armenian lives. In turn, this organization became a model for the much wider post–World War I European reconstruction program, which was congressionally supported and led by Herbert Hoover (1874–1964). This effort also became significant in the long-term development of international humanitarian relief.

A mural in Los Angeles commemorating the 1915 Armenian genocide. *Americans of Armenian descent have held annual rallies calling for official US recognition of the Armenian genocide perpetrated by Turkey in 1915.* DAVID MCNEW/GETTY IMAGES NEWS/GETTY IMAGES

Nevertheless, American foreign relations took an entirely different turn from late 1919 onwards. This was not simply a consequence of Wilson's political eclipse or the American retreat into isolationism. The attempt to create post-Ottoman polities favoring Armenian, Greek, and other groups as envisaged at Sèvres was nullified by the military resistance of the Turks under their new nationalist leader, Mustafa Kemal, later Atatürk (1881–1938). The subsequent 1923 Treaty of Lausanne between the Allies and the new Republic of Turkey not only acknowledged a sovereign Turkey but also contained the corollary that an Armenian entity or Armenian minority rights within Turkey were expunged from the record. A residual Armenian state was created in 1918 on the Russian side of the international border. This state survived, however, only because of the Soviet takeover of this region two years later, not because of any American, British, or French help. The visible denouement of this new reality came during mass evacuations of Greeks and Armenians from the port of Smyrna (İzmir) in September 1922. The actions of individual US naval officers notwithstanding, no US or other Allied ship present intervened to prevent one of the last great Armenian massacres of this period.

LONG-TERM IMPACT

More keenly, the new US high commissioner to Turkey, Admiral Mark L. Bristol (1868–1939), was intent on forging a constructive diplomacy with Kemal largely motivated by potential oil reserves or other concessions that might have benefited US businesses. This dollar diplomacy also fed into a longer-term political shift. US-Turkish political friendship and eventual alliance were not properly cemented until Turkey became a member of NATO in 1952. But a quid pro quo for Turkey's hosting of a major US Air Force base and Cold War listening stations was American diplomatic avoidance of the Armenian genocide or issues of survivor compensation.

This silence has led to a curious ongoing political oddity in US attitudes to Armenian issues. Working from the United States, Raphael Lemkin (1900–1959), the creator of the term *genocide* and the prime mover behind a genocide convention initially sponsored by the United States, was strongly impelled by the events of 1915, while today the US administration provides substantial humanitarian assistance to Yerevan, the capital of Armenia. Yet at the same time the United States offers no official recognition of the genocide, nor is it involved in the annual April 24 commemoration events. Moreover, repeated efforts by US Armenian organizations seeking congressional recognition have failed not least because of equally vociferous US Turkish organizational lobbying. Turkey also currently funds posts in Turkish studies at key US universities, part of whose aim is to refute the belief that what happened in 1915 was genocide. One side effect is that Armenian frustration at nonrecognition of the genocide led in the late 1970s and 1980s to a spate of terrorist attacks on Turkish targets by the now dissolved Armenian Secret Army for the Liberation of Armenia (ASALA), some of which took place in the United States. On the other side of the coin, foreign policy shifts over the last decade may suggest that one hundred years after the genocide the political stalemate on US acknowledgment may be broken.

SEE ALSO *Contemporary Genocides and US Policy; Ethnic Cleansing; Genocide; Holocaust; Human Rights; United Nations; Universal Declaration of Human Rights; World War I*

BIBLIOGRAPHY

Adalian, Rouben Paul, ed. *Guide to the Armenian Genocide in the U.S. Archives, 1915–1918.* Alexandria, VA: Chadwyck-Healey, 1994.

Balakian, Peter. *The Burning Tigris: The Armenian Genocide and America's Response.* New York: HarperCollins, 2003.

Bloxham, Donald. *The Great Game of Genocide: Imperialism, Nationalism, and the Destruction of the Ottoman Armenians.* Oxford: Oxford University Press, 2005.

Davis, Leslie A. *The Slaughterhouse Province: An American Diplomat's Report on the Armenian Genocide 1915–1917,* edited by Susan Blair. New Rochelle, NY: A.D. Caratzas, Orpheus Publishing, 1989.

Hovannisian, Richard G., ed. *The Armenian Genocide in Perspective.* New Brunswick, NJ: Transaction Publishers, 1986.

Hovannisian, Richard G., ed. *Remembrance and Denial: The Case of the Armenian Genocide.* Detroit, MI: Wayne State University Press, 1999.

Kévorkian, Raymond H. *The Armenian Genocide: A Complete History.* London and New York: I.B. Tauris, 2011.

Miller, Donald E., and Lorna Touryan Miller. *Survivors: An Oral History of the Armenian Genocide.* Berkeley: University of California Press, 1993.

Morgenthau, Henry, Sr. *Ambassador Morgenthau's Story.* New York: Doubleday, Page, 1918.

Winter, Jay, ed. *America and the Armenian Genocide of 1915.* Cambridge: Cambridge University Press, 2003.

Mark Levene
Reader in Comparative History
Member of Parkes Centre for Jewish/Non-Jewish Relations
University of Southampton

ARMSTRONG, LOUIS

SEE *Jazz.*

ARMY, US

As one of the oldest national institutions in the United States, the US Army has a direct lineage to the Continental Army, which was established in 1775 by the Continental Congress. Civilian control of the army is mandated by the US Constitution, which designates the president as commander in chief of the army and navy, while Congress is delegated the sole power of creating and funding these institutions, as well as the responsibility to declare war. The president appoints army officers, but the US Senate, serving as a further check on executive power over the military, must confirm even the lowliest lieutenant.

Founded by the first federal Congress in 1789, the US Army supported continental expansion in the nineteenth century and projected American power globally in the twentieth century. Initially, the War Department, headed by the secretary of war, exercised immediate civilian control of the US Army until the formation of the Department of Defense in 1947. With defense unification, the institutional character of the army continued, even though the secretary of defense remained, next to the president, the preeminent civilian leader of the army and other branches of the armed services.

THE COMPOSITION OF THE US ARMY

Traditionally, the United States in peacetime maintained a small regular army made up of volunteers. During major wars, the army relied on US Volunteers, locally raised and officered regiments accepted into federal service for the duration of a conflict. Conscription has proved highly controversial, and its first use to fill the ranks of the army during the American Civil War (1861–1865) led to an uprising in New York City in 1863. After considerable debate the United States jettisoned the volunteer system during World War I (1914–1918) and adopted conscription for this conflict. In 1940, President Franklin D. Roosevelt (1882–1945) convinced Congress to reinstate conscription, and this system for raising troops remained in place for World War II (1939–1945), as well as the Korean War (1950–1953) and the Vietnam War (1954–1975). Responding to growing opposition to the draft, especially by the antiwar movement, President Richard M. Nixon (1913–1994) implemented the "all-volunteer army" in 1973. This shift away from conscription required a massive upgrading of salary and benefits for soldiers, combined with a robust advertising campaign to fill the ranks in the closing years of the Cold War and during the wars in Afghanistan and Iraq.

As an institution, the US Army has embraced ethnic diversity, and foreign-born soldiers often made up a significant proportion of the enlisted ranks. African Americans served in the US Army during the American Revolution (1775–1783) and the War of 1812, but they would be excluded during the antebellum era due to political pressure from white southerners. During the Civil War, African Americans would again become a part of the military, albeit serving in segregated units until the early 1950s. The armed services, including the army along with other branches, would be the first major national institution to desegregate as result of President Harry S. Truman's (1884–1972) Executive Order of 1948 and the outbreak of the Korean War in 1950.

Like racial barriers, gender barriers would also fall. Until the twentieth century, military service was closed to women, but the world wars brought the limited inclusion of women in noncombatant roles. Women became a permanent fixture of the military after 1945. Under the all-volunteer army, they saw their placement into wider occupational specialties, with significant combat in the wars in Iraq and Afghanistan.

The Continental Army and later the US Army in the early Republic remained highly dependent on foreign trained officers, especially engineers. The founding of the US Military Academy in West Point, New York, in 1802, with a curriculum focused on engineering, served to meet this need. West Point officers played a crucial role in developing coastal fortifications deemed necessary to prevent a foreign invasion. In addition, the US Army Corps of Engineers has contributed significantly to infrastructure development since the nineteenth century.

A range of foreign military thinkers and ideas has significantly influenced the US Army. During the American Revolution, Prussian-born Friedrich Wilhelm Von Steuben (1730–1794) wrote an influential training manual and played an instrumental role in training George Washington's (1732–1799) army in European-style drill. After surveying European armies following the American Civil War, Emory Upton (1839–1881) argued that the United States should end the practice of relying on volunteers and instead form a professional force. The creation of the position of army chief of staff and a general staff in 1903 would be styled after the general staff system of Germany and other European military powers. Initially composed of the chief of staff of the army and heads of the navy and the army air forces, the Joint Chiefs of Staff emerged as a result of interactions with the British chiefs of staff during World War II.

THE ARMY'S ROLE IN THE FORMATION OF AMERICAN NATIONAL IDENTITY

The US Army has played a central role in the formation of American national identity. Veterans of American wars have been accorded special benefits from the federal government. Beginning with the American Civil War, veterans have formed a series of mass membership organizations to preserve wartime comradeship, promote favorable governmental policies, and foster patriotism. Countless works of popular and literary fiction, as well as motion pictures, have often drawn on the US Army for plots and characters. The western, a genre of fiction and motion pictures that reached a peak in the mid-twentieth century, often dealt with the role of the army on the Great Plains. After World War I and the Vietnam War, a genre emerged that portrayed the US Army in a more sinister light. Overall, one of the most enduring images of the US Army is that of citizen soldiers who have chafed at regimentation and iron discipline.

Until the 1890s, the United States remained primarily an insular power and the US Army primarily served as a frontier constabulary subduing successive Native American tribal nations. The US Army played a pivotal role in supporting manifest destiny, especially under President James K. Polk (1795–1849). The threat of war forced territorial concessions from Great Britain in disputed Oregon Territory, and Polk persuaded Congress to declare war against Mexico. Under the leadership of General Winfield Scott (1786–1866), the US Army succeeded in capturing Mexico City in 1847, forcing a negotiated settlement that led to Mexico's cession of vast stretches of territory in what became the southwestern United States. Drawing heavily on US volunteers, the US Army ended efforts by southern states to forge an independent Confederacy in 1865. In the aftermath of the war, Congress made the army the principal institution to administer Reconstruction of the South. This decision provoked significant resistance on the part of white Southerners, and the year after Reconstruction ended, Congress enacted the Posse Comitatus Act (1878), which placed strict limits on the use of the army in enforcing civil laws.

The Spanish American War (1898) and the subsequent Philippine insurrection (1899–1902), along with the building of the Panama Canal, fundamentally altered the role of the US Army. Deployed to fight overseas wars, the army served as a colonial army subduing indigenous peoples and proved vital in administering overseas possessions. Acquiring overseas possessions led to the establishment of permanent foreign bases in Asia and Central America.

MILITARY ALLIANCES WITH OTHER NATIONS

Since World War I, the US Army has fought major wars as part of military alliances with other nations. For instance, most American soldiers in 1917 to 1918 would fight in France, and the supreme military commander would be a French general. White American soldiers stationed in France often had strained relationships with France's civilian population, whom they charged with price gouging and incidents of vandalism directed at private property. African American troops in France encountered a less restrictive racial climate and often forged friendly relations with French civilians to the point where a significant number settled in the country after 1918.

When deployed abroad during World War II, US soldiers often fought in multinational commands made up of troops from the British Commonwealth and other Western allies. This pattern continued in the Cold War when, during the Korean War, the US Army and other armed forces served under the United Nations Command led by an American general. In Vietnam, US Army officers provided the bulk of advisors used to sustain the South Vietnamese Army before American involvement escalated. Even when the United States took a dominant role in this conflict (1965–1973), the US Army depended on South Vietnamese troops and smaller contingents from Australia, South Korea, and elsewhere to bear the burden of war. The Cold War and the subsequent wars following the terrorist attacks of September 11, 2001, fostered the development of an extensive network of military bases around the world.

AMERICA'S REPRESENTATIVE ABROAD

Not only has the US Army been the first line of defense in protecting American interests at home and abroad, it has also been the first introduction to Americans and US culture for many around the world. Whether through military combat or humanitarian aid, the US Army represents the United States overseas, where it shapes international perceptions of Americans in the world.

SEE ALSO *Air Force, US; Department of Defense, US; Department of Homeland Security; Department of State; The Influence of Sea Power upon History (Alfred Thayer Mahan, 1890); Joint Chiefs of Staff; Marine Corps, US; Navy, US*

BIBLIOGRAPHY

Bailey, Beth. *America's Army: Making the All-Volunteer Force.* Cambridge, MA: Belknap Press of Harvard University Press, 2009.

Chambers, John Whiteclay, II. *To Raise an Army: The Draft Comes to Modern America.* New York: Free Press, 1987.

Coffman, Edward M. *The Old Army: A Portrait of the American Army in Peacetime, 1784–1898.* New York: Oxford University Press, 1986.

Keene, Jennifer D. *Doughboys, the Great War, and the Remaking of America.* Baltimore, MD: Johns Hopkins University Press, 2001.

Linn, Brian McAllister. *Guardians of Empire: The U.S. Army and the Pacific, 1902–1940.* Chapel Hill: University of North Carolina Press, 1997.

Weigley, Russell F. *History of the United States Army.* New York: Macmillan, 1967.

G. Kurt Piehler
Director and Associate Professor of History
Institute on World War II and the Human Experience
Florida State University

ASHE, ARTHUR

1943–1993

Arthur Robert Ashe Jr. was a world-class tennis player, civil rights and human rights activist, public intellectual, and author. He grew up in segregated Richmond, Virginia, and learned to play tennis after taking lessons from Ronald Charity, a student at Virginia Union University. At age ten, Ashe began attending the American Tennis Association's (ATA) Junior Development Program run by Robert Walter Johnson, a Lynchburg, Virginia, physician and mentor of tennis player Althea Gibson. Johnson taught Ashe how to negotiate racism by avoiding confrontation with whites. Ashe lived in St. Louis with Richard Hudlin, a tennis coach and former ATA star, during his senior year of high school.

Ashe attended the University of California, Los Angeles (UCLA), on a tennis scholarship from 1961 to 1966, leading the Bruins in 1965 to the NCAA team championship and capturing the singles and doubles titles. In 1963, he became the first African American selected to the US Davis Cup team. At UCLA, Ashe was challenged by black activists, such as Maulana Karenga, the founder of Organization US, who encouraged him to lend his voice to the black freedom movement. As an ROTC cadet, Ashe graduated from UCLA and was commissioned as a second lieutenant in the US Army and sent to the United States Military Academy in West Point, New York.

In 1968, Ashe dazzled the tennis world, winning the US Nationals and inaugural US Open and guiding the US Davis Cup team to a victory over Australia. He entered the civil rights debate as well, giving a speech at the Church of the Redeemer in Washington, DC, and appearing on CBS's *Face the Nation.* Fusing the approaches of Booker T. Washington, Dr. Martin Luther King Jr., and Whitney Young Jr., Ashe focused his message on personal responsibility, economic empowerment, open dialogue among the races, and the need for federal enforcement of the Civil Rights and Voting Rights Acts.

Nowhere was Ashe's commitment to racial justice more felt than in South Africa during the apartheid era. In 1969, the South African government denied Ashe's visa request to compete in the South African Open, citing his public opposition to apartheid. He responded with a campaign to isolate South Africa from world sport, which included testimony before the US Congress and the United Nations, as well as frequent statements to the press. High-ranking government officials in the United States and South Africa, especially US secretary of state William Rogers, negotiated Ashe's visa. Despite his hatred of apartheid, Ashe refused to forfeit matches against South African players or support the banning of South African athletes from the United States. In 1973, in reaction to intense pressure from the international community, South Africa finally granted Ashe a visa. He made a number of trips to South Africa in the remaining two decades of his life, advocating for an end to apartheid, meeting with black and colored leaders and government officials, and establishing the Black Tennis Foundation.

Ashe balanced tennis and activism throughout the 1970s. He won his second Grand Slam singles title, the Australian Open, in 1970, reached the finals of the US Open in 1972, and took home the World Championship Tennis (WCT) crown in 1975. Also in 1975, he defeated the world's top-ranked player, Jimmy Connors, in a stunning upset at Wimbledon. Ashe suffered from injuries and ineffective play in the late 1970s, culminating in his retirement in 1979 following a heart attack.

Although he served as captain of the US Davis Cup team from 1981 to 1985, winning two championships in 1981 and 1982, Ashe devoted the rest of his life to public service. He wrote columns for the *Washington Post,* gave speeches on a variety of topics, was arrested in 1985 for protesting outside of the South African embassy, and authored the first-ever history of black athletes, titled *A Hard Road to Glory* (1988).

Ashe contracted HIV from a blood transfusion in 1983 and was diagnosed with full-blown AIDS in 1988. He kept his diagnosis private until 1992, when *USA Today* learned of his condition. In the year before his death, Ashe was a strong voice for AIDS research and awareness, sex education, and dispelling myths about the disease. He addressed the UN General Assembly on December 1, 1992, World AIDS Day, and died two months later.

SEE ALSO *Acquired Immunodeficiency Syndrome (AIDS); Ali, Muhammad; Apartheid; Human Rights; Olympics*

BIBLIOGRAPHY

Ashe, Arthur Robert, Jr., and Neil Amdur. *Off the Court.* New York: New American Library, 1981.

Ashe, Arthur Robert, Jr., and Arnold Rampersad. *Days of Grace: A Memoir.* New York: Knopf, 1993.

Hall, Eric Allen. *Arthur Ashe: Tennis and Justice in the Civil Rights Era.* Baltimore, MD: Johns Hopkins University Press, 2014.

Morgan, Eric J. "Black and White at Center Court: Arthur Ashe and the Confrontation of Apartheid in South Africa." *Diplomatic History* 36, 5 (2012): 815–841.

Eric Allen Hall
Assistant Professor of History and Africana Studies
Georgia Southern University

ASHMUN, JEHUDI

SEE *Liberia.*

ASIA

The vital relationship between Asia and the United States was established at the moment of the nation's founding. Engagement with Asia during the pre- and postrevolutionary periods shaped the development of the British North American colonies and the early American Republic. American maritime expansion from the mid-eighteenth to the mid-nineteenth centuries influenced the transpacific world and, conversely, the development of colonial America and later the United States.

The United States was established during a period of European expansion into the Asia-Pacific region (c. 1764–1806). It is not surprising, therefore, that the history of the nation has been intertwined with that of Asia from its inception. While this engagement was enduring, attitudes toward the region have changed over time as a result of political and economic developments in both societies. Freed from colonial constraints, American merchants arrived in Canton immediately upon gaining their independence. From these early beginnings, the United States increased its presence in Asia over the course of the nineteenth century. During the twentieth century, political, economic, and social engagement between America and Asia occurred through wars, trade, and immigration networks that brought the people of Asia to America's shores.

AMERICANS' EARLY ENCOUNTERS WITH ASIA

Long before direct contact was made with Asia, the continent and its people figured significantly in the American imaginary. Throughout the eighteenth century, Western consumers in Europe and its New World colonies coveted Chinese products, such as tea, silk, and porcelain. The Chinese carefully guarded the processes that produced these commodities, keeping the global demand for them extremely high. In contrast, Chinese society was materially self-sufficient. Therefore, any Europeans who wished to obtain Chinese goods were compelled to pay for them in specie. This, paired with the popularity of Chinese goods, created a global drain of silver into China during the eighteenth century.

Throughout the colonial period, British laws forbade Americans from trading directly with foreign nations. According to the economic principles of mercantilism that informed British policy during this time, colonies were expected to contribute first and foremost to the economic prosperity of the mother country by supplying raw materials to its industries. In addition, colonial American consumers were required to purchase all manufactured goods—including coveted Chinese products—from British merchants.

With their victory in the Revolutionary War (1775–1783), Americans were released from British mercantile laws. Thus, their presence in Asia and the entire Pacific region was a direct result of their newly won freedom from the British Empire. The early China trade (c. 1784–1842) was important both economically and symbolically to the newly independent American nation. It represented new and potentially lucrative fiscal opportunities at the same time that vital colonial trade routes to other British possessions, such as the West Indies, were closed to Americans. Americans wasted little time in sending ships to China. The *Empress of China*, the first American ship to reach China, was launched in 1784, just months after the Paris Peace Treaty officially granted Americans their freedom.

In this initial period of US trade in Asia, China was ruled by the powerful Qing (Ching) ruler Qianlong (1711–1799), who imposed a series of restrictive mandates, collectively referred to as the *Canton system*, on all foreign merchants. European traders, which at this time included Great Britain, Sweden, the Netherlands, and Denmark, were only allowed into the port city of Canton during trading season. Once there, they were compelled to work under the close supervision of specially appointed Chinese merchants known as *hongs*, who were responsible for overseeing all foreign trade. Although the number of individuals holding this powerful and lucrative position varied over the years, their number stabilized at thirteen over the course of the eighteenth century. Each foreign ship would have to engage a *hong* merchant to oversee its business in Canton.

The quest for goods that would appeal to Chinese tastes encouraged exploration and exploitation of natural resources and indigenous peoples throughout the Pacific world. Merchants depended upon Native Americans and Pacific Islanders to provide them with the natural products that were the only commodities that could turn a profit in Canton. Among these items were ginseng from the hinterlands surrounding the Adirondack to the

Appalachian Mountains, pelts from the Pacific Northwest, sandalwood from Hawai'i, sea slugs from Fiji, and birds' nests from Borneo. Entanglement in global networks of trade with Asia commonly disrupted, and even destroyed, the social organization of the native peoples who harvested these items and prepared them for sale.

CONNECTING OCEANS: LINKAGES BETWEEN THE ATLANTIC AND PACIFIC

The quest for goods that would turn a profit in Canton inspired Americans to establish new trade routes that connected the Atlantic and Pacific Oceans. Enterprising citizens recognized early on that the serendipity of North America's position between the two oceans provided them with the potential to create linkages between them. Initially, American ships bound for Canton traversed the Atlantic Ocean before following established British routes to China. However, within three years of Americans' initial voyage to Canton, the *Columbia* became the first American ship to arrive in China via the Pacific. Other ships would soon follow. Merchants from New England would sail around Cape Horn and then traverse the northwest coast of North America to Nootka Sound in search of animal pelts, before finally crossing the Pacific to China.

The early maritime fur trade along North America's West Coast preceded Americans' settlement in that region. China traders en route to Canton established clandestine trading relations with native tribes, such as the Haida, Salish, Chinook, Nootka, and Tlingit. This activity violated the prohibitions of the Spanish government, which at the time laid claim to trading rights in the region. This conflict of interest would portend later incursions into Spanish territory on the West Coast. America's commercial interests in the Pacific would later be linked to the continental expansion of the United States as the nation moved westward over the course of the nineteenth century. Asian markets provided an impetus for terrestrial expansion of American territory, as well as for the development of new aquatic routes across the Pacific.

Long before the tenants of "manifest destiny" were formally articulated, Americans involved in the China trade were looking westward from their settlements along the East Coast and imagining a national territory that would span the entire North American continent. When this was accomplished, the United States would enjoy the enviable position of connecting Asia with Europe. Thus, overland expansion across the North American continent was driven in part by the desire to connect these two major aquatic systems.

During this initial period of US presence in Asia and the Pacific world, Americans gained valuable knowledge about conducting trade under the Canton system. They also established innovative new routes to China that allowed them to trade with Native Americans on the northwest coast before traversing the Pacific. From this moment forward, Americans began to consider the Pacific Ocean as their gateway to Asia. Despite these accomplishments, their presence and economic engagement in the region remained minimal.

INCREASED US ENGAGEMENT WITH ASIA DURING THE NINETEENTH CENTURY

Relations between the United States and Asia intensified and expanded over the nineteenth century, with the most pronounced growth occurring after midcentury. Many influential sectors in American society believed that the Asia-Pacific region was vital to the nation's development. Their efforts were successful; over the course of this century, the United States became the largest Western presence in the Pacific region. Increased American activity in Asia was also encouraged by US acquisition of territory along the Pacific coast of North America.

Prior to the mid-nineteenth century, the nation's engagement with Asia was, for the most part, limited to China traders and some Christian missionaries. However, after the Civil War (1861–1865), America's presence in Asia and especially in the North Pacific increased significantly, and economic engagement in the region intensified. This development was facilitated by technological advancements, such as the introduction of the clipper ship and later steam navigation and the telegraph, which made regular communication between the Atlantic and Pacific coasts more convenient, closing what had formerly been a vast geographical distance between the United States and Asia.

Americans' increased involvement in Asia and the Pacific encouraged the nation's military and political growth. For instance, it compelled the federal government to establish a stronger navy, as well as a more robust foreign policy to protect the country's interests in the region. Beginning in the early decades of the nineteenth century, citizens involved in trade with Asia filed petitions to Congress, urging the government to support their commercial activities more actively. These petitions asked for military and diplomatic protection for Americans working in distant lands. During the first half of the century, the US government also supported exploratory missions in the region, most notably the American Expedition to the Pacific (1838–1842), led by Charles Wilkes (1798–1877).

By the third decade of the nineteenth century, the balance of power in China was shifting in favor of foreign interests at the same time that internal conflict shook the stability of this ancient society. The British had long been frustrated by strict trade restrictions and extortion at the hands of the all-powerful *hong* merchants. In order to address the trade imbalance, the British began engaging in the illicit trade in opium, which they grew on their plantations in India. They simultaneously turned to their government for an increased military presence in Canton.

Chinese efforts to stop the importation of the highly addictive substance and to resist these military actions eventually led to the First (1839–1842) and Second (1856–1860) Opium Wars. British victory in these military conflicts caused a severe weakening of the Qing dynasty and, eventually, the opening of China to the Western world. Upon their defeat, the Chinese were forced to submit to a series of what became known as "unequal treaties," which included the opening of additional trading ports, most-favored-nation status for the United Kingdom, and promises for British extraterritoriality. Americans benefitted greatly from the British victory and the vulnerable state of the Qing dynasty. In 1844, the United States and China signed the Treaty of Wanghia (Wangxia), which granted Americans the same rights and privileges that were conceded to the British, in addition to other favorable provisions. The Treaty of Tianjin, signed in 1858, granted the United States even more concessions regarding the opium trade, as well as acceptance of missionaries and Christianized Chinese.

The forced opening of numerous Chinese ports to trade after the Opium Wars and the US acquisition of California in the Mexican-American War (1846–1848) promised to significantly increase the volume of trade between North America and Asia. Around this time, American interests in Asia began to focus on Japan and specifically on efforts to compel its leaders to "open" the island nation to outside contact. Since the seventeenth century, Japanese leaders pursued a policy of isolation from what they believed were dangerous and corrupting foreign influences.

American motivations for compelling Japan to allow contact with the outside world were multifold. American whalers trolling the waters of the North Pacific had looked to Japan in their quest for safe harbors, assistance for shipwrecked sailors, and provisioning centers. The transition from the use of sailing ships to steam-powered vessels over the course of the nineteenth century increased the need to make contact with Japan. Steam-powered ships required access to coaling stations, and Japan was considered a crucial location for this purpose.

The US government sent Commodore Matthew Perry (1794–1858) on two missions to Japan in the mid-nineteenth century. In July 1853, Perry led four American ships into the waters of Tokyo Bay. There he met with the Tokugawa shogunate, a feudal military government that ruled Japan between 1603 and 1868. Perry returned to Japan the following spring, bringing with him an even larger display of American military power that included nine steam-powered frigates, 1,775 men, and over one hundred guns. Confronted with America's advanced technology and military power, the Japanese signed the Treaty of Kanagawa in March 1854. This treaty promised protection of shipwrecked American sailors, gave the United States access to two ports, and granted the right to appoint consuls in these two cities. Importantly, the treaty included a most-favored-nation clause that ensured that other foreign governments would not supplant the United States as the dominant Western presence in Japan.

THE AGE OF IMPERIALISM

At the end of the Civil War, American interests again turned to Asia. Among other things, American leaders set out to acquire strategically located naval bases throughout the Asia Pacific region in order to maintain both their Asiatic and Pacific squadrons, which were deployed to protect US interests in the region. In 1864, Japan granted the US government a perpetual lease in Yokohama Bay, where a coaling station was established.

The years roughly between 1870 and 1940 marked the height of imperialism as the most powerful European nations circled the globe in search of new areas of exploitation. During these years, overseas investments in the Pacific region grew considerably. Although some Americans hoped to benefit from opportunities for expansion and exploitation, the nation's anticolonial origins generated mixed feelings among citizens about the acquisition of formal overseas territories, including those in Asia. At this time, China was experiencing a period of extreme instability, economic depression, and domestic strife. Its defeat in the Sino-Japanese War (1894–1895) opened the way for imperial powers, such as Japan, Great Britain, Russia, Italy, and Germany, to establish spheres of interest around vital port cities.

In America, there were growing concerns at the possibility of China being divided among other foreign powers. In response to this threat, the United States adopted what became known as the Open Door policy in US foreign affairs in the late nineteenth and early twentieth centuries. Secretary of State John Hay (1838–1905) first articulated the main tenants of this approach in 1899. The Open Door policy was designed to protect US business interests in China, while promising to support the preservation of Chinese sovereignty against foreign encroachment.

The Open Door policy provided a compromise between American anti-imperialists and annexationists by allowing business interests to trade in China, while at the same time pledging to respect Chinese sovereignty and protect it from formal colonial division. This policy allowed the United States to create and maintain an "informal empire" in the underdeveloped world through economic influence and commercial development, rather than formal imperialism. According to some scholars, the United States became a major foreign presence in Asia due to its success in ensuring the free flow of capital around the globe without the need for formal political control.

The increasingly frequent and regular transpacific networks of exchange that connected the United States to Asia carried goods, ideas, and people in both directions across the Pacific Ocean. Since the late eighteenth century, Protestant missionaries had been traveling to Asia and the Pacific Islands in search of converts. Beginning in the mid-nineteenth century, large numbers of Chinese migrants began immigrating to America, drawn by the promise of the California Gold Rush, as well as jobs in the agriculture and manufacturing sectors. Immigrants escaping hardship in China also made vast contributions to the monumental project of building the first transcontinental railroad.

In areas of heavy Asian immigration, such as California, virulent anti-Chinese sentiment arose. This fear of the so-called "Yellow Peril" was a reaction to competition from Chinese immigrants who were willing to work for lower wages than native-born American workers. As a result of this widespread animosity, the Chinese Exclusion Act prohibiting the immigration of all Chinese laborers was passed in 1882. This was the first law that barred the entry of an entire group on the basis of their racial and ethnic identity.

After the Chinese were barred from entry into the country, Americans in need of laborers looked to Japan for recruits. Japanese immigration to the United States initially began as a result of political and social upheaval following the Meiji Restoration of 1868, which restored imperial rule to Japan. These newcomers took jobs as migrant laborers and farmers on the West Coast and in Hawai‘i, which was heavily controlled by American business interests and missionaries. In 1908, anti-Asian sentiment against the Japanese compelled the United States and Japan to sign what became known as the "Gentlemen's Agreement." By this time, Japan had emerged as an increasingly powerful nation and therefore had some say in the fates of its citizens living abroad. Although in the end Japan conceded to US demands, the Japanese were able to assert some influence in the negotiations. For their part, the Japanese agreed to limit emigration of unskilled laborers to the United States, while Americans agreed to grant admission to businessmen, students, wives, children, and in some cases relatives of resident Japanese. The influence of geopolitics on the lives of Asians living abroad, as well as their American-born children, would be even more apparent in the mass incarceration of more than one hundred thousand innocent Japanese (approximately two-thirds of whom were American citizens) living in the United States during World War II.

The rise of Japan as an imperial power over the course of the late nineteenth century and the first half of the twentieth century influenced political relations between the United States and Asia. Prior to 1905, the two nations enjoyed a relatively harmonious relationship. During the Russo-Japanese War (1904–1905), for instance, American sympathies clearly were behind the Japanese. However, American sentiment toward the rapidly modernizing, militarizing, and industrializing island nation began to change to suspicion and fear, especially when Japan began to assert imperial control over mainland Asia and in particular Korea and China.

In 1914, Japan entered World War I (1914–1918) by declaring war on Germany. Japanese leaders hoped that Germany's defeat in the war would allow Japan to expand its sphere of interest in the Pacific and China. At the war's conclusion and with the defeat of the Central powers, Japanese officials hoped their nation would be recognized as an equal by the major Western powers. Japanese representatives called for inclusion of a clause supporting racial equality in the League of Nations Covenant at the Paris Peace Conference in 1919. The clause was summarily dismissed by influential Western nations and never made it to full debate. After this humiliating rejection, Japan entered a path of nationalistic development and imperial expansion.

In the years following World War I, both the United States and Japan continued to establish their presence in the Pacific. The United States controlled the eastern half of the North Pacific and Japan controlled the western half. Japan's bombing of Pearl Harbor on December 7, 1941, brought the United States and Japan into direct conflict. With Japan's military defeat at the conclusion of this "war without mercy," the United States emerged as the dominant power in the region.

The postwar years marked the establishment of a close relationship between the United States and Japan. During this period, Asian immigrants in the United States continued to fight for equal treatment and acceptance within American society. The Immigration and Nationality Act of 1965 abolished the national origins quota that had served to limit immigration from Asia and Africa. A product of the civil rights movement, this landmark law created more opportunities for Asians to immigrate to the United States. The post-1965 era saw increased immigration from Asian countries such as Korea, Vietnam, Cambodia, and India.

SEE ALSO *Canton; China; Coolies; Foreign Mission Movement; Foreign Mission School (Cornwall, CT); Immigration Quotas; Indian Ocean; The Mikado (Arthur Sullivan and W. S. Gilbert, 1885); Nast, Thomas; Opium War; Pacific Ocean; Passport; Vivekananda, Swami*

BIBLIOGRAPHY

Barnhart, Michael A. *Japan and the World since 1868: International Relations and the Great Powers.* London: Edward Arnold, 1995.

Cohen, Warren I. *America's Response to China: A History of Sino-American Relations.* 5th ed. New York: Columbia University Press, 2010.

Duus, Peter. *Modern Japan.* 2nd ed. Belmont, CA: Wadsworth, Cengage Learning, 1998.

Fairbank, John King. *The United States and China.* 4th ed., revised and enlarged. Cambridge, MA: Harvard University Press, 1983.

Heffer, Jean. *The United States and the Pacific: History of a Frontier.* W. Donald Wilson, trans. Notre Dame, IN: University of Notre Dame Press, 2002.

Hutchison, William R. *Errand to the World: American Protestant Thought and Foreign Missions.* Chicago: University of Chicago Press, 1987.

LaFeber, Walter. *The Clash: U.S.–Japanese Relations Throughout History.* New York: Norton, 1997.

Lee, Erika. *The Making of Asian America: A History.* New York: Simon & Schuster, 2015.

Wiley, Peter Booth. *Yankees in the Land of the Gods: Commodore Perry and the Opening of Japan.* New York: Penguin, 1991.

Wills, John E., Jr., ed. *China and Maritime Europe, 1500–1800: Trade, Settlement, Diplomacy, and Missions.* New York: Cambridge University Press, 2011.

Kariann Akemi Yokota
Associate Professor
University of Colorado Denver

ASSIMILATION

SEE *Americanization.*

ATLANTIC CHARTER (1941)

Issued on August 14, 1941, by US president Franklin Roosevelt (1882–1945) and British prime minister Winston Churchill (1874–1965), the Atlantic Charter proclaimed "common principles in the national policies of their respective countries on which they base their hopes for a better future for the world." These principles, affirmed and accepted in September by the Soviet Union, Charles de Gaulle's (1890–1970) Free French, and the governments-in-exile of the nations of occupied Europe, represented an agreement on the basis for the type of world for which the Second World War was fought. The charter helped lay the foundation for the United Nations and provided a firm moral basis for the Allied effort against the Axis powers.

The Atlantic Charter originated during a secret meeting between Roosevelt and Churchill on American and British warships off the coast of Canada. As the United States was not a belligerent in August 1941, the emergence of a document outlining a common set of goals for the war effort reaffirmed the American commitment to an Allied victory while potentially facilitating eventual American entry into the war. Committing the British, and subsequently the other Allies, to Wilsonian goals for the postwar world prevented the possibility that America would enter the war as an associated power rather than as a member of the Allies, as had happened in 1917. As such, the document specifically renounced territorial aggrandizement as a goal for the Allied effort.

The charter itself put forth both practical and idealistic goals for the Allies, with the world's largest empire (Britain) and only communist dictatorship (USSR) stating that they supported the creation of a world free from want, fear, or oppression, where all people could select their own rulers (self-determination). The document explicitly referred to the "destruction of Nazi tyranny" as a necessary precursor to the creation of this freer world.

In the immediate aftermath of the charter's acceptance, Roosevelt authorized the US Navy to convoy Lend-Lease aid to the British as far as Iceland. This action shortened the distance for British transport ships to bring the aid home, reducing the amount of time German U-boats had to strike at them. Additionally, Roosevelt ordered the navy to "shoot on sight" any U-boat within the declared neutral zone surrounding North and South America or any that posed a threat to American shipping. For isolationists, the combination of the Atlantic Charter and these naval orders meant American entry into the war was inevitable and deliberately planned. In fact, Roosevelt was not sure he had sufficient public support for intervention, a problem not solved until the attack on Pearl Harbor.

In the long run, the Atlantic Charter provided some of the impetus for the creation of the United Nations. Indeed, the UN itself lists the Atlantic Charter as one of its founding documents, citing in particular its sixth and eighth clauses. The sixth clause elucidated the commitment to the postwar goal of peace with freedom from want and fear. The eighth clause called for the maintenance of peace through disarmament and the creation of a permanent system of general security and international justice, which the United Nations hoped to provide.

Economically, the charter called for significant economic collaboration as a means of providing freedom from want. Specifically, the fifth clause called for such collaboration to provide universally improved labor standards and social security. Additionally, the charter called for equal access to raw materials for all nations. This sort of economic framework undergirded the creation of the Marshall Plan, the European Economic Community/European Union, and the General Agreement on Tariffs and Trade.

Although not a legally binding treaty or alliance document, the Atlantic Charter provided a framework at the time for the United States to support the goals of the Allies' war effort while justifying the provision of material assistance to them. Further, it committed the Allies even before American entry to a morally based future for international relations, territorial and colonial settlements, and economic relations. Although the postwar world did not entirely fulfill the idealistic vision provided by the charter, the creation of the United Nations, the World Court, and the World Trade Organization can at least in part be traced to the authors and words of the Atlantic Charter.

SEE ALSO *Britain; Roosevelt, Franklin D.; Self-Determination; Tariff; United Nations; Wilson, Woodrow; World Trade Organization; World War II*

BIBLIOGRAPHY

Avalon Project, Yale Law School. Atlantic Charter, August 14, 1941. http://avalon.law.yale.edu/wwii/atlantic.asp

Borgwardt, Elizabeth. *A New Deal for the World: America's Vision for Human Rights*. Cambridge, MA: Harvard University Press, 2007.

Brinkley, Douglas, and David R. Facey-Crowther, eds. *The Atlantic Charter*. London: Macmillan, 1994.

Divine, Robert A. *The Reluctant Belligerent: American Entry into World War II*. New York: Wiley, 1979.

Richard M. Filipink
Associate Professor
Western Illinois University

ATLANTIC OCEAN

The Atlantic Ocean has been a zone of cultural, biological, and commercial exchange since long before the United States became a nation. Beginning in the fifteenth century, European exploration and imperialism linked the American and Afro-Eurasian hemispheres by bringing people, goods, and diseases across the ocean (Crosby 1972). The existence of the United States in fact is a product of this Atlantic exchange. Its population has origins in Europe, Asia, Africa, and the Americas, and plants and animals from overseas have forever altered its landscape. Still today, the Atlantic Ocean remains a conduit of people, politics, and goods.

PEOPLE

The United States owes its population diversity in part to the centuries-long migration of people across the Atlantic. European colonialism carried white settlers and African slaves to a continent peopled by descendants of Paleo-Indians, who had migrated to the Americas thousands of years prior to Europeans' arrival (Pauketat 2012, 86). From the colonial era up through the first decades of the nineteenth century, the majority of immigrants came from Great Britain, France, Spain, the Netherlands, Germany, Ireland, and the West Coast of Africa. Europeans traveled across the Atlantic as both indentured servants and voluntary settlers seeking economic opportunity and political and religious freedom. Thousands of Africans, too, entered the Americas against their will, as slave traders transported them across the Atlantic from the sixteenth century up through the closing of the international slave trade in 1808 (Rawley and Behrendt 2009). In the second half of the nineteenth century, the numbers of German and Irish migrants crossing the ocean increased, followed by central, eastern, and southern Europeans around the turn of the twentieth century. From 1892 to 1954, the federal immigration center at Ellis Island served as a hub of Atlantic immigration, with waves of newcomers entering New York Harbor. Immigration tapered off during the Great Depression and World War II, and in the second half of the twentieth century, the majority of Atlantic newcomers to the United States hailed from Latin America.

Throughout its history, the United States has also witnessed an outflow of its population to other Atlantic nations. Following the Revolutionary War (1775–1783), many loyalists moved to Canada and other British colonies. During the nineteenth century, enslaved Americans and free blacks migrated to Canada and Mexico, as well as to the African colony of Liberia, which was founded by the American Colonization Society in 1821 as a place to resettle free-born blacks and former slaves (Jasanoff 2011; Yarema 2006). And although the US government does not keep track of emigrants, over the past two centuries, American-born citizens have moved throughout the Atlantic region for personal, political, and economic reasons.

WAR AND DIPLOMACY

Since it declared independence from England in 1776, the United States has engaged in war and diplomacy with other Atlantic nations. Indeed, its Revolutionary War was an Atlantic event, as it was fought throughout North America and the Caribbean and involved not only Great Britain but France and Spain as well. It also marked the first conflict of what would become known as the age of revolutions, a series of wars that lasted from 1776 to 1848 throughout Europe and the Americas, which were sparked in part by Enlightenment ideals of freedom, rationality, and individualism (Hobsbawm 1996). Just as the American Revolution was influenced by European political philosophy, its success inspired revolutionary leaders in France, Haiti, and Latin America, and American citizens were keenly interested in their struggles. Throughout its first decades of independence, the United States battled with England, France, and Spain over territorial claims and fishing and shipping rights and went to war with Britain for a second time in 1812. Although many historians have described the early United States as "isolationist," the United States in fact signed a host of treaties with other Atlantic nations throughout the nineteenth century and waged war in Mexico in 1846 and in Cuba in 1898 (Rossignol 1995). It also cooperated with Great Britain in policing the transatlantic slave trade; from 1819 to 1861, the United States maintained the Africa Squadron as a unit of the US Navy to suppress the slave trade along the coast of West Africa.

Even domestic events generated Atlantic involvement. The American Civil War (1861–1865), for example, reverberated across the ocean, as both the Union and Confederacy sought military support from England and France. European nations remained officially neutral, although private citizens provided material support to both sides. Following the war, diplomatic ties between the United States and Great Britain strengthened, and the two nations have remained allies ever since.

During the twentieth century, the United States' Atlantic involvement intensified. The commencement of World War I (1914–1918) prompted American journalist Walter Lippmann (1889–1974) to refer to the Western world as an "Atlantic community" that was threatened by Germany and its allies. He advocated US military involvement as a means of protecting the "Atlantic Highway" (Bailyn 2005, 6–7). In 1917, the United States entered World War I by declaring war on Germany and supporting the Allied powers of England, France, and Russia. Following the war, President Woodrow Wilson (1856–1924) attempted to solidify the United States' relationship with other Atlantic powers by promoting its involvement in the League of Nations, an international organization dedicated to maintaining peace. The US Senate, though, voted against membership, and the United States remained relatively uninvolved in events across the Atlantic until World War II (1939–1945). Instead, it spent the interwar years cultivating its relationships with the nations to its south by providing financial assistance to the Latin American governments that it deemed amenable to US interests. In the 1930s, the administration of Franklin Delano Roosevelt (1882–1945) established the Good Neighbor Policy in the region, including the creation of the Office of Inter-American Affairs. When World War II broke out in Europe, the United States continued its cultural diplomacy in Latin America in order to combat the influence of the Axis powers—Germany, Italy, and Japan—in the region (Smith 2005; Sadlier 2012, 10). It also provided military supplies to England before officially entering World War II in 1941.

Following its victory in the war, the United States strengthened its diplomatic position as a supplier of aid to its war-torn neighbors across the Atlantic. It also established itself as a bulwark against communism during the Cold War against its former ally, the Soviet Union. The United States entered into the North Atlantic Treaty Organization (NATO) in 1949, recognizing that collective defense was the surest way to protect the Atlantic community from Soviet incursions. The United States used its military and economic power to police the Atlantic, which included a series of military interventions in Latin America. Following the Cold War, the "Atlantic community" remained important to US interests, and in 1991 NATO established the North Atlantic Cooperation Council, which later became the Euro-Atlantic Partnership Council. These organizations aimed at consultation and cooperation on military, diplomatic, and humanitarian issues around the Atlantic. While Atlantic relations were no longer polarized around communism and democracy, the United States continued to cooperate with Atlantic nations on issues relating to terrorism and national security. As the twenty-first century progresses, the United States continues to act as both a partner and a bully in foreign affairs.

TRADE

While politics and national security have informed much of the United States' relationships around the Atlantic, nothing has been perhaps as important as commerce. From its beginnings as a colonial supplier to the British Empire, to its current position as a major trade partner, the United States has always been actively engaged in commerce beyond its borders. The United States commenced international trade by participating in a "triangular trade" in which it exported foodstuffs and lumber to Britain's Caribbean colonies in exchange for island sugar and British manufactured goods. It also participated in the transatlantic slave trade, both by purchasing slaves and by capturing, transporting, and selling slaves throughout the Atlantic (Rawley and Behrendt 2009). America's legal participation in the transatlantic slave trade ended in 1808, but it continued to be involved in transatlantic commerce. During the early nineteenth century, Britain generally absorbed around 20 to 25 percent of America's produce, while the provisioning of Britain's colonies in the West Indies was particularly important for American merchants (Carter et al. 2006). Additionally, the Napoleonic Wars (1803–1815) gave the United States the opportunity to serve as a neutral provider to European nations at war.

The United States was also actively involved in the South Atlantic. In addition to whaling, which it did off the coasts of both North and South America, the United States began sailing to Latin America to trade raw produce, manufactured wares, and luxury goods. The region's independence wars ushered in new trading opportunities: with the termination of its colonial relationships with Spain and Portugal came the opening of ports to foreign nations (Lynch 1998). Silver, which constituted the majority of legal tender in the United States, could now be procured directly from Latin American mines. And beginning in the 1830s, US merchants also began trading domestic manufactures for raw materials, such as hides and dyestuffs. Although Cuba remained a Spanish colony, it was permitted to engage in Atlantic trade. The United States sent lumber and foodstuff to Cuba in exchange for sugar and coffee, which it sold on the Baltic coast for bar iron—an important product for the United States' burgeoning industry.

Most significant was the United States' status as the preeminent Atlantic supplier of cotton (Beckert 2014). Although the American Civil War and the abolition of slavery in the United States disrupted cotton production, by the 1870s, the United States regained its status as the main supplier of English, French, and German cotton manufacturers, even as foreign nations turned to other Atlantic regions, such as Brazil and West Africa, for new sources of supply. While cotton and other agricultural goods remained important exports into the twentieth century, the United States increasingly sent industrial goods, and eventually financial products and information services, across the ocean. The twentieth century brought new levels of globalization and with the advent of the shipping container, patterns of commerce shifted worldwide (Levinson 2006). Regardless, the Atlantic Ocean continues to serve as a major thoroughfare of US trade.

Recognizing the Atlantic basin's long history as a region of cross-cultural exchange and geopolitical conflict and cooperation, scholars made "Atlantic history" a subject of study in the second half of the twentieth century (Games 2004). While the "Atlantic" as a mode of inquiry emerged in the specific context of the Cold War, it continues to remain relevant, despite shifting geopolitics. And even as the predominance of the Atlantic Ocean as a highway of exchange has diminished in an age of increased global contact, the ocean's dynamic past resonates in the present and will continue to inform the United States' transoceanic interactions.

SEE ALSO *Africa; Africa Squadron; Atlantic Slave Trade; Britain; Caribbean; Cuba; Europe; France*

BIBLIOGRAPHY

Armitage, David. "Three Concepts of Atlantic History." In *The British Atlantic World, 1500–1800*, edited by David Armitage and Michael J. Braddick. 2nd ed. Basingstoke, UK: Palgrave Macmillan, 2009.

Bailyn, Bernard. *Atlantic History: Concept and Contours.* Cambridge, MA: Harvard University Press, 2005.

Beckert, Sven. *Empire of Cotton: A Global History.* New York: Knopf, 2014.

Carter, Susan B., Scott Sigmund Gartner, Michael R. Haines, Alan L. Olmstead, Richard Sutch, and Gavin Wright, eds. *Historical Statistics of the United States.* Millennial ed. New York: Cambridge University Press, 2006.

Crosby, Alfred W. *The Columbian Exchange: Biological and Cultural Consequences of 1492.* Santa Barbara, CA: Greenwood Press, 1972.

Evans, Chris, and Göran Rydén. *Baltic Iron in the Atlantic World in the Eighteenth Century.* Leiden, Netherlands: Brill, 2007.

Fichter, James R. *So Great a Proffit: How the East Indies Trade Transformed Anglo-American Capitalism.* Cambridge, MA: Harvard University Press, 2010.

Games, Alison. "From the Editor: Introduction, Definitions, and Historiography: What Is Atlantic History?" *OAH Magazine of History*, "The Atlantic World," 18, 3 (2004): 3–7.

Hobsbawm, Eric J. *The Age of Revolution: 1789–1848.* New York: Vintage, 1996.

Jasanoff, Maya. *Liberty's Exiles: American Loyalists in the Revolutionary World.* New York: Vintage, 2011.

Levinson, Marc. *The Box: How the Shipping Container Made the World Smaller and the World Economy Bigger.* Princeton, NJ: Princeton University Press, 2006.

Lynch, John. *The Spanish American Revolutions, 1808–1826.* 2nd ed. New York: Norton, 1986.

Pauketat, Timothy R. *The Oxford Handbook of North American Archaeology.* London: Oxford University Press, 2012.

Rawley, James A., and Stephen Behrendt. *The Transatlantic Slave Trade: A History.* Rev. ed. Lincoln: University of Nebraska Press, 2009.

Rossignol, Marie-Jeanne. "Early Isolationism Revisited: Neutrality and Beyond in the 1790s." *Journal of American Studies* 29, 2 (1995): 215–227.

Sadlier, Darlene J. *Americans All: Good Neighbor Cultural Diplomacy in World War II.* Austin: University of Texas Press, 2012.

Smith, Joseph. *The United States and Latin America: A History of American Diplomacy, 1776–2000.* New York: Routledge, 2005.

Yarema, Allan. *The American Colonization Society: An Avenue to Freedom?* Lanham, MD: University Press of America, 2006.

Lindsay Schakenbach Regele
Assistant Professor
Miami University

ATLANTIC SLAVE TRADE

The phrase "US slave trade" has three main meanings. One is the traffic that brought slaves into the territories that either were or became the United States. A second is the traffic carried on in slaving expeditions organized in those territories, regardless of the port of disembarkation. A third is the traffic carried on under the US flag, which in the nineteenth century became a flag of convenience for slave traders based outside North America, especially Cubans and Brazilians. The Trans-Atlantic Slave Trade Database (www.slavevoyages.org) indicates that an estimated 389,000 captives arrived in North America directly from Africa. This figure does not include slaves carried from the Caribbean to the mainland, which amounted to a further 67,000 before 1808 (when the Act Prohibiting Importation of Slaves, a federal law passed by the US Congress in 1807, took effect). The traffic into the United States from the rest of the Americas after 1808 is unlikely to have exceeded 50,000.

THE IMPORTATION OF SLAVES TO NORTH AMERICA

Thus, the most recent voyage-based data for the intra-American and transatlantic slave trade point to total arrivals of 389,000 directly from Africa down to 1860 and 67,000 from other parts of the Americas by 1808. If we add to this, say, 50,000 for the years after 1808, then the total inflow into the North American mainland amounted to slightly more than half a million people. Given that 10.7 million slaves came to the Americas directly from Africa, the United States received less than 4 percent of all slaves that survived the Atlantic crossing—fewer than the tiny island of Barbados. Ninety percent of the half million arrived before 1808, yet by 1860, just half a century later, the black population of the United States was four million. Given that nearly five million captives arrived in Brazil directly from Africa, and another million arrived in Jamaica alone, it is clear the North American mainland was very much on the periphery of the Atlantic slave trade, and that natural population growth began earlier in North America than elsewhere in the black Americas.

The peripheral status of the mainland trade emerges in other ways. There is no recorded instance of a slave vessel sailing directly from Africa to a port on the North American mainland. The three best-known Africans to survive the Middle Passage to colonial North America were Ayuba Suleiman Diallo (Maryland, c. 1701–1773), the poet Phillis Wheatley (Boston, c. 1753–1784), and Venture Smith (Rhode Island, c. 1729–1805). The voyages of each were interrupted when their vessel anchored in the eastern Caribbean. Every slaver captain sought the best market for his captives, and St. Kitts, Antigua, Martinique, and especially Barbados would provide both price information and final instructions from owners. Slave traders would usually choose to sell in the Caribbean first. The major driving force behind the transatlantic slave trade was the rapid expansion of sugar plantations in the Caribbean and Brazil (and the insatiable demand for sugar among European consumers). The United States grew little sugar (the Louisiana sugar industry beginning after the slave trade ended).

Slaves nevertheless arrived in every British colony and US state prior to 1808. Almost three-quarters of the African component of the US population arrived before 1776. By that time, the Chesapeake had received all its captives, and the northern states 98 percent of their eventual total. But even the lower South had received over half of those who would eventually disembark. Overall, 55 percent of Africans entering North America arrived in Charleston and Savannah, with a further one-third scattered across a wide range of Chesapeake entry points. In the Chesapeake, the York River received at least twice as many slaves as any disembarkation district in the region. In the North, New York received five times as many captives as Rhode Island.

On the African side, captives arrived from a wide variety of coastal regions. But a small area extending just 100 miles (161 kilometers) north of the Congo River supplied almost one-quarter of the captives arriving in North America, with present-day western Nigeria contributing a further sixth. But the striking pattern is the preponderance of slaves from the region now comprised of Senegal, the Gambia, Guinea-Bissau, Guinea, Sierra Leone, and Liberia. This region contributed just one in ten of all captives carried across the Atlantic to the Americas, yet it accounted for two out of five US arrivals. There were also very few arrivals from southeast Africa. During the colonial era, the slave ships sailed mostly from British ports, usually London, Liverpool, and Bristol, but thereafter US-based merchants brought in nearly two-thirds of all African arrivals.

SLAVING EXPEDITIONS ORGANIZED IN THE UNITED STATES

The second definition of the US slave trade concerns traffic carried on under the US flag, and, before 1776, organized in ports that eventually formed part of the United States. The first such voyage probably left Boston in 1644, and the last left New York in 1863. Between these years, US-owned vessels carried over 300,000 slaves from Africa. Nevertheless, a far greater number were carried off on vessels leaving Caribbean ports and many more again left from Brazil—the location of two of the biggest slaving ports in the Atlantic World (Salvador and Rio de Janeiro). Overall, fewer than 7 percent of all slave voyages sailing to Africa from the Americas as a whole cleared from ports located on the North American mainland. Here too the adjective *peripheral* is appropriate and the amount of capital involved in the US business—and, by implication, its effects on the US economy—cannot have been great. If there is a connection between industrialization and the slave trade, it is more likely to have occurred in Brazil than North

America. The United States was very much among the ranks of the minor transatlantic slave-trading powers, well behind the Netherlands but more important than Denmark. Most strikingly, however, almost one-quarter of slaves carried on US vessels arrived in just one four-year period, 1804 to 1807.

The US-owned traffic was not just smaller than that of most other nations; it drew on a quite different range of trade goods. Trading for slaves on the African coast required a well-mixed trading cargo and a different range of merchandise for each region—sometimes, indeed, for ports within a given region. All slave traders based in the Americas relied heavily on the produce of the Americas for their trade goods. Brazilians used gold, *cachaça* (liquor), and tobacco rolls. In colonial America, by contrast, the options were more limited. Virginian tobacco did not do well in Africa. Manufactured goods were expensive, and there was no gold. This left rum. For seventy years, from the 1730s to early 1800s, US slavers carried little but rum to Africa. On the African coast, they were known simply as "rum ships." Ports in the Americas that could offer a combination of low-cost rum and efficient shipping facilities were most likely to be centers of the slave trade.

All Rhode Island ports together accounted for almost half (48.6 percent) of the slave vessels leaving the North American mainland for Africa. But expeditions left from Portland, Marblehead, Salem, Portsmouth, the whaling center of New Bedford, New Haven, Perth Amboy, Annapolis, Norfolk, and Mobile, in addition to every larger port on the East Coast, of course. The larger ports dominated. Newport, Boston, New York, and Charleston accounted for more than 80 percent of voyages. But even when the slave trade was at its height between 1804 and 1807, it formed a tiny fraction of total US external commerce.

Once on the African coast, vessels bringing rum could not often trade directly for captives. They first needed access to trading factories, castles, or rivers frequented by slave ships from Europe so that they could obtain a mixed trading cargo. US slave merchants found these in the Gambia, in the Sierra Leone estuary, and on the Gold Coast. The castles of the Gold Coast, Cape Coast Castle, and Anomabu were the most important. From the late eighteenth century, however, US slave traders shifted the distribution of their purchasing activities to a pattern more in line with the other major slaving nations of the North Atlantic. In the nineteenth century, one in five slaves obtained by US vessels came from what was always the largest source of captives on the African littoral for other national slave-trader groups—west-central Africa, mainly Loango, Cabinda, and Malimbo north of the Congo River.

In the Americas, US slave ships carried well over twice as many slaves to the Caribbean and Spanish America as they did to the mainland. The most striking feature of the geographic distribution of US slave sales is the rapid diversification of markets after 1783. Before the Revolution, colonial US slave traders sold 60 percent of their slaves in the British Caribbean and most of the remainder on the mainland. After the Revolution, the British Caribbean took only 4 percent, and the proportion going to US slave markets also fell as US states restricted slave trading. For a quarter century after independence, US slave traders therefore carried thousands of slaves into the Río de la Plata, the Dutch Americas, the Danish West Indies, and the Mascarene Islands in the Indian Ocean, as well as Cuba. They were clearly able to compete with anyone internationally. For US slave traders, abolition of the slave trade constituted a missed opportunity.

THE US FLAG AS A FLAG OF CONVENIENCE

Abolition conveniently divides the second definition of US slave trade from the third—a slave trade, mainly to Brazil and Cuba, that used the US flag as a flag of convenience. After 1820, when slave trading became a capital offence, there is little hard evidence of US *ownership* of slaving ventures to Cuba and Brazil, as opposed to US participation in the form of supplying ships, crew, fraudulent papers, and port facilities. By contrast, there is abundant evidence of Cuban, Spanish, Portuguese, and Brazilian ownership. There were certainly slave vessels owned by US citizens that carried slaves to the Americas after 1820. The two best-known ships are probably the *Wanderer* and the *Clotilda*, which brought captives into Georgia in 1858 and Alabama in 1860, respectively. But to describe a significant part of the post–1820 transatlantic slave trade as American is to misunderstand its nature.

There were two American links with the illicit traffic to Brazil and Cuba. US shipbuilders sent a steady stream of fast sailing vessels into the slave trade after 1830, but country of construction is clearly not the same as country of ownership. In addition, slave traders in Cuba and Brazil began to use the US flag as a way of escaping the attention of the British anti-slave-trade squadron. By this time, the British had switched from being the major Atlantic slave-trading power to the leader of the campaign to suppress the slave trade. The United States rarely had the naval resources to police the use of its own flag, but it also refused to cooperate with British efforts to end the traffic, prior to the Civil War at least. The great advantage of the US flag was that only US naval vessels could legally interfere with a vessel flying it, and US naval coverage on the coast was intermittent at best. In this limited sense, the US slave trade continued until the Civil War began in 1861.

SEE ALSO *Act Prohibiting Importation of Slaves (1807); Africa; American Colonization Society; Colonization Movement; Liberia*

BIBLIOGRAPHY

Coughtry, Jay. *The Notorious Triangle: Rhode Island and the African Slave Trade, 1700–1807.* Philadelphia: Temple University Press, 1981.

Eltis, David. "The U.S. Transatlantic Slave Trade, 1644–1867: An Assessment." *Civil War History* 54, 4 (December 2008): 347–378.

Eltis, David, and David Richardson. *Atlas of the Transatlantic Slave Trade.* New Haven, CT: Yale University Press, 2010.

Howard, Warren S. *American Slavers and the Federal Law, 1837–1862.* Berkeley: University of California Press, 1963.

Marques, Leonardo. *The United States and the Transatlantic Slave Trade to the Americas, 1776–1867.* New Haven, CT: Yale University Press, forthcoming.

Trans-Atlantic Slave Trade Database. http://www.slavevoyages.org

David Eltis

Robert W. Woodruff Emeritus Professor of History
Emory University

ATOMIC BOMB

Atomic bombs are massive explosive weapons powered by nuclear fission. Although atomic and nuclear weapons formed the core of the US and Soviet arsenals for most of the Cold War, as of 2015 only two atomic weapons have been used in warfare, in both cases by the United States against Japan in the closing days of World War II (1939–1945). The dawn of the atomic age in 1945 ushered in an arms race between the United States and the Soviet Union that governed many aspects of international relations in the late twentieth century and continues to have repercussions for global security today.

THE DEVELOPMENT AND USE OF THE ATOMIC BOMB

The splitting of an atomic nucleus—a process known as fission—releases large amounts of energy. In certain configurations, the neutrons ejected by this process can trigger a chain reaction in neighboring atoms, thereby creating explosions ranging from 1 to 500 kilotons. Any fissile material undergoing such a chain reaction is said to have "gone critical." Atomic bombs are usually based on one of two designs. In a gun-type assembly design, one piece of subcritical uranium-235 (colloquially known as enriched uranium) is shot toward a second piece. The more sophisticated implosion method uses carefully calibrated small explosions to compress a sphere of subcritical fissile material, usually plutonium-239. In either case, the conventional, triggering detonation is followed by an exponentially larger explosion that in turn releases energy and produces radioactive fallout. Nuclear weapons, in contrast to atomic bombs, gain most of their power from nuclear fusion, in which atomic nuclei are fused rather than split.

The United States used both kinds of atomic bombs against Japan. On August 6, 1945, the *Enola Gay,* a B-29 bomber, dropped "Little Boy," a uranium-based gun-type device, over Hiroshima. Three days later, *Bockscar,* also a B-29, dropped "Fat Man," a plutonium-based implosion device, over Nagasaki. Together, the bombs are estimated to have killed more than 200,000 people, primarily through burns and radiation sickness. The vast scale of the destruction, combined with the Soviet Union's entry into the war against Japan on August 8, forced Japan to announce its surrender on August 15.

THE AFTERMATH

Given the proximity of these events, most commentators at the time credited Japan's surrender to the bombs. According to this interpretation, their use rendered a ground invasion of Japan in October 1945 unnecessary, saving anywhere from forty thousand to a million American and countless Japanese lives. Since that time, however, historians have debated whether the bombs' use was justified on moral, military, and political grounds. The vast majority of those killed at Hiroshima and Nagasaki were civilians; the United States issued no warning before unleashing this new, secret weapon. In retrospect, given intelligence intercepts that indicated that the Japanese government was considering surrender in the summer of 1945, many military leaders felt that the bombings were unnecessary and indiscriminate. Some historians have additionally argued that the United States used the bomb to intimidate the Soviet Union, from whom military leaders had hoped to keep the bomb's development secret.

US leaders saw the atomic bomb as a propaganda coup in the immediate postwar years. The bomb seemed to offer the United States a special kind of postwar leadership, with its development representing the culmination of American scientific genius and technical know-how. The crash program to develop the weapon, known as the Manhattan Project, involved more than 150,000 scientists, engineers, and technicians at dozens of sites in the United States, Canada, and the United Kingdom, at a cost of more than $2 billion.

In late August 1945 the US government released significant details on the bombs' technical aspects in an attempt to control public speculation about their mechanisms. This controlled release was followed by a much larger publicity campaign associated with Operation

Crossroads in 1946, the first of several tests in the Marshall Islands designed to explore the effects of atomic weapons on ships, planes, and animals. The second detonation of this series, Test Baker, blanketed the seventy-one ships in the fleet with so much radioactive fallout that they could not be repaired; the failed cleanup effort exposed almost five thousand sailors to dangerous levels of plutonium. Crossroads established a pattern that would characterize US and Soviet atomic testing for most of the rest of the Cold War: an enthusiasm for documenting a given weapon's destructive powers without fully anticipating the dangers it posed to workers or the environment. Perhaps more to the point for postwar foreign policy, however, Crossroads also demonstrated the unilateral strength of US power.

POPULAR CULTURE AND THE ATOMIC BOMB

Postwar popular culture embraced the ambiguity of the atomic bomb as simultaneously something to be protected and feared. US government officials assured the public that atomic research would produce not only winning weaponry but also cures for cancer and electricity "too cheap to meter." Press coverage of Operation Crossroads sparked enthusiasm for all things atomic, from popular music to the two-piece swimsuit—dubbed the "bikini" after the Bikini Atoll where the tests took place. Radioactive mutants, from Godzilla to Spider-Man, have remained fixtures in popular culture ever since.

The United States maintained its atomic monopoly for only four years after the Hiroshima and Nagasaki bombings. In the months immediately following the end of World War II, a number of American scientists, including physicist J. Robert Oppenheimer (1904–1967), who had spearheaded the scientific and technical effort on the bomb's development at Los Alamos, New Mexico, advocated for some sort of international agency to prevent the proliferation of atomic weapons. Their efforts, however, met fierce opposition from military leaders, and atomic weaponry remained a national prerogative. Moreover, unbeknownst to US authorities, Soviet spies had infiltrated American weapons labs. On August 29, 1949, the Soviet Union detonated its first atomic bomb, and the nuclear arms race officially began. By 1964, China, France, and the United Kingdom had joined the nuclear club. Eventually, India, Pakistan, South Africa, and North Korea announced successful atomic detonations. Although it does not officially confirm or deny their existence, the state of Israel is widely assumed to possess nuclear weapons. Twenty-five years after the collapse of the Soviet Union in 1991, the difficulty of tracking and controlling the fissile materials associated with the more than 100,000 warheads produced during the Cold War continues to bedevil efforts at global security.

SEE ALSO *Bikini Atoll; Einstein, Albert; Manhattan Project; World War II*

BIBLIOGRAPHY

Boyer, Paul. *By the Bomb's Early Light: American Thought and Culture at the Dawn of the Atomic Age.* Chapel Hill: University of North Carolina Press, 1994.

Rhodes, Richard. *The Making of the Atomic Bomb.* New York: Simon & Schuster, 1986.

Walker, J. Samuel. *Prompt and Utter Destruction: Truman and the Use of Atomic Bombs against Japan,* rev. ed. Chapel Hill: University of North Carolina Press, 1997.

Audra J. Wolfe
Philadelphia, Pennsylvania

AUSTIN, STEPHEN F.

SEE *Texas Republic.*

AUTOMOBILES

In 1896, Charles Duryea (1861–1938) and Frank Duryea (1869–1967) produced the first American-made gasoline automobile sold in the United States. By the outbreak of World War I in 1914, the United States was producing more automobiles per year than the rest of the world combined (Flink 1988, 23–25). Since then, the automobile has taken on a central role on par with few other consumer goods in American culture, symbolizing at turns manufacturing might, freedom through mobility, and material excess. The rise of the automobile to the level of cultural symbol depended on a number of American domestic advantages combined with a long history of robust international trade. The American automobile industry, from the beginning, has depended on global networks of labor, materials, commerce, and ideas.

THE GROWTH OF THE AMERICAN AUTO INDUSTRY

Though he did not invent the automobile or the assembly line, Henry Ford (1863–1947) is most commonly associated with the introduction of both into the American landscape. The Ford Motor Company first produced the seminal Model T in 1908 and sold more than fifteen million units before discontinuing the model in 1927 (Watts 2005, 372). The factors that contributed to the Model T's success were the same factors that allowed for the massive expansion of the American automobile industry relative to the auto industries of

Poster advertising the Ford Anglia car, circa 1950, featuring people in a variety of national costumes. *The Ford Motor Company supported a robust worldwide sales network, as the allure of the American automobile extended to Europe and elsewhere.* NATIONAL MOTOR MUSEUM/HERITAGE IMAGES/HULTON ARCHIVE/GETTY IMAGES

France, Germany, and the United Kingdom, which arose contemporaneously. Prior to World War I (1914–1918), the United States saw a higher average wage than other industrialized nations, ready access to cheap raw materials, and a majority of its consumers living in rural areas with a need for inexpensive, reliable transportation (Flink 1988, 43–44). The Model T became the first truly mass-market automobile by combining a low price, attained through newly efficient modes of production, with a simple and durable design ideal for rural consumers traveling over the nation's network of rugged, largely unimproved roads.

The improvement of American roads was a crucial factor in the rising success of the automobile. Originating with nineteenth-century bicyclists, the good roads movement gained force in the first decades of the twentieth century as it united the interests of farmers, city boosters, Progressive Era social reformers, and motorists of all stripes in the push for a reliable and extensive road network for automobile travel (Jakle and Sculle 2008, 33–35). Though early automobile manufacturers were forced to adapt their designs to inhospitable operating conditions, Americans gradually remade the landscape into one ideal for high-speed auto travel. Federal highway bills in 1916 and 1921 began a tradition of federal standards, state administration, and public funding for roads that reached its fullest expression in the Eisenhower Interstate Highway System after World War II (Jakle and Sculle 2008, 53–54, 153–155). Meanwhile, the United States' widespread adoption of low-density, automobile-dependent suburban landscapes provided an enticing, though deeply problematic, model of development for other industrialized nations to follow.

The expansion of auto manufacturing in Detroit, Michigan, in the early twentieth century by Ford and competitors like Chrysler and General Motors was dependent on a massive inflow of labor, including African American workers from the American South and foreign-born workers from Poland, Canada, Germany, and Russia (Bates 2012, 15–16). Additionally, American manufacturers were quick to expand their growing operations into other countries. By 1917, the Ford Motor Company had manufacturing plants in Canada, England, and Argentina, supporting a robust worldwide sales network (Brinkley 2003, 131, 201–203). From an early date, the success of the automobile industry relied on inexpensive labor and ready access to foreign markets for the import of raw materials and export of finished goods. As the twentieth century progressed, the United States became more and more dependent on access to large quantities of cheap oil, specifically, to support the rising energy needs of its increasingly mobile consumers (Wells 2012, 173–174).

THE CENTRAL ROLE OF CARS IN AMERICAN CULTURE

After the United States emerged from World War II (1939–1945) in a position of relative economic and manufacturing dominance, American concepts of citizenship and consumerism became increasingly intertwined. Both culturally and politically, American rhetoric began to posit a unity of interest between the consumer and the nation (Cohen 2004, 7–12). The automobile formed a key part of this equation. Americans with access to cheap gasoline, publicly funded superhighways, and affordable suburban housing demanded cars attuned to their new surroundings. By the 1970s, American automobiles were generally larger, less efficient, and more powerful than their foreign counterparts.

The 1973–1974 Organization of Arab Petroleum Exporting Countries (OAPEC) oil embargo and resultant oil crisis exposed the depth of American dependence on cheap oil from foreign markets. After a subsequent oil shock in 1979, gasoline prices in the United States were roughly 80 percent higher than they had been in 1970 (Flink 1988, 388–391). Since most Americans were still dependent on car ownership, demand for smaller, more efficient automobiles skyrocketed. American manufacturers rushed to comply with new models, such as the compact Ford Pinto and Chevrolet Vega, but they struggled to compete with the growing popularity of import models from Japanese and European manufacturers, including Toyota, Volkswagen, and Datsun. In 1982, Honda moved to capitalize on American demand for fuel-efficient, reliable Japanese cars and began producing the Accord sedan at its plant in Marysville, Ohio, making it the first "import" car to be mass produced in the United States (Flink 1988, 339–343).

In the second decade of the twenty-first century, the American automobile market is rife with contradictions. Consumer spending points to an interest both in increased efficiency and in the space afforded by large vehicles, such as sport utility vehicles (SUVs), crossover vehicles, and full-size trucks. Manufacturers now devote a large part of their research and development efforts into hybrid gasoline-electric, fully electric, and hydrogen fuel-cell power plants designed to help maintain automobile demand in the face of rising fuel costs, as the United States continues efforts to increase domestic and foreign oil production. As an increasing majority of Americans now live in urban environments, the country is seeing a renewed interest in public transportation, as well as new technology-focused models for car- and ride-sharing, including Zipcar and Lyft. American auto manufacturers, meanwhile, anticipate increasing demand among expanding middle classes in countries like India and China while developing models for global, rather than just American, markets. Nonetheless, it seems likely that, moving forward, the absolute dominance of the automobile as the primary mode of American transportation will be understood as a twentieth-century phenomenon.

SEE ALSO *Airplanes; Americanization; Cold War; Exceptionalism; Exports, Exportation; Industrialization; Internationalism; Isolationism; Trains; World War I; World War II; World's Fairs*

BIBLIOGRAPHY

Bates, Beth Tompkins. *The Making of Black Detroit in the Age of Henry Ford.* Chapel Hill: University of North Carolina Press, 2012.

Brinkley, Douglas. *Wheels for the World: Henry Ford, His Company, and a Century of Progress, 1903–2003.* New York: Viking, 2003.

Cohen, Lizabeth. *A Consumers' Republic: The Politics of Mass Consumption in Postwar America.* New York: Knopf, 2003.

Flink, James J. *The Automobile Age.* Cambridge, MA: MIT Press, 1988.

Jakle, John A., and Keith A. Sculle. *Motoring: The Highway Experience in America.* Athens: University of Georgia Press, 2008.

Watts, Steven. *The People's Tycoon: Henry Ford and the American Century.* New York: Knopf, 2005.

Wells, Christopher W. "The Road to the Model T: Culture, Road Conditions, and Innovation at the Dawn of the American Motor Age." *Technology and Culture* 48, 3 (2007): 497–523.

Wells, Christopher W. *Car Country: An Environmental History.* Seattle: University of Washington Press, 2012.

Aaron Hatley
PhD Candidate
Harvard University

B

BACK-TO-AFRICA MOVEMENT

From the beginning of the Atlantic slave trade, when Africans threw themselves over the sides of ships in the belief that death would return them to their ancestral land, the promise of a back-to-Africa movement has held persistent and often popular appeal in Africa's diaspora. Emigrationist sentiment in the United States waxed during eras of instability—during the turbulent 1850s, following the withdrawal of federal troops from the South in 1877, during the "nadir" of the 1890s—and waned during moments of optimism and opportunity. But the back-to-Africa idea was not merely reactive. Proponents argued that the scattered members of the race had been called to a higher destiny than simply staking their claim to American rights and citizenship. Providence dictated that the sons and daughters of the slave trade return to rebuild their fallen homeland, armed with the skills and faith acquired during their long years of exile. The appeal of "Africa for the Africans" illustrated the extent to which black families desired security, stability, and opportunity. But it also reflected the prophetic faith that sustained African American politics during the long years of enslavement, and that underpinned popular understandings of Pan-Africanism, anticolonialism, and liberationist politics in the decades that followed.

THE ANTEBELLUM PERIOD

In 1815, wealthy African American shipbuilder and captain Paul Cuffe (1759–1817) carried thirty-eight emigrants to the young British colony of Sierra Leone. But early efforts at large-scale black emigration were typically given possibility and place in the United States by the establishment of the American colony of Liberia in 1819, and under the auspices of the American Colonization Society (ACS). By the first decades of the nineteenth century, white boosters of black repatriation were driven by a complex mix of motivations that blended philanthropic sentiment, antislavery zeal, racial panic, and practical expediency. Under the leadership of Robert Finley (1772–1817), the ACS viewed Liberia as a site that would at once encourage the spread of Western civilization, commerce, and Christianity through the region; offer a space for free blacks to develop and demonstrate their capacity for self-government; and provide slaveholders a means to manumit their slaves without creating a large and potentially destabilizing free black population at home.

Although the ACS promoted voluntary emigration, many of its southern supporters viewed the society as a means to forcibly expatriate the nation's most vocal antislavery advocates. One of the society's early champions, Thomas Jefferson (1743–1826)—who expressed an antipathy for forced bondage and for African Americans in equal measure—viewed emigration as the only means to rid the United States of slavery without inviting an all-out race war. Little wonder then that despite some important collaborators—Daniel Coker (1780–1846), John Russwurm (1799–1851), Edward Wilmot Blyden (1832–1912), Alexander Crummell (1819–1898)—the ACS was generally viewed with mistrust and suspicion by free blacks.

The most important advocate of African emigration during the antebellum period was the freeborn physician, writer, antislavery activist, and all-around Renaissance man Martin Delany (1812–1885). By the 1850s, several important shifts—Liberian independence (1848), Mexican cession (1848), the passage of the Fugitive Slave Act

(1850), and later the *Dred Scott* decision (1857)—had given renewed impetus to the prospect of emigration among free blacks. In *The Condition, Elevation, Emigration, and Destiny of the Colored People of the United States* (1852), Delany argued that African Americans, trapped as a "nation within a nation" in the United States, would be better served building their own nation in Central America. By the end of the decade, Delany had turned his focus to Africa. In 1859 and 1860, along with his fellow "commissioner" Robert Campbell (1829–1884), Delany toured Liberia, Lagos, and Yorubaland. He returned with a signed treaty granting him land for an African American colony at Abeokuta (in present-day Nigeria). But the Civil War and the tantalizing prospect of emancipation brought a practical halt to emigrationist aspirations. Delany joined his longtime rival—and leading critic of back-to-Africa sentiment—Frederick Douglass (c. 1818–1895) in stumping and recruiting for the Union cause.

HENRY MCNEAL TURNER'S EMIGRATIONIST PROJECT

The war effort also attracted the service of a rising minister in the African Methodist Episcopal (AME) Church, Henry McNeal Turner (1834–1915). After working as a chaplain for an all-black regiment, Turner won election to the Georgia state legislature following the war. But Turner's faith in American politics was dashed by the wave of violence, intimidation, and fraud that spread across the South following emancipation. By the end of Reconstruction, convinced that African Americans would never be treated as equal partners in the United States, he had emerged as the nation's most vocal and successful proponent of emigration. The timing was propitious. In 1878, when the upstart Liberian Exodus Joint Stock Company chartered a ship, the *Azor*, to carry 206 men, women, and children to Liberia, ten thousand people gathered to send them off. By the early 1890s, as the Jim Crow regime began to cast its shadow over the South, emigration clubs operated across the region, and the ACS enjoyed a brief revival.

Turner, perhaps more than anyone before or after, captured the particular combination of black pride, Western chauvinism, prophetic faith, and Victorian gender sensibilities that propelled the back-to-Africa movement. European colonialists, he argued, were not wrong to view Africa as backward, uncivilized, and undeveloped. But the land had been given to men with black skin, and God had brought Africans to the New World so that in their suffering they might reclaim the faith lost to Africa in antiquity, and so that they might fashion for themselves the civilizational tools necessary for Africa's return to glory. The great cause of uniting a scattered flock in a renewed Africa offered a "theater for manhood" denied in the United States, and a proper opportunity for black women to assume idealized, domestic, and subordinate positions beside their men.

Turner viewed the European scramble for Africa in the late nineteenth century with dismay and horror. Nevertheless, his extensive organizing and religious work around the country on behalf of black nationhood sustained the traditions of black pride, economic self-sufficiency, and political autonomy that gave the back-to-Africa idea its enduring appeal. And his work facilitating the merger of the Ethiopian Church in South Africa and the AME Church in the United States established a diasporic pipeline of political, educational, and religious exchange that reverberated well into the twentieth century.

TWENTIETH-CENTURY BACK-TO-AFRICA EFFORTS

Efforts to establish an African American colony in West Africa also continued into the twentieth century, first under the auspices of Chief Alfred C. Sam's Akim Trading Company in 1915 and then, more spectacularly, under the direction of Marcus Garvey's Harlem-based Universal Negro Improvement Association (UNIA) following World War I (1914–1918). Guided by the grander vision of restoring colonized Africa to black rule, the Jamaican-born Garvey (1887–1940) pursued a wide range of political, organization, educational, business, and diplomatic schemes that brought the UNIA millions of worldwide members and supporters by the early 1920s. In 1919 Garvey announced plans to relocate the UNIA's parent body from New York to Monrovia, and he sent envoys to Liberia to negotiate conditions. Like his emigrationist forebears, Garvey viewed Liberia—along with Abyssinia (Ethiopia), one of two remaining independent nations on the continent—as a felicitous theater for the establishment of black Atlantic commercial relations and the reclamation of black political manhood. He also imagined Liberia as a staging ground for an active assault on European rule of the continent. The Liberian government, at first receptive to the idea of a UNIA colony, quickly backtracked amid pressure from France and Britain, and amid growing fears of what a strong Garveyite presence would mean for its own claim to sovereignty. The UNIA's colonization scheme was repelled in 1921, and an effort to revive relations in 1923 and 1924 also came to naught.

In 1966, Garvey's dream was realized posthumously when the UNIA was granted two thousand acres of land in Liberia by the paramount chief of Tchien. That same year, Ghanaian president Kwame Nkrumah (1909–1972) was ousted in a coup that brought the last great migration of African diasporic subjects to an end. Nkrumah's

Ghana, which won independence in 1957, attracted a generation of prominent expatriates—among them W. E. B. Du Bois (1868–1963), Maya Angelou (1928–2014), Julian Mayfield (1928–1984), Vicki Garvin (1915–2007), Alphaeus Hunton (1903–1970), St. Clair Drake (1911–1990), and David Levering Lewis (b. 1936)—drawn to the euphoric project of building an independent African state and an indigenous Pan-Africanism. More recently, the Ghanaian government's successful efforts to promote "heritage" or "roots" tourism has highlighted the enduring appeal of West Africa in the imaginations and aspirations of African Americans. Calls across the centuries for Westernized blacks to claim their manhood and statehood in Africa have been replaced by more modern and more culturally collaborative projects. But the back-to-Africa spirit lives on.

SEE ALSO *Africa; American Colonization Society; An Appeal to the Coloured Citizens of the World (David Walker, 1829); Caribbean; Colonization Movement; Liberia*

BIBLIOGRAPHY

Campbell, James T. *Middle Passages: African American Journeys to Africa, 1787–2005*. New York: Penguin, 2006.

Ewing, Adam. *The Age of Garvey: How a Jamaican Activist Created a Mass Movement and Changed Global Black Politics*. Princeton, NJ: Princeton University Press, 2014.

Redkey, Edwin S. *Black Exodus: Black Nationalist and Back-to-Africa Movements, 1890–1910*. New Haven, CT: Yale University Press, 1969.

Adam Ewing
Assistant Professor
Virginia Commonwealth University

BALDWIN, JAMES

SEE *Lost Generation.*

BALFOUR DECLARATION (1917)

On November 2, 1917, Lord Arthur James Balfour (1848–1930), the British foreign secretary, drafted a single-page letter to Lord Rothschild proclaiming his "sympathy with Jewish Zionist aspirations." The official declaration supported "the establishment in Palestine of a national home for the Jewish people." The language of "a national home" rather than "the national home" for Jews reflected a diplomatic strategy on the part of Balfour and the British government, a deliberate alteration of the language submitted by Chaim Weizmann (1874–1952) and Nahum Sokolow (1859–1936) on behalf of the World Zionist Organization. Balfour added, "nothing shall be done which may prejudice the civil and religious rights of existing non-Jewish communities in Palestine," nor should the creation of this new Jewish national home affect "the rights and political status enjoyed by Jews in any other country." The short document at once acknowledged Jewish territorial peoplehood and aspirations on the international stage and left to interpretation the exact form of their future territorial rights and how these would be balanced with those of other peoples and nations.

BACKGROUND

The Balfour Declaration emerged partially as a result of cooperation between Britain and France, along with the United States; this cooperation was formalized in the Sykes-Picot Agreement (1916). The United States had not yet entered World War I (1914–1918), and British politicians perceived Zionist Americans as allies who could help convince the United States to join the war. In May 1917, prior to the publication of the Balfour Declaration, Balfour traveled to the United States and met with Louis Brandeis (1856–1941), the leader of the Zionist Organization of America. Brandeis and other Zionists gained an ongoing audience with President Woodrow Wilson (1856–1924) and influenced his foreign policy regarding Palestine.

THE AMERICAN RESPONSE

After the release of the Balfour Declaration and Britain's capture of Jerusalem, many Jewish Americans expressed enthusiasm about the future of Palestine. As public expression of their excitement over the statement, fifteen thousand Jews congregated at Carnegie Hall in New York City on December 23, 1917, and twenty-five thousand paraded in Newark, New Jersey. Some—such as some Reform rabbis, Bundists, and others who continued to perceive Zionism as excessively utopian—continued to express reservations. For example, the well-known anti-Zionist Reform rabbi Samuel Schulman (1864–1955) wrote in the *New York Times* that he opposed language describing Palestine as a homeland for Jews "because such a phrase implies the idea of present homelessness of the Jewish people" (Schulman 1917, XX3). Jewish American "anti-Zionists," such as Schulman, did not object to protecting Jewish rights in Palestine. They saw Jewish rights in Palestine as parallel to Jewish rights in the United States, rights to be extended to all citizens of a liberal democracy, rather than to privileged members of an ethnic democracy. The Jewish anti-Zionist movement considered the Balfour Declaration and the ensuing diplomacy based on it in tension with their commitment to Jewish life in the United States.

The Balfour Declaration marked a turning point in the political struggle for territorial claims in Palestine. It also marked a shift in alliances within the US political climate among non-Jewish American politicians who had previously opposed Zionism because of their perception that it represented a minority of Jews. Wilson was concerned with a delicate balance of creating a coalition among Britain, America, and Jews, as well as not appearing to take a belligerent position toward Turkey. By 1919, once the Ottoman Empire's power had dissolved, Wilson was able to wholeheartedly support the British Mandate and its commitment to Jewish sovereignty in Palestine. The Balfour Declaration, its incorporation into the mandate, and the political approval of the United States solidified both British political claims in the region and recognition of "the Jewish people" as an official entity in international law (Friedman 1973, 122). The Balfour Declaration marked an expansion of Zionist American campaigns and a more concrete national American political project regarding Palestine, though the exact nature of the plans for Jewish sovereignty in Palestine remained in flux.

If the Balfour Declaration walked a tightrope between offering a Jewish homeland in Palestine and balancing that promise with Arab-Palestinian rights, the Paris Peace Conference in 1918 to 1919 interpreted the phrasing of "Jewish national home" explicitly to mean that the entire territory would become a Jewish state. However, the King-Crane Commission—which was made public in 1922, having been undertaken in 1919 to inform America of Arab understanding of the Balfour Declaration and the future of Palestine—presented the Arab opposition to a Jewish state. At times, Zionist Americans, citing the Balfour Declaration, would press for Jewish rights to a self-determined state. But Jews remained the numerical minority throughout the first half of the twentieth century, so Zionists frequently refrained from calling openly for a state, strategically waiting for a larger Jewish population to take root. Arab or Palestinian American responses rarely gained a national platform or voice in the United States. A general commitment to a Jewish homeland in Palestine characterized American policy until the late 1930s; however, the potential political and territorial contours of this commitment varied. After the 1937 Peel Commission and 1939 White Paper, a greater number of Jewish Americans began explicitly and consistently to support the formation of a state.

PALESTINE AS A REFLECTION OF AMERICAN IDEALS

Zionist Americans not only imagined Palestine as a place of refuge for Jewish refugees from Europe, but they also projected their ideals of democracy and progressivism onto the romanticized space. Arthur Balfour and the Balfour Declaration gained mythic status for Zionist culture in the United States. A Zionist visual culture—as appeared, for example, in the pages of the Zionist Organization of America's journals the *Maccabaean* and the *New Palestine*—with Western figures such as Balfour sought to connect Zionism with images that emphasized democratic values and civility. Furthermore, Jewish and Christian Americans perceived Palestine through the lens of "the Holy Land," so dreams of social justice and self-determination were colored by their expectations rooted in religious backgrounds. Some scholars have argued that this led to the firm commitment of the Christian American public and the government to favor Jews because of their identity with ancient Israelites, while others have suggested that the seeming antiquity of Arab ways of life led to the perception that they most closely represented biblical life. Either way, conceptions of religious heritage, as well as contemporary political questions, weighed heavily on how Americans responded to the Balfour Declaration and its ensuing political era.

Zionist Americans were so convinced of the transformative, civilizing force that Jewish presence would bring to Palestine, many could not imagine Arabs rejecting Jewish benevolence and rights to the land. After the League of Nations officially ceded Palestine to Britain in the spring of 1920, despite the Balfour Declaration's rhetoric ensuring Jewish and Arab rights, a trajectory toward some measure of Jewish autonomy seemed more certain. Some Palestinian Arabs began to revolt. However, the *New York Times* and the Zionist journal the *Maccabaean* explained that the violence was not evidence of Arab dissatisfaction with growing Jewish settlement but the result of criminals or nomads not representative of majority Arab sentiment. As a result of the British Mandate and the Balfour Declaration, Jews and Zionists became entangled with the image of imperialism. Though most Americans understood Jews as seeking to liberate themselves from imperial persecution, the situation on the ground in Palestine was much more complicated and perceived quite differently by the diverse local population. Zionist alliances to the United States and Britain ultimately shaped Jewish territory and statehood, but also left the imprint of imperialism on the Zionist project.

SEE ALSO *Holocaust; Judaism; League of Nations; Paris Peace Conference (1919); Treaty of Versailles; United Nations; World War I; World War II; Zionism*

BIBLIOGRAPHY

Ahmed, Hisham. "From the Balfour Declaration to World War II: The U.S. Stand on Palestinian Self-Determination." *Arab Studies Quarterly* 12, 1–2 (Winter/Spring 1990): 9–41.

Balfour, Arthur James. "The Balfour Declaration." November 2, 1917. http://www.jewishvirtuallibrary.org/jsource/History/balfour.html

Berkowitz, Michael. *Western Jewry and the Zionist Project, 1914–1933.* Cambridge: Cambridge University Press, 1997.

Cohen, Naomi. *The Americanization of Zionism, 1897–1948.* Hanover, NH: Brandeis University Press, 2003.

Davidson, Lawrence. *America's Palestine: Popular and Official Perceptions from Balfour to Israeli Statehood.* Gainesville: University Press of Florida, 2001.

Diner, Hasia. *The Jews of the United States, 1654 to 2000.* Berkeley: University of California Press, 2004.

Fischer, Louis. "In Upper Galilee." *Maccabaean* 33 (April 1920): 135.

Friedman, Isaiah. "Response to the Balfour Declaration." *Jewish Social Studies* 35, 2 (1973): 105–124.

F.O. 371/3054/84173, Sykes to Picot, 12 December 1917, tel. no. 1181; minutes by Graham, Hardinge, and Balfour, p. 233438.

Kalmar, Ivan Davidson, and Derek J. Penslar, eds. *Orientalism and the Jews.* Waltham, MA: Brandeis University Press, 2005.

Medoff, Rafael. *Zionism and the Arabs: An American Jewish Dilemma, 1898–1948.* Westport, CT: Praeger, 1997.

Mendes-Flohr, Paul, and Jehuda Reinharz, eds. *The Jew in the Modern World: A Documentary History.* 3rd ed. New York: Oxford University Press, 2011.

Sarna, Jonathan. "A Projection of America as It Ought to Be: Zion in the Mind's Eye of American Jews." In *Envisioning Israel: The Changing Ideals and Images of North American Jews,* edited by Allon Gal, 41–59. Detroit, MI: Wayne State University Press, 1996.

Schulman, Samuel. "Jewish Nation Not Wanted in Palestine: The Views of Those Who are Opposed to Zionism Expressed by a Leading American Rabbi." *New York Times,* November 25, 1917, XX3.

Stein, Leonard. *The Balfour Declaration.* London: Simon and Schuster, 1961.

"10 Killed in Jerusalem." *New York Times,* April 8, 1920, 5.

Jessica Carr
Assistant Professor in Religious Studies
Lafayette College

BALKAN WARS

SEE *Yugoslav Wars.*

BANANA REPUBLICS

Early in the twentieth century, the term *banana republic* came to articulate a range of clichés and caricatures that framed US diplomatic relations with Central America and the Caribbean. Coined by American author O. Henry (1862–1910) in *Cabbages and Kings* (1904), *banana republic* referred to countries ruled by dictators, oligarchs, and "strongmen" who oversaw economies based on agricultural exports—usually coffee, bananas, or sugar—and dependent on the labor of Indians, mixed-race peasants, or members of the African diaspora, who were often engaged in imperial struggles against Spanish colonialism. Early on, banana republics were linked to racial and cultural legacies left by Spanish colonialism in Cuba, the Dominican Republic, Puerto Rico, and Panama.

Large-scale Caribbean and Central American banana exports to the United States began in the 1870s, first to Boston and later to New Orleans and other southern coastal ports. Honduras began cultivating commercial bananas after the 1870s. US citizens, diplomats, and military men who ventured into these regions brought a vision of their country's place in the world grounded in the history and myths associated with westward expansion. This vision included Americans' sense of a white "manifest destiny" to bring order and "progress" to the remnants of Spanish colonialism in the United States, its mixed-race populations, and remaining Indians. This view of the United States' destiny led to the Monroe Doctrine (1823), which declared much of the Western Hemisphere an exclusive US sphere of influence, as well as war with Mexico in 1848, and later efforts to purchase Cuba from Spain.

US investments in the Caribbean and Central America were minor between the declaration of the Monroe Doctrine and the 1890s. Economic relations mostly consisted of imports of fruits and loans for infrastructure projects, particularly railroads and a canal through Nicaragua or Panama. Such initiatives produced individual colonialist projects, such as the alliance between Cornelius Vanderbilt (1794–1877) and the filibuster William Walker (1824–1860) in Nicaragua in the 1850s.

In the 1830s, US citizens who settled in Mexican territory declared independence and withstood Mexican efforts to recover Texas, inspiring others in the practice of filibustering, including Walker. Walker sailed to Nicaragua in 1855 and embroiled himself in a civil war among elites who were facing Vanderbilt's efforts to control transit across Nicaragua and transportation via ocean freight to California during the gold rush. Walker declared himself president of Nicaragua, reestablished slavery, and ruled from 1856 to 1857, until Central American armies defeated him and Hondurans executed him in 1860.

By 1929, Honduras had become the main exporter of bananas in the world as enterprises owned by two US corporations—the United Fruit Company and the Standard Fruit Company—financed wars among Honduran elites to secure concessions. By the 1930s, United Fruit, headed by Sam "the Banana Man" Zemurray (1877–1961), dominated the banana republics with operations in many Central American and Caribbean countries. Zemurray enjoyed close relations with the US State Department and the Central Intelligence Agency (CIA), which he leveraged in 1954 to engineer a coup against the president of Guatemala, Jacobo Arbenz Guzmán (1913–1971), who challenged United Fruit's monopolies.

US diplomats appeared to function as either active agents of US corporations or as passive observers of the neocolonial American empire, particularly when US marines protected economic or geopolitical interests. From 1898 to 1959, between the US defeat of Spain in Cuba and the overthrow of General Fulgencio Batista (1901–1973) by Fidel Castro (b. 1926), US diplomatic relations with so-called banana republics were framed by doctrines of imposition articulated in the 1904 Roosevelt Corollary to the Monroe Doctrine, dollar diplomacy, and the Good Neighbor Policy of the 1930s and 1940s.

After 1950, the Good Neighbor approach succumbed to struggles of the Cold War between the United States and the Soviet Union and their allies. Between the 1960s and the fall of the Soviet Union in 1989, a period that also saw the decolonization in Africa, Asia, and the Middle East, US diplomacy often drew on the caricature of banana republics. The US invasion of Panama in 1989, authorized by President (and former CIA chief) George H. W. Bush, apprehended Panamanian dictator Manuel Noriega (b. 1934), who had served as a paid informant of the CIA for decades. The invasion framed US–Latin American relations in clichés that US citizens, corporations, and diplomats had used since the 1910s.

American filmmaker DeeDee Halleck's documentary *The Gringo in Mañanaland* (1995) explored the banana republic stereotypes presented in travelogues, Hollywood and industrial films, newsreels, military documentaries, and textbooks. Films from the 1950s to the 1980s incorporated the banana republic caricature in the service of myth making and parody, as exemplified by Jacques Tourneur's *Appointment in Honduras* (1953) and Woody Allen's *Bananas* (1969). Alex Cox's biographical film *Walker* (1987) served as a critique of intervention in Nicaragua by the Ronald Reagan administration in the 1980s. In 1978 a new retail clothing store expressed its image of "wild" adventure with the name Banana Republic. Today, Banana Republic is a chain with hundreds of stores throughout the world.

Banana republic tropes often frame assessments of resistance to US hegemony in the Americas. For example, when Manuel Zelaya Rosales (b. 1952), the president of Honduras from 2006 to 2009, questioned US intervention in his country's affairs, his populism appealed to a century of Honduran resentment at being reduced by US diplomats and corporations to a classic banana republic. In doing so, Zelaya aligned himself with Latin America's historic anti-US nationalism and contemporary leftist leaders, despite the fact that he is descended from elite Spanish colonial families dating back to the eighteenth century. Zelaya, who often clashed with US foreign policy makers, was ousted in a military coup in 2009. Former secretary of state Hillary Rodham Clinton characterized Zelaya as "a throwback to the caricature of a Central American strongman, with his white cowboy hat, dark mustache, and fondness for Hugo Chavez and Fidel Castro" (Clinton 2014, 222), a description grounded in long-standing US myths about banana republics.

SEE ALSO *Caribbean; Colonialism; Colonization Movement; Guatemala; United Fruit Company*

BIBLIOGRAPHY

Clinton, Hillary Rodham. *Hard Choices.* New York: Simon and Schuster, 2014.

Cohen, Rich. *The Fish That Ate the Whale: The Life and Times of America's Banana King.* New York: Picador, 2012.

Colby, Jason M. *The Business of Empire: United Fruit, Race, and U.S. Expansion in Central America.* Ithaca, NY: Cornell University Press, 2011.

Euraque, Darío A. *Reinterpreting the Banana Republic: Region and State in Honduras, 1870–1972.* Chapel Hill: University of North Carolina Press, 1996.

Soluri, John. *Banana Cultures: Agriculture, Consumption, and Environmental Change in Honduras and the United States.* Austin: University of Texas Press, 2005.

Darío A. Euraque
Professor of History and International Studies
Trinity College, Hartford, Connecticut

BANDUNG CONFERENCE (1955)

From April 18 to 24, 1955, twenty-nine Asian, African, and Middle Eastern nations participated in the Afro-Asian Conference in Bandung, Indonesia. Organized the previous year under the sponsorship of India, Pakistan, Ceylon (later Sri Lanka), Indonesia, and Burma (later Myanmar), this gathering—popularly known as the Bandung Conference—marked a new international era in which former Asian and African colonies sought to amplify the global fight against colonialism, white supremacy, and the continued threat of nuclear war. Bandung marked the beginning of the Non-Aligned Movement in which the "Third World" challenged the United States and the Soviet Union through proclaiming to be politically neutral as a counterweight to the Cold War divide.

Indonesian President Sukarno (1901–1970) declared on opening day: "We are united … by a common detestation of colonialism in whatever form it appears. We are united by a common detestation of racialism. And we are united by a common determination to preserve and stabilize peace in the world." In addition, Sukarno warned that although the edifice of colonialism was crumbling, new forms of imperial control were emerging in its wake. With nuclear war still looming and the reign of the US dollar underwriting underdevelopment in the Third World, Sukarno offered that conference delegates could "inject the voice of reason into world affairs ... [and] mobilize all the spiritual, all the moral, all the political strength of Asia and Africa on the side of peace" (Prashad 2007, 34).

Sukarno, along with Prime Ministers Jawaharlal Nehru (1889–1964) of India, Gamal Abdel Nasser (1918–1970) of Egypt, and U Nu (1907–1995) of Burma led the Third World solidarity initiatives and established the importance of nonalignment during the conference. Though Bandung was ideologically diverse and contained delegates from across the political spectrum, none had a more pronounced presence than Zhou Enlai (1898–1976) of the People's Republic of China (PRC). Zhou was ebullient, conciliatory, and desperately in search of new allies. With a packed schedule he wined and dined delegates of all political persuasions and effectively established China as a principled ally of the Third World. Conversely, Bandung offered China a way out of its global isolation following the Sino-Soviet divide and the ever-growing hostility of the United States after the establishment of the Southeast Asia Treaty Organization (SEATO), a regional security initiative that "institutionalize[d] a bipolar order in Asia" (Fraser 2003, 116) with the help of Japan, South Korea, Australia, and New Zealand.

The United States and the Soviet Union were not invited to the conference. US State Department officials believed that this intentional snubbing provided a real opportunity for China to have an outsized influence on delegates. Initially, US policy makers suggested that Bandung be treated with a "cold shoulder." Later, analysts suggested that a more effective strategy would be to deploy a diplomacy of "encouragement" in an effort to mobilize US allies in attendance to challenge the presence of Communist China. Secretary of State John Foster Dulles (1888–1959) was particularly concerned that the Bandung Conference was serving as a springboard for "communist success and Asian autonomy" (Fraser 2003, 121). For the United States, "fear of the newly assertive world of color was proving to be contagious among Western powers, and the PRC had become the symbol of that assertiveness that so threatened the West" (122). This was particularly salient following the 1954 *Brown v. Board of Education* decision, where domestic race relations continuously compromised the United States' international image as the chief purveyor of democracy, particularly in the decolonizing world of Asia and Africa.

Although the United States was not invited, New York congressman Adam Clayton Powell Jr. (1908–1972) attended the conference to the consternation of the US State Department. During the 1940s, Powell had been a member of the Council on African Affairs (CAA) and was at the forefront of the anticolonial left/liberal coalition that challenged the United States to live up to its democratic principles at home and abroad. Powell later abandoned the CAA in 1948 and became a staunch supporter of American foreign policy under the Truman Doctrine. Consistent with his political shifts under President Harry S. Truman (1884–1972), Powell went out of his way during the conference to defend the United States and invoke "the dominant Cold War pro–civil rights argument that 'America must "clean up" her own race problem as swiftly as possible in order to reassure the people of Asia'" (Von Eschen 1997, 170).

Powell's interests in the Bandung Conference were both political and personal. Reflecting on his experience, Powell believed that the gathering of peoples of color at Bandung was both "divine" and representative of "a new Mecca" (Fraser 2003, 134) that demanded his presence. Similarly, African American writer Richard Wright (1908–1960) attended the conference precisely because it appeared to be a gathering that was beyond ideology and steeped in an almost "extra-human" desire to bring together the dispossessed to sort out their challenges on their own terms and set the stage for a new international order (Wright 1956, 14; Fraser 2003, 134). Wright's emotional sentiments were shared by many African Americans. Both Martin Luther King Jr. (1929–1968) and Malcolm X (1925–1965) would reference the Bandung Conference as a watershed event that marked the beginning of a "new world order." As twenty-first-century globalization reconfigures economic and political relationships between the Global North and South, the Bandung Conference remains an important symbol of postcolonial liberation and the quest for equality and human rights throughout the world.

SEE ALSO *Cold War; Decolonization; Third World*

BIBLIOGRAPHY

Fraser, Cary. "An American Dilemma: Race and Realpolitik in the American Response to the Bandung Conference, 1955." In *Window on Freedom: Race, Civil Rights, and Foreign Affairs, 1945–1988*, edited by Brenda Gayle Plummer, 115–140. Chapel Hill: University of North Carolina Press, 2003.

Mullen, Bill V. *Afro Orientalism*. Minneapolis: University of Minnesota Press, 2004.

Prashad, Vijay. *The Darker Nations: A People's History of the Third World*. New York: New Press, 2007.

Von Eschen, Penny M. *Race against Empire: Black Americans and Anticolonialism,1937–1957*. Ithaca, NY: Cornell University Press, 1997.

Wright, Richard. *The Color Curtain: A Report on the Bandung Conference.* New York: World Publishing Company, 1956.

Fanon Che Wilkins
Associate Professor of African American History and Culture
Graduate School of Global Studies, Doshisha University

BARBARY WARS

From the end of the American Revolution to the War of 1812, North Africa presented the new United States with its first non-European policy crisis and its most persistent and frustrating international entanglements. The capture of roughly 450 American sailors by North African corsairs beginning in 1784 and the Barbary Wars of the early nineteenth century left lasting imprints on American culture and influenced diplomatic and military history.

AMERICA'S FIRST NON-EUROPEAN POLICY CRISIS

American ships were vulnerable to North African corsairs following the Revolution because they were no longer protected by the British navy. North African leaders—particularly in Morocco, Tripoli, Tunis, and Algiers—maintained that they had the right to capture ships belonging to Christian nations with whom they had not signed treaties and with whom they were, in their view, at war. The emperor of Morocco had made efforts to negotiate a treaty with the United States during the American Revolution, but in October 1784, with negotiations bogging down, Moroccan corsairs captured the American merchant ship *Betsy* and its crew, thereby spurring a quick resolution of the treaty and the equally rapid release of ship and crew. In late July 1785, Algerian corsairs captured two more American ships, the *Dauphin* and *Maria*, and imprisoned twenty-one crew members. Eight years later in October and November 1793, with no progress made in negotiations between the two nations, Algiers captured eleven more American ships, enslaving 105 crew members.

These events had a powerful impact on the national psyche. They revealed the new nation's weakness in the most embarrassing fashion and threatened to destroy hopes that an enlarged Mediterranean trade would compensate for the loss of the British trade during the postwar depression. The Continental Congress's inability to raise the money to ransom the captives and placate the North Africans exacerbated dissatisfaction with the Articles of Confederation and factored into some Americans' decisions to support ratification of the Constitution. The remarkable ineptitude of the early treaty negotiations by the American agent, John Lamb, did not improve morale.

By 1795, the United States finally managed to sign a treaty with Algiers stipulating a tribute payment of $600,000 to the dey to avoid further captures, plus $200,000 ransom for the captives and smaller ongoing payments in subsequent years. These costs and the dey's additional demand that he be supplied with a new frigate would be the single-largest item in the national budget that year, and the United States proved incapable of raising the necessary funds expeditiously. This failure further delayed the release of the captives, most of whom would not return home until early 1797, in some cases nearly a dozen years after they had been captured. During the crisis, Congress also determined to build a navy in order to prevent future captures. Although slow and costly, this initiative eventually resulted in construction of the US Navy's first three frigates.

CULTURAL IMPACT

This encounter with the Islamic world also had an important cultural impact on the new nation. The exotic notion of American captives in North Africa influenced a number of novels, plays, and poems. One of the first important American novels, Royall Tyler's *The Algerine Captive* (1797), incorporated some of the actual events and captives into its narrative. David Humphreys, a diplomat and member of the group known as the Connecticut Wits, wrote a number of poems that made use of the captives' plight to encourage American patriotism, such as "On the Happiness of America" (1787). Susanna Rowson's influential play, *Slaves in Algiers* (1794), was perhaps the most famous work to come out of the crisis. Additionally, a number of captivity and travel accounts written by the captives themselves (or in one case based on some of their experiences) attempted to familiarize American readers with the history and geography of North Africa while providing lurid tales of captivity.

These cultural productions, often considered the earliest examples of American orientalism, reflected inward at the same time that they promised exposure to exotic locales. Several, such as the anonymous poem "The American in Algiers, or the Patriot of Seventy-Six in Captivity" (1797) and David Everett's play, *Slaves in Barbary* (1797), were concerned as much with American slavery as Barbary captivity. These works compared American slave owners unfavorably to the so-called barbarians. Others, such as Susanna Rowson, used their readers' fascination with harems and sodomy as a means to prompt Americans to reflect on their own imperfect gender system.

Burning of the frigate* Philadelphia *in Tripoli Harbor in 1804 (engraving). *Commodore Stephen Decatur's daredevil burning of the captured US frigate helped turn the tide of war after an initial lackluster performance by the US military.* **ROGER VIOLLET/GETTY IMAGES**

WARS WITH TRIPOLI AND ALGIERS

The War with Tripoli (1801–1805), which was prompted by the United States' refusal to pay tribute to Tripoli as part of an earlier treaty negotiation and the bashaw's subsequent declaration of war on the United States, kept North Africa in the public eye. The US military's initially lackluster performance and the disastrous capture of the *Philadelphia*, one of the navy's new frigates, with its 307-man crew in 1803 reinforced the general impression that the new nation was unable to deal with foreign threats. However, Stephen Decatur's daredevil action of burning the captured frigate in Tripoli Harbor in 1804 and a remarkable campaign in which the US Navy met up with a rebel band of Tripolitans led by the American William Eaton in Derne (now Derna) turned the tide of the war and public opinion.

A final war with Algiers in 1815 solidified the emerging sense of triumphalism. Prompted by another ship's capture in 1812 but delayed due to the War of 1812, the United States sent its largest naval fleet ever into the Mediterranean. The fleet quickly won a complete victory over Algiers and then went on to Tunis to force that country to reimburse the United States for earlier captures. For good measure, Decatur also sailed into Tripoli, where he freed a number of European captives. The United States forced treaties on all three Barbary powers that ended the tributary system. This turn of events prompted a sense of exceptionalism as the United States, no longer forced to pay tribute or ransoms to North Africa, was now perceived as victor rather than victim. One newspaper writer crowed, "This is a glory which never encircled the brow of a Roman pontiff; nor blazed from an imperial diadem" (Peskin 2009, 202). Coupled with Andrew Jackson's belated victory over the British at the Battle of New Orleans in the same year, this final Barbary war replaced the earlier sense of weakness with a new sense of strength and competence that would mark the new nation's increasing engagement outside of its continental boundaries during the rest of the nineteenth century.

SEE ALSO *Africa; Jefferson, Thomas*

BIBLIOGRAPHY

Allison, Robert J. *The Crescent Obscured: The United States and the Muslim World, 1776–1815.* New York: Oxford University Press, 1995.

Lambert, Frank. *The Barbary Wars: American Independence in the Atlantic World.* New York: Hill and Wang, 2005.

Parker, Richard B. *Uncle Sam in Barbary: A Diplomatic History.* Gainesville: University Press of Florida, 2004.

Peskin, Lawrence. *Captives and Countrymen: Barbary Slavery and the American Public, 1785–1816.* Baltimore, MD: Johns Hopkins University Press, 2009.

Lawrence A. Peskin
Professor of History
Morgan State University

BARNUM, P. T.
1810–1891

Long before Walt Disney and Euro Disney, there was Phineas T. Barnum and his "dime museum" show that traveled across Europe. Renowned for his American Museum in New York City with its exhibits of "human oddities" and mechanical wonders, Barnum played a key role in exporting American popular entertainments overseas and in exposing American audiences to foreign people and places. Widely regarded in antebellum America as its premier showman, Barnum also saw the rest of the world as a theater of operations, embracing especially the idea that America and Americans could and should provide the world with an endless source of amusement (Harris 1973).

Barnum launched his first overseas tour in England in 1844 with his star performer, the 25-inch-tall Charles Stratton (1838–1883), better known to the public as General Tom Thumb. When Edward Everett (1794–1865), the American minister to England, helped arrange an audience with Queen Victoria at Buckingham Palace, Barnum's celebrity status overseas was secured. Over the next three years, Barnum's show traveled around the United Kingdom, Spain, France, Germany, the Netherlands, and Belgium. Barnum and Stratton met heads of state and performed before large audiences. Never one to miss an opportunity to promote his show, Barnum purchased a miniature carriage emblazoned with American frontier hero David Crockett's motto, "Go Forward." Barnum's purchase paid dividends when French king Louis-Philippe added Stratton, riding in his miniature carriage and pulled by four Shetland ponies, to a royal parade in Paris (Cook 2005).

Because Barnum needed to return periodically to the United States to handle domestic business affairs, he organized a commercial management operation in Europe that impressed observers with its attention to publicity. Barnum and his agents also acquired and sold European shows and exhibits, bringing performers, like singer Jenny Lind (1820–1887), the "Swedish Nightingale," back to the United States for a tour that included a brief trip to Cuba. No less important, Barnum made his American Museum a tourist destination for European notables, including an 1860 visit by the prince of Wales, who had met Barnum and Stratton in London. In an interview with American journalist and poet Walt Whitman (1819–1892), Barnum presented himself as an authority on cultural contrasts between America and Europe, declaring: "There, everything is frozen—kings and *things*—formal, but absolutely *frozen*, here it is life. Here it is freedom, and here are *men*" (Saxon 1989, 150).

Exporting American popular culture, not to mention importing foreign dignitaries to take in American popular amusements on their travels to the United States, proved so profitable that once the Civil War ended, Barnum began seeking new ways to expand his business achievements, both at home and abroad, especially after fire destroyed the American Museum in 1865. Between 1851 and 1870, his interest in outdoor entertainment grew, and he dabbled in multiple outdoor wagon (later railroad) shows, including traveling "ethnological congresses" featuring alleged "primitive" people from around the world. His interest in traveling shows drew him into multiple circus partnerships, most famously with James A. Bailey (1847–1906) to organize "The Greatest Show on Earth." In the 1870s and 1880s, Barnum sent versions of his shows to the Middle East, East Asia, and South Asia, as well as to Australia and New Zealand. Always on the lookout for performers and animals to bring back to the United States, Barnum's agents kept him supplied with a steady stream of acts and exhibits, including an enormous elephant, Jumbo, acquired from the London Zoological Gardens in 1881 (Adams 1997).

With its "exotic" animal and human performers, Barnum's shows reflected and shaped views of much of the world along Orientalist lines, making it clear that Americans, no less than Europeans, had the capacity for thinking about the world in ways that would be conducive to imperialism. In an era when the United States was often viewed in Europe as a cultural backwater, Barnum helped redefine American culture in commercial and global terms, suggesting that world markets would be as open to American entertainment culture as they were to wheat and reapers. Often ridiculed for his "humbug" shows both in the United States and overseas, Barnum is better remembered for ushering in the shift from popular culture to mass culture and for advancing a version of

Poster for Barnum & Bailey Circus, 1889. *"The Greatest Show on Earth," a circus partnership formed by P. T. Barnum with James Bailey, featured "exotic" human and animal performers traveling throughout the United States and around the world.* APIC/HULTON ARCHIVE/GETTY IMAGES

imperial cosmopolitanism in both Europe and the United States that prized transnational entertainment as a defining feature of the modern world.

SEE ALSO *Americanization; Buffalo Bill's Wild West*

BIBLIOGRAPHY

Adams, Bluford. *E. Pluribus Barnum: The Great Showman and the Making of U.S. Popular Culture.* Minneapolis: University of Minnesota Press, 1997.

Cook, James W., ed. *The Colossal P. T. Barnum Reader: Nothing Else Like It in the Universe.* Urbana: University of Illinois Press, 2005.

Harris, Neil. *Humbug: The Art of P. T. Barnum.* Chicago: University of Chicago Press, 1973.

Saxon, A. H. *P. T. Barnum: The Legend and the Man.* New York: Columbia University Press, 1989.

Walker, David. "The Humbug in American Religion: Ritual Theories of Nineteenth-Century Spiritualism." *Religion and American Culture: A Journal of Interpretation* 23, 1 (2013): 30–74.

Robert W. Rydell
Professor of History
Montana State University

BASEBALL

Since the mid-nineteenth century, Americans have exported baseball across the globe to promote the national image; make money; expand US influence and power; and "improve" the morals, character, manliness, health, and work ethic of foreign peoples who were considered inferior. Baseball has been exported to the Pacific basin and Latino populations in the Caribbean and Central America, where it has prospered as a culturally and politically significant sport. The spread of baseball globally reveals a great deal about American imperial reach during the nineteenth and twentieth centuries.

The first recipient nation was Canada, where sons of American immigrants were playing an early regional version of baseball known as the Massachusetts game by 1838. It differed from the New York game (modern baseball), codified in 1845, in significant ways: the field was not shaped like a diamond, there was no foul territory, putouts by hitting runners with thrown balls were allowed, and a hundred runs were needed to win. Canadians adopted modern baseball by 1859, preferring it to cricket because it required less skill, was more adaptable to local customs, had frequent shifts between offense and defense, and ended more quickly. By 1914, baseball was Canada's national summer sport.

BASEBALL IN THE PACIFIC

Baseball made its way overseas first to the Kingdom of Hawai'i, where in 1819 Protestant missionaries arrived to convert, educate, and uplift the indigenous population. In the early 1840s, Captain James H. Black introduced the Massachusetts game, which was seen as a moral substitute for traditional pastimes. Modern baseball was first played at the Pinahou School, which educated the children of missionaries and the indigenous elite. Plantation owners taught baseball to their foreign laborers in the late nineteenth century to teach them time and work discipline and teamwork, to provide a positive alternative to other amusements that were regarded as vile, and to Americanize them. By around 1900, racially integrated plantation all-star teams played teams from rival farms, undercutting management's plan to divide workers by ethnicity and leading to greater employee solidarity. Chinese and Japanese teams promoted both acculturation and ethnic pride.

Baseball was brought to China in the 1850s by Chinese students studying in the United States. By 1863, there were baseball clubs in Shanghai. Not only was the game fun, but it also demonstrated Chinese manliness, which fit into the government's interest in westernizing its citizenry. Three Chinese colleges had ball clubs by 1895, and one year later, the Tianjin YMCA introduced baseball. High schools soon took up the game. American-educated Chinese remained the sport's main advocates in the early twentieth century. They believed that physical culture promoted modernization, manliness, and national pride. The revolutionary leader Sun Yat-sen (1866–1925) enjoyed baseball as a student in Hawai'i and envisioned it as a means to infiltrate the establishment and undermine its authority. His United League formed a ball club in Changsha, the capital of Hunan, that secretly promoted revolutionary activities, including the throwing of hand grenades.

Japan was closed to the West until 1853, but with the coming of the Meiji era in 1868, the nation was opened to Western culture. Japan had a long history of individual sports but little familiarity with team sports. Baseball arrived in Japan via American teachers and Japanese engineering and education students returning from the United States. In 1873, Horace E. Wilson (1843–1927), a teacher at Tokyo's Daigaku Minamiko, introduced the game. High school students and fans preferred it over cricket because baseball was more exciting and easier to play, the equipment was more accessible, and games took less time. Railroad engineer Hiraoka Hiroshi (1856–1934), who became a Red Stockings fan when he studied in Boston, was Japan's most important baseball supporter. He organized the Shimbashi Athletic Club, the nation's first private baseball team, in 1878. Hiroshi's connections to railroading fused baseball with the concept of modernity in the minds of fans. The game appealed to a society that sought social experimentation and cultural innovation but still wished to maintain traditional Bushido values. Baseball taught loyalty, courage, order, harmony, perseverance, and self-restraint. The national government supported baseball by approving a primary textbook that included baseball rules.

Baseball in Japan remained segregated. For years, Japanese athletes were barred from playing at the prestigious Yokohama Athletic Club (YAC), where American businessmen and sailors played baseball. Japanese high school students wanted to play the Americans to gain recognition as social equals to Americans and to demonstrate national honor. Finally, in 1896 the YAC hosted a game between students and American sailors. The students won, 29–4, becoming national heroes by defeating the Americans at their own game. The Japanese quickly made baseball their own, and even exported it to occupied Korea in 1905. The imperial government used sports, particularly baseball, along with education to inculcate Japanese culture in Korea and undermine traditional local values.

THE BASEBALL TOURS

The diffusion of baseball overseas was abetted by tours made by American professionals starting in 1874, when manager Harry Wright (1835–1895) led his National Association Boston Red Stockings and the Philadelphia Athletics to his native England to promote baseball there. However, those games got little publicity and had little impact. Then in 1888, Albert G. Spalding (1850–1915), the owner of the Chicago White Stockings, arranged a more ambitious trip to Australia that expanded into a world tour. His players competed against a select group of National Leaguers known as the "All-Americas." Spalding's goals were to spread baseball internationally and expand the market for his sporting goods business. The journey covered 32,000 miles, with 56 games in 13 different countries, drawing 200,000 people. The tour did not win many converts to the game, but the returning players were considered heroes who displayed manly spirit, drive, fair play, and a belief in American superiority, the latter a reflection of the United States' view of itself as a rising world power.

There were subsequent tours to Asia by college teams, and in 1913–1914, the New York Giants and the Chicago White Sox toured the world, including stops in Australia, Japan, and Great Britain. Negro League teams toured Japan in the 1920s and 1930s. The most important tour, which occurred in 1934, was promoted by Japanese newspaper publisher Matsutaro Shoriki, who put together an all-star Japanese team to play eighteen games against Major Leaguers led by Babe Ruth. In total, 500,000 fans attended the games. The Japanese squad became the Yomiuri Tokyo Giants, the nation's first professional team, which was followed by the creation of the professional Japanese Baseball League in 1936.

BASEBALL IN LATIN AMERICA

The first baseball game in Mexico was played in 1877 by American marines, and ten years later railroad workers employed by American firms formed the first Mexican team. The sport initially gained popularity in border towns, where middle-class Mexicans adopted it as a measure of national economic and cultural progress and the privileged status of whiteness. Still, by the early 1900s, the border divided American baseball culture, characterized by Anglo exclusivity and a commitment to the ideology of white superiority, and the emerging Mexican baseball community. This divide was further compounded by the 1910 Mexican Revolution, which curtailed interest in the American sport. However, the sport's popularity returned, and in 1925 the Liga Mexicana de Béisbol was founded.

American sailors brought baseball to Cuba in 1866, but the main impetus was from young Cubans residing in New York City and Key West, Florida, who admired baseball and other elements of American

A US Navy sailors' baseball team poses for a photo, Buenos Aires, Argentina, 1890. *Baseball, a popular American export in Latin America and elsewhere beginning in the mid-nineteenth century, took root to become a significant national sport in many countries.* MARK RUCKER/TRANSCENDENTAL GRAPHICS/GETTY IMAGES SPORT/GETTY IMAGES

culture. In 1868 Nemesio Guilló, who studied at Spring Hill College in Mobile, Alabama, founded the Habana baseball club. Two years later, Havana's Esteban Bellán (1849–1932), who attended New York's Fordham Preparatory School, played for the professional Troy (New York) Haymakers, which from 1871 to 1873 played in the National Association, the first American professional league. Bellán helped arrange the first organized game in Cuba on December 27, 1874, between Habana and Matanzas, and he served as Habana's player/manager in the professional Liga General de Baseball de la Isla de Cuba (1878–1886).

Many of the first Cuban players were middle-class whites. For them, baseball was a symbol of Spanish opposition. Cubans made baseball their own, promoting it as a symbol of progress, democracy, social mobility, cooperation, and national integration, while the colonial government saw baseball as subversive and briefly halted play in 1869 and 1873. By the 1890s, over two hundred amateur teams, including teams composed of Afro-Cubans, competed regularly. Owners of factories, mines, and rural sugar mills sponsored most teams. Those sponsored by American firms often used baseball as a way to control their workforce.

In 1895, during the Cuban War for Independence, Spanish leaders banned the sport again because it was identified with *Cuba libre.* Afterward, baseball became the national sport, even though the occupying Americans used baseball to promote political order and social control. In 1900 Cubans formed the Liga Cubana, which drew players from lower-class backgrounds, and exported baseball to the Dominican Republic and Venezuela.

Major league teams regularly visited Cuba, going back to the Philadelphia Athletics in 1886. Such tours certified the abilities of top Cuban players, especially in 1910 when Cubans defeated the American League champion Detroit Tigers. The next year, the Cincinnati Reds signed "white Castilians" Rafael Almeida (1887–1968) and Armando Marsans (1887–1960). However, no overtly Afro-Cuban entered Major League Baseball (MLB) until Minnie Miñoso (1925–2015) in 1949. For years, Latino ballplayers were "strangers in the land" whose teams made no effort to help them adjust to a lonely life in America, where they encountered negative stereotypes and widespread discrimination and had to contend with a different language, new foods, and alien social habits. MLB took a big step forward in welcoming them when the San Diego Padres hired the first Spanish-speaking manager, Cuban Preston Gómez (1923–2009), in 1969.

GLOBALIZATION AND MAJOR LEAGUE BASEBALL TODAY

Less than 1 percent of MLB players in 1880 were foreign born, and as recently as 1960, just 1 percent were born abroad. However, by 1970, the proportion had risen to 12.3 percent, as MLB sought cheaper sources of labor. The growing presence of Latinos in baseball, and the rapid growth of Latino communities, significantly increased the comfort of Spanish-speaking Major Leaguers. As of 2015, all MLB teams had baseball academies in the impoverished Dominican Republic, where baseball is perceived as one of the few ways to escape poverty. In 2014, 27.4 percent of MLB players came from sixteen foreign countries, including 10.7 percent from the Dominican Republic and 12.7 percent from other Latino nations, often earning multimillion-dollar salaries. There have been sixty-one Japanese players in MLB, starting with pitcher Masanori Murakami (b. 1944) in 1964.

MLB lags behind other pro sports in promoting globalization, having until 2000 left the job to individual teams like the Seattle Mariners. Currently MLB sponsors baseball overseas to license baseball products, lease broadcasting rights, and expand its impact around the globe. As of 2015 men's baseball leagues could be found in at least forty countries, including twenty in Europe, and women's leagues could be found in twenty countries. In 2006 the professional World Baseball Classic was initiated, employing national teams. Japan won the championship in 2006 and 2009, and the Dominican Republic won in 2013. The United States has never medaled. This event supplanted the Baseball World Cup, which ran from 1938 to 2011 and was exclusively amateur until 1998. Cuba won twenty-five titles, the United States four.

SEE ALSO *Globalization; National Basketball Association (NBA); Olympics*

BIBLIOGRAPHY

Gems, Gerald R. *The Athletic Crusade: Sport and American Cultural Imperialism.* Lincoln: University of Nebraska Press, 2006.

Guthrie-Shimizu, Sayuri. *Transpacific Field of Dreams: How Baseball Linked the United States and Japan in Peace and War.* Chapel Hill: University of North Carolina Press, 2012.

Klein, Alan M. *Baseball on the Border: A Tale of Two Laredos.* Princeton, NJ: Princeton University Press, 1997.

Klein, Alan M. *Growing the Game: The Globalization of Major League Baseball.* New Haven, CT: Yale University Press, 2006.

Regalado, Samuel. *Viva Baseball!: Latin Major Leaguers and Their Special Hunger.* 3rd ed. Urbana: University of Illinois Press, 2008.

Riess, Steven A. *Sport in Industrial America, 1850–1920*. 2nd ed. Chichester, UK: Wiley, 2013.

Zeiler, Thomas W. *Ambassadors in Pinstripes: The Spalding World Baseball Tour and the Birth of the American Empire*. Lanham, MD: Rowman & Littlefield, 2006.

Steven A. Riess
Bernard Brommel Research Professor, Emeritus
Northeastern Illinois University

BAY OF PIGS

In April 1961 disaster struck in Cuba. In two short years Fidel Castro's (b. 1926) dictatorial methods, his nationalization program, his clear ties to the Soviet bloc, his support of burgeoning revolutionary movements elsewhere in Latin America, and his constant and intemperate denunciations of US "imperialism" brought Cuban-American relations to the breaking point. Indeed, President Dwight D. Eisenhower (1890–1969) had broken diplomatic relations with Cuba in 1960. As president, John F. Kennedy (1917–1963) inherited a carefully planned counterrevolutionary movement, organized and designed by the Central Intelligence Agency (CIA), to overthrow the Castro regime in the spring of 1961. At the time of Kennedy's inauguration, some two thousand to three thousand rebel Cuban soldiers were training in the United States and Guatemala for an invasion of the island. By threatening to withdraw its support, the CIA, in February, managed to fuse all anti-Castro elements into a single, promising effort.

CIA planners had simply assumed that the Castro regime had lost its appeal. With the Cuban people anticommunist and living under duress, the guerrilla invasion would assuredly ignite a revolution and free the country from communist domination. Kennedy himself had doubted the wisdom of the invasion, but so insistent were his advisers associated with the planning that he granted a grudging consent.

On April 17, 1961, approximately thirteen hundred Cuban assault troops struck the Ciénaga de Zapata swamps of Las Villas Province (Bay of Pigs) on the south coast of Cuba. There was no popular uprising. Kennedy's refusal to back the invasion with US airpower ensured Castro's control of the skies. Cuban regulars quickly demolished the invading forces. The president accepted blame for the fiasco with good grace. The invasion's failure, however, demonstrated both that the Castro regime enjoyed substantial national support and that guerrillas, operating in hostile territory, had had little assurance of victory. Upon reflection, Kennedy and his staff agreed that the decision not to use American forces was the correct one. Washington's growing obsession with Castro received considerable impetus when the Cuban leader, basking in the prestige of victory, began to convert Cuba into a Soviet-style state with a single governing party, a command economy, and stronger economic ties to the Soviet bloc. The Soviets, in exchange, rewarded Castro with shipments of tanks and artillery, along with the necessary advisers and technicians.

For the Kennedy administration, then, Castro's ties to the Kremlin rendered him the ideal agent of international communism in the Western Hemisphere. On November 30, 1961, the president issued a memorandum committing the United States to help the Cuban people overthrow Castro. Thereafter, the administration sent sabotage units made up of Cuban émigrés into Cuba under a covert action plan called Operation Mongoose, with General Edward Lansdale (1908–1987) in command. A planning document of February 20, 1962, set the target dates of the operation. After the necessary internal preparations, guerrilla operations would begin in August and September 1962; during October, an open revolt would establish the new government. Another document dated March 14, 1962, declared that "the U.S. will make maximum use of indigenous resources, internal and external, but recognizes that final success will require decisive U.S. military intervention" (Keller 1989).

Attorney General Robert Kennedy (1925–1968), determined to eliminate Castro after the Bay of Pigs, was Mongoose's driving force. During 1962, the Kennedy administration embarked on a variety of maneuvers to weaken the Castro regime. In January, the foreign ministers of the Organization of American States (OAS) met in Punta del Este, Uruguay, to deal with the issue of Castro's alliance with the Soviet bloc. Secretary of State Dean Rusk (1909–1994) sought diplomatic sanctions against Cuba. Seven Latin American states, including the larger ones, issued a memorandum on January 24, recognizing that the alliance between Castro and the Soviets "excludes the present Government of Cuba from participation in the inter-American system" but opposed sanctions. Rusk now limited his objective to the suspension of Cuba from the Permanent Council of the OAS. In his plea to the delegates on January 25, he declared that the United States had no quarrel with the Cuban people, or even with the principles of the Cuban Revolution, but rather "with the use of Cuba as a 'bridgehead in the Americas' for Communist efforts to destroy free governments in this hemisphere" (Graebner, Burns, and Siracusa 2010, Vol. 1, 261–262). On January 31, the conference adopted the seven-nation memorandum. On the resolution excluding Cuba, the vote was a bare two-thirds majority, fourteen to one (Cuba) with six abstentions. The convention also recognized the right of any country to sever trade relations with Cuba. On

February 2, the United States instituted a complete embargo. During succeeding weeks the administration undermined Cuban trade negotiations with Israel, Jordan, Iran, Greece, and Japan.

Kennedy's misadventure with the Bay of Pigs, which even the CIA's own internal postmortem concluded had exceeded the agency's capabilities and responsibilities, cost American prestige dearly. As well, the president took the failure personally, harboring a sensitivity to the issue for the remainder of his presidency, and it became an important factor in how he viewed his options in the foreign policy crises of the remainder of his time in office. Most important, Kennedy learned from his bitter experience to keep tight control from the Oval Office and remain skeptical of military advice.

SEE ALSO *Castro, Fidel; Central Intelligence Agency (CIA); Cuba; Kennedy, John Fitzgerald*

BIBLIOGRAPHY

Avalon Project, Yale Law School. Resolutions Adopted at the Eighth Meeting of Consultation of Ministers of Foreign Affairs, Punta del Este, Uruguay, January 22–31, 1962. http://avalon.law.yale.edu/20th_century/intam17.asp

Bissell, Richard M. *Reflections of a Cold Warrior: From Yalta to the Bay of Pigs.* New Haven, CT: Yale University Press, 1996.

Graebner, Norman A., Richard Dean Burns, and Joseph M. Siracusa. *America and the Cold War, 1941–1991: A Realist Interpretation.* 2 vols. Santa Barbara, CA: Praeger, 2010.

Higgins, Trumbull. *The Perfect Failure: Kennedy, Eisenhower, and the CIA at the Bay of Pigs.* New York: Norton, 1987.

Keller, Bill. "Papers Show 1962 U.S. Plan against Castro." *New York Times,* January 27, 1989. http://www.nytimes.com/1989/01/27/world/papers-show-1962-us-plan-against-castro.html

Joseph Siracusa
Professor of Human Security and International Diplomacy
Royal Melbourne Institute of Technology

BEAT GENERATION

The Beat generation is a term that refers to a group of writers who met in the late 1940s and early 1950s and who would go on to produce a body of stylistically innovative work that offered alternatives to the staid thinking of the times. The core of the group centered around Jack Kerouac (1922–1969), Allen Ginsberg (1926–1997), and William S. Burroughs (1914–1997), but quickly expanded to include other like-minded writers, such as Gary Snyder (b. 1930), Michael McClure (b. 1932), and Diane di Prima (b. 1934), who were interested in exploring new ways of thinking that were in direct opposition to postwar American culture. For these writers, life in postwar America was too confining. The rise of mass media tended to send a single, dominant message that preached conformity in the face of a perceived Soviet threat to freedom and capitalist values. Beat writers were part of a larger zeitgeist of writers, painters, and musicians that championed the idiosyncratic, personal, and spontaneous as an antidote to such group thinking.

While the Beats were deeply indebted to the American culture they both celebrated and castigated, from the very beginning Beat writers and their works were a global phenomenon. The willingness of the Beats to question authority meant that their work touched a chord with those across the globe disenchanted with the postwar status quo. Beat works like Kerouac's *On the Road* (1957), Ginsberg's *Howl* (1956), and Burroughs's *Naked Lunch* (1959) were quickly translated into various European languages and became part of a globalized counterculture that culminated in the youth protests of 1968. Ginsberg's work was an important element in struggles for drug decriminalization, ecological issues, and homosexual rights, while Burroughs became an icon throughout the world for those interested in technology, addiction, and systems of "control."

Much of the Beats' global influence was the result of their willingness to look beyond US borders for inspiration. The Beats, as well as their texts, journeyed throughout the world. Kerouac, best known for his automobile trips across America, traveled extensively, including several trips to Mexico, where he celebrated what he called the "fellaheen" lifestyle of drug and alcohol use and antimaterialism. Ginsberg, whose time in Mexico also deeply influenced his work, spent time in Paris at the "Beat Hotel" before journeying to India, where he solidified his Buddhist practice with his lover and fellow Beat poet Peter Orlovsky (1933–2010). Ginsberg would continue to travel throughout most of his life, giving readings, promoting his social causes, and always making a point of seeking out other artists, often in the company of other Beats like Lawrence Ferlinghetti (b. 1919). Asia was an important destination for Beat poets interested in Buddhist literary practices, most notably Gary Snyder, Joanne Kyger (b. 1934), and Philip Whalen (1923–2002). Burroughs, perhaps the most peripatetic of all the Beats, left the United States for Mexico and traveled into South America in search of the drug "yage," before settling in Tangier, Morocco, where he was attracted to the freedom to use drugs and indulge in sex with young males. Burroughs would continue on to Paris, where he stayed at the "Beat Hotel" with Ginsberg and Beat poet Gregory Corso (1930–2001), and spent considerable time in London as well. As writers who drew on their personal experiences, it is unsurprising that these international experiences find echo in the work of Beat writers.

Critical of the conformism that swept the United States and indeed the globe in the postwar years, the Beats drew on their international experiences to craft a critique of prevailing thinking that found adherents in both America and abroad. In recent years, with the rise of the Internet and the penetration of American media into all corners of the globe, the Beats and their works have only gained more international exposure and continue to be translated and read worldwide.

SEE ALSO *Expatriate Artists; Lost Generation; New Left*

BIBLIOGRAPHY

Grace, Nancy M., and Jennie Skerl, eds. *The Transnational Beat Generation.* New York: Palgrave Macmillan, 2012.

Mackay, Polina, and Chad Weidner, eds. "The Beat Generation and Europe." Special issue, *Comparative American Studies: An International Journal* 11, 3 (2013).

Mortenson, Erik. "Importing Counterculture: *On the Road*'s Turkish Reception." In *The Transnational Turn in American Studies: Turkey and the United States,* edited by Tanfer Emin Tunc and Bahar Gursel, 119–40. Bern, Switzerland: Peter Lang, 2012.

Myrsiades, Kostas, ed. *The Beat Generation: Critical Essays.* New York: Peter Lang, 2002.

Tietchen, Todd F. *The Cubalogues: Beat Writers in Revolutionary Havana.* Gainesville: University Press of Florida, 2010.

Erik Mortenson
Assistant Professor
Koç University

BERLIN AIRLIFT

On June 24, 1948, officials in the Soviet occupation zone in Germany announced that "technical difficulties" had closed land and water routes between the Western zones and the German capital, Berlin. Within a matter of days, British and American officials hurriedly organized all available aircraft to ferry food and other supplies to Berlin's Western sectors. Before this airlift ended in September 1949, 277,682 flights had delivered 2,325,652 tons of supplies to the city. When the transportation restrictions ended, Berliners celebrated a Western victory and proclaimed, "Hurray, we're still alive!" But for all its power, this image of a besieged city that held out against Soviet threats to starve it into submission misrepresents the complexity of the first open clash of the Cold War.

After the defeat of Nazi Germany in 1945, the victorious Allies divided the country into four occupation zones. Berlin was located more than 100 miles into the Soviet zone, and it was similarly divided into sectors: Soviet, US, British, and French. At the 1945 Potsdam Conference, the four victors anticipated that this political and administrative division would prove temporary and reiterated that Germany should continue to function as a single economic unit.

Conflicts over how to rebuild the German economy, however, proved a critical component in the escalating tensions between the Soviets and the three Western powers. In February 1947, when the Moscow meeting of the Council of Foreign Ministers failed to reach an agreement on a German peace settlement, US secretary of state George Marshall (1880–1959) became convinced that the Soviets had little interest in facilitating a German recovery and rather hoped that the continued economic crisis would push Germans into the arms of the Communists. While Marshall most famously proposed the Marshall Plan to aid European economic recovery and thus bolster opposition to communism, in Germany, that policy was but one part of the increasing separation between economic and political developments in the Western and Soviet zones.

Already in December 1946, the British and Americans had linked the economies of their zones, creating the so-called Bizone. In June 1947, German authorities in the Soviet zone created a German Economic Commission in an effort to centralize their administrative control. By 1948, these institutional structures were looking more and more like separate German states. The decisive political split came with the declaration of separate Eastern and Western currency reforms in June 1948. Although the transportation restrictions that came to constitute the blockade are generally understood to have emerged as a Soviet response to the Western currency reform and plans to create a West German state, Soviet zone restrictions on trade and transport evolved as part of increasingly desperate Soviet efforts to maintain control over political and economic development within their zone of occupation. In fact, the Berlin blockade occurred at a moment of Soviet weakness in Germany, not Soviet strength.

The control measures that comprised the blockade depended on cooperation among a wide range of Soviet zone officials and security agencies in and around Berlin: municipal, rail, and water police, at times in conjunction with Soviet military police. They expanded the system of checkpoints that comprised the "ring around Berlin" and carried out additional raids at rail stations and sector crossing points, and even in subway cars. Despite these efforts, a steady flow of goods continued to make its way into West Berlin.

Berliners were used to improvising survival strategies in a black market economy, and they integrated airlift supplies into the bartering, illicit trade, and foraging trips into the surrounding countryside, with which they had managed since the end of World War II. In August 1948

Berlin residents under Soviet blockade await supplies brought in by American and British planes, 1948–1949. *For all its achievements in delivering needed food and supplies, the airlift was most important for transforming the relationship between the Western Allies and the Germans they had fought against only a few years before.* GAMMA-KEYSTONE/GETTY IMAGES

one Communist official complained to the Soviets that, despite the blockade, fresh vegetables continued to arrive in West Berlin, delivered by truck from the Western zones. That fall, Communist leaders asserted that each day, some 200,000 Berliners headed out of the city into the surrounding Soviet zone to forage for foodstuffs. A US intelligence report described such a level of continued trade between West Berlin businesses and the Soviet zone that it asked, "Is Berlin blockaded?" As late as February 1949, one American political adviser in Berlin noted that the Western-sector economy continued to be sustained by ongoing trade with the Soviet zone.

In fact, rather than the Soviet blockade, it was the Western powers' currency reform in March 1949 that ended these economic connections between West Berlin and the Soviet zone. Until that point, West Berliners could use both East and West marks to pay for many goods and services. But the second currency reform decreed the West mark the sole currency in the city's Western sectors. West Berlin politicians, especially the Social Democratic mayor Ernst Reuter (1889–1953), had been pushing for this reform as a means to help signal the Western powers' ongoing commitment to the city.

For Berliners, the steady hum of planes taking and off and landing as part of the airlift was audible evidence of that dedication. For all of its logistical achievements, the airlift was most important for transforming the relationship between the Western Allies and the Germans they had fought only a few years before. Pilots, who had once dropped bombs on Berlin, now risked their lives to bring supplies, even to drop chocolate-laden parachutes to German children waiting at the end of the runways at Berlin's Tempelhof Airfield. Thirty-nine British personnel died during the airlift, along with thirty-two Americans and thirteen Germans.

The diplomatic agreement that ended the blockade guaranteed the continued existence of West Berlin, but it also marked the Western acceptance of a Stalinist state in the Eastern half of Germany. Even this ambiguous

Western victory depended on much more than the airlift, but concealing Berliners and their actions behind a totalizing narrative of Soviet blockade and Anglo-American airlift helps to hide the unintentional collusion with which the East and West maintained the Cold War's hegemonic power for the next forty years.

SEE ALSO *Cold War; Domino Theory; Iron Curtain; Marshall Plan; Potsdam Conference (1945); Truman, Harry S.*

BIBLIOGRAPHY

Cherny, Andrei. *The Candy Bombers: The Untold Story of the Berlin Airlift and America's Finest Hour.* New York: Putnam, 2008.

Harrington, Daniel F. *Berlin on the Brink: The Blockade, the Airlift, and the Early Cold War.* Lexington: University Press of Kentucky, 2012.

Koop, Volker. *Kein Kampf um Berlin? Deutsche Politik zur Zeit der Berlin-Blockade 1948/1949.* Bonn, Germany: Bouvier Verlag, 1998.

Shlaim, Avi. *The United States and the Berlin Blockade, 1948–1949: A Study in Crisis Decision-Making.* Berkeley: University of California Press, 1983.

Steege, Paul. *Black Market, Cold War: Everyday Life in Berlin, 1946–1949.* New York: Cambridge University Press, 2007.

Stivers, William. "The Incomplete Blockade: Soviet Zone Supply of West Berlin, 1948–49." *Diplomatic History* 21, 4 (1997): 569–602.

Trotnow, Helmut, and Bernd von Kostka, eds. *Die Berliner Luftbrücke: Ereignis und Erinnerung.* Berlin: Frank and Timme, 2010.

Tusa, Ann, and John Tusa. *The Berlin Airlift.* New York: Athenaeum, 1988.

Paul Steege
Associate Professor, Department of History
Villanova University

BERLIN CONFERENCE (1884–1885)

The Berlin Conference, held in the winter of 1884 to 1885, inaugurated what the British newspaper the *Times* called the "scramble for Africa." Convened by Otto von Bismarck (1815–1898), chancellor of the recently unified Germany, dignitaries representing the United States, Belgium, Spain, Denmark, France, Italy, the United Kingdom, Austria-Hungary, the Netherlands, Russia, Portugal, the Ottoman Empire, and the United Kingdoms of Norway and Sweden gathered to reach an international agreement regarding the free navigation of the Congo and Niger Rivers and the abolition of slave trading in Africa. The General Act of the Berlin Conference, signed on February 26, 1885, recognized the legitimacy of King Leopold II (1835–1909) of Belgium's Congo Free State and established procedures for future European claims to protectorates and territories in Africa. To these ends, the act dictated that railroads, roads, and "lateral canals" connected to the rivers be zones of free commerce and navigation, outlining the boundaries of the Congo basin and forbidding commercial monopolies in the region. The act also required the signatories to protect "natives," travelers, and missionaries, as well as guarantee "liberty of conscience" and "religious toleration" for these persons.

The General Act, in many ways, recognized what had been occurring in Africa since the early nineteenth century—increased European exploration of and nonindigenous claims to land after the abolition of the transatlantic slave trade (sometimes referred to as "the African trade"). The United States abolished the trade in 1807, but subsequently facilitated the founding of settler colonies in present-day Liberia to "repatriate" free-born and freed African Americans. In 1847, Liberia declared its independence; however, the United States did not diplomatically recognize the republic until 1862. From 1847 to 1862, the United States believed that it had officially ended its direct involvement in Africa. In 1876 the United States intervened in a clash between the African American settlers (the so-called Americo-Liberians) in Maryland County and the indigenous Grebo peoples. The Grebo objected to the settlers' attempts to purchase their land or claim it by right of treaty and took up arms against them. Fueled by rumors and evidence that Europeans were arming the Grebo, the US government sent the USS *Alaska* to Monrovia, Liberia, to suppress Grebo resistance and broker peace in the Liberian-Grebo War. By the time of US intervention in this conflict, European involvement in Africa had intensified.

Events such as Britain's punitive expedition against Abyssinia (1867–1868) and King Leopold II's claim to the Congo Free State in 1876 harbingered the "scramble for Africa." In 1876, supporters of King Leopold established the African International Association (Association Internationale Africaine) to facilitate the "civilization" of Central Africa through exploration, missionary activity, the establishment of trading posts, and the abolition of the internal slave trade. By 1877, there existed an American Branch of the International Association for the Civilization of Central Africa under the presidency of John H. B. Latrobe (1803–1891)—a lawyer who had been active in the Liberian colonization project. Delegates from this group attended the annual meetings of the African International Association alongside members from "National Committees" representing Belgium, Switzerland, the Netherlands, France, Austria, Germany, and Spain. With the help of

British-born and self-fashioned American explorer Henry Morton Stanley's (1841–1904) Anglo-American Expedition of 1878, the African International Association and its affiliates laid the groundwork for the official founding of the Congo Free State after the Berlin Conference.

John Kasson (1822–1910), diplomat and US envoy to Germany, and Henry S. Sanford (1823–1891), former minister to Germany, represented President Chester A. Arthur (1829–1886) at the conference. (Sanford's membership in the American Branch of the International Association for the Civilization of Central Africa, coupled with his ambassadorial experience, credentialed him as a representative.) Although Kasson and Sanford signed the General Act, the US House and Senate debated whether the two men and the president possessed constitutional powers to bind the United States to that agreement. Congress determined that they did not, and the United States never deposited a ratification of the act with the Berlin Foreign Office by the April 1886 deadline. Nevertheless, President Grover Cleveland (1837–1908) recognized the sovereignty of the Congo Free State in September 1885.

European dignitaries noted the presence of the United States at the Berlin Conference as a clear sign that the nation had entered a new phase in its foreign policy. Despite its adherence to the Monroe Doctrine, America had engaged one of the most pressing world issues at the time, the "African question"—Africa under European control and the status of Africans subject to imperial rule. American citizens recognized that the United States had sanctioned or at least opened the door for continued involvement in African affairs.

SEE ALSO *Africa; Colonialism; Exceptionalism*

BIBLIOGRAPHY

Abingbade, Harrison Ola. "The Settler-African Conflicts: The Case of the Maryland Colonists and the Grebo, 1840–1900." *Journal of Negro History* 66, 2 (1981): 93–109.

Förster, Stig, Wolfgang J. Mommsen, and Ronald Robinson, eds. *Bismarck, Europe, and Africa: The Berlin Africa Conference, 1884–1885, and the Onset of Partition.* Oxford: Oxford University Press, 1988.

"General Act of the Conference of Berlin concerning the Congo." *American Journal of International Law* 3, 1 (1909): 7–25.

Hertslet, Edward, R. W. Brant, and H. L. Sherwood, eds. *The Map of Africa by Treaty,* Vol. 2. London: Cass, 1967. Originally published by HMSO in 1909.

Pakenham, Thomas. *The Scramble for Africa: The White Man's Conquest of the Dark Continent from 1876 to 1912.* New York: Avon, 1992.

Jeannette Eileen Jones
Associate Professor of History and Ethnic Studies
University of Nebraska–Lincoln

BERLIN WALL

The Berlin Wall was a 96-mile-long barrier that ringed democratic West Berlin, closing it off from East Berlin and the surrounding Communist state of the German Democratic Republic (GDR). The GDR began construction on August 13, 1961, constantly improving the 26-mile-long portion of the wall that bisected Berlin until the 1980s, with its 11-foot-tall concrete slabs, 116 integrated guard towers that overlooked a no-man's-land of anti-vehicle trenches, motion sensors, razor wire, and land mines (Large 2000, 452). The wall would stand as a symbol of the Cold War until November 9, 1989, when the border between East and West Germany opened once again.

BACKGROUND TO THE WALL'S CONSTRUCTION

Instead of keeping people out, the Berlin Wall was intended to keep in GDR citizens. Between 1949 and 1961, around 2.8 million East Germans and East Berliners defected for Western countries through West Berlin (Kempe 2011, xix). Crucially, half of those who left were under the age of twenty-five, amounting to a crippling drain of professionals, skilled workers, and intellectuals from GDR society. In order to prevent the potential for social and economic collapse, General Secretary Walter Ulbricht (1893–1973) ordered the border closed on August 12, 1961, claiming it necessary for national security (Harrison 2003, 205). When Berliners awoke the next day, they found the western half of the city cut off from the GDR.

At the core of the issue was the failure of the four powers—the United States, Great Britain, France, and the Soviet Union—to find a permanent political solution for Germany after World War II (Zubok and Pleshakov 1996, 195). The temporary plan was to divide Germany into four zones and Berlin into four sectors. Due to the way in which the map was drawn, Berlin fell 110 miles inside the Soviet Union's zone. Suspicion and competition between the erstwhile allies led to the first crisis in Berlin, when Soviet leader Joseph Stalin (1879–1953) ordered the western boroughs of the city blockaded on June 24, 1948, in a bid to stop the West from creating a democratic republic from their occupation zones. The allies mounted a successful airlift that supplied their sectors, prompting Stalin to relent on May 12, 1949 (Harrington 2012, 274). The temporary divisions of Germany became permanent on May 23, 1949, when the Federal Republic of Germany (FRG) was founded. Moscow responded on October 7, 1949, with the FRG's counterpart, the German Democratic Republic. East Berlin became the GDR's declared capital, while West Berlin was affiliated with but not part of the FRG. The city's unique status meant it was

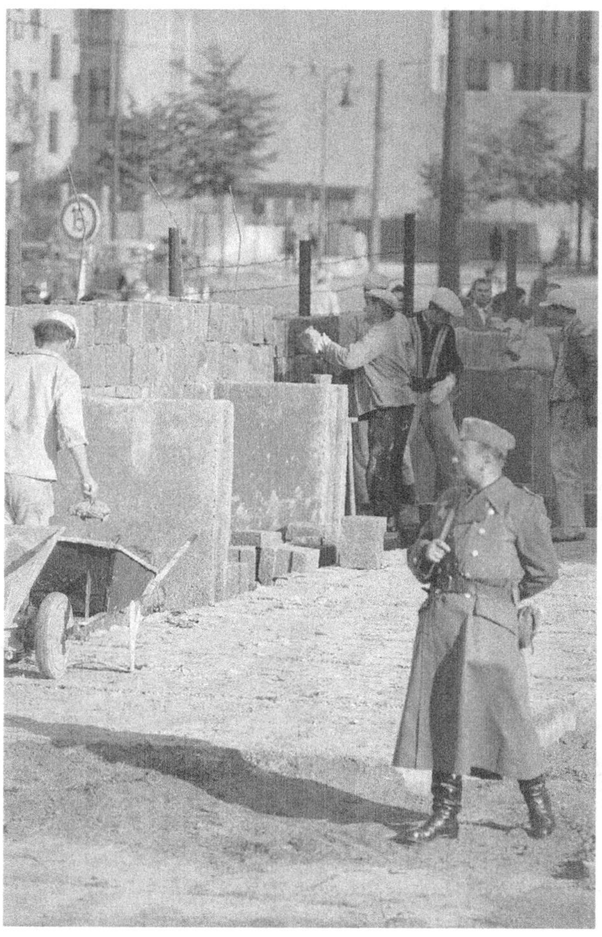

Construction of the Berlin Wall, 1961. *The Berlin Wall, erected in 1961 to close off democratic West Berlin from East Berlin and the surrounding Communist state of the German Democratic Republic, stood until 1989 as a symbol of Communist repression during the Cold War.* PATRICE HABANS/PARIS MATCH/ GETTY IMAGES

the Western allies' most vulnerable position in the Cold War; for disaffected citizens in the GDR, it was an escape hatch out of an otherwise closed bloc.

THE BERLIN CRISIS

By 1958, it was clear to the East German leadership and Soviet premier Nikita Khrushchev (1894–1971) that something had to be done to stem the tide of defectors and the FRG's rising military power (Trachtenberg 1999, 253). In a November 10 speech and a November 28 note, Khrushchev demanded that the Western powers leave Berlin and threatened to conclude a separate peace treaty with East Germany unless the West recognized the GDR. The culmination of the three-year crisis was the building of the Berlin Wall, which caught US officials off guard, as they had expected the Soviets to interfere with Western access to Berlin (Smyser 2010, 104).

Since 1945, US officials had been granted entry into East Berlin without presenting identification. By fall 1961, East German border police began stopping American-flagged vehicles. Washington recognized the four-power status of the city, not GDR sovereignty, which prompted officials to argue that the situation was an infringement on Allied rights of access. John F. Kennedy (1917–1963) and his special representative in Berlin, Lucius D. Clay (1897–1978), sought to prove that East German sovereignty was a fiction by provoking a tense situation in the city, thereby forcing the Soviet authorities to take control of all Communist operations in Berlin (Trauschweizer 2006, 212). Moreover, the United States could bring the Soviet Union to the negotiating table to settle open questions while buoying West Berlin morale. Clay forced the test of will on October 27, when he ordered ten M-48 tanks to the Friedrichstrasse border crossing, known as Checkpoint Charlie. The Soviets responded with ten tanks of their own, and a sixteen-hour showdown ensued. After Clay had induced the Red Army to react, officials in Washington opened up back-channel communications with Moscow and negotiated a Soviet withdrawal. Ultimately, one of the tensest moments of the Cold War yielded the results the United States sought: proof that the GDR had to answer to the Soviet Union and confirmation that the city's four-power status remained, at least in part.

A SYMBOL OF THE COLD WAR

The wall inspired some of the US presidency's most iconic Cold War moments. On June 26, 1963, Kennedy gave his famous "Ich bin ein Berliner" (I am a Berliner) speech on the steps of the Schöneberg city hall to 450,000 Berliners, where he juxtaposed communism and democracy, remarking that "we never had to put a wall up to keep our people in" (Daum 2008, 142–143). By the 1980s, the Berlin Wall had lost none of its former symbolism. On June 12, 1987, Ronald Reagan (1911—2004) used the Brandenburg Gate as the backdrop for his challenge to Soviet leader Mikhail Gorbachev (b. 1931) to "tear down this wall" if he truly sought peace and prosperity (Mann 2009, 199). Lesser known are two other presidential visits, Richard Nixon's (1913–1994) in 1969 and Jimmy Carter's (b. 1924) in 1978, both intended as symbolic gestures of American support for West Berlin and the FRG.

THE 1989 OPENING

Since the Berlin Wall was such an enduring symbol of the Cold War, its opening on November 9, 1989,

President John F. Kennedy on a platform overlooking the Berlin Wall, 1963. *On June 26, Kennedy gave his famous "Ich bin ein Berliner" speech to 450,000 Berliners, where he juxtaposed communism and democracy, remarking that "we never had to put a wall up to keep our people in."* BETTMANN/CORBIS

seemed to signal the coming end of the contest between the superpowers. In summer 1989, a series of liberalization policies within the Eastern bloc changed the political landscape, making it possible for East Germans to escape to the West by way of Hungary and Czechoslovakia (Tusa 1997, 366–368). By autumn, East German protestors in Leipzig and Berlin demanded that the GDR regime enact its own reforms. Officials sought to control the situation and appease protestors by updating travel regulations, though changes were mostly cosmetic.

On November 9, Günter Schabowski (b. 1929), the Communist Party boss in East Berlin, offhandedly announced at the end of an hour-long news conference that travel to West German territory was now possible (Sarotte 2014, 127). Though GDR leaders had not intended such a literal statement, television reports quickly spread the news and thousands of East Germans converged at checkpoints, where they told confused guards that the border was now open. A stunned world watched as East Berliners celebrated and hammered away at the wall's concrete slabs. Demolition began in summer 1990 and was completed in 1992, a year after the Cold War ended. In its thirty-year lifetime, the Berlin Wall had been a symbol of the Iron Curtain, of Germany's division, and of the animosity and distrust between East and West, as well as a monument to the 136 people who died in its shadow.

SEE ALSO *Berlin Airlift; Cold War; Domino Theory; Kennedy, John Fitzgerald; Reagan, Ronald Wilson*

BIBLIOGRAPHY

Daum, Andreas W. *Kennedy in Berlin.* Translated by Dona Geyer. Cambridge: Cambridge University Press, 2008.

Harrington, Daniel F. *Berlin on the Brink: The Blockade, the Airlift, and the Early Cold War.* Lexington: University Press of Kentucky, 2012.

Harrison, Hope M. *Driving the Soviets Up the Wall: Soviet–East German Relations, 1953–1961.* Princeton, NJ: Princeton University Press, 2003.

Kempe, Frederick. *Berlin 1961: Kennedy, Khrushchev, and the Most Dangerous Place on Earth.* New York: Putnam, 2011.

Large, David Clay. *Berlin.* New York: Basic Books, 2000.

Mann, James. *The Rebellion of Ronald Reagan: A History of the End of the Cold War.* New York: Viking Penguin, 2009.

Sarotte, Mary Elise. *The Collapse: The Accidental Opening of the Berlin Wall.* New York: Basic Books, 2014.

Smyser, W. R. *Kennedy and the Berlin Wall.* Lanham, MD: Rowman and Littlefield, 2010.

Trachtenberg, Marc. *A Constructed Peace: The Making of the European Settlement, 1945–1963.* Princeton, NJ: Princeton University Press, 1999.

Trauschweizer, Ingo. "Tanks at Checkpoint Charlie: Lucius Clay and the Berlin Crisis, 1961–62." *Cold War History* 6, 2 (2006): 205–228.

Tusa, Ann. *The Last Division: A History of Berlin, 1945–1989.* Reading, MA: Addison-Wesley, 1997.

Zubok, Vladislav, and Constantine Pleshakov. *Inside the Kremlin's Cold War, from Stalin to Khrushchev.* Cambridge, MA: Harvard University Press, 1996.

Seth Givens
PhD Candidate
Ohio University

BIKINI ATOLL

After the nuclear attacks on Hiroshima and Nagasaki, Japan, in 1945, the United States was intent on exploring the attributes of this revolutionary new weapon and decided to begin conducting a series of atomic tests. On January 15, 1946, President Harry Truman (1884–1972) declared that the United States was the sole trustee of all Pacific islands captured from the Japanese during World War II, including the Marshall Islands. That summer, the United States began to plan Operation Crossroads, the first series of nuclear tests to be conducted at Bikini Atoll, which consists of twenty-three separate islands in the northern Marshall Islands. To conduct the tests the United States relocated the population of 167 Bikinians to other islands and atolls in the Marshall Islands, an exile from which they have never returned. Although the United States obtained permission from Bikini's King Juda to remove the Bikinians from their home, in reality he had no alternative but to comply. The army staged a filmed event in which King Juda "granted permission" to the United States to use Bikini for nuclear tests (eight takes were necessary). The American commodore told the Bikinians that the goal of the tests was to turn the new weapon into a force for peace and that they were for the "good of mankind." At first most Bikinians were moved to Rongerik Atoll, then Kwajalein Atoll, and then the islands of Kili and Jaluit. Starvation and deprivation plagued the Bikinians at these sites, and eventually most settled on the capital atoll of Majuro, where Bikini City Hall stands today.

From 1946 to 1958 the United States conducted twenty-three nuclear tests at Bikini, including numerous hydrogen bomb tests (a total of sixty-seven weapons would be detonated in the Marshall Islands). Initially the tests were conducted to explore the capacities of this revolutionary new weapon, but over time the rationale for ongoing tests would shift. During the Crossroads tests in 1946 the United States detonated the first underwater nuclear weapon, explored radioactive decontamination techniques, and measured the effects of detonating the weapon at various altitudes. Eventually the site was a primary location for developing components of thermonuclear weapons and eventually testing these weapons; the Marshall Islands remains the only location where the United States has tested hydrogen bombs, which are thousands of times more powerful than atomic bombs.

The most devastating nuclear test ever conducted at Bikini Atoll was the Castle Bravo test, which took place on March 1, 1954. This was the first test of a deliverable thermonuclear bomb. The Bravo bomb was twice as powerful as its designers had anticipated, and it created a vast radioactive fallout cloud that extended for hundreds of miles downwind. Radiation levels on Rongelap Atoll, 95 miles away, were so intense that two days later the United States forcibly evacuated all its residents. All suffered from radiation sickness and many later died from their exposure. The Bravo fallout cloud also blanketed hundreds of fishing boats. One, the *Daigo Fukuryū Maru* (the *Lucky Dragon No. 5*), located over 80 miles away, was so contaminated that all of its crew became sick and one crew member died six months later. The Bravo test put the word *fallout* into common usage.

Unlike the Rongelapese, the Bikinians were spared the devastations of suffering from radiation sickness because they were forcibly removed before the nuclear testing began at Bikini. However, their community suffered terribly as a result of this testing and their forced migration. The displaced Bikinians continued to live for generations as guests on the atolls of others, without land to call their own. They suffered from starvation and poverty on the atolls and islands where they were relocated because of the inferiority of these locations compared to Bikini. The inability to live according to traditional customs resulted in dependence on processed, packaged foods brought in from abroad and small payment subsidies for their lost land, eroding the independence and self-reliance of the community. Several generations grew up never knowing their home islands, and their identity is maintained through the sustained efforts of community elders rather than through the organic processes of daily living.

Bikini Atoll was so heavily contaminated with radionuclides (such as cesium 137) from the tests that it was deemed permanently uninhabitable. In 1977 the US government formally ruled that Bikini was too radioactive for human habitation because radiation readings were still too high for long-term exposure to be risked. In 2010 the United Nations Educational, Scientific and Cultural Organization (UNESCO) officially designated Bikini Atoll as a World Heritage Site.

SEE ALSO *Cold War; Nuclear Weapons*

BIBLIOGRAPHY

Barker, Holly M. *Bravo for the Marshallese: Regaining Control in a Post-nuclear, Post-colonial World.* Belmont, CA: Wadsworth/ Thomson, 2004.

Kiste, Robert C. *The Bikinians: A Study in Forced Migration.* Menlo Park, CA: Cummings, 1974.

Ōishi, Matashichi. *The Day the Sun Rose in the West: Bikini, the Lucky Dragon, and I.* Honolulu: University of Hawai'i Press, 2011.

Weisgall, Jonathan M. *Operation Crossroads: The Atomic Tests at Bikini Atoll.* Annapolis, MD: Naval Institute Press, 1994.

Robert Jacobs
Associate Professor
Hiroshima Peace Institute, Hiroshima City University

BIN LADEN, OSAMA

SEE *War on Terror.*

BLACK ATLANTIC

Since Europeans' earliest contacts with West African societies in the fifteenth century, Africans and the African diaspora have played important roles in shaping historical trajectories, transatlantic cultures, and intellectual thought in the Atlantic world.

In the seventeenth century and beyond, certain regions of the New World were ostensibly African. For example, in seventeenth-century Cartagena de Indias (in present-day Colombia)—one of the largest slave ports in the Spanish Americas—links between large urban, free black populations and powerful runaway-slave maroon societies in the hinterlands demonstrate the important legacy of African kingship and power structures in the New World. Similarly, highly sought-after free and enslaved African healers in Cartagena and the Caribbean mixed indigenous American, European, and African curing techniques, resulting in the development of important healing practices in the Atlantic world. The emergence of African Catholicism through the veneration of black saints in religious brotherhoods across the Iberian world mirrors late seventeenth-century Catholicism in the Kongo, where religious movements arose to venerate black saints and claim Jesus as Kongolese. In the south, a Lusophone (Portuguese-speaking) Black Atlantic also emerged. Generations of Eurafrican trading families circulated throughout the Lusophone world between Luanda, Lisbon, and Bahia in the seventeenth century, and later also between Benguela, Ouidah, and Rio. African traders operated on both sides of the Atlantic, and many Brazilians and former slaves established residency in Portuguese ports in Africa. Some elite Africans sent their children to be educated in Brazil and hired out their slaves to work in Brazil. Such intense communication between these spaces meant that reverberations from changing African power structures were acutely felt in Brazil.

Similarly, seventeenth- and eighteenth-century plantation societies in the Americas were arguably as African as they were English, French, Dutch, Spanish, or Portuguese. Even in extremely harsh living conditions, enslaved men and women often deployed practices of measuring time, religious observance, ethnic identities, kinship, healing, and death rituals that originated in varied African and Eurafrican societies. For example, naming practices in seventeenth-century Anglo and Dutch plantations demonstrate how enslaved men and women drew on syncretic Central African cultural heritages that mixed Catholicism and European languages with local African cultures.

Amid interimperial and revolutionary wars, African diaspora fought for Spanish, English, Portuguese, French, and Dutch militias, and were active agents in the circulation and development of ideas and culture across imperial and national boundaries. After the British wrested control of Jamaica from Spain in 1655, enslaved, free, and maroon black populations maintained knowledge of Spanish imperial legal cultures, which they deployed as important tools for negotiating privileges under Anglo rulers. During the American Revolutionary War (1775–1783), many enslaved men and women escaped plantation slavery in Anglo colonies in order to seek Spanish royal protection or to fight for British loyalists, demonstrating significant fluency in legal structures across different imperial systems.

African diaspora also shaped the late eighteenth- and early nineteenth-century British abolitionist movement—a campaign that achieved the passing of the Slave Trade Act of 1807 in Britain—by writing compelling autobiographical slave narratives and developing an interpretation of Christianity that incorporated biting attacks on slavery. African diaspora who settled in Sierra Leone in the late eighteenth century—under British protection—represented the reification of national African linguistic and ethnic identities in all of West Africa. And the Haitian Revolution (1789–1804) demonstrated the redeployment of African kingship and French republicanism all over the Caribbean, in turn shaping nationhood across the Americas.

In the nineteenth century and beyond, massive migrations of African diaspora within the United States and across political spheres in the Atlantic world resulted in important transnational circulations in intellectual and political thought and cultural expression. For example, it is impossible to conceive of the Jazz Age or the Harlem Renaissance in the early twentieth century as a US phenomenon occurring in a vacuum separate from large-scale migrations across the Caribbean region. People on the move sparked intense cultural exchanges and the emergence of new forms of music, art, and intellectual thought across the different national and linguistic boundaries, including those of the United States. As such, these cultural phenomena represent amalgamations and innovations of varied African diasporic cultures across the entangled and multilingual Caribbean region of the late nineteenth and early twentieth centuries. Similarly, African American diaspora who settled in Africa drew on the survival and reinvention of varied forms of Yoruba culture across Anglo, French, Spanish, and Portuguese regions of the Americas to spearhead the development of pan-Yoruba identities in West Africa.

SEE ALSO *Act Prohibiting Importation of Slaves (1807); Africa Squadron; Antislavery; Atlantic Slave Trade; Back-to-Africa Movement; Emancipation Day; Haitian Revolution; Slave Regimes*

BIBLIOGRAPHY

Brooks, George E. *Eurafricans in Western Africa: Commerce, Social Status, Gender, and Religious Observance.* Athens: Ohio University Press, 2003.

Brown, Vincent. *The Reapers' Garden: Death and Power in the World of Atlantic Slavery.* Cambridge, MA: Harvard University Press, 2008.

Candido, Mariana P. *An African Slaving Port and the Atlantic World: Benguela and Its Hinterland.* New York: Cambridge University Press, 2013.

Cañizares-Esguerra, Jorge, Matt D. Childs, and James Sidbury, eds. *The Black Urban Atlantic in the Age of the Slave Trade.* Philadelphia: University of Pennsylvania Press, 2013.

Carretta, Vincent, and Philip Gould, eds. *"Genius in Bondage": Literature of the Early Black Atlantic.* Lawrence: University Press of Kentucky, 2001.

Ferreira, Roquinaldo. *Cross-Cultural Exchange in the Atlantic World: Angola and Brazil during the Era of the Slave Trade.* New York: Cambridge University Press, 2012.

Gómez, Pablo F. "The Circulation of Bodily Knowledge in the Seventeenth-Century Black Spanish Caribbean." *Social History of Medicine* 26, 3 (2013): 383–402.

Heywood, Linda M., and John K. Thornton. *Central Africans, Atlantic Creoles, and the Foundation of the Americas, 1585–1660.* New York: Cambridge University Press, 2007.

Landers, Jane. *Atlantic Creoles in the Age of Revolutions.* Cambridge, MA: Harvard University Press, 2010.

Matori, J. Lorand. *Black Atlantic Religion: Tradition, Transnationalism, and Matriarchy in the Afro-Brazilian Candomblé.* Princeton, NJ: Princeton University Press, 2005.

Palmié, Stephen. *The Cooking of History: How Not to Study Afro-Cuban Religion.* Chicago: University of Chicago Press, 2013.

Putnam, Lara. *Radical Moves: Caribbean Migrants and the Politics of Race in the Jazz Age.* Chapel Hill: University of North Carolina Press, 2013.

Sweet, James F. *Domingos Álvares, African Healing, and the Intellectual History of the Atlantic World.* Chapel Hill: University of North Carolina Press, 2011.

Chloe Ireton
Doctoral Candidate
The University of Texas at Austin

BLACK POWER MOVEMENT

The Black Power movement (BPM) was an important dimension of the black American struggle for equal rights and social justice through the mid-twentieth century. The BPM encompassed more militant and radical forms of cultural and political activism than did the more heralded and generally older generation of activists involved with the civil rights movement, which mainly advocated for federal recognition of legal citizenship rights. The BPM arose especially in American urban areas from the mid-1960s through the early 1970s but drew much of its inspiration from black American affinities for global anticolonialism during the early Cold War era.

Many contemporary observers have misinterpreted the BPM as simply a reaction to the slow pace of social change in the wake of the 1964 and 1965 civil rights and voting rights legislation passed by the Lyndon Johnson (1908–1973) administration and to the urban rebellions that occurred over the same period in many US cities around issues of poverty. Black Power activists, however, offered some of the most trenchant and far-reaching critiques of US "democracy" in their time and were among the first groups of Americans to vehemently oppose Western-led military interventions in Cuba, the Congo, and Vietnam. Indeed, many Black Power leaders, such as Huey P. Newton (1942–1989) and Bobby Seale (b. 1936), who founded the Black Panther Party for Self-Defense (later the Black Panther Party), sustained valuable economic and global critiques of US power and empire in the world as they spoke about police brutality and racial discrimination at home. Proponents of Black Power at the local level also established independent schools, community centers, and soup kitchens to provide alternative infrastructures and organizations for black American communities seeking social justice through education, cultural production, self-policing, and civic advocacy.

The term *Black Power* in the American context is frequently ascribed to a 1966 speech by Student Nonviolent Coordinating Committee (SNCC) chair Stokely Carmichael (later Kwame Turé, 1941–1998). The coining of this term certainly aligns with the shifting contours of black American struggles for rights and justice through the latter half of that decade toward greater demands for democracy, increased militancy, and political representation. As an itinerant minister of the nationalist Nation of Islam, Malcolm X (1925–1965) was a forerunner of the late 1960s forms of Black Power. Malcolm's pilgrimage to Mecca in 1964 led him to an increasingly international perspective that advocated for Third World liberation alongside calls for social revolution in the United States, which echoed past and future calls for global black political solidarities.

Other early forerunners of Black Power in America were African American icons like the singer and activist Paul Robeson (1898–1976) and the radical intellectual W. E. B. Du Bois (1868–1963). Each worked diligently from the 1930s through the 1950s with such organizations as the Council on African Affairs, which promoted Pan-African independence against ongoing forms of European colonialism. As members of the radical black Left, Du Bois and Robeson also worked against restrictions in the early years of the Cold War that sometimes required uncritical allegiance to American interests at home and abroad. As civil rights leader Martin Luther King Jr. (1929–1968) said shortly before his assassination (and after his simultaneously expressed opposition to the Vietnam War and advocacy for economic racial justice), Du Bois "exemplified Black power in achievement and he organized Black Power in action. It was not an abstract slogan to him" (King 1968, 110). Black Power as a concept clearly crossed generations and modes of African American political thought and practice.

A frequent symbol of the early BPM was the black panther, first used by the Lowndes County Freedom Organization in Alabama—an offshoot of SNCC when it was directed by Carmichael/Turé. The panther symbol was also used by Newton and Seale when, as community college students in 1966, they founded the Black Panther Party for Self-Defense (BPP) in Oakland, California, and by the many BPP chapters that soon spread across the country from Los Angeles, to Chicago, to New York and whose memberships reached tens of thousands nationwide by the end of the decade. Amid growing unrest and repression in the United States, BPP Central Committee member Eldridge Cleaver (1935–1998) moved to Algeria in 1969, where he and other BPP delegates participated in a Pan-African Cultural Festival. From there, the BPP was able to open an Afro-American Information Center and its international section from afar while connecting to nonaligned Third World activists and struggles.

An important dimension of the BPM through the 1960s was its complex appeal to African American working classes, ghetto dwellers, and prisoners. This appeal was often cultural in form, expressing itself through the adornment of black leather clothing and the open wielding of automatic weapons. Such optics offered an important, if mainly symbolic, form of resistance to white supremacy and American power in the world. While actual instances of violent resistance were rare, the optics of armed self-defense undertaken by the Black Panthers in particular—such as when they stormed the California state legislature in May 1967—helped channel both the very real and psychological frustrations of black American communities with persistent racial inequalities in American urban life and culture. As such, while critics of the BPM have suggested that the movement was simply a form of "reverse discrimination," most proponents of Black Power were in fact affirming the sanctity of black life and culture and the right to collective self-definition in a period when the American state (from local police departments to the Federal Bureau of Investigation [FBI] and the Central Intelligence Agency) did much to elide such affirmations. Such elisions were highlighted by the use of excessive force against urban rebellions, as racial segregation and associated forms of poverty increased without any redress for those most afflicted.

Moreover, unlike their predecessors in the civil rights establishment, Black Power activists consistently offered fundamental critiques of America's racial history, as well as its current roles in global military "conflicts," such as the Vietnam War. During the late 1960s and early 1970s especially, the BPP (and indeed much of the BPM) was subjected to a widespread FBI-led Counterintelligence Program that included targeted surveillance, intimidations, infiltrations, and assassinations and that ultimately succeeded in outlawing, exiling, or discrediting many of the movement's main leaders, such as Carmichael/Turé, Newton, and Angela Davis (b. 1944). Such forms of repression did much to dissolve the momentum that the BPM had gained from the insurgent 1960s.

SEE ALSO *Ali, Muhammad; Malcolm X; Pan-Africanism; Powell, Adam Clayton, Jr.; Student Nonviolent Coordinating Committee (SNCC)*

BIBLIOGRAPHY

Bloom, Joshua, and Waldo E. Martin Jr. *Black against Empire: The History and Politics of the Black Panther Party.* Berkeley: University of California Press, 2013.

Joseph, Peniel E. *Waiting 'til the Midnight Hour: A Narrative History of Black Power in America.* New York: Holt, 2006.

King, Martin Luther, Jr. "Honoring Dr. Du Bois." *Freedomways* 8, 2 (1968): 104–111.

Singh, Nikhil Pal. *Black Is a Country: Race and the Unfinished Struggle for Democracy.* Cambridge, MA: Harvard University Press, 2004.

Van Deburg, William L. *New Day in Babylon: The Black Power Movement and American Culture, 1965–1975.* Chicago: University of Chicago Press, 1992.

Ian Rocksborough-Smith
Visiting Assistant Professor of History
Saint Francis Xavier University

BLACK POWER SALUTE

SEE *John Carlos and Tommie Smith, Mexico City Olympics (John Dominis, 1968).*

BLY, NELLIE
1864–1922

Newspaper reporter Elizabeth Jane Cochrane Seaman, known to the world by the pen name Nellie Bly, became an American icon in 1890 when she circled the globe in seventy-two days, six hours, eleven minutes, and fourteen seconds. Bly was on assignment for the *New York World,* Joseph Pulitzer's brash mass-circulation newspaper, which promoted the venture as an American triumph made possible by modern technology and one young woman's extraordinary verve. Traveling alone and with a single gripsack so small she could barely stuff her jar of cold cream into it, Bly made the whole world seem smaller—and safer—than many Americans had ever imagined it could be. Because her access to cables was limited, she could not file many reports along the way, so the *World* sparked interest in her journey with a guessing contest. Entrants had to estimate, down to the second, how long it would take Bly to get home. The grand prize was a trip to Europe. By the time the paper stopped accepting entries, it had received 927,433 guesses. During the final leg of her trip, a dash from San Francisco to New Jersey, crowds greeted Bly at every railway station. The book she wrote about her journey sold out in six months, and advertisers adapted the image of Bly in her traveling outfit (a checked wool coat and an English cap) to sell dresses, caps, gloves, dolls, schoolbags, pens, and traveler's checks. Her exploits inspired a board game, "Round the World with Nellie Bly," featuring a colorful spiral of seventy-two illustrated squares with notes like "Suez Canal/Lose Next Throw" and "Yokohama/Go Ahead 1 Day." At the board's center was an oversized island of Manhattan, where a flag waved from the *New York World* building, a visual emblem of the nation's and the newspaper's conviction that they were, in fact, the center of the globe.

More Americans traveled abroad in the late nineteenth century than ever before, and many worked as foreign correspondents, particularly in Europe. The amenities of new ocean liners and the growth of railroads made far-flung

An advertisement for pills featuring the world-traveling Nellie Bly, circa 1890. *Nellie Bly, on assignment for the* New York World, *gained fame in 1890 when, traveling alone, she circled the globe in seventy-two days. Advertisers seized on the image of the audacious Bly to sell a variety of products.* POPPERFOTO/GETTY IMAGES

travel easier. For women journalists, writing from abroad also offered escape from the constraints of women's-page work and opportunities, denied at home, to cover politics and culture. Bly had already done this when she left the *Pittsburgh Dispatch* in 1886 and, with her mother, went to Mexico, where she spent several months reporting on local customs and politics. But her globe-trotting trip was a different endeavor entirely. With the *World*'s publicity machine pumping out daily, breathless reports about her progress, Bly injected a populist energy into the genteel tradition of writing from abroad. Other travelers had toured the world before. Bly was not even the first woman to do it alone: Austrian traveler Ida Pfeiffer (1797–1858) made the trip by herself twice, once in 1848 and again in 1851 (Scatamacchia 2003). But Bly's solo trip resonated in unique ways with readers in the United States, which was on the brink of emerging as a world power and already engaging in imperialist conflicts with Cubans, Filipinos, Hawaiians, and others. As white newspaperwomen like Bly mapped the world and, implicitly, argued for the United States' right to new territories, they embraced American expansionism (Fahs 2011).

Bly focused more on hurtling through space than experiencing the countries she passed through. In this, she embraced the same ethic as the fictional hero whose time she was trying to beat: British gentleman Phileas Fogg, the protagonist of Jules Verne's best seller *Around the World in Eighty Days* (1873). Verne's wry narrator explains that the single-minded Fogg, "being one of those Englishmen who are wont to see foreign countries through the eyes of their domestics," never wanted to sight see (26). Bly sailed from Hoboken, New Jersey, without a maid, but she shared Fogg's priority: speed. Observed the *World* correspondent who reported on Bly's arrival in Southampton: "If she attempts any description at all of what she saw in England, it will be much the same as a man describing Broadway if he were shot through a pneumatic tube from the Western Union Building to the Twenty-Third Street Uptown Office" (Greaves 1889). Bly's travelogue often focused more on railroad cars, steamship cabins, and her fellow passengers than on the people or customs of the countries through which she barreled. It showcased her daring, determination, and willingness to laugh at herself, even as it revealed her relative lack of interest in cultures not her own, her unshakable conviction that Americans already had the best of everything, and her racist views, particularly of the Chinese and South Asians.

SEE ALSO *Africa; Asia; Atlantic Ocean; Europe; Gender; Pacific Ocean*

BIBLIOGRAPHY

Bly, Nellie. *Around the World in Seventy-Two Days and Other Writings,* edited by Jean Marie Lutes. New York: Penguin, 2014.

Chaplin, Joyce. *Round about the Earth: Circumnavigation from Magellan to Orbit.* New York: Simon and Schuster, 2012.

Fahs, Alice. *Out on Assignment: Newspaper Women and the Making of Modern Public Space.* Chapel Hill: University of North Carolina Press, 2011.

Goodman, Matthew. *Eighty Days: Nellie Bly and Elizabeth Bisland's History-Making Race around the World.* New York: Ballantine, 2013.

Greaves, Tracey. "Nellie Bly's Trip." *World,* December 8, 1889.

Lutes, Jean Marie. "Journalism, Modernity, and the Globe-Trotting Girl Reporter." In *Transatlantic Print Culture, 1880–1940: Emerging Media, Emerging Modernisms,* edited by Ann Ardis and Patrick Collier, 167–181. Basingstoke, UK: Palgrave Macmillan, 2008.

Roggenkamp, Karen. *Narrating the News: New Journalism and Literary Genre in Late Nineteenth-Century American Newspapers and Fiction.* Kent, OH: Kent State University Press, 2005.

Ruddick, Nicholas. "Nellie Bly, Jules Verne, and the World on the Threshold of the American Age." *Canadian Review of American Studies* 29, 1 (1999): 1–12.

Scatamaccchia, Cristina. "From the Grand Tour to the *Tour du Monde*: Nellie Bly and the Metamorphosis of Women's Travels at the End of the Nineteenth Century." In *America and the Mediterranean,* edited by Massimo Bacigalupo and Pierangelo Castagneto, 507–513. Torino, Italy: Otto Editore, 2003.

Verne, Jules. *Around the World in Eighty Days.* Mineola, NY: Dover, 2015.

Jean Marie Lutes
Associate Professor, Department of English
Villanova University

BOEING COMPANY

On July 15, 1916, along the shores of Lake Washington in Seattle, a small aircraft manufacturing company was formed. William E. Boeing (1881–1956) and US Navy commander George Conrad Westervelt (1879–1956) set up Pacific Aero Products to build their first aircraft: a wood-and-fabric B&W biplane. From this modest beginning rose one of the world's largest aerospace enterprises: the Boeing Company.

EARLY YEARS

William Boeing was the son of a wealthy timber magnate whose family owned vast holdings of iron ore in the famous Mesabi Range in northern Minnesota. After leaving Yale before his graduation, Boeing looked to the Northwest to open his own lumber business. When he became interested in aviation after flying in a Martin biplane, he diversified his investments, borrowed from the bank he controlled, and started building aircraft for the US military during World War I (1914–1918).

Seattle was an ideal location for the manufacture of aircraft because, at that time, airplanes were built primarily of high-grade spruce, which abounds in the Pacific Northwest.

The immediate postwar years were difficult, to the point where the Boeing Airplane Company, as it was renamed in 1917, was forced to build furniture to make ends meet. After moving to the "Red Barn" on the Duwamish River, south of Seattle, the company eventually received contracts from the US Army Air Service to build Thomas Morse fighters and rebuild de Havilland DH-4 light bombers. Boeing remanufactured the DH-4s with metal-tube fuselages, not wood. From the 1920s onward, despite the company's proximity to vast spruce supplies, Boeing became a world leader in the construction of all-metal aircraft.

INNOVATIONS IN AIRCRAFT DESIGN

Boeing quickly developed a reputation for designing innovative yet reliable military aircraft. Throughout the 1920s, Boeing was a principal supplier of rugged biplane fighters to the US Navy, particularly the F4B series of wood-and-metal aircraft. Through William Boeing's connections with the US Navy, he became acquainted with Frederick Rentschler (1887–1956), the president of the Pratt & Whitney Company, which produced powerful air-cooled radial engines. Boeing and Rentschler pooled their resources in late 1928 and established the United Aircraft and Transport Corporation, the first large aviation holding company, which soon controlled 50 percent of the nation's aviation assets, including several airlines that they would merge into United Air Lines in 1931. This holding company put Boeing in a strong financial position, which would help the company weather the Great Depression. It exists today as United Technologies Corporation.

Boeing was in the forefront of the technological revolution that occurred between 1927 and 1933. With the advent of anodization of aluminum alloys and the invention of Alclad aluminum alloys, metal aircraft that were highly resistant to corrosion could be made. Other advances, such as internally braced, cantilevered wings and monocoque, single-shell fuselage construction, set the stage for the emergence of a new generation of high-performance civil and military aircraft. Boeing took the lead in this revolution, producing the aircraft that featured these innovations and more, including the B-9 bomber (1931), which was as fast as a contemporary fighter, and the Boeing 247 (1933), the world's first modern airliner.

The Boeing 247, built at the request of the US Post Office to carry mail and passengers more efficiently, was 60 percent faster than the Ford Tri-Motors it replaced. The Boeing Company's shortsighted decision to sell all of them to United Air Lines before offering the aircraft to competing airlines forced TWA to turn to Douglas, which quickly built an even better airliner, the DC-2 and later the DC-3, which outperformed the Boeing 247. Boeing attempted to counter this mistake by building the world's first pressurized airliner, the Boeing 307 Stratoliner, but it entered service in 1940 just as World War II (1939–1945) caused the market for civil aircraft to evaporate.

BOEING BOMBERS

Following the airmail crisis of 1934, which led to the breakup of the aviation holding companies and the retirement of William Boeing from his firm, the Boeing Airplane Company was left in a precarious financial position. The company gambled all of its resources to answer a request by the US Army Air Corps to build a long-range strategic bomber. The result was the graceful Model 299, which first flew in 1935. It immediately set numerous speed and performance records and was the clear choice of the air corps until a fatal crash in October gave the award to a lesser Douglas design. Undaunted, the air corps prevailed upon the army to purchase a test squadron of these remarkable bombers, now designated the B-17 Flying Fortress.

The B-17 made Boeing famous. More than twelve thousand were built during World War II, and the B-17 earned a reputation for strength and survivability as waves of these aircraft took the war deep into the heart of Nazi Germany, destroying factories and cities and crippling Axis war production. Shortly thereafter, using the latest technologies available, Boeing created the most advanced bomber in the world, the B-29 Superfortress, which entered service in 1944. Pressurized, capable of carrying 10,000 pounds (more than 4,500 kilograms) of bombs over 3,000 miles (4,828 kilometers) and protected by computer-controlled gun turrets, Superfortresses leveled Japan and in August 1945 delivered the two atomic bombs that ended the war.

Boeing continued its success in building bombers after the war when the company combined two captured German technologies—the swept-wing and the axial-flow jet engine—into the revolutionary B-47 Stratojet, which played a significant role in protecting America during the Cold War. A larger bomber based on this aircraft, the B-52 Stratofortress, became the iconic symbol of American strategic airpower. First flown in 1952 as a delivery vehicle for nuclear weapons, the B-52 gained a reputation for its immense lifting capability and range. It excelled at the delivery of conventional bombs during the Vietnam conflict and into the twenty-first century in several Middle Eastern wars.

BOEING AIRLINERS

Today Boeing is known for its airliners, but that was not the case until 1958, when the revolutionary Boeing 707 entered service. In the early 1950s Boeing once again gambled the company's resources on building a jet-powered aerial tanker to refuel the B-47s and B-52s on long-range missions. At the time, the Boeing KC-97, which was based on the popular but poorly selling 377 Stratocruiser airliner and used the engines and wings of the B-29, was the standard tanker. Propeller-driven and significantly slower than jet-powered bombers, the KC-97 labored on until Boeing convinced the US Air Force to purchase its 367-80, known as the Dash 80. This gamble paid off handsomely when the air force bought 829 KC-135s and C-135s. In October 1958, Boeing would go on to sell a widened version, known as the Boeing 707, to Pan American World Airways and other airlines.

In October 1958, the Boeing 707 introduced the world to the Jet Age. Flying at almost 600 miles (965 kilometers) per hour—the same speed airliners fly today—the 707 dramatically decreased long-range travel time while lowering operating costs and increasing productivity. This, in turn, allowed for cheaper airfares, which created a massive expansion of air travel worldwide. US airlines, such as Pan Am and TWA, used the 707 to expand jet travel and American influence around the world. With the United States still riding the post–World War II wave of prosperity, US tourists and businesspeople traveled throughout the world on the wings of the 707. The 707 sealed the fate of ocean liners and railroads for long-distance passenger travel. As the 1960s and 1970s advanced, new Boeings filled short- and medium-range markets, particularly the beautiful three-engine 727 and the squat 737. The Boeing 737 was a slow seller until the deregulation of the US airline industry in 1978 made it the ideal choice for a new generation of airlines that were free to compete on fares. Fitted with the latest turbofan engines, a new series of 737 came to dominate the national and international narrow-bodied, medium-range market. Today, the latest 737 can fly transcontinentally at unprecedented levels of efficiency. It is the best-selling jet airliner of all time.

This success was made possible by Boeing's unceasing efforts to improve by incorporating the latest technologies. Another Boeing revolution occurred in 1970, when the massive 747 entered service. Two-and-a-half times larger than the 707, the so-called jumbo jet introduced wide-bodied, twin-aisle comfort and efficiency to the world's airlines. The airliner of choice for decades for international air travel, the 747, with its distinctive humped fuselage, was a clear symbol of America's presence throughout the globe. Air Force One, the airplane that carries the president of the United States, is a Boeing 747.

This advanced aircraft was sold throughout the free world and, because of its range and massive payload, helped expand global commerce. Because it could carry more than four hundred passengers over immense ranges, the 747 drastically lowered seat-mile costs, further lowering fares to the point where just about anyone could afford to fly, democratizing air travel. Designed initially as a cargo plane, the 747 could carry a huge payload and do so effectively because of a new type of engine, the high bypass turbofan, which produced unheard of levels of power and efficiency. That engine type is now the dominant engine on today's airliners.

Subsequent Boeing airliner designs have sold well for decades. The efficient narrow-bodied Boeing 757 was well suited to low-volume, long-range routes, while the twin-engine 767 came to dominate transatlantic travel in the 1990s.

In 1997, following the end of the Cold War and the marked decline in defense spending, Boeing gained control over North American and McDonnell Douglas, forming one of the largest aerospace corporations in the world. For decades the leader in civil aircraft production, Boeing faced strong competition from its European competitor, Airbus. Boeing rose to the challenge with numerous improvements to existing designs, including the 777 twin-engine wide-body that carries the same payload as the first generation of 747s. The Boeing 777 is now the airliner of choice for many of the world's longer, heavier-traveled routes.

More recently, Boeing led the world in another revolution, this time in construction. As Boeing did in the 1920s when it embraced all-metal construction, the company gambled again to produce the world's first all-composite airliner, the Boeing 787. Despite teething pains that delayed introduction, the 787 is delivering on its promise of 20 percent greater efficiency than the aircraft it replaces. The Boeing 787 is already a best seller that is bringing direct service between numerous new city pairs, obviating the need for lengthy delays through major hub airports. Boeing continues to be a world leader in aerospace as it enters its second century.

SEE ALSO *Globalization; Pan American World Airways*

BIBLIOGRAPHY

Bowers, Peter M. *Boeing Aircraft since 1916.* London: Putnam Aeronautical, 1989.

Mansfield, Harold. *Vision: A Saga of the Sky.* New York: Duell, Sloane, and Pearce, 1956.

Rodgers, Eugene. *Flying High: The Story of Boeing and the Rise of the Jetliner Industry.* New York: Atlantic Monthly Press, 1996.

Serling, Robert J. *Legend and Legacy: The Story of Boeing and Its People.* New York: St. Martin's Press, 1991.

Sutter, Joe, with Jay Spenser. *747: Creating the World's First Jumbo Jet and Other Adventures from a Life in Aviation*. New York: HarperCollins for Smithsonian Books, 2006.

van der Linden, F. Robert. *The Boeing 247: The First Modern Airliner*. Seattle: University of Washington Press, 1991.

F. Robert van der Linden
Curator of Air Transportation
Smithsonian National Air and Space Museum

BOLÍVAR, SIMÓN

1783–1830

Simón Bolívar was a central figure in the Latin American wars of independence (1810–1825), particularly in the northern theater from Venezuela to Peru. Born into one of Venezuela's richest families, his early life was both privileged and tragic. His father died before he was three; his mother before he was ten. He was married at eighteen and a widower at nineteen. An early admirer of the British political and social tradition, he blamed Spanish rule for Spanish America's backwardness. Napoleon Bonaparte's usurpation of the Spanish throne in 1808 triggered a guerrilla war in Spain and civil war in Spanish America in 1810 between those favoring restoration of the Spanish throne and more radical elements favoring independence.

Bolívar became an early proponent of Venezuelan independence and fought to defend the first Venezuelan republic, which was declared in July 1811 and composed of seven sovereign states. In April 1812, in the midst of a savage civil war, Francisco de Miranda (1750–1816) became general of the armies and virtual dictator. Bolívar, an early admirer of Miranda, served under his command. When the republic fell in August 1812, Miranda was arrested but Bolívar was spared and went into exile in Cartagena. In the Cartagena Manifesto (December 15, 1812), Bolívar blamed the republic's failure on its tolerance and its federalist structure, a US model that he believed ill-suited Spanish American realities.

Bolívar determined to liberate Venezuela with support from the Congress of New Granada (modern Colombia), and began his "Admirable Campaign" of liberation. To create a sense of Venezuelan national identity yet give opponents of the republic an opportunity to change sides, he issued a "War to the Death" decree, which pardoned European Spaniards and Canary Islanders who joined the fight for independence and forgave American Spaniards (Creoles) *regardless* of their loyalties, but sentenced to death other European Spaniards, even if they were neutral. In the restored Venezuelan republic, established in August 1813, Bolívar ruled as virtual dictator, justifying his actions on the grounds that royalist forces had mobilized slave and mulatto troops against the republic. When the second republic fell in July 1814 Bolívar was driven into exile, first to Cartagena and then to Kingston, Jamaica.

This time Bolívar decided to make his war a continental struggle. Faced with a fierce Spanish counterrevolution after the final defeat of Napoleon in 1815, Bolívar made a compelling argument for Spanish American independence in the Jamaica Letter (September 15, 1815) and appealed for aid from European liberals, the United States, and especially the British government. When it was not forthcoming, Haitian president Alexandre Pétion (1770–1818) offered support after Bolívar pledged to wage war not only for independence but to end slavery. With the help of black and mulatto troops and foreign mercenaries, Bolívar commenced a successful campaign of liberation from Venezuela to Peru.

In the process, he had also become a popular, albeit controversial, figure in the United States. Henry Clay (1777–1852) made a passionate plea on behalf of the Spanish American cause in a famous address to Congress in March 1818. At the time, Secretary of State John Quincy Adams (1767–1848) was mired in negotiations with the Spanish over Florida, complicated by Andrew Jackson's (1767–1845) raid into Florida, as well as Spanish fears that the United States might recognize the republics established by the patriot forces in Spanish America. Bolívar's name figured prominently in this discussion.

Adams was understandably cautious about recognition for political reasons, but he also shared a growing sentiment among some US political leaders that Bolívar's use of black and mulatto troops and his antislavery pledge set a dangerous precedent. In a famous address at Angostura (present-day Ciudad Bolívar, Venezuela) in February 1819, Bolívar called for the mixing of Venezuela's diverse peoples in the name of unity. The coincidence of such rhetoric at the time of Missouri's application for statehood as a slave state and debates over the role of free blacks in US society made Bolívar suspect not only among white Venezuelans but among some US leaders.

Actually, Bolívar's views on the volatile issue of race were nuanced. Although Bolívar believed the common people of the new republics could, through guidance and education, be prepared for the role of citizen, he often referred to the dangers of rule by people of color. Many North Americans, even those who opposed slavery, were unsettled by the Bolivarian example of waging war with the help of slaves and free blacks who then took a place in the new republic. These critics were less mindful of Bolívar's qualities as a statesman, particularly his role in the creation of Colombia, the union of Venezuela, New

Granada (modern Colombia and Panama), and Quito (modern Ecuador) from 1819 to 1822.

In the aftermath of a revolt within the Spanish military in 1820 and a six-month truce in the war, British and US leaders began to acknowledge the inevitability of Spanish American independence. In June 1822, the United States became the first country to recognize Colombian independence. From 1822 to the decisive battle at Ayachucho, Peru, in December 1824, Bolívar's army and that of the Argentine José de San Martín (1778–1850) brought an end to Spanish rule in South America. Bolívar was now an acclaimed figure in the United States and in Europe. Nevertheless, in 1825, US officials were concerned that Bolívar might try to liberate Spanish Cuba, rousing apprehension that the British would gain influence as a protector of the island. US officials also feared that he intended to give the British a privileged role as a de facto protector of former Spanish colonies in the creation of a defensive confederation at the Congress of Panama in 1826. His dictatorial rule during his last years in power was further cause for concern. His move toward dictatorship was the result of pressure from his followers to keep Colombia from splitting into three separate countries. His postwar behavior somewhat sullied his recognition as the "South American George Washington."

Bolívar resigned the presidency in April 1830 and agreed to go into exile, perhaps in England or in the Caribbean. His body wasted by tuberculosis, he died in December 1830 in Santa Marta, Colombia. In time, the man remembered by some for his cynical remark that "those whose serve a revolution plow the sea" would become a cult figure whose life and legacy continue to inspire and divide Venezuelans and Latin Americans.

SEE ALSO *South America*

BIBLIOGRAPHY

Bushnell, David, and Lester D. Langley, eds. *Simón Bolívar: Essays on the Life and Legacy of the Liberator.* Lanham, MD: Rowman and Littlefield, 2008.

Chasteen, John Charles. *Americanos: Latin America's Struggle for Independence.* New York: Oxford University Press, 2008.

Langley, Lester D. *The Americas in the Age of Revolution, 1750–1850.* New Haven, CT: Yale University Press, 1996.

Langley, Lester D. *Simón Bolívar: Venezuelan Rebel, American Revolutionary.* Lanham, MD: Rowman and Littlefield, 2009.

Lynch, John. *Simón Bolívar: A Life.* New Haven, CT: Yale University Press, 2006.

Lester D. Langley
Professor Emeritus of History
University of Georgia

BOLSHEVISM

Bolshevism, derived from the Russian word for "majority," originally referred to V. I. Lenin's (1870–1924) majority faction in the Russian Social Democratic Workers Party. It became the prominent Marxist movement throughout the world, but it was torn in the 1920s between the followers of Joseph Stalin (1879–1953) and those of Leon Trotsky (1879–1940) and split in the 1950s by rivalries between the Soviet Union, China, and Yugoslavia. In 1952 the Moscow branch of the movement dropped the word *Bolshevik* and renamed itself the Communist Party of the Soviet Union.

BOLSHEVISM IN THE UNITED STATES

After seizing power in the Russian Revolution (1917), the Bolsheviks came into conflict with the United States by withdrawing Russia from its World War I alliance against Germany and for advocating worldwide revolution against the capitalist order. Along with other members of the Western alliance, the United States intervened militarily in the Russian Civil War on the side of anticommunists. With the Bolshevik victory in 1920, the United States withdrew its forces and refused to recognize the Union of Soviet Socialist Republics (USSR) until 1933.

The success of the Bolshevik Revolution, along with a wave of terrorist bombings, stirred anxiety in the United States over radical activists. The news media branded them all as "Reds," regardless of their ideology. During the first Red scare (1918–1920), which brought Federal Bureau of Investigation director J. Edgar Hoover (1895–1972) to prominence, the United States jailed political activists and deported foreign-born militants. Although xenophobia and political conservatism played a part in the Red scare, anti-Bolsheviks were correct in assessing the Communist Party USA (CPUSA) as a front for the Soviet Union. Like all Bolshevik parties at that time, American Communists took their ideology and strategy from Moscow under the direction of Comintern, the Russian Bolshevik Party's international arm. Although Lenin's successor, Stalin, spoke of building "socialism in one nation," the Marxist dream of a global communist utopia was never abandoned even if it took second place to the security of the Russian-dominated Soviet Union.

The CPUSA shifted positions according to Stalin's calculations. During the 1930s the party participated in "popular front" coalitions with New Deal supporters and liberal reformers around such issues as civil rights for African Americans. When Stalin signed a non-aggression pact (the 1939 Treaty of Non-aggression between Germany and the Union of Soviet Socialist Republics) with Germany, the CPUSA ceased protests against pro-Nazi groups and advocated US neutrality. When the United States entered World War II against Germany alongside the Soviet Union, the CPUSA supported the war effort.

Bolshevism was politically negligible in the United States until the Great Depression triggered widespread unemployment and disillusionment. During the 1930s, CPUSA membership swelled to 100,000. Communists infiltrated unions and progressive organizations, and many concealed their membership under instructions from Comintern. Prominent cultural figures such as Theodore Dreiser (1871–1945) and John Dos Passos (1896–1970) lent their support. However, the shock of Stalin's non-aggression pact with Adolf Hitler caused a precipitous decline from which the CPUSA never recovered. Even if many leftists remained in denial over the extent of Stalinist brutality and clung to the hope that the Soviet Union represented a better future, the CPUSA was increasingly discredited. Although mass support eluded them, the party's disciplined cadres exerted influence over Henry Wallace's (1888–1965) Progressive Party presidential campaign (1948), and some unions affiliated with the Congress of Industrial Organizations (CIO), until Walter Reuther (1907–1970) secured control of the CIO (1946–1949) and expelled Communists from leadership.

COLD WAR DEVELOPMENTS

With the onset of the Cold War, Bolshevism became America's foreign and domestic enemy. The second Red scare (1947–1957), a concerted effort to drive real or suspected Bolsheviks from public life, involved blacklists by private companies, loyalty oaths for government and other employees, congressional and state investigations, and espionage trials. Communists were imprisoned under the Alien Registration Act, which criminalized membership in organizations advocating the overthrow of the government. The Red scare mixed paranoia and political opportunism with genuine national security concerns. In a case that became an international cause célèbre, CPUSA members Julius (1918–1953) and Ethel (1915–1953) Rosenberg were executed in 1953 for passing atomic secrets to the Soviets. Soviet archives opened after the Cold War dispelled doubt over Julius Rosenberg's guilt.

As a member of the House Un-American Activities Committee (HUAC), Representative Richard M. Nixon (1913–1994) became a nationally recognized political figure after leading an investigation resulting in the espionage-related conviction in 1950 of diplomat Alger Hiss (1904–1996). Soviet archives later confirmed Hiss's guilt. One of the most publicized actions against domestic Bolshevism was HUAC's investigation of Communist influence in Hollywood. HUAC subpoenaed movie industry figures. "Uncooperative" directors and screenwriters such as Dalton Trumbo (1905–1976) and Edward Dmytryk (1908–1999) were imprisoned and forced to work anonymously. Others went into exile. Senator Joe McCarthy (1908–1957) seized the spotlight by conducting a reckless campaign against government employees suspected of being covert Communists. After his televised Senate hearing on the US Army in 1954 triggered public dismay over his tactics, *McCarthyism* entered the dictionary as a synonym for *witch hunt.*

Communism became anathema in American life, yet the excesses of McCarthyism eventually brought sympathy for its victims and awareness of the danger of outlawing dangerous ideas in a free society. During the 1960s, New Left activists attempted to rehabilitate the CPUSA's reputation, but if Marxism became a safe topic in academia, few New Leftists submitted to party discipline. Black activist Angela Davis (b. 1944), who ran for vice president on the CPUSA ticket, was among the few 1960s radicals to join the party.

During the Cold War, the United States defined itself as the worldwide opponent of Bolshevism and defender of democracy and capitalism against the Soviet bloc, which by 1950 encompassed Eastern Europe and mainland China, and supported "wars of national liberation" against colonial regimes. US diplomat George Kennan (1904–2005) proposed a strategy of "containment" (1946) to halt the spread of communism without the cost of directly attacking the Soviet bloc. Kennan's strategy was adopted by President Harry Truman (1884–1972) and continued as the pillar of American foreign policy during the Eisenhower, Kennedy, Johnson, and Nixon administrations. Containment began with aid to anticommunists in Greece's civil war (1946–1949) and the Berlin Airlift (1948), and resulted in the North Atlantic Treaty Organization (1949) and other military alliances, a chain of US military bases encircling the communist world, and aid to undemocratic but anticommunist regimes in Asia, Africa, and Latin America. The Korean and Vietnam Wars were fought in the name of containment, as was US support to anticommunist mujahideen in Afghanistan (1979–1989).

While the US military record during the Cold War was mixed, America decisively defeated Bolshevism on the battlefields of economics and culture. Communist state planning could not compete with postwar America's regulated capitalism, which promoted the unprecedented expansion of the middle class and stimulated the war-shattered economies of Western Europe and Japan through the Marshall Plan. Communist regimes lagged behind the West in producing consumer goods. Although the USSR challenged US technological prowess by orbiting the first artificial satellite and amassing a powerful nuclear arsenal, it was unable to satisfy the material desires of its citizens. While the Soviet bloc was admired for preserving classic art forms, America took the lead in shaping an increasingly globalized popular culture through Hollywood filmmaking and a music industry that gave the world blues, jazz, rock, funk, and rap. The United States was able to present an appealing and prosperous image to the world in contrast to the dour subsistence of Bolshevik-dominated nations.

SEE ALSO *Empire, US; Exceptionalism; Internationalism; Isolationism; League of Nations; Paris Peace Conference (1919); Roosevelt, Theodore; Spanish-American War; Wilson, Woodrow; World War I*

BIBLIOGRAPHY

Bell, Daniel. *Marxian Socialism in the United States*. Ithaca, NY: Cornell University Press, 1996.

Lewy, Guenter. *The Cause That Failed: Communism in American Political Life*. New York: Oxford University Press, 1990.

Starobin, Joseph R. *American Communism in Crisis, 1943–1957*. Cambridge, MA: Harvard University Press, 1972.

Glen Jeansonne
Professor of History
University of Wisconsin–Milwaukee

David Luhrssen
Editor
Shepherd Express

BORDERLANDS

Borderlands are spaces at the edges of empires and nations in which heightened levels of cultural mixing occur and where central states exert weak control. In North America, interimperial European rivalries, European empires rubbing up against Indian homelands, and the expansion of Indian empires formed the first borderlands. Whether it was the Great Lakes region, the Lower Missouri Valley, or the Rio Grande basin, the French, British, and Spanish empires faced off against one another and against Indians who had lived in these regions prior to the arrival of Europeans. More recently, scholars have begun to recognize the presence of Indian empires that formed their own distinct Indian borderlands.

NORTH AMERICAN BORDERLANDS

The first borderlands and the ones most associated with the term in North America were formed when Spanish missionaries, soldiers, and settlers invaded the region that is today the US Southwest in the late sixteenth and early seventeenth centuries. The Spanish confronted various Indian groups, including Pueblos, Apaches, and Comanches, on their northern frontier, but they also traded with and battled French and British settlers. Although most historians have tended to view Indians as bit players in the borderlands drama, Pekka Hämäläinen (2008) has shown how the Comanche empire's domination from the southern Great Plains to New Mexico in the mid-eighteenth to mid-nineteenth centuries was central to the history of this borderlands region. By the early to mid-nineteenth century, the borderlands between European empires became bordered lands between nation-states—Mexico to the south, the United States in the middle, and Canada to the north. Some scholars (Adelman and Aron 1999) argue that this transformation closed off the possibilities and cultural exchange that existed in the borderlands, while others (Truett and Young 2004) maintain that the cultural mixing and trading relationships continued into the national period and up to today.

In the seventeenth and early nineteenth centuries, several important borderlands regions formed where various European settlers converged with Indian settlements on the frontier. In the Great Lakes region, British, French, Native American, and African American settlers formed a Creole multiethnic community. Spurred by the fur trade in the seventeenth century, Europeans traded with each other and Indians. Through periods of conflict, warfare, and collaboration, this area remained a borderlands where Indians played various European rivals and the Anglo-Americans against one another into the early nineteenth century.

The Missouri and Mississippi River valleys became an important "middle ground" in the eighteenth and early nineteenth centuries as French inhabitants moved into a region that had been occupied by Indians and explored tentatively by the Spanish. As in the Great Lakes region, fur provided the initial impetus for French settlement and trade with Indians. Unlike in the Great Lakes, where an international border between Canada and the United States divided the territory, after 1812, the United States established dominance over the Mississippi and Missouri River regions. However, Louisiana continued to be a Creole society with strong French, Spanish, and Caribbean influences.

THE STUDY OF BORDERLANDS

Borderlands are places, but the study of borderlands has also become an important field in the discipline of history. As a conceptual lens, the study of borderlands has gone from a marginal field of history to become the defining metaphor for cultural interactions across many disciplines. In 1902 the historian Herbert Eugene Bolton (1870–1953) coined the term *borderlands* to refer to the northern frontier region of New Spain and as a response to Frederick Jackson Turner's (1861–1932) totalizing "frontier thesis." Since the 1990s, borderlands has become a metaphor to understand identity formation at the edges of empires and nations where cultures blend, conflict, and create unique hybrid forms.

Bolton's borderlands highlighted the Spanish legacy in the US Southwest and led him to a broader vision of a transcontinental history of the Americas. Bolton and his legion of students reminded North American historians about the other America south of the Rio Grande and its impact on the United States. Even though Turner's master narrative reigned supreme, Bolton's views, along with a host of critiques from south and north of the border, began to chip away at the frontier thesis.

Latin American intellectuals like Edmundo O'Gorman (1906–1995) dismissed Bolton's Pan-Americanist-inflected effort to write a continental history of the Americas as an overly romanticized vision that neglected a long history of US imperialism. Although they did not use the term *borderlands*, Latin American intellectuals also theorized the cultural contact zone between Anglo and Latin America. Cuban poet, journalist, and independence hero José Martí (1853–1895) famously compared "our America" to that of the Anglos, highlighting differences but also aspiring for continental harmony. The borderlands as seen from the south took on a less rosy hue, especially for Mexicans who had half of their territory taken in the mid-nineteenth century.

In the 1960s, Native Americans in the United States challenged the racism in the descriptions by Bolton and his students of Indians as little more than uncivilized "savages." Chicano historians picked up on this critique as well, condemning Bolton and his acolytes for glorifying Spanish conquistadors who raped and pillaged their way through the northern frontier. For Chicano historians, the borderlands were not a remote frontier region but the center of their homeland, called Aztlán. Although Chicanos were mestizo (mixed race) people, they increasingly identified with their indigenous over their Spanish ancestry.

In the late 1960s and 1970s, Chicanas brought a feminist critique to the Chicano nationalist vision of Aztlán and highlighted the oppression of Indian and mestiza women at the hands of Spanish conquistadors, Anglo invaders, and Chicano militants. These multiple critiques were encapsulated in Gloria Anzaldúa's (1942–2004) powerful 1987 book, *Borderlands/La Frontera*. In this poetic treatise, Anzaldúa articulated the concept of the "new mestiza" as someone who at once identified with all parts of her identity: Anglo, indigenous, Spanish, Texan, lesbian, and female. For Anzaldúa, "a consciousness of the Borderlands" stemmed from the realization that people participated in several cultures simultaneously. "Cradled in one culture, sandwiched between two cultures, straddling all three cultures and their values systems, la mestiza (the hybrid woman) undergoes a struggle of flesh, a struggle of border, and inner war … a cultural collision" (Anzaldúa 1987, 77–78). The borderlands was no longer simply a place, but it was a process by which individuals could shape their identity out of multiple strands from their past.

In the 1980s, New Western history emerged as a critique of the Turner thesis and the Boltonian borderlands. It was around this time that postmodern theories of identity formation converged with a neoliberal economy where goods and communications whizzed across global borders with increasing speed. Along with Anzaldúa, anthropologist Roger Rouse (1991) and performance artist Guillermo Gómez-Peña (1996) began to explore the idea of the border as a postmodern third space that existed both within national territories and beyond them. The border was no longer just found at the boundary line between nations, but it existed anywhere two or more cultures butted against one another. Gómez-Peña asked readers to look beyond the political map with fixed territorial borders and imagine one that depicted "a more complex system of overlapping, interlocking, and overlaid maps … [one] that [belonged] to the homeless, and to nomads, migrants, and exiles" (Gómez-Peña 1996, 6).

Since the 1990s borderlands and borders have become some of the key metaphors used across various humanistic and social science disciplines to explain cultural mixing and interaction. Moving beyond the focus on the paradigmatic US-Mexico border, scholars have begun to explore the US-Canadian borderlands and borderlands all over the globe. Borderlands as a conceptual lens helps historians to understand national as well as transnational formations and individual as well as group identities. In a century, the borderlands concept has moved from the fringe to the center.

SEE ALSO *Canada; Mexico; North America; Texas Republic*

BIBLIOGRAPHY

Adelman, Jeremy, and Stephen Aron. "From Borderlands to Borders: Empires, Nation-States, and the Peoples in Between in North American History." *American Historical Review* 104, 3 (1999): 814–841.

Anzaldúa, Gloria. *Borderlands/La Frontera: The New Mestiza*. San Francisco: Spinsters/Aunt Lute, 1987. 4th ed., 2012.

Bolton, Herbert Eugene. *The Spanish Borderlands: A Chronicle of Old Florida and the Southwest*. New Haven, CT: Yale University Press, 1921.

Bolton, Herbert Eugene. "The Epic of Greater America." *American Historical Review* 38, 3 (1933): 448–474.

Gómez-Peña, Guillermo. *The New World Border: Prophecies, Poems, and Loqueras for the End of the Century*. San Francisco: City Lights, 1996.

Hämäläinen, Pekka. *The Comanche Empire.* New Haven, CT: Yale University Press, 2008.

Hurtado, Albert L. *Herbert Eugene Bolton: Historian of the American Borderlands.* Berkeley: University of California Press, 2012.

Johnson, Benjamin H., and Andrew R. Graybill, eds. *Bridging National Borders in North America: Transnational and Comparative Histories.* Durham, NC: Duke University Press, 2010.

Rouse, Roger. "Mexican Migration and the Social Space of Postmodernism." *Diaspora* 1, 1 (1991): 8–23.

Truett, Samuel. "Epics of Greater America: Herbert Eugene Bolton's Quest for a Transational American History." In *Interpreting Spanish Colonialism: Empires, Nations, and Legends,* edited by Christopher Schmidt-Nowara and John M. Nieto-Phillips, 213–248. Albuquerque: University of New Mexico Press, 2005.

Truett, Samuel, and Elliott Young, eds. *Continental Crossroads: Remapping U.S.-Mexico Borderlands History.* Durham, NC: Duke University Press, 2004.

Elliott Young
Professor of History
Lewis & Clark College

BORLAUG, NORMAN

1914–2009

Norman Ernest Borlaug is known as the father of the Green Revolution because of his research to develop new high-yielding, disease-resistant wheat varieties to help small-scale farmers improve the food supply for their families and the general population in Mexico, India, and Pakistan.

Born to Norwegian American parents, Borlaug grew up on a farm near Cresco, Iowa. He attended a one-room rural school through the eighth grade. In 1932, upon graduation from Cresco High School, Borlaug attended the University of Minnesota, where he majored in forestry and graduated five years later. He remained at the university, where he studied plant pathology and earned an MS in 1940 and a PhD in 1942.

Borlaug first took a position as a microbiologist with the DuPont Corporation. In 1944 he joined the Cooperative Mexican Agricultural Program as an employee of the Rockefeller Foundation, which financed its research to help Mexico improve wheat production. As the scientist in charge of the wheat-improvement program, Borlaug and his team pursued an interdisciplinary approach to increasing production by integrating the research of geneticists, agronomists, chemists, and plant pathologists. They conducted research to develop wheat varieties that would bear heavy heads of grain. Borlaug released his first hybrid wheat variety in 1948 and sixteen additional high-yielding and disease- and drought-resistant varieties by 1956, which made Mexico self-sufficient in wheat production.

Borlaug's success as a scientist brought administrative appointments. From 1960 to 1963, he served as an associate director of the Rockefeller Foundation, where he led the Inter-American Food Crop Program. In 1966 Borlaug's genetic research led to the creation of the International Maize and Wheat Improvement Center, known by its Spanish acronym CIMMYT (for Centro Internacional de Mejoramiento de Maíz y Trigo), where he directed the wheat program until 1980. Borlaug's work provided a model for other nations to increase wheat production. He pursued applied, rather than theoretical, research. He wanted results and insisted that the development of new wheat varieties be suitable for distribution and immediate improvement of agricultural production.

Hunger and famine in India and Pakistan during the late 1940s brought Borlaug to the South Asian subcontinent. In 1963, the governments of India and Pakistan invited him to evaluate their agricultural research programs. Borlaug met with government officials and agricultural scientists and convinced them to adopt the high-yielding wheat varieties that he had developed in Mexico. He emphasized that government subsidies for fertilizer, irrigation, and road development were crucial to expanding agricultural production. Borlaug argued that governments had to support applied agricultural science, because subsistence farmers in food-deficient nations could not afford to adopt new agricultural techniques to improve grain production without government assistance. Borlaug advocated the creation of state-supported agricultural demonstration projects, where farmers could observe the benefits of new agricultural technology.

By 1968, Pakistan, using Borlaug's Green Revolution technologies, including new seed varieties, became self-sufficient in wheat. India followed in 1972 for wheat and by 1975 for all cereal grains. The United Nations Food and Agriculture Organization and the Rockefeller Foundation encouraged Borlaug to inform government leaders in the Middle East, East Asia, and Africa about the benefits of Green Revolution agricultural technology and persuade them to support the development and adoption of high-yielding grain varieties that would help subsistence farmers feed their families and produce a surplus to ease hunger in urban areas.

In 1970, Borlaug received the Nobel Peace Prize for agricultural research that helped end the possibility of famine in India and Pakistan. As yet, he is the only agricultural scientist to receive that award. Upon acceptance of the prize, Borlaug reminded the audience that 50 percent of the world's population remained undernourished and 65 percent remained malnourished. He believed that population control was essential to enable agricultural science to help farmers solve the problem of world hunger. Access to adequate food, he contended, enabled people to pursue a meaningful, peaceful life, and he noted that access to food was a human right. Borlaug argued that agricultural scientists had a responsibility to develop crop varieties that would produce abundantly and prevent hunger. He did not believe the choice was between feast (guaranteed by agricultural science, including genetically modified seed varieties) or famine (ordained by the environment), but rather that agricultural science could help farmers maintain sustainable productivity that would keep the food supply ahead of population growth in developing nations. Borlaug never assumed that the Green Revolution would end world hunger or that it would solve socioeconomic problems, but rather that it would help fight hunger.

Borlaug received the Presidential Medal of Freedom (1977) and the World Food Prize (2000), among many other honors. He also served as distinguished professor of international agriculture at Texas A&M University (1984–2009) and as senior consultant to the director general of CIMMYT (1980–2009).

SEE ALSO *Department of Agriculture, US; Green Revolution; Rockefeller Foundation*

BIBLIOGRAPHY

Borlaug, Norman E. "The Impact of Agricultural Research on Mexican Wheat Production." *Transactions of the New York Academy of Sciences*, Ser. II, 20, 3 (1958): 278–295.

Borlaug, Norman E. "The Green Revolution, Peace, and Humanity; Speech Delivered upon Receipt of the 1970 Nobel Prize, Oslo, Norway, December 11, 1970." CIMMYT Reprint and Translation Ser. no. 3 (January 1972).

Hurt, R. Douglas. "Norman Borlaug: Geneticist of the Green Revolution." *Iowa Heritage* 84 (Summer 2003): 78–84.

"Living History Interview with Dr. Norman E. Borlaug." *Transnational Law and Contemporary Problems* 1 (Fall 1991): 539–554.

Phillips, Ronald L. *Norman E. Borlaug, 1914–2009*. Biographical Memoir. Washington, DC: National Academy of Sciences, 2013. http://www.nasonline.org/publications/biographical-memoirs/memoir-pdfs/borlaug-norman.pdf

World Food Prize Foundation. "Norman Borlaug: Curriculum Vitae." http//www.worldfoodprize.org/en/dr_norman_e_borlaug/cirriculun_vitae/

R. Douglas Hurt
Professor and Department Head
Department of History, Purdue University

BOURNE, RANDOLPH, "TRANSNATIONAL AMERICA"

SEE *Melting Pot.*

BOXER REBELLION

The Boxer Rebellion was an anti-Christian uprising that swept through North China as the nineteenth century ended. The term, however, is misleading: The insurgents involved—mostly young men from North China villages who blamed the coming of the foreign religion for angering local gods and thereby precipitating a horrific drought—did not "box," though they did use martial arts techniques. More important, they were not "rebels"—they did not seek to overturn but rather to buttress the position of the ruling Qing dynasty (1644–1912). One of their main slogans was "support the Qing, exterminate the foreigners"; the most common Chinese name for them was Yihetuan (Righteous and Harmonious Militia), so they might best be seen as a kind of self-organized loyalist militia.

It is hard to say precisely when the insurrection began or pinpoint the origins of the groups involved, as sporadic anti-Christian incidents took place throughout the preceding decades and the Yihetuan evolved out of various preexisting bands. What is clear is that the insurrection gained momentum in the early months of 1900, which was also when the term *Boxer* gained currency in the foreign-language press, and that it peaked during the famous fifty-five-day siege, from late June to mid-August, by the Yihetuan of the foreign legation quarters of Beijing. Qing officials were initially divided over whether to treat the group as bandits to be suppressed or loyalists to be supported, but those arguing for the latter persuaded Empress Dowager Cixi, the most powerful member of the ruling family, to send imperial troops to support the siege of the legations.

That siege was finally lifted when a contingent of foreign fighters made up of thousands of soldiers from many lands—what would now be called an international peacekeeping force—moved on Beijing. This force freed the foreigners, as well as Chinese Christians who had taken refuge in or near the legation quarter. An amazingly cosmopolitan army, it contained American, Austro-Hungarian, Russian, Italian, German, and Japanese troops, as well as soldiers of the British Empire, many of whom were South Asian, and of the French Empire, many of whom were Southeast Asian. This force, which in Chinese was known as the Baguo Lianjun (Eight-Country Allied Army), drove the Qing rulers into exile north of Beijing and took control of and looted the treasures housed in the dynasty's Beijing palaces. Over the following year the soldiers went on to carry out campaigns of reprisal

American troops marching near the Temple of Agriculture, Beijing, China, 1900. *Thousands of foreign fighters from many lands—what would now be called an international peacekeeping force—moved on Beijing to free foreigners and Chinese Christians threatened by an anti-Christian uprising by Chinese insurgents.* BETTMANN/CORBIS

and revenge, during which they killed many Chinese men, women, and children, some of whom had had no connection to the Yihetuan. These campaigns dramatically increased the death toll of a bloody struggle, likely costing hundreds of thousands of lives in all, whose earliest victims had been the small number of foreigners and much larger number of Chinese Christians killed by the Yihetuan. The fighting finally ended in September 1901 with the signing of the Boxer Protocol, a treaty that required the Qing to pay an enormous indemnity for all damages to foreign property and losses of foreign lives.

These events were the biggest international news story of the time. And this was no small feat, given how many other dramatic events—the Boer War in South Africa, battles between American troops and Filipino insurgents in Southeast Asia, and a spectacular World's Fair in Paris—took place in 1900.

Knowing what happened in China during the decades prior to 1900 helps to explain the motivations of members of the Yihetuan and the debates within the government over suppressing or backing the group. China had been wracked by a series of foreign incursions, which saw the Qing dynasty's military defeated, in turn, by troops and warships of the British Empire (1839–1842); the combined armies of Britain and France (1858–1860); and, most humiliatingly, given Chinese traditional views of Japan as a minor neighboring state, by Japanese forces (1894–1895). China had also undergone a fair measure of domestic unrest, including a series of insurrections that were genuinely rebellious and involved sects whose members embraced various sorts of millenarian ideas—that is, beliefs, tied to various eschatological religious notions, that the faithful could call on supernatural powers to magically right the world and usher in a new era. The Yihetuan, whose members—though not rebels—thought that incantations could make them invulnerable to bullets and that they could call on their ancestors and local gods to come down and fight beside them as spirit soldiers, fit in with this millenarian tradition.

When the so-called Boxer Rebellion and international invasion took place, many Chinese saw the events as replays of things that had happened before. Qing officials who wanted to see the Yihetuan suppressed argued that the groups were a second coming of the Buddhist White Lotus millenarians who had challenged the dynasty a century before; when foreign troops moved into Beijing, some in China saw this as a replay of what had happened in 1860, when British and French soldiers seized the capital and burned the Old Summer Palace. Some Britons held captive in Beijing thought instead of parallels to the Indian Mutiny of 1857. And some Americans saw similarities between Chinese events and the Ghost Dance risings of the Sioux in 1890–1891.

The Boxer Rebellion and the invasion that quelled it have had a rich afterlife in popular culture, inspiring everything from reenactments in Buffalo Bill's Wild West shows to Hollywood and Hong Kong films. The events have also endured in the realm of political analogy. Western and Japanese officials and journalists would sometimes dismiss protests of later periods as nothing but new "Boxerism"—that is, as violent and xenophobic—even when the protesters were staging nonviolent demonstrations and boycotts. Chinese officials and journalists, meanwhile, have sometimes invoked the memory of the brutal Eight-Country Allied Army invasion even when actions by foreign powers do not involve violence. The biggest international news story of 1900, in short, continues to cast a long and complex shadow.

SEE ALSO *China; Open Door Policy*

BIBLIOGRAPHY

Bickers, Robert, and R. G. Tiedemann, eds. *China, the Boxers, and the World.* Lanham, MD: Rowman and Littlefield, 2007.

Cohen, Paul A. *History in Three Keys: The Boxers as Event, Experience, and Myth.* New York: Columbia University Press, 1997.

Esherick, Joseph W. *The Origins of the Boxer Uprising.* Berkeley: University of California Press, 1987.

Wasserstrom, Jeffrey N. "Terror and War at the Turn of Two Centuries: The Boxer Crisis Revisited." In *Empire, Nation, and Beyond,* edited by Joseph W. Esherick, Wen-Hsin Yeh, and Madeleine Zelin, 192–210. Berkeley, CA: Institute of East Asian Studies, 2006.

Jeffrey Wasserstrom
Professor of History
University of California, Irvine

BRACERO PROGRAM

As men and women poured into American cities to take up manufacturing jobs in war industries during World War II (1939–1945), agriculturalists in the Southwest worried about the possibility of labor shortages at harvest time. At their request, officials from the Departments of Agriculture, Labor, and State met with their counterparts in Mexico to discuss a temporary labor-importation program between the two countries. The Emergency Farm Labor Supply Program, the first of a series of laws and international agreements that came to be known as the bracero (laborer) program, was formalized by an exchange of diplomatic notes in August 1942. Four weeks later, five hundred guest workers arrived by train from Mexico City to the sugar-beet fields of Stockton, California. Over the next twenty-two years, nearly 5 million contracts were signed by Mexican men to work in farms and, briefly, on railroads throughout the United States. The bracero program reignited migration patterns that had existed since the turn of the century but which had been forcibly halted by the large-scale repatriation of ethnic Mexicans during the Great Depression.

The bracero program was not the first time that American immigration officials had recruited Mexican nationals for temporary employment in the United States. From 1917 to 1921, the US Immigration Service operated a guest-worker program that oversaw the importation of more than 700,000 Mexican nationals for work in agriculture. Nor were Mexicans the only foreign guest workers brought into the country. Jamaicans, Bahamians, Barbadians, and Hondurans were all imported under a special wartime agreement with Great Britain. Smaller guest-worker programs also brought in French-Canadian, Navajo, and Japanese workers to fill regional labor needs.

Unlike its 1917 counterpart, the World War II–era bracero program counted on the participation of Mexican officials in negotiating the terms of the international agreement. American labor demands, coupled with the desire to promote hemispheric unity under the Good Neighbor Policy, gave Mexican diplomats considerable leverage during these negotiations. They used this leverage to secure the US government's endorsement of bracero contracts, guarantee a minimum wage, and grant braceros the right to elect representatives. Just as importantly, Mexican officials used the diplomatic opening created by the Good Neighbor Policy to condition bracero employment on the fair and equal treatment of Mexicans in the United States. Mexico made good on this threat by barring braceros from working in Texas, a state with the long history of anti-Mexican discrimination, until 1948.

By then, however, the rapid growth of undocumented migration, caused in part by the unavailability of bracero labor in Texas and the formation of migrant networks by braceros elsewhere in the United States had drastically eroded Mexico's bargaining power over the program. Mexican officials refused to renew the bracero accords in 1948, but the program continued, albeit unilaterally and on terms favorable to US employers. During this period, the bracero program also served as a way of legalizing Mexican nationals who had entered the country illegally, a process that both growers and government agents referred to as "drying out wetbacks." The practice of legalizing unauthorized migrants by converting them into braceros would be used again during Operation Wetback, the infamous deportation campaign carried out by the US Border Patrol in 1954.

Acting on the recommendations of the President's Commission on Migratory Labor, Congress authorized a massive overhaul of the bracero program in 1951. The commission's report had argued that the presence of Mexican guest workers depressed the wages of American farmworkers and likely encouraged prospective braceros to enter the country illegally. Lawmakers responded by bringing Mexico back into the agreement and reintroducing the federal government as the guarantor of individual work contracts. The spirit of cooperation was short-lived, however, and, in January 1954, the US Border Patrol unilaterally opened the border and circumvented Mexican oversight of the bracero program by paroling migrants directly to employers.

The bracero program ended in 1964 when Public Law 78 was allowed to expire without extension. Advances in mechanical harvesting technology, together with mounting criticisms by church, union, and civil rights organizations, contributed to the program's demise. Six months after the bracero program expired, President Lyndon B. Johnson (1908–1973) signed the Immigration and Nationality Act of 1965, which for the first time placed numerical limits on immigration from the Western Hemisphere. The closing of legal avenues for Mexican migration, bracero or otherwise, precipitated a new wave of unauthorized migration that saw the number of illegal entrants from Mexico triple between 1965 and 1972. While the bracero program formally ended in 1964, a smaller guest-worker program continued under the H-2 visa system authorized by the Immigration and Nationality Act.

SEE ALSO *Good Neighbor Policy; Mexico*

BIBLIOGRAPHY

Calavita, Kitty. *Inside the State: The Bracero Program, Immigration, and the I.N.S.* New York: Routledge, 1992.

Cohen, Deborah. "Caught in the Middle: The Mexican State's Relationship with the United States and Its Own Citizen-Workers, 1942–1954." *Journal of American Ethnic History* 20, 3 (2001): 111–132

Henderson, Timothy J. "Bracero Blacklists: Mexican Migration and the Unraveling of the Good Neighbor Policy." *Latin Americanist* 55, 4 (2011): 199–217.

Israel Pastrana
PhD Candidate, History
University of California, San Diego

BRETTON WOODS

The July 1944 Bretton Woods international monetary conference was the most important international gathering since the Paris peace talks of 1919. Convened by the US Department of the Treasury under the administration of President Franklin D. Roosevelt (1882–1945), the conference, beginning just three weeks after the D-day landings at Normandy, involved more than seven hundred delegates from forty-four Allied nations. Its most notable achievements were the establishment of the International Monetary Fund (IMF), to preside over a new fixed exchange-rate system based on the US dollar, and the International Bank for Reconstruction and Development (now known as the World Bank), set up mainly to help finance postwar European reconstruction.

The conference was the brainchild of Secretary of the Treasury Henry Morgenthau's (1891–1967) deputy, Harry Dexter White (1892–1948), who had begun strategizing about such a gathering as early as 1936. The 1930s were marked by, among other problems, a collapse in international trade and monetary relations. White wanted to repair both by, first and foremost, establishing a mechanism and institution to prevent competitive devaluations of currencies—a stratagem by which, White believed, governments tried to gain unfair advantage over other nations by making their exports cheaper in terms of US dollars. The importance of the dollar in international trade derived from the fact that the United States controlled about two-thirds of the world's monetary gold; given that gold was considered the ultimate form of payment, the dollar was its most credible surrogate.

The Treasury under Morgenthau and White had another important geopolitical aim for which it used the conference: eliminating the United Kingdom as a rival economic power in the postwar world. At Bretton Woods, Morgenthau wanted, in his own words, "to move the financial center of the world from London and Wall Street to the United States Treasury" (Steil 2013a, 216). Part of this involved undermining any compulsion or incentive for other countries to hold pound sterling balances. As Britain was rapidly headed toward insolvency trying to finance its war effort against Germany and the Axis powers, the United States was able to condition its material and financial assistance, through programs such as Lend-Lease, on Britain accepting American terms at Bretton Woods.

The head of the UK Bretton Woods delegation, the renowned economist John Maynard Keynes (1883–1946), negotiated with White for two years leading up to the conference over the terms that would form the core of the Bretton Woods agreement. Their visions were very different. White wanted the dollar to be the foundation of the new international monetary arrangement; Keynes, in contrast, wanted this to be a new supranational currency managed by the IMF—*bancor*. White wanted countries to devalue only with permission from the IMF; Keynes wanted countries to be compelled to devalue or revalue according to set rules. White wanted a strong IMF, in which the United States would have veto power; Keynes wanted a passive IMF that acted as a more or less automatic source of concessionary financing for countries running balance-of-payments deficits (like the United Kingdom). White wanted IMF quotas and voting power to be determined by the cash, gold, and securities that each country contributed; Keynes wanted these determined by each country's share of international trade—a formula copacetic to the United Kingdom, which traded a lot while having little of value in terms of financial assets. White wanted both the IMF and World Bank to be domiciled in Washington; Keynes wanted one of the institutions in London and the other in New York (which had less political symbolism than Washington).

The other participating nations had only modest influence over the details of the agreement, and were mainly concerned with getting higher IMF quotas than their rivals. The Soviet delegation stood out as the only obstructionist one, Joseph Stalin (1879–1953) having granted it little negotiating room. The Soviets signed on at the very end of the conference, but never ratified the agreement and therefore never joined the IMF. White would go on to become a highly controversial figure over allegations, many of which were borne out decades later in decrypted wartime international communications, that he had over many years acted as an agent for Soviet intelligence. Though there is no evidence of Soviet influence over White's design for the Bretton Woods monetary and financial system (as there was no Soviet monetary thinking to speak of), President Harry S. Truman (1884–1972) allowed a European—Belgian Camille Gutt (1884–1971)—to be appointed as the IMF's first managing director in order to prevent Federal Bureau of Investigation director J. Edgar Hoover (1895–1972) from revealing details of the White allegations publicly. A European has continued to head the IMF ever since.

Although the so-called Bretton Woods era of fixed exchange rates, from 1946 to 1971, was one marked by a robust global economic recovery and revival of international trade, it is important to note that it was actually not until 1961 that the first nine European countries formally adopted the IMF's convertibility requirements, and the IMF was largely moribund throughout much of the 1940s and 1950s. If any single initiative deserves major credit for stimulating this recovery, it is the Marshall Plan—an initiative launched three years after Bretton Woods.

SEE ALSO *International Monetary Fund; World Bank*

BIBLIOGRAPHY

Clarke, Peter. *The Last Thousand Days of the British Empire: Churchill, Roosevelt, and the Birth of the Pax Americana.* New York: Bloomsbury Press, 2008.

James, Harold. *International Monetary Cooperation since Bretton Woods.* New York: Oxford University Press, 1996.

Skidelsky, Robert. *John Maynard Keynes: Fighting for Britain, 1937–1946.* London: Macmillan, 2000.

Steil, Benn. *The Battle of Bretton Woods: John Maynard Keynes, Harry Dexter White, and the Making of a New World Order.* Princeton, NJ: Princeton University Press, 2013a.

Steil, Benn. "Why There Will Be No New Bretton Woods." *Wall Street Journal,* February 27, 2013b.

Steil, Benn. "Red White: Why a Founding Father of Postwar Capitalism Spied for the Soviets." *Foreign Affairs* 92, 2 (March/April 2013c): 115–129.

Benn Steil
Director of International Economics
Council on Foreign Relations

BRITAIN

When the American commissioners signed and affixed their seal to a parchment in Ghent, Belgium, in late December 1814, they had little reason to expect that, when ratified the following year, the document would become historic as the *last* treaty of peace between the United States and Great Britain. Anglo-American relations had begun in war, and in war's aftermath portended perpetual suspicion and animosity. Nevertheless, this dysfunctional start evolved into a rapprochement that over time would yield one of the strongest and most secure relationships in the history of nations. This evolution progressed through fits and starts from crisis to crisis until, by the middle of the twentieth century, crises had waned and the notion of an Anglo-American "special relationship" had become the assumed order of the Atlantic world. By this juncture, however, roles had reversed and circumstances had forced the patriarchal posture of John Bull to defer to the superpower status of Brother Jonathan. Allied in a common effort to defeat Nazism and then to frustrate the ambitions of communism, the two nations celebrated victories over both in the second half of the twentieth century, only to be confronted by the twenty-first-century threat of militant Islam in the global war on terror.

EARLY ANGLO-AMERICAN RELATIONS

The term *Anglo-American relations* could not properly be applied before 1782, when Benjamin Franklin and the American delegation secured generous concessions from the Lord Shelburne ministry that led to formal recognition of American independence in the Paris peace treaty the following year. During the period from Thomas Jefferson's Declaration of Independence in 1776 to the surrender of Lord Cornwallis to George Washington at Yorktown in 1781, Anglo-American relations might have referred simply to a violent domestic altercation within the British Empire. With independence, however, the thirteen North American colonies elevated the transatlantic relationship to a state-to-state interaction.

Independence hardly meant that Great Britain was prepared to treat the upstart republic as a sovereign nation. It would not be until Chief Justice John Jay's special mission in 1794 that the British welcomed an American representative with suitable decorum, and even then it was prompted by expediency resulting from Britain's conflict with revolutionary France. The 1794 American effort, nevertheless, produced the first peacetime treaty between the two nations. Commonly referred to as Jay's Treaty, the negotiation was seen by many at the time as an embarrassing capitulation that won neither respect for the rights of neutrals, the disavowal of the practice of impressment, nor any significant progress toward a favorable trade arrangement. The treaty did, however, secure a British commitment to finally withdraw troops from the northwestern territories of the United States, where they had remained since the Revolution. And, more importantly, Jay's effort calmed relations somewhat and postponed an altercation that could have cost the young republic autonomy if not independence.

After a brief respite in Britain's conflict with the French, British harassment of American ships and sailors resumed with renewed hostilities in 1803, this time with Napoleon's France. Despite depredations by the French, the pain inflicted on America by the British was considerably worse, as the Crown's transgressions confirmed the criticism that Britain "not only rules the waves, she waives the rules." Issuing onerous Orders in Council to starve Napoleon of essential materials, Britain boxed America in with little or no latitude to peacefully engage in Atlantic trade. Escalating pressure and insults to the United States set off a public outcry when the British attacked the USS *Chesapeake* in 1807. But the Jefferson administration knew that the United States was far too weak to do more than withdraw from Atlantic trade through the adoption of the Embargo Act later that year. Two years later, Congress lifted Jefferson's failed embargo and passed the dilemma to James Madison who found it necessary to again war with Britain or sacrifice US sovereignty to the heavy hand of London. The War of 1812 was far from successful for the United States, ending as it did with none of the prewar issues resolved at Ghent. In the broader picture, however, the war proved highly beneficial for the young republic. This second war finally forced London's acknowledgment of the United States not only as a sovereign nation, but, indeed, as rising and potentially useful. Likewise, the United States began to appreciate the potential protection a friendly British fleet might offer—a benefit that could ease the cost of defending an expanding continental republic.

Between Ghent and the onset of America's Civil War in 1861, commercial issues and border disputes dominated Anglo-American relations. Trade was not a new issue but rather the outgrowth of America's withdrawal from the British imperial system and consequent struggle to find a path through reciprocity to a favorable balance. This path was steep, and apart from negotiations, such as Andrew Jackson's reciprocity accommodation in 1830, and occasional moments of free trade, such as the effort to draw down protectionist impediments in the 1840s, this issue remained a point of contention through much of Anglo-American history. Meanwhile, a number of agreements and an appreciation for the benefits of good relations, cultivated by statesmen such as John Quincy Adams and Lord Castlereagh, demonstrated a newfound willingness to resort to the pen rather than the sword. The demilitarization of the Great Lakes in the Rush-Bagot Treaty of 1817 was followed the next year by the most important of the postwar negotiations. The Convention of 1818 addressed a number of outstanding issues ranging from American fishing rights off the Canadian Maritimes (a perennial controversy that would ebb and flow until 1912) to the disputed boundary between the United States and Canada. Although the Convention was not successful in all areas, it contributed to a new pattern of peacefully addressing differences.

THE POSITIVE POTENTIAL OF ANGLO-AMERICAN COOPERATION

In the early 1820s, European talk of restoring to Spain its Latin American colonies sparked shared Anglo-American concern over their interests in the Western Hemisphere. Although the James Monroe administration declined a British offer to join in a bilateral pronouncement defending the autonomy of the Latin American republics, Britain's tacit approval of the American declaration (the 1823 Monroe Doctrine) indicated both a common interest and a cooperative spirit. On a number of occasions, Anglo-American competition for influence threatened this alignment over the status of Latin America. The pattern of peaceful remedy by negotiation continued, however, as reflected by the Clayton-Bulwer Treaty of 1850, which promised Anglo-American cooperation in any future isthmian canal.

Meanwhile, border disputes threatened friendly relations, commercial or otherwise. The most serious flared up along the ill-defined northern boundary between the United States and Canada. In 1842, Daniel Webster and Lord Ashburton resolved the squabble over the northeastern line between Maine and New Brunswick, along with a number of other issues that had festered since the late 1830s. The treaty that customarily bears their names (the Webster-Ashburton Treaty) was instrumental in a developing rapprochement between the two nations. Sadly, Webster and Ashburton were unable to resolve the conflict over the northwestern boundary and left it to James Polk, whose administration threatened war to assert America's claim to the entire Oregon Territory from California to Alaska. Once again, a growing appreciation for the commercial interdependence between the two nations overcame the rhetoric of national honor to produce a compromise in the Oregon Treaty of 1846. Both nations now understood that each benefited from friendly relations. The final border issue would not be resolved until gold discoveries in America's Russian acquisition provoked a dispute over the line between Alaska's panhandle and British Columbia at the turn of the century. A defiant demonstration of resolve by Theodore Roosevelt notwithstanding, few moments in Anglo-American history better reflect the determination to maintain an amicable association: Britain, at arbitration in 1902, voted *with* America *against* Canada.

TENSION DURING THE AMERICAN CIVIL WAR

The American Civil War (1861–1865) produced a host of problems for Anglo-American relations. London was inclined to support the antislavery United States, but also needed southern cotton. After Abraham Lincoln's administration announced a blockade of southern ports in 1861, Queen Victoria, quite logically, declared neutrality in the American conflict—a declaration that, Lincoln complained, legitimized the Confederate States. As tension increased between Washington and London, an American sea captain provoked the Lord Palmerston government by seizing two Confederate envoys from the British mail steamer RMS *Trent.* Although resolved peacefully with the release of the envoys and a tepid apology, tension over the status of the Confederate States and potential British recognition continued into 1863.

While the notion simmered, the US minister in London held close a directive from Lincoln that threatened war if London intervened. By late 1862, this possibility had faded as the Union finally began to show promise on the battlefield. Also, despite the surprisingly negative reception in Britain of the Emancipation Proclamation (1863), the sign that Lincoln had recalibrated the rationale for the war helped to restrain British interventionists. The final Anglo-American conflict arose from Confederate agent James Bulloch's acquisition of "warships" for the Confederate navy from British yards. The most famous of these, the CSS *Alabama*, not only caused tension during the war, but lent its name to a legal battle between Washington and London after the war that was not resolved until Britain acknowledged the error and paid damages in the *Alabama* Claims dispute. The Treaty of Washington that codified the resolution of the *Alabama* controversy in 1871 also addressed a number of outstanding issues and contributed to warming Anglo-American relations.

THE GREAT RAPPROCHEMENT

The event that established what is commonly called the "Great Rapprochement" at the dawn of the twentieth century involved another boundary, but this time not between British and American territory. The Venezuela boundary dispute of the 1890s was sparked by the US resuscitation of the near-dormant Monroe Doctrine to block London from unilaterally forcing a boundary between British Guiana and Venezuela. Despite his lack of standing in an argument between Europeans and South Americans, President Grover Cleveland wedged his way in and, in fact, issued through Secretary of State Richard Olney an ultimatum to London that the boundary be submitted to arbitration. A dismissive initial reaction from London provoked Cleveland to raise the ante by threatening to have an American team draw the boundary. In the jingoistic atmosphere of the 1890s, Americans were keen to twist the British lion's tail. London, in a watershed moment in Anglo-American relations, conceded to the American pressure and submitted to arbitration—an arbitration that, at any rate, favored the British position.

The boundary incident was not about defending Venezuela but had become simply a vehicle for projecting increased US involvement in world affairs and hemispheric hegemony. To the American press, it was a patriotic win. London, however, had merely made a pragmatic calculation that, with Germany on the rise and the power balance in Europe shifting, it might be useful to be flanked by a friendly rather than a hostile United States. British priorities were trending toward Europe, then the Middle East, Asia, and Africa, and they seemed content to leave the general maintenance of much of the Western Hemisphere to the United States. The developing Great Rapprochement between the two English-speaking nations reflected in the Venezuela saga yielded almost immediate dividends to both. The British supported the United States in its "splendid little war" with Spain in 1898, and the United States backed Britain in its South African conflict with the Boers the following year.

TENTATIVE RELATIONS DURING WORLD WAR I

If either side expected warming relations to trigger an automatic alliance if and when Europe drifted into war, this illusion dissipated quickly when the "guns of August" opened the Great War in 1914. President Woodrow Wilson, in fact, declared strict neutrality and directed the American people to remain detached, even in attitude, from the European conflagration. But this detachment did not extend to trade, as Washington planned to exploit commerce with all European markets; this, ironically, placed Americans, ships, and cargo in similar circumstances to those faced by Jefferson a century earlier. And, as with Jefferson, the British resorted to provocative Orders in Council in an attempt to block supplies to Germany and the Central powers. Expanding the list of contraband items, Britain began to harass American shipping and, in summer 1916, "blacklisted" American companies allegedly trading with Germany. This infuriated Wilson, who was "at the end of his patience with Britain and the Allies." British Prime Minister David Lloyd George knew the risk of violating American neutrality but was determined to walk as close to the line as possible without crossing it.

The tension in Anglo-American relations ultimately was relieved by the more provocative actions of Germany as Berlin initiated submarine warfare to seal off British waters. After the German sinking of the passenger liner *Lusitania* in 1915, with the loss of over a thousand souls, the ire of Americans shifted to Germany, and Britain's image improved from bully to victim. When the more staid secretary of state William Jennings Bryan resigned after Wilson's unbalanced *Lusitania* response, he was replaced by the pro-British Robert Lansing. Almost all motion now was toward Britain and the Allies, including the relaxation of Washington's restrictive loan policy, the benefits of which were skewed overwhelmingly toward London.

In April 1917—after Germany ended its pledged pause in unrestricted submarine warfare and the public learned of the tactless German Foreign Minister Arthur Zimmermann telegram encouraging Mexico to ally against the United States—Wilson took America to war. He did not, however, officially join Britain as an ally but designated the United States an "associated" power. This reserved posture, along with his determination to press for more draw than victory, put US and British goals at odds. The British had suffered. The United States was tardy to the war. London saw no reason to defer to Wilson, whose contribution to the land war came so late and whose idealism was incompatible with the pragmatic goals of victory and the expansion rather than contraction of the empire. Still, Wilson knew when he arrived in Europe after Germany had yielded to armistice in November 1918 that America's role had been essential to Allied success. His detachment from the realities faced by his European colleagues at Versailles, however, joined with his insistence on forcing a "new world order" to strain Anglo-American relations.

THE INTERWAR YEARS

The tensions between London and Washington at the peace conference carried into the interwar years. US failure to join the League of Nations seemed to indicate a desire to return to isolation. Americans might have wished, in their disillusionment, to go back to the safety of geographic isolation, but the shift from a debtor to a creditor nation, increasing global influence, and the epicenter of global finances pivoting from London to New York made withdrawal into the American cocoon impossible. America was, by circumstance, engaged and insistent on recovering its financial investment in the war—a contentious bone in the form of the Allied war debt that persisted through the interwar period. London felt it had paid with blood. The fiscally conservative Americans insisted that the debt be satisfied, but implausibly did so while closing off the American markets with renewed trade barriers. As the Great Depression rocked the Atlantic world in the 1930s, Washington compounded the problem by rejecting calls to stabilize currency internationally in favor of focusing on America's domestic health.

The passage of the neutrality acts in the mid-1930s seemed to confirm America's retreat from responsibility. The strain of the interwar years on Anglo-American relations again was relieved by the Germans. In fact, the "common enemy" element now set the formula for harmony between Washington and London. To stop Adolf Hitler, Franklin Roosevelt circumvented the neutrality acts to assist Britain. His first effort came in 1937 when Congress agreed that belligerents might be supplied on the basis of "cash and carry," an arrangement that would obviously favor the dominant sea power.

THE ANGLO-AMERICAN ALLIANCE OF WORLD WAR II

After the war began in 1939, Roosevelt stepped up efforts to dilute neutrality and to support the British, now led by Winston Churchill, who was quick to exploit his pedigree as the product of "an English-Speaking Union" (Churchill's mother was American). The most important example of Roosevelt's dismantling of neutrality came in March 1941, when he piloted the Lend-Lease Act through Congress. The "lion's" share of the initial appropriation of $7 billion went to the British. The imagery of developing Anglo-American "harmony" was on display in August as Churchill and Roosevelt met off the coast of Newfoundland amid American and British sailors singing "Onward Christian Soldiers" from, it was noted, the same English hymnals. The meeting produced more than sentiment; the two leaders articulated unified war aims in the Atlantic Charter. The agreement did not, as Roosevelt hoped, convince Britain to finally end imperial preference, but

President Franklin D. Roosevelt and Prime Minister Winston Churchill on board the HMS* Prince of Wales, *August 1941. *The meeting off the coast of Newfoundland produced more than sentiments of Anglo-American harmony, as the two leaders articulated unified war aims in the Atlantic Charter.* **HULTON ROYALS COLLECTION/KEYSTONE/GETTY IMAGES**

the charter *did* pledge freedom of the seas and a shared determination to disarm aggressor states.

When Churchill and Roosevelt met again in late December 1941, America was at war and, for the first time, a British ally. This was the beginning of unprecedented cooperation as the Combined Chiefs of Staff set up headquarters in Washington to coordinate war plans, American intelligence operatives worked closely and openly with their British counterparts, and British officers and American officers became colleagues under the same command structure, ultimately in a chain that reported to American general Dwight D. Eisenhower. The tone of cooperation flowed from the top, with Roosevelt and Churchill meeting nine times formally and accounting for more than seventeen hundred direct communications, either by letter, phone, or telegraph.

Of course, communication was not without controversy. For example, although Roosevelt and his advisers were responsive to Joseph Stalin's plea for a western front, Churchill overruled it in favor of his "soft underbelly" strategy, staging from North Africa. Also, after Stalin joined the wartime conferences, Roosevelt began to court the Soviet partner and, at the Yalta Conference in early 1945, the American president famously excluded Churchill from peripheral talks with the Russian. Nevertheless, the general pattern was overwhelmingly characterized by the friendly association between the two Atlantic allies. Perhaps the most striking example of wartime cooperation came with the Quebec Agreement in 1943, under which the Americans and British committed to cooperate in the development of an atomic weapon.

During the war, the United States and Britain worked on postwar plans for both economic and political stability. In 1944 in Bretton Woods, New Hampshire, a currency stabilization scheme was finally established that would peg exchange to the dollar. At Dumbarton Oaks in Washington, DC, the same year, British and Americans cooperated in the first stages of an international organization that would become the United Nations.

THE "SPECIAL RELATIONSHIP" OF THE COLD WAR ERA

In the aftermath of the Allied victory in 1945, it was clear that the role reversal between the United States and Britain was complete. Britain was devastated at home, was heavily in debt, and could no longer manage its vast empire. The United States, while suffering comparable losses on the battlefield, was unscathed at home and emerged from the war with a resurgent economy and astounding power. Pax Britannica was no more. Pax Americana was rising and would be called upon to lift the British out of their postwar devastation and to fill the vacuum left by British abdication of commitments, such as those to Greece and Turkey. In 1947 the United States, in what would become the Truman Doctrine, announced its intention to take up the mantel not just in Greece and Turkey but throughout the world. The following year, the Marshall Plan began to disperse billions to rebuild and stabilize Britain and the rest of Western Europe. While sorting out economic relief, the United States finally broke into the imperial preference by insisting that all currencies in the empire be convertible to dollars.

In 1946, Churchill issued his most famous pronouncement of the "special relationship" as part of his "Sinews of Peace/Iron Curtain" speech in Fulton, Missouri. By this time, Anglo-American relations again benefited from the threat of a common enemy, Soviet communism. The success of former ally Joseph Stalin's powerful Red Army to extend communism into Eastern Europe undermined any thought of relaxing defenses after the war. Instead, a combined Anglo-American front proved necessary to contain the spread of communism. The most famous examples of cooperation in the early Cold War were over the breaking of the Berlin blockade in the late 1940s and the establishment of the North Atlantic Treaty Organization (NATO) in 1949. Perhaps the most graphic illustration of the openness of the relationship was British willingness to "permanently" host American forces in Britain, including, over time, nuclear forces.

Cooperation did not mean that the British would willingly assume the role of second to the Americans. The British intended rather to play the part of elder statesman, mentoring the sometimes impetuous younger power. London especially hoped to restrain America's atomic muscle. This was made problematic by the US implementation of the McMahon Act (1946), which excluded Britain from continued nuclear collaboration. Britain could do no more than advise and caution American presidents on any possible military use of the bomb. Cooperation returned in the nuclear defense arena during President Eisenhower's second term with the US-UK Mutual Defense Agreement (1958).

During the Cold War, the Anglo-American relationship, while consistently important, was not always "special." For example, Britain opposed the United States over which China—Communist or Nationalist—should be seated at the United Nations. Britain recognized the People's Republic of China in 1950. The United States would not do so for almost three decades. And, while Britain supported the United States in the Korean conflict, the British refused to back America's war in Vietnam. In 1956 Prime Minster Anthony Eden dealt a serious blow to Anglo-American relations by joining the French in an invasion of Egypt to secure the Suez Canal. Eisenhower chastised Eden for not consulting Washington before this impetuous action and forced (with economic pressure) an end to the Suez fiasco. Personalities at the top would gradually repair the relationship, beginning with the efforts of John Kennedy and Harold Macmillan. And, of course, the simpatico Ronald Reagan and Margaret Thatcher—surviving an occasional test, such as Britain's 1982 altercation with Argentina over the Falklands and America's 1983 military incursion on Grenada—formed what can be described as the high tide of Anglo-American relations as the two collaborated to help end the Cold War.

AFTER THE COLD WAR

With the Soviet adversary departing the stage at the end of the 1980s, Anglo-American cooperation was no longer critical. For years, the British had been torn between strengthening relations with their European partners and maintaining a crucial connection to the United States. The end of the Cold War freed Britain to invest more in the current iteration of European union and to combat its image as America's "fifty-first state." Nevertheless, when George H. W. Bush constructed a coalition for the 1991 Gulf War, Britain was the most essential and willing partner. Likewise, when London wanted to address the genocide in the Balkans, Bill Clinton, although reticent, agreed to engage the power of the United States in a multinational effort.

After the terrorist attacks on New York and Washington in 2001, London was the first to express concern and a willingness to join in a "moral crusade" against terrorism. Prime Minister Tony Blair and President George W. Bush formed a partnership to root out al-Qaeda in Afghanistan and—based on shared intelligence convincing both capitals that the Iraqis were developing weapons of mass destruction—to remove the Saddam Hussein regime in Baghdad. President Barack Obama's initial inclination was to relegate the Anglo-American relationship to merely one of many important to US interests. Nevertheless, as long as Washington and London continue to share common concerns, especially those that involve "common enemies," such as the threat of militant Islam, Obama and Prime Minster David Cameron, as well as their successors, will continue to massage the "special" nature of Anglo-American relations.

SEE ALSO *American Revolution; Anglophobia; Atlantic Charter (1941); Balfour Declaration (1917); The Civil War; Europe; League of Nations; Monroe Doctrine (1823); Paris Peace Conference (1919); Secularization; United Nations; Universal Declaration of Human Rights; War of 1812; Whiteness; World War I; World War II*

BIBLIOGRAPHY

Adams, Iestyn. *Brothers across the Ocean: British Foreign Policy and the Origins of the Anglo-American "Special Relationship," 1900–1905.* New York: Tauris, 2005.

Allen, H. C. *Great Britain and the United States: A History of Anglo-American Relations (1783–1952).* New York: St. Martin's Press, 1955.

Allen, H. C. *Conflict and Concord: The Anglo-American Relationship since 1783.* New York: St. Martin's Press, 1959.

Bartlett, C. J. *"The Special Relationship": A Political History of Anglo-American Relations since 1945.* New York: Longman, 1992.

Bourne, Kenneth. *Britain and the Balance of Power in North America, 1815–1908.* Berkeley: University of California Press, 1967.

Brauer, Kinley J. "The United States and British Imperial Expansion, 1815–60." *Diplomatic History* 12, 1 (1988): 19–38.

Burk, Kathleen. *Britain, America, and the Sinews of War, 1914–1918.* London: Allen and Unwin, 1985.

Burk, Kathleen. *Old World, New World: The Story of Britain and America.* London: Little, Brown, 2007.

Burton, David H. "Theodore Roosevelt and the 'Special Relationship' with Great Britain." *History Today* 23 (August 1973): 527–535.

Campbell, Charles S., Jr. *Anglo-American Understanding, 1898–1903.* Baltimore, MD: Johns Hopkins University Press, 1957.

Campbell, Charles S., Jr. *From Revolution to Rapprochement: The United States and Great Britain, 1783–1900.* New York: Wiley, 1974.

Charmley, John. *Churchill's Grand Alliance: The Anglo-American Special Relationship, 1940–57.* New York: Harcourt Brace, 1995.

Crapol, Edward P. "From Anglophobia to Fragile Rapprochement: Anglo-American Relations in the Early Twentieth Century." In *Confrontation and Cooperation: Germany and the United States in the Era of World War I, 1900–1924,* edited by Hans-Jürgen Schröder, 13–31. Providence, RI: Berg, 1993.

Dobson, Alan P. *Anglo-American Relations in the Twentieth Century: Of Friendship, Conflict, and the Rise and Decline of Superpowers.* New York: Routledge, 1995.

Dumbrell, John. *A Special Relationship: Anglo-American Relations from the Cold War to Iraq.* New York: Palgrave Macmillan, 2006.

Ellis, Sylvia. *Historical Dictionary of Anglo-American Relations.* Lanham, MD: Scarecrow Press, 2009.

Hogan, Michael J. *Informal Entente: The Private Structure of Cooperation in Anglo-American Economic Diplomacy, 1918–1928.* Chicago: Imprint, 1991.

Jones, Howard. *Blue and Gray Diplomacy: A History of Union and Confederate Foreign Relations.* Chapel Hill: University of North Carolina Press, 2010.

Jones, Howard, and Donald A. Rakestraw. *Prologue to Manifest Destiny: Anglo-American Relations in the 1840s.* Wilmington, DE: SR Books, 1997.

Jones, Wilbur D. *The American Problem in British Diplomacy, 1841–1861.* Athens: University of Georgia Press, 1974.

Louis, William Roger, and Hedley Bull, eds. *The Special Relationship: Anglo-American Relations since 1945.* Oxford: Oxford University Press, 1986.

Moser, John E. *Twisting the Lion's Tail: American Anglophobia between the World Wars.* New York: New York University Press, 1999.

Orde, Anne. *The Eclipse of Great Britain: The United States and British Imperial Decline, 1895–1956.* New York: St. Martin's Press, 1996.

Ovendale, Ritchie. *Anglo-American Relations in the Twentieth Century.* New York: St. Martin's Press, 1998.

Perkins, Bradford. *Castlereagh and Adams: England and the United States, 1812–1823.* Berkeley: University of California Press, 1964.

Perkins, Bradford. *The Great Rapprochement: England and the United States, 1895–1914.* New York: Atheneum, 1968.

Riddell, Peter. *Hug Them Close: Blair, Clinton, Bush, and the "Special Relationship."* London: Politico's, 2003.

Svendsen, Adam D. M. *Intelligence Cooperation and the War on Terror: Anglo-American Security Relations after 9/11.* New York: Routledge, 2010.

Watt, D. Cameron. *Succeeding John Bull: America in Britain's Place, 1900–1975: A Study of the Anglo-American Relationship and World Politics in the Context of British and American Foreign-Policy-Making in the Twentieth Century.* New York: Cambridge University Press, 1984.

Woods, Randall Bennett. *A Changing of the Guard: Anglo-American Relations, 1941–1946.* Chapel Hill: University of North Carolina Press, 1990.

Woodward, David R. *Trial by Friendship: Anglo-American Relations, 1917–1918.* Lexington: University Press of Kentucky, 1993.

Donald A. Rakestraw
University College Professor of American Studies
Winthrop University

BUCHANAN, JAMES

1791–1868

Best known as a doughface politician whose presidency exacerbated sectional tensions, James Buchanan's influence on American foreign policy in the antebellum period has often been underestimated. For more than three decades in public office, as a congressman, diplomat, secretary of state, and president, Buchanan championed the cause of American empire. Buchanan's commitment to America's manifest destiny was as integral to his political identity as was his strict constructionist position on domestic issues.

Born in rural central Pennsylvania in 1791 and educated at Dickinson College, Buchanan moved to Lancaster, Pennsylvania, in 1809 to study law. Soon thereafter, he commenced a political career that culminated with his election to the presidency.

By the mid-1820s, as a young congressman, Buchanan advocated the acquisition of Cuba on the premise that it would diffuse slavery from the Upper South, thereby easing sectional tensions and preventing "Africanization" (servile insurrection and black control, as in Haiti) on the doorstep of the United States. Unlike southern fire-eaters and filibustering adventurers, Buchanan never embraced the forcible annexation of Cuba. For him, the logic of a negotiated sale was irrefutable. However, the Spanish government was unprepared to make a deal when Buchanan was in a position to offer one, first as secretary of state (1845–1849) and later as president (1857–1861).

As secretary of state, Buchanan embraced President James K. Polk's (1795–1849) expansionist agenda in the

Northwest and in Mexico. Concerned about his political standing, as well as a possible war with Britain, Buchanan tacked from aggressive to moderate on negotiations over Oregon. In nearly simultaneous cabinet deliberations over Mexican policy, Buchanan opposed the "All Mexico" option. Yet when Polk's emissary, Nicholas Trist (1800–1874), concluded the Treaty of Guadalupe Hidalgo in 1848, Buchanan insisted that Trist had given away too much to the defeated Mexicans. In this Buchanan was overruled.

Regarding Oregon, Buchanan advised Polk that the American people would not support a war for territory beyond the forty-ninth parallel, but he followed Polk's instruction to demand more from the British. In the ongoing diplomatic dance over Oregon, Buchanan served as a moderating force in cabinet deliberations. Yet in the end, when a compromise along the forty-ninth parallel emerged, Buchanan stood alone in the cabinet opposing it. Buchanan's final lurch in favor of 54°40′ was almost certainly a matter of political posturing.

Having failed twice (1848 and 1852) to capture his party's nomination for president, Buchanan's decision to accept appointment as US minister to the Court of St. James proved politically advantageous, but his tenure in London (1853–1855) was not markedly productive. Although he forged a good working relationship with the British foreign secretary, Lord Clarendon (1800–1870), and forcefully articulated the precepts of the Monroe Doctrine, Buchanan failed to ease Britain out of Central America. Neither did he advance prospects for American expansion in that region. Buchanan's forceful protest of illegal British recruitment of American citizens for its armed forces—and his subsequent efforts to mitigate the intemperate statements made by British and American representatives in London and Washington, respectively—once again demonstrated his diplomatic skills. All the same, Buchanan departed London late in 1855 with little to show for his service beyond avoiding armed conflict and securing British acknowledgment of his argument that "free ships make free goods."

Buchanan's service in London insulated him from toxic polemics over slavery expansion and made him the most available Democrat for president in 1856. Having won a narrow victory in a three-way contest, Buchanan's next four years would prove tempestuous and frustrating, culminating in the election of a Republican president and the secession of Deep South states.

Hoping as president to revive and update his old theme of America's manifest destiny, Buchanan achieved modest success at best. Serving in effect as his own secretary of state, he once more engaged the British on sensitive Central American issues, winning small concessions and avoiding escalation of tensions in the far northwest. Buchanan also pursued a vigorous policy against filibusters and did his best to contain the international slave trade, with mixed results. Further efforts to purchase Cuba from Spain made no headway. Buchanan's attempt to buy Alaska from Russia for $5 million also failed, but it did lay the groundwork for William Seward's (1801–1872) success in 1867.

Buchanan's vision of an imperial America never faded, but as his energies and his political capital diminished during his presidency, and as the sectional crisis took center stage in American policy debates, his foreign policy initiatives lost rather than gained momentum. He continues to be remembered less as a leading agent of manifest destiny than as a blundering executive whose policy choices contributed materially to the breakdown of the Union.

SEE ALSO *Manifest Destiny; Polk, James K.*

BIBLIOGRAPHY

Belohlavek, John M. "In Defense of Doughface Diplomacy: A Reevaluation of the Foreign Policy of James Buchanan." In *James Buchanan and the Coming of the Civil War*, edited by John W. Quist and Michael J. Birkner. Gainesville: University Press of Florida, 2013.

Binder, Frederick Moore. *James Buchanan and the American Empire.* Selinsgrove, PA: Susquehanna University Press, 1994.

Donovan, Theresa A. "President Pierce's Ministers at the Court of St. James." *Pennsylvania Magazine of History and Biography* 91 (1967): 457–470.

Klein, Philip S. *President James Buchanan: A Biography.* University Park: Pennsylvania State University Press, 1962.

May, Robert E. "James Buchanan, the Neutrality Laws, and American Invasions of Nicaragua." In *James Buchanan and the Political Crisis of the 1850s*, edited by Michael J. Birkner. Selinsgrove, PA: Susquehanna University Press, 1996.

Smith, Elbert B. *The Presidency of James Buchanan.* Lawrence: University Press of Kansas, 1975.

Michael J. Birkner
Professor of History
Gettysburg College

BUDDHISM

Buddhists traditionally ascribe the teachings of their tradition to an ancient Indian prince named Siddhārtha Gautama, who renounced his worldly position to become the Buddha in the fifth or sixth century BCE. Buddhists do not consider dharma, or the teachings of Buddhism, to be the result of divine revelation but rather the natural law of the universe. Periodically, a being is able to awaken to this dharma and teach the world, making that person a Buddha. Buddhism does not have a creator deity, and it pronounces three characteristics of all existence: impermanence (*anitya*), no-self (*anātman*), and suffering (*duḥkha*). The only way to rid oneself of the suffering that characterizes the persistent rounds of rebirth (*saṃsāra*) is to attain *nirvāṇa*. The exact meaning of *nirvāṇa* has been debated throughout history, but it is agreed that it is a state of ultimate bliss. By the first century CE, Buddhism had spread well beyond its point of origin along the Ganges River. The Silk Roads and other travel routes helped to spread Buddhism west to China and Japan, although it could be argued that pilgrimage sites such as Bōdh Gayā or trade routes such as Gandhāra equally brought differing lineages together. This vast geographical scope resulted in a variety of Buddhist traditions practiced around the world.

EARLY AMERICAN BUDDHISM

There is very little information on Buddhists or Buddhism and the United States prior to the latter part of the nineteenth century. Such writers as Ralph Waldo Emerson (1803–1882) and Henry David Thoreau (1817–1862) publicized their interest in Buddhist thought and texts for over a generation prior to the arrival of Asian immigrants who practiced Buddhism. In 1844 Elizabeth Palmer Peabody (1804–1894) published an excerpt of the Lotus Sūtra in the *Dial*, beginning what Thomas Tweed (2000, 14) has described as the earliest Buddhist "fad." Prior to this, a culture of religious experimentation had laid the groundwork for North American interest in Buddhism as well as acceptance of Asian culture over a century later. The first Chinese Buddhist temples, called Tin Hou Temple and Kong Chow Temple, were established in San Francisco in 1853. However, these temples did not have long-standing organizational strength. The first well-established Buddhist lineage in the United States was the Japanese Jōdo Shinshū Buddhists, arriving in Hawai'i in 1889 and San Francisco in 1899. The Jōdo Shinshū immigrants began to adapt themselves to the religious styles they found in the United States while continuing to make changes and uphold traditions established in the denominational headquarters in Kyoto, Japan. These changes include renaming themselves the Buddhist Churches of America, the addition of pews and hymns, and the removal of many traditional temple elements. These changes reflected transnational adaptations happening in the Jōdo Shinshū organizational structure in Japan at the time as well.

BUDDHISM IN THE FIRST HALF OF THE TWENTIETH CENTURY

Very little has been written about Buddhism in America between 1900 and 1955. This is due in large part to the limitations placed on Asian immigration at the end of the nineteenth century. In the first half of the twentieth century, especially during World War II, American Buddhists experienced racial, ethnic, and religious persecution. Japanese American temples and Buddhist churches were emptied and citizens detained following Executive Order 9066, which authorized the relocation and detention of Japanese Americans. However, from February 19, 1942, to the end of the war, Buddhism continued to grow as Japanese Buddhists kept their traditions alive while incarcerated in the detention camps. Americans were also engaging Buddhist ideas and practices in their own way. Numerous seekers came to Buddhism during this time and began to write about their own viewpoints regarding their new religious tradition. Some of the most active were Anagarika Dharmapala (1864–1933) and Colonel Henry Steel Olcott (1832–1907), the cofounder and first president of the Theosophical Society.

The biggest changes for Buddhism in the United States came through the Immigration and Nationality Acts of 1952 and 1965, which liberalized immigration from Asian countries. Concordantly, interest in Buddhism and particularly Zen began in the 1950s with Beat generation writers such as Jack Kerouac (1922–1969), Alan Watts (1915–1973), and Gary Snyder (b. 1930) and carried through the 1960s hippie counterculture movement and communalism. After the 1960s, numerous Buddhist groups that had not had an institutional presence in the United States, including the Vietnamese, Tibetans, and Sri Lankans, began to immigrate and set up lasting temples. The inclusion of diverse groups from all over the world that were still connected to their home countries gave American Buddhism a transnational character.

LATER DEVELOPMENTS IN AMERICA

Beginning in the 1950s, and becoming more predominant in the 1960s, Americans began to embrace Buddhism as a legitimate religious tradition. The most predominant forms at this early stage were Zen- and Theravāda-influenced forms such as insight meditation (*Vipassanā*). Zen is a meditation-based form of Buddhism found mainly in East Asia, while *Vipassanā* is a form of meditation utilizing concentration on the body and mental processes. In the 1960s, numerous seekers traveled to Japan, Thailand, India, and various other locations to ordain as monks and nuns. The Chinese invasion of Tibet in 1950 also began Tibetan immigration to the United States, although the first Tibetan Buddhist Temple was founded in 1958 in New Jersey for the Kalmyk community there.

Since the 1960s, Buddhist communities have flourished across the United States. Intra-Buddhist communication and organizations have been prevalent, as has dialogue with other religions. This led to the creation of regional organizations such as the Buddhist Council of the Midwest, which organizes celebrations and fosters unity among various lineages. As Richard Hughes Seager (1999) has pointed out, North America represents one of the first locations in modern history where so many various forms of Buddhism have come together in such proximity. The intermingling of different forms of Buddhism in the United States has allowed for interreligious dialogue, the creation of interfaith organizations, and the development of Buddhist hybridity. Writings such as Thích Nhất Hạnh's (b. 1926) *Living Buddha, Living Christ* are not only on the *New York Times* best-seller list but they also demonstrate the fluidity of Buddhist American identities. Multiple religious identities are common in the United States. Jewish Buddhists make up large proportions of Buddhist groups and include some of the most prominent names in American Buddhist communities, such as Joseph Goldstein (b. 1944), Jack Kornfield (b. 1945), and Sharon Salzberg (b. 1952).

Buddhism in the United States reflects a wide variety of lineages, practices, and countries of origin. This variety includes "Buddhism without Beliefs," Soka Gakkai International (SGI), and the Fo Guang Shan. Such organizations as Fo Guang Shan, SGI, and the Tzu Chi Foundation are international organizations with central leadership in Asia but branches and hierarchies across North America as well. Since 1991, SGI-USA, with roots in Japanese Nichiren, has become one of the most popular Buddhist organizations in the United States. Fo Guang Shan is a Taiwan-based Chán Humanistic Buddhism movement founded in 1967 by Venerable Master Hsing Yun (b. 1927).

Buddhism in the United States has been a fixture of popular culture over the past few decades, with movies such as *Kundun* and *Seven Years in Tibet,* as well as appearances on *The Simpsons* and conversions by celebrities such as Orlando Bloom (b. 1977) and Tina Turner (b. 1939). Since the turn of the millennium Buddhism's public visibility has increased through the rise of the mindfulness movement. Mindfulness is an ancient Buddhist meditation practice whereby the subject deeply focuses on every task and every process of both body and mind while it is performed. As Jeff Wilson (2014) explains, in many cases mindfulness has been completely removed from Buddhism and placed within Western cultural constructs such as mindfulness for sex and mindfulness for CEOs. As Wilson describes, the mindfulness movement has mutually transformed Buddhism and American culture. Buddhists have taken on the language of science and transformed some traditional teachings in order to include mindfulness theories and practices. American culture has begun to use mindfulness practice in nearly every aspect of life. The practice is recommended by psychologists to patients and school administrators to elementary-age children. The pervasive use of mindfulness beyond Buddhists is evidence of the way Buddhism has influenced American culture and how American culture has influenced Buddhism.

SEE ALSO *China; India; Japan; World's Parliament of Religions (1893)*

BIBLIOGRAPHY

Albanese, Catherine L. *A Republic of Mind and Spirit: A Cultural History of American Metaphysical Religion.* New Haven, CT: Yale University Press, 2007.

Ama, Michihiro. *Immigrants to the Pure Land: The Modernization, Acculturation, and Globalization of Shin Buddhism, 1898–1941.* Honolulu: University of Hawai'i Press, 2011.

Schmidt, Leigh Eric. *Restless Souls: The Making of American Spirituality: From Emerson to Oprah.* San Francisco: HarperSanFrancisco, 2005.

Seager, Richard Hughes. *Buddhism in America.* New York: Columbia University Press, 1999.

Tweed, Thomas A. *The American Encounter with Buddhism, 1844–1912: Victorian Culture and the Limits of Dissent.* Chapel Hill: University of North Carolina Press, 2000.

Wilson, Jeff. *Mindful America: The Mutual Transformation of Buddhist Meditation and American Culture.* Oxford: Oxford University Press, 2014.

Ryan Anningson
Doctoral Candidate
Wilfrid Laurier University–University of Waterloo, Joint PhD Program in Religious Diversity in North America

BUFFALO BILL'S WILD WEST

At the dawn of the twentieth century, William F. "Buffalo Bill" Cody (1846–1917) was the one of the most famous Americans in the world, and his path from poverty and obscurity to international celebrity is one of the most remarkable stories of America's Gilded Age. While Cody made his mark on American culture through popular media versions of his frontier experiences in settling, hunting, scouting, and developing the American West, it is his efforts to celebrate the region's history as a nationalistic movement through thousands of performances of *Buffalo Bill's Wild West* within the United States, Canada, and Europe that created an enduring global legacy. Cody and his colleagues did not refer to their product as a "show" but rather as an historical exhibition, distinguishing it from circuses and other spectacles and emphasizing its authenticity and educational quality in an attempt to market the event to a middlebrow clientele. From 1883 to 1916, Cody presented an idealized image of the American West to large audiences in more than 2,800 American locales and 550 European towns and cities, entertaining and educating millions of attendees. Intriguingly, Cody initially planned an international production, and *Buffalo Bill's Wild West* performed equally in Europe and America during its first ten years.

ORIGINS

Cody's "Buffalo Bill" persona and his reputation as the premiere Western frontiersman had been established as early as 1869 when Ned Buntline's *Buffalo Bill, the King of Border Men* appeared serially in Street and Smith's *New York Weekly*, followed by hundreds of other Buffalo Bill dime novels over the next forty years. The authentic frontier mise-en-scène that Cody arranged for the celebrity buffalo hunts he guided in the 1870s, the more than 350 performances of the *Buffalo Bill Combination* melodramas in the 1870s and 1880s, and the publication of his autobiography in 1879 each contributed elements to the development of an enormously successful grand Western spectacle that would come to be known as *Buffalo Bill's Wild West.*

The concept of *Buffalo Bill's Wild West,* showcasing horsemanship and cowboy culture, was born with the 1882 Independence Day celebration produced by Cody in his hometown of North Platte, Nebraska. The following year, Cody partnered with North Platte dentist and expert marksman William Frank "Doc" Carver (1851–1927) to produce *The Wild West, Hon. W. F. Cody and Dr. W. F. Carver's Rocky Mountain and Prairie Exhibition* for one season before Cody teamed with actor-manager Nathan Salsbury (1846–1902) to create *Buffalo Bill's Wild West.* Along with general manager and publicist John M. Burke (1842–1917),

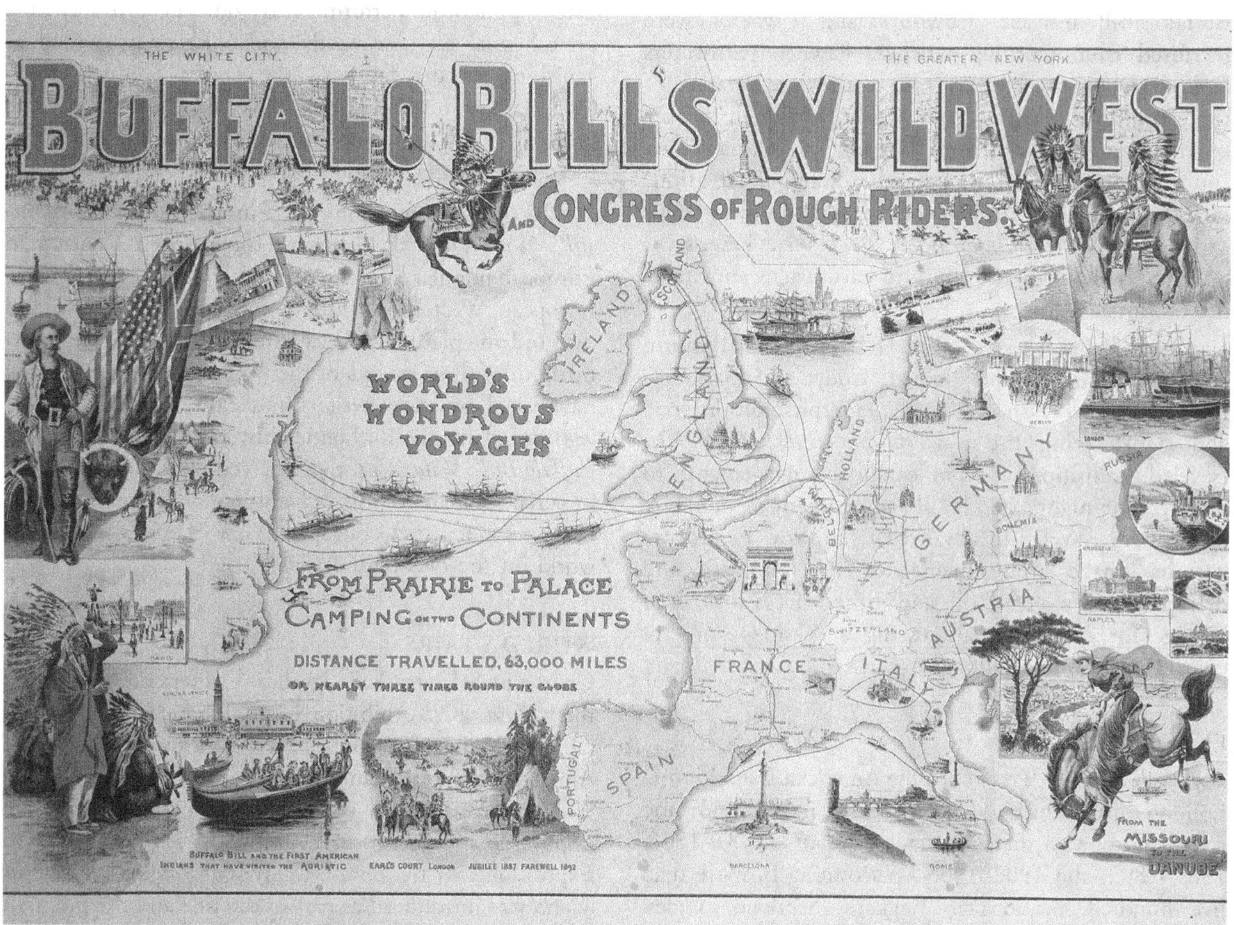

***Map from a program for* Buffalo Bill's Wild West and Congress of Rough Riders.** *Buffalo Bill Cody and his theatrical partner successfully presented their Wild West exhibition in conjunction with world's fairs. At the World's Columbian Exposition in Chicago in 1893, the phrase "Congress of Rough Riders of the World" was introduced as part of the title and the program revised to feature mounted military troops from many nations alongside celebrated sharpshooters.* **BUFFALO BILL CENTER OF THE WEST**

the co-owners exhibited the production regularly from 1884 to 1908, first in the United States and then in Europe. Eventually more than one hundred different Wild West–style shows copied Cody's model and toured widely both nationally and internationally between 1885 and 1950.

ELEMENTS OF THE PROGRAM

Featuring exhibitions of skill and bravery associated with popular figures inhabiting the American West, a typical *Buffalo Bill's Wild West* program included feats of marksmanship, races between American cowboys, Mexican *vaqueros*, and Native Americans, along with demonstrations of performers riding bucking horses, roping wild Texas steers, and hunting buffalo. More complex stagecraft resulted in dramatic "illustrations" of Indian attacks on the Old Deadwood Stagecoach, emigrant wagons, and a homestead cabin, as well as reenactments of iconic historical events, such as Custer's Last Stand, with the entire program presided over by Buffalo Bill himself. Cowboys and *vaqueros* were recruited from working ranches. Pawnee performers from Oklahoma were a key part of the first iteration of the exhibition in 1883. Later, Cody petitioned the US government to allow him to employ Lakota Sioux Indians from the Pine Ridge and Rosebud reservations in South Dakota. Indian performers enjoyed their experiences with *Buffalo Bill's Wild West* because it afforded them an opportunity to earn wages and travel internationally.

In 1895, James A. Bailey (1847–1906) of Barnum & Bailey Circus fame joined Cody and Salsbury, injecting needed cash to keep the enterprise on the road and transforming the way *Buffalo Bill's Wild West* traveled, transitioning from extended engagements to mostly one-night stands. The company's publicity department traveled in advance of the show to procure permits, make arrangements for the purchase and delivery of tons of food and other necessities, and arrange for newspaper advertising and the posting of colorful posters and billboards.

EUROPEAN TOURS

Buffalo Bill's Wild West joined the American Exhibition in London during Queen Victoria's Jubilee in May 1887 and toured Europe on three separate occasions—1887–1888, 1889–1892, and 1902–1906—performing in more than five hundred locations in England, Scotland, Wales, France, Spain, Italy, Germany, Austria-Hungary, and Belgium. These performances confirmed European conceptions of the American West (and the United States) and ignited what contemporaries called a "Wild West Fever" that erupted from the ideas, characters, and settings that people in Europe had read and dreamed about for decades. Cody and Salsbury understood that cosmopolitan London in particular, and Europe in general, was the ideal location for a spectacle based on America's provincial Western frontier to make a valid statement of American authenticity. Europeans scorned late nineteenth-century American culture as a crassly commercial and inauthentic mixing of the lowbrow and the highbrow, the vulgar and the sublime. Emphasizing authenticity, Cody successfully wedded history and romantic nostalgia, making his program appealing to its audiences.

While each country held its own image of the American West and the meanings conveyed by it, *Buffalo Bill's Wild West* spoke to the specific desires and general anxieties of its European audiences. British audiences, including Queen Victoria (1819–1901) herself, saw the Native American performers as both authentic exotic ethnographic subjects in a social Darwinist manner and as dramatic foils to a recognizable imperial impulse toward progress. German and Italian audiences marveled at the Native American performers as romantic symbols of a preindustrial era that Cody and Salsbury presented as vanishing in the face of "the drama of civilization" (American manifest destiny). This trope aligned with the idea of the "white man's burden," one of the dominant themes of the era's world's fairs.

In the years following the European tours of *Buffalo Bill's Wild West*, the images it popularized recurred in European popular literature, Buffalo Bill dime novels, new European Western adventure novels, Italian opera, and the Indian picture and Western genres of the new medium of film. Images of the American frontier initially established by travel writers and early novelists became legitimized by the authentic, historical performances of *Buffalo Bill's Wild West*, then merged with the celebratory imperialistic expansionist adventures of European countries to create a new European view of America and the world for the twentieth century.

WORLD'S FAIRS

Cody and Salsbury had significant experience presenting their *Wild West* exhibition in conjunction with world's fairs, including the fair in New Orleans in 1884, the American Exhibition in London in 1887, the Exposition Universelle in Paris in 1889, and the World's Columbian Exposition in Chicago in 1893. It was at the Columbian Exposition that the phrase *Congress of Rough Riders of the World* was introduced as part of the title and the program was revised to feature mounted military troops from many nations alongside celebrated sharpshooters like Annie Oakley (1860–1926) and Johnny Baker (1869–1931) and American cowboys and Native American performers. In 1899, in yet another example of Cody's emphasis on

Colored lithograph poster announcing "je viens" (I'm coming), c. 1889. *From 1883 to 1916, Buffalo Bill Cody presented an idealized image of the American West to large audiences in more than 2,800 American locales and 550 European towns and cities, entertaining and educating millions of attendees.* BUFFALO BILL MUSEUM/BUFFALO BILL CENTER OF THE WEST

authenticity, sixteen of Theodore Roosevelt's Rough Riders joined the *Wild West* and participated in a dramatization of the taking of San Juan Hill, a clear demonstration of American imperialism.

FINAL YEARS AND LASTING IMPACT

After Bailey died in 1906, Cody found himself entangled in Bailey's estate litigation, leaving him in dire financial straits. Major Gordon W. "Pawnee Bill" Lillie (1860–1942) purchased the interest in *Buffalo Bill's Wild West* held by the Bailey estate in 1909, and the following year the two men created *Buffalo Bill's Wild West Combined with Pawnee Bill's Great Far East.* This exhibition toured America until 1913, when once again Cody found himself financially strapped and his *Wild West* enterprise forced into bankruptcy. Cody was relegated to touring America in a series of final performances with the *Sells-Floto Circus* in 1914 and 1915 and *Miller Brothers and Arlington 101 Ranch Real Wild West* in 1916.

Cody died on January 10, 1917, at the age of seventy in Denver, Colorado. The Wild West that he popularized cemented the stereotypical images of the American frontier in popular culture both in America and across the globe—an image frequently reappearing in literature and film in the century following Buffalo Bill's final performance. *Buffalo Bill's Wild West* also began an American tradition that continues today at almost every public function: the playing of "The Star-Spangled Banner," which became the official national anthem in 1931, partly due to the popularization of the song through the *Wild West* performances.

SEE ALSO *Americanization; Empire, US; Exceptionalism; Roosevelt, Theodore; Spanish-American War*

BIBLIOGRAPHY

Cody, William F. *The Wild West in England.* Edited by Frank Christianson. Lincoln: University of Nebraska Press, 2012. Originally published in 1888.

Griffin, Charles Eldridge. *Four Years in Europe with Buffalo Bill.* Edited by Chris Dixon. Lincoln: University of Nebraska Press, 2010. Originally published in 1908.

Kasson, Joy S. *Buffalo Bill's Wild West: Celebrity, Memory, and Popular History.* New York: Hill and Wang, 2000.

Kroes, Rob. "European Responses to American Mass Culture: The Case of Buffalo Bill's Wild West." *European Contributions to American Studies* 54 (January 2005): 51–71.

Lottini, Irene. "When Buffalo Bill Crossed the Ocean: Native American Scenes in Early Twentieth-Century European Culture." *European Journal of American Culture* 31, 3 (2012): 187–203.

Warren, Louis S. *Buffalo Bill's America: William Cody and the Wild West Show.* New York: Knopf, 2005.

The William F. Cody Archive: Documenting the Life and Times of Buffalo Bill. http://codyarchive.org

Douglas Seefeldt
Assistant Professor, Department of History, Ball State University
Senior Digital Editor, The Papers of William F. Cody

BUNDY, McGEORGE
1919–1996

McGeorge Bundy served as special assistant for national security affairs during the John F. Kennedy (1917–1963) and Lyndon B. Johnson (1908–1973) administrations. Bundy, by reconceptualizing this role, became the president's primary foreign policy adviser during the middle period of the Cold War.

Following Kennedy's election in November 1960, he asked Bundy, dean of the Faculty of Arts and Sciences at Harvard University, to join his administration as special assistant for national security affairs. After the inauguration, Bundy, in a memorandum to Kennedy, provided an overview of the National Security Council (NSC) as it had functioned during the Dwight D. Eisenhower (1890–1969) administration, adding that the body had grown too large. In a subsequent memorandum, he stressed that the NSC should mirror Kennedy's management style, not Eisenhower's. Bundy reorganized the NSC based on Kennedy's decision-making preference. Both the Operations Coordinating Board and the Planning Board were abolished (Preston 2006, 40). Bundy instituted the National Security Action Memorandum, which informed the executive branch agencies of "new policy directives" (Preston 2006, 41). In place of the Planning Board, Bundy, instead, organized NSC staffers in positions along geographic or functional lines. These staff members, such as Walt Rostow (1916–2003), Carl Kaysen (1920–2010), Robert Komer (1922–2000), and Michael Forrestal (1927–1989), also enjoyed "direct access" to the president (Preston 2006, 43).

After Kennedy's assassination on November 22, 1963, Johnson asked Bundy to remain as national security adviser. When others questioned Bundy's decision to stay on in a Johnson administration, Bundy believed that his "loyalties should be to the office of the presidency" and not with a specific individual (Bird 1998, 268). In contrast to the Kennedy administration, Johnson held fewer NSC meetings, preferring to discuss issues with Bundy, Secretary of State Dean Rusk (1909–1994), Secretary of Defense Robert McNamara (1916–2009), and other senior officials in what would become known as the "Tuesday lunch." In early 1966, Bundy resigned and accepted the presidency of the Ford Foundation, where he served until 1979. He then taught in the history department at New York University.

Bundy played key roles in three of the major foreign policy crises of the Kennedy and Johnson administrations. He supported the April 1961 Cuban Bay of Pigs invasion, for he believed that the United States must act decisively against Premier Fidel Castro. The invasion's failure led Bundy to offer his resignation to Kennedy, even as Bundy blamed the Central Intelligence Agency and the Joint Chiefs of Staff for the debacle. Kennedy refused to accept the resignation and instead moved Bundy and his staff from the Old Executive Office Building to the White House, opting to have Bundy in closer proximity to the Oval Office (Bird 1998, 197). After the administration initiated Operation Mongoose, a covert program directed at Cuba, Bundy joined the "Special Group Augmented" and served as its chair.

On October 15, 1962, Bundy learned of the existence of Soviet medium-range and intermediate-range ballistic missiles in Cuba. Soviet premier Nikita Khrushchev (1894–1971) had reached a secret agreement with Castro to provide missiles as a deterrent to any future US invasion. As a member of the Executive Committee (ExComm) of the NSC, Bundy was present for the deliberations concerning the shape the American response would take; all US officials agreed that the missiles had to be removed. By his own later admission, Bundy served as the "straw boss" for all three options—diplomacy, blockade, and airstrike—concluding that the president would be "ill-served" if "all reasonable options" were not explored (Bundy 1988, 400). Kennedy ultimately opted for a naval quarantine of Cuba.

Bundy believed that the United States should reject any neutralization of South Vietnam and supported South Vietnamese efforts to inculcate democratic reform. Following the assassination of South Vietnamese president Ngo Dinh Diem on November 2, 1963, Bundy drafted and issued NSAM 273. The memorandum reaffirmed the US objective in South Vietnam to assist its people and government against an externally directed Communist conspiracy. As the situation deteriorated in the spring of 1964, Bundy recommended that Johnson make a decision to use "selected and carefully graduated" military force against North Vietnam. Following the February 1965 Vietcong attack on the US military billet at Pleiku, Bundy, who was in South Vietnam at the time, pushed for immediate, sustained reprisals against North Vietnam. He argued that defeat seemed inevitable unless the United States stepped up its commitment to the South Vietnamese government. He also later pressed Johnson to elucidate a broader program of economic reform, which Johnson outlined in an April 7, 1965, speech at Johns Hopkins University.

SEE ALSO *Bay of Pigs; Cuban Missile Crisis; Ford Foundation; Johnson, Lyndon Baines; Kennedy, John Fitzgerald; McNamara, Robert S.; Vietnam War*

BIBLIOGRAPHY

Bird, Kai. *The Color of Truth: McGeorge Bundy and William Bundy, Brothers in Arms: A Biography.* New York: Simon and Schuster, 1998.

Bundy, McGeorge. *Danger and Survival: Choices about the Bomb in the First Fifty Years.* New York: Random House, 1988.

Clausen, Paul, Evan M. Duncan, and Jeffrey A. Soukup, eds. *Foreign Relations of the United States, 1961–1963,* Vol. 25: *Organization of Foreign Policy; Information Policy; United Nations; Scientific Matters.* Washington, DC: GPO, 2001.

Giglio, James N. *The Presidency of John F. Kennedy.* Lawrence: University Press of Kansas, 1991.

Humphrey, David C., Ronald D. Landa, and Louis J. Smith. *Foreign Relations of the United States, 1964–1968,* Vol. 2: *Vietnam, January–June 1965.* Washington, DC: GPO, 1996.

Kaysen, Carl. "McGeorge Bundy (30 March 1919–16 September 1996)." *Proceedings of the American Philosophical Society* 142, 3 (1998): 458–465.

Keefer, Edward C., and Charles S. Sampson. *Foreign Relations of the United States, 1964–1968,* Vol. 1: *Vietnam, 1964.* Washington, DC: GPO, 1992.

Patterson, Thomas G., and William J. Brophy. "October Missiles and November Elections: The Cuban Missile Crisis and American Politics, 1962." *Journal of American History* 73, 1 (1986): 87–119.

Preston, Andrew. *The War Council: McGeorge Bundy, the NSC, and Vietnam.* Cambridge, MA: Harvard University Press, 2006.

Kristin L. Ahlberg
Office of the Historian
US Department of State

The views expressed in this essay are those of the author and are not necessarily those of the US Department of State or the US government. This essay is based on fully declassified and publicly available sources.

BUSH, GEORGE H. W.

1924–

George Herbert Walker Bush, the forty-first president of the United States, commenced his career in foreign affairs during the presidency of Richard M. Nixon. Nixon tapped Bush, who had earlier served two terms in the US House representing Texas's seventh congressional district, to be ambassador to the United Nations in 1971. Heeding the call of Nixon again in 1973, Bush chaired the Republican National Committee amid revelations of the Watergate scandal. President Gerald Ford rewarded Bush for his efforts to sustain the Republican Party by appointing him liaison to China in late 1974 as the two superpowers sought to normalize bilateral relations. Bush remained in the position until 1976, when Ford asked him to direct the Central Intelligence Agency (CIA), which was reeling from a series of scandals, internal mismanagement, and congressional scrutiny.

PATHWAY TO THE WHITE HOUSE

Bush exited national politics in 1976 upon the election of Democratic president Jimmy Carter. He reemerged on the national stage in 1980 in an unsuccessful bid for the Republican presidential nomination against former California governor Ronald Reagan. Faced with a host of prominent Republican candidates for vice president, including former president Ford, Reagan announced the choice of Bush as his running mate on the eve of the convention in Detroit, Michigan. Bush's assurance of unequivocal support of Reagan's agenda, his historical loyalty and sense of duty to past presidents, and his foreign policy credentials buttressed Reagan's ultimate decision.

As vice president during Reagan's first term, Bush chaired the President's Task Force on Deregulation and another task force on drug smuggling. His antidrug efforts would later culminate in the creation of the Office of National Drug Control Policy (ONDCP) by Congress in 1988 as part of a war on drugs. As president, Bush named the first director of the ONDCP in 1989. In 1983, Bush traveled to El Salvador in a bid to halt death squads utilized by the interim leader of the war-torn Central American country, Álvaro Magaña, to eliminate dissidents.

In Reagan's second term, Bush traveled abroad frequently as the president's foreign policy emissary, making invaluable contacts with world leaders that would solidify his coalition-building skills during the First Gulf War (1990–1991). Nonetheless, when news broke in 1986 that the Reagan administration had sold arms to Iran in exchange for the release of US nationals held in the Middle East, and that aides had funneled money to counterrevolutionaries in Central America in violation of congressional legislation, Bush was implicated in the

Iran-Contra scandal. Conclusive evidence of Bush's involvement never emerged.

BUSH'S PRESIDENCY AND THE FIRST GULF WAR

In the absence of a far-reaching domestic agenda, foreign policy dominated Bush's four years in office. The unforeseen collapse of the Berlin Wall in 1989 marked the end of Soviet domination of the former Warsaw Pact countries in Eastern and Central Europe. That same year, Bush engineered the successful invasion and liberation of the Central American nation of Panama, deposing dictator and alleged drug-smuggler Manuel Noriega. By 1991, Bush met with Soviet leader Mikhail Gorbachev to assuage Cold War tensions, and in July he signed the Strategic Arms Reduction Treaty (START), which reduced the nuclear stockpiles of both countries in advance of the disintegration of the Soviet Union on December 26, 1991. While many anticipated a "peace dividend" or decreased defense spending following the Soviet Union's demise, Bush worked immediately on an aid bill to the new Commonwealth of Independent States in order to secure the Russian nuclear arsenal.

The pivotal foreign policy event in Bush's presidency was Iraqi dictator Saddam Hussein's invasion of the tiny emirate of Kuwait in summer 1990. Hussein claimed that Kuwait had engaged in "horizontal drilling" of Iraqi oil fields and further contended that Kuwait was a rightful province of Iraq. In August 1990 Bush issued an ultimatum to Hussein to remove Iraqi troops from Kuwait and restore the status quo ante or face military action by January 1991.

Bush assembled an impressive international coalition of thirty-four countries that lent logistical, hardware, and troop support for the invasion of Iraq, which was sanctioned by the United Nations. The invasion commenced on January 17, 1991, and major damage to the Iraqi air force and army was inflicted within ninety-six hours under the steadfast command of the chairman of the Joint Chiefs of Staff, Colin Powell. The hostilities terminated on February 28, 1991. The exact number of Iraqis killed in the conflict remains disputed, with figures ranging from 20,000 to 100,000 (troops and civilians). Approximately 1,000 Kuwaiti civilians were killed, along with 303 American troops. Additionally, the ecological disaster precipitated by retreating Iraqi forces' burning of oil fields created an untold cost to the regional environment for decades.

On March 11, 1991, Bush gave a speech in which he referred to a "new world order." Critics charged that his design was for a "one world government." A closer reading, however, underscores the elaboration of a set of principles to guide US foreign policy that comprised a security plan for the Persian Gulf region, a commitment to preclude the Iraqi regime from developing weapons of mass destruction, a broad-brush plan for peace under United Nations resolutions, and regional economic development. Bush's leadership in the Persian Gulf War and the United States' continued, influential role in the region underscored his commitment to the notion of American exceptionalism in foreign affairs.

THE 1992 CAMPAIGN AND AFTER

As the electorate turned to domestic issues following the Gulf War, Bush came under increased scrutiny for rising unemployment and an economic slowdown. The entry of Reform Party candidate and millionaire H. Ross Perot confounded Bush's reelection bid in 1992, as Perot and Democratic candidate William J. Clinton indefatigably criticized Bush on the economic downturn, with allegedly no plan for a turnaround. Perot also condemned Bush's negotiation of the North American Free Trade Agreement (NAFTA) with Canada and Mexico. Perot's candidacy cost Bush a sizable number of votes among disaffected Republicans, and ultimately enabled Clinton to emerge victorious with a plurality of the popular vote.

Upon leaving office, Bush made the controversial decision to pardon six key figures in the Iran-Contra scandal. He granted pardons to Caspar Weinberger, Elliott Abrams, and Robert McFarlane, along with three employees of the CIA. In his postpresidency, Bush remained active in foreign affairs and philanthropy, joining with former president Clinton in disaster relief for victims of the 2004 tsunami in the Indian Ocean and Hurricane Katrina in 2005. The legacy of his presidency is enshrined at the George Bush Presidential Library and Museum on the campus of Texas A&M University in College Station, Texas, which opened in 1997.

SEE ALSO *Bush, George W.; Central Intelligence Agency (CIA); Cheney, Dick; Cold War; Exceptionalism; New World Order; Powell, Colin; Reagan, Ronald Wilson; War on Drugs*

BIBLIOGRAPHY

Barilleaux, Ryan J., and Mark J. Rozell. *Power and Prudence: The Presidency of George H. W. Bush.* College Station: Texas A&M University Press, 2004.

Bose, Mena, and Rosanna Perotti, eds. *From Cold War to New World Order: The Foreign Policy of George Bush.* Westport, CT: Greenwood Press, 2002.

Bush, George, and Brent Scowcroft. *A World Transformed.* New York: Knopf, 1998.

Duffy, Michael, and Dan Goodgame. *Marching in Place: The Status Quo Presidency of George Bush.* New York: Simon and Schuster, 1992.

Gilboa, Eytan. "The Panama Invasion Revisited: Lessons for the Use of Force in the Post Cold War Era." *Political Science Quarterly* 110, 4 (1995–1996): 539–562.

Greene, John Robert. *The Presidency of George H. W. Bush*. 2nd ed. Lawrence: University Press of Kansas, 2015.

Hess, Gary R. *Presidential Decisions for War: Korea, Vietnam, the Persian Gulf, and Iraq*. 2nd ed. Baltimore, MD: Johns Hopkins University Press, 2009.

Ruggie, John Gerald. "Third Try at World Order? America and Multilateralism after the Cold War." *Political Science Quarterly* 109, 4 (1994): 553–570.

Richard S. Conley
Associate Professor of Political Science
University of Florida

BUSH, GEORGE W.

1946–

George Walker Bush, the forty-third president of the United States, was born in New Haven, Connecticut, on July 6, 1946, to George H. W. Bush (forty-first president of the United States) and Barbara Bush, but spent the majority of his childhood in Midland, Texas. While his parents were transplants to the region, George W. Bush viewed Midland as home. As a result, many of his conservative values can be traced to Midland. As Bush got older, he followed his father's path, attending Phillips Academy in Andover, Massachusetts, and Yale University. After graduation from Yale, Bush served in the Texas Air National Guard. Later, he attended Harvard Business School, where he obtained his MBA.

EARLY CAREER

In 1975, Bush headed back to Midland, where he got involved in the oil business. By 1986, his company, Spectrum 7, was facing serious losses; Harken Oil and Gas took the company over and assumed its debts. In 1988 Bush served as the "loyalty thermometer" in his father's presidential campaign, monitoring leaks, dealing with media, and mediating staff disputes. Following the successful campaign, Bush became part owner of the Texas Rangers baseball franchise. After his father's unsuccessful bid for reelection in 1992, Bush was free to pursue his own political career. In 1994, he ran against the popular Democratic governor of Texas, Ann Richards (1933–2006), defeating her and serving two terms as governor of the state.

INITIAL OPPOSITION TO INTERVENTIONIST FOREIGN POLICY

In 2000 Bush defeated Vice President Al Gore in a narrow and controversial presidential election. As with most presidential campaigns, the focus was on domestic politics. Bush promised a humble foreign policy and was opposed to nation building in general, citing failed interventionist policies in Somalia and Haiti; his view was largely based on the ideas of his primary foreign policy adviser, Condoleezza Rice. Rice took a dim view of military interventions, particularly for humanitarian reasons, but never clearly outlined when military force might be justified. Instead, Bush suggested that the United States should strengthen its military, scale back military commitments, and focus on great powers like China and Russia.

The vision he expressed throughout the campaign and into his presidency emphasized American exceptionalism. Backed by a strong military, the United States could promote democracy and democratization throughout the world. Most notably, American values would promote stability and order in the international system, particularly in the post–Cold War world. Bush was especially critical of the Clinton administration's lack of vision during the decade after the end of the Cold War.

9/11 AND THE WARS IN AFGHANISTAN AND IRAQ

Once in office, the Bush foreign policy became mired in interagency reviews, as the administration focused its attention on domestic issues. On September 11, 2001, the administration was forced to refocus its energies toward foreign rather than domestic policy after al-Qaeda terrorists led by Osama bin Laden (1957–2011) attacked the World Trade Center and the Pentagon. Bin Laden and his terrorist network were being protected by the Taliban government in Afghanistan. On September 20, President Bush delivered a speech to Congress that amounted to a declaration of war. Bush demanded that Afghanistan surrender to the United States not only bin Laden, but all members of al-Qaeda currently operating in the country. "They will hand over the terrorists," Bush stated, "or they will share in their fate." On October 7, Bush launched the war with Afghanistan, beginning what would become a larger war on terror. The war removed the Taliban from the country, established a fledgling democracy, and put al-Qaeda on the run. Even before the war was over, however, Bush had turned his attention to an old adversary, Iraq and Saddam Hussein (1937–2006).

Iraq had not been implicated in the September 11 attacks, but Bush linked the decision to oust Saddam Hussein to the newly declared war on terror. Most significantly, Bush emphasized the potentially dangerous combination of terrorism, regimes sponsoring terrorism, and weapons of mass destruction. Following the Iraqi invasion of Kuwait in 1990 and the subsequent eviction of Iraq from Kuwait in 1991, the international community, led by the United States, mandated that Iraq destroy its caches of biological and chemical weapons and dismantle its nuclear weapons research program. On January 29,

2002, Bush made it clear that he would not allow Iraq to acquire these weapons or deliver them into the hands of terrorists, launching a wider war on terror against what Bush termed the "axis of evil," which also included Iran and North Korea. On March 19, 2003, Bush launched the invasion of Iraq, which ousted Hussein's regime.

Bush's decision to invade Iraq was the most controversial decision of his presidency. The October 2002 resolution authorizing the invasion of Iraq that he presented to Congress received bipartisan support. On November 8, 2002, Bush secured a unanimous vote in the United Nations Security Council authorizing the return of weapons inspectors and promising "serious consequences" if Iraq did not cooperate (Resolution 1441). On March 17, 2003, Bush issued an ultimatum to Hussein, demanding that he give up power within forty-eight hours. On March 19, the United States launched its invasion of Iraq. On April 9, Baghdad fell, symbolically marking the end to Hussein's regime. In July, US forces killed Hussein's sons, Uday and Qusay, and on December 13 they captured Saddam Hussein.

Despite declaring the "mission accomplished" on May 1, 2003, chaos reigned in Iraq for years as the US occupation force faced an insurgency. To counter the insurgency, Bush authorized the "New Way Forward" in 2007, a strategy more commonly referred to as the "surge" because it increased the number of troops in Iraq in order to provide more security in Baghdad and Anbar Province. The surge proved effective, although the controversy over the war in Iraq did not end.

In 2003, the Abu Ghraib torture scandal emerged. During the war, there were allegations of physical and sexual abuse, torture, rape, sodomy, and murder by members of the US Army and Central Intelligence Agency. Although the Bush administration attempted to portray the abuses as isolated incidents, it soon became clear that this was not the case. Later, documents known as the Torture Memos came to light and confirmed the authorization of "enhanced interrogation techniques." A 2014 Senate inquiry into the matter also confirmed the human rights abuses. While the memos argued that international humanitarian laws, such as the Geneva Conventions, did not apply to American interrogators overseas, subsequent US Supreme Court cases, including *Hamdan v. Rumsfeld* (2006), ruled that the Geneva Conventions did apply.

SEE ALSO *Abu Ghraib; Cheney, Dick; Exceptionalism; Gore, Albert, Jr.; Guantánamo Bay; Neoliberalism; September 11, 2001; War on Terror*

BIBLIOGRAPHY

Bush, George W. "Address to a Joint Session of Congress and the American People." September 20, 2001. http://georgewbush-whitehouse.archives.gov/news/releases/2001/09/20010920-8.html

Bush, George W. "President Delivers State of the Union Address." January 29, 2002. http://georgewbush-whitehouse.archives.gov/news/releases/2002/01/20020129-11.html

Bush, George W. *Decision Points*. New York: Crown, 2010.

Cairo, Michael F. *The Gulf: The Bush Presidencies and the Middle East*. Lexington: University Press of Kentucky, 2012.

National Commission on Terrorist Attacks upon the United States. *The 9/11 Commission Report: Final Report of the National Commission on Terrorist Attacks upon the United States*. Chaired by Thomas H. Kean and Lee H. Hamilton. Washington, DC: GPO, 2004. http://www.9-11commission.gov/report/911Report.pdf

Peleg, Ilan. *The Legacy of George W. Bush's Foreign Policy: Moving beyond Neoconservatism*. Boulder, CO: Westview Press, 2009.

Rice, Condoleezza. "Campaign 2000: Promoting the National Interest." *Foreign Affairs* 79, 1 (January/February 2000): 45–62. http://www.foreignaffairs.com/articles/55630/condoleezza-rice/campaign-2000-promoting-the-national-interest

The Torture Archive. National Security Archives. George Washington University. http://www2.gwu.edu/~nsarchiv/torture_archive/

United Nations Security Council. Resolution 1441. November 8, 2002. http://www.un.org/depts/unmovic/documents/1441.pdf

Michael F. Cairo
Professor of Political Science
Transylvania University

BUSH, VANNEVAR

1890–1974

On the eve of World War II, Vannevar Bush was a celebrated designer of the world's most powerful mechanical computers and, as president of the influential Carnegie Institution of Washington, DC, he was a science leader in the US capital. As Europe descended into war in 1940, Bush emerged as a singular advocate for mobilizing university-based science on behalf of national defense. Seeking to overcome a legacy of mistrust between soldiers and scientists, Bush declared in May 1940 at a conference on security, "For war or peace, we must leave no stones unturned in research" (Zachary 1997, 110). Two weeks later, Bush met with President Franklin D. Roosevelt (1882–1945), who quickly approved his plan to have government contract with universities and industrial labs in order for "brains for hire" to work on behalf of the US Army and Navy.

With Roosevelt's backing, Bush revolutionized science-military relations as director of the National Defense Research Committee and its successor, the Office of Scientific Research and Development. Harvesting his personal network of elite researchers, Bush orchestrated rapid advances in radar, explosives, and other technologies that proved decisive once the United States formally entered World War II in December 1941. As Roosevelt's adviser on science, Bush became a national hero, lionized on the cover of *Time* magazine in 1944 as the "general of physics." Though a mathematician and an electrical engineer by training, Bush inherited, at Roosevelt's urging, the chaotic campaign by physicists to build an atomic bomb. Once convinced that the bomb could make a difference in the current war—and that German physicists might be pursuing this superweapon—Bush played a central role in the organization of the Manhattan Project. As the ultimate boss of both General Leslie Groves (1896–1970) and J. Robert Oppenheimer (1904–1967)—the military and scientific leaders of the project—Bush alone decided with Roosevelt to pursue the production of a weapon. In September 1944, Bush and his key aide on atomic matters, James Conant (1893–1978), advised Roosevelt that US atomic leadership might be short-lived and that some kind of discussions with the Soviet Union was wise.

With the death of Roosevelt in April 1945, President Harry Truman (1884–1972) relied on Bush to help decide whether to use the bomb against the Japanese. Bush backed the decision, though he voiced concerns that the Soviets might feel threatened by the new weapon. The bombings of Hiroshima and Nagasaki in August 1945 reinforced the widespread belief that science and technology were decisive to national security and the American way of life. Seeking to ensure strong federal support for research after the end of World War II, Bush issued a seminal report, *Science: The Endless Frontier*, in July 1945. The report proposed the creation of a national research agency, run independently by academic scientists, that would address both military and civilian aspects of national needs. Bush crafted a grand bargain in which mission-oriented outcomes in public welfare and defense could be joined by unprecedented federal support for unfettered "basic" research. The compelling "frontier" metaphor created a new master narrative about science and American society. While the report was hugely influential, Bush misjudged the political strength of scientists and provoked intense opposition from Truman and populist Democrats, who wanted any new science agency to come under full executive and legislative control. By the time the National Science Foundation was born in 1950, Bush's vision of scientific autonomy was weakened.

In the early years of the Cold War, Bush emerged as a theorist of nuclear weapons strategy and the Cold War, presenting his views in *Modern Arms and Free Men* (1949). While Bush lost his role as Truman's science adviser, he remained such a respected figure that when the Soviets tested their first atomic bomb in 1949, Truman asked Bush to chair the committee that reviewed the scientific evidence and ultimately confirmed what the Soviets had achieved. While never regretting the use of atomic weapons, Bush favored an agreement with the Soviets to restrain the arms race. In late 1952, Secretary of State Dean Acheson (1893–1971) tapped Bush as chair of a panel that advised the president to delay the first H-bomb test, which was scheduled shortly before a national election to determine Truman's successor. "If the test is conducted, and if it succeeds," the panel concluded, "we will lose what may be a unique occasion to postpone or avert a world in which both sides pile up constantly larger stockpiles of constantly more powerful weapons." Despite opposition to the test from Bush, Conant, and Oppenheimer—essentially the top scientific leadership of the Manhattan Project—Truman refused to delay. Bush saw the decision to test as a missed opportunity for the world—and the end of his direct influence on American politics and policies.

SEE ALSO *Cold War; Manhattan Project; Nuclear Weapons; Roosevelt, Franklin D.*

BIBLIOGRAPHY

Bush, Vannevar. *Modern Arms and Free Men: A Discussion of the Role of Science in Preserving Democracy*. New York: Simon and Schuster, 1949.

Kevles, Daniel J. *The Physicists: The History of a Scientific Community in Modern America*. Cambridge, MA: Harvard University Press, 1995. Originally published by Knopf in 1977.

"Memorandum by the Panel of Consultants on Disarmament." Undated. Disarmament files, lot 58 D 133. In *Foreign Relations of the United States, 1952–1954*, Vol. 2, Pt. 2: *National Security Affairs*, edited by Lisle A. Rose and Neal H. Petersen, Doc. 49. Washington, DC: GPO, 1983. http://history.state.gov/historicaldocuments/frus1952-54v02p2/d49

Zachary, G. Pascal. *Endless Frontier: Vannevar Bush, Engineer of the American Century*. New York: Free Press, 1997.

G. Pascal Zachary
Professor of Practice
Arizona State University

C

CALHOUN, JOHN C.

SEE *War Hawks.*

CAMP DAVID ACCORDS (1978)

The Camp David Accords paved the way for a separate peace treaty between Israel and Egypt but in the end failed to produce the intended comprehensive peace treaty pertaining to the Arab-Israeli conflict. Although signed at the White House on September 17, 1978, the Camp David Accords were named for the presidential retreat in Maryland where Egyptian president Anwar Sadat (1918–1981) and Israeli prime minister Menachem Begin (1913–1992) conducted negotiations, with US president Jimmy Carter (b. 1924) presiding. The intensive negotiations lasted nearly two weeks before the two main agreements were signed: a Framework for Peace in the Middle East and a Framework for the Conclusion of the Peace Treaty between Israel and Egypt.

The impetus for peace talks came primarily from Sadat, who declared he would "go to the ends of the earth for peace, even to the Knesset itself," referring to the Israeli parliament (Shlaim 2014, 367). In November 1977, Sadat accepted an invitation and indeed appeared before the Knesset, where he was received with prolonged applause. Carter then orchestrated the meetings in Maryland to forge an agreement between the longtime adversaries who had fought major, albeit brief, wars in 1967 and 1973. In the wake of the Camp David Accords, Sadat and Begin received the 1978 Nobel Peace Prize. The following year, Egypt and Israel signed a peace treaty under which Israel withdrew from the Sinai Peninsula, which was demilitarized, and the two states established normal diplomatic relations.

Begin, the Likud Party leader, welcomed a separate peace with Egypt, but he rejected calls for Israeli withdrawal from Arab territories occupied in the 1967 war, nor would he recognize a Palestinian state. Begin agreed to an Israeli withdrawal from the Sinai Peninsula in order to relieve Israel of a security threat from Egypt, which had marked some early success against Israeli forces before being turned back in the 1973 war. Begin, however, opposed an Israeli withdrawal from the West Bank of the Jordan River, the Golan (or Syrian) Heights, and the Gaza Strip, all of which Israel had occupied in the June 1967 war. In its 1977 platform, the Likud Party declared, "The right of the Jewish people to the Land of Israel is eternal, and is an integral part of its right to security and peace" (Shlaim 2014, 360). The "Land of Israel" included the West Bank, which some Israelis referenced by the biblical names Judea and Samaria, rather than as United Nations–demarcated Arab territory. Other Israelis, including a newly formed activist group called Peace Now, favored returning the occupied territories in order to achieve a comprehensive peace with Palestinians and other Arabs.

Pressed hard by Carter and Sadat amid the prolonged Camp David negotiations, Begin reluctantly agreed in the Framework for Peace in the Middle East to resolve the conflict based on United Nations General Assembly Resolution 242 (1967), which called for the return of the occupied territories to the Arab residents. Begin refused to endorse a Palestinian state, but the comprehensive plan signed at Camp David did provide for creation of a "self-governing authority" and envisioned "the resolution of the Palestinian problem in all its aspects." Under this accord, Begin became the first Israeli leader to acknowledge "the legitimate rights of the Palestinian people," yet he had no intention of ending the Israeli occupation of territories that he considered part of the biblical Greater Israel. Moreover, despite the pledge, Begin remained opposed to the creation and recognition of a Palestinian state. For these reasons, many Arabs, including the Palestine Liberation Organization, opposed the accords and condemned Sadat as a traitor. Egypt was expelled from the Arab League, and in 1981 Islamic fundamentalists assassinated Sadat in the midst of a military parade in Cairo.

Although he was a fundamentalist Christian and strong supporter of Israel, Carter blamed Begin and his Likud followers for undermining the Camp David Framework for Peace in the Middle East. In November 1979 the Iran hostage crisis, followed the next month by the Soviet invasion of Afghanistan, diverted attention from the Arab-Israeli conflict. Meanwhile, Begin authorized new Jewish settlements in the occupied West Bank. Carter lost the 1980 presidential election to Ronald Reagan (1911–2004), who had criticized the incumbent president for putting pressure on Israel. Once in office, Reagan showed little interest in pursuing the Camp David accord for a broader Middle East peace agreement. Begin served as Israel's prime minister until 1983, but his claim to a Greater Israel endured and remained a central stumbling block in the path of a comprehensive Middle East peace.

SEE ALSO *Arab-Israeli Conflict; Carter, James Earl, Jr.; Israel*

BIBLIOGRAPHY

Shlaim, Avi. *The Iron Wall: Israel and the Arab World.* Updated and expanded ed. New York: Norton, 2014: 359–394.

Smith, Charles D. *Palestine and the Arab-Israeli Conflict: A History with Documents.* 8th ed., 351–356. Boston: Bedford St. Martin's, 2013.

Wright, Lawrence. *Thirteen Days in September: Carter, Begin, and Sadat at Camp David.* New York: Knopf, 2014.

Walter L. Hixson
Distinguished Professor
University of Akron

CANADA

Canada and the United States have had one of the closest bilateral relations of any two countries in the world. They share the North American continent and to a considerable extent a common political heritage, although French Canada, with distinct cultural, legal, and political traditions and institutions, sets Canada apart from the predominantly English heritage of the United States. Long after Canada's confederation in 1867, US policy toward its northern neighbor was conducted with the British in London. It was not until the Balfour Declaration in 1926 that Canada, along with the other dominions in the British Commonwealth, was declared equal and autonomous with Great Britain, and Canada and the United States began to engage in a more clearly bilateral relationship. In 1927, the United States appointed its first minister to Ottawa.

NINETEENTH-CENTURY RELATIONS

US relations with British North America and Canada in the nineteenth century were concerned primarily with border disputes occasioned by the westward expansion of both countries. In the early nineteenth century, the government of President James Madison (1751–1836) declared war against Great Britain. The causes of the war were disputes over territorial expansion, alleged British support of North American Indians in areas claimed by the United States, and bitter disagreements over neutrality of the seas during the Napoleonic Wars. The two-year War of 1812 was fought on the Atlantic coast and in the Great Lakes, as well as in the American Gulf coast. Many Americans viewed the conflict as the second war of independence, stimulating a surge of nationalism. The war actually resolved little. The Treaty of Ghent (1814) returned territorial boundaries to their prewar status.

The Webster-Ashburton Treaty of 1842 resolved the boundary dispute between Maine and New Brunswick, set the border between Lake Superior and Lake of the Woods, and established the border westward to the Rocky Mountains at the forty-ninth parallel. The two parties agreed to the shared use of the Great Lakes. The treaty also called for the abolition of the slave trade on the high seas. Four years later, the Oregon Treaty extended the border to the Pacific, with the exception of Vancouver Island, which remained in its entirety British territory. In 1903, arbitration resolved the controversy over the border between Alaska and Canada in favor of the United States.

Prior to and during the American Civil War, there were tensions over slavery. After the American Revolution, some African Americans secured their freedom in Canada. Then, as early as the 1820s, Canadians were active in the antislavery movement. The Canadian Anti-Slavery Society maintained contacts with leading abolitionists in the United States and assisted the Underground Railroad to bring escaped slaves across the border. By 1861, some thirty-five thousand former slaves had made their homes in Upper Canada.

In the aftermath of the Civil War, tensions arose over perceived annexationist ambitions by the United States and raids into Canada by US-based members of the Irish Republican Fenian Brotherhood. There were five raids between 1866 and 1871 with the objective of pressuring Great Britain to withdraw from Ireland. The Battles of Ridgeway and Fort Erie in 1866 involved more than one thousand Fenian fighters, many of them Civil War veterans, who crossed the Niagara River and engaged an inexperienced Canadian militia. The raids were inconclusive. The Andrew Johnson (1808–1875) administration guaranteed the border, and the US Army detained those Fenians it was able to capture.

ECONOMIC INTEGRATION IN THE TWENTIETH CENTURY

In the twentieth century, the bilateral economic relationship matured and the two economies became increasingly integrated. Trade policy had always been controversial. In 1854, the US Congress and the legislatures of Upper and Lower Canada concluded a ten-year reciprocity trade agreement, but in 1911 Canada rejected economic reciprocity with the United States in a hotly contested election. Canada slowly moved away from protectionism. In 1965 the Liberal government of Lester Pearson (1897–1972) and the Lyndon Johnson (1908–1973) administration concluded the Auto Pact, the Canada–United States Automotive Products Agreement, which removed tariffs on cars, trucks, buses, tires, and automotive parts. In 1989, the George H. W. Bush administration and the Conservative government of Brian Mulroney signed the Canada–United States Free Trade Agreement, and in 1994 the Bill Clinton administration brought Mexico into the North American Free Trade Agreement (NAFTA).

THE RISE OF CANADIAN NATIONALISM

As Canada gained autonomy from the British, Canadian governments pursued policies of cultural nationalism, in part to distinguish Canada from its southern neighbor. The establishment of the Canadian Broadcasting Corporation (CBC) in 1936 as a Crown corporation was one manifestation of that orientation. Its mandate was to reflect Canada and its regions to national and regional audiences, while serving the special needs of those regions. The English-language CBC and its French counterpart, Radio-Canada, have sought to provide a distinctly Canadian cultural perspective by promoting the work of Canadian artists, writers, performers and dramatists when confronted by the omnipresence of American popular culture.

Canadian nationalism was also manifest in economic policy in response to the high level of US direct foreign investment in Canada. The Liberal governments of Pierre Elliott Trudeau (1919–2000) in the 1970s and early 1980s institutionalized economic nationalism with the establishment of the Foreign Investment Review Agency and the state-owned Petro Canada and the National Energy Policy, both designed to provide Canada with more energy independence and reduce the influence of US corporations in the natural resource sector. The Richard Nixon (1913–1994) administration opposed the Foreign Investment Review Agency, established in 1973. In the 1980s, the Ronald Reagan (1911–2004) administration strongly protested against the National Energy Policy as discriminatory.

DEFENSE, FOREIGN POLICY, AND THE ENVIRONMENT

With World War II and the Cold War, defense collaboration intensified, although there was strong opposition in Canada to the placement of nuclear weapons on Canadian soil. Nonetheless, the two countries were founding members of the North Atlantic Treaty Organization (NATO), and in 1958 they established the North American Aerospace Defense Command. Canada participated along with the United States in the Korean War. The Canadian governments in the 1960s and 1970s of John Diefenbaker (1895–1979), Pearson, and Trudeau sought to set themselves apart from the Vietnam War and the US-Soviet confrontations, as much as Canada closely adhered to the foreign policy values of the West. Canada maintained its diplomatic relationship with revolutionary Cuba after the United States broke ties, and the Trudeau government moved to accommodate the People's Republic of China earlier than the Nixon administration.

In the 1980s, the Conservative government of Mulroney pursued more collaborative relations with the United States, concluding an agreement on acid rain and the Canada–United States Free Trade Agreement. The Mulroney government did press the Reagan administration to pursue a peaceful resolution of the Central American conflict in Nicaragua and El Salvador. There was not always consensus on Middle East policies, although both countries are firm supporters of Israel. Canada supported the United States in the First Gulf War and, following the terrorist attacks on the United States in 2001, supported the US intervention in Afghanistan. The Liberal government of Jean Chrétien did not, however, support the George W. Bush administration's invasion of Iraq in 2003, in part arguing that the international weapons inspectors needed more time to complete their mandate. That decision brought the bilateral relationship to its lowest level in the post–World War II era. Senior US officials, including President Bush, canceled official visits to Canada, and senior US officials publicly and frequently criticized the Canadian government and to an extent the Canadian people for their excessively pacifist approach to the global threat of terrorism and their failure to pull their weight in international defense. With the election of the Conservative Party government of Stephen Harper in 2006, Canadian policy returned to a more pro-US orientation, although tensions persisted over the failure of the Barack Obama administration to approve the controversial Keystone XL pipeline to facilitate the movement of Canadian oil to the Gulf coast.

SEE ALSO *Antislavery; North America; War of 1812*

BIBLIOGRAPHY

Borneman, Walter R. *1812: The War That Forged a Nation.* New York: HarperCollins, 2004.

Bothwell, Robert. *Alliance and Illusion: Canada and the World, 1945–1984.* Vancouver: University of British Columbia Press, 2007.

Granatstein, John L. *Yankee Go Home? Canadians and Anti-Americanism.* Scarborough, ON: HarperCollins, 1996.

Granatstein, John L., and Norman Hillmer. *For Better or for Worse: Canada and the United States into the 21st Century.* Toronto, ON: Thomson/Nelson, 2007.

Hillmer, Norman. *Partners Nevertheless: Canadian-American Relations in the Twentieth Century.* Toronto, ON: Copp Clark Pitman, 1989.

Ramirez, Bruno. *Crossing the 49th Parallel: Migration from Canada to the United States, 1900–1930.* Ithaca, NY: Cornell University Press, 2001.

Ross, Douglas. *In the Interests of Peace: Canada and Vietnam, 1954–1973.* Toronto, ON: University of Toronto Press, 1984.

Senior, Hereward. *The Fenians and Canada.* Toronto, ON: Macmillan, 1978.

Stewart, Gordon T. *The American Response to Canada since 1776.* East Lansing: Michigan State University Press, 1992.

Stuart, Reginald C. *United States Expansionism and British North America, 1775–1871.* Chapel Hill: University of North Carolina Press, 1988.

Thompson, John H., and Stephen J. Randall. *Canada and the United States: Ambivalent Allies.* 4th ed. Athens: University of Georgia Press, 2008.

Upton, Leslie. *The United Empire Loyalists: Men and Myths.* Toronto, ON: Copp Clark, 1967.

Stephen J. Randall
Faculty Professor, Emeritus Professor of History
University of Calgary

CANTON

Canton (**廣東**, pinyin Guǎngdōng), now known as Guangzhou, served as the only Chinese port open to foreign trade for most of the seventeenth through the nineteenth centuries. During this period, an intricate system of strict regulations and formal practices that became known in the West as the Canton system regulated all commerce between the Chinese Empire and the outside world. American merchants first entered into the China trade after the end of the Revolutionary War in 1783.

Canton is located in the Pearl River delta of southern China. It was built several miles upriver from the mouth of an estuary that flows into the South China Sea. Its strategic placement rendered Canton an ideal trading center because it could be easily protected from sea attacks. In order to further buttress security, the Chinese built a wall around the city and erected a series of fortresses along the river leading up to it.

THE CANTON SYSTEM

The trade regulations that collectively became known as the Canton system were established during the Qing dynasty (1644–1912). This series of strict mandates was developed in response to Chinese fears about the adverse effects of foreign influence on their society. Beginning in the mid-eighteenth century, foreign ships were forbidden from sailing directly into Canton. Instead, foreigners were required to stop at Macao, where they would hire a local river pilot to guide them to Whampoa Reach, located at the mouth of the Pearl River estuary, approximately 18 miles (29 kilometers) away from the city.

Foreign ships were only allowed in Canton during trading season, and foreign women were strictly forbidden from entering the city at any time. While in residence, Westerners were physically separated from the general population. They were confined to a specially designated area outside of the city wall, where each trading nation established headquarters or factories that served both as residences and business offices for their employees.

The Qianlong emperor (1711–1799) decreed that only specially appointed Chinese merchants known as *hongs* would be sanctioned to oversee all purchases and sales made in Canton. Although the number of hong merchants varied over the years, the number was established at thirteen in the early nineteenth century. These powerful Chinese middlemen constituted a guild collectively known as the *cohong*. The captain of every foreign vessel trading in China was required employ a member of the *cohong*, who would serve as the guarantor for the ship's business dealings, as well as the proper conduct of its crew, supercargo, and captain.

By the eighteenth century, several European nations, including Great Britain, the Netherlands, France, Denmark, and Sweden, had established regular trade with China. There was a high demand in the West for various refined Chinese goods, such as porcelain and silk. However, the most sought-after Chinese commodity was tea, which at the time was grown exclusively in China.

In contrast, the Chinese had little desire for products from the outside world. The Chinese refused to enter into formal trade relations with foreign nations. Instead, foreign traders were required to offer "tribute" to the emperor in the form of specie in exchange for the privilege of gaining access to highly coveted Chinese goods. The popularity of tea drinking in the West compelled foreign merchants to continue to make the journey to Canton, despite the adverse trade regulations imposed upon them. During this period, the demand for Chinese goods was so great that it caused a global silver shortage.

THE AMERICAN ENTRANCE INTO THE CHINA TRADE

Americans first entered Canton during this restrictive and highly formalized period. Enterprising citizens of the newly independent American nation placed great economic and symbolic importance on their entrance into the China trade. Throughout the colonial period, Americans were forbidden to trade directly with foreign nations. According to the economic principles of mercantilism, colonies were expected to supply raw materials to the mother country. Furthermore, colonial subjects were compelled to purchase all of their manufactured goods—including coveted Chinese products—from Great Britain. Under British law, Crown-chartered companies, such as the British East India Company, were granted exclusive access to lucrative foreign markets.

Given these adverse circumstances, Americans were eager to send their own ships to China after gaining their freedom in the Revolutionary War. The former colonials immediately began making plans to send trading vessels to Canton. The earliest voyages to China were led by veterans of the war for independence, such as John Barry (1745–1803), Samuel Shaw (1754–1794), John Green (1736–1796), and Thomas Truxtun (1755–1822). Additionally, privateers used in the Revolutionary War were recommissioned for the China trade.

The *Empress of China* was the first American ship to reach Canton. On February 22, 1784, just six months after the Paris Peace Treaty granting America its independence was signed, the *Empress* left New York Harbor. The launch of the *Empress* was celebrated throughout the nation as a symbol of America's newly won freedom from Great Britain and the promise of the nation's prosperous future. Upon their arrival in Whampoa Reach on August 28, 1784, Americans faced several challenges. Their lack of funds and inexperience were readily apparent. Unsure of what goods would be of value in China, the *Empress* was loaded with trade goods that were of little interest to Chinese buyers. These products included turpentine, planks, tin, tar, cordage, wire, broadcloths, lead ballast, and Teneriffe and Madeira wines. Eventually, Americans learned to simplify their outward loads and limit them to the few commodities that were valued by the Chinese. These included natural commodities procured in North America, such as ginseng and fur pelts.

Initially, Americans struggled to establish an identity that was separate from their British counterparts. Apart from merchant and custom receipts, Americans did not appear in official Chinese records until three years after their initial arrival in China. Alarmed by the threat of American competition in the trade, British diplomats and merchants made several attempts to disabuse Chinese officials of the assumption that Americans and Britons were one in the same. For their part, many Chinese, suspcious of outsiders, tended to lump all foreigners into a group known as *fan guei* (foreign devils). Although there was fierce competition among Westerners in Canton, they often found it was in their interest to cooperate because Chinese officials often treated all outsiders in a similar manner.

THE CHALLENGES OF THE CHINA TRADE

In the first several years after their arrival, Americans were minor players in Canton. They were largely unaware of the complex customs, such as presenting "gifts" or bribes to officials, that were part of doing business in the city. Shaw, the captain of the *Empress*, recorded the humiliation he suffered because of his failure to bring the customary gift to the appointed customs supervisor, commonly referred to as the *hoppo*. Traditionally, upon entering Canton, foreigners would present offerings, such as mechanical gadgets and clockworks, as a token of their appreciation for the honor of exchanging goods with China.

During these early years, the volume of American trade was insignificant compared to the long-established European houses and especially to the British East India Company, which at the time was the most powerful foreign presence in Canton. In the first years, Americans had some difficulty finding hong merchants who would be willing to sponsor their vessels. Chinese merchants were wary of sponsoring ships that had the potential to make less profit after various duties were paid. Their hesitations were also due in part to pressure from British diplomats and merchants, who discouraged Chinese hong merchants from working with their American rivals.

Early American merchants who were new in Canton were faced with the challenge of purchasing the best quality goods on the market for a fair price. The supercargo was given the crucial mandate of supervising

The English Factories at Canton ***(drawing based on a painting, 1847).*** *From the 17th through the 19th centuries, a system of trade regulations governing commerce between the Chinese Empire and the outside world became known in the West as the Canton system. American merchants first entered into the China trade in 1783.* PRINT COLLECTOR/HULTON ARCHIVE/GETTY IMAGES

all purchases. In order for a China trade voyage to be profitable, supercargoes had to have a deep understanding of both the complex system of trade with the Chinese Empire and their customers' desires. Unscrupulous merchants often took advantage of inexperienced buyers by passing off shoddy goods and adulterated products such as tea.

Eventually, Americans found a way to compete against European merchants. Initially, American ships traveled to China by crossing the Atlantic Ocean and then proceeding to follow the same route British ships took around the Cape of Good Hope in Africa. Eventually, however, Americans established a Pacific route that brought them around Cape Horn in South America. From there, ships would ply the northwest coast of North America collecting valuable natural resources, such as furs, from indigenous tribes in exchange for manufactured goods.

For Westerners trading in China, the biggest challenge was finding products that would pique the interest of Chinese buyers. To the delight of American traders, otter and seal pelts garnered large profits on the Chinese market. Wealthy Chinese customers wanted the furs to line their silk garments. Over the years, Americans adopted various sailing routes that included stops in Hawai'i, Borneo, Île de France (Mauritius), Batavia (Jakarta), Calcutta (Kolkata), Bombay (Mumbai), and other ports throughout the region. In each of these locations, they would acquire products that they hoped would turn a profit on the Chinese market.

THE IMPACT OF OPIUM

The power of the Chinese Empire began to decline due to widespread smuggling of opium into the country. Over the course of the eighteenth century, intense Western demand for tea created a serious monetary deficit for Great Britain. To counter the trade imbalance, in the 1780s the British began to import opium grown on their plantations in India into China. By the early decades of the nineteenth century, sales of this highly addictive drug increased dramatically. To the delight of Western merchants, the balance of trade with China was reversed as the Chinese demand for opium increased.

The Charter Act of 1833 ended the British East India Company's monopoly on the China trade. This momentous change in British law opened the door to more enterprising British merchants who wished to enter the lucrative trade in opium. In addition, American merchants began importing opium of lesser quality from Turkey. Chinese administrators began to try to block the importation of opium into their country when the deleterious effects of this drug on China's people and its economy became clear. In 1838 China passed a law sentencing native Chinese sellers to death. The following year, a special commissioner was charged with the task of eradicating opium from China altogether.

The First Opium War (1839–1842) was fought between Britain and China over issues of trade and diplomacy. In 1842 the Treaty of Nanking officially ended the war and put an end to the Canton system and thus to Canton's monopoly on foreign trade. Five new ports were opened to foreign trade, the opium trade was legalized, Hong Kong was given to the British, and Britons were granted indemnity and extraterritoriality. In the wake of China's defeat, other foreign nations, including the United States, demanded equal concessions from the Chinese administration. American merchants in particular wanted to prevent Great Britain from establishing dominance in the trade. In 1844, the Treaty of Wanghia was signed, granting Americans their demands.

In the wake of the Chinese defeat in the First Opium War and even more dramatically after the Chinese defeat in the Second Opium War (1856–1860), Americans were poised to establish dominance in the China trade. Around this time, American merchants also began to use clipper ships to make the trip to China shorter. In fact, these swift vessels were in part developed because of the high demand for tea. By the mid-nineteenth century, Americans had established dominance in the foreign trade.

SEE ALSO *Asia; China; Economics*

BIBLIOGRAPHY

Blussé, Leonard. *Visible Cities: Canton, Nagasaki, and Batavia, and the Coming of the Americans.* Cambridge, MA: Harvard University Press, 2008. See especially chap. 2, "Managing Trade across Cultures," 50–58.

Downs, Jacques M. *The Golden Ghetto: The American Commercial Community at Canton and the Shaping of American China Policy, 1784–1844.* Bethlehem, PA: Lehigh University Press, 1997.

Dulles, Foster Rhea. *The Old China Trade.* Boston: Houghton Mifflin, 1930.

Goldstein, Jonathan. *Philadelphia and the China Trade, 1682–1846: Commercial, Cultural, and Attitudinal Effects.* University Park: Pennsylvania State University Press, 1978.

Latourette, Kenneth Scott. *The History of Early Relations between the United States and China, 1784–1844.* New Haven, CT: Yale University Press, 1917.

Marshall, P. J., and Glyndwr Williams. *The Great Map of Mankind: British Perceptions of the World in the Age of Enlightenment.* London: Dent, 1982. Includes information regarding Europeans' first contact with the Chinese Empire.

Matsuda, Matt K. *Pacific Worlds: A History of Seas, Peoples, and Cultures.* Cambridge: Cambridge University Press, 2012. See especially chap. 13, "The World That Canton Made," 176–196.

Kariann Akemi Yokota
Associate Professor
University of Colorado Denver

CAPTAIN AMERICA

Captain America is a fictional superhero created in 1940 by Joe Simon (1913–2011) and Jack Kirby (1917–1994) for Timely (now Marvel) Comics. Clad in an American-flag-themed costume and wielding an indestructible shield, he both embodies the ideal of America and fights for American interests. Comic books describing Captain America's first battles against German saboteurs were published ten months before the Japanese attack on Pearl Harbor on December 7, 1941. Therefore, Captain America cannot be understood as a mere reflection of American identity or foreign policy; the character is, rather, a creative intervention in those fields. More than 1 million copies of *Captain America* comics were sold each month during World War II, but sales declined soon after the war ended in 1945. An attempt to revive the title in the early 1950s during the Korean War, with communists replacing Nazis, was canceled due to poor sales.

Captain America was revived in *The Avengers* #4 (1964) as that team's leader, a role he has generally occupied up to the present. Beyond the Avengers, he first shared a comic with Iron Man (*Tales of Suspense*) and then received his own eponymous title in 1968, which has been published continually since then. The post-1964 Captain America, however, shared little with the World War II and 1950s iterations. Rather, he was a "man out of time," providing his creators with a lens through which to examine the changing meaning of America. For example, in the 1970s, Captain America teamed up with the Falcon, arguably the first African American superhero. The Falcon was by day a Harlem social worker who introduced the complex politics of race into Captain America's narrative of American progress. Indeed, Captain America has generally been interpreted as embodying a New Deal–era liberal progressivism in which American ideals are necessarily flawed in practice, but nevertheless define American exceptionalism. This attempt to occupy the "middle" of a liberal consensus has been challenged in recent years by the fragmentation of that consensus, and now the creators often feel pressure from both sides of the political spectrum to conform to vastly different visions of America.

Another difference between the pre- and post-1964 Captain America is the relative absence of explicit foreign policy–related issues in the later comics. While critics outside the United States often see Captain America as embodying imperialism, the hero has generally ignored contemporary conflicts, such as the wars in Vietnam and Iraq, that have been domestically divisive. In fact, the 1950s anticommunist version of the hero was retroactively exposed as a psychotic imposter, excising the McCarthyite era from the American narrative and drawing a direct link between the progressivism of the New Deal and the civil rights era.

After 9/11, Captain America seesawed through various orientations toward both American domestic and foreign affairs. Initial story lines had Captain America fighting the war on terror, even as villains were given space to critique American foreign policy. However, Marvel Comics pulled back from this controversial stance. Subsequently, Captain America was "killed" in a story line that had the hero leading the resistance against a Patriot Act proxy. This story received international media attention as a perceived critique of the George W. Bush administration. The hero was later revived, and since 2011 can be found in the cinematic universe of the Avengers as well.

SEE ALSO *Americanization; Cold War; Exceptionalism; World War II*

BIBLIOGRAPHY

Dittmer, Jason. "Captain America's Empire: Reflections on Identity, Popular Culture, and Post-9/11 Geopolitics." *Annals of the Association of American Geographers* 95, 3 (2005): 626–643.

Dittmer, Jason. "America Is Safe While Its Boys and Girls Believe in Its Creeds!: Captain America and American Identity prior to World War 2." *Environment and Planning D: Society and Space* 25, 3 (2007): 401–423.

Dittmer, Jason. "Retconning America: Captain America in the Wake of WWII and the McCarthy Hearings." In *The Amazing Transforming Superhero! Essays on the Revision of Characters in Comic Books, Film, and Television*, edited by Terrence Wandtke, 33–51. Jefferson, NC: McFarland, 2007.

Dittmer, Jason. "Captain America in the News: Changing Mediascapes and the Appropriation of a Superhero." *Journal of Graphic Novels and Comics* 3, 2 (2012): 143–157.

Dittmer, Jason. *Captain America and the Nationalist Superhero: Metaphors, Narratives, and Geopolitics*. Philadelphia: Temple University Press, 2013.

Jason Dittmer
Reader in Human Geography
University College London

CAPTIVITY NARRATIVES

Captivity narratives—stories of capture by an "other"—have been a mainstay in North America since the earliest days of European settlement. These narratives often contained the details of the captive's trials and tribulations, the captive's fortitude in the face of "cruel and barbarous" treatment, and ultimately of the captive's redemption and triumphant return home. From the earliest days of the American Revolution, captivity narratives helped Americans define what they were fighting for. Although they initially drew on Puritan captivity narratives of the colonial era, citizens of the young United States quickly began to produce their own harrowing accounts of captivity. In the decades that followed, Americans produced and consumed myriad accounts of imprisonment at the hands of an alien other as they sought to define what it meant to be an American.

Generally speaking, these nineteenth-century narratives dealt with captivity at the hands of one of three groups: the British, Native Americans, and North African "pirates." While the narratives all share a similar structure, each offered readers insight into a distinct world. Stories of British captivity helped define what Americans were rebelling against, Native American captivity helped to define what Americans were becoming, and North African captivity helped to define the United States' position relative to a foreign other. Collectively, these varying narratives helped triangulate the position of the young United States in the larger nineteenth-century Atlantic world.

In the earliest days of the Revolution, the colonial-era captivity narratives of Mary Rowlandson (1637–1711) and John Williams (1664–1729) were reprinted and sold to a ready audience. When originally published, these colonial narratives helped to define the "Englishness" of British North America colonists in the face of Native American threats. Half a century later, Revolutionary-era Americans repurposed these narratives allowing the Indian captors in Rowlandson's and Williams's works to serve as metaphors for the British with whom they were at war. As the conflict dragged on, American prisoners began to offer their own accounts of British cruelty, which served to facilitate the transition from British subjects to independent citizens of the new United States. Ethan Allen (1738–1789) and John Dodge (1751–1800) were the first Americans to offer stand-alone narratives of their time in British captivity. Like their colonial predecessors and reflective of the larger American effort to cast the British as "other," Allen and Dodge presented narratives that highlighted their own virtue during their captivity, while decrying the British as a savage enemy. These narratives served as a powerful metaphor for the Revolution itself, as the American people were tested in the face of a cruel enemy, only to emerge from the ordeal a stronger and more virtuous people.

Immediately on the heels of the Revolution, Americans returned to the Indian captivity narrative of the colonial era, reformulating the earlier experiences of captivity and attempting to integrate the frontier experience into American identity. Best embodied in John Filson's (1747–1788) *The Adventures of Col. Daniel Boone*, first published in 1784, these narratives attempted to romanticize American Indians as part of a perceived historical legacy distinct from a British colonial past. In these narratives, the captive Americans not only maintained their "civilized" identity, but they also mastered the skills of their captives, allowing them to triumph over the wilderness. The end result was the creation of the myth of the American frontiersman who straddled the border between civilization and wilderness.

Even as Americans attempted to claim mastery of the frontier, they were reminded of their vulnerability in the larger Atlantic world as accounts of American sailors held captive in North Africa began to reach the United States. Throughout the 1780s, American sailors found themselves vulnerable to enslavement in the Barbary states of North Africa (Morocco, Algiers, Tunis, and Tripoli). The capture of dozens of American sailors and their subsequent enslavement in these North African states left many Americans feeling insecure about the future of their young republic. Newspaper accounts of American captives in North Africa gave way to stand-alone accounts, such as Susanna Rowson's (1762–1824) fictional *Slaves in Algiers; or, A Struggle for Freedom* (1794) and John Foss's (d. 1800) *Journal of the Captivity and Sufferings of John Foss, Several Years a Prisoner in Algiers* (1798). In addition to the traditional themes of American virtue in the face of a savage other, these works also provided readers with a glimpse into the alien world of North African states under Muslim rule. Rowson's work, in particular, added an additional twist to the captivity narrative by portraying American women as the paragon of American virtue and using the genre to make the case for greater rights for women in the United States.

By 1816, many of the threats of the previous decade had disappeared, but the popularity of captivity narratives remained. Through the nineteenth century, these narratives retained a central position in American literature as works of fiction, history, and folklore, continuing to inform the development of American identity and character.

SEE ALSO *Barbary Wars*

BIBLIOGRAPHY

Baepler, Paul. *White Slaves, African Masters: An Anthology of American Barbary Captivity Narratives.* Chicago: University of Chicago Press, 1999.

Bowman, Larry G. *Captive Americans: Prisoners during the American Revolution.* Athens: Ohio University Press, 1976.

Burnham, Michelle. *Captivity and Sentiment: Cultural Exchange in American Literature, 1682–1860.* Hanover, NH: University Press of New England, 1997.

Derounian-Stodola, Kathryn Zabelle, and James Arthur Levernier. *The Indian Captivity Narrative, 1550–1900.* New York: Twayne, 1993.

Dzurec, David. "Prisoners of War and American Self-Image during the American Revolution." *War in History* 20, 4 (2013): 430–451.

Lepore, Jill. *The Name of War: King Philip's War and the Origins of American Identity.* New York: Vintage, 1998.

Peskin, Lawrence A. *Captives and Countrymen: Barbary Slavery and the American Public, 1785–1816.* Baltimore, MD: Johns Hopkins University Press, 2009.

Sieminski, Greg. "The Puritan Captivity Narrative and the Politics of the American Revolution." *American Quarterly* 42, 1 (1990): 35–56.

Slotkin, Richard. *Regeneration through Violence: The Mythology of the American Frontier, 1600–1860.* Middletown, CT: Wesleyan University Press, 1973.

David J. Dzurec
Associate Professor of History
University of Scranton

CAREY, LOTT

SEE *Liberia.*

CARIBBEAN

US interest in the Caribbean was primarily commercial in the eighteenth century, before shifting to economic and territorial domination in the nineteenth century. Strategic concerns, such as the struggle against communism and the drug trade, along with close cultural ties fostered by immigration, have proved dominant since the twentieth century.

EIGHTEENTH-CENTURY COMMERCIAL INTERESTS

In colonial times, various mercantilist trade restrictions imposed by Britain (Navigation Acts) and other nations (such as the French *exclusif* or the Spanish *flota*) sought to prevent trade between North America and the Caribbean. But market forces provided a powerful incentive to violate these laws. Many Caribbean islands were focused on the production of tropical crops like sugar and were in dire need of North American products, such as timber, cod, and flour, which were exchanged for coffee, sugar, and molasses. Privateers and pirates, such as the notorious Blackbeard (Edward Teach), also preyed on Caribbean trade routes from North American ports.

The Caribbean played a significant role in the American Revolution (1775–1783). France and Spain entered the war in 1778 and 1779, respectively, in part because they feared that a reconciliation between patriots and loyalists would be sealed by an attack on Caribbean colonies; for this reason, the 1778 French-American treaty of alliance required that the United States help France defend its Caribbean outposts. Islands such as St. Eustatius were used to funnel contraband weapons into the United States. Caribbean troops, such as the mixed-race *chasseurs volontaires* from Saint-Domingue (Haiti), fought in the siege of Savannah (1779). The fleet of Admiral François-Joseph-Paul de Grasse (1722–1788) also transited through the Caribbean before taking part in the Battle of the Capes (1781).

The issue of slavery, of central importance in the early US republic, was made all the more timely by the outbreak of the Haitian Revolution (1791–1804). The Haitian Revolution was contemporary with the Quasi-War with France (1798–1800), much of which was fought in Caribbean waters. Though concerned by the possibility that the Haitian slave revolt might spill into southern states, US statesmen proved unwilling to sever links with this French colony, which was the second-largest US commercial partner after Britain at the time. President John Adams (1735–1826) thus signed a diplomatic agreement with Haitian revolutionary Toussaint Louverture (1743–1803) in 1799 to continue bilateral trade as long as Haiti did not promote privateering or labor unrest. Thomas Jefferson (1743–1826) largely continued in his footsteps, though Congress imposed a short-lived embargo after Haiti's 1804 independence (1805–1807). Haitian exiles of all colors also settled in US ports, most notably a nine-thousand-strong group that reached New Orleans in 1809 and gave this city a lasting Caribbean flair. Conversely, there were attempts to resettle US freed people in Haiti and elsewhere. These peaked under the presidency of Jean-Pierre Boyer (1776–1850) in Haiti (1818–1843) but did not significantly dent the African American population.

NINETEENTH-CENTURY ECONOMIC AND TERRITORIAL DOMINATION

Neutrality laws normally disallowed US meddling in the Latin American wars of independence that raged in the 1810s and 1820s. US interest in Spanish Florida also precluded official US support for the rebels so as to avoid offending Spain. But some revolutionaries, notably Venezuela's Francisco de Miranda (1750–1816), were assisted through private channels. Private meddling in Caribbean affairs would culminate in various filibustering expeditions, such as that of William Walker (1824–1860) in Nicaragua (1855).

US interest in the Caribbean region continued despite the decline of the Caribbean sugar industry in the nineteenth century (Cuba excepted). Economic interests remained paramount: in addition to the Cuban sugar industry, American industrialists also controlled railroads in Central America and oil interests in Mexico and Venezuela. The United Fruit Company (UFCo) controlled the Central American banana industry.

In a political context dominated by manifest destiny and the Monroe Doctrine (1823), US interest in the Caribbean region also took on an expansionist role. There were advanced diplomatic negotiations to take over Samaná Bay (Dominican Republic), Môle Saint-Nicolas (Haiti), and the Yucatán (Mexico), or even to annex entire Caribbean islands, but these were eventually abandoned because the US Senate was unwilling to incorporate large mixed-race populations into the Union.

US imperialism, which peaked around 1900, thus employed indirect means: economic domination, customs receivership, brief military occupations, puppet dictators, or acquisition of strategic points. (These contrasted with the outright colonization of much of Africa and Asia by European powers around the same time.) The first notable US intervention took place in 1898, when the United States took part in the Cuban war of independence. Bound by the Teller Amendment, the United States did not take over Cuba outright after defeating Spain, but it leased a base in Guantánamo Bay and tightly controlled Cuban politics through the Platt Amendment. Puerto Rico also became a US protectorate. Theodore Roosevelt (1858–1919), well known for his advocacy of preemptive US interventions (Roosevelt Corollary to the Monroe Doctrine), acquired a canal zone in Panama in 1903 (Hay–Bunau-Varilla Treaty). The canal, completed in 1914, remained the linchpin of the United States' quasi-empire in the Caribbean until it was ceded in 1999 (per the 1977 Carter-Torrijos Treaty). Other notable US interventions included Nicaragua (1909), Haiti (1915), and the Dominican Republic (1916).

TWENTIETH-CENTURY RELATIONS

A post–World War I isolationist backlash saw the United States withdraw its troops from most aforementioned countries, leaving them instead in the hands of friendly regimes backed by US-trained constabularies. The policy was formalized in 1933 at the Montevideo Conference and came to be known as Franklin Roosevelt's Good Neighbor Policy. The policy also led Hollywood to employ Caribbean locales, notably in *Week-End in Havana* (1941).

US noninterventionism was severely tested with the outbreak of the Cold War in 1946 to 1947. To preclude communist infiltration in a region often described as an "American lake" or "backyard," the US enrolled Caribbean and Latin American countries in the Organization of American States, founded in 1948. In 1954 the Central Intelligence Agency (CIA) assisted in the overthrow of Guatemalan President Jacobo Arbenz Guzmán (1913–1971), seen as procommunist and inimical to UFCo interests. A similar operation in 1961 in Cuba, aimed at Fidel Castro (the Bay of Pigs invasion), badly backfired, leading to a trade embargo, the Cuban missile crisis of 1962, and decades of enmity between Cuba and the United States. Other US regime changes conducted under the banner of anticommunism included the Dominican Republic (1965) and Grenada (1983).

The US interventions in Panama (1989) and Haiti (1994) marked a shift to different priorities as the Cold War drew to an end (1989–1991). The Panama operation was ostensibly designed to curtail drug trafficking, notably the use of the Caribbean as a transit point for Colombian cocaine, as part of the war on drugs. The Haiti intervention, officially known as Operation Restore Democracy, was presented as an exercise in nation-building; fears that Haitian immigrants would flock to Florida also played a role.

Immigration from the Caribbean has become an important subtext of US-Caribbean relations in recent decades. The United States has generally proved unwilling to accept economic refugees, such as Haitian boat people, though many came illegally anyway. To foster local growth and reduce emigration pressures, the United States has promoted free-trade agreements, such as the United States–Caribbean Basin Trade Partnership Act (2000). Humanitarian aid provided through official channels (such as the United States Agency for International Development) or private channels (such as church missions) is also notable. Much money is also provided by Caribbean exiles (workers' remittances) and tourism, notably the cruise industry.

By contrast with economic migrants, Caribbean political refugees received preferential treatment, especially when they came from countries under communist rule, such as Cuba (1980 Mariel boatlift) and Nicaragua. Puerto Rico and the Dominican Republic have also created significant immigrant communities in the United States. Caribbean immigrants have played an important role in the United States. Notable first- and second-generation Caribbean implants include baseball players like David Ortiz and Sammy Sosa (Dominican Republic); singers like Rihanna (Barbados), Shakira (Colombia), and Wyclef Jean (Haiti); actors like Harry Belafonte (Jamaica-Martinique) and Sidney Poitier (Bahamas); writers like Edwidge Danticat (Haiti); and statesmen like Colin Powell (Jamaica).

SEE ALSO *Cuba; Haitian Revolution*

BIBLIOGRAPHY

Boot, Max. *The Savage Wars of Peace: Small Wars and the Rise of American Power.* New York: Basic Books, 2003.

Brown, Gordon S. *Toussaint's Clause: The Founding Fathers and the Haitian Revolution.* Jackson: University Press of Mississippi, 2005.

McCullough, David. *The Path between the Seas: The Creation of the Panama Canal, 1870–1914.* New York: Simon and Schuster, 1977.

Schoultz, Lars. *Beneath the United States: A History of U.S. Policy toward Latin America.* Cambridge, MA: Harvard University Press, 1998.

Philippe R. Girard
Professor of Caribbean History
McNeese State University

CARNEGIE ENDOWMENT FOR INTERNATIONAL PEACE

The Carnegie Endowment for International Peace (CEIP) describes itself as "the oldest international affairs think tank in the United States." Founded in 1910 with a gift of $10 million by industrialist Andrew Carnegie (1835–1919), the CEIP claims to be both a nonpartisan and nonprofit organization dedicated to "advancing cooperation between nations and promoting active international engagement by the United States" (CEIP 2015). In Carnegie's own words, the ultimate aim of the endowment was "to hasten the abolition of international war, the foulest blot upon our civilization" (Lutzker 1972, 150).

The endowment's initial trustees shared a general worldview, and from its inception the endowment supported a conservative or "practical" internationalism that avoided the radicalism and emotional tone of other turn-of-the-century peace movements. Instead, the endowment sought global peace through bureaucratic means: arbitration, international law, and international organization. This was most clearly seen in its support for the Permanent Court of Arbitration and the Hague Conventions. Embodying characteristics typical of contemporary progressive thought, early endowment presidents such as former secretary of state Elihu Root (1845–1937) and Columbia University president Nicholas Murray Butler (1862–1947) believed that rigorous study and scientific inquiry offered the clearest path to international peace (the most obvious example of this inquiry being the endowment's 152-volume *Economic and Social History of the World War*).

This practical internationalism survived World War I (1914–1918) and remained the hallmark of the CEIP through the interwar years, alongside calls for lower tariffs and greater international trade. In 1940, Butler argued that "a world built upon the principles of economic cooperation and international organization is the only guarantee of an enduring peace" (*Year Book, 1940,* 45). Such attitudes guided the activity of the CEIP through the war years, with emphasis increasingly placed on the need for a new international organization. The CEIP worked to educate the American public about the need to engage with world affairs, as well as attempting to influence the government directly. The endowment's James T. Shotwell (1874–1965) was part of US postwar planning during World War II (1939–1945), most notably as an assistant to the State Department and as a consultant at the United Nations Conference on International Organization in San Francisco.

A focus on the United Nations after 1945, however, ultimately limited the endowment's influence in the Cold War years, a fact reinforced by its move to New York in 1947. Only in 1971 did the CEIP move back to Washington, DC, in an attempt to reengage more directly with the US foreign-policy-making process. However, it does not take institutional positions or engage in lobbying, although it sees itself as a centrist institution along the American political spectrum. Its public profile was raised by its part in the creation of *Foreign Policy* magazine, which the endowment published from 1978 to 2008. Seeking to expand its influence and reflecting global trends, the endowment in 2007 moved beyond a purely American focus, and with research centers in China, Russia, and Israel, it now describes itself as the world's first global think tank.

SEE ALSO *Think Tanks*

BIBLIOGRAPHY

Carnegie Endowment for International Peace (CEIP). http://carnegieendowment.org/

Carnegie Endowment for International Peace (CEIP). *Year Book, 1940.* Washington, DC: Carnegie Endowment, 1940.

Carnegie Endowment for International Peace (CEIP). "Carnegie at 100: A Century of Impact." 2015. http://carnegieendowment.org/about/?fa=centennial

Lutzker, Michael A. "The Formation of the Carnegie Endowment for International Peace: A Study of the Establishment-Centered Peace Movement, 1910–1914." In *Building the Organizational Society: Essays on Associational Activities in Modern America,* edited by Jerry Israel, 143–162. New York: Free Press, 1972.

Patterson, David S. *Toward a Warless World: The Travail of the American Peace Movement 1887–1914.* Bloomington: Indiana University Press, 1976.

Andrew Johnstone
Senior Lecturer in American History
University of Leicester

CARSON, RACHEL

SEE *Silent Spring (Rachel Carson, 1962).*

CARTER, JAMES EARL, JR.

1924–

James Earl "Jimmy" Carter Jr. was the thirty-ninth president of the United States. Carter won the 1976 election on a platform of morality and reform in the aftermath of the Watergate scandal, and served a single term as president from January 20, 1977, to January 20, 1981. During his presidency, Carter dealt with a number of foreign policy issues, including human rights, the Israeli/Egyptian peace process, the collapse of détente and the escalation of the Cold War, the establishment of diplomatic relations with the People's Republic of China, and the Iranian Revolution and subsequent hostage crisis. After leaving office, Carter continued to play a high-profile role in world affairs, promoting democracy and humanitarian causes, engaging in diplomatic missions, and receiving the Nobel Peace Prize in 2002 for his "effort to find peaceful solutions to international conflicts, to advance democracy and human rights, and to promote economic and social development."

CARTER'S CONTROVERSIAL FOREIGN POLICY

Coming into office, Carter sought to pursue a Wilsonian foreign policy, calling for the United States to base its policy decisions on human rights, morality, and the promotion of democracy rather than reflexive anticommunism. Carter sought to help American allies develop democratic governments and curb human rights abuses following the principles of the Helsinki Accords, signed in 1975.

His record, in practice, was mixed, and generated significant criticism from both supporters and opponents of his policies at home. Carter's actions helped accelerate the success of democracy in South Korea, but his decision to defund the Somoza regime in Nicaragua led to its overthrow and the seizure of power by the Marxist Sandinistas led by Daniel Ortega (b. 1945) in 1979. Republicans and many Democrats condemned Carter's policies as detrimental to containment and a threat to American allies. A number of Democratic policy makers, such as Paul Nitze (1907–2004) and Jeane Kirkpatrick (1926–2006), left the party and formed the core of the neoconservative movement, which guided American foreign policy during the Ronald Reagan (1911–2004) and George W. Bush (b. 1946) administrations.

Supporters of the human rights–based policies condemned Carter for not going far enough, as he continued to support the regimes of Filipino dictator

Ferdinand Marcos (1917–1989) and Iranian ruler Mohammad Reza Pahlavi (1919–1980). Further highlighting the inconsistency, Carter regularly condemned the human rights violations of the Soviet Union, accusing the Soviets of violating the Helsinki Accords. At the same time, Carter completed the process of normalizing relations with the People's Republic of China, formally exchanging diplomatic recognition on January 1, 1979, while resolutely ignoring accusations of human rights violations by the Chinese government.

THE CAMP DAVID ACCORDS

Carter's most notable success came amid growing tension in the Middle East. Egyptian president Anwar Sadat (1918–1981) sought improved relations with Israel as a means of stabilizing the Egyptian economy. After Sadat's speech before the Israeli Knesset on November 19, 1977, Carter believed real progress could be made with American assistance. Carter invited Sadat and Israeli prime minister Menachem Begin (1913–1992) to conduct talks at the presidential retreat at Camp David in Maryland. Originally scheduled for three days, the talks lasted thirteen (September 5–17, 1978). Carter was the driving force behind the talks, meeting with the two men separately and preventing them from leaving until an agreement was reached. The subsequent Camp David Accords (ratified in 1979) formally ended the state of war between the two nations. Additionally, Egypt granted diplomatic recognition to Israel, Israel returned the Sinai Peninsula, the two sides agreed to future talks regarding the Palestinian question, and the United States agreed to maintain a listening post on the peninsula to monitor the two sides. Sadat and Begin were awarded the 1978 Nobel Peace Prize; Carter, despite his massive efforts, was snubbed.

Although the agreements eventually led to normalized relations between Jordan and Israel and to more than three decades of peace between Israel and Egypt, in the immediate short term, the impact was largely negative. Terrorist attacks and kidnappings of Americans increased, along with renewed violence between Israel and the Palestine Liberation Organization (PLO). Sadat was assassinated by Islamic fundamentalists in the Egyptian military on October 6, 1981. Although in 1993 the Oslo Accords appeared to fulfill the requirement of settling the Palestinian question by granting control of the West Bank and the Gaza Strip to the Palestinians in return for an end of terrorism and recognition of Israel, the subsequent two decades saw a failure to finalize an agreement. The Palestinian Authority refused to recognize Israel and denounce terrorism, while the Israelis restricted access to Hamas-controlled Gaza. Carter later emerged as a

Egyptian president Anwar Sadat, President Jimmy Carter, and Israeli prime minister Menachem Begin* (left to right), *peace treaty signing ceremony, 1979. *When Egypt sought improved relations with Israel as a means of stabilizing the Egyptian economy, Carter hosted talks between Sadat and Begin in the United States and facilitated the 1979 Camp David Accords, which formally ended the state of war between the two Mideast nations.* DIRCK HALSTEAD/THE LIFE IMAGES COLLECTION/GETTY IMAGES

consistent critic of Israeli policies toward Lebanon and the Palestinian Authority.

THE IRANIAN HOSTAGE CRISIS

Carter's greatest failure also came amid the growing tension in the Mideast. Despite his commitment to democracy and civil rights, Carter maintained a close personal relationship with Shah Mohammad Reza Pahlavi. The shah maintained a brutal secret police force (SAVAK) that repressed internal dissent, and he played a leading role in the Organization of the Petroleum Exporting Countries' increase of oil prices (a major source of inflation for the United States), but Carter maintained that the shah was a staunch ally and the sort of leader the United States should support. As the shah's health failed due to advancing prostate cancer, his control over the country diminished. Protests and strikes in 1978, led in part by the recently returned-from-exile Ayatollah Ruhollah Khomeini (1902–1989), led to the shah's abdication and flight from the country on January 16, 1979.

Initially, the new government in Iran sought to maintain economic ties with the United States, and an initial seizure of the US embassy by militants on February 14, 1979, was settled peacefully. Carter's decision eight months later to allow the shah entry into the United States for cancer treatments and his subsequent refusal to extradite him led to the seizure of the American embassy in Tehran and its remaining staff on November 4, 1979. The subsequent hostage crisis overshadowed the remainder of Carter's presidency and contributed both to the perception that he was weak and to his eventual defeat in 1980.

Carter initially responded to the seizure by freezing Iranian assets and vowing not to campaign until the hostages were freed. As the crisis dragged on and public support waned, Carter sought a way out. Despite assuring North Atlantic Treaty Organization allies and his secretary of state, Cyrus Vance (1917–2002), that he would not resort to a military solution and would allow diplomacy to take its course, Carter approved a rescue attempt by American Special Forces. On April 24, 1980, eight helicopters flew into Iran to rendezvous with transport planes in the Persian desert. The plan called for the helicopters to land on the embassy roof, after which Special Forces would liberate the hostages and the choppers would fly to the transport planes for exit from the country. Due to poor weather, a helicopter collided with a transport plane, killing both crews, and the mission was scrubbed.

Vance immediately resigned, and the Iranians vowed to hold the hostages until Carter left the White House. The Iranians made good on the vow. Although an agreement to exchange the hostages for the unfreezing of Iranian assets was generally agreed to by October, the hostages were held until January 20, 1981, the day Reagan was inaugurated president.

US-SOVIET RELATIONS

Carter's attempts to maintain détente with the Soviet Union diminished as his presidency progressed. Coming into office, Carter initially pursued the negotiation of a new Strategic Arms Limitation Treaty (SALT II), which would have capped the number of strategic delivery systems (missiles and bombers), banned the construction of new land-based intercontinental ballistic missiles (ICBMs), and limited the deployment of multiple warheads on missiles. Although an agreement was reached by negotiators on June 18, 1979, Carter lacked the necessary two-thirds majority in the Senate for ratification.

At the same time, relations between the two countries were deteriorating, in part due to Carter's consistent criticism of the Soviets' human rights record. Ultimately, détente completely collapsed when the Soviets invaded Afghanistan on December 25, 1979. In response to what Carter termed "Soviet aggression," the president withdrew SALT II from consideration by the Senate. The president also conflated the Soviet invasion with the Iranian seizure of hostages, seeing the two as an attempt to destroy American influence in the region.

Carter responded by declaring the Carter Doctrine during the State of the Union address on January 23, 1980. Authored by National Security Advisor Zbigniew Brzezinski (b. 1928), the Carter Doctrine stated that "An attempt by any outside force to gain control of the Persian Gulf region will be regarded as an assault on the vital interests of the United States of America, and such assault will be repelled by any means necessary, including military force." Additionally, Carter increased defense spending, announced an American boycott of the 1980 Summer Olympics in Moscow, and began to funnel a small amount of money and supplies to the Afghans to help them resist Soviet occupation.

POSTPRESIDENCY

Carter's response to the Soviets, coupled with the seizure of American hostages in Iran, produced a "rally around the flag" effect in the United States in late 1979 to early 1980, and Carter's approval ratings spiked. However, as the hostage crisis dragged on, oil prices and inflation increased, and the Soviets appeared to establish control of Afghanistan, Carter's popularity waned. Although he held off a challenge by Massachusetts senator Ted Kennedy (1932–2009) for the Democratic nomination, Carter was soundly defeated by the Republican candidate, Ronald Reagan. The Republicans also won control of the Senate, though the Democrats held on to the House.

After his presidency, Carter maintained an active role both at home and overseas. In 1982 he created the Carter Center, a nongovernmental organization headquartered in Atlanta and dedicated to the promotion of democracy, human rights, and the alleviation of suffering around the globe. During its existence, the Carter Center has served as election monitor for more than ninety elections worldwide, contributed to the eradication of guinea worm disease, and sought to publicize and prevent human rights abuses. Carter has personally engaged in several diplomatic missions, some with and some without the support of the US government. For example, in 1994 Carter led a mission to Haiti to restore the democratically elected government of Jean-Bertrand Aristide (b. 1953). Accompanied by Georgia senator Sam Nunn (b. 1938) and former chairman of the Joint Chiefs of Staff general Colin Powell (b. 1937), Carter successfully brokered an agreement that prevented military intervention and restored the government.

Also in 1994, at the behest of President Bill Clinton (b. 1946), Carter traveled to North Korea to negotiate with Kim Il Sung (1912–1994) regarding a reversal of the latter's expulsion of inspectors from the International Atomic Energy Agency (IAEA). Clinton saw it as an opportunity to allow the North Koreans to back down in private, resume IAEA inspections, avoid international sanctions, and save face. Carter exceeded his instructions and negotiated a draft treaty, subsequently known as the Agreed Framework, whereby the North Koreans would dismantle their nuclear weapons program and comply with nonproliferation agreements in return for oil, assistance building nuclear power plants, and talks regarding the restoration of diplomatic recognition. The agreement lasted until 2002. In 2010 Carter returned to North Korea and secured the release of an American arrested for illegally entering the country.

More controversially, Carter has been a consistent critic of both President George W. Bush and President Barack Obama (b. 1961) regarding their policies in Iraq and Afghanistan. Throughout Bush's presidency, Carter derided the invasion of Iraq, calling its justification groundless and based on lies while calling for immediate American withdrawal. Carter further condemned the administration's human rights violations, especially those conducted at the prison camp at Guantánamo Bay, Cuba. He also criticized the British government for supporting the American policy. Although Carter supported Obama's nomination and election, he blasted the new president for continuing to maintain the Guantánamo Bay prison. He further slammed Obama's use of drone aircraft to kill suspected terrorists and condemned the surveillance programs conducted under the auspices of the 2001 Patriot Act by the National Security Agency as destructive to democratic government in the United States.

Carter and the Carter Center continue to advocate for peace in the Middle East and around the globe, and Carter's commitment to environmental issues also continues. In many ways, Carter's postpresidential actions have surpassed those of his presidency.

SEE ALSO *Arab-Israeli Conflict; Camp David Accords (1978); Deindustrialization; Iran Hostage Crisis; Organization of the Petroleum Exporting Countries (OPEC); Strategic Arms Limitation Talks (SALT I and SALT II)*

BIBLIOGRAPHY

Brinkley, Douglas. *The Unfinished Presidency: Jimmy Carter's Journey beyond the White House.* New York: Viking, 1998.

Carter, Jimmy. "State of the Union Address." January 23, 1980. http://www.jimmycarterlibrary.gov/documents/speeches/su80jec.phtml

Carter, Jimmy. *Keeping Faith: Memoirs of a President.* New York: Bantam, 1982.

Kaufman, Burton I. *The Presidency of James Earl Carter Jr.* Lawrence: University Press of Kansas, 1993. 2nd rev. ed., with Scott Kaufman, 2006.

Norwegian Nobel Committee. "The Nobel Peace Prize for 2002 to Jimmy Carter—Press Release." October 11, 2002. http://www.nobelprize.org/nobel_prizes/peace/laureates/2002/press.html/

Smith, Gaddis. *Morality, Reason, and Power: American Diplomacy in the Carter Years.* New York: Hill and Wang, 1986.

Strong, Robert A. *Working in the World: Jimmy Carter and the Making of American Foreign Policy.* Baton Rouge: Louisiana State University Press, 2000.

Richard M. Filipink
Associate Professor
Western Illinois University

CASH AND CARRY

Cash and carry was a practice whereby foreign purchasers of American goods had to pay cash for supplies and carry them away in their own vessels. The scheme was designed to avoid US ensnarement in World War II.

In the 1930s American ships were exposing themselves to attack by entering the ports of belligerent nations, and the United States was extending massive loans to enable nations at war to pay for its shipments. In 1935 Congress passed the first Neutrality Act, which included a mandatory embargo on "arms, armaments and implements of war" once the president declared that a war existed. A year later Congress passed a similar law, adding a ban on loans to belligerents (with Latin American nations being made an exception). In the spring of 1937, faced with the expiration of the existing law on May 1, the United States again turned its attention to neutrality. In light of international upheavals, Congress was convinced the law needed strengthening. In 1936 Germany had denounced the Locarno agreements, invaded the Rhineland, and formed the Rome-Berlin Axis. In the same year, the Italian government had annexed Ethiopia, civil war had broken out in Spain, and hostilities had erupted between Japan and China—all increasing public anxiety concerning American ensnarement overseas. Although it was clear that Congress would retain the arms embargo and prohibition on loans, the United States faced the dilemma of continuing trade in civilian commodities. As munitions were only part of a belligerent's needs and as American ships could still legally carry nonmilitary cargoes to belligerent ports, the danger of involvement in war remained. Yet, as an embargo on all goods would injure the US economy, Americans searched for a way to foster both peace and prosperity.

The financier and statesman Bernard M. Baruch (1870–1965), writing in the June 1936 issue of *Current History*, came up with a solution: "We will sell to any belligerent anything except lethal weapons, but the terms are '*cash on the barrel-head and come and get it*' " (emphasis in the original). Congress added such a provision to the pending neutrality bill, which would remain in force until May 1, 1939, and would apply to civil strife as well as international war. On March 18 the House approved the measure 374 to 12; on April 29 the Senate backed it 41 to 15; and on May 1 President Franklin D. Roosevelt signed the Neutrality of Act of 1937 into law, fully realizing that cash and carry would favor Britain and France, nations that dominated the seas, over Germany and Italy.

Because the cash-and-carry provision of the 1937 Neutrality Act was due to expire on May 1, 1939, in the spring of that year the administration sought a new bill that would retain cash and carry while repealing the arms embargo. On June 30 the House voted 200 to 188 in favor of a bill embodying both cash and carry and the arms embargo, but the Senate failed to act.

On September 21, 1939, three weeks after Adolf Hitler invaded Poland, Roosevelt sought to reinstitute cash and carry. Addressing a special session of Congress, Roosevelt claimed that the current legislation threatened peace, for existing legislation permitted American merchantmen to enter belligerent waters with nonmilitary cargoes; hence it could not prevent the kind of "incident" most likely to involve America in war. US ships, he continued, must be banned from entering "danger zones." Furthermore, belligerents must pay cash for supplies secured in the United States and carry them away in foreign vessels. Privately, Roosevelt told aides, "foreign orders mean prosperity in this country, and we can't elect the Democratic party unless we get prosperity." The president never mentioned the true reason for revising the neutrality law, namely that it would help Britain and France; rather, he stressed that his scheme would keep America out of the conflict. Congress passed the administration measure by large margins, the Senate voting 63 to 30 on October 27, the House voting 243 to 181 on November 2, and Roosevelt signing the Neutrality Act of 1939 two days later.

Quite naturally, the news caused much rejoicing in London. Prime Minister Neville Chamberlain claimed that the bill "reopens for the Allies the doors of the greatest storehouse of supplies in the world." The French immediately placed orders for munitions and war supplies. At first the British held off, believing that the temporary standstill in fighting and the assumption that the conflict would last three years would give them sufficient time to produce their own arms. Beginning in March 1941, the lend-lease bill dominated all transactions.

On November 7, 1941, with the United States already escorting British convoys for three-quarters of the Atlantic, the Senate voted 50 to 37 to repeal commercial restrictions, hence permitting the United States to carry cargoes to belligerent ports. Six days later, by a vote of 212 to 194, the House responded similarly, and the measure became law on November 17.

SEE ALSO *Lend-Lease Act (1941); Roosevelt, Franklin D.; Tariff; World War II*

BIBLIOGRAPHY

Divine, Robert A. *The Illusion of Neutrality*. Chicago: University of Chicago Press, 1962.

Doenecke, Justus D. *Storm on the Horizon: The Challenge to American Intervention, 1939–1941*. Lanham, MD: Rowman and Littlefield, 2000.

Schwarz, Jordan A. *The Speculator: Bernard M. Baruch in Washington, 1917–1965*. Chapel Hill: University of North Carolina Press, 1981.

Justus D. Doenecke
Emeritus Professor of History
New College of Florida

CASTRO, FIDEL
1926–

Born in eastern Cuba on August 13, 1926, Fidel Alejandro Castro Ruz became prime minister of Cuba in 1959, ushering in a new era of relations between that island nation and the United States. The son of a wealthy Spanish planter, Castro studied at Jesuit boarding schools, attending prep school at the Colegio de Belén and eventually studying law at the prestigious University of Havana.

By the late 1940s, Castro had become an active member of the anticommunist Orthodox Party. His early political ambitions were truncated by a military coup led by Fulgencio Batista (1901–1973), a political and military strongman who installed himself as dictator with US recognition in 1952, canceling the upcoming elections. Castro and 150 others planned an insurrection against Batista, which culminated in the failed assault against the Moncada military barracks on July 26, 1953. Most of the surviving rebels were imprisoned, including Castro, who recorded his frustrations in *History Will Absolve Me*, a railing indictment against the Batista regime, leading to the consolidation of the July 26 Movement (M-26-7).

Upon his release from prison on amnesty in 1955, Castro resumed his insurrectionary activities, this time in Mexico. He led an expedition of eighty-two men on board the *Granma* to eastern Cuba on December 2, 1956. After two years of guerrilla warfare in the Sierra Maestra, Castro and his men marched on Havana on January 1, 1959. This marked the triumph of the Cuban Revolution, a nationalist, anti-imperialist insurrection that aimed to fulfill the broken promises of Cuba's first independence, which had been truncated by US intervention in the independence war against Spain (1898), military occupation (1899–1902), and the imposition of the Platt Amendment (1901), which enabled subsequent US intervention.

By April 1959, then–Cuban prime minister Castro visited the United States, but US president Dwight D. Eisenhower refused to meet with him. In May Castro signed the first agrarian reform law, which prohibited foreign land ownership and set strict size limits for privately owned property. The US government initiated trade restrictions, which pushed Castro toward the Soviet Union.

Castro's term as prime minister was also plagued by a Central Intelligence Agency–backed movement to arm Cuban exiles, which culminated in the catastrophic Bay of Pigs invasion in April 1961. Subsequently, Soviet leader Nikita Khrushchev (1894–1971) negotiated to install nuclear missiles in Cuba to deter further American aggression, leading in 1962 to a nuclear standoff known as the Cuban missile crisis. For decades thereafter, the two defining features of US-Cuba policy were economic embargo and diplomatic isolation. The United States also sponsored dozens of assassination attempts against Castro.

Between 1976 and 2008, Castro served as president of Cuba. Despite a brief period of détente under the Jimmy Carter administration, relations with the United States remained tense. With the fall of the Soviet Union in 1991, Cuba entered a severe economic downturn, causing Castro to declare a "Special Period in time of Peace." The United States strengthened the economic embargo with the 1992 Cuba Democracy Act and the 1996 Helms-Burton Act. The crisis forced Castro to reach out to sympathetic governments in Venezuela, Brazil, Bolivia, and others, some of which became known as the New Left.

In summer 2006, Castro stepped down from power temporarily due to health problems, and in 2008 he ceded power permanently to his brother, Raúl Castro. In 2015, Fidel Castro remains an important public figure in Cuba, even with the re-establishment of diplomatic relations between the United States and Cuba.

SEE ALSO *Baseball; Bay of Pigs; Cuban Missile Crisis*

BIBLIOGRAPHY

Alarcón, Ricardo. *Fidel Castro, Cuba, y los Estados Unidos: Conversaciones con Ricardo Alarcón de Quesada, presidente de la Asamblea Nacional del Poder Popular.* Havana: Editorial José Martí, 2007.

Álvarez Mola, Martha Verónica, Sergio Ravelo López, and Norma Castillo Falcato, eds. *Fidel Castro: Selección de documentos, entrevistas, y artículos (1952–1956).* Havana: Editora Política, 2007.

Blanco, Katiuska. *Fidel Castro Ruz, guerrillero del tiempo: Conversaciones con el líder histórico de la Revolución Cubana.* Havana: Casa Editora Abril, 2011.

Castro, Fidel. *History Will Absolve Me: Fidel Castro's Self-Defense Speech before the Court in Santiago de Cuba on October 16, 1953.* Havana: Guairas, 1967.

Castro, Fidel. *Reflexiones del comandante en jefe Fidel Castro Ruz.* Caracas: Ediciones de la Presidencia de la República, 2007.

Ramonet, Ignacio, and Fidel Castro. *Fidel Castro: My Life: A Spoken Autobiography.* Translated by Andrew Hurley. New York: Scribner's, 2006.

Sweig, Julia E. *Inside the Cuban Revolution: Fidel Castro and the Urban Underground.* Cambridge, MA: Harvard University Press, 2002.

Bonnie A. Lucero
Department of History and Philosophy
University of Texas–Pan American

CATHOLICISM

The imperial rivalries, religious wars, and developments in political and economic thought that excited Europe from the late fifteenth century into the seventeenth century encouraged rulers in Spain, France, and England to support overseas expansion. Catholics were among the first Europeans to execute these initiatives in the Americas.

CATHOLICISM IN EARLY AMERICA

Spanish exploration of the Florida peninsula by Juan Ponce de León (c. 1471–1521) in 1513 eventually produced the city of Saint Augustine, the first European settlement in the land later known as the United States, in 1565. Settlements in New France began in the seventeenth century, and French Franciscan and Jesuit missionaries had established mission stations from the Saint Lawrence Seaway to the Great Lakes region and down the Mississippi River to New Orleans by 1700.

English Catholics arrived in the Americas not as missionaries to Native Americans, as were the French and Spanish, but as planters and laborers. Receiving a royal charter from King Charles I (1600–1649) in 1634, the Calvert family established Maryland as a haven for English Catholics but also as a colony where the state's protection of religious liberty would allow Catholics and Protestants to coexist peacefully. In 1649, Maryland's colonial assembly passed the Act of (Religious) Toleration; however, Catholics remained a minority in the population and saw their religion outlawed in 1654 after Puritans assumed control of the colony as part of the English Civil War. Maryland's subsequent colonial assemblies outlawed Catholic religious practice (1689), required Catholics to pay taxes to support the Church of England (1692), and stripped Catholics of their rights to hold political office and to vote (1718), leaving many to maintain secret chapels in their homes where itinerant priests could celebrate mass.

The American Revolution restored religious toleration and rights for Catholics in Maryland. Charles Carroll (1737–1832), a wealthy Catholic planter, was a delegate to the Continental Congress and the sole Catholic to sign the Declaration of Independence. His cousin, Jesuit priest John Carroll (1735–1815), became chief administrator of the Catholic Church in the United States in 1784 at the urging of Benjamin Franklin (1706–1790). Five years later and just several weeks after George Washington (1732–1799) was inaugurated president, Pope Pius VI (1717–1799) confirmed the election of John Carroll by American clergy as the nation's first bishop.

From his location in Baltimore, Carroll was responsible for thirty thousand Catholics in the United States, slightly more than half of whom resided in Maryland. Along with his fellow Jesuits, he founded Georgetown College (later University) in 1789. In 1791 Carroll encouraged French priests of the Society of Saint Sulpice (Sulpicians) to establish Saint Mary's Seminary in Baltimore for the local training of clergy.

Carroll also supported the fledgling Catholic parochial school system through his support of Elizabeth Ann Bayley Seton (1774–1821). A wealthy convert to Catholicism, Seton opened a girl's school in Baltimore in 1806 and established the Sisters of Charity, a religious congregation of women devoted to teaching, in 1813.

Although Bishop Carroll seemingly embraced American republicanism and its influence on Catholic practice, including the election of bishops, lay participation and responsibility for trustee parishes, and religious liberty, he discouraged marriage between Catholics and Protestants and attempted, with little success, to regulate such unions. Carroll's influence and the success of Anglo-American politics, economics, and culture in the new nation spurred on English Catholicism in the United States as Spanish and French Catholicism waned with the relative decline of France and Spain as imperial powers.

NINETEENTH-CENTURY ETHNIC DIVERSITY

The American Catholic Church experienced internal and external pressures as a result of significant waves of European immigration in the nineteenth century. Ethnic diversity transformed the organization and practice of Catholicism in the United States. In Philadelphia, for example, German American Catholics formed their own national parish (Holy Trinity) in 1787 out of frustration with Anglo-Catholic leadership. Ethnic struggles intensified as Irish American Catholics emerged as a dominant force in the American Catholic Church. Arriving poor and starving during the potato famine of the 1840s, Irish immigrants took advantage of their English language, educated clergy, parochial schools staffed largely by Irish nuns, and sheer numbers to survive and ultimately thrive in the United States by the end of the nineteenth century. In contrast, African American Catholics in the American South enjoyed far less freedom to define themselves; however, individuals and groups did break through, among them "free woman of color" Henriette DeLille (1813–1862), who founded the Sisters of the Holy Family in New Orleans in the mid-nineteenth century.

Still, Irish Americans, particularly priests and bishops but also politicians, gave Catholicism its public face in America well into the twentieth century. Their tendency for legalism positioned Irish Americans for an important role in the revival of the concept of papal authority in the second half of the nineteenth century. Pope Pius IX (1792–1878), long embroiled in conflict with Italian nationalists, enacted a series of measures that reinforced papal authority, including: the doctrine that Jesus's mother, Mary, had been conceived without original sin, known as the Immaculate Conception (1854); the *Syllabus of Errors* (1864), which took the form of a list of "condemned propositions" of the modern era and included moderate rationalism, socialism, communism, secret societies, and modern liberalism; and, the First Vatican Council (1869–1870), which declared papal infallibility.

American Catholics, led largely by Irish American clergy, enthusiastically supported Pope Pius IX, or "Pio Nono." When Italian nationalists took control of Rome in 1870, effectively making the pope a prisoner in the Vatican, tens of thousands of American Catholics attended mass meetings and organized parades in protest. They donated to "Peter's pence," a medieval practice of offering the pope financial support, which had been revived in 1850. In 1884, American bishops affirmed and formalized their own authority over dioceses, parishes, and schools in the Third Plenary Council of Baltimore, a national meeting of Catholic bishops that had previously met in 1852 and 1866.

German American Catholics were also influential in the United States during the nineteenth century. They were generally more affluent and better educated than the Irish and other immigrant groups and so they more readily ventured beyond the Eastern Seaboard and into the Midwest for settlement, such as the triangle created by Cincinnati, St. Louis, and Milwaukee. They were protective of their language and traditions, building parishes and schools organized by nationality rather than by territory. German American Catholics took their demands for a multilingual and multinational American Catholic Church and their frustrations with Irish American Catholics to the pope. In 1871, Peter Paul Cahensly (1838–1923), a German businessman, organized an international aid society for German immigrants called Sankt (Saint) Raphaels Verein, and in 1891, the society presented a petition to the pope, which detailed their concern that Catholicism was not taking root in the United States for a lack of clergy from immigrant groups beyond Ireland. "Cahenslysim" garnered support from Germany for German Catholics in the United States.

From 1880 until World War I, Catholic immigrants arrived from southern and eastern Europe. Italians from southern Italy and Sicily settled in eastern cities and seemed to identify their faith with extended family and neighborhood culture rather than with ecclesiology or national parishes. Polish Catholics, on the other hand, followed the German pattern as they supported national parishes and schools in cities like Chicago, Milwaukee, Detroit, and Cleveland. In 1904, Polish Americans in Scranton, Pennsylvania, who were upset with the non-Polish Catholic hierarchy founded a separate Polish National Catholic Church. Most Polish Catholics did not leave the Roman Catholic Church. Many Polish American Catholics entered religious communities, which supported the bourgeoning Catholic parochial school system. They also introduced new devotions in the United States, such as that of the Black Madonna of Częstochowa.

Catholics in America met with varying degrees of nativist hostility. In 1830, an anti-Catholic weekly newspaper called the *Protestant* began printing stories about Roman corruption. Anti-Catholic mobs set fire to church buildings around the same time; one of the more notable incidents occurred in 1834, when a mob burned down a convent of Ursuline sisters in Charlestown, Massachusetts. Associations formed for the purpose of coordinating an aggressive campaign against Catholicism in the United States, including the American Protestant Association (1842), the Know-Nothing Party (1854), the American Protective Association (1887), and a revived Ku Klux Klan (1920s).

In 1884 American bishops at the Third Plenary Council of Baltimore pronounced that every Catholic parish should establish its own parochial school. Catholic immigrants, led by conservative bishops such as Michael A. Corrigan (1839–1902) of New York and Bernard McQuaid (1823–1909) of Rochester, sought to isolate themselves from a society and particular institutions, specifically public schools, that they believed had been hostile to them. In addition to the Catholic school system, Catholic leaders formed the Knights of Columbus (1882), a fraternal service organization that provided charitable services, promoted Catholic education, and defended Catholicism against the nativists.

In contrast to the separationist response to nativism, another camp of bishops, led by James Cardinal Gibbons (1834–1921) of Baltimore, Archbishop John Ireland (1838–1918) of St. Paul, Minnesota, and Bishop John J. Keane (1839–1918) of Richmond, Virginia, encouraged a Catholic culture that was more open to American ideas and customs. In 1887, Cardinal Gibbons defended the Knights of Labor, founded largely by Irish American Catholics and one of the first labor organizations in the United States, when the pope, instigated by German American Catholics, considered issuing a condemnation of the labor union. Cardinal Gibbons and Archbishop Ireland joined Bishop John Lancaster Spalding (1840–1916) of Peoria, Illinois, in advocating for an American graduate program in theology; in 1889, the Catholic University of America was founded in Washington, DC, with Bishop Keane as its first rector.

The bishops participated in the World's Parliament of Religions at the Columbian Exposition in 1893, refrained from condemning the public school system, and spoke favorably about the separation of church and state, which had been anathema in Europe.

In 1899, the Vatican intervened in this heady time in the American Catholic Church when Pope Leo XIII (1810–1903) issued *Testem Benevolentiae Nostrae* (Concerning new opinions, virtue, nature, and grace, with regard to Americanism), an encyclical letter that condemned a number of opinions under the collective label of "Americanism." The pope alleged that a group of liberal bishops in America had erred in at least three ways: they privileged natural or active virtues (which Protestant Americans regarded highly) over supernatural virtues (such as passive obedience practiced by the saints); they too readily adapted to modern popular culture; and they devalued the role of the Catholic Church in salvation in their emphasis on (American) individualism. Gibbons, Ireland, and the group of so-called liberal bishops quickly disavowed the errors enumerated in the papal letter and argued that they had never carried the banner of "Americanism" nor knew any Catholic who had. The real controversy occurred in France, where liberal French Catholics sought to use their understanding of American political liberalism, and specifically the figure of an American priest and founder of the Missionary Society of St. Paul the Apostle (Paulists), Isaac Hecker (1819–1888), who they argued had championed a Catholic rapprochement with liberalism and modernity, to further their reform agenda for French Catholicism.

The "Americanist controversy," which was actually a French impression of the American Catholic Church, is therefore often referred to as "the phantom heresy." And yet, *Testem Benevolentiae*, which was preceded in 1895 by *Longinqua Oceani* (Wide expanse of the ocean), a papal critique of the separation of church and state, and a separate papal letter that condemned interdenominational congresses, effectively halted any efforts directed toward the rapid assimilation of Catholics in America or a liberal Catholicism that sought to adapt to new ideologies. Although American Catholics would, in fact, climb American political, economic, corporate, and social ladders in the late nineteenth and early twentieth centuries, the American Catholic Church did not reassert itself in matters of church theology until the Second Vatican Council of the 1960s.

The last two decades of the nineteenth century marked a time of radical change in the United States as decades of immigration, urbanization, and industrialization motivated transformations in American politics, economics, and culture as well as encouraged an expansionist US foreign policy. American Catholics were prominent in the foreground of this change and would remain there for much of the twentieth century.

In 1898 the United States declared war on Spain over European imperialism in Cuba and the Philippines. Although Catholics were concerned about the war's impact on church property and the advancement of Protestant missionaries in Spain's former colonies, Catholics in the United States generally supported the war against Spain. However, by 1901, when the US government signaled its desire to retain control of the Philippines in its effort to defeat Filipino nationalist insurgents, American Catholic newspaper editors, bishops, and politicians largely withdrew their support of US foreign policy, equating American imperialism with Protestant triumphalism and anti-Catholicism.

AMERICAN CATHOLICISM'S ROLE IN THE NEW CENTURY

In the first half of the twentieth century, Catholic bishops sought to consolidate their membership and to play a more transformative, public role in American society, and internationally as well. They were spurred on by the Vatican's office for the Propagation of the Faith (Propaganda Fide), which officially removed the United States as mission territory in 1908. When Pope Leo XIII issued *Rerum Novarum* (On the condition of the working classes), an encyclical that declared the Catholic Church's concern for social issues and introduced a Catholic social doctrine that could be taken seriously by bishops, corporations, labor unions, and heads of state around the world, reformers in the United States, such as Father John A. Ryan (1869–1945), began to engage American governmental bureaucracy and politics from a more confident position. Ryan's advocacy for minimum-wage laws, public housing, and government programs to support the unemployed, the elderly, and the disabled is emblematic of the Catholic response to the excesses of industrialization that defined Catholic thought for much of the twentieth century.

In 1917, American Catholic bishops established the National Catholic War Council to coordinate the church's role in America's effort in World War I, which they staunchly supported. Two years later, the bishops established the National Catholic Welfare Council (NCWC), which they renamed the National Catholic Welfare Conference in 1923, to administer the bishop's pronouncements on political, economic, and social issues.

The contribution of Father Ryan and the NCWC helped to shape generations of Catholic public servants in the early twentieth century who attempted to apply Catholic social teaching in the public sphere. Alfred E. Smith (1873–1944), the Democratic politician from New York who in 1928 became the first Catholic to win a national party nomination for the presidency, is the most well known. Smith lost to the Republican nominee, Herbert Hoover (1874–1964) (444 to 87 electoral college votes), but he shored up an urban, Catholic base for the Democratic Party.

The years after World War I initiated a period of robust institution building for the American Catholic Church, which included Catholic periodicals, academic and professional organizations, and a so-called American hour for overseas mission. The war prevented Europe from reviving its missionary enterprise abroad in a way that would match its endeavors in previous centuries. By this time, America's new geopolitical prominence had motivated a desire around the world for English-speaking missionaries. In 1911 the Catholic Foreign Mission Society of America was established as the first Catholic organization of priests specifically devoted to overseas missions. The society was soon joined by the Maryknoll Sisters of St. Dominic (and, in 1975, by the Maryknoll Lay Missionaries), which all shared the name of Maryknoll and headquarters in Ossining, New York. In 1918 the Catholic Students' Mission Crusade attracted thousands of seminarians and college and high school students from across the United States for prayer and evangelization. Religious congregations of men and women devoted increasing numbers of their membership to overseas mission. Forty-five US Catholic mission magazines were in circulation in 1930.

American Catholics during World War II (1939–1945) once again demonstrated their patriotism through their military service, appearances in the popular films of John Ford (1894–1973) and Leo McCarey (1898–1969), success in sports such as the University of Notre Dame Fighting Irish football team, and as the subjects of photographs and journalism in Henry Luce's (1898–1967) influential *LIFE* magazine. Catholic tropes of innocence and suffering informed an American culture that elevated examples of American endurance during the Cold War. In 1955, sociologist Will Herberg (1901–1977) published *Protestant-Catholic-Jew,* which suggested that the United States could no longer be considered a Protestant nation because Catholics and Jews had, through their commitment to their own fervent religious identity, asserted a substantial influence on mainstream American culture.

CATHOLICISM IN THE POSTWAR PERIOD

Catholic missionaries were seen as serving on the front lines in the American confrontation with communism in Asia. In the early days of the Cold War, Catholic missionaries had already stationed themselves in the world's communist zones: China, Korea, Vietnam, Cuba, and Latin America. Dr. Thomas A. Dooley (1927–1961) captured America's imagination by his medical missionary work and anticommunist activities in Southeast Asia until his death from cancer. There was a simultaneous and connected movement of anticommunist fervor in the United States, led largely by Catholics such as Senator Joseph McCarthy (1908–1957), television personality Bishop Fulton J. Sheen (1895–1979), Francis Cardinal Spellman (1889–1967) of New York, and Richard Cardinal Cushing (1895–1970) of Boston. Throughout the 1960s, Catholics in the United States responded to their fears of the expansion of communism, as well as the spread of Protestantism, in Latin America with increased support for overseas mission. In 1961, Pope John XXIII (1881–1963) called for all American Catholic religious congregations to commit 10 percent of their personnel for service in Latin America. New organizations formed for this purpose, such as the Papal Volunteers for Latin America.

The early 1960s stimulated even greater American Catholic involvement in the international Catholic Church through the Second Vatican Council (1962–1965)—a meeting of the world's bishops called by Pope John XXIII and ultimately concluded by Pope Paul VI (1897–1978). The meeting affirmed aspects of American Catholic life, including engagement with social issues, ecumenism, and modern liturgical worship. The role of an American Jesuit, Father John Courtney Murray (1904–1967), in crafting Vatican II's "Declaration on Religious Freedom" is perhaps the best example of the American Catholics' experience with pluralism asserting a decisive role in influencing Vatican teaching. The campaign rhetoric of America's first Catholic president, John F. Kennedy of Massachusetts (1917–1963; president, 1961–1963), and the "Land O' Lakes Statement" by an assemblage of Catholic universities regarding academic freedom (1967) exhibit the manifestations of American Catholic confidence in the 1960s.

The late 1960s was a time of upheaval across the globe. Vatican II brought confusion along with reform as many Catholics balked at the demands of the new vernacular liturgy and theological innovations. Priests and sisters left religious life in droves. Ideological divisions, as well as the Vietnam War, led to polarization between Catholics of varying theological and political positions.

In 1967 Monsignor Ivan Illich (1926–2002) published "The Seamy Side of Charity" in the Jesuit magazine *America.* The article challenged North American Catholic missionaries to extricate themselves from Latin America and instead focus on changing unjust political, economic, and social structures. A "Catholic Left" solidified that challenged America's involvement in Vietnam. Liberation theology, which emerged from the Latin American Bishops Conference (CELAM) at Medellín, Colombia, in 1968 and appeared in the United States through the writings of Peruvian theologian Father Gustavo Gutiérrez (b. 1928), argued for new approaches to mission and social issues that was informed by the experiences of the poor.

The papacy of John Paul II (1920–2005; pope, 1978–2005) coincided with tidal waves of change internationally and nationally that had serious implications for American Catholics. The final years of the Cold War and the US Supreme Court decision in *Roe v. Wade* (1973), which legalized abortion, saw a substantial number of conservative Catholic elites and rank-and-file citizens aligning with the presidential administration of Ronald Reagan (1911–2004; president, 1981–1989). However, American Catholic bishops expressed their concern with the American status quo in pastoral letters about war and nuclear weapons in the *The Challenge of Peace* (1983) and on systemic inequality in *Economic Justice for All* (1986).

In 2002 the clergy sexual abuse crisis rocked the American Catholic Church as allegations and convictions, first in the Archdiocese of Boston, consumed media attention, ignited lay advocacy networks, and caused financial pressures that led to parish closings and the sale of church property. In 2012 American Catholic bishops expressed resistance to policies of President Barack Obama (b. 1961; in office 2009–) on health care coverage for contraception and on gay marriage in their advocacy campaign on religious liberty, "Fortnight for Freedom." As fewer Americans identified as Catholics in the twenty-first century, immigration from Catholic regions in Latin America, Africa, and Asia was on the rise. Pope Francis (b. 1936; pope 2013–), the world's first pope from Latin America, criticized American consumerism. He also argued for a new day of international cooperation and played a crucial role in restoring US relations with Cuba in 2014.

Since the colonial period, American Catholic identity has been historically multivalent. Similarly, geopolitics, the role and influence of the Vatican in the world, and US foreign policy and international status have shaped and continue to shape the American Catholic experience.

SEE ALSO *Kennedy, John Fitzgerald; Knights of Columbus; Protestant-Catholic-Jew (Will Herberg, 1955)*

BIBLIOGRAPHY

Appleby, R. Scott, and Kathleen Sprows Cummings, eds. *Catholics in the American Century: Recasting Narratives of U.S. History.* Ithaca, NY: Cornell University Press, 2012.

Clark, Emily. *Masterless Mistresses: The New Orleans Ursulines and the Development of a New World Society, 1727–1834.* Chapel Hill: University of North Carolina Press, 2007.

Curtis, Sarah Ann. *Civilizing Habits: Women Missionaries and the Revival of French Empire.* New York: Oxford University Press, 2010.

D'Agostino, Peter R. *Rome in America: Transnational Catholic Ideology from the Risorgimento to Fascism.* Chapel Hill: University of North Carolina Press, 2004.

Dries, Angelyn. *The Missionary Movement in American Catholic History.* Maryknoll, NY: Orbis Books, 1998.

Farrelly, Maura Jane. *Papist Patriots: The Making of an American Catholic Identity.* New York: Oxford University Press, 2012.

Gleason, Philip. *Contending with Modernity: Catholic Higher Education in the Twentieth Century.* New York: Oxford University Press, 1995.

Kane, Paula M. *Sister Thorn and Catholic Mysticism in Modern America.* Chapel Hill: University of North Carolina Press, 2013.

Linden, Ian. *Global Catholicism: Diversity and Change since Vatican II.* New York: Oxford University Press, 2009.

Matovina, Timothy M. *Latino Catholicism: Transformation in America's Largest Church.* Princeton, NJ: Princeton University Press, 2011.

McDannell, Colleen. *The Spirit of Vatican II: A History of Catholic Reform in America.* New York: Basic Books, 2011.

McGreevy, John T. *Catholicism and American Freedom: A History.* New York: Norton, 2003.

O'Toole, James M. *The Faithful: A History of Catholics in America.* Cambridge, MA: Belknap Press, 2008.

Charles T. Strauss
Assistant Professor
Mount St. Mary's University

CENTRAL INTELLIGENCE AGENCY (CIA)

The Central Intelligence Agency (CIA) was created by the National Security Act of 1947, charged with the functions of foreign intelligence analysis and (following confirmation by the National Security Council) overseas covert operations. Its creation marked a victory for American internationalists who desired an expanded role for the United States in global affairs, including enhanced powers to combat international communism, and a defeat for isolationists and opponents of government secrecy. Due to the seeming paradox of a secret government agency existing within the world's largest democracy, the CIA has remained an object of scrutiny, hostility, and fantasy among Americans and non-Americans alike down to the present day.

COVERT OPERATIONS DURING THE COLD WAR

In the first years of its existence, the CIA focused its attention on Europe, where it sought both to "liberate" Eastern European nations under Soviet control and to contain the further spread of communism to Western European countries weakened by World War II. Several operations in this period involved the secret funding of private citizen groups within the United States, among them labor officials, intellectuals, and students who enjoyed nonofficial channels to counterpart groups in Europe, ensuring that CIA covert action had an impact on American as well as foreign societies.

By the early 1950s, with Western Europe stabilized and Eastern Europe apparently impervious to US penetration, the focus of CIA operations moved to "Third

World" nations perceived as susceptible to communist influence. This shift coincided with the 1952 election of Dwight D. Eisenhower (1890–1969), an advocate of covert operations as a noncostly, plausibly deniable means of waging the Cold War, and the appointment of covert action enthusiast Allen W. Dulles (1893–1969) as director of central intelligence.

Dulles oversaw the two most important CIA operations of the early Cold War era. In 1953, the agency conspired with Britain's secret intelligence service, MI6, to depose Iran's democratically elected prime minister, Mohammad Mossadegh (1882–1967), after he had nationalized British-controlled Iranian oil fields and inspired American fears that he might succumb to a communist takeover. The following year, the CIA planned the overthrow of Guatemalan president Jacobo Arbenz Guzmán (1913–1971), who had redistributed land owned by the US United Fruit Company to peasant farmers and purchased arms from communist Czechoslovakia. Both operations reflected a mix of US political and economic concerns; both owed their successful outcomes to the actions of local elites as well as those of the CIA; and both resulted in the installation of highly repressive regimes, provoking profound resentment of the United States in the countries concerned, and later leading in the case of Iran to acts of terrorism against American targets, a phenomenon known as blowback.

Nevertheless, the Iran and Guatemala operations were regarded in Washington at the time as major Cold War victories, causing successive administrations to rely on covert action intended either to remove Third World leaders perceived as inimical to US interests (for example, in Indonesia, the Congo, Cuba, Iraq, the Dominican Republic, Guyana, Brazil, and Chile) or strengthen governments considered strategic assets (in Egypt, South Vietnam, and those countries where CIA-instigated regime change had already taken place, such as post-1953 Iran). Some observers, including analysts within the CIA, argued that this emphasis on covert operations was causing the agency to neglect its intelligence function, leading to failures, such as the lack of warning of the Iranian Revolution of 1979. Meanwhile, opposition to the United States and its intelligence arm grew within the countries subjected to CIA intervention.

OPPOSITION TO CIA ACTIVITY

Although US Cold War foreign policy commanded a remarkable degree of support from American society, the unease about official secrecy expressed at the time of the agency's creation never disappeared altogether, and during the 1960s the US media showed an increased tendency to question the propriety of CIA covert action. Several factors contributed to this development, among them the undeniable failure of some operations, such as the botched invasion of Cuba at the Bay of Pigs in 1961, which caused the resignation of Allen Dulles (ironically, the detection of Soviet missiles on Cuba the following year represented an outstanding intelligence success for the CIA); growing public opposition to the Vietnam War; and the influence of overseas protests against US interventionism.

Starting with the exposure of the covert funding of US student groups in 1967, a series of American newspaper reports revealed CIA involvement in such questionable activities as Operation Phoenix, a program to neutralize Vietnamese communists by methods such as assassination, and MH-CHAOS, a domestic campaign to spy on the anti–Vietnam War movement. Following the Watergate scandal, congressional investigations resulted in further revelations, such as the existence of an internal dossier of CIA abuses known as the "Family Jewels." Senator Frank Church (D-Idaho; 1924–1984) famously likened the agency to a "rogue elephant," but defenders of the CIA insisted that it had never acted without presidential approval.

REVIVAL UNDER REAGAN

The CIA's fortunes revived in the 1980s when President Ronald Reagan (1911–2004), committed to a policy of renewed confrontation with the communist powers, appointed the hard-line anticommunist William J. Casey (1913–1987) as director of central intelligence. Under Casey, the CIA intervened vigorously in the Central American state of Nicaragua and provided support to mujahideen fighters resisting the Soviet invasion of Afghanistan. Again, however, the agency was mired in controversy when it faced allegations of wrongdoing in its support of the Nicaraguan Contras (including complicity in the Iran-Contra scandal and tolerance of drug trafficking) and incompetence in its failure to predict the disintegration of the Soviet Union and the end of the Cold War.

Similarly, after the rise of Islamist terrorism and the start of the war on terror, the CIA was criticized for various alleged shortcomings in its intelligence performance—for example, failing to avert the 9/11 attacks and erroneously affirming the existence in Iraq of weapons of mass destruction—and, at the same time, abusing suspected terrorists by means of extraordinary rendition, "enhanced interrogation," and targeted killings, then obstructing congressional investigation of these activities. The enemy might be different from that of the Cold War, but the CIA still faces the same struggle to balance the contradictory elements of its mission as the secret intelligence service of a democratic global superpower.

SEE ALSO *Bush, George H. W.; Bush, George W.; Covert Wars; Dulles, Allen W.; Guatemala; Iran*

BIBLIOGRAPHY

Immerman, Richard H. *The Hidden Hand: A Brief History of the CIA*. Chichester, West Sussex, UK: Wiley-Blackwell, 2014.

Jeffreys-Jones, Rhodri. *The CIA and American Democracy*. 3rd ed. New Haven, CT: Yale University Press, 2003.

Johnson, Loch K. *America's Secret Power: The CIA in a Democratic Society*. New York: Oxford University Press, 1989.

Mazzetti, Mark. *The Way of the Knife: The CIA, a Secret Army, and a War at the Ends of the Earth*. New York: Penguin, 2013.

Prados, John. *Safe for Democracy: The Secret Wars of the CIA*. Chicago: Ivan R. Dee, 2006.

Thomas, Evan. *The Very Best Men: Four Who Dared: The Early Years of the CIA*. New York: Simon and Schuster, 1995.

Wilford, Hugh. *The Mighty Wurlitzer: How the CIA Played America*. Cambridge, MA: Harvard University Press, 2008.

Hugh Wilford
Professor of History
California State University, Long Beach

CHENEY, DICK
1941–

Few Americans have compiled a political résumé as extensive as that of Richard B. Cheney (Dick Cheney, born January 30, 1941). Over a thirty-five-year period, he served as White House deputy chief of staff, chief of staff, a five-term member of the House of Representatives (including service as House minority whip), secretary of defense, and vice president of the United States. Although he initially focused on domestic and political matters, Cheney increasingly became deeply engaged in national security and international concerns. This involvement culminated during the George W. Bush (b. 1946) administration, when he helped create and implement policies for the war on terror and the war against Iraq.

Cheney's association with Donald Rumsfeld (b. 1932) brought him to power when Rumsfeld became the top White House aide of Gerald R. Ford (1913–2006) in late September 1974. As Rumsfeld's deputy, Cheney had extensive exposure to Ford, and when Rumsfeld became secretary of defense in October 1975, Cheney succeeded him as chief of staff. The thirty-four-year-old Cheney had little standing to participate in deliberations regarding global matters, an area dominated by Secretary of State Henry Kissinger (b. 1923).

Two years after Ford's defeat in the 1976 presidential election, Cheney was elected to the House of Representatives from Wyoming, where he soon procured a spot on the Republican leadership ladder. He supported the Nicaraguan Contra rebels and the defense programs of Ronald Reagan (1911–2004) and opposed sanctions against South Africa's apartheid regime. In 1984, after reelection to a fourth term, he was appointed to the House Intelligence Committee, where he developed national security expertise. He achieved prominence as the ranking House Republican on the committee created in early 1987 to investigate the Iran-Contra scandal during the Reagan administration. On that committee he defended support for the Contras and robust presidential power against congressional assertions.

After the Senate rejected former Texas senator John Tower (1925–1991) as George H. W. Bush's (b. 1924) secretary of defense in March 1989, Cheney was nominated and confirmed for that position. Cheney, among the more conservative members of Bush's national security team, was skeptical regarding the commitment of Soviet leader Mikhail Gorbachev (b. 1931) to reform. Iraq's invasion of Kuwait presented the occasion for the first major conflict in the post–Cold War era. Cheney traveled to Saudi Arabia to obtain permission to deploy American troops there; he also traveled to other Arab nations to obtain logistical support. Cheney's portfolio was more concerned with military operations than diplomacy. He rejected economic sanctions as a strategy to expel Iraq from Kuwait and, as an early advocate of military action, worked to develop a substantial ground and air offensive. Cheney opposed seeking authorization from Congress to use force against Iraq, a course Bush nonetheless followed.

After Bush's defeat in 1992, Cheney returned to private life, where he considered, but rejected, a presidential run in 1996. He became chief executive officer of Halliburton, a large oil services company, in late 1995. During his nearly five years in that position, he expanded the company through mergers and increased federal business and opposed unilateral sanctions that prevented American companies from doing business with such countries as Iran.

George W. Bush (b. 1946) enlisted Cheney to run his vice presidential search in the spring of 2000 and ultimately chose Cheney as his running mate. They were elected that year in a disputed election and reelected in 2004. The defining moment of Bush's presidency, and Cheney's vice presidency, occurred on September 11, 2001, when the terrorist group al-Qaeda hijacked commercial airliners and crashed them into New York's World Trade Center and also the Pentagon in Washington. In Bush's absence from Washington, DC, that day, Cheney directed the nation's response from the Presidential Emergency Operations Center. In the following weeks and months, Cheney assumed a pivotal role in planning the response to al-Qaeda. He spearheaded development of various programs to identify and combat terrorists, obtained presidential approval of them, and often remained involved in their implementation. He advocated the war on Iraq based on the premise that its president, Saddam Hussein (1937–2006), was developing weapons of mass destruction and was linked to terror. He argued against seeking authorization from Congress or further United Nations resolutions subjecting Iraq to inspections before initiating hostilities. He remained a steadfast defender of the Iraq War after no weapons of mass destruction or link to al-Qaeda was found and after other politicians withdrew support. He also defended the administration's antiterror policies, including those that became controversial. In internal discussions he generally took a harder line and opposed some of Bush's second-term initiatives to pursue negotiated resolutions with Iran and North Korea.

Cheney gave high priority to protecting American security and viewed a strong presidency and Bush's antiterror policies as means to achieving that end. After leaving office, he continued his vocal defense of "enhanced interrogation" methods, denying that they constituted torture and claiming that they yielded valuable intelligence.

SEE ALSO *Abu Ghraib; Bush, George H. W.; Bush, George W.; Exceptionalism; Guantánamo Bay; Multinational Corporations; Nixon, Richard Milhous; Powell, Colin; War on Terror*

BIBLIOGRAPHY

Baker, Peter. *Days of Fire: Bush and Cheney in the White House.* New York: Doubleday, 2013.

Cheney, Dick, with Liz Cheney. *In My Time: A Personal and Political Memoir.* New York: Threshold Editions, 2011.

Gellman, Barton. *Angler: The Cheney Vice Presidency.* New York: Penguin, 2008.

Goldstein, Joel K. "Cheney, Vice Presidential Power and the War on Terror." *Presidential Studies Quarterly* 40, 1 (March 2010): 102–139.

Hayes, Stephen F. *Cheney: The Untold Story of America's Most Powerful and Controversial Vice President.* New York: Harper-Collins, 2007.

Joel K. Goldstein
Vincent C. Immel Professor of Law
Saint Louis University School of Law

CHEROKEE NATION V. GEORGIA (1831)

On March 18, 1831, the US Supreme Court issued its opinion in *Cherokee Nation v. Georgia.* The court decided neither for nor against the Cherokee Nation's right to protest Georgia's claims to its territory. The Cherokee Nation was *not* a foreign nation; instead it was a "domestic dependent nation" and could not represent itself in an American court of law. Chief Justice John Marshall (1755–1835) wrote the opinion for the four to two majority, while Smith Thompson (1768–1843) and Joseph Story (1779–1845) dissented. The opinion was a victory of sorts for the Cherokee Nation. For the first time, an Indian nation stood before the US Supreme Court.

BACKGROUND

In 1802 President Thomas Jefferson (1743–1826) promised Indian removal through westward expansion. He signed the Compact of 1802 to remove all Indian tribes within Georgia's designated borders as soon as possible by "reasonable and peaceable" means. However, the Cherokee Nation had been unusually resistant to removal efforts from its southeastern homelands. The treaties of 1817 and 1819 limited the Cherokee Nation's remaining territory to an area claimed predominantly by Georgia. State leaders became increasingly impatient as Georgia's population increased. Wanting to remove all Native Americans to land west of the Mississippi, the newly elected president, Andrew Jackson (1767–1845), promoted his Indian Removal bill from 1829 until its passage in May 1830. Yet the constitutionality of the bill was in question because it gave unilateral control to the chief executive over powers expressly delegated to Congress in the US Constitution, Article I, Section 8: "Congress shall have Power … To regulate Commerce with foreign Nations, and among the several States, and with the Indian Tribes." The bill passed through the House of Representatives by a slim margin of 102 to 97. Jackson signed the bill into law, and the Cherokee Nation turned to the courts.

Cherokee Principal Chief John Ross (1790–1866) hired the influential and recently retired attorney general William Wirt (1772–1834) to promote their cause. Before accepting, Wirt asked a mutual friend, Dabney Carr (1773–1837), to assess Marshall's position (Kennedy 1856, II: 254). The chief justice responded to Carr's question by indicating his appreciation for the Cherokee Nation's plight, wishing that "both the Executive and legislative departments had thought differently on the subject" (Hobson 2006, 11:381). Although Marshall refrained from definitive support, Wirt and Ross felt encouraged to pursue legal options.

THE EVOLUTION OF MARSHALL'S VIEWS

Marshall's opinion in *Cherokee Nation v. Georgia* demonstrates a complex mix of support for and resistance to recognizing Cherokee sovereignty. "If courts were permitted to indulge their sympathies, a case better calculated to excite them can scarcely be imagined," he wrote. Marshall, however, restrained the bench's authority: "Before we can look into the merits of the case, a preliminary inquiry presents itself. Has this Court jurisdiction of the cause?" Although the court declined to render an opinion, Marshall simultaneously kept the issue alive. Well known for preferring moderate and unanimous opinions, Marshall had taken the "middle road" of his time and barely held the majority opinion in the case. Indeed, fellow justices Henry Baldwin (1780–1844) and William Johnson (1771–1834) concurred with Marshall in denying Cherokee jurisdiction, but as Marshall also expounded upon US responsibilities, these justices felt compelled to write separate and less expansive opinions. Uncharacteristically, Marshall encouraged Justices Thompson and Story to publish dissenting opinions through court reporter Richard Peters Jr. (1780–1848). Significantly more pages were written in favor of Cherokee sovereignty than against.

Cherokee Nation v. Georgia demonstrates Marshall's evolving interpretation of Emmerich de Vattel's (1714–1767) treatise, *The Law of Nations* (1758), justifying US expansion policies into Native American territory. Vattel, a Swiss philosopher, argued for the dominance of European powers over Native Americans and for the rights accorded first conquest, also known as the Doctrine of Discovery. European powers that first discovered and settled Indian lands assumed preemptive rights over them. In this way, Vattel justified the European conquest of America. In *Johnson and Graham's Lessee v. M'Intosh* (1823), Marshall applied Vattel's ideas to demonstrate that the United States had won the right of conquest of Indian lands on the American continent over the European powers. In accord with Vattel's doctrine, he wrote in *Johnson* that the United States "hold and assert in themselves the title by which it was acquired." This "discovery gave [the United States] an exclusive right to extinguish the Indian title of occupancy, either by purchase or by conquest; and gave also a right to such a degree of sovereignty, as the circumstances of the people would allow them to exercise." After rendering the *Johnson* decision, however, the chief justice became increasingly disturbed by the rapacious violence of westward expansion and the misuse, in his mind, of his opinion in *Johnson.*

In the same year as Marshall's *Johnson* decision, Chancellor James Kent (1763–1847) of New York offered a new interpretation of US-Indian relations, based on the concept of "domestic dependent nation," in his New York Supreme Court decision in *Goodell v. Jackson* (1823). In *Cherokee Nation v. Georgia,* Marshall combined the ideas of Vattel and Kent. Marshall explained that the validity of conquest was limited solely to acts of warfare: "The preemptive right, and exclusive right of conquest in case of war, was never questioned to exist in the States which circumscribed the whole or any part of the Indian grounds or territory." But, in cases where war was not a factor, to have taken Indian land "by direct means would have been a palpable violation of their rights."

Through *Cherokee Nation* Marshall explained the responsibilities of the United States as the more powerful nation. The Cherokees "look to our government for protection; rely upon its kindness and its power; appeal to it for relief to their wants; and address the President as their great father." The Cherokee Nation was "in a state of pupilage"; the United States held the responsibilities of a "ward to his guardian." The application of "ward" and "guardian" to respective nations was a question of national power, not personal maturity. Indeed Chief Ross expressed optimism over the *Cherokee Nation* decision, despite the court's refusal to grant the Cherokees full rights as a foreign nation. He wrote, "I sincerely believe that a foundation is laid upon which our injured rights may be reared and made permanent" (Moulton 1985, 920). The subsequent imprisonment of two Cherokee missionaries, the Reverend Samuel Austin Worcester (1798–1859) and Dr. Elizur Butler (b. 1794) in the Georgia penitentiary provided Marshall with the opportunity to express his more expansive opinion on behalf of Cherokee sovereignty rights in *Worcester v. Georgia* one year later on March 3, 1832.

SEE ALSO *Civilization Fund; Foreign Mission Movement; Indian Removal Act (1830); Reservation; Worcester v. Georgia (1832)*

BIBLIOGRAPHY

Burke, Joseph C. "The Cherokee Cases: A Study in Law, Politics, and Morality." *Stanford Law Review* 21, 3 (February 1969): 500–531.

Cherokee Nation v. Georgia, 30 U.S. 5 Pet. 1 (1831).

de Vattel, Emmerich. *Le droit des gens.* 1758. Published as *The Law of Nations,* edited by Joseph Chitty. Philadelphia: T. & J.W. Johnson, 1883.

Garrison, Tim Alan. "United States Indian Policy in Sectional Crisis: Georgia's Exploitation of the Compact of 1802." In *Congress and the Emergence of Sectionalism: From the Missouri Compromise to the Age of Jackson,* edited by Paul Finkelman and Donald R. Kennon, 97–132. Athens: Ohio University Press, 2008.

Goodell v. Jackson, 20 Johns. 693 (N.Y. Sup. Ct. 1823).

Hobson, Charles F., Susan Holbrook Perdue, and Joan S. Lovelace, eds. John Marshall to Dabney Carr, June 26, 1830. *The Papers of John Marshall.* Vol. 11. Chapel Hill: University of North Carolina Press, 2002.

Johnson and Graham's Lessee v. M'Intosh, 21 U.S. 8 Wheat. 543 (1823).

Kennedy, John Pendleton, ed. William Wirt to Dabney Carr, June 21, 1830. *Memoirs of the Life of William Wirt, Attorney-*

General of the United States. Vol. 2. Philadelphia: Blanchard and Lea, 1856.

Morgan, Nancy. "Jeremiah Evarts: The Cherokees' Forgotten Counsel." In *"Our Cause Will Ultimately Triumph": Profiles in American Indian Sovereignty,* edited by Tim Alan Garrison, 27–38. Durham, NC: Carolina Academic Press, 2014.

Moulton, Gary E., ed. John Ross to the Cherokees, April 14, 1831. In *The Papers of Chief John Ross*. Vol. 1. Norman: University of Oklahoma Press, 1985.

White, G. Edward. *Marshall Court and Cultural Change, 1815–1835*. New York: Macmillan, 1988.

Nancy Morgan
Instructor, School of Historical, Philosophical and Religious Studies
Arizona State University

CHICANO MOVEMENT

Despite its common classification as the Mexican American subset of the larger American civil rights movement that defined the 1960s, there is actually no specific date of origin that marks the beginning of the Chicano movement. Rather, like the cultural identity it represents, the roots of the movement are found in important but scattered events throughout a history that transcends national borders, encompassing many noteworthy cultural and philosophical traits that are better understood in a transnational context. While the cultural identity behind the term *Chicano* can be traced back to important dates like 1848—the year the Treaty of Guadalupe Hidalgo was signed, ending the Mexican-American War and establishing an undeniable "Mexican American" lineage in the process—the Chicano movement was equally influenced by various international struggles for social justice, including student-led protests in France and Mexico during the 1960s.

The Chicano movement can be divided into four overlapping spheres—economic, political, cultural, and social—representing the demands for justice and equality at the heart of the movement. The one struggle that touched the individual lives of most Chicanos was the fight for economic justice. Federally sanctioned labor practices like the bracero program underscored the economic expendability of most Mexicans and Chicanos. While their labor was important and necessary for the US economy, their inclusion into the larger national collective was continually forestalled and undermined. Such economic exploitation was nowhere more evident than in the plight of migrant farmworkers. Considered an invisible labor pool even today, Chicanos who work in the fields are subjected to discriminatory practices deemed illegal by US law yet commonly exercised without repercussions.

Cesar Chavez (1927–1993) and Dolores Huerta (b. 1930) led the struggle against such economic discrimination by founding the National Farm Workers Association, later known as the United Farm Workers, in 1962. Together, they helped attain higher wages and better working conditions for farmworkers across California. Chavez in particular emerged as a national icon for farmworker rights, gaining notoriety through his nonviolent approach to political protest, a strategy learned from figures like Mahatma Gandhi (1869–1948) and Martin Luther King Jr. (1929–1968). Famous for his self-sacrifice and spiritual hunger fasts used to promote nonviolence, peace, and hope, Chavez's fame reached its pinnacle when he met privately with Robert Kennedy (1925–1968) and won his support for farmworker rights.

The farmworker struggle for economic justice also shed light on the political disenfranchisement of Chicanos, which was challenged by activists like Reies Lopez Tijerina (1926–2015) and Oscar Acosta (b. 1935), who battled unlawful land seizures and systemic discrimination in courtrooms across the Southwest. In New Mexico, Tijerina engaged in a Zapatista-like politics of land reclamation, often confronting US government authorities with force. Using the knowledge he gained while conducting research in Mexico and Spain, Tijerina argued that many lands in the Southwest had been illegally appropriated by the federal government. In 1966, he occupied part of the Carson National Forest, reclaiming it as the "Republic of San Joaquín del Río de Chama." In a similar vein of radical activism, Acosta gained notoriety as a confrontational Chicano lawyer who openly challenged what he deemed to be a corrupt and racist US legal system. In addition to working on several prominent civil rights cases in California, Acosta is well-known for his provocative legal practices, like calling on judges as witnesses in order to highlight the racist prejudice that defined the grand jury selection process.

The Chicano movement also included important social and cultural leaders, such as Rodolfo "Corky" Gonzales (1928–2005). Founder of Denver's Crusade for Justice in 1966, Gonzales gained national attention for his mobilization of Chicano youth. Using a platform built on Chicano nationalism, Gonzales advocated for a collective identity grounded in Aztec myths like that of Aztlán. This emphasis on cultural consciousness was echoed in many Chicano artistic works, from the plays of El Teatro Campesino to the poetry of Alurista (b. 1947) and, more recently, Gloria Anzaldúa (1942–2004). Inspired by this newfound identity, Chicano youth rallied to become a major component of the movement.

Led by student organizations, such as MEChA (Movimiento Estudiantil Chicano de Aztlán), Chicano students participated in a variety of school "walkouts" in

1968 to protest their educational curriculum. Embodying the intersection of social and cultural demands, students complained about the lack of educational opportunities available to them, including the absence of Chicano history and culture in public school curricula and the underrepresentation of Chicano teaching faculty. Students were also instrumental in larger sociopolitical interventions, exemplified in the Chicano moratoriums against the Vietnam War from 1969 to 1971. Comprising a large contingency within the movement, these students would prove instrumental in the future development, articulation, and redefining of what it means to be Chicano.

SEE ALSO *Bracero Program; Mexico*

BIBLIOGRAPHY

Gómez-Quiñones, Juan, and Irene Vásquez. *Making Aztlán: Ideology and Culture of the Chicana and Chicano Movement, 1966–1977.* Albuquerque: University of New Mexico Press, 2014.

Haney-López, Ian F. *Racism on Trial: The Chicano Fight for Justice.* Cambridge, MA: Belknap Press of Harvard University Press, 2003.

Herrera-Sobek, María, ed. *Reconstructing a Chicano/a Literary Heritage: Hispanic Colonial Literature of the Southwest.* Tucson: University of Arizona Press, 1993.

Rosales, F. Arturo. *Chicano: The History of the Mexican American Civil Rights Movement.* Rev. ed. Houston, TX: Arte Público Press, 1997.

Carlos Gallego
Associate Professor, English Department
St. Olaf College

CHINA

On the eve of the American Revolution, the North American colonists had long enjoyed the benefits of British trade with China. Many colonial homes were filled with "Chinese Chippendale" furniture and Chinese wallpapers, silks, and porcelains. Cheap "chinaware" dishes and pots could be found in homes, taverns, and forts from Philadelphia to the Mackinac Straits of Michigan. Above all, there was Chinese tea, such as that dumped in Boston Harbor one night in December 1773.

SINO-AMERICAN RELATIONS IN THE EARLY REPUBLIC

Immediately after winning their independence, freed from the British East India Company's monopoly, the Americans leapt into the China trade. Commercial interests on the eastern seaboard, no longer permitted to trade with the British West Indies, anticipated enormous profits in this new cross-Pacific venture. For the first fifty years of direct contact with China, American interests were wholly commercial. There were no government-to-government relations.

At the close of the eighteenth century and in the early years of the nineteenth, China—the Qing dynasty—was the dominant power in East Asia. The Chinese dictated the terms of contact with the "barbarians" who came by sea. Conditions for Western merchants were unpleasant, their movements and opportunities restricted under the Canton system, a coastal version of the tribute system the Chinese applied to all foreigners. They had no recourse when confronted by arbitrary Chinese actions, such as the execution in 1821 of one Terranova, a seaman from an American vessel. Terranova had allegedly swept debris off the deck that struck and killed a Chinese boat passenger. Threatened with the loss of trade privileges if they did not comply, the American merchants turned him over to local authorities, who strangled him.

Unnoticed by Chinese leaders, the locus of power in the world was shifting toward Europe. In particular, the British, strengthened by the Industrial Revolution and military modernization spurred by the Napoleonic Wars of the early nineteenth century, were ready to challenge Chinese practices, to demand a relationship between equals. A confrontation arose from Chinese determination to end the sale of opium, a moral and financial problem for their empire. British merchants appealed to their government, which responded by sending ships and troops from its Indian colony in 1839, triggering what came to be known as the Opium War.

China was defeated and in 1842 was forced to sign the Treaty of Nanjing, opening several ports to British merchants and granting the British most-favored-nation status for their trade. In addition, the British imposed limits on Chinese import tariffs, spared their citizens from China's legal jurisdiction through the concept of extraterritoriality, and seized Hong Kong.

Despite Chinese efforts to enlist the Americans on their side—their traditional policy of using barbarians to control barbarians—the United States was not involved. Many Americans, most notably John Quincy Adams (1767–1848), were appalled by the idea of fighting in order to sell opium. But American merchants quickly gained all of the privileges exacted by London for its merchants. This practice, later labeled "jackal diplomacy," served American purposes for most of the nineteenth century. The British and other powers fought the Chinese and won privileges, while the Americans stood by and shared in the spoils.

The US government made a perfunctory and unsuccessful effort to obtain a trade treaty with China in 1832. The decade of the 1830s was marked most significantly by the arrival of the first American missionaries, whose influence in Washington came to rival that of the merchants. Businessmen were often leery of antagonizing their host government. Missionaries, in China contrary to Chinese law, were not. They lobbied for an American treaty, obtained with considerable effort in 1844 by Caleb Cushing (1800–1879), aided by Peter Parker (1804–1888), a medical missionary related by marriage to Daniel Webster (1782–1852), the secretary of state. The Treaty of Wangxia (now part of Macao) confirmed the privileges the Americans already enjoyed as a result of British treaties.

In 1850, China was wracked by the Taiping Rebellion, a struggle that lasted fifteen years and took at least 20 million lives. Unfazed by his domestic troubles, the Qing emperor ignored British demands in 1858 for treaty revision as stipulated in the original British and American treaties. Ultimately British and French forces overcame Chinese resistance and forced the Beijing regime to accept the Treaties of Tianjin, stripping the Chinese of all protection against foreign exploitation. China was forced to open eleven new ports, allow navigation up the Yangtze (also Yangzi and in modern times Chang), and permit missionaries and other foreigners to roam the country and diplomats to reside in Beijing. Although there was some unauthorized American naval participation in the fighting, the United States remained neutral—and once again shared in the spoils.

Although Parker and Commodore Matthew Perry (1794–1858) contemplated territorial acquisitions comparable to the British entrepôt in Hong Kong, there was no interest in Washington. For the remainder of the nineteenth century, the American government and those of its citizens with interests in China contented themselves with the leavings of British and other imperial powers—what has been called "multilateral imperialism."

THE EXPANDING US ROLE IN EAST ASIA

William Seward (1801–1872), Abraham Lincoln's secretary of state, envisioned a larger role in East Asia for the United States, but first his country had to survive its Civil War. He sent Anson Burlingame (1820–1870) to China to assure the British and French of American cooperation there, determined not to offend nations who could intervene in the American Civil War to the detriment of the Union. After the war, Seward instructed Burlingame to ask the Chinese to send an envoy to Washington. Eventually, the Chinese asked Burlingame to lead a Chinese delegation to major European capitals, as well as to the United States. Seward and Burlingame signed a treaty with which the United States promised not to interfere in China's internal development and allowed Chinese immigrants to enter the United States. The latter clause created a series of crises for years afterward as the Chinese were mistreated and ultimately, in 1882, excluded from entry—in violation of the treaty.

In 1894 and 1895, the Japanese easily defeated China militarily, and the weakness thus exposed led the Japanese and several European powers to contemplate carving up the Chinese "melon." The handful of Americans with interests in China urged action by their government to prevent being shut out of trade or denied scope for their missionary work. President William McKinley (1843–1901) and John Hay (1838–1905), his secretary of state, resisted these pressures, but in 1899 and 1900 Hay issued his "Open Door" notes. Sent to the capitals of all of the major powers involved in China, Hay asked that they respect the territorial integrity and independence of China and the rights of other nationalities in their spheres of influence. Danger to China's existence as a sovereign state was very great after the Boxer War of 1900—when American troops from the Philippines joined those of other nations to rescue their citizens under siege in Beijing. When the various powers, for reasons of their own, chose not to carve up China, some Americans perceived their country as China's champion.

As evident in their subsequent victory over Russia in 1905, the Japanese had come to dominate East Asia. The British quickly came to terms with them, and President Theodore Roosevelt (1858–1919) understood that the United States was powerless to confront Japan when it threatened minor American interests in Manchuria, where Japanese interests were vital. He explained to his successor, William Howard Taft (1857–1930), that the United States would have to have an army comparable to the German and a navy comparable to the British to confront Japan.

Despite Roosevelt's arguments for appeasing Japan in China while Americans mistreated Japanese immigrants in the United States, Taft and Woodrow Wilson (1856–1924), his successors in the White House, were appalled by increasingly rapacious Japanese imperialism and groped unsuccessfully for a means to counter it. Taft's weapon of choice was "dollar diplomacy." Wilson, failing to persuade the Japanese by faulting their behavior, attempted to use the League of Nations to contain them and to draw them into a new international order in which there was no place for imperialism.

The Chinese did little to help themselves. In 1912, the Qing dynasty was overthrown and replaced by a republic, nominally led initially by Sun Yat-sen (1866–1925). The years that followed were chaotic as an effort to establish a parliamentary democracy was thwarted by Yuan Shikai (1859–1916), a former Qing general who wielded real power and attempted to establish a new dynasty with himself as emperor. His failure and death led to an era in which various Chinese military men, the "war lords," struggled for control of parts of the country. Eventually, in the 1920s, Sun's followers, supported by the Soviet Union, battled the war lords in an attempt, largely successful, to unite the country—and less successfully, to drive out foreign imperialists.

THE RISE OF CHINESE NATIONALISM AND JAPANESE IMPERIALISM

The United States welcomed the creation of the Republic of China, imagining that its system of government might approximate that in Washington. In 1921 and 1922, nations with interests in China—and for the first time, Chinese representatives—met in Washington to relieve tensions among them and to protect China from further infringement of its sovereignty. Among the treaties signed was the Nine Power Treaty, designed by the United States, with which the signatories promised not to interfere in China's internal affairs and to allow the Chinese to modernize in their own way.

The United States looked favorably upon the rise of Chinese nationalism, expecting it to be advantageous to American interests there. Never perceiving themselves as imperialists but rather as China's champions, Americans assumed they would be exempted from Chinese anti-foreignism. Neither the Guomindang, Sun's party, whose military leader was Chiang Kai-shek (1887–1975), nor the Chinese Communists, initially allied with Chiang, shared America's self-image. Eventually, in 1928, Chiang, having outmaneuvered the Soviets and having split with the Communists, won recognition and some concessions to Chinese sovereignty from the United States and the other foreign powers with interests in China.

The Japanese military, unhappy with concessions civilian leaders had made to Chiang, was determined to resist further incursions by the Chinese into what it considered its sphere of influence in China, specifically in Manchuria. In 1931, as much of the world was mired in the Great Depression, the Japanese army in Manchuria created an incident that it used to justify driving all semblance of Chinese authority out of the region. Ultimately, Japan created the puppet state of Manchukuo. The League of Nations, which the United States had not joined, condemned Japan's action but was powerless to reverse it.

In Washington, Henry Stimson (1867–1950), President Herbert Hoover's (1874–1964) secretary of state, groped for a way to stop the Japanese, to preserve Chinese sovereignty over Manchuria and protect American interests there. Military force was never an option: American interests, defined narrowly as trade and investments, were not sufficiently important. The president opposed economic sanctions, fearing they would lead to war. Instead they settled on the "Stimson-Hoover doctrine," indicting Japan for violating the Nine Power Treaty—to no avail.

WORLD WAR II

Throughout the 1930s, the United States struggled with the Depression and watched the rising threat of Adolf Hitler's Germany. American leaders were Atlanticists, much more concerned with events in Europe than those in Asia. Nazi Germany was perceived as a greater danger to American security than was Japan. The outbreak of full-scale war between China and Japan in 1937 was troubling, but Washington was more responsive to the plight of Great Britain when war broke out in Europe in 1939. American support for China was modest until 1940, when the Germans, Japanese, and Italians formed an alliance with the Tripartite Pact aimed at intimidating the United States, threatening a two-front war should the Americans intervene in either Europe or Asia.

The American response to the Tripartite Pact was to increase its aid to both Britain and China and to begin economic sanctions against Japan. Attempts to negotiate a *modus vivendi* between the United States and Japan broke down in November 1941. On December 7, 1941, the Japanese bombed Pearl Harbor. In China, Chiang's beleaguered government cheered the attack, knowing it would bring the United States into the war on their side, providing hope for victory.

China had become an ally, but only a second-class ally for President Franklin D. Roosevelt (1882–1945) and his advisers. They hoped the Chinese would keep the Japanese occupied while the United States, Great Britain, and the Soviet Union concentrated their efforts on the defeat of Hitler and his allies. Chiang hoped the Americans would defeat the Japanese while his forces focused on their internal enemy, the Chinese Communists. Neither Roosevelt nor Chiang was satisfied with his ally's contribution, and tensions arose between them before the end of the war. Americans in China, military and diplomatic, were troubled by the apparent unwillingness of Chiang's troops to fight and by the repressiveness of his government. They were more favorably impressed by the efforts of the Chinese Communists, who seemed more aggressive in their confrontations with the Japanese.

POSTWAR US RELATIONS WITH TAIWAN AND COMMUNIST CHINA

After the Japanese surrendered in August 1945, civil war erupted between the Chinese government and the Chinese Communists. American leaders, eager to see the emergence of a unified strong China that was able to contain Japan, tried unsuccessfully to mediate. Considering the effort to assist Chiang in the defeat of the

Communists beyond American means, especially as the United States sought to contain the Soviet Union in Europe, Washington eventually abandoned him. The National Security Council concluded that although a Communist victory in China was undesirable, a Communist China did not constitute a threat to the United States and probably could not for another fifty years. The Americans, perceiving tensions between Moscow and Beijing, tried merely to prevent Beijing from becoming an adjunct to Soviet power.

Defeated on the mainland, Chiang and the remnants of his forces fled to Taiwan in 1949. On October 1, 1949, Communist leader Mao Zedong (1893–1976) proclaimed the establishment of the People's Republic of China (PRC). The United States withheld recognition, largely for domestic political reasons, a response to residual support for a wartime ally. American analysts expected the PRC to finish off Chiang's forces on Taiwan in the next year or so. Once Chiang's defeat was final, President Harry Truman (1884–1972) would extend diplomatic recognition to the only surviving Chinese government.

In January 1950 China and the Soviet Union signed an alliance, disappointing Washington. The differences between the two Communist states had been put aside temporarily. Also in January, Secretary of State Dean Acheson (1893–1971) described the defensive perimeter of the United States, excluding Taiwan and the Asian mainland. In June, Joseph Stalin (1879–1953) and Mao, assuming the United States would not respond, supported the desire of the North Korean Communist leader, Kim Il Sung (1912–1994), to invade South Korea and unite Korea under his rule. To their dismay, the Americans not only led the United Nations to the defense of South Korea, but also acted to prevent the PRC from attacking Taiwan. The United States surrendered the idea of abandoning Taiwan and recognizing the PRC.

Having intervened in the Chinese civil war, ultimately engaging troops of the PRC in Korea, the United States, despite displeasure with Chiang's repressive regime, began to support the buildup of Taiwan's defenses. Eventually, in 1954, the administration of President Dwight D. Eisenhower (1890–1969) signed a mutual defense treaty with the Republic of China (ROC) on Taiwan. Nominally committed to supporting Chiang's hopeless efforts to reclaim the mainland, Washington in fact promoted the idea of two Chinas, one ruled from Beijing and the other from Taipei—a notion acceptable to neither side of the Taiwan Strait.

In 1954 and again in 1958, Mao initiated crises in the strait, attacking islands near the mainland coast that remained under the control of Chiang's forces. In neither instance was Beijing prepared to invade Taiwan, and Eisenhower took only such action as would indicate that an invasion would not be tolerated. There was little support in the United States or among America's allies for a war with China over the offshore islands, of which the two most important were Jinmen and Mazu.

By the time John F. Kennedy (1917–1963) entered the White House in January 1961, tensions between Moscow and Beijing had undermined their alliance. The Sino-Soviet split gave the United States an enormous advantage in the Cold War, but the Cuban missile crisis of 1962, the assassination of Kennedy, the Cultural Revolution in China, and America's war in Vietnam delayed any significant effort toward a Chinese-American rapprochement in the 1960s. It was clear, however, that elite opinion in the United States favored normalization of relations with China. The policy recommendation that emerged out of Senate hearings in the mid-1960s was for "containment without isolation."

The Normalization of Relations with the PRC. Richard Nixon (1913–1994), with a reputation as a hard-line anticommunist and Red-baiter, was elected president in 1968. Aware of the Sino-Soviet split, intensified by two serious border clashes in March 1969, he perceived the easing of Chinese-American tensions as a means of strengthening the United States in its confrontation with the Soviet Union. He also hoped the Chinese would press North Vietnam to facilitate an end to America's war in Vietnam. In 1971, he sent Henry Kissinger, his national security adviser, on a secret mission to Beijing. Mao and Zhou Enlai (1898–1976), his principal adviser, eager for American support against Moscow, welcomed Kissinger.

Kissinger's talks with Zhou and Mao revealed Nixon's willingness to abrogate Washington's mutual defense treaty with Taiwan, reduce its commitment to Taipei, end the American effort to create two Chinas, and acknowledge that both Beijing and Taipei insisted there could be only one China. The Chinese invited Nixon to visit China, which he did in 1972, to discuss further cooperation against the Soviets and movement toward the establishment of diplomatic relations between the United States and China. This rapprochement constituted a major shift in the Cold War balance of power from which the Soviet Union never recovered.

Nixon's intention to shift American recognition of China from Taipei to Beijing was thwarted by his impeachment because of the cover-up of the Watergate break-in and his subsequent resignation in 1974. His successor, Gerald Ford (1913–2006), retained Kissinger as his secretary of state. The two men were eager to proceed with recognition of the PRC but chose not to act, fearing that retribution from the Republican Right would cost Ford his party's presidential nomination in 1976. Ford won the nomination but lost the election to Jimmy Carter.

President Richard Nixon toasts Prime Minister Zhou Enlai during a state banquet in Beijing, 1972. *Zhou Enlai, Mao's principal adviser, was eager for US support against the Soviet Union and welcomed a 1971 visit by Secretary of State Henry Kissinger, which set the stage for Nixon's visit the following year.* UNIVERSALIMAGESGROUP/GETTY IMAGES

In China, Deng Xiaoping (1904–1997), who had become China's leader after the deaths of Mao and Zhou, was becoming impatient, eager for the Americans to follow through on the promises made by Nixon and Kissinger, especially the abandonment of Taiwan. Carter and Zbigniew Brzezinski, his national security adviser, were prepared to move ahead, but were slowed by resistance in the Department of State by men who had other priorities and by strong support for Taiwan in Congress. In December 1978, Leonard Woodcock (1911–2001), head of the American liaison office in Beijing (the de facto embassy), and Deng finessed the Taiwan issue and reached agreement on normalization. In January 1979, nearly thirty years after its establishment, the PRC gained recognition by the United States. To achieve this, Washington had to agree to end its recognition of the Taipei government and abrogate the mutual defense treaty signed with it in 1954.

Relations with Taiwan. Aware of the likely reaction from friends of Taiwan, the Carter administration insisted on maintaining "unofficial" relations with Chiang's government and most importantly, on continuing to supply it with arms. Deng expressed his unwillingness to accept the continuation of arms sales, but he did not let disagreement on the issue prevent the establishment of diplomatic ties, which were important to him in China's dealings with the Soviet Union.

The American Congress, however, insisted on strengthening ties to Taiwan and in 1979 passed the Taiwan Relations Act (TRA). The act required the US government to permit Taiwan to enjoy the privileges of a sovereign country, although it was no longer recognized as one. It also required the United States to provide Taiwan with whatever "defense articles and defense services" would be necessary to defend itself. In addition, it declared that any coercive action against Taiwan would be considered a threat to the region and of "grave concern" to the United States. Deng was outraged, and Carter could only promise to interpret the TRA in a manner consistent with the normalization agreement. The arms sales issue created tensions between Beijing and Washington forever after.

Chairman Mao Zedong welcomes President Richard Nixon at his house in Beijing, 1972. *The Chinese invited Nixon to China to discuss cooperation against the Soviets and movement toward the establishment of US-China diplomatic relations, signaling a major shift in the Cold War balance of power.* AFP/GETTY IMAGES

THE PRC UNDER DENG XIAOPING

Ronald Reagan (1911–2004), elected president in 1980, refused to accept the normalization agreement and announced his desire to resume official relations with Taipei. Chinese leaders were shaken and began to back away from cooperation with the United States. Reagan ultimately retreated from hostility to the PRC and visited China in 1984, and relations between the two countries, especially trade, strengthened in his second term. Deng's economic reforms—his concept of "socialism with Chinese characteristics"—moved China toward a market economy, becoming a major trading partner for Americans.

Reagan's successor, George H. W. Bush, had headed the liaison office in Beijing in the 1970s and perceived good Chinese-American relations as vital to the security of the United States. Although horrified by the Tiananmen massacres of 1989, when Chinese troops killed protesting civilians across the country, Bush was unwilling to weaken the relationship. Forced by Congress and public opinion to impose sanctions on China and to demand that China live up to its obligations on human rights, he sent secret missions to Beijing to assure Deng of his goodwill. When knowledge of these missions became public, Bush was accused of coddling the "butchers of Beijing."

Deng resisted international pressures, and businesspeople in Japan, Europe, and the United States were eager to resume activities in China. In the 1990s, the administration of Bill Clinton initially pledged to press the Chinese on human rights, but quickly caved to demands of the business community. The United States granted the PRC most-favored nation treatment for its exports, without gaining any concessions in return. The Chinese economy soared, and China entered the twenty-first century as one of the world's great economic powers.

THE US RESPONSE TO TENSIONS BETWEEN THE PRC AND THE ROC

There were also dramatic changes on Taiwan. The ROC slowly evolved into a democracy in the 1990s, greatly increasing its support in the United States—especially after the Tiananmen massacres. Lee Teng-hui, a native Taiwanese, succeeded Chiang Kai-shek's son as president, and appeared to inch his government toward establishing an independent Taiwan that was not a part of China, as both Beijing and Taipei had previously insisted. In 1996, on the eve of Lee becoming the first popularly elected president in Chinese history, the PRC, attempting to intimidate the islanders, created a crisis in the Taiwan

Strait. The People's Liberation Army massed troops on the coast across from Taiwan and bracketed the island with missile fire. Forced to respond, the Clinton administration warned the Chinese not to attack and sent two carrier battle groups to the strait. The crisis passed, but it was clear that the United States was going to have difficulty accommodating the rise of Chinese power.

In 2000, there was an extraordinary, peaceful transfer of power on Taiwan, from the Guomindang (Nationalist) Party, which had controlled the government of the ROC as a one-party dictatorship since 1928, to the Democratic Progressive Party (DPP). The DPP was a predominantly native Taiwanese party, committed to establishing an independent Taiwan. In both Beijing and Washington, there was great unease about the intentions of Chen Shuibian, the new president. The US government feared Chen would provoke a crisis in the Taiwan Strait, and it did not want to be drawn into conflict with the PRC. Eventually, the actions of the mercurial Chen forced President George W. Bush, also elected in 2000, to stand by the side of the PRC prime minister and issue a warning to Chen against taking steps toward Taiwan's independence. Chen's successor, the Guomindang's Ma Ying-jeou, did much to ease cross-Strait relations.

US-CHINA RELATIONS IN THE TWENTY-FIRST CENTURY

Early in Bush's administration, a crash between an American reconnaissance plane and a Chinese interceptor, misplayed by both sides, caused considerable tension. Eventually, a face-saving solution evolved, and relations between the PRC and the United States, although occasionally stressed, remained amiable for the remainder of Bush's term of office. After 9/11, Beijing was quick to announce its support for the American struggle against terrorism.

Nonetheless, the future of the relationship was fraught with peril. China's economy continued to boom and its military buildup posed a threat to its neighbors and to American interests in the western Pacific. The PRC was clearly emerging as the second-greatest power in the world and was apparently determined to dominate East Asia. Nationalism had replaced communism as the central ideology in the country, and its leaders chose to pursue a more assertive foreign policy—and perceived the United States as attempting to contain China, to prevent its rise. In the second decade of the twenty-first century, the relationship was frequently strained. The American desire for a friendly, democratic China seemed unattainable.

SEE ALSO *Angel Island; Buddhism; Canton; Chinese Exclusion Act (1882); Dollar Diplomacy; Immigration; Immigration Quotas; Manchuria; Missionary Diplomacy; Open Door Policy; Orient; Orient Express; Orientalism; United Nations*

BIBLIOGRAPHY

Borg, Dorothy. *American Policy and the Chinese Revolution, 1925–1928.* New York: Octagon Press, 1968. First published in 1947.

Cohen, Warren I. *America's Response to China: A History of Sino-American Relations.* 5th ed. New York: Columbia University Press, 2010.

Hachigan, Nina, ed. *Debating China: The U.S.-China Relationship in Ten Conversations.* New York: Oxford University Press, 2014.

Hunt, Michael H. *The Making of a Special Relationship: The United States and China to 1914.* New York: Columbia University Press, 1983.

Lampton, David M. *Same Bed, Different Dreams: Managing U.S.-China Relations, 1989–2000.* Berkeley: University of California Press, 2001.

Mann, James. *About Face: A History of America's Curious Relationship with China, from Nixon to Clinton.* New York: Knopf, 1999.

Mann, James. *The China Fantasy: How Our Leaders Explain Away Chinese Repression.* New York: Viking, 2007.

May, Ernest R., and John K. Fairbank, eds. *America's China Trade in Historical Perspective: The Chinese and American Performance.* Cambridge, MA: Harvard University Asia Center, 1986.

Qing, Simei. *From Allies to Enemies: Visions of Modernity, Identity, and U.S. China Diplomacy, 1945–1960.* Cambridge, MA: Harvard University Press, 2007.

Tucker, Nancy Bernkopf. *Patterns in the Dust: Chinese-American Relations and the Recognition Controversy, 1949–1950.* New York: Columbia University Press, 1983.

Tucker, Nancy Bernkopf. *The China Threat: Memories, Myths, and Realities in the 1950s.* New York: Columbia University Press, 2012.

Warren I. Cohen
University Distinguished Professor Emeritus, Michigan State University, and Distinguished University Professor Emeritus, University of Maryland, Baltimore County
Senior Scholar, Woodrow Wilson Center

CHINESE EXCLUSION ACT (1882)

By the late 1870s, a movement to radically curtail the immigration of Chinese into the United States, which had begun and for a time been restricted to California and the American West, had taken on a decidedly national character. It had also achieved considerable political momentum, scoring a striking legislative success in 1879 when Congress passed a bill captioned "An act to restrict the immigration of Chinese to the United States," limiting the number of Chinese who might be brought into the country in a single ship to fifteen. The bill, however, was vetoed by President Rutherford B. Hayes

(1822–1893), who found it to be in violation of the Burlingame Treaty, which was negotiated in 1868 between the United States and China and which affirmed a mutual right of free immigration.

REVISION OF THE BURLINGAME TREATY

Several congressional resolutions had called for the revision or outright abrogation of the Burlingame Treaty, and similar calls were to be found in the 1880 platforms of both the Democratic and Republican Parties, each concerned to garner the electoral votes of the Pacific states in what was expected to be a close presidential election. As it happened, the executive branch had begun to take steps aimed at treaty revision as early as the spring of 1879. In April, Secretary of State William Evarts (1818–1901) instructed his minister to China, George Seward (1840–1910), to begin negotiations with the Chinese aimed at removing what he called the embarrassments and mischiefs caused by the free emigration clauses of the Burlingame Treaty. There was soon evidence that the time might be ripe for reaching such an agreement. In June Ulysses Grant (1822–1885), then in Asia at the tail end of a round-the-world trip, was approached by the Chinese with a request that he mediate a dispute between China and Japan concerning the Ryukyu Islands. In exchange, they suggested that they might be willing to make concessions on Chinese immigration to the United States, a fact that Seward communicated to Evarts in July.

Seward proceeded with his assignment, but from the outset it was clear that it would not be easy. The Chinese seemed willing to make concessions regarding the immigration of certain problematic classes, lewd women, criminals, and contract laborers (by which term they seem to have meant Chinese lured abroad under false pretenses) but not to go any further. They also sought a quid pro quo in the form of a US pledge to grant greater protection to the Chinese against the sort of unfriendly discriminatory legislation that increasingly dotted the California law books. The Chinese observed that in 1879 the state had seen fit to include anti-Chinese provisions in its new constitution. Seward, for his part, seemed unwilling to press the Chinese to go any further, stressing the need for proceeding cautiously.

Impatient with this approach, Evarts decided someone new needed to be put in charge if progress were to be made. In February, he asked James Angell (1829–1916), then president of the University of Michigan, to head a special mission to China to negotiate a new treaty. Angell and two others arrived in China in August (Angell had replaced Seward as minister earlier in the summer) and commenced work. They took a much harder tack than Seward, at one point telling the Chinese that the United States was prepared to act unilaterally should the discussions not prove fruitful. In relatively short order they reached their goal, concluding an agreement to modify the Burlingame Treaty on November 17, 1880. It gave the United States the right at its discretion to regulate, limit, or suspend, but not prohibit, the immigration of Chinese laborers. Chinese laborers then in the United States and other Chinese—teachers, students, merchants, and tourists were instanced—were to be permitted to remain in the country and to go and come at will. In something of a concession, the United States promised to devise measures for the protection of Chinese who should meet with ill treatment here. The treaty was ratified by the Senate on July 10, 1881.

THE MILLER BILL

It was a foregone conclusion that Congress would move quickly to exercise the powers granted by the treaty, and on December 5, 1881, the opening day of the Forty-Seventh Congress, Senator John F. Miller (1831–1886) of California introduced a bill to do so. Captioned "An Act to execute certain treaty stipulations relating to Chinese," it suspended the entry of Chinese laborers into the United States for twenty years, exempting laborers who were present in the United States at the time of the treaty or who should have come into the country within sixty days after the bill's passage. By implication it exempted nonlaborers.

Because those exempted from the law's provisions had the right to go and come at will, a system of identification needed to be established. The bill, a cumbrously worded measure, divided the Chinese into two classes: those who had arrived in the United States up to the expiration of the time frame just described, *whether or not laborers,* and those who had not. Those in the first class were to register with customs officials before leaving the country and to obtain certificates permitting them to return. The certificates were to contain sufficient information to identify the holders. Those in the second class, Chinese entitled and seeking to enter the United States for the first time after the expiration of the time frame, a class limited to nonlaborers, were to obtain "passports" from the Chinese government affirming their entitlement. These people were to be granted a visa by a US representative in China, to be presented on arrival and to be kept thereafter and produced to US authorities on demand. Masters of vessels carrying Chinese passengers were, before arrival in a US port, to compile lists of all Chinese with their names and identifying particulars, as shown by the certificates and passports, and no Chinese vessel was to be permitted to land before a customs official had boarded the vessel and confirmed a right to land. Chinese entering the United States illegally and persons knowingly assisting them were declared guilty of a misdemeanor.

Two provisions would be added during debates in the Senate. The first made clear that the term *laborer* included the skilled as well as the unskilled; the second prohibited the naturalization of Chinese by any state or federal court, made necessary, it was said, because some state courts had done just this, notwithstanding federal law limiting naturalization to whites and persons of African descent.

CONGRESSIONAL DEBATE

In support of the measure Senator Miller trotted out arguments that by this time had become the common coin of the anti-Chinese movement. The Chinese were servile laborers, Miller declared, held in virtual bondage by the Chinese Six Companies, the coordinating council of the several place-of-origin associations to which Chinese immigrants belonged (a widely purveyed canard). Their competition was degrading white labor and driving laborers into penury. They were incapable of assimilation and were totally unfit for the duties and privileges of citizenship. They were bringing in strange, loathsome diseases. Others echoed similar views. Images of hordes of Chinese flooding the country were bandied about. Numerous memorials, primarily though not exclusively from the West, were introduced into the record, all calling for either the outright prohibition or radical restriction of Chinese immigration.

A few senators spoke up in opposition. Senator George F. Hoar (1826–1904) of Massachusetts reprimanded his colleagues for singling out one ethnic group for discrimination, an example, he said, of "the old race prejudice which has so often played its hateful and bloody part in our history" (13 Cong. Rec. 1518 [1882]). The same arguments against the Chinese were heard previously against blacks and other ethnic groups, the Irish, for example. Memorials in opposition from religious groups that were afraid of the bill's possible impact on missionary work in China, and from business groups fearful of its impact on trade, were also entered in the record. A few voiced support for the bill but objected to the twenty-year suspension as too long. Still, there was never any doubt that the bill would be passed. And indeed it did, by a vote of twenty-nine to fifteen, but with thirty-two recorded as absent, in the Senate, and later by a larger margin in the House. But President Chester Arthur (1829–1886) returned the measure to the Senate with his veto.

ARTHUR'S VETO

The president affirmed his support for restriction but voiced strong objections to the Miller bill, first and foremost to its twenty-year limit. Citing the record of treaty negotiations, he said he had no doubt that neither of the parties contemplated prohibiting immigration for so long, "nearly a generation," as he put it. It was, he declared, a "breach of our national faith." In addition he objected to the system of registration and passports that the law established. Chinese whose immigration was not prohibited were entitled to the same privileges as those afforded to citizens of most favored nations, he noted. If Americans did not impose such requirements on other foreigners, he doubted whether Americans could impose them on the Chinese. In addition, he characterized the system as "undemocratic and hostile to the spirit of our institutions" (13 Cong. Rec. 2552 [1882]).

THE EXCLUSION ACT, FINAL VERSION

Probably because the two-thirds majority necessary to override the veto was not to be had in the Senate, a decision was made to draft a bill the president could accept. The new bill preserved some of the language and the general structure of the Miller bill but included some significant changes. It suspended the entrance of Chinese laborers into the United States for ten years rather than twenty. As in the Miller bill, laborers present at the time of the treaty or who had arrived before the expiration of the grace period (extended to ninety days in the new bill) were permitted to reside here and to leave and return as they wished.

For purposes of regulating travel rights, the drafters now distinguished between the rights of laborers and nonlaborers. With respect to the exempt class of laborers, the collector of customs was to go on board any China-bound ship, identify such laborers by physical characteristics, occupation, age, and place of residence, inscribe their names in registry books, and offer them, free of charge, certificates, with information corresponding to the entries in the registry books. The certificates were to entitle them to reenter the United States. Chinese other than laborers, entitled to and about to come to the United States, were to procure certificates from the Chinese government (the term *passports* was dropped) identifying them and confirming their right to enter. There was no requirement that these people have a visa or that documents be produced whenever demanded by American authorities after arrival. As in the Miller bill, no Chinese was to be permitted to land in a US port before a customs official had examined a list prepared by the ship's master and examined individual certificates that confirmed each person's right to enter. Persons seeking to enter the United States by land were required to obtain and produce the same certificates as those seeking to enter by sea. The definition of *laborer* and the bar on naturalization were left unchanged from the Miller bill. As in the Miller bill, it was made a crime for anyone knowingly to bring into the United States Chinese not authorized to enter. Chinese entering the country illegally were liable to deportation, but, unlike in the Miller bill, were not made subject to criminal prosecution. The new bill was signed by Arthur and became law on May 6, 1882.

The law was the first break with what had been an historical American commitment to open immigration. It was also the first immigration measure to target a particular nationality or ethnic group (or class for that matter) for invidious treatment. More generally, as the eminent immigration historian Roger Daniels (2005) put it, it proved "the pivot on which all American immigration policy turned" (232), initiating a period of growing restriction, increasingly based on race or ethnicity. The law, too, or perhaps more precisely the law and the treaty that lay behind it, marked a watershed in the history of US-China relations, introducing, as historian Michael Hunt (1983) notes, a new element of tension in ties between the two countries. It would only intensify in succeeding years as US exclusion policy hardened, as anti-Chinese hostility, often erupting in violence, increased in the West, and as China came to realize that the US government seemed unwilling to take decisive measures to stem it.

PRESS REACTION

The San Francisco papers greeted passage of the act with jubilation and optimism. "The Chinese question is not settled but it is fairly on the way to settlement," the *Morning Call* editorialized in its May 4, 1882, edition. The act, the *San Francisco Chronicle* declared in its May 9, 1882, edition, while not perfect, was as good as could be gotten, and, it said, "leaves no further excuse for injecting the Chinese question into either State or national politics." Such optimism proved premature. Enforcement, in part because of Chinese litigation in the federal courts, proved difficult, and Congress found it necessary to amend the act three times during the next decade, each time making its provisions more onerous for the Chinese, in one amendment unilaterally abrogating rights guaranteed Chinese laborers under the 1880 treaty. In 1902, the twentieth anniversary of the 1882 act, the ban on the immigration of Chinese laborers was made permanent, lifted only in 1943 when, given the wartime alliance with China, it seemed at the very least an embarrassment.

SEE ALSO *American Protective Association; Angel Island; China; Immigration; Immigration and Nationality Act of 1965; Immigration Quotas; Immigration Restriction League; Know-Nothings; Nativism; "The New Colossus" (Emma Lazarus, 1883); Passport; Whiteness*

BIBLIOGRAPHY

Chan, Sucheng. *Entry Denied: Exclusion and the Chinese Community in America, 1882–1943.* Philadelphia: Temple University Press, 1991.

Daniels, Roger. *Guarding the Golden Door: American Immigration Policy and Immigrants since 1882.* New York: Hill and Wang, 2005.

Gold, Martin B. *Forbidden Citizens: Chinese Exclusion and the U.S. Congress: A Legislative History.* Alexandria, VA: TheCapitol .Net, 2012.

Gyory, Andrew. *Closing the Gate: Race, Politics, and the Chinese Exclusion Act.* Chapel Hill: University of North Carolina Press, 1998.

Hunt, Michael H. *The Making of a Special Relationship: The United States and China to 1914.* New York: Columbia University Press, 1983.

Lee, Erika. *At America's Gates: Chinese Immigration during the Exclusion Era, 1882–1943.* Chapel Hill: University of North Carolina Press, 2003.

McClain, Charles J. *In Search of Equality: The Chinese Struggle against Discrimination in Nineteenth-Century America.* Berkeley: University of California Press, 1994.

Salyer, Lucy E. *Laws Harsh as Tigers: Chinese Immigrants and the Shaping of Modern Immigration Law.* Chapel Hill: University of North Carolina Press, 1995.

Charles J. McClain
Chair (emeritus), Jurisprudence and Social Policy Program, and Lecturer in Residence, School of Law
University of California, Berkeley

THE CIVIL WAR

When the American Civil War began in April 1861, officials in both the Union and the Confederacy realized that successful management of foreign affairs would play a central role in deciding the war's outcome. Confederates hoped that their new nation would receive prompt recognition, support, and military aid from abroad, as the colonists had received during the American Revolution. Abraham Lincoln (1809–1865) and his secretary of state, William Henry Seward (1801–1872), worked hard to prevent foreign intervention, especially from Great Britain and France. As the war lengthened, observers in the United States and abroad realized that the impact of the conflict would be felt around the world. The fighting held the potential to disrupt global patterns of trade, and the issues at stake, including the future of slavery, the nature and meaning of nationalism, and the rights of citizens and neutrals in wartime, attracted attention across the globe.

EARLY CONFEDERATE AND UNION DIPLOMATIC EFFORTS

In the first few months of the war, Americans in the North and in the South expected a brief and decisive conflict. Confederate officials, consequently, pushed for speedy recognition of their nation's independence. To that end, during the early spring of 1861, even before the commencement of hostilities, the Confederate government dispatched William Lowndes Yancey (1814–1863), Pierre Rost (1797–1868), and Ambrose Dudley Mann (1801–1889) to Europe to advocate for recognition of the Confederate government. Before the end of the year, James Murray Mason (1798–1871) and John Slidell (1793–1871) were sent to replace them as official emissaries to Britain and France, respectively. The Confederacy's commissioners abroad came prepared to make two principal arguments in support of national independence. First, they pointed out the importance of Southern cotton supplies to the textile industries in Britain and France, a supply they believed would be disrupted by war. Second, they argued that all aggrieved peoples anywhere in the world had the right to self-government and national independence. They offered precedents derived from world history, including French recognition of the United States during the American Revolution and British support for nationalist uprisings in Europe in 1848 and in Italy during the late 1850s and early 1860s.

The Union's diplomats faced a more complicated set of questions. Lincoln and his supporters insisted that the Confederacy was not a nation, and that the war should be seen as a domestic insurrection. In April 1861, however, the president declared a blockade of Southern ports, a measure usually reserved for wars between nations. Queen Victoria's government responded with a declaration of British neutrality. Though Britain's declaration recognized the legality of the blockade, it angered many Unionists because it also implied that the Confederates held rights as belligerents.

These tensions reached their height in the *Trent* affair. In November 1861, a Union naval vessel stopped a British mail steamer, the *Trent*, and seized the Confederate diplomats, Mason and Slidell, who were on their way to Europe to carry out their instructions. The British people and the British government responded with outrage, claiming that the seizure insulted the British flag and violated Great Britain's rights as a neutral power. American Unionists celebrated the capture and arrest of the two diplomats, believing them to be rebel criminals. The crisis drove the United States and Great Britain to the brink of war. In early 1862, however, the Lincoln administration relented, releasing the prisoners and issuing an apology to the British government. Though no one knew it at the time, the Union's diplomats had staved off the most serious threat of British intervention that would arise at any time during the war.

THE ISSUE OF SLAVERY

The issue of slavery proved more difficult to resolve. Though public opinion in France and Britain proved generally hostile to slavery, for the first year of war, US officials insisted that the war had nothing to do with the peculiar institution. In fact, the Union's most important diplomat abroad, Charles Francis Adams (1807–1886), who was the American minister to Great Britain, carried dispatches instructing him to explain that the war had been caused by disagreements over the nature of national sovereignty, not over slavery. The situation changed dramatically in September 1862, when Lincoln issued his Preliminary Emancipation Proclamation, the final version of which took effect on January 1, 1863. For some European observers, the proclamation stirred fears of slave rebellion and memories of insurgencies in Haiti and the Caribbean. In general, though, the move toward the abolition of slavery allowed Union officials to enlist the sympathies of European liberals. A Union victory would now result in the destruction of the world's most powerful slaveholding regime, potentially portending an end to human bondage throughout the hemisphere.

DISRUPTIONS IN GLOBAL TRADE

In the meantime, the war began to have an increasingly important effect on the global economy. Since the beginning of hostilities, Confederates had deliberately withheld cotton supplies from the world market in an attempt to force Britain and France into intervention. By 1863, the Union's tightening blockade would have prevented most of the South's cotton from getting to Europe, whether white Southerners had wanted it to or not. As Confederates had predicted, the cotton shortage damaged British and French industries. Once stores saved up from a series of bumper crops that had been produced during the prewar years had been depleted, factories cut production, and textile workers lost their jobs. To the dismay of Confederates, however, the crisis proved temporary. The British, in particular, found new sources of cotton production in Egypt and India. The subsequent shift in global trade would undermine the position of Southern planters for decades to come.

THE FRENCH INCURSION INTO MEXICO

By 1863, the Confederacy's best hope for foreign intervention lay with France. The French emperor, Napoleon III (1808–1873), had long hoped to reestablish a French empire in the Americas. He took advantage of the war in the United States to further his imperial designs. In 1861, the French prevailed upon Britain and Spain to join a punitive expedition against Mexico aimed at forcing the liberal government of Benito Juárez (1806–1872) to pay debts the nation had contracted abroad. Though the British and the Spanish quickly abandoned the endeavor, the French, encouraged by Mexican conservatives, pushed on with the invasion. In June 1863, French troops entered Mexico City.

In early 1864, Napoleon installed the Austrian archduke Ferdinand Maximilian Joseph (1832–1867) as the new emperor of Mexico. The Confederates welcomed the new government on their southern border. Confederate officials hoped that a show of support for Maximilian might entice Napoleon III to intervene in the Civil War. White Southerners also harbored racist doubts about the fitness of nonwhite peoples for self-government. They believed that a European imperial government would impart stability, which they believed Mexico lacked.

Unionists, for their part, viewed the French incursion into Mexico as a violation of the Monroe Doctrine. The future of the New World belonged to republics, most Northerners believed, not to imperial monarchies. The position of the United States prevailed. Despite Confederate overtures, neither Napoleon nor Maximilian ever recognized the independence of the Confederacy. As the armies of the South disintegrated during the spring of 1865, the US military rushed troops to the Mexican border. In 1866 the French army withdrew from Mexico, intimidated by the American show of force. The French withdrawal weakened Maximilian and empowered Juárez's liberal insurgents. In May 1867 Maximilian was captured at Querétaro by the rebels. He was tried and executed the following month, thus ending the European intervention in Mexico.

THE ROLE OF THE AMERICAN WEST

The US government's concern over affairs in the Southwest should prove unsurprising. The nation's expansion to the Pacific Ocean played a major role in precipitating the Civil War. During the antebellum years, Northern and Southern politicians had especially disagreed over the future status of slavery in the territories acquired as a result of the Mexican War. The Compromise of 1850 had admitted California into the Union as a free state, thereby angering many Southerners, but also opening the prospect of imperial expansion into the Pacific. Immigrants and laborers from across Asia and Latin America arrived in the United States through ports on the Gulf of Mexico and on the West Coast, especially after the discovery of gold at Sutter's Mill in 1848. Chinese Americans fought in the Civil War in both the Union and Confederate armies in small but proportionately significant numbers when counted as a percentage of the Asian-born population. The distinguished military service of several Chinese Americans, however, did not help cement claims to citizenship, as it had for African Americans and the Irish. In 1882 the Chinese Exclusion Act forbade the naturalization of Chinese immigrants, an injustice that would not be remedied until well into the twentieth century.

INTERNATIONAL LAW

Questions related to international law also proved difficult to resolve. In the years after the war, Great Britain's positions and actions as a neutral power especially came into question. During the war, Confederate Lieutenant James Bulloch (1823–1901) contracted with private shipyards in Britain to build vessels for the Confederate service, including the ship that would be christened the CSS *Alabama.* Charles Francis Adams protested that Great Britain, as a neutral power, had a duty to prevent the *Alabama* from sailing. The British government declined to take action, however, and, after leaving port and arming for war while docked in the Azores, the *Alabama* began a successful career as a commerce raider, seizing and sinking scores of US merchant vessels. In 1869, several years after the Confederate surrender, the US government sued the British government for damages inflicted by the *Alabama* and other Confederate ships built in British shipyards. The *Alabama* Claims, as the cases were called, required international arbitration. The cases were eventually resolved in favor of the United States, with the British paying more than $15 million in damages. The ruling helped clarify the roles and responsibilities held by neutrals in wartime and furthered the development of the emerging field of international law.

CONCLUSION

The federal victory in the Civil War destroyed slavery in the United States and preserved the unity of the American republic. In the following two decades, slavery disappeared everywhere in the hemisphere and the United States took on a growing role in world affairs. Some historians have suggested that the confirmation of the power of the federal government furthered a trend toward the development of bigger and more powerful nation-states, as the unification of Germany later in the century suggested. In the Western Hemisphere, the victorious Union army upheld the Monroe Doctrine, an action that, in the case of Mexico, helped to shape at least one nation's future. The American Civil War engaged issues that held importance for the future of the entire nineteenth-century world.

SEE ALSO *Antislavery; Confederate States of America; Lincoln, Abraham; Seward, William H.*

BIBLIOGRAPHY

Beckert, Sven. "Emancipation and Empire: Reconstructing the Worldwide Web of Cotton Production in the Age of the American Civil War." *American Historical Review* 109, 5 (2004): 1405–1438.

Fleche, Andre M. *The Revolution of 1861: The American Civil War in the Age of Nationalist Conflict.* Chapel Hill: University of North Carolina Press, 2012.

Jones, Howard. *Union in Peril: The Crisis over British Intervention in the Civil War.* Chapel Hill: University of North Carolina Press, 1992.

Jones, Howard. *Abraham Lincoln and a New Birth of Freedom: The Union and Slavery in the Diplomacy of the Civil War.* Lincoln: University of Nebraska Press, 1999.

Jones, Howard. *Blue and Gray Diplomacy: A History of Union and Confederate Foreign Relations.* Chapel Hill: University of North Carolina Press, 2010.

McCunn, Ruthanne Lum. "Chinese in the Civil War: Ten Who Served." *Chinese America: History and Perspectives* (1996): 149–181.

Schoonover, Thomas David. *Dollars over Dominion: The Triumph of Liberalism in Mexican–United States Relations, 1861–1867.* Baton Rouge: Louisiana State University Press, 1978.

Sexton, Jay. "The Funded Loan and the *Alabama* Claims." *Diplomatic History* 27, 4 (2003): 449–478.

Andre M. Fleche
Associate Professor of History
Castleton College

CIVILIZATION FUND

On March 3, 1819, Congress established the Civilization Fund to support the cultural assimilation of the nation's Indians. The fund annually provided $10,000 to subsidize their schooling, especially as it related to agriculture, reading, writing, and arithmetic.

The premise for the Civilization Fund had its origins in some of the Indian policies of the early Republic. Beginning in 1795 the United States established a federal factory system to regulate trade and maintain allegiances with American Indians. In 1796 the United States hired former senator Benjamin Hawkins (1754–1816) to establish the Creek agency in Georgia. Hawkins, who directed the agency until 1816, pursued what he called the "plan of civilization." This plan used gifts, education, and encouragement to convince Creeks to grow and spin cotton, herd cattle, codify their laws in writing, and otherwise become a community of market-oriented farmers. Such a transformation would end their reliance on hunting, eliminate the sovereignty of Indian communities, and otherwise open up the Creek hunting grounds to western settlers.

As Hawkins's tenure among the Creeks came to an end, Superintendent of Indian Trade Thomas L. McKenney (1785–1859) began to push to make the "plan of civilization" a national one. He called upon Congress to provide $100,000 per year to fund the process. The goal was to create a generation of civilized Indian citizens who embraced the private ownership of land and accepted federal jurisdiction. As he campaigned for the program, McKenney urged Indian agents to provide agricultural tools to help Indians assimilate to the American norm and asked agents to forge alliances with various religious missionaries.

McKenney soon found an ally in Henry Southard (1747–1842), the chairman of the House Committee on Indian Affairs, and Secretary of War John C. Calhoun (1782–1850). With their assistance, Congress passed the Indian Civilization Fund Act in 1819. The act fell short of McKenney's lofty expectations. By providing only one-tenth of the proposed budget and leaving implementation decisions to the president, the program necessarily subsidized preexisting programs rather than create new ones. As a result, most of the nation's tribes went virtually untouched. A disproportionate number of students came from the largest southeastern nations—the Cherokees, Choctaws, Chickasaws, and Creeks.

In a few instances, President James Monroe (1758–1831) provided tribes the option to select which schools they would send their children to and thereby determine how the funds would be spent. This was especially true when tribal governments agreed to augment the expenditure with funds owed to them from earlier treaties. The government sent most of the money directly to Protestant religious organizations that contributed their own assets to the enterprise and were already involved in missionizing Indian country. Even with these additional resources, the programs had a limited reach. At its height, around 1830, the Civilization Fund took credit for subsidizing fifty-two schools and educating 1,512 students. The fund had its greatest notoriety with the Choctaw Academy—a school with mostly Choctaw students but one that educated young men from various tribes. Established in 1825, the academy stretched its federal allocation by drawing on funds from the Baptist General Convention and from the Choctaw tribe. After a decade of operation, the academy enrolled 188 students.

SEE ALSO *Cherokee Nation v. Georgia (1831); General Allotment Act (Dawes Severalty Act, 1877); Indian Removal Act (1830); Reservation*

BIBLIOGRAPHY

Green, Michael D. *The Politics of Indian Removal: Creek Government and Society in Crisis.* Lincoln: University of Nebraska Press, 1982.

Prucha, Francis Paul. *The Great Father: The United States Government and the American Indians.* Lincoln: University of Nebraska Press, 1984.

Andrew K. Frank
Allen Morris Associate Professor of History
Florida State University

CLASH OF CIVILIZATIONS (SAMUEL HUNTINGTON)

Political scientist Samuel P. Huntington (1927–2008) first introduced his clash of civilizations thesis in a 1992 lecture. With support from foundations that also funded conservative think tanks, he expanded the thesis to book length. He proposed that, due to the end of the Cold War, the eight civilizations of the world established a new global dynamic. These civilizations were defined primarily by culture, which he associated very strongly with religion. He labeled them Western, Confucian, Japanese, Islamic, Hindu, Slavic-Orthodox, Latin American, and African, and he argued that they formed a new multipolar world in which power would follow culture. In such a world, conflict would arise from cultural differences and was inevitable. He added "in this new world, local politics is the politics of ethnicity," while "global politics is the politics of civilizations" (Huntington 1996, 28). This new pattern would be distinct from the Cold War era, when, he said, conflicts arose mainly due to ideological differences or because of nationalism.

Huntington's thesis immediately engendered controversy and debate. He contradicted some think tank authors who asserted their own theses—namely, that the end of the Cold War meant the "end of history" or the end of major periods of conflict. Still other critics of Huntington identified numerous problems within his thesis, including how he defined the terms *civilization*, *culture*, and *religion*. In particular, critics noted that religion and culture are not bound by geography or civilization, and that religion is but one aspect of culture that varies regionally in significance. Huntington's thesis was also contested by scholars of globalization, who asserted a model of the world based upon complicated and rapidly increasing cultural and economic flows that lead to extreme cultural interactivity and great diversity around the world. Compared to their liquid analogy, Huntington's argument asserted an older world of solids that invariably bumped into each other, resulting in conflict.

Another criticism that emerged was that Huntington was preoccupied with the relationship between the West and Islamic cultures. Presidents George W. Bush and Barack Obama each rejected the idea that the conflicts they faced were due to a clash of civilizations. Regarding the war on terror, Bush stated in 2006 that "this struggle has been called a clash of civilizations," but "in truth, it is a struggle for civilization." In 2014 Obama argued that the world is not defined by a clash of civilizations, but the United States should nonetheless be wary of those who might exploit the clash narrative for their own anti-US purposes, suggesting that the narrative might still capture the mind-set of a few. The presidents' statements revealed their view that nation-states, not civilizations, remained the dominant organizing entities in the world.

Criticism of Huntington is often associated with Edward Said (1935–2003), who wrote, after September 11, 2001, that the thesis was "belligerent" and essentially ideological. Said claimed Huntington did not allow for plurality or diversity in non-Western culture, a point that is reinforced by the complexity of the momentous events of the Arab Spring. Similarly, the regional conflicts raging in 2015 in Syria, Yemen, and Libya, or those that involve ISIS, cannot be explained as a clash of civilizations. Examining conflicts more broadly, studies have shown that international terrorism is not primarily a problem limited to conflicts between Western and Islamic cultures. Indeed, international terrorism before and after the Cold War followed recognizable patterns, indicating that the significant break that Huntington believed necessitated a new global theory had not, in fact, occurred.

SEE ALSO *Foreign Affairs (Magazine); Said, Edward; Think Tanks*

BIBLIOGRAPHY

Appadurai, Arjun. *Fear of Small Numbers: An Essay on the Geography of Anger*. Durham, NC: Duke University Press, 2006.

Barber, Benjamin R. *Jihad vs. McWorld*. New York: Times Books, 1995.

Goytisolo, Juan. *Landscapes of War: From Sarajevo to Chechnya*. Translated by Peter Bush. San Francisco: City Lights, 2000.

Halper, Stefan, and Jonathan Clarke. *America Alone: The Neo-Conservatives and the Global Order*. Cambridge: Cambridge University Press, 2004.

Huntington, Samuel P. *The Clash of Civilizations and the Remaking of World Order*. New York: Touchstone, 1996.

Neumayer, Eric, and Thomas Plümper. "International Terrorism and the Clash of Civilizations." *British Journal of Political Science* 39, 4 (2009): 711–734.

Said, Edward. "The Clash of Ignorance." *Nation*, October 22, 2001, 1–5.

Peter A. McCord
Professor of History
State University of New York, Fredonia

CLAY, HENRY

SEE *War Hawks.*

CLEMENS, SAMUEL LANGHORNE

SEE *Twain, Mark.*

CLEVELAND, GROVER
1837–1908

Discussion of Grover Cleveland and his presidencies rarely dwells on his foreign policy, and it is true that Cleveland's goals as president were primarily domestic. Despite its lower priority, his foreign policy articulated a clear vision of America's role in the world. In a unique juxtaposition, Cleveland was at once a nationalist, defending the United States against all threats in the Americas, and a firm isolationist, opposed to the expansionist and imperial impulses of his time. In his own words, "our duty in the present instructs us to address ourselves mainly to the development of the vast resources of the great area committed to our charge and to the cultivation of the arts of peace within our own borders, though jealously alert in preventing the American hemisphere from being involved in the political problems and complications of distant governments" (Cleveland 1885).

Cleveland's interpretation and application of the Monroe Doctrine demonstrate his nonexpansionist view of national security. Cleveland routinely invoked the doctrine to justify intervention in disputes in South America. For instance, he used the Monroe Doctrine as a justification to force Great Britain and Venezuela to accept American arbitration of a boundary dispute. Similarly, he asserted the right to insist that Nicaragua grant to Great Britain a settlement for the mistreatment of British citizens. While Cleveland's preferred intervention was always diplomatic, not military, his insistence that the United States had the right to step into disputes in South America is significant in "reviving" and legitimizing the practical application of the Monroe Doctrine for subsequent presidents. It is also worth noting that Cleveland was willing to back up his diplomatic "requests" by placing military forces close to the territory at issue.

Given Cleveland's willingness to use the Monroe Doctrine as a tool to intervene in the affairs of South American countries, his anti-expansionist convictions are striking and uncharacteristic of his era. For Cleveland, protecting national security required only that the United States prevent foreign interference in its affairs (which included all of the Americas). He faced much criticism for his isolationist strategy; his foreign policy was labeled "un-American," but he was not deterred (Blake 1942, 272). This is remarkable given the expansionist mood of the time. One scholar argues, "In point of actual fact, to no president more than to him was presented the opportunity of converting the republic into an empire" (Blake 1942, 11).

The best example of his opposition to imperialism is his unpopular refusal to proceed with the annexation of Hawai'i. In 1893 Cleveland withdrew a treaty annexing Hawai'i because he opposed pursuing what he considered imperial ambitions to acquire the territory of others. In a Special Message (1893) he explained his opposition, saying,

> I believe that a candid and thorough examination of the facts will force the conviction that the Provisional Government [in Hawai'i] owes its existence to an armed invasion by the United States.… It has been the settled policy of the United States to concede to people of foreign countries the same freedom and independence in the management of their domestic affairs that we have always claimed for ourselves.

Cleveland is not considered a foreign policy president, but his perspective on America's role in the world reflects enduring American foreign policy principles. Cleveland's application of the Monroe Doctrine confirmed and strengthened the precedent justifying American involvement in the Americas, and even as America has become a world power with a more interventionist foreign policy strategy, Cleveland's articulation of isolationism retains its appeal.

SEE ALSO *Americanization; Anti-imperialism; Chinese Exclusion Act (1882); Empire, US; Exceptionalism; Immigration; Immigration Quotas; Imperialism; Manifest Destiny; Monroe Doctrine (1823); Tariff*

BIBLIOGRAPHY

Blake, Nelson M. "Background of Cleveland's Venezuelan Policy." *American Historical Review* 47, 2 (January 1942): 259–277.

Cleveland, Grover. Special Message, December 18, 1893. *Messages and Papers of the Presidents*. The American Presidency Project, edited by John Woolley and Gerhard Peters. http://www.presidency.ucsb.edu/ws/index.php?pid=70788

Cleveland, Grover. First Annual Message, December 8, 1885. *Messages and Papers of the Presidents*. The American Presidency Project, edited by John Woolley and Gerhard Peters. http://www.presidency.ucsb.edu/ws/index.php?pid=29526

Dulebohn, George R. "Principles of Foreign Policy under the Cleveland Administrations." PhD diss., Wharton School, University of Pennsylvania, 1941.

Gerhardt, Michael J. *The Forgotten Presidents: Their Untold Constitutional Legacy*. Oxford: Oxford University Press, 2013.

Sykes, Patricia Lee. *Presidents and Prime Ministers: Conviction Politics in the Anglo-American Tradition*. Lawrence: University Press of Kansas, 2000.

Karen S. Hoffman
Visiting Assistant Professor and Director of Undergraduate Studies
Marquette University

CLINTON, HILLARY RODHAM
1947–

As the third American woman appointed secretary of state, Hillary Rodham Clinton engaged in activities abroad that mirrored both her own commitment to the empowerment of women and her belief in the vital role the United States plays on the world stage.

The early life of Clinton provides slight foreshadowing of her prominence on the international stage. The oldest child of Hugh and Dorothy (Howell) Rodham, Hillary Rodham was born in Chicago in 1947. Her early political views were shaped by her parents' allegiance to the Republican Party, as well as the social justice ministry of her church youth group. After graduating from high school, she traveled east to Wellesley College in Massachusetts, where she rose to prominence among her classmates. Selected to deliver their commencement address in 1969, Rodham introduced a theme that has remained constant across the decades: "We also know that to be educated, the goal of it must be human liberation. A liberation enabling each of us to fulfill our capacity" (Clinton 1969). She met her future husband, Bill Clinton, while pursuing a law degree at Yale. Several years after graduating, Hillary joined Bill in Arkansas, and they married in 1975. In 1978, Bill was elected governor, and in 1980 they became parents to their only child, Chelsea.

The Clintons emerged onto the national political scene as Bill sought the Democratic nomination for the presidency in 1992. Proud of his spouse's intellect and abilities, Bill touted the couple as a "buy one, get one free" bonanza for voters, immediately causing a backlash among a public more comfortable with a less active potential First Lady (Rosenberg 2000). Despite the campaign's difficulties, Bill Clinton was elected to two terms. One of his first acts as president was to appoint Hillary Clinton as chair of the President's Task Force on National Health Care Reform, where she again experienced a hostile response from the press and the public. Rather than retreating to a more traditional role, Clinton shifted to less visible forms of activism, at least in terms of American audiences (Mattina 2003).

Clinton launched her own political career on the world stage at the 1995 United Nations Fourth World Conference on Women in Beijing, China. Her famous assertion "that human rights are women's rights … and women's rights are human rights" resonated through her time as First Lady (Clinton 1995). Seeking to make women's advancement a US foreign policy goal, she launched the Vital Voices Democracy Initiative with then–secretary of state Madeleine Albright. For the next four years, Clinton traveled the world spreading the message of the necessity of women's empowerment to democracy's advancement, an undertaking that received scant attention by the American press (Mattina 2003).

As her time in the White House came to a close, Clinton declared her candidacy for the US Senate from New York. She was elected and won high praise from both sides of the aisle for her work ethic and collegiality (Jacobs 2014). Among other assignments, she served on the Committee on Armed Services, working both on emerging threats and capabilities and on troop readiness and management support. In 2002, she voted in favor of sending troops to Iraq, a position that she defended as necessary to America's safety. However, Clinton later expressed disappointment in President George W. Bush's handling of the war (CNN Politics 2004). She visited troops in both Afghanistan and Iraq, personally assessing the on-the-ground situations in each country.

Reelected to the Senate in 2006, Clinton used her experience to launch a presidential campaign in 2007. After losing a difficult primary fight with Barack Obama, Clinton offered conciliatory messages to her opponent in her concession speech. She was appointed secretary of state by President Obama in 2009.

Clinton's tenure in that role began with a foreign policy "pivot" for the United States when her first official visit was to Asia. She would later make the case that "harnessing Asia's growth and dynamism is central to American economic and strategic interests," and she spent a significant amount of time and energy in the region (Clinton 2011). Visiting 112 countries, she did much to restore America's prominence in world affairs, a position that had been damaged during the previous administration.

Further, Clinton consistently argued that "democracy without the participation of women is a contradiction in terms" (Clinton 2012). Because of this focus on women (and children), Clinton has been criticized for spending too much time on "soft issues" while secretary of state (Glasser 2013). Regardless, her accomplishments across three decades of international prominence demonstrate a consistent worldview and commitment to improving the lives of all people. On April 12, 2015, Clinton announced what many political observers had predicted: she was indeed running again for the American presidency, signaling another chapter in her remarkable life.

SEE ALSO *Arab-Israeli Conflict; Clinton, William Jefferson; Feminism, Women's Rights; Obama, Barack Hussein; War on Terror*

BIBLIOGRAPHY

Clinton, Hillary Rodham. "Hillary D. Rodham's 1969 Student Commencement Speech." Wellesley College, Massachusetts, 1969. http://www.wellesley.edu/events/commencement/archives/1969commencement/studentspeech

Clinton, Hillary Rodham. "Remarks for the United Nations Fourth World Conference on Women." Beijing, September 5, 1995. http://www.un.org/esa/gopher-data/conf/fwcw/conf/gov/950905175653.txt

Clinton, Hillary Rodham. *Living History.* New York: Simon & Schuster, 2003.

Clinton, Hillary Rodham. "America's Pacific Century." *Foreign Policy*, October 11, 2011. http://foreignpolicy.com/2011/10/11/americas-pacific-century/

Clinton, Hillary Rodham. "Remarks to the International Women's Leadership Forum." Ulaanbaatar, Mongolia, July 9, 2012. http://www.state.gov/secretary/20092013clinton/rm/2012/07/194696.htm

Clinton, Hillary Rodham. *Hard Choices.* New York: Simon & Schuster, 2014.

Glasser, Susan B. "Was Hillary Clinton a Good Secretary of State? And Does It Matter?" *Politico*, December 8, 2013. http://www.politico.com/magazine/story/2013/12/was-hillary-clinton-a-good-secretary-of-state-john-kerry-2016-100766.html#.VRYXB7l0xjo

Gutgold, Nichola D. *Almost Madame President: Why Hillary Clinton "Won" in 2008.* Lanham, MD: Lexington, 2009.

"Hillary Clinton: No Regret on Iraq War Vote." CNN Politics. April 21, 2004. http://www.cnn.com/2004/ALLPOLITICS/04/21/iraq.hillary/

Jacobs, Ben. "Remember When Republicans Loved Hillary Clinton?" *Daily Beast*, December 1, 2014. http://www.thedailybeast.com/articles/2014/12/01/remember-when-republicans-loved-hillary-clinton.html

Mattina, Anne F. "Hillary Rodham Clinton: Using Her Vital Voice." In *Inventing a Voice: The Rhetoric of American First Ladies of the Twentieth Century*, edited by Molly N. Wertheimer, 417–434. Lanham, MD: Rowman & Littlefield, 2004.

Parry-Giles, Shawn. *Hillary Clinton in the News: Gender and Authenticity in American Politics.* Urbana: University of Illinois Press, 2014.

Rosenberg, Debra. "Inside Hillary's DC Game." *Newsweek*, February 14, 2000, 44.

Anne F. Mattina
Professor and Chair, Department of Communication
Stonehill College

CLINTON, WILLIAM JEFFERSON
1946–

William Jefferson "Bill" Clinton, former governor of Arkansas, was inaugurated the forty-second president of the United States in January 1993. He thus became the first chief executive to enter the White House following the end of the Cold War. Much of Clinton's presidency was taken up with efforts to devise a new basis for American internationalism for the new era. Clinton lacked any direct foreign policy experience, though he had studied international politics at a postgraduate level at Oxford University in the United Kingdom. His international outlook was also molded by his response to the conflict in Vietnam, which he seems to have interpreted as demonstrating the folly of far-flung military adventures with unclear objectives. His failure to serve in Vietnam contributed to the poor relations with the US military that characterized his presidency.

FIRST-TERM RELUCTANCE TO DEPLOY THE MILITARY

During the 1992 presidential election, in which Clinton defeated both President George H. W. Bush and the independent, anti-free-trade candidate Ross Perot, debates about foreign policy were dominated by international economic agendas. Reflecting the mood of the campaign, Clinton gave his principal attention to domestic affairs in his early period in office. His main foreign policy preoccupation related to the US commitment to Somalia, which President Bush had instigated following the 1992 election. Initially conceived as a post–Cold War humanitarian intervention, the Somalian operation developed under Clinton into a wider, nation-building commitment. Following the killing of nineteen Americans in the "Black Hawk Down" incident of October 1993, the administration—now under severe pressure from Congress—effectively began the process of exiting Somalia.

The shadow of Somalia made it difficult for the administration to contemplate major military commitments, especially in Africa, for the remainder of Clinton's presidency. The massacres in Rwanda (April–May 1994) thus proceeded without anything approaching significant armed intervention, either on the part of the United States or the United Nations (UN). The only other significant US military intervention during Clinton's first term concerned the deteriorating security situation in Haiti, whose elected leader was ousted by a military coup in 1991, triggering a regional refugee crisis. A US invasion in October 1994 was preempted by a deal to restore democratic leadership in Haiti. The experience of the first term appeared to indicate that the United States would contemplate post–Cold War military action only in contexts that impinged directly on US security or economic interests.

THE PROMOTION OF FREE TRADE AND GLOBALIZATION

The first term also saw the clear emergence of what was perhaps the central preoccupation of the Clinton presidency: the promotion of free trade and the embrace of economic globalization. Key developments included: the passage through Congress of the North American Free Trade Agreement (NAFTA) and the General Agreement on Tariffs and Trade (GATT), both in 1994; the negotiation of more than three hundred bilateral free-trade deals during the entire Clinton presidency; and the setting up of the World Trade Organization (WTO) in 1995. The US rescue of the Mexican *peso* in 1995 was a marked success. Often criticized for lacking consistency and clear direction in his foreign policy, Clinton's commitment to free trade was his guiding compass. The free-trade agenda faced a few setbacks, notably the denial by the Republican Congress in 1997 of free- (fast track) trade-deal negotiating authority. However, Clinton deserves to be remembered as "the globalization president."

The working out of an intellectual basis for post–Cold War internationalism was largely the work of Tony Lake, Clinton's first-term national security adviser. Administration thinking was influenced by democratic peace theory, the view that the spread of democracy was bound to facilitate global peace. Lake developed the doctrines of rogue states, democratic enlargement, and engagement and enlargement to denote the US commitment to global democracy, free trade, and human rights. Rogue states that refused to conform to the emerging globalized norms would be regarded as potential or indeed actual enemies. In his second inaugural address (January 1997), Clinton declared that, for the first time in human history, more people on Earth now lived under democracy than under dictatorship.

THE BALKAN WAR

At a more practical level, debates about the parameters within which American internationalism should operate in post–Cold War conditions centered on the disorder that had broken out in the Balkans as the former Communist state of Yugoslavia collapsed. Clinton's two secretaries of state, Warren Christopher (served 1993–1997) and Madeleine Albright (served 1997–2001), differed radically in their approach to post–Cold War intervention. Christopher exuded caution, while Albright promoted strongly activist democracy- and peace-promotion agendas.

The Christopher-Clinton policy toward the civil war in Bosnia during the first term involved only a very limited military response to what was widely interpreted in Washington as Serbian aggression. The massacre at Srebrenica in July 1995, combined with pressure from the new Republican Congress in the later part of 1995, impelled the Clinton administration on a new course of diplomatic activism in the Balkans. Assistant Secretary of State Richard Holbrooke (1941–2010) successfully negotiated a Bosnian agreement at Dayton, Ohio; the agreement included a commitment to deploy US forces to oversee its implementation. The Kosovo campaign of 1999, undertaken without United Nations approval, constituted a highly controversial use of air power on the part of the United States and the United Kingdom. It culminated in the exit from power (following pressure from Moscow) of Slobodan Milošević (1941–2006) and the issuing of guarantees to ethnic Albanian Muslims living in the Serbian province of Kosovo.

POLICY TOWARD COMMUNIST AND FORMER COMMUNIST STATES

Clinton's policy toward the old Communist enemy in Moscow was organized around a strategic alliance with the cause of Russian reform. In practice, this policy meant support not only for political reform in Russia, but also endorsement of its headlong rush toward capitalist economics. Washington sought to bind Russia into the program of expanding the North Atlantic Treaty Organization (NATO) into Eastern Europe by negotiating with Russian leader Boris Yeltsin (1931–2007) an arrangement whereby Moscow would itself participate in the "Partnership for Peace" on the fringes of NATO. Both Yeltsin and his successor, Vladimir Putin, who became Russian president in 2000, signaled the extreme Russian disquiet at the setting in motion of a NATO expansion dynamic that would probably lead to NATO forces being deployed on Russia's borders.

Policy toward China brought together a containment of Chinese power (notably with the sending of two US aircraft carriers to the seas near Taiwan in 1996) with the integration of China into world economic networks, culminating in Beijing's 2001 entry into the WTO. The problem of North Korean nuclear weapons was the subject of a (flawed) agreement between Washington and Pyongyang in 1994. The Clinton administration achieved normalization of relations of the old Communist foe in Vietnam, though domestic US political dynamics prevented a similar outcome in Cuba.

PEACE-PROMOTION DRIVE

The Clinton peace-promotion drive had a major success in Northern Ireland. President Clinton was intimately involved in the diplomacy, which resulted in the 1998 Belfast Agreement. Northern Ireland was consciously seen by the White House as a dry run for the much more challenging task of achieving a settlement for peace between Israel and the Palestinians. The early Clinton years saw various regional agreements (notably the Oslo Accords of 1993) in which the United States took the role of sponsor rather than central director.

Intense personal presidential diplomacy in the Middle East was a feature of Clinton's second term. Diplomacy leading to the 1997 Wye River Accords, essentially ceding land to the Palestinian Authority in return for security guarantees to Israel, was one product of this activity. In 2000, President Clinton personally directed an extraordinary program of negotiation between Israeli and Palestinian leaders. Clinton issued detailed "parameters" to light the path toward a solution. Eventual failure was variously ascribed to Palestinian intransigence and to the Clinton team's inability to establish presidential credibility as an evenhanded facilitator of peace.

In respect of another regional conflict, that between Iran and Iraq, the US administration followed a policy of "double containment." Iraqi dictator Saddam Hussein (1937–2006), in particular, was to be kept "in his box."

Hussein's failure to cooperate with UN weapons inspection prompted significant use of US air power, notably the Desert Fox bombing campaign over Iraq in late 1998.

TWENTY-FIRST-CENTURY REPUTATION

Into the twenty-first century, Clinton's presidential reputation became linked to the debate over the degree to which he had left America vulnerable to international terrorism. Any charge that Clinton ignored international terror is absurd. The president regularly referred to the "borderless threats" of the post–Cold War era. Following the first World Trade Center bombing in 1993, the issue of Islamic terror made its way up to the top of the bureaucratic tree. Associated military action—missile attacks on Sudan and Afghanistan in 1998—was ineffective, however, as were efforts to assassinate al-Qaeda leader Osama bin Laden (1957–2011).

In general terms, Clinton's foreign policy reputation has survived reasonably well. President Clinton can reasonably be seen as a leader who set America on a coherent path of internationalism within the increasingly globalized post–Cold War context. As an ex-president, Clinton has been active in the promotion of international public health, antipoverty, environmental, and peace-promotion causes under the auspices of the Clinton Foundation and the associated Clinton Global Initiative.

SEE ALSO *Albright, Madeleine; Clinton, Hillary Rodham; Contemporary Genocides and US Policy; Gore, Albert, Jr.; North American Free Trade Agreement (NAFTA); World Trade Organization; Yugoslav Wars*

BIBLIOGRAPHY

Boys, James D. *Clinton's Grand Strategy: US Foreign Policy in a Post–Cold War World.* London: Bloomsbury Academic, 2015.

Chollet, Derek, and James Goldgeier. *America between the Wars: 11/9 to 9/11: The Misunderstood Years between the Fall of the Berlin Wall and the Start of the War on Terror.* New York: PublicAffairs, 2008.

Clinton, Bill. *My Life.* New York: Knopf, 2004.

Dumbrell, John. *Clinton's Foreign Policy: Between the Bushes.* New York: Routledge, 2009.

Harris, John F. *The Survivor: Bill Clinton in the White House.* New York: Random House, 2005.

Schier, Steven E., ed. *The Postmodern Presidency: Bill Clinton's Legacy in US Politics.* Pittsburgh, PA: University of Pittsburgh Press, 2000.

White, Mark, ed. *The Presidency of Bill Clinton: The Legacy of a New Domestic and Foreign Policy.* London: Tauris, 2012.

John Dumbrell
Professor of Government
Durham University, UK

COCA-COLA

Many people think of Coca-Cola as the quintessential American product, but its origins belie this patriotic branding. After all, the product was essentially a temperance adaptation of a popular French patent medicine called Vin Mariani, originally developed in the 1870s. This product, which was essentially Bordeaux wine mixed with cocaine-containing coca leaves, captured the attention of John Pemberton (1831–1888), an Atlanta pharmacist who took great pride in being up to date on the latest international pharmaceutical trends. Pemberton produced his own version of Vin Mariani in the 1880s, calling it Pemberton's French Wine Coca, but when temperance agitation emerged in Atlanta, he decided to develop a nonalcoholic alternative, replacing wine with carbonated water in the finished beverage. Thus was born Coca-Cola in 1886.

Coca-Cola was truly a global product from the start, as the vast majority of the ingredients that went into the soft drink came from overseas suppliers. Originally, the company sourced much of its sugar from Caribbean producers and derived caffeine from tea leaves and cocoa waste discarded by European tea and chocolate firms. Other ingredients found in Coke had international origins, including the Peruvian coca leaves that gave the soft drink its distinctive name and which remained a key component of the company's secret formula for years. Around 1903, Coke president Asa G. Candler (1851–1929) made the decision to remove cocaine from Coca-Cola, but the company continued to use Peruvian leaves, albeit decocainized versions, throughout the twentieth century.

As Coke's supply network spread far and wide across the globe, so too did its distribution network. Beginning in 1886 Coca-Cola relied on a host of independently owned distributors to peddle its products. In the early years, the company partnered with regional soda-fountain operators in the American Southeast, selling gallon jugs of concentrated syrup to local soda jerks, who then added water—80 percent of the finished product—at the point of sale. This enabled Coke to save lots of money on shipping costs, since concentrated syrup was lighter than bottles of finished beverages. In 1899 Candler radically expanded the firm's distribution network, granting two Chattanooga lawyers the rights to bottle Coca-Cola throughout the United States.

The decision to farm out bottling responsibilities to independent franchisees enabled Coca-Cola to rapidly spread across the nation and the globe. By 1920, more than one thousand Coca-Cola bottlers serviced US markets, and the company began to identify bottling partners in Cuba, Canada, and a few European markets. But it was not until the 1940s and World War II that the

Billboard advertising Coca-Cola on the outskirts of Bangkok, Thailand. *In the 1940s Coca-Cola's foreign sales took off, with the company head eager to place Coke "within an arm's reach of desire" in every country around the world.* DMITRI KESSEL/TIME LIFE PICTURES/GETTY IMAGES

company's foreign sales took off. At that time, Robert W. Woodruff (1889–1985) ran the company and was eager to place Coke "within an arm's reach of desire" in every country around the world. Through the Coca-Cola Export Corporation, organized in 1930, Woodruff aggressively pursued foreign markets, extending franchising contracts to independent bottlers in both developing and developed nations. The US military aided this international expansion in the 1940s, offering Coke exclusive contracts to sell its products to American troops and local citizens in both the European and Pacific theaters of war.

Coke's US military connections helped solidify the company's cultural appeal in new markets overseas after World War II. For many people living in war-torn countries, Coke was a symbol of American freedom, carried in the hands of American GIs that liberated bombed and battered towns. To be sure, not everyone welcomed the arrival of this new product—most notably French winemakers who viewed the bubbly beverage as unwelcome competition—but for others, this was a drink inseparably tied to the Allied forces and the promise of democracy they held out in open rebellion to authoritarian Nazi rule. Over time, Coke realized that it sold more

Coca-Cola advertisements on the transit checkpoint gates of La Paz, Bolivia, circa 1955. *By the middle of the twentieth century, in many places around the world, the Coke logo had become a symbol of the American dream.* THREE LIONS/HULTON ARCHIVE/GETTY IMAGES

than just a sugary syrup; it also sold the American dream in places around the world where freedom was under fire. In short, piggybacking on the US Army to get to new markets was not just a smart way to save on bottling costs (the military, after all, helped transport and set up Coke's distribution machinery), it also enabled the company to accrue valuable cultural capital it could use to attract new consumers to their brand.

But it was foreign businesspeople, not just the US government, that made Coca-Cola a success overseas. For one, the company's independent bottlers—often wealthy and politically connected elites—knew how to lobby local and regional governments in order to gain access to valuable public resources. They also understood local customs and were therefore able to advertise Coke products using language and metaphors that spoke to local people. Finally, Coke's foreign bottling franchisees also assumed costs that Coke did not want to bear, including the cost of sweeteners. For example, Coke sold overseas bottlers a sugarless concentrate beginning in the 1920s, thereby outsourcing one of the most expensive ingredient costs to outside distributors.

Thus, what made Coke the most recognized global brand in 2012—"the global high sign" in over two hundred countries worldwide that year—was not necessarily what it did, but what it did not do. Coke made lots of money not by vertically integrating into ownership of its production and distribution networks but by embedding itself in technological infrastructure built, maintained, and financed by others. This franchising strategy made millionaires of many independent bottlers, but it also placed heavy burdens on the natural capital of host communities. For example, Coke's twenty-first-century spread into arid regions of the world, especially Southeast Asia, taxed already stressed underground aquifers. As of 2014, consumer resistance to corporate capture of such precious water resources remained a serious public relations problem for the company.

SEE ALSO *Disney; Globalization; Rock 'n' Roll; Television*

BIBLIOGRAPHY

Allen, Frederick. *Secret Formula: How Brilliant Marketing and Relentless Salesmanship Made Coca-Cola the Best-Known Product in the World.* New York: HarperBusiness, 1994.

Blanding, Michael. *The Coke Machine: The Dirty Truth behind the World's Favorite Soft Drink.* New York: Avery, 2010.

Elmore, Bartow. *Citizen Coke: The Making of Coca-Cola Capitalism.* New York: Norton, 2014.

Hays, Constance. *The Real Thing: Truth and Power at the Coca-Cola Company.* New York: Random House, 2004.

Kuisel, Richard F. "Coca-Cola and the Cold War: The French Face Americanization, 1948–1953." *French Historical Studies* 17, 1 (Spring 1991): 96–116.

Pendergrast, Mark. *For God, Country, and Coca-Cola: The Definitive History of the Great American Soft Drink and the Company That Makes It.* 3rd ed. New York: Basic Books, 2013.

Bartow J. Elmore
Assistant Professor of History
University of Alabama

CODE TALKERS

Although not developed until near the end of World War II, the term *code talker* refers to Native Americans who used their tribal languages to send communications for the US Armed forces during World Wars I and II. Members of thirty-four distinct tribal communities have been identified as having served in this fashion.

ORIGINS IN WORLD WAR I

During World War I (1914–1918), Germans readily broke American codes and killed many pedestrian couriers. Frustrated with the lack of a secure method of communication, officers thought to use Native Americans in their units on the odds that Germans would be unable to understand their languages. The practice is first documented in early October 1918 during World War I among Eastern Band Cherokee serving in the Thirtieth Division and later that month among Oklahoma Choctaw in the Thirty-Sixth Division. Following the use of Choctaw in the taking of Forest Farm in France in October 26–28, 1918, a number of Choctaw soldiers developed code terms, but they were unable to use them before the war ended.

From these experiences, two forms of code talking developed: type one, or individuals using specially encoded vocabulary within native languages; and type two, or individuals sending messages in their everyday language without a coded lexicon.

THE CODE TALKER PROGRAM OF WORLD WAR II

Prior to World War II (1939–1945), the US Army recruited seventeen Comanche, seventeen Oneida and Chippewa, and eight Meskwaki, who were trained as signal personnel and directed to develop coded vocabularies within their native languages. In April 1942, the marines began a similar but much larger program with the Navajo, eventually training around 420 men, from which an estimated 285 served in combat from Guadalcanal through Okinawa in all six marine divisions in the Pacific theater. Some also took part in the occupation of Japan. In 1943, eight Hopi were pulled together for a similar program in the Eighty-First Division. These groups were all type one code talkers.

Codes were based on newly created terms for military or other items that were inserted into the code talkers' everyday tribal languages. Code terms were typically descriptions using common vocabulary, such as *wakaree* ("turtle" in Comanche to mean "tank"), *paaki* ("house on water" in Hopi to mean "ship"), and *gini* ("chicken hawk" in Navajo to mean "dive bomber"). The Comanche and Navajo also developed coded alphabets for spelling out proper names by using the first letter of each code word translated into English. For example, when translated, the Comanche words for "pray," "ant," "rain," "ice," and "snow" would convey "Paris." While non–Native American officers assembled the lists of necessary terminology, Native American soldiers devised the actual code terms and alphabets.

Around three hundred other Native Americans provided type two code talking. They were formed into de facto groups of two to seven or more men by local unit commanders, typically in the field during combat situations. Non-Navajo code talkers served in North Africa, Europe, and the Pacific.

By using languages that were not based on Indo-European structures, were largely unwritten and unfamiliar to enemy forces, and often contained additional coded vocabulary for military items, code talkers provided important military communications that could be immediately translated back into English and implemented. Code talkers could convey messages in one to two minutes that would have taken military signals intelligence hours to encode, send, and decode. By ensuring secure and faster communications, code talkers contributed to Allied success in several campaigns in both world wars and were publicly lauded by their commanding officers and fellow soldiers for their service.

Perhaps the greatest paradox of the code talker experience is that the majority of these men had attended assimilation-oriented, government-run, military-style boarding schools that prohibited the use of their native languages, with school authorities often meting out physical punishment for infractions. Ironically, because many Native American men had been acculturated at a young age at such schools, boot camp was generally easy for them. Yet, with the exception of large numbers of Native American recruits in some locally formed companies and regiments, the formation of all–Native American units was discouraged in an attempt to further assimilate Native Americans into mainstream society through military service. At a time when the US government emphasized assimilation into a Euro-American mainstream, Native American code talkers provided an important example of the value of cultural and linguistic diversity. In contrast, during World War II African Americans were kept in segregated military units, while Japanese Americans were placed in internment camps, eventually allowing men to serve in the all Japanese-American 442 Regimental Combat Team. In both instances inclusion and integration with mainstream Euro-American troops was limited. After the war, returning code talkers entered a wide range of careers in such fields as politics, federal service, ranching, and education, including the teaching of native languages.

BELATED RECOGNITION

While the Navajo have enjoyed great renown since their code was declassified in 1968, other tribal nations with smaller numbers of code talkers are only recently receiving long-overdue recognition. Overall, recognition of many Native American code talkers came only after the majority of them had died. Since the 1980s, a number of tribes have begun recognizing their own code talkers with ceremonies, awards, and memorials. In 2001 the first twenty-nine Navajo were awarded Congressional Gold Medals; the remainder later received silver medals. On September 23, 2004, a Senate committee hearing on "The Contributions of Native American Code Talkers in American Military History" considered evidence on code talking by non-Navajo groups. This effort contributed to the passage of the Code Talkers Recognition Act of 2008. On November 20, 2013, at the US Capitol, thirty-three tribes received Congressional Gold Medals, with surviving code talkers or their families receiving silver medals.

Code talkers contributed to the American identity by drawing global attention to their unique service during World Wars I and II and by raising awareness of the military contributions of Native Americans and other minority veterans. The story of the code talkers has attracted interest around the world, especially in France and England, where many served during both world wars. In the United States, code talkers have intersected with popular culture through the GI Joe Navajo Code Talker doll, Pendleton Woolen Mills' Code Talker Blanket, the 2002 film *Windtalkers*, several documentary films, numerous publications, and lectures delivered by surviving code talkers and such scholars as William C. Meadows and Zonnie Gorman. Since 2006, the Smithsonian Institution's interactive traveling exhibition Native Words, Native Warriors has educated the public on the service of Native American code talkers.

SEE ALSO *Cherokee Nation v. Georgia (1831); Civilization Fund; Department of State; Empire, US; Exceptionalism; Frontier Wars; Indian Citizenship Act (1924); Jackson, Andrew; World War II*

BIBLIOGRAPHY

Bloor, Colonel Alfred W., 142nd Infantry commanding officer. "Transmitting Messages in Choctaw." Letter to the commanding general, Thirty-Sixth Division (Attention Capt. Spence), January 23, 1919. APO No. 796. National Archives, AGO REC, World War I, File 236–32.5.

Holiday, Samuel T., and Robert S. McPherson. *Under the Eagle: Samuel Holiday, Navajo Code Talker*. Norman: University of Oklahoma Press, 2013.

Meadows, William C. *The Comanche Code Talkers of World War II*. Austin: University of Texas Press, 2002.

Meadows, William C. "North American Indian Code Talkers: Current Developments and Research." In *Aboriginal Peoples and Military Participation: Canadian and International Perspectives*, edited by P. Whitney Lackenbauer, R. Scott Sheffield, and Craig Leslie Mantle, 161–213. Kingston, ON: Canadian Defense Academy Press, 2007.

Meadows, William C. "Honoring Native American Code Talkers: The Road to the Code Talkers Recognition Act of 2008 (Public Law 110–420)." *American Indian Culture and Research Journal* 35, 3 (2011): 3–36.

Native Words, Native Warriors. National Museum of the American Indian companion website to the traveling Smithsonian Institution exhibition. 2007. http://nmai.si.edu/education/codetalkers/html/

Paul, Doris A. *The Navajo Code Talkers*. Philadelphia: Dorrance, 1973.

Stanley, John W. "Personal Experiences of a Battalion Commander and Brigade Signal Officer, 105th Field Signal Battalion, in the Somme Offensive, September 29–October 12, 1918." Infantry School, Fourth Section, Committee H, Fort Benning, GA, advanced course, 1930–1931.

William C. Meadows
Department of Sociology-Anthropology
Missouri State University

COLD WAR

The Cold War, which lasted from the end of World War II in 1945 to the dissolution of the Soviet Union (USSR) in 1991, took the form of a global competition between two ideologies, that of the free world, led by the United States and its allies, and that of the communist world, led by the Soviet Union. It was fought with propaganda; proxy wars that destroyed lives on every continent; CIA covert activities around the world, including Iran, Chile, and Nicaragua; and the political use of military and economic aid. Before the fall of the infamous Berlin Wall in 1989, it was also a time of relentless and institutionalized tragedy, with showdowns in Korea, Berlin, and Cuba. Most of all it was fought against the background of the nuclear arms rivalry that dominated the second half of the twentieth century.

That the American-Soviet relationship as World War II allies would disintegrate to a status of animosity was not preordained. Yet for some Americans the euphoria of victory and peace evaporated quickly. The Soviet Union's total victory over Germany, upsetting the historical European balance of power, mattered little to Americans who had lauded the USSR for its costly and necessary contributions to Allied success. But for a small minority of US officials and writers, all conditioned by their wartime experience, the continuing postwar Soviet occupation of Eastern Europe enhanced that country's strategic position, especially in the Balkans, and rendered bordering regions vulnerable to further Soviet expansion. It required only the Kremlin's postwar demands on Iran and Turkey to unleash visions of Soviet military expansion reminiscent of the Italian, German, and Japanese aggressions that, so recently, had brought war to the world. Responding to Soviet pressures on Turkey for a new settlement of issues surrounding the Turkish Straits in August 1946, Acting Secretary of State Dean Acheson (1893–1971) and the Joint Chiefs of Staff, with advice from State Department experts, prepared a memorandum on Turkey for President Harry Truman (1884–1972). The memorandum warned:

> If the Soviet Union succeeds in its objective of obtaining control over Turkey, it will be extremely difficult, if not impossible, to prevent the Soviet Union from obtaining control over Greece and over the whole Near and Middle East ... [including] the territory lying between the Mediterranean and India. When the Soviet Union has once obtained full mastery of this territory it will be in a much stronger position to obtain its objectives in India and China. (quoted in Graebner, Burns, and Siracusa 2010, Vol. 1, 111)

Adviser Clark Clifford's (1906–1998) September 1946 report to Truman, reflecting the views of top Washington officials, described a deeply threatened world with similar language.

When suspected Soviet ambitions in early 1947 seemed to focus on Greece as well as Turkey, the Truman administration framed the famed Truman Doctrine, with its corresponding rhetorical predictions of falling dominoes across Europe, Africa, or Asia should Greece fall to its communist-led guerrillas. Senator Arthur Vandenberg (1884–1951) of Michigan accepted the administration's dire predictions uncritically. "Greece," he wrote on March 12, "must be helped or Greece sinks permanently into the Communist order. Turkey inevitably follows. Then comes the chain reaction which might sweep from the Dardanelles to the China Sea" (quoted in Graebner, Burns, and Siracusa 2010, Vol. 1, 116). Never before, critics noted, had US leaders described external dangers in such limitless, imprecise terms. Despite some bitter opposition to the Truman Doctrine in Congress, the measure, with its $400 million package of military aid to Greece and Turkey, passed both houses of Congress by wide margins.

The rhetorical portrayals of Soviet territorial ambitions that underwrote the Truman Doctrine far exceeded Soviet military capabilities and intentions. The Kremlin had already demonstrated its extreme reluctance to confront the West militarily along the Iranian and Turkish borders, where its strategic advantage was profound. Confronted by the predictable resistance of the non-Soviet world, Kremlin leaders understood that any military venture would end in disaster. Indeed, US military officials concluded as early as 1946 that the Soviet Union had no intention of embarking on a career of military aggression. But what seized the country's emerging anticommunist elite was the fear that the real Soviet danger, one that rendered military aggression irrelevant, lay in the limitless promise of Soviet ideological expansion. For those Americans who took the Soviet rhetoric seriously, the USSR, as the self-assigned leader of world communism, possessed the power and will to incite or support communist-led revolutions everywhere, imposing on them its influence, if not its direct control. Such notions of ideological conquest attributed to the Kremlin the power to extend its influence over vast areas without military force.

THE WEST AND THE SOVIET THREAT

Rhetorical depictions of the Soviet Union's expansive power took slight measure of the West's economic, political, and diplomatic predominance. During the two years that followed Congress's approval of the Truman Doctrine, the Western powers achieved an unbroken succession of diplomatic triumphs that demonstrated their total superiority. The sometimes astonishing successes began in 1948 with the elimination of communists from the French government, severing any possible ties to the Kremlin. Similarly, Washington's varied electioneering efforts in Italy triumphed in an election that freed the

Russian propaganda poster "Phrases and ... Bases," 1952. *The Russian cartoon shows a US Army General placing flags on NATO bases in Europe and the Middle East, while a tiny radio announcer in his pocket holds a staff of wheat and says: "Peace, defense, disarmament." The Truman Doctrine rested on the assumption that the Soviet Union had territorial ambitions across Europe, Africa, and Asia. The United States sought to shore up various countries against possible invasion, but overestimated Soviet military capabilities and intentions.* FINE ART IMAGES/HERITAGE IMAGES/GETTY IMAGES

government of all communists and socialists. In June, Marshal Josip Broz Tito (1892–1980), Yugoslavia's staunch communist leader, broke with the Kremlin to demonstrate that communism could not erode the power of nationalism, and that Kremlin control extended only as far as the reach of Soviet armies.

During subsequent months, America's varied policies aimed at the containment of Soviet power emerged victorious. In Greece, the US-supported government, in August 1949, eliminated the communist-led insurgency, driving the surviving guerrillas into Albania. Truman proclaimed victory on November 28. Meanwhile, US officers organized and modernized the Turkish army, vastly improved the country's military capabilities with shipments of equipment and aircraft, and constructed new roads and airstrips. Even greater triumphs for European stability came in response to the Czech coup of February 1948, which established a communist regime in Czechoslovakia and created a momentary threat to European security. Amid that crisis, Congress, which had long resisted the cost, adopted the Marshall Plan to launch Europe on a course of unparalleled economic growth. During May 1949, Joseph Stalin lifted the Berlin blockade, which had been instituted a year earlier to prevent the unification of Germany's three western zones. The meeting of the Council of Foreign Ministers in Paris one month later announced the formation of the Federal Republic of Germany, an achievement long opposed by the Kremlin. Finally, in April 1949, again in response to the Czech war threat, twelve Western countries formed the North Atlantic Treaty Organization (NATO) to underwrite the stability and security of Western Europe.

Washington, with the complete cooperation of the European powers, gained the full spectrum of its immediate objectives, in large measure because Europe's postwar challenges gave the economic supremacy of the

United States a special relevance. With Europe in ruins and the Soviet Union reeling in near disaster, US economic power was absolute.

The war had rained destruction on every major power of Europe and Asia, destroying countless cities, factories, and rail lines. By contrast, the United States, with its many accumulating elements of power, had escaped unscathed. Its undamaged industrial capacity now matched that of the rest of the industrialized world. Its technological superiority was so obvious that the world assumed its existence and set out to acquire or copy American products. During the immediate postwar years, the United States reached the highest point of world power achieved by any nation in modern times.

Abroad, the United States gained its marvelous triumphs where it mattered: the economic rehabilitation of Western Europe and Japan, the promotion of international trade and investment, and the maintenance of a defense structure that underwrote the containment effort and played an essential role in Europe's political development and burgeoning confidence. These contributions to the world's unprecedented security and prosperity comprised the essence of the nation's postwar international achievement.

In the events of 1948 and 1949, especially in the Czech and Berlin crises, the Cold War in Europe reached its peak. At the same time, the rapid succession of Western victories and Soviet retreats, added to Western Europe's astonishing recovery, created the foundations of a profound East-West stability across Europe. If American purpose in Europe was the stability of a divided continent—beyond which no policy would be effective—the United States, in 1949, had achieved its goal. The United States, alone or with its allies, would not assume the risk of war by seeking to change the status quo of Europe; the Soviets had no power to do so. With the major antagonists compelled to accept existing conditions, Britain's Winston Churchill (1874–1965), American diplomat George Kennan (1904–2005), journalist Walter Lippmann (1889–1974), and countless informed observers called for negotiations to adjust differences, relieve tensions, and perhaps stall an arms race. For Churchill, delay would serve no purpose. But for Secretary of State Acheson and much of official Washington, the object of diplomacy was not compromise but the measuring of changing conditions. Settlements, when they came, would simply record the corroding effect of Western power on the ambitions and designs of the Kremlin. Meanwhile, NATO, backed by the power of the United States, would sustain the military division—and thus the stability—of Europe with a vengeance.

Western superiority and unending diplomatic triumphs offered reassurance only to those who believed the Soviet Union well contained, physically and diplomatically. For those whose concern was Soviet ideological expansion, the danger was only emerging. By 1948, the official American worldview could detect no visible limits to the Kremlin's expansive power. A National Security Council study, NSC-7 ("The Position of the United States with Respect to Soviet-Directed World Communism"), dated March 30, 1948, defined the Soviet challenge in global terms: "The ultimate objective of Soviet-directed world communism," the document warned, "is the domination of the world. To this end, Soviet-directed world communism employs against its victims in opportunistic coordination the complementary instruments of Soviet aggressive pressure from without and military revolutionary subversion from within." With its control of international communism, NSC-7 continued, the USSR had engaged the United States in a struggle for power "from which we cannot withdraw short of national suicide" (quoted in Graebner, Burns, and Siracusa 2010, Vol. 1, 147–148). The more pervading NSC-20/4 ("U.S. Objectives with Respect to the USSR to Counter Soviet Threats to U.S. Security"), which enshrined Kennan's containment policy, was approved by the president on November 24, 1948. It defined the danger in similar terms: "Communist ideology and Soviet behavior clearly demonstrate that the ultimate objective of the leaders of the USSR is the domination of the world."

Designed specifically to kindle the nation's insecurities, NSC-68 ("United States Objectives and Programs for National Security"), of April 1950, represented the final and most elaborate attempt of the Truman Cold War elite to define a national defense policy. This document, like its predecessors, described the Soviet danger in global, limitless terms. It concluded that the USSR, "unlike previous aspirants to hegemony, is animated by a new fanatic faith, antithetical to our own, and seeks to impose its absolute authority over the rest of the world." For the Soviets, conflict had become endemic, waged through violent and nonviolent means in accordance with the dictates of expediency. "The issues that face us," NSC-68 continued, "are momentous, involving the … destruction not only of the Republic but of civilization itself." Defeat at the hands of the Soviets would be total (Siracusa 1980, 4–14).

PERCEPTIONS OF FALLING DOMINOES IN ASIA: 1948–1950

Events in East Asia, where the United States faced two unwanted, powerfully led communist revolutions in China and Indochina, seemed to confirm the fears of Soviet expansionism.

Washington officials simply presumed that both revolutions were under Kremlin control. The State

Department's China experts, in a memorandum of October 1948, concluded that the Soviets, through their alleged role in the coming communist victory in China, had acquired control of that country as firmly "as in the satellite countries behind the Iron Curtain." The USSR, apparently, had acquired control of China without one soldier. Secretary of State Acheson claimed no less. "The Communist leaders," he declared, "have foresworn their Chinese heritage and have publicly announced their subservience to a foreign power, Russia." With the final Chinese communist victory in late 1949, NSC-48/1 ("The Position of the United States with Respect to Asia") declared: "The USSR is now an Asiatic power of the first magnitude with expanding influence and interests extending throughout continental Asia and into the Pacific" (quoted in Graebner, Burns, and Siracusa 2010, Vol. 1, 171).

In late 1949, Chiang Kai-shek (1887–1975), with a powerful coterie of American Chinese Nationalist supporters, went into exile on the island of Formosa (Taiwan), eliminating the final barrier to the communist conquest of Asia. This rendered those held responsible for Washington's refusal to launch an effective rescue mission guilty of treason. Among those who shared this absolute, unshakable devotion to the Nationalist cause were businessmen, missionaries, members of Congress, and the press, who had strong ties to the old China that they loved. Their position at the core of American anticommunism gave them incredible access to the country's fears and emotions. It was left for Senator Joseph McCarthy (1908–1957) of Wisconsin to launch the crusade against the alleged communists in government who were responsible for the demise of China's Nationalist regime. The undying crusade for Chiang's return to the mainland sustained Washington's decision to avoid recognition of the new communist government.

Meanwhile, the supposition that the Soviets controlled Asia's communist movements brought the United States into direct confrontation with Ho Chi Minh (1890–1969) and the communist-led struggle for Indochinese independence. Ho assumed command of Indochina's independence movement in 1945 and proclaimed his country's freedom from French rule. When France subsequently reestablished control over its former colony, the United States, in April 1946, announced its support of France. What governed this decision was the evolving US conception of Ho, not as a nationalist seeking the independence of his country, but as a communist serving the interests of the Kremlin. In February 1947 Secretary of State George C. Marshall (1880–1959) warned Paris that the old empires were doomed, and that the French Empire was no exception. "On the other hand," he continued, "we do not lose sight of the fact that Ho Chi Minh has direct Communist connections and it should be obvious that we are not interested in seeing colonial administrations supplanted by [the] philosophy and political organizations emanating from and controlled by the Kremlin" (quoted in Graebner, Burns, and Siracusa 2010, Vol. 1, 157–158). Marshall's rationale for supporting the French faced a serious challenge from officials in the State Department's Division of Southeast Asian Affairs, as well as US diplomats in East Asia, who argued that Ho was a native nationalist, not tied to the Kremlin, no danger to American security, and destined to win.

In 1949 France, in its search for a native nationalist who could challenge Ho for the support of Indochinese nationalism, selected Bao Dai (1913–1997), former king of Annam, as spokesman for the new state of Vietnam. Some US officials doubted that the maneuver would succeed. It was too late, observed State Department adviser Raymond Fosdick (1883–1972), to establish a cheap substitute for French colonialism in the form of the Bao Dai regime. "For the United States to support France in this attempt," he wrote, "will cost us our standing and prestige in all of Southeast Asia" (quoted in Graebner, Burns, and Siracusa 2010, Vol. 1, 160). Because Ho was independent of both Russia and China, there was nothing to be gained by supporting French policy. However, Washington, viewing Ho as an agent of the Kremlin, had eliminated all choices except that of following the French to disaster.

With the French withdrawal in 1954 and the perennial failure of the Vietnamese government in Saigon to rid the country of its communist-led insurgency, the United States, in 1965, at the direction of Secretary of Defense Robert S. McNamara (1916–2009), assumed command of the disintegrating struggle to save Vietnam. Meanwhile, the alleged dangers emanating from Vietnam reached eastward across Asia to Europe, as well as throughout the Pacific. It became increasingly clear to President Lyndon B. Johnson (1908–1973) that Ho's campaign against South Vietnam was part of a larger, much more ambitious strategy being conducted by the communists. "What we saw taking place rapidly," recalled Johnson in his memoirs, "was a Djakarta-Hanoi-Beijing-Pyongyang axis, with Cambodia probably to be brought in as a junior partner and Laos to be absorbed by the North Vietnamese and Chinese" (quoted in Siracusa 1998, 114). For the Joint Chiefs of Staff the war in Vietnam was "a planned phase in the Communist timetable for world domination." Visions of falling dominoes continued to discount the power of nationalism or the individuality of nations that in reality rendered the states of East Asia resistant to external encroachments. No Washington official could define the enemy that, having acquired Saigon, would spread communist conquest across Asia and the Pacific. If Moscow and Beijing were the enemy, fighting Hanoi in the defense of Saigon was

Children in a Florida classroom during a disaster drill, 1962. *In the event of a sudden Soviet nuclear attack, schoolchildren were taught to practice the "duck and cover" method, seeking protection under their desks and covering their heads with their hands.* BETTMANN/CORBIS

irrelevant. If Hanoi's defeat assured the peace and stability of Asia, what was the meaning of falling dominoes? Hanoi, driven by Vietnamese nationalism, possessed the power and will to unite Vietnam; it possessed neither the power nor the intent to expand across Asia and the Pacific.

American policy in East Asia faced its ultimate test in Korea. When North Korea's communist forces invaded the South on June 25, 1950, Washington officials simply presumed that the Kremlin ordered the attack. Moscow maintained a powerful, unwanted influence in North Korean affairs. It approved the North Korean invasion reluctantly, and only when Kim Il-sung (1912–1994), the North Korean leader, assured an easy victory. The Soviets promised aid and advice, but nothing more. Yet Secretary Acheson, following the attack, addressed a note to the US embassy in Moscow that accused the Soviets of possessing "controlling influence over [the] North Korean regime." The note demanded that the Kremlin press the North Korean authorities to withdraw the invading forces immediately. When the American ambassador advised Washington to avoid any identification of the USSR with the invasion, Truman, in his June 27 address, defined the Soviet danger more vaguely: "The attack upon Korea makes it plain beyond all doubt that Communism has passed beyond the use of subversion to conquer independent nations and will now use armed invasion and war" (quoted in Siracusa 1998, 112). Americans agreed with the president that the North Korean attack, unless challenged, presaged another world war. As US forces entered Korea, Washington officials again presumed that they could defeat the Korean enemy, soon threatening rhetorically all Southeast Asia as well as the Pacific, without engaging Soviet military forces.

General Douglas MacArthur (1880–1964), following his success at Inchon, received permission to advance to the Yalu River and thereby eliminate the North Korean regime. Soon the administration received warnings from American advisers as well as observers throughout Asia that MacArthur's advance would bring China into the war. Again Washington refused to confront the Kremlin when it attributed the predicted Chinese invasion, in late November 1950, to Soviet influence and expansionism. Because of that terrifying judgment, East Asia would long remain the core of the Cold War, where the United States continued to face such perennial antagonists as North Vietnam, China, and the Soviet Union.

CONTAINMENT AND COEXISTENCE: 1960s–1990

By the mid-1960s, the continuing Cold War, especially in Asia, began to cool somewhat amid the changing realities of international life. Europe had long recovered from the damages of war and had achieved levels of wealth and prosperity unprecedented in its history. Its very stability erased fears of Soviet aggression. The earlier crises over Berlin had long become history. The USSR and China, the communist giants, had become the world's most bitter rivals, demonstrating that a Communist bloc no longer existed. Revolts behind the Iron Curtain demonstrated the reality that Soviet power and influence in

Eastern Europe was limited. Finally, the rhetoric of Soviet expansionism, driven by the alleged quest for world domination, was never reflected in actual Soviet behavior. Despite anticommunist warnings that the communist and noncommunist worlds could not coexist, in actuality, they coexisted with sufficient success to create one of the world's golden ages. The two foundations of Western policy—containment and coexistence—emerged triumphant.

Much of the United States' predominant realism had become soft, emphasizing less the demands of security and defense than the need for accommodation with the realities of coexistence. European stability and Asian nationalism presented few options beyond maximizing international relationships in a divided but fundamentally unchallenging world. Convinced that previous administrations had exaggerated the Soviet threat, President James Earl (Jimmy) Carter (b. 1924) set out, in 1977, to establish a more relaxed, flexible, nonideological relationship with both China and the USSR. After the American failure in Vietnam, the country could no longer maintain the illusion of global power. Carter responded by lessening the strategic importance of Asia, Africa, and Latin America. Nationalism, he believed, limited both Soviet and American influence in the Third World. In his Notre Dame speech of May 1977, he rejected the traditional notion that American interests were global. "Being confident of our own future," he said, "we are now free of that inordinate fear of communism which once led us to embrace any dictator who joined us in that fear" (quoted in Graebner, Burns, and Siracusa 2010, Vol. 2, 393–395). Dismissing the Cold War commitment to global containment, Carter accepted Soviet activity in the Afro-Asian world with profound indifference.

But the Soviet Union's Leonid Brezhnev (1906–1982), in power since 1964, not only perfected the Soviet structure of centralized power but also diverted his country's newfound wealth from oil and natural gas into new weaponry. What the enhanced military sophistication contributed to Soviet prestige and ambition remained elusive, but its contrast with Carter's readiness to accommodate communist Third World advances, especially in Africa, launched many Democrats who had favored soft realism into an anticommunist crusade, as neoconservatives, to restore America's Cold War role as the world's defender against communist expansionism. The neoconservatives found themselves aligned with the traditional Republican anticommunist right.

Already facing open challenges to its alleged loss of will, the Carter administration reacted to the Soviet invasion of Afghanistan in late December 1979 with bewilderment and rage. On January 4, the president revealed his new anti-Soviet mood to the nation. "A Soviet-occupied Afghanistan," he declared, "threatens both Iran and Pakistan, and is a stepping stone to possible control over much of the world's oil supplies" (quoted in Graebner, Burns, and Siracusa 2010, Vol. 2, 343–47). Soviet dominance over Afghanistan and adjacent countries, he warned, would threaten "the stable, strategic and peaceful balance of the entire world." Actually, the Soviets, recognizing the nature of their Afghan opposition, were already seeking an escape. But the widespread assumption that the Soviet invasion of Afghanistan exposed South and Southeast Asia to further Soviet encroachment pushed American hawkishness to a new high.

Ronald Reagan (1911–2004) caught the country's post-Afghanistan alarms at full tide, embellished them, and rode them to presidential victory. He entered office in January 1981 with an advisory team committed to the recovery of the country's global leadership. Despite the new administration's tough rhetoric and massive military expansion, it maintained the defense posture of previous administrations. It made no effort to recover the alleged losses of the Carter years—in Afghanistan or elsewhere. Even before Reagan's inauguration, the Soviet Union had entered its long, predictable disintegration that, in 1985, produced Mikhail Gorbachev (b. 1931) and the possibility of a genuine US-Soviet détente, one that Reagan and Gorbachev achieved in their four summits. The processes of Soviet disintegration culminated in the collapse of the Soviet satellite empire in Eastern Europe in 1989 and exit from the Cold War during the following year. Reagan supporters attributed the Soviet collapse to the rhetorical toughness and military buildup of the Reagan years. For Soviet experts, the communist regime's collapse flowed naturally from its internal flaws, its political erosion, and its ideological rejection. After forty-five years, the Cold War died quietly and without celebration.

THE NUCLEAR LEGACY

The nuclear arms race, together with arms control, was a major component of the Cold War as the United States and the Soviet Union vied for more and more sophisticated weaponry. Nuclear weapons, as well as new delivery systems, were a central feature of this contest, as each nation invested heavily in what became a game of technological escalation aimed at producing more and better military devices. The United States' successful test of a hydrogen bomb in 1952 made possible the creation of warheads smaller than the World War II atom bombs but twenty-five hundred times more powerful. These developments were followed in the 1960s with improved delivery systems that included short range (SRBM), medium range (MRBM), and intercontinental (ICBM) ballistic missiles. Initially, these missiles and their nuclear warheads were land based, but in 1960 the United States launched its first submarine armed with sixteen Polaris missiles, only to be followed by the Soviet submarines equipped with nuclear-tipped missiles. The submarine-launched ballistic missile (SLBM), with the ability to elude detection, was a game changer. Also, the growth in the number of targeted warheads grew dramatically with the introduction of multiple independently targetable reentry vehicles (MIRVs), ballistic missiles that could carry ten or more warheads. In an attempt to defend against these new threats, both nations experimented with antiballistic missile (ABM) systems.

By the 1960s, the superpowers now possessed enough nuclear weapons to obliterate each other's cities and cause tens of millions of causalities; indeed, Washington and Moscow had within their capability enough weapons to destroy the world many times over. Recognition of this fact meant that each nation dare not use its weapons for fear of being destroyed itself by retaliatory attacks. The concept of nuclear deterrence was born from the fact that there could be no winners in a nuclear war. Secretary of Defense McNamara labeled this situation one of "assured destruction," more popularly known as mutual assured destruction (Siracusa 2015, 67). Determining that they could not find security through technology alone, leaders in Washington and Moscow slowly turned to mechanisms referred to as arms control agreements.

In 1969, the superpowers' delegations began bilateral talks focused on limitations of both defensive and offensive strategic weapons systems—essentially ICBMs and SLBMs. These negotiations continued, intermittently, resulting in two Strategic Arms Limitation Treaties (SALT I and II); the Intermediate-Range Nuclear Forces Treaty (INF), the only treaty that actually reduced the number of nuclear warheads during the Cold War; and the Strategic Arms Reduction Talks (START I) that were finally concluded in 1991.

During the Cold War, the United States entered into several important arms accords with the Soviet Union, beginning with the 1963 Limited Test Ban Treaty, which banned signatories from testing new nuclear devices in the atmosphere, space, territorial waters, or at sea, while permitting underground tests. The Outer Space Treaty (1967) outlawed national claims of sovereignty or military activities in space. Most important was the Nuclear Non-Proliferation Treaty (NPT) of 1968. President Johnson regarded the NPT as one of the most significant accomplishments of his administration. The NPT's basic objective was to help halt the spread of nuclear weapons by banning the sale or distribution of any major nuclear weaponry to nonnuclear states. For their part, nonnuclear states had the right to obtain the materials to build civilian nuclear power plants without being charged research and development costs. The endgame was to pursue general disarmament in the future.

SEE ALSO *Air Force, US; Allende, Salvador; Bandung Conference (1955); Bay of Pigs; Berlin Airlift; Berlin Wall; Castro, Fidel; Central Intelligence Agency (CIA); Covert Wars; Cuban Missile Crisis; Department of Defense, US; Détente; Deterrence; Domino Theory; Guatemala; Gulf of Tonkin Resolution; Ho Chi Minh; Iran-Contra Scandal; Kennan, George F.; Kitchen Debate; Laos; Limited Test Ban Treaty; Marshall Plan; McCarthyism; McNamara, Robert S.; Modernization Theory; Mossadegh, Mohammad; Mutual Assured Destruction (MAD); North Atlantic Treaty Organization (NATO); Point Four; Potsdam Conference (1945); Rand Corporation; Spies and Espionage; Strategic Arms Limitation Talks (SALT I and SALT II); Strategic Defense Initiative (Star Wars)*

BIBLIOGRAPHY

Gaddis, John Lewis. *We Now Know: Rethinking Cold War History.* New York: Oxford University Press, 1997.

Graebner, Norman A., Richard Dean Burns, and Joseph M. Siracusa. *Reagan, Bush, Gorbachev: Revisiting the End of the Cold War.* Westport, CT: Praeger Security International, 2008.

Graebner, Norman A., Richard Dean Burns, and Joseph M. Siracusa. *America and the Cold War, 1941–1991: A Realist Interpretation.* 2 vols. Santa Barbara, CA: Praeger, 2010.

LaFeber, Walter. *America, Russia, and the Cold War, 1945–1996,* 8th ed. New York: McGraw-Hill, 1997.

Mann, James. *The Rebellion of Ronald Reagan: A History of the End of the Cold War.* New York: Viking, 2009.

Siracusa, Joseph M. "NSC 68: A Re-appraisal." *Naval War College Review* 33, 6 (November–December 1980): 4–14.

Siracusa, Joseph M. *Into the Dark House: American Diplomacy and the Ideological Origins of the Cold War.* Claremont, CA: Regina Books, 1998.

Siracusa, Joseph M. *Nuclear Weapons: A Very Short Introduction.* 2nd ed. Oxford: Oxford University Press, 2015.

Wilson, James Graham. *The Triumph of Improvisation: Gorbachev's Adaptability, Reagan's Engagement, and the End of the Cold War.* Ithaca, NY: Cornell University Press, 2014.

Zubok, Vladislav. *A Failed Empire: The Soviet Union in the Cold War from Stalin to Gorbachev.* Chapel Hill: University of North Carolina Press, 2007.

Joseph Siracusa
Professor of Human Security and International Diplomacy
Royal Melbourne Institute of Technology University

COLD WAR: RACE AND THE COLD WAR

The idea of "race" is relatively new in human history. At heart, the concept of race actually refers to varieties of phenotypes (skin color, hair texture, facial features, etc.) and connects those superficial differences to cultural, religious, economic, or political differences, whether real or perceived. Race supported a hierarchical organization of humanity—with white people at the summit—shaped by supposedly "natural" proclivities and limitations, with the implication that biology equaled destiny. However, this school of thought faced several challenges in the early twentieth century from scholars like W. E. B. Du Bois (1868–1963), Franz Boas (1858–1942), Zora Neale Hurston (1891–1960), Margaret Mead (1901–1978), and Melville Herskovits (1895–1963).

In the late 1930s Gunnar Myrdal (1898–1987), a Swedish economist and sociologist, came to the United States to undertake a massive social study. His work built on or incorporated the findings of noted black scholars like Du Bois, Charles S. Johnson (1893–1956), and others. In 1944 Myrdal published *An American Dilemma: The Negro Problem and Modern Democracy* to much acclaim. Although not a direct attack on the concept of race, Myrdal's study pointed out centuries-old white advantages and underscored generations of black protest and petition by highlighting the limits of American democratic practice. Myrdal's work appeared as American soldiers were fighting in a racially segregated military against a Nazi foe that widely trumpeted its white supremacist ethos. Despite this intellectual intervention, as well as the brave service of black women and men in the war effort, the spike in lynchings immediately after the war made 1946 one of the grimmest years for blacks in America since the founding of the National Association for the Advancement of Colored People (NAACP) in 1909. Many of those lynched or brutally beaten—including a young Hosea Williams, later a key member of the Southern Christian Leadership Conference—were uniformed black veterans.

RACE AS A WAY OF SEEING THE WORLD

Once American policy makers determined that it was necessary to wage a "cold war" against the Soviet Union, they had to articulate the matters at stake to a war-weary nation. American planners argued that the only force that could hope to defeat the march of global communism was the combined might of Western capitalist, democratic nations of Europe (and its colonies), Australia, and most importantly the United States—the so-called Free World, which asserted its commitment to meritocracy, independence, and civil liberties. Yet this model was problematic.

Although the concept of a free world was appealing to many Americans, large sections of black, Latino, and Asian American communities could not reconcile their discrete histories with the notion of America as part of it. For many people in these communities, America was the place of slavery, racial discrimination, and brutal, violent marginalization. Similarly, the restive populations of Africa and Asia puzzled over this construction, because the United States, Great Britain, Spain, France, and others represented the world of forced labor, colonization, and economic exploitation. Accordingly, for billions of people in the world, the idea of a free world made no sense because it implied that America and its allies occupied a place outside of time, a place in which the great slave powers and hoarders of global wealth had no history and no accountability.

Convinced of the viability of the concept, Western planners and politicians often dismissed the claims of Africans, Asians, and Latin Americans as hysterical or unworthy; for Africans or Asians to insist on self-determination was both irrational and dangerous. Yet most Western policy makers knew that Jim Crow segregation was a strategic liability in the effort to woo the emerging nations of the so-called Third World. Consequently, in a number of lawsuits that sought to end overt forms of racial discrimination, the US government filed "friend of the court" briefs siding with litigants who fought for racial justice and described the damage that racism had done to America's diplomacy with a wary world. The foremost example was the Supreme Court case of *Brown v. Board of Education* (347 U.S. 483 [1954]; referred to as *Brown I*).

The court's ruling in the initial phase of the case (that public, racially segregated schools violated the Constitution) was just the declaration that American statesmen needed. The decision seemed to verify the claim that America was making progress in race relations and that democracy could work for everyone. However, a year later in *Brown II* (349 U.S. 294 [1955])—the remedy phase of the case—the court avoided telling racial segregationists that they would have to immediately admit black students to previously all-white schools. Instead, the court gave white officials and school boards the power to control the process of desegregation and simply instructed the defendants to fix their constitutional violation "with all deliberate speed." Thus it was no surprise that the clarion call of *Brown I* was drowned out by school closings and bombings; the Southern Manifesto, a congressional resolution condemning the 1954 decision in *Brown*; or the abortive attempt, in 1956, of Autherine Lucy to desegregate the University of Alabama by becoming its first black student, only to be expelled days later.

Beginning in the mid-1950s, the State Department's Bureau of Educational and Cultural Relations (now known as the Bureau of Educational and Cultural Affairs [ECA]) arranged global tours by such prominent jazz artists as Duke Ellington, Dave Brubeck, Dizzy Gillespie, and Louis Armstrong. Although by the late 1960s these tours waned as a result of the ascendance of rock and roll, the jazz tours represented a significant effort by the United States to present a distinctly American culture to the peoples of the world, whether ally, adversary, or ambivalent.

Lisa Davenport (2015) explores how the ECA used jazz as a cultural representation of America's self-proclaimed commitment to individual freedom, equality, and civil liberties. Of course, this representation rubbed up against the nation's history of slavery and discrimination and its troubled contemporary reality. State Department officials were of two minds about using black jazz performers as "jambassadors." It was not uncommon for officials to monitor closely what the artists were saying to audiences or to warn European women to avoid interacting with black musicians. As a result, cultural diplomacy had a somewhat limited impact on foreign opinions regarding the United States because it could not overcome (and, at times, reflected) the many facets of racial privilege that manifested in everyday life. As Davenport observes,

> the goal of containing communism remained paramount in shaping the course of jazz diplomacy and prevailed over America's policy of redefining relations with emerging new nations in Africa, Asia, and Latin America. The United States addressed the issues of race and jazz in a global context only to align its cultural policies with its anticommunist agenda—to win the Cold War, counter Soviet cultural propaganda, and defeat communism. (2015, 143)

The dissonance between a projection of American cultural superiority in the world and the facts of American behavior at home illuminates the various ways in which the concept of race inflected the Cold War.

THE COLD WAR AS RACIAL CRUCIBLE

The Cold War had a profound impact on the modern civil rights movement and vice versa. In important ways the treatment some Americans meted out to black and brown diplomats reinforced the struggle for racial justice and embarrassed official Washington. Dark-skinned emissaries who moved to New York for work at the United Nations faced rampant discrimination in their efforts to find suitable housing. Others were jailed or beaten for breaches of Jim Crow etiquette in the South. One of the more infamous incidents occurred in October 1957 when white workers at a Howard Johnson's restaurant in Delaware refused to serve a glass of orange juice to Komla Gbedemah, Ghana's finance minister. President Dwight Eisenhower, stung by international condemnation of the Little Rock Nine crisis a few weeks earlier, in which Arkansas's governor had attempted to bar nine black students from a racially segregated school until the president intervened, hosted Gbedemah at a hastily convened meeting at the White House.

Many Americans of color saw the Cold War as an ideal moment in which to more effectively bargain their long-standing national loyalty for some sense of inclusion, or the freedom of other peoples. Others were inspired by worldwide freedom struggles. Concomitantly, many whites across the country regarded the movement with suspicion, even as some recognized that success within the struggle would aid in the battle against communism.

For example, years before the Montgomery bus boycott of 1956–1957, a protest against racial segregation in the public transit system of the Alabama city, the civil rights activist James Lawson spent time in India studying *satyagraha*, an element of nonviolent resistance, to use as a tool of direct action in America. In 1964 Malcolm X (1925–1965), influenced by the pan-racial solidarity he had seen in Africa and Mecca, Saudi Arabia, as well as countries of the Non-Aligned Movement, created the Organization of Afro-American Unity and spoke of collaboration with nonviolent activists in the South. Many black power activists took a cue from global liberation struggles and reconceived the position of blacks in the United States as akin to an internal colony. Yet fears of communism also constrained black action. Although the NAACP valued Justice Department support in its desegregation litigation, accusations that Du Bois, the singer Paul Robeson (1898–1976), the dancer and singer Josephine Baker (1906–1975), and other prominent African Americans were communists or sympathizers led the NAACP to shun many powerful activists. Although the civil rights leader the Reverend Martin Luther King Jr. (1929–1968) had visions of creating a better place for all Americans through grassroots movements, his critics dogged him with charges of being a communist. This Red-baiting survived King's death and served as a pretext for those who opposed a national holiday in his honor.

In one of the major victories of the civil rights movement, Congress passed the Voting Rights Act of 1965. White elites supported the legislation in part as a means of demonstrating America's devotion to progress in race relations. Yet the emphasis that elites placed on fighting communism caused many social justice advocates to doubt the strength of that devotion. For instance, King became a public critic of America's role in the Vietnam conflict, in part because the expansive military budget overwhelmed the much smaller allotments to fight racism and poverty at home. Moreover, white fears of mass movements led to widespread, unconstitutional surveillance, infiltration of activist groups, the use of agent provocateurs to foment dissent within these groups, and political assassinations. The activities of state-run spy agencies like the Mississippi State Sovereignty Commission and the federal government's COINTELPRO mirrored the American-supported coups, plots, and assassinations that marred the development of countries like Iran, Guatemala, the Congo, Indonesia, and Chile. Accordingly, white distrust in the sincerity and validity of social protest movements everywhere acted as a brake on racial progress.

The easing of tensions between East and West, followed by the collapse of the Soviet Union in 1991, ushered in a sense of both triumphalism and paradox. Jesse Jackson's efforts to gain the Democratic Party's nomination for president in 1984 and 1988 had stood in stark contrast to the politics of abandonment that marginalized communities in urban America. Minority income and wealth gains stagnated, some school systems reverted to a de facto segregation, and incarceration rates for blacks and other minorities increased alarmingly. As the Cold War ended, racial justice remained a fraught concept in American life.

SEE ALSO *An American Dilemma: The Negro Problem and Modern Democracy (Gunnar Myrdal, 1944); An Appeal to the World! (NAACP, 1947); Black Power Movement; Cold War; Decolonization; Human Rights; Jazz; King, Martin Luther, Jr.; Malcolm X; Non-Aligned Movement; Robeson, Paul Leroy; Student Nonviolent Coordinating Committee (SNCC)*

BIBLIOGRAPHY

Alexander, Michelle. *The New Jim Crow: Mass Incarceration in the Age of Colorblindness.* New York: New Press, 2012.

Anderson, Carol. *Eyes off the Prize: The United Nations and the African American Struggle for Human Rights, 1944–1955.* Cambridge: Cambridge University Press, 2003.

Anderson, Carol. *Bourgeois Radicals: The NAACP and the Struggle for Colonial Liberation, 1941–1960.* New York: Cambridge University Press, 2014.

Bell, Derrick. *Silent Covenants:* Brown v. Board of Education *and the Unfulfilled Hopes for Racial Reform.* Oxford: Oxford University Press, 2004.

Borstelmann, Thomas. *The Cold War and the Color Line: American Race Relations in the Global Arena.* Cambridge, MA: Harvard University Press, 2001.

Davenport, Lisa. "The Paradox of Jazz Diplomacy: Race and Culture in the Cold War." In *African Americans in U.S. Foreign Policy: From the Era of Frederick Douglass to the Age of Obama*, edited by Linda Heywood, Allison Blakely, Charles Stith, and Joshua C. Yesnowitz. Urbana: University of Illinois Press, 2015.

Dudziak, Mary L. *Cold War Civil Rights: Race and the Image of American Democracy.* Princeton, NJ: Princeton University Press, 2000.

Fraser, Cary. *Ambivalent Anti-colonialism: The United States and the Genesis of West Indian Independence, 1940–1964.* Westport, CT: Greenwood Press, 1994.

Glick, Brian. *War at Home: Covert Action against U.S. Activists and What We Can Do about It.* Boston: South End Press, 1989.

Krenn, Michael L. *Fall-Out Shelters for the Human Spirit: American Art and the Cold War.* Chapel Hill: University of North Carolina Press, 2005.

Krenn, Michael L. *The Color of Empire: Race and American Foreign Relations.* Washington, DC: Potomac Books, 2006.

Lauren, Paul G. *Power and Prejudice: The Politics and Diplomacy of Racial Discrimination.* 2nd ed. Boulder, CO: Westview Press, 1996.

Monson, Ingrid. *Freedom Sounds: Civil Rights Call Out to Jazz and Africa.* Oxford: Oxford University Press, 2007.

O'Reilly, Kenneth. *Racial Matters: The FBI's Secret File on Black America, 1960–1972.* New York: Free Press, 1991.

Plummer, Brenda Gayle. *Rising Wind: Black Americans and U.S. Foreign Affairs, 1935–1960.* Chapel Hill: University of North Carolina Press, 1996.

Plummer, Brenda Gayle, ed. *Window on Freedom: Race, Civil Rights, and Foreign Affairs, 1945–1988.* Chapel Hill: University of North Carolina Press, 2003.

Von Eschen, Penny M. *Race against Empire: Black Americans and Anticolonialism, 1937–1957.* Ithaca, NY: Cornell University Press, 1997.

Von Eschen, Penny M. *Satchmo Blows Up the World: Jazz Ambassadors Play the Cold War.* Cambridge, MA: Harvard University Press, 2004.

White, George, Jr. *Holding the Line: Race, Racism and American Foreign Policy toward Africa, 1953–1961.* Lanham, MD: Rowman & Littlefield, 2005.

George White Jr.
Associate Professor of History and Chair,
Department of History & Philosophy
York College, City University of New York

COLLECTIVE SECURITY

SEE *Internationalism; Interventionism; League of Nations.*

COLOMBIA

US-Colombian relations overall rank among the warmest between the United States and any other South American republic. In 1820, as Spain's Latin American colonies were seeking independence, the US House of Representatives passed a resolution in support of the newly independent republics, and representatives of the region were received in Washington. The United States formally recognized Colombia on June 19, 1822, before any European power did so. The first US consulates were established in Cartagena and Santa Marta in 1823, with the first embassy established in Bogotá in 1939.

As was the case across the hemisphere, Colombian constitutionalism was heavily influenced by the US Constitution of 1789—given both the lack of other examples around the world as well as the affinity between the United States and Latin American nations as former European colonies. Most prominently, Colombia adopted American presidentialism (i.e., an executive elected separately from the legislature) and symmetrical bicameralism (in terms of legislative power).

1820s–1950s

At first, the United States had minimal relations with Colombia, as was typical of its role in the region during the nineteenth century. These relations were largely linked to US economic interests. During this period Colombia was embroiled in a series of civil wars and constitutional orders (between 1821 and 1886 the country had eight constitutions, many of them promulgated in the context of civil war). As such, foreign policy was not a major focus for the government in Bogotá. Still, during this period the Mallarino-Bridlack Treaty of 1846 was signed allowing North Americans freedom of transit on the isthmus of Panama (then a province of Colombia). In this context a New York company secured the rights to construct a trans-isthmian railroad, an early indication of the geostrategic importance of the region to the United States.

The nadir of US-Colombian relations was in the early 1900s over the issue of Panama. When the Colombian government rejected the 1903 Hay-Herrán Treaty, which would have allowed the construction of a US canal across Panama, the administration of Theodore Roosevelt (in office 1901–1909) supported a local rebellion that led to Panamanian independence and the construction of the canal. The Colombian diplomat Tomás Herrán lacked the authority to negotiate the treaty, and the terms were quite favorable to the United States. Roosevelt, who considered the Colombian government to be populated with "contemptible little creatures," used the Mallarino-Bridlack Treaty as a legal pretense for supporting the Panamanian rebellion. These events froze US-Colombian relations for over a decade. There was no formal break, but relations were such that attempts at thawing the relationship contributed to the early exit from office of two Colombian presidents, Rafael Reyes in 1909 and Marco Fidel Suárez in 1921.

Lured by the potential of Colombian oil and other trade prospects, the United States entered into negotiations in 1914 for what would become the Thomson-Urrutia Treaty of 1921. This treaty, which paid Colombia a $25 million indemnity and led to recognition by Colombia of Panama and its canal arrangement with the United States, set the stage for stronger relations, first linked to trade (especially coffee) and later to various geopolitical considerations. Although Colombia remained neutral during World War I, it did support US and Allied actions in World War II (but did not send troops). In a significant instance of US-Colombian military cooperation, Colombia was the only Latin American country to send troops to the multinational effort in the Korean War in the 1950s. These troops were funded, trained, and outfitted by the United States.

1960s–1990s

The Fulbright Commission was established in Colombia in 1957 and since then has facilitated the educational interchange of over three thousand American and Colombian students. In the 1960s Colombia was an early partner in the United States' Alliance for Progress program, and it was also the first Latin American country to receive Peace Corps volunteers. The major factors in the US-Colombian relations of the 1960s were those of trade and national security—specifically US support for Colombia's fight against leftist guerrilla groups, involving a combination of development and military aid.

US policy toward Colombia from the mid-1970s until the turn of the twenty-first century was, as Russell Crandall (2008) put it, "driven by drugs." Colombian smugglers had a long history in both marijuana and cocaine dating back to the 1930s, although these did not emerge as major issues until the 1970s, when President Richard M. Nixon (in office 1969–1974) declared a "war on drugs" with a major focus on marijuana and heroin, and into the 1980s, when President Ronald Reagan (in office 1981–1989) re-declared that war with a focus on powder and crack cocaine. President George H. W. Bush (in office 1989–1993) renewed the war on drugs yet again. If US citizens at the time were aware of Colombia, it was likely for one of two reasons: coffee or cocaine. Indeed, cocaine's influence on US popular culture was significant, as characters in many US movies (such as *Clear and Present Danger*) and television programs (such as *Miami Vice*) were patterned on Colombian drug lords, especially Pablo Escobar and his Medellín Cartel. The focus on drugs led to a number of policies, including the Andean Initiative in 1989, which was a $2.2 billion plan to increase military assistance to Bolivia, Colombia, and Peru.

As the drug war escalated, the issue of extradition of accused drug criminals from Colombia to the United States became a major political and legal issue in Colombia. This included a violent campaign by drug lords (who called themselves "the extraditables") to block all such extraditions. For a time, extradition was unconstitutional. The 1990s started with the dismantling of the Medellín Cartel and the death of the infamous Escobar, in 1993; but the election of Ernesto Samper to the presidency (1994–1998) led to serious difficulties with Washington. Samper was accused of taking large campaign contributions from the Cali Cartel (which had taken over as the major trafficker after the demise of the Medellín Cartel). At the same time the outgoing head of the US Drug Enforcement Administration (DEA) in Bogotá, Joe Toft, stated in an interview in the Colombian press that Colombia was a "narco-democracy" where cartels had a huge influence over politicians and the legal system. During the Samper administration Colombia was twice "decertified" (i.e., legally declared to be not cooperating in the drug war, with cuts to funding as a result), and Samper himself was denied a visa to enter the United States. Despite the troubles between Washington and Bogotá, the Colombian government did crack down on and dismantle the Cali Cartel.

TWENTY-FIRST CENTURY

The most significant drug-war policy was Plan Colombia, which was initiated in 2000 and arose out of proposals by the administration of President Andrés Pastrana (in office 1998–2002). With an initial $1.3 billion allocation, this policy eventually cost roughly $8 billion. The stated goal was to develop a two-pronged strategy of focused interdiction against the Colombian cocaine production and trafficking industry while also aiding in alternative development programs. Both areas were funded, but the primary focus was on interdiction, especially crop eradication. Prior to the US involvements in Iraq and Afghanistan, Colombia ranked as receiving the third-highest amount of US foreign aid (after Israel and Egypt); after those US wars began, Colombia ranked fifth.

US-Colombian ties deepened considerably with the election of Álvaro Uribe (in office 2002–2010). The George W. Bush administration (2001–2009) saw Uribe as a key ally in the war on terror and, in a policy shift from previous administrations, Colombia's fight against leftist guerrillas and drug cartels were treated by the United States as one and the same. During this period extraditions of suspects in the drug war increased, and negotiations for US use of Colombian air bases (for drug interdiction) were undertaken. Most significantly, the two countries negotiated and signed the US-Colombia Free Trade Agreement, which went into effect on May 15, 2012. Relations with the administration of Juan Manuel Santos (elected in 2010) remained strong as of 2015.

SEE ALSO *Panama Canal*

BIBLIOGRAPHY

Crandall, Russell. *Driven by Drugs: U.S. Policy toward Colombia.* 2nd ed. Boulder, CO: Lynne Rienner, 2008.

La Rosa, Michael J., and Germán R. Mejía. *Colombia: A Concise Contemporary History.* Updated ed. Lanham, MD: Rowman and Littlefield, 2013.

Marcella, Gabriel. *The United States and Colombia: The Journey from Ambiguity to Strategic Clarity.* US Army War College: Strategic Studies Institute, 2003. http://www.strategicstudiesinstitute.army.mil/pubs/display.cfm?pubID=10

Safford, Frank, and Marco Palacios. *Colombia: Fragmented Land, Divided Society.* New York: Oxford University Press, 2002.

Shifter, Michael. "Plan Colombia: A Retrospective." *Americas Quarterly* 6, 3 (2012): 36–42. http://www.americasquarterly.org/node/3787

Steven L. Taylor
Professor and Chair, Department of Political Science
Troy University

COLONIALISM

The United States is both a product of colonialism and a colonial society. Colonialism thus permeates American history. Colonialism has been variously defined, often in close association with imperialism, but essentially entails the taking of colonies and the establishment of relations of control or dependence. Typically, the colonizer justifies the assertion of power over the colonized through perceptions of cultural, and especially racial and religious, superiority. Colonialism has also been justified as a necessity in a context of geopolitical competition among states. Finally, colonialism is inseparable from economic motives insofar as the purpose of colonies is to access land, labor, wealth, and profit, or some admixture thereof, to the benefit of the colonizer.

Colonialism ultimately depended on the binary logics of civilization over primitivism, godliness over heathenism, progress over regression, and often light over dark skin color and the pseudoscience associated with such racial categorizations. The colonizer did not, however, possess all of the power under colonialism. The colonized engaged in resistance but could also adopt positions of accommodation, acculturation, assimilation, and alliance. Colonial relationships are thus complex and vary in place and time. Nonetheless, colonialism is at its core an exploitative relationship backed by the potential for the use of force and the actual application of violence, which often becomes systemic and indiscriminate in application.

VARIETIES OF COLONIZATION

Varieties of colonization include *settler colonialism,* of which the United States was a product. England (Great Britain after 1707) spawned settler colonies in Australia, New Zealand, South Africa, and North America, including the future United States and Canada. Settler colonialism refers to a history in which settlers drove indigenous populations from the land in order to construct their own ethnic and religious national communities. Settler colonies pursued policies of elimination rather than exploitation as they pushed indigenous populations further into the interior. Invariably, indigenous resistance produced often-indiscriminate violence and removal policies justified through tropes of racial superiority and national destiny.

A triangular relationship between settlers, the metropolitan authority, and the indigenous population distinguished and defined US and other settler colonies. Over time, as settlers sought to remove and replace indigenous people on the land, they gradually cast aside the authority of the "mother" country. Settler colonies such as the United States thus created their own national identities through a long-term process of eliminating both indigenous people and metropolitan authority. While disease, demographic swamping, and removal policies drove out indigenous peoples, political revolt culminating in the American Revolution cast aside British authority.

Following independence, the United States implemented another variety of colonialism through the *internal colonization* of indigenous people and minorities. Internal colonization refers to various forms of economic and political authority or privileging at the expense of ethnic minorities. Indians were forced onto reservations, their cultures and economic arrangements broken up through initiatives culminating in the Dawes Act (1887), a program authorizing seizures of Indian land and division of reservations into individual plots rather than traditional communal arrangements. Internal colonization also applied to Hispanics, first centered in the Southwest and California, areas annexed by the United States in the Mexican War (1846–1848), but gradually spreading throughout the country. African Americans, most arriving through compulsion via the African slave trade, were first enslaved and later relegated to internal colonization through segregation and economic and political marginalization. Internal colonization might also be applied to Asian Americans and other immigrant communities at various times and places in American history.

HISTORICAL DENIAL

The United States, like other settler societies and indeed nearly all nations, constructed a national narrative emphasizing the positive aspects of the nation's history and thus de-emphasizing the colonial past. Indian removal and slavery, for example, could not be ignored, but the fullness of their implications for national identity was inconsistent with the narrative of American exceptionalism. The dominant narrative emphasized freedom, inclusion, and individual opportunity. Under this framework, slavery was acknowledged as a mistake, which had been rectified through the blood purge of the Civil War, whereas continental expansion could be glossed as the inevitable product of "manifest destiny."

Historical denial or elision of settler colonization fueled the misperception that American colonialism began near the turn of the twentieth century as a consequence of the Spanish-American War (1898). The arbitrary separation of continental and overseas empires thus obscures the continuities of colonialism. After defeating Spain in the war, the United States took colonies in the Caribbean and across the Pacific Ocean. The late-nineteenth-century US colonial empire arose in the context of an "age of imperialism" in which the modernized European nations established colonial authority over most of the world's landed surface, especially in Asia and Africa, while competing for island possessions and sea power.

US COLONIZATION IN CENTRAL AMERICA AND THE CARIBBEAN

In the wake of the Spanish-American War, the United States established what amounted to a colonial empire in Central America and the Caribbean Sea. Washington held indirect control over Cuba, including a right under the Platt Amendment (1901) that it exercised to intervene militarily whenever it chose to do so. The United States established a military base at Guantánamo Bay and dominated Cuba economically and politically until the Cuban Revolution of 1959, which began a long conflict with the regime of Fidel Castro. In 1898, Puerto Rico came under direct US control and remained a colony subject to congressional fiat. Puerto Ricans have exercised various levels of accommodation and resistance, including debates and referenda over both independence and statehood, either of which would require congressional approval.

Asserting US hegemony over the Caribbean, President Theodore Roosevelt (1858–1919) pronounced his "corollary" to the Monroe Doctrine in 1904, pledging to European nations that Washington would police the hemisphere on behalf of "civilization" and that accordingly they should stay out. The subsequent regime of "dollar diplomacy" entailed US colonial supervision of the economies of several Caribbean and Central American states, as well as ongoing military interventions and occupations. In 1903, following the rejection of an isthmian canal treaty by the Colombian senate, the United States fomented a coup in which the province of Panama gained independence from Colombia. Roosevelt later admitted he "took the canal zone" in order to sign an agreement with a French canal builder in a "treaty that no Panamanian ever signed," as it became known in Panama.

The United States occupied and dominated Panama, including frequent military interventions, until Panama received full authority over the canal in 1999.

The United States asserted colonial authority backed by military occupation from 1916 to 1924 in the Dominican Republic and from 1915 to 1934 in Haiti. In 1917, the United States purchased the Virgin Islands (St. Thomas, St. Croix, and St. John), located south of Puerto Rico, from Denmark. The United States had considerable economic investment and influence in Mexico, but proved unable to establish colonial authority despite repeated military interventions in the 1910s. Dollar diplomacy and military intervention characterized US relations with the Central American states, including Nicaragua, which US marines occupied from 1912 to 1925 and 1927 to 1933, after which a puppet regime was established. It fell in 1979, precipitating a bloody power struggle that radiated to neighboring states and intensified as it became part of the broader global Cold War. According to subsequent United Nations (UN) tribunals, US-backed anticommunist military regimes were complicit in the killings of tens of thousands of people in Guatemala and El Salvador. Washington intervened militarily to topple governments in Grenada (1983) and Panama (1989).

US EXPANSION ACROSS THE PACIFIC

US expansion across the Pacific began in the nineteenth century and included the taking of colonies, as well as incorporation in 1959 of the states of Hawai'i and Alaska. The United States purchased Alaska from Russia in 1867 and thereafter established colonial authority over the indigenous people, the Aleuts, Inupiat, Athabascans, Tlingit, and Haida, among them. The United States, led by Protestant missionaries and plantation owners and investors, gradually dispossessed indigenous Hawaiians and established a US settler colony in the islands. Americans overthrew the Hawaiian monarchy in 1893 (for which the United States formally apologized a century later) and annexed the islands in 1898.

The US Navy, aided by Filipino rebels, drove Spain out the Philippines in 1898. Washington thereafter waged a brutal counterinsurgency war from 1899 to 1902, culminating in the defeat of the guerrillas, who suffered hundreds of thousands of casualties, mostly from disease but also as a consequence of the United States' indiscriminate warfare. Resistance continued, especially in the predominately Muslim southern portions of the archipelago, until the 1910s. The Filipinos allied with the United States against Japanese occupation during World War II, and received independence thereafter in 1946. The United States maintained two major military bases in the Philippines until the 1990s and maintained close security ties with Philippine leaders and the military and police forces of the islands.

The peace treaty with Japan in 1951, sanctioning the ongoing US military occupation of Okinawa, solidified US naval domination of the North Pacific. The United States maintained political control and military bases in Guam, Samoa, Hawai'i, and the Philippines. In 1947, a year after the atomic bomb test on Bikini Atoll in the Marshall Islands, Washington took control of the former Japanese mandate islands, generally known as Micronesia, under a UN trusteeship. In the 1990s, the US-UN trusteeship formally ended with the establishment of three independent but still heavily US-influenced states of Micronesia, the Marshall Islands, and Palau, as well as a US territory, the Commonwealth of the Northern Mariana Islands.

SEE ALSO *Berlin Conference (1884–1885); Caribbean; Colonization Movement; Cuba; Empire of Liberty; Exceptionalism; General Allotment Act (Dawes Severalty Act, 1877); Hawai'i; Insular Possessions; Northwest Ordinance (1787)*

BIBLIOGRAPHY

Goldstein, Alyosha, ed. *Formations of United States Colonialism.* Durham, NC: Duke University Press, 2014.

Hixson, Walter L. *American Settler Colonialism: A History.* New York: Palgrave Macmillan, 2013.

Langley, Lester D. *The Banana Wars: United States Intervention in the Caribbean, 1898–1934.* Wilmington, DE: SR Books, 2002.

Loomba, Ania. *Colonialism/Postcolonialism.* 2nd ed. New York: Routledge, 2005.

Taylor, Alan. *American Colonies.* New York: Penguin, 2001.

Thompson, Lanny. *Imperial Archipelago: Representation and Rule in the Insular Territories under U.S. Dominion after 1898.* Honolulu: University of Hawai'i Press, 2010.

Walter L. Hixson
Distinguished Professor
University of Akron

COLONIZATION MOVEMENT

The colonization movement encompassed a broad array of efforts aimed at creating settlements for African Americans outside of the United States in the decades following the American Revolution through the era of the US Civil War. In the United States, the colonization movement was primarily concentrated within the American Colonization Society, which created the colony of Liberia in West Africa. However, during this era there were numerous proposals to create colonies in both North and South America, as well as in other parts of Africa. Although only a small number of African Americans ever left the United States for any of these settlements, the movement had a profound impact on US political culture and African American activism during the antebellum era.

EARLY COLONIZATION PROPOSALS

The earliest attempts to create colonies for African Americans grew from the crises of the North American slave system during the Revolutionary era. Concerned about the persistence of slavery in his state, Thomas Jefferson (1743–1826) in 1776 drafted a version of Virginia's new constitution that would have provided for the colonization of emancipated slaves to an unspecified region outside of the state. Although these sections were omitted from the final constitution, a few years later they would be included in Jefferson's influential book *Notes on the State of Virginia*, which helped disseminate his ideas about colonization. In subsequent decades, this basic idea was extended through proposals to colonize African Americans somewhere within North America, in part due to fears of slave revolts after uprisings in the French Caribbean colonies and after Gabriel Prosser's (c. 1776–1800) rebellion in Virginia in 1800.

As these proposals for North American colonies were beginning to circulate, the concept of an African colony was gaining ground as a result of British efforts to establish a colony for freed slaves in Sierra Leone. Founded in 1787, the colony was conceived under the guidance of the British abolitionist Granville Sharp (1735–1813) as a way to counteract the slave trade in West Africa and resettle former slaves throughout the British Empire, many of whom had been emancipated for aiding the British in their war with American colonists. The colony's anti–slave trade purpose would later be influential in the United States among colonizationists who would follow this model for a colony aimed at disseminating civilization, Christianity, and commerce in West Africa. Although few Africans Americans emigrated to Sierra Leone during this period, the colony's existence helped facilitate the first major black-led colonization effort, headed by the prominent New England merchant and ship captain Paul Cuffe (1759–1817). In 1811 and 1815, Cuffe led two expeditions to transport African American settlers to Sierra Leone. Cuffe also hoped to stimulate the economic development of Africa by forging political ties between Africa and the United States. Although Cuffe's efforts were largely unsuccessful, they inspired many Americans interested in colonization to focus their efforts on creating a colony in Africa.

AMERICAN COLONIZATION SOCIETY

In 1816, the American Society for Colonizing Free People of Color (later shortened to the American Colonization Society, or ACS) became the first US organization explicitly devoted to establishing colonies for African Americans. Beyond attracting new attention to the cause of African colonization, the ACS provided an institutional framework for a movement that had been scattered and disorganized. President James Monroe (1758–1831) supported the organization with limited funding through the 1819 Slave Trade Act. In 1821, the ACS used US military resources to pressure the Gola people of Cape Mesurado in West Africa to accept the founding of a settlement that would eventually be called Liberia.

From its beginnings, the ACS appealed to diverse, and sometimes conflicting, constituencies, including southern slaveholders, northern antislavery leaders, and evangelical Christians. Some ACS members used paternalistic rhetoric to argue that the colony could uplift African Americans by removing them from the debilitating effects of discrimination in the United States. Other members of the ACS were more focused on the task of removing from the United States "corrupt" and "degraded" free African Americans who were seen as troublesome populations in both the slaveholding South and the northern states where slavery had been recently abolished.

The racist and paternalistic language used by many ACS members signaled a definite shift in the colonization project away from the earlier efforts of Cuffe, which had been focused on the needs of black communities. Prominent black leaders who had previously supported various colonization plans, such as James Forten (1766–1842) and Richard Allen (1760–1831), now rallied northern black communities to oppose the movement. Opposition to African colonization schemes played a crucial role in defining northern black activism. This would be evident in the attention devoted to the issue in the pages of the first African American newspaper, *Freedom's Journal*, and in the influential pamphlet *Appeal to the Coloured Citizens of the World* (1829), by the black abolitionist David Walker (1796–1830).

The steadfast opposition of black northern activists eventually pushed many white colonizationists to condemn the movement as a vehicle for ending slavery. This shift was dramatically symbolized by the publication in 1832 of William Lloyd Garrison's (1805–1879) *Thoughts on African Colonization*, which encouraged fellow activists to abandon the colonization movement, as he had, and support the immediate abolition of slavery. Although the ACS suffered from these attacks and from financial setbacks in the 1830s, it would remain the dominant movement to colonize African Americans up through the Civil War.

ALTERNATIVES TO LIBERIA

The polarization created by the ACS would come to define debates within African American communities as they pursued colonization plans outside the framework offered by Liberia. These projects were often described as "emigration" plans to distinguish them from the stigma attached to the mainstream African colonization movement. One of the first of these alternatives was proposed by the president of Haiti, Jean-Pierre Boyer (1776–1850), who encouraged African Americans to become citizens of the first black republic. Other African Americans pursued plans to relocate to parts of the British Empire where slavery had been abolished, such as Upper Canada in the 1820s and 1830s and the West Indies in the 1840s and 1850s.

Only small numbers of African Americans actually migrated as a result of these proposals. However, after the passage of the Fugitive Slave Act in 1850, many African Americans reconsidered both emigration and the African colonization scheme as they lost hope for improving their situation in the United States. In 1852, Martin Delany (1812–1885) published the most robust African American proposal for emigration in his *Condition, Elevation, Emigration, and Destiny of Colored People of the United States*, which suggested possible colonization sites in the Caribbean, Central America, and Africa. Following Delany's proposals, and those advanced by other black leaders, such as Henry Highland Garnet (1815–1882), emigration became a subject of heated debate in many of the black political conventions of the era. Despite the rising interest in these plans among African Americans, none resulted in large-scale migration of African Americans.

While the number of black-led emigration plans rose in the 1850s, white colonizationists continued to promote Liberia. At the same time, they envisioned the founding of new colonies in the Americas. In the late 1850s and early 1860s, national politicians in the recently formed Republican Party, including Frank Blair Jr. (1821–1875) and James Doolittle (1815–1897), popularized plans to create colonies in Central America that would enable the end of slavery while allowing the United States to gain an economic foothold in the region.

As president, Abraham Lincoln (1809–1865) aggressively pursued similar proposals, eventually signing a contract with an American businessman who promised to help colonize freed slaves in territory he had purchased on the isthmus of Panama. Although the course of slave emancipation shifted Lincoln's focus away from colonization, he continued to entertain various colonization schemes until late in the war. After the end of the Civil War in 1865, colonization and emigration efforts would diminish significantly. Although the ACS continued to send emigrants to Liberia until the late nineteenth century, the society functioned more as a philanthropic organization, and its decline signaled the end of significant efforts among white Americans to establish colonies for black Americans. However, in the late nineteenth century, after the failure of Reconstruction to meaningfully incorporate African Americans as full citizens of the United States, schemes for emigration to Africa reemerged. These ideas continued to have a significant impact on the development of black nationalist and Pan-Africanist thought well into the twentieth century.

SEE ALSO *Africa; American Colonization Society; An Appeal to the Coloured Citizens of the World (David Walker, 1829); Back-to-Africa Movement; Liberia*

BIBLIOGRAPHY

Bilotta, James D. *Race and the Rise of the Republican Party, 1848–1865*. New York: Peter Lang, 1992. 2nd ed., Philadelphia, Xlibris, 2002.

Burin, Eric. *Slavery and the Peculiar Solution: A History of the American Colonization Society*. Gainesville: University Press of Florida, 2005.

Byrd, Alexander X. *Captives and Voyagers: Black Migrants across the Eighteenth-Century British Atlantic World*. Baton Rouge: Louisiana State University Press, 2008.

Clegg, Claude A. *The Price of Liberty: African Americans and the Making of Liberia*. Chapel Hill: University of North Carolina Press, 2004.

Guyatt, Nicholas. "'The Outskirts of Our Happiness': Race and the Lure of Colonization in the Early Republic." *Journal of American History* 95, 4 (2009): 986–1011.

Miller, Floyd John. *The Search for a Black Nationality: Black Emigration and Colonization, 1787–1863*. Urbana: University of Illinois Press, 1975.

Newman, Richard S. *The Transformation of American Abolitionism: Fighting Slavery in the Early Republic*. Chapel Hill: University of North Carolina Press, 2002.

Onuf, Peter S. "'To Declare Them a Free and Independent People': Race, Slavery, and National Identity in Jefferson's Thought." *Journal of the Early Republic* 18 (1998): 1–46.

Sidbury, James. *Becoming African in America: Race and Nation in the Early Black Atlantic*. New York: Oxford University Press, 2007.

Staudenraus, P. J. *The African Colonization Movement, 1816–1865*. New York: Columbia University Press, 1961.

Brandon Mills
Lecturer, Department of History
University of Colorado Denver

COMMUNISM

SEE *Cold War; Marx, Karl; Russia.*

COMMUNITARIAN SOCIALISM

Communitarian socialism, the larger reform movement organized around theories of ideal communities, became an important part of the reform landscape in the United States and Europe in the period between the 1820s and 1850s. In these planned communities, living spaces, occupations, and sometimes wages were shared among the group's members. Often characterized as utopian socialism by the movement's detractors, communitarians like the Fourierists shared many of their members with the other growing reform movements of the 1840s and 1850s, including abolition, women's rights, and those interested in free love (marital and sexual reform).

The ideas of the Scottish communitarian socialist Robert Owen (1771–1858) inspired some of the first planned communities organized along communitarian socialist lines in the United States (New Harmony, Indiana, 1825–1829). The theories of the French communitarian socialist Charles Fourier (1772–1837), however, produced the greatest flurry of communitarian activity and reflected a cosmopolitan network of European and North American reformers.

Fourier's theories centered on the creation of carefully organized communal living arrangements known as phalanxes. Each phalanx was supposed to house 1,400 to 1,600 individuals, many of whom would share living space in the large communal building known as the phalanstery. Functioning phalanxes were designed to be joint-stock corporations, with each member earning shares based on individual labor.

Fourier believed that the establishment of functioning phalanxes throughout the world would reorganize labor, eradicate poverty, and even reorder marriage and sexual relationships. In the phalanxes, labor would be shared and individuals would be free to try numerous vocations. The movement reached its peak in the United States in the mid-1840s when the American reformer Albert Brisbane (1809–1890) and the New York newspaper editor Horace Greeley (1811–1872) publicized Fourier's theories. In the United States, reformers, intellectuals, wealthy land speculators, southern plantation owners, and average Americans alike all expressed interest in the movement.

Fourierism emerged as a transnational movement—there was distinct interplay between the United States and Europe. Networks of Fourierists were created by American travel abroad, European emigration to the United States, the growth of communication and transportation technologies, and the rise of the radical press.

Fourier's ideas of secular communitarianism were brought to the United States by Brisbane, whose travels in Europe during the 1820s and 1830s brought him into Fourier's orbit. While Brisbane was in Europe studying, he sent letters about Fourier's theories to his former French tutor, Jean Manesca (1778?–1838), in New York City. Manesca and a group of Francophone expatriates created a social group dedicated to Fourier's ideas, the New York Fourierienne Society in the 1830s.

By the 1840s, Fourierism grew in popularity in the United States and Europe. Known as associationists in the United States and phalansteriens in France, Fourierists founded dozens of phalanxes during the 1840s, more than two dozen in the United States alone. The conversion of the Brook Farm Institute of Agriculture and Education from a transcendentalist community to a Fourierist phalanx was one of the most famous of the Fourierist experiments. These Fourierist communities spanned from the Northeast to the burgeoning West—places like Ohio and Indiana—and ultimately as far south as Texas. The larger international movement included a network of active acolytes and small phalanxes in parts of France, England, and even in French colonial outposts in Algeria.

Brisbane and the leadership of the organized American Fourierist movement remained in contact with French Fourierist leaders in Paris, including Victor Considerant (1808–1893). There was also a growing conversation between the North American Fourierist leadership and the British Fourierist leadership in the 1840s. British Fourierist reformers like J. J. Garth Wilkinson (1812–1899), and Hugh Doherty (1810?–1891) were central in expanding Fourierism's reach.

American Fourierists traveled in Europe throughout the 1840s and 1850s, and frequently met with their Fourierist counterparts while abroad. During the French Revolution of 1848, American and British Fourierists arrived in Paris on the eve of the bloody June Days. The revolution inspired a distinct moment of solidarity between the Europeans and Americans.

European Fourierists also traveled to the United States and visited Fourierist communitarian experiments like Brook Farm (West Roxbury, Massachusetts 1841–1847) and the North American Phalanx (Monmouth County, New Jersey 1843–1853), sometimes settling and living at these communities for extended periods. In 1855, Considerant helped establish a Fourierist community near Dallas, Texas, with a group of French, Belgian, and Swiss émigrés (La Reunion, 1855–1860).

International contact increased exponentially with the establishment of a Fourierist press. From the 1830s to the 1850s, dozens of Fourierist newspapers emerged in Europe and the United States, some with an intense commitment to sectarianism, and others, like the French *Démocratie Pacifique* and the sympathetic American newspaper the *New-York Tribune*, hoping to reach a wider audience. The use of more advanced communication and transportation technology, such as faster steamships and the telegraph, enabled increased communication between Fourierists on both sides of the Atlantic. Fourierists in the United States frequently read excerpts from European Fourierist newspapers at their weekly meetings.

The cosmopolitanism of the Fourierist movement was highlighted by the annual celebration of Fourier's birthday. Each April 7, Fourierists in the United States, Europe, and Algeria would celebrate Fourier's birthday, often reading congratulatory notes and updates from the Fourierists abroad. Fourierism ultimately waned in the 1850s and 1860s as phalanxes continued to fail and members became absorbed in other reform movements, such as the free love movement, or in the field of politics.

SEE ALSO *Transatlantic Reform*

BIBLIOGRAPHY

Beecher, Jonathan. *Charles Fourier: The Visionary and His World.* Berkeley: University of California Press, 1987.

Beecher, Jonathan. *Victor Considerant and the Rise and Fall of French Romantic Socialism.* Berkeley: University of California Press, 2001.

Delano, Sterling F. *Brook Farm: The Dark Side of Utopia.* Cambridge, MA: Belknap Press, 2004.

Guarneri, Carl J. *The Utopian Alternative: Fourierism in Nineteenth-Century America.* Ithaca, NY: Cornell University Press, 1991.

Megan Perle Bowman
Georgia State University

CONFEDERATE STATES OF AMERICA

Confederate efforts to obtain formal recognition from the international community catapulted the American Civil War into an international event. The war that broke out in 1861 after southern Americans separated from the United States and created the Confederate States of America had an impact on European and Latin American nations, particularly those with colonies or commercial interest in the Caribbean and North America. Although the American war had global implications because of European possessions around the world, Confederate diplomats limited their efforts to the European powers. The decisions and responses of foreign governments to both Confederate and Union actions not only influenced events in Europe, but affected the course and outcome of the war.

THE QUESTION OF FORMAL RECOGNITION

The Confederate States of America was organized with remarkable speed. By February 1861, Jefferson Davis (1807–1889) had been selected as the interim president. Davis immediately pursued formal recognition from the international community. Formal recognition would allow the fledgling nation to negotiate defense alliances and favorable commercial treaties. Moreover, recognition legitimized the existence of a nation as part of the international community.

Nineteenth-century international law provided that new governments merited recognition when they establish de facto independence. The definition of *de facto independence* was vague, but nevertheless presented the Confederates with an early diplomatic opportunity. Davis immediately dispatched three envoys to the capitals of Europe to pursue recognition. William Lowndes Yancey (1814–1863), a fire-eating radical from Alabama who advocated the reestablishment of the international slave trade, was the nominal leader of the group. Despite several meetings with Lord John Russell (1792–1878), the British foreign minister, Yancey returned home in the late summer of 1861 after failing to accomplish his mission.

EXPANSION INTO LATIN AMERICA

The American Civil War presented the imperial powers of Europe with an opportunity to advance their territorial and commercial ambitions in North America. Napoleon III (1808–1873), the emperor of France, wasted little time in mounting an expedition into Mexico, but the desperate struggle in America prevented both North and South from confronting the French incursion. French troops captured Mexico City and soon controlled over half of Mexico. With little more than token diplomatic resistance from the United States, Napoleon III created a puppet government and installed Austrian archduke Ferdinand Maximilian Joseph (1832–1867) as emperor of Mexico.

Throughout the 1850s, the United States and particularly those slave states now composing the Confederacy had pursued expansionist ambitions in Latin America. In 1861, the Confederates had visions of increasing the size of their "slaveholding republic" by annexing parts of Mexico, Latin America, and particularly Cuba. The French intervention required the Confederates to reexamine their priorities. Southerners needed French support to secure access to the port of Matamoros to exchange cotton for arms, medicine, and other necessities. This superseded any expansionist ambitions, and the Confederates, however reluctantly, tolerated the French presence in Mexico.

THE UNION BLOCKADE

The Confederates were presented with a diplomatic opportunity in April 1861, when Abraham Lincoln (1809–1865) issued the blockade proclamation. A blockade was illegal under international law unless it was declared against a nation at war. Moreover, a legitimate blockade could only be recognized if the blockading country possessed sufficient naval power to enforce it. The United States could not meet these requirements because the US government did not recognize the Confederate States of America and the US Navy was incapable of enforcing a blockade.

The British stopped short of formally recognizing the Confederacy, but Britain did declare it a belligerent party. Technically, belligerent status would allow the British and other neutral nations to engage in normal commercial activity with the Confederate States. However, the Confederates were ineffective in pressing the British to reject the blockade and forcibly open Confederate ports. The United States had traditionally supported commercial activity by neutral nations in times of war, but in 1861 the circumstances dictated a change in their interpretation of international maritime law. The British grudgingly agreed not to force the issue and accepted, if not formally, the blockade.

THE *TRENT* INCIDENT

The question of recognition was complicated for the Europeans, particularly the British and French. Despite the apparent justification for recognition presented by the Confederates, the Europeans were reluctant to risk armed confrontation with the United States. The Confederates decided to send two special envoys, John Slidell (1793–1871) and James Murray Mason (1798–1871), to lobby in Paris and London, respectively, for recognition and assistance. The two men departed and, after running through the Union blockade, transferred to the British mail-packet ship *Trent*. On November 8, 1861, the American warship *San Jacinto*, under the command of Charles Wilkes (1798–1877), intercepted the *Trent* and removed Mason and Slidell from the ship. When word reached London, the British authorities demanded an apology and the return of the two Confederates to the protection of the British flag, demands that were accompanied by threats of military action. After intensive deliberations, the Lincoln administration complied with British demands, and European intervention was averted. Although the Confederates had little control over the incident with the *Trent*, it was the closest that the British came to intervening directly in the American Civil War.

COTTON DIPLOMACY

With the arrival of Mason and Slidell, Confederate hopes for foreign recognition accelerated into requests for military aid. From the outset, Confederate leaders had decided to withhold cotton to create an economic crisis in Europe that would force Britain and France to aid the Confederacy, a strategy known as "cotton diplomacy." In 1860, finished textiles accounted for one-third of British exports. Britain's textile mills employed millions directly and sustained numerous peripheral commercial activities. The possibility of a cotton famine in Europe was a real threat to economic stability. Confederate operatives thought their strategy would force the British to at least recognize the "cotton kingdom," even if they did not intervene militarily. However, for a variety of reasons, including European warehouses filled with large stockpiles of cotton that had been purchased in 1860, withholding cotton as a diplomatic strategy failed to collapse an integrated and diverse British economy.

Slidell and Mason used cotton to collateralize a $3 million loan arranged through the Erlanger investment bank in Paris. The proceeds from the sale of the bonds were used to support the clandestine efforts of Captain James Dunwoody Bulloch (1823–1901) to purchase and construct ships for the Confederate navy in the shipyards of both England and France. Both European countries had neutrality laws to prevent such activities, but Bullock was effective in circumventing the British Foreign Enlistment Act of 1819, at least for a while. The construction and escape of the Confederate raiders *Alabama* and *Florida* provoked international controversy that continued until 1872, when arbitration settled US claims against Great Britain for $15 million.

CONCLUSION

For more than four years, the Confederate States of America operated as an independent sovereign nation with a functioning central government, an active foreign policy, and a large and well-equipped army. The Confederacy never received formal recognition from the international community and was never legitimized by the Lincoln administration. Nevertheless, Southern diplomatic efforts contributed to the escalation of the American conflict into a war with international implications. Confederate dependence on a cotton strategy elevated economic coercion as a diplomatic tactic to unprecedented levels of acceptance within the community of nations. Confederate purchases of war materials in Europe and the transportation of embargoed supplies led to new interpretations of international law for the protection of neutral shipping. With the collapse of the Confederacy in the spring of 1865, the United States could again engage in a unified diplomatic outreach. For their part, Southerners rejoined the Union and cooperated with their former adversaries to expel the French from Mexico and return the United States to a position of influence and prestige in North America.

SEE ALSO *The Civil War*

BIBLIOGRAPHY

Case, Lynn M., and Warren F. Spencer. *The United States and France: Civil War Diplomacy*. Philadelphia: University of Pennsylvania Press, 1970.

Crook, D. P. *The North, the South, and the Powers, 1861–1865.* New York: Wiley, 1974.

Delaney, Robert W. "Matamoros, Port for Texas during the Civil War." *Southwestern Historical Quarterly* 58, 4 (1955): 473–487.

Ferris, Norman. *The Trent Affair: A Diplomatic Crisis.* Knoxville: University of Tennessee Press, 1977.

Foreman, Amanda. *A World on Fire: An Epic History of Two Nations Divided.* London: Allen Lane, 2010.

Gentry, Judith F. "A Confederate Success in Europe: The Erlanger Loan." *Journal of Southern History* 36, 2 (1970): 157–188.

Hubbard, Charles M. *The Burden of Confederate Diplomacy.* Knoxville: University of Tennessee Press, 1998.

Jones, Howard. *Blue and Gray Diplomacy: A History of Union and Confederate Foreign Relations.* Chapel Hill: University of North Carolina Press, 2011.

Lester, Richard I. *Confederate Finance and Purchasing in Great Britain.* Charlottesville: University Press of Virginia, 1975.

Merli, Frank. *Great Britain and the Confederate Navy, 1861–1865.* Bloomington: Indiana University Press, 1970.

Owsley, Frank L. *King Cotton Diplomacy: Foreign Relations and the Confederate States of America.* 2nd ed. Revised by Harriet Chappell Owsley. Chicago: University of Chicago Press, 1959.

Romero, Matías. *The Mexican Lobby: Matías Romero in Washington, 1861–1867.* Edited and translated by Thomas D. Schoonover, with Ebba Wesener Schoonover. Lexington: University Press of Kentucky, 1986.

Spencer, Warren F. *The Confederate Navy in Europe.* Tuscaloosa: University of Alabama Press, 1983.

Charles M. Hubbard
Professor of History and Lincoln Historian
Lincoln Memorial University, Harrogate, Tennessee

CONGRESS FOR CULTURAL FREEDOM

The Congress for Cultural Freedom (CCF) was founded following its inaugural conference held in West Berlin on June 26 to 29, 1950. For the next seventeen years, it coordinated and supported conferences, exhibitions, and journals around the world with the purpose of defending and expanding freedom of thought and expression in opposition to totalitarian threats. Representative of the "noncommunist left," the CCF opposed neutralism as much as it did Soviet-style communism. A permanent Secretariat was established in Paris, and an Executive Committee took care of the running of the organization. Financing for the CCF was publicly declared to come from the Ford Foundation and various private philanthropies, such as the Farfield Foundation, but in 1966 to 1967 it was revealed via the *New York Times* and *Ramparts* that large-scale funding had also come from the Central Intelligence Agency (CIA). This revelation led to questions concerning the credibility of the CCF as an organization devoted to freedom of expression, although the debate among historians continues as to how far the CIA actually "controlled" the CCF. After many prominent members resigned, the CCF was reformed in September 1967 as the International Association for Cultural Freedom (IACF). Grants from the Ford Foundation sustained the IACF for several more years, but in 1979 the IACF too was closed, its purpose no longer clear.

The American input and influence in the CCF was strong from the beginning. The CIA may have provided a large amount of the financial support, but the CCF's contribution to the field of culture and ideas was sustained by a community of anti-Stalinist (often ex-communist) intellectuals, who saw it as their mission to expose the repressiveness and falsities of the communist cause. As a supportive arm for the Paris Secretariat, the American Committee for Cultural Freedom (ACCF) was created in 1951, involving influential writers, philosophers, scientists, and cultural figures, such as Sidney Hook, James Burnham, Daniel Bell, Arthur Schlesinger Jr., Lionel Trilling, Reinhold Niebuhr, Elia Kazan, John Dos Passos, Robert Oppenheimer, and Mary McCarthy. Abstract expressionist artists Jackson Pollock and Robert Motherwell were also members for a time. The American Committee wanted to run a combative campaign against communist propaganda, and some of its members were less willing to accept criticism of US policies than others associated with the CCF. This resulted in major conflicts with the Paris Secretariat in 1952 to 1953 over the trial and execution of Julius and Ethel Rosenberg, the anticommunist campaign of Senator Joseph McCarthy, and lastly the anti-Americanism of Bertrand Russell, one of the CCF's honorary chairmen. As a result, the ACCF was effectively disbanded in 1957.

The CCF began as a transatlantic network, with nineteen of the twenty-one nationalities represented at the inaugural conference being European. This complexion changed after the mid-1950s, as the Cold War stalemate in Central Europe and the decline of the communist threat in the West moved the ideological contest between capitalist democracy and communist collectivism to the rapidly decolonizing Third World. Between 1951 and 1966, the CCF organized major conferences and seminars in Bombay (Mumbai), Rangoon (Yangon), Mexico City, Tokyo, Ibadan, Canberra, Cairo, Khartoum, Freetown, Dakar, Manila, Montevideo, Nairobi, and Kuala Lumpur. In this way, it hoped to overcome any North-South divide by building a transnational community of intellectuals committed to protecting the freedom of cultural expression. Only this, in their view, could ensure cultural excellence and progress.

The CCF pursued this agenda in various ways. Firstly, it benefited from its structural power as a source of philanthropic funding and organization. The CCF created a kind of cultural "habitus" for a generation of intellectuals who had migrated or been displaced by war and totalitarian repression. Part of the CCF's lasting legacy was exactly in being able to provide support for this intellectual diaspora.

Secondly, the CCF solidified its cultural presence by establishing and sponsoring an array of cultural-literary journals around the world, starting with *Preuves* in France. These publications avoided direct confrontation with left-wing opponents, and editorials chose a middle-ground position that mixed political analysis with cultural review essays to ensure a broader public appeal. Most notorious was *Encounter* in London, a high-profile literary review that ran from 1954 to 1991 and was edited by Irving Kristol, Stephen Spender, and Melvin Lasky. By the mid-1960s, the CCF could point to a wide network of publications in various languages, including *Tempo Presente* (Italy), *Der Monat* (West Germany), *Cuardernos* (Latin America), *Quest* (India), *Quadrant* (Australia), *Hiwar* (Lebanon), and *Black Orpheus* (Nigeria). Some, such as *Minerva* (originally set up by Chicago philosopher Edward Shils) and *China Quarterly* (established by Harvard emeritus Rod MacFarquhar), have adapted and continued beyond the CCF years.

Thirdly, the CCF pursued various intellectual campaigns that sought to engage with and interpret social and political change in the modern world. For CCF General Secretary Nicolas Nabokov, this involved linking up cultural developments in different parts of the world and broadening awareness and appreciation of modernist culture in literature, music, and the arts in general. The Frenchman Raymond Aron and the Americans Daniel Bell, Edward Shils, and Seymour Martin Lipset argued for the "end of ideology," whereby politics was considered no longer a contest between rival ideological movements because the forces of industrialization were causing both democratic capitalist and authoritarian collectivist systems to adopt similar methods of socioeconomic management. The evolution of societies down similar technocratic paths of urbanization and development, and what this meant for democracy, individuality, worker participation, and elite formation, attracted more attention in the 1960s.

Operating as a global cultural philanthropist, the CCF attempted to connect intellectual debate across the different continents and shift the debate away from simplistic observations on East-West competition. In doing so, it not only aimed to merge North American and European opinion into a definable "Western," transatlantic tradition, but also to open up and strengthen intellectual channels with the newly independent, industrializing states of Asia and Africa. Although the issue of CIA funding has gathered the most attention, the intellectual-cultural output of the CCF and the networks it maintained undoubtedly stretch beyond any simplistic accusations of propaganda.

SEE ALSO *Central Intelligence Agency (CIA); Ford Foundation*

BIBLIOGRAPHY

Berghahn, Volker R. *America and the Intellectual Cold Wars in Europe: Shepard Stone between Philanthropy, Academy, and Diplomacy.* Princeton, NJ: Princeton University Press, 2001.

Coleman, Peter. *The Liberal Conspiracy: The Congress for Cultural Freedom and the Struggle for the Mind of Postwar Europe.* New York: Free Press, 1989.

Grémion, Pierre. *Intelligence de l'anticommunisme: Le Congrès pour la liberté de la culture à Paris, 1950–1975.* Paris: Fayard, 1995.

Saunders, Frances Stonor. *Who Paid the Piper? The CIA and the Cultural Cold War.* London: Granta, 1999.

Scott-Smith, Giles. *The Politics of Apolitical Culture: The Congress for Cultural Freedom, the CIA, and Postwar Hegemony.* London: Routledge, 2002.

Giles Scott-Smith
Professor of Diplomatic History
Leiden University

CONTEMPORARY GENOCIDES AND US POLICY

This essay considers US foreign policy as it pertains to three late twentieth-century instances of genocide: Cambodia, Rwanda, and Bosnia. The main findings from these cases suggest that the sources of US foreign policy in response to genocide during this period can be found in the realm of domestic politics. The policies were largely dictated by public war-weariness, whereby politicians had little to gain and much to lose electorally by committing the United States to potentially controversial and costly military involvement abroad. Importantly, this trend began to change in the mid-1990s in the aftermath of the Bosnia crisis, when failing to respond to genocide became increasingly electorally important for US presidents.

CAMBODIA

A prominent instance of genocide in contemporary history occurred in Cambodia between 1975 and 1979, when the Communist Khmer Rouge (KR) regime led by Pol Pot (1925–1998) sought to create a regime of agrarian socialism that was founded on communist principles advanced by Joseph Stalin (1879–1953) and Mao Zedong

(1893–1976). Once the KR took power in 1975, it began forcibly evacuating the urban populations to the countryside and cut off virtually all contact with the outside world. For the next three years, the KR would implement their plan of returning Cambodia to its "mythic past," which included purifying Cambodian society along ethnic, racial, and social lines, eventually resulting in 2 million deaths. Children were taken away from their parents and sent to labor camps; schools, universities, factories, and hospitals were shut down; religion was banned; and religious leaders, intellectuals, and other educated people were tortured and murdered along with their extended families. Various ethnic minorities were also targeted for destruction, including Chinese, Vietnamese, and Thai, as well as thousands of Christians and Cham Muslims (Etcheson 2005, chap. 2).

The reaction of the US government to these atrocities was significantly influenced by the US role in neighboring Vietnam during the 1960s, where in its quest to oppose the spread of communism, the United States welcomed the 1970 overthrow of Cambodian Prince Norodom Sihanouk (1922–2012) by the prime minister, Lon Nol (1913–1985), who was staunchly anticommunist and pro-American, but also corrupt, despotic, and incompetent (Power 2003, 92). Thus, when Pol Pot (then known as Saloth Sar) and his exiled followers sought to depose Lon Nol's regime, they had significant assistance from supporters of Prince Sihanouk, as well as Vietnamese Communists. When the KR's victory seemed imminent, and alarming reports of atrocities made their way to Washington, few in the US Congress and public trusted the warnings of officials from the Richard Nixon (1913–1994) and Gerald Ford (1913–2006) administrations, whose reputations had been tainted by the unpopular Vietnam conflict and the Watergate scandal. Further US military involvement in Indochina—even to stop a genocide in progress—was thought by many in Congress to be likely to do more harm than good (*Washington Post* 1975). This was despite the fact that in May 1975, Henry Kissinger (b. 1923) testified to the US Congress that once in power, the KR would attempt to eliminate all political opponents (Williams et al. 1985, 316). Although the United States had finally begun to officially condemn the KR in 1978, Vietnam's invasion of Cambodia in late 1978 caused the United States to side with the genocidal KR against its (former) enemy, although it was Vietnam's military victory over the KR that ultimately dislodged the regime's grip on power and halted the genocide (Power 2003, 141).

RWANDA

Nearly twenty years later in the Great Lakes region of Africa, a civil war between rival ethnic groups in Rwanda—Hutus and Tutsis—was briefly paused in 1993 by a United Nations (UN) brokered peace agreement, which authorized a peacekeeping force to patrol the region. The conflict had escalated in previous years when an exiled Tutsi rebel group called the Rwandan Patriotic Front (RPF) invaded and attempted to depose the Hutu-led government of Rwanda. The peace agreement quickly broke down when, in April 1994, the Hutu-dominated government began implementing its plan for the extermination of all members of the Tutsi ethnic group in Rwanda. The plan involved empowering local Hutu militia, called Interahamwe, to locate and murder Tutsis, as well as inciting civilian Hutus over the radio waves to identify and murder their Tutsi neighbors. In a matter of one hundred days, nearly 800,000 Tutsis and sympathetic Hutus were murdered—many by being hacked to death with machetes (Dallaire 2003, 263–421).

Like the US response to the Cambodian genocide, the US response to Rwanda was heavily influenced by prior unpopular military involvement in the region—in this case, the controversial US action in Somalia less than a year before. In short, the political backlash against the failed US operation in Somalia, which included the so-called Black Hawk Down incident, led the Bill Clinton (b. 1946) administration to develop a policy that made military involvement in Rwanda virtually impossible unless it could be demonstrated that it would advance US interests (Heinze 2007, 363). Not only did the United States not want to get pressured into "another Somalia," US and UN officials both reasoned that UN intervention should be reserved for when it could have a reasonable chance for success. If Somalia was any indication, intervention in Rwanda was bound to fail (Barnett 2002, 163). In fact, US officials were so careful to avoid creating any expectation for a US intervention that they avoided using the term *genocide* to describe the situation, out of a fear that a finding of genocide might force the US government to act pursuant to its obligations in the 1948 Genocide Convention (Heinze 2007, 366). In the end, the genocide was only halted with the military victory of the RPF, which eventually deposed the Hutu leadership and forced the main perpetrators of the genocide into neighboring Zaire (now the Democratic Republic of the Congo), causing significant instability there for years to come.

BOSNIA

Around this same time, the US and its partners in the North Atlantic Treaty Organization (NATO) had been involved in trying to halt the violence that broke out when Yugoslavia began to disintegrate in 1991, an episode characterized by ethnic violence among the region's Serbian, Croatian, and Bosnian Muslim populations. The multiethnic republic of Bosnia and Herzegovina was the site of some of the most brutal atrocities—most notably the Srebrenica massacre of 1995, which the International Criminal Tribunal for the former Yugoslavia found in 2004 to have constituted genocide (Milanović 2007, 669–694). The genocide consisted of the execution of more than seven thousand Bosnian men and boys and the forcible transfer of nearly thirty thousand Bosnian women by military and paramilitary units of the short-lived Republika Srpska—the Serb-controlled portion of Bosnia (Power 2003, 392).

The city of Srebrenica had been designated a "UN safe area" since 1993, with the idea that peacekeepers would patrol the city and could call upon NATO air support if needed under an elaborate "dual key" system, wherein any NATO military action had to be approved by both UN civilian leadership and NATO military officials. So while US policy was to rely on air power and not use ground troops, European NATO partners were additionally reluctant to deploy air power out of concern for civilian casualties and the safety of their own ground forces (Chollet 2005, 8–9, 184–185). In addition, US policy during the time was focused on gaining access to the Serb prison camps, rather than military coercion, due to continued domestic squeamishness in light of US casualties in Somalia, and Belgian casualties in Rwanda. Thus, when the commander of the peacekeepers protecting Srebrenica called for air support, the "dual key" arrangement left NATO unable to respond in time.

For its part, the United States was abiding by preexisting policy constraints in place since Somalia, while the "dual key" arrangement that put the onus on European partners provided the political cover to remain uninvolved. Importantly, once the horrors of Srebrenica became publicized and seized upon by President Clinton's political opponents, the US policy of noninvolvement became increasingly untenable, paving the way for a US-led air campaign against the Serbs that helped end the conflict (Power 2003, 406–422). This marked an important turning point in US politics where, unlike in Cambodia or Rwanda, allowing genocide to continue was perceived to be sufficiently politically costly to impel a more decisive response.

SEE ALSO *Clinton, William Jefferson; Human Rights; Interventionism; Yugoslav Wars*

BIBLIOGRAPHY

Barnett, Michael. *Eyewitness to a Genocide: The United Nations and Rwanda.* Ithaca, NY: Cornell University Press, 2002.

"Cambodian Aid: Administration's Choice." *Washington Post,* March 17, 1975.

Chollet, Derek H. *The Road to the Dayton Accords: A Study of American Statecraft.* New York: Palgrave Macmillan, 2005.

Dallaire, Roméo, with Brent Beardsley. *Shake Hands with the Devil: The Failure of Humanity in Rwanda.* New York: Carroll and Graf, 2003.

Etcheson, Craig. *After the Killing Fields: Lessons from the Cambodian Genocide.* Lubbock: Texas Tech University Press, 2005.

Heinze, Eric A. "The Rhetoric of Genocide in US Foreign Policy: Rwanda and Darfur Compared." *Political Science Quarterly* 122, 3 (2007): 359–383.

Milanović, Marko. "State Responsibility for Genocide: A Follow-Up." *European Journal of International Law* 18, 4 (2007): 669–694.

Power, Samantha. *"A Problem from Hell": America and the Age of Genocide.* New York: Perennial, 2003.

Williams, William Appleman, Thomas McCormick, Lloyd C. Gardner, and Walter LaFeber. *America in Vietnam: A Documentary History.* London: Norton, 1985.

Eric A. Heinze
Associate Professor of Political Science and International Studies
University of Oklahoma

COOLIES

The debate over "coolie labor" in the United States was central to struggles over freedom and slavery. Although coolies signed contracts indenturing them for periods of three to eight years, and contracts were supposed to symbolize freedom in liberal societies, abolitionists and white labor unions argued that coolie labor was a thinly disguised form of slavery.

The derogatory term *coolie* refers to low-paid manual laborers from Asia. The word *coolie* derives from Tamil (*kuli*), Urdu (*quli*), Chinese (*kuli*), and possibly from the Turkish word *qui*, meaning "slave," but Europeans first started using it in the eighteenth century to refer to low-paid Asian manual laborers. Although *coolie* never has had a legal definition, it was used widely from the mid-nineteenth through the early twentieth century throughout the Americas.

The trade in Asian labor began in the sixteenth century as millions of workers from China and India migrated to Southeast Asia to work on plantations. By the early nineteenth century, the British began transporting Indian contract laborers to their colonies in the Caribbean to fill the labor vacuum after the abolition of the African slave trade. As many as 430,000 Asians, mostly Indians, were brought to the British West Indies as indentured laborers from 1831 to 1920. From 1847 to 1874, 150,000 Chinese contract laborers were brought to Cuba, and another 100,000 were transported to Peru. In all, three-quarters of a million Asian indentured laborers were imported to Latin America and the Caribbean.

Unlike in Latin America, where imperial and national governments regulated the coolie trade and oversaw contracts, in the United States, Chinese migrants signed private agreements with employers; it is thus hard to count accurately the number of "coolies" in the United States. Before exclusion in 1882, 258,000 Chinese were admitted to the United States, while afterward (1882–1943), there were at least 300,000 registered entries. An equal number of Chinese sneaked across the Canadian or Mexican border or entered by boat from Cuba during the exclusion era (Young 2014, 160). From 1885 to 1949, more than 97,000 Chinese entered Canada. In both the United States and Canada, it may be assumed that the majority of these Chinese were manual laborers. However, counting coolies is beside the point. Some Chinese came to the United States as contract laborers, others came on the credit-ticket system or as "free" migrants, but for the general public, they were all viewed as coolies.

Opposition to Chinese coolies came from white labor unions concerned about competition with cheap Asian workers and from slave abolitionists who feared the reintroduction of slavery by other means. In 1862 President Abraham Lincoln (1809–1865) signed an "Act to Prohibit the 'Coolie Trade' by American Citizens in American Vessels." The Anti-Coolie bill left it vague as to who counted as a "coolie," but it reaffirmed the right of "free and voluntary emigration of any Chinese subject." This bill was simultaneously the last slave-trade law and the first federal immigration regulation (Jung 2006, 37).

Notwithstanding the Anti-Coolie bill or the 1885 Foran Act prohibiting all contract laborers from entering the country, efforts to recruit Chinese contract laborers continued into the twentieth century. In the late 1860s, Chinese coolies were imported to the United States to work on railroads in New Jersey and plantations throughout the South, especially Louisiana. Some of the schemes failed but several succeeded in importing hundreds of Chinese coolies from plantations in Cuba (Cohen 1984, 53–55).

Cornelius Koopmanschap (1828–1882), a Dutch-born recruiter of Chinese laborers, spearheaded the most far-reaching campaign to import 100,000 coolies to the United States. In July 1869, Koopmanschap met in Memphis with five hundred delegates from all over the South to establish the Mississippi Valley Immigration Labor Company. After the Tennessee legislature voted to prohibit importation of Chinese workers, Koopmanschap moved his operation to Louisiana, where he found more support for his plan. In spite of a State Department ruling that prohibited his scheme, Koopmanschap succeeded in bringing in a few shipments of several hundred Chinese (Jung 2006, 113–117).

Although overt attempts to import Asian contract laborers ended in the 1870s, Asians continued to come under various forms of indenture that were not visible to state authorities. The 1882 Chinese Exclusion Act helped to cast all Chinese as undesirable coolies. In newspapers and popular magazines, low-paid Asian workers were depicted as coolies well into the twentieth century whether they came as free laborers or not. Thus, even though anti-coolie legislation was supposed to end bonded labor, it served to cast Chinese and other Asians as perpetual aliens unfit for citizenship.

SEE ALSO *Alien Contract Labor Law/Foran Act (1885); China; Chinese Exclusion Act (1882); Immigration Quotas*

BIBLIOGRAPHY

Cohen, Lucy M. *Chinese in the Post–Civil War South.* Baton Rouge: Louisiana State University Press, 1984.

Jung, Moon-Ho. *Coolies and Cane: Race, Labor, and Sugar in the Age of Emancipation.* Baltimore, MD: Johns Hopkins University Press, 2006.

Meagher, Arnold J. *The Coolie Trade: The Traffic in Chinese Laborers to Latin America, 1847–1874.* Philadelphia: Xlibris, 2008.

Northrup, David. *Indentured Labor in the Age of Imperialism, 1834–1922.* New York: Cambridge University Press, 1995.

Young, Elliott. *Alien Nation: Chinese Migration in the Americas from the Coolie Era through World War II.* Chapel Hill: University of North Carolina Press, 2014.

Yun, Lisa. *The Coolie Speaks: Chinese Indentured Laborers and African Slaves in Cuba.* Philadelphia: Temple University Press, 2008.

Elliott Young
Lewis & Clark College

COPLEY, JOHN SINGLETON

1738–1815

The artist John Singleton Copley, born on Boston's Long Wharf in 1738, was connected to the Atlantic from his youth. Amid the hustle and bustle of a colonial port, Copley witnessed the goods and people of the Atlantic world on the move. His mother's remarriage to Peter Pelham (c. 1695–1751), an English-born painter and engraver, after his father's death, connected Copley to the cultural as well as economic circuits of the British Empire.

EARLY CAREER IN AMERICA AS A PORTRAIT PAINTER

Following in his stepfather's footsteps, the Boston colonial picked up the paintbrush as a teenager and began the lifelong process of fashioning himself as a British artist. He

The Death of Major Peirson, 6 January 1781, ***oil painting by John Singleton Copley depicting the French invasion of the British island of Jersey.*** *With a subject ripped from the London headlines, Copley's painting pays tribute to the sacrifice of an English major killed while defending the island of Jersey—situated in the English Channel—from French invasion during the American Revolutionary War. Copley may have shared his personal concerns regarding the war in the composition, as the fleeing women and children are actually portraits of his wife and family. The painting also features a representation of a black African that is unusual for the eighteenth century: Peirson's servant, Pompey, is at the center of the action, raising a gun to avenge his master's death.* UNIVERSAL HISTORY ARCHIVE/UNIVERSALIMAGESGROUP/GETTY IMAGES

learned his trade by copying black-and-white engraved prints of old master paintings that found their way across the Atlantic from Europe to the colonies. He would later complain, "In this Country … there is no examples of Art, except what is to [be] met with in a few prints indiferently exicuted, from which it is not possable to learn much" (Copley [1766] 1914, 51). Absorbing what lessons he could from these works, Copley created for himself the classical training of British artists.

In the 1760s, Copley earned a reputation as a painter of portraits for the men and women of Boston's elite. Copley represented his colonial sitters as genteel participants in a transatlantic society. Surrounded with luxury imports as well as the tools of their trades, the subjects of these portraits perform a British imperial identity that emphasizes cultural kinship with those in the metropole. Copley's talent opened doors to a more elevated rank in society, allowing the artist to mold himself into the image of his patrons. His advancement was further enhanced by his marriage to Susanna "Sukie" Clarke, whose father was an agent of the East India Company.

Despite professional success, Copley chafed against the confined opportunities for the ambitious artist in the colonies. He aspired to a grander form of painting than the copying of likenesses and to a wider appreciation for his talents within the empire. Copley struck up a correspondence with Benjamin West (1738–1820), his fellow American artist and contemporary, who had left Pennsylvania to establish himself in London in 1763. West was active in the Royal Academy and enjoyed the patronage of the king; he encouraged Copley in his ambitions.

Copley first came to the attention of the London art world in 1766 with the exhibition of a portrait of his stepbrother, Henry Pelham (1749–1806), known as *A Boy with a Flying Squirrel* (1765). With its dazzling surfaces and sure handling of detail, the painting made quite a stir, winning praise from the president of the Royal Academy—Joshua Reynolds (1723–1792)—among others. The flying squirrel, a species native to North America, is a subtle nod to the artist's birthplace, as well as a clever metaphor for the painting's own "flight" across the Atlantic.

The increasing political unrest of the early 1770s profoundly affected Copley's family. The tea dumped into the harbor in December 1773 by the "Sons of Liberty" at the Boston Tea Party had been consigned for sale to Copley's father-in-law, among other Loyalist merchants. During this period, Copley painted prominent members of the Patriot cause, most famously Paul Revere (1735–1818) and Samuel Adams (1722–1803). However, he also painted British officers and Loyalists. Copley's loyalties as a transatlantic figure in the period of American independence have been a perennially debated aspect of the artist's biography. Claiming Copley as a patriotic American or a loyalist Briton, and assessing his work accordingly, was the central thrust of early studies of the man. However, his family and friendships, his written correspondence, his art, and his eventual departure for England, suggest a profound and painful ambivalence on the subject, similar to that of many colonists with ties to both sides of the ocean.

MOVE TO LONDON AND SHIFT TO HISTORY PAINTING

Copley set sail for London on June 10, 1774, nine days before the British set up a blockade on Boston Harbor. While he expected to eventually return to America, it was in fact the last time he would see the land of his birth. After a season in London, Copley embarked on a European Grand Tour, taking in Paris and Italy. Traveling to ancient classical sites and seeing in vivid color the works of Titian (c. 1488–1576) and Raphael (1483–1520) that he had copied from black-and-white prints as a youth, Copley absorbed the elements of a British artistic education of which he had always dreamed. During these travels, Copley learned of the outbreak of war in America through delayed and fragmented news reports and letters. His own letters to his family suggest that he weighed a profound pride in his native country alongside a desire for a unified empire.

Returning to London in 1775, Copley went to work incorporating the lessons of his Grand Tour into his art. His painting shifted both in style and subject matter as he sought to make a place for himself within the intense competition of the London art world. In the same year, Copley's family joined him in England, part of the wave of Loyalists fleeing hostilities in the colonies to other parts of the empire.

Like his fellow American Benjamin West, Copley turned to history painting, with a particular focus on contemporary events impacting the Atlantic world. His earliest, and perhaps the most famous of these, is *Watson and the Shark* (1778). Painted as a commission for a prominent London merchant, Brook Watson (1735–1807), the thrillingly suspenseful picture represents an event from the subject's youth, when he was attacked by a shark and lost his leg as a young sailor in Cuba's Havana Harbor. The painting's violent action, and the uncertainty of its outcome, serves as a potent metaphor for the conflict tearing apart England and America at that very moment.

Copley's successful history paintings, like *The Death of the Earl of Chatham* (1781), *The Siege of Gibraltar* (1783–1791), and *The Death of Major Peirson* (1783), captured moments of high drama and British national pride during the American Revolutionary War. Copley continued to paint portraits throughout his career, including among his sitters Americans visiting London, as well as English people. Copley's growing artistic success in London led to more commissions, membership in the Royal Academy, and patronage from King George III (1738–1820). It also led to his falling out with West as the two frequently found themselves in competition for work.

Having left America at the outset of the war, Copley was never a citizen of the United States; he identified himself as a British subject his entire life. After his move to England, Copley's life and career fit the mold of any great British painter, regardless of place of birth. He continued working and painting up to his death in 1815. His children continued his transatlantic legacy: his daughter returned to the United States to marry a Boston merchant, while his son went on to a position in British politics and became a peer of the realm. Copley's importance as an artist of the Atlantic world is confirmed through his seminal contribution to the development of art in both America and England.

SEE ALSO *American Revolution; Expatriate Artists; Loyalists; West, Benjamin*

BIBLIOGRAPHY

Barratt, Carrie Rebora, ed. *John Singleton Copley in America.* New York: Metropolitan Museum of Art, 1995.

Boime, Albert. "Blacks in Shark-Infested Waters: Visual Encodings of Racism in Copley and Homer." In *Race-ing Art History: Critical Readings in Race and Art History*, edited by Kymberly N. Pinder, 169–190. New York: Routledge, 2002.

Copley, John Singleton. "Copley to Benjamin West." November 12, 1766. In *Letters and Papers of John Singleton Copley and Henry Pelham, 1739–1776*, 50–52. Boston: Massachusetts Historical Society, 1914.

McInnis, Maurie D. "Cultural Politics, Colonial Crisis, and Ancient Metaphor in John Singleton Copley's *Mr. and Mrs.*

Ralph Izard." *Winterthur Portfolio* 34, nos. 2/3 (1999): 85–108.

Neff, Emily Ballew. *John Singleton Copley in England*. Houston, TX: Houston Museum of Fine Arts, 1995.

Neff, Emily Ballew, with Kaylin H. Weber. *American Adversaries: West and Copley in a Transatlantic World*. Houston, TX: Houston Museum of Fine Arts, 2013.

Prown, Jules David. *John Singleton Copley*. Cambridge, MA: Harvard University Press, 1966.

Rather, Susan. "Carpenter, Tailor, Shoemaker, Artist: Copley and Portrait Painting around 1770." *Art Bulletin* 79, 2 (1997): 269–290.

Roberts, Jennifer L. "Dilemmas of Delivery in Copley's Atlantic." In *Transporting Visions: The Movement of Images in Early America*, 13–69. Berkeley: University of California Press, 2014.

Emily Clare Casey
Department of Art History
University of Delaware

COTTON

The close relationship in the nineteenth century between the American supply of cotton and Britain's industrial demand for the fiber obscures how late the crop grew in the newly independent colonies. When eight bags of cotton from the United States landed at Liverpool in 1784, a customs officer seized them in surprise. He did not expect such an import from a region not known for growing cotton. In the decades that followed, however, American production increased. Contrary to popular opinion, Eli Whitney's (1765–1825) 1793 patent for a cotton gin does not explain the expansion of production; it ripped up the cotton, and Britain's manufacturers took decades to accustom themselves to the lower-quality upland type of cotton torn up by Whitney-style gins. However, the increasing demand of Britain's factories and the disruption of their usual supplies by the Napoleonic Wars justified to manufacturers the eventual adoption of cotton from the US South. After 1820 the crop found its footing, and when it did, the southern states expanded across the West, the region committed further to plantation production using slave labor, and in 1861 the conflicts between the North and the South would spark a civil war.

Exporting cotton provided a crucial source of capital to the expanding nation. Cotton represented 16 percent of the entire US export trade in 1800 and 36 percent in 1810; by 1850 cotton was 53 percent of total US exports and by 1860 had reached 59 percent; after the war, in 1870, the proportion again reached 60 percent. By 1900, however, cotton represented only 18 percent of total exports, and despite an uptick during World War I (1914–1918), the crop had lost its dominance in the export trade of the United States. During the nineteenth-century export boom, most of the crop went to northwest England, which had industrialized textile production in the last decades of the eighteenth century and relied on American-grown cotton for its dramatic increase in the nineteenth century. As British manufacturers captured markets from India's spinners, weavers, and cloth printers, factories replaced domestic production, and they made cotton cloth for the world.

By 1860, more than 75 percent of the cotton consumed in British factories came from the American South. But England was not the only customer for American cotton. Industrialists in France, Switzerland, Germany, Russia, Spain, and Mexico borrowed textile technology from Britain, and most bought American cotton to be worked in their factories. They were joined by Japan after the Meiji Restoration in the last decades of the nineteenth century. The flow of cotton from America shaped the world economy and international relations between industrializing nations and colonial consumers of their products. Cotton cloth from European factories dressed people around the world and formed the basis for global trade patterns. For example, antebellum merchants traded cloth from British factories for slaves in West Africa, and many of those slaves were then sold to planters in the American South whose plantations grew cotton for British factories. This particular set of economic relationships became known as the "triangle trade," and its proceeds contributed to Britain's commercial dominance as the "workshop of the world." Between 40 and 60 percent of nineteenth-century British exports were textile cloths made from cotton grown in America.

The US Civil War disrupted the supply of cotton to the world's spindles from 1861 to 1865. Confederate leaders withheld cotton from the market, hoping to force diplomatic recognition of their nation. They did not succeed; Britain stayed neutral in the conflict. By the time the Confederates released cotton, the Northern blockade of Southern ports limited exports and made factory inputs unpredictable. British manufacturers sought other supplies, and the shortfall stimulated cotton production in India, Egypt, and Brazil. These new sources did not immediately succeed in replacing American supplies, and the cotton famine threw hundreds of thousands of English operatives out of work. After the war, new growths continued and the British mill owners drew more of their raw materials from the new suppliers. As a result, the US South now had new competitors.

The importance of US cotton in world history persisted into the twentieth century. From 1900 to 1913, Booker T. Washington's (1856–1915) Tuskegee Institute in Alabama collaborated with the German imperial government to bring American cotton types and cultivation to Togo in West Africa. That effort to spread cotton agriculture from the US South to a German colony demonstrated that world supply and demand for cotton was shifting again, just as it had done when American cotton first landed in Britain.

SEE ALSO *Atlantic Slave Trade; Britain; The Civil War*

BIBLIOGRAPHY

Beckert, Sven. "Emancipation and Empire: Reconstructing the Worldwide Web of Cotton Production in the Age of the American Civil War." *American Historical Review* 109, 5 (December 2004): 1405–1438.

Beckert, Sven. *Empire of Cotton: A Global History.* New York: Knopf, 2014.

Ellison, Thomas. *The Cotton Trade of Great Britain.* London: Effingham Wilson, 1886.

Federal Reserve Board. *Federal Reserve Bulletin.* Washington, DC: Government Printing Office, 1923.

Gates, Paul W. *Agriculture and the Civil War.* New York: Knopf, 1965.

Lakwete, Angela. *Inventing the Cotton Gin: Machine and Myth in Antebellum America.* Baltimore, MD: Johns Hopkins University Press, 2003.

Riello, Giorgio. *Cotton: The Fabric That Made the Modern World.* Cambridge: Cambridge University Press, 2013.

Wright, Gavin. *The Political Economy of the Cotton South: Households, Markets, and Wealth in the Nineteenth Century.* New York: Norton, 1978.

Zimmerman, Andrew. *Alabama in Africa: Booker T. Washington, the German Empire, and the Globalization of the American South.* Princeton, NJ: Princeton University Press, 2012.

Barbara Hahn
Associate Professor, Department of History
Texas Tech University

COUNCIL ON FOREIGN RELATIONS

The Council on Foreign Relations (CFR), a private group of foreign policy experts who have constituted an extremely influential US foreign policy think tank, was founded immediately after World War I. In May 1919 expert advisers from the British and American delegations at the Paris Peace Conference established the American Institute of International Affairs, and a parallel British organization, the London-based Royal Institute of International Affairs. In 1921, the struggling American Institute merged with and took the name of the Council on Foreign Relations, a foreign policy discussion group established by New York bankers and lawyers in 1918.

Based in New York, the CFR had a small group of salaried permanent staff answering to a board of directors. Members included an elite, closely knit group of government officials, past and present, top businesspeople, media representatives, and academics, chosen through nomination. The CFR organized meetings featuring prominent American and foreign speakers, discussion and study groups, and conferences, with proceedings normally kept strictly confidential. Its books on international issues and its influential journal, *Foreign Affairs*, established in 1922, were widely circulated among top-level decision makers. Although supposedly committed to no specific policies, between the world wars the CFR provided a base for Americans who believed the United States should be more active internationally. From the late 1930s onward, with Carnegie Corporation funding, the CFR established affiliated committees in thirteen major cities around the United States, a number that had expanded to thirty-seven by the late twentieth century.

Before the United States entered World War II, prominent CFR members were leaders in pro-Allied and interventionist groups working closely with the administration of President Franklin D. Roosevelt (1882–1945). Even before the attack on Pearl Harbor in December 1941, the CFR, in collaboration with the State Department, had launched a major project, the War-Peace Studies, funded by the Rockefeller Foundation, to begin planning for the postwar world. This venture anticipated that when the war ended the United States would remain far more internationally engaged than before. From around 1940, many CFR members held key positions in the wartime and postwar national security bureaucracy.

From 1945 onward, the CFR organized many study and discussion groups to craft recommendations on international policy. Their members included leading government officials, such as George F. Kennan (1904–2005), General Dwight D. Eisenhower (1890–1969), Allen W. Dulles (1893–1969), Dean Acheson (1893–1971), and John J. McCloy (1895–1989). Topics included aid to Europe, American-Russian relations, Europe's economic and political reconstruction, US foreign economic policies, military and alliance strategy, and the United Nations. These groups, meeting in strict confidentiality, helped to hammer out an elite consensus on Cold War foreign policy, developing initiatives that would result in the Marshall Plan, the regeneration of Germany, the North Atlantic Treaty Organization (NATO), and US encouragement of European economic union.

Resembling a comfortable club, the CFR was a sheltered arena where diplomats, military personnel, intelligence operatives, and foundation representatives, as well as the academics, businesspeople, and lawyers who circulated through the official apparatus, unobtrusively encountered and vetted each other. In some respects, the CFR functioned almost as an annex to the government's national security bureaucracy. It helped to launch the policy-making careers of such academics as future secretary of state Henry Kissinger (b. 1923) and national security adviser Zbigniew Brzezinski (b. 1928). In 1957 a CFR study group produced a best-selling volume on nuclear strategy by Kissinger. In the mid-1960s a major study program on China chaired by Dulles recommended that the United States reopen relations with the communist mainland, helping prepare the ground for President Richard Nixon's (1913–1994) subsequent moves toward China.

During the 1960s the CFR began to attract substantial public attention. It became and remained a favorite target of fierce criticism from populist extremists and conspiracy theorists of both right and left, who excoriated it as the home of an undemocratic elite committed to promoting the interests of international capitalism and global world government. Like other American institutions, the CFR was deeply divided over the Vietnam War, with some of its members at least partially responsible for American policies in Indochina. Some longtime CFR officials, notably McCloy, its chairman during the 1960s, were reluctant to publish studies or appoint visiting researchers who might be overly unsympathetic toward US government policies. The visiting fellow appointment in 1965 of the realist scholar Hans J. Morgenthau (1904–1980), who insisted on attending anti–Vietnam War events in Europe, caused considerable heartburn within the CFR, as top CFR officers were clearly disturbed that Morgenthau's position might be seen as reflecting CFR views. Critics also charged that the CFR was stuffy, outdated, narrow, remote, unrepresentative, and irrelevant, and that its directors were a small, self-perpetuating, and out-of-touch oligopoly, automatically elected to multiple terms on a near lifetime basis.

In response, the CFR, under the energetic chairmanship of banker David Rockefeller (b. 1915), launched initiatives to broaden its membership geographically; include minorities, women, and younger Americans; and set limits to directors' terms in office. Facing increasing competition from newer rival think tanks on both right and left, in the early 1970s the CFR opened a Washington office to facilitate communication with government officials. As American politics turned more conservative in the late 1970s and 1980s, assorted right-wingers and neoconservatives were invited to become CFR members. The number of study and discussion groups and meetings increased and their topics broadened, with more attention devoted to Asia and Africa and to nontraditional security issues, such as immigration, terrorism, the environment, and climate change. The CFR's journal and other print and electronic publications were recognized as key venues for seminal discussions of the most salient issues on the international agenda. This pattern continued throughout the Cold War and beyond. As its centenary approached, the CFR continued to be one of the most prestigious American foreign policy think tanks.

SEE ALSO *Carnegie Endowment for International Peace; Foreign Affairs (Magazine); Think Tanks*

BIBLIOGRAPHY

Armstrong, Hamilton Fish. *Peace and Counterpeace from Wilson to Hitler: Memoirs of Hamilton Fish Armstrong.* New York: Harper and Row, 1971.

Barber, Joseph. *These Are the Committees.* New York: CFR, 1964.

Bundy, William P. "Notes on the History of *Foreign Affairs.*" 1994. http://www.cfr.org/about/history/foreign_affairs.html

Campbell, John D. "The Death Rattle of the Eastern Establishment." *New York Times Magazine*, September 20, 1971, 1–7ff.

Council on Foreign Relations (CFR). *The Council on Foreign Relations: A Record of Twenty-Five Years, 1921–1946.* New York: CFR, 1947.

Dye, Thomas R. "Oligarchic Tendencies in National Policy-Making: The Role of the Private Policy-Planning Organizations." *Journal of Politics* 40, 2 (1978): 309–331.

Grose, Peter. *Continuing the Inquiry: The Council on Foreign Relations from 1921 to 1996.* New York: CFR, 1996.

Lukas, J. Anthony. "The Council on Foreign Relations—Is It a Club? Seminar? Presidium? 'Invisible Government'?" *New York Times Magazine*, November 21, 1971, 34, 123–131, 138, 142.

Parmar, Inderjeet. *Think Tanks and Power in Foreign Policy: A Comparative Study of the Role and Influence of the Council on Foreign Relations and the Royal Institute of International Affairs, 1939–1945.* Basingstoke, UK: Palgrave Macmillan, 2004.

Perloff, James. *Shadows of Power: The Council on Foreign Relations and the American Decline.* Boston: Western Islands, 1988.

Roberts, Priscilla. "'The Council Has Been Your Creation': Hamilton Fish Armstrong, Paradigm of the American Foreign Policy Establishment?" *Journal of American Studies* 35, 1 (2001): 65–94.

Roberts, Priscilla. "Underpinning the Anglo-American Alliance: The Council on Foreign Relations and Britain between the Wars." In *Twentieth-Century Anglo-American Relations*, edited by Jonathan Hollowell, 25–43. Basingstoke, UK: Palgrave, 2001.

Santoro, Carlo. *Diffidence and Ambition: The Intellectual Sources of U.S. Foreign Policy.* Translated by Andrew Ellis and Leslie Gunn. Boulder, CO: Westview, 1991.

Schulzinger, Robert D. *The Wise Men of Foreign Affairs: The History of the Council on Foreign Relations.* New York: Columbia University Press, 1984.

Shoup, Laurence H., and William Minter. *Imperial Brain Trust: The Council on Foreign Relations and United States Foreign Policy.* New York: Monthly Review Press, 1977.

Wala, Michael. *The Council on Foreign Relations and American Foreign Policy in the Early Cold War.* Providence, RI: Berghahn, 1994.

Zimmer, Louis B. *The Vietnam War Debate: Hans Morgenthau and the Attempt to Halt the Drift into Disaster.* Lanham, MD: Lexington, 2011.

Priscilla Roberts
Associate Professor History
University of Hong Kong

COVERT WARS

The US Central Intelligence Agency (CIA) guards its archives with tenacity. We know a great deal about some covert operations during the Cold War. Of others, we know only the bare outlines. And there are surely operations about which we are totally unaware.

There are different types of covert operations—propaganda, political action, economic influence, paramilitary. This essay focuses on paramilitary operations. It does not examine operations launched in Indochina because they were ancillary to the larger war effort in Vietnam. Some paramilitary operations sought the overthrow of a foreign government; others sought to crush revolts that threatened friendly regimes or to harass unfriendly foreign governments without expecting to overthrow them.

With the exception of Gerald Ford (1913–2006) and Jimmy Carter (b. 1924), during the Cold War every US president launched at least one covert operation to unseat a foreign government. With the exception of Harry Truman (1884–1972), none launched a covert paramilitary operation in Europe. "The Cold War was a contest that consisted of shadow-boxing in areas of marginal significance," historian Nancy Mitchell writes, "because real war in places that really counted—Berlin, Washington, and Moscow—was unwinnable" (Mitchell 2010, 67). As President Dwight Eisenhower (1890–1969) understood when senior CIA officials urged him to help the Hungarian rebels fighting against communist rule in late 1956, the risk of triggering a war with the Soviet Union was too great. Europe was out of bounds. US paramilitary operations during the Cold War were launched in the Third World.

TRUMAN AND ALBANIA

Despite claims to the contrary (e.g., Brands 1993, 60), President Truman embraced paramilitary operations. As former director of central intelligence (DCI) Richard Helms (1913–2002) noted, "Truman okayed a good many decisions for covert operations that in later years he said he knew nothing about" (Helms 1989). These decisions included many paramilitary operations behind the Iron Curtain that were intended to strengthen resistance forces and harass the Soviet Union, as well as operations to harass China during the Korean War. One had a more grandiose goal: to overthrow the government of Albania.

Joseph Stalin's (1879–1953) break with Yugoslav leader Tito (Josip Broz, 1892–1980) in 1948 seemed to present the West with a great opportunity; the Albanian regime remained loyal to the Soviet Union and launched a bloody purge against Tito's numerous supporters within the Albanian Communist Party and armed forces. Albania became an isolated Soviet outpost in the Mediterranean: its only land borders were with Yugoslavia, suddenly hostile, and Greece, a US client. Across the Adriatic Sea was another US client, Italy.

The British concocted the plan, and they convinced the Americans to join: together they would train Albanian exiles and infiltrate them into Albania, where they would galvanize the strong anticommunist movement and inspire a population eager to revolt. The operation, which began in 1949, was based on faulty intelligence and wishful thinking: the resistance forces were weak and the population passive. Disaster was inevitable. One after another the teams sent by the Americans and British were wiped out, but more were sent. Hundreds of Albanians died. "Seldom has an intelligence operation proceeded so resolutely from one disaster to another," a scholar noted (Winks 1987, 399). In 1953 the Eisenhower administration terminated the foolhardy endeavor.

PARAMILITARY OPERATIONS IN LATIN AMERICA

The Eisenhower years were a golden age for the CIA. Eisenhower shared Truman's penchant for paramilitary operations, poured resources into the agency, and appointed Allen Dulles (1893–1969) as DCI. Allen was the younger brother of John Foster Dulles (1888–1959), Eisenhower's secretary of state and most trusted foreign policy adviser. The two brothers were in constant, easy communication; often, after a day's work, Allen would drop by Foster's house to go over unfinished business. Never have a secretary of state and a CIA director enjoyed so close a relationship. It bothered some people: "It is a relationship that it would be better not have to exist," remarked the chair of a committee appointed by Eisenhower to investigate the agency. Eisenhower disagreed: "Part of CIA's work is extension of work of State Department" (Doolittle 1954).

Whereas under Truman covert paramilitary operations consistently failed, under Eisenhower two of the three operations to overthrow governments succeeded: in Iran in 1953 and Guatemala in 1954. These two successes enhanced the CIA's prestige among those in the know. The agency's failure to oust the government of Indonesia in 1957 to 1958 did not dim its luster.

The overthrow of President Jacobo Arbenz Guzmán (1913–1971) of Guatemala is one of the few covert paramilitary operations about which the US government has declassified a rich trove of documents. These documents prove that US intelligence on Guatemala during the Eisenhower years was very good. The CIA reported that Arbenz was either a communist or a fellow traveler, that his closest advisers were communists, and that they were the engine behind Arbenz's successful agrarian reform program. (One hundred thousand families—one-sixth of Guatemala's population—received the land they desperately needed.) US intelligence also reported that there was no communist infiltration in the Guatemalan armed forces. This, too, was right.

The CIA did not assert that there was the danger of a communist takeover in Guatemala—and there is no indication that US policy makers even posed the question. Given the imbalance of power between the United States and Guatemala, the cost of destroying the Arbenz government was so low that they did not bother to contemplate any alternative—such as learning to coexist with the pro-communist government that respected political freedoms to a degree unusual in Latin America.

A force of about 250 CIA-sponsored exiles invaded Guatemala in June 1954. The Guatemalan army could have crushed them easily, but it did not dare: the exiles were the proxies of the United States, and if the Guatemalan army defeated them, what would Eisenhower do next? He would send in US troops—this is what the CIA station in Guatemala, the US embassy, and the US military mission told the Guatemalans. The same message was trumpeted by the Guatemalan opposition media day after day. "How could the leaders of Guatemala imagine that the United States would tolerate a nest of enemies on its very doorstep?" asked a prominent Guatemalan journalist who worked closely with the CIA. "Germany … is still occupied, and so is Japan—and we will be too, we poor fools who don't even produce fireworks, much less the ammunition for a token resistance" (Marroquín Rojas 1954, 1). In the United States, no organ of the mainstream press and no member of Congress—Democrat or Republican—advocated trying to coexist with Arbenz's Guatemala.

When the exile invasion began, the Guatemalan army refused to fight; it turned instead against Arbenz and forced him to resign. The leader of the invaders, who had been handpicked by the CIA, became the new president of Guatemala.

The overthrow of Arbenz reassured the Eisenhower administration that the hemisphere was safe—until 1959, when Fidel Castro (b. 1926) seized power in Cuba. The United States responded to Castro's challenge in the way it always dealt with nuisances in its backyard: with violence. On Eisenhower's orders, the CIA began plotting the overthrow of Castro. In April 1961, three months after the inauguration of President John Kennedy (1917–1963), 1,300 CIA-trained insurgents stormed a Cuban beach at the Bay of Pigs, only to surrender en masse.

Defeat at the Bay of Pigs added an element of personal venom to Kennedy's crusade against Cuba. Rejecting Castro's offer of conversations about a modus vivendi between the two countries, he "chewed out" the CIA deputy director for plans, Richard Bissell (1909–1994), for "sitting on his ass and not doing anything about getting rid of Castro and the Castro regime" (US Senate 1975, 141). CIA paramilitary operations against Cuba did not taper off until 1965.

Haunted by the fear of a second Cuba, the Kennedy and Lyndon Johnson (1908–1973) administrations engaged in covert operations in several other Latin American countries to undermine groups or governments they considered soft on communism. By the end of the Johnson administration, the specter of a second Cuba in the hemisphere had waned, but then, in 1970, Salvador Allende (1908–1973) won the Chilean presidential election. Allende was a sincere democrat, but he was a socialist, he headed a coalition that included the Communist Party, and he was a friend of Castro. For President Richard Nixon (1913–1994) and Henry Kissinger (b. 1923), Allende's accession to the presidency was an affront to the United States and a terrible example for Latin America. They vowed to bring him down. Technically, the Chilean military acted on its own when it overthrew Allende on September 11, 1973, but, as Kissinger said, by undertaking a destabilization campaign and aiding antigovernment groups, the CIA had "created the conditions as great as possible [for a coup]" (Kissinger 1973).

PARAMILITARY OPERATIONS IN AFRICA

From the late 1950s through the early 1970s, the focus of CIA paramilitary operations was in Indochina against the North Vietnamese and in the Western Hemisphere against Castro. But when sixteen African countries became independent in 1960, a new front opened. Africa became, in the words of Secretary of State Christian Herter (1895–1966), "a battleground of the first order" (Gleijeses 2002, 6).

Over the next two decades, the United States engaged in two major paramilitary operations in Africa. In 1964 and 1965, President Johnson sought to defeat a revolt in the former Belgian Congo against the corrupt and repressive regime that Eisenhower and Kennedy had imposed on the country. The CIA recruited an army of one thousand white mercenaries, armed them, provided indispensable logistic support, and even organized a mercenary air force to bomb and strafe the rebels. The mercenaries perpetrated massive atrocities, and they crushed the revolt.

The other major paramilitary operation was in 1975 in Angola, where the Ford administration worked with the government of South Africa to crush a left-wing movement. With Washington's collusion, South African troops invaded the country and almost succeeded in installing friendly leaders in Luanda, the Angolan capital—but then thirty-six thousand Cuban soldiers poured into Angola and pushed the South African troops out.

REAGAN, THE PRESS, AND THE CONTRA WAR

Jimmy Carter did not launch major paramilitary operations until the Soviet invasion of Afghanistan in December 1979. He then expanded the program of nonlethal aid to the Afghan mujahideen that he had approved in July 1979, to a grand total of $60 million that included "all manner of weapons and military support" (Gates 1996, 251). The goal of the operation was to raise the cost of the invasion for the Soviets.

For the CIA, the presidency of Ronald Reagan (1911–2004) was another golden age, a return to the Eisenhower years. Money and manpower flowed to the agency. Furthermore, for the first time since Eisenhower, the DCI, William Casey (1913–1987), was a member of the president's inner circle. There were, however, two significant differences between the Eisenhower and Reagan eras. Congress, whose oversight of the agency had been lax, now wanted to be in the loop, and the US press was no longer silent.

No laws had prevented the American press from reporting on covert operations, but its silence in the first three decades of the CIA's existence is striking. Take, for example, the overthrow of Arbenz in Guatemala. The hand of the United States was obvious. The CIA itself reported that the Western European press was virtually unanimous in concluding that the agency had engineered Arbenz's downfall. In the words of the CIA inspector general, "The fig leaf was very transparent, threadbare" (Kirkpatrick 1989). Not threadbare enough, however, for the US press. When it came to exploring the US role in the fall of Arbenz, US newspapers either ignored the issue or rejected out of hand any insinuation that the US government had assisted the rebels. This was the pattern: the same "discipline" was evident in 1958 during the operation against Indonesia, in the weeks before the Bay of Pigs, in 1964 and 1965 during the operation in the former Belgian Congo, and in 1975 in Angola.

Even more striking than the silence of the US press is the failure of historians to take note of it. With the exception of analyses of the Bay of Pigs and of one book about the Indonesian operation, no historian ever mentions the connivance of the press. Therefore, there is no explanation of this self-censorship.

By the 1980s, the press had changed. There were three major paramilitary operations in the Reagan years—in Afghanistan, Angola, and Nicaragua—and the press reported all three. The most controversial was against Nicaragua. The Contra war against the Sandinista government was never popular with American public opinion or Congress, but Reagan pursued it, undeterred. He believed that the Sandinistas were Marxist-Leninists and that the United States could not tolerate a Marxist-Leninist regime in Central America. While the administration waged economic warfare on Nicaragua, the CIA nurtured the anti-Sandinista army—the Contras. It armed them, paid them, and provided them sanctuaries in neighboring Honduras. Thousands flocked to join the Contras, believing that victory was inevitable because Reagan stood behind them and, if needed, would send in US troops. This confidence—that the United States would win the war for them—swelled the Contras' ranks but eviscerated their will to fight.

Very early, in 1982, the US press began to report on the US role in the Contra war. For the first time in the history of the United States there was a debate—a vigorous debate—on a paramilitary operation while it unfolded (not after it had failed, as had been the case for the Bay of Pigs). The debate took place in the media, among large sectors of public opinion, and in the US Congress. There were bitter clashes between the congressional intelligence committees and the CIA. DCI Casey and his closest associates dissembled and obfuscated when informing Congress of what the CIA was doing for the Contras.

After Reagan's landslide reelection in November 1984, many Americans feared he might approve an invasion of Nicaragua, and perhaps he would have, had the Iran-Contra scandal not weakened him. When Reagan left the White House, the Sandinistas were still in power.

"THE BALANCE SHEET"

CIA paramilitary operations during the Cold War did not strain the US treasury; Afghanistan, by far the most expensive, cost about $2 billion spread over more than a decade—a small sum for a country as rich as the United States. Nor were they costly in American lives. The CIA kept US personnel away from combat zones. No more than a dozen Americans were killed in the operations reviewed in this essay.

Several of these operations failed, but failure entailed little cost for the United States, even in diplomatic terms. Relations with Albania, for example, would have been execrable even without Truman's paramilitary operation. Being a superpower helped cushion the price of defeat. The CIA's assault on Cuba in the 1960s poisoned relations between the two countries, but Cuba still sought a modus vivendi with the Kennedy and Johnson administrations—only to be rebuffed. From the perspective of the US government, the most costly failure may have been the 1975 operation in Angola, because it drew 36,000 Cuban soldiers to that country. And yet, with hindsight, the Cuban troops, who remained fifteen years, did not hurt any significant US interests; they protected Angola from apartheid South Africa and forced Pretoria to grant independence to Namibia.

Success—achieving the goals set by US policy makers—was often more costly than failure. The fact that the CIA could solve a problem at low cost made it easy for US policy makers to avoid hard thinking. Many Americans date the beginning of US-Iranian enmity to the triumph of the Iranian Revolution in 1979 and the capture of the hostages. It would be more accurate, however, to cite 1953—the overthrow of Iranian prime minister Mohammad Mossadegh (1882–1967). He posed no threat to the United States. A modus vivendi with him might have better served Washington's long-term interests. But why bother trying when it was so easy to destroy him?

CIA covert paramilitary operations were rarely a secret outside the United States. In the Third World, they reinforced the image of the United States as a chauvinistic bully. But they did more. When ordering the agency to launch paramilitary operations, US policy makers did not intend to harm the people of the countries they targeted—they believed they were acting in the US national interest, and any collateral damage was unfortunate. All too often, however, these operations did not serve the national interest of the United States, and they inflicted a devastating toll on the people of the countries that were targeted. This is the most grave liability of the paramilitary operations that the CIA launched during the Cold War, and it is a stain on the record of the United States, even if most Americans are blissfully unaware of it.

SEE ALSO *Central Intelligence Agency (CIA); Freedom Fighters; Mossadegh, Mohammad; United Fruit Company*

BIBLIOGRAPHY

Barrett, David M. *The CIA and Congress: The Untold Story from Truman to Kennedy.* Lawrence: University Press of Kansas, 2005.

Bernstein, Victor, and Jesse Gordon. "The Press and the Bay of Pigs." *Columbia University Forum* (Fall 1967): 5–18.

Brands, H. W. *The Devil We Knew: Americans and the Cold War.* Oxford: Oxford University Press, 1993.

Burke, Michael. *Outrageous Good Fortune: A Memoir.* Boston: Little, Brown, 1984.

Cogan, Charles. "Partners in Time: The CIA and Afghanistan." *World Policy Journal* 10, 2 (1993): 73–82.

Conboy, Kenneth, and James Morrison. *Feet to the Fire: CIA Covert Operations in Indonesia, 1957–1958.* Annapolis, MD: Naval Institute Press, 1999.

Crocker, Chester A. *High Noon in Southern Africa: Making Peace in a Rough Neighborhood.* New York: Norton, 1992.

Cullather, Nick. *Secret History: The CIA's Classified Account of Its Operations in Guatemala, 1952–1954.* Stanford, CA: Stanford University Press, 1999.

Doolittle: Memcon (Gen. Doolittle and President Eisenhower), October 19, 1954. Whitman File, Adm. Series, Box 13, Dwight D. Eisenhower Library, Abilene, KS.

Dorril, Stephen. *MI6: Inside the Covert World of Her Majesty's Secret Intelligence Service.* New York: Free Press, 2000.

Dravis, Michael. "Storming Fortress Albania: American Covert Operations in Microcosm, 1949–54." *Intelligence and National Security* 7, 4 (1992): 425–442.

Dujmović, Nicholas. "Drastic Actions Short of War: The Origins and Application of CIA Covert Paramilitary Function in the Early Cold War." *Journal of Military History* 76, 3 (2012): 775–808.

Esterline, Jacob, interviewed by Piero Gleijeses, Hendersonville, NC, November 18–19, 1992.

Gates, Robert. *From the Shadows: The Ultimate Insider's Story of Five Presidents and How They Won the Cold War.* New York: Simon and Schuster, 1996.

Gleijeses, Piero. *Shattered Hope: The Guatemalan Revolution and the United States, 1944–1954.* Princeton, NJ: Princeton University Press, 1991.

Gleijeses, Piero. "Ships in the Night: The CIA, the White House and the Bay of Pigs." *Journal of Latin American Studies* 27, 1 (1995): 1–42.

Gleijeses, Piero. *Conflicting Missions: Havana, Washington, and Africa, 1959–1976.* Chapel Hill: University of North Carolina Press, 2002.

Gleijeses, Piero. *Visions of Freedom: Havana, Washington, Pretoria and the Struggle for Southern Africa, 1976–1991.* Chapel Hill: University of North Carolina Press, 2013.

Godson, Roy. *Dirty Tricks or Trump Cards: U.S. Covert Action and Counterintelligence.* New Brunswick, NJ: Transaction, 2008. Originally published by Brassey's in 1995.

Grose, Peter. *Operation Rollback: America's Secret War behind the Iron Curtain.* Boston: Houghton Mifflin, 2000.

Guthman, Edwin O., and Jeffrey Shulman, eds. *Robert Kennedy in His Own Words.* New York: Bantam, 1988.

Helms, Richard, interviewed by Piero Gleijeses, Washington, DC, September 7, 1989.

Holly, Susan K., ed. *Foreign Relations of the United States, 1952–1954: Guatemala.* Washington, DC: US Department of State, 2003.

Holt, Pat, interviewed by Piero Gleijeses, Bethesda, MD, February 19, 1992.

Immerman, Richard. *The CIA in Guatemala: The Foreign Policy of Intervention.* Austin: University of Texas Press, 1982.

Kahin, Audrey, and George Kahin. *Subversion as Foreign Policy: The Secret Eisenhower and Dulles Debacle in Indonesia.* New York: New Press, 1995.

Kirkpatrick, Lyman, interviewed by Piero Gleijeses, Middleburg, VA, June 2, 1989.

Kissinger, Henry. Memo TelCon, Nixon and Kissinger, September 16, 1973. The Declassified Record, National Security Archive, Washington DC.

Kissinger, Henry. *Years of Renewal.* New York: Simon and Schuster, 1999.

Kornbluh, Peter. *The Pinochet File: A Declassified Dossier on Atrocity and Accountability.* Rev. ed. New York: New Press, 2013.

Leogrande, William M. *Our Own Backyard: The United States in Central America, 1977–1992.* Chapel Hill: University of North Carolina Press, 1998.

Marroquín Rojas, Clemente. "Y usted: ¿Qué deduce, señor ministro?" *La Hora* (Guatemala City), January 14, 1954, 1.

Michaels, Jeffrey. "Breaking the Rules: The CIA and Counterinsurgency in the Congo 1964–1965." *International Journal of Intelligence and Counterintelligence* 25, 1 (2012): 130–159.

Mitchell, Nancy. "The Cold War and Jimmy Carter." In *Cambridge History of the Cold War,* edited by Melvyn Leffler and Odd Arne Westad, Vol. 3, 66–88. New York: Cambridge University Press, 2010.

Powers, Thomas. *The Man Who Kept the Secrets: Richard Helms and the CIA.* New York: Knopf, 1987.

Prados, John. *Safe for Democracy: The Secret Wars of the CIA.* Chicago: Ivan R. Dee, 2006.

Rabe, Stephen. *U.S. Intervention in British Guiana: A Cold War Story.* Chapel Hill: University of North Carolina Press, 2005.

Ranelagh, John. *The Agency: The Rise and Decline of the CIA.* New York: Simon and Schuster, 1986.

Rositzke, Harry. *The CIA's Secret Operations: Espionage, Counter-espionage, and Covert Action.* New York: Reader's Digest Press, 1977.

Schlesinger, Stephen, and Stephen Kinzer. *Bitter Fruit: The Untold Story of the American Coup in Guatemala.* Garden City, NY: Doubleday, 1982.

Smist, Frank. *Congress Oversees the United States Intelligence Community, 1947–1989.* Knoxville: University of Tennessee Press, 1990.

Snider, L. Britt. *The Agency and the Hill: CIA's Relationship with Congress, 1946–2004.* Washington DC: CIA Center for the Study of Intelligence, 2008.

Thomas, Evan. *The Very Best Men: Four Who Dared: The Early Years of the CIA.* New York: Simon and Schuster, 1995.

US Senate, Select Committee to Study Government Operations with Respect to Intelligence Activities. *Alleged Assassination Plots Involving Foreign Leaders: An Interim Report of the Select Committee to Study Governmental Operations with Respect to Intelligence Activities.* Washington, DC: GPO, 1975.

Warner, Michael. "The CIA's Internal Probe of the Bay of Pigs Affair." *Studies in Intelligence* 42, 5 (1998–1999): 93–101.

Weiner, Tim. *Legacy of Ashes: The History of the CIA.* New York: Doubleday, 2007.

Winks, Robin W. *Cloak and Gown: Scholars in the Secret War, 1939–1961.* New York: Morrow, 1987.

Yousaf, Mohammed, and Mark Adkin. *Bear Trap: Afghanistan's Untold Story.* London: Cooper, 1992.

Piero Gleijeses
Professor of American Foreign Policy
School of Advanced International Studies
Johns Hopkins University

CROWE, EYRE

1824–1910

English painter Eyre Crowe visited America in 1852 and 1853 as the secretary to English author William Makepeace Thackeray (1811–1863). When Crowe returned to England, he created a series of sketches later published as wood engravings in the *Illustrated London News* and three oil paintings that depict the domestic trade in enslaved African Americans just before the American Civil War (1861–1865). An act of Congress had abolished the international slave trade in the United States effective 1808, but a domestic trade accounted for the sale of hundreds of thousands of people from the Upper South to the Deep South, where the cotton boom led to a near-bottomless market for enslaved labor. Crowe's images provide some of the only eyewitness visual renderings of the slave trade in Richmond, Virginia, and Charleston, South Carolina, two of the largest slave-trading centers in the American South.

Together these images played an important role in spreading antislavery awareness in both Britain and America, and they tell the story of the American slave trade. Describing himself as an "abolitionist," Crowe published the images along with articles in the *Illustrated London News* and *Household Words,* and he exhibited three paintings made from his sketches, two in 1854 and a third in 1861. Importantly, these images moved away from the caricatured representations prevalent in much antislavery material, such as that related to Harriet Beecher Stowe's novel *Uncle Tom's Cabin* (1852).

Exhibited at the Royal Academy in London in 1861, *Slaves Waiting for Sale, Richmond, Virginia,* 1861 (Heinz Family Collection), was previously published in the *Illustrated London News* in 1856. Critics did not fail to notice the timeliness of the subject, given that the

American Civil War had just begun. Seeing the painting as a moving depiction of the "appalling guilt of that accursed system," they were quite struck by what they saw as the verisimilitude of the picture, perhaps guided by the unusual subject (Crowe 1861, 165). Rather than depicting a slave auction, a popular subject in abolitionist materials, Crowe instead depicted enslaved people seated on benches in the moments before the sale. Critics declared it "one of the most important pictures of the exhibition" (Crowe 1861, 165). All were particularly struck by the figure of the male slave on the right of the picture. Viewers were at the time accustomed to seeing images of slaves who accepted their position with a happy complacency, as famously depicted by Stowe in her characterization of Uncle Tom in *Uncle Tom's Cabin.* Crowe chose instead to depict a very different figure, a man described as expressing "suffused indignant scorn, mingled with defiance" (Crowe 1861, 165). In the figure of this man, Crowe had depicted a slave who could resist, rebel, or run away at any moment. It was his most powerful statement about slavery and the slave trade.

Exhibited in 1854 at the Royal Scottish Academy in Edinburgh, *A Slave Sale: Charlestone* [*sic*], *South Carolina,* 1854 (Museo della Belle Artes, Havana, Cuba), was based on the slave auction he witnessed when he visited that city; it was later published in the *Illustrated London News* in 1856. It showed an event more commonly depicted in abolitionist imagery: a slave auction. On the day of the sale he attended, ninety-six people from the same plantation were being sold, "in families, with the exception of a few who are single," according to the newspaper ad (*Charleston Mercury*, March 10, 1853). His image is a visual jumble, a chaotic density of bodies, creating a scene he described as a "spectacle." His image highlights the red flags used by auctioneers to advertise an auction, and the masts of ships in the background. Those "cotton-laden ships," as he described them, tied England to American slavery through the textile industry (Crowe 1856, 556). The critics described it as "crammed with action and varied character," which they thought appropriate to a scene representing "the unholy traffic of human gore" ("Exhibition of the Royal Scottish Academy, Seventh Notice" 1854).

The third image in Crowe's cycle on the American slave trade was a painting exhibited at the Society of British Artists in London: *Going South: A Sketch from Life in America,* 1854 (Chicago History Museum). In this image, Crowe depicted what happened to slaves after they were purchased in the city's salesroom. Centered at a railroad terminal in Richmond with the city's skyline visible in the background, *Going South* shows a scene of extraordinary confusion as slaves are marched to the railroad cars for their journey South. Some may have had short journeys to nearby locations, but most were at the beginning of a migration that would conclude in another auction room hundreds of miles away in South Carolina, Alabama, Mississippi, or Louisiana.

SEE ALSO *Antislavery*

BIBLIOGRAPHY

Bancroft, Frederic. *Slave Trading in the Old South.* Columbia: University of South Carolina Press, 1996. Originally published by J. H. Furst in 1931.

Charleston Mercury, March 10, 1853.

Crowe, Eyre. "Sketches in the Free and Slave States of America." *Illustrated London News,* September 27, 1856, 313–314.

Crowe, Eyre. "Sale of Slaves at Charleston, South Carolina." *Illustrated London News,* November 29, 1856, 556.

Crowe, Eyre. "Sketching at a Slave Auction." *Household Words* 15, 360 (February 14, 1857): 154.

Crowe, Eyre. "Exhibition of the Royal Academy." *Art-Journal* 23 (June 1, 1861): 165.

Deyle, Steven. *Carry Me Back: The Domestic Slave Trade in American Life.* New York: Oxford University Press, 2005.

"Exhibition of the Royal Scottish Academy, Seventh Notice." *Caledonian Mercury,* March 23, 1854.

Gudmestad, Robert H. *A Troublesome Commerce: The Transformation of the Interstate Slave Trade.* Baton Rouge: Louisiana State University Press, 2003.

Johnson, Walter. *Soul by Soul: Life inside the Antebellum Slave Market.* Cambridge, MA: Harvard University Press, 1999.

McInnis, Maurie D. *Slaves Waiting for Sale: Abolitionist Art and the American Slave Trade.* Chicago: University of Chicago Press, 2011.

Tadman, Michael. *Speculators and Slaves: Masters, Traders, and Slaves in the Old South.* Madison: University of Wisconsin Press, 1996.

Maurie D. McInnis
Professor of Art History
University of Virginia

CUBA

Cuba exemplifies the futility of drawing clear lines between the "domestic" and the "foreign" in US history. It has figured prominently in US national politics since long before the 1959 Cuban Revolution made Fidel Castro (b. 1926) and Che Guevara (1928–1967) household names across North America. Cuban immigrants and exiles have helped shape everything from the US national pastime and presidential politics to the television sitcom and American popular music. Listen, for example, to that quintessentially "American" pop song, "Louie, Louie," for the Cuban cha-cha beat that drives it (Sublette 2007, 70).

In fact, until the outbreak of the US Civil War in 1861, many Americans saw Cuba as an inevitable part of the future United States. In 1809 Thomas Jefferson (1743–1826) described it as the southern outpost of an "empire for liberty" spanning the continent (Jefferson, as quoted in Smith 1995, 1586). For John Quincy Adams (1767–1848), Cuba's proximity made it a "natural appendage" to the US mainland (Adams 1963, 27). James Buchanan (1791–1868), secretary of state under the annexationist president James K. Polk (1795–1849), agreed. He wrote in 1849 that "Cuba is already ours. I can feel it in my finger ends" (Buchanan 1960, 360–361).

CUBAN ANNEXATION

The so-called annexationist movement enjoyed broad support in the antebellum United States, especially in the expansionist decade after the 1846–1848 Mexican-American War. Cuba, where slavery was legal and lucrative, would have been a tantalizing prize for southern states seeking to expand slavery. Yet Cuban annexation also enjoyed a strong northern constituency (May 1972, 30). A bilingual annexationist newspaper, *La verdad* (The truth), was published in New York from 1848 to 1856. Even "free soilers" opposed to slavery's spread into new western states hoped that Cuban annexation might pacify the South and avert a war over slavery. And Cuba's strategic position in the Gulf of Mexico and near the Central American isthmus (a popular route to California) would boost American commerce and speed the settlement of the West. Spain, however, bluntly rejected Polk's offer of $100 million for the island: Polk's ambassador in Madrid wrote to Washington with the response of Spanish officials: "sooner than see the Island transferred to any power, they would prefer seeing it sunk in the Ocean" (Rauch 1948, 97). Buchanan's "finger ends" had deceived him.

Militant annexationists were undeterred, however. Private, proslavery mercenary expeditions, called filibusters, were organized in the United States throughout the 1840s and 1850s to capture Latin American territory. William Walker's (1824–1860) short-lived 1856 conquest of Nicaragua (where he reintroduced slavery) was the most famous, but Cuba was the biggest prize. The Venezuelan-born filibuster Narciso López (1797–1851) led two failed filibuster campaigns to annex Cuba to the United States as a slave state; he was executed in Havana after his final defeat in 1851.

The 1861–1865 US Civil War and the abolition of slavery spelled the end of hopes for Cuban annexation, and in Cuba, anti-Spanish sentiment had shifted from annexation to independence: in 1868, Cuba's first war for independence broke out. The 1873 capture and execution of the crew of the *Virginius*, a US ship smuggling weapons to the rebels, revived US interest in Cuban resistance to Spain. Yet as with annexationism, US sympathy for Cubans' republican aspirations was difficult, if not impossible, to separate from American ambitions for control over the island. This dynamic came to a head in 1898, when the United States intervened in Cuba's final, successful war of independence, which had begun three years earlier.

1898 AND THE PLATT AMENDMENT

On February 15, 1898, the US warship *Maine* exploded in Havana's harbor. The explosion was widely attributed to Spanish sabotage and provided a convenient pretext for invasion. (A 1976 investigation by the US Navy attributed the explosion to an accidental fire.) War fever swept the nation, with slogans like "Remember the *Maine*, to Hell with Spain" auguring an age of American imperialism in the Caribbean and Pacific, as US troops invaded the Spanish colonies of Puerto Rico, the Philippines, and Cuba. Yet from the beginning, what Americans have called the Spanish-American War was framed as a humanitarian intervention.

Most historians now agree that while the US invasion hastened Spain's capitulation, the decisive damage to the empire's hold on Cuba had already been done. And so Máximo Gómez (1836–1905), the leader of the Cuban Liberation Army, pointedly refused to attend the ceremonial lowering of the Spanish flag over Havana in 1898. Almost four centuries after it was first raised over the island, and after three decades of bloody struggle for independence, the flag of Castile finally came down, only to be swiftly replaced by the Stars and Stripes.

Cuba was now effectively a US protectorate. A four-year military occupation laid city sewers and worked to eradicate yellow fever, although it was a Cuban physician, Carlos Finlay (1833–1915), whose research first identified the disease's transmission by infected mosquitoes (Espinosa 2009, 100–113). When the occupation formally ended in 1902, the Platt Amendment—passed first by the US Congress and narrowly approved by the new Cuban assembly—compromised Cuba's new independence. The amendment restricted the new government's power to negotiate international treaties and to organize its domestic finances. Most notoriously, it granted to the United States the "right to intervene for the preservation of Cuban independence" and "the maintenance of a government adequate for the preservation of life, property, and individual liberty." The requirement that Cuba lease land for the construction of US military bases led to the construction of the Guantánamo Bay Naval Base. The Platt Amendment was finally repealed in 1934, when Franklin Roosevelt's (1882–1945) administration sought improved relations

"The First Steps Alone," showing "Columbia," symbolizing America, letting go of a child, symbolizing the newly independent nation of Cuba, 1902. *After nearly four centuries as a Spanish colony, Cuba became a US protectorate in 1898. Four years later Cuba gained independence, though with some restrictions, through the Platt Amendment as passed by the US Congress and approved by the new Cuban assembly.* STOCK MONTAGE/ARCHIVE PHOTOS/GETTY IMAGES

with Latin America. Yet the US naval base at Guantánamo remains, the long-lived fruit of the "humanitarian" militarism of 1898.

THE CUBAN REVOLUTION AND THE BEGINNING OF THE EMBARGO

After a three-year guerrilla war, the rebels led by Fidel Castro entered Havana on January 1, 1959, overthrowing a US-allied dictator, Fulgencio Batista (1901–1973). It may surprise readers today that Castro was initially popular in the United States; the politically shrewd *comandante* was viewed even by many anticommunists as a liberal who was friendly to the United States, an impression Castro was content to encourage (Gosse 1993, 49). As they had long done, Anglo-Americans looking at Cuba tended to see whatever they wanted—a reflection of themselves, or of their fears.

Yet Castro's politics may have been opaque even to him in these early years. His early sympathies to Marxism and the Soviet Union have been a subject of fierce, likely unresolvable, debate. On April 17, 1961, Cuba quickly repelled an invasion by a US-armed militia of Cuban exiles at the Bay of Pigs, which was intended to incite popular revolt against Castro. It was a humiliating defeat for President John F. Kennedy (1917–1963) and the US Central Intelligence Agency (CIA), who had planned the attack, and a political triumph for Castro, which he followed two days later with a defiant speech that declared

Cuba's revolution to be "socialist." Later, during the Cuban missile crisis of 1962, the island became a proxy battleground for the United States and the Soviet Union, which placed nuclear-armed missiles on Cuban soil and then struck a deal with Kennedy to remove them without Castro's approval. Popular American support for the revolutionaries was now restricted to the growing Black Power and radical student movements, whose adherents would continue to view Cuba as an ally against racism, colonialism, and poverty.

Cuba's move to the Soviet camp during the Cold War must be considered in the context of its escalating confrontation with the United States. The US embargo is a case in point. Less the single, coherent policy that the name implies, "the embargo" is instead a patchwork of sanctions first issued by Dwight D. Eisenhower (1890–1969) and strengthened under President Kennedy and, after passage of the 1996 Helms-Burton Act, Bill Clinton. In June 1960, Eisenhower responded to Cuba's imports of Soviet oil by canceling the US sugar quota, which had for decades set the market for Cuba's biggest export. Cuba retaliated by nationalizing US-owned firms, banks, and property in its territory. By February 1962, virtually all trade, travel, and diplomatic ties between the two countries had been cut. US observers tempting to read the embargo's escalation simply as a Cold War skirmish, however, might miss the long-standing roots of the revolutionaries' resolve to defy the United States, which reached far back into the island's history of anticolonial revolt. As one 1960 slogan put it, "Sin cuota, pero sin amos" (Without a quota, but without masters), using an old term, *amo*, that slaves had used for their owners (Gott 2005, 184).

As many critics have charged, however, the revolution exchanged one set of rulers for another. Sugar continued to dominate Cuba's economy, with the Soviet Union assuming the quota abandoned by the United States. Meanwhile, the revolutionary energies of the early 1960s hardened into the Soviet-style single-party police state that persists. What has remained consistent is the embargo. Conservative Cuban exiles and their supporters have for decades argued that the embargo weakens the Cuban regime by battering its economic base. Yet it also serves a convenient political purpose in Cuba itself, where the government has long defied US interference. In 2014, US president Barack Obama and Cuban president Raúl Castro initiated a rapprochement, through which the embargo—which had paradoxically served the political establishments of both countries for so long—was to be loosened. What type of relationship would succeed the long separation remained unclear. In 1891, the Cuban revolutionary and poet José Martí (1853–1895) argued that ignorance would pay dearly, warning that "the disdain of the formidable neighbor who does not know her is our America's greatest danger, and it is urgent—for the day of the visit is near—that her neighbor come to know her, and quickly, so that he will not disdain her" (Martí 2002, 295).

SEE ALSO *Caribbean; Castro, Fidel; Cuban Missile Crisis*

BIBLIOGRAPHY

Adams, John Quincy. "Letter to Hugh Nelson, April 28, 1823." In *What Happened in Cuba? A Documentary History*, by Robert Freeman Smith. New York: Twayne, 1963.

Buchanan, James. *Works of James Buchanan*, Vol. 8. Edited by John Bassett Moore. New York: Antiquarian Press, 1960.

Chaffin, Tom. *Fatal Glory: Narciso López and the First Clandestine U.S. War against Cuba.* Charlottesville: University Press of Virginia, 1996.

Espinosa, Mariola. *Epidemic Invasions: Yellow Fever and the Limits of Cuban Independence, 1878–1930.* Chicago: University of Chicago Press, 2009.

Gosse, Van. *Where the Boys Are: Cuba, Cold War, and the Making of a New Left.* New York: Verso, 1993.

Gott, Richard. *Cuba: A New History.* New Haven, CT: Yale University Press, 2005.

Martí, José. "Letters from New York: Our America" (1891). In *José Martí: Selected Writings.* Translated by Esther Allen. New York: Penguin, 2002.

May, Robert E. *The Southern Dream of a Caribbean Empire, 1854–1861.* Baton Rouge: Louisiana State University Press, 1972.

Rauch, Basil. *American Interest in Cuba: 1848–1855.* New York: Columbia University Press, 1948.

Smith, James Morton, ed. *The Republic of Letters: The Correspondence between Thomas Jefferson and James Madison, 1776–1826*, Vol. III. New York: Norton, 1995.

Sublette, Ned. "The Kingsmen and the Cha-Cha-Chá." In *Listen Again: A Momentary History of Pop Music*, edited by Eric Weisbard. Durham, NC: Duke University Press, 2007.

Treaty between the United States and the Republic of Cuba Embodying the Provisions Defining Their Future Relations as Contained in the Act of Congress. Signed May 22, 1903. General Records of the US Government, 1778–2006, RG 11, National Archives. http://www.ourdocuments.gov/doc.php?flash=true&doc=55

John Patrick Leary
Assistant Professor, Department of English
Wayne State University

CUBAN MISSILE CRISIS

The Cuban missile crisis of 1962 emerged from two historical developments: the Cold War between the United States and the Soviet Union, which had begun after World War II, and the national liberation struggles of developing countries. In light of the protagonists' growing nuclear arsenals, several international crises over the course of the Cold War had the potential for global calamity, and in the early 1960s the conflict intensified. John F. Kennedy was narrowly elected president in 1960 in part by promising a more assertive stance against the Soviets than had been taken by the administration of Dwight Eisenhower (in office 1953–1961). Soviet foreign policy under Premier Nikita Khrushchev, who emerged as leader of the Soviet Union in the mid-1950s, appeared to be entering an especially aggressive phase. Khrushchev sought gains at the West's expense globally, beyond the Eurasian landmass, where a chain of US-led alliances kept Soviet power in check.

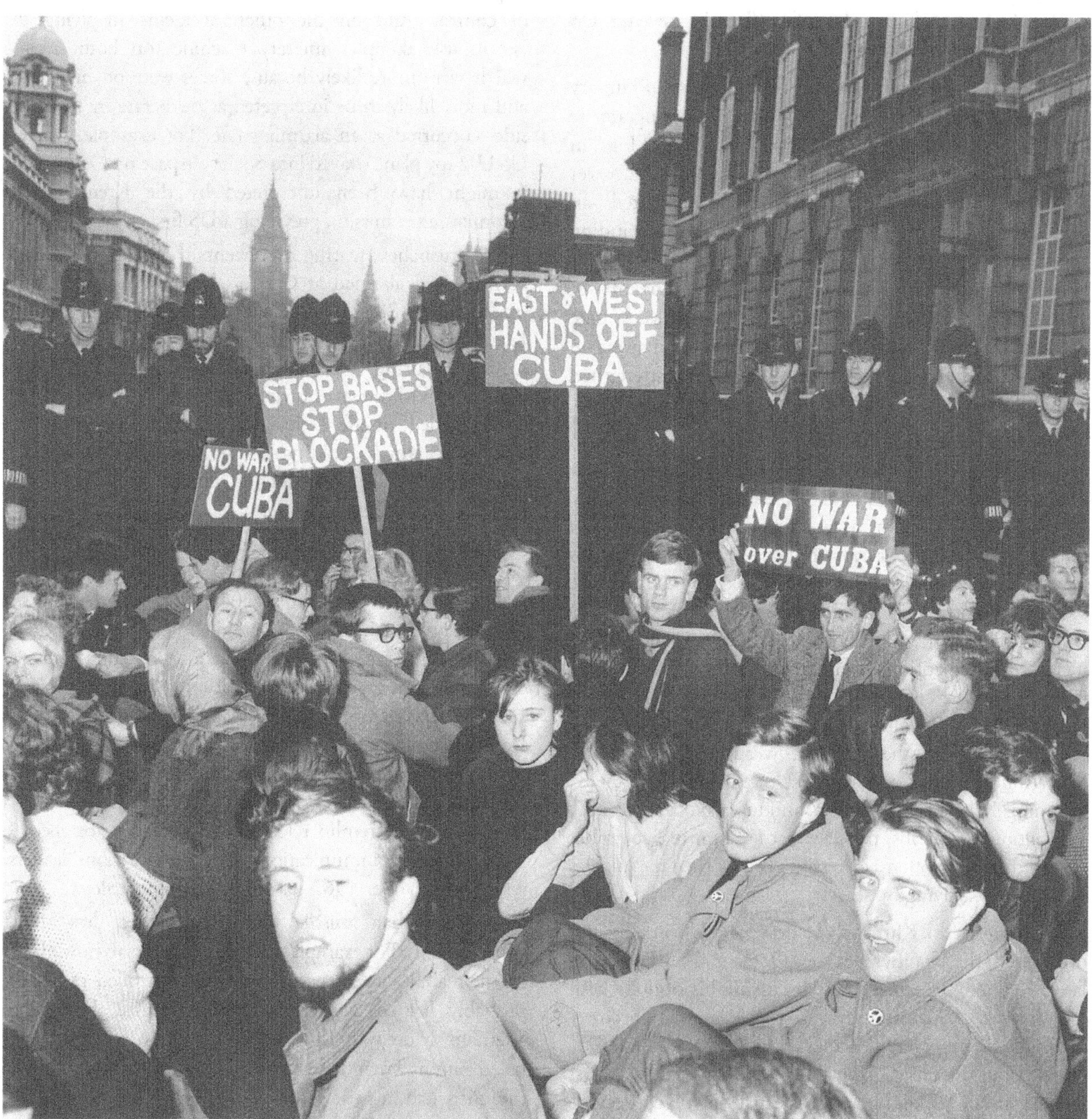

Demonstrators in London protest the United States' handling of the Cuban missile crisis, October 1962. *During the tensest week of the Cold War, massive US and Soviet arsenals were on high alert and World War III seemed a genuine possibility. Though neither President John F. Kennedy nor Soviet premier Nikita Khrushchev was ever close to deliberately ordering a nuclear strike, as the historical record has shown, the danger was inadvertent war.* KEYSTONE/HULTON ARCHIVE/GETTY IMAGES

An opportunity for Khrushchev presented itself with the guerrilla war led by Fidel Castro against Cuban president Fulgencio Batista. Castro's nationalist and communist revolution was intended in part to break decades of American domination. After Castro seized power in January 1959, US-Cuban relations worsened quickly as he nationalized American-owned property and built a communist dictatorship. Eisenhower responded by turning the economic screws and ordering the Central Intelligence Agency (CIA) to plan an invasion using anti-Castro Cuban exiles; as he left office, he severed US diplomatic relations with Cuba.

When Kennedy entered the White House in January 1961, he signed off on the CIA Cuban exile program he had inherited. The resulting invasion at the Bay of Pigs, in mid-April, failed miserably. But Kennedy persisted. Over subsequent months his administration executed an aggressive policy aimed at overthrowing Castro, including an ever-tightening economic embargo; the CIA's Operation Mongoose, a major covert action program of propaganda and sabotage; a series of plots to assassinate the Cuban leader; and large-scale military maneuvers in the Caribbean. This policy only served to strengthen Cuban-Soviet defense cooperation.

Indeed, Khrushchev decided in the spring of 1962 to launch Operation Anadyr, the secret deployment of nuclear medium- and intermediate-range ballistic missiles in Cuba. He had several motives: he was anxious to catch up in a nuclear arms race he was now losing, bent on defending his new communist ally against US attack, irked by the presence of similar North Atlantic Treaty Organization (NATO) Jupiter missiles near his borders in Turkey, and feeling increased competition from Mao Zedong's China for leadership in the communist world. Castro, likewise intent on defending his revolution and strengthening the "socialist camp," welcomed the powerful weapons, which could reach much of the continental United States. Kennedy, assuming Khrushchev's Cuban buildup would entail only conventional weapons, publicly warned him in September against deploying offensive missiles. But by then the missiles were already arriving by sea.

Unknown to Khrushchev, however, US intelligence discovered the deployment on October 14. Two days later, Kennedy began secretly discussing his options with his Executive Committee of the National Security Council. Members agreed they must secure the missiles' removal but disagreed on the means. The president at first favored an air strike, but once the risks involved became clear, he decided on a naval blockade of Cuba. This would forestall further Soviet shipments while signaling American resolve and preserving his options. He announced this move, as well as the existence of the crisis itself, to a national television audience on October 22.

The tensest week of the Cold War followed. In this confrontation between the two sides, massive arsenals were on high alert and World War III seemed a genuine possibility. Neither of the two leaders was ever close to deliberately ordering a nuclear strike; the latest evidence suggests a profound cautiousness on the part of both Kennedy and Khrushchev (though not some of their advisers). Rather, the danger was inadvertent war. On one hand, US conventional military action in Cuba might provoke a Soviet military response elsewhere, and events might quickly escalate out of control. And on the other, accidents involving the enormously complex military machines on both sides—which were more likely because forces were on high alert, and more likely to be interpreted as deliberate by the other side—occurred at an alarming rate. For example, when a US U-2 spy plane strayed into Soviet airspace on October 27, it might have been interpreted by the Kremlin as a reconnaissance mission presaging a US first strike.

Khrushchev, fearing that events were spinning out of control, and alarmed at Castro's bellicosity, agreed early on October 28 to withdraw his missiles. In return, Kennedy pledged never to invade Cuba, along with secretly assuring Moscow that the Jupiters in Turkey would be withdrawn shortly. Americans and Soviets had both decided, in effect, that strained relations with junior allies were worth avoiding all-out war. Castro especially was outraged when Khrushchev settled.

Difficult US-Soviet and Soviet-Cuban negotiations, over ancillary issues such as inspections and removal of Soviet IL-28 bombers also in Cuba, delayed a final settlement until November 20. Afterward the United States continued its covert program and economic blockade against Cuba, and US-Cuban relations remained hostile. US-Soviet relations thawed significantly, however. Having prevailed and demonstrated his toughness, as many saw it, Kennedy now enjoyed the latitude to pursue improved ties with Moscow; these were manifested, most importantly, in the Limited Test Ban Treaty of 1963. That same year a White House–Kremlin teletype "hotline" was installed to improve crisis communication between the nations' leaders, which in October 1962 had been alarmingly slow.

The Cuban missile crisis had other, less direct consequences. For example, the faith US officials now placed in their ability to manage crises via controlled escalation probably helped lead them to Americanize the war in Vietnam. Moreover, Khrushchev's Kremlin rivals cited his failed gambit when they ousted him in 1964. Beyond these, the crisis had at least some lasting, sobering effect. Other crises, some of them quite dangerous, would follow, but generally the superpowers tried mightily to avoid a repeat of October 1962. Since then the crisis has been the subject of intensive study—and not surprisingly, as historians agree it was the most dangerous moment in the Cold War.

SEE ALSO *Bay of Pigs; Castro, Fidel; Cold War; Kennedy, John Fitzgerald; Nuclear Weapons*

BIBLIOGRAPHY

Dobbs, Michael. *One Minute to Midnight: Kennedy, Khrushchev, and Castro on the Brink of Nuclear War.* New York: Knopf, 2008.

Fursenko, Aleksandr, and Timothy Naftali. *"One Hell of a Gamble": Khrushchev, Castro, and Kennedy, 1958–1964.* New York: Norton, 1997.

Munton, Don, and David A. Welch. *The Cuban Missile Crisis: A Concise History.* 2nd ed. New York: Oxford University Press, 2012.

White, Mark J., ed. *The Kennedys and Cuba: The Declassified Documentary History.* Rev. ed. Chicago: Ivan R. Dee, 2001.

Philip Nash
Associate Professor of History
Penn State University, Shenango Campus

D

DAWES SEVERALTY ACT

SEE *General Allotment Act (Dawes Severalty Act, 1877).*

DEBS, EUGENE V.

1855–1926

Eugene Victor Debs, born and raised in Terre Haute, Indiana, is most famous for his leadership of the American socialist movement in the early twentieth century. But Debs was not born a socialist, and he would infuse his socialist advocacy with values recognizable from the Terre Haute of his youth. In this sense, he was a quintessential American socialist.

Born to Alsatian immigrant parents who ran a small grocery store, Debs grew up in the charged political climate of the Civil War (1861–1865), where the Union victory carried with it an expanded sense of the possible in this small city. By age fourteen, Debs left school, hired on as a paint scraper for the local railroad, and dreamt of becoming a master mechanic in time. Laid off during the depression in 1874, he traveled to St. Louis in search of work, writing to his sister of his deepest concerns: "I don't expect to stay away from home forever, nor even for an unreasonable length of time; I only want to stay long enough and to prove that I can act manly when must be" (Salvatore 2007, 190).

Three years later, the devastating depression sparked the first national strike wave against the nation's railroads; but in Terre Haute, Debs, then the secretary-treasurer of the local branch of the Brotherhood of Locomotive Firemen, condemned the strike as anarchy. He supported William Riley McKeen (1829–1913), the Terre Haute native and president of the railroad. In 1879, following Debs's first election as Terre Haute's city clerk on the Democratic ticket, even the local Republican paper extolled him as "the blue-eyed boy of destiny."

Slowly, the events of the 1880s forced Debs to reconsider his positions. His experience in the Indiana legislature in 1885 as a new assemblyman revealed an inner core of corruption that shocked him. Then, too, he discovered that local entrepreneurs, such as McKeen, had increasingly been absorbed into national corporations headquartered in eastern financial urban centers that cared little about the local impact of their corporate decisions. Debs became a strong union supporter, urged his Brotherhood to adapt the strike as a tactical weapon, and began to develop a powerful critique of corporate capitalism. By 1894, Debs had left the Brotherhood, cofounded the American Railway Union (an industrial union of all skills and crafts united in one organization), and led them in the great Pullman strike of that year. The combined forces of the railroad corporations, backed by the legal power of the federal government and the widespread use of federal troops against striking workers, broke the strike, and Debs and other leaders received jail sentences.

During his six-month incarceration, Debs received numerous requests to head various socialists organizations. Although he scorned concentrated capital's power in a jailhouse interview, he insisted that the ballot was the only remedy to ensure that "every man is entitled to all he produces with his brains and hands" (Salvatore 2007, 151). This evocation of American producer ideology structured as well his paean to the promise of American democracy delivered to a crowd of some 100,000 in Chicago on his release from jail in November 1895. It was this Eugene Debs who, a short two years later at age forty-two, announced himself an American socialist.

As a socialist, Debs's critique of the corporation grew sharper, and his encouragement of working-class democratic protest more urgent. Debs repeatedly crisscrossed the county on grueling speaking tours, supporting strikes and socialist candidates for office and urging citizens to defend their nation's democratic promise against corporate power. Five times between 1900 and 1920, Debs ran for president on the Socialist ticket, and in 1912 he gained his highest total, some 6 percent of the vote in the four-way contest with Woodrow Wilson (1856–1924), the victor; Theodore Roosevelt (1858–1919) on the Progressive Party platform; and the incumbent Republican, President William Howard Taft (1857–1930). Throughout his incessant public engagement, the core of his message as the Socialist standard-bearer remained constant. As he expressed it in 1910:

> I am not a Labor Leader; I do not want you to follow me or anyone else; if you are looking for a Moses to lead you out of this capitalist wilderness, you will stay right where you are. I would not lead into the promised land if I could, because if I could lead you in, some one else would lead you out. YOU MUST USE YOUR HEADS AS WELL AS YOUR HANDS, and think yourself out of your present condition. (Salvatore 2007, 229–30)

Individualism, responsibility, and the promise of opportunity yet to come remained core aspirations in Debs's socialism as he articulated the constrictions on those possibilities imposed by the new corporate industrial society. Fighting that behemoth required new approaches and tactics, including a broader collective identity to contest the corporate redirection of America's political tradition.

In June 1918, Debs gave a speech interpreted by the government as a violation of the Espionage Act as World War I (1914–1918) was yet in progress. At his Cleveland trial, Debs again extolled the American revolutionaries—"the rebels of their day"—and warned that it was not he, but "American institutions," that were on trial. Unmoved, the jury found him guilty and the judge sentenced him to a ten-year sentence. It was from Atlanta Federal Penitentiary, as prisoner number 9653, that Debs last ran for president of the United States in 1920. President Warren Harding commuted Debs's prison sentence, as well as that of twenty-three other political prisoners, on December 23, 1921. Debs died on October 20, 1926, and is buried in Terre Haute.

SEE ALSO *Socialism*

BIBLIOGRAPHY

Bell, Daniel. "The Background and Development of Marxian Socialism in the United States." In *Socialism and American Life*, edited by Donald Drew Egbert and Stowe Persons. Princeton, NJ: Princeton University Press, 1952.

Buhle, Paul. *Marxism in the United States: Remapping the American Left*. London: Verso, 1987.

Dubofsky, Melvyn. *We Shall Be All: A History of the Industrial Workers of the World.* Chicago: Quadrangle, 1969.

Freeberg, Ernest. *Democracy's Prisoner: Eugene V. Debs, the Great War, and the Right to Dissent.* Cambridge, MA: Harvard University Press, 2008.

Howe, Irving. *Socialism and America.* New York: Harcourt Brace Jovanovich, 1985.

Kraditor, Aileen S. *The Radical Persuasion, 1890–1917: Aspects of the Intellectual History and the Historiography of Three American Radical Organizations.* Baton Rouge: Louisiana State University Press, 1981.

Laslett, John H. M., and Seymour Martin Lipset, eds. *Failure of a Dream? Essays in the History of American Socialism.* Garden City, NY: Anchor Press, 1974.

Salvatore, Nick. *Eugene V. Debs: Citizen and Socialist.* Urbana: University of Illinois Press, 1982. 2nd ed., 2007.

Nick Salvatore
Maurice and Hinda Neufeld Founders Professor of Industrial and Labor Relations
Cornell University

DECLARATION OF INDEPENDENCE

When the Continental Congress established a committee to draft the Declaration of Independence on June 11, 1776, the thirteen colonies had already been coordinating armed resistance against the British military for more than a year. Royal government had been under siege for almost two years. The Declaration, therefore, did not initiate the American Revolution. Instead, it marked a transformation in the revolutionaries' collective self-conception of their armed enterprise. What began as resistance had quickly transformed into rebellion and then became a civil war. By the summer of 1776, the revolutionaries viewed their enterprise as a war for national independence. They wanted others, at home and abroad, to see it as they did, too. The Revolution, they claimed, was no longer a domestic rebellion between king and colonies. There could be no honorable reconciliation of the provinces back into the British Empire. It was now an international war.

The drafters stated their international ambitions clearly in the Declaration's first sentence. "When in the Course of human events, it becomes necessary for one people to dissolve the political bands which have connected them with another," they began, "and to assume among the powers of the earth, the separate and equal station to which the Laws of Nature and of Nature's God entitle them, a decent respect to the opinions of mankind requires that they should declare the causes which impel them to the separation." Thomas Jefferson (1743–1826), the principal drafter of the Declaration, emphasized in this opening sentence that the conflict was existential, involving the fundamental question of political allegiance and collective independence as international states. No longer a haphazard sequence of intraimperial conflicts, the Revolution was now imagined as an epochal series of "*human* events" that justified the American people's claim to assume their "*equal* station" as one of "the *powers* of the earth." The thirteen colonies proclaimed themselves to be independent states—international states in what they saw as a preexisting European system of states.

ROOTS IN THE LAW OF NATIONS

The source of authority for this claim was "the Laws of Nature and of Nature's God." What precisely Jefferson meant by these laws is disputed, but a fair interpretation is that he was referring at least (if not exclusively) to the law of nations, which in the eighteenth century was frequently titled "the Law of Nature and Nations." It was common for lawyers and commentators to equate, to one degree or another, some parts of the law of nations with the law of nature, and then the latter with divine law. As such, the drafters were invoking a body of legal principles superior to that in the British Empire: the law among nations, of which that empire was only one. There was a higher law governing even nations that justified a body of people to separate from one polity and form another.

Emmerich de Vattel (1714–1767), in his influential treatise on the law of nations in the eighteenth century, argued that a declaration of war was necessary for offensive wars and advisable for all others because it provided notice to a state's own citizens, the enemy, and neighboring states and their subjects. Declarations activated the laws of war and neutrality; they might call into play preexisting treaty guarantees; and they presented a series of decisions for bystanding states. In the summer of 1776, the Continental Congress wanted to send strong signals to all these audiences. At home, it wished to draw the line between patriot and royalist more clearly and force people to choose sides. In Britain, it wished to explain its actions and rally sympathetic Britons to its cause. Elsewhere in Europe, and particularly in France, it hoped to negotiate treaties of commerce, alliance, and financial assistance.

The Continental Congress drew on the law of nations to supply two critical premises beneath the Declaration. The first premise was that the law of nations condoned just wars, most of which were defensive wars. States could wage war against other states that infringed their basic rights—rights enjoyed as polities and as individuals. That is how Jefferson framed the American case: it was a war to protect Americans and their governments from British tyranny and abuse, hence the need to specify specific grievances that justified defensive action, as well as the failure of all attempts to redress those grievances. This was a familiar form for colonial Americans. When Great Britain declared war on France in 1756, for example, it listed numerous grievances against France, and it claimed that it had repeatedly tried to redress those grievances through diplomacy. Those attempts having failed, declarations framed war as a last, desperate measure.

The second useful premise derived from the law of nations was state equality. International states were equal under the law of nations, despite the very real imbalances of power between them. Contemporaries often spoke of a world divided between strong and weak states; in the eyes of the law of nations, however, all states were equally entitled to both the rights and powers of nationhood. Legal equality meant that the revolutionary states, when claiming independence, could demand that Britain respect their sovereignty, and they could ask other independent nations to do so as well. Along with the powers to wage war on land and sea, they could also negotiate treaties of commerce and military alliance to assist in those efforts. This sequence—public statement of claims, exasperation at grievances unanswered, and the assertion of legitimate self-help under the law of nations—was almost a generic form for declarations of war in the eighteenth-century Atlantic world. The American revolutionaries embraced it for their own Declaration.

They also made it their own. Theirs was a special kind of declaration of war, designed for a civil war, which the revolutionaries wanted other Atlantic states to recognize as an international war. The Declaration thereby inaugurated, as David Armitage (2007) has observed, a new genre of independence declarations within the law of nations, which has become a template for colonial revolutionaries ever since. In the context of a colonial revolution, the Declaration of Independence was also a direct retort to the King's Proclamation of Rebellion of August 1775, which accused the colonists of "traitorous conspiracies" and put them outside the bounds of the civil law. In effect, through the Declaration, the Continental Congress declared that the turmoil that George III (1738–1820) proclaimed a domestic insurrection, thus activating martial law, was actually an international conflict, thereby invoking the laws of war and neutrality.

COMPANION FOUNDATIONAL DOCUMENTS

Congress quickly sent a copy of the Declaration to its secret agent in France, Silas Deane (1737–1789), and instructed him to present it to the courts of France and "the other Courts of Europe," and publish a French translation in the newspapers. However, the revolutionaries realized that *declaring* independence was hardly enough to accomplish the goal itself. At the very same time that Congress appointed a committee to draft the Declaration, it appointed two other committees to draft the Articles of Confederation and a model commercial treaty. A few weeks earlier, it had circulated a resolution to the thirteen states, recommending that they establish new governments—effectively, write new state constitutions. The four types of documents together—the state constitutions, the Declaration of Independence, the Articles of Confederation, and the Model Treaty—combined to form a revolutionary portfolio, which Congress collected and sent to France with its most powerful diplomat, who happened also to be the most recognizable American in Europe: Benjamin Franklin (1706–1790). Together, these foundational documents of the American nation played a substantial role in revolutionary diplomacy.

CONTINUING INFLUENCE

The Declaration continued to have influence long after the end of the American Revolution as a template for revolutionary and especially colonial independence movements. As Armitage has demonstrated, independence seekers borrowed the form and even language of the Declaration as early as 1790, in the Austrian Netherlands, and continue to do so today. In 2008, for example, the Kosovo Assembly declared their republic "to be an independent and sovereign state." There too, as two and a quarter centuries earlier, mere statement of the claim did not make it fact. It did, however, initiate a diplomatic process that continues to this day.

SEE ALSO *Adams, John; American Revolution; Franklin, Benjamin; Jefferson, Thomas*

BIBLIOGRAPHY

Armitage, David. *The Declaration of Independence: A Global History*. Cambridge, MA: Harvard University Press, 2007.

Billias, George Athan. *American Constitutionalism Heard Round the World, 1776–1989: A Global Perspective*. New York: New York University Press, 2009.

Hulsebosch, Daniel J. "The Revolutionary Portfolio: Constitution-Making and the Wider World in the American Revolution." *Suffolk University Law Review* 47 (2014): 759–822.

Maier, Pauline. *American Scripture: Making the Declaration of Independence*. New York: Knopf, 1998.

Onuf, Peter S. "A Declaration of Independence for Diplomatic Historians." *Diplomatic History* 22, 1 (1998): 71–83.

Daniel J. Hulsebosch
The Charles Seligson Professor of Law
New York University School of Law

DECOLONIZATION

Decolonization is often defined as the retreat of European colonialism. Coined in an academic encyclopedia in the early 1930s, the term gained traction among politicians and intellectuals after World War II as it became synonymous with the end of European colonial rule. In a strict sense, the phrase refers to the process where an imperial power, having conquered and imposed its will upon a territory, transfers control of that land to a legally sovereign national state.

DECOLONIZATION'S MEANING AND LEGACY

Decolonization's precise contours and legacy are the subject of considerable debate. Some scholars see the process's origins in the American hemisphere during the eighteenth and nineteenth centuries, but most associate the phrase with events in Asia and Africa between 1945 and 1975. Nationalists of this era took cues from one another—more so than their American forebears—and their efforts changed the international system, leading to the creation of approximately 195 nation-states, a dramatic expansion of the fifty or so nation-states that existed at the dawn of the twentieth century. This transformation changed international politics, but it did not result in the redistribution of power and wealth. In the twenty-first century, scholars variously celebrate decolonization as the harbinger of postcolonial liberation or denounce it as a tool of neocolonial domination.

What accounts for this disagreement, and what does it reveal about twentieth-century decolonization? In part, the problem stems from terminology, which has changed considerably since the 1930s. When decolonization reached its apogee in the mid-twentieth century, social scientists and nationalist politicians shaped the phrase's meaning. Both groups tended to see progress as universal and inevitable, and assumed that economic modernization would spread naturally to colonized peoples if indigenous nation-states replaced European empires. These nation-states, the argument went, would possess distinct personalities, but they would advance together on a shared path of development.

These assumptions came under attack after the 1960s. As the optimism of decolonization faded, postcolonial scholars and statesmen, drawing often upon the writings of Frantz Fanon (1925–1961), Edward Said (1935–2003), and Walter Rodney (1942–1980), among others, turned a critical eye toward nationalism itself, critiquing everything from the institutions that colonialism left behind to the practices that curtailed freedom after independence. These critiques moved hand in hand with questions: Was secular nationalism a European invention? Did imperialism require territory or might it take subtler forms? Was liberation possible in a world defined by Western ideas? Each query hinted at anxieties about the end of empire and dissatisfaction with the intellectual tools of midcentury social science.

Beyond terminology, decolonization was complicated by the fact that historical actors had defined the concept differently. Some viewed European power through the prism of global governance. John A. Hobson (1858–1940), for instance, who authored influential tomes about modern empire during the early twentieth century, felt that colonialism was distinct from imperialism. He equated the former with European migration and resettlement—the supposed engines of American nationalism—and viewed the latter as a neologism for war in Asia and Africa. Although the violence of Europe's "small wars" was innately unjust, he championed reform over liberation, and equated anti-imperialism with the creation of a rule-based international system rooted in peace, prosperity, and common values.

This formula did not impress all of Hobson's contemporaries. Vladimir Lenin (1870–1924) argued that colonialism and imperialism were separated by time not violence, and he drew upon the writings of Karl Marx (1818–1883) to suggest that both processes grew from the vagaries of capitalism. It was a farce, therefore, to equate decolonization—that is, the retreat of imperialism—with membership in a rule-based community that codified the power of the powerful. Both Hobson and Lenin lamented the West's industrialized militarism, yet they articulated different visions about empire's logic and future. Whereas Hobson saw no alternative to world interdependence—and expressed the outlines of what would become liberal internationalism—Lenin embraced revolution and dedicated his life to freeing Russia from industrial capitalism.

Subsequent anti-imperialists struggled to reconcile this tension. India's Rabindranath Tagore (1861–1941) critiqued aspects of Hobson's thinking, especially his Eurocentrism, but similarly suggested that education and self-empowerment, not anticapitalist revolution, would liberate his countrymen. In his travels around the world, Tagore proselytized a vision of global interdependence where goods and ideas moved across borders, and people—irrespective of their backgrounds—fostered a common, multicultural civilization. China's Sun Yat-sen (1866–1925), in contrast, fought to overthrow the Qing dynasty because it had failed to control the spread of European technology and trade after the Opium Wars of the mid-nineteenth century. Although China was not formally colonized in the nineteenth century, Sun Yat-sen's supporters saw themselves as the victims of Western exploitation, and pointed to Japan as proof that a thoroughly modern government, dedicated to economic and political reform, could emancipate and unify the Chinese people. Although Tagore and Sun Yat-sen were visionaries who similarly rejected the hubris of Europe's civilizing mission, they defined imperial retreat differently, with the former pushing for greater equality in an interdependent age and the latter emphasizing autonomy, so China could pursue an independent path abroad.

REFORM, REVOLUTION, OR A THIRD WAY?

By the time academics invented the word *decolonization*, European imperialism was beset differently on several fronts. Within Europe after World War I (1914–1918), reformers saw the League of Nations as an instrument to establish common standards of global governance. The mandate system, in theory, promised to replace imperial exploitation with universal progress, thereby spreading economic modernity to non-European people while legitimizing the West's centrality to development everywhere. Some colonized people attacked this mind-set through the league's petition system, which allowed colonial peoples to document colonial practices, while others mobilized mass movements in the streets. In South Asia, Mahatma Gandhi (1869–1948) organized the peaceful drive for indigenous democracy, lamenting British chauvinism while insisting that Indians become equal partners in a federated world system. Farther north, Mao Zedong (1893–1976) spearheaded a communist revolution among China's northern peasants, drawing inspiration from the Soviet Union and anger from Sun Yat-sen's successors. The line between formal and informal empire remained murky, as did decolonization's precise meaning. For some, it signified reform and interdependence; for others, it indicated freedom and power.

Regardless, European imperialism buckled after World War II (1939–1945). The ascension of the United States and Soviet Union heralded the birth of a Cold War, which refracted the debate about decolonization. On one side, Washington tried to walk a tightrope, rebuilding Western Europe and Japan in its image while tentatively promoting the end of Europe's empires in Asia Pacific and the Middle East. American policy makers sought a political order where nation-states traded freely and interacted peacefully, and Washingtonians used security pacts, foreign aid, and United Nations (UN) diplomacy to promote their own multicultural alternative to the civilizing mission. Decolonization challenged this formula profoundly, and as new countries became UN members, it became harder to avoid the critique that the "free world" was nothing more than a rule-based community Washington defined.

Opposite the United States, the Soviet Union remained anticapitalism's lodestar. Despite the devastation wrought by the policies of Joseph Stalin (1879–1953) and the wars of Adolf Hitler (1889–1945), Moscow had apparently industrialized without Western investment, making it a potent symbol at a time when decolonization appeared increasingly synonymous with UN membership and US money. Encouraged by Stalin, Mao's first act as China's premier was to wage war against the UN in Korea. He then launched a series of Stalinist land programs that transformed Chinese society. His actions terrified some, inspired others, and raised the questions: Had the superpowers hijacked the terms of decolonization? Did options exist beyond capitalism and communism?

An answer came at the Asia-Africa Conference of 1955. India, China, and other countries put their differences aside to articulate a "third way" between the United States and Soviet Union. This tentative alliance promoted racial equality and regional trade, and massaged earlier tensions about the proper contours of Europe's retreat. In theory, Asian and African countries would work in lockstep within and beyond the UN, taking control of that organization's agenda while renegotiating the terms of world trade. This development created angst in Washington, nudging some policy makers to confront America's own race problem, and it inflated Moscow's ambitions, leading to overstretch in Latin America and Africa. Europe's statesmen, for their part, responded to this "third way" with bluster—invading the Suez region in 1956 while recasting empire as a cooperative enterprise—but in the words of Britain's Harold Macmillan (1894–1986), a "wind of change" had arrived, which culminated in the creation of dozens of national states in Africa, the Caribbean, and Asia Pacific after 1960.

THE FRAGILITY OF POSTCOLONIAL SOVEREIGNTY

This transformation was a triumph. Decolonization empowered the fight against racism worldwide, which added urgency to America's own civil rights movement, and it remade politics at the UN General Assembly and the International Court of Justice. However, tensions remained. War erupted along the Sino-Indian border in 1962, and the regional trade prophesized in the mid-1950s failed to materialize during the 1960s. Washington's decision to send soldiers into Vietnam, coming on the heels of the UN's multilateral (unsuccessful) Congo mission, seemed to confirm the fragility of postcolonial sovereignty, even as antiwar passions distracted from the deeper truth that governments everywhere were struggling to establish their legitimacy after independence. By the mid-1970s, African and Asian nation-states were experiencing déjà vu all over again. They were being subjected regularly to interventions from superpowers, multinational corporations, and international institutions—trends that have only accelerated since the end of the Cold War.

Was decolonization a chimera? Some pundits blame disillusionment on indigenous corruption; others point toward neocolonialism. Both sides are equipped with theories and data, yet their debate, which tends to focus on events after the 1960s, elides the fact that these disagreements were woven into the decolonization process from the very beginning. Depending on one's vantage point, the movement against imperialism was either a campaign to redefine the terms of membership in a rule-based international community or a revolution against the economic and political sinews of that community. The Cold War gave this debate its trajectory—neither Washington nor Moscow wanted to perpetuate European rule after the 1940s—but this deeper tension is as alive today as it was in the mid-twentieth century, as seen in conversations about inequality, rights, law, and terrorism. Who governs our world and how can they do it better? More than a definition, this *question* is at the heart of decolonization.

SEE ALSO *Bandung Conference (1955); League of Nations; Modernization Theory; Non-Aligned Movement; Orientalism; United Nations*

BIBLIOGRAPHY

Aydin, Cemil. *The Politics of Anti-Westernism in Asia: Visions of World Order in Pan-Islamic and Pan-Asian Thought.* New York: Columbia University Press, 2007.

Cooper, Frederick. *Colonialism in Question: Theory, Knowledge, History.* Berkeley: University of California Press, 2005.

Irwin, Ryan. "Decolonization and the Cold War." In *Routledge Handbook of the Cold War,* edited by Artemy Kalinovsky and Craig Daigle. London: Routledge, 2014.

Shipway, Martin. *Decolonization and Its Impact: A Comparative Approach to the End of the Colonial Empires.* Oxford: Wiley-Blackwell, 2008.

Westad, Odd Arne. *The Global Cold War: Third World Interventions and the Making of Our Times.* Cambridge: Cambridge University Press, 2005.

Ryan Irwin
Assistant Professor
University at Albany–SUNY

DEINDUSTRIALIZATION

Deindustrialization, a process of social and economic change caused by the removal or reduction of industrial capacity or activity in a country or region, is the opposite of industrialization. Deindustrialization is not a recent phenomenon. The word has its origins in World War II (1939–1945) when the Nazis stripped occupied areas of their industry. In the midst of the economic crisis of the 1970s and 1980s, however, the term *deindustrialization* resurfaced in the work of a growing number of economists, labor historians, and geographers as an explanation for economic change, and, in particular, the sharp decline of basic industries. During this period, North America and Western Europe hemorrhaged tens of millions of industrial jobs. Once proud manufacturing centers around the Great Lakes and across New England were hollowed out.

American industry, undamaged by World War II, accounted for close to half of global manufacturing output in the mid-1950s. Productivity rose, and workers enjoyed rising standards of living and benefited from the protections of the liberal state and Keynesian fiscal and monetary policy. However, this premier position as "manufacturer to the world" was not sustained as Japan, continental European countries, and, in the 1970s and 1980s, several developing Asian nations challenged US preeminence in textiles, cars, steel, major household appliances, machine tools, and consumer electronics. Much of this work went to newly industrialized areas with cheap labor, including Mexico, South Korea, Hong Kong, and Taiwan. Free-trade agreements hastened the flow of work from the United States.

As US firms went global with their production, seeking out low-wage regions of the world to get their basic manufacturing done, industries like textiles and apparel suffered devastating employment losses, while countries like Bangladesh, Jamaica, and the Dominican Republic constructed massive free-trade zones and offered incentives for US corporations to relocate. Over time, the globalizing activities of US corporations that used world markets to outsource production entailed sending more complex work like automobile and computer production abroad.

At the end of World War II, 51 percent of workers in the United States were employed in manufacturing-based jobs. Now, 75 percent are employed in the service sector. From the 1970s forward, as key US industries globalized their business, decision making revolved less around long-term domestic investments and far more toward enhancing shareholder value. By comparison, Japan's and Germany's continued successes into the twenty-first century in the manufacture of things like machine tools were based on investments in a skilled workforce, shop-floor decision making by front line workers, and interfirm collaborations.

Across the decade of the 1980s, one in five American workers saw his or her job disappear. Among the Fortune 500's largest manufacturers, employment dropped to 12.4 million from 15.9 million in the decade of the 1980s. General Motors, Ford Motor Company, Boeing, and General Electric eliminated 208,500 more jobs between 1990 and 1995. The scale of decline, evidenced by the search for the next cheap place to get things made, supplanted the "golden age" of rising working-class living standards. The number of US manufacturing jobs continues to shrink: between January 2000 and April 2009, 5 million manufacturing jobs were lost, with globalization and increased productivity to blame. White-collar and professional jobs are also being lost. Forrester Research, a consulting firm, estimated that 3.4 million white-collar jobs would be outsourced between 2003 and 2015, including 542,000 computer jobs, 259,000 management jobs, 191,000 architectural jobs, 79,000 legal jobs, and 1.6 million backoffice jobs. In a reversal of the positive socioeconomic trends in the twenty years after World War II, the outsourcing of well-paying industrial jobs contributed to a national wage depression and increased income inequality. Inflation-adjusted median income in the mid-1990s was roughly 5 percent lower than in the late 1970s. As the twentieth century ended, nearly 20 percent of US households had a zero or negative net worth.

In the introduction to *Beyond the Ruins: The Meanings of Deindustrialization*, Joseph Heathcott and Jefferson Cowie point out:

> Deindustrialization is not a story of a single emblematic place, such as Flint or Youngstown, or a specific time period, such as the 1980s; it was a much broader, more fundamental, historical transformation. What was labeled deindustrialization in the intense political heat of the late 1970s and early 1980s turned out to be a more socially complicated, historically deep, geographically diverse, and politically perplexing phenomenon than previously thought. (Cowie and Heathcott 2003, 2)

Now deindustrialization is even affecting countries that were the beneficiaries of waves of US factory closing. For example, companies are moving factories from China to Indonesia, where they can pay less and face fewer environmental regulations. Meanwhile, in the garment sector, firms like Wal-Mart push their producers to manufacture ever-cheaper baby clothes and T-shirts, hastening the tendency of firms in the Philippines to subcontract work to factories in Sri Lanka and

Bangladesh. Thus the historical process of deindustrialization reflects ongoing changes in the global economy.

SEE ALSO *AFL-CIO: Labor's Foreign Policy; Globalization; Keynesian Economics; Neoliberalism*

BIBLIOGRAPHY

Bluestone, Barry, and Bennet Harrison. *The Deindustrialization of America: Plant Closings, Community Abandonment, and the Dismantling of Basic Industry.* New York: Basic Books, 1982.

Chen, Xiangming, and Nick Bacon, eds. *Confronting Urban Legacy: Rediscovering Hartford and New England's Forgotten Cities.* Lanham, MD: Lexington, 2013.

Cowie, Jefferson, and Joseph Heathcott, eds. *Beyond the Ruins: The Meanings of Deindustrialization.* Ithaca, NY: Cornell University Press, 2003.

Forrant, Robert. *Metal Fatigue: American Bosch and the Demise of Metalworking in the Connecticut River Valley.* Amityville, NY: Baywood, 2009.

High, Steven. *Industrial Sunset: The Making of North America's Rust Belt, 1969–1984.* Toronto, ON: University of Toronto Press, 2003.

Mah, Alice. *Industrial Ruination, Community, and Place: Landscapes and Legacies of Urban Decline.* Toronto, ON: University of Toronto Press, 2012.

Massey, Doreen, and Richard Meegan. *The Anatomy of Job Loss: The How, Why, and Where of Employment Decline.* New York: Methuen, 1982.

McCarthy, John C. "3.3 Million U.S. Services Jobs to Go Offshore," TechStrategy Research Brief. Forrester Research, Inc. November 11, 2002.

Walley, Christine J. *Exit Zero: Family and Class in Postindustrial Chicago.* Chicago: University of Chicago Press, 2013.

Robert Forrant
Professor of History
University of Massachusetts Lowell

DELANY, MARTIN

SEE *Back-to-Africa Movement.*

DEMOCRACY IN AMERICA (ALEXIS DE TOCQUEVILLE, 1835–1840)

Since its two-volume publication in 1835 and 1840 (with English translations following in 1838 and 1840), *De la Démocratie en Amérique,* or *Democracy in America,* by French count Alexis de Tocqueville (1805–1859) has forcefully affirmed the equation of the United States with social equality and popular sovereignty to American, European, and ultimately global publics. While providing US readers with external validation of their self-image, it has invited non-Americans to triangulate democracy, the United States, and their own societies as a model of debating their political future. As such, the text has confirmed, amplified, and modified extant discourses on America as a utopian or dystopian other.

Amid a vast body of antebellum European travel literature ethnocentrically censuring the United States as a barbaric or infant nation of absences, lacking order, culture, morals, and manners, Tocqueville's account stuck out as the first theory-minded study of modern democracy, a detached and multivocal survey of the political, social, and cultural mechanisms of a societal order prefiguring (and revealing the tools to productively channel) what he believed to be the inevitable progress of equality in France and the world.

Tocqueville's method of exploring an issue from all sides opened *Democracy in America* to highly selective and contingent readings. He was enthusiastically embraced by Americans convinced of their political superiority over European regimes, yet anxious over their continued cultural dependency on the Old World. He thus served as an authoritative French voice that could be read as confirming the providential nature of American democracy as a beacon to the world as well as its exceptional quality in transforming the European antagonism of liberty and religion into the mutually reinforcing foundation of freedom. Yet they summarily rejected one of *Democracy in America*'s central tenets, egalitarianism's subversion of individual liberty by the tyranny of a conformist majority. Tocqueville nonetheless became an honorary American as the first volume of *Democracy* was adopted as a standard textbook on US government and society and was referenced in a number of state constitutional conventions. His argument on the tensions between liberty and equality acquired a new urgency during the rising conflict over slavery, secession, and American identity culminating in the Civil War (1861–1865), after which *Democracy* became a respected but little studied classic surpassed by the new industrial order and its deep social antagonisms.

English Whig Henry Reeve's (1813–1895) translation of the *Démocratie,* which Tocqueville considered antidemocratically biased, met with great interest in Britain among conservatives and radicals alike, who read it either as an indictment or an endorsement of democratic politics and reformist agendas. Its greatest intellectual impact was on English liberalism and particularly on John Stuart Mill (1806–1873), who integrated and adapted aspects such as the danger of majority tyranny into his thought. The French viewed *Démocratie* as a mere report and apologia for the United States, and Tocqueville consistently failed as a parliamentarian and minister to constructively apply its insights to French politics. It was discussed by French liberals of the Third Republic but had little real impact, in the same way that German republicans used it as a reference when debating federalism during the constitutional assembly of 1848 without much consequence, after which it fell out of view together with democracy.

The book's revival in the 1930s once again occurred in a transatlantic context of a United States seeking to position and define its society in relation to the failing European democracies giving way to fascism and communism. The darker second volume in particular was read as a prophecy of the mass age that could help explore the dynamics of corporatist conformity, privatism, and the interventionist state. It guided American sociologists since the 1950s, as well as transatlantic philosophers such as Hannah Arendt (1906–1975) concerned with totalitarianism and the revival of the polis or libertarian economists such as Friedrich Hayek (1899–1992). Firmly ensconced among the sacred scriptures of American civil religion in negotiating the key issues of individualism and community, liberty, and equality, and the limits of a materialistic pursuit of happiness, the book has served liberals, conservatives, communitarians, libertarians, and progressives alike to validate their particular visions of US society as well as their criticism of the status quo. Beyond the United States its discourse on the ambivalence of democracy and the challenges of civil society could be argued to have a continuing potential for evoking strong resonances during periods of social transformation or acute crisis in which democratization becomes a political issue and America a potential role model, whether in postsocialist Eastern Europe, the societies of the Arab Spring, or Asian and African threshold countries.

SEE ALSO *Transatlantic Reform*

BIBLIOGRAPHY

Amos, Sigrid Karin. *Alexis de Tocqueville and the American National Identity: The Reception of* De la Démocratie en Amérique *in the United States in the Nineteenth Century.* Frankfurt am Main, Germany: Peter Lang, 1995.

Clark, Thomas. "Die *Démocratie* in Amerika: Zur Wirkungsgeschichte Tocquevilles in den Vereinigten Staaten." In *Alter Staat–Neue Politik. Tocqueville's Entdeckung der modernen Demokratie,* edited by Karlfriedrich Herb and Oliver Hidalgo, 155–75. Baden Baden, Germany: Nomos, 2004.

Clark, Thomas. "The American Democrat Reads *Democracy in America:* Tocqueville and Cooper in the Transatlantic Hall of Mirrors." *Amerikastudien/American Studies* 52, 2 (2007): 187–208.

Marti, Urs. "Tocquevilles Wirkungsgeschichte in Europa." In *Alter Staat–Neue Politik: Tocqueville's Entdeckung der modernen Demokratie,* edited by Karlfriedrich Herb and Oliver Hidalgo, 135–53. Baden Baden, Germany: Nomos, 2004.

Mélonio, Françoise. *Tocqueville and the French.* Charlottesville: University Press of Virginia, 1998.

Tocqueville, Alexis de. *Democracy in America: Historical-Critical Edition of De la Démocratie en Amérique,* edited by Eduardo Nolla, translated from the French by James T. Schleifer. Indianapolis, IN: Liberty Fund, 2010.

Zunz, Olivier. "Tocqueville and the Americans: Democracy in America as Read in Nineteenth-Century America." In *The Cambridge Companion to Tocqueville,* edited by Cheryl B. Welch, 359–396. Cambridge: Cambridge University Press, 2006.

Thomas Clark
Visiting Associate Professor of American Studies
University of Tübingen, Germany

DEPARTMENT OF AGRICULTURE, US

The US Department of Agriculture (USDA) was formed on May 15, 1862, a time when the United States was largely an agrarian nation. President Abraham Lincoln, who called the USDA "the people's department," did not grant the department cabinet status, but President Grover Cleveland signed a bill that did so in 1889.

Inspiration for a USDA dates back to the 1830s, when American farmers became interested in experimenting with seed varieties and animal breeds from overseas, mostly Europe. US Commissioner of Patents Henry Ellsworth (1791–1858) began to work closely with agricultural societies to acquire those seeds and breeds. His work was influential in the establishment of an Agricultural Division within the US Patent Office, and Ellsworth himself became known as the father of the Department of Agriculture.

The USDA maintained a strongly domestic focus from its founding through the Great Depression in the 1930s. Its role, as exemplified in the Hatch Act of 1887 and the Smith-Lever Act of 1914, was largely to inform farmers about the latest trends in agricultural science and help them to implement new strategies. The Hatch Act funded a national network of agricultural experiment stations—research centers that focused on food production—while Smith-Lever provided for cooperative extension services—agricultural education outlets located at land-grant universities. During the Depression the USDA played a role in helping farmers secure low interest and federally backed loans in order to stay afloat during economically difficult times.

By mid-century the USDA's role (with the notable exception of setting nutritional standards) had assumed a more global perspective, focusing in particular on crop yields and trade policies. President Harry S. Truman initiated this transition with the Point Four Program (so named because it happened to be the fourth point in his 1949 inaugural speech). Designed primarily to curry favor with developing nations during an era of impending Soviet domination, the nation's first international economic development program aimed to provide far-ranging technical assistance and economic support to underdeveloped countries potentially ripe for a communist takeover. The USDA became an integral element of this policy by overseeing Point Four's agricultural training programs.

The USDA's foreign involvement continued when the Agricultural Trade Development and Assistance Act of 1954 established a program to foster global trade in American foodstuffs. The act's intention, according to President Dwight D. Eisenhower, was to "lay the basis for a permanent expansion of our exports of agricultural products, with lasting benefits to ourselves and peoples in other lands." In 1961 President John F. Kennedy renamed the program Food for Peace, noting that "food is a helping to people around the world whose good will and friendship we want." In 1966 Congress upgraded the act by passing the Food for Peace Act. With this law there was a shift from unloading surplus grain to promoting humanitarian aid. In 2008 the Food for Peace Act officially replaced the original Agricultural Trade Development and Assistance Act.

Other key developments ensured that the USDA remained a federal department with international influence. Kennedy furthered the USDA's global focus when he created the United States Agency for International Development (USAID). USAID works closely with the USDA's Foreign Agricultural Service to foster global food security and in so doing "enable resilient, democratic societies to realize their potential." This goal is pursued by bringing several USDA innovations—such as extension services, farmer loan programs, and developing food markets—to other parts of the world.

Work supported by the USDA on wheat breeding in the 1940s helped make possible the work of the biologist Norman Borlaug (1914–2009) and the Green Revolution, an agricultural initiative starting in the 1960s that would dramatically increase crop yields throughout the developing world. In 1945 the USDA sent the agronomist Samuel Cecil Salmon (1885–1975), a wheat specialist, to Japan to deal with postwar food shortages there. Salmon's work provided the bridge between the semidwarf Japanese wheat and the traditional wheat strains that breeders such as Borlaug would engineer to create unprecedented yield explosions. Between 1960 and 1990, China's wheat production went from 19.1 million to 90.1 million metric tons. South Asia saw increases from 15.5 million to 63.5 million metric tons.

The USDA's active engagement in global agribusiness has brought the department its fair share of criticism. A 2004 report called "USDA Inc." roundly condemned the USDA for working as a corporate handmaiden of a chemically driven and ecologically unsound approach to agriculture. The USDA's direct and indirect support of agricultural biotechnology, concentrated animal feeding operations, and corporate consolidation has been met with substantial blowback from a sustainable food movement that is currently challenging USDA authority with calls for a national food policy.

The USDA's future is one in which it will have to balance the traditional demands of global agribusiness with the decentralized efforts of small farmers serving local markets through nonindustrial methods of production.

SEE ALSO *Green Revolution; Point Four; United States Agency for International Development (USAID)*

BIBLIOGRAPHY

Conkin, Paul. *A Revolution down on the Farm: The Transformation of American Agriculture since 1929*. Louisville: University Press of Kentucky, 2009.

Hurt, R. Douglas. *American Agriculture: A Brief History*. West Lafayette, IN: Purdue University Press, 2002.

Mattera, Philip. "USDA Inc.: How Agribusiness Has Hijacked Regulatory Policy at the U.S. Department of Agriculture." Corporate Research Project of Good Jobs First. 2004. http://www.nffc.net/Issues/Corporate%20Control/USDA%20INC.pdf

James McWilliams
Ingram Professor of History
Texas State University, San Marcos

DEPARTMENT OF DEFENSE, US

The United States Department of Defense (DoD) is by far the largest of the fifteen cabinet-level departments of the executive branch of the US government. DoD is responsible for directing the armed forces of the United States as well as several defense-related agencies. DoD is headed by the secretary of defense, who is nominated by the president and confirmed by the US Senate.

The DoD has an estimated 3 million employees, including members of the branches of the armed services. The DoD includes the three military services (army, navy, and air force), the Joint Chiefs of Staff, nine Combatant Commands, and seventeen individual agencies, the largest of which is the National Security Agency (NSA). The NSA's budget and number of employees are classified, but they are known to be significantly larger than those of the entire Department of State, including all of the latter's embassies worldwide. Other sizable agencies within the DoD are the National Geospatial-Intelligence Agency, the National Reconnaissance Office, the Defense Intelligence Agency, and the Missile Defense Agency.

Although the DoD's official annual budget for 2015 was approximately $600 billion, this figure did not include numerous defense and military expenditures that are counted separately. An estimated total for all defense-related expenses, including veterans' affairs, supplemental budgeting for the war in Iraq, and payments on the national debt, brings the amount closer to more than $900 billion per year.

HISTORY OF THE DOD

Prior to the adoption of the National Security Act of 1947, the armed forces of the United States were divided between two cabinet-level departments of the executive branch: the Department of War (for practical purposes the command of the US Army and the Army Air Forces) and the Department of the Navy (including the Marine Corps). Separate laws enacted by the Continental Congress in 1775 created the original army, navy, and Marine Corps of the United States. In the decade following the conclusion of the Revolutionary War, the three military services largely fell into disuse. When the First Congress convened in New York in 1789, one of its first acts was to create a cabinet-level War Department whose secretary would be responsible for overseeing all the equipment and personnel from the three armed services. A decade later, with Congress having become increasingly displeased with the War Department's management of the fledgling navy, a law was enacted that created a new and separate Navy Department and that placed the Marine Corps under its purview. Thus, between 1798 and 1947, the War Department (effectively the army) and the Navy Department were two separate cabinet-level departments of the executive branch that operated independently, albeit under the ultimate authority of the president. The divided military command between the War Department and Navy Department historically was marked by bouts of rivalry (symbolized in sport by the annual Army-Navy football game), jealousy, and sometimes hostility, although during the 1920s and 1930s the two departments developed a joint-action plan to be used in the event of war (known as FTP-155).

In 1941, with World War II already raging in Europe and the Pacific, but prior to the bombing of Pearl Harbor, military leaders developed plans through which the two rival armed forces might better coordinate to strengthen the defensive capabilities of the United States in the event of war. The military adopted in 1941 (and revised in 1942) a system of regional "Defense Commands" that divided the US mainland into four territories (Western Defense Command, Central Defense Command, Northeast Defense Command, and Southern Defense Command). The navy's Atlantic and Pacific fleets (based in Norfolk, Virginia, and San Diego, California, respectively) fell under separate commands. The experiences of World War II prompted the movement toward a more integrated battle command structure. Although the army (including the Army Air Forces) and the navy (including the marines) were not themselves united under a joint American command, they were placed under the authority of a "supreme" commander who had authority over the armed services of all allied nations in specific theaters of operation. The most famous (but not the sole) example during the war was that of General Dwight D. Eisenhower (1890–1969) as the Supreme Commander of the Allied Expeditionary Force for the invasion of Normandy in 1944. In this position, Eisenhower held combined command authority over the British and American navies, armies, and air forces.

The Pentagon building, the construction of which began on September 11, 1941—sixty years to the day before it was attacked in 2001—is today the physical and symbolic headquarters of the US Department of Defense. It was built on land once owned by Confederate general Robert E. Lee (1807–1870) that was located between what later became Arlington National Cemetery and the Washington National Airport. The Pentagon, built in only seventeen months, is the largest office building in the world, boasting more than seventeen miles of corridors and three times as much office space as the Empire State Building. The outermost corridor of the building, E Ring, is almost a mile in circumference. Because of the uneven terrain beneath the building, it alternates between four and five stories in height. The Pentagon was originally designed to house between twenty thousand and thirty-five thousand employees. During World War II, the Pentagon housed only the War Department (i.e., the US Army and the Army Air Forces). The navy and marines continued their operations from other facilities in the Washington, DC, area.

THE POST–WORLD WAR II ERA

In the two years following the war, President Harry S. Truman (1884–1972) proposed that the American military be reorganized in order to facilitate better coordination in military planning, operations, intelligence gathering, and weapons acquisition. Seizing on the examples of supreme commanders from the war, and recognizing the increasingly significant global role of the

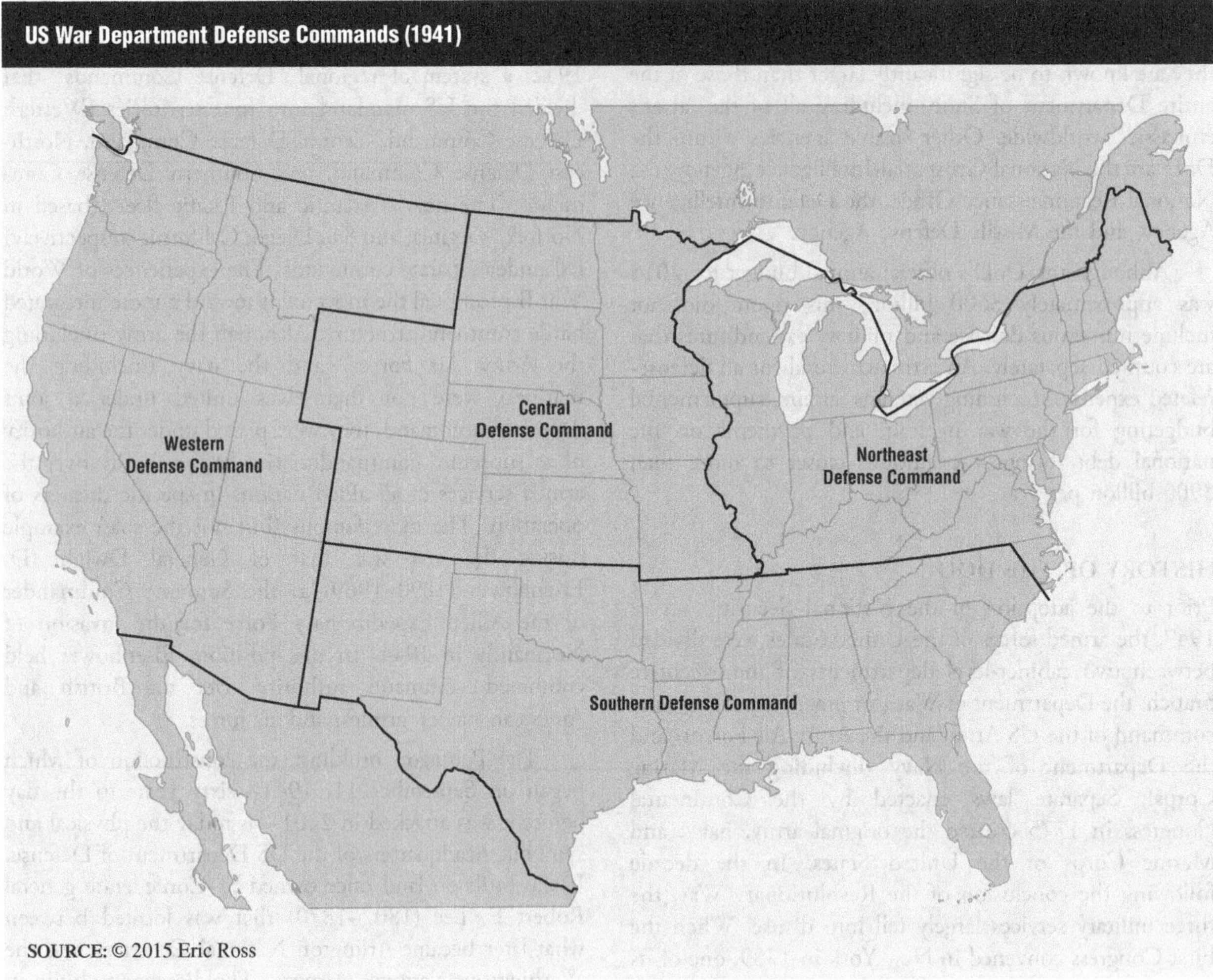

Figure 1. *With World War II already raging in Europe and the Pacific, but prior to the bombing of Pearl Harbor, military leaders developed plans through which the US Army and Navy might better coordinate to strengthen US defensive capabilities. The military adopted a system of regional "Defense Commands," dividing the mainland into four territories, with the Navy's Atlantic and Pacific fleets under separate commands.* © ERIC ROSS

United States, the president, certain members of Congress, military leaders, and other prominent officials spent two years debating alternate plans to reorganize national defense. These combined efforts ultimately led to the adoption of the National Security Act of 1947, the single most important restructuring of the national security apparatus in American history. In addition to creating the Central Intelligence Agency and the National Security Council, the 1947 act significantly revised the military community. The law eliminated the cabinet-level positions of secretary of war and secretary of the navy and created the new position of secretary of defense with command authority over all of the armed services of the United States under a single cabinet-level department. (The new department originally was called the "National Military Establishment" before being renamed the Department of Defense in 1949.) The 1947 act established three armed services within the Department of Defense: the US Army, the US Navy (including the Marine Corps), and a new US Air Force. During the following five years, the signals intelligence and cryptological activities of the military were reorganized within the Department of Defense, culminating in Truman's signing in 1952 of the classified National Security Council Intelligence Directive No. 9, which created the NSA within the Department of Defense.

With the adoption of the National Security Act of 1947, the new secretary of defense, former secretary of the navy James Forrestal (1892–1949), moved into the Pentagon and began the difficult process of attempting to bring the three rival armed forces under one roof. Two years later, with the appointment of a forceful new secretary of defense, Louis Johnson (1891–1966), the navy leadership and the Joint Chiefs of Staff began to move into the third and fourth floors of the E Ring facing the Potomac River. Secretary Johnson commandeered Room 3E-880 for himself—a room that has been occupied by every secretary of defense since that time. In August 1949 the 1947 act was amended to further strengthen the authority of the secretary of defense over the individual armed services that increasingly occupied different sections of the Pentagon. The Marine Corps, however, did not begin its move from the nearby Navy Annex, built at the same time as the Pentagon in 1941, until 1996. (The Navy Annex, demolished in 2012 to make additional room for Arlington National Cemetery, is the site of the Air Force Memorial.)

The National Military Command Center (NMCC), known in popular culture as the "War Room," is located within the Joint Staff area of the Pentagon. The NMCC coordinates the military's communications, command, and control systems and monitors events worldwide. Unlike the striking image portrayed in the film *Dr. Strangelove,* the NMCC (which has had different locations within the Pentagon over time) is a series of rooms filled with desks, computers, television screens, and electronic equipment.

Following the Soviet Union's detonation of an atomic bomb in 1949, concern increased regarding the potential vulnerability of the Pentagon to Soviet attack. The decision was taken to create a backup military command headquarters at Raven Rock Mountain in Pennsylvania (Site R), near Camp David, Maryland, that would become the alternate and emergency headquarters of the DoD in the event of war. (Site R was one of the "undisclosed locations" that Vice President Dick Cheney [b. 1941] repeatedly occupied following the attacks of September 11, 2001.) Additional "continuation of government" sites for other parts of the federal government were built in Virginia at Mount Weather and in an underground bunker for Congress at the Greenbrier resort.

LATER REORGANIZATION

The last significant legislative change to the DoD's organizational structure to reduce the long-standing problem of interservice rivalry occurred with the adoption of the Goldwater-Nichols Department of Defense Reorganization Act of 1986. The Goldwater-Nichols law increased the focus on what has become six regional Unified Combatant Commands (UCC)—US Africa Combatant Command, US Central Combatant Command, US European Combatant Command, US Northern Combatant Command, US Pacific Combatant Command, and US Southern Combatant Command—and three functional commands (Special Operations, Strategic, and Transportation). Each UCC is headed by a single combatant commander (CCDR), typically headed by the service that has a preponderance of forces in the region, who has combined authority over the army, navy, and air force personnel in the designated region. The chain of command now bypasses the three departmental secretaries (army, navy, and air force) as well as the chiefs of the four services (i.e., army and navy chiefs of staff, the commandant of the Marine Corps, and the chief of naval operations) and descends instead from the president, to the secretary of defense, to the CCDR. The chairman of the Joint Chiefs has no command authority but serves instead as the principal military adviser to the president, the secretary of defense, and the National Security Council. Thus, the military service leadership and their rivalries—a defining characteristic of the US military since the eighteenth century—has been cut out of the chain of command over soldiers and sailors in the field.

By the 1990s, much of the Pentagon building was in a serious state of decay and the decision was made for it to undergo a thorough renovation. With an appropriation of $4.5 billion, work began in 1994 and was completed in 2011, interrupted by the attacks of September 11. In addition to its revamped offices and work spaces, the Pentagon now houses metro and bus stops, a post office, banks, more than a dozen fast-food restaurants and a cafeteria, a drugstore, a florist shop, clothing stores, a chocolate store, an electronics store, barbers and hair dressers, laundry and shoe repair services, and facilities for dental and eye care.

THE DOD AND AMERICAN CULTURE

The US military has played important roles in American culture since the 1940s. One institution within the DoD, the Defense Advanced Research Projects Agency, was largely responsible for the early stages of development of the modern Internet, ARPANET (a packet-switching network), TCP/IP, and e-mail. The Pentagon also has been the subject of one of the most dramatic episodes in American history regarding secrecy in government and the deception of the American people. During the 1960s, Secretary of Defense Robert McNamara (1916–2009) ordered that a classified history of the Vietnam War be compiled. Daniel Ellsberg (b. 1931), who had contributed to the history, and his colleague Anthony Russo (1936–2008), secretly made photocopies of the history and leaked them to the *New York Times, Washington Post,* and other newspapers. When the *New York Times* published portions of these documents, which became known as the Pentagon Papers, the administration of President Richard Nixon (1913–1994) went all the way to the US Supreme Court in an unsuccessful attempt to prevent further publication (*New York Times Co. v. United States,* 403

U.S. 713 [1971]). Although the secret history was completed before the beginning of the Nixon administration, its publication significantly undermined the credibility of the presidency and the Pentagon as it was revealed that the US government had systematically lied to the American people about the Vietnam War.

Because of its size and reach, the DoD played both real and symbolic roles in American cultural battles regarding nondiscrimination, particularly with regard to the racial integration of the military services in the 1940s and integrating women into the military academies and services. It has also been at the center of the hot-button culture-war issue of gays in the military, most notoriously with regard to the since-abandoned "Don't Ask, Don't Tell" policy instituted during the Clinton administration.

Aside from its organizational structure, the physical building, and the operations that take place within, the Pentagon both symbolizes and exemplifies competing themes in national security policy and American popular culture. Three of these interrelated and competing themes are considered here: American global military power, Americans' self-image as exemplified by the military, and American violence.

AMERICAN GLOBAL MILITARY POWER

The Pentagon is the quintessential symbol of the United States' global military power and reach. There is a significant consensus in American politics, including both major political parties, that the United States should have a military "second to none." For years the United States has spent almost as much on military operations as all other countries of the world combined. The nation possesses as many aircraft carriers as all other countries of the world combined. The US Navy has separate fleets permanently based in the Atlantic, Pacific, Mediterranean, and Persian Gulf and operates more than two dozen bases outside the United States.

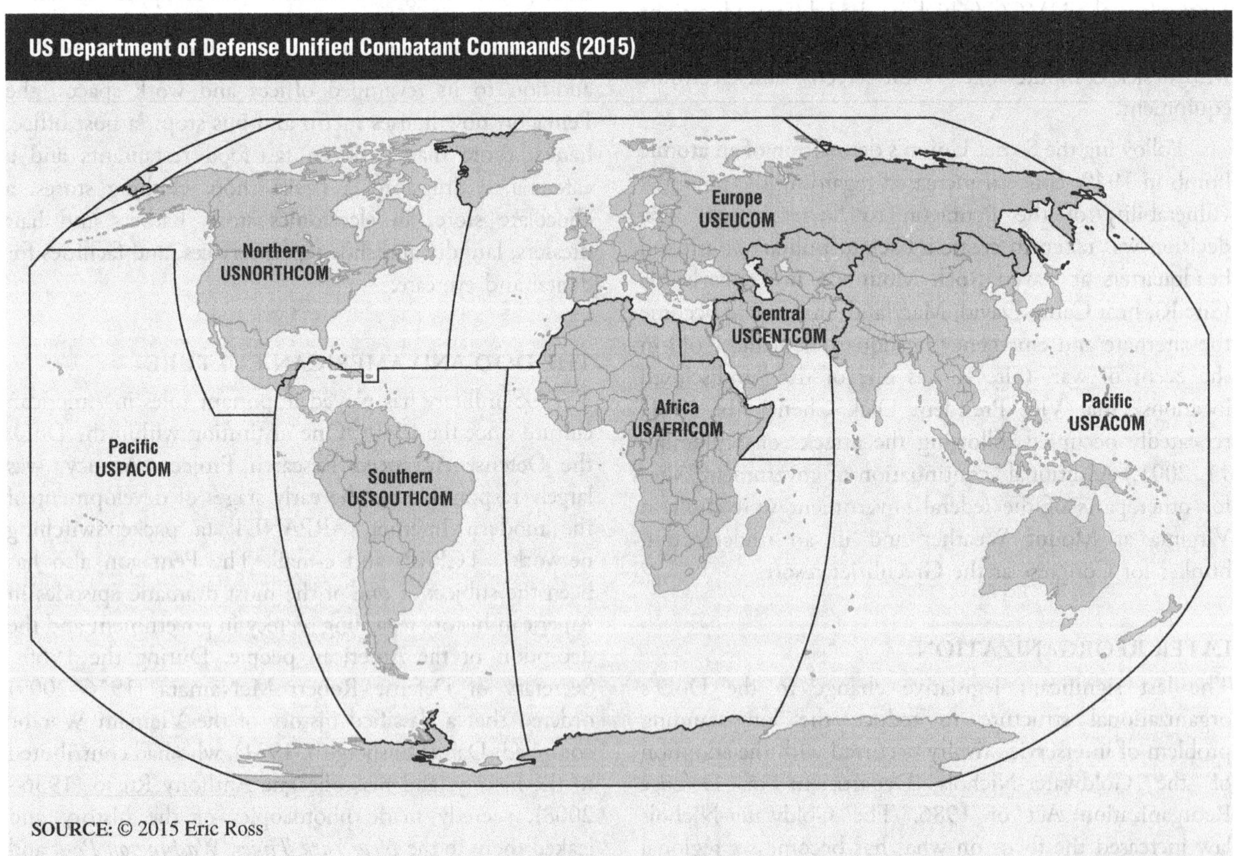

Figure 2. *The increased global reach of American military power can be seen by contrasting the US War Department's Defense Commands in 1941, which were centered on the continental United States (see figure 1), with that of the current Unified Combatant Commands system, which places the entire world within the Pentagon's purview. In 1941, Central Command referred to fewer than ten states in the American Midwest. By 2015, Central Command oversees almost 20 countries in the Middle East, Central Asia, and the Persian Gulf.* © ERIC ROSS

While the number of American soldiers in uniform is only the second largest in the world (after China), American military capacity is by far the most significant. While there are debates in the United States about particular weapons systems and strategies, virtually no prominent politicians openly challenge the consensus that the United States should have (and pay for) the most powerful military in the world. The accompanying map graphically illustrates how the US government in the twenty-first century perceives its global interests, reach, and military role. Whereas the War Department's "Central Command" at the beginning of World War II referred only to nine states in the American Midwest, by 2015 the DoD's Central Command referred to almost twenty countries in the Middle East, Central Asia, and the Persian Gulf.

This modern consensus in favor of a global military presence is relatively new in American history. For the greater part of US history, the consensus was opposed to a large military. The leading statement of the original consensus was the Farewell Address of President George Washington (1732–1799), who warned of "entangling alliances" and standing armies and who advocated commerce and trade with nations as the path to prosperity. While there certainly were significant exceptions to this long-standing preference for a small military, most notably with regard to westward expansion, the Mexican-American War of 1846–1848, the Spanish-American War, and the recurrent use of gunboat diplomacy (particularly in the Western Hemisphere), the United States was a much more reluctant actor with regard to colonialism than any other comparably powerful country. The United States was an active supporter of disarmament during the interwar period and entered into World War I and World War II relatively late. After both world wars, the United States immediately and massively demobilized.

With the beginning of the Cold War, however, particularly in 1947, the United States abandoned its long-standing belief in maintaining only a small military presence in peacetime and in eschewing military alliances in peacetime. The North Atlantic Treaty Organization (NATO), the Southeast Asia Treaty Organization (SEATO), and the Rio Pact (more formally, the Inter-American Treaty of Reciprocal Assistance) became new models for peacetime military alliances. After a dramatic decline in the number of soldiers in uniform from 1945 to 1947, the trend reversed. The United States increasingly saw itself as the bulwark against worldwide communism and sought to make its military second to none. Even with the end of the Cold War by 1991, the new consensus was not abandoned and is now a foundational principle in American politics.

THE PENTAGON AND THE MILITARY AS THE EMBODIMENT OF POSITIVE AMERICAN IDEALS AND VALUES

In political speeches and commercial advertising since the 1980s, the US military has been broadly depicted as embodying positive American values. American soldiers are typically portrayed as being heroes who are strong, brave, religious ("there are no atheists in foxholes"), clean-cut, responsible, honor-bound, self-sacrificing, and the protectors of "our freedoms" and the "American way of life." The military can be trusted to "carry out its mission," act decisively, and "get the job done." This official depiction of the US military is reinforced in movies, television shows, and novels. In the popular media that supports this vision of the military, even the soldiers who disobey orders, or who show some lack of discipline, or who behave as mavericks, ultimately will come to have the greater interests of their country and comrades at heart and can be trusted in the end to do their duty and become heroes.

Since the beginning of cinema, the US military and Hollywood have collaborated on films that portray the military and American servicemen in this positive and heroic light. The War Department provided equipment and technical advice for the first film to win the Academy Award for Outstanding Picture, *Wings* (1927), which told the fictional story of two Army Air Corps pilots in World War I. At the beginning of World War II director Frank Capra (1897–1991) made a series of seven short films titled *Why We Fight* that explained the importance of the free peoples' of the world (identified as Americans, the British, the Russians, and the Chinese) taking up arms against the governments that enslaved people (Germany, Japan, and Italy). The first of the *Why We Fight* films quotes Vice President Henry A. Wallace (1888–1965): "This is a fight between a free world and a slave world." During World War II several major films were released that depicted heroic, freedom-loving Americans at war against the barbarians of the East and West, including *A Yank on the Burma Road* (1942), *Wake Island* (1942), *Gung Ho!* (1943), *Bataan* (1943), *Guadalcanal Diary* (1943), *Thirty Seconds over Tokyo* (1944), *The Fighting Seabees* (1944), *Marine Raiders* (1944), and *God Is My Co-pilot* (1945).

The fact that Hollywood produced flattering images of the US military at war does not mean that the American public was unaware of the darker and less inspiring aspects of military life. Immediately after World War II, the American military was widely denounced in the American press, particularly by religious leaders, because of its corrupting influence on the moral life of soldiers. In 1947, as American troops were continuing their occupation of Europe and Japan, President Truman sent a fact-finding commission to determine the accuracy of press claims about alcoholism and decadence in the military. The commission and its individual members reported the pervasiveness of alcohol; prostitution; syphilis; gambling; vulgarity; and the crimes of rape, assault, and theft. The war and the military experience were seen as having undermined young men's moral values. Military life did not build character; it undermined it. When veterans returned to America, a tidal wave of syphilis spread across the country, just as it had after World War I. The very successful film *The Best Years of Our Lives* (1947) touched upon the difficulties of the postwar period and treated returning veterans not as conquering heroes but as wounded and sometimes bitter human beings undergoing the painful steps of readjustment.

In response to such reports, in the late 1940s the military began an ideological campaign to promote greater morality in the military. Booklets were prepared for servicemen that stressed religious and moral values. Many evangelical Christian groups that had long been pacifist or antimilitary took upon themselves the new mission of promoting religion in the military and focused their efforts particularly on the new US Air Force and its new academy: Colorado Springs became a headquarters not only for the Air Force Academy and the North American Aerospace Defense Command (NORAD) but also for the American evangelical community. During the 1950s, an active campaign both within and outside the Pentagon promoted the link between God, the United States, and the military. Rather than being perceived as a threat to the moral values of young men, as was the case during and immediately following the war, the military increasingly came to be seen as a character-building institution where troubled youth could be sent to learn self-discipline. When the American public responded critically to the Ribbon Creek incident in 1956 on the marine base at Parris Island, South Carolina, where a drunken drill instructor negligently caused the deaths of six recruits, Hollywood responded with the film *The D.I.* (1957), which omitted the actual incident that prompted the making of the film and praised instead the character-building role of Marine Corps drill instructors on undisciplined youths. The final credits of the film state: "We wish to express our gratitude to the United States Marine Corps—not only for their assistance in the making of this film, but for … Tripoli, Belleau Wood, Guadalcanal, Tarawa, Saipan, Iwo Jima, Korea." The actual problem was swept under a metaphorical rug.

Only two feature films released during the 1950s and 1960s depicted the Vietnam War. The first, *The Quiet American* (1958), was in theory based on the Graham Greene novel of the same title that described Vietnam during the last days of French occupation and the arrival of American intelligence officials. Like *The D.I.*, *The Quiet American* completely inverted the meaning of the original. In the Hollywood version, Americans are portrayed as a positive moral force in a poor country struggling against communism, unlike Greene's novel, which presented Americans as naive, moralistic, and dangerous. John Wayne's *The Green Berets* (1968), a prowar film, was produced with the assistance of the Pentagon. During the 1960s and early 1970s, the positive values of military life continued to be conveyed in the American media. Some films raised the specter of the dangers of nuclear war, including highly successful films in 1964 that raised the possibility of an accidental nuclear war (*Fail Safe* and the dark comedy *Dr. Strangelove*), as well as the potential threat to the Republic from a charismatic military leader as depicted in *Seven Days in May*. Nevertheless, most of the films about the military from the 1950s to 1970 continued to be nostalgic, and many used the "good war," as World War II was called, as the topic of the film: *From Here to Eternity* (1953), *The Bridge on the River Kwai* (1957), *The Guns of Navarone* (1961), *The Longest Day* (1962), *PT-109* (1962), *Merrill's Marauders* (1962), *The Dirty Dozen* (1967), and *Patton* (1970).

Although documentary films questioning the Vietnam War appeared in the 1960s, it was not until the 1970s that a series of films appeared that used humor to challenge the premises of prior American military actions with veiled references to Vietnam: *Little Big Man* (the US Cavalry at the Battle of Little Big Horn), *M*A*S*H* (the Korean War), and *Catch-22* (World War II). After the Vietnam War ended in 1975, several films were released that probed the darker, morally destructive, and violent aspects of the war, including, most famously, *The Deer Hunter* (1978), *Apocalypse Now* (1979), *Platoon* (1986), and *Born on the Fourth of July* (1989). These films, among the first direct motion-picture attacks on the US military, received many artistic awards.

In an effort to burnish the image of the military after Vietnam, the Pentagon's Office of Public Affairs (as had its predecessors) used its liaison relations with Hollywood and provided logistical assistance for several films and television programs that depicted the military in a favorable light and that emphasized the military values of honor, duty, and accountability. Examples of such films and television programs that have received technical and logistical support from the DoD since the 1980s include *Top Gun, Black Hawk Down, The Hunt for Red October, Pearl Harbor, Zero Dark Thirty, Thirteen Days, Patriot Games, An Officer and a Gentleman, Clear and Present Danger,* and *JAG*.

While the American public is sharply divided about the use of the military to solve challenging political and security dangers from abroad, the military has been very successful in helping to shape a broadly positive image of itself at home. Whatever public disagreements politicians on the political left and right may have about the use of the military abroad, they compete with each other in their praise for soldiers, who are universally described as being heroic, freedom-loving, and positive role models for society.

AMERICAN VIOLENCE AND THE AMERICAN PURSUIT OF GLOBAL MILITARY POWER

Many American presidents, including Truman, John F. Kennedy (1917–1963), Nixon, Ronald Reagan (1911–2004), George H. W. Bush (b. 1924), and George W. Bush (b. 1946), typically before sending troops off to combat, referred to Americans as being a "peaceful people." Wartime propaganda films repeat the same trope to emphasize American reluctance to engage in combat and the belief that war for Americans is always a last resort. Outside of the United States, however, there is a widely accepted counter-stereotype that Americans are particularly prone to violence and are warlike, as exemplified in the American gun culture, murder rate, imprisonment rate, gangsters, and violent movies. One of the salient symbols of American violence for foreigners is the Pentagon. Many Americans find military briefings in wartime to be reassuring, as exemplified during the First and Second Gulf Wars in spokesmen Norman Schwarzkopf (1934–2012), Colin Powell (b. 1937), and Donald Rumsfeld (b. 1932), who spoke calmly and assuredly about precision-guided missiles, minimal collateral damage, and "shock and awe." Others, however, saw such briefings as glorifying violence while deliberately obfuscating the misery that occurs on the ground. In addition to the Pentagon's role in sponsoring the violence of war, it is also perceived as being responsible for promoting, encouraging, and supporting violence throughout the world through its support of repressive and violent regimes. The most notorious example is the DoD's School of the Americas (renamed in 2001 the Western Hemisphere Institute for Security Cooperation) at Fort Benning, Georgia, which has long been portrayed as a school for the training of foreign soldiers in methods of torture and assassination. While the extent to which its sixty thousand graduates have engaged in torture, gratuitous violence, or assassination might be debated, there is no question that many of its alumni, including Manuel Noriega (b. 1934), Roberto D'Aubuisson (1944–1992), Hugo Banzer (1926–2002), Vides Casanova (b. 1937), and Héctor Gramajo (1938–2004), have been shown to be responsible for murders, assassinations, death squads, and torture.

Because of its symbolic role as a center of American violence, the Pentagon has been an obvious symbolic target for opposition to perceived American militarism. Three particularly salient protests have been directed specifically at the Pentagon. The first was an anti–Vietnam War protest by a Quaker named Norman Morrison (1933–1965) in 1965. As had some pacifist Buddhist monks in South Vietnam, Morrison poured kerosene over his body and lit himself aflame under the window of Secretary of Defense McNamara. Two years later, on October 21, 1967, a mass rally of tens of thousands of opponents of the war in Vietnam marched from the Lincoln Memorial to the Pentagon. The DoD braced itself for the demonstration by stationing more than two thousand soldiers inside the walls of the Pentagon. Hundreds of demonstrators, including Norman Mailer (1923–2007), were arrested. The March on the Pentagon was one of the first mass rallies in protest against the escalation of the war in Vietnam. The most famous attack on the Pentagon was, of course, that of September 11, 2001, staged by al-Qaeda. Although Osama bin Laden (1957–2011) did not state explicitly why the Pentagon had been his target, the world certainly perceived it as both a symbolic and actual attack on the center of American military power. For many, the subsequent abuses by American soldiers at the Abu Ghraib prison in Iraq and the Haditha massacre in November 2005, also in Iraq, simply confirmed the stereotype.

THE "MILITARY-INDUSTRIAL COMPLEX" AND PENTAGON WASTE

In popular culture and the political world, the Pentagon is frequently seen as a symbol of the "military-industrial complex" as well as of waste. Although scandals erupt from time to time over grossly inflated prices for items such as wrenches or toilet seats, or the enormous cost overruns for weapons systems, including the now infamous examples of the M-14 rifle, the Bradley Fighting Vehicle, the M-247 Sergeant York air defense artillery, and the Lockheed Martin F-35, there has been no political will to systematically and definitely bring the waste under control.

Apart from the US president and the White House, the DoD and the Pentagon are the most striking and visible symbols of the United States throughout the world.

SEE ALSO *Air Force, US; Army, US; Central Intelligence Agency (CIA); Department of Homeland Security; Department of State; Deterrence; Joint Chiefs of Staff; Military-Industrial Complex; National Security Agency (NSA); National Security Council (NSC); Navy, US; Nuclear Weapons; World War II*

BIBLIOGRAPHY

Bacevich, Andrew J. *The New American Militarism: How Americans Are Seduced by War.* New York: Oxford University Press, 2005.

Bacevich, Andrew J., ed. *The Long War: A New History of U.S. National Security Policy since World War II.* New York: Columbia University Press, 2007.

Burton, James G. *The Pentagon Wars: Reformers Challenge the Old Guard.* Annapolis, MD: Naval Institute Press, 1993.

Fussell, Paul. *Wartime: Understanding and Behavior in the Second World War.* New York: Oxford University Press, 1989.

Goldberg, Alfred. *The Pentagon: The First Fifty Years.* Washington, DC: Historical Office, Office of the Secretary of Defense, 1992.

Greenfield, Kent Roberts, and Robert R. Palmer. *Origins of the Army Ground Forces General Headquarters U.S. Army, 1940–1942.* Washington, DC: Historical Section, Army Ground Forces, 1946.

Gunn, T. Jeremy. *Spiritual Weapons: The Cold War and the Forging of an American National Religion.* Westport, CT: Praeger, 2009.

Koppes, Clayton R., and Gregory D. Black. *Hollywood Goes to War: How Politics, Profits, and Propaganda Shaped World War II Movies.* Berkeley: University of California Press, 1990.

Suid, Lawrence H. *Guts and Glory: The Making of the American Military Image in Film.* Rev. ed. Lexington: University Press of Kentucky, 2002.

Vogel, Steve. *The Pentagon: A History: The Untold Story of the Wartime Race to Build the Pentagon—and to Restore It Sixty Years Later.* New York: Random House, 2008.

T. Jeremy Gunn
Professor of Political Science and Law
International University of Rabat, Morocco

DEPARTMENT OF FOREIGN AFFAIRS

The establishment of a successful foreign policy, especially as it related to commerce and national security, mattered deeply to the men of the American Revolution. On January 10, 1781, two years before the fledgling United States achieved its formal independence, the Congress under the new Articles of Confederation established a "Department for Foreign Affairs" with a secretary elected as administrator. The secretary's role included handling the correspondence of American diplomats abroad and foreign ministers resident in Philadelphia, as well as attending Congress and keeping that body informed as to recent international developments.

After contentious debate and considerable intrigue, Robert R. Livingston (1746–1813) was chosen as the first secretary, his tenure lasting from August 1781 to August 1783. The thirty-four-year-old prominent New Yorker had served with distinction in the Continental Congress. A lawyer by profession, he focused on financial matters in the Congress, and developed close relations with the "nationalist" faction. These ties produced enemies among the "states' rights" element. Virginian Arthur Lee (1740–1792) competed equally with Livingston for the post, until the French minister, the Chevalier de la Luzerne (1741–1791), intervened, claiming he used loans and bribes to secure the votes needed to elect Livingston by the narrow margin of one state.

Livingston's major contribution focused on his role in guiding the American commissioners negotiating the Peace of Paris with Great Britain in 1782 to 1783. He offered advice on topics ranging from protecting the Florida boundary and guarding fishing rights to opposing the repatriation of Loyalists. The secretary also embarked on the unrewarding task of establishing a bureaucracy and order in a new department, creating systems of filing information, and developing lines of communication within the government. A meddlesome Congress and poor salary likely prompted his resignation in December 1782.

When Livingston finally departed the office in May 1783, Congress left the post in a vacant and confused state until selecting another New Yorker, John Jay (1745–1829), in July 1784. Jay, who served through March 1790, dealt with numerous problems with only a dozen staff members, including a doorkeeper, messengers, and clerks. Major issues existed with Britain, including the payment of prewar debts, persistence of Crown garrisons in the Old Northwest, restrictions of trade, and compensation for Loyalists. These would go unresolved in spite of the exertions of John Adams (1735–1826), appointed as first minister in 1785. In a treaty with Spanish diplomat Diego de Gardoqui (1735–1798) in 1786, Jay agreed to limited restrictions on navigation of the Mississippi River in exchange for a commercial treaty, a proposal rejected by the Congress. The Barbary corsairs complicated matters by commencing attacks on American shipping in 1784. A treaty with Morocco was quickly signed, but Jay wanted war with troublesome Algiers. Congress refused, and the pirate problem persisted until 1815. Capable Secretaries Livingston and Jay experienced limited success. A feeble Congress, military, and image of the United States abroad hindered their work. The department did, however, lay the groundwork for a new, stronger iteration under the Constitution.

SEE ALSO *Department of State; Jay, John*

BIBLIOGRAPHY

Bemis, Samuel Flagg. *Pinckney's Treaty: A Study of America's Advantage from Europe's Distress, 1783–1800.* Rev. ed. New Haven, CT: Yale University Press, 1960.

Dangerfield, George. *Chancellor Robert R. Livingston of New York, 1746–1813.* New York: Harcourt Brace, 1960.

Giunta, Mary A., ed. *The Emerging Nation: A Documentary History of the Foreign Relations of the United States under the Articles of Confederation, 1780–1789.* 3 vols. Washington, DC: NHPRC, 1996.

Jensen, Merrill. *The New Nation: A History of the United States during the Confederation, 1781–1789.* New York: Knopf, 1950.

Morris, Richard B. *The Forging of the Union, 1781–1789.* New York: Harper and Row, 1987.

Reuter, Frank T. "The Diplomacy of an Emerging Nation." *Journal of the Early Republic* 17, 3 (1997): 493–502.

Ritcheson, Charles R. *Aftermath of Revolution: British Policy toward the United States, 1783–1795.* New York: Norton, 1969.

Stahr, Walter. *John Jay: Founding Father.* New York: Hambledon and London, 2005.

John M. Belohlavek
Professor of History
University of South Florida

DEPARTMENT OF HOMELAND SECURITY

The US Department of Homeland Security (DHS) has its genesis in the aftermath of the September 11, 2001, terrorist attacks. Those events triggered a new period of US involvement on the world stage, as well as a corresponding increase in attention to US domestic security. The DHS has been a part of both elements of this response since shortly after the attacks took place. The roots of the department lie in the Office of Homeland Security, a cabinet-level position established by President George W. Bush and announced during an address to a joint session of Congress on September 20, 2001. In his address, Bush spoke of homeland security as a "defensive measure" that would combine intelligence, law enforcement, government policy, and citizen vigilance. Bush's comments were representative of the dual nature of homeland security. The DHS is an agency tasked with securing domestic affairs through attention to activities and events beyond the borders of the United States.

The DHS is a cabinet-level department of the federal government charged with protecting the United States from domestic emergencies. These emergencies include terrorist attacks as well as natural and manmade disasters. As a result, the DHS is responsible for a wide range of security and law-enforcement activities. DHS operations range from cybersecurity, customs, antiterrorism, border security, immigration, transportation security, and disaster relief. The department is empowered to work in these disparate areas through its control of other major federal agencies, such as the US Secret Service and the US Coast Guard (in peacetime). This makes the DHS one of the largest single components of the federal government. As of 2014, the DHS's core responsibilities pertain to five "homeland security missions": (1) preventing terrorism; (2) securing and managing US borders; (3) enforcing and administering immigration laws; (4) safeguarding and securing cyberspace; and (5) assisting disaster recovery.

The DHS's various missions mean the department frequently acts in an international capacity. The DHS is often in a position to shape perceptions of the United States through its work with foreign nationals. Due to its control of the borders and customs services, the DHS oversees the security of billions of dollars of international trade per day. This includes security operations at international airports and seaports, as well as an extensive security program at numerous land crossings on the Mexican and Canadian borders. Given its responsibility for borders and customs, the DHS is often the first federal agency that international visitors meet upon their arrival in the United States. The border security and transportation functions of the DHS are among its largest and most important tasks, and these activities comprise 50 percent of DHS personnel.

The DHS has not been immune to legal concerns regarding the balance between security and the privacy of American citizens, especially as it relates to citizens' interactions with the rest of the world. As with other far-reaching government initiatives like the National Security Agency's (NSA) warrantless wiretapping programs, these DHS programs have been a function of the post-9/11 international context in which these agencies operate. Concerns have arisen over DHS programs, such as the seizure and opening of international mail destined for delivery to American citizens in the United States (Meeks 2006). As this particular program was conducted by US Customs and Border Protection, it illustrates the wide reach of the DHS in the aftermath of its incorporation of many previously separate federal agencies.

The Office of Homeland Security was formalized as its own cabinet-level department, the Department of Homeland Security, through the Homeland Security Act of 2002. As originally envisioned in Bush's announcement, the DHS would have four core areas of responsibility: (1) border and transportation security; (2) emergency preparedness and response; (3) chemical, biological, radiological, and nuclear countermeasures; and (4) information analysis and infrastructure protection. Twenty-two preexisting federal agencies were consolidated under the DHS as part of this reorganization. Since the department's founding, a number of domestic and foreign developments have pushed the DHS to further refine the department's goals, though "preventing terrorism" remains central to the department's identity and mission.

The creation of the DHS required a massive restructuring of the federal government, the largest such undertaking since the National Security Act of 1947 that created the Department of Defense, the Central Intelligence Agency (CIA), and the National Security Council (Andreas 2003, 92). As part of these broader changes, the federal government for the first time defined *homeland security*, deciding that it was "a concerted national effort to prevent terrorist attacks within the United States, reduce America's vulnerability to terrorism, and minimize the damage and recover from attacks that do occur" (Office of Homeland Security 2002).

While the DHS has some similarities with security organizations within the US federal government, its sprawling responsibilities and enforcement options present the department with unique challenges. Whereas information produced by the CIA or NSA will often remain secret, information produced by the DHS has a wider and more public consumer base. By law, the DHS is required to share information about foreign threats with not only other parts of the federal government but also with government and law enforcement at the state and local levels (Greenberg 2009, 221–222). The DHS's information-distribution functions put the department in a position to influence international relations at a variety of sites, such as the US border, on a daily basis.

The DHS is the only cabinet-level department that has spent its entire institutional existence in the twenty-first century. In both domestic and international contexts, the DHS embodies much of the American relationship with the broader world since 2001. The DHS is both a first line of defense against extraordinary threats—such as terrorist attacks—and a regular, mundane feature of American lives, as with the Transportation Security Administration at airports.

The functions of the DHS represent the changing place of the United States in the twenty-first-century world. While the concept of "homeland security" would be crystallized in the department's name, the idea of protecting the homeland was not new. Americans had practiced civil defense drills in wartime since World War II (1939–1945), and with the advent of atomic weapons, these readiness practices spread into peacetime. Such activities provided iconic images of backyard bomb shelters and schoolchildren crawling under desks. Yet the shift from "civil defense" to "homeland security" represented more than a change in terminology. It represented a change in the nature of America's relationship with the world, and in the perception of its enemies. No longer would American security be threatened solely by foreign countries. The 9/11 attacks made clear the threat posed by nonstate actors. The DHS played a leading role in shaping the first decade of the American response to these challenges to international order.

SEE ALSO *Department of Defense, US; Department of State; National Security Agency (NSA); Security Council, UN; September 11, 2001*

BIBLIOGRAPHY

Andreas, Peter. "Redrawing the Line: Borders and Security in the Twenty-First Century." *International Security* 28, 2 (2003): 78–111.

Department of Homeland Security, History Office. *Brief Documentary History of the Department of Homeland Security, 2001–2008.* 2008. https://www.hsdl.org/?view&did=37027

Greenberg, Harold M. "Is the Department of Homeland Security an Intelligence Agency?" *Intelligence and National Security* 24, 2 (2009): 216–235.

Knight, Judson. "United States Department of Homeland Security." In *Encyclopedia of Espionage, Intelligence, and Security*, edited by K. Lee Lerner and Brenda Wilmoth Lerner. Detroit, MI: Thomson/Gale, 2003.

Meeks, Brock N. "Homeland Security Opening Private Mail." *NBC News*, January 6, 2006. http://www.nbcnews.com/id/10740935/ns/us_news-security

Office of Homeland Security (OHS). *National Strategy for Homeland Security.* 2002. http://www.dhs.gov/sites/default/files/publications/nat-strat-hls-2002.pdf

Michael Graziano
PhD Candidate
Florida State University

DEPARTMENT OF STATE

The US Foreign Service originated in 1775 under the Continental Congress with the use of secret agents to gather information in Europe about the American colonies. A congressional resolution formed the Department of Foreign Affairs in 1781, and in 1789 the US Constitution created the Department of State and gave the president the authority to appoint ambassadors, ministers, and consuls, with Senate approval, as official representatives abroad. In 1790, President George Washington (1732–1799) appointed Thomas Jefferson (1743–1826), already serving as minister to France, as the first secretary of state. The department was small, but it boasted some important achievements in foreign affairs during the early years of the Republic, including normalization of relations with England and Spain. During these years, however, the new American democratic ideology and values clashed occasionally with traditional European court protocol. Jefferson, for instance, refused to follow diplomatic seating etiquette at formal dinners.

EARLY DEPENDENCE ON INDIVIDUAL ENVOYS

Through the nineteenth century, American diplomacy continued to depend heavily on the talents of individual envoys who, due to the department's consistent budgetary constraints, relied on personal wealth and influence to work effectively in foreign aristocratic circles. During the American Civil War (1861–1865), for instance, Charles Francis Adams (1807–1886), the son and grandson of US presidents, served as the American envoy in London. At a time when communication between London and Washington was slow and cumbersome, he essentially single-handedly convinced the British government that the American government would not fall to the Confederates. The British foreign minister noted that the British government "had every reason to be satisfied with the language and conduct of Mr. Adams." Many other appointees were not nearly so capable, however, and the department struggled to limit the power of the spoils system while attempting to project the ideals of American democratic pluralism throughout the world.

EXPANSION AND REORGANIZATION

The need for more effective representation "on the ground" became more important as American economic influence expanded after the Civil War. In 1908, recognizing the growing need for expertise in specific areas of the world, the department created the first geographic divisions. Meanwhile, the American people became generally more interested in "foreign affairs" with the outbreak of war in Europe in 1914 and the eventual participation of Americans in that war. The department's need for greater efficiency and expansion became even more apparent when employees abroad were called upon to aid American citizens caught abroad and to collect information needed by the US military and policy makers. Despite important logistical and practical work performed during the war years, the State Department played a nearly negligible role in wartime decision making, a phenomenon that would be replayed in World War II (1939–1945) and beyond.

World War I (1914–1918) did provide additional impetus for reform in the department, and in 1924 the Rogers Act merged the diplomatic service, responsible for political representation, and the consular service, responsible mainly for commercial issues abroad. It also formalized language training for overseas personnel. In 1924 the State Department hired a professional historian to head the Division of Publications, which had been created to edit and publish the Foreign Relations of the United States series (FRUS). FRUS is the official documentary record of major US foreign policy decisions and diplomatic activity and has been in continuous publication (with just a few exceptions) since 1861. The Division of Publications was later subsumed under the Office of the Historian, which retains the responsibility for producing FRUS. By the 1950s, publication of FRUS lagged almost twenty years behind the events being documented, so FRUS has evolved from an operational resource to an official historical record for scholars.

World War II further strained the resources of the department both at home and abroad. Further expansion and reorganization of the department reflected a growing understanding that the work of the department would need to more explicitly include areas such as international organizations and economic affairs, somewhat beyond the scope of "traditional" diplomacy. Even as the complexity of the institution increased, the department's influence waned. Presidents assumed greater control and centralization of foreign policy from the White House, and a new national security structure, including the Defense Department, the National Security Council, and the Central Intelligence Agency, emerged to confront the Cold War, as did new organs of foreign policy, including economic and military aid, cultural exchanges, propaganda, covert operations, and media relations. All of this competition for primacy in foreign affairs placed additional strains on the State Department, as did the political attacks of the McCarthy era in the 1950s, which seriously discredited the institution and destroyed morale at a time when the department still carried on the day-to-day work of diplomacy all over the world.

PUBLIC DIPLOMACY

The first efforts at "cultural relations," or what came to be called "public diplomacy," by the State Department occurred as part of President Franklin Roosevelt's (1882–1945) Good Neighbor Policy, in an effort to improve relations with Latin America. These efforts continued through World War II, and in 1945, President Harry S. Truman (1884–1972) transferred operations undertaken by the Office of War Information to the State Department. That same year, the new assistant secretary of state for public affairs, William Benton (1900–1973), told Congress that "the relations between nations ha[d] constantly been broadened to include not merely governments but also peoples" (Hart 2013, 111).

The State Department's education and cultural exchange programs, intended to improve international understanding through individual exchange experiences, reveal a growing recognition that perceptions abroad of the United States mattered in important ways to US foreign relations. Through the Bureau of Educational and Cultural Affairs, thousands of foreigners began visiting the

United States every year, while Americans began traveling abroad under the same program. The cultural exchange program included performing artists and athletes, as well as students, teachers, and professionals. The exchange programs expanded greatly after the passage of the 1946 Fulbright Act. In 1949 Secretary of State George Marshall (1880–1959), appearing on a television program intended to explain to the American public the role of the State Department, announced that "Foreign Policy has entered the American home and taken a seat at the family table" (Hart 2013, 13). All of these efforts were intended to increase American awareness of foreign affairs issues, to improve the department's image both at home and abroad, and to improve the American image abroad.

THE IMPACT OF SOCIAL CHANGE

By the 1960s and 1970s, the State Department belatedly began to reflect decades of social change within the United States, as well as the folly of sending such a homogenous (elite white male) corps of diplomats out into the world to represent the country. The department made a concerted effort to recruit African American Foreign Service officers and appointed, between 1961 and 1965, eight African American ambassadors and an African American head of the US Information Agency. By the 1960s, discrimination against Catholics and Jews had mostly disappeared (although Jews were not permitted to work in Arab countries under an informal agreement until the late 1970s). The number of women Foreign Service officers doubled in the 1970s, and by the end of the 1980s, almost 25 percent of Foreign Service officers were women.

TWENTY-FIRST-CENTURY CHALLENGES

Recent assessments of the Department of State generally agree, however, that the department continues to underperform in the area of policy leadership, at least partly due to the militarization of American foreign policy in the post–Cold War era, but especially since the terrorist attacks of September 11, 2001. Yet successes and reforms often go underreported. For instance, the department successfully created twenty new embassies in Europe after 1991 without adding additional personnel. Also in the 1990s, the Bill Clinton administration created a new undersecretary for global issues, reflecting an increased awareness of global concerns, including the environment and population growth. The State Department budget remains miniscule in relation to other federal agencies, and its labyrinthine bureaucratic structure, as well as new challenges to American security after 9/11 and the creation of another new federal agency, the Department of Homeland Security, further complicated the State Department's primary purpose—advancing American objectives and interests throughout the world, promoting and protecting the interests of American citizens, and implementing presidential foreign policy.

After 9/11, George W. Bush's administration promised to more effectively promote public diplomacy through the State Department in order to more favorably shape the image of the United States in the wider world. These efforts had stalled significantly after the end of the Cold War. During Barack Obama's first term (2009–2013), the department raised the level of public awareness of its efforts largely due to the "personal diplomacy" and high-profile status and travel schedule of Secretary of State Hillary Clinton. Clinton practiced grassroots and community diplomacy, with a special focus on issues concerning women and girls. In 2013 the Department of State created a new Office of Faith-Based Community Initiatives to better engage with faith communities around the world, recognizing the leadership role of women in faith-based communities in many parts of the world. This move reflects the stated goal of the Obama administration to pursue a foreign policy of engagement and cooperation, though the relevance of the department in policy making remains subordinate to the White House and the national security apparatus.

SEE ALSO *Department of Defense, US; Department of Homeland Security; National Security Agency (NSA); Security Council, UN*

BIBLIOGRAPHY

Barnes, William, and John Heath Morgan. *The Foreign Service of the United States: Origins, Development, and Functions.* Washington, DC: Historical Office, Department of State. 1961.

Estes, Thomas S., and E. Allan Lightner, Jr. *The Department of State.* New York: Praeger, 1976.

Hart, Justin. *Empire of Ideas: The Origins of Public Diplomacy and the Transformation of U.S. Foreign Policy.* New York: Oxford University Press, 2013.

Rubin, Barry. *Secrets of State: The State Department and the Struggle over U.S. Foreign Policy.* New York: Oxford University Press, 1985.

US Department of State, Office of the Historian. https://history.state.gov/departmenthistory

Molly Wood
Professor of History
Wittenberg University

DEPARTMENT OF VETERANS AFFAIRS

Since its inception shortly after World War I (1914–1918), the functions and structure of the Department of Veterans Affairs (VA) have changed according to the nature and impact of military engagements, veterans' demands, and fiscal, political, and social circumstances, but its core mission has been relatively consistent: manage a set of entitlements conditionally available to former service members. The United States is hardly unique in offering post-service support—governments the world over have done so for centuries—but the VA represents a unique approach in comparison with other developed nations, which provide their military veterans with health care and other benefits in part via more expansive welfare states.

In a nation where centralized, federally sponsored social assistance has been viewed with skepticism, elected officials, bureaucrats, and advocacy groups have justified veterans' entitlements in a variety of ways. Following military drafts during the nineteenth and twentieth centuries, government funded benefits were heralded as a necessary means of offering recompense to individuals who may have been compelled by the state to serve. Some entitlements were aimed at allowing disabled veterans to maintain independence in civilian society. Since conscription was discontinued in 1973, veterans' benefits have also been used as a means of increasing and prolonging voluntary enlistments.

Veterans' access to unique entitlements in the United States predates the creation of the VA. Early efforts took place at the local level even before the nation was established. British colonial governments in North America, for example, offered pensions and land grants to settlers who fought Indian tribes. Disparate local efforts were followed by the passage of the first national pension law in 1776 and the establishment throughout the nineteenth century of state and federally sponsored Soldiers' Homes, which offered residents room, board, and the camaraderie of fellow veterans.

The modern-day VA is rooted in the World War I era, when veterans' advocates, elected officials, and bureaucrats reconceptualized, expanded, and consolidated post-service benefits with the goal of bolstering rehabilitation and self-reliance. Great War veterans had access, through a variety of federal agencies, to vocational education, disability and life insurance, and medical care. But influential advocacy organizations argued that the system was disorganized and inadequate. Joined by bureaucrats and medical professionals, they successfully argued in 1921 for the creation of an independent agency, called the Veterans' Bureau (VB), to foster greater coordination. During the interwar years the VB grew into a diverse social service organization, administering pension, insurance, and medical care programs through a central office in Washington, DC, as well as state-based regional offices. In 1930, again at the behest of bureaucrats and advocates who equated consolidation with efficiency, the Bureau of Pensions and National Home for Disabled Volunteer Soldiers, which had been created in the nineteenth century, were combined with the VB to form the Veterans Administration.

As the bureaucracy grew and the Great Depression brought economic hard times, demand for services escalated. By 1941, approximately 58,000 veterans of Indian wars, the Civil War (1861–1865), the Spanish-American War (1898), and World War I were receiving care in more than ninety veterans' hospitals across the country—the majority suffering from "neuropsychiatric" conditions. That year, pension, disability compensation, and life insurance payments totaling more than $433 million were made to 856,000 veterans and their dependents.

With the passage of the 1944 GI Bill, the government signaled its commitment to providing new veterans with middle-class opportunities by offering them access to publicly funded university education, guarantees of home loans, employment assistance, and unemployment compensation. By 1947, the VA employed approximately 200,000 people to administer those benefits and oversaw a budget of more than $500 million. More than 12 million World War II (1939–1945) veterans reported gaining directly from the GI Bill. Although some women and men of color reaped its benefits, many faced additional, occasionally insurmountable, barriers in accessing them.

Throughout the VA's existence, government officials have attempted to display gratitude to those who served while maintaining fiscal responsibility. GI bills passed after military conflicts in Korea and Vietnam were somewhat less generous than their World War II counterparts. Questions that had long plagued legislators, veterans' advocates, and VA administrators regarding how to determine access to benefits—by considering, for example, length of service, extent of disability, and income—came to the fore and shaped an era of veterans' activism. President Ronald Reagan's stance on the VA in the 1980s encapsulated the simultaneous skepticism and embrace of the organization's mission. In 1988, after mandating that some veterans pay for a portion of their medical care, Reagan elevated the VA from being an independent agency to a cabinet-level office that would be known as the Department of Veterans Affairs. According to an Associated Press report, Reagan's White House spokesman maintained that the change in status "would not necessarily increase its size or budget but would give it a greater say in the councils of government."

Increased benefits and VA restructuring have typically been spurred not strictly by public generosity but by larger changes in the health and welfare landscape and perceived crises. Following World War II, for example, when veterans' hospitals were maligned as antiquated institutions, new VA leadership dictated that the institutions would be affiliated with academic medical centers and cease relying on the civil service system. Later, the well-publicized struggles of Vietnam veterans helped create an awareness of the unique challenges of readaptation to civilian life, giving the VA reason to expand access to community-based mental health counseling and programs aimed at combating substance abuse, homelessness, and the long-term consequences of exposure to chemical weapons, such as Agent Orange. In the 1990s, building on that diversification and responding to the needs of a new cadre of veterans of the First Gulf War, VA leadership replaced the agency's hospital-centered model with "integrated service networks," which relied on a variety of in- and outpatient facilities in particular regions. In 2014, as service members returning from wars in Iraq and Afghanistan placed fresh demands on the system, and news reports revealed that both elderly and new veterans were enduring long wait times for medical appointments, legislation was hastily passed authorizing some beneficiaries to seek care from private providers.

Between 1940 and 2012 the VA's inflation-adjusted share of the federal budget increased at an average of 3.8 percent per year, peaking during and after World War II, the Vietnam War, and the wars in Iraq and Afghanistan. The costs of military engagements—for veterans, and for their government—evidently extend well beyond the battlefield.

SEE ALSO *Central Intelligence Agency (CIA); Department of Defense, US; Department of Homeland Security; Department of State; Embassies, Consulates, and Diplomatic Missions; Joint Chiefs of Staff; National Security Council (NSC)*

BIBLIOGRAPHY

Kelly, Patrick J. *Creating a National Home: Building the Veterans' Welfare State, 1860–1900.* Cambridge, MA: Harvard University, 1997.

Oliver, Adam. "The Veterans Health Administration: An American Success Story?" *Milbank Quarterly* 85, 1 (2007): 5–35.

Ridgway, James D. "Recovering an Institutional Memory: The Origins of the Modern Veterans' Benefits System from 1914 to 1958." *Veterans Law Review* 5 (2013). http://www.bva.va.gov/docs/vlr_vol5/ridgway.pdf

Rostker, Bernard. *Providing for the Casualties of War: The American Experience through World War II.* Santa Monica, CA: Rand, 2013.

Scott, Christine. "Veterans Affairs: Historical Budget Authority, FY1940–FY2012." Congressional Research Service Report for Congress, June 13, 2012. https://www.fas.org/sgp/crs/misc/RS22897.pdf

Severo, Richard, and Lewis Milford. *The Wages of War: When America's Soldiers Came Home—from Valley Forge to Vietnam.* New York: Simon and Schuster, 1989.

Skocpol, Theda. *Protecting Soldiers and Mothers: The Political Origins of Social Policy in the United States.* Cambridge, MA: Belknap Press of Harvard University Press, 1992.

Stevens, Rosemary A. "The Invention, Stumbling, and Reinvention of the Modern U.S. Veterans Health Care System, 1918–1924." In *Veterans' Policies, Veterans' Politics: New Perspectives on Veterans in the Modern United States,* edited by Stephen R. Ortiz. Gainesville: University Press of Florida, 2012.

Jessica L. Adler
Assistant Professor, Departments of History and Health Policy and Management
Florida International University

DÉTENTE

Détente is a French word that refers to an easing of tension. The word was used particularly in the 1970s to describe calming interactions between the United States and the Soviet Union.

By contrast with the tension that characterized Soviet-American relations after the end of World War II, during the early 1970s the relationship between Moscow and Washington improved remarkably. The two countries engaged in arms control agreements (the Strategic Arms Limitation Talks, or SALT I, in 1972) and summitry that represented a marked shift in superpower relations. As the United States simultaneously broke from its earlier nonrecognition policy vis-à-vis the People's Republic of China (PRC)—while the Soviets and the Chinese exchanged blows along their border in 1969—the view of the Cold War as a bipolar confrontation had, it seemed, become a thing of the past. In Europe, the division of Germany moved toward stabilization with the advent of inter-German relations, a four-power agreement on the status of Berlin, and a series of bilateral treaties between the Federal Republic of Germany on the one hand and the Soviet Union, Poland, and other Soviet bloc countries on the other. In the early 1970s, moreover, the talks that eventually led to the Conference on Security and Cooperation in Europe (CSCE)—culminating in the signing of the Helsinki Final Act in August 1975—finally got under way.

The principal American policy makers behind this shift were President Richard Nixon (1913–1994) and National Security Advisor and Secretary of State Henry Kissinger (b. 1923). Their often secretive diplomacy and open advocacy of realpolitik aimed at minimizing ideological conflict in superpower relations. Their initial success was most clearly in evidence in 1972 when Nixon visited both China and the Soviet Union. A few years later, however, the Watergate scandal had caused Nixon to resign, while Kissinger's apparent disregard for human-rights concerns was prompting widespread domestic criticism against their policies.

Détente also failed to have a positive impact on the many regional crises that occurred, or continued, in the early 1970s. In October 1973, for example, the outbreak of the Yom Kippur War between Israel and its Arab neighbors produced a potentially dangerous proxy confrontation between the United States (which supported Israel) and the Soviet Union (which armed Egypt and Syria). Kissinger's frantic "shuttle diplomacy" eventually preempted a major confrontation. In Southeast Asia, despite the Paris Agreements of January 1973, the war in Vietnam continued until the eventual unification of North and South Vietnam in 1975.

By the late 1970s, Soviet-American détente was all but dead. Although the Jimmy Carter (b. 1924) administration negotiated a SALT II agreement, the Soviet invasion of Afghanistan in late 1979 prevented its ratification by the US Congress. The Iranian Revolution of 1979 and the subsequent hostage crisis that overshadowed the last year of Carter's presidency served to increase demands inside the United States for a more robust American foreign policy. The 1980 election of Ronald Reagan (1911–2004), who openly called for a more belligerent American foreign policy, signaled the final end of the era of negotiations that Nixon had announced a decade earlier. In short, within a few years the optimistic climate of the early part of the decade had given way to the so-called second Cold War.

SEE ALSO *Cold War; Kissinger, Henry; Nixon, Richard Milhous*

BIBLIOGRAPHY

Garthoff, Raymond L. *Détente and Confrontation: American-Soviet Relations from Nixon to Reagan*. 2nd ed. Washington, DC: Brookings, 1994.

Hanhimäki, Jussi M. *The Rise and Fall of Détente: American Foreign Policy and the Transformation of the Cold War*. Washington, DC: Potomac Books, 2013.

Sargent, Daniel J. *A Superpower Transformed: The Remaking of American Foreign Relations in the 1970s*. New York: Oxford University Press, 2015.

Zanchetta, Barbara. *The Transformation of American International Power in the 1970s*. New York: Cambridge University Press, 2014.

Jussi M. Hanhimäki
Professor of International History
Graduate Institute of International and Development Studies, Geneva, Switzerland

DETERRENCE

Deterrence builds upon a timeless concept of human interactions: one party influencing the choice of another by threatening consequences that outweigh gains. This concept assumed a special meaning with the advent of nuclear weapons, and it was refined and elevated to a cornerstone of American foreign and defense policies during the Cold War.

As the early Cold War intensified, the United States faced challenges in how to compensate for Soviet conventional military superiority in Europe and how to make use of the US nuclear monopoly to protect American vital interests abroad. One of the first to articulate a solution to the problem was American military strategist Bernard Brodie (1910–1978). In a 1946 book titled *The Absolute Weapon*, Brodie wrote that, "Thus far the chief purpose of our military establishment has been to win wars. From now on its chief purpose must be to avert them" (76). In short, the real power of nuclear weapons lay in the threat to use them rather than actually using them.

As other military strategists built upon the theory of deterrence Brodie had articulated, President Harry Truman (1884–1972) began applying it in specific foreign policy challenges, such as the Berlin blockade (1948–1949). It also became a guiding principle in the Truman administration's broader efforts to contain Soviet power and was a key consideration in Truman's decision to proceed with development of the thermonuclear bomb, a class of weapons thousands of times more powerful than the atomic bombs dropped on Hiroshima and Nagasaki in 1945. They were so powerful that their actual use was practically unthinkable. Their only purpose was to deter.

The 1952 presidential election brought a new flavor of deterrence to the fore, one that put heavier emphasis on the calculated ambiguity of whether the United States might retaliate with nuclear strikes to any provocation, especially those like the Korean War (1950–1953). Once implemented by President Dwight Eisenhower (1890–1969), it became known as massive retaliation.

In the 1960 presidential election, Democratic candidate John F. Kennedy (1917–1963) challenged the credibility of this all-or-nothing approach, proposing instead a new deterrence policy known as flexible response that put greater emphasis on the credibility of proportional responses to deter the adversary.

By the mid-1960s, the Soviets had built their nuclear arsenal to relative parity with that of the United States in terms of numbers of nuclear warheads and the means of their delivery, such as bombers and missiles. That reality ushered in a new phase, where both superpowers could guarantee the utter destruction of the other. This era of mutually assured destruction and the arms race that it brought with it was dangerous, but the era also proved relatively stable and lasted through the end of the Cold War without an outbreak of open war between the superpowers.

The end of the Cold War challenged entrenched ideas about deterrence. Critics of deterrence policy point out that its effectiveness depends on factors that are less applicable after the Cold War: that decision makers will act rationally and that the adversary can be readily identified and held accountable. These limitations have led to a marked reduction in the prominence of deterrence in US defense policy.

SEE ALSO *Cold War; Intercontinental Ballistic Missiles; Military-Industrial Complex; Mutual Assured Destruction (MAD)*

BIBLIOGRAPHY

Brodie, Bernard, ed. *The Absolute Weapon: Atomic Power and World Order.* New York: Harcourt, Brace, 1946.

Freedman, Lawrence. *The Evolution of Nuclear Strategy.* 3rd ed. New York: Palgrave Macmillan, 2003.

George, Alexander L., and Richard Smoke. *Deterrence in American Foreign Policy: Theory and Practice.* New York: Columbia University Press, 1974.

Kaplan, Fred. *The Wizards of Armageddon.* New York: Simon and Schuster, 1983.

David Coleman
Senior Research Fellow
National Security Archive

DICKENS, CHARLES

1812–1870

British author Charles Dickens arrived in America as a literary celebrity in the winter of 1842. The author of *The Pickwick Papers* (1836–1837) and the creator of *Oliver Twist* (1837–1839) and the beloved Little Nell of *The Old Curiosity Shop* (1840–1841), he first toured Boston, Cambridge, and the Lowell mills in Massachusetts before heading to New York. On February 18, 1842, Dickens was given a public dinner in New York at which eight hundred people were present, many from publishing and journalistic establishments.

Even before Dickens journeyed to the United States, his stories had been serialized in periodicals and appeared in inexpensive publications, books, and theater adaptations. While the constant reprinting of Dickens's works makes it difficult to quantify his overall circulation in the United States, it is clear that they sparked intense commercial competition. In 1837, the public response to the serialization of *The Pickwick Papers* indicated the emergence of a mass readership that would revolutionize publishing in the United States. Within the tensions of competitive commerce and American nationalism, Dickens's fiction earned a wide and lasting readership and had a profound impact on American life. Despite attacks on Dickens's character by some American newspapers and a backlash against his *American Notes* (1842), Dickens remained one of the most popular authors in the United States.

By the time of Dickens's visit in 1842, however, tensions had entered into his relationship with the American press and with US publishers over the issue of international copyright. At this time, American publishers freely reprinted articles and stories from Europe, and British authors received no payment for the reprinting of their work. Dickens had circulated among authors a petition that urged copyright protection and royalties for British authors whose works were reprinted in the United States. American publishers like Park Benjamin and Harper Brothers firmly opposed proposals for international copyright, sometimes arguing their commercial interests in nationalistic terms.

In Philadelphia, Dickens investigated the Pennsylvania system of solitary confinement for prisoners. Edgar Allan Poe (1809–1849) met with him in his rooms at the United States Hotel. Dickens also visited the nation's capital and witnessed the institution of slavery in nearby Virginia. In *American Notes*, which he composed upon his return to England, Dickens revealed a mixed response to America, and he was often critical. Readers in Europe noted that Dickens appreciated many things about the United States, but he also expressed distaste for certain rough and uncultivated aspects of American life, particularly Americans' habit of spitting. He discussed his opposition to slavery and slaveholders in chapter seventeen of *American Notes*.

Dickens's fiction was received within this ideological context of American nationalism and business competition. While many readers approached him as a beloved friend, he could also be construed as representing the British enemy in the wake of the American Revolution and the War of 1812. Dickens's novel *Martin Chuzzlewit* (1843–1844), set in both Britain and the United States, further angered American critics with its sharp satire on business malpractice, corruption, and the American press, as well as a satirical account of his character's purchase of swampland along the Mississippi River in Illinois.

Dickens returned to the United States in 1867 for a public reading tour, and he was greeted warmly. Americans' attitude toward Dickens had changed over time, and the disputes of previous years were forgotten. Dickens again visited the major cities of the eastern

United States, reading selections from *A Christmas Carol* (1843), *Oliver Twist*, and other stories. Despite suffering from a cold, shingles, and other ailments, Dickens drew large audiences, reading in the company of more than 114,000 people. Dickens averaged about four readings per week in the United States between December 1867 and April 1868. His public readings evoked intense feelings, and many who attended agreed that they were lively pieces of theater.

Dickens's popularity among American audiences has been sustained by numerous stage and film adaptations of his fiction. Notable among these are David Lean's *Great Expectations* (1946), several film versions of *A Tale of Two Cities*, David O. Selznick and George Cukor's *David Copperfield* (1935), the Broadway musical *Oliver!* by Lionel Bart, and the many film and stage adaptations of *A Christmas Carol*.

SEE ALSO *Transatlantic Reform*

BIBLIOGRAPHY

Claybaugh, Amanda. "Toward a New Transatlanticism: Dickens in America." *Victorian Studies* 48, 3 (2006): 439–460.

Dickens, Charles. *The Public Readings*. Edited by Philip Collins. Oxford: Oxford University Press, 1975.

Dickens, Charles. *American Notes for General Circulation*. London: Chapman and Hall, 1842. Reprint, edited by Patricia Ingham, New York: Penguin, 2000.

Dickens, Charles. *Martin Chuzzlewit*. London: Chapman and Hall, 1843–1844. Reprint, edited by Patricia Ingham, New York: Penguin, 2000.

Glavin, John, ed. *Dickens on Screen*. Cambridge: Cambridge University Press, 2003.

Meckier, Jerome. *Innocent Abroad: Charles Dickens's American Engagements*. Lexington: University Press of Kentucky, 1990.

Slater, Michael, ed. *Dickens on America and the Americans*. Austin: University of Texas Press, 1978.

Tambling, Jeremy. *Lost in the American City: Dickens, James, and Kafka*. New York: Palgrave, 2001.

Robert McParland
Professor of English
Felician College

DISNEY

The Walt Disney Company is a transnational entertainment and media conglomerate based in Burbank, California. It is one of six such conglomerates composing the configuration of the Hollywood media oligopoly in the early twenty-first century. More than the other Hollywood companies, however, Disney is also a globally recognized, distinct corporate brand with an immediate meaning for consumers around the globe. Combining a self-styled reputation for innocuous, wholesome family amusements with international consumer capitalist success, Disney is an important emblem of US cultural values around most of the world.

THE DISNEY BRAND AND BUSINESS STRATEGY

Since beginning in the 1920s, the Disney brand has colonized the imaginations of successive generations of children around the world. The Disney brand signals a reputation for children's and family entertainment that is pleasant and safe, presented by reliable, clean, highly professional, inevitably happy personnel. This reputation has been extraordinarily effective and consistent across generations and throughout the world. One major study, the Global Disney Audiences Project, for example, surveyed more than one thousand people in eighteen countries and found that nearly every respondent reported having seen a Disney film. Asked to describe Disney, people across the globe repeated terms such as: family, imagination, magic, happiness, and fun (Wasko, Phillips, and Meehan 2001).

This enviable reputation, moreover, is enhanced by association with the particularly American ideologies of individualism and entrepreneurialism embodied in the mythologized figure of Walter Elias Disney (1901–1966), who founded and ran the company for more than four decades with his brother, Roy Oliver Disney (1893–1971). After starting the Disney Brothers Cartoon Studio in 1923, Walt emerged as the primary "creative" force while Roy attended to business and financial concerns. The Walt Disney Studio, as it was soon renamed, was a creative, at times innovative, animation studio in its formative years. Walt, in particular, seems to have been eager to incorporate new technologies into filmmaking, including synchronized sound, cell animation, and color film. What turned out to be especially innovative, however, was the brothers' leveraging of intellectual-property licensing and merchandising as a significant means of revenue. Later, they would also become industry innovators by expanding their company into a horizontally structured entertainment conglomerate, years ahead of other Hollywood studios (Wasko 2001; Epstein 2005).

A strategy of merchandising animated characters began in earnest following the first Mickey Mouse short films in 1928. As soon as 1929, Mickey began appearing on children's toys and books, soon expanding to include everything from wristwatches to handkerchiefs to shoe polish. By 1935, during the depths of the Great Depression, Disney's revenue from licensing deals exceeded that of its movies (Epstein 2005). This strategy extended beyond the United States from almost the beginning. In 1932, Disney's official fan clubs, the Mickey Mouse Clubs, were already established in more than thirty countries and had more than 1 million members worldwide (Wasko 2001). Animation—especially simply drawn, anthropomorphic animals—was well suited to translate across linguistic and cultural borders during these early days of synchronized sound (Epstein 2005).

DISNEY'S ALLIANCE WITH THE US GOVERNMENT

During World War II (1939–1945), Disney contracted with the government to produce films to support the war effort and train troops and civilians, keeping the company solvent during the war years. By 1943, 94 percent of the film produced by Disney was for the government (Giroux and Pollock 2010). Disney worked with the Franklin D. Roosevelt administration to produce films supporting the State Department's Good Neighbor Policy, such as *Saludos Amigos* (1943) and *The Three Caballeros* (1945). Disney was further contracted to produce a series of propaganda and educational short films (some distributed on 16 millimeter) for Latin American audiences. These were intended to help keep Latin American countries allied with US interests—or at least neutral—during the war (Kaufman 2009). Some of the films, however, came to be interpreted by many within the intended audience as efforts at American colonial indoctrination (Giroux and Pollock 2010).

From the wartime Donald Duck propaganda short *Commando Duck* (1944) to the 1950s nuclear advocacy film *Our Friend the Atom* (1957), some of Disney's filmmaking reflected what became an ongoing alliance with the US government. Still fuming from a contentious Screen Cartoonists Guild strike in 1941 and pumped full of patriotism, Walt Disney took on more explicit and more reactionary politics. He was the first vice president of the Motion Picture Alliance for the Preservation of American Ideals, which laid the basis for the Hollywood blacklist. In 1947, he testified before the House Un-American Activities Committee as a friendly witness, explaining that communism was "an un-American thing" (Giroux and Pollock 2010; Wasko 2001).

EXPANSION

In 1953, the Disney brothers formed their own distribution arm, Buena Vista Distribution, which included Buena Vista International. Now a full Hollywood studio, Disney was particularly aggressive in its efforts at international distribution, with nearly one-third of the world's population having seen at least one Disney film by 1954 (Wasko 2001). At the same time, rather than view television as a threat to their business, the Disney brothers saw it as an opportunity to expand their marketing directly into people's homes. In 1954, Disney began a lengthy collaboration with the ABC television network in the United States, producing a weekly anthology series, *Disneyland*, which recycled the library of existing material and also introduced new characters and products. In a further branding coup, each episode was introduced by Walt himself, every inch the charming, small-town American businessman, cementing an accessible, endearing public persona.

In an early example of corporate synergy, each division of the company was being used to advertise and promote the others. This was nowhere clearer than with Disney's next endeavor, the construction of a themed amusement park in Anaheim, California, to be called Disneyland. The park opened in 1955, debuting to the entire country at once in a special television event on ABC (an initial investor and co-owner). Inside the 160-acre park, amusements were divided into four separate areas: Adventureland, Frontierland, Fantasyland, and Tomorrowland, united by Main Street, U.S.A., a nostalgic, sanitized image of small-town American commerce. Disneyland was instantly successful, bringing the company's branded characters and imaginary cinematic settings to life, surrounded by rides and activities for all ages, as well as acres of merchandise for sale. By the start of the 1960s, well before other major studios began to do so, Disney was integrating film, television, theme park, and merchandising businesses.

In 1971, a second, much larger theme park, Walt Disney World, opened in Florida. The initial Magic Kingdom soon expanded into a "resort destination" that included multiple hotels, theme parks, and attractions. Eventually, Disney even built the actual town of Celebration nearby (Ross 1999). Disneyland and Disney World are visited by millions from around the world each year. Combining carefully curated, wholly sanitized fun and entertainment with abundant consumption and commodification, they promote a vision of American prosperity and entertainment while strengthening the corporate global brand (Wasko 2001).

DISNEY'S GLOBAL EMPIRE

In the 1980s, Michael Eisner, CEO of Disney from 1984 to 2005, began rereleasing the considerable library of Disney properties and rejuvenated the animation division with Disney-branded interpretations of fairy tales and traditional stories from around the world, including *The Little Mermaid* (1989), *Beauty and the Beast* (1991), *Aladdin* (1992), and *The Lion King* (1994). Eisner helped Disney regain the commercial success that had floundered following the deaths of the Disney brothers.

Eisner used the strength of the Disney brand to launch new undertakings, including a new theme park, Euro Disneyland, which opened in 1992. (A Tokyo

Visitors at the Disneyland Paris Resort, January 2015. *Euro Disneyland, which opened in 1992, met with some initial resistance, including disdain for American-style consumerism, objections to the prohibition of alcohol sales in the park, and confusion over the meaning of "Euro." By 1995 the park—which had begun serving beer and wine in 1993—was renamed Disneyland Paris.* GONZALO FUENTES/REUTERS/CORBIS

Disneyland had opened in Japan in 1983, but was a licensed endeavor not owned or operated by Disney). Even while Euro Disneyland attracted 11 million visitors in its first year, disdain for American-style consumerism and concerns about cultural imperialism led to the colorful description of Euro Disneyland as a "cultural Chernobyl" (Gomery 2005; Neate, Sylt, and Reid 2012). The Euro Disneyland labor force, for example, resisted initial requirements to speak English and adhere to strict appearance codes; Disney's American understanding of "family friendly" prohibited the sale of alcohol; and even the relative meaning of "Euro" was misunderstood. "As Americans, the word 'Euro' is believed to mean glamorous or exciting. For Europeans it turned out to be a term they associated with business, currency, and commerce," Eisner later conceded (Giroux and Pollock 2010). By 1995, Disney had financially reorganized the park and renamed it Disneyland Paris. It began serving wine and beer in 1993 (Disney's US parks followed suit in 2012).

Learning from these events, in 2005 Disney opened the Hong Kong Disneyland Resort in strategic collaboration with the local government (which is the majority owner in this arrangement). In addition to having an invested local collaborator, Disney avoided much of the backlash experienced in France by paying closer attention to cultural specificity, with design adhering to guidelines of feng shui and employees speaking Cantonese, Mandarin, and English (Giroux and Pollock 2010). In 2011 construction began on the next theme park, Shanghai Disney Resort, slated to open in 2016.

In 2015, Disney's overall business comprised five divisions: media networks, theme parks and resorts, studio entertainment, consumer products, and interactive media. Disney's studios include Disney, Pixar, Marvel, Lucasfilm, and Touchstone (which also distributes DreamWorks). Disney media networks include music, print, theater, and television. Disney now owns the ABC television network, ESPN, and a stake in A&E, Hulu, and Fusion. Disney Channels Worldwide are distributed through cable, satellite, and digital television; through Disney Media Distribution to local broadcasters across the globe; and via online and mobile components. These channels reach more than 600 million viewers worldwide. Recent global expansion for Disney media includes India, where it has acquired Indiagames and UTV, which produce branded games, films, television, and mobile content locally. Disney Channel Malaysia serves as the basis for online and mobile programming across Southeast Asia, including an interactive virtual world known as *Club Penguin*. In China, Disney operates all five of its business divisions across economic and political divides, including the mainland, Hong Kong, and Taiwan. Disney has been established in Russia since 2006, primarily in media, studio, and consumer goods. In addition to Disney's theme parks in California, Florida, Paris, Tokyo, Hong Kong, and Shanghai, it also operates a cruise line with four ships and a privately owned island in the Bahamas, thirteen properties composing the Disney Vacation Club, and a guided family-adventure vacation agency.

THE CONSEQUENCES OF DISNEYFICATION

This global reach is impressive but not without consequence. Disney is a leader in antipiracy enforcement around the world. Disney is also a global employer. In addition to its offices, theme parks, and retail stores around the world, Disney outsources animation and production labor and merchandise manufacturing. The Disney Company has been accused of operating sweatshops, employing children, overlooking safety violations, and paying below minimum wage, in the process becoming an emblem of US industrial exploitation of global labor (Budd 2005; Giroux and Pollock 2010; Tschang and Goldstein 2010). Simultaneously, Disney's global reach represents for many an explicit form of cultural imperialism, in which US national influence is equated with the Disneyfication of culture and commerce.

The term *Disneyfication* describes the company's approach to cultural appropriation. Disney produces a sanitized, homogenized, and Americanized product based on folk tales and fairy tales, then forcefully protects it as intellectual property. The related term *Disneyization* describes social practices that seem to emulate Disney corporate practices. These include the development of themed environments, multiple forms of hybrid consumption, ubiquitous brand merchandising, affective and performative labor, and surveillance control of consumers and workers (Budd 2005; Bryman 2004). Disney's synthesis of its global corporate practice with an endearing brand image has proven to be both a successful business strategy and a symbol of the excesses of US economic and cultural imperialism.

SEE ALSO *Coca-Cola; Globalization; Good Neighbor Policy; Hollywood; Jazz; Musicals; Rock 'n' Roll; Television*

BIBLIOGRAPHY

Bryman, Alan. *The Disneyization of Society*. London: Sage, 2004.

Budd, Mike. "Introduction: Private Disney, Public Disney." In *Rethinking Disney: Private Control, Public Dimensions*, edited by Mike Budd and Max H. Kirsch, 1–36. Middletown, CT: Wesleyan University Press, 2005.

Epstein, Edward Jay. *The Big Picture: The New Logic of Money and Power in Hollywood*. New York: Random House, 2005.

Giroux, Henry A., and Grace Pollock. *The Mouse that Roared: Disney and the End of Innocence*. Rev. ed. Lanham, MD: Rowman and Littlefield, 2010.

Gomery, Douglas. *The Hollywood Studio System: A History*. London: BFI, 2005.

Kaufman, J. B. *South of the Border with Disney: Walt Disney and the Good Neighbor Program, 1941–1948*. New York: Walt Disney Family Foundation Press, 2009.

Neate, Rupert, Christian Sylt, and Caroline Reid. "Disneyland Paris Celebrates 20th Birthday €1.9bn in Debt." *Guardian* (London), April 11, 2012. http://www.theguardian.com/world/2012/apr/11/disneyland-paris-20th-birthday-debt

Ross, Andrew. *The Celebration Chronicles: Life, Liberty, and the Pursuit of Property Values in Disney's New Town*. New York: Ballantine Books, 1999.

Taylor, John. *Storming the Magic Kingdom: Wall Street, the Raiders, and the Battle for Disney*. New York: Knopf, 1987.

Tschang, Feichin Ted, and Andrea Goldstein. "The Outsourcing of 'Creative' Work and the Limits of Capability: The Case of the Philippines' Animation Industry." *IEEE Transactions on Engineering Management* 57, 1 (2010): 132–143.

Walt Disney Company. http://thewaltdisneycompany.com

Wasko, Janet. *Understanding Disney: The Manufacture of Fantasy*. Cambridge: Polity Press, 2001.

Wasko, Janet, Mark Phillips, and Eileen R. Meehan. *Dazzled by Disney? The Global Disney Audiences Project*. London: Leicester University Press, 2001.

Shawn Shimpach
Associate Professor, Department of Communication and Interdepartmental Program in Film Studies
University of Massachusetts, Amherst

DOLLAR DIPLOMACY

Dollar diplomacy, a term first used in a derogatory sense around 1910, refers to the early twentieth-century American foreign policy that enlisted loans from US banks to achieve political ends in less-developed nations. The policy actually predated the coining of the term: President Theodore Roosevelt (1858–1919) pioneered the strategy when he faced a crisis in the Dominican Republic in late 1904.

THE EMERGENCE OF THE POLICY IN US-DOMINICAN RELATIONS

Dollar diplomacy emerged just as the United States became the world's greatest industrial power. With economic supremacy came new interest in foreign trade and the projection of American power abroad. In 1898 the United States easily won the Spanish-American War, took possession of Puerto Rico and the Philippines, and exercised special powers over Cuba. Americans saw these acquisitions as a new departure in US history—a turn toward imperialism. A savage guerrilla war in the Philippines and political conflict in Cuba, however, killed the American appetite for taking direct control of foreign territories.

Despite this change in mood, many Americans still believed their country was destined to dominate the poor, weak, and unstable nations of the Caribbean and Central America. That belief grew stronger when Panama, with American help, split off from Colombia in 1903 and gave the United States permission to build a canal across the isthmus. The question became, what sort of control over the "revolution-ridden countries" south of the Rio Grande was possible, short of outright annexation and imperial rule?

Roosevelt's 1905 intervention in the Dominican Republic provided one answer. Political turbulence in that nation had led to default on foreign loans; by late 1904, several European nations threatened to intervene, in violation of the Monroe Doctrine. To end the crisis, Roosevelt combined three elements that became "classic" dollar diplomacy: first, strong diplomatic pressure to allow American officials to collect customs duties, the source of nearly all Dominican government income; second, reform of the Dominican fiscal system by an American economist; and third, a large loan from American banks to refinance the Dominican foreign debt.

In the Dominican case, the arrangement was not imposed by force. In fact, Dominican president Carlos Morales (1868–1914) welcomed US intervention. "We have saved the republic from anarchy," Morales told his countrymen. The American plan "is almost paternal" and the advantages "are ours, all ours, since they [the Americans] will be forced by the duty and moral obligation which they have assumed before the whole world to help us with the project of political and social regeneration" (Veeser 2002, 135). For a time, the Dominican customs receivership stopped revolutions and increased government revenue, and American policy makers saw it as a model for stabilizing other Caribbean and Central American nations. Under Roosevelt's successor, William Howard Taft (1857–1930), dollar diplomacy became official policy.

THE FINANCIAL ARM OF TAFT'S PEACE-BUILDING STRATEGY

Taft saw dollar diplomacy as an effective way to bring peace and stability to countries near the Panama Canal. There, he noted, political disorder had led to "chaotic national finances" and "heavy foreign debt." By turning their custom houses over to US officials, these nations could thwart "would-be dictators" and "remove at one stroke the menace of foreign creditors and … revolutionary disorder." Taft applauded "American bankers … willing to lend a helping hand to the financial rehabilitation of such countries" (Taft 1912). By improving living conditions in the region through economic growth, dollar diplomacy would end civil wars and reduce the need for American intervention. Taft and his secretary of state, Philander Knox (1853–1921), thus saw dollar diplomacy as the financial arm of a peace-building strategy that included the creation of the Central American Court of International Justice in 1907.

During Taft's term in office, *dollar diplomacy* began to refer to this policy. As the original pejorative meaning of the term suggests, however, dollar diplomacy was not only about promoting peace and stability. Policy makers fully expected that making loans to Central American and Caribbean nations would increase American trade with them. As the *Wall Street Journal* put it in 1912, "give us dollar diplomacy, good and strong, and we shall secure our commercial dominion." Critics of the policy condemned the mixture of government policy with private profit-seeking as "squalid," "mean," and "un-American" ("Dollar Diplomacy" 1913).

In theory, dollar diplomacy would use financial leverage rather than gunboats to achieve US goals, but in practice military power always stood behind the policy, as the cases of Nicaragua and Honduras demonstrate. To overcome instability in Honduras, Taft and Knox pressured President Miguel Dávila (1856–1927) to accept a Dominican-style custom receivership, with the promise of loans from US banks. They urged a similar arrangement on President Adolfo Díaz (1875–1964) in neighboring Nicaragua. Both men hesitated, fearing that accepting American control would spark revolutions. (Carlos Morales, the Dominican president who accepted the first customs receivership, had indeed been quickly overthrown.)

Meanwhile, treaties to ratify both plans stalled in the US Senate, where critics denounced Taft's alliance with Wall Street bankers. Dávila finally signed off on the US customs receivership in 1911—only to be chased from office in short order by an outraged Honduran people. In Nicaragua, Díaz also faced a rebellion after agreeing to the US plan, leading Taft to land some 2,600 marines to keep the friendly president in power. American marines would remain in Nicaragua until 1932.

Even the model arrangement in the Dominican Republic collapsed. After Dominican president Ramón Cáceres was assassinated in 1911, that country plunged into the kind of disorder that the receivership had supposedly ended forever. President Woodrow Wilson (1856–1924), who had denounced dollar diplomacy as immoral, sent several hundred marines to the island to "secure" the US embassy. When they failed to restore order, Wilson ordered a full-scale military occupation of the Dominican Republic that lasted from 1916 to 1924. Once seen as a magic wand that could quell disorder and spur progress, dollar diplomacy regained the negative connotation that characterized the term when it was first coined.

THE ASSESSMENT OF HISTORIANS

Earlier historians largely took dollar diplomacy at face value. In 1943 Samuel Flagg Bemis (1891–1973) noted that Roosevelt's Dominican intervention was "benevolent imperialism" that reflected a genuine concern for the well-being of the people (Bemis 1943, 157, 161). After 1960 revisionist historians took the rhetoric of peace and uplift as so much window dressing. Walter LaFeber (1993, 217), a leading revisionist, refers to dollar diplomacy's marriage of the US government to powerful bankers as a dangerously incestuous relationship. More recently, historians have emphasized race and gender in their understanding of the policy. Emily Rosenberg (1999, 33) notes that to the exclusively white and male elites who made US foreign policy at the time, Latin Americans had "feminine" characteristics, including an inability to control spending by their government.

Though Wilson ended the practice of dollar diplomacy as official policy, the conditions that gave rise to it continued, as did efforts to combine loans with oversight in order to stabilize struggling nations. Rosenberg (1999, 2) notes that, since World War II, the International Monetary Fund has often conditioned its loans to developing nations on their acceptance of financial supervision. Lars Schoultz (1998, 188) argues that US policy makers in the 1990s believed that only American financial guidance, known as the Washington Consensus, could avert economic chaos in Latin America. And Brian Loveman (2010, 189) contends that dollar diplomacy "anticipated the missionary zeal" of American policy makers who promote global free trade as the foundation of peace and democracy today. Like those later US strategies, the original dollar diplomacy allowed policy makers to believe they were fostering world peace and prosperity, even as they benefited American banks and businesses.

SEE ALSO *Interventionism; Open Door Policy; Roosevelt Corollary (1904); Roosevelt, Theodore; Taft, William Howard; Wilson, Woodrow*

BIBLIOGRAPHY

Bemis, Samuel Flagg. *The Latin American Policy of the United States: An Historical Interpretation.* New York: Harcourt, Brace, 1943.

"Dollar Diplomacy." *Wall Street Journal,* March 21, 1913, 1.

"First Installment of Message Sent to Congress by President." *Wall Street Journal,* December 4, 1912, 6.

LaFeber, Walter. *Cambridge History of American Foreign Relations,* Vol. 2: *The American Search for Opportunity, 1865–1913.* New York: Cambridge University Press, 1993.

Loveman, Brian. *No Higher Law: American Foreign Policy and the Western Hemisphere since 1776.* Chapel Hill: University of North Carolina Press, 2010.

Rosenberg, Emily. *Financial Missionaries to the World: The Politics and Culture of Dollar Diplomacy, 1900–1930.* Cambridge, MA: Harvard University Press, 1999.

Schoultz, Lars. *Beneath the United States: A History of U.S. Policy toward Latin America.* Cambridge, MA: Harvard University Press, 1998.

Taft, William Howard. Fourth Annual Message. December 3, 1912. http://millercenter.org/president/taft/speeches/speech-3786

"Success in South America." *Wall Street Journal,* June 26, 1912, 1.

Veeser, Cyrus. *A World Safe for Capitalism: Dollar Diplomacy and America's Rise to Global Power.* New York: Columbia University Press, 2002.

Cyrus Veeser
Professor of History
Bentley University

DOMINO THEORY

President Dwight D. Eisenhower (1890–1969) first articulated the domino theory at a press conference on April 7, 1954, as the nine-year Franco–Viet Minh War was winding down amid an ignominious French defeat at Dien Bien Phu, Vietnam. The president, convinced that the United States must step in to replace France as the guarantor of freedom in Indochina, sought to explain to the American people the strategic importance of the former French colonies of Vietnam, Laos, and Cambodia. The falling domino principle held that Southeast Asian countries were like a fragile row of dominos, and that one country falling to communism would send its neighbors cascading one-by-one into the Soviet camp. According to Eisenhower, then, the potential consequences of communist victory extended far beyond the borders of Indochina. Indeed, the falling dominos would "not only multiply the disadvantages that you would suffer through loss of materials, sources of materials, but now you are talking really about millions and millions and millions of people" (Eisenhower 1958, 383). The result, he argued, would be nothing less than a total reversal of the Cold War balance of power in the region, threatening American positions in Japan, Taiwan, the Philippines, and eventually Australia and New Zealand.

The imperative to resist such an outcome served as the justification for direct American intervention in South Vietnam following the July 1954 Geneva Agreement that ended the Franco–Viet Minh War. Based on the logic of the domino theory, Eisenhower's administration threw its support behind the staunchly anticommunist leader Ngo Dinh Diem (1901–1963), a Catholic modernizer whom the United States helped install and keep in power for nearly a decade. The always-tense relationship between Diem and his American patrons was, in the words of one historian, a "misalliance" (Miller 2013). Yet despite frequent disputes between Diem and his American advisers over competing visions for governance and reform, and in the face of Diem's increasing unpopularity with his own constituents, the premises of the domino theory continued to fuel a close relationship between Diem and the United States. It was not until late 1963 that the John F. Kennedy (1917–1963) administration saw no alternative but to lend tacit support to a military coup against its longtime ally. This move did not signal a renunciation of the domino theory but recognition that the continuing goal of propping up a stable, noncommunist South Vietnamese government would require new Vietnamese partners.

The domino theory persisted as the primary justification for American involvement in Vietnam for two decades. It figured prominently in Lyndon B. Johnson's (1908–1973) explanation for his decision to escalate and Americanize the war in 1965 and endured throughout the full-scale war that ended in 1973 with the Paris Peace Agreement. Throughout this period, the theory took on a logic of its own and proved elastic enough to accommodate shifting geopolitical realities and perceptions. By the time President Kennedy replaced Eisenhower in 1961, a "doctrine of credibility" emerged to reconfigure how American policy makers conceived of the domino theory. Kennedy administration officials were less concerned than their predecessors had been that a country falling to communism would automatically imperil its immediate neighbors on the basis of geographic proximity. Instead, they feared a psychological domino theory, in which one country's fall would lead others around the world to lose faith in the credibility of American commitments, thereby driving them into the communist camp. Thus, Vietnam became a critical test case for the United States to demonstrate its resolve to noncommunist allies the world over.

Following the Vietnamese communist victory in April 1975, a few regional dominos did fall. Cambodia's five-year civil war concluded on April 17, 1975, with the Khmer Rouge seizure of power, and in August 1975 the communist Pathet Lao took power in Laos. However, by this late date in the Cold War, the Sino-Soviet split was complete and the communist bloc had fractured beyond repair. These ostensibly communist takeovers were by no means victories for the Soviet Union, much less for the precepts of Marxist-Leninism. To a limited extent, American concerns about credibility proved justified. The US defeat in Southeast Asia emboldened the Soviet Union to challenge American interests in Africa and Latin America, and movements to resist American imperialism following the heroic Vietnamese example gained steam throughout the Third World. However, such misguided Soviet adventurism would prove more of a blessing than a curse to the United States, which suffered few significant geopolitical setbacks and emerged victorious in the Cold War when the Soviet bloc crumbled in 1989. The lie given to the domino theory by the outcome of the Vietnam War wrought greatest damage on the domestic life of the United States. Since 1975, the resulting "Vietnam syndrome" has fueled heated debates over the proper role of American power in the world, and the underlying conflicts show few signs of resolution.

SEE ALSO *Cold War; Eisenhower, Dwight D.; Kennedy, John Fitzgerald; Vietnam War*

BIBLIOGRAPHY

Anderson, David L. *Trapped by Success: The Eisenhower Administration and Vietnam, 1953–1961.* New York: Columbia University Press, 1991.

Eisenhower, Dwight D. "The President's News Conference of April 7, 1954." *Public Papers of the Presidents of the United States: Dwight D. Eisenhower, 1954*, 381–390. Washington, DC: GPO, 1958.

Logevall, Fredrik. *The Origins of the Vietnam War.* New York: Routledge, 2001.

Miller, Edward G. *Misalliance: Ngo Dinh Diem, the United States, and the Fate of South Vietnam.* Cambridge, MA: Harvard University Press, 2013.

Jessica M. Chapman
Associate Professor, Department of History
Williams College

DOUGLASS, FREDERICK

c. 1818–1895

In 1845 Frederick Douglass's autobiography, *Narrative of the Life of an American Slave, Written by Himself,* was published in Boston, exposing him as the fugitive

"Frederick Baily," who had escaped the house of his master, Hugh Auld, in Baltimore in 1838. Fearing Auld's reprisal and keen to continue his antislavery activism, Douglass took passage to the United Kingdom aboard the Cunard Line vessel *Cambria,* docking in Liverpool on August 28, 1838, and landing in Dublin two days later. His arrival marked the beginning of an eighteen-month sojourn that was to prove personally and professionally transformative. In 1847 Douglass would return to his wife and family in the United States a free man rather than a fugitive, a major figure in transatlantic abolitionism with a supportive network of British and Irish friends, financially solvent and carrying with him the funds to set up his own newspaper, the *North Star.*

THE AUTOBIOGRAPHY IN THE UNITED KINGDOM

Douglass's time in Ireland and Britain was significant on literary, political, artistic, economic, and personal fronts. Shortly after his arrival in Dublin, Douglass's autobiography was republished by Dublin Quaker printer Richard Webb (1805–1872). The work sold quickly and widely, providing Douglass with a significant income from his writing, one augmented by what he earned on his speaking tour as a member of the American Anti-Slavery Society. A second Irish edition was published in early 1846, with several British editions following over the next year, making the *Narrative* the first widely read first-person account of American slavery.

The Irish and British *Narratives* are formally distinctive, illustrating the ways in which the work responded to the political geographies of its transatlantic mediation. The American edition was framed by a preface and a letter from eminent white abolitionists William Lloyd Garrison (1805–1879) and Wendell Phillips (1811–1884), respectively. Douglass, however, wrote his own preface to the Irish editions and included a wide variety of paratextual material on topics religious, economic, and organizational in appendices that locate the modified work firmly in its UK social context and confirm his growing network of local alliances. The preface demonstrates Douglass's growing self-confidence as an author, as well as the greater intellectual and political independence possible outside the immediate constraints of American abolitionism.

DOUGLASS AND THE BRITISH AND IRISH PUBLICS

This transatlantic refashioning of the African American fugitive narrator and political activist speaks volumes about the developing relationship between Douglass and his new British and Irish publics, for whom he quickly became a cause célèbre. His sojourn was characterized by an unprecedented freedom from race prejudice, as well as by considerable social and economic success. He was spared the day-to-day dangers and ignominies that attended his life in America. The absence of discrimination generally was compounded by the "negrophilia" he encountered in middle- and upper-class British social circles, which allowed him to cross class boundaries in ways that would have been otherwise inconceivable. It sparked Douglass's corresponding Anglophilia: he lionized British political culture, repeatedly drawing comparisons unfavorable to America by casting monarchy and empire as champions of freedom, and democracy and republicanism as defenders of slavery. The letters he wrote to Garrison during his time overseas, many of which he subsequently published in the *Liberator,* confirm his role not just as an advocate for abolition in the United Kingdom but in producing a particular political image of the United Kingdom for a US audience. His admiration for Britain and the empire was to last throughout his life and lies at the heart of his sometime ambivalence to conditions in Ireland—he was present during the Great Famine of 1845–1847—and later in North Africa.

On his tour around Britain and Ireland, Douglass made many new acquaintances and friends, with local abolitionist chapters springing up in response to his presence and public appearances. This was particularly true of ladies' abolitionist societies, through which Douglass made several important and long-lasting friendships, including with Isabel Jennings in Cork, and with Ellen Richardson and her sister-in-law, Anna Richardson, in Newcastle. It was at Summerhill, the Richardsons' house, that Douglass reputedly met Julia Griffiths (1811–1895) during the Christmas of 1846. Douglass enjoyed a lifelong friendship with Griffiths, who was later to move to the United States to work closely with him on the the *North Star* and on *Frederick Douglass' Paper* in the years leading up to the Civil War.

Religious matters loomed large throughout Douglass's visit. In Ireland and England, he moved largely in the company of Nonconformists and members of the established church. Tensions arose between Douglass and the Methodist churches in the south of Ireland after controversy was provoked when he singled out southern Methodist slaveholders for public criticism. In Scotland, the financial support received by the Free Church of Scotland from southern Presbyterians provoked a political storm, sparking the famous "Send Back the Money" campaign in which Douglass was active throughout 1846. It was during his time in Scotland that Douglass considered emigrating permanently to the United Kingdom and settling in Edinburgh. However, his wife, Anna Murray (1813–1882), who had remained in Lynn, Massachusetts, with their four children while Douglass was overseas, was not in favor of the plan. When their daughter Rosetta fell ill, Anna petitioned Douglass to return to the United States. It was safe to do so after 1846, when the Richardsons arranged for the purchase of Douglass's freedom, despite the considerable debate this sparked in abolitionist circles concerning the morality of compensating slaveholders for the manumission of their property.

If Douglass had arrived in the United Kingdom a little-known fugitive, he returned to the United States in 1847 a fully fledged political and literary force, experienced on the abolitionist platform and matured as a journalist following two years of letter writing and reportage in the *Liberator.* He was leaving behind an enduring network of friends and allies who would remain part of his social circle, even at a distance, as supporters and readers of his newspapers. Douglass was to make two additional visits to Britain in later years: one in 1859, shortly after John Brown's raid on Harpers Ferry; the last in 1886 with his second wife, Helen Pitts (1838–1903), as part of a longer tour that included France, Italy, and Egypt. This was to be the Douglass's final overseas trip, marking the end of a forty-year relationship—with Britain, the empire and with UK friends—of immeasurable personal, professional, and political importance.

SEE ALSO *Antislavery; Transatlantic Reform*

BIBLIOGRAPHY

Blassingame, John W., and John R. McKivigan, eds. *Frederick Douglass Papers, Series One: Speeches, Debates, and Interviews.* Vol. 1, *1841–46.* New Haven, CT: Yale University Press, 1979.

Douglass, Frederick. *Narrative of the Life of Frederick Douglass, an American Slave, Written by Himself.* 2nd Irish ed. Dublin, Ireland: Webb and Chapman, 1846.

Douglass, Frederick. *Life and Times of Frederick Douglass, Written by Himself.* Boston: De Wolfe & Fiske, 1892.

McKivigan, John R., ed. *Frederick Douglass Papers, Series Three: Correspondence,* Vol. 1, *1842–52.* New Haven, CT: Yale University Press, 2009.

Rice, Alan J., and Martin Crawford, eds. *Liberating Sojourn: Frederick Douglass and Transatlantic Reform.* Athens: University of Georgia Press, 1999.

Sweeney, Fionnghuala. *Frederick Douglass and the Atlantic World.* Liverpool, UK: Liverpool University Press, 2007.

Fionnghuala Sweeney
Senior Lecturer in American Literature
School of English Literature, Language and Linguistics
Newcastle University, United Kingdom

DRUGS

Use of psychoactive substances to alleviate pain, enhance quality of life, and alter consciousness has always played an integral part in human existence. During the period that encompasses the colonial and national experience of the United States, profound changes in both society and pharmacology fundamentally altered this long-standing homo-chemical relationship.

TRADITIONAL ATTITUDES: PRE-COLUMBIAN TO THE LATE NINETEENTH CENTURY

Until roughly the 1880s, the concept of "drugs" as it is typically used today did not exist in the United States or anywhere else. Societies across the globe did not draw stark distinctions between foods, refreshments, herbs, spices, medicines, and substances of abuse.

When the Spanish introduced cacao from Mesoamerica, most considered it a medicinal. Only later, when mixed with sugar, did "chocolate" gravitate toward categorization as a confection. The use and cultivation of tobacco quickly spread around the planet from its New World homeland, becoming a significant cash crop supporting the British North American colonies. Tobacco enjoyed this rapid ascent to a world commodity, no doubt largely because of the addictive characteristics of nicotine. Nevertheless, since the substance did not cause obvious inebriety, it was both prescribed by physicians and enjoyed by habitués without the assumption that it must have some medicinal effect.

Even the most common psychoactive substance, alcohol, was not easily or consistently categorized. Many viewed beer simply as a beverage, or even a staple because it had long been considered a type of liquid bread. Most segments of society consumed at least some wine, not least because doing so appeared a healthful alternative to avoid waterborne diseases. State authorities and religious leaders often tried to suppress the use of hard liquors, especially among the lower classes, because cheap inebriants, such as gin and rum, generated social disruption and facilitated political revolt. Nevertheless, the revenues governments derived from taxing increasingly popular "stimulants," such as alcohol, tobacco, coffee, and tea (as well as the sugar necessary to make the latter two palatable), proved sufficiently attractive to counteract draconian consumption-limitation efforts.

Preparations derived from opium played an important role in pharmacopeias. The poppy's analgesic and other qualities were well known to the unregulated array of medical practitioners of the era, including "physicks," homeopaths, barber-surgeons, shaman-healers, and patent medicine purveyors. The most common approach to medico-drug regimens consisted of self-treatment according to whatever home remedies one inherited or invented. Essentially, until a few decades after the Civil War, "drugs" permeated a more-or-less open market featuring a continuum of substances ranging from the innocuous and ubiquitous, such as coffee, to exotic rarities like coca. Most of those preparations might or might not be consumed for a medicinal purpose, depending on the circumstances and practices of the particular time and place.

PHARMACOLOGICAL REVOLUTION, DIFFERENTIATION, AND GATEKEEPING: LATE NINETEENTH CENTURY TO THE PRESENT

The modern era that began in the decades around 1880 as a constellation of factors, including industrialized pharmaceutical production and marketing, medical and governmental professionalization, and multiple alterations in societal norms, combined to profoundly reshape conceptions about drugs. The emergence of professional medicine, characterized by Western scientific methods, a specialist literature, the limiting of authorized practice to those with adequate training, and certain key technologies, such as the hypodermic needle, made it possible for physicians to diagnose and treat with increasing authority. The advent of scientific pharmacology, pursued most successfully by emerging multinational pharmaceutical corporations that competed for sales globally, facilitated increasingly sophisticated research methodologies that generated development of a breathtaking array of products.

The vast majority of these twentieth- and twenty-first-century pharmaceutical concoctions are nonaddicting substances, created to treat all manner of deadly diseases, nonlethal complaints, and minor annoyances. Both to ensure proper usage of this massively expanded formulary and to support further research and development by securing adequate profit for pharmaceutical companies, a thoroughgoing system of prescription controls rapidly developed by the early twentieth century. For those able to afford it, this cornucopia of relief and quality-of-life enhancement represents one of the marvels of the era.

By the early twentieth century, concerns about addiction also increased, resulting in the imposition of stringent controls on distribution of habit-forming drugs. Reports of burgeoning drug use among minorities and the urban poor fostered fears about societal breakdown. Contamination of the mainstream population by substances that caused a fundamental loss of personal control appeared increasingly threatening. A negative view of "recreational" use of psychoactive substances, defined as nonmedicinal consumption only for pleasure, became common among medical, police, and government officials wielding increasing authority as they gained professional status. Moreover, the burgeoning explosion of pharmaceutical substances required periodic expansion of the definition of addiction: "miracle drugs," such as cocaine (introduced in the 1880s), amphetamines (in frequent use by the 1950s), and certain types of reuptake inhibitors (designed in recent decades to effect targeted synaptic functions in the brain), presented habituating characteristics that differed from opium-based narcotics.

Concern about all those issues resulted in domestic legislation and US support for international agreements intended to limit supplies of addicting substances to the amount deemed necessary for "legitimate" medical purposes. As the national/international drug regulatory regime matured by the 1940s, US pro-control advocates attempted periodically to suppress supplies, distribution, and illicit usage by imposing a variety of strategies including strict(er) border controls, crop-eradication programs, crackdowns on illicit manufacturers, prosecution of illegal suppliers, arrests of individual users, enhanced monitoring of "ethical" pharmaceutical companies and prescribers, and support for overseas antitrafficking initiatives. Tobacco escaped significant regulatory attention until the 1960s, when scientific researchers demonstrated its debilitating effects. Since that time, domestic measures that focused on education rather than punishment have resulted in a significant decrease in national consumption. Severe proscription of alcohol use occurred during the period the Eighteenth Amendment was in force (1920–1933). Thereafter, owing in part to a patchwork of local and state controls supported by a majority of the electorate, per-capita consumption of alcohol did not return to pre-Prohibition levels for a generation.

The modern era revolves largely around questions of authority and access—who possesses the power to make determinations about what sort of use is legitimate? By the 1960s, upheavals in American society concerning the balance between socially imposed restrictions and the liberties of individual citizens rose to prominence: young people, in particular, challenged racial discrimination, dissented from US participation in the Vietnam War, advocated for women's rights, and decried environmental degradation. Recreational drug use provided an important symbolic tool for protestors because illicit psychoactive substance use constituted a direct affront to authority.

In subsequent decades, access-limitation preferences undulated between more and less regulation according to prevailing views about the extent to which the individual's responsibility to society should inhibit personal choice. By the later 1970s, the recurrence of increased per-capita alcohol use generated a backlash against drunk driving and underage drinking. Use of coca-based substances flared in popularity intermittently until the drug's negative effects became evident to the latest cohort of habitués. The battle over whether to redefine marijuana use as legitimate surfaced repeatedly, featuring shifting coalitions of pro- and anti-criminalization advocates. The extent to which patients suffering significant pain could utilize the tremendous analgesic properties of narcotics, or what types of psychological maladies merit pharmacological intervention, remain under considerable debate.

The historical evidence suggests that humans will continue to consume mind-altering chemicals according to their conscious and unconscious desires (and, for some, regardless of prevailing legal strictures). Nevertheless, no society has tolerated totally unfettered access to drugs or imposed complete proscription. How to calculate "harm reduction" will remain a permanent issue of debate, especially in a world featuring an ever-increasing array of substances designed to cater to our every psycho-physiological need.

SEE ALSO *Afghanistan; Americanization; China; Colombia; Cuba; Exceptionalism; Exports, Exportation; Global South; Immigration; Immigration Quotas; India; Industrialization; Internationalism; Interventionism; Isolationism; Mexico; Nativism; War on Drugs; World Health Organization; World's Fairs*

BIBLIOGRAPHY

Burnham, John C. *Bad Habits: Drinking, Smoking, Taking Drugs, Gambling, Sexual Misbehavior, and Swearing in American History.* New York: New York University Press, 1993.

Courtwright, David T. *Forces of Habit: Drugs and the Making of the Modern World.* Cambridge, MA: Harvard University Press, 2002.

Inciardi, James A., and Karen McElrath, eds. *The American Drug Scene: Readings in a Global Context.* 7th ed. Oxford: Oxford University Press, 2014. See also previous editions for a wide variety of chapter topics.

McAllister, William B. *Drug Diplomacy in the Twentieth Century: An International History.* New York: Routledge, 2000.

Weimer, Daniel. *Seeing Drugs: Modernization, Counterinsurgency, and U.S. Narcotics Control in the Third World, 1969–1976.* Kent, OH: Kent State University Press, 2011.

Zinberg, Norman. *Drug, Set, and Setting: The Basis for Controlled Intoxicant Use.* New Haven, CT: Yale University Press, 1984.

William B. McAllister
Special Projects Division Chief, Office of the Historian
United States Department of State
Adjunct Associate Professor, Graduate School of Foreign Service
Georgetown University

The views here are the author's and do not necessarily represent those of the US government or the Department of State.

DULLES, ALLEN W.

1893–1969

The appointment in 1953 of Allen Welsh Dulles as director of the Central Intelligence Agency (CIA) highlights how American traditions of engagement with the global arena were affected by the evolving environment of the twentieth century. While the impact of espionage and covert operations on earlier diplomacy—as well as economic and cultural interactions—had been minimal, these approaches had a powerful influence on US foreign policy in the post-1945 era. Dulles's career provides a window onto controversies surrounding the transformation, some of which remain relevant to this day.

As the son of an intellectual Presbyterian minister and the grandson of a secretary of state, John Watson Foster (1836–1917), Allen Dulles would have seemed destined to carry traditional attitudes and behaviors into a new century. His early life choices would have been familiar to earlier generations of policy makers: Princeton (entering shortly after Woodrow Wilson's years there), a year of teaching in India before joining the Foreign Service, initial postings in Vienna, Bern (after US entry into World War I in 1917), the Paris Peace Conference, and Constantinople. He served as head of the Department of State's Near East Division (1922–1926) while earning a law degree part time at George Washington University, then joined the Wall Street firm of Sullivan & Cromwell, headed by his brother, John Foster Dulles (1888–1959). While working with globally oriented business clients (as did his brother), he remained routinely involved in foreign policy matters. He served on delegations to disarmament conferences throughout the interwar years, and participated in public debates about neutrality and interventionism after the mid-1930s.

Historic concerns always colored Dulles's career, especially his belief in the need for full-bodied involvement in international affairs and attentiveness to global economic opportunities. Yet interests less familiar to his predecessors gradually became more prominent. Dulles was attracted to "intelligence" as early as his Bern posting (1917–1918), when he began cultivating a source network throughout central Europe. A dramatic escalation came with his involvement with the Office of Strategic Services (OSS) after the Japanese attack on Pearl Harbor in December 1941. He spent most of World War II (1939–1945) back in Switzerland, building a legendary record: running a network of anti-Hitler German agents that provided valuable information about the Berlin Foreign Office and V-rocket research, for instance, and coaxing "Operation Sunrise" toward the surrender of German forces in Italy.

Dulles returned to Sullivan & Cromwell in 1945, but was barely offstage during the early Cold War years when OSS capacities were shifted to the new CIA. The Harry Truman (1884–1972) administration regularly consulted him about organizational matters before and after the passage of the 1947 National Security Act. He eventually made a formal move to become deputy director of the

CIA in 1950. The election of Dwight Eisenhower (1890–1969) in 1952 and John Foster Dulles's appointment as secretary of state in 1953 brought Allen Dulles's elevation to the CIA director's position.

The CIA developed a broad range of approaches under Dulles's leadership. Namesake "intelligence" efforts certainly continued, including building a tunnel into East Berlin to access Soviet communication lines, nabbing a copy of Soviet leader Nikita Khrushchev's famous 1956 "secret speech" about Joseph Stalin, and developing U-2 spy plane capabilities. But Dulles pushed in other directions too. Aided by Eisenhower's concern for "long haul" budget sustainability, for example, covert operations seen as low cost were greenlighted with enthusiasm. These included the training and supplying of dissident groups involved in overthrowing Iranian prime minister Mohammad Mossadegh (1882–1967) in 1953 and Guatemalan president Jacobo Arbenz Guzmán (1913–1971) in 1954; "Red Sox/Red Cap" operations encouraging anti-Soviet agitation in Eastern Europe; and the development of psychological warfare and paramilitary capabilities in the Philippines, Vietnam, and Indonesia.

Dulles's CIA operations sparked controversy even when deemed successful. (That this was fully expected is evidenced by the advance concern for maintaining "plausible deniability" for the United States and the White House.) American values were seen by some as severely tarnished by campaigns against the elected leaders of sovereign states, especially when they were more reasonably seen as reformers or nationalists rather than communist cat's-paws. Even worse for some, such actions could turn the United States into a protector and abettor of regimes that would foster brutality and corruption. Mohammad Reza Pahlavi (1919–1980), the shah of Iran, became a particularly notorious case of the time bombs sometimes planted by covert operations.

The controversies were greater yet when operations quickly took problematic turns. There were angry accusations of irresponsibility when the rousing of freedom fighters in Hungary led to their abandonment during the 1956 Hungarian uprising, and the Soviet downing of an American U-2 spy plane in 1960 led to the embarrassing cancellation of a Paris summit. Most notorious of all was the 1961 Bay of Pigs fiasco in Cuba. Planning and execution of this anti-Castro effort proved so weak—and was so globally publicized—that Dulles's position in the new John F. Kennedy (1917–1963) administration was fatally undermined.

Dulles was eased into retirement within months of the Cuban disaster. He worked at burnishing his legendary status with several books (especially *The Craft of Intelligence* [1963]), but he never succeeded in ending debate about the nature of the work for which he was emblematic.

SEE ALSO *Central Intelligence Agency (CIA); Cold War; Covert Wars; Dulles, John Foster; Eisenhower, Dwight D.; Kennedy, John Fitzgerald*

BIBLIOGRAPHY

Dulles, Allen W. *The Craft of Intelligence.* New York: Harper and Row, 1963.

Grose, Peter. *Gentleman Spy: The Life of Allen Dulles.* Boston: Houghton Mifflin, 1994.

Ranelagh, John. *Agency: The Rise and Decline of the CIA.* New York: Simon and Schuster, 1986.

Ronald W. Pruessen
Professor of History
University of Toronto

DULLES, JOHN FOSTER
1888–1959

John Foster Dulles's tenure from 1953 to 1959 as President Dwight Eisenhower's secretary of state serves as a window onto the global range of challenges that would confront the United States for the balance of the twentieth century and beyond. The Dulles of those years also provides an early example of the highly mixed, ongoing record of policy makers as they sought to meet those challenges over subsequent decades.

Dulles was well prepared for the global scale of the responsibilities he encountered at the Department of State. The grandson and nephew of two secretaries of state—John Watson Foster (1836–1917) and Robert Lansing (1864–1928), respectively—Dulles had worked on reparations issues at the 1918–1919 Paris Peace Conference before building a highly successful legal career representing banking and corporate clients with interests in Europe, Asia, and Latin America. By the 1940s, he had become a key foreign policy adviser within the Republican Party.

The Harry S. Truman administration's concern for bipartisanship brought Dulles significant responsibilities on early post–World War II issues. Dulles worked closely with Democratic secretaries of state when he was regularly appointed an "adviser" to US delegations at international meetings, including the 1945 San Francisco Conference that founded the United Nations and the 1947 Council of Foreign Ministers meetings in Moscow and London that attempted to draft peace settlements with some of the defeated enemies. His 1947 discussions with Truman's secretary of state, George Marshall, about using European integration as a key means of avoiding future problems with Germany were an important part of Washington's deliberations leading up to the Marshall Plan, for example. By 1950, the perceived value of Dulles's contributions was sufficient to generate his appointment as "special representative of the president," with a personal rank as "ambassador": he was given primary responsibility for the negotiation of a peace treaty with Japan and successfully navigated a task made especially complicated by the outbreak of war on the Korean peninsula.

Dulles's influence reached its peak after the 1952 election. As Eisenhower's secretary of state, essentially all foreign policy matters required his engagement—and that engagement had full impact because of Dulles's strong, mutually respectful relationship with the president. He devoted the lion's share of his time and energy to an intertwined cluster of issues: Cold War tensions with the Soviet Union and the People's Republic of China; the postwar recovery of Europe; and the unrest in Asia, Africa, the Middle East, and Latin America caused by anticolonial agitation and revolution.

There were definite achievements to Dulles's credit. He energetically supported the evolution of the European Coal and Steel Community into the Common Market and worked creatively to see the Federal Republic of Germany integrated into the North Atlantic Treaty Organization (NATO). Such US efforts helped to expand opportunities for continental economic growth while alleviating the Franco-German tensions that had plagued the world for almost a century. Dulles also managed to increasingly separate the United States from European imperial traditions in both Southeast Asia, where there was a gradual break with French policies in Indochina, and the Middle East, where the United States pressured Great Britain and France (as well as Israel) to find ways of accommodating the rise of "Arab nationalism"—with a flashpoint coming during the 1956 Suez crisis, when Washington used the United Nations to force London, Paris, and Tel Aviv to end their military campaign against Egypt.

The Eisenhower administration's success was undercut by more problematic policies, however. Hints of détente with Moscow (e.g., the Geneva Summit Conference of 1955) never gathered steam, with efforts sometimes limited by Dulles's occasional tendency to firebrand public rhetoric ("godless communism," "massive retaliation") and sometimes by the administration's resistance to compromise on issues like German reunification. There were not even hints of détente with the People's Republic of China, thanks to a conviction that toughness in places like the Taiwan Straits and Indochina would eventually force concessions by Beijing. Nor was Dulles able to move beyond a limited break with traditional imperial pretensions: US policies tended to favor engagement with so-called Third World nationalists as a means of managing them. When they proved recalcitrant, as they often did, a shift to paternalistic condescension and what can be described as neocolonial strategies was common (e.g., covert operations in Iran, Guatemala, and Indonesia; "state building" efforts in South Vietnam).

As with any high-level policy maker, Dulles faced challenges and circumstances that would not be precisely duplicated over time. His complex record of successes and failures, however—particularly the attitudes and inclinations that helped produce the latter—remain relevant to an understanding of how US foreign policy evolved from John F. Kennedy's presidency onward.

SEE ALSO *Cold War; Dulles, Allen W.; Eisenhower, Dwight D.; Kennedy, John Fitzgerald*

BIBLIOGRAPHY

Immerman, Richard H., ed. *John Foster Dulles and the Diplomacy of the Cold War.* Princeton, NJ: Princeton University Press, 1992.

Immerman, Richard H. *John Foster Dulles: Piety, Power, and Pragmatism in U.S. Foreign Policy.* Lanham, MD: Rowman and Littlefield, 1998.

Pruessen, Ronald W. *John Foster Dulles: The Road to Power.* New York: Free Press, 1982.

Ronald W. Pruessen
Professor of History
University of Toronto

DUNCAN, ISADORA

SEE *Lost Generation.*

DYLAN, BOB

1941–

Bob Dylan is an American singer-songwriter, musician, and author. He has released thirty-six studio albums, eleven live LPs, and numerous compilation and rarities collections over the course of a more than fifty-year career. Dylan's records have sold over 125 million copies worldwide, and other artists have recorded his songs an astounding thirty-three thousand times and counting. His autobiography, *Chronicles, Volume One*, was published in 2004 and spent nineteen weeks on the *New York Times* best-seller list for nonfiction. He has received the Presidential Medal of Freedom (2012), the Ordre des Arts et des Lettres (1990) from France, and a Pulitzer Prize Special Arts Award (2008) for his profound impact on popular music and American culture.

LIFE, CAREER, AND MAJOR WORKS

Bob Dylan was born Robert Allen Zimmerman in Duluth, Minnesota, on May 24, 1941, and was raised in the Iron Range town of Hibbing, Minnesota. He played in a number of short-lived bands as a teenager, influenced by Elvis Presley (1935–1977) and Buddy Holly (1936–1959) and the explosion of rock 'n' roll, as well as by country, western, and blues, including music by Hank Williams (1923–1953) and Jimmy Reed (1925–1976), which he heard on long-range radio broadcasts at night. After graduating high school in 1959, Dylan enrolled at the University of Minnesota. In Minneapolis, he immersed himself in a bohemian scene, reading Beat generation writers, listening to folk music of Woody Guthrie (1912–1967) and others, and performing in coffee shops. After a year and a half, Dylan left the University of Minnesota for Greenwich Village, which was then the epicenter of the American folk revival, arriving in New York City in January 1961. Later that year, he signed with Columbia Records, and an eponymous album of folk music was released in March 1962.

His second album, *The Freewheelin' Bob Dylan*, established Dylan as an internationally renowned folk artist. Original Dylan compositions from this record, including "Blowin' in the Wind," "Masters of War," and "A Hard Rain's A-Gonna Fall," would become anthems of 1960s' protest movements around the world. Significantly, songs from this era of his career—with themes touching on racism and inequality and war and destruction—are what much of the world continues to identify as quintessential Dylan. *The Freewheelin'* record was particularly popular in England, and its sophisticated lyrical content had a profound influence on many popular recording artists, including the Beatles, who, after listening to it repeatedly, began writing more mature, introspective, and lyrically complicated songs (*Beatles Anthology* 2000, 112, 158).

Dylan's most important composition came about, however, after he decided to move beyond the restrictive conventions of acoustic folk music and the subject matter of topical or protest songs. "Like a Rolling Stone" (1965) was a raucous, six-minute-long electric rocker featuring

Bob Dylan performing in Spain, July 2012. *Dylan, who has had a profound impact on popular music and American culture, has sought to bring his Americana sound to the rest of the world with a relentless touring schedule since the late 1980s. By 2015, he had performed concerts in more than fifty countries.* © CHRISTIAN BERTRAND/SHUTTERSTOCK.COM

emotionally charged lyrics about resentment and vengeance. Prior to "Like a Rolling Stone," love was the dominant theme in popular American music, and songs had to be under three-minutes long to gain airplay on radio stations. With its unique subject matter, sound, and length, "Like a Rolling Stone" forever changed the course of popular music—expanding what was possible to accomplish in song for songwriters the world over. The song reached number two on *Billboard*'s Hot 100 chart in the United States, making it the highest charting single of Dylan's career. Numerous songwriters and musicians have cited "Like a Rolling Stone" as a critical influence, and in 2004 and again in 2011 *Rolling Stone* magazine listed it as the greatest song of all time.

Dylan's 1966 *Blonde on Blonde* LP pushed further at the boundaries of the recording industry by being the first double album in popular American music. *Blonde on Blonde* also included a song that occupied an entire record side at over eleven minutes long. The influence of these innovations on other artists cannot be overstated.

As much of the English-speaking rock world embraced psychedelia in 1967, Dylan bucked convention, and in doing so, once again became a trendsetter. That summer, with musicians who would eventually become the Band, Dylan recorded approximately 140 traditional songs, standards, and original compositions in a style that blended country, blues, folk, and bluegrass, and which has since been termed *Americana*. As a musical genre, Americana has become so influential and popular that the National Academy of Recording Arts and Sciences began offering a Grammy Award in this category beginning in 2010. In the period when Dylan and the Band invented Americana, often referred to as the "Basement Tapes" era, Dylan began mining songs from the nineteenth and early twentieth centuries for inspiration for his own original tunes, in addition to recording a number of cover versions. Traditional ballads from rural America, along with material from the Great American Songbook, have been a significant influence on Bob Dylan's work ever since. Moreover, he has played a leading role in resurrecting often forgotten traditional songs for new audiences at home and abroad. In many ways, Bob Dylan considers himself to be a crucial modern link to the great songs of the American past.

INTERNATIONAL IMPACT

Dylan has sought to bring his Americana sound to the rest of the world with a relentless touring schedule since the late 1980s. By 2015, he had performed concerts in over fifty countries, spanning the four corners of the globe, though he had yet to play in Africa. Some locations for Dylan concerts have been groundbreaking, such as his September 1987 performance before eighty thousand people in East Berlin, a full two years before the fall of the Berlin Wall. A 1994 show in Kraków, Poland, saw concertgoers holding signs that read, "We waited 30 years!" (Maymudes and Maymudes 2014, 246). More recently, Dylan has played concerts in Vietnam and China. The China shows, in April 2011, were met with criticism from those who thought Dylan should not perform in a country guilty of human rights violations, while others criticized him for failing to play his most overt 1960s-era protest songs at these concerts.

Indeed, despite his enormous output of songs dealing with love, death, salvation, and other nonpolitical topics, and his own desire to avoid being characterized as merely a protest singer, Dylan continues to be linked to political and social movements aiming for greater equality in the world. Indicative of this enduring association of Dylan with the politics of change and the global resonance of his music, Amnesty International, the human rights organization headquartered in Great Britain, issued a collection of seventy-five new cover versions of his songs in 2012 to celebrate their fiftieth anniversary. Eighty artists from twelve different countries contributed to this record, titled *Chimes of Freedom*. *Chimes of Freedom*, at once a tribute to Dylan and a fundraiser for such an important organization, is perhaps an apt testament to his influential place in the world and a fitting legacy for his extraordinary career in music.

SEE ALSO *Beat Generation; Presley, Elvis Aaron; Rock 'n' Roll*

BIBLIOGRAPHY

The Beatles Anthology. San Francisco: Chronicle, 2000.

"500 Greatest Songs of All Time." *Rolling Stone*, May 31, 2011.

Maymudes, Victor, and Jacob Maymudes. *Another Side of Bob Dylan: A Personal History on the Road and off the Tracks*. New York: St. Martin's Press, 2014.

Sounes, Howard. *Down the Highway: The Life of Bob Dylan*. Updated ed. New York: Grove Press, 2011.

Wilentz, Sean. *Bob Dylan in America*. New York: Doubleday, 2010.

Noah L. Gelfand
Adjunct Assistant Professor
University of Connecticut at Stamford

E

EARTH DAY

Each year on and around April 22, people all over the world participate in environment-themed events under the name "Earth Day." The tradition goes back to an America-wide day of action held on April 22, 1970. Originally conceived by US Senator Gaylord Nelson (1916–2005) as a nationwide teach-in on the environment, the first Earth Day comprised more than twelve thousand events with an estimated twenty million participants. No other country held a similar event, even though environmentalism was on the upswing all over the West at the time. By way of comparison, West Germany held 106 events in 1970 in celebration of the European Conservation Year. Moreover, the European Conservation Year was an initiative of the Council of Europe and thus adhered to a top-down model of environmental education, whereas Earth Day thrived on grassroots dynamism. While the European Conservation Year is largely forgotten, Earth Day is a fixture in American environmental memory.

Earth Day 1970 was the culmination of several years of environmental protests. It shaped, and in turn mirrored, the flourishing of environmental sentiments and influenced a generation of activists. It also helped in the passage and enactment of landmark legislation, though Earth Day maintained a certain distance toward specific agendas, parties, and organizations. With a strong presence in schools and universities, Earth Day was more about raising awareness and spotlighting the general significance of environmental policies. While annual Earth Day celebrations stood as a symbol of American interest in environmental affairs, they remained somewhat disconnected from political events throughout the 1970s and 1980s.

Earth Day received a boost with Earth Day 1990 when a professional campaign, led by the national coordinator of the original event, Denis Hayes (b. 1944), brought attendance figures on a par with 1970. The campaign also marked the breakthrough of Earth Day as a global event, helped by the inspiring Earth Summit in Rio de Janeiro in 1992. The Earth Day Network, headquartered in Washington, DC, now works with twenty-two thousand partners in 192 countries. Schools and other educational institutions remain key arenas of activities.

Over the years, Earth Day mirrored the changing agenda of environmentalism in national and international politics. While the annual event became more amenable to mainstream environmental groups and corporate funding, it retained its openness for different groups, activities, and concerns. In fact, its nonpartisan character may have been an important factor for the event's broad acclaim ever since the first Earth Day, which served as a unifying moment for a society torn apart over the Vietnam War and civil rights. Some activists have criticized this attitude toward environmental campaigning. For instance, the 1984 Bhopal disaster inspired calls to replace Earth Day with a "Corporate Clean-Up Day" on December 3, the day of the catastrophic gas leak in a Union Carbide plant in India. Earth Day thus mirrors the worldwide concern for the environment while also highlighting the tensions and divisions that are just as much part of global environmentalism.

SEE ALSO *Deindustrialization; Earthrise (Bill Anders, 1968); Silent Spring (Rachel Carson, 1962)*

BIBLIOGRAPHY

Fortun, Kim. *Advocacy after Bhopal: Environmentalism, Disaster, New Global Orders.* Chicago: University of Chicago Press, 2001.

Rome, Adam. *The Genius of Earth Day: How a 1970 Teach-in Unexpectedly Made the First Green Generation.* New York: Hill and Wang, 2013.

Frank Uekötter
Reader in Environmental Humanities
University of Birmingham

EARTHRISE (BILL ANDERS, 1968)

On Christmas Eve 1968, the crew of *Apollo 8* became the first people to orbit the moon, and so the first to see Earth rise above the lunar horizon. The sight had been anticipated, but on that day it took the busy crew by surprise. They scrambled for their cameras, and Bill Anders (b. 1933) took the famous color image, since named *Earthrise.* He later recalled: "I looked up and saw the Earth coming up on this very stark, beat-up lunar

Earthrise, *photograph by astronaut William Anders.* *When prints of the image taken during the* Apollo 8 *mission were released to the press, the image of Earth as a blue planet, miraculously alive in the sterile blackness of space, created a sensation. As Anders said, "We came all this way to the moon, and yet the most significant thing we're seeing is our own home planet."* LWM/NASA/ALAMY

horizon, an Earth that was the only color that we could see, a very fragile looking Earth … we came all this way to the moon, and yet the most significant thing we're seeing is our own home planet" (Anders 2008, 2).

When prints of the image were released to the press a few days later (this was before digital photography), they created a sensation. At a time when the attention of both the National Aeronautics and Space Administration (NASA) and the media was focused on the outward journey to space, the sight of the whole Earth in color, visibly a planet but also visibly unique, provided a dramatic reversal of perspective—a reversal underlined by the crew's powerful reading on Christmas morning of the opening verses from the book of Genesis describing the creation of the heavens and Earth. On their subsequent international goodwill tours, the astronauts presented prints of *Earthrise* to heads of state the world over.

The image of Earth as a planet, miraculously alive in the sterile blackness of space, proved inspirational. For the biologist Lewis Thomas (1913–1993) and the independent scientist James Lovelock (b. 1919), it came as dramatic visual confirmation that Earth could be understood as a self-regulating network of living systems—the core of Lovelock's Gaia hypothesis that "Earth … is actively made fit and comfortable by the presence of life itself" (Lovelock 1979, intro.). In Britain, David Bowie (b. 1947) was inspired by *Earthrise* to compose "Space Oddity," a 1969 song about a doomed astronaut that became an elegy for the space age ("Planet Earth is blue, and there's nothing I can do") (Broackes and Marsh 2013, 42). In the United States, the global citizenship campaigner John McConnell (1915–2012) used another *Apollo 8* Earth image as an Earth flag. He went on to found the first Earth Day in San Francisco on March 21, 1970, shortly followed by its more enduring East Coast cousin on April 22.

The years of the Apollo program (1968–1972) were also the years of the environmental renaissance, which culminated in the first United Nations "Earth summit," held in Stockholm, Sweden, in 1972. Friends of the Earth, founded in 1969, became part of a new environmentalism that rejected the old divide between humanity and its environment and took the whole Earth as its symbol. The widespread assumption that Earth could not be fundamentally altered by human activity lost credibility in the face of photographs that clearly showed that Earth had limits, defined by an atmosphere no thicker (relatively speaking) than the skin of an apple.

NASA eventually embraced the new perspective in its "mission to Earth" program of the mid-1990s, and in time would proclaim these first color images of Earth as one of the great benefits of the space program. But it was the journalist Norman Cousins (1915–1990) who put it best: "what was most significant about the lunar voyage was not that men set foot on the Moon, but that they set eye on the Earth" (quoted in Poole 2008, 3).

SEE ALSO *Apollo Program; Earth Day; National Aeronautics and Space Administration (NASA)*

BIBLIOGRAPHY

Anders, Bill. Interviewed for "To the Moon," an episode of *NOVA*, produced by WGBH Boston for PBS, 1999. Quoted in *Earthrise: How Man First Saw the Earth*, by Robert Poole, 2. New Haven, CT: Yale University Press, 2008.

Broackes, Victoria, and Geoffrey Marsh, eds. *David Bowie Is*. London: V&A, 2013.

Cosgrove, Dennis. *Apollo's Eye: A Cartographic Genealogy of the Earth in the Western Imagination*. Baltimore, MD: Johns Hopkins University Press, 2001.

Höhler, Sabine. *Spaceship Earth in the Environmental Age, 1960–1990*. London: Pickering and Chatto, 2015.

Lovelock, James. "Introduction." In *Gaia: A New Look at Life on Earth*. Oxford: Oxford University Press, 1979.

Oliver, Kendrick. *To Touch the Face of God: The Sacred, the Profane, and the American Space Program, 1957–1975*. Baltimore, MD: Johns Hopkins University Press, 2013.

Poole, Robert. *Earthrise: How Man First Saw the Earth*. New Haven, CT: Yale University Press, 2008.

Poole, Robert. "What Was Whole about the Whole Earth? Cold War and Scientific Revolution." In *The Surveillance Imperative: The Rise of the Geosciences during the Cold War*, edited by Simone Turchetti and Peder Roberts, 213–235. New York: Palgrave Macmillan, 2014.

Robert Poole
Guild Research Fellow, History
University of Central Lancashire, United Kingdom

ECONOMICS

From the colonial period forward, the United States has been imbricated in international markets, and economic development has occurred within an international context of trade, finance, and diplomacy. Initially, the American colonies provided Europeans access to bountiful natural resources and land. In the northeastern United States, logging, fur trading, potash and pearl ash production, and shipbuilding were key industries. Fishing and whaling were profitable as well. In contrast, southern states relied upon slave labor to produce commodities for sale in an international marketplace. These included indigo, sugar, tobacco, rice, and, after the American Revolution (1775–1783), cotton. These early specializations can be viewed as examples of comparative advantage, yet both regions worked in concert with one another as an integrated economy after the Revolution, but with financial concerns often driving political considerations, a recurring pattern in American history.

THE UNIFIED MARKET OF THE EARLY AMERICAN REPUBLIC

The US Constitution, adopted in 1787, established the entire nation as a unified market. There were to be no tariffs or taxes on interstate commerce. The Constitution stipulated that the federal government could regulate commerce with foreign nations and among the states, establish uniform bankruptcy laws, create money and regulate its value, fix standards of weights and measures, establish post offices and roads, and fix rules governing patents and copyrights. Alexander Hamilton, the first secretary of the treasury, advocated an economic development strategy in which the federal government would nurture infant industries by providing subsidies and imposing protective tariffs on imports. He also urged the federal government to create a national bank and assume the public debts the colonies had incurred during the Revolutionary War, in large measure to ensure that the young nation would be able to secure credit. He succeeded in building a reliable financial reputation for the United States by taking over state debts and bundling them with the national debt into new securities sold to investors. He funded the debt with tariffs on imported goods and a highly controversial tax on whiskey. Additionally, Hamilton was granted congressional authority to create the First Bank of the United States in 1791, which remained in operation through 1811. In 1816 the bank was succeeded by the Second Bank of the United States, which remained in operation through 1836.

THE RISE OF THE COTTON INDUSTRY

After the Revolution, the United States sought to develop trade relationships with other European nations. Unfortunately, many remained committed to restrictive mercantilist policies, and Americans were left with few alternatives to the British. They offered the best terms on credit and were open to forming trade relationships with the former colony. Because of these factors, southern planters embraced cotton cultivation, as well as slavery, in order to gain access to British credit and markets. With the development of Eli Whitney's cotton gin in 1793 and the Louisiana Purchase in 1803, cotton production expanded rapidly through the American South. By 1815, the United States was the world's largest cotton producer, and Great Britain was the largest consumer of American cotton. The rise of the British cotton manufacturing industry and the invention of the cotton gin changed the trajectory of economic and political development in the United States, while the demand for field hands to pick cotton reinvigorated slavery in the South. An acknowledgment and understanding of this relationship is pivotal to a full understanding of American economic development, which occurred within the context of international trade and finance.

The commitment to cotton production in the South and efforts to develop industries in northern states created opposing interests between the regions that eventually resulted in the Civil War (1861–1865). Southern planters were committed to free trade and state's rights. Since they produced commodities for sale in an international market this made sense, but these views were antithetical to those that supported the use of tariffs and protectionist policies to aid the development of industry domestically. In the northeastern United States, where finance and the production of goods and provision of services drove economic growth, different concerns prevailed, and protectionist policies designed to nurture American industry were widely supported. Textile production was the leading industry, with the manufacture of shoes, clothing, and machinery also expanding. The political tensions between North and South were further exacerbated by the incorporation of western states into the Union and the corresponding creation of new markets and investment opportunities. These included the development of cattle and grain markets, as well as the California gold rush in 1849.

THE IMPACT OF INDUSTRIALIZATION

By 1860, 16 percent of the US population lived in urban areas, and a third of the nation's income came from manufacturing. Cotton was no longer king, and the concerns of planters no longer drove political decisions, resulting in southern states seceding from the Union. In 1861, after many southern states had left the Union for the Confederacy, the remaining states passed the Morrill Tariff. In 1863 and 1864, a national bank code was drafted. After the Civil War, northern industry, which had expanded rapidly because of the demands of the war, surged ahead, and industrialists came to dominate many aspects of American life, including social and political affairs. For better or worse, from the Civil War forward, business interests acquired increasingly significant political influence and power, while also contributing to wide disparities in wealth.

The increasing gap between rich and poor gave rise to violent protests through the remainder of the nineteenth century. Although this was an era characterized by industrialization and economic growth, the United States was prevented from reaching its true economic potential due to labor unrest, racial tension, corruption, and an unstable financial system. As Adam Tooze makes clear, before World War I, "America was a byword for urban graft, mismanagement and greed-fuelled politics, as much as for growth, production and profit" (2014, 9). A European-inflected solution was found in many of the innovations of the Progressive Era, but it was the outbreak of war in Europe that eased many of the tensions of the Gilded Age.

THE ECONOMIC CONSEQUENCES OF WORLD WAR I

World War I (1914–1918) gave a decisive boost to the American economy, as the Western Allies, most notably Britain, again availed themselves of American resources, relying on the United States to outfit their troops. In 1916 Britain purchased more than half of its shell casings, two-thirds of its grain supply, and nearly all of its oil from foreign suppliers, with the United States filling the majority of orders. These purchases were paid for through the offering of increasingly large bond issues to Americans, denominated in dollars. By the end of 1916, Americans had invested over $2 billion in the Allied war effort (American gross domestic product at the time was $50 billion—roughly equivalent to $560 billion today). Additionally, the sheer volume of Allied purchases from the United States led to an unprecedented mobilization of resources in the United States as private enterprise converted to military production to meet European demand. The stimulus provided to the American economy tilted the international balance of power decisively toward the United States, but also left Americans deeply invested in an Allied victory. In spite of Woodrow Wilson's reluctance to enter the war, the United States mobilized troops in 1917.

By the end of the war, the United States had developed into a global power based largely on this newfound financial might. Now a force to be reckoned with, the United States possessed the unprecedented ability to direct the financial and security concerns of other nations. Wilson sought to utilize this power to suppress European rivalries, but in his attempts to do so he failed to cooperate with the efforts of other nations to create a stable global economy and establish effective institutions to ensure international security. The United States, which had been the largest creditor during the war, insisted that both France and Britain pay their debts in full, yet pressed the French and Belgians to relent in their demands for reparations from Germany. The problem was that France owed money to both Britain and the United States, and could not meet its debt obligations unless Germany paid. If France did not pay Britain, then Britain could not meet its obligations to the United States. At this moment, the United States controlled international economic stability but demanded payment in full instead of offering aid to Europe, thereby determining the fate of Germany.

Germany would only have been able to meet its obligations if the Germans had found a market for their exported goods. Being able to sell products to the United States, which after the war had the largest and wealthiest market for consumer goods, would have alleviated much of the pressure on Germany. Unfortunately, after the war, in an effort to reduce inflation and restore prices to prewar levels, American monetary authorities restricted access to credit and created a depression. This dashed European hopes tied to American market share, with consumer demand plummeting right when Europe generally, and Germany in particular, needed access to robust markets. In large measure, this misguided policy was dictated by the gold standard.

With the exception of the United States, every other country had abandoned the gold standard at the outbreak of hostilities. Doing so allowed these governments to print more money, as opposed to tying their currency to the amount of gold held in their coffers. This meant that their currency effectively depreciated, relative to gold. When the war ended, each country was faced with the choice of whether or not to return to the gold standard, and at what rate. After 1920 the decision became more complex: return to the gold standard at 1913 levels, matching the deflationary moves of the United States with even steeper deflationary pressure on their own currencies, which would create increased unemployment and more difficulty for debtors, or repeg the country's currency at a diminished rate. The admission of the loss of value in a national currency came at a cost to the country's citizens, who would now receive a lower return on the bonds they had purchased to support their country's war effort while the Americans were repaid at a much higher rate because they had lent in dollars. Britain chose the former route, and all the others chose the latter, with uniformly disastrous results. These decisions also had pronounced consequences for the United States: European imports were now underpriced and remarkably cheap in comparison to domestically produced goods. The United States subsequently raised tariffs on European imports in 1921 and 1923, leading to a hyperinflationary spiral in Germany.

The end result was yet more debt. The hyperinflation of 1923 rectified Germany's debt problem, since

Germany's creditors were easier to pay off with inflated currency. Repayment made the country appear to be creditworthy. However, this further exacerbated the daisy chain of debt. From 1924 to 1930, the Germans borrowed from the Americans to pay reparations to France and Belgium. The French and Belgians correspondingly repaid their war debts to the British and Americans. The British then used their French and Italian payments to reimburse the United States. The only player that could restore any sanity to this system was the United States, and it failed to do so.

THE GREAT DEPRESSION AND WORLD WAR II

In 1929, the world became embroiled in a global depression that brought international markets to a standstill. Numerous parliamentary-style governments were overturned and replaced with totalitarian regimes committed to territorial expansion and rapid modernization of their nations. Adolf Hitler's Germany, Benito Mussolini's Italy, and Joseph Stalin's Russia are a few examples. Each country sought a return to greater prosperity and global economic power after years of struggle to repay debts from the previous war. Germany in particular also sought a transformation of the new world order, hoping to supplant the United States as a global economic power.

Fortunately, the end of World War II (1939–1945) followed a different script, and it seems the United States learned from earlier mistakes. In contrast to the financial chaos generated in the wake of World War I by America's facile insistence on full payment from European allies, the United States poured $13 billion (approximately $120 billion today) into Europe to aid with economic recovery through the European Recovery Program, commonly known as the Marshall Plan. Thus, after World War II, Europe recovered quickly, in large measure because of American aid. This created a more stable global economy and a robust market for goods produced in both the United States and Europe. In conjunction with the 1944 Bretton Woods agreement, which established the International Monetary Fund and the International Bank for Reconstruction and Development (now part of the World Bank group), these actions created a new global order, with a liberal democratic European political system under American protection and a financial world tied to both gold and the US dollar.

The American postwar boom is partially attributable to these developments, as well as the postwar "military industrial complex." At the end of the war, the United States continued to aggressively fund military development based partially on the evolution of the Cold War and the arms race with the Soviet Union. Military spending accelerated further with American intervention in Vietnam. Spending on war and social programs contributed to short-term prosperity but at a high cost in the later 1960s. The government's failure to raise taxes to pay for these efforts led to accelerating inflation at the dawn of the 1970s. This inflation was further exacerbated by the United States unilaterally terminating use of the gold standard, which ended the Bretton Woods accord and made the US dollar a fiat currency, as well as a reserve currency, used by many nation-states.

RISING LEVELS OF DEBT

Unfortunately, increased borrowing has fueled American recovery from economic stumbles since the 1970s. Since 1973, rising levels of consumer debt have characterized the economy and fueled increasing levels of international debt. As a result, the United States had been transformed, partially through an abundance of consumer debt, from an international creditor to the world's foremost debtor nation. This shift, and the holding of the majority of this debt by China, have given China an incredible amount of leverage over the United States, with correspondingly increased power internationally. China's eventual economic parity with the United States will likely result in a transference of global economic and political might.

CONCLUSION

This history of the United States highlights the international nature of economics and development generally. An understanding of the need for finance and the role of trade and markets are integral to historical understanding. It is clear that any national history must be viewed within an international context. Even in the United States, economic concerns often drive political choices and shape national policy. Further, economic concerns also frequently determine diplomatic policies. To pretend otherwise and focus solely on national factors results in at best a partial understanding of the past that lacks explanatory rigor.

SEE ALSO *Exports, Exportation; Gender; Race; Tariff*

BIBLIOGRAPHY

Hyman, Louis. *Debtor Nation: The History of America in Red Ink.* Princeton, NJ: Princeton University Press, 2011.

Rodgers, Daniel T. *Atlantic Crossings: Social Politics in a Progressive Age.* Cambridge, MA: Harvard University Press, 1998.

Schoen, Brian. *The Fragile Fabric of Union: Cotton, Federal Politics, and the Global Origins of the Civil War.* Baltimore, MD: Johns Hopkins University Press, 2009.

Sexton, Jay. *Debtor Diplomacy: Finance and American Foreign Relations in the Civil War Era, 1837–1873.* Oxford: Clarendon Press, 2005.

Tooze, Adam. *The Wages of Destruction: The Making and Breaking of the Nazi Economy*. London: Penguin, 2006.

Tooze, Adam. *The Deluge: The Great War, America, and the Remaking of the Global Order, 1916–1931*. New York: Viking, 2014.

Kathryn Boodry
Instructor of History
University of Oregon

1848 REVOLUTIONS

Most Americans greeted news of the 1848 Revolutions early in the year enthusiastically, because they understood the revolutions to be a sign that the traditional monarchies of continental Europe were about to give way to republican regimes, and so took them as a salute to the American example. Some Americans even called for US military intervention on behalf of the revolutions. Initially, then, the European revolutions, which spawned fledgling republics, calls for limited monarchy, and independence movements from Ireland to eastern Europe, boosted American nationalism. That consensus of enthusiasm, however, fractured by late 1848 because of additional news that the revolution in France was in socialist hands, and news that some conflicts in central and southern Europe had devolved into ethnic cleansing.

By 1850, the revolutions were largely defeated, further splintering American opinion. The American response to the 1848 Revolutions came to be a measure of domestic political divisions, particularly over slavery and radical reform. Some conservative Americans, especially merchants and southerners, grew more convinced that Europeans had little capacity for liberal democracy. These groups used news of the European counterrevolution to justify the maintenance of the American social order. On the other hand, more liberal Americans, especially in New England and on the western frontier, the home of many new immigrants from Europe, feared the "despots" of both Europe and the proslavery United States, to whom they compared forces of European counterrevolution.

INITIAL CONSENSUS OF ENTHUSIASM

Americans entered the year 1848 flushed with confidence from military success in Mexico. The US Senate ratified the Mexican peace treaty only a few days before transatlantic steamers brought the first news of the 1848 upheavals in Europe. Much of the news Americans read about events in Europe came from conservative British newspapers, such as the *Times* of London. But the *New-York Tribune*, edited by Horace Greeley (1811–1872), also ran stories by American war correspondents Margaret Fuller (1810–1850) and Charles Dana (1819–1897), which were more enthusiastic. The US-Mexican War and the 1848 Revolutions together seemed to symbolize rising American power. It was easy to envision an American republican mission unfolding not only in Mexico but also in the Old World.

Some northern journalists and Democratic politicians, expressing the ideology of "Young America," saw the time as ripe for an aggressive American policy in Europe. They called for an official US response to support revolutionary movements in German and Italian states and Hungary. Indeed, besides hastily recognizing the French Second Republic, US diplomats also accorded official recognition to short-lived regimes in Sicily and Frankfurt. The Frankfurt Assembly, in attempting to organize an all-German republic, was also the only regime to receive the congratulations of President James Polk (1795–1849), as well as, briefly, military advice and training from the US Navy. George Bancroft (1800–1891), the US minister to Great Britain, a historian, and Young American, excitedly predicted privately that even the British monarchy might give way to a republic. Bancroft and the US minister to France, Richard Rush (1780–1859), distributed literature about the US Constitution to the French Second Republic, established in February 1848, hoping it would adopt American-style political institutions.

Outside official channels, moreover, support for radical Europe showed in various ways. Americans paraded, wore revolutionary cockades, and staged banquets to evince sympathy with European rebels. Protestant ministers preached that news of the ousting of Pope Pius IX (1792–1878) from the Vatican and establishment of a Roman republic led by Giuseppe Mazzini (1805–1872) and Giuseppe Garibaldi (1807–1882), which guaranteed freedom of religion, suggested the downfall of all Catholicism, and perhaps the beginning of the millennium. Several American towns and counties changed their names to those of European revolutionary celebrities. Although they arrived too late to make any difference in the short term, various Mexican war veterans and recent Irish and German immigrants organized volunteers and gathered arms and money to return to Europe to assist in its liberation.

OPPOSITION TO AMERICAN INTERVENTION

Support for vigorous pro-revolutionary American action in Europe was not universal. In politics, most Whigs and many southern Democrats opposed all but the most symbolic of American shows of support. American businessmen took interest in European turbulence, but mainly in hopes that shaken European financiers would buy American securities, and that American exports of cotton and tobacco would grow in more open European markets. Apologists for American slavery frowned on support for European liberation movements, especially with the abolition in 1848 of feudal labor in central Europe and slavery in the French West Indian colonies. The French Second Republic underwent the "June Days" in the summer of 1848, when thousands of unemployed workers and socialist leaders sought to force the government to extend welfare and guarantee work. This showdown was crushed by the French military in the streets of Paris, and some five thousand casualties and its bloodshed horrified many American observers concerned for law and order.

Zachary Taylor (1784–1850), elected president in November 1848 as a southern Whig (though he had little prior political experience), in his inaugural address invoked the warning of George Washington (1732–1799) against US involvement in European political affairs. With the collapses of the 1848 Revolutions, many Americans took comfort in the idea that the United States was different from Europe in its stability achieved via a republican revolution that had not threatened property or been excessively violent.

CALLS FOR REFORMS IN THE UNITED STATES

While the 1848 Revolutions did not trigger American intervention in Europe and for some Americans confirmed their national superiority, the revolutions also encouraged American reform. Advocates of various causes—international pacifism, women's rights, workers' rights, and most prominently, antislavery—perceived that transatlantic reform was indeed gaining momentum, and used upheavals in Europe to argue that analogous change should occur in the United States. Revolutionary Europe, these groups declared, was an indicator of American defects, and a warning of what awaited the United States if militarization, paternalism, and slavery continued unabated.

Elihu Burritt (1810–1879) and the former slave William Wells Brown (1814–1884) led an American delegation to attend a Paris peace conference in 1849 that, in debates to limit armaments and outlaw war, anticipated the later League of Nations and United Nations. Elizabeth Cady Stanton (1815–1902) and Lucretia Mott (1793–1880) organized the Seneca Falls Convention of July 1848, where they expressed a demand for women's rights of suffrage, education, wages, and divorce, partly to respond to news of women's revolutionary and political activities in Europe. After passage of the Fugitive Slave Law in 1850, requiring the national government to help recapture runaway slaves, the *Liberator*, the leading abolitionist newspaper, described episodes of slaves' flight and apprehension in terms of Hungarian freedom fighters succumbing to Austrian oppression, and said American slavery and European counterrevolution were linked.

In 1848 a coalition of liberal European immigrants, northern workingmen, and antislavery supporters formed the Free Soil Party, inspired by concerns that the US western territories were jeopardized by the spread of land monopoly and plantation slavery. Land reform in the western United States, later leading to the Homestead Act of 1862, was their main platform. The Free Soilers' showing in the 1848 election ironically helped Taylor defeat the Democrat Lewis Cass (1782–1866), who called for American support for the European revolutions. On the other hand, that same coalition would lead the formation in the mid-1850s of the Republican Party, which shared its values.

LOUIS KOSSUTH

Many European revolutionary refugees came to America, some to settle permanently, others to raise funds to rejoin the struggle in Europe. Of the latter type, the most celebrated was the Hungarian lawyer Lajos "Louis" Kossuth (1802–1894), whose speaking and fund-raising tour during the first part of 1852 was sensational, if somewhat quixotic. Kossuth led the Hungarian independence movement against the Habsburg Empire before the movement was defeated by Austrian and Russian forces, forcing his asylum in the Ottoman Empire (against Austrian protest) until the USS *Mississippi*, authorized by Congress, rescued him and his followers and brought them across the Atlantic. In America, Kossuth pleaded for both private financial support for the Hungarian struggle, which he received, and military intervention in Europe, which was refused. Some critics pointed out that Serb and Croat minorities would suffer under Hungarian rule, and proslavery southerners were suspicious of Kossuth's advocacy of universal liberty. But Americans displayed their sympathy for Hungary by donning "Kossuth" hats and cloaks, and, among men, growing beards. On his way to Washington to take up the presidency in 1861, Abraham Lincoln (1809–1865) put on a Kossuth hat to disguise and protect himself against would-be assassins.

POLITICAL FRACTURING

The secession crisis that Lincoln's election triggered, in fact, signaled the replication in the United States of earlier events in Europe beginning in 1848. Intellectuals and diplomats in support of the Confederate States of America likened the Confederacy not only to the American revolutionaries of 1776 but also to rebels in Ireland, the German and Italian states, Poland, and Hungary. Meanwhile, Lincoln and the defenders of the Union interpreted the 1848 Revolutions differently, as inspiration to unify the country without "despotic" slavery and in order to compensate for the defeat of popular government in Europe a decade earlier. The ultimate impact of the 1848 Revolutions in the United States, then, was to contribute to the fracturing of American politics between proslavery and antislavery groups, who embraced different legacies of the European upheavals.

SEE ALSO *Garibaldi, Giuseppe; Kossuth, Louis*

BIBLIOGRAPHY

Curti, Merle. "Impact of the Revolutions of 1848 on American Thought." *Proceedings of the American Philosophical Society* 93, 3 (1949): 209–215.

Eyal, Yonatan. *The Young America Movement and the Transformation of the Democratic Party, 1828–1861.* Cambridge: Cambridge University Press, 2007.

Fleche, Andre M. *Revolution of 1861: The American Civil War in the Age of Nationalist Conflict.* Chapel Hill: University of North Carolina Press, 2012.

Gazley, John. *American Opinion of German Unification, 1848–1871.* New York: Columbia University Press, 1926.

Marraro, Howard. *American Opinion on the Unification of Italy, 1846–1861.* New York: Columbia University Press, 1932.

Reynolds, Larry J. *European Revolutions and the American Literary Renaissance.* New Haven, CT: Yale University Press, 1988.

Roberts, Timothy M. *Distant Revolutions: 1848 and the Challenge to American Exceptionalism.* Charlottesville: University of Virginia Press, 2009.

Spencer, Donald. *Louis Kossuth and Young America: A Study of Sectionalism and Foreign Policy, 1848–1852.* Columbia: University of Missouri Press, 1977.

Tuchinsky, Adam. *Horace Greeley's* New-York Tribune: *Civil War–Era Socialism and the Crisis of Free Labor.* Ithaca, NY: Cornell University Press, 2009.

Timothy M. Roberts
Western Illinois University

EINSTEIN, ALBERT
1879–1955

Even before Albert Einstein arrived in the United States, most Americans knew his name and recognized the much-photographed German-born physicist from his shock of unkempt hair. In 1919, when photographs of a solar eclipse confirmed his revision of Newtonian physics, Einstein was acclaimed in newspaper headlines around the world. Einstein's engaging manner and distinct persona captured the attention of the public, although few claimed to understand his general theory of relativity.

Reporters, photographers, and newsreel cameramen greeted him as a celebrity upon his first visit to New York in 1921. The *New York Times* described his "geniality, kindliness and interest in the little things of life." The image clung to him. Thronged by crowds and sought out by quote-seeking journalists, Einstein embodied the popular idea of genius as eccentric and incomprehensible. His name became a synonym for brilliance.

Shocked by the carnage of World War I, Einstein became active in peace movements. The rise of Nazism in Germany in the 1920s forced him to ponder the limits of pacifism. Although falsely accused of Bolshevism by far-right American groups, he was already in the United States on a speaking tour when Adolf Hitler assumed power in Germany in 1933. Einstein was granted a professorship at the nascent Institute for Advanced Study, a research center in Princeton, New Jersey. He remained at the institute for the rest of his life, never leaving the United States except for a short trip to Bermuda, and became an American citizen in 1940. Relieved of the responsibility of teaching, Einstein was given uninterrupted time for thought.

In the first years of his American exile, Einstein was reticent in public about Nazi Germany and the plight of the Jews, while privately aiding refugees with money and affidavits to facilitate visas. In 1938, as conditions in Germany worsened, Einstein became more vocal, but his public call to "conscience of all well-disposed people" had no effect on restrictive US immigration policies (Fölsing 1997, 691).

As early as the 1905 paper that introduced the equation $E=mc^2$, Einstein alluded to the possibility of releasing the energy of atoms. He voiced concerns in 1920 over the potential destructiveness of atomic energy. However, Einstein was not at the forefront of nuclear research and was left behind in physics after refusing to accept the validity of quantum mechanics. Encountering him at Princeton in the 1930s, the theoretical physicist J. Robert Oppenheimer (1904–1967) remarked, "Einstein is completely cuckoo." After World War II, Oppenheimer became director of the Institute for Advanced Study and helped develop the hydrogen bomb in rooms directly above Einstein's office without involving the elder scientist.

Einstein did, however, play a role in launching the Manhattan Project. In an August 1939 letter to President Franklin D. Roosevelt, he warned that uranium "may be turned into a new and important source of energy" that could "lead to the construction of bombs" capable of destroying entire cities, and added that Germany was prepared to develop such weapons. Despite his prestige, Einstein was deemed a security risk by the Federal Bureau of Investigation and US Army Intelligence because of past political associations and thus did not participate in the Manhattan Project. Einstein's only contribution to the war as a scientist was to advise the US Navy on explosives.

In 1945, when his letter to Roosevelt became public, reporters sought Einstein's opinion on the atom bomb. He responded with an idea that had preoccupied him for years, the necessity for a world government to maintain peace by monopolizing military force. He regarded war as the problem, and hoped that the bomb would "intimidate the human race" into putting its affairs in order. Not unlike his unsuccessful quest to find a unified field theory in physics, Einstein worked without result for a unified world order.

Einstein was not alone in considering a world federation based on the United Nations, but Cold War tensions soon rendered as politically untenable any surrender of sovereignty, including control over the "secret" of the atom bomb. Einstein chaired the Emergency Committee of Atomic Scientists, which tried to promote understanding of the bomb's implications, but by 1948 the committee had ceased to meet because of internal divisions and was unable to move public policy. Einstein often spoke on the radio and signed declarations on the atomic program that attracted attention but inspired no action.

When declining health prevented Einstein from traveling about the United States, his Princeton home became a place of pilgrimage for American and foreign dignitaries. His comments against the abuses of McCarthyism brought calls from the far right to strip him of citizenship, but he was secure in the knowledge that no US government would deport one of its most renowned citizens for his political statements. With wry self-deprecation, Einstein acknowledged that he remained universally admired but was seldom listened to.

SEE ALSO *Manhattan Project; World War II*

BIBLIOGRAPHY

Balibar, Françoise. *Einstein: Decoding the Universe.* Translated by David J. Baker and Dorie B. Baker. New York: Harry N. Abrams, 2001.

Fölsing, Albrecht. *Albert Einstein: A Biography.* Translated by Ewald Osers. New York: Viking, 1997.

Isaacson, Walter. *Einstein: His Life and Universe.* New York: Simon and Schuster, 2007.

Sayen, Jamie. *Einstein in America: The Scientist's Conscience in the Age of Hitler and Hiroshima.* New York: Crown, 1985.

Glen Jeansonne
Professor of History
University of Wisconsin–Milwaukee

David Luhrssen
Editor
Shepherd Express

EISENHOWER, DWIGHT D.

1890–1969

Dwight D. Eisenhower, nicknamed "Ike," served as the thirty-fourth president of the United States and general of the army. Prior to becoming president, he served in World War II (1939–1945) as the supreme commander of the Allied Expeditionary Force (1943–1945), planned the successful invasion of Normandy and the liberation of Western Europe from Nazi control (1944–1945), and served as the North Atlantic Treaty Organization's (NATO's) first supreme Allied commander (1950–1952).

Born in Denison, Texas, Eisenhower moved at an early age to Abilene, Kansas. The third of seven sons born to David Jacob and Ida Elizabeth Eisenhower, he entered the US Military Academy at West Point in 1909, where he finished near the middle of his class. After receiving his commission, he met and married Mamie Geneva Doud (1896–1979) in 1916. Their first son, Doud "Ickey" Eisenhower, died of scarlet fever in 1921. Their second son, John Sheldon Doud Eisenhower (1922–2013), entered the military, eventually serving in World War II and the Korean conflict.

Most Eisenhower biographies divide his life into three episodes: the formative years between World War I and World War II, his time as Allied commander during World War II, and his presidency. Of the three, only in his presidency did Eisenhower live continuously within the United States.

FORMATIVE YEARS

During his formative years Eisenhower's life fell under the influence Brigadier General Fox Conner (1874–1951), who provided Eisenhower with his fundamental outlook on political and military matters. Eisenhower became close to Conner when, in 1922, the army assigned him to the Panama Canal Zone, then under Conner's command. Conner thought a second world war was inevitable; thus, he began to seek out and mentor those officers best able to lead the military in a future European conflict with Germany (he also mentored George Marshall [1880–1959] and George Patton [1885–1945]). While in Panama, Conner convinced Eisenhower that infighting among the Allies had hampered the war effort. The great challenge of the coming war lay in leading the Allies to overcome national interests to sustain a coordinated war effort.

After two years in Panama, Conner arranged for Eisenhower to enroll in the army's Command and General Staff School at Fort Leavenworth, Kansas. Eisenhower finished first in his class. From there, Conner helped arrange for Eisenhower to travel to Europe as he compiled a guidebook for the American Battle

Monuments Commission. On its surface, the task seemed thankless, but its real purpose lay in familiarizing Eisenhower with the terrain for the next world war.

Eisenhower next enrolled in the army's War College, where he completed a thesis on wartime economic "mobilization." The thesis linked military success to industrial technology and provided the groundwork for many of his subsequent policy views as president—especially the limits that can be placed on an economy. The report impressed General of the Army Douglas MacArthur (1880–1964), who, in the late 1920s, brought Eisenhower to Washington as his aide. From there, Eisenhower had a front-row seat for viewing the unfolding New Deal in the early 1930s. He largely supported Franklin Roosevelt's (1882–1945) experiments with using government to bring about industrial recovery because they fit the conclusions that followed his own study of industrial mobilization.

WORLD WAR II

In 1935 the Philippines (until then an American colony) obtained semi-independent status and asked MacArthur to create a Philippine army. MacArthur agreed, resigned his position in Washington, and left for Manila, bringing Eisenhower with him. Shortly after Eisenhower returned to the United States in 1939, Adolf Hitler (1889–1945) ordered the invasion of Poland, initiating World War II. Two years later, when the Japanese attacked Pearl Harbor, Marshall, who had replaced MacArthur as general of the army, brought Eisenhower to Washington, where Eisenhower's organizational abilities and diplomatic acumen led Marshall to conclude that he should command the American army in Europe. Promoted over sixty-six more senior generals, Eisenhower arrived in London in June 1942.

British prime minister Winston Churchill (1874–1965) remarked that the night Pearl Harbor was attacked he "slept the sleep of the saved and thankful" knowing that American forces would soon join the British in their desperate fight against Nazi Germany (Churchill 1948–1954, 540). At the same time, though, many British officers viewed America as a kind of bumbling giant, powerful but unwise to the ways of European war. Eisenhower's first command effort, Operation Torch (aimed at dislodging Nazi forces from Africa) seemed to confirm their suspicions. Launched in November 1942, the campaign ultimately succeeded after many delays and only because of massive material advantages. Overall, Eisenhower's planning proved weak and American forces performed poorly. Moreover, the setbacks in Africa ultimately dashed American hopes of a quick cross-channel invasion of France in 1943—a fact particularly aggravating to Soviet Union Premier Joseph Stalin (1879–1953), who frantically hoped for an American invasion of France to drag Germany's military away from its fight with Soviet forces.

Still, Eisenhower succeeded in developing good relationships with many of his British counterparts, who forgave his strategic errors because of his evenhandedness in balancing British and American interests. He also eventually developed a working relationship with Charles de Gaulle (1890–1970), who by 1943 had become the de facto leader of the French resistance, despite his difficult personality and thin skin. Indeed, Eisenhower's diplomatic abilities ultimately persuaded President Roosevelt to appoint him commander of the cross-channel invasion of 1944, a responsibility all had assumed would fall to Marshall.

Taking a chance that weather conditions would allow for success, Eisenhower ordered nearly 160,000 troops to land in Normandy, France, on June 6, 1944. By the end of August, more than 1 million troops had entered Europe, and Paris had been liberated. Despite a brief but bloody German counteroffensive in the winter of 1944 to 1945 (the Battle of the Bulge), Germany had collapsed by the following spring. On May 7, 1945, Eisenhower accepted the German surrender from General Alfred Jodl (1890–1946) (Hitler had committed suicide at the end of April).

Throughout the campaign, Eisenhower pursued a broad-front strategy, allowing both British and American forces to advance in step. In retrospect, some have questioned whether his diplomatically prudent strategy may have been a strategic error—a single rapid thrust at Berlin might have ended the war sooner. For that to work, however, the Allies would have had to solve the supply shortages that plagued their advance throughout late 1944.

THE PRESIDENCY

With victory in war, Eisenhower achieved a lasting legacy. His prestige and public charisma led both Democrats and Republicans to court him as a presidential candidate, despite his oft-stated disinterest in politics. After serving as army chief of staff (1945–1948) and then president of Columbia University (1948–1950), Harry S. Truman (1884–1972) appointed him supreme allied commander of NATO in December 1950. During his time in that post, Eisenhower grew disillusioned with Truman's presidency, as well as the isolationist politics of Senator Robert Taft (1889–1953)—the leading Republican presidential candidate in 1952. By June of that year, Eisenhower had left Europe and declared his candidacy for the Republican Party nomination, later winning the general election in a landslide.

President Dwight D. Eisenhower* (center), *with Vice President Richard M. Nixon and Soviet official Nikita Khrushchev* (right), *at the White House on September 16, 1959, holding a copy of an object deposited on the Moon by a Soviet lunar probe. *Eisenhower, fearing the consequences of American overextension if the Cold War were fought on too many fronts, developed a less-expensive strategy of Soviet containment. Dubbed the "New Look," his policy, announced in 1953, declared that the United States reserved the right to respond to any communist provocation disproportionately with a massive nuclear strike.* SOVFOTO/UIG/GETTY IMAGES

Eisenhower focused his presidency on foreign affairs. Like many American leaders of both parties, he viewed the Cold War as an ideological fight between American freedom and communist "slavery" and considered it the overriding conflict of the modern age. Unlike Truman, John F. Kennedy (1917–1963), and Lyndon Johnson (1908–1973), however, Eisenhower recognized economic and military limits to American power, fearing the consequences of American overextension if the Cold War were fought too zealously. (These concerns culminated in his 1961 farewell address, when he warned against the unwarranted influence of the "military-industrial complex.") Upon becoming president, he hoped to quickly end the Korean War (1950–1953) and then develop a less-expensive strategy to "contain" Soviet expansion.

Stalin's death in March 1953 allowed for a negotiated settlement to the Korean War. Later in 1953 Eisenhower unveiled his own policy, dubbed the "New Look," for containing communist aggression. Under Truman, American policy meant to contain Soviet provocations proportionally, meeting any communist aggression with an equal American resolve. But this approach inadvertently committed the United States to engage where, when, and how the communists chose, allowing them the initiative. By contrast, Eisenhower's New Look announced that the United States reserved the right to respond to any communist provocation disproportionately with a massive nuclear strike. Eisenhower intentionally remained vague about what actions might trigger such a nuclear response, however. While his approach made the Cold War more dangerous, it left the Soviets uncertain what actions would incite a nuclear attack, making them reticent to do anything that might provoke Eisenhower. His approach also reduced expenses, since nuclear weapons cost less than conventional forces. On the whole the New Look succeeded in giving Eisenhower more strategic flexibility and keeping the United States out of a "shooting" war.

Consistent with his tutelage under Conner, Eisenhower also sought allies who could help carry the burdens of the Cold War, arguing that the cause of global freedom should trump national interests. Europe remained Eisenhower's top strategic priority; foreign policy here amounted to holding the British and French together under American leadership and convincing those two countries to accept a rehabilitated and rearmed West Germany as part of the Western alliance. While the British and French resisted some of Eisenhower's efforts, for the most part Western Europe remained committed to American strategy during his presidency.

But Eisenhower's appeal to global over national interests largely failed in the Third World. Exhausted by World War II, England and France struggled to reassert dominance over their colonies during the 1950s, a dominance that American leaders (Eisenhower included) largely opposed anyway. As a result, throughout the Global South, a growing chorus of independence movements demanded national self-determination. Ideally, Eisenhower hoped to keep both the former imperial powers and former colonies on the American side of the Cold War. His efforts were complicated, however, by the fact that many colonial people interpreted their forced subservience as an expression of Western racism and consistent with the experience of black Americans. Asians and Africans watched the slow progress of America's civil rights movement carefully as a bellwether for judging Eisenhower's claims to fight for global freedom. Complicating matters even further, many independence leaders either embraced communism (such as Ho Chi Minh [1890–1969] in Vietnam) or sought neutrality in the Cold War (such as Jawaharlal Nehru [1889–1964] in India). Eisenhower's New Look approach and its threat of massive nuclear retaliation offered little guidance in this context.

As a result, Eisenhower followed an ad hoc approach to colonial independence, relying on some combination of (1) propaganda (what he called psychological warfare), (2) Central Intelligence Agency (CIA)–sponsored covert operations, and (3) the use of local proxies to influence other countries in their region—each of which he employed on a case-by-case basis. He hoped thereby to achieve an ordered end to European empires and a gradual transition to Third World independence that would leave former colonies and declining empires on good terms with each other and the United States.

The results were (at best) mixed. While Eisenhower generally succeeded in placating his European allies, much of the Third World remained wary of American influence. Psychological warfare warned that communists hoped to implement "Red colonialism" in the Third World; but this hypothetical danger paled in comparison to the lived colonialism most revolutionaries knew too well. The CIA successfully sponsored coups in Iran (1953) and Guatemala (1954), deposing leftist regimes and replacing them with US-friendly dictators. But these successes encouraged future, disastrous attempted coups in Indonesia (1957–1958) and Cuba (1961). Moreover, in the long run and in almost every case, the CIA also created deep resentments in the countries where it operated.

Local proxies proved particularly difficult to work with. Some countries, such as the Philippines and Pakistan, often advanced American policy within their region during the Eisenhower years. But the logic behind this approach—that one nation could affect the politics of its neighbors—ran in both directions, leading Eisenhower to fear a "domino effect" of former colonies turning communist once one did so. Eisenhower followed this logic most tragically in the case of South Vietnam, where the United States found itself increasingly entangled in that country's destiny, an entanglement that subsequent presidents, less cautious than Eisenhower, would find strangling.

Despite these shortcomings Eisenhower remained very popular while in office, and his reputation continues to grow among academics and foreign policy experts. He remained first and foremost a war hero for many Americans. While his presidency had its share of failures, in an era marked by leaders prone to overestimating American power and prestige, Eisenhower's legacy offers an example of constraint and circumspection.

SEE ALSO *Bandung Conference (1955); Cold War; Deterrence; Military-Industrial Complex*

BIBLIOGRAPHY

Ambrose, Stephen E. *Eisenhower: Soldier and President.* New York: Simon and Schuster, 1990.

Churchill, Winston S. *The Second World War*, Vol. 3. London: Cassell, 1948–1954.

Eisenhower, Dwight D. *Crusade in Europe.* Garden City, NY: Doubleday, 1948.

Eisenhower, Dwight D. *Mandate for Change, 1953–1956: The White House Years.* Garden City, NY: Doubleday, 1963.

Eisenhower, Dwight D. *Waging Peace, 1956–1961: The White House Years.* Garden City, NY: Doubleday, 1965.

Eisenhower, Dwight D. *At Ease: Stories I Tell to Friends.* Garden City, NY: Doubleday, 1967.

Holland, Matthew F. *Eisenhower between the Wars: The Making of a General and Statesman.* Westport, CT: Praeger, 2001.

Osgood, Kenneth A. *Total Cold War: Eisenhower's Secret Propaganda Battle at Home and Abroad.* Lawrence: University of Kansas, 2006.

Smith, Jean Edward. *Eisenhower: In War and Peace.* New York: Random House, 2012.

Statler, Kathryn C., and Andrew L. Johns. *The Eisenhower Administration, the Third World, and the Globalization of the Cold War.* Lanham, MD: Rowman and Littlefield, 2006.

Grant Madsen
Assistant Professor
Brigham Young University

ELLIS ISLAND

Ellis Island, a small island in New York Harbor, opened as a federal immigration inspection station on January 1, 1892. Prior to the 1880s, the regulation of immigration was largely left up to individual states. The main processing station before Ellis Island was Castle Garden, run by New York State in conjunction with German and Irish immigrant aid societies. Beginning in the 1880s, the US Congress began to play a larger role in the regulation of immigration and started to delineate categories for exclusion. The 1891 Immigration Act excluded "idiots, insane persons, paupers or persons likely to become public charges, persons suffering from a loathsome or a dangerous disease, persons who have been convicted of a felony or other infamous crime or misdemeanor involving moral turpitude, [and] polygamists." Ellis Island's role was to weed out so-called undesirable immigrants who fell into one of those categories.

THE PRIMARY US IMMIGRANT INSPECTION STATION

Ellis Island would serve as the primary facility regulating immigrants into the United States until the mid-1920s. During this period, some 20 million immigrants arrived in America; Ellis Island processed roughly three-quarters of those arrivals. This period saw not only an increase in immigrants but also a shift in their demographics, with increasing numbers of southern and eastern Europeans arriving. Italy, Russia, and the Austro-Hungarian Empire were the largest countries of origin for Ellis Island immigrants. Even though most immigrants came from Europe, Ellis Island also witnessed immigrants from the Middle East (Lebanon, Turkey, Syria) and black immigrants from the Caribbean.

Over the years, the island would steadily expand through landfill; eventually there would be more than two dozen buildings on the site, many of them medical facilities. A commissioner, appointed by the US president, ran Ellis Island with a workforce composed of civil service inspectors and interpreters, as well as doctors from the US Public Health Service. With so many immigrants arriving daily, individual examinations were impossible. Instead, immigrants formed single-file lines and passed by inspectors and doctors who looked for signs of medical problems. After the line inspection, registry clerks interviewed immigrants to gain more information about whether they might fall into one of the categories for exclusion.

Around 80 percent of immigrants passed through Ellis Island in a matter of hours. The other 20 percent were set aside for further inspection or a hearing with the island's Board of Special Inquiry. Those individuals would be detained on the island until the resolution of their cases. Immigrants ordered excluded could appeal their cases to government officials in Washington. Ultimately, fewer than 2 percent of all immigrants arriving at Ellis Island were ordered excluded and returned home—this amounts to about 150,000 individuals between 1892 and 1921. Immigration officials also had the ability to deport immigrants already residing in the country within a certain number of years after their arrival if they were found to fall under one of the categories of exclusion.

Physical examination of women immigrants at Ellis Island, New York, circa 1910. *From 1892 until the mid-1920s, Ellis Island served as the primary facility regulating immigrants into the United States. During this period, Ellis Island processed roughly three-quarters of the 20 million immigrants who arrived in America.* © EVERETT HISTORICAL/SHUTTERSTOCK.COM

More than half of excluded immigrants were deemed "likely to become a public charge." Immigrants with health problems were also detained and sent to the island's hospital. Ellis Island's doctors were some of the first in the United States to experiment with intelligence testing, hoping to weed out arrivals who were "mentally defective."

Ellis Island officials worked closely with steamship companies—many of them British and German-owned—that carried immigrants across the Atlantic. Even though many Americans accused the steamship companies of encouraging immigration, those companies created their own inspection facilities in European ports to weed out passengers who might not pass inspection at places like Ellis Island. They had a financial incentive to do so, since American immigration officials would fine them for every excluded immigrant they brought.

Activities at Ellis Island could bring officials into conflict with other nations. US government officials sometimes toured Europe to understand why immigrants left their homelands. A 1909 investigation by an Ellis Island official of possible forced prostitution among immigrants led French government officials to complain to the American embassy. Ellis Island made news when immigration officials detained former Venezuelan ruler Cipriano Castro (1858–1924) in 1912 on charges of moral turpitude based on his alleged involvement in the murder of a political opponent. In 1922, acting on the complaints of British nationals who had been detained at Ellis Island, the British ambassador toured the facility and reported his findings to Parliament.

CHANGES DURING WORLD WAR I AND AFTER

During World War I (1914–1918), immigration to the United States slowed as German U-boats made transatlantic travel difficult. Ellis Island became a temporary home for some 1,500 German enemy aliens detained in the early days after America's entry into the war in April 1917. Later in the war, Ellis Island served as a station for American troops waiting to be sent to Europe, as well as for wounded troops returning from the front.

The war heightened anti-immigrant feelings. Criticism of "hyphenated Americans" and proclamations of "100 percent American" grew louder. After the war, support increased among the American public for greater restrictions on immigration. The immigration quotas imposed by Congress in 1921 and 1924 reduced the overall number of immigrants arriving in the United States. The introduction of visas in 1924 meant that the primary place for immigrant screening would be American consulates abroad. This reduced the importance of Ellis Island, which was now used increasingly as a detention facility. During World War II (1939–1945), Ellis Island housed German and Italian enemy aliens suspected of being fascist sympathizers. After the war, aliens who were suspected of communist sympathies under the 1950 Internal Security Act were detained there. Two of those detainees appealed their cases to the US Supreme Court, including German-born war bride Ellen Knauff, who spent nearly twenty-seven months in detention at Ellis Island.

In 1954 the Dwight Eisenhower administration moved the New York immigration office to Manhattan and shut down Ellis Island. The facilities would lie abandoned for three decades. With a revival of ethnic identity in the 1970s and 1980s, Americans became more interested in their immigrant past. During this time, the Statue of Liberty–Ellis Island Foundation was created to raise money to restore both sites. In 1990 the newly restored main building on Ellis Island was opened to the public. It also contained a new immigration museum. Despite the reopening, most of the buildings on the island were still in a state of disrepair and remained closed to the public. Ellis Island has since become a popular tourist site, although the island was severely damaged by Hurricane Sandy in 2012. Along with the Statue of Liberty, Ellis Island has been transformed into a national icon symbolizing the role of immigration in American society.

SEE ALSO *Alien Contract Labor Law/Foran Act (1885); Chinese Exclusion Act (1882); Immigration and Naturalization Service; Immigration Quotas; Nativism*

BIBLIOGRAPHY

Bayor, Ronald H. *Encountering Ellis Island: How European Immigrants Entered America.* Baltimore, MD: Johns Hopkins University Press, 2014.

Cannato, Vincent J. *American Passage: The History of Ellis Island.* New York: HarperCollins, 2009.

Fairchild, Amy L. *Science at the Borders: Immigrant Medical Inspection and the Shaping of the Modern Industrial Labor Force.* Baltimore, MD: Johns Hopkins University Press, 2003.

Vincent J. Cannato
Associate Professor of History
University of Massachusetts Boston

EMANCIPATION DAY

Emancipation Day celebrations honor the end of enslavement for people of African descent in the Atlantic world. The holiday is just as diverse today as the experience of emancipation was in the nineteenth century. Celebrations across the Atlantic world illustrate the transnational and intercultural elements of Atlantic world slavery.

THE CARIBBEAN AND LATIN AMERICA

Most Caribbean nations celebrate Emancipation Day on August 1, in honor of the Slavery Abolition Act passed by the British Parliament. While the official year of the act is 1833, enforcement did not begin until August 1, 1834, hence the selection of August 1 for contemporary celebrations. The full title of the act, however, reveals the complicated history of emancipation in the British Caribbean. The title reads, "An Act for the Abolition of Slavery throughout the British Colonies; for promoting the Industry of the manumitted Slaves; and for compensating the Persons hitherto entitled to the Services of such Slaves."

The word *freedom* is conspicuously absent, while the words *industry* and *compensating* illustrate the restrictive nature of the act. Slave owners were heavily compensated, while formerly enslaved workers were not offered any remuneration. Instead, these workers were labeled apprentices and the vast majority were forced to work for their former enslavers. Apprenticeship offered a step away from slavery, but it was not yet freedom.

Once again, August 1 would be the day for a second emancipation, as the apprentice system was abolished permanently on August 1, 1838. Black workers were now able to negotiate labor contracts with greater freedom or pursue their own independent economic ventures. August 1, therefore, looms large in Emancipation Day celebrations. Each year on that date, events are held in Barbados, Bermuda, Guyana, Jamaica, Trinidad and Tobago, Turks and Caicos, and St. Lucia to celebrate the end of slavery. Other Caribbean nations hold celebrations on other days of the month. For example, Antigua and Barbuda, the British Virgin Islands, and Grenada all hold celebrations on the first Monday of the month regardless of the particular date.

The means of celebrating these holidays in the Caribbean often draw on a host of African, British, and French influences. The French influence can be seen by the adoption of large street parties known as *J'ouvert.* J'ouvert is traditionally held prior to Lent as a component of Carnival, but Emancipation Day celebrations, including the August 1 celebration in Barbados and first Monday celebration in Anguilla, draw upon French J'ouvert party traditions. J'ouvert parties, like other Emancipation Day holidays, include parades, music performances, and feasts.

Latin American nations hold fewer Emancipation Day celebrations. Puerto Rico is the only nation that maintains an active annual holiday. On March 22, 1866, the Spanish Parliament responded favorably to a petition campaign and abolished slavery on the island. In Brazil, no national holiday commemorates the end of slavery, but in the state of Bahia, women of the Imandade da Boa Morte (Sisterhood of the Good Death) have their own celebrations. These women draw on Catholic and Candomblé religious traditions on the Friday closest to August 15 to honor the Lady of the Good Death's role in ending slavery.

Only one nation combines celebrations of national independence with celebrations of the end of slavery. That nation is Haiti, the first nation in the Western Hemisphere to abolish slavery. Haitians celebrate both independence and emancipation on January 1 by eating a pumpkin soup known as *soup joumou.* Under French law, slaves were forbidden from eating soup on New Year's Day. On January 1, 1804, Marie-Claire Heureuse Félicité (1758–1858), wife of Emperor Jean-Jacques Dessaline (1758–1806), served the soup publicly, and a long-standing tradition was born.

EMANCIPATION DAY IN THE UNITED STATES

Emancipation in the United States occurred in less uniform fashion. Northern states began abolishing slavery during the American Revolution, and burgeoning new communities of black Americans and their abolitionist allies held Emancipation Day ceremonies on August 1. The ultimate demise of slavery in the United States required the death of 750,000 Americans. Enslaved persons in the United States escaped bondage in fits and starts throughout the messy contingency of the Civil War. Many enslaved persons emancipated themselves during the war by running to the Union army or simply seizing the turmoil of the war to escape. These freedom seekers forced the Union army to develop policies on the fly. The resulting policies, which designated former slaves as contraband of war, unintentionally transformed the Union army into an agent of liberation.

On April 16, 1862, several months prior to the Emancipation Proclamation, President Abraham Lincoln (1809–1865) issued the Compensated Emancipation Act, which freed all enslaved persons in the District of Columbia. Residents of Washington, DC, continue to celebrate Emancipation Day on April 16 and commemorate the event with concerts, parades, public lectures, and more. The majority of American slaves, however, earned their freedom well after the Emancipation Proclamation took effect on January 1, 1863. Many were not liberated until the war was nearly over.

The most widespread emancipation celebration commemorates the moment when slavery was finally outlawed in Texas. Several months after Robert E. Lee's (1807–1870) surrender at Appomattox Court House, Virginia, emancipation remained but a rumor for the nearly 250,000 slaves in Texas. However, on June 19,

1865, federal troops arrived in Galveston and announced that slavery was abolished in the state. Celebrations on June 19, called Juneteenth, continue both in Texas and beyond. In 1968 civil rights leader Ralph Abernathy (1926–1990) encouraged participants in the Poor People's March to Washington, DC, to take up the holiday, and Juneteenth celebrations now occur throughout the United States.

Juneteenth is not the only emancipation holiday in the United States, however. For example, Florida recognizes May 20 as Emancipation Day, honoring the day in 1865 when Brigadier General Edward M. McCook (1833–1909) read aloud the Emancipation Proclamation in Tallahassee. Kentucky and Tennessee hold Emancipation Day celebrations on August 8, and eastern Mississippi celebrates the Eighth o' May, which remembers when Union troops crossed the border from Alabama in 1865, proclaiming freedom to slaves.

Recent attempts have been made to extend Juneteenth abroad, and black members of the US Armed Forces have been active in holding and publicizing celebrations in South Korea, Afghanistan, Israel, Japan, Guam, and elsewhere. International organizations with American ties, such as the W. E. B. Du Bois Center for Pan-African Culture in Accra, Ghana, have recently begun holding Juneteenth celebrations as well.

SEE ALSO *Act Prohibiting Importation of Slaves (1807); Africa Squadron; Amistad; Antislavery; Atlantic Slave Trade; Haitian Revolution; Race; Slave Regimes*

BIBLIOGRAPHY

Abnernethy, Francis E., Patrick B. Mullen, and Alan B. Govenar, eds. *Juneteenth Texas: Essays in African-American Folklore.* Denton: University of North Texas Press, 1996.

Beckles, Hilary McD., ed. *Inside Slavery: Process and Legacy in the Caribbean Experience.* Kingston, Jamaica: Canoe Press, the University of the West Indies, 1996.

Drescher, Seymour. *Abolition: A History of Slavery and Antislavery.* New York: Cambridge University Press, 2009.

Kerr-Ritchie, Jeffrey R. *Rites of August First: Emancipation Day in the Black Atlantic World.* Baton Rouge: Louisiana State University Press, 2011.

Walker, Sheila S. "The Feast of Good Death: An Afro-Catholic Emancipation Celebration in Brazil." *Sage: A Scholarly Journal on Black Women* 3, 2 (Fall 1986): 27–31.

White, Richard. "Civil Rights Agitation: Emancipation Days in Central New York in the 1880s." *Journal of Negro History* 78, 1 (Winter 1993): 16–24.

Ben Wright
Assistant Professor of History
University of Texas at Dallas

EMBARGO ACT (1807)

The Embargo Act of 1807 was Thomas Jefferson's experiment in economic coercion during the Napoleonic Wars (1803–1815). He and Secretary of State James Madison hoped that embargoing American trade with Britain and France would compel both to respect US neutral rights. As in the neutrality crisis of the 1790s, the United States intended to remain neutral while trading with both powers as the primary carrier of foodstuffs to the belligerents' West Indian colonies. Both Britain and France, however, aimed to deny American supplies to the other side. An alternative to Napoleon Bonaparte's continental system, the embargo would enable the United States to avoid war while punishing Britain in particular: Britain restricted American participation in neutral trade between France and Spain and their Caribbean colonies, and impressment of American seamen into the British navy violated US sovereignty.

The *Leopard-Chesapeake* affair was a significant lead-up to the embargo, engendering American outrage and clamors for war. On June 22, 1807, the British warship HMS *Leopard* attacked the American frigate USS *Chesapeake* off the coast of Norfolk, Virginia. A boarding party subsequently removed four sailors as deserters, impressing the three Americans among them. Amid war fever, Jefferson favored an embargo, believing threats of war unlikely to force British respect for US sovereignty or trade. British pressure on American commerce escalated: strict interpretation of the Rule of 1756, where Britain would not trade with neutrals also trading with the enemy, would stifle the American reexport (carrying) trade in the West Indies. The Orders in Council of November 1807, subjecting French and allied ports to a Royal Navy blockade, were the last of a series of provocations.

The US Congress approved the Embargo Act on December 22, 1807. For fourteen months, it prohibited American vessels from sailing to foreign ports and prohibited foreign vessels from loading any cargo in the United States. The embargo primarily targeted Britain, its control of the seas, and its apparent goal of monopolizing world trade. Reflecting neither idealism nor mere moralism, Jefferson's decision did not reject or disengage from the Atlantic system. Rather, Jefferson chose between three limited options, which he described as "War, Embargo, or Nothing" (Cogliano 2014, 240). The strength of British sea power made the war option unfavorable. The Orders in Council and Napoleon's decrees meant that inaction would force the United States to choose between Britain and France, alienating one or the other. Accepting impressment meant violations of US sovereignty—effectively repudiating the American Revolution's republican legacy. Embargo seemed the least bad option as a coercive act that allowed the United States time to prepare for a seemingly inevitable war. In addition, it would protect a republican political economy, which Jeffersonian Republicans saw in agricultural terms. A republic's survival demanded virtue; an agricultural political economy would protect Americans from the Old World luxury and corruption deadly to republican government. In theory, the United States would experience only temporary deprivation of markets, feeding itself while the European belligerents and their colonies suffered from want of necessities.

But the embargo failed to exact concessions from either Britain or France. Flawed design and poor implementation did not prohibit British exports to the United States. Moreover, Jefferson used the power of the state to enforce its terms. The embargo undermined US war preparedness economically, while leaving Britain largely unaffected. New England, New York, New Jersey, and Pennsylvania merchants suffered from loss of maritime trade. Southern and western farmers lost their British market. The British merchant marine appropriated trade routes that American shipping had relinquished. Smuggling increased across the northern and southern borders of the United States. Illegal shipments allowed American goods to reach Britain nonetheless. Despite an initial rise in the price of American goods, a growing South American demand for British goods offset decreased commerce with North America. Within the United States, a backlash against the embargo exacerbated sectional differences over a commercial policy that threatened the Union, making it difficult for Jefferson's administration to enforce its own foreign policy. Jefferson's use of the coercive power of the state to enforce the embargo alienated supporters, given Republican aversion to centralized federal power.

In late 1808 the House Foreign Affairs Committee, after much debate, pushed for legislation exempting all nations but Britain and France from the embargo and banning British and French ships from American waters. On March 1, 1809, Jefferson signed the new Non-Intercourse Act, which replaced the Embargo Act of 1807 and permitted US trade with nations other than France and Britain. Its failure led to Macon's Bill No. 2 (1810). Worsening Anglo-American relations would eventually lead to the War of 1812.

SEE ALSO *Jefferson, Thomas; Non-Intercourse Act (1809); War of 1812*

BIBLIOGRAPHY

Brown, Gordon S. *Toussaint's Clause: The Founding Fathers and the Haitian Revolution.* Jackson: University Press of Mississippi, 2005.

Cogliano, Francis D. *Emperor of Liberty: Thomas Jefferson's Foreign Policy.* New Haven, CT: Yale University Press, 2014.

McCoy, Drew R. *The Elusive Republic: Political Economy in Jeffersonian America.* Chapel Hill: University of North Carolina Press, 1980.

Perkins, Bradford. *Prologue to War: England and the United States, 1805–1812.* Berkeley: University of California Press, 1961.

Sadosky, Leonard J. "Jefferson and International Relations." In *A Companion to Thomas Jefferson*, edited by Francis D. Cogliano, 199–217. Malden, MA: Blackwell, 2012.

Spivak, Burton. *Jefferson's English Crisis: Commerce, Embargo, and the Republican Revolution.* Charlottesville: University Press of Virginia, 1979.

Wendy H. Wong
Research Associate
McNeil Center for Early American Studies

EMBASSIES, CONSULATES, AND DIPLOMATIC MISSIONS

The exchange of diplomatic personnel has been an important marker of sovereignty in European and then global politics since the mid-fifteenth century, signaling governments' mutual recognition of one another's legitimacy. Originally, *embassy* or *mission* referred to the people who were sent abroad to represent their government, and a new set of rules to govern their exchange emerged from the Congress of Vienna in 1815. From roughly 1890 until the end of World War II in 1945, those rules were gradually altered, in part because governments began to acquire property abroad. Since 1945, *embassy* has typically referred to a building, rather than the people who work in it. Consular activities have altered with those diplomatic changes, though the core mission of providing aid to a government's citizens abroad has remained constant. The US government's changing use of embassies, diplomatic missions, and consulates reflects shifts in foreign policy goals and the government's power to achieve those goals.

THE CONSULAR SERVICE

After securing aid for their independence struggle against Britain, Americans were more interested in expanding their commerce abroad than engaging in other aspects of international politics. George Washington (1732–1799) reinforced this view in his 1796 Farewell Address, a revered prescription for US foreign policy that was consistently invoked to guide—and limit—US involvement abroad until the North Atlantic Treaty Organization was formed in 1949. As a result, the Consular Service, created with the Department of State in 1789, grew far more quickly than the diplomatic corps. While diplomats dealt with high politics and representation, early consuls facilitated commercial exchange and provided aid to

Americans in peril abroad, which, in the early years, primarily meant sailors. Consuls secured their own office and living space, and they were most often based at port cities. There could be multiple consuls serving in any given country.

Over the course of the nineteenth century, the US government followed the lead of European powers in securing trading rights in the Ottoman, Chinese, and Japanese empires. Those "unequal treaties" gave the Western powers jurisdiction over their citizens in those empires, generating the legal practice of extraterritoriality; consuls posted there operated courts for US citizens. As international tourism increased from the 1870s with the advent of new transportation technologies, providing aid to Americans abroad required more time. After the Bureau of Immigration was created in 1891, consuls were increasingly involved in screening potential migrants, and, from World War I (1914–1918), issuing visas. With the 1924 passage of the Rogers Act, the diplomatic corps and consular service were combined into the US Foreign Service. Within the Foreign Service, some officers specialized in consular work, defined as aiding Americans abroad and issuing visas; this practice continues today. The number of consular posts steadily decreased over the twentieth century as consular services were shifted to newly acquired capital-city embassy buildings.

DIPLOMATIC MISSIONS

While consular work was considered important and necessary, if not glamorous, in the nineteenth century, diplomatic missions faced more criticism in the United States. Many Americans viewed diplomatic practices as quintessentially European and thus inherently un-American. Though Americans did not participate in the Congress of Vienna, they gradually adopted the rules laid out there, which included the establishment of a ranking system for diplomatic missions that reflected the distribution of power across the international system. The governments of great powers would exchange ambassadors, while other relationships could be served by envoys, ministers, or agents. Early US diplomats usually served at the rank of minister or envoy. Diplomats of all ranks were responsible for securing office space and living quarters, often at their own expense. Given the general lack of government financial support, American and European diplomatic missions were typically headed by people of independent means, contributing to the aristocratic cast of the diplomatic service and opening it to criticism in the United States.

In 1890, the US and British governments agreed to raise their diplomatic missions to the rank of ambassador, signaling the importance of Anglo-American relations and a tentative US claim to great power status. In 1898, the US and Mexican governments exchanged ambassadors, starting a wave of elevations in US–Latin American relations. These exchanges did symbolize the importance of relations with Latin American countries to the United States, but they also destabilized the symbolism of the broader system, as US officials rarely viewed those Latin American governments as equals; exchanging diplomats with the ambassadorial rank no longer signaled great power status. The general trend, realized after 1945, was to eliminate the post ranking system and instead make all chiefs of diplomatic missions ambassadors. In the post-1945 system, the rank was supposed to symbolize that all legitimate governments were equal, which, of course, did not align with actual distributions of power.

DIPLOMATIC BUILDINGS

As the US government engaged more regularly in relations with governments across the globe, some Americans argued for the purchase or construction of diplomatic and consular buildings. Those buildings would provide continuity, increase efficiency, and signal the global reach of US power and economic interests. The 1911 Lowden Act provided money for acquiring diplomatic buildings but did not create a body to implement the program, a problem remedied with the 1926 Porter Act, which created the Foreign Service Buildings Committee to approve plans and the Foreign Buildings Office to carry them out. By 1932, the US government had roughly forty properties abroad.

World War II disrupted most aspects of international interactions, creating a blank slate for a newly internationally minded US government to present its power. Nearly three hundred diplomatic buildings were built or purchased between 1945 and 1960, including embassies, libraries, and cultural centers. Host governments provided materials and labor in exchange for reductions in their war-induced debts to the United States. Typically built in a modernist style that aimed to display superlative American building techniques—especially with reinforced concrete and glass—and signal that the United States was the wave of the future, these embassies increasingly became targets of vandalism as local residents expressed opposition to US policies. The attacks escalated; embassy personnel were killed in Saigon in 1965, and between 1975 and 1985, there were 243 attacks on US diplomatic buildings.

Following congressional investigations in the 1980s, the State Department altered its approach to embassy design, favoring self-contained compounds at a distance from city centers in an effort to improve security. Embassy compounds today are more apt to house employees of a variety of federal agencies, not just those of the State Department.

SEE ALSO *Americanization; Central Intelligence Agency (CIA); Department of State; Empire, US; Exceptionalism; Foreign Service, US; National Security Council (NSC)*

BIBLIOGRAPHY

Anderson, Matthew Smith. *The Rise of Modern Diplomacy, 1450–1919.* London: Longman, 1993.

Kennedy, Charles Stuart. *The American Consul: A History of the United States Consular Service, 1776–1914.* Westport, CT: Greenwood Press, 1990.

Loeffler, Jane C. *The Architecture of Diplomacy: Building America's Embassies.* New York: Princeton Architectural Press, 1998.

Morgan, William D., and Charles Stuart Kennedy, eds. *The U.S. Consul at Work.* Westport, CT: Greenwood Press, 1991.

Nicolson, Harold. *The Evolution of Diplomatic Method.* London: Constable, 1953.

Plischke, Elmer. *U.S. Department of State: A Reference History.* Westport, CT: Greenwood Press, 1999.

Robin, Ron Theodore. *Enclaves of America: The Rhetoric of American Political Architecture Abroad, 1900–1965.* Princeton, NJ: Princeton University Press, 1992.

Nicole M. Phelps
Associate Professor of History
University of Vermont

EMPIRE, US

The status of the United States as an empire has oscillated from an assumed fact to a contested controversy since the nation's founding. Despite ongoing dissent, however, the United States has continually functioned as an empire through various means since its founding. The reservation system has been central to the nation's imperial architecture. Early in the republic's history, it became a means through which the United States administered political control over indigenous nations of North America. More than one hundred years before the United States entered the so-called age of overseas imperialism, moreover, the nation functioned as a racial state that principally excluded Native Americans and blacks from its political body and displaced millions of American Indians from sovereign lands onto concentrated regions known as Indian reservations. This created a system of internal colonies, located and controlled within the geopolitical borders of the United States (Hixson 2013). By the twentieth century, however, the United States had developed significant control over various overseas polities, such as Cuba and the Philippines. This created important changes in the form and function of US empire as the imperial republic rapidly developed a global garrison presence. Throughout the history of US empire, moreover, institutional forms of religion have undergirded the exercise of imperial power, while religious frameworks have served to rationalize empire.

CONCEPTS AND TERMINOLOGY

Empires result from a specific type of political order: colonialism. The form and function of colonialism result when one polity (a state) dominates and controls a population that exists outside of the political community of the dominant polity (a metropole). Most simply, this is "foreign" control of a population that is regarded as a colony. But the actual history of colonialism is more complicated, sometimes involving what experts have termed *internal colonialism.* By either of these means, empires have historically held colonies that are, in political terms, possessed by and dependent on the metropole (Benjamin 2007; Colás 2007). Finally, empires are a political genre constituted through a difference in social power, not necessarily physical location. So, although the literature on empires commonly assumes that a great physical distance or an ocean must separate the metropole and colony, it is the difference in *power* and not spatial distance that enables the political order of empires (Porter 2006; Immerman 2010).

AN IMPERIAL REPUBLIC: INDIAN CONQUEST, SLAVERY, AND COLONIAL RULE

The United States functioned as an actual empire from the very time of its formation as a republic primarily because of its relationship to American Indian populations (and, to a lesser extent, to Africans who were mostly enslaved) (Immerman 2010). The polities that first formed the US republic, in turn, had existed as a network of colonies controlled by the British Crown. These colonies existed alongside the imperial holdings of France and Spain. Amid the network of European colonies was a much larger population of hundreds of American Indian nations throughout North America. Although Indians collectively outnumbered Europeans, their shifting alliances were not race-based but rooted instead in strategic political advantage. As a result, Native polities often allied with white settler polities against other Native nations, a pattern that enabled settler colonies to increase their advantage over Indian defenses and to progressively dispossess indigenous peoples of their land (Byrd 2011; Hixson 2013).

Of major importance to this process were the religious formations of settler colonialism. Christianity, specifically, promoted an ardent theology of conquest by divine right through chosenness, to which Anglo-American settlers and government officials repeatedly made recourse. Biblical narratives such as the Exodus legend, European philosophies of imperialism over so-called heathens, and Christian political theology arrogating sovereignty as the exclusive right of Christian rulers all functioned to endow US empire with a mantle of divine imperative and moral authority (Horsman 1981).

Race was a key component of US empire. The United States of America was formally organized as a racial state, as a nation for white citizens only. As early as 1790, in fact, US naturalization law stipulated racial whiteness as a prerequisite for becoming a US citizen. This condition created the foundations for a lasting architecture of white imperial domination over Indian and black populations, who were deemed incapable of authentic membership in the nation's political community. Linking citizenship to whiteness was inherent to the formation of the imperial republic as a racial state. In fact, this condition demonstrates the nature of race itself as a state practice of governing populations, regarding some as members of the state's political community (body politic) while regulating others as perpetually incapable of belonging to the political community of the state that governs (Goldberg 2002; Omi and Winant 2015).

Because race governance is created through colonialism, the historical symbiosis of racialization and US empire should not be surprising. Throughout the 1800s, architects of racism ranged from public officials, such as Thomas Jefferson (1743–1826) and John C. Calhoun (1782–1850), to military leaders, such as Andrew Jackson (1767–1845), to private capitalists who consolidated and commoditized the debts Native Americans owed to white settlers. These racial architects employed a variety of means to justify the political project of racial empire. Jefferson, for instance, insisted that blacks differed from whites because of differences in phenotypic appearance, physiology, and intelligence. Both Jefferson and Jackson, moreover, insisted that American Indians lacked the ability to participate in self-governance, a very common claim that was further promoted by the French author Alexis de Tocqueville (1805–1859) after his historic visit to the United States during the 1830s. The racial studies that began to proliferate at the hands of white scientists, moreover, drew on an almost endless array of claims—these varied from putative differences in skeletal structure or the flow of certain "humors" within the body to linguistic structures that endowed or constrained intellectual or affective capacities—all to justify the political project of governing human populations as racial entities (Hixson 2013).

US empire, moreover, comprised staggering advantages in material wealth for Anglo-Americans. The burgeoning imperial state fostered initiatives for building railroad networks, expanding farmlands for Anglo-American settlers, and dispossessing millions of American Indians and thereby forcing them into dependence on white-controlled commodities and markets. The racist structures and institutions created during the 1800s enabled the United States to develop as a racial state that expanded onto lands of American Indians while simultaneously excluding indigenous peoples from the imperial nation. Thus, the United States was extending its political control over an increasing array of geographies while strengthening the institutional force of the exclusionary practices that ensured its continuation as a racial settler state (Smith 2015; Hixson 2013).

Expansion onto the lands of American Indian nations was not the only factor in the making of US empire. Slavery was equally important to the imperial structures of the United States. Although slavery is frequently viewed reductively as a labor practice or theorized through the principle of chattel (reducing persons to property), the institution has actually functioned as a central means of governing populations as distinct and set apart from legitimate members of a society's political community. This condition was certainly the case in the United States. This political role of slavery—enabling whites to control the movements, practices, and organizing of blacks as an effectively colonized population—was frequently recognized and enjoined by defenders of slavery who warned that, in the absence of the institution, blacks would either take control of political institutions or terrorize white citizens by retaliating for the injustices of slavery. By this disingenuous logic, white supremacists equated politically dominating blacks through slavery with defending against antiwhite discrimination. Given the fact that blacks outnumbered whites in Mississippi and South Carolina and in scores of regions throughout the South, defenders of slavery were keen to emphasize that preserving slavery was essential to governing blacks as an excluded group to prevent them from becoming members of the nation's body politic (Johnson 2015).

OVERSEAS IMPERIALISM: THE WAR OF 1898

Among the most important developments in US empire was the so-called Spanish-American War of 1898. When the various peoples colonized by Spain fought revolutionary wars to win their sovereignty, the United States declared war against Spain, claiming to support the anticolonial aspirations of colonies such as Cuba and the Philippines. But the United States actually aimed to increase its own imperial status and seized control of Spain's colonies: Cuba, Puerto Rico, Guam, and the Philippines. Since the Philippines had become a sovereign state as a result of resisting Spanish rule, the United States started a war against the new republic in order to reduce it to a colonial status. A similar pattern emerged in other colonies. As a consequence, in just a few years the United

States shifted from being an empire chiefly of internal colonies to controlling overseas colonies and establishing permanent garrisons from the Pacific to the Caribbean regions (McCoy 2009; Immerman 2010).

Acquiring overseas territories was not the only significant result of the war. In addition, military conquest in the Philippines engendered important changes in US governing practices at home and abroad. For instance, the United States implemented systematic torture—particularly in the Philippines—to extract information from enemy captives. During and after the war against the Filipino military, US personnel spied on Filipinos and infiltrated their military and civic institutions. During the early twentieth century, these practices of surveillance and repression, developed to destroy Filipino democracy, began to manifest domestically as the US government began to repress citizens and to engage them not as mere criminals but as enemies of the state (McCoy 2009).

A special challenge factored into the formation of US colonialism in this period: the nation-state. By the time the United States began to colonize overseas polities, the phenomenon of nationalism was soundly established as a commonsense mode for organizing a state. In contrast to the monarchical states that dominated previously, the political community of a nation-state was conceived through the notion of a people as an ethnos or race. Such political order stood in sharp contrast to imagining the political community through the body of a monarch. This was precisely the issue that led Anglo-American colonies to revolt against the British monarch. Nationalism bred revolution, and revolutionary zeal was stridently anticolonial (Porter 2006; Cooper 2005).

Older empire-states, such as Britain, France, and Spain, had enjoyed a long history of imperial dominion without the renegade ambitions stoked by nationalism. Their colonies could easily conceive of freedom through imperial citizenship—membership in the empire with undifferentiated benefits of submission to a monarch. The United States, by contrast, was acquiring overseas colonies in the age of nationalism. By the accounting of the nation-state, even the benefits that might accrue in consequence of colonial rule seemed a pittance absent home rule. The feasibility of US empire depended on curbing or taming nationalism. As a result, US colonialism featured a distinctive emphasis on satellite states—ostensibly sovereign polities under a ruler who was local or indigenous but who was nevertheless controlled from without (Cooper 2005).

The colonization of Cuba is an instructive example. From the early 1900s until the Cuban Revolution of 1959, the United States controlled Cuba as a colony of the satellite variety. This was done by organizing Cuba as a polity with its own governing officials, military, constitution, and so on. But the nation's constitution guaranteed that the United States would enjoy extensive control over Cuba's domestic and foreign policy, its economic practices, and virtually every major aspect of political authority. Similar measures were obtained throughout Latin America under US hegemony (Grandin 2007).

Corporatism was a major element of US empire. The US-based United Fruit Company, for instance, controlled land, politics, and economic policy in multiple Caribbean and Latin American states. Ford Motor Company likewise enjoyed substantial control beyond the formal borders of the United States. In Liberia, the Firestone Corporation functioned extensively as a state, overseeing the creation and implementation of public policy, deciding fiscal policy, establishing normative labor practices, and even deciding Liberia's foreign policy. The fact that corporatism was an indirect means of governing should not distract attention from its historical lineage or its efficacy (Grandin 2007).

AMERICAN ASCENDENCY: FROM THE GREAT WARS THROUGH THE COLD WAR

During the greater part of the twentieth century, the United States became a superpower, eventually exceeding even the greatest European empires in its capacity to dominate. This was a direct consequence of establishing a global presence through military occupation; achieving economic domination through corporatism; and administering a massive, international program of counterintelligence to undermine the capacity of non-Western states to implement programs to exercise sovereignty. By the 1980s, which brought the end of the Cold War, the US empire was left with no true rival (Porter 2006; Johnson 2000).

One could view the creation of US overseas colonies as laying the foundation for this rise to power. But the more immediate origin was US involvement in World War I (1914–1918) and World War II (1939–1945). These so-called Great Wars were chiefly a crisis of European colonialism, a competition among Western empires. World War II in particular was rooted in Germany's departure from a centuries-long tradition whereby European nations colonized only non-Europeans. Germany aspired to colonize a range of European nations, beginning with Poland and eventually conquering France. As with World War I, the United States entered World War II as a major balancing force, bringing urgently needed cash, weapons technology, and soldiers. Before the 1940s, Britain was the most powerful Western empire. By the time the Paris Peace Treaties of 1947 were signed, even the British were forced to acknowledge that the United States was economically more powerful, and, along with other European nations, Britain eagerly accepted US financial assistance through the Marshall Plan (Porter 2006).

It was no accident that in the same year the US Congress passed the National Security Act, under Harry Truman's (1884–1972) administration. This watershed legislation created a permanent organization to administer covert military operations and counterintelligence: the Central Intelligence Agency (CIA). This new federal agency replaced the experimental, temporary Office of Strategic Services (OSS), which had enabled the United States to operate globally to surveil, influence, and redirect the actions of foreign government officials during World War II (Immerman 2010).

Equally important was President Truman's decision to create the School of the Americas in 1946 in the Panama Canal Zone, which eventually served to train militias and military dictators who would govern under the direction of the United States. This was a critical element for creating satellite states—ostensibly sovereign polities that were actually controlled by the United States. This indirect form of rule was by no means a novelty. For many centuries, empires have appointed local leaders to administer colonies. This was a standard practice of the Ottoman Empire, for instance. It also became the norm for British colonialism in South Asia (Blum 2000). There was one important difference, however, that magnified the significance of satellite states in the twentieth century: the overwhelming dominance of nationalism. In earlier periods, polities were monarchical states. But the rise of the nation-state (a state conceptualized as rooted in the identity of an ethnic or racial population instead of a sovereign monarch or royal family) changed everything. Virtually every state was affected by this new form of political order. Most importantly, nationalism became the primary instrument for decolonization movements, which began to multiply profusely by the mid-twentieth century (Cooper 2005).

The United States' investment in the national security paradigm and strategies of foreign intervention came to fruition in many ways throughout the twentieth century, particularly as a means for defying the sovereignty of other nations. In 1953 the CIA coordinated with Britain to overthrow Iran's newly elected democracy. By establishing a military coup, the CIA successfully removed that nation's president, Mohammad Mossadegh (1882–1967), from power. The CIA then installed a monarch (the shah) to govern the country and to ensure that Western corporations enjoyed cheap and easy access to Iran's oil reserves. Equally important, the CIA engineered an elaborate system of torture and abduction that targeted democratic activists who opposed Western control of Iran. Once in place, this torture system was maintained by the Iranian government to ensure the shah could remain in power. As a result, Iran functioned as a satellite state—ostensibly sovereign while actually controlled politically by the United States (Rejali 2007; Immerman 2010; Blum 2000).

To guarantee its primacy over the Soviet Union and its array of communist satellite states, the United States also implemented multiple forms of state terrorism. For instance, under the Ronald Reagan (1911–2004) administration, the United States trained, armed, and funded a range of Islamist movements, most notably the Taliban of Afghanistan, in order to administer a proxy war against the Soviet Union. After Cuba's successful revolution of 1959 ended its status as a US satellite state, the United States directed an unprecedented scale of terrorism against the island nation. This included destroying Cuban bridges, refineries, and chemical plants; paying European manufacturers to produce defective equipment that was then sold to Cuba; breeding disease-carrying mosquitos to target human populations in Cuba; and executing more than 630 assassination attempts against Fidel Castro (b. 1926). In 1971, the CIA even injected Cuban swine herds with a virus to undermine the nation's agricultural economy. As a result, Cuba was forced to euthanize more than 500,000 pigs (Blum 1995, 186–189).

Such informal methods of influence and control were by no means limited to Cuba, moreover. By 1959, the United States had trained at least 550 students from thirty-six countries in chemical and biological warfare at the US Army's Chemical School at Fort McClellan, Alabama. The aim was to equip US allies to target popular democratic movements that challenged Western colonialism. During Richard Nixon's (1913–1994) administration, the United States devoted millions of dollars to stymie Salvador Allende's (1908–1973) presidential campaign. When Allende prevailed in the election, the US implemented a coup, resulting in Allende's assassination in 1973. With the dissolution of Chile's democracy, the US then supported Augusto Pinochet's (1915–2006) leadership of a military dictatorship whose violent rule was crucial to promoting US influence throughout Latin America (Blum 1995, 189).

Throughout the Cold War era, moreover, US empire was stridently marked by both implicit and explicit appeals to religious authority to promote American vigilance against communism, which was reductively portrayed as atheistic and in staunch opposition to a Christian or God-fearing United States. Throughout Latin America, a range of religious activists, such as Christian liberation theologians, promoted communist reform to end centuries of Western colonialism, genocide, and labor exploitation, but this religious dimension of communism was decisively elided by religious activists and government officials. US legislators added the phrase "under God" to the national Pledge of Allegiance. Popular ministers, such as Billy Graham (b. 1918), became cultural icons as they promoted evangelical revivalism as the rightful response to the threat of secularism supposedly emanating from domestic and foreign sources of communism. Even the National Security Council equated the imperial ambitions of the United States with a religious struggle between Western theism and communism as a state religion (Herzog 2011).

US EMPIRE AFTER 9/11

Following the destruction of the World Trade Center in New York City on September 11, 2001, administration officials prioritized the pursuit of political Islam as the chief threat to US national security. As a result, the global footprint of US military occupation was intensified and expanded. In addition to invading Afghanistan in 2001, the United States invaded Iraq in 2003, dissolved its government, and installed a US military command until a government friendly to Western interests could be composed. Most notably, the paradigm of "regime change"—changing the governmental leadership of sovereign nations—became a publicly articulated policy of the US administration.

The US response to the September 11 attacks occasioned both denials and assertions of the nation's imperial status. Avid supporters of US unilateralism, such as historian Niall Ferguson, even argued that the United States needed to increase the scale of its international influence, for the sake of global security. This ambivalent mode of public debate mirrored previous historical moments. But 9/11 was not simply a repetition of previous eras. It was especially distinctive not least because it was the first time US civilians were victims of a foreign attack on domestic soil. The resulting sense of urgency and aggressive response was unprecedented. One evidence of this was the US government's new practice of publicly announcing the assassination of hundreds of foreigners (and, occasionally, US citizens, such as Anwar al-Awlaki [1971–2011]), even when such killings were administered through officially covert means (Johnson 2000; McCoy 2009).

In addition to these factors was the serendipity of technological advances in machine intelligence within military applications. What had been the occasional use of unmanned aerial vehicles (commonly known as drones) for surveillance in the 1990s advanced to the level of missile-armed fighter drones flying thousands of missions per month for both classified CIA operations and those of conventional military branches. Drone warfare, combining both intelligent machines and remote human operators, drastically reduced the risk to US personnel and, with drones capable of flying eight miles above Earth's surface for days at a time, radically upscaled American capacity for surveillance and stealth warfare.

Empires have always depended on the ability to synthesize intensive and extensive power, where the former concerns the scale at which they can compel adherence and the latter, the geographical expanse or distance from the metropolitan sphere of authority at which force can be delivered. Technological changes, such as sea-power and aviation advances, have dramatically altered the scope of both the intensive and extensive powers of US empire. In the years following 9/11, the US military complex benefited from a vigorous pace of developments, enabling cyberwarfare to hamper and disable military and civilian operations of sovereign nations, drone warfare to kill personnel and destroy property in unilateral strikes in nations such as Yemen and Pakistan, and intelligence gathering to intercept data, communications, and financial transactions by state and nonstate actors on a global scale.

Most importantly, the US empire in the post-9/11 world has enjoyed structural and ideological departures from classical empires that, far from diminishing the imperial status of the United States, have enabled a scale of dominance and force deployment across ideological, military, economic, and political domains that would have been impossible for previous empires to achieve. In multiple important ways, therefore, the United States differs from so-called traditional imperial polities because it is an empire of the present age that has achieved an unmatched ability to control populations and territories beyond the boundaries of its own political community.

SEE ALSO *Americanization; Anti-imperialism; Cold War; Exceptionalism; Foreign Affairs (Magazine); Haiti; Hawai'i; Hollywood; Imperialism; Internationalism; Interventionism; Isolationism; League of Nations; Paris Peace Conference (1919); Philippines; Puerto Rico; Race; Roosevelt, Theodore; September 11, 2001; Spanish-American War; Twain, Mark; United Nations; Whiteness; Wilson, Woodrow; World War I; World War II*

BIBLIOGRAPHY

Benjamin, Thomas, ed. "Introduction." *Encyclopedia of Western Colonialism since 1450*. Detroit: Macmillan Reference, 2007.

Blum, Edward J. *Reforging the White Republic: Race, Religion, and American Nationalism, 1865–1898*. Baton Rouge: Louisiana State University Press, 2005. Updated ed., 2015.

Blum, William. *Killing Hope: U.S. Military and CIA Interventions since World War II*. Monroe, ME: Common Courage Press, 1995.

Blum, William. *Rogue State: A Guide to the World's Only Superpower*. Monroe, ME: Common Courage Press, 2000.

Byrd, Jodi A. *The Transit of Empire: Indigenous Critiques of Colonialism.* Minneapolis: University of Minnesota Press, 2011.

Colás, Alejandro. *Empire.* Malden, MA: Polity Press, 2007.

Cooper, Frederick. *Colonialism in Question: Theory, Knowledge, History.* Berkeley: University of California Press, 2005.

Deloria, Vine, Jr. *Custer Died for Your Sins: An Indian Manifesto.* New York: Macmillan, 1969.

Goldberg, David Theo. *The Racial State.* Malden, MA: Blackwell, 2002.

Grandin, Greg. *Empire's Workshop: Latin America, the United States, and the Rise of the New Imperialism.* New York: Owl Books, 2007.

Herzog, Jonathan P. *The Spiritual-Industrial Complex: America's Religious Battle against Communism in the Early Cold War.* New York: Oxford University Press, 2011.

Hesse, Barnor. "Im/Plausible Deniability: Racism's Conceptual Double Bind." *Social Identities* 10, 1 (2004): 9–29.

Hixson, Walter L. *American Settler Colonialism: A History.* New York: Palgrave Macmillan, 2013.

Horsman, Reginald. *Race and Manifest Destiny: The Origins of American Racial Anglo-Saxonism.* Cambridge, MA: Harvard University Press, 1981.

Immerman, Richard H. *Empire for Liberty: A History of American Imperialism from Benjamin Franklin to Paul Wolfowitz.* Princeton, NJ: Princeton University Press, 2010.

Johnson, Chalmers. *Blowback: The Costs and Consequences of American Empire.* New York: Metropolitan Books, 2000. New ed., Holt, 2004.

Johnson, Sylvester A. *African American Religions, 1500–2000: Colonialism, Democracy, and Freedom.* New York: Cambridge University Press, 2015.

Mamdani, Mahmood. *Good Muslim, Bad Muslim: America, the Cold War, and the Roots of Terror.* New York: Doubleday, 2004.

McCoy, Alfred W. *Policing America's Empire: The United States, the Philippines, and the Rise of the Surveillance State.* Madison: University of Wisconsin Press, 2009.

Omi, Michael, and Howard Winant. *Racial Formation in the United States.* 3rd ed. New York: Taylor and Francis, 2015.

Porter, Bernard. *Empire and Superempire: Britain, America, and the World.* New Haven, CT: Yale University Press, 2006.

Rejali, Darius. *Torture and Democracy.* Princeton, NJ: Princeton University Press, 2007.

Smith, Andrea. *Conquest: Sexual Violence and Native American Genocide.* Durham, NC: Duke University Press, 2015.

Sylvester A. Johnson
Associate Professor of African American Studies and Religious Studies
Northwestern University

EMPIRE OF LIBERTY

The American Revolution changed the way that people thought about empire throughout the Atlantic world. Thomas Jefferson's (1743–1826) vision of an "Empire of Liberty" was not a uniquely American creation. Rather, his scheme for founding a transcontinental empire according to republican principles was shaped by his experience of the British Empire and the civil war that eventually divided Great Britain's North American colonies between the independent United States and the other thirteen provinces that remained loyal to the Crown. As a former American subject of the British Crown, Jefferson believed that the British Empire was a federative entity with sovereignty divided between the imperial government in London and the provincial assemblies in North America. As a revolutionary, he abandoned the subordination of the colonial periphery to the imperial metropole in favor of a republican association between equal polities. Jefferson's Empire of Liberty, then, simultaneously rejected and idealized the prerevolutionary British Empire.

THE COLONIAL INHERITANCE OF AMERICAN EMPIRE

While American and British policymakers broadly agreed that a failure of imperial governance had led to the American Revolution, they disagreed about the Revolution's causes and they drew different lessons for the future of North American empire. British imperial officials generally blamed the Revolution on the imperfect replication of English constitutional forms in the American colonies: overpowerful provincial assemblies had produced a democratic excess that was dangerously out of balance with the aristocratic and monarchical elements of England's mixed constitution. For Jefferson, the leading architect of American empire in the early years of the Republic, the rigid political subjection of the American periphery to the British center was responsible for the Revolution. He intended to replace these brittle bonds with the more subtle and supple ties of republican empire. His concept of an Empire of Liberty replaced political subordination with a harmonious association of reciprocal interests between free and equal states. The great paradox underlying republican empire was that its members had to be completely independent of one another to allow them to spontaneously create consensual bonds of union with one another.

From the beginning, advocates of an Empire of Liberty saw it as a transcontinental enterprise that was central to asserting the sovereignty of the United States on the global stage. The New World empire spawned by the American Revolution was not an inward-looking or exceptional project that reflected Americans turning away from Europe. Rather, the American colonization of a vast swath of North America was tied up with US ambitions to engage in the European world as an equal power. Great Britain had ceded the vast territory of the trans-Appalachian West to the United States by the Treaty of

Paris (1783), which ended the War of Independence. Home to thousands of native peoples and only a handful of American colonists in 1783, the trans-Appalachian West presented both opportunities and dangers for the fledgling Republic. Conscious of the historical fragility of republics, proponents of American imperialism hoped that the colonization of Indian homelands by US citizens would promote the virtue of the body politic and protect liberty. The founders believed that a virtuous citizenry was essential to safeguard the Republic from tyranny by ensuring that corrupt politicians could not monopolize political power. Colonizing the Ohio and Illinois countries promised to provide the expanding population of American citizens in the eastern states with a means of maintaining their political virtue by becoming independent farmers, rather than wage laborers beholden to their employers. The United States' imperial inheritance from the British Empire promised to secure the future of the American Revolution.

FORMING THE SINEWS OF TRANSCONTINENTAL EMPIRE

North America remained a site of interimperial competition after the American Revolution, ensuring that Jefferson's Empire of Liberty was only one of many imperial players. Notably, the Spanish and British Empires, which shared land borders with the United States on all sides, competed for the military alliance of native peoples and the political attachment of American colonists. The geography of North America did not easily support connections between the eastern states and the trans-Appalachian West. In an era when rivers functioned as commercial and communication highways, the Appalachian Mountains raised a significant barrier between people living on either side of the range. Moreover, the St. Lawrence River and the Great Lakes to the north, and the Ohio River and Mississippi River to the west, both offered trans-Appalachian colonists easier access to British Canada and Spanish Louisiana. While Jefferson conceived of a republican empire formed through "spontaneous" bonds of union between like-minded citizens on both sides of the Appalachian Mountains, the stakes involved in creating an Empire of Liberty meant that American policymakers could not leave the formation of these intersectional east-west political ties to chance. The federal state would play a critical role in creating the conditions for an expanding union.

The political economy of American empire depended as much on the United States' international trade as it did on the conquest and colonization of native homelands in the trans-Appalachian West. Jefferson and the architects of the Empire of Liberty expected that intersectional commerce between western farmers and eastern merchants would form the sinews of union, tying together the two sections through mutual interest. American imperialism looked westward, across the continent, and eastward, toward Europe. In the West, the American soldiers and diplomats would need to conquer native homelands in the Ohio River valley and extract territorial cessions from the defeated Indian nations. While the republican theory underpinning an Empire of Liberty emphasized friendship and individual liberty, the violence essential to realizing this imperial project offers a stark reminder that the founders envisioned the United States as a white republic. The federal state would then survey and sell parcels of land to industrious farmers, who would be keen to bring their crops to market to recoup the expense of their land purchases. In the East, American policy makers had to ensure that merchants in the Atlantic port cities could access international markets that would consume the produce and supply the material wants of western farmers.

Securing the United States' place in the Atlantic marketplace was a guiding principle of Jeffersonian foreign policy in large part because Jefferson recognized that international trade helped to connect western farmers and eastern Atlantic merchants. Consequently, from his appointment as secretary of state in George Washington's cabinet in 1789 to his retirement from the presidency in 1809, Jefferson championed a range of policies to protect American maritime trade. As secretary of state, Jefferson proposed using US naval power to protect American merchant shipping in the Mediterranean from capture by Barbary states in North Africa, a policy he pursued within weeks of assuming the presidency in 1801.

THE IMPACT OF ATLANTIC GEOPOLITICS

As a minor power in the geopolitics of the Atlantic world, the United States could only go so far in shaping its own destiny; rival empires and outside events played a significant role in determining the fortunes of American imperialism during the early years of the American Republic. In particular, the French and Haitian Revolutions had a profound effect on the course of American empire. French émigrés, who arrived in the United States in the 1790s, excited fears of separatist schemes to restore the French Empire in the trans-Appalachian West at the same time that they also helped to supply the foreign capital necessary for Americans to purchase western lands. The Haitian Revolution made possible the Louisiana Purchase, arguably Jefferson's greatest achievement as president. The retrocession of Louisiana from Spain to Napoleonic France in 1800 threw into doubt the right of American citizens to move goods through the port of New Orleans, sparking renewed rumors of western secession from the American Union. Jefferson instructed James Monroe (1758–1831) to purchase the port of New Orleans, but mounting French losses from Napoleon's attempt to suppress the Haitian Revolution convinced him to offer the United States the entire territory of Louisiana in 1803.

The United States did not always benefit from conflict in the revolutionary Atlantic world. The efforts of the British and French Empires to starve one another into submission through rival economic blockades posed a significant threat to the Empire of Liberty by denying Americans access to foreign markets. The War of 1812, which brought the United States to the brink of disunion, was ultimately a war for American empire, which President James Madison (1751–1836) thought necessary to prevent British interference with native resistance to American colonization in the West and the Royal Navy's obstruction of American commerce in the Atlantic. While the prosecution of the war threw into doubt the future of the Empire of Liberty, the United States again benefited from foreign events with the end of the Napoleonic Wars. Peace reopened European markets, while American diplomats managed to extend American imperial claims over the peoples and territory of North America when negotiating the Treaty of Ghent (1815) with British diplomats who were distracted by discussions about the future of Europe at the Congress of Vienna. By the time that President Monroe issued the so-called Monroe Doctrine, opposing European colonization in the Americas in 1823, the United States had firmly established its own Empire of Liberty.

SEE ALSO *Jefferson, Thomas; Louisiana Purchase; Northwest Ordinance (1787)*

BIBLIOGRAPHY

Cogliano, Francis D. *Emperor of Liberty: Thomas Jefferson's Foreign Policy.* New Haven, CT: Yale University Press, 2014.

Furstenburg, François. *When the United States Spoke French: Five Refugees Who Shaped a Nation.* New York: Penguin, 2014.

Gould, Eliga H. *Among the Powers of the Earth: The American Revolution and the Making of a New World Empire.* Cambridge, MA: Harvard University Press, 2012.

Griffin, Patrick. *American Leviathan: Empire, Nation, and Revolutionary Frontier.* New York: Hill and Wang, 2007.

Hatter, Lawrence B. A. "The Narcissism of Petty Differences? Thomas Jefferson, John Graves Simcoe, and the Reformation of Empire in the Early United States and British-Canada." *American Review of Canadian Studies* 42, 2 (2012): 130–141.

Lewis, James E., Jr. *The American Union and the Problem of Neighborhood: The United States and the Collapse of the Spanish Empire, 1783–1829.* Chapel Hill: University of North Carolina Press, 1998.

Onuf, Peter S. *Statehood and Union: A History of the Northwest Ordinance.* Bloomington: Indiana University Press, 1987.

Sexton, Jay. *The Monroe Doctrine: Empire and Nation in Nineteenth-Century America.* New York: Hill and Wang, 2011.

Taylor, Alan. *The Divided Ground: Indians, Settlers, and the Northern Borderland of the American Revolution.* New York: Knopf, 2006.

Tucker, Robert W., and David C. Hendrickson. *Empire of Liberty: The Statecraft of Thomas Jefferson.* New York: Oxford University Press, 1990.

Wallace, Anthony F. C. *Jefferson and the Indians: The Tragic Fate of the First Americans.* Cambridge, MA: Belknap Press, 1999.

Weeks, William Earl. *The New Cambridge History of American Foreign Relations,* Vol. 1: *Dimensions of the Early American Empire, 1754–1865.* New York: Cambridge University Press, 2013.

Lawrence B. A. Hatter
Assistant Professor of History
Washington State University

ETHNIC CLEANSING

Ethnic cleansing is the forcible removal of a particular group of people from a specific territory. There is no formal legal definition of the term because it is, strictly speaking, not a crime in and of itself, although it does fall under the category of *crimes against humanity* according to the International Criminal Tribunal for the former Yugoslavia (ICTY) and the Rome Statute of the International Criminal Court (ICC). In February 1993 the United Nations Security Council's Commission of Experts defined ethnic cleansing as:

> Rendering an area wholly homogenous by using force or intimidation to remove persons of given groups.... by means of murder, torture, arbitrary arrest and detention, extra-judicial executions, rape and sexual assault, confinement of civilians in ghetto areas, forcible removal, displacement and deportations of civilians, deliberate military attacks or threats of attacks on civilians and civilian areas, and wanton destruction of property. (Power 2002, 483)

The main difference between ethnic cleansing and genocide is the perpetrators' intent. According to international law as codified in the Genocide Convention (1948) and the Rome Statute (1998), the crime of *genocide* requires "intent to destroy, in whole or in part, a national, ethnical, racial, or religious group, as such." *Ethnic cleansing,* in contrast, entails the intent to remove the group but not necessarily to eliminate or destroy it. For example, the Holocaust of World War II and the 1994 Rwandan genocide certainly count as ethnic cleansings, but not all ethnic cleansings amount to genocide, as these events do. Many scholars accept the distinction between the two terms while admitting significant overlap. Those who support the distinction point to examples of ethnic cleansing that were undertaken relatively peacefully and argue that proving intent remains critical for convictions when prosecuting other crimes, such as first-degree murder. Others argue that fixating on intent obfuscates the overall effect of ethnic cleansing because it often results in death and destruction since no group voluntarily leaves its homeland. It is important that both camps claim their views are consistent with the understanding of genocide according to the term's originator, Raphael Lemkin (1900–1959).

The term *ethnic cleansing* derives from the words *ethnos* (Greek) and *chishenie* (Russian) or *čišćenje* (Serbo-Croatian), and entered the international vocabulary in 1992 when Serbs referred to their own actions in the former Yugoslavia as *etničko čišćenje*. But the concept of driving a population out of one's territory was hardly novel. The Nazis sought to make the Third Reich *Judenrein* (Jew free), and in 1939 Adolf Hitler (1889–1945) and other leading Nazis coined the term *völkische Flurbereinigung* (ethnic cleansing). The practice itself dates back to the ancient Assyrian ruler Tiglath-Pileser III (r. 745–727 BCE), who enforced resettlement of multiple conquered groups as state policy, including in the northern Israelite kingdom during campaigns in Syria and Palestine (Roth 1971–1972, 1034). Other examples include the murder of the Albigensians (1209–1222) in the south of France (Languedoc) by Pope Innocent III, the expulsion of Jews from Spain (1492), and the German massacres of the Herreros (1904–1905), although many more instances could be listed. In American history, the Trail of Tears following passage of the Indian Removal Act of 1830 qualifies as a campaign of ethnic cleansing, since many Native Americans were forcibly driven from their homelands.

Much of the attention regarding ethnic cleansing has focused on the former Yugoslavia due to former Serbian president Slobodan Milošević's (1941–2006) campaign to drive Muslims and Croats from Bosnia and ethnic Albanians from Kosovo. The efforts included expulsions, summary executions, rapes, torture, looting, beatings, and forced marches. Many were simply told to "leave or die" and given only minutes to collect their belongings. Often homes, property, and religious sites were burned to the ground, and streets were renamed in an attempt to erase any memory of the people who had until just recently lived there. Because the men were off fighting, women were left relatively defenseless and became the target of mass rapes. The ICTY found that rape had been widespread and systematically used as a tool of war, and the tribunal was among the first to convict perpetrators for such actions. US officials avoided using the term *genocide* to describe events in Bosnia because doing so carried an imperative to act. President Bill Clinton authorized air strikes but did not commit troops due in large part to events in Somalia at the time.

While the Balkans are no longer facing ethnic cleansing, Darfuris in Sudan have been suffering since 2003 from genocide and ethnic cleansing at the hands of Arab militias known as the Janjaweed, sanctioned by President Omar al-Bashir. He is the first sitting head of state to be indicted by the ICC on charges of genocide, crimes against humanity, and war crimes.

SEE ALSO *Armenian Genocide; Genocide; Holocaust; Human Rights; United Nations; Universal Declaration of Human Rights*

BIBLIOGRAPHY

Andreopoulos, George J., ed. *Genocide: Conceptual and Historical Dimensions*. Philadelphia: University of Pennsylvania Press, 1994.

Bell-Fialkoff, Andrew. "A Brief History of Ethnic Cleansing." *Foreign Affairs* 72, 3 (1993): 110–121.

Convention on the Prevention and Punishment of the Crime of Genocide. Adopted by the General Assembly of the United Nations on December 9, 1948. https://treaties.un.org/doc/Publication/UNTS/Volume%2078/volume-78-I-1021-English.pdf

International Tribunal for the Prosecution of Persons Responsible for Serious Violations of International Humanitarian Law Committed in the Territory of the Former Yugoslavia since 1991. Updated Statute of the International Criminal Tribunal for the Former Yugoslavia. September 9, 2009. First adopted May 25, 1993. http://www.icty.org/x/file/Legal%20Library/Statute/statute_sept09_en.pdf

Jones, Adam. *Genocide: A Comprehensive Introduction*. 2nd ed. New York: Routledge, 2011.

Kiernan, Ben. *Blood and Soil: A World History of Genocide and Extermination from Sparta to Darfur*. New Haven, CT: Yale University Press, 2007.

Mann, Michael. *The Dark Side of Democracy: Explaining Ethnic Cleansing*. New York: Cambridge University Press, 2005.

Naimark, Norman M. *Fires of Hatred: Ethnic Cleansing in Twentieth-Century Europe*. Cambridge, MA: Harvard University Press, 2001.

Power, Samantha. *"A Problem from Hell": America and the Age of Genocide*. New York: Basic Books, 2002.

Robertson, Geoffrey. *Crimes against Humanity: The Struggle for Global Justice*. 4th ed. New York: New Press, 2012.

Rome Statute of the International Criminal Court. Adopted on July 17, 1998, by the UN Diplomatic Conference of Plenipotentiaries on the Establishment of an International Criminal Court. http://www.icc-cpi.int/NR/rdonlyres/ADD16852-AEE9-4757-ABE7-9CDC7CF02886/283503/RomeStatutEng1.pdf

Roth, Cecil, ed. *Encyclopaedia Judaica*. Vol. 6. New York: Macmillan, 1971–1972.

Schabas, William A. *Genocide in International Law: The Crime of Crimes*. 2nd ed. New York: Cambridge University Press, 2009.

Scheffer, David. *All the Missing Souls: A Personal History of the War Crimes Tribunals*. Princeton, NJ: Princeton University Press, 2012.

Sémelin, Jacques. *Purify and Destroy: The Political Uses of Massacre and Genocide.* Translated by Cynthia Schoch. New York: Columbia University Press, 2007.

Shaw, Martin. *What Is Genocide?* Malden, MA: Polity Press, 2007.

Jeff Gottlieb
PhD Candidate in Religion, Ethics, and Philosophy
Florida State University

EUROPE

In the Revolutionary era, some of the most significant connections between the United States and Europe were economic. The primary financial backers for the American Revolution (1775–1783) were Spanish, Dutch, and French, making Europeans the first holders of American debt. When George Washington (1732–1799) took office in 1789, foreign-held debt equaled 29 percent of the total federal debt. Recognition of American independence by France in 1778 and England in 1783 allowed for the resumption of transatlantic commerce, which proved important for American growth, although the Napoleonic Wars complicated matters.

EUROPE'S ECONOMIC RELATIONS WITH THE UNITED STATES

The US Constitution, ratified in 1788, gave the federal government authority over national finances. This improved America's credit on European capital markets, as demonstrated by the Dutch and British bankers' loans that financed the 1803 Louisiana Purchase. Foreign-held debt continued to be significant throughout the antebellum era, while America enjoyed sizable investment from and trade with Europe. With the Civil War (1861–1865), however, European distrust of the United States grew, and many Europeans began to dump their American investments, with the exception of the British, many of whom sympathized with the South and lent the Confederacy money. After the Civil War, foreign direct investment (FDI) into the United States grew, as did transatlantic business in general. Britain invested the most, with the steel, coal, and railroad industries being the largest beneficiaries. Other Europeans, including many Germans and French, also traded readily with the United States.

Although transatlantic trade grew between 1896 and 1913, many European financial leaders perceived US regulations as lax. For example, the United States had no central bank until 1913, while major European partners had been operating such banks for decades—the British since 1694. When Europeans did invest in the United States in the early twentieth century, their investments tended to take one of two forms. First, some freestanding companies that were established and capitalized in Europe but had investments abroad transferred a European management presence to the United States. Other companies remained headquartered in Europe but devised new goods, services, products, and economic activities for the US market.

World War I (1914–1918) brought a new era of confusion for foreign investors. By 1914, there was $7.1 billion in foreign investment into the United States. US investments abroad totaled half that sum. Europeans were frantically seeking safe investments in the summer of 1914, by the end of which European investments equaled about 20 percent of US gross domestic product. But Europeans soon began selling assets to pay for their wartime expenses. The process was so frantic that the New York exchange shut down for several days to avoid European dumping.

The interwar period saw mixed levels of transatlantic economic interaction. The United States began more actively investing in Europe, but the recession had, by 1929, led to a considerable slowing of investment by both sides. Stateside, legislation vis-à-vis foreign ownership of American companies also constrained European-American economic cooperation. By the 1930s, however, European capital flowed into American corporate securities due to the stability the United States offered European markets. Additionally, American investment attracted further European investment, especially in telecommunications.

European investment in the United States continued during World War II (1939–1945), even after the United States passed regulations to control foreign funds. The British, who were exempted from these regulations, invested the most, although others, like the Netherlands, continued to invest as well. As for the Germans, embargoes against them made US economic ties virtually impossible. In the face of such regulations, companies that engaged in transatlantic business tried to either circumvent the embargoes or create new products, as when Coca-Cola in Germany created Fanta, or IG Farben, a German chemical company, moved around its assets in the late 1930s.

The decades immediately following World War II saw substantial increases in US-European economic cooperation. US investment in Europe substantially exceeded FDI into the United States, although British insurance companies continued their stateside investments, as did Swiss companies (e.g., Ciba, Sandoz, and Geigy) and Dutch companies (e.g., Shell and Seagrams).

A considerable challenge confronted the transatlantic economic relationship in 2008 to 2009, with the collapse of the investment firm Lehman Brothers and the ensuing financial crisis. US federal intervention, including the nationalization of US insurance giant American

International Group and the deep recession that followed, also had an impact on the European Union (EU). The European banks' problems led to bailouts and subsequently a sovereign debt crisis, the origin of which some European leaders blamed on US speculators.

The Transatlantic Trade and Investment Partnership (TTIP) negotiations were launched in 2013 to reenergize and further intensify transatlantic relations. However, political wrangling on both sides and at all levels have made the process challenging.

EUROPEAN DIPLOMATIC RELATIONS WITH THE UNITED STATES

In November 1776, the Dutch become the first foreign nation to officially recognize the US flag. As for relations with other European powers, Benjamin Franklin (1706–1790), America's first foreign minister, succeeded in convincing France to recognize American independence in 1778 after the US victory at Saratoga in the fall of 1777, and the two countries concluded an alliance. The Spanish and Dutch also became involved in the fight for American independence, though to different degrees. Because of the Pacte de Famille between Bourbon France and Spain, Spain declared war against Britain alongside the French. However, Spain refused to officially recognize American independence due to the fear that its colonies west of the Mississippi might also rebel. Although the Dutch Republic's *stadtholder*, William V (1748–1806), sided with Britain, Amsterdam refused to do so and renegotiated trade relations with America in 1778, plans that were discovered by the English, complicating Anglo-Dutch relations.

American relations with Britain and France were in flux until after 1815, in part due to the complications of the aftermath of the American Revolution, and in part due to warfare between the two European parties. Demarking a policy of neutrality that the United States maintained for decades, George Washington warned of America becoming involved in permanent alliances with Europe in his 1796 Farewell Address. That policy did not preclude mutually beneficial treaties that did not embroil the United States in European affairs. Disputes over whether early French aid to the United States was a loan or a gift led to the 1797 XYZ Affair, resulting in the Quasi-War (1798–1800) between France and the United States. European refusal to recognize Americans' claims of their rights to neutral trade during the Napoleonic Wars led to tensions with both Britain and France in the first decades of the nineteenth century, culminating in a war between the United States and Britain from 1812 to 1814.

In the following decades, several treaties supported US land protection and expansion. The Rush-Bagot Treaty (1817) between Britain and the United States limited armaments in Lake Champlain and the Great Lakes. During the same period, Spain, signed the Adams-Onís (Transcontinental) Treaty (1819), which granted Oregon Country and Florida to the United States, while Spanish control of Florida was firmly acknowledged. Elsewhere, Spain's fragile hold on Texas had collapsed by 1821; the United States annexed the territory in 1845.

The American Civil War and Spanish-American War. The American Civil War (1861–1865) also proved a formidable test to US-European relations. The Union blockaded southern cotton and other goods from being traded with Britain and other European states. Great Britain and Spain officially recognized the Confederacy as a belligerent in 1861, while other European governments remained either neutral or quiet Confederate supporters. The French, for example, took interest in Mexico, which presented a challenge to the administrations of Abraham Lincoln (1809–1865) and Ulysses S. Grant (1822–1885).

Following the Civil War, America debated whether to endorse isolationism or imperialism. The Spanish-American War partially answered that question. From 1895 to 1898, Cuban resistance forces embroiled themselves in skirmishes for independence from Spanish rule. The British initially supported Spain, but negotiations conducted by US foreign secretary John Hay (1838–1905) and British foreign minister Edward Grey (1862–1933) led to Britain solidifying its friendship with the United States and not meddling in its dispute with Spain. This agreement coincided with what historian Bradford Perkins (1968) called the "Great Rapprochement," a term referring to the period from 1895 to 1914 when Anglo-American relations depended on British preparedness to accept America's rise on the global stage. After the US battleship *Maine* was destroyed in Havana Harbor in February 1898, America launched a ten-week war against Spain in Cuba, ending with the 1898 Treaty of Paris. The terms of it and other agreements over the next five years pursuant to it brought an end to the Spanish presence in North America, and granted Guam to the United States, along with a 999-year lease of Guantánamo Bay in Cuba. Spain also surrendered the Philippines to the United States for $20 million.

World War I. Initially, the United States remained out of World War I. Despite the sinking of the *Lusitania* in 1915, with 128 American casualties, by a German U-boat, the United States remained isolationist, and President Woodrow Wilson (1856–1924) was reelected in 1916 with the campaign slogan "He kept us out of the war." The interception of a telegram from German foreign minister Arthur Zimmermann (1864–1940) encouraging Mexico to ally with Germany and possibly wage war against the United States, along with the resumption of Germany's unrestricted submarine warfare in the Atlantic, changed Wilson's stance by 1917, and the United States entered the war. Within sixteen months, the bloody affair had drawn to a close, and Wilson, with the support of French premier Georges Clemenceau (1841–1929) and British prime minister David Lloyd George (1863–1945), advocated for the Treaty of Versailles (1919), which incorporated Wilson's Fourteen Points and his proposal for the League of Nations.

Despite Wilson's noble aims, the United States sought to isolate itself from European military affairs in the ensuing years, signing agreements with European nations to that effect, including the Kellogg-Briand Pact (1928). In the end, the US Senate refused to ratify the League of Nations (as did Russia), and the league failed to enforce the Treaty of Versailles or help rebuild Germany. This coincided with a strong sense of American isolationism, codified by four Neutrality Acts, passed in 1935, 1936, 1937, and 1939.

World War II. In 1933, in the face of a depressed economy, the United States was reluctant to involve itself in another European war, though Americans were generally wary of Adolf Hitler's National Socialism. Germany hoped solidarity with the Jim Crow South would strengthen America's isolationist position. However, southern American newspapers ignored the similarities between southern Negrophobia and Nazi racial policy, and Americans otherwise ideologically open to Hitler's policies shunned them, if only for nativist reasons.

In January 1941, President Franklin D. Roosevelt's (1882–1945) plan to lend armaments to nations vital to American interests, with the expectation of payment-in-kind after the war (Lend-Lease), became the first diplomatic support for Europe during the war. After Germany's Blitzkrieg in Poland, the Nazis' march across Europe, and ten months of bombings over Britain, Winston Churchill (1874–1965) asked Roosevelt for help. However, Roosevelt held firm to the promise he made in an October 1940 campaign speech, insisting that American "boys are not going to be sent into any foreign wars." As with Wilson during World War I, external events, particularly the bombing of Pearl Harbor on December 7, 1941, made Roosevelt renege on his campaign promise, a move welcomed by America's European allies. Three days after the United States declared war on Japan, Germany declared war on the United States, again embroiling America in a European conflict.

The Yalta and Potsdam negotiations toward the end of World War II redefined the transatlantic relationship for decades. They made clear that: (1) the victors would divide Germany into four zones (French, British, Russian, and American); and (2) the Russian vision for Europe differed from that of the United States and its allies, with the latter unwilling to support communism's spread while Russia hoped for it. Against this backdrop, Roosevelt endeavored to establish a body stronger than the League of Nations that could ensure a more peaceful world order through consensus-driven dialogue. In 1945, the United Nations Charter was signed. As tensions with the Soviets increased, the need for further security for the United States and its European allies became apparent. In 1949, ten European nations and the United States and Canada signed the North Atlantic Treaty, America's first peacetime military alliance with any European nation since the late eighteenth century and the basis for the North Atlantic Treaty Organization (NATO).

The Cold War Period. In 1946, Winston Churchill verbalized what many feared when he declared that "an iron curtain has descended across the Continent." Like Churchill, US president Harry Truman (1884–1972) distrusted the Soviets and their expansionist intentions. That shared distrust of the Soviets became the catalyst for stalwart transatlantic relations throughout the Cold War era, as the United States and its Western European allies signed agreements aimed at stabilizing international economic and political relations. The Anglo-French Treaty of Dunkirk (1947) for mutual defense and the Treaty of Brussels (1948) bringing the Benelux countries into the alliance signified to the United States that Europe was serious about its self-sufficiency.

Truman also feared that communism was taking too strong a hold in Greece. By 1947, he convinced Congress to provide military and economic aid for Greece, as well as for Turkey, which was in a similar situation. The Truman Doctrine, combined with the Marshall Plan and George Kennan's (1904–2005) policy of containment, proved welcome to Western Europe, which fell largely under US influence through treaties and shared ideological beliefs. The nations of Eastern Europe, like Poland, were encompassed within the Soviet sphere.

The outbreak of hostilities in Korea in June 1950 prompted a reassessment of European-American relations, since Truman had announced that he would substantially increase US troop levels in Europe, with the expectation that the Europeans would follow suit. This meant that West Germany needed to be rearmed because its geographic location served as a bulwark between communism and freedom. Thus, NATO sanctioned a "forward strategy," which established an integrated military force under a centralized command structure headed by SACEUR (the supreme allied commander Europe).

The level of German military involvement in the allied force troubled the French, so in 1950 France proposed the Pleven Plan for a common European defense. Although the plan passed, the French vetoed the defense treaty in 1954 after a domestic election produced a more skeptical parliament. By 1955, West Germany and Italy were integrated into NATO and the Western European Union (WEU), which had been created by the Treaty of Brussels. The Soviets responded with the Warsaw Pact, formed in 1955 to counteract NATO's military influence, further demarcating the European East-West divide. With a sizable amount of the WEU's costs for the military protection covered by the United States, many Europeans became concerned about their reliance on US aid. The United States, for its part, remained frustrated that Europe was not covering more of its own defense costs. Some of these concerns were assuaged with the creation in 1957 of the European Economic Community (EEC) and European Atomic Energy Committee.

The administration of President John F. Kennedy (1917–1963) announced a new vision for transatlantic relations as Europe drew closer together and wanted to develop a more equal partnership with US leadership, rather than domination. Free trade and the shared burden of security for the West were part of this vision. French President Charles de Gaulle (1890–1970) differed, instead championing European independence from US influence. Given that the EEC had become less dependent on US goods, Kennedy pushed through a Trade Expansion Act in 1962 and undertook talks on the General Agreement on Tariffs and Trade (GATT) with Europe the same year.

In the 1960s the US-European relationship had to withstand three considerable challenges: (1) fear among Europeans that their socioeconomic culture was being Americanized; (2) US engagement in Vietnam; and (3) distrust among Europeans in US military and economic support. During that decade, West German foreign minister Willy Brandt (1913–1992) made positive overtures toward Eastern Europe, especially East Germany, a move that made the United States, Britain, and France fear that Germany's West-leaning affinities were waning. Thus, the twentieth anniversary of NATO in 1969 was marred with American concerns about Europe and its position on the war in Southeast Asia. Nevertheless, the East-West binary, demarcating the Cold War's primary divide, held the alliance together.

The 1970s started with President Richard Nixon (1913–1994) deciding not to raise interest rates to boost investment in the US economy in 1970. The Nixon administration took the United States off the gold standard the following year, which led the other Group of Ten (G10) nations, seven of them European, to realign their currencies, allowing them to float within ±2.25 percent relative to the dollar. This was an essential move given that some European currencies had been pegged to the dollar.

Nixon's overtures to China, coupled with Europe's visceral reaction to the level of US engagement in the Vietnam War, compounded tensions. The Arab-Israeli (Yom Kippur) War in October 1973 deepened the divide further. NATO allies, with the exception of Portugal and the Netherlands, refused to join the United States in an airlift of supplies to Israel due to European fears of Arab retribution. In 1973 Arab members of the Organization of the Petroleum Exporting Countries (OPEC) embargoed oil to the United States and the Netherlands, which led to a quadrupling of global oil prices. Instead of working with the United States, major European countries attempted to make bilateral oil agreements with Arab oil producers. The Watergate crisis (1972–1974) further increased Europeans' reluctance to engage in dialogue with the American government. Nevertheless, security was paramount, and in June 1974, NATO's government chiefs signed the Declaration on Atlantic Relations, a statement declaring that US nuclear forces and troops in Europe remained necessary for the mutual security of NATO members. The Strategic Arms Limitation Talks/Treaty (SALT) I (1972) and SALT II (1979) between the US and Soviet governments led to the Conference on Security and Cooperation in Europe beginning in 1973 and the 1975 Helsinki Accords (Final Act), which recognized the territorial borders and sovereign control of European countries and created a possibility for freer exchanges between Eastern and Western Europe.

In the 1980s, President Ronald Reagan (1911–2004) affirmed his commitment to Western European alliances. However, his American and European detractors challenged his success. French and the British leaders, for example, questioned US leadership in the Middle East, maintaining that Britain's years of experience in the region gave them insights that Americans lacked.

During this period, Europeans wished to avoid opposing the United States on Afghanistan, as they already disagreed with US involvement in Nicaragua, Grenada, and Libya. To avoid greater Americanization of European affairs, in 1984, French President François Mitterrand (1916–1996) led the move toward revivifying the WEU for security matters. The 1987 Single European Act opened up the internal European market, which, after the 1991 signing of the Maastricht Treaty, established the EU with a common currency, the euro. These developments left the United States fearing discriminatory measures against American products.

At the same time, the United States and the European Community were participating in new defense policies, such as the suggestion from the Reagan administration that it was willing to negotiate an armaments deal with the Soviets. Though Mitterrand

and British prime minister Margaret Thatcher (1925–2013) endorsed Reagan's position, others in Europe were concerned the United States had not gone far enough on arms control. To this, the Reagan administration retorted that Europeans should capitulate to Soviet pressure. Just as problematic was Reagan's Strategic Defense Initiative, also known as Star Wars.

In June 1987 Reagan's "tear down this wall" speech in Berlin drew significant European support. In December 1987 Reagan and Soviet leader Mikhail Gorbachev (b. 1931) signed the Intermediate-Range Nuclear Forces Treaty. The following year, West German chancellor Helmut Kohl (b. 1930) initiated talks between the European Community and Soviet Union on increasing cooperation between the Eastern and Western blocs. This move enhanced the American view that Germany and Europe on the whole sought an independent stance in regional matters. The following year, the Cold War drew to a close, and the tumultuous events that followed necessitated a redefining of the transatlantic relationship.

Redefining the Transatlantic Relationship after the Cold War. While many European leaders, including Thatcher, were uncomfortable with the prospect of German reunification, the United States did not see it as a threat. In the end, the reunification was handled within the Two-Plus-Four negotiations—the two Germanys plus the four Allied powers of World War II. The European Community voted to allow a unified Germany to remain a member. Keenly aware of the country's history, Chancellor Kohl aided European acceptance of German reunification by engaging Germany in a restructured Conference on Security and Cooperation in Europe and a stronger European Community.

In this spirit, US Secretary of State James Baker (b. 1930) called for a "New Atlanticism," culminating in November 1990 with the United States and the European Community signing the Transatlantic Declaration. This agreement established regular summit meetings, with a view to cooperation on cross-border issues, such as illicit drug proliferation and terrorism. These efforts proved essential to the transatlantic relationship, as debates broke out about NATO and America's role in it. The United States viewed the Yugoslav wars of the 1990s to be a European problem. However, the United States did pledge troops, and Americans were appalled by the deaths of more than eight thousand Bosniaks in the July 1995 Srebrenica massacre. These wars made plain that America was necessary for NATO's success.

Transatlantic political dialogue at various levels led to the New Transatlantic Agenda, established in 1995 with the aim of improving transatlantic relations and promoting democracy globally. An outgrowth of this agreement concluded in 1998 with the Transatlantic Economic Partnership, which addresses bilateral and multilateral trade. European and American businesses and diplomats embraced these efforts to strengthen transatlantic trade. But new challenges emerged with George W. Bush's neoconservative foreign policy and the US war on terror in the aftermath of the 9/11 attacks. European governments were initially supportive of the United States, and the Taliban-led Afghani government was vilified on both sides of the Atlantic. The United States' intervention in Iraq, however, presented serious challenges to the transatlantic relationship. Half of current and soon-to-be EU members considered the American-led invasion of Iraq an imposition of American ideals that smacked of imperialism. Some Americans, especially Republicans, saw the European opposition as weak and outdated. For example, Defense Secretary Donald Rumsfeld (b. 1932) described France and Germany as part of "old Europe," while those supporting the United States (e.g., Poland) were part of "new Europe." Disagreement between the United States and European countries decreased as the Iraq War drew to a close, and many Europeans rallied behind Bush's commitment to ending the AIDS epidemic in Africa.

Anti-Bush sentiment among Europeans lingered through 2008. Barack Obama's presidential candidacy was very much welcomed in Europe, with many considering it a sign of American progress. More than 200,000 people attended Obama's July 2008 speech at the Brandenburg Gate in Berlin. Europeans embraced Obama's message of pluralism, but some Americans were concerned that the speech negated American exceptionalism.

Once in office, Obama, like his predecessors, voiced concerns about Europe's limited contributions to NATO. The transatlantic relationship remained tenuous through early 2010, but Europeans found Obama's toned-down war-on-terror rhetoric more acceptable than Bush's more assertive position, and both sides were generally cooperative. Europe and the United States agreed to continued collective defense via NATO and to joint intervention in Libya. However, America's focus on Asia disappointed some European leaders. In addition, the surreptitious interception of phone conversations, including those of German chancellor Angela Merkel (b. 1954), raised the ire of Europeans, once again straining the transatlantic relationship.

CULTURAL EXCHANGE BETWEEN EUROPE AND THE UNITED STATES

The exchange of ideas and customs between America and Europe began with European colonization of North America. Europeans constituted over half of foreign-born

Americans through the 1980 census. However, by 2014, that number had shrunk to about 12 percent.

Until the nineteenth century, cultural influence generally flowed from but not to Europe. European Enlightenment thinking, for example, had a major impact on early America, especially in politics. In the nineteenth century, immigration to the United States as a result of the wave of wars and revolutions in Europe between 1830 and 1914 led to 54 million Europeans crossing the Atlantic. European immigrants brought their values, views, and traditions with them. Some of the ideas transported to the United States posed challenges to Americans, including German immigrant Francis Daniel Pastorius's antislavery declaration (1688) and the German 1848ers, who eventually migrated to the Midwest and Texas, where they spread their antislavery views. The best-known publication detailing the European take on nineteenth-century American culture was Alexis de Tocqueville's adept *Democracy in America* (1835/1840), based on the Frenchman's nine-month visit to the United States in 1830.

At the eve of World War I, the cultural ties between Europe and the United States were relatively strong, largely due to mass immigration. Immigrants of this period were interested in Americanizing themselves and their families once they arrived in the United States, indicated by their general reluctance to speak languages other than English. They conformed partly to attain upward mobility in the workforce. Arguably, this era marked a turning point in European perceptions of America: Europeans were increasingly accepting of American norms, though sometimes norms were forced upon European émigrés. For example, anti-German instruction in some states, such as Iowa, presented the only reason for many German-speaking university faculty to learn English at all.

The relationship between the United States and Great Britain during this period suffered other difficulties. Many Americans of Irish, Italian, or German decent, who comprised a large percentage of immigrants to the United States, took issue with England. The English, especially the well-educated and affluent, still held American culture in contempt. When the Rhodes scholarships were founded in 1902, many at Oxford University expressed consternation that Americans were unlikely to study the classics because they were "uncultured."

Accompanying this disrespect from the British and continentals alike was a fear that the world was becoming "Americanized" by the 1920s, as the journalist W. T. Stead (1849–1912) phrased it in 1902. Intellectuals saw this process as the downfall of Occidental influence on culture, if not the demise of all things decent and good, for many Europeans perceived the United States as a simplistic, uncultured nation. Until the 1930s Americans considered expatriates living in Europe to be traitors, a belief that evolved after educated people on both sides of the Atlantic grew to recognize that Europeanization of the United States was happening in parallel to an Americanization of Europe. The acceptance of the United States as a great power after World War I played a significant role in that ideological shift, as demonstrated by the advent of film, the acceptance of American literary works, and the rise of American artists. The notion of high culture and low culture, which gained traction with modernist and postmodernist art, provided evidence of a mutual acceptance of European and American culture, creating an invisible barrier not between Americans and Europeans but between social classes throughout much of the twentieth century.

Beginning in 1950, transatlantic cultural relations became more complicated. Educated circles in Europe often frown upon America's rugged representation, as manifested in its gun laws, school-free days for hunting, and even its love for American football rather than soccer. Europeans also scrutinize American diets, as obesity in America has increased significantly. This fact has led to a flood of films and books that have justified many Europeans' view that Americans are generally simple and unfit, a seeming reemergence of Europeans' nineteenth-century skepticism regarding American culture in general.

Regardless, student exchanges have increased the flow of culture across the Atlantic. Of the top ten 2011–2013 study-abroad destinations for US students, six are European countries. About 13 percent of students at American colleges and universities in 2013 were European (Institute of International Education 2015). In education, the Bologna harmonization process and its related Tuning project, both aiming to mutualize recognition of educational standards in EU member states, have gained the attention of American educators and policy makers, furthering the depth of exchange. According to a 2007 Institute of International Education white paper, the United States remains a top international-exchange destination for students from most EU nations, and 81 percent of European institutions want more American students to enhance campus culture, but the relationship is lopsided.

SEE ALSO *Atlantic Ocean; Atlantic Slave Trade; Britain; Cold War; Democracy in America (Alexis de Tocqueville, 1835–1840); Expatriate Artists; Foreign Performing Artists; France; Grand Tour; Immigration; Monroe Doctrine (1823); War of 1812; World War I; World War II*

BIBLIOGRAPHY

Adams, James Truslow. "Americans Abroad: A Study in Evolution." *New York Times*, June 21, 1931.

Churchill, Winston. "The Sinews of Peace" (the Iron Curtain speech). Westminster College, Fulton, MO, March 5, 1946. https://www.nationalchurchillmuseum.org/sinews-of-peace-iron-curtain-speech.html

Dyal, Donald H., Brian Carpenter, and Mark Thomas, eds. *Historical Dictionary of the Spanish-American War.* Westport, CT: Greenwood Press, 1996.

Eliasson, Johan. *America's Perceptions of Europe.* New York: Palgrave Macmillan, 2010.

Etzioni, Amitai. "A Grand Design? A Review." *Journal of Conflict Resolution* 7, 2 (1964): 155–163.

Ferguson, Niall. *The Cash Nexus: Money and Power in the Modern World, 1700–2000.* New York: Basic Books, 2002.

Gibson, Campbell, and Kay Jung. *Historical Census Statistics on the Foreign-Born Population of the United States: 1850 to 2000.* US Census Bureau, Population Division, Working Paper No. 81. 2006. http://www.census.gov/population/www/documentation/twps0081/twps0081.pdf

Gordon, Philip H., and Karen E. Donfried. "The U.S.-Europe Partnership." Transcript and audio of a discussion with Philip Gordon, assistant secretary of state for European and Eurasian affairs, and Karen Donfried of the German Marshall Fund. Council on Foreign Relations, Washington, DC, December 9, 2009. http://www.cfr.org/eu/us-europe-partnership/p20980

Grosser, Alfred. *The Western Alliance: European-American Relations since 1945.* New York: Continuum, 1980.

Herring, George C. *From Colony to Superpower: U.S. Foreign Relations since 1776.* New York: Oxford University Press, 2008.

Howard, Michael. "A European Perspective on the Reagan Years." *Foreign Affairs* 66 (1988): 478–493.

Institute of International Education (IIE). *Meeting America's Global Education Challenge: Current Trends in U.S. Study Abroad and the Impact of Strategic Diversity Initiatives.* IIE Study Abroad White Paper Series, Issue 1. New York: Author, 2007.

Institute of International Education (IIE). *Open Doors 2014: Report on International Educational Exchange.* New York: Author, 2015.

Kilbride, Daniel. *Being American in Europe, 1750–1860.* Baltimore, MD: Johns Hopkins University Press, 2013.

Kissinger, Henry. *Years of Upheaval.* Boston: Little, Brown, 1982.

Klautke, Egbert. "Anti-Americanism in Twentieth Century Europe: Historiographical Review." *Historical Journal* 64, 4 (2011): 1125–1139.

Kobrak, Christopher. *Banking on Global Markets: Deutsche Bank and the United States, 1870 to the Present.* Cambridge: Cambridge University Press, 2008.

Kohl, Helmut. "Helmut Kohl's Ten-Point Plan for German Unity (November 28, 1989)." Translated by Jeremiah Riemer. 1989. http://germanhistorydocs.ghi-dc.org/sub_document.cfm?document_id=223

Kohl, Wilfrid L. "The Nixon-Kissinger Foreign Policy System and U.S.-European Relations: Patterns of Policy Making." *World Politics* 29, 1 (1975): 1–43.

Kolodziej, Edward A. *French International Policy under de Gaulle and Pompidou: The Politics of Grandeur.* Ithaca, NY: Cornell University Press, 1974.

Mokyr, Joel. *The Oxford Encyclopedia of Economic History.* Oxford: Oxford University Press, 2003.

NATO Public Policy Division. *Towards the New Strategic Concept: A Selection of Background Documents.* Brussels, Belgium: NATO Public Policy Division, 2010. http://www.nato.int/nato_static_fl2014/assets/pdf/pdf_publications/20120412_Towards_the_new_strategic_concept-eng.pdf

Pederson, William D. *Presidential Profiles: The FDR Years.* New York: Facts on File, 2006.

Perkins, Bradford. *The Great Rapprochement: England and the United States, 1895–1914.* New York: Atheneum, 1968.

Peterson, John. *Europe and America: The Prospects for Partnership.* 2nd ed. New York: Routledge, 1996.

Pilcher, Jeffrey M. *The Oxford Handbook of Food History.* New York: Oxford University Press, 2012.

Roger, Philippe. *The American Enemy: A Story of French Anti-Americanism.* Translated by Sharon Bowman. Chicago: University of Chicago Press, 2005.

Roosevelt, Franklin D. "Campaign Address at Boston, Massachusetts." October 30, 1940. American Presidency Project, edited by John T. Woolley and Gerhard Peters. http://www.presidency.ucsb.edu/ws/?pid=15887

Stead, W. T. *The Americanization of the World; or, The Trend of the Twentieth Century.* New York: Markley, 1902.

Wansbrough Jones, Llewelyn, Acting Deputy Chief of Staff, Supreme Headquarters, Allied Powers Europe. "Planning for Forward Strategy." September 6, 1954. http://www.nato.int/nato_static/assets/pdf/pdf_archives/20140410_planning_for_forward_strategy.pdf

Wilkins, Mira. *The History of Foreign Investment in the United States to 1914.* Cambridge, MA: Harvard University Press, 1989.

Wilkins, Mira. *The History of Foreign Investment in the United States, 1914–1945.* Cambridge, MA: Harvard University Press, 2004.

Christopher Brooks
Associate Professor, Department of History
East Stroudsburg University

EVANGELICALISM

SEE *Protestantism.*

EXCEPTIONALISM

With the recent global turn in the study of American history, the concept of American exceptionalism has come under close scrutiny by scholars critical of the idea that America has a unique role to play in human history. New attention has been paid to historical phenomena earlier considered uniquely American, which have been reinterpreted as part of hemispheric or global patterns. Historians of colonialism and empire, "frontiers," international labor and reform movements, immigration, and the environment, for example, have particularly challenged the assumptions of American exceptionalism. The new debate about American exceptionalism and its consequences for US foreign policy call for review of the evolution of the idea of exceptionalism over American history. Its meanings have hardly remained static, and, indeed, its latest interpretation has helped to precipitate antiexceptionalist criticism.

ORIGINS OF THE CONCEPT AND TERM

Claims for American exceptionalism are often traced to its first usage by Alexis de Tocqueville (1805–1859) in *Democracy in America*: "The position of the Americans is therefore quite exceptional, and it may be believed that no democratic people will ever be placed in a similar one" (Tocqueville 1840, 2:36–37). Tocqueville perceived that Americans preferred material, not intellectual, achievement, given their distance from Europe and what today is called a "middle-class" society. He predicted that other societies would also become democratic, but not like what he perceived in the early American Republic. The term *American exceptionalism* emerged in the 1930s when socialist thinkers, most notably a German sociologist, Werner Sombart (1863–1941), pondered why the United States, despite its industrialization, had not exhibited a strong class consciousness, much less a broad socialist political movement, in contrast to European patterns. In the era of World War II, the "consensus" school of history writing, including scholars Daniel Boorstin (1914–2004), Louis Hartz (1919–1986), and Arthur Schlesinger Jr. (1917–2007), similarly emphasized Americans' lack of ideological and class conflict, in contrast to the threats of international communism and fascism.

COLONIAL AND REVOLUTIONARY ERAS

Yet long before the word *exceptional* appeared in arguments for American exceptionalism, Europeans brought the concept to the New World, at least from the founding of "New England." The American land, both in its supposedly primitive state upon Europeans' arrival and in its yield for colonists' sustenance and commercial trade, seemed evidence of God's revealing his plan to the "new Israelites," a common moniker of the settlers. John Winthrop (c. 1587/8–1649), a founder of the Massachusetts Bay Colony, expressed his exceptionalist vision of the colony as a "City upon a Hill," meaning an example of an uncompromising Bible-based society (Winthrop 1985, 82). Winthrop's metaphor, from Matthew 5:14, is perhaps the most famous metaphor in American history.

Puritan Massachusetts was unique in its uniformity, not diversity, on account of excluding people who did not fit the profile of white Protestant dissenters from the Church of England. Until the civil rights movements of the twentieth century, in fact, claims for American exceptionalism, meaning ordinary people's unusual economic prosperity and equality under the laws, were really opportunities often open only to white men. British North America and the early United States, in their restraints of gender, race, and caste that denied rights to women, Native peoples, and African Americans, resembled most other areas of European colonial conquest and settlement. Critics of American treatment of native peoples and of slavery, in fact, considered claims of exceptionalism ironic, not authentic. The Seneca Indian Handsome Lake (1735–1815), for example, inverted Euro-Americans' explanation of "How America Was Discovered" and argued that the devil, not God, had sent them to the New World (Madsen 1998, 47). The British writer Samuel Johnson (1709–1784) asked memorably, "How is it that we hear the loudest yelps for liberty among drivers of negroes?" (Hodgson 2010, 60). And on Independence Day 1852, the abolitionist Frederick Douglass (c. 1818–1895), a former slave, asked plaintively, "What to the slave is the Fourth of July?" (Edwards and Weiss 2011, 130). These historical critiques have informed recent arguments against American exceptionalism.

Nonetheless, promoters of immigration and settlement such as Benjamin Franklin (1706–1790) described America as a place of boundless economic opportunity for those willing to work, regardless of their ethnic and religious backgrounds. Franklin, a "self-made man," illustrated the promise of success implicit in the "American Dream," a phrase coined by the writer James Truslow Adams (1878–1949), and, until recently, a synonym for exceptionalism implying the likely, but peculiar, chances for prosperity for ordinary Americans, both native born and immigrant (Adams 1931, 317).

In the late eighteenth century, and partly under Franklin's influence, America's unique economic purpose took the form of a radically new political arrangement when thirteen of the British colonies united and fought for independence from England. These colonists asserted ideas of the English philosopher John Locke (1632–1704), particularly natural rights to liberty and property—"pursuit of happiness" in the Declaration of Independence—which British colonialism jeopardized. Most radically of all, Thomas Jefferson (1743–1826), the Declaration's main author, asserted that, following the American example, all people have a right of revolution against tyranny.

Subsequent revolutionaries, including Czech peoples during World War I, Vietnamese people at the conclusion of World War II, and even white Rhodesians in the 1960s, used Jefferson's language to assert independence from imperial government. Anticipating this modern reverberation, radical pamphleteers of the American Revolution argued that global destiny hinged on Americans' fate in their colonial rebellion, establishing it as an unprecedented event in human history. In the pamphlet *Common Sense*, Thomas Paine (1737–1809), like the Puritans earlier in New England, described America as the world's asylum. But while American Puritans demanded religious fidelity among a community of saints, and drove out or made war on nonconformists, for Paine America was for anyone who loved liberty and hated kings.

EARLY NINETEENTH TO MID-TWENTIETH CENTURIES

Following the Revolution, American exceptionalism took on a political connotation, highlighting the new nation's unique form of government and ability to maintain stability. Both of these achievements were secured by dramatic expansion of territory in the nineteenth century and projection of global military and cultural power in the twentieth. In the early twentieth century and again in the early twenty-first, in fact, critics of the idea of American exceptionalism argued that such American expansion and power made the United States into an empire, little different from the historical empires of ancient and modern Europe.

Advocates of exceptionalism, however, keen to distinguish the country especially from Europe (even as American relations and conflicts in other areas of the world, especially Asia, became more important) emphasized not only the development of republican government, but also the nature of American expansion—it allegedly occurred in "empty space," that is, areas not heavily populated. Exceptionalists thus understood US growth west of the Mississippi River during the mid-nineteenth century, and of overseas territories at the turn of the twentieth century, not as military conquests but as anticolonial fact-finding missions in support of peaceful annexation. Beginning with the Corps of Discovery expedition across the Louisiana Territory from 1804 to 1806, the practice was established of benign incorporation of territory into the American sphere in order to transplant democratic institutions.

In 1839, the journalist John L. O'Sullivan (1813–1895) wrote of America as "destined to manifest to mankind the excellence of divine principles," coining what is now known as *manifest destiny* (McDougall 1997, 77). O'Sullivan predicted that the United States would overspread the Western Hemisphere with republicanism, thus civilizing it with locally elected government and encouragement of global trade. This method of empire—in Jefferson's phrase, an "empire for liberty"—distinguished the American way from European cutthroat imperialism and colonial exploitation in India, the Caribbean, and Africa (McDougall 1997, 83).

An analogous argument developed during the Cold War, when Americans competed for developing world allies and engaged in a space race with the Soviet Union. President John Kennedy (1917–1963) advocated the space program not to achieve or reflect US defeat of the Soviet Union but simply because "the moon and planets are there, and new hopes for knowledge and peace are there" (Kennedy 1962). For American exceptionalists, if the post–World War II United States was an empire, it was an empire by invitation, not, as in the Soviet bloc, by imposition. Indeed, between the two superpowers, the United States was often, if hardly always, the stronger supporter of human rights, bolstering equation of exceptionalism with superiority.

AMERICAN INVOLVEMENT IN FOREIGN WARS

Meanwhile, the memory of the American Revolution's accomplishment of a federal republic, without excessive violence that destroyed property or collapsed separation of church and state, shaped Americans' often critical judgments of foreign upheavals. Other revolutionary places, including, over time, France, Haiti, Latin America, Habsburg Europe, Mexico, Russia, China, and postcolonial Africa and the Middle East, proclaimed popular government but then failed to implement democratic institutions and fell into chaos or dictatorship. Thus, from the early nineteenth to the mid-twentieth centuries, the meaning of exceptionalism emphasized the *unique* case of American revolutionaries—stressing that their accomplishment could not be replicated overseas—more than the *universalist* message of the revolutionary era, welcoming the American Revolution's reverberation and global replication. This interpretation dampened Americans' interest in intervening abroad to help political upheavals, effectively enacting the early warnings of presidents George Washington (1732–1799) and Jefferson against foreign entanglements.

Americans have waged foreign wars, of course, but in accordance with exceptionalist ideology, US military action has often been justified as liberation of others from tyrannical government or backward cultural practices, and not ending in permanent occupation or colonization. In calling for US entry into World War I, President Woodrow Wilson (1856–1924) abjured all material compensation and welcomed the "sacrifices we shall freely make" to make the world "safe for democracy" (Wilson 1917). Thus American expansion or projection of force was selfless not selfish, and in accordance with manifest destiny, ordained by God. This argument emerged in the US-Mexico War of 1846 to 1848, and was reiterated intermittently thereafter. During the Spanish-American-Filipino War and then the Vietnam War, for example, supporters of American exceptionalism opposed nationalist resistance movements led by Emilio Aguinaldo (1869–1964) and Ho Chi Minh (1890–1969) as a rejection of Americans' sacrifices to defend civilization. This attitude, to critics, showed the hypocrisy of exceptionalist claims: American origins in popular revolution were an important justification for policy makers' assertion of the country's unique global role, yet during the twentieth century the United States often opposed popular revolutions in the developing world.

TWENTY-FIRST CENTURY

Both of the first US presidents of the twenty-first century came to trumpet American exceptionalism. Before his election, President George W. Bush (b. 1946) disavowed any US mission for foreign nation building. Yet in response to the September 11, 2001, terrorist attacks, the Bush administration launched the Iraq War in 2003, in the president's words, to "spread the peace that freedom brings" and, echoing the Puritans, as his generation's step on "the road of providence" (Bush 2005). Likewise, President Barack Obama (b. 1961) in 2009 dismissed American exceptionalism as no different from other countries' similar claims, but in 2013 urged US intervention in war-torn Syria as a prerogative of American exceptionalism, especially a tradition of humanitarian use of force. In 2015, it remained unclear whether Bush's and Obama's exceptionalist justifications of US disinterested power signaled the concept's last hurrah in US policy making—Congress rejected Obama's appeal for Syrian intervention—or its persistence.

Outside the White House, however, by the early twenty-first century the meaning of American exceptionalism had lost complexity and, perhaps as a result, credibility. In the colonial and revolutionary eras, exceptionalism implied American exclusion from ordinary historical patterns of corruption and dangers presented by foreign conflicts and peoples. From the early nineteenth to the mid-twentieth centuries, this meaning existed alongside a second interpretation, which was that the United States could expand, in both immigrant population as well as distant territories, without jeopardizing either its own institutions or the fate of other peoples. During the Cold War and thereafter, exceptionalism took on the more controversial meaning of equation with and justification for military intervention.

SEE ALSO *Colonialism; Empire of Liberty*

BIBLIOGRAPHY

Adams, James Truslow. *Epic of America.* Boston: Little, Brown, 1931.

Armitage, David. *The Declaration of Independence: A Global History.* Cambridge, MA: Harvard University Press, 2007.

Bender, Thomas. *Nation among Nations: America's Place in World History.* New York: Hill and Wang, 2006.

Bush, George. "Address before a Joint Session of the Congress on the State of the Union." February 2, 2005. The American Presidency Project. http://www.presidency.ucsb.edu/ws/?pid=58746

Davis, David Brion. *Revolutions: Reflections on American Equality and Foreign Liberations.* Cambridge, MA: Harvard University Press, 1990.

Edwards, Jason A., and David Weiss, eds. *Rhetoric of American Exceptionalism: Critical Essays.* Jefferson, NC: McFarland, 2011.

Gaddis, John Lewis. *We Now Know: Rethinking Cold War History.* Oxford: Oxford University Press, 1997.

Greene, Jack P. *The Intellectual Construction of America: Exceptionalism and Identity from 1492 to 1800.* Chapel Hill: University of North Carolina Press, 1993.

Hietala, Thomas R. *Manifest Design: American Exceptionalism and Empire.* Rev. ed. Ithaca, NY: Cornell University Press, 2003.

Hodgson, Godfrey. *Myth of American Exceptionalism.* New Haven, CT: Yale University Press, 2010.

Ignatieff, Michael, ed. *American Exceptionalism and Human Rights.* Princeton, NJ: Princeton University Press, 2005.

Kammen, Michael. *Season of Youth: The American Revolution and the Historical Imaginative.* Ithaca, NY: Cornell University Press, 1988.

Kammen, Michael. "Problem of American Exceptionalism: A Reconsideration." *American Quarterly* 45 (1993): 1–43.

Kennedy, John. Address at Rice University, Houston, Texas. September 12, 1962. Presidential Papers, President's Office Files, Speech Files. http://www.jfklibrary.org/Asset-Viewer/Archives/JFKPOF-040-001.aspx

Lipset, Seymour. *American Exceptionalism: A Double-Edged Sword.* New York: Norton, 1996.

Lovestone, Jay. *American Labor Movement: Its Past Present and Future.* New York: Workers Age, 1932.

Madsen, Deborah. *American Exceptionalism.* Jackson: University Press of Mississippi, 1998.

McDougall, Walter. *Promised Land, Crusader State: The American Encounter with the World since 1776.* New York: Houghton Mifflin, 1997.

McEvoy-Levy, Siobhán. *American Exceptionalism and U.S. Foreign Policy: Public Diplomacy at the End of the Cold War.* New York: Palgrave Macmillan, 2001.

Ninkovich, Frank. *Global Republic: America's Inadvertent Rise to World Power.* Chicago: University of Chicago Press, 2014.

Roberts, Timothy M. *Distant Revolutions: 1848 and the Challenge to American Exceptionalism.* Charlottesville: University of Virginia Press, 2009.

Schuck, Peter H., and James Q. Wilson, eds. *Understanding America: The Anatomy of an Exceptional Nation*. New York: PublicAffairs, 2008.

Tocqueville, Alexis de. *Democracy in America*. 2 vols. Translated by Henry Reeve. New York: Langley, 1840.

Tyrrell, Ian. "American Exceptionalism in an Age of International History." *American Historical Review* 96 (1991): 1031–1055.

Wilentz, Sean. "Against Exceptionalism: Class Consciousness and the American Labor Movement, 1790–1920." *International Labor and Working Class History* 26 (Fall 1984): 1–24.

Wilson, Woodrow. Joint Address to Congress Leading to a Declaration of War against Germany. April 2, 1917. Records of the US Senate, Record Group 46, National Archives. http://www.ourdocuments.gov/doc.php?doc=61

Winthrop, John. "A Model of Christian Charity" (1630). In *Puritans in America: A Narrative Anthology*, edited by Alan Heimert and Andrew Delbanco, 81–92. Cambridge, MA: Harvard University Press, 1985.

Timothy M. Roberts
Associate Professor, Department of History
Western Illinois University

EXPATRIATE ARTISTS

At the beginning of the nineteenth century, America was a young nation, still forging its identity and establishing its place in the world. Its days of war and conflict were far from over; much of the country was still undeveloped, major cities were just taking shape, and cultural institutions were in their early stages of conception. As a result, Americans had little access to information about or imagery of Europe beyond that which was available in travel guides. This lack of information was often supplemented by overly romanticized literary accounts. The presentation of such destinations as Spain, Italy, and England framed them as classical, exotic, culturally superior, and full of rich history that one must experience. Many guidebooks of the time also featured similarly exaggerated accounts of these places. Americans began to consider visits to Europe as essential to a complete understanding of the world as a whole; Rome, for example, was seen as a cautionary tale for the young American nation. Rome was a vast, powerful empire brought to an end as a result of internal conflict. The US has often been compared to Rome as it became a powerful nation in relatively little time; what happened in Rome was an example of what not to do.

THE LURE OF EUROPE

The absence of cultural institutions and lack of accurate accounts ensured a limited knowledge of events happening around the world. News of innovations and developments reached American shores sometimes as much as a decade later, as was the case with the arrival of impressionism. As a result, many American artists and writers sought to bolster their knowledge, experience, and exposure by traveling abroad. This journey across the Atlantic afforded them the opportunity to experience firsthand the avant-garde art scene of Paris, to interact with the English writers, to travel to exotic locales in Spain and northern Africa. For Americans, Europe was the epicenter of fine arts, history, and refinement. Indeed, accomplished nations were born in Europe, and the histories of the countries on the European continent were long and rich, spanning hundreds if not thousands of years. In comparison, America seemed infantile and uncivilized.

Artists and writers of early America often received informal, if any, training in their field. Many of them learned from family members or through years of independent study. For colonial artists in particular, publications containing prints, drawings, and other reproductions frequently served as a source of style and technique. As a child and a young artist, John Singleton Copley (1738–1815) regularly observed his stepfather, an engraver making mezzotint plates, and Copley methodically copied images from encyclopedias.

For some artists, such as Copley, the value of study abroad was obvious but impractical. For others, such as Benjamin West (1738–1820), their greatest training and ultimate success was found while traveling and ultimately residing in London and Rome, which at the time served as major art centers in Europe. West was the first American to travel to Italy for the purpose of studying art. It was there that he gained what was likely his first exposure to old masters and ancient civilization. Though travel to Europe for the purpose of personal and professional improvement seemed essential, it was out of reach for most Americans. The cost of such a trip was, by contemporary standards, extraordinary and afforded only to those of substantial means. As the century progressed, the practice of sponsorship emerged as a viable option for those without independent financial resources. In these arrangements, a person of more abundant means—often a patron—financially supported the artist or writer while he or she lived and studied abroad.

The practice of going abroad for professional enrichment was certainly known early in the nineteenth century, but it did not reach its peak until after the Civil War (1861–1865). It was at this time that Americans traveled to Europe in droves to experience the ever-more modern climate of such cities as Düsseldorf and Rome. Many of the great American artistic and literary figures of this time were born abroad, while others were born in America and traveled with their families, as was the case for Henry James and Mary Cassatt.

Portrait of the novelist Henry James, by John Singer Sargent (1913). *Many of the great American artistic and literary figures of the late nineteenth and early twentieth centuries were born abroad, while others were born in America and traveled extensively or took up residence abroad. Both Sargent and James considered themselves Americans but saw Europe as offering the greatest chance for artistic success.* APIC/HULTON FINE ART COLLECTION/GETTY IMAGES

HENRY JAMES

Henry James (1843–1916), born in New York City, spent the majority of his childhood traveling extensively throughout Europe with his father and brothers. They returned to America for relatively short periods throughout his youth, but all of his formal education was conducted in Europe. His return to America as a young adult was difficult for him; while his father and other siblings found themselves well suited to the change, James is reported to have felt uncomfortable and restless in a place that seemed foreign to him. By the 1870s, James had permanently settled in London, where he would remain until his death in 1916. For Henry James, America was a restrictive environment that did not allow him to reach his full potential as a writer. He saw Americans as incapable of appreciating truly great literary work. James felt stifled in New York and longed to be back in Europe in the world of literary greats like Charles Dickens (1812–1870). He saw America as a place where American artists went to die, an escape to Europe was their only means of salvation.

MARY CASSATT

Mary Cassatt (1844–1926), born in Pennsylvania, traveled with her family to Europe as a young child. Although her early exposure was more limited than that of James, she did receive a great deal of her education during her time abroad. Her early art training took place in Philadelphia at the Pennsylvania Academy of Art, but the method of art instruction in America, based on the study of plaster casts, left her discontented. In 1866 she decided to continue her studies in Paris, where she would have access to live models, as well as collections of important artworks by such artists as Diego Velázquez (1599–1660) and Frans Hals (1580–1666), considered essential to the mastery of the art of painting. While in Paris, she studied privately under the artist Jean-Léon Gérôme (1824–1904) because the École des Beaux-Arts did not yet admit women. Yet Paris afforded Cassatt a climate much less restrictive for women, which allowed her to study painting with almost complete freedom. She was not confined to working only with other women, but was free to employ models outside of her family and to study the nude body.

Cassatt began to work closely with the impressionists, befriending Edgar Degas (1834–1917) and taking much influence from him. She is the only American to formally align herself with the impressionists and is in this regard the first American impressionist. During this time in Paris, the influence of Japanese wood-block prints became widespread and can be seen in the work of many artists living and working in Paris—Cassatt was no exception. This firsthand exposure to Japonisme would not have been possible had she remained in America. Indeed, this element is absent from much of the work of the American impressionists of the late nineteenth century, which consists largely of landscape scenes.

Rather than return home, Cassatt remained in Paris through the end of her life. She saw Paris as a place where she could experience the rapidly changing world of art in real time, with relative freedom, rather than the disconnected and shielded experience she would surely have had in America.

JOHN SINGER SARGENT

In contrast to James and Cassatt, John Singer Sargent (1856–1925) was born in Florence, Italy, to American parents but spent his entire childhood in Europe, visiting America for the first time when he was twenty years old. The entirety of his art training took place in Europe. In Paris, he studied under the painter Carolus-Duran

(1837–1917), who encouraged his students to travel and study great works of art in person. As a result, Sargent traveled to Spain, Italy, and North Africa to copy artworks in museums and to observe local culture. His work is unique in that it combines influences from a wide array of sources, all synthesized into a style that is unmistakably Sargent's. The beginning of his professional life as an artist was spent in Paris, where he had free access to avant-garde circles, the tradition of the Paris Salon, and important collections of artworks. Sargent, like Cassatt and James, considered himself an American but recognized that Europe was the place that offered the greatest chance for success.

THOMAS EAKINS

Reconstruction-era America was much less focused on supporting the arts than it was on rebuilding a nation destroyed by the Civil War. The social issues plaguing America during this time created a harsh and restrictive climate for artists and writers who wished to push the boundaries of tradition. Consider, for example, the work of Thomas Eakins (1844–1916), who was born in Philadelphia, educated in Paris, and studied the masters of Spanish painting before returning to America to live and work. When he returned home, his work reflected his experience. He painted scenes that were unconventional in the tradition of American painting and often not well received. A well-known example is Eakins's *The Gross Clinic* (1875, Jefferson Medical College of Thomas Jefferson University, Philadelphia), an impeccable work that was considered gruesome and inappropriate for viewing by the general public because of its depiction of blood. This work was directly influenced by Rembrandt (1606–1669), but this connection was neither understood nor appreciated by the American public.

Furthermore, Eakins struggled both with his employer and with tradition over his theories concerning the study of the human form and his belief that an understanding of and access to the human figure were a necessary part of an artist's basic training. By contrast, Sargent's adaptation of the techniques of such artists as Velázquez was both appreciated and admired, such that Sargent became one of the foremost society painters not only in Paris and London but in America as well.

CONCLUSION

James, Cassatt, and Sargent, among others, felt that living and working in Europe was essential to their success, and that they would not have been given the same freedoms to explore and develop had they remained in or returned to America. The great lack of access to cultural resources, coupled with the tumultuous postwar climate, created an environment not conducive to the opportunities desired by artists and writers of the time. It was a common assumption among artistic and literary circles that everyday Americans could not appreciate great works and lacked the taste and refinement of the European public. These groups were harshly outspoken in their criticisms of Americans, and they often felt out of place among their own countrymen. It was for this reason that many of them made the journey across the Atlantic to a climate more suited to their ambitions and desire for professional growth and exploration.

SEE ALSO *Copley, John Singleton; Crowe, Eyre; Europe; Grand Tour; West, Benjamin*

BIBLIOGRAPHY

Bardazzi, Francesca. "American Forever." In *Americans in Florence: Sargent and the American Impressionists*, edited by Francesca Bardazzi and Carlo Sisi, 20–43. Venice, Italy: Marsilio, 2011.

Cantor, Jay E. *Beyond Native Shores: A Widening View of American Art, 1850–1975.* New York: Adelson Galleries, 2003.

Craven, Wayne. *American Art: History and Culture.* Boston: McGraw-Hill, 2003.

Earnest, Ernest P. *Expatriates and Patriots: American Artists, Scholars, and Writers in Europe.* Durham, NC: Duke University Press, 1968.

Evans, Dorinda. *Benjamin West and His American Students.* Washington, DC: Smithsonian Instiution Press, 1980.

McGuigan, Mary K. "'This Market of Physiognomy': American Artists and Rome's Art Academies, Life Schools, and Models, 1825–1870." In *America's Rome: Artists in the Eternal City, 1800–1900*, edited by Paul S. D'Ambrosio, 39–72. Cooperstown, NY: Fenimore Art Museum, 2009.

Vance, William L. "America's Rome." In *America's Rome: Artists in the Eternal City, 1800–1900*, edited by Paul S. D'Ambrosio, 9–38. Cooperstown, NY: Fenimore Art Museum, 2009.

Stephanie W. Kowalczyk
Instructor
Kent State University

EXPORTS, EXPORTATION

The terms *exports* and *exportation* refer to the shipping of goods and services out of a country to an import destination. American exports became a major element of the global economy in the late nineteenth century, although the United States was not yet the world's major trade power. The country had focused much more attention on imports, and thus had protected itself behind tariff walls (both to aid infant industries and as a source of revenue). In the 1890s, launching a trend that exists to this day, the United States became the world's most dynamic trader of exported goods.

Even though the value of British and German exports exceeded those of the United States before World War I, because America traded in primary, semiprocessed, and industrial goods by 1910, its diversity overcame the dominance of the two European nations, which imported raw materials and exported manufactures. This Americanization capitalized on the growing interdependence of the Atlantic world and continued into the next century as well. European consumers fell in love with US inventions—typewriters, sewing machines, phonographs, automobiles (including peripherals such as tires, provided by the Firestone and Harvey/American Rubber companies), telephones, elevators, and incandescent lights. The US reputation for mass-produced consumer exports was well deserved, as overseas buyers looked to this colossus for state-of-the-art technology and quality products. The "Made in America" label meant affordable, high-value goods.

The substance and means of this export boom revealed the diversity, and power, of the American presence abroad. For instance, the Baldwin Locomotive Works, a capital goods firm, symbolized speed and progress, American-style. In 1900, the company exported an average of one engine a day, shipping to South America, Africa, Asia, Australia, and Europe. As Baldwins sped across the Argentine Pampas or hauled freight on the Trans-Siberian Express, they—and the United States—became known for strength and dynamism. American companies also exported materials to Uganda to build railroad bridges and rails to construct the Cape-to-Cairo Railway that boosted British trade in Africa.

Some Europeans worried about the Americanization of the world, but clearly, much of Europe was soon dependent on US products for everyday use—safety razors from Connecticut, corsets from Illinois, and bacon from Kansas City. Americans drew on a maturing patent system to retain rights to these goods, but also built and benefited from emerging, expanding, and sophisticated transportation (the Panama Canal) and communications (transatlantic cable) to market and ship US exports. Especially British restrictions on trade competition provoked American business complaints, but concerted export promotion by US manufacturing associations and the rising power of transnational, private traders (rather than government-sponsored exporters) boosted trade abroad.

While the Great Depression and World War II dramatically slowed trade, new institutional structures to govern trade and finance—the World Bank and International Monetary Fund and the General Agreement on Tariffs and Trade (and ultimately, the World Trade Organization)—led to a surge in exports (both American and worldwide) in the postwar period and the era of modern-day globalization. An internationalist, open-door foreign policy that turned America away from isolationism, joined by trade liberalization and lower tariffs, regional integration of national economies, and legal norms and practices encouraged an export boom.

Decades later, these and other products—blue jeans, computers, airplanes, Disney Worlds, and insurance and banking services—would add to the American export powerhouse. Many of these were cultural exports, which were critical elements in the American export dynamo. World's fairs showed millions of people the ingenuity and affordability of American export goods. Improvements in transportation had facilitated exports of entertainment. For instance, Buffalo Bill Cody took his popular Wild West Show to London after the Civil War. In the twentieth century, American films flooded Europe, perpetuating stereotypes of cowboys and Indians, and then later promoting a youth culture. With heightened migration of people arose "exports" of American brides, married to European diplomats and aristocrats, which gave rise to further fears of Americanization of societies abroad.

To avoid barriers to trade after World War II in the face of European (particularly French) protests of Americanization as such competitive exporters as Firestone tried to break into markets by offering discounts, US multinationals invested in overseas plants to circumvent tariff walls. Soon Americans would face severe competition of their own, as European and Asian exporters, such as Germany, Japan, and China, turned the historic US trade surplus into a deficit in 1971. Since then, the government has tried to boost exports, which have reached nearly 14 percent of gross domestic product in recent times, up from an average of 3.5 percent from 1920 to 1970.

SEE ALSO *Americanization; Barnum, P. T.; Buffalo Bill's Wild West; Exceptionalism; Firestone Tire and Rubber Company; Ford, Henry; Hollywood; Industrialization; Internationalism; Isolationism; Singer Manufacturing Company; Tariff; World's Fairs*

BIBLIOGRAPHY

Dür, Andreas. *Protection for Exporters: Power and Discrimination in Transatlantic Trade Relations, 1930–2010.* Ithaca, NY: Cornell University Press, 2010.

Eckes, Alfred E., Jr., and Thomas W. Zeiler. *Globalization and the American Century.* Cambridge: Cambridge University Press, 2003.

Topik, Steven C., and Allen Wells. "Commodity Chains in a Global Economy." In *A World Connecting, 1870–1945,* edited by Emily S. Rosenberg. Cambridge, MA: Belknap Press of Harvard University, 2012.

Zeiler, Thomas W. "Opening Doors in the World Economy." In *Global Interdependence: The World after 1945*, edited by Akira Iriye. Cambridge, MA: Belknap Press of Harvard University, 2014.

Thomas W. Zeiler
Professor of History
University of Colorado Boulder

EXTRATERRITORIALITY

Understood in its broadest terms, *extraterritoriality* refers to an exemption from local law that is enjoyed by particular persons or nationalities as they travel abroad. Typically, this privileged status is granted through a process of diplomatic negotiation, and spelled out in the terms of a treaty. And while extraterritoriality is often depicted as a nineteenth-century phenomenon—and even then, almost always in the context of Western imperialism in China—the concept has a much longer history. Beginning with the ancient Mediterranean world (most thoroughly codified by the Roman Empire), there have been myriad examples of local sovereigns granting certain legal exemptions to foreign merchants and diplomats as a means to facilitate trade and forestall the erosion of indigenous cultural practices.

And yet, when later communities of European and American colonizers claimed that their own extraterritorial rights were rooted in long-standing precedent, they could do so only disingenuously. Earlier versions of extraterritorial privileges were less often imposed than granted, more often voluntarily conjured than militarily mandated. By the time the nineteenth century rolled around, the exemption from native law enjoyed by white sojourners in China and other places was, unlike preceding models, buttressed by gunboats, virtually irrevocable, and not in any way reciprocal. And, more importantly, "modern" extraterritoriality (or *extrality*, as it was known at the time) was rooted in a racialized worldview characteristic of post-Enlightenment romantic-nationalist discourse. The world's nonwhite races (and non-Christian people), this logic went, were demonstrably "inferior" and thus unfit for entrance into the community of "civilized" nations. As such, no member of the superior white race could be expected to suffer prosecution and punishment at the hands of people thought to lack the capacity for reason, considered intellectually unequipped to understand concepts like law or due process, and so fundamentally incapable of meting out justice. Nineteenth-century extraterritorial legal theory was, therefore, both a reinforcing mechanism of and a rationale for racism.

Americans abroad during the nineteenth century tended to enjoy immunity from local justice as a result of what is known as *hitchhiking imperialism*. Typically, some more powerful European state would militarily extract extraterritorial privileges for its subjects, and the United States would quickly negotiate similar exemptions for its own citizens. This was certainly the case in China, which, while not the only place where Americans exercised extrality, was arguably the most significant for the scope of privileges claimed by Euro-American sojourners. As a result of decisive British victory in the First Opium War (1839–1842), the largely "closed" society of China was forcibly opened, with extraterritorial rights a key provision of the 1842 peace negotiations. American diplomats, in the Treaty of Wangxia (ratified in 1845), quickly snatched matching concessions for themselves. By the terms of that agreement, US citizens in China could only be tried by American consular or military officers. Chinese litigants bringing suit against Americans, meanwhile, would be forced to do so in so-called mixed courts containing both local and foreign judges. This was only the first in what were a series of "unequal treaties" that, over the course of the nineteenth century, gradually carved up the Chinese Empire into a series of colonial spheres of influence that enjoyed practical sovereignty from Qing authority. For many, this created the impression that foreign nationals could effectively elude punishment for crimes committed overseas.

But while it is difficult to understate the ways in which extraterritoriality came to symbolize for Chinese nationalists and communist revolutionaries alike the abject humiliation of their country, it is also useful to acknowledge that it was more than a tool designed to facilitate the imperialistic domination of another people. Indeed, studies of courtrooms run by American diplomats in China (what later became the "US Court for China," an appendage of the Justice Department's Ninth Circuit) reveal that the preponderance of cases involved the punishment of poor, working-class US citizens for vagrancy, drunkenness, gambling, and prostitution. These extraterritorial courts, in other words, were used not so much to dominate "lesser races" as to corral and control the "lower sort" of Americans whose rowdy behavior jeopardized both business interests and the national image overseas. Indeed, "progressive" American imperialists argued that the extraterritorial courtroom would be a tool of uplift: by punishing rapacious citizens, it preserved order within China, thus assuring the continued survival of the Qing state and, by extension, an East Asian market for US goods. It was designed to demonstrate for pro-Western Chinese the virtues of American jurisprudence, which, in turn, might inspire internal reform within China.

But even if extrality was not a blunt tool of imperial domination (as it can be caricatured), nor was it the righteous instrument its defenders imagined. Simply put, more and more people overseas came to see themselves as victims of a fundamentally unequal international legal system, one which in turn seemed to give free rein to invading armies of foreign capitalists and missionaries. The former used legal cover to extract resources and abuse native workers, while the latter hid behind extraterritoriality to promulgate what indigenous authorities often described as heretical doctrines. Nationalist movements in China and around the world fixated on extraterritoriality not only as degrading in and of itself, but also for the further abuses that system had helped facilitate. By the late 1950s, the US State Department, bowing to shifting international mores, had closed the last of its extraterritorial courts—those in Morocco and Tangier. But the issue would not disappear. Even to this day, protests against various status-of-forces agreements between the United States and foreign governments, which exempt American military personnel from local law enforcement, channel that same resentment against a potentially abusive imperial instrument.

SEE ALSO *Foreign Mission Movement; Passport*

BIBLIOGRAPHY

Cassel, Pär Kristoffer. *Grounds of Judgment: Extraterritoriality and Imperial Power in Nineteenth-Century China and Japan.* Oxford: Oxford University Press, 2012.

Ruskola, Teemu. *Legal Orientalism: China, the United States, and Modern Law.* Cambridge, MA: Harvard University Press, 2013.

Scully, Eileen P. *Bargaining with the State from Afar: American Citizenship in Treaty Port China, 1844–1942.* New York: Columbia University Press, 2001.

Brian Rouleau
Assistant Professor of History
Texas A&M University

F

FAR EAST

SEE *Orientalism.*

FEDERAL COUNCIL OF CHURCHES

Few institutions have demonstrated the interlinking of American nationalism and internationalism better than have ecumenical Christian organizations like the Federal Council of Churches (FCC). The FCC was born in 1908 out of decades of Protestant cooperation in foreign and home missions. Its thirty-three member denominations formed the vital center of what was termed the "new home missions," a movement to engineer vibrant Christian personalities through the restructuring of rural and urban-industrial environments. FCC objectives traversed familiar categories of foreign and domestic. "United and concerted actions" were needed, according to one initial planning meeting, "if the Church is to lead effectively in the conquest of the world for Christ" (Cavert 1968, 42).

FROM THE SOCIAL GOSPEL TO CHRISTIAN INTERNATIONALISM

The FCC's social gospel message reflected a transatlantic progressive outlook. The organization's widely circulated *Social Creed of the Churches* (1908) wedded state welfare policies emanating from England and Germany to a homespun moral establishment informed by social scientific expertise. Ecumenical Protestants' outreach to the working class mirrored that of their friends overseas in the British Forward Movement and Wesleyan Methodist Union for Social Service. The FCC preached "equal rights" for the American working classes secured through collective bargaining and federal regulations. Its pleas for more comprehensive social service, however, also underscored armies of Christian middle-class women reforming urban "delinquents," Americanization policies for new immigrants, and Prohibition. FCC faith in class control would frustrate younger churchmen like H. Richard Niebuhr (1894–1962) and Reinhold Niebuhr (1892–1971). They instead joined mentors Sherwood Eddy (1871–1963), Harry F. Ward (1873–1966), and other FCC veterans in searching for a more radical social Christianity. Through their leadership, FCC circles became both receptacles for and disseminators of the British Labour Party's democratic socialism.

World War I (1914–1918), meanwhile, drew the ecumenical American churches out into the borderless realms of Christian internationalism. The FCC partnered with the Andrew Carnegie–funded Church Peace Union from its start and worked through its own Commission on International Justice and Goodwill to "abolish war" (Cavert 1968, 58). FCC churches were crucial supporters of American entry into World War I for the same reasons that most progressives were: because they saw it as an opportunity to build a more just and peaceful world. Initial postwar setbacks did not discourage FCC leaders from picturing a global ecumenical community through new and old Protestant networks like the Universal Conference on Life and Work, the International Missionary Council, and the World's Student Christian Federation (WSCF).

Burgeoning Christian internationalism coincided with mainstream Anglo-American internationalism, including grassroots Protestant support for global disarmament, for the United States to join the Permanent Court of International Justice, and for the movement to outlaw war. Internationalist engagement also stimulated new domestic FCC projects in interfaith cooperation and rural rehabilitation everywhere from Texas and Arkansas to Puerto Rico and Alaska. Armed with the conviction that "the spirit of Christian brotherliness can remove every unjust barrier of trade, color, creed and race," the overwhelmingly white FCC churches and leadership created their first Commission on Race Relations in 1921 and began sponsoring "Race Relations Sundays" (Cavert 1970, 175). Ecumenical Americans would not fully embrace transnational over transatlantic alliances until after World War II (1939–1945). Still, interwar Christian internationalism challenged the very Anglo-Saxon exceptionalism it had emanated from.

TOWARD A WORLD CHRISTIAN COMMUNITY DURING THE 1930s

The FCC's universal nationalist spirit matured in response to the specter of global totalitarianism. Franklin Roosevelt (1882–1945) endorsed the American ecumenical churches for their bearing of the progressive cross after World War I when he confessed that he was "as radical as the Federal Council of Churches" (Cavert 1968, 143). The FCC, like the president, faced constant attack from anticommunist, pro-business sectors for its support for Social Security, public works, and the modernization programs of the Tennessee Valley Authority and National Resources Planning Board. Yet while most FCC leaders and churches applauded parts of the New Deal, several feared the whole of its bureaucratic machinery.

This subtle fracture helps explain the FCC's later attraction to nonstatist radicalism, such as the Social Credit program of British social Christians, or to the international "Kingdom of God" cooperative movement led by Japanese evangelist Toyohiko Kagawa (1888–1960). Fascist advances also fueled the "trifaith" endeavors of the National Conference of Christians and Jews (later the National Conference for Community and Justice), formed by FCC members and Jewish affiliates in 1928 and with branches in more than one hundred cities ten years later. Christian nationalism still trumped interreligious civil religion, though, as the FCC labored to shore up Western Protestant culture through mass evangelistic campaigns like the National Christian Mission (1937), the University Christian Mission (1938), and new military chaplaincy programs.

The FCC's championship of world ecumenism further revealed its amalgam of internationalist solidarity and Protestant tribalism. It was no accident that the FCC's executive secretary, Samuel McCrea Cavert (1888–1976), was one of the founders of the Yale-based Theological Discussion Group (1933), an offshoot of the WSCF that included America's best and brightest ecumenical minds, including the Niebuhrs and Paul Tillich (1886–1965). Cavert and other members ensured that the FCC would play a decisive role in determining the shape and scope of a World Council of Churches (WCC)—Cavert even bragged that he coined the name. Theological Discussion Group members teamed with British ecumenical leaders at the 1937 Oxford Conference on Life and Work to launch the WCC-in-Formation a year later. Oxford attendees followed Reinhold Niebuhr and others in identifying fascism as the first fruit of failed secular age.

While ecumenical Protestants in America and in the WCC co-opted traditionally Roman Catholic universalism—Cavert called Theological Discussion Group members "Evangelical Catholics" (Edwards 2012, 55)—they still resented and resisted supposed papal encroachment on their spiritual territories. FCC personnel helped block multiple presidential attempts to appoint an ambassador to the Vatican, and ecumenical Protestants more generally endorsed Paul Blanshard's (1892–1980) liberal anti-Catholic treatise, *American Freedom and Catholic Power* (1949). At its inaugural meeting in 1948, the WCC would toast Cavert and the FCC for their pioneering work in global Christian union. The "World Christian Community" imagined at Oxford would nevertheless struggle to live up to its name until at least Vatican II (1962–1965).

THE FCC'S WAR FOR HUMAN RIGHTS

By that time, the FCC's greatest internationalist accomplishments—and indeed the FCC itself—had largely been forgotten. During World War II, FCC concerns moved seamlessly between evangelistic and humanitarian endeavors, ranging from the Christian Commission for Camp and Defense Communities to the Church Committee on Overseas Relief and Reconstruction. That latter group would be superseded in 1946 by the Church World Service, the largest international Protestant relief agency of the era (although its work has been supplanted today by the conservative evangelical-based World Vision). The FCC also took a bolder stand for civil rights in response to the racial violence of World War II. Ecumenical Christians were outspoken critics of Japanese American internment and helped resettle victims after the camps closed. Following the lead of African American churches, the FCC finally confronted Jim Crow wisdom directly. A 1948 report, *The Church and Human Rights*, argued that segregation was "a violation of the Gospel" (Cavert 1970, 158). Acting as guardians of the free world at home, many FCC churches helped to advance postwar open housing and colorblind employment movements.

The title of the 1948 report pointed to the ecumenical community's wish to expand democratic governance at home as well as globally. During the war, the FCC leadership eschewed pacifism for international organization, as reflected in their Just and Durable Peace Commission. Chaired by John Foster Dulles (1888–1959), the committee produced several statements on behalf of the United Nations, anticolonialism, development, demilitarization, and religious liberty—which included a widely circulated *Six Pillars of Peace* pamphlet reflecting and rivaling similar Vatican publications. If all that the Dulles Commission could hope for in light of growing Soviet-American tensions was a "just endurable peace" (H. Richard Niebuhr's quip), ecumenical Christians such as O. Frederick Nolde (1899–1972) would still take pride in their helping to draft the United Nations' Universal Declaration of Human Rights (1948). Nolde and American associates enjoyed privileged access to the United Nations and the US State Department as agents of the WCC-affiliated think tank, the Commission of the Churches on International Affairs.

BECOMING THE NATIONAL COUNCIL OF CHURCHES

The FCC finally merged with longtime home missions partners in 1950 to form an ecumenical powerhouse, the National Council of Churches (NCC). The FCC's universal nationalism lived on in the new organization, as its leaders boasted of "building a Christian America in a Christian world" (Barstow et al. 1951, 143). Ecumenical alumni feared that the NCC would abandon the FCC's "prophetic" ministry for technocratic efficiency. Yet it was precisely the NCC's bold, interrelated stances on the Vietnam and culture wars that led many Protestant laity to give up on the ecumenical dream of a united liberal America. The several remaining voices of cooperative Christianity—as the historic products as well as shapers of American internationalism—are hard to hear in a resiliently anti-internationalist evangelical age.

SEE ALSO *Carnegie Endowment for International Peace; Catholicism; Cold War; Hague Conferences (1899, 1907); Jewish Welfare Board; Judaism; Knights of Columbus; Protestantism; Religions; Secularization; World War I; World War II; World's YWCA/YMCA*

BIBLIOGRAPHY

Barstow, Robins W., Luther Wesley Smith, and Norman E. Tompkins, eds. *Christian Faith in Action: Commemorative Volume: The Founding of the National Council of Churches in Christ in the United States of America.* New York: NCCC, 1951.

Burnidge, Cara. *A Peaceful Conquest: Woodrow Wilson, the League of Nations, and the Great War of the Protestant Establishment.* Chicago: University of Chicago Press, forthcoming.

Cavert, Samuel McCrea. *The American Churches in the Ecumenical Movement, 1900–1968.* New York: Association Press, 1968.

Cavert, Samuel McCrea. *Church Cooperation and Unity in America: A Historical Review, 1900–1970.* New York: Association Press, 1970.

Edwards, Mark Thomas. *The Right of the Protestant Left: God's Totalitarianism.* New York: Palgrave Macmillan, 2012.

Gill, Jill K. *Embattled Ecumenism: The National Council of Churches, the Vietnam War, and the Trials of the Protestant Left.* DeKalb: Northern Illinois University Press, 2011.

Gorman, Daniel. *The Emergence of International Society in the 1920s.* New York: Cambridge University Press, 2012.

Hollinger, David A. *After Cloven Tongues of Fire: Protestant Liberalism in Modern American History.* Princeton, NJ: Princeton University Press, 2013.

Nurser, John S. *For All Peoples and All Nations: The Ecumenical Church and Human Rights.* Washington, DC: Georgetown University Press, 2005.

Phillips, Paul T. *A Kingdom on Earth: Anglo-American Social Christianity, 1880–1940.* University Park: Penn State University Press, 1996.

Preston, Andrew. *Sword of the Spirit, Shield of Faith: Religion in American War and Diplomacy.* New York: Knopf, 2012.

Rodgers, Daniel T. *Atlantic Crossings: Social Politics in a Progressive Age.* Cambridge, MA: Belknap Press, 1998.

Schultz, Kevin. *Tri-Faith America: How Catholics and Jews Held Postwar America to Its Protestant Promise.* New York: Oxford University Press, 2011.

Sluga, Glenda. *Internationalism in the Age of Nationalism.* Philadelphia: University of Pennsylvania Press, 2013.

Thompson, Michael G. *For God and Globe: Christian Internationalism in the United States between the Great War and the Cold War.* Ithaca, NY: Cornell University Press, 2015.

Warren, Heather A. *Theologians of a New World Order: Reinhold Niebuhr and the Christian Realists, 1920–1948.* New York: Oxford University Press, 2015.

Zubovich, Gene. "The Global Gospel: Protestant Internationalism and American Liberalism, 1940–1960." PhD diss., University of California, Berkeley, 2014.

Mark Edwards
Associate Professor, History
Spring Arbor University

THE FEMININE MYSTIQUE (BETTY FRIEDAN, 1963)

First published in 1963, *The Feminine Mystique* by Betty Friedan (1921–2006) has been heralded as a foundational text of the US "second-wave" women's movement in the 1960s and 1970s. The book is central to the "liberal feminist" branch of thought and activism that emphasized women's economic, legal, and political equality. In the wildly popular text, Friedan criticized the idea that women were naturally fulfilled by devoting their lives to being housewives and mothers, an idea she termed the "feminine mystique." The book analyzes the roots of the feminine mystique in popular and scientific thought, explains its negative impact on women, and argues that meaningful work is vital to women's fulfillment. The conditions Friedan describes most closely resembled the lives of educated middle-class women, the group that was the book's largest readership and the most visible segment of US second-wave feminism.

The book and the gender roles it challenged were rooted in the particular global location of the United States in the 1960s. The post–World War II ideology, economy, and built environment gave rise to the experiences of Friedan and her female readers. Specifically, the baby boom, the development of massive suburbs, and economic development based on the manufacturing of consumer goods fueled the concentration of white, middle-class women in homogenous suburbs isolated from employment. The Cold War also played a role. A former socialist labor journalist, Friedan sought refuge from anticommunism and Red-baiting in suburban motherhood. As biographer Daniel Horowitz remarks, "The feminine mystique may also have been a coded phrase for what else was capturing America—the fear of atomic war, Cold War suspicion, and, most immediately, McCarthyism" (Horowitz 1998, 244).

Given that *The Feminist Mystique* was written for and about educated women, the book has been most popular in countries where large numbers of middle-class women are full-time homemakers. In Australia, for example, *The Feminine Mystique* had a substantial effect on women and was a foundational text in the formation of a liberal branch of feminism. It also influenced a large number of liberal men concerned about women's issues, including Pope John XXIII (1881–1963). His 1963 encyclical *Pacem in terris* endorses the central argument in *The Feminine Mystique* that women need the opportunity to develop their talents and contribute to the wider community.

Although the book was widely available in Western Europe, its influence was eclipsed by the large outpouring of European feminist thought and the dominance of socialist feminism. In Spain, however, *The Feminine Mystique* was very influential. One of the first international ideological books allowed after decades of Francoist censorship, it was quickly translated into Spanish, Catalan, and Galician. Despite the differences in the context of women's lives, the book was so well received that a version adapted to the Catalan reality was commissioned. Although the political context prohibited the development of a strong feminist movement, the book is credited with fostering a change in consciousness and the development of a feminist perspective in Spain.

Friedan emerged as one of the most visible leaders of US second-wave feminism, and one of its most frequent targets. In Latin America, *The Feminist Mystique* was critiqued as exemplifying an imperialist brand of feminism that isolated women's issues from larger struggles for justice. Such criticism found a global audience at the United Nations' 1975 International Women's Year Conference in Mexico City. One of the founders of the National Organization for Women (NOW), Friedan secured consultative status for the organization, which enabled her to play a leadership role in the nongovernmental organization tribune accompanying the official meetings. In a conference characterized by tensions between "Third World women" focused on structural inequalities and "Western feminists" focusing on sex-specific issues, such as reproductive rights and women's employment, Friedan became almost a caricature of the West. She was even attacked for the feminist focus on sexual rights and lesbianism, emphases opposed by Friedan and not discussed in *The Feminine Mystique* (Olcott 2010, 739).

More recent criticism has highlighted problems stemming from the emphasis placed by *The Feminine Mystique*—and by American liberal feminism in general—on women becoming self-sufficient through employment. As neoliberal globalization has advanced through the very low-wage employment of women and ideologies of individual self-sufficiency, critics have pointed out the use of Friedan's ideas to legitimate, if not support, this transition. Hester Eisenstein, for example, calls Friedan's brand of feminism "the handmaiden to capitalism" (Eisenstein 2005, 511).

SEE ALSO *Feminism, Women's Rights; International Women's Year (IWY), 1975*

BIBLIOGRAPHY

Eisenstein, Hester. "A Dangerous Liaison? Feminism and Corporate Globalization." *Science and Society* 69, 3 (2005): 487–518.

Friedan, Betty. *The Feminine Mystique.* New York: Norton, 1963.

Godayol, Pilar. "Three Feminist Classics in Catalan, Galician, and Spanish: Charlotte Perkins Gilman, Virginia Woolf, and Betty Friedan." *Women's Studies International Forum* 42 (January–February 2014): 77–86.

Horowitz, Daniel. *Betty Friedan and the Making of* The Feminine Mystique*: The American Left, the Cold War, and Modern Feminism.* Amherst: University of Massachusetts Press, 1998.

McGrath, Sophie. "Vatican II and Feminism." *Compass* 47, 3 (2013): 9–13.

Olcott, Jocelyn. "Cold War Conflicts and Cheap Cabaret: Sexual Politics at the 1975 United Nations International Women's Year Conference." *Gender and History* 22, 3 (2010): 733–754.

Doreen J. Mattingly
Associate Professor, Department of Women's Studies
San Diego State University

FEMINISM, WOMEN'S RIGHTS

US feminism and campaigns for women's rights have been among the most self-consciously transnational social movements in the country's history. Many scholars refer to US feminism in the plural—feminisms—because of its many strands and incarnations that since the eighteenth century have drawn inspiration and support from allies abroad. Indeed, the very term *feminism* is generally credited to the French utopian socialist Charles Fourier (1772–1837), whose ideas inspired communities in the early nineteenth-century United States; to Fourier and his acolytes, women's status served as a metric of more general social progress. Over the past two and a half centuries, US feminism has found expression through many social movements and intellectual engagements with ties beyond the United States, including liberalism, socialism, utopianism, pacifism, anti-imperialism, antislavery, temperance, labor rights, and civil rights. Early nineteenth-century US suffragists looked to late eighteenth-century writers such as Mary Wollstonecraft (1759–1797) and Olympe de Gouges (1748–1793), who in turn had been galvanized as much by abolition efforts as by revolutions in France and the Americas to establish citizenship rights. Other strands of US feminism have emerged from struggles for labor rights, social justice, family rights, and sexual liberation. Although different iterations of feminism have held sway in different contexts, this polysemy has contributed to the durability and elasticity of US feminism.

The role of US feminism in the world in many ways has followed the arc of US influence more generally: emerging in the late nineteenth century, increasing in a more aggressive fashion during the first decades of the twentieth century, peaking during the decades after World War II, and on the defensive in the wake of decolonization. US feminist movements during these phases have been alternately—even simultaneously—admired and resented but rarely ignored. Through friendships and organizations, the women who populated these movements often maintained ties to like-minded activists around the world.

EMERGENCE IN NINETEENTH-CENTURY SOCIAL MOVEMENTS

As the historian Bonnie Anderson (2000) has demonstrated, feminist movements and women's rights movements more generally were born out of internationalism—emerging from the socialist, antislavery, and free-congregation movements of the early nineteenth century. Suffragists Elizabeth Cady Stanton (1815–1902) and Lucretia Mott (1793–1880), for example, met at the 1840 Anti-Slavery Society Convention in London, which notoriously sidelined women participants, and formed part of a network of women who kept in close contact via letters and then telegraph. When they organized the Seneca Falls Convention eight years later, the resulting declaration appropriated the language of the US Declaration of Independence, but the speeches drew inspiration from the revolutionary movements that had spread throughout Europe that spring and fostered Karl Marx and Friedrich Engels's *Communist Manifesto* (1848). Like the earlier revolutionary moment that had inspired Wollstonecraft and de Gouges, the upheaval that brought barricades to Europe and Civil War to the United States still left women without voting rights.

When the United States finally granted full citizenship rights to former male slaves with the ratification of the Fourteenth and Fifteenth Amendments to the US Constitution but did not extend voting rights to women, prominent women among the abolitionists expressed bitter disappointment. Women like Stanton, Susan B. Anthony (1820–1906), and Sojourner Truth (c. 1797–1883) insisted that the amendments should include women, and the failure of these efforts generated a lasting rift that drove some feminists to establish organizations focused more squarely on women's rights—particularly suffrage rights—as well as other issues that generally came under the umbrella of family and social welfare.

The latter decades of the nineteenth century witnessed the creation of a handful of what would become important and enduring international women's organizations in which US women had substantial influence. The International Council of Women (ICW), founded in 1888, emerged directly from the split over the citizenship amendments, as Stanton and Anthony built a network of Anglophone and Western European women focused on women's reform issues, including suffrage. The World Woman's Christian Temperance Union, founded in 1891, had its origins in Ohio and exemplified both the missionary impulses shared by many international women's organizations as well as the effort to link core issues (such as temperance) to broader concerns such as suffrage, living wages, and pacifism. Similarly, the World Young Women's Christian Association, founded in 1894 by a coalition of British, Canadian, Western European, and US national YWCAs, served as a vehicle for many progressive US women to connect social reform with Christian values.

THE SUFFRAGE MOVEMENT

In 1904, frustrated by these diffuse efforts and desiring an international organization more squarely focused on securing women's voting rights, the US suffragist Carrie Chapman Catt (1859–1947) helped found the International Woman Suffrage Alliance (later renamed the International Alliance of Women) as a breakaway group from the ICW. While pacifist and antiwar campaigns had figured prominently in all these organizations, the outbreak of World War I in 1914 galvanized women to create an international peace network. The prominent US reformer Jane Addams (1860–1935) presided over a 1915 congress in The Hague that created the International Committee of Women for Permanent Peace (later renamed the Women's International League for Peace and Freedom, or WILPF) with the US pacifist Emily Greene Balch (1867–1961) as its secretary. As the historian Leila Rupp (1997) has pointed out, WILPF was the first of these women's organizations that was born international and created national chapters, rather than assembling national chapters into an international organization.

Following the success of the US suffragist movement with the passage of the Nineteenth Amendment in 1920, leaders from the US women's movement stepped up their missionary zeal in promoting women's suffrage and women's rights around the world and particularly in the Americas, through organizations such as the Inter-American

Alice Paul* (left)*, an American, conferring with English members of the newly formed International Advisory Committee of the National Woman's Party at the American Women's Club of London, 1925. *Following the success of the US suffragist movement with the passage of the Nineteenth Amendment in 1920, leaders from the US women's movement continued to advocate globally for political, economic, and social equality for women.* UNIVERSAL HISTORY ARCHIVE/GETTY IMAGES

Commission of Women, a subsidiary of the Pan-American Union, presided over initially by the US suffragist Doris Stevens (1892–1963). While many Latin American suffragists welcomed solidarity from US women, they also resisted efforts to impose a particular women's agenda and expressed dismay that the granting of women's suffrage in the United States seemed to have done little to curb US imperialism in Latin America and the Caribbean.

THE POST–WORLD WAR II FEMINISM AND DECOLONIZATION

Following World War II, a new women's international organization, the Women's International Democratic Federation (WIDF), was founded in response to US policies. Established in Paris in December 1945, the WIDF founders cited the devastation of Hiroshima and Nagasaki as inspiration for its campaign for disarmament and an end to colonialism. The US State Department persistently sought to marginalize the organization, denying visas for WIDF representatives to attend United Nations sessions, for example. In 1949, the House Un-American Activities Committee attacked the WIDF's US affiliate, the Congress of American Women founded by Susan B. Anthony II (1916–1991), the grandniece of the famous suffragist. The publication of Simone de Beauvoir's *The Second Sex* that same year would launch what is often called second-wave feminism, inspiring US authors such as Betty Friedan (1921–2006) and Kate Millett (b. 1934).

Organizations such as the WIDF spoke more directly to emerging connections between the US civil rights movement and campaigns for national liberation and decolonization that erupted throughout the world in the decades following World War II. Both within and outside the United States, many women questioned the universalist claims of the established women's organizations and influential thinkers, claims that rested on assumptions that all women shared a core set of perspectives and experiences. US women of color—many of whom came to call themselves "Third World women"—sought alliances with like-minded women from Asia, Africa, and Latin America who similarly experienced exclusion and oppression along lines of race and class, as well as sex. By the 1970s, organizations such as the Third World Women's Alliance had begun to shape debates within US feminist circles more broadly. If feminist debates of the late nineteenth century bore the imprint of global concern with industrialization and the "social question," those of the late twentieth century returned their attention to the legacies of imperialism, slavery, and white supremacy.

A new generation of US feminists, who had come of age politically amid racist violence and deepening US involvement in Vietnam, were inspired to seek alliances with women around the world and returned to many of the concerns that had animated feminist thinkers and activists since the late eighteenth century. They made common cause with human rights campaigns in Latin America and antiapartheid efforts in South Africa. Efforts to control their own sexuality, reproduction, and family formations loomed large in women's activism both in the United States and abroad. Socialist feminists drew attention to the ways that capitalist modes of production particularly exploited women's labor, including their unpaid household labor. The women's liberation movement, which inspired similar movements as far away as Australia and as close as Mexico, sought to completely upend conventional power structures through consciousness-raising sessions, decentered and antihierarchical configurations of authority, and the privileging of experience over expertise. Its mantra, "The personal is political," gained traction in diverse settings throughout the world as women in widely disparate circumstances examined the structural and political aspects of what they has previously seen as their personal or intimate forms of oppression. Many of the ideas and practices that came out of women's liberation took on lives of their own as they took root in new settings. The anthropologist Kathy Davis (2007) has shown, for example, how the widely read women's liberationist text, *Our Bodies, Ourselves*, first published in the United States in 1970, was translated and adapted to women's health practices around the world.

The decentered nature of this movement generally makes it impossible to determine where exchanges across borders originated. In an example of the feminist cosmopolitanism that characterized such campaigns, the Brooklyn-born Selma James, who had lived in Trinidad for many years before returning to London, paired up with the Italian feminist Mariarosa Dalla Costa to launch the Wages for Housework campaign, which found followers in the United States and beyond. By the 1970s, societies around the world had developed some expression of the term *double shift* or *double day* to describe the compounded burden of women's commodified and uncommodified labors. While one strain of feminism in the United States—often dubbed *liberal feminism*—stressed the importance of women gaining educational and professional opportunities, many women in the United States and beyond questioned why the substantial skills and labor that they already performed did not garner greater recognition and support.

As had been the case in the early decades of the twentieth century, advances in reproductive technologies and concerns about global population growth made strange bedfellows of feminists, who sought women's control of their own fertility, and population-control advocates concerned about fertility among poorer (and often darker) populations. The alliance frayed, however, as news surfaced of both government and private-sector support for forced sterilizations and mandatory birth control both in the United States and abroad, often with the blessing (and funding) of the same organizations advocating for abortion and contraception rights. While women around the world launched their own efforts to decriminalize abortion and gain access to birth control, many also rejected the implication that only wealthy women had the right to have children.

GRASSROOTS COSMOPOLITANS

The United Nations (UN) Decade for Women (1975–1985) fostered countless networks and organizations that strengthened ties among geographically separated like-minded women. Transnational organizations—often sponsored by nongovernmental organizations (NGOs) based in the United States or northern Europe—mobilized around not only long-standing "women's issues," such as reproductive control and political rights, but also around issues such as environmental justice, antinuclear proliferation, and economic development. In many ways, these newer organizations resembled the late nineteenth-century organizations, with their mingling of women-specific concerns and broader questions of social justice. However, technological developments and the geopolitical transformation brought by decolonization meant that these new-model NGOs enjoyed much more diverse membership and leadership and consequently took up a broader array of issues from more locally rooted perspectives.

While the UN Decade for Women intensified contact among diverse groups of women, it also set in relief the differences that still divided women's movements. When an international group of lesbians organized a solidarity demonstration during the first UN Women's Conference in 1975 in Mexico City, for example, many participants saw demands for sexual rights as a distraction from other concerns. Concomitantly, as ethnic studies and postcolonial studies took root in US academies, more feminist intellectuals pointed to the radical heterogeneity—even impossibility—of womanhood. These thinkers and writers highlighted the ways in which widely held US feminist ideas often rested upon the presumption that all other cultures and societies should seek to emulate the United States. The philosopher Uma Narayan (1997) points out that, even amid this growing self-awareness, US feminists often ignored domestic violence rates in the United States and focused instead on what she calls "death by culture" in places like Africa, South Asia, and Latin America.

Such positions highlight the ambivalent embrace of US feminism around the world by the 1980s. While many women's organizations applauded US feminists' deconstruction of gender essentialism, they deployed what critical theorist Gayatri Spivak famously dubbed "strategic essentialism" to claim particular feminine authority on issues that had galvanized women's organizations for nearly two centuries—issues such as war, food security, environmental degradation, state violence, and the protection of women and children from labor abuses. French feminists countered with the development of a school of feminist thought more deeply rooted in psychoanalytic theory and stressing gender difference. Latin American feminists, who had successfully used maternalist arguments to challenge dictatorships throughout the region, selectively took up the ideas of US-based feminist theorists who described gender as infinitely malleable and contingent. Women throughout the Third World challenged the idea that women's concerns could be separated out from larger social and economic issues.

The decades since the UN's world conferences of women—the Mexico City conference was followed by those in Copenhagen (1980), Nairobi (1985), and Beijing (1995)—have witnessed dramatic changes in the US role in geopolitics, and the influence of US feminism in the world has followed a similar trajectory. The ideal of a "global sisterhood"—most explicitly articulated by US feminist Robin Morgan—has given way to the recognition that US feminism reflects not universalism but rather particular historical and cultural contingencies. As transnational networks grew over these decades, US feminists increasingly recognized the specificities of their own perspectives as they built networks with allies around the world. This radical diversification of the US women's movement—bringing into contact activists and intellectuals from increasingly disparate backgrounds—transformed its role both inside and outside the United States from one in which women's concerns were known in advance to one that reflected the political and social struggles of a particular time and place.

SEE ALSO *The Feminine Mystique (Betty Friedan, 1963); Gender; International Women's Year (IWY), 1975; New Woman; Paul, Alice Stokes; Roosevelt, Eleanor; Rosie the Riveter; Suffrage; Wollstonecraft, Mary*

BIBLIOGRAPHY

Anderson, Bonnie S. *Joyous Greetings: The First International Women's Movement, 1830–1860.* New York: Oxford University Press, 2000.

Basu, Amrita. *The Challenge of Local Feminisms: Women's Movements in Global Perspective.* Boulder, CO: Westview Press, 1995.

Berkovitch, Nitza. *From Motherhood to Citizenship: Women's Rights and International Organizations.* Baltimore, MD: Johns Hopkins University Press, 1999.

Bolt, Christine. *Sisterhood Questioned? Race, Class, and Internationalism in the American and British Women's Movements, c. 1880s–1970s.* London and New York: Routledge, 2004.

Cott, Nancy F. *The Grounding of Modern Feminism*. New Haven, CT: Yale University Press, 1987.

Davis, Kathy. *The Making of* Our Bodies, Ourselves*: How Feminism Travels across Borders*. Durham, NC: Duke University Press Books, 2007.

Fernandes, Leela. *Transnational Feminism in the United States: Knowledge, Ethics, and Power*. New York: New York University Press, 2013.

Ferree, Myra Marx, and Aili Mari Tripp. *Global Feminism: Transnational Women's Activism, Organizing, and Human Rights*. New York: New York University Press, 2006.

Freedman, Estelle B. *No Turning Back: The History of Feminism and the Future of Women*. New York: Ballantine, 2002.

Garner, Karen. *Shaping a Global Women's Agenda: Women's NGOs and Global Governance, 1925–85*. Manchester, UK: Manchester University Press, 2010.

Kaplan, Temma. *Crazy for Democracy: Women in Grassroots Movements*. New York: Routledge, 1997.

Margolis, Diane Rothbard. "Women's Movements around the World: Cross-Cultural Comparisons." *Gender and Society* 7, 3 (1993): 379–399.

McFadden, Margaret H. *Golden Cables of Sympathy: The Transatlantic Sources of Nineteenth-Century Feminism*. Lexington: University Press of Kentucky, 1999.

Moghadam, Valentine M. *Globalizing Women: Transnational Feminist Networks*. Baltimore, MD: Johns Hopkins University Press, 2005.

Mohanty, Chandra Talpade. *Feminism without Borders: Decolonizing Theory, Practicing Solidarity*. Durham, NC: Duke University Press, 2003.

Narayan, Uma. *Dislocating Cultures: Identities, Traditions, and Third World Feminism*. New York: Routledge, 1997.

Orleck, Annelise. *Rethinking American Women's Activism*. New York: Routledge, 2014.

Rupp, Leila J. *Worlds of Women: The Making of an International Women's Movement*. Princeton, NJ: Princeton University Press, 1997.

Thayer, Millie. "Transnational Feminism: Reading Joan Scott in the Brazilian *Sertão*." *Ethnography* 2, 2 (2001): 243–271.

Wu, Judy Tzu-Chun. *Radicals on the Road: Internationalism, Orientalism, and Feminism during the Vietnam Era*. Ithaca, NY: Cornell University Press, 2013.

Jocelyn Olcott
Associate Professor of History
Duke University

FENIAN BROTHERHOOD

The term *Fenians* was contemporaneously applied to members of both the Fenian Brotherhood, an Irish nationalist organization established in the United States in 1858 and the focus of this discussion, and the Irish Republican Brotherhood (IRB), its Ireland-based counterpart. Although the two groups together composed a transatlantic revolutionary movement that aimed to end British rule in Ireland, they did not always act in harmony. The Brotherhood was responsible for three serious raids on British North America from 1866 to 1870 and was a major factor in pushing for the 1867 Irish rebellion, which ended in failure.

FOUNDING AND SPREAD OF THE FENIAN BROTHERHOOD

The Fenian Brotherhood was founded at the end of a decade of mass migration prompted by the Great Famine. Experience of the famine sharpened anti-British sentiment among many Irish emigrants in the late 1840s and early 1850s and led to a strengthened nationalist movement in the United States. In addition, many early Brotherhood members, including John O'Mahony (1815–1877), the Brotherhood's first leader, had taken part in the failed Irish uprising of July 1848 and were convinced of the need to build an organizationally sophisticated, covert, Mazzinian nationalist movement. Historians have also suggested that a feeling of alienation among immigrant communities, vulnerable to nativist attacks, fuelled nationalist associational life in American cities.

Although there was less of a premium on secrecy in the United States than there was for the IRB, it is still hard to reach a precise assessment of the Fenians' numerical strength in the United States. Lists of active Fenian groups, or "circles," were often noted in newspapers and correspondence, although the composition of these circles was rarely elucidated. Whatever the number of actively engaged Fenians, it seems plausible to suggest that there were a great many more sympathizers outside the Brotherhood who attended public speeches, lectures, and picnics. The Brotherhood received additional moral and financial strength from various auxiliary groups that historians have described as a "Fenian sisterhood." Although clerical opposition worked against popular support among Irish American communities, its relative impact is hard to gauge; at any rate, it is highly likely that papal proscription had less impact in the United States than it did in Ireland.

The Brotherhood drew its strength from the major cities of the northern United States, although there were notable Fenian circles in the states of the Confederacy, too. Those in the North tended to view their Union service as consonant with their aspirations for Irish freedom, although those in the South were sometimes critical of the notion that one might support secession and national self-determination in an Irish context but deny those same principles in an American one. Although the Civil War undercut any hopes of a coordinated transatlantic movement in support of Irish revolution in the early 1860s, Union and Confederate army camps proved fertile recruitment grounds for the Brotherhood. In addition, service in the war provided military training and expertise for many who would go on to occupy prominent roles in the Brotherhood after the Civil War.

INTERNAL DIVISIONS AND DECLINE

The Fenian Brotherhood divided in late 1865 over two issues. First, there were internal concerns about O'Mahony's use of Fenian funds. Second, there was disagreement over the expediency of attacking British North America. Ironically, each resulting faction ended up launching its own northbound expeditions in 1866. Neither was successful, and money and effort directed at Canadian operations meant less time and attention spent on supporting operations in Ireland. Factionalism in the United States was mirrored in Ireland, where James Stephens (1824–1901) was eventually deposed as leader of the IRB in December 1866 after repeatedly failing to deliver the Irish uprising he had promised. By the time of that uprising, in spring 1867, the Fenian Brotherhood was already beginning to sputter out.

The extent of the US government's sympathy for the Fenian movement is debatable. The Anglophobic climate of the post–Civil War years undoubtedly encouraged Fenian leaders to believe that they would be supported by the American public at large. Politicians in both the Democratic and Republican Parties courted the Irish vote through expressions of sympathy with Irish nationalism, spurred as they were by the desire to buttress their support in the confused and conflicted political environment of Reconstruction. Assertions that the Fenians had secured a promise of support from President Andrew Johnson's (1808–1875) administration rest on very limited evidentiary foundations. By contrast, recent work by historian Peter Vronsky (2011) suggests that American authorities actively colluded with British officials in order to stymie the Brotherhood. In the abstract, the American public exhibited sympathy for Irish nationalist aspirations, and there were many who saw toleration of the Fenians as due revenge for the toleration of Confederate organizers on British soil during the Civil War. Sympathy was broader than it was deep, however, and few native commentators had positive things to say about the Brotherhood after its attempted raids on Canada.

An improvement in Anglo-American relations, symbolized by the successful arbitration of outstanding Civil War–era claims at Geneva in 1872, fostered an environment that was less sympathetic to Fenian activity. In addition, failures in Canada, persistent concerns about finance, and the good-faith efforts of the first Gladstone ministry (1868–1874) to address Irish discontent, led to a decline in the Brotherhood's stock. By the early 1870s, it had been largely superseded by the Clan na Gael as the primary North American organization advocating Irish revolution. At its founding, members of the Clan disavowed the Fenians' interest in Canada and emphasized the new organization's centralization and subservience to the needs of would-be revolutionaries in Ireland.

The Fenian Brotherhood's apparently quixotic existence continues to attract scholarly attention, but it is important not to overstate its significance. The Brotherhood's brief vitality illustrates the tensions of the Anglo-American relationship in the years following the end of the Civil War, the fluidity of Reconstruction-era US politics, and contemporary assumptions about British North America.

SEE ALSO *Anglophobia; Atlantic Ocean; Europe; Great Famine; Nativism; Transatlantic Reform*

BIBLIOGRAPHY

Devoy, John. *Recollections of an Irish Rebel.* [1929.] Shannon, Ireland: Irish University Press, 1969.

Gleeson, David T. *The Irish in the South, 1815–1877.* Chapel Hill: University of North Carolina Press, 2001.

Jenkins, Brian. *Fenians and Anglo-American Relations during Reconstruction.* Ithaca, NY: Cornell University Press, 1969.

Miller, Kerby. *Emigrants and Exiles: Ireland and the Irish Exodus to North America.* New York: Oxford University Press, 1985.

Sim, David. *A Union Forever: The Irish Question and U.S. Foreign Relations in the Victorian Age.* Ithaca, NY: Cornell University Press, 2013.

Steward, Patrick, and Bryan McGovern. *The Fenians: Irish Rebellion in the North Atlantic World, 1858–1876.* Knoxville: University of Tennessee Press, 2013.

Vronsky, Peter. *Ridgeway: The American Fenian Invasion and the 1866 Battle That Made Canada.* Toronto: Allen Lane Canada, 2011.

Wilson, David A. *Thomas D'Arcy McGee.* 2 vols. Montreal, Quebec: McGill-Queen's University Press, 2008–2011.

David Sim
Lecturer in US History
University College, London

FERDINAND, ARCHDUKE FRANCIS

SEE *World War I.*

FILIBUSTER

In the Atlantic world during the 1850s, the noun/adjective/verb *filibuster* (spelled sometimes with two *l*'s) commonly denoted criminal private armed expeditions from the United States that invaded foreign territory, as well as the organizers of such enterprises. The term, derived from a Dutch word for "freebooters," came into common English-language usage immediately following the Mexican-American War (1846–1848), when several such armed parties left US soil for Mexico and Spain's colony of Cuba. However, filibustering antedated the term's coining, and the United States was by no means the only nation that incubated such plots.

Filibustering violated US and international law. Under the US Neutrality Act of 1818, persons implicated for organizing or participating in such affairs were punishable by fines of up to $3,000 and imprisonment for up to three years. US presidents enforced these strictures by issuing proclamations warning Americans against joining expeditions and by ordering US Army, Navy, and Revenue Cutter Service personnel to prevent filibusters from leaving US territory. Additionally, federal officials arrested and prosecuted suspected conspirators. In 1857 a US naval commodore, Hiram Paulding (1797–1878), even violated Nicaraguan sovereignty in deploying troops on its Caribbean coast to thwart an American filibuster landing. However, filibusters used secret codes and other subterfuges to elude detection prior to their departures, and some federal officers lacked enthusiasm for carrying out their antifilibuster instructions from Washington. Consequently, enough expeditions escaped interdiction to convince foreign and domestic critics alike that the invaders had covert federal support. Many observers charged that plans to extend America's borders by means of filibustering surrogates lay behind Washington's laxity in fulfilling its international responsibilities. This was the same period when the expansionist philosophy of manifest destiny—a belief that God specially favored America's territorial extension—gained traction in much of the United States, especially within the Democratic Party, one of the nation's major political organizations. That all Democratic presidents from the Mexican-American War to the American Civil War (1861–1865) had expansionist agendas gave fodder to suspicions that they encouraged or at least tolerated filibustering.

NUMBERS AND IMPACT

Because filibusters maintained few records, their total number during the 1850s remains indeterminate, though an estimate of between five thousand and ten thousand persons, including significant numbers of European and Cuban immigrants, seems reasonable for those conspirators actually leaving or attempting to leave US soil for foreign destinations. Most filibuster incursions abroad involved relatively small numbers of men, in the tens or hundreds. However, they had an impact out of proportion to their size. On several occasions, filibuster plots, rumors, and invasions so complicated American foreign relations that they risked entangling the US government in unwanted wars, especially with European powers with economic, strategic, or colonial interests in the Gulf-Caribbean basin. Significant disputes occurred between the United States and Spain over the execution and imprisonment of American filibusters captured near and on Cuban soil during the Narciso López (1797–1851) expeditions of 1850 to 1851 and over an anti-Spanish riot that erupted in New Orleans in 1851 in reaction to executions of captured American filibusters. Tensions complicated by Anglo-American competition for control of potential canal routes across Central America escalated between the United States and Great Britain in the mid-1850s when Royal Navy vessels interfered with US commercial vessels bearing filibusters to Central American shores.

Most filibuster attacks in the 1850s were perpetrated against Mexico, Cuba, and Central American states, though US filibusters were also engaged in Ecuador and were rumored to be planning incursions in such disparate places as Ireland, Canada, Haiti, the Dominican Republic, and the Hawaiian Islands. Earlier, in 1837 to 1838, several thousand American sympathizers crossed US borders with Lower and Upper Canada in support of the so-called Patriot uprisings there against British rule. Most filibuster expeditions failed, often with much loss of life, as was the case with the Henry A. Crabb (1823?–1857) expedition to Mexico in 1857 and López's landings in Cuba. However, the most infamous filibuster, the native Tennessean William Walker (1824–1860), achieved considerable if temporary success, holding Nicaragua's presidency from his inauguration in July 1856 after a manipulated election into the next year. Walker's conquests posed so serious a threat to other Central American states that they joined together with antifilibuster elements in Nicaragua in an alliance that expelled the so-called Gray-eyed man of destiny and his followers in the spring of 1857. Walker subsequently organized new invasion plots against Central America, claiming he remained Nicaragua's legitimate president. These efforts culminated with his execution by a Honduran firing squad on September 12, 1860, after a British naval officer took him and his accomplices into custody on Honduras's behalf.

FILIBUSTERS' MOTIVATION

Typically, American filibusters were motivated by hopes of adventure and financial gain from promised salaries, bonuses, and spoils of war. However, widely shared beliefs in the promise of American territorial expansion, the superiority of American governmental forms, and the racial and religious inferiority of supposedly benighted Catholic peoples of Latin America also helped foster the expeditions, as did residual Texan hatreds of Mexicans from the Texas Revolution of 1835 to 1836. Several plots, like the 1853–1855 aborted John A. Quitman (1799–1858) conspiracy to filibuster Cuba, originated in the desires of southern slaveholders to protect and spread slavery. Quitman—a slaveholding former governor of Mississippi—and his mostly southern collaborators shared fears that Spain, under British pressure, was on the verge of "Africanizing" Cuba by abolishing slavery there, which would make the island permanently undesirable to southern slaveholders. Walker legalized slavery in Nicaragua during his tenure there and gained support in the South after his expulsion by advocating the spread of slavery throughout Central America, including the subjugation of native peoples.

AFTER THE CIVIL WAR

US filibustering, which mostly subsided during the American Civil War, resumed with "Fenian" invasions into Canada in 1866, 1870, and 1871, as well as filibuster activity involving Cuba throughout the postwar decades and a number of inconsequential plots and invasions in the twentieth century. All the while, the word *filibustering* morphed into a term for legislative stalling, and the expeditions of the 1850s faded from the nation's collective historical memory. They left their greatest legacy in Central America, where suspicions long persisted that the US government fostered Walker's invasions and where the allied campaign in 1856 to 1857 to expel the filibusters is remembered as the region's "National War."

SEE ALSO *Manifest Destiny; Mexican-American War; South America*

BIBLIOGRAPHY

Brown, Charles H. *Agents of Manifest Destiny: The Lives and Times of the Filibusters.* Chapel Hill: University of North Carolina Press, 1980.

Greenberg, Amy S. *Manifest Manhood and the Antebellum American Empire.* New York: Cambridge University Press, 2005.

May, Robert E. *Manifest Destiny's Underworld: Filibustering in Antebellum America.* Chapel Hill: University of North Carolina Press, 2002.

Robert E. May
Professor of History
Purdue University

FIRESTONE TIRE AND RUBBER COMPANY

Harvey Firestone (1868–1938) founded the Firestone Tire and Rubber Company in 1900 in Akron, Ohio, where the company's major competitors were also based. At the time, the Dutch and British monopolized production of raw rubber, which requires a tropical climate to grow, in Southeast Asia. By 1915, America consumed approximately 70 percent of the world's raw rubber, which was vital to an industrialized economy. Firestone's son, Harvey Firestone Jr. (1898–1973), took over the company in the mid-1920s as the price of raw rubber was rising. In need of a raw rubber outlet of his own, he eventually found one in the sub-Saharan nation of Liberia.

Liberia was established in 1822 as a colony for freed American slaves by the paternalistic—if not outright racist—American Colonization Society, in the belief that integration into American society was futile. The so-called Americo-Liberians' "return" to Africa was physical rather than spiritual. Essentially ignoring Liberia's hinterland, Americo-Liberians formed and maintained a small, isolated English-speaking political cadre centered in the coastal capital, Monrovia, named for James Monroe (in office 1817–1825), the American president at the time of settlement. Liberia became an independent republic in 1847. Although American aid to the nation was sporadic until World War II (1939–1945), when Liberia gained strategic status because of its location and raw materials, Liberian elites fostered the notion of a "special relationship" with the United States.

At the same time that Firestone Jr. was searching for new raw rubber sources, Liberia was deeply in debt to Britain, which had already grabbed Liberian land for its colony Sierra Leone, and other colonial powers, and thus sought aid from the US government. Encouraged by the Warren G. Harding administration (1921–1923), Firestone stepped in, providing aid in exchange for extremely favorable terms for opening and operating a Firestone rubber plant in Liberia.

Mutually beneficial cooperation between Washington and Firestone deepened during World War II, with access to rubber critical to the Allied effort, and continued after the war. When President Harry Truman (in office 1945–1953) extended systematic aid to the developing world for the first time under his Point Four Program in 1949, he appointed Firestone Jr. as an adviser to the program.

At the time, Firestone was the only corporation contributing to Liberia's national revenue. Such relationships between American businessmen and the American government were common, as the former could often offer valuable insight into developing areas. This was certainly the case with Firestone and Liberia.

Americans, rather than the Liberian government, pushed for Liberian development. Firestone and the US government provided aid to native Liberians, including healthcare and sanitation, education, infrastructure, and communications. Although such improvements benefited Liberians, they also improved conditions for American extraction of strategic materials, spurred production, enticed further American investment, and created better living situations for American technicians.

Although Washington upheld Firestone as a bastion of development ideals for its work improving Liberian infrastructure, health, and sanitation, and increasing Liberia's trained manpower, the company was not free from the tarnish of racism and abuse. In the 1930s the scholar and civil rights activist W. E. B. Du Bois (1868–1963) and the National Association for the Advancement of Colored People (NAACP) lodged a complaint against Firestone for its low payments to the Liberian government under the terms negotiated with the help of the US government, the meager wages it paid to its employees, and the company's support of a "dictator king" who amassed wealth while doing nothing for ordinary Liberians. The State Department deflected the allegations. In the late 1950s the Liberian government, still heavily reliant on Firestone for internal revenue and still disinterested in Liberians outside of elite circles, charged the company and the American government with discrimination against Liberians. Such complaints, though not unfounded, were little more than posturing for more American aid by the Liberian government. Ultimately, the Firestone company's role in Liberian development trumped concerns over questions of monopolization, abuse of power, or racism by the governments of both the United States and Liberia. Firestone Jr. continued to be a key contact for those in Washington concerned with development in Africa.

The Firestone company remained the largest single employer in Liberia in the 1980s, when the exploitation of native Liberians by the Americo-Liberian minority led to a coup d'état. Nine years later another coup d'état led to a protracted civil war that was one of Africa's bloodiest. Firestone's facilities, purchased in 1988 by its rival Bridgestone—also founded in Akron, Ohio, but by then Japanese-owned—were ravaged. In 2005 the Liberian government stabilized, and in 2010 Firestone remained a major employer and contributor to Liberian government revenue. Although the company remained a major job provider at a time when unemployment remained at 75 percent, and continued investing in the development of Liberian infrastructure, health, and education, it also continued to face serious allegations of labor violations lodged by American- and Liberian-based organizations.

SEE ALSO *Americanization; Cold War; Exports, Exportation; Industrialization; World War I; World War II*

BIBLIOGRAPHY

Du Bois, W. E. B. "Liberia, the League and the United States." *Foreign Affairs* 11, 4 (1933): 682–695. https://www.foreignaffairs.com/articles/liberia/1933-07-01/liberia-league-and-united-states

Higgin, Hannah Nicole. "Disseminating American Ideals in Africa, 1949–1969." PhD diss., University of Cambridge, 2014.

Lee, Daniel E., and Elizabeth J. Lee. "Liberia and Firestone: A Case Study." In *Human Rights and the Ethics of Globalization*. New York: Cambridge University Press, 2010.

Marinelli, Lawrence A. "Liberia's Open Door Policy." *Journal of Modern African Studies* 2, 1 (1964): 91–98.

Tully, John. *The Devil's Milk: A Social History of Rubber*. New York: Monthly Review Press, 2011.

Hannah Nicole Higgin
History Faculty
University of Cambridge

FLU EPIDEMIC, 1918–1919

In 1918 a new and virulent strain of influenza circled the globe in pandemic form. Scholars continue to disagree about the time and location of its origins. Though misnamed the Spanish flu by contemporaries, many today identify a first wave of influenza that originated in the American Midwest in the early spring. With the nation at war, the illness passed largely unnoticed but soon emerged on the battlefields of Europe during World War I, likely carried there by American troops, and circulated through the late spring and summer. In late August, the pandemic exploded in its second and most deadly wave, striking on three continents simultaneously and soon infecting even the most isolated communities worldwide. As the war in Europe continued, soldiers on both sides of the conflict were soon stricken in massive numbers. A third wave followed in many regions, including the United States, in early 1919, and illness from influenza persisted in some areas into 1920, though the connection of these late deaths to the pandemic remains unclear.

THE PANDEMIC

Perhaps one in four people worldwide were sickened by pandemic influenza, with approximately 2.5 percent of those dying from the disease or its sequelae, yet mortality rates could vary even city to city. Though hard figures are impossible to reach due to the lack of data, scholars today suggest that between 50 million and 100 million people died, including between 2 million and 3 million in both Europe and Africa, and perhaps 1.5 million in the Americas. China may have suffered between 4 million and 9.5 million deaths, and India as many as 17 million. In comparison, World War I claimed roughly 16 million deaths. By the pandemic's end, over 25 million Americans, more than one-quarter of the nation's population, had suffered from the disease, and 675,000 had died, lowering life expectancy figures for 1918 in the United States by twelve years.

This was a shockingly new influenza virus. Patients suffered from some combination of very high fevers, significant pain in the muscles and joints, piercing headaches, coughing and difficulty breathing, delirium, unconsciousness, nosebleeds, and a discoloration of their face and extremities as their lungs filled with fluid. While many died from influenza, secondary infections, especially bacterial and viral pneumonia, also claimed many. Patients could sicken and die within hours, and in the United States the pandemic claimed nearly half of its victims in a brief month and a half. While seasonal influenza is generally fatal among the very young and the elderly, the 1918 pandemic claimed almost half of its victims in the United States among those between twenty and forty years of age, a pattern repeated worldwide.

With most soldiers in this age group as well, the prosecution of the war was disrupted by the pandemic, even as wartime conditions and the constant movement of troops facilitated the spread of the disease. Among soldiers, Germany likely suffered the greatest impact from influenza. Americans' greatest military engagement in Europe corresponded exactly with the pandemic's worst months, disrupting supply lines and sickening soldiers in shocking numbers at the front and also back home in training camps. While some 50,000 American soldiers died as a result of combat, the pandemic claimed 43,000.

THE AMERICAN RESPONSE

Americans initially faced the pandemic with confidence in the power of science to protect them. Recent developments in bacteriology, beginning in Europe in the mid-nineteenth century, had produced stunning successes in controlling many infectious diseases, such as cholera, diphtheria, and smallpox, and had fostered broad acceptance of germ theory and great optimism. Urban reform associated with Progressivism, too, produced a belief in the power of the state to improve Americans' lives. Though scientists worked desperately to identify the causal agent and to produce a vaccine during the pandemic, neither effort succeeded.

Though Progressivism had also facilitated the growth of the American public health movement, in 1918 public health structures were still limited. The US Public Health Service would offer guidance and the American Red Cross would play a substantial role in providing and coordinating human and material resources. Still, responses were largely determined and facilitated by local and state governments and health boards, the power of which varied dramatically. While some cities employed every tool available—offering extensive education, closing schools and public amusements, prohibiting public gatherings, requiring public masking, staggering work schedules, employing quarantines and vaccines, and prosecuting violations of these measures, for instance—other communities lacked the necessary public health infrastructure. Recent research makes clear that those communities that employed social distancing practices early in the pandemic fared best. In a rare concession to the pandemic, the October military draft call did not take place, though the Fourth Liberty Loan Drive continued as planned, worsening the scourge. Celebration of the war's end, too, interfered with efforts to control the disease's spread.

In many nations, including the United States, the war complicated health-care provision, with domestic medical and nursing personnel depleted by military service. Many communities created emergency hospitals and mobilized to aid the sick. But there was little physicians could offer beyond basic caregiving. Although the virus did not discriminate, American individuals and systems often did. Social identity shaped the experiences of patients and their families: poorer families faced the risk of destitution and homelessness when wage earners sickened; access to health care was sometimes shaped by economic status; and people of color faced a segregated health-care system that offered them only limited support during the emergency.

THE LONG-TERM IMPACT

Surprisingly, the catastrophe had little long-term impact in American public life. While in Canada the crisis contributed to the creation of the federal Department of Health in 1919, and in Britain to the Ministry of Health, in the United States the pandemic's mark was largely private. Though the pandemic lived on in the memories of those most affected by the crisis, the historian Alfred Crosby fittingly declared it *America's Forgotten Pandemic* (2003). Scholars have offered many theories for this public amnesia, including, for instance, the pandemic's sudden arrival and uncertain departure; its tendency to kill the young, rather than the leadership class; Americans' experience of it as a local rather than national event; the peacetime prosperity that followed; and its failure to create systemic or cultural change.

Perhaps most important among the explanations are two others. First, the pandemic's conflation with the war sped the process of forgetting. Though the pandemic's cost in lives for Americans was more than ten times that of battle deaths in the war, even during the height of the influenza crisis it was often overshadowed in the public sphere by international events. While the war would be remembered, the pandemic became a part of the war best forgotten, suggesting a second crucial explanation: the divergence between the nation's sense of itself and the experience of the influenza catastrophe. In a nation finding new power on the world stage, and embracing a public narrative of strength, progress, and promise for the future, the pandemic's story of helplessness and loss had little place.

SEE ALSO *Empire, US; Exceptionalism; Internationalism; Interventionism; Isolationism; League of Nations; Paris*

Peace Conference (1919); Treaty of Versailles; United Nations; World Health Organization; World War I

BIBLIOGRAPHY

Barry, John M. *The Great Influenza: The Story of the Deadliest Pandemic in History.* New York: Viking, 2004.

Bristow, Nancy K. *American Pandemic: The Lost Worlds of the 1918 Influenza Epidemic.* New York: Oxford University Press, 2012.

Byerly, Carol R. *Fever of War: The Influenza Epidemic in the U.S. Army during World War I.* New York: New York University Press, 2005.

Crosby, Alfred W. *America's Forgotten Pandemic: The Influenza of 1918.* 2nd ed. New York: Cambridge University Press, 2003.

"Influenza Pandemic in the United States." Suppl. 3, *Public Health Reports* 125 (2010): 1–144.

Johnson, Niall P. A. S., and Juergen Mueller. "Updating the Accounts: Global Mortality of the 1918–1920 'Spanish' Influenza Pandemic." *Bulletin of the History of Medicine* 76, 1 (2002): 105–115.

Markel, Howard, Harvey B. Lipman, J. Alexander Navarro, Alexandra Sloan, Joseph R. Michalsen, Alexendra Minna Stern, and Martin S. Cetron. "Nonpharmaceutical Interventions Implemented by US Cities during the 1918–1919 Influenza Pandemic." *Journal of the American Medical Association* 298, 6 (2007): 644–654.

Opdycke, Sandra. *The Flu Epidemic of 1918: America's Experience in the Global Health Crisis.* New York: Routledge, 2014.

University of Michigan Center for the History of Medicine. *Influenza Encyclopedia: The American Influenza Epidemic of 1918–1919: A Digital Encyclopedia.* http://www.influenzaarchive.org

Nancy K. Bristow
Professor of History
University of Puget Sound

FORD, GERALD R.

1913–2006

Gerald Rudolph Ford was a US congressman from Michigan, minority leader of the US House of Representatives, vice president of the United States, and president.

Ford was born on July 14, 1913, in Omaha, Nebraska, and was raised in Grand Rapids, Michigan. He flirted with isolationist tendencies as a young man but became a committed internationalist after serving as a naval officer during World War II. In 1948, he won a seat in Congress representing Michigan's Fifth District, and he became House minority leader in 1965. In 1973, after Vice President Spiro Agnew (1918–1996) resigned amid scandal, President Richard Nixon (1913–1994) nominated Ford to replace him. Ford served eight months as vice president. As the Watergate scandal consumed the White House, on August 9, 1974, Nixon resigned, making Ford the nation's first nonelected president.

ENERGY POLICY

In his 1975 State of the Union address, Ford proposed a tax cut to stimulate the recession-plagued economy. He also targeted another policy conundrum, the energy crisis. The problem's roots lay in price controls, which Congress and the Nixon administration had imposed to restrain inflation. But controls discouraged oil exploration and production and thereby created energy shortages. Ford's program proposed to end oil controls by May 1975, but Congress pushed back, fearing that higher oil prices would hurt consumers and exacerbate inflation. In December 1975 Ford signed the Energy Policy and Conservation Act (EPCA), which rolled back oil prices—the opposite of what he wanted—followed by phased decontrol over thirty-nine months. Although Ford considered vetoing it, EPCA contained provisions that made it palatable enough to approve, such as a strategic petroleum reserve, right-on-red traffic laws, and corporate average fuel economy (CAFE) standards for automakers.

INTERNATIONAL DIPLOMACY

Just as in energy policy, a reinvigorated Capitol Hill tried to assert itself in diplomacy, and Ford later lamented the "unfortunate encroachment by the Congress on foreign power action by the United States" (quoted in Mieczkowski 2005, 281). The Vietnam War's frenetic conclusion illustrated Ford's frustrations. In early 1975, as communist North Vietnam overran South Vietnam, Ford asked Congress for $722 million in economic and military aid to help the South resist a takeover. Congress rejected the request, and in April 1975 South Vietnam fell to the North. In what Ford later termed his presidency's saddest day, he ordered the evacuation of the US embassy in Saigon, and refugees streamed onto American aircraft carriers offshore. At home, Ford supported the entry of South Vietnamese refugees into the United States when they faced racism and fears of job competition from Americans who succumbed to xenophobic emotions. Ford's sympathy for the displaced South Vietnamese, press secretary Ron Nessen recalled, "was one of the best examples of moral leadership" during his presidency (quoted in Mieczkowski 2005, 294).

South Vietnam's collapse seemed to symbolize a worldwide retreat of American power. Smaller countries challenged US authority, and soon after South Vietnam's surrender, the Ford administration saw an opportunity to reassert strength. In May 1975, Cambodian pirates seized the US merchant ship *Mayaguez* and took its thirty-nine crew members hostage. Secretary of State Henry Kissinger argued that forceful action would boost America's world prestige, and Ford launched punitive air strikes against Cambodia and ordered US marines to storm an island where intelligence sources believed the crew was located. Forty-one Marines died during the operation, but in the end, the Cambodians released the *Mayaguez* crew unharmed.

Ford's attention to the Pacific reflected Asia's growing power and influence. In November 1974, he became the first president to visit Japan, and the following year, he became the second president to visit China. An advocate of personal diplomacy, Ford also enjoyed warm relations with European allies. In a May 1975 conclave outside Paris, he met with the leaders of France, Britain, Germany, Italy, and Japan, marking the first such meeting of America and its industrialized allies. In 1976 Ford hosted these leaders plus the Canadian prime minister in Puerto Rico for a G7 (Group of Seven) summit, beginning a diplomatic tradition that continued after Ford left office.

THE COLD WAR

Both the greatest foreign policy disappointment and success of Ford's presidency involved the Soviet Union and the Cold War. He embraced Nixon's policy of détente, which involved lessening tensions with communist foes, and in November 1974, he met with Soviet premier Leonid Brezhnev (1906–1982) in Russia to negotiate a new strategic arms limitation treaty. While the two leaders reached a framework for a new agreement, the Senate never ratified it, constituting Ford's biggest diplomatic setback. But in July 1975 he met Brezhnev again in Helsinki, Finland, during the Conference on Security and Cooperation in Eastern Europe (CSCE). Altogether, thirty-four nations plus the Vatican participated in the meeting, which approved provisions to ease the exchange of people and information with the Soviet Union and its satellite nations. Ford considered the Helsinki Accords his biggest diplomatic achievement because it encouraged the independence of Eastern Europe and helped to accelerate the Cold War's end.

CHALLENGES FROM REAGAN AND CARTER

At the time, few observers realized the Helsinki Accords' importance. Instead, critics—especially conservatives in Ford's own party—lambasted the agreement as a capitulation to the Soviet Union. The barbs of former California governor Ronald Reagan (1911–2004) were conspicuous, and the onetime actor mounted a primary challenge against Ford for the 1976 Republican nomination using foreign policy as an attack theme. He charged Ford with being soft on the Soviets and allowing the United States to slip behind Russia in military strength. While false, the accusations seemed believable given the Cold War's duration and toll on America, and Reagan remained formidable throughout the Republican primary season. At the Republican National Convention, Ford finally clinched the nomination.

The Reagan challenge compromised Ford's strength, and he trailed the Democratic presidential nominee, former Georgia governor Jimmy Carter, in polls. Ford made up ground by challenging Carter to televised debates, performing well in their first face-off. But his momentum stalled after a gaffe in the second debate (devoted to foreign policy) in which he declared that there was "no Soviet domination of Eastern Europe" during his administration. His intended meaning was that Soviet rule failed to dominate the spirit of Eastern Europeans, but his wording was infelicitous. Ultimately, Ford narrowly lost the election to Carter by 50 percent to 48 percent.

ASSESSMENT

After Ford left office, observers credited him with restoring integrity to the executive branch after the Watergate scandal. His economic record was also important, as he presided over a significant reduction in inflation, which fell from 11 percent in 1974 to 5.7 percent by 1976. In foreign policy, Ford was true to his international activism, helping to establish the G7 summitry tradition and asserting US strength when it appeared to ebb after the Vietnam War.

SEE ALSO *Carter, James Earl, Jr.; Deindustrialization; Kissinger, Henry; Nixon, Richard Milhous; Reagan, Ronald Wilson; Vietnam War*

BIBLIOGRAPHY

Cannon, James. *Gerald R. Ford: An Honorable Life.* Ann Arbor: University of Michigan Press, 2013.

Firestone, Bernard, and Alexej Ugrinsky, eds. *Gerald R. Ford and the Politics of Post-Watergate America.* Westport, CT: Greenwood Press, 1993.

Ford, Gerald. *A Time to Heal: The Autobiography of Gerald R. Ford.* New York: Harper and Row, 1979.

Kaufman, V. Scott, ed. *A Companion to Gerald R. Ford and Jimmy Carter.* New York: Wiley-Blackwell, 2015.

Kissinger, Henry. *Years of Renewal.* New York: Simon and Schuster, 1999.

Mieczkowski, Yanek. *Gerald Ford and the Challenges of the 1970s.* Lexington: University Press of Kentucky, 2005.

Mount, Graeme, with Mark Gauthier. *895 Days That Changed the World: The Presidency of Gerald R. Ford.* Montreal: Black Rose, 2006.

Nessen, Ron. *It Sure Looks Different from the Inside.* New York: Simon and Schuster, 1978.

Yanek Mieczkowski
Professor
Dowling College

FORD, HENRY

1863–1947

Henry Ford was a US automobile manufacturer who cofounded Ford Motor Company (FMC) and later became its principal stockholder and president. He emerged in the early twentieth century as an emblem of the automotive industry and is best remembered for the popularization of mass production.

FAMILY AND EARLY CAREER

Ford's family immigrated to the United States from Ireland during the Great Irish Famine of the mid-nineteenth century. The second child of William Ford and Mary Litogot, he began his life on a prosperous farm in Wayne County, Michigan. Ford's formal education introduced him to Anglo-American imperialism in the pictures and prose of the McGuffey Readers, which were used for instruction in the Scotch Settlement School that Ford attended for six years in the town of Dearborn.

As a young man, Ford gained a reputation as an amateur watch repairer and mechanical tinkerer. He worked in several machine shops in Detroit and as an engineer for Edison Illuminating Company. In 1888, Ford married Clara Bryant. By the end of 1893, the same year his only son, Edsel, was born, Ford had built his first engine in the kitchen sink of his Detroit home. At the turn of the century, Ford helped establish two companies, Detroit Automobile Company (1899) and Henry Ford Company (1901). At the age of forty, Ford became vice president and chief engineer of FMC, the organization he established in 1903 with eleven other investors.

Rows of Model Ts, Britain's best-selling car from 1913 to 1923, in the Ford factory at Trafford Park, Manchester, England. *By 1928 Ford Motor Company, driven by Henry Ford's mass production ideals, had assembly plants in twenty-one countries on six continents.* NATIONAL MOTOR MUSEUM/HERITAGE IMAGES/GETTY IMAGES

MODEL T AND THE ASSEMBLY LINE

In 1906, Ford became president of FMC. Two years later, the company introduced its most famous product, the Model T. In 1913, Ford implemented assembly-line techniques and technologies in his Highland Park plant, increasing production exponentially and insisting that the new methods and machines be publicly observable. People from around the world were further introduced to Ford's brand of mass production when visiting the 1915 Panama-Pacific International Exposition in San Francisco, where Ford displayed a fully functioning Model T assembly line in the FMC exhibition hall.

Designed and priced to appeal to a broad spectrum of buyers, FMC printed sales catalogs and advertisements for the Model T, or the "Tin Lizzie," in English, French, Spanish, and German. By 1927, when the new Model A was publicly introduced, FMC had sold 15 million Model Ts globally and paved the way for later designs, like the Model Y, which sold exclusively in Ford's foreign markets.

FMC EXPORTS AND ASSEMBLY ABROAD

In less than one year of business, Ford Motor Company reached an agreement with Gordon McGregor (1873–1922), a prominent Canadian businessman, to share production and branding rights. Ford-Canada became the primary manufacturer and exporter of Ford products throughout the British Empire, excepting Great Britain and Ireland, which Ford-US supplied. Ford-US also exported cars and parts to nations outside the Dominion.

As the Ford brand grew markets in the United States and Canada, the two organizations shared similar trajectories of global expansion, at first through export houses, international agents, and foreign dealerships, and later through direct investment in branch assembly plants abroad. Ford was soon selling cars in Denmark, Russia, Germany, India, Japan, Brazil, South Africa, and Australia, among others. By 1928, there were Ford assembly plants in twenty-one countries on six continents. In the 1930s Ford advocated and experimented with vertical integration in his factories, using raw materials extracted from around the globe.

FORD'S IDEOLOGY: AMERICANIZATION, PACIFISM, ANTISEMITISM

As business expanded, Ford announced policies that increased workers' hourly wages, nearly doubling the going rate, and initiated profit sharing for eligible employees. Widely heralded, FMC's new wage and labor policies came to be known as the Five-Dollar Day, and workers from around the world poured into the burgeoning city of Detroit to secure jobs. To qualify for profit sharing, employees underwent rigorous financial and domestic examination, and for many recent immigrants, Ford required regular attendance at the company's English school. Ford also helped lead many of the city's Americanization efforts, including the establishment of municipal language programs and public ceremonies of US citizenship.

Despite his company's considerable wartime production, Ford was an ardent pacifist and argued vehemently against US entrance into both world wars. In 1915 Ford joined a group of antiwar crusaders on a voyage to negotiate peace in war-torn Europe. Dubbed the Peace Ship, the ultimately unsuccessful journey became a public relations nightmare for Ford, who left the trip early amid widespread ridicule about his naive efforts at political intervention. Ford later attributed the Peace Ship's failure to a set of nefarious forces at play in global politics, deploying populist and antisemitic tropes about a cabal of "international bankers" that sought to profit from the war.

Ford further pronounced his antisemitism in a series of articles and essays published in the *Dearborn Independent*, a newspaper he purchased in 1918. By 1927, Ford was persuaded to issue a public apology and retraction of antisemitic statements published under his name and in his newspaper. However, concerns about Ford's antisemitism were publicly rekindled in 1938 when he refused to return the Grand Cross of the German Eagle, which was awarded to him by the Nazi regime on his seventy-fifth birthday.

Ford's mass-production ideals spread significantly during his lifetime, spurred in part by his ghostwritten autobiography, *My Life and Work* (1922). The book sold widely and was translated into several languages. Prompted by Ford's life and career, people around the globe were soon debating "Fordism" and questioning whether its effects on the world were worth its costs.

SEE ALSO *AFL-CIO: Labor's Foreign Policy; Americanization; Fordlândia; Great Depression; Industrialization; International Labor Organization; Judaism; Nativism; Robber Barons; Socialism; Whiteness; World War I*

BIBLIOGRAPHY

Baldwin, Neil. *Henry Ford and the Jews: The Mass Production of Hate.* New York: PublicAffairs, 2001.

Brinkley, Douglas. *Wheels for the World: Henry Ford, His Company, and a Century of Progress, 1903–2003.* New York: Viking, 2003.

Nevins, Allan, and Frank Ernest Hill. *Ford: The Times, the Man, the Company.* New York: Scribner's, 1954.

Nye, David E. *America's Assembly Line.* Cambridge, MA: MIT Press, 2013.

Watts, Steven. *The People's Tycoon: Henry Ford and the American Century.* New York: Knopf, 2005.

Wilkins, Mira, and Frank Ernest Hill. *American Business Abroad: Ford on Six Continents.* Detroit, MI: Wayne State University Press, 1964. Reprint, New York: Cambridge University Press, 2011.

Kati Curts
PhD Candidate
Yale University

FORD FOUNDATION

Like the robber barons of the late nineteenth century, such as John Rockefeller (1839–1937) and Andrew Carnegie (1835–1919), who used their accrued wealth to create private philanthropic organizations, the Ford family bequeathed its vast fortune to a foundation designed to further the cause of humanity. To that end, the Ford Foundation makes grants to ease poverty, promote international cooperation, and advance creative achievement. Since 1936, when Henry Ford (1863–1947) and his son Edsel (1893–1943) endowed the foundation, over $400 million in grants have supported the construction of hospitals, research at educational institutions, projects in the arts, environmental causes, and the civil rights movement.

After Henry Ford's death in 1947, the foundation inherited his shares in Ford Motor Company, making it for many years the largest endowed nongovernmental charity in the world. Grandson Henry Ford II (1917–1987) sold the stock and gradually decoupled the automobile company from the charity. They became entirely separate entities by 1975, giving the foundation's trustees a greater degree of independence to fund worthy projects. High-profile successes of the foundation include the Edison Institute (now known as The Henry Ford) in Dearborn, Michigan, which collects and displays American artifacts; the endowment of public broadcasting and children's television shows like *Sesame Street*; aid for demographic and agricultural research in developing counties; support for environmental research; funding for legal opposition to apartheid in South Africa; financing for the arts and humanities, including the construction and operation of New York's Lincoln Center as a site for performing arts; and socioeconomic innovations that include microfinancing, community revitalization, and the raising of public awareness for the struggles of minorities and women. Like the Rockefeller and Carnegie foundations, the Ford Foundation also funds peace initiatives and relief for epidemic diseases, such as AIDS.

Despite these successes, the Ford Foundation's grants have sometimes drawn criticism. Both conservatives and liberals have periodically censured the foundation as politically motivated. For example, the Republican Party condemned the foundation's voter drives for minorities who traditionally cast ballots for Democrats. Awards given to developing countries have also come under scrutiny, particularly grants to Palestinian groups. But perhaps the most serious criticism comes from those, like Inderjeet Parmar (2012), who see the foundation as an instrument of the US government for influencing the global community. Regardless of the success or failure of the projects the foundation funds, Parmar argues that it has fostered a socioeconomic plane in which the values and ideals of the United States can pervade through a network of like-minded individuals. Whether funding creative artists who promoted American liberty and cultural prosperity during the Cold War or subsidizing Third World financing projects to extend the reach of capitalist markets, critics of the Ford Foundation have called attention to the inherent conflict of interest facing private charities.

Today, the Ford Foundation has ten worldwide offices and funds projects in more than fifty countries. Regardless of how its activities are interpreted, the foundation has used the Ford family's fortune to make a demonstrable impact on the world, and the foundation has become a model for the private charities of the twenty-first century, including the Bill and Melinda Gates Foundation.

SEE ALSO *Gates Foundation; Nongovernmental Organizations (NGOs); Rockefeller Foundation; United States Agency for International Development (USAID)*

BIBLIOGRAPHY

Berman, Edward H. *The Ideology of Philanthropy: The Influence of the Carnegie, Ford, and Rockefeller Foundations on American Foreign Policy.* Albany: State University of New York Press, 1983.

Bresnan, John. *At Home and Abroad: A Memoir of the Ford Foundation in Indonesia, 1953–1973.* Jakarta, Indonesia: Equinox, 2006.

Guilhot, Nicholas. *The Democracy Makers: Human Rights and the Politics of Global Order.* New York: Columbia University Press, 2005.

Klein, Naomi. *The Shock Doctrine: The Rise of Disaster Capitalism.* New York: Holt, 2007.

Macdonald, Dwight. *The Ford Foundation: The Men and the Millions.* New Brunswick, NJ: Transaction, 1989. Originally published in 1955 by Reynal.

Magat, Richard. *The Ford Foundation at Work: Philanthropic Choices, Methods, and Styles.* New York: Springer, 1979.

Parmar, Inderjeet. *Foundations of the American Century: The Ford, Carnegie, and Rockefeller Foundations in the Rise of American Power.* New York: Columbia University Press, 2012.

Michael Patrick Cullinane
Senior Lecturer in US History
Northumbria University

FORDLÂNDIA

Fordlândia was a 2.5-million-acre rubber plantation in Brazil's Amazon River basin established by Henry Ford (1863–1947) and Ford Motor Company. It featured running water, an elaborate sanitation system, a hospital, a dining hall, swimming pools, a golf course, sidewalks with fire hydrants, and rows of clapboard cottages. Fordlândia's legacy is controversial, as was its creation. It is remembered by some as an inchoate beginning to and a potent symbol of modernization efforts in one of Brazil's remotest regions. It is also remembered for its ambivalent contribution to the task of uplifting some of the country's most impoverished populations, and for its involvement in national unification amid a history of extreme regionalism. Fordlândia also stands as a reminder of Henry Ford's efforts to export an idealized small-town America and as a tragic ruin of capital hubris, extractive industry, and the coming of mass production in the twentieth century.

Prompted in part by the rising price of latex in Southeast Asia, American businessman and tire magnate Harvey Firestone (1868–1938) urged his friend, Henry Ford, to join him in developing alternative rubber supplies for American industry. While Firestone established plantations in Liberia, Ford looked to the jungles of Brazil, the region to which the superior rubber tree, *Hevea brasiliensis*, was native.

The South American country was familiar to Ford, as Brazil had proven to be a successful international market for his company's growing automotive empire. Politicians, authors, and other supporters argued that Ford would help modernize the interior backwoods of the country, where they located Brazil's history of slavery, racial discord, imperial oppression, violent uprising, and subsequent repression. The dense jungle region's raw materials enticed Ford with the possibility to further integrate his company's global supply chain. It also seemed to offer Ford the opportunity to transform the region's inhabitants into productive members of an emerging Brazilian middle class.

In 1927 the governor of Pará signed a land concession permitting Ford's newly established subsidiary, Companhia Ford Industrial do Brasil, legal access to all land, lumber, mineral, and water rights on a plot of steeply sloping terrain in the country's interior. The concession also included significant tax exemptions and granted the company the ability to develop its own physical structures and infrastructure, including any banking, police, medical, and educational institutions it deemed necessary. In return, Ford's emissaries agreed to plant a thousand acres of the ceded land by the end of the rubber plantation's first year and, after twelve years of operation, to return a percentage of its profits to the Brazilian government.

Ford's plantation had a number of vocal critics. Antônio Emiliano de Souza Castro, a senator in Pará, was among those who argued against the plan, denouncing the unequal nature of the government grant. Critics also worried that the relative leniency of the concession would enable Ford to violate Brazil's sovereignty. Some in the press condemned the deal's lack of transparency and speculated about whether Ford's interests went beyond reform and rubber to oil and gold securities. Despite Ford's contentious place in the Brazilian imagination, the state legislature approved the governor's agreement in 1927, though federal approval was never secured, a fact that would continue to cause tax and tariff troubles for Ford in the coming years.

Fordlândia was more successful as an idea and ideal than as a reality. Managerial incompetence, environmental complications, and volatile labor relations engulfed the plantation from its earliest years. Political changes in Brazil also proved ambivalent toward Ford's Amazonian endeavor. Additionally, Fordlândia never actually managed to produce much rubber, lumber, or other resources for manufacture or sale. By 1935, leaf blight and predatory insects had increasingly ravaged Fordlândia's crops, and its operations were scaled back. When the United States entered World War II in late 1941, the American government effectively nationalized Ford's endeavors to cultivate wild Brazilian rubber. Yet Fordlândia's output remained significantly lower than that of other global latex suppliers.

If Fordlândia was relatively inadequate to the task of producing rubber, it was considerably more successful in helping the US government promote the American dream to Americans. Three years after traveling to Ford's Brazilian plantation on a 1941 promotional tour with the US Office of Inter-American Affairs, Walt Disney (1901–1966) produced *The Amazon Awakens*, a documentary featuring Fordlândia, using film from Ford Motor Company.

Given its turbulent history and general lack of success, it is unsurprising that, in November 1945, as synthetic rubber became increasingly available, Ford Motor Company, under the new leadership of Henry Ford's grandson, Henry Ford II (1917–1987), sold Fordlândia to the Brazilian government and divested its Brazilian subsidiary of all land and resource rights in Pará.

SEE ALSO *Americanization; Ford, Henry*

BIBLIOGRAPHY

Galey, John. "Industrialist in the Wilderness: Henry Ford's Amazon Venture." *Journal of Interamerican Studies and World Affairs* 21, 2 (1979): 261–289.

Grandin, Greg. *Fordlandia: The Rise and Fall of Henry Ford's Forgotten Jungle City*. New York: Picador, 2009.

Lewis, David L. *The Public Image of Henry Ford: An American Folk Hero and His Company.* Detroit, MI: Wayne State University Press, 1987.

Wilkins, Mira, and Frank Ernest Hill. *American Business Abroad: Ford on Six Continents.* Detroit, MI: Wayne State University Press, 1964. Reprint, New York: Cambridge University Press, 2011.

Wolfe, Joel. *Autos and Progress: The Brazilian Search for Modernity.* New York: Oxford University Press, 2010.

Kati Curts
PhD Candidate
Yale University

FOREIGN AFFAIRS (MAGAZINE)

Foreign Affairs, the journal of the leading US foreign policy think tank, the Council on Foreign Relations (CFR), was established in 1922. The previous year, the New York–based CFR had merged with the American Institute of International Affairs, an organization established by expert advisers in the US delegation at the Paris Peace Conference, to encourage policy-oriented research and discussion on international affairs.

The new CFR appointed Archibald Cary Coolidge (1866–1928), a Harvard-based academic specializing in diplomatic history, to be founding editor of its journal. Coolidge was assisted by an energetic young Princeton graduate, Hamilton Fish Armstrong (1893–1973). Son of a New York artist and an admirer of President Woodrow Wilson, Armstrong had been a military attaché in Serbia during World War I and a *New York Evening Post* reporter in Europe thereafter. Armstrong and Coolidge immediately succeeded in persuading a wide slew of eminent European statesmen, together with top American politicians of every stripe, to contribute to the new journal. They sought to ensure that *Foreign Affairs* covered all points of view on international affairs, both within and beyond the United States. The first issue included an article by former secretary of state Elihu Root (1845–1937). The quarterly gave extensive coverage to developments in Soviet Russia. It attempted to review all new books of any significance to international affairs. By 1927, its circulation had risen from 1,500 to 11,000, an influential and elite group of readers.

On Coolidge's death in 1928, Armstrong succeeded him as editor, a position he held for forty-five years until retiring in 1972. Every year he traveled abroad, soliciting articles from leading international figures. Though officially committed to no policy, prominent CFR officers, including Armstrong, broadly favored an expanded US role in international affairs, and they backed US intervention in World War II. With the CFR heavily involved in developing Cold War policy, in 1947 the journal published the article "The Sources of Soviet Conduct" by the young American diplomat George F. Kennan (1904–2005), a piece that would become a key text publicizing the guiding US strategy of "containing" the Soviet Union. The 1967 article "Asia after Viet Nam" by Republican presidential hopeful Richard Nixon (1913–1994) implied that the United States should move to open diplomatic relations with communist China.

By 1970, the venerable CFR seemed ossified, outdated, and complacent, causing younger foreign affairs writers and intellectuals to establish the rival journal *Foreign Policy*. In 1972, the decision of CFR chairman David Rockefeller (b. 1915) to appoint one of the major architects of US policies toward Vietnam, former undersecretary of state for East Asia William P. Bundy (1917–2000), as Armstrong's successor provoked fierce though ultimately ineffective protests from CFR members opposed to his stance on Vietnam. Bundy, who remained editor until 1984, gave greater prominence to economic issues, oil, and energy policy. The former diplomat William G. Hyland (1929–2008), editor from 1984 to 1992, reemphasized political and strategic issues.

With the end of the Cold War, *Foreign Affairs* continued to be the premier US journal on international affairs, publishing such seminal articles as Samuel Huntington's (1927–2008) "The Clash of Civilizations" (1993), predicting that cultural differences would drive post–Cold War international conflicts. James F. Hoge Jr. (b. 1935), editor from 1992 to 2010 and an experienced journalist, moved to bimonthly publication, modernized the journal's appearance, production, and management structure, and introduced a popular online version in 2009, policies that Hoge's successor, Gideon Rose, a former National Security Council staffer with ten years of prior experience as managing editor of *Foreign Affairs*, had helped to implement and built upon. The journal also introduced several foreign-language versions, in Spanish, Japanese, Russian, and Greek. It was, the CFR proclaimed, "the most widely circulated journal on international politics and economics in the world" (CFR 2000). By the mid-1990s, circulation had risen to 110,000. Over the next two decades, it continued to grow, especially after the terrorist attacks of September 11, 2001, reaching 163,000 in 2013. Through the years, *Foreign Affairs* has published many of the most globally influential and widely discussed articles on international affairs, contributing significantly to the CFR's status as one of the world's most important and influential think tanks.

SEE ALSO *Clash of Civilizations (Samuel Huntington); Council on Foreign Relations*

BIBLIOGRAPHY

Armstrong, Hamilton Fish. *Peace and Counterpeace from Wilson to Hitler: Memoirs of Hamilton Fish Armstrong.* New York: Harper and Row, 1971.

Armstrong, Hamilton Fish, with James Chace, Carol Kahn, and Jennifer Whittaker, eds. *Fifty Years of Foreign Affairs.* New York: Praeger, 1972.

Bird, Kai. *The Color of Truth: McGeorge Bundy and William Bundy: Brothers in Arms.* New York: Simon and Schuster, 1998.

Bundy, William P. "Notes on the History of *Foreign Affairs.*" Council on Foreign Relations, 1994. http://www.cfr.org/about/history/foreign_affairs.html

Byrnes, Robert F. *Awakening American Education to the World: The Role of Archibald Cary Coolidge, 1866–1928.* Notre Dame, IN: University of Notre Dame Press, 1982.

Campbell, John D. "The Death Rattle of the Eastern Establishment." *New York Times Magazine,* September 20, 1971, 1–7ff.

Coolidge, Harold Jefferson. *Archibald Cary Coolidge: Life and Letters.* Boston: Houghton Mifflin, 1932.

Council on Foreign Relations (CFR). "*Foreign Affairs* Announces the Appointment of Gideon Rose as Managing Editor." October 16, 2000. http://www.cfr.org/world/foreign-affairs-announces-appointment-gideon-rose-managing-editor/p5386

Hyland, William G. "Foreign Affairs at 70." *Foreign Affairs* 71, 4 (1992): 171–193.

Lukas, J. Anthony. "The Council on Foreign Relations—Is It a Club? Seminar? Presidium? 'Invisible Government'?" *New York Times Magazine,* November 21, 1971, 34, 123–131, 138, 142.

Roberts, Priscilla. "'The Council Has Been Your Creation': Hamilton Fish Armstrong, Paradigm of the American Foreign Policy Establishment?" *Journal of American Studies* 35, 1 (2001): 65–94.

Wala, Michael. *The Council on Foreign Relations and American Foreign Policy in the Early Cold War.* Providence, RI: Berghahn, 1994.

Priscilla Roberts
Associate Professor of History
University of Hong Kong

FOREIGN MISSION MOVEMENT

The earliest American foreign missions were established in the seventeenth-century colonies from Virginia to New England. The missionaries, primarily Puritans, were guided by what was viewed as a special obligation to carry out foreign missions under the Great Commission, or the biblical injunction to "go into all the world and preach the gospel." Thomas Mayhew's (1593–1682) mission to native tribes on Martha's Vineyard and Roger Williams's (c. 1603–1683) work among the Algonquin Indians in what is today Rhode Island were exemplary of these earliest missions. From the early 1800s through the 1870s, foreign missions among Native Americans expanded as the nation acquired new, territorial possessions. With territorial expansion came a growth in the denominations that served among Native American tribes. Working along strict denominational lines, Presbyterians, Episcopalians, American Baptists, the United Church of Christ, and Disciples of Christ all participated in various mission efforts in the American Far West.

AMERICAN BOARD OF COMMISSIONERS FOR FOREIGN MISSIONS

In addition to these continental missions, American evangelical Christians participated in foreign missionary movements abroad. Organized in 1810 by Massachusetts Congregationalists, the American Board of Commissioners for Foreign Missions (also known simply as the American Board or ABCFM) became the largest organizing body for American international missions. Between 1812 and 1845, the American Board sponsored projects in India, East Asia, the Middle East, Africa, and the Pacific Rim. By 1910, it was responsible for 102 mission stations and a missionary staff of six hundred in India, Ceylon, West Central Africa (Angola), South Africa and Rhodesia, Turkey, China, Japan, Micronesia, the Philippines, Mexico, Spain, and Austria (Global Ministries 2010). The American Board's collaboration with Britain's largest foreign missionary society, the London Missionary Society, began in 1812 and suggested the interdenominational and transnational cooperation that would mark mainline Protestant missionary efforts going forward.

NINETEENTH-CENTURY REVIVALISM

Diverse theological trends have shaped the methods of American foreign missions since the 1790s when the Second Great Awakening first inspired an evangelical revival in the United States. Postmillennialism, or the belief that Christians had a duty to purify and prepare society for the return of Christ, and interdenominational cooperation helped popularize foreign missionary service abroad. These newer missions minimized theological distinctions, voiced an aversion to formal or detailed creed, and emphasized the reconstruction of entire societies over individual conversion. The postmillennial revivalism led to another upsurge in the American foreign mission movement following the Civil War (1861–1865) and through the turn of the twentieth century. Mainline Protestant denominations became especially influential in foreign missions in the post–Civil War era. Drawn to the movement by outspoken revivalists like Dwight Moody (1837–1899) and John R. Mott (1865–1955) and through recruitment efforts on college campuses, a new generation of young Americans joined mainline Protestant organizations like the Student Volunteer Movement and the YMCA, which offered youth the opportunity to serve missions both at home and abroad.

The revivalism of the mid- to late nineteenth century was not limited to mainline Protestant denominations or to those preaching a postmillennial theology. Premillennial denominations, including Assemblies of God and Brethren in Christ, and more marginal religious denominations, including the Church of Jesus Christ of Latter-Day Saints, or Mormons, established foreign missionary efforts abroad as well. The Catholic Church also established missionary projects in China and Korea in the early twentieth century, while nondenominational organizations, like the World Woman's Christian Temperance Union, operated missions in East and South Asia, as well as in Europe, in the same period.

INTERDENOMINATIONAL AND TRANSNATIONAL COOPERATION

Since the mid-nineteenth century, American foreign missionaries carried out their work in collaboration with diverse European organizations. Inspired by the revivalist spirit of the 1860s, American missionaries helped the London Missionary Society establish missions in India, while others would go on to serve with the China Inland Mission, founded in 1875 by British-based Hudson Taylor (1832–1905). American and British foreign missionaries and the ABCFM played an important role in expanding collaborative efforts in China, Ceylon (Sri Lanka), and Japan by the dawn of the twentieth century. American women and young people were particularly influential in the expansion of cooperative efforts abroad. Founded in the 1860s, the Woman's Foreign Missionary Society drew American Congregationalists and Methodist women into cooperative partnerships with Canadian and British women's mission agencies in China. Voluntary youth organizations like the Canadian Intercollegiate Missionary Alliance and the Student Volunteer Missionary Union of Great Britain flourished into the early twentieth century and encouraged additional cooperative movements among American and foreign missionaries. In the case of the latter, British and American evangelicals bolstered missionary efforts ranging from East Asia to Africa.

Shifting theological views also encouraged the growth of cooperative efforts with non-European nations and their missionary representatives. Beginning in the 1840s ABCFM senior secretary Rufus Anderson (1796–1880) began calling for missionaries to withdraw from foreign missions as soon as practicable. Influenced greatly by democratic and Congregational ideologies, Rufus proposed what came to be known as the Great Compromise, whereby foreign missionaries would enter a nation and impose a set of moral values that would serve as a model for indigenous Christian leaders to follow. Once established and tested, foreign missionaries were then encouraged to turn churches and mission institutions over to native officials. While debates over indigenization continued through the early twentieth century, Rufus's ideology nonetheless became a foundation for mainline Protestant missionaries in an era when American missionaries and organizations were becoming influential in shaping global Christian missionary efforts. The inclusion of non-Western representatives in previously Western European and American efforts expanded further in the decades following World War I (1914–1918). Part of a larger internationalist movement, American and European missionaries began to encourage representatives from formerly marginalized nations, including representatives from Asia, Africa, and Latin America, to join organizations like the World's Parliament of Religions and World Missionary Conferences and attend annual conferences like the Jerusalem Conference of World Missions held in 1928.

SHAPING THE US IMAGE ABROAD

Given the global nature of their efforts, American foreign missions played a crucial role in shaping the United States' image abroad since at least the early nineteenth century. From their cooperation with the London Missionary Society in India and the China Inland Mission to the internationalism that drove YMCA secretaries in Japan following World War I, American foreign missions have frequently complemented the efforts of foreign policy makers and the American nation-state generally. American missionaries were not uncommonly associated with modern European and American empire building, colonial rule, and especially "cultural imperialism," whereby missionaries imposed colonial religious and moral systems on indigenous subjects. Missionaries also frequently held racist or condescending views toward the people with whom they worked. This was particularly true in the late nineteenth-century imperialist era, when social Darwinism penetrated Western culture.

Despite their being an important force for American cultural imperialism, American missionaries abroad also served as mediators between diverse cultures and managed to cross cultural divides depending on personalities, theology, adaptability, language facility, and time in country. American missionary women used varied methods to reinterpret the meanings of American nationalism and imperialism in the colonial settings in which they served. Those who served in Bulgaria in the mid-nineteenth century, for instance, promoted an American discourse of domesticity, female domestic responsibility, female education, and national progress to Bulgarian Orthodox Christians in the Ottoman Empire. Despite their imposition of such ideals, American female missionaries invariably bridged diverse cultures by appealing to educated urban Bulgarians who rearticulated a language of domesticity in their protests against Ottoman reform and their promotion of Bulgarian nationalism. Likewise, American missionary women at Kobe College in Japan used female education to facilitate cross-cultural dialogue between American women missionaries and Japanese students from 1873 and 1909. Many of the earliest Japanese converts would go on to pressure Meiji-era social and industrial reform in the era leading up to World War I.

THE LIBERAL CONSENSUS

American foreign missions have rarely been guided by a single theological principle. Since the Republican period and through today, denominational differences, disagreements over the purpose and methods of foreign missions, and divergences in theological interpretations divided Protestant, Catholic, liberal, fundamentalist, and nondenominational missions. While these divisions never entirely went away, there did exist certain periods when something bordering on consensus emerged. In the late nineteenth and early twentieth centuries, mainline Protestant churches aligned behind the liberal watchword the "evangelization of the world in this generation" and shared a commitment to the promotion of interorganizational cooperation and ecumenism. Inspired by the promise to affect social and moral reform abroad, liberal Protestant organizations like the YMCA and Student Volunteer Movement drew a new generation of young people to the foreign missionary movement.

Despite their ability to find consensus in the late nineteenth and early twentieth centuries, the growth of cooperative efforts slowed in the decades following World War I, when critics of postmillennialism began to question the merits of American foreign missionary efforts. Fundamentalists criticized postmillennial theology for turning biblical belief and doctrinal rigor into little more than social evangel. The emergence of totalitarianism and global warfare led to additional critiques of postmillennial American foreign missionary efforts. Particularly influential in the 1940s and 1950s and popularized by outspoken theologian Reinhold Niebuhr (1892–1971), Christian realism argued against the possibility of a realization of a Kingdom of God given the innately corrupt tendencies that shaped modern nation-states and societies. Historians generally agree that the American foreign mission movement never regained the influence or the liberal consensus seen between the 1890s and 1930s. Even without consensus, the presence of American foreign missionary efforts remained influential in the post–World War II (1939–1945) era and continues to operate in nations around the world today.

POST–WORLD WAR II REVIVAL OF AMERICAN FOREIGN MISSIONARY EFFORTS

Even with the downturn in the liberal movement, a revival of American foreign missionary efforts occurred after World War II and continued through the Cold War as the nation expanded its fight against the spread of communism around the globe. While postmillennial liberalism characterized earlier revivals, the Cold War saw the growth of more evangelical, conservative, and fundamentalist efforts. These efforts to combat "godless communism" allied well with US foreign policy agendas and spread more rapidly with the emergence of powerful evangelical figures like Billy Graham (b. 1918). Conservatives, including various evangelical and charismatic, or Pentecostal, denominations, continued to swell the ranks of American foreign missions through the Ronald Reagan (1911–2004) era and into the 1990s. Up to fifty thousand American foreign missionaries were reported to be serving abroad at the end of the decade.

In addition to these conservative evangelical efforts, liberal and nondenominational missions remained influential in the post–World War II era. Mainline Protestants, including divisions of the Methodist, Presbyterian, and Episcopalian Churches, rallied behind a shared commitment to promoting greater freedom in former colonized nations following World War II. As organizational structures became decentralized and more informal in the 1990s, nondenominational missions witnessed new popularity. The proliferation of small mission associations, short-term mission trips organized by churches and universities, and a decline in the long-term mission of earlier periods has also led to a greater number of American foreign missionaries serving abroad.

SEE ALSO *Africa; American Board of Commissioners for Foreign Missions; Asia; Hawai'i; Middle East; Pacific Islands; Student Volunteer Movement for Foreign Missions; Transatlantic Reform*

BIBLIOGRAPHY

"ABCFM American Board of Commissioners for Foreign Missions 200th Anniversary." Global Ministries, 2010. http://www.globalministries.org/resources/mission-study/abcfm/abcfm-american-board-200.html

Ahlstrom, Sydney E. *A Religious History of the American People.* 2nd ed. New Haven, CT: Yale University Press, 2004.

Amstutz, Mark R. *Evangelicals and American Foreign Policy.* New York: Oxford University Press, 2013.

Dunch, Ryan. "Beyond Cultural Imperialism: Cultural Theory, Christian Missions, and Global Modernity." *History and Theory* 41, 3 (2002): 301–325.

Hunter, Jane. *The Gospel of Gentility: American Missionary Women in Turn-of-the-Century China.* New Haven, CT: Yale University Press, 1984.

Hutchison, William R. *Errand to the World: American Protestant Thought and Foreign Missions*. Chicago: University of Chicago Press, 1987.

Ishii, Noriko Kawamura. *American Women Missionaries at Kobe College, 1873–1909: New Dimensions in Gender*. New York: Routledge, 2004.

Porter, Andrew. *The Imperial Horizons of British Protestant Missions, 1880–1914*. Grand Rapids, MI: Eerdmans, 2003.

Reeves-Ellington, Barbara, Kathryn Kish Sklar, and Connie A. Shemo, eds. *Competing Kingdoms: Women, Mission, Nation, and the American Protestant Empire, 1812–1960*. Durham, NC: Duke University Press, 2010.

Ruble, Sarah E. *The Gospel of Freedom and Power: Protestant Missionaries in American Culture after World War II*. Chapel Hill: University of North Carolina Press, 2012.

Tyrrell, Ian. "Woman, Missions, and Empire: New Approaches to American Cultural Expansion." In *Competing Kingdoms: Women, Mission, Nation, and the American Protestant Empire, 1812–1960*, edited by Barbara Reeves-Ellington, Kathryn Kish Sklar, and Connie A. Shemo. Durham, NC: Duke University Press, 2010.

Sarah M. Griffith
Assistant Professor of History
Queens University of Charlotte

FOREIGN MISSION SCHOOL (CORNWALL, CT)

In 1816 the American Board of Commissioners for Foreign Missions (ABCFM) began preparations for a foreign mission school. The move was prompted by several New England ministers who were aware that young men from Asia and the Pacific islands had been arriving in the United States on merchant ships. They believed that creating a boarding school for such youths would aid the cause of Protestant missions overseas. First, the school would draw attention to foreign missions by gathering these young men from so-called heathen or pagan cultures into one place and educating them in the values of New England society. Stories about exotic youths within their midst would be used as propaganda to encourage New Englanders to donate funds to the ABCFM. American young men who planned to become missionaries could go to the school to learn about the cultures and languages of the countries to which they were assigned.

The school would also train the foreign students to return to their native countries as Protestant missionaries. The board believed that most Westerners who traveled abroad did not behave as good Christians and therefore created prejudices against both Christianity and its Western representatives. Natives would not have to overcome such prejudices when returning to their home country, and as converts to a foreign religion they would be especially qualified to profess the advantages of Christianity over the beliefs of their ancestors. The board also believed that spreading knowledge of Western civilization would help them spread religion. The school would train its students in mechanics, agriculture, commerce, and medicine as well as Protestant Christianity. The recent assimilation of several Sandwich Islanders (Hawaiians), including Henry Obookiah (c. 1787–1818), was seen as evidence that cultural transformations were possible among non-Westerners.

The school began operations in May 1817 with twelve students. Two were missionary candidates from New England. Seven were from the Sandwich Islands, including Obookiah, while two were from India and one was a Canadian Indian. The school soon admitted students from China; the Society Islands; and the Cherokee, Choctaw, and Delaware tribes of American Indians. By 1819, it had thirty-two students, including seventeen American Indians and six American missionary candidates, as well as students from Malacca and Sumatra. In 1823 the population peaked at thirty-five students, including a Tahitian, a New Zealander, and a Malay, as well as Sandwich Islanders, Cherokees, Choctaws, an Oneida, two Stockbridge Indians, two Tuscaroras, one Narragansett, and two Caughnawagas.

The school relied on donations, supplemented by the students' efforts at farming. It held public examinations and exhibitions that displayed the achievements of students. The board published observers' accounts, as well as letters from graduates, to publicize the students' decorum and accomplishments in language and theology as well as scientific subjects such as astronomy. At least three became assistant missionaries for the ABCFM in the Sandwich Islands. By 1826 the school had trained about sixty students for varying lengths of time.

The school thus encouraged New Englanders' interest in various Asian societies as well as in American Indians, whom the board was trying to Christianize and assimilate. The board believed that converting to Christianity and learning English would help Indians become integrated into white society (otherwise they feared the tribes' extinction). Most supporters of the board shared its goals of protecting and converting American Indians but not of integrating them as equals. When two Cherokee students, John Ridge (1802–1839) and Elias Boudinot (c. 1804–1839), married white women, they provoked an uproar. The leaders of the ABCFM privately affirmed their support for the marriages, believing that intermarriage would help American Indians assimilate, but publicly they did not take a strong stance. The controversy was one factor leading to the closing of the school in 1827. Other challenges to the school's assimilation strategy included students' difficulties adjusting to the new culture or climate (some, like Obookiah, sickened and died) or readjusting to their native societies upon returning. The board also concluded that students would be better off enrolled in American colleges rather than sequestered on their own and treated as an exhibition. And as missionaries established schools in many of their native countries, the board told supporters that the Cornwall school duplicated other efforts. The school, which had seventeen pupils when it closed, was considered successful at advertising foreign missions and exposing New Englanders to talented young Indians and Asians, among whom they would continue to promote religious conversions.

SEE ALSO *American Board of Commissioners for Foreign Missions; Cherokee Nation v. Georgia (1831); China; Foreign Mission Movement; Hawai'i; Indian Removal Act (1830)*

BIBLIOGRAPHY

Andrew, John A., III. *Rebuilding the Christian Commonwealth: New England Congregationalists and Foreign Missions, 1800–1830.* Lexington: University Press of Kentucky, 1976.

Demos, John. *The Heathen School: A Story of Hope and Betrayal in the Age of the Early Republic.* New York: Knopf, 2014.

Hutchison, William R. *Errand to the World: American Protestant Thought and Foreign Missions.* Chicago: University of Chicago Press, 1987.

The Missionary Herald, Containing the Proceedings of the American Board of Commissioners for Foreign Missions. Boston: American Board of Commissioners for Foreign Missions, 1821–1906.

The Panoplist, and Missionary Herald. Boston: Samuel T. Armstrong, 1818–1820.

The Panoplist, and Missionary Magazine. Boston: Samuel T. Armstrong, 1808–1817.

Ashley E. Moreshead
Visiting Assistant Professor, Department of History
University of Central Florida

FOREIGN PERFORMING ARTISTS

Lewis Hallam's London Company presented the earliest professional theatrical performances in the American colonies, beginning with William Shakespeare's *The Merchant of Venice* in Williamsburg, Virginia, in 1752. From that time, European actors, musicians, dancers, writers, composers, circus performers, and impresarios who toured or immigrated to the United States influenced the development of American performing arts. Americans imported European talent, adapting their performance methods to create distinctively American traditions.

With the rise of the star system as a replacement for the stock system in the American theater in the early nineteenth century, English and Irish star performers began to tour the United States in great numbers, peaking with such influential tragedians as George Frederick Cooke (1756–1812), Edmund Kean (1789–1833), Junius Brutus Booth (1796–1852), Tyrone Power (1795–1841), and William Macready (1793–1873). These actors ensured that developments in European performance traditions reached the United States and influenced the tastes of American audiences. Cooke, in the early nineteenth century the most popular foreign actor in the United States, along with Kean and Booth, aided a shift toward an emphatic, tumultuous, romantic style of acting from the more subdued neoclassical style. Significantly, Booth, who immigrated to America in 1821, fathered both Edwin Booth (1833–1893), America's most celebrated actor of the era, and John Wilkes Booth (1838–1865), Abraham Lincoln's assassin. A rivalry between English actor Macready, the favorite actor of elite American audiences, and American-born populist actor Edmund Forrest (1806–1872) culminated in the class-based Astor Place riot in 1849, in which working-class Americans asserted a distinction between British and American values and cultural identities. Twenty-two individuals protesting Macready's performances outside the Astor Place Opera House in Manhattan were killed, and 144 were injured by the state militia. These events demonstrated the significance of the urban nineteenth-century theater as a space for civic and political unrest and debate.

In the mid-nineteenth century, as international travel from Europe became more feasible and impresarios saw the opportunity to capitalize on the international fame of star performers, influences from non-English-speaking performing artists escalated. The most notable actress to appear in nineteenth-century America was Mademoiselle Rachel (1821–1858), of the Comédie-Française, known for an understated, psychologically motivated approach to acting. She toured the United States without popular success in 1855, but she made an impression on American critics and actresses, who began to imitate her performance style. Her rival, Italian actress Adelaide Ristori (1822–1906), toured America in 1866, with both popular and critical success.

In addition to developments in traditional theatrical performance, English and non-English-speaking European artists began to have an impact on the development and direction of popular performance forms. The Scottish popular performer John Bill Ricketts, for example, presented the first complete circus performance in 1793, later establishing permanent circus buildings in Philadelphia and New York, where the circus industry would begin to flourish. With a growth in the popular entertainment industry during the mid-nineteenth century, American impresarios invited performers from throughout Europe, including dancers, such as the French Madame Céline Céleste (1815–1882) and the Viennese Fanny Elssler (1810–1884); mimes, such as the French Ravel family; and singers, such as Henry Russell (1812–1900) from England and Philippe Musard (1792–1859) from France. In 1850, P. T. Barnum's "Swedish Nightingale," Jenny Lind (1820–1887), took America by storm, popularizing vocal performance for the masses. Significantly, too, the popular Irish melodramatic actor-playwright Dion Boucicault (1822–1890), who worked in the United States from 1854 to 1860, led the charge to create the first American copyright law, a move that helped elevate involvement in the arts to a professional, and more respectable, endeavor.

The twentieth century saw the arrival in the United States of international artists who garnered greater respectability and signified refinement in the performing arts. Foreign-born producers and impresarios, notably German-born Otto H. Kahn (1867–1934) and the Russian-born Morris Gest (1875–1942), Max Rabinoff (1877–1966), and Sol Hurok (1888–1974), imported talented composers, dancers, singers, and actors from Italy, Germany, Russia, and elsewhere in eastern Europe. By the 1920s, producers had cultivated an appreciation of Russian theatrical performance as the epitome of high culture through the tours of elite performers and troupes, such as the dancers Anna Pavlova (1882–1931) and Mikhail Mordkin (1880–1944), opera star Fyodor Chaliapin (1873–1938), the Ballet Russes, the Chauve-Souris led by Nikita Balieff (1877–1936), and the Moscow Art Theatre under the direction of Konstantin Stanislavsky (1863–1938). American actors, dancers, designers, and singers began studying their craft in the many studios and schools that were established by Russian émigrés. Most notably, the enduring impact of Stanislavsky's "system" on the training of American actors highlights the significance of Russian influence on the American performing arts. Additionally, European modernist performance was introduced to the United States by the German director Max Reinhardt (1873–1943) and performances by the Yiddish Art Theatre under the direction of Maurice Schwartz (1889–1960), the Habima Troupe from Russia, and the Yiddish-speaking Vilna Troupe. These international artists diversified the landscape of the American performing arts and helped American cities develop thriving cultural centers that established the prominence of the United States in artistic and cultural creativity.

SEE ALSO *Crowe, Eyre; Dickens, Charles; Grand Tour*

BIBLIOGRAPHY

Hohman, Valleri J. *Russian Culture and Theatrical Performance in America, 1891–1933.* New York: Palgrave Macmillan, 2011.

Postlewait, Thomas. "The Hieroglyphic Stage: American Theatre and Society, Post–Civil War to 1945." In *The Cambridge History of American Theatre,* Vol. 2: *1870–1945,* edited by Don B. Wilmeth and Christopher Bigsby, 107–195. New York and Cambridge: Cambridge University Press, 1998.

Williams, Simon. "European Actors and the Star System in the American Theatre, 1752–1870." In *The Cambridge History of American Theatre,* Vol. 1: *Beginnings to 1870,* edited by Don B. Wilmeth and Christopher Bigsby, 303–337. New York and Cambridge: Cambridge University Press, 1998.

Wilmeth, Don B., and Christopher Bigsby, eds. *The Cambridge History of American Theatre,* Vol. 1: *Beginnings to 1870.* New York and Cambridge: Cambridge University Press, 1998.

Valleri Robinson
Associate Professor, Department of Theatre
University of Illinois at Urbana-Champaign

FOREIGN SERVICE, US

Members of the US Foreign Service represent the US government abroad, either as Foreign Service officers (FSOs), who are professional diplomats, or as Foreign Service specialists (FSSs), who are professionals in other fields, such as medicine or information technology, and provide services to US personnel at diplomatic posts. Members of the Foreign Service contribute to the formation and implementation of US foreign policy and personify the US government when they interact with leaders and citizens of other countries. The Foreign Service is part of the Department of State and was created via the Rogers Act of 1924. Entry is based on a multipart examination, presidential appointment, and Senate confirmation.

THE PRE-1924 DIPLOMATIC CORPS AND CONSULAR SERVICE

Prior to the Rogers Act, the Department of State included a diplomatic corps, whose members engaged in high politics and representational duties, and the consular service, whose members facilitated international trade and assisted Americans in peril abroad, among numerous other duties. Diplomatic and consular appointments were made by the president and confirmed by the Senate, and they were often made based on service to the president's political party, rather than on any particular fitness for the demands of the job. (It was, for example, fairly rare for diplomats and consuls to have relevant foreign language skills.) Republican control of the White House for the majority of the time between the Civil War (1861–1865) and the start of Woodrow Wilson's (1856–1924) administration in 1913 meant that many people were able to build de facto careers representing the US government because they continued to receive appointments.

Civil service reform was slow to arrive at the State Department, however. Party leaders were reluctant to give up one of the few remaining sources of patronage positions, and Congress was reluctant to raise diplomatic and consular salaries to a level that would allow people without independent means to serve. It fell to presidents with personal commitments to civil service reform to introduce a merit system. Grover Cleveland (1837–1908) and Theodore Roosevelt (1858–1919) put many diplomatic and consular positions on the merit system via executive orders in 1895, 1905, 1906, and 1909. Top positions could still go to political appointees, however, and State Department leaders often overlooked low scores on written examinations for candidates who interviewed well.

In 1915, Congress confirmed many of these changes via legislation, putting all but the very top diplomatic and consular posts on the merit system (though those top posts were open and frequently given to career personnel). Under the 1915 law, diplomats and consuls were appointed to classes of service, rather than to specific posts, as had been the previous practice; personnel transfer without presidential and Senate action became possible. That change allowed State Department leaders to demand "worldwide availability" from diplomats and consuls, which has remained the most fundamental requirement for service ever since. Invocation of that rule was often used into the 1970s to deny positions to women, African Americans, and naturalized citizens (many of whom were Jews).

THE ROGERS ACT OF 1924

The experiences of World War I (1914–1918), the introduction of immigration quota laws and a visa system, and the business community's interest in expanding American trade abroad finally created the correct circumstances for more far-reaching congressional action in reforming US representation abroad. The Rogers Act of 1924 combined the diplomatic corps and consular service into a single US Foreign Service. The law perpetuated the requirement of an examination for entry and a merit system for promotion, and it introduced retirement benefits and an improved salary scale that allowed for (somewhat) broader participation. Career FSOs would rotate through three-to-four-year postings, with the possibility of tours in Washington, DC. The rotation system meant that postings in the new system were of comparable length to those in the earlier election-based system. Rotations also encouraged FSOs to be generalists, rather than specialists in a given area or country. The State Department did recognize the need for expertise, however, and they created a program for area specialists; Russia and China were given particular attention. The broad contours of the Rogers Act remained in place through subsequent reforms in 1946 and 1980.

Arguably, the Rogers Act professionalized American diplomacy, but the State Department never managed to secure a monopoly on creating and implementing foreign policy. The military, the Department of Commerce, and, after its creation in 1947, the National Security Council offered the stiffest competition. The law also allowed approximately half the chief-of-mission positions to be held by political appointees rather than career FSOs. However, the Rogers Act did make stable careers in diplomacy possible, and for a broader range of people.

AFRICAN AMERICANS AND WOMEN IN THE FOREIGN SERVICE

That broader range was still predominantly white men, although increasingly from beyond the northeastern Ivy League establishment. A handful of African American men had received political appointments since the Civil War, including Ebenezer Don Carlos Bassett (1833–1908), who was appointed US minister to Haiti in 1869. Liberia was the other common posting for African American appointees. The first African American professional at the State Department was Clifton Wharton (1899–1990), who worked as a law clerk before passing the diplomatic examination in 1924. He was posted to Liberia and became the first African American career FSO to reach the rank of ambassador when he was accredited to the Liberian government in that capacity in 1961. The first African American political appointee at the ambassadorial rank was Edward R. Dudley (1911–2005), who was appointed to Liberia in 1949. The few African American FSOs who served before the 1970s were usually posted to Liberia, the Azores, the Canary Islands, and Madagascar.

Lucile Atcherson (1894–1986) was the first woman to pass the diplomatic examination. She was kept in Washington for three years before finally being sent to Bern, Switzerland, in 1925. She resigned shortly after being transferred to Panama in 1927. The first woman to pass the foreign service exam was Pattie Field (b. 1902), who was posted to Amsterdam in 1925. She resigned in 1929 to take a job at the National Broadcasting Company. The first female career FSO was Frances E. Willis (1899–1983), who began her career in Valparaiso, Chile, in 1927 and became the first female career ambassador in 1962. The first female political appointee was Eugenie Anderson (1909–1997), who became ambassador to Denmark in 1949.

Between 1931 and 1945, no women passed the foreign service exam. One deterrent to women's service was the rule, in place until 1971, that they had to resign their jobs when they married. Their male counterparts only had to suspend their work if they wanted to marry a foreign citizen, and then only temporarily. Although very few women were FSOs before the 1970s, women were essential to the conduct of US diplomacy, living abroad with their FSO husbands and serving as hostesses and volunteer workers. They were not paid, but they were assessed as part of their husbands' performance evaluations. This controversial practice ceased in 1972, when the State Department issued its Policy on the Wives of Foreign Service Employees, which explicitly categorized spouses as private citizens with no representational duties. In 1978 the Family Liaison Office was created to help Foreign Service spouses find employment abroad, and those efforts have continued to expand.

QUALIFICATIONS AND CAREER TRACKS

To enter the USFS today, one needs to be a US citizen between the ages of twenty-one and sixty. Successful candidates pass a written exam and must undergo a review of paperwork submitted to the Qualifications Evaluation Panel, an oral interview, medical and security clearances, and a final panel evaluation before being placed on the register of eligible officers, which is then approved by the Senate. According to recruiting materials, Foreign Service personnel have to demonstrate composure, cultural adaptability, experience and motivation, initiative and leadership, judgment, objectivity and integrity, resourcefulness, and skills at information integration and analysis, written and oral communication, planning and organizing, quantitative analysis, and working cooperatively. This description reflects the long-standing State Department preference for representatives who have broad general knowledge, strong interpersonal skills, and administrative competence. Most FSOs have undergraduate degrees, and many have advanced degrees or work experience, but there are no specific educational requirements to be an FSO; indeed, foreign languages are still not a requirement, as the State Department provides necessary language training.

Upon applying for the service, potential FSOs choose one of five career tracks. Those focusing on consular affairs provide assistance to Americans abroad and issue visas. Economic officers promote trade and engage with environmental issues. Political officers conduct negotiations and advise policy makers. Public diplomacy specialists interact with the media, build and maintain a presence on the Web, and administer cultural programs. Management specialists deal with the operation of embassies and other posts abroad, including managing personnel, budgets, and real estate, and helping family members find employment. In addition to FSOs, the USFS also includes Foreign Service specialists, who serve in a range of positions falling into eight broad categories: administration, construction engineering, facility management, information technology, international information and English-language programs, medical and health, office management, and security. Professionally credentialed FSSs facilitate the smooth running of US diplomatic posts abroad, serving not only State Department employees, but also employees of other parts of the US government who live and work abroad. The expansion in the number of FSSs, especially since the 1980s, reflects security concerns and a heightened interest in using US citizens rather than local employees to run posts abroad.

SEE ALSO *Americanization; Central Intelligence Agency (CIA); Cold War; Department of Homeland Security; Department of State; Embassies, Consulates, and Diplomatic Missions; Empire, US; National Security Council (NSC); Peace Corps; World War I; World War II*

BIBLIOGRAPHY

Barnes, William, and John Heath Morgan. *The Foreign Service of the United States: Origins, Development, and Functions.* Washington, DC: US Department of State, 1961.

Calkin, Homer L. *Women in the Department of State: Their Role in American Foreign Affairs.* Washington, DC: GPO, 1978.

Fenzi, Jewell, and Carl L. Nelson, eds. *Married to the Foreign Service: An Oral History of the American Diplomatic Spouse.* New York: Twayne, 1994.

Ilchman, Warren Frederick. *Professional Diplomacy in the United States, 1779–1939: A Study in Administrative History.* Chicago: University of Chicago Press, 1961.

Krenn, Michael L. *Black Diplomacy: African Americans and the State Department, 1945–1969.* Armonk, NY: Sharpe, 1999.

Plischke, Elmer. *U.S. Department of State: A Reference History.* Westport, CT: Greenwood Press, 1999.

Schulzinger, Robert D. *The Making of the Diplomatic Mind: The Training, Outlook, and Style of United States Foreign Service Officers, 1908–1931.* Middletown, CT: Wesleyan University Press, 1975.

US Department of State. *Becoming a Foreign Service Officer/ Specialist.* 2014. https://careers.state.gov/uploads/82/8d/828dd9d3767f997acb7de795e62a55a3/Foreign-Service-Selection-Process-Brochure-for-Officers-and-Specialists.pdf

Weil, Martin. *A Pretty Good Club: The Founding Fathers of the U.S. Foreign Service.* New York: Norton, 1978.

Werking, Richard Hume. *The Master Architects: Building the United States Foreign Service, 1890–1913.* Lexington: University Press of Kentucky, 1977.

Nicole M. Phelps
Associate Professor of History
University of Vermont

FOUR FREEDOMS

President Franklin Delano Roosevelt (1882–1945) first articulated the Four Freedoms in his State of the Union address on January 6, 1941. They attained iconic status as a summary declaration of American war aims in World War II. Through the Cold War and beyond, they continued to serve as a kind of charter and measuring rod for American foreign policy and, indeed, as a lodestar for much of the world's political and social aspirations. President Roosevelt's widow, Eleanor Roosevelt (1884–1962), succeeded in stitching the language of the Four Freedoms into the Preamble of the Universal Declaration of Human Rights, adopted by the United Nations in 1948.

The path to the formulation of the Four Freedoms began with a singularly importunate letter from British prime minister Winston Churchill (1874–1965) to President Roosevelt dated December 8, 1940, laying out Britain's desperate need for massive infusions of American matériel and money if Britain were to continue fighting the war against Nazi Germany that had begun in September 1939. Roosevelt had long since made known his support for Britain's cause, though he had stopped well short of advocating American belligerency. But to provide assistance on the scale that Churchill now requested required that he ask Congress for an initial appropriation of some $7 billion. "Lend-Lease," as Roosevelt's initiative soon came to be called, would eventually send some $50 billion of munitions to Britain and America's other allies in World War II.

Convincing a still largely isolationist Congress and country to shoulder that burden—and thereby increase the risk of ensnaring the United States in a shooting war—was the challenge Roosevelt faced as he took to the podium in the House chamber.

The United States, he said, hoped to shape "a world founded upon four essential human freedoms":

> The first is freedom of speech and expression—everywhere in the world.
>
> The second is freedom of every person to worship God in his own way—everywhere in the world.
>
> The third is freedom from want—which, translated into world terms, means economic understandings which will secure to every nation a healthy peacetime life for its inhabitants—everywhere in the world.
>
> The fourth is freedom from fear—which, translated into world terms, means a world-wide reduction of armaments to such a point and in such a thorough fashion that no nation will be in a position to commit an act of physical aggression against any neighbor—anywhere in the world.

That ringing peroration helped to secure passage of the Lend-Lease Act in March 1941.

Grounded in inherited conceptions of individual rights and liberties—as recently enhanced in the New Deal—Roosevelt's language distilled much of the essence of America's political creed. Perhaps for that reason the Four Freedoms have often been rendered by artists and writers as describing values that Americans would fight, defensively, to protect at home. Norman Rockwell's (1894–1978) pictorial depictions of the Four Freedoms, first published in the *Saturday Evening Post* in 1943, exemplified that interpretation. But the context of Roosevelt's remarks makes clear that he intended them primarily as foreign-policy goals to be pursued in the wider world. He was defining an international agenda, not a domestic one.

Fittingly, the words are inscribed on the wall of the final "room" of the Roosevelt Memorial in Washington, DC, in the space dedicated not to the Great Depression and the New Deal but to the wartime years. The Franklin D. Roosevelt Four Freedoms Park on Roosevelt Island in New York City, designed by architect Louis Kahn, offers powerful artistic testimony to the enduring legacy of the Four Freedoms.

SEE ALSO *"The American Century" (Henry Luce, 1941); Cold War; Roosevelt, Franklin D.; World War II*

BIBLIOGRAPHY

"FDR and the Four Freedoms Speech." Franklin D. Roosevelt Presidential Library and Museum. http://www.fdrlibrary.marist.edu/fourfreedoms

Kennedy, David M. *Freedom from Fear: The American People in Depression and War, 1929–1945*. New York: Oxford University Press, 1999.

Powers of Persuasion: Poster Art from World War II. "Four Freedoms." National Archives and Records Administration. http://www.archives.gov/exhibits/powers_of_persuasion/four_freedoms/four_freedoms.html

David M. Kennedy
Donald J. McLachlan Professor of History Emeritus
Stanford University

FOURTEEN POINTS

SEE *Wilson, Woodrow.*

FRANCE

Except for brief hostilities during the Quasi-War of 1798 to 1800, when American naval ships battled French privateers, and in 1942, when American troops encountered Vichy

French forces during Operation Torch in North Africa, France and the United States have avoided going to war against one another. France's sale of the Louisiana Territory in 1803 facilitated American expansion westward, and its gift of the Statue of Liberty, dedicated in 1886, became a symbol of Franco-American amity. Following the September 11, 2001, terrorist attacks, the French newspaper *Le Monde* declared "Nous sommes tous américains" (We are all Americans).

RECIPROCAL ADMIRATION AND CRITICISM

Since 1776, when the French government intervened to help the Americans gain independence, cultural relations between the two countries have had their ups and downs, with positive and negative perceptions often surfacing at the same time or even in the same observer. Alexis de Tocqueville (1805–1859), for example, voiced both admiration for American democracy and dynamism, and suspicion of American egalitarianism in *Democracy in America* (1835–1840). Americans have valued the philosophy of Jacques Derrida (1930–2004), the elegance of Coco Chanel (1883–1971), and expressions such as *à la mode.* Envisioning the Paris of Pigalle, known as the city's red light district, and the Folies Bergère, they have also viewed France as a site of immorality and excessive sexuality. French critics of America have, in turn, targeted "Coca Colonization," rock-and-roll music, and McDonald's. Euro Disney, opened near Paris in 1992, set off additional alarm over Americanization in France, as did French celebrations of Halloween in the late 1990s. The American post-Thanksgiving "Black Friday" is now also catching on in France.

Early Franco-American exchanges included Thomas Paine (1737–1809), who supported the American Revolution in *Common Sense* (1776) and the French Revolution in *The Rights of Man* (1791), and de Tocqueville. Thomas Jefferson (1743–1826) and other early American leaders also visited France. The inventor and artist Samuel F. B. Morse (1791–1872) traveled to Paris, where he painted *The Gallery of the Louvre* (1831–1833). With larger numbers of visitors to France by 1904, Henry Adams's (1838–1918) *Mont Saint-Michel and Chartres* became an iconic American view of medieval France. American art critic Walter Pach (1883–1958) helped introduce Americans to European modern art by bringing what many viewed as shocking paintings by Marcel Duchamp (1887–1968) and Henri Matisse (1869–1964) to New York for the 1913 International Exhibition of Modern Art. Today, the French Heritage Society, established in 1982, with chapters in the United States and France, works to restore historic buildings and gardens in both countries.

Favorable currency exchange rates after World War I brought American literati, including William Faulkner (1897–1962), F. Scott Fitzgerald (1896–1940), Sylvia Beach (1887–1962), Gertrude Stein (1874–1946), and Ernest Hemingway (1899–1961), to Paris, which also welcomed black American artists, such as Josephine Baker (1906–1975) and Sidney Bechet (1897–1959), who helped establish jazz there. Anti-Americanism, however, fueled by resentment of the dollar's strength, led to physical assaults on American tourists in Paris in 1926.

Following the unexpectedly quick military defeat of France by Nazi Germany in 1940, the United States maintained diplomatic relations with the new Vichy government in an attempt to minimize its collaboration with the Germans. The Allied invasion of French North Africa in November 1942, however, led to a rare case of French and American forces exchanging fire, even if briefly. While most French welcomed D-day and the liberation in June 1944, disagreements between American policy makers and Charles de Gaulle (1890–1970) over the role of France in the postwar world led to tensions after the war as France fought to maintain its empire in Indochina and Algeria, and after France withdrew from the North Atlantic Treaty Organization in 1966. American tourism to France, however, increased with the coming of jumbo jets and cheaper air travel after 1978, when airlines were deregulated in the United States. The US Department of Commerce estimated that, in 2013, 2 million Americans visited France and 1.5 million French visitors came to the United States.

CULTURAL EXCHANGE THROUGH FILM AND GASTRONOMY

Two key areas of cultural exchange have been film and gastronomy. American films of the 1890s focused on the cancan, a high-stepping dance popular from the late nineteenth through the mid-twentieth centuries. The silent films *French Can-Can* and *An Impromptu Can-Can at the Chorus Girls' Picnic*, both released in 1898, typified the first American-made films about France, followed by two more about the Folies Bergère in the mid-1930s. *They Had to See Paris* (1929) featured an Oklahoma visitor's homespun common sense against the perceived pretentiousness he encountered in France. *Casablanca* (1942), set in Rick's Café Américain in French Morocco, became the iconic story of the French Resistance during World War II. D-day was the inspiration for several American epic films, notably *The Longest Day* (1962) and *Saving Private Ryan* (1998).

An American in Paris (1951), accompanied by George Gershwin's (1898–1937) music, reflected popular American tourist images of Paris taxis, the Eiffel Tower, Notre Dame, the Folies Bergère, and 1890s Montmartre cancan dancers. *Funny Face* (1957), in which Audrey Hepburn (1929–1993) plays a young woman visiting Paris to meet a spiritual beatnik guru, depicted the city as a tourist icon in the era of Jean-Paul Sartre (1905–1980). By the 1970s, however, French motifs appeared less frequently, replaced in part by adult or pornographic films associated with Paris, such as *Paris Porno* (1976) and *From Paris with Lust* (1985).

In the United States, where high-end taste meant French food, the most enduring images of France are culinary. Again, ambivalences existed. An eighteenth-century fashion for French food coexisted with the fear that it included mysterious and suspect ingredients. In Boston, a French restaurant named Julien's Restorator, opened by Jean-Baptiste Paypalt (c. 1753–1805) in 1794, served truffle dishes, cheese fondues, and soups. In 1833 Delmonico's established the French restaurant as a high-end destination in New York. Tourist circuits adopted French service styles, and in 1876 the Harvey railway-station restaurant network hired a French chef from the Palmer House in Chicago at the then-high salary of $5,000 per year.

During the 1930s the young American writer Mary Frances Kennedy Fisher (1908–1992) drove through France and acquainted American readers with newly "discovered" French regional cuisine, facilitated by the coming of the automobile. Writing for *Gourmet* magazine, established in 1941, Fisher, André Simon (1877–1970), and Samuel Chamberlain (1895–1975) helped revitalize American tastes for France's cuisine after World War II. The American chef Julia Child (1912–2004) popularized French food for homemakers in the United States with her cookbook *Mastering the Art of French Cooking* (1961), written with her French colleagues Simone Beck (1904–1991) and Louisette Bertholle (1905–1999).

Even in the 1970s, when interest in French gastronomy was high, Americans sometimes defined their own cultural identity in contrast to a perceived French pretentiousness. A 1971 article in *Holiday* magazine advised readers "how to get and keep the upper hand with a French menu." French restaurants clustered in areas of affluence, education, and leisure: the Northeast, the California coast and wine country, and the Seattle-Vancouver region. A subsequent shift away from classic Parisian fare was marked by negative images that appeared in such works as *Real Men Don't Eat Quiche* (1982), a satirical book by screenwriter and humorist Bruce Feirstein. In a 1991 *Newsweek* article titled "An American Revolution," journalist Laura Shapiro argued "our love affair with French food is over, done in by new passion for our own chefs and ingredients" (Shapiro 1991, 54). Shapiro pointed to the spread of McDonald's in France to suggest that the French culinary scene itself was changing. Political issues intruded in 2003 when French moves to block a United Nations resolution calling for the military overthrow of Saddam Hussein in Iraq led to a brief but bitter anti-French campaign in the United States that included an abortive campaign to rename french fries as freedom fries. On the other side of the Atlantic, the opening of a McDonald's in the Louvre food court sparked protests in France in 2009, and in 2014 French foreign minister Laurent Fabius ordered a diplomatic offensive against an "Anglo-Saxon" plot to "dethrone" French cuisine.

Although Americans continue to use French culinary terms, France's integration into Europe and its consequent decline in distinctiveness represent the closing of an era of French iconicity in the United States. According to the Modern Languages Association, nearly 360,000 American college students studied French in 1970, a number that had fallen to 205,000 by 1998, before increasing slightly to 216,000 in 2009. The rise of the ready-to-wear industry in the 1960s and 1970s cut into the French domination in fashion as well.

SEE ALSO *Europe; Napoleon Bonaparte; World War I; World War II*

BIBLIOGRAPHY

Benstock, Shari. *Women of the Left Bank, Paris 1900–1940.* Austin: University of Texas Press, 1986.

Duroselle, Jean-Baptiste. "Relations between Two Peoples: The Singular Example of the United States and France." *Review of Politics* 41, 4 (1979): 483–500.

Gordon, Bertram M. "Going Abroad to Taste: North Americans, France, and the Continental Tour from the Late Nineteenth Century to the Present." In *Proceedings of the Western Society for French History: Selected Papers of the Annual Meeting,* 156–170. Greeley: University Press of Colorado, 1998.

Gordon, Bertram M. "The Decline of a Cultural Icon: France in American Perspective." *French Historical Studies* 22, 4 (1999): 625–651.

Hemingway, Ernest. *A Moveable Feast.* New York: Scribner's, 1964.

Kuisel, Richard F. *The French Way: How France Embraced and Rejected American Values and Power.* Princeton, NJ: Princeton University Press, 2011.

Levenstein, Harvey. *Seductive Journey: American Tourists in France from Jefferson to the Jazz Age.* Chicago: University of Chicago Press, 1998.

Levenstein, Harvey. *We'll Always Have Paris: American Tourists in France since 1930.* Chicago: University of Chicago Press, 2004.

McCullough, David G. *The Greater Journey: Americans in Paris.* New York: Simon and Schuster, 2011.

Portes, Jacques. "France and the United States." In *France and the Americas: Culture, Politics, and History,* edited by Bill Marshall, 37–46. Santa Barbara, CA: ABC-Clio Press, 2005.

Roger, Philippe. *The American Enemy: The History of French Anti-Americanism.* Translated by Sharon Bowman. Chicago: University of Chicago Press, 2005.

Shapiro, Laura. "An American Revolution." *Newsweek* 118, 25 (December 16, 1991): 54–57.

Stovall, Tyler. *Paris Noir: African Americans in the City of Light.* Boston: Houghton Mifflin, 1996.

Wall, Irwin M. *The United States and the Making of Postwar France, 1945–1954.* Cambridge: Cambridge University Press, 1991.

Bertram M. Gordon
Professor of History
Mills College

FRANKLIN, BENJAMIN

1706–1790

Benjamin Franklin was the leading American diplomat of the American Revolution and one of the most famous and influential Americans of his century, both at home and abroad.

COLONIAL AT THE HEART OF EMPIRE

The Revolution came late in Franklin's life—he was seventy when he signed the Declaration of Independence, with a long career in business, civic leadership, and public affairs behind him. He had spent most of the two decades preceding the Revolution in London as an agent for Pennsylvania and, later, three other colonies. As the tensions between the colonies and the metropole mounted in the years after the Seven Years' War (1756–1763), he had served as an advocate for the colonies and a voice of conciliation to both sides. From late 1774 to early 1775, as the crisis came to a head, Franklin met with representatives of the ministry in secret last-ditch negotiations to reach a settlement but without success. When Franklin left Britain for home that spring, convinced that the ministry and Parliament were beyond the reach of reason, he still had many friends and admirers in Britain and Europe. But others in the government and among its supporters had come to see him as an arch conspirator, a representative abroad of the cabal they believed had fomented rebellion in the colonies. By the time Franklin reached home, fighting had begun in Massachusetts. He immediately began work in the offices and numerous committees to which he was named in the Pennsylvania government and the Continental Congress to prepare the defenses and plan for the future of the colonies.

REVOLUTIONARY IN A WIDER WORLD

Franklin was deeply involved in foreign policy and diplomacy from the beginning. He served on the committees for drafting the Declaration of Independence and the Model Treaty, principally authored by Thomas Jefferson (1743–1826) and John Adams (1735–1826), respectively. Franklin was sent in early 1776 as one of the commissioners of the ultimately unsuccessful mission to persuade the Canadian colonists to join the Revolution, and he was appointed one of the representatives who met with Lord Howe (1726–1799) on Staten Island in September 1776 to discuss his last-minute terms for peace. Franklin served on the Secret Committee, established in September 1775, charged with procuring munitions and supplies from abroad. He was one of the initial members of the Committee for Secret Correspondence formed in November to establish contact with potential friends and allies abroad. And he helped draft the instructions to the first congressional agent to France, Silas Deane (1737–1789), who was directed to Franklin's own European connections and correspondents for help. In late 1776, Franklin was himself sent to join Deane and Arthur Lee (1740–1792) as a commissioner to the French court. After the French alliance was secured in 1778, Franklin was made sole US minister plenipotentiary to France.

In his diplomatic capacity, Franklin secured a series of loans from France, coordinated French military aid to the United States, and maintained French confidence in American credit, unity, and resolve. He worked on his own initiative to arrange prisoner exchanges with Britain and to provide aid to American prisoners of war. In conjunction with other US diplomats, he managed US finances and credit in Europe. At the same time, he functioned for much of the war as de facto US consul general in Europe, providing aid to Americans in distress and fielding numerous inquiries, applications, and proposals from Europeans.

Franklin worked to further US interests in less formal ways as well. Both in concert with the French ministry and on his own, he orchestrated the publication of American public documents, favorable news reports, ripostes to British propaganda, and a few of his own satirical, polemical, and philosophical writings. He likewise used his own public image to bolster that of his country. He had arrived in France already a celebrity for his scientific achievements and his philosophical, political, and literary works. He immediately found himself the focus of public curiosity, admiration, and even adulation, and was hailed, as well, as the embodiment of New World republican virtue, simplicity, and wisdom—fashionable and idealized among an influential segment of the elite of Enlightenment France and Europe. Franklin selectively embraced and played up this image and his popularity, while, through his wit, sophistication, and sociability, so congenial and agreeable to the French aristocratic salon culture in which he moved, he helped to diffuse any sense

Illustration of Benjamin Franklin at the French court, 1778. *As an American diplomat, Franklin arrived in France already a celebrity for his scientific achievements and his philosophical, political, and literary works. The focus of public curiosity, admiration, and adulation, he was hailed as the embodiment of New World republican virtue, simplicity, and wisdom.* AMERICAN STOCK ARCHIVE/ ARCHIVE PHOTOS/GETTY IMAGES

that the republican revolution he represented posed a threat to European political and social order. He attended meetings of scientific societies, wrote papers, served on royal scientific commissions, and corresponded with leading scientists and philosophers throughout Europe. He was active in an eminent lodge of Freemasons. In the process, he bolstered both his own and his country's reputation.

At the same time, Franklin worked to dispel European misconceptions about his country and compatriots. Americans were neither naive nor backward; they did not share European aristocratic values; and they would have little use for European immigrants seeking sinecures, feudal estates, or markets and patrons for fine arts and luxury goods. Conversely, he warned his fellow Americans against imitating or allowing themselves, their politics, and their society to be corrupted by the luxury and aristocratic values of their Old World allies.

Franklin and his conduct in France were not always viewed with favor by all of his American colleagues abroad or constituents at home, some of whom believed or charged, variously, that he was dissolute, lazy, corrupt, careless, too submissive to France, too fond of peace, or simply too old (an opinion he was inclined to share). Nevertheless, Franklin retained many supporters and considerable influence, and he was kept at his post in France for the duration of the war and well beyond, despite his repeated requests to be recalled and allowed to retire.

PEACEMAKER AMONG THE NATIONS

At the close of the war, Franklin was appointed one of the five peace commissioners. He, John Adams, and John Jay (1745–1829), the three principally involved in the negotiations, successfully concluded a treaty securing independence and granting expansive boundaries for the

United States, albeit without consulting or taking much account of the Native American nations who inhabited and claimed much of the trans-Appalachian West located in these boundaries. Franklin and his colleagues were unable to bring the British to conclude an acceptable commercial treaty.

Franklin shared with his colleagues and many of his compatriots the conviction, embodied in the 1776 Model Treaty, that liberal, equitable trade among all nations, with comprehensive protections for neutral shipping in wartime, would form the best basis for lasting peace and prosperity, for the United States and for all. To such principles Franklin hoped to add humanitarian provisions that, if established in international law, might further reduce the risk and mitigate the rigors of war. These included the proscription of privateering and protections for noncombatants engaged in work, like farming, fishing, or scientific pursuits, necessary to sustain the civilian population or of benefit to humankind in general. Franklin tried, fruitlessly, to persuade the British to accept such provisions in the treaty of peace. He would have more success persuading other powers.

Following the preliminary peace with Britain, Franklin concluded a commercial treaty with Sweden, which included a provision forbidding the citizens and subjects of each power to engage in privateering against the people, ships, or property of the other. Franklin was subsequently commissioned with Adams and Jefferson to negotiate treaties of amity and commerce with other European powers. Before Franklin left France in the summer of 1785, they signed a treaty with Prussia, which included Franklin's proposed articles prohibiting privateering and protecting noncombatants.

STATESMAN ON THE WORLD STAGE

Even after his return to America in the fall of 1785, Franklin maintained an extensive social and scientific correspondence with friends and intellectuals in Europe. At home, he continued in public service and remained active in public and scientific discourse. In these last years of his life, he capped his career in diplomatic service as a delegate to the 1787 Constitutional Convention, where he helped to negotiate the new compact among the thirteen American states. Though his substantive proposals for the new government were largely dismissed by his younger colleagues, Franklin, like George Washington (1732–1799), lent considerable added prestige and authority to the Convention and the Constitution. He brought, as well, an influential voice in favor of compromise, conciliation, and unanimity.

Abroad, Franklin continued to enjoy great prestige as an individual, as an emblem of American republican virtue, and as an embodiment of American potential. Upon his death, French luminaries eulogized Franklin one after the other and the French revolutionaries of the National Assembly put on mourning in his honor.

SEE ALSO *Adams, John; American Revolution; Declaration of Independence; Jay, John; Jefferson, Thomas*

BIBLIOGRAPHY

Chaplin, Joyce E. *The First Scientific American: Benjamin Franklin and the Pursuit of Genius.* New York: Basic Books, 2006.

Dull, Jonathan R. "Franklin the Diplomat: The French Mission." *Transactions of the American Philosophical Society* 72 (1982): 1–76.

Dull, Jonathan R. *Benjamin Franklin and the American Revolution.* Lincoln: University of Nebraska Press, 2010.

Labaree, Leonard W., et al., eds. *The Papers of Benjamin Franklin.* 41 vols. as of 2015. New Haven, CT: Yale University Press, 1959– .

Stourzh, Gerald. *Benjamin Franklin and American Foreign Policy.* Chicago: University of Chicago Press, 1954.

Wood, Gordon S. *The Americanization of Benjamin Franklin.* New York: Penguin, 2004.

John M. Huffman
Assistant Editor, The Papers of Benjamin Franklin
Yale University

FREEDOM FIGHTERS

"Freedom fighters" was a common description during the Cold War for opponents of communist rule. The term became highly popular in the 1980s when President Ronald Reagan (1911–2004) used it to bolster support for the Contras in Nicaragua, who tried to overthrow a leftist government that allegedly posed a communist danger to neighboring countries in Central America.

US officials often framed the Cold War as a struggle between freedom and authoritarianism, as President Harry S. Truman (1884–1972) did in March 1947 in his Truman Doctrine speech when he declared, "It must be the policy of the United States to support free peoples who are resisting attempted subjugation by armed minorities or by outside pressures" (Truman 1947). Neither Truman, however, nor President Dwight D. Eisenhower (1890–1969) used the term *freedom fighters* in his public rhetoric, even though it became a familiar way to characterize anticommunist resistance movements. *Time* magazine, for example, chose the Hungarian Freedom Fighter as its Man of the Year for 1956. This symbolic figure represented the "anonymous thousands" of revolutionaries who struggled to "end the long night of Communist dictatorship" in Eastern Europe (*Time* 1957). John F. Kennedy (1917–1963) was the first president to use "freedom fighters" in a public statement when he lauded the Cuban exiles the Central Intelligence Agency (CIA) had trained and equipped to topple the government of Fidel Castro (b. 1926) during the disastrous Bay of Pigs invasion in April 1961. By the last year of his presidency, Kennedy had broadened the term to include Latin American citizens engaged in political organizing to build democracy and thwart communism.

During the 1980s, conflicts in Afghanistan and Nicaragua made "freedom fighters" a controversial part of Cold War rhetoric. Jimmy Carter (b. 1924) applied that term to forces in Afghanistan that battled Soviet troops, which had invaded in December 1979 to protect a faltering communist government. Carter's rhetoric was misleading, as the mujahideen, or guerrilla resistance, consisted of a diverse coalition of warlords and tribal groups, some of whom wished to establish an Islamic state. Carter authorized covert CIA assistance to the mujahideen, and Reagan increased aid to the Afghan resistance that he, too, called "freedom fighters." Their battlefield success was a major reason for the Soviet troop withdrawal in 1988 and 1989.

Reagan quite frequently called the counterrevolutionaries in Nicaragua "freedom fighters," a term he preferred to "Contras." He even insisted they were the moral equivalent of America's Founding Fathers. Such statements were highly controversial, as critics charged that the Contras were human rights violators who tortured and executed civilians. Other opponents of Reagan's policy maintained that the president exaggerated Soviet influence in Nicaragua and that the Contras, rather than the Nicaraguan government, constituted the greatest threat to peace and security in Central America. In what became known as the Reagan Doctrine, the president proclaimed that the United States "must not break faith" with freedom fighters against "Soviet-supported aggression" from Afghanistan to Nicaragua (Reagan 1985). Congress, however, limited aid to the Contras, and Reagan's desire to sustain the Nicaraguan "freedom fighters" in the face of those restrictions led to the Iran-Contra scandal.

SEE ALSO *Central Intelligence Agency (CIA); Reagan, Ronald Wilson; Truman Doctrine*

BIBLIOGRAPHY

Higgins, Trumbull. *The Perfect Failure: Kennedy, Eisenhower, and the CIA at the Bay of Pigs.* New York: Norton, 1989.

"HUNGARY: Freedom's Choice." *Time* 69, 1 (January 7, 1957).

LeoGrande, William M. *Our Own Backyard: The United States in Central America, 1977–1992.* Chapel Hill: University of North Carolina Press, 1998.

Reagan, Ronald. Address before a Joint Session of the Congress on the State of the Union, February 6, 1985. *Messages and Papers of the Presidents.* The American Presidency Project, edited by John T. Woolley and Gerhard Peters. http://www.presidency.ucsb.edu/ws/?pid=38069

Truman, Harry. Special Message to the Congress on Greece and Turkey: The Truman Doctrine, March 12, 1947. *Messages and Papers of the Presidents.* The American Presidency Project, edited by John T. Woolley and Gerhard Peters. http://www.presidency.ucsb.edu/ws/?pid=12846

Chester J. Pach
Associate Professor, Department of History
Ohio University

FREMONT, JOHN C.

SEE *Mexican-American War.*

FRENCH REVOLUTION

Between 1789 and 1804 the French Revolution and its resulting wars engulfed the Atlantic world. The impetus of the French Revolution in the late 1780s was rooted in an ideological conflict over the proper form of government, coupled with a fiscal crisis that originated with the extensive loans required to prosecute French involvement in the American Revolution (1775–1783). Initial efforts at political reform of the ancien régime and the destruction of the old feudal order ushered in a brief period of constitutional monarchy (1789–1792), the creation of a republic (1792), the execution of Louis XVI and the beginning of global conflict (1793), the Terror against domestic "enemies" (1793–1794), and finally a more moderate Directory expanding the territorial ambitions of the republic (1795–1799). After a decade of internal conflict and turmoil within France, the ascension of Napoleon Bonaparte (1769–1821) to power in 1799 through a military coup, and his self-proclaimed elevation to the position of "emperor of the French" in 1804, ushered in the end of the revolution through the institution of a government that was primarily interested in maintaining law and order rather than furthering revolutionary change. The French Revolution, in addition to its wide-ranging effects upon the European continent, also had major ramifications for the political and economic development of the early American Republic.

INITIAL AMERICAN SUPPORT

At the outset of the French Revolution in 1789, most Americans believed that the French were following their example of the previous decade. The Marquis de Lafayette (1757–1834), a central player in the early phase of the

French Revolution and a veteran of the American War for Independence, worked with Thomas Jefferson (1743–1826) to craft the Declaration of the Rights of Man and Citizen and later granted George Washington (1732–1799) the key to the Bastille as a token of his gratitude for being able to serve in the dual causes of liberty. Between 1789 and 1793, American support for the reforms of the French Revolution, including trade liberalization and representative government, was strong. American citizens were apt to wear French tricolor cockades, publicly celebrate French military victories, and claim that the two revolutions were part of the same inexorable spread of liberty. The Washington administration even provided military aid to the French West Indian colony of Saint-Domingue at the outset of its slave revolt in August 1791.

American attitudes toward the French Revolution began to change in 1793. In August 1792 the Parisian crowd rose up against King Louis XVI and massacred his Swiss Guard after French émigré (nobles who fled the revolution), backed by Prussian and Austrian armies, announced that they would fight until the king was restored to his ancient privileges. The formation of the French Republic in September 1792, the massacres of those deemed enemies of the revolution, and the January 1793 execution of Louis XVI marked an important departure for the American response to the French Revolution. News of these events arrived in the United States in the spring of 1793, at the same time that the French Republic's first minister arrived: Citizen Edmond-Charles Genêt (1763–1834). The foreign ministry tasked Genêt with encouraging the Americans to openly support France in its war against Britain and other European powers. When Citizen Genêt arrived in Charleston, South Carolina, he slowly made his way to the American capital in Philadelphia by land and was widely celebrated. Many Americans flocked to the French minister, and some outfitted privateer vessels to raid British shipping. The Washington administration, on the other hand, chose to take a careful position with regard to France's wars. Realizing that American support for France could bring it into a second war with Great Britain, Washington issued a proclamation of neutrality on April 22, 1793, and officially maintained that the 1778 Treaty of Alliance only required the United States to aid France in defensive wars, not offensive ones that it had started.

GENÊT'S POLARIZING MISSION TO AMERICA

Upon Genêt's arrival in Philadelphia, his actions and news of the radical turn of the French Revolution quickly polarized American politics and alienated even Genêt's closest supporter in Washington's cabinet, Jefferson. Washington's secretary of state had been the United States' minister to France in the late 1780s, and was a strong supporter of the French Revolution. Jefferson believed that "the liberty of the whole earth was depending on the issue of the contest" (Wood 2009, 180). Treasury Secretary Alexander Hamilton (1755–1804), on the other hand, largely opposed the social change and violence occurring in France and explained that the difference between the American and the French Revolutions was the difference "between Liberty & Licentiousness" (Wood 2009, 177). It was little wonder then that Jefferson initially supported Genêt, while Hamilton recommended that the United States abrogate its treaty obligations.

Broad swaths of the American public quickly fell into the Hamiltonian and the Jeffersonian camps. The Jeffersonian Republicans initially supported Genêt and openly favored the French while generally preferring to remain out of their wars. The Republicans viewed the American Revolution in similar terms to that of the French: both revolutions overthrew feudal institutions and brought forth a modern republic based upon natural rights. The Hamiltonian Federalists, conversely, were convinced that the ideological forces of the French Revolution would bring social disorder to the United States and sought to delegitimize the revolution in the eyes of Americans. For the Federalists, the American Revolution was an independence movement that recreated in America great institutions that could provide liberty and security under a constitutionally defined government and a strong commitment to a national commonwealth.

Genêt's provocative actions in the United States ultimately helped the Federalists in their political fight with the Republicans. Despite orders from the Washington administration to stop outfitting privateers in American ports, Genêt continued in his mission and announced that if Washington opposed him then he would go over his head and take the French cause directly to the American people. Even Jefferson could not abide this interference in American domestic politics, and soon the State Department requested that the French Republic recall Genêt. The French Republic agreed to Genêt's recall, and, fearing the guillotine, Genêt successfully applied to Washington for political asylum.

THE JAY TREATY AND THE QUASI-WAR

In the year following Genêt's mission, the British began to openly attack American commerce with the French West Indies in an attempt to cut off the French from their sugar-and coffee-producing colonies. Rejecting the neutral principle that free ships make free goods, British admiralty courts accepted any vessel carrying enemy produce as a legal prize. With war clouds on the horizon, the Washington administration delegated the chief justice of the Supreme Court, John Jay (1745–1829), to negotiate a treaty with Britain. The resulting 1794 Jay Treaty addressed few American grievances, such as neutral shipping rights, but did avert a war with Britain.

France, however, believed that the Jay Treaty marked a diplomatic turn toward the principal enemy of their revolution and an abandonment of the 1778 treaties. Soon, France too began to authorize the seizure of American merchant vessels trading with enemy powers. After his inauguration as president in 1797, John Adams (1735–1826) authorized a diplomatic commission to France to negotiate an end to their hostile trade policy and privateering against American vessels. Upon arriving in Paris, the American diplomats were informed by representatives of foreign minister Charles Maurice de Talleyrand (1754–1838) that the United States would have to first agree to a large bribe in order to begin negotiations. The XYZ Affair—so named due to the redaction of French names when news of the attempted bribe was released to Congress in early 1798—propelled the United States into an undeclared naval war with France. During the Quasi-War (1798–1800), Federalist majorities in Congress were able to expand the country's military capacity and officially annulled the 1778 French treaties. Adams's secretary of state even met with representatives of Toussaint Louverture's (1743–1803) regime in Saint-Domingue, and considered recognizing the colony as independent from France. With the passage of the Alien and Sedition Acts, the Federalists targeted foreign supporters of the French Revolution residing within the United States who published newspapers that were highly critical of the Adams administration. The unpopular nature of these acts, viewed by many as an assault on civil liberties, helped propel Jefferson's election to the presidency in 1800.

THE IMPORTANCE OF THE FRENCH REVOLUTION FOR US DEVELOPMENT

In addition to the effects of the French Revolution upon American domestic politics and foreign relations, émigré from the revolution facilitated the transfer of people, goods, and capital across the Atlantic. Refugees from the violence of the French Revolution, such as Louis-Marie, vicomte de Noailles (1756–1804), and Éleuthère Irénée du Pont de Nemours (1771–1834), employed their personal and family fortunes in the United States. Noailles, for example, provided capital and personal connections with other refugees to found a town for exiles from the French and Haitian Revolutions in northern Pennsylvania, while du Pont employed his family wealth and knowledge of chemistry to begin a highly successful gunpowder factory in Delaware. As Hamilton had noted in his 1791 "Report on Manufactures," the lack of capital had long inhibited American economic development. During the 1790s French émigré readily solved this deficiency and, in so doing, helped to develop lands in the American backcountry and introduce new manufacturing techniques.

Napoleon Bonaparte's overthrow of the Directory in 1799 hastened the end of the French Revolution but not the importance of Franco-American relations for the development of the United States. Bonaparte's diplomats were ready to renounce the Directory's hostility to the United States and in the 1800 Treaty of Mortefontaine readily agreed to end the war and normalize trade relations.

Following the cessation of hostilities with the United States, and with the European powers in the 1802 Treaty of Amiens, Bonaparte turned France's imperial attentions to its colony of Saint-Domingue. Since 1791 the colony had undergone civil war, slave revolt, British occupation, and an end to the institution of slavery, with control of the island ultimately resting under Toussaint Louverture, a former slave. In 1802, the French invaded the island and arrested Toussaint in the hopes of reasserting control of the island's plantation economy and the revenues derived from it. In Bonaparte's view for a new French empire in the new world, the territory of Louisiana in the interior of the North American continent would supply foodstuffs to the sugar and coffee plantations in Saint-Domingue. That colony, in turn, would supply French citizens with its produce, which the government could then tax.

Over the course of the next year, tropical disease and a brutal war with Toussaint's lieutenants destroyed the French army and Bonaparte's colonial vision. Realizing that the expedition was a failure, Bonaparte offered to sell all French land claims in North America to the United States in 1803. Seizing the opportunity, the Jefferson administration effectively doubled the size of the country with the Louisiana Purchase and secured a continental republic through the acquisition of the port of New Orleans with the stroke of a pen.

SEE ALSO *American Revolution; France; Haitian Revolution; Jefferson, Thomas; Lafayette, Marquis de; Toussaint Louverture; Wollstonecraft, Mary*

BIBLIOGRAPHY

Bradburn, Douglas. *The Citizenship Revolution: Politics and the Creation of the American Union, 1774–1804.* Charlottesville: University of Virginia Press, 2009.

Brown, Howard G. *Ending the French Revolution: Violence, Justice, and Repression from the Terror to Napoleon.* Charlottesville: University of Virginia Press, 2006.

DeConde, Alexander. *The Quasi-War: The Politics and Diplomacy of the Undeclared War with France, 1797–1801.* New York: Scribner's, 1966.

Doyle, William. *The Oxford History of the French Revolution.* 2nd ed. New York: Oxford University Press, 2002.

Dubois, Laurent. *Avengers of the New World: The Story of the Haitian Revolution.* Cambridge, MA: Harvard University Press, 2004.

Dunn, Susan. *Sister Revolutions: French Lightning, American Light.* New York: Faber and Faber, 1999.

Furstenberg, François. *When the United States Spoke French: Five Refugees Who Shaped a Nation.* New York: Penguin, 2014.

Palmer, R. R. *The Age of the Democratic Revolution: A Political History of Europe and America, 1760–1800.* Princeton, NJ: Princeton University Press, 2014.

Popkin, Jeremy D. *A Concise History of the Haitian Revolution.* Chichester, UK: Wiley-Blackwell, 2012.

Wood, Gordon. *Empire of Liberty: A History of the Early Republic, 1789–1815.* New York: Oxford University Press, 2009.

Andrew J. B. Fagal
The Papers of Thomas Jefferson
Princeton University

FRIEDMAN, MILTON
1912–2006

Milton Friedman was an economist and educator with unusual influence in American policy-making circles during the late twentieth century. The son of Jewish dry-goods merchants, he was born in New York and grew up in New Jersey. Friedman hoped to become an actuary, but his undergraduate mentors at Rutgers University nudged him instead toward the emerging field of economics and, after attaining an MA from the University of Chicago in 1933, he joined the Franklin Roosevelt administration, bouncing between several New Deal agencies during the 1930s and 1940s. As a midlevel bureaucrat, Friedman became interested in the nature of income and in 1946 submitted a PhD thesis on the topic to Columbia University. Shortly thereafter, he took a teaching position at the University of Chicago, where he spent three decades training students, networking with like-minded economists, and writing scholarly tomes about the monetary dimensions of US economic policy. His efforts resulted in a Nobel Prize in Economic Sciences in 1976. The following year, he and his wife, Rose Director Friedman (1910–2009), an esteemed economist in her own right, retired to San Francisco. As an affiliate of Stanford University's Hoover Institution, Friedman collaborated with the nearby Federal Reserve Bank and popularized his ideas about the money supply on television. During the 1980s he served on President Ronald Reagan's Economic Policy Advisory Board. Until his death in 2006, Friedman wrote columns and advised leaders around the world.

Friedman changed the way scholars understand economic recessions. When he began his career, the prevailing view among economists was that economic downturns resulted from unregulated markets, which, according to British economist John Maynard Keynes (1883–1946), were incubators for underemployment, underinvestment, and instability. In a series of articles and books, Friedman rejected Keynes's ideas about employment, consumption, and wages. Economic downtowns, he argued, grew not from markets but from the supply of money in the economy.

Friedman's most popular book, *A Monetary History of the United States, 1867–1960* (1963), cowritten with Anna Schwartz (1915–2012), explored the historical relationship between the United States' economic fluctuations and the country's money supply. On the basis of his findings, Friedman elaborated what would become his signature policy insight: both consumption and output could be maintained if governments regulated the growth rate of an economy's monetary base. This argument was not new; it stemmed from a school of thought known as monetarism, but Friedman substantiated his ideas using novel statistical methods and coupled his conclusions with colorful attacks on Keynesianism, specifically the premise that government investment and spending effected employment and output positively. Government, in his mind, was the barrier, not the lubricant, of economic prosperity.

Friedman's ideas did not find an audience in Washington, DC, until after his retirement. During his academic career, he toiled mostly at the periphery of the economics profession, cultivating an energetic community of monetarists in Chicago that lived in the shadow of their Keynesian colleagues from Harvard University and the Massachusetts Institute of Technology. Everything changed after the Vietnam War, when government investment and spending failed to stem the rise of unemployment and inflation. Friedman's 1976 Nobel Prize came for his theoretical writings about the natural rate of unemployment, but policy makers flocked to him in these years because he correctly predicted the arrival of stagflation. His views on inflation, specifically his suggestion that the Federal Reserve could remedy the situation by preventing fluctuations in the US money supply, helped organize Paul Volcker's approach as chairman of the Federal Reserve during the late 1970s and 1980s. In retirement, Friedman and his wife produced a ten-part Public Broadcasting Service television series and wrote an accompanying general-interest book, *Free to Choose: A Personal Statement* (1980). Friedman also traveled widely in Asia and Europe, proselytizing deregulation, lower tax rates, privatization, and monetarism. By the time of his death, he was arguably the intellectual lodestar of modern economic conservatism in the United States.

Today, Friedman's legacy is contested along predictable lines. Even his staunchest critics recognize that his predictions about stagflation represent one of the great intellectual achievements of postwar economics. However, liberals mostly reject Friedman's wider conclusions about Keynesianism, and many see the boom of 1982 to 1990, which overlapped with Friedman's time on the Economic Policy Advisory Board, as the result of government spending and lower taxes, making it a prototypical example of an expansionary budget deficit, fully in line with Keynes's general theories. Moreover, among younger conservatives, the nuances of Friedman's ideas are occasionally lost, specifically monetarism's role in preventing economic downturns. Unlike Friedrich Hayek (1899–1992), Friedman promoted active, albeit constrained, government. Regardless, Friedman gave depth and substance to the conservative movement after World War II.

SEE ALSO *Bush, George W.; Clinton, William Jefferson; Keynesian Economics; Neoliberalism; Reagan, Ronald Wilson; Think Tanks; World Trade Organization*

BIBLIOGRAPHY

Burgin, Angus. *The Great Persuasion: Reinventing Free Markets since the Depression.* Cambridge, MA: Harvard University Press, 2012.

Ebenstein, Alan O. (Lanny). *Milton Friedman: A Biography.* New York: Palgrave Macmillan, 2007.

Friedman, Milton. *A Monetary History of the United States, 1867–1960.* Princeton, NJ: Princeton University Press, 1963.

Friedman, Milton, and Rose D. Friedman. *Two Lucky People: Memoirs.* Chicago: University of Chicago Press, 1998.

Jones, Daniel Stedman. *Masters of the Universe: Hayek, Friedman, and the Birth of Neoliberal Politics.* Princeton, NJ: Princeton University Press, 2012.

Ryan Irwin
Assistant Professor of History
University at Albany–SUNY

FRIEDMAN, THOMAS L.

SEE *The World Is Flat (Thomas L. Friedman, 2005).*

FRONTIER WARS

From the beginnings of European settlement through the late nineteenth century, colonists fought, swindled, and in many cases massacred the North American indigenous population throughout the continent. Most of these tragic encounters occurred in frontier regions, or areas outside of immediate Euro-American legal, political, or military control. Although numerous American Indian nations and confederations combatted the Spanish, French, Dutch, and English settlers, in some cases coming close to wiping out entire colonial populations (King Philip's War, Yamasee War), the most protracted and geographically widespread conflicts between American Indians and Euro-Americans occurred on the Great Plains during the second half of the nineteenth century.

THE PLAINS WARS: EARLY YEARS

Known as the Frontier Wars, or the Plains Indian Wars, these struggles challenged long-held Euro-American assumptions regarding settler colonialism, agricultural development, land distribution, and frontier warfare. Plains Indian combatants, including tens of thousands of Lakota, Cheyenne, Arapaho, and Comanche participants, were often better armed than other Indian fighters farther east, and fast-evolving equestrian cultures throughout the Plains region equipped their defenders for mobile warfare with infantry and light cavalry units in the US Army. The most successful equestrian nations on the Plains fueled their economic, demographic, and military expansion by converting the half million square miles of grassland across the Plains into biofuel for their growing horse herds, which in turn expanded opportunities for and returns on bison hunting.

The relative isolation of the Great Plains insulated the region's indigenous population from European expansionism to a degree, but by the early nineteenth century the eastern Plains and prairies transformed into a vast borderland between the growing equestrian nations to the west and south and the ambitious new American republic to the east. Initially, the prospects for cooperation and coexistence seemed promising, as the Plains Indian nations provided a buffer against Spain, and the United States offered cheaper goods. However, tensions rose when the Oregon Trail opened to settlers in the early 1840s. Immigrants to Oregon, California, and Utah denuded the landscape of trees and grass, and bison grew scarce in some areas. In an effort to mollify the land's rightful owners, the United States recognized Lakota sovereignty over portions of Nebraska, Wyoming, the Dakotas, and Montana in the 1851 Fort Laramie Treaty. Nevertheless, war broke out in 1854 when a standoff between Sicangu Lakota Chief Scattering Bear and US Army Lieutenant John Grattan (1830–1854) over the theft of a Mormon migrant's cow erupted in gunfire. The Sicangu killed Grattan and twenty-nine of his soldiers; the following year Colonel William Harney (1800–1889) retaliated by assaulting a Sicangu and Oglala village near

Ash Hollow, Nebraska, killing eighty-six Indians and capturing another seventy women and children.

1860s

Intermittent warfare on the Plains continued for the next two decades. Relations between the Lakota and the US government hit a new low in 1863 when Lincoln approved the execution of thirty-eight Dakota prisoners in Mankato, Minnesota, following a short but bloody war between several Mdewakanton and Sisseton bands and whites who settled in the region. Meanwhile, in the South, Texas Rangers used recently invented revolvers to drive Comanches and Kiowas out of the state.

Until the late 1860s Euro-American domination was not always manifest or predestined. The Lakota, Northern Cheyenne, and others successfully resisted American military control for decades, although their growing reliance on manufactured goods and the concomitant decline of the bison population gradually pushed tribes into varying degrees of economic dependency. For one, the US Army did not have the money or the manpower to subdue the Plains Indian nations until the late 1870s. It faced an enemy that was better armed and more mobile and that had more fresh mounts at its disposal than the frontier cavalry. Secondly, although waves of homesteaders and other settlers arrived on the Plains to colonize the region, the region's aridity prevented them from establishing roots. Instead of turning the Plains into prairies, they fought ranchers for access to water and overleveraged their credit in order to keep their farms afloat.

In spite of farmers' mixed success on the Plains, the Homestead Act, the construction of the Union Pacific railroad, and a string of gold rushes in the Rockies together established the legal and transportation infrastructure that led to the settling of the Plains. The expanding rail network promised farmers and ranchers access to eastern markets. Gold rushes in Colorado, Montana, and South Dakota attracted thousands of argonauts, while rising demand for beef in the East and an abundance of grass across the Great Plains combined to create the great open-range cattle boom of the 1860s and 1870s. Within a decade following the end of the Civil

Sioux and Arapaho delegations to Washington, DC, circa 1865–1880, by the photographer Mathew Brady. *During the second half of the nineteenth century, the Frontier Wars, or the Plains Indian Wars, challenged long-held assumptions regarding American settlement of the West, agricultural development, land distribution, and frontier warfare.* BUYENLARGE/ARCHIVE PHOTOS/GETTY IMAGES

War, a region that was known only a generation earlier as the "Great American Desert" was suddenly blooming.

Meanwhile, wary of Euro-American economic, military, and demographic pressure, Plains Indians divided over how to contend with the United States. Some leaders, including Sicangu Lakota Chief Spotted Tail (c. 1823–1881), pleaded for diplomacy and restraint, while Oglala Lakota Chief Red Cloud (1822–1909) and others demanded war. Their split grew deeper when Colonel John M. Chivington (1821–1894) and seven hundred soldiers attacked a Southern Cheyenne village near Sand Creek in northeastern Colorado. On November 29, 1864, Chivington and his men killed between 150 and 600 American Indian men, women, and children in response to scattered livestock raids in and around Denver. The massacre enraged thousands of Plains Indians, many of whom joined Red Cloud's campaign against the United States that killed settlers in Nebraska and burned down Fort Sedgwick in Colorado Territory.

This conflict, known variously as Red Cloud's War and the Colorado War, spread into Wyoming in 1866 when the United States established three forts along the Bozeman Trail to protect gold seekers traveling to Montana. Red Cloud attacked all three, and on December 21, 1866, he ambushed US Captain William J. Fetterman's (1833–1866) command near Fort Phil Kearny in Wyoming, killing all eighty-one men. Exhausted after five years of Civil War and facing an open-ended military occupation of the South, the United States invited Red Cloud to peace talks. In another brief moment of diplomatic triumph, the federal government and several (but certainly not all) Lakota and Cheyenne leaders signed the Fort Laramie Treaty of 1868, which established a permanent Lakota reservation in South Dakota, secured indigenous hunting rights, and notably guaranteed Lakota ownership of the Black Hills.

1870s

In spite of the treaty, the conflict intensified. In 1868 the army expelled the Northern Cheyenne from the Republican River valley after the Battle of Summit Springs in Colorado, and that same year General George Custer (1839–1876) defeated Black Kettle (c. 1803–1868) and allied tribes at the Battle of Washita in Oklahoma. President Ulysses S. Grant's (1822–1885) so-called Peace Policy actually worsened the fighting by declaring all nonagency Indians to be enemy combatants. Finally, in 1874 Custer led an unauthorized expedition into the Black Hills. He found gold, and shortly thereafter whites invaded the region. Incensed by this brazen incursion into sacred Lakota lands, thousands of Plains Indians prepared for war.

The United States invaded the Great Plains in 1876, sending three columns of men to force Crazy Horse (c. 1840–1877), Sitting Bull (c. 1831–1890), and their men to surrender and move to federal reservations. The war did not begin well. On June 17, General George Crook (1828–1890) won a pyrrhic victory against Crazy Horse and nearly eighteen hundred fighters at the Battle of Rosebud in Montana. Although Crook survived Crazy Horse's surprise attack, Custer and the Seventh Cavalry Regiment were not so lucky. Crazy Horse destroyed Custer's regiment at the Battle of Little Bighorn on June 25, killing 212 soldiers. In response, Congress passed legislation authorizing the army to raise twenty-five hundred additional troops and prohibiting the distribution of food or money to the Lakota until they agreed to sell their land. By 1877, military pressure, starvation, and poor morale forced Crazy Horse and other chiefs to surrender. Although Sitting Bull's band escaped to Canada, they returned in 1881 and surrendered themselves to US authorities. By 1879, the Plains Indian Wars were over, and their survivors were confined to reservations.

Unfortunately, although Plains Indian military resistance ended, the US Army continued to impose the government's will on indigenous people and, in some cases, brutally attack them. Perhaps the most notorious incident occurred near Wounded Knee Creek, South Dakota, in 1890, when soldiers murdered as many as three hundred men, women, and children after attempting to disarm a Lakota camp. Although political activism, legal wrangling, and cultural renewal defined Lakota and other Plains Indian struggles throughout the twentieth century and into the twenty-first, Wounded Knee also signified how Lakota autonomy had by that time been subordinated to military and economic control by the US government.

SEE ALSO *Cherokee Nation v. Georgia (1831); General Allotment Act (Dawes Severalty Act, 1877); Indian Removal Act (1830); Reservation; Wounded Knee (1890 and 1973)*

BIBLIOGRAPHY

Bray, Kingsley M. *Crazy Horse: A Lakota Life.* Norman: University of Oklahoma Press, 2008.

Brown, Dee. *Bury My Heart at Wounded Knee: An Indian History of the American West.* New York: Holt, Rinehart & Winston, 1970.

Hämäläinen, Pekka. *The Comanche Empire.* New Haven, CT: Yale University Press, 2008.

McGinnis, Anthony. *Counting Coup and Cutting Horses: Intertribal Warfare on the Northern Plains, 1738–1889.* Evergreen, CO: Cordillera Press, 1990.

Ostler, Jeffrey. *The Plains Sioux and U.S. Colonialism from Lewis and Clark to Wounded Knee.* New York: Cambridge University Press, 2004.

Utley, Robert M., and Wilcomb E. Washburn. *The American Heritage History of the Indian Wars.* Edited by Ann Moffat and Richard Snow. New York: American Heritage Books, 1977.

West, Elliott. *The Contested Plains: Indians, Goldseekers, and the Rush to Colorado.* Lawrence: University Press of Kansas, 1998.

White, Richard. *The Roots of Dependency: Subsistence, Environment, and Social Change among the Choctaws, Pawnees, and Navajos.* Lincoln: University of Nebraska Press, 1983.

Matthew Luckett
Dean's Lecturer on Social Research
Department of History, University of California Los Angeles

FUERZAS ARMADAS DE LIBERACIÓN NACIONAL (FALN, ARMED FORCES OF PUERTO RICAN NATIONAL LIBERATION)

The Fuerzas Armadas de Liberación Nacional (FALN) was an armed, clandestine organization that operated in the United States from 1974 to the early 1980s. The FALN considered Puerto Rico a US colony and sought its independence. It also called for the release of the five Puerto Rican Nationalist Party prisoners who had been in US jails since the 1950s.

From 1974 to 1980, the FALN carried out a number of bombings directed at US corporations, financial institutions, and government offices in Chicago, New York City, and Washington, DC (Committee in Solidarity with Puerto Rican Independence, et al. 1979, 40–50). The group published communiqués, which it delivered to media outlets or left in public places like phone boxes, that stated the reasons for the action. For example, on August 3, 1977, the FALN bombed Mobil Oil Company and US Defense Department offices in New York City. In its communiqué, the FALN wrote, "our actions today are part of our campaign to dramatize and to intensify our just struggle for the independence of Puerto Rico and the unconditional freedom of five Puerto Rican Nationalists. We have chosen these multinational corporations" because they are "using underhanded and barbaric tactics to explore and exploit our natural resources" (Committee in Solidarity with Puerto Rican Independence, et al., 1979, 70).

The FALN did not generally target individuals; to prevent people being killed it issued warnings so that those present could be evacuated. However, on January 24, 1975, it bombed Fraunces Tavern in lower Manhattan and killed four people. It did so "in retaliation for the CIA-ordered bomb that murdered" two pro-independence workers in Puerto Rico (Committee in Solidarity with Puerto Rican Independence, et al. 1979, 61). This bombing remains the FALN's most controversial action.

The FALN saw itself as part of the hemispheric struggle against what it called US imperialism. In many of its communiqués, it expressed solidarity with people fighting the military dictatorships that dominated much of South America; it also supported the Panamanian people's demand for control of the canal. Equally, the FALN expressed its opposition to the police brutality and exploitative living conditions many Puerto Ricans living in the United States experienced.

Because the FALN was a clandestine organization, members did not declare their affiliation with it. However, on April 1, 1980, eleven accused members of the organization were arrested in Evanston, Illinois. By 1983, four other Puerto Ricans were arrested and accused of membership in the FALN. The fifteen declared themselves prisoners of war, refused to recognize the right of the US government to try them, and did not participate in their trials. They were convicted on a variety of criminal charges and one eminently political one, seditious conspiracy, which means conspiring to overthrow the US government by force. Individuals, organizations, and governments, especially the Cuban, defined the Puerto Ricans as political prisoners and advocated their release. In 1999 President Bill Clinton granted twelve of the still-incarcerated activists clemency. Haydée Beltran Torres, who was convicted of murder for her role in the death of a janitor in the 1977 bombing of the Mobil Oil Building in New York City, was not released until 2009. Carlos Alberto Torres, a reputed leader of the FALN, was not released until 2010. Following his arrest in 1980, Alfredo Mendez, one of the eleven, became a government witness and has not been heard of since. As of 2015, only one FALN prisoner, Oscar López, remains in jail.

SEE ALSO *Colonialism; Imperialism; Puerto Rico*

BIBLIOGRAPHY

Committee in Solidarity with Puerto Rican Independence, et al. *Towards People's War for Independence and Socialism in Puerto Rico: In Defense of Armed Struggle.* Chicago: Committee in Solidarity with Puerto Rican Independence, et al., 1979.

Fernández, Ronald. *Prisoners of Colonialism. The Struggle for Justice in Puerto Rico.* Monroe, ME: Common Courage Press, 1994.

Power, Margaret. "From Freedom Fighters to Patriots: The Successful Campaign to Release the FALN Political Prisoners." *Centro Journal* 25, 1 (2013): 146–179.

Susler, Jan. "Puerto Rican Political Prisoners in U.S. Prisons." In *Puerto Rico under Colonial Rule. Political Persecution and the Quest for Human Rights.* Edited by Ramón Bosque Pérez and José Javier Colón Morera. Albany: State University of New York Press, 2006.

Margaret Power
Professor of History
Illinois Institute of Technology

FULBRIGHT, J. WILLIAM
1905–1995

At the outset of his public career, James William Fulbright had an extraordinary vision: an American-sponsored international exchange program that would educate thousands of scholars and students from every part of the globe. Such a program, he believed, would do much to help rid the world of the twin evils of parochialism and nationalism. Fulbright began his tenure in the US Senate near the close of World War II (1939–1945), when much of Europe and Asia lay in ruins. Two new superpowers, Russia and the United States, faced each other across a devastated world. One already possessed atomic weapons and the other, it was commonly agreed, would shortly develop a nuclear-strike capability. Like many of his generation, Bill Fulbright believed that humanity had been given a second chance and that the heritage and largess of the United States imposed upon it a special responsibility to lead the world into a new era. He did not argue that it was America's destiny to force its culture on others. Rather, its mission was to make the world safe for diversity.

Fulbright recognized that in a democracy an enlightened foreign policy depends upon an educated electorate. He saw clearly that xenophobia breeds intolerance and aggression. The ability of the United States, the most powerful nation in the world in 1946, to protect its democratic institutions and to facilitate the establishment of a peaceful and stable world in the atomic age depended in large part on the nation's ability to learn about and appreciate foreign cultures. To this end, he founded the program that was to bear his name.

In this sense, the Fulbright exchange program was an integral part of the internationalist movement that swept America during and after World War II. Fulbright was a primary actor and a major intellectual contributor to that movement. His speeches traced isolationism and nationalism to a common source and claimed that in the modern world, with its technologically advanced communications and armament systems, national sovereignty was impossible. Only if the international community accepted collective security and economic interdependency could the endless cycle of aggression and war be broken. An international exchange program was a prime method, Fulbright believed, of weaning the peoples of the world away from the sacred cow of national sovereignty.

At the same time, however, the genesis of the exchange program grew out of Fulbright's disillusionment with the selfsame internationalism, or, rather, with America's commitment to it. He was alarmed by the intense opposition in Congress to the Bretton Woods legislation creating the International Monetary Fund and the International Bank for Reconstruction and Development, and to the Anglo-American Loan of 1946, an opposition spearheaded, he believed, by isolationists and economic nationalists. Fulbright was concerned about the Harry Truman (1884–1972) administration's increasingly obvious intent to get tough with the Soviet Union in 1945 to 1946. The administration's unwillingness to internationalize atomic energy was particularly disturbing. When the State Department and White House agreed to a United Nations Charter that seemed to preserve rather than diminish national sovereignty, he began to wonder if America's leaders really understood what Woodrow Wilson (1856–1924) had been talking about. Perhaps his countrymen, particularly those in power, did not comprehend the obligations and requirements that a "parliament of man" would entail.

In September 1945 Fulbright, then a first-term senator, introduced an amendment to the Surplus Property Act of 1944 that would use proceeds from the sale of US surplus property overseas to fund an educational exchange program. In the process of defeating the Axis, the US military and its civilian appendages had built more than $6.5 billion worth of manufacturing industries in various countries and had stockpiled $2.8 billion in goods, including everything from machine tools and rolling stock to raw cotton and jeeps. Although various domestic groups sought to either distribute these products free or allow them to be bought at cut rates within the United States, Congress resisted. The cost of reimportation would be immense, and the dumping of large quantities of stocks on the domestic market would cripple the private sector in its efforts to convert from a wartime to a peacetime footing.

Fulbright's short, thirty-line bill authorized the use of proceeds from the sale of surplus property overseas for educational exchange in the areas of science, culture, and education. The junior senator from Arkansas believed that the juxtaposition of surplus property, a shortage of dollars abroad with which to purchase that property, and widespread sympathy in the United States for a more active role in world affairs would be sufficient to overcome a tightfisted Congress and the historic indifference of official Washington to international educational exchange. The impetus for the program came almost solely from Fulbright. In 1945, there was no organized pressure from educators and certainly not from the Truman administration to launch such a program.

In November 1945, Fulbright abandoned his first proposal in favor of a second, broader bill that made more explicit his ideas on international education. Under this second measure, which was finally adopted, the State Department was to be the sole disposal agency for surplus property located outside the United States and its possessions. The Division of Cultural Affairs could accept dollars, foreign currency, or promissory notes, and it could enter into agreements with foreign governments to use the proceeds from these transactions to finance educational activities for Americans in other countries, study by foreign nationals in overseas US institutions, and transportation of visitors from abroad to study in America. As finally amended, the legislation established a nonpartisan Board of Foreign Scholarships to administer the project and limited the amount that could be spent in any one country to $1 million. After obtaining Truman's offhand endorsement of the bill, the Arkansan quietly secured the support of the Democratic and Republican leadership of both houses of Congress. As a result, his pet scheme passed without opposition. On August 1, 1946, President Truman signed the bill into law, and the Fulbright scholarship program came into being.

SEE ALSO *Cold War; Marshall Plan*

BIBLIOGRAPHY

Johnson, Haynes, and Bernard M. Gwertzman. *Fulbright: The Dissenter.* Garden City, NY: Doubleday, 1968.

Kellerman, Henry J. *Cultural Relations as an Instrument of U.S. Foreign Policy: The Educational Exchange Program between the United States and Germany, 1945–1954.* Washington, DC: Department of State, 1978.

Woods, Randall B. *Fulbright: A Biography.* New York: Cambridge University Press, 1995.

Randall B. Woods
Distinguished Professor, John A. Cooper Professor of History
University of Arkansas

G

GALLATIN, ALBERT

SEE *Jefferson, Thomas.*

GARIBALDI, GIUSEPPE

1807–1882

Giuseppe Garibaldi was a leading figure in the Italian struggles for political unity and independence. His involvement in a revolutionary conspiracy organized by the Italian democrat and nationalist Giuseppe Mazzini (1805–1872) in 1834 forced him into exile in South America, where he fought in wars in Brazil's Rio Grande do Sul (1837) and in Uruguay (1842–1846). In 1848 he returned to Italy to take part in the revolutions and acquired fame above all for his part in the defense of the Roman republic (February–June 1849). The American writer Margaret Fuller (1810–1850) was in Rome throughout the revolution, and it was the admiring accounts that she published in the *New-York Daily Tribune* that brought Garibaldi's heroic exploits to the attention of American readers.

When Garibaldi was in exile again after the revolutions, Mazzini persuaded him to visit New York to promote and raise funds for the Italian nationalist cause. On July 30, 1850, Horace Greeley (1811–1872), the publisher of the *Tribune*, announced the arrival of "the world-renowned Garibaldi, the hero of Montevideo and the defender of Rome." A major public reception had been planned to welcome the "Hero of the Two Worlds," but this was canceled on the grounds that Garibaldi was unwell and suffering from exhaustion. There were other reasons, however. Fuller's accounts of Garibaldi's exploits in Rome had not escaped the attention of John Joseph Hughes (1797–1864), who had recently been appointed the first Catholic Archbishop of New York by Pope Pius IX. Outraged, Hughes mobilized Catholics, including many of the estimated three thousand Italian immigrants in New York, to protest the presence in the city of the pope's great enemy.

Many American democrats had doubts about Garibaldi's politics too, and when his supporters tried to organize a reception in Hastings-on-Hudson, just north of New York City, Eleuterio Felice Foresti (1793–1858), a fellow Italian exile and democrat, warned him against accepting because "Red Republicanism was not in good standing with the American People" (Marraro 1946). A local magistrate, Judge Edmonds, repeated the advice, commenting that "although Americans are in favor of freedom all over the world, the American propensity is for bloodless revolutions through the ballot-box and public opinion" (Marraro 1946).

Garibaldi remained in New York as the guest of Foresti and then at the house of an Italian scientist in Staten Island before resuming his trade as a merchant sea captain. In 1854 he left America for the last time and on returning to Europe he disappointed his republican admirers on both sides of the Atlantic by declaring his support for King Victor Emmanuel II (1820–1878) of Piedmont-Sardinia in the struggle for Italian independence. When in April 1859 Piedmont, in secret alliance with the Emperor Louis Napoleon III (1808–1873) of France, went to war with Austria, Garibaldi's mounted volunteers fought in support of the regular Piedmontese army. A year later Garibaldi led the fabled "Expedition of the Thousand" to Sicily that triggered the collapse of the Bourbon Kingdom of the Two Sicilies.

In March 1861 Victor Emmanuel II became Italy's first king, but unification was incomplete. The Austrians still held Venice, and the Pope, under French protection, still ruled Rome. Garibaldi wanted to attack Rome immediately, but fearing this would lead to war with France, Victor Emmanuel refused. At the height of his military fame, Garibaldi was inactive and impatiently waiting on the island of Caprera for an opportunity to launch an expedition against Rome when in June 1861 he received an unofficial letter from a junior American diplomat in Antwerp inquiring about his willingness to accept a command in the Union army. Following the humiliating defeat of the Union forces at the First Battle of Bull Run (July 21, 1861) in Virginia, Secretary of State William H. Seward (1801–1872) made a more formal offer and instructed the US minister in Brussels to meet secretly with Garibaldi on Caprera. They met on September 7, but the discussions came to nothing. Garibaldi would accept only the position of commander in chief and demanded authorization to declare the abolition of slavery. The demands were impossible, leading to speculation that Garibaldi was simply using the American offer and rumors of his departure to persuade Victor Emmanuel to allow him to move against Rome. But that did not happen either (Gay 1907).

Garibaldi, who did publicly praise the struggle for emancipation, featured in the US Civil War in name at least. In June 1861 two Italian exiles, one a founder of the first English-language Italian-American weekly in New York, the other a former Piedmontese army officer, raised an Italian Legion, which became the 39th New York Infantry but was better known as the Garibaldi Guard. The unit recruited as many Hungarians, Poles, Germans, Spaniards, and Portuguese as Italians, and took part in the major battles of the war. In 1888, following his death six years earlier, Garibaldi was commemorated with a bronze statue in New York's Washington Square Park and, in the US Capitol, a marble bust donated to the US Senate by a group of Italian-American citizens "as a link in the chain of sympathy that all free men feel for the champions of liberty and free government."

SEE ALSO *1848 Revolutions*

BIBLIOGRAPHY

Capper, Charles. *Margaret Fuller: An American Romantic Life*, Vol. 2: *The Public Years*. New York: Oxford University Press, 2007.

Doyle, Don H. "'Bully for Garibaldi.'" *New York Times*, September 26, 2011. http://opinionator.blogs.nytimes.com/2011/09/26/bully-for-garibaldi/

Doyle, Don H. *The Cause of All Nations: An International History of the American Civil War*. New York: Basic Books, 2014.

Fuller, Margaret. *"These Sad but Glorious Days": Dispatches from Europe, 1846–1850*, edited by Larry J. Reynolds and Susan Belasco Smith. New Haven, CT: Yale University Press, 1991.

"Italian Americans in the Civil War." In *The Civil War Society's Encyclopedia of the Civil War*. http://www.civilwarhome.com/italian.html

Gay, H. Nelson. "Lincoln's Offer of a Command to Garibaldi: Light on a Disputed Point of History." *Century Magazine* 75 (1907): 63–74.

Marraro, Howard R. "Garibaldi in New York." *New York History* 27, 2 (1946): 179–203.

Riall, Lucy. *Garibaldi: Invention of a Hero*. New Haven, CT: Yale University Press, 2007.

United States Senate Art. Bust of Giuseppe Garibaldi, by Giuseppe Martegana. https://www.senate.gov/artandhistory/art/artifact/Sculpture_21_00007.htm

John A. Davis

Emiliana Pasca Noether Chair in Modern Italian History

University of Connecticut

GARRISON, WILLIAM LLOYD

SEE *Transatlantic Reform.*

GARVEY, MARCUS

SEE *Universal Negro Improvement Association (UNIA).*

GATES FOUNDATION

As the cofounder and chief executive officer of the computer software company Microsoft, William Henry Gates III (b. 1955) became a billionaire in 1987, just before turning thirty-two years old. Not long after, he emerged as a major philanthropist, creating a foundation in 1994. Six years later, with his wife, he turned it into what is now the Bill and Melinda Gates Foundation, the largest grant-making organization in the world, with assets of more than $40 billion at the end of 2014.

Headquartered in Seattle, Washington, the Gates Foundation made grants totaling $3.6 billion in 2013. Its income comes from the endowment established by the Gateses, as well as from donations from investor Warren E. Buffett (b. 1930), who also serves as a trustee. Bill Gates's father, William H. Gates Sr. (b. 1925), cochairs the foundation and is a director of an associated organization that manages the foundation's assets. Sue Desmond-Hellmann (b. 1958) became chief executive officer of the foundation in 2014 after a career in higher education and industry.

The Gates Foundation has nearly four times as much wealth as the second-biggest grant-making foundation in the United States, the Ford Foundation, and more than ten times the assets of the Rockefeller Foundation. In addition to its wealth, the Gates Foundation is notable for its commitment to international philanthropy. In 2013, over 80 percent of its grants—more than $3 billion—were made in three programs:

- Global development, which seeks to help developing countries overcome problems of poverty and poor nutrition. Examples of programs receiving support include efforts by BRAC, a Bangladeshi organization, to help the poor use mobile technology for money transfers, and by the Alliance for a Green Revolution in Africa to enhance agricultural productivity through the development of improved seeds and soil.
- Global health, which focuses on using science and technology to cure chronic diseases—especially those that kill children—in developing countries. Grantees have included the GAVI Alliance, an organization that aims to increase rates of childhood immunization against polio and other illnesses, and SWASTI, which fosters community-based services in Asia for people at risk of acquiring HIV/AIDS.
- Global policy and advocacy, which builds relationships with governments, philanthropists, and others around the world to help the Gates Foundation achieve its objectives. For example, support has gone to a variety of antismoking coalitions, such as the Southeast Asia Tobacco Control Alliance, and efforts to identify successful antipoverty programs, such as those carried out by the International Initiative for Impact Evaluation.

In the United States, the Gates Foundation is best known for its programs in education, which accounted for 83 percent of the $500 million spent domestically in 2013. From its initial focus on using digital technology in education, the foundation has moved to funding programs to promote charter schools and to reform curricula, sponsored by organizations such as the National Alliance for Public Charter Schools and the Council of Chief State School Officers.

These education grants have been among the Gates Foundation's most controversial. Critics have charged that they are harming public education by diverting government funding to private—and less effective—schools. The Gates Foundation's support for a "Common Core" curriculum has also been viewed as a threat to the tradition of local control in American education.

The foundation's international work has attracted critics too. With so much money behind the Gates Foundation's priorities, concerns have been raised that it has too much influence over developing countries. Others have charged that its endowment includes investments in companies, such as in the energy industry, whose business practices are worsening the problems the foundation is trying to solve.

The Gates Foundation is often portrayed as exemplifying "philanthro-capitalism," a grant-making strategy applying the techniques of venture capitalists to philanthropy (Bishop and Green 2008). Thus, it has laid down a series of "Grand Challenges," or goals for improving global health and development, and sought to adapt its support to the success of its grantees in achieving them. However, largely because of the complexity of and limited knowledge about many social and health problems, the effectiveness of this approach continues to be debated.

Unlike other large grant makers, the Gates Foundation plans to spend its entire endowment within twenty years of its founders' deaths, rather than continue indefinitely. Gates has also used his stature as the world's leading donor to promote, with Buffett, "The Giving Pledge," according to which very wealthy individuals and families pledge to commit half of their fortunes to philanthropy. By the end of 2014, 128 had done so.

SEE ALSO *Ford Foundation; Nongovernmental Organizations (NGOs); Rockefeller Foundation; United States Agency for International Development (USAID)*

BIBLIOGRAPHY

Bill and Melinda Gates Foundation. http://www.gatesfoundation.org/

Bishop, Matthew, and Michael Green. *Philanthro-capitalism: How the Rich Can Save the World.* New York: Bloomsbury Press, 2008.

The Giving Pledge. http://givingpledge.org/

Leslie Lenkowsky
Professor of Practice in Public Affairs and Philanthropic Studies
Indiana University

GENDER

Gender is generally defined as the social construction of categories of masculinity and femininity. Scholarship on gender issues in international relations has followed the general trajectory of US historiography. Initially, much of the history of foreign relations focused on diplomats and international laws. In the 1970s and 1980s, historians added prominent and elite women into this picture, particularly with the women's rights movement. In a 1990 *Journal of American History* article, Emily Smith Rosenberg listed several more ways that women and gender could be more broadly incorporated into the study of international relations. In addition to focusing on elite women, scholars could study women who had done "women's work" in an international context, look at the ways that gendered discourses shaped hierarchies, and include women as a part of other categories. Recently, historians have drawn upon feminist and gender theory to include masculinity, especially within formal diplomacy. In scholarship today, gender is therefore a very broad lens through which historians can examine a diverse range of topics.

GENDER IN THE COLONIAL ERA AND THE EARLY REPUBLIC

In initial European colonization, gender roles, sex, and sexuality were often at the forefront when people came into contact. In the northeast, English settlers engaged in protracted conflicts, such as King Philip's (Metacomet's) War with Native Americans in the 1670s. As Jill Lepore (1998) contends, the English viewed Native American raids as symbolic attacks on the individual body and the body of the community, in ways that were central to the formation of American identity. Jennifer Morgan's *Laboring Women* (2004) traces the ways that gender informed initial contact in the emerging Atlantic slave system. Explorers and colonizers used language to reduce African women to their reproductive abilities and dehumanize them in order to justify racial inequality and slavery. In the American Southwest, the primary point of contact was between Spanish priests and conquistadores and native men and women. Scholars such as James Brooks (2002) and Ramon Gutierrez (1991) have studied the ways that gender influenced notions of honor, shame, and proper gender roles, particularly in terms of social institutions such as marriage.

Historians of gender in the revolutionary period have tended to focus on elite women's discourse, which led to calls for women's rights from such intellectuals as Mary Wollstonecraft (1759–1797). Recently, scholars have focused on the lives of lower-class people and elite masculinity. Works such as Sarah Pearsall's *Atlantic Families* (2008) examine nonelites to argue that the lines between public and private were fluid as a shared set of "Atlantic values" about domesticity was placed in crisis by political and social upheaval. For masculinity, the work of Thomas Foster (2013) and Trevor Burnard (2004) on founding father Gouverneur Morris (1752–1816) and Jamaican planter Thomas Thistlewood (1721–1786) is illustrative of the interweaving of gender, sexuality, and national identity.

Gender continued to be a factor as the early republic expanded westward, particularly as Euro-Americans came into increasing contact with Native Americans in the Mississippi and Great Lakes regions. Richard White's landmark study *The Middle Ground* (1991) illustrates the central role of women in creating the cultural space between Europeans and Native Americans in the Great Lakes region. Case studies by Theda Perdue (1998) and Tiya Miles (2005) show the complex intertwining of race, class, and gender within the Cherokee community in the Southeast.

NINETEENTH- AND EARLY TWENTIETH-CENTURY REFORM MOVEMENTS

In the mid-1800s, transatlantic and global reform movements grew rapidly. Women's suffrage is probably the best known of the movements that explicitly addressed gender disparity. In addition to work on individual leaders, such as Sandra Stanley Holton's 1994 article on Elizabeth Cady Stanton (1815–1902), historians have also studied women's rights as part of the gendered discourse of the time period. For example, Allison L. Sneider (2008) situates the movement in the context of imperialism, particularly the question of who had the right to determine voting and citizenship privileges not only for women but also for minority groups within the United States and colonized people abroad.

Scholars have tended to focus on elite men and women leaders of global reform movements such as emancipation and temperance (see Sklar 1990). However, more recent work, such as Pamela Scully and Diana Paton's transnational anthology *Gender and Slave Emancipation in the Atlantic World* (2005), reveals the ways that emancipation itself was gendered. The mid-nineteenth century was also a time of global religious and moral reform movements, and the Women's Christian Temperance Union (see Tyrell 1991), the Young Men's Christian Association, and the Young Women's Christian Association had local, national, and international components. Jane Hunter's *Gospel of Gentility* (1984), and the anthology *Competing Kingdoms* (2010), explore the ways that American missionary women interacted with the local communities they were placed within, even though the national boards of many foreign missionary societies were headed by men. In addition to these broader movements, there were groups that fostered transnational cooperation and dialogue, such as those that Leila J. Rupp discusses in *Worlds of Women* (1997)—the International Council of Women (founded 1888), the International Alliance of Women (founded 1904), and Women's International League for Peace and Freedom (founded 1915).

In the Gilded Age and Progressive Era, masculinity and foreign policy came to the forefront in several ways. As Gail Bederman argued in *Manliness and Civilization* (1995), gender—particularly Theodore Roosevelt's "strenuous life"—was deeply intertwined with domestic and foreign policy. Kristin Hoganson (1998) illustrated the ways that masculinity shaped calls for US involvement in the Spanish-American War among US political leaders. Scholars have also argued that gender was integral to understanding race, nation, and class, for both Anglo-Americans and local peoples, within the colonies and areas under US control, such as Puerto Rico, the Philippines, Haiti, and Cuba. As Mary Renda (2001) contends, paternalism was a key part of American occupation in Haiti. In these places, gender and racial categories were often connected to medical issues, with local people classified as dirty, diseased, or promiscuous. For example, Vincente Rafael (2000) focuses on white women and the role of the domestic sphere in imperialism in the Philippines. Warwick Anderson (2006) discusses white scientific and governmental men's concerns about their own health and the use of public health to portray Filipinos as diseased, while Eileen J. Suarez Findlay (1999) addresses US conceptions of Puerto Rican women's sexuality. Laura Briggs (2002) looks at the ways that US officials used these racial and imperialist categories of difference to focus on birth control (including eugenics) for working-class women in Puerto Rico in the interwar period.

TWENTIETH-CENTURY WARS

World War I disrupted traditional gender roles for both men and women. Women increasingly moved into the work force and joined the military, as Kimberly Jensen (2008) illustrates. The 1917 Selective Service Act (the draft), and men's enlistment in the armed forces brought masculinity and national service to the forefront of national consciousness. As Gerald Shenk (2005) explains, the draft was not equitable, but instead promoted a system that divided men, and their capacity for manhood, by racial categories, therefore perpetuating a system of white patriarchy. In *Disloyal Mothers and Scurrilous Citizens* (1999), Kathleen Kennedy examines the ways that women violated the image of the patriotic mother by protesting the war, and were subsequently prosecuted under the Espionage Act of 1917.

Scholars of World War II mobilization have studied the impact of large numbers of male soldiers—and the women with whom they formed relationships abroad—on international relations during and after the war. As Petra Goedde examines in *GIs and Germans* (2003), US soldiers began relationships with German women and feminized the defeated Germany. This transformed the way that Americans saw Germans—from enemies to victims of the Nazi regime. Mary Louise Roberts (2013) paints a grimmer picture of sex in wartime, arguing that the US military portrayed French women as sexually available, and the resulting (sometimes violent) exploitation of women soured the relationship between the US and French governments. Katharine H. S. Moon (1997) focuses on similar issues in Korea, where leaders in the 1970s sought to use prostitutes as "political ambassadors" to Americans during the Cold War.

THE COLD WAR AND AFTER

When examining the Cold War, historians have also looked at the ways that domestic notions of acceptable gender roles shaped foreign policy. In *Cold War Orientalism* (2003), Christina Klein discusses the ways that US political and cultural leaders used sentimental tropes to make Asia seem less foreign, so that the public would support US interests in the region. In *Imperial Brotherhood* (2001), Robert D. Dean examines the ways gender shaped US involvement in the Vietnam War. Mirroring the war hawks of the Spanish-American War, white male leaders tapped into longstanding discourses on masculinity to assert both their own right to lead within the United States and the right of the United States to be in Vietnam. On the other side of the "imperial brotherhood" were the people Judy Tzu-Chun Wu discusses in *Radicals on the Road* (2013). This group of Americans and international peace activists—including African Americans, Asian Americans, and women antiwar activists—traveled widely to Vietnam and Southeast Asia, forming a "radical Orientalism" that critiqued US Cold War culture and the war in Vietnam.

In the wake of the Cold War, gender roles have continued to shape the ways that the United States interacts with the world. Cynthia Enloe (1993) has applied a gendered lens to a wide variety of case studies, particularly dealing with the militarization of masculinity and femininity. During the Cold War, gender was infused with notions of security, in which men served as soldiers and women were supportive from within the domestic sphere.

Since 2000, US government and aid agencies have also been interested in the rights of women, particularly in areas of conflict or natural disaster. For example, United States Agency for International Development (USAID) programs in Afghanistan have attempted to advance the role of women in different areas of society, from the private sector to politics. USAID efforts have also included maternal care, safe housing, vaccines, and family-planning programs. While these programs generally meet with approval within the United States, they often receive a more complicated reception abroad, and can be advanced or stymied by local political and religious factors.

SEE ALSO *Captivity Narratives; Cuba; Foreign Mission Movement; Spanish-American War; Suffrage; Transatlantic Reform; Wollstonecraft, Mary*

BIBLIOGRAPHY

Anderson, Warwick. *Colonial Pathologies: American Tropical Medicine, Race, and Hygiene in the Philippines.* Durham, NC: Duke University Press, 2006.

Bederman, Gail. *Manliness and Civilization: A Cultural History of Gender and Race in the United States, 1880–1917.* Chicago: University of Chicago Press, 1995.

Briggs, Laura. *Reproducing Empire: Race, Sex, Science, and US Imperialism in Puerto Rico.* Berkeley: University of California Press, 2002.

Brooks, James F. *Captives and Cousins: Slavery, Kinship, and Community in the Southwest Borderlands.* Chapel Hill: University of North Carolina Press for the Omohundro Institute of Early American History and Culture, 2002.

Burnard, Trevor G. *Mastery, Tyranny, and Desire: Thomas Thistlewood and His Slaves in the Anglo-Jamaican World.* Chapel Hill: University of North Carolina Press, 2004.

Dean, Robert D. *Imperial Brotherhood: Gender and the Making of Cold War Foreign Policy.* Amherst: University of Massachusetts Press, 2001.

Enloe, Cynthia. *Bananas, Beaches, and Bases: Making Feminist Sense of International Politics.* Berkeley: University of California Press, 1990. 2nd ed., 2014.

Enloe, Cynthia. *The Morning After: Sexual Politics at the End of the Cold War.* Berkeley: University of California Press, 1993.

Findlay, Eileen J. Suárez. *Imposing Decency: The Politics of Sexuality and Race in Puerto Rico, 1870–1920.* Durham, NC: Duke University Press, 1999.

Foster, Thomas. "Reconstructing Libertines and Early Modern Heterosexuality: Sex and American Founder Gouverneur Morris." *Journal of the History of Sexuality* 22, 1 (2013): 65–84.

Goedde, Petra. *GIs and Germans: Culture, Gender, and Foreign Relations, 1945–1949.* New Haven, CT: Yale University Press, 2003.

Gutiérrez, Ramón A. *When Jesus Came, the Corn Mothers Went Away: Marriage, Sexuality, and Power in New Mexico, 1500–1846.* Stanford, CA: Stanford University Press, 1991.

Hoganson, Kristin L. *Fighting for American Manhood: How Gender Politics Provoked the Spanish-American and Philippine-American Wars.* New Haven, CT: Yale University Press, 1998.

Hoganson, Kristin L. "What's Gender Got to Do with It? Women and Foreign Relations History." *OAH Magazine of History* 19, 2 (2005): 14–18.

Holton, Sandra Stanley. "'To Educate Women into Rebellion': Elizabeth Cady Stanton and the Creation of a Transatlantic Network of Radical Suffragists." *American Historical Review* 99, 4 (1994): 1112–1136.

Hunter, Jane. *The Gospel of Gentility: American Women Missionaries in Turn-of-the-Century China.* New Haven, CT: Yale University Press, 1984.

Jensen, Kimberly. *Mobilizing Minerva: American Women in the First World War.* Champaign: University of Illinois Press, 2008.

Kennedy, Kathleen. *Disloyal Mothers and Scurrilous Citizens: Women and Subversion during World War I.* Bloomington: Indiana University Press, 1999.

Klein, Christina. *Cold War Orientalism: Asia in the Middlebrow Imagination, 1945–1961.* Berkeley: University of California Press, 2003.

Lepore, Jill. *The Name of War: King Philip's War and the Origins of American Identity.* New York: Knopf, 1998.

Miles, Tiya. *Ties That Bind: The Story of an Afro-Cherokee Family in Slavery and Freedom.* Berkeley: University of California Press, 2005.

Moon, Katharine H. S. *Sex among Allies: Military Prostitution in U.S.-Korea Relations.* New York: Columbia University Press, 1997.

Morgan, Jennifer. *Laboring Women: Reproduction and Gender in New World Slavery.* Philadelphia: University of Pennsylvania Press, 2004.

Pearsall, Sarah. *Atlantic Families: Lives and Letters in the Later Eighteenth Century.* Oxford: Oxford University Press, 2008.

Perdue, Theda. *Cherokee Women: Gender and Culture Change, 1700–1835.* Lincoln: University of Nebraska Press, 1998.

Rafael, Vicente L. *White Love and Other Events in Filipino History.* Durham, NC: Duke University Press, 2000.

Reeves-Ellington, Barbara, Kathryn Kish Sklar, and Connie A. Shemo, eds. *Competing Kingdoms: Women, Mission, Nation, and the American Protestant Empire, 1812–1960.* Durham, NC: Duke University Press, 2010.

Renda, Mary. *Taking Haiti: Military Occupation and the Culture of U.S. Imperialism, 1915–1940.* Chapel Hill: University of North Carolina Press, 2001.

Roberts, Mary Louise. *What Soldiers Do: Sex and the American GI in World War II France.* Chicago: University of Chicago Press, 2013.

Rosenberg, Emily S. "Gender." *Journal of American History* 77, 1 (1990): 116–124.

Rupp, Leila J. *Worlds of Women: The Making of an International Women's Movement.* Princeton, NJ: Princeton University Press, 1997.

Scully, Pamela, and Diana Paton, eds. *Gender and Slave Emancipation in the Atlantic World.* Durham, NC: Duke University Press, 2005.

Shenk, Gerald E. *"Work or Fight!" Race, Gender, and the Draft in World War One.* New York: Palgrave Macmillan, 2005.

Sklar, Kathryn Kish. "'Women Who Speak for an Entire Nation': American and British Women Compared at the World Anti-Slavery Convention, London, 1840." *Pacific Historical Review* 59, 4 (1990): 453–499.

Sneider, Allison L. *Suffragists in an Imperial Age: U.S. Expansion and the Woman Question, 1870–1929.* New York: Oxford University Press, 2008.

Tyrell, Ian. *Woman's World, Woman's Empire: The Women's Christian Temperance Union in International Perspective, 1880–1930.* Chapel Hill: University of North Carolina Press, 1991.

White, Richard. *The Middle Ground: Indians, Empires, and Republics in the Great Lakes Region, 1650–1815.* Cambridge: Cambridge University Press, 1991.

Wu, Judy Tzu-Chun. *Radicals on the Road: Internationalism, Orientalism, and Feminism during the Vietnam Era.* Ithaca, NY: Cornell University Press, 2013.

Karen Phoenix
Instructor
Washington State University

GENERAL AGREEMENT ON TARIFFS AND TRADE (GATT)

SEE *World Trade Organization.*

GENERAL ALLOTMENT ACT (DAWES SEVERALTY ACT, 1877)

On February 8, 1877, the US Congress passed the General Allotment Act, also known as the Dawes Act or the Dawes Severalty Act after its sponsor, Massachusetts senator Henry Dawes (1816–1903). The act divided Indian reservations into individual parcels of land and opened the remaining lands to white settlers whose proximity would supposedly provide a "civilizing" influence. It granted heads of families and single people over eighteen years old 160 acres. Married women were allotted with their husbands, but single, divorced, or widowed women over age eighteen received their own full allotments. Single people under eighteen were allotted 40 acres. The federal government held these allotments in trust for twenty-five years (or longer if deemed necessary) so that the owners could neither sell the land nor be taxed on it. The division of tribal lands reflected government officials' belief that communal tribal land holdings were hindering the assimilation of indigenous peoples into mainstream American culture.

The dispossession that occurred under the Dawes Act was part of a global conquest of indigenous peoples and lands called *settler colonialism* and is best understood as only one component of a broader agenda of asserting European hegemony over native peoples in order to create a culturally homogeneous settler state on indigenous lands.

SETTLER COLONIALISM IN THE UNITED STATES, CANADA, AND AUSTRALIA

The Dawes Act was the centerpiece of the US government's efforts to dispossess and assimilate Native Americans in order to replace aboriginal cultures with that of the colonizers. Politicians framed this legislation as an enlightened attempt to "uplift" their poor degraded neighbors, whom they saw as "savages." Such stereotypes held across the lands where English settlers dispossessed the aboriginal inhabitants—the United States, Canada, and Australia. In each of these nations, analysis of dispossession and forced assimilation uncovers similar dynamics of power that help illuminate processes of settler colonialism. Similarly, analysis of how the colonized peoples in each of these nations responded to the assaults on their cultures reveals the limitations of such programs of conquest and absorption. The indigenous peoples of the United States, Canada, and Australia survived similar assaults on their cultures, and their continued presence in each of these countries reveals the tenacity of the human spirit in the face of colonial oppression.

Examination of settler colonialism in the United States, Australia, and Canada reveals several common themes: appropriation of indigenous lands, forced assimilation of indigenous children, and suppression of indigenous culture. The governments of all three nations took indigenous land and forced children into boarding or mission schools or placed them with nonindigenous families. Although the processes of this compulsory assimilation differed somewhat according to location, the United States, Canada, and Australia had once been colonies of the British Empire, and British jurisprudence shaped their interactions with the aboriginal populations. Each of these settler societies sought to erase the original inhabitants of the land in order to consolidate their claims upon it. Thus legislation such as the Dawes Act was only a small part of the assault on aboriginal culture in these former British colonies.

APPROPRIATION OF INDIGENOUS LANDS

Appropriation of indigenous lands lay at the heart of policies such as the Dawes Act. In North America, British colonizers based their claims to indigenous lands on the doctrine of discovery, a legal construct derived from Pope Nicholas V's 1452 call for the conquest of non-Christian territories. The governments of both the United States and Canada recognized aboriginal land claims in theory and signed treaties with indigenous peoples exchanging land in return for various promises. Both nations also set aside territory for indigenous peoples, called reserves in Canada and reservations in the United States. The two nations differed in their legal assessments of these lands, however. The Canadian government declared in 1823 that indigenous peoples were subjects of the British Crown with no separate juridical status, while the US Supreme Court ruled in *Cherokee Nation v. Georgia* (1831) that Indians constituted "domestic dependent nations." The following year, in *Worcester v. Georgia*, the Court acknowledged Indians' rights to their lands. Despite these rulings, American Indians were dispossessed and pushed onto reservations that were promised to them forever. Although the First Nations of Canada resisted allotment of their communally held lands in the 1860s, the Dawes Act broke this promise in the United States, transferring millions of acres of land out of Indian hands.

Settler colonialism in Australia proceeded from a different premise regarding the land, but the end results were similar to what happened in North America. Australian authorities did not recognize aboriginal land rights, operating from the idea of *terra nullius*—the land is empty—despite human habitation dating back roughly forty thousand years. After the British colonized Australia in the eighteenth century, colonial administrators apportioned lands to colonizers in freehold titles (which granted title) or pastoral leases (which granted use rights); aborigines were pushed onto marginal lands and, in the process, settlers carried out numerous massacres of indigenous peoples. The decentralized nature of Australian colonialism meant that policies regarding indigenous peoples varied across regions, but in general, the Australian government responded to settler violence against Aborigines by setting aside remote reserves for native peoples. In the late nineteenth and early twentieth centuries, different regions appointed a "protector of the Aborigines," whose job was to encourage indigenous peoples to assimilate for their own "protection." Thus, while indigenous Australians never had a reservation to allot, they suffered dispossession and forced assimilation programs similar to aboriginal peoples in North America. For all indigenous peoples, one of the most traumatic aspects of enforced assimilation was child removal.

BOARDING SCHOOLS AND CHILD REMOVAL

In the late nineteenth century, government officials in the United States, Canada, and Australia removed indigenous children from their families in order to "civilize" them. In each nation, policy makers believed that indigenous peoples were dying out and that they should abandon their fading culture and assimilate. North American officials established boarding or residential schools as a means of removing children from the influences of their native culture and educating them in "civilized" ways. Both the United States and Canadian governments mandated this education and removed children to these institutions by force when necessary. North American residential schools implemented a curriculum designed to indoctrinate indigenous children in mainstream history and culture, punished students harshly for speaking their native tongue, and regimented these schools with a strict military model that most students found oppressive.

In Australia, authorities divided Aborigines into "full blood" and "half caste" and removed "half caste" children to white homes or missions, hoping to "rescue" children with "white blood" from the "degrading" influences of Aboriginal settlements. Policy makers argued that this approach allowed "half-caste" children to be absorbed into white culture while their darker families died out on Aboriginal reserves. Unlike in North America, where authorities assumed that children would bring their education back to their communities after graduation, child removal in Australia was permanent. However destructive such practices were, indigenous peoples in each of these nations selectively adapted elements of assimilation according to their own agendas and used education to advance their own self-determination.

SEE ALSO *Frontier Wars; Indian Removal Act (1830); Reservation; Wounded Knee (1890 and 1973)*

BIBLIOGRAPHY

Atwood, Bain, and S. G. Foster, eds. *Frontier Conflict: The Australian Experience.* Canberra: National Museum of Australia, 2003.

Central Land Council (A council of ninety aboriginal people elected from communities in the southern half of Canada's Northern Territory). "The Aboriginal Land Rights Act." http://www.clc.org.au/articles/cat/land-rights-act/

Hanson, Erin. "Aboriginal Rights." *Indigenous Foundations.* http://indigenousfoundations.arts.ubc.ca/home/land-rights/aboriginal-rights.html

Hanson, Erin. "The Residential School System." *Indigenous Foundations.* http://indigenousfoundations.arts.ubc.ca/home/government-policy/the-residential-school-system.html

Hoxie, Fredrick E. *A Final Promise: The Campaign to Assimilate the Indians, 1880–1920.* Lincoln: University of Nebraska Press, 1984. Reprint, New York: Cambridge University Press, 1989.

Jacobs, Margaret D. *White Mother to a Dark Race: Settler Colonialism, Maternalism, and the Removal of Indigenous Children in the American West and Australia, 1880–1940.* Lincoln: University of Nebraska Press, 2009.

Lomawaima, K. Tsianina, Brenda J. Child, and Margaret L. Archuleta, eds. *Away from Home: American Indian Boarding School Experiences, 1879–2000.* Phoenix, AZ: Heard Museum, 2002.

Mainville, Robert. *An Overview of Aboriginal and Treaty Rights and Compensation for their Breach.* Saskatoon, SK: Purich, 2001.

Tennant, Paul. *Aboriginal Peoples and Politics: The Indian Land Question in British Columbia, 1849–1989.* Vancouver: University of British Columbia Press, 1990.

University of British Columbia. *Indigenous Foundations.* An information resource on key topics relating to the histories, politics, and cultures of the aboriginal peoples of Canada. http://indigenousfoundations.arts.ubc.ca/home.html

Wolfe, Patrick. *Settler Colonialism and the Transformation of Anthropology: The Politics and Poetics of an Ethnographic Event.* New York and London: Cassell, 1999.

Katherine M. B. Osburn
Associate Professor of History
Arizona State University

GENEVA CONVENTIONS

In 1859, Henri Dunant (1828–1910), a Swiss businessman, witnessed the aftermath of the Battle of Solferino. The battle, an engagement in the second Italian war of independence, pitted the victorious allied French–Sardinian army against the Austrian army in Lombardy. Profoundly shocked by the treatment of wounded soldiers left on the field, Dunant cofounded in 1863 the International Committee for Relief to the Wounded, renamed the International Committee of the Red Cross in 1876. In 1864, the committee organized a sixteen-nation conference that produced the Geneva Convention for the Amelioration of the Condition of the Wounded in Armed Forces in the Field. This convention obligated signatories to respect medical facilities, personnel, and civilians caring for the wounded. Twelve nations signed initially; the United States ratified the convention in 1882.

Changes in the nature of warfare prompted modifications to the convention. In 1899, Hague Peace Conference declarations revised the Geneva Convention to prohibit "asphyxiating gases" and "expanding bullets." In 1906, a second conference produced the Second Geneva Convention for the Amelioration of the Condition of Wounded, Sick, and Shipwrecked Members of Armed Forces at Sea, extending the 1864 convention to maritime warfare.

In July 1929, a third conference considered the treatment of prisoners of war (POWs). The resulting agreement, the Geneva Convention relative to the Treatment of Prisoners of War, defined POWs, and detailed obligations for their protection, treatment, and captivity. The convention also recognized the Red Crescent and Red Lion alongside the Red Cross.

The Second World War (1939–1945) demonstrated the necessity of extending the conventions' protections to civilians. Consequently, the Fourth Geneva Convention relative to the Protection of Civilian Persons in Time of War, signed in August 1949, bound signatories when engaged in war or occupation, whether declared or otherwise. Further, the agreement defined "protected persons," both civilian and combatant, and detailed their protections, status, and treatment. The agreement also proscribed such actions as hostage taking, murder, mutilation, humiliation, experimentation, execution, collective punishment, and population transfers. The convention was also registered with the United Nations. In 1955, the United States signed the convention with attached reservations applicable to the death penalty.

While the 1949 convention represents the last complete revision, two additional amendments were accepted in 1977. Acknowledging that post-1945 warfare bore little resemblance to previous conflicts, the protocols formalized efforts, begun in 1949, to extend the convention beyond those affected by wars between states. Protocol I stated that struggles against "colonial domination, alien occupation or racist regimes" were international conflicts and provided protections to insurgents, deemed "combatants," as well as formalizing a definition of armed forces. Other additions afforded civilian medical personnel, women, and children special protections and reconfirmed prohibitions against the general targeting of civilians and infrastructure.

Protocol II encompassed those endangered by noninternational conflicts. Specifically, it clarified and expanded Common Article 3 dealing with internal wars. Consequently, representatives were required to balance victim protection with the inviolability of state sovereignty. The resultant Protocol II ensured that the convention's protections and prohibitions encompassed internal conflicts. Although the United States signed the protocols, Congress declined to ratify them.

In 2005, a final amendment, the Protocol Additional to the Geneva Conventions of 12 August 1949, and relating to the Adoption of an Additional Distinctive Emblem established the Red Crystal alongside the Red Cross and Red Crescent. Supported and confirmed in 2007 by the United States, the protocol provided nations such as Israel an alternative to the Red Cross or Red Crescent.

The Geneva Conventions, ratified by 196 states including the United States, represent a key feature of international law. Indeed, since ratification, the US has consistently applied the conventions, from the Korea War (prior to signing the 1949 convention) through the 1991 Gulf War. However, after September 11, 2001, US-led invasions of Afghanistan and Iraq produced controversy around their principles and application. While initially the George W. Bush administration determined that aspects of the conventions did not encompass Taliban and al-Qaeda fighters, in February 2002 the United States acknowledged that Afghanistan's signatory status extended protections to captured Taliban but not al-Qaeda. However, detainees were classified as unlawful combatants rather than prisoners of war.

In 2006, the US Supreme Court decided in *Hamdan v. Rumsfeld* that Common Article 3 of the Geneva Conventions applied to al-Qaeda, with particular reference to the prohibition of "torture and inhuman or degrading treatment." In July 2006, the Bush administration conformed to the ruling, applying the conventions to all terrorism detainees. Subsequently, in 2009, the Barack Obama administration reinterpreted Article 3 and altered US policy, restricting certain interrogation techniques. In 2010, President Obama reaffirmed a commitment to the Geneva Conventions. As of 2015, however, the United States continued to detain and classify Taliban and al-Qaeda members as enemy combatants rather than POWs or "protected persons" as defined by the Geneva Conventions.

SEE ALSO *United Nations*

BIBLIOGRAPHY

Callen, Jason. "Unlawful Combatants and the Geneva Conventions." *Virginia Journal of International Law* 44 (2003): 1025–1072.

Flaherty, Martin S. "Human Rights Law, American Justice, and the 'War on Terror.'" *OAH Magazine of History* 25, no. 3 (2011): 35–40.

Jinks, Derek. "Applicability of the Geneva Conventions to the Global War on Terrorism." *Virginia Journal of International Law* 46 (2005): 165–196.

Jinks, Derek, and David Sloss. "Is the President Bound by the Geneva Conventions." *Cornell Law Review* 90 (2004): 97–202.

Kolb, Robert. "The Relationship between International Humanitarian Law and Human Rights Law: A Brief History of the 1948 Universal Declaration of Human Rights and the 1949 Geneva Conventions." *International Review of the Red Cross* 38, 324 (1998): 409–419. https://www.icrc.org/eng/resources/documents/misc/57jpg2.htm#header

Matheson, Michael J. "The United States Position on the Relation of Customary International Law to the 1977 Protocols Additional to the 1949 Geneva Conventions." *American University Journal of International Law and Policy* 2 (1987): 419–427.

Moorehead, Caroline. *Dunant's Dream: War, Switzerland, and the History of the Red Cross.* London: Harper Collins, 1998.

Noone, Gregory P. "History and Evolution of the Law of War Prior to World War II." *Naval Law Review* 47 (2000): 176–207.

Pictet, Jean, ed. *The Geneva Conventions of 12 August 1949: Geneva Convention Relative to the Protection of Civilian Persons in Time of War.* Geneva, Switzerland: International Committee of the Red Cross, 1958.

Shumate, Brett. "New Rules for a New War: The Applicability of the Geneva Conventions to Al-Qaeda and Taliban Detainees Captured in Afghanistan." *New York International Law Review* 18 (2005): 1–68.

Yingling, Raymund T., and Robert W. Ginnane. "The Geneva Conventions of 1949." *American Journal of International Law* 46, 3 (1952): 393–427.

CONVENTIONS AND PROTOCOLS

1949 Conventions and Additional Protocols, and their Commentaries. https://www.icrc.org/applic/ihl/ihl.nsf/vwTreaties1949.xsp

Convention for the Amelioration of the Condition of the Wounded in Armies in the Field. Geneva, 22 August 1864. https://www.icrc.org/applic/ihl/ihl.nsf/Treaty.xsp?documentId=477CEA122D7B7B3DC12563CD002D6603&action=openDocument

Convention for the Amelioration of the Condition of the Wounded and Sick in Armies in the Field. Geneva, 6 July 1906. https://www.icrc.org/applic/ihl/ihl.nsf/Treaty.xsp?documentId=C64C3E521F5CC28FC12563CD002D6737&action=openDocument

Convention relative to the Treatment of Prisoners of War. Geneva, 27 July 1929. https://www.icrc.org/applic/ihl/ihl.nsf/Treaty.xsp?documentId=0BDEDDD046FDEBA9C12563CD002D69B1&action=openDocument

Protocol Additional to the Geneva Conventions of 12 August 1949, and relating to the Protection of Victims of International Armed Conflicts (Protocol I), 8 June 1977. https://www.icrc.org/applic/ihl/ihl.nsf/Treaty.xsp?documentId=D9E 6B6264D7723C3C12563CD002D6CE4&action=open Document

Protocol Additional to the Geneva Conventions of 12 August 1949, and relating to the Protection of Victims of Non-International Armed Conflicts (Protocol II), 8 June 1977. https://www.icrc.org/applic/ihl/ihl.nsf/Treaty.xsp?document Id=AA0C5BCBAB5C4A85C12563CD002D6D09&action=openDocument

Protocol Additional to the Geneva Conventions of 12 August 1949, and relating to the Adoption of an Additional Distinctive Emblem (Protocol III), 8 December 2005. https://www.icrc.org/applic/ihl/ihl.nsf/Treaty.xsp?documentId=8BC1504B556D2F80C125710F002F4B28&action=open Document

Stephen Connor
Assistant Professor of History
Nipissing University

GENOCIDE

As a nation that began as a result of settler colonialism, the United States has its own long history in relation to genocide. And while the word *genocide* itself may continue to be a source of scholarly debate, there remains only one internationally recognized legal definition, that of the 1948 United Nations Convention on the Prevention and Punishment of the Crime of Genocide (Art. II):

In the present Convention, genocide means any of the following acts committed with intent to destroy, in whole or in part, a national, ethnical, racial or religious group, as such:

1. Killing members of the group;
2. Causing serious bodily or mental harm to members of the group;
3. Deliberately inflicting on the group conditions of life calculated to bring about its physical destruction in whole or in part;
4. Imposing measures intended to prevent births within the group;
5. Forcibly transferring children of the group to another group.

Whether the United States acts as a complicit participant or a seemingly indifferent bystander, US responses to genocide have followed three mindsets. The first is the notion of the "city on the hill," a phrase taken from Jesus's Sermon on the Mount in the Gospel of Matthew 5:14 ("You are the light of the world. A city that is set on a hill cannot be hidden."). Historically, the phrase was first used by Puritan John Winthrop

(1587–1649) in a sermon titled "A Model of Christian Charity." It was later used by President John F. Kennedy (1917–1963) on January 9, 1961, and President Ronald Reagan (1911–2004) on January 11, 1989. All three boldly stated the applicability of divine favor and greatness to the United States through its world-superior status vis-à-vis other nation-states and its predominantly white Protestant citizens.

The second mindset is that of *manifest destiny*, a nineteenth-century term understood to sanction the right of American citizens to settle throughout the land under their governance. According to this view, Americans (primarily white Protestants) possessed favor from God and "special virtues" to remake the American West in their own image. The recipients of this "adventure" would be Native Americans, with whom American settlers would fight wars and later displace onto "reservations," defying Native American cultural traditions. This mindset extended beyond the continental United States to affect Americans' understanding of the world. Evidence of this orientation can be seen in the War of 1812, the conflict with Mexico over Texas (1846–1848), the Spanish-American War (1898), and the war with the Philippines (1899–1902). Similar nationalistic and providential sentiments can be found elsewhere in world history. The German Nazi concept of *Lebensraum* (living space), or the *right* of the German people to occupy and displace other peoples—including Jews—was also used to their territorial and cultural advantage.

The third mindset is that of the Monroe Doctrine (1823). The doctrine, intended to be a bulwark against European expansion in the Americas, held that the United States would consider any further colonization in the Americas as an act of aggression against the United States and its neighbors to the south. This doctrine, like the above positions, reflects the notion of American superiority in relation to other nation-states and Americans' willingness to make decisions for territories beyond their own borders.

This history and these orientations contributed to Americans' forty-year reluctance to ratify the UN Convention on the Punishment and Prevention of the Crime of Genocide. Passed by the United Nations on December 9, 1948, the Genocide Convention remains the *only* legally defined understanding of this "crime of crimes," with genocide the only crime punishable by the international community. And while the convention has received heavy criticism in some quarters for its inclusion of only four victim groups: national, ethnical, racial, or religious, it has given rise to the Rome Statute of the International Criminal Court (ICC, 1998), the International Criminal Tribunal for the former Yugoslavia (ICTY, 1993), and the International Criminal Tribunal for Rwanda (ICTR, 1994). The latter two have been supported by the United States. Although the Bill Clinton administration signed the Rome Statute, the George W. Bush administration withdrew the signature.

Despite the convention, the twentieth century came to be known as the "century of genocide." In addition to the Holocaust of World War II, genocides have occurred in Southwest Africa, Turkey, Japan (Hiroshima and Nagasaki), Guatemala, Cambodia and Laos, Bosnia, Rwanda, Indonesia and East Timor, and the Sudan. The United States responded to each case differently. Considered as a whole, there is no clear, consistent principle that guides the United States with regard to genocide. US actions have been contradictory, revealing a deep ambivalence in American culture about intervention. America's history and dominant mindsets toward its historical treatment of both Native Americans and African Americans reveal the consequences of ambivalence toward the difficult, uncomfortable, and complicated topic of genocide.

SEE ALSO *Armenian Genocide; Ethnic Cleansing; Holocaust; Human Rights; Manifest Destiny; Monroe Doctrine (1823); United Nations; Universal Declaration of Human Rights*

BIBLIOGRAPHY

Alvarez, Alex. *Native America and the Question of Genocide.* Lanham, MD: Rowman and Littlefield, 2014.

Bartrop, Paul R. "Genocide and War." Unpublished working paper, 2013.

Bass, Gary J. *The Blood Telegram: Nixon, Kissinger, and a Forgotten Genocide.* New York: Knopf, 2013.

Dunbar-Ortiz, Roxanne. *An Indigenous Peoples' History of the United States.* Boston: Beacon Press, 2014.

Fein, Helen. "Genocide and Other State Murders in the Twentieth Century." Lecture delivered October 25, 1995, at the United States Holocaust Memorial Museum. http://www.ushmm.org

Fournet, Caroline. *The Crime of Destruction and the Law of Genocide: Their Impact on Collective Memory.* Burlington, VT: Ashgate, 2007.

Gitlin, Todd, and Liel Leibovitz. *The Chosen Peoples: America, Israel, and the Ordeals of Divine Election.* New York: Simon and Schuster, 2010.

Graybill, Lyn. "'Responsible … by Omission': The United States and Genocide in Rwanda." *Seton Hall Journal of Diplomacy and International Relations* 3, 1 (2002): 86–103.

Hutchinson, William R., and Hartmut Lehmann, eds. *Many Are Chosen: Divine Election and Western Nationalism.* Harrisburg, PA: Trinity Press International, 1994.

Jacobs, Steven Leonard. "We Charge Genocide: An Historical Petition All But Forgotten and Unknown." Conference Presentation: "Understanding Atrocities," Mount Royal University, Calgary, Alberta, Canada, February, 2013.

Kakel, Carroll P., III. *The American West and the Nazi East: A Comparative and Interpretative Perspective.* New York: Palgrave Macmillan, 2013.

Kaufmann, Chaim. "See No Evil: Why America Doesn't Stop Genocide." *Foreign Affairs* 81, 4 (2002): 142–149.

Kornbluh, Peter. *The Pinochet File: A Declassified Dossier on Atrocity and Accountability.* New York: New Press, 2003.

LeBlanc, Lawrence J. *The United States and the Genocide Convention.* Durham, NC: Duke University Press, 1991.

Lindberg, Tod. "How to Prevent Atrocities: There's No Substitute for Presidential Leadership." *Weekly Standard* 18, 25 (March 11, 2013): 26–29.

Mann, Michael. *The Dark Side of Democracy: Explaining Ethnic Cleansing.* Cambridge: Cambridge University Press, 2005.

Model, David. *State of Darkness: US Complicity in Genocides since 1945.* Bloomington, IN: AuthorHouse, 2008.

Moorhead, James H. "The American Israel: Protestant Tribalism and Universal Mission." In *Many Are Chosen: Divine Election and Western Nationalism,* edited by William R. Hutchison and Hartmut Lehmann, 145–195. Harrisburg, PA: Trinity Press International, 1994.

Power, Samantha. *"A Problem from Hell": America and the Age of Genocide.* New York: Basic Books, 2002

Ronayne, Peter. *Never Again? The United States and the Prevention and Punishment of Genocide since the Holocaust.* Lanham, MD: Rowman and Littlefield, 2001.

Smith, Anthony D. *Chosen Peoples: Sacred Sources of National Identity.* Oxford and New York: Oxford University Press, 2003.

Stephanson, Anders. *Manifest Destiny: American Expansion and the Empire of Right.* New York: Hill and Wang, 1995.

United Nations. Convention on the Prevention and Punishment of the Crime of Genocide. Adopted by the General Assembly of the United Nations on December 9, 1948. https://treaties.un.org/doc/Publication/UNTS/Volume%2078/volume-78-I-1021-English.pdf

Waxman, Matthew C. *Intervention to Stop Genocide and Mass Atrocities: International Norms and U.S. Policy.* New York: Council on Foreign Relations, 2009.

Winter, Jay, ed. *America and the Armenian Genocide of 1915.* Cambridge: Cambridge University Press, 2003.

Steven Leonard Jacobs
Aaron Aronov Endowed Chair of Judaic Studies
University of Alabama, Tuscaloosa

GERMANY

After the United States of America declared independence on July 4, 1776, numerous Germans who had immigrated from various German principalities to North America since 1683 fought for their new home country. They saw the United States as a democratic state where man would triumph over tyranny and prejudice. The United States maintained good relations with the German kingdom of Prussia and subsequently with the nation of Germany throughout the nineteenth century. Following the catastrophic world wars of the twentieth century, Germany and the United States resumed a relationship of cooperation and pursuit of mutual interests.

THE UNITED STATES AND PRUSSIA

In its first bilateral treaty with a German principality, in 1785, the United States concluded a trade agreement with Frederick the Great (1712–1786), the king of Prussia. Such trade agreements remained the ideal, and in 1796 diplomatic relations between the United States and Prussia were established. The United States for many decades followed President George Washington's advice in his 1797 Farewell Address "to steer clear of permanent alliances." As President Thomas Jefferson more precisely stated in his First Inaugural address in 1801, the nation's goal was to ensure "peace, commerce, and honest friendship with all nations, entangling alliances with none."

In 1848 revolutionary Germans in various German principalities called for a federal nation-state organized as a constitutional monarchy. To no one's surprise, the United States government welcomed this initiative, becoming the only foreign power to recognize the short-lived 1848 Frankfurt government by sending an emissary. During the great European conflict of the 1850s, the Crimean War, both the United States and Prussia remained neutral and increased their mutual trade volume.

Regarding commerce the United States cooperated closely with the Kingdom of Prussia. Both countries tried to observe the common right of freedom of the seas. Denmark's requirement that all ships sailing through the Danish straits to enter or leave the Baltic Sea pay a toll was oppressive to both US and Prussian commerce, though a greater number of Prussian ships were affected by it. Through US-Prussian cooperation and the support of other nations, in 1857 Denmark was persuaded to abolish the toll. After the US Department of State successfully concluded a trade agreement with Japan, German merchant ships were provided with nautical charts by the US government and could therefore sail to Japanese harbors safely. The United States and Prussia also cooperated closely in China, opposing France's expansionist moves there.

When the US Civil War broke out in 1861, the Prussian prime minister Otto von Bismarck (1815–1898) declared, in contrast to statements by other Western European countries, that from Prussia's viewpoint the war was not an international conflict but rather an internal matter of the United States. Taking sides with the Union officially, Prussia consequently referred to the Union's opponent as "the so-called Confederacy." Germany's abortive revolution of 1848 and economic problems had caused a new wave of German emigration to the United States. Thousands of those immigrants now fought on the side of the North, Carl Schurz (1829–1906) being a prominent example. Bismarck's open sympathy for the Union also made it easier for Prussian officers to obtain a leave of absence in case they wanted to join the Union Army. The Civil War resulted in a boom in the importation of German products, including weapons. In addition, the US Department of the Treasury was relieved of its concerns about the acceptance of the Union's war bonds. The credit for the greenback, resting mainly on these bonds, was in great demand on the Frankfurt Stock Exchange and helped to prevent the dollar's loss in value through depreciation.

After the 1867 creation of the North German Confederation, the United States was finally able to settle the longstanding problem of naturalization. German emigrants to the United States visiting their former German home principality risked being forced to serve in that principality's army for two or three years. Bismarck, now the chancellor of the Prussian-dominated North German Confederation, prepared a treaty respecting US citizenship. He saw to it that King Wilhelm I (1797–1888) and US envoy to Berlin George Bancroft (1800–1891) signed the treaty on February 22, Washington's birthday, in 1868.

When the Franco-Prussian War started in 1870, Count Bismarck approached the US government to secure the support of the US embassy in Paris for the purpose of protecting the Germans living in France. During the war US generals Ambrose E. Burnside (1824–1881) and Philip H. Sheridan (1831–1888) visited German troops on the battlefields.

THE UNITED STATES AND THE GERMAN EMPIRE

In 1871 the United States immediately established diplomatic relations with the new German nation-state. A year later the United States and Great Britain accepted King Wilhelm I, now also Kaiser Wilhelm I of the German Empire, as arbitrator in the Northwest Boundary Dispute. In 1872 both countries accepted his awarding of the San Juan Islands west of the Haro Straits to the United States.

In 1889 the United States sent diplomats to Berlin to participate for the first time in a European conference. There the American diplomats, supported by Bismarck, successfully insisted on the use of English instead of French, to that point the common diplomatic language. The conference resulted in the Samoa Act, a condominium over the Samoan Islands negotiated by the German Empire, Great Britain, and the United States.

During the Spanish-American War of 1898 the German Empire adopted a position of "benevolent neutrality." In 1902 Harvard University established an exchange program for professors with Prussia. It was in US interests for American officers to graduate from Prussian military schools and serve with Prussian regiments. American officers were welcomed frequently as maneuver guests by Kaiser Wilhelm II (1859–1941), and US Navy units often visited Kiel Week, an annual sailing event of the Imperial German navy, which in return visited US harbors.

The strong friendship with Germany, however, in no way dominated US interests in foreign policy. The German Empire failed to create an entente among itself, the United States, and China that intended to break the close cooperation of France, Russia, and the United Kingdom, which the imperial government perceived as "encirclement." Minor frictions between Germany and the United States in Manila Bay in the Philippines, Venezuela, and Samoa in the South Pacific sparked rumors in Washington that the German Empire planned to violate the Monroe Doctrine. Germany's recognition of the Mexican government under General José Victoriano Huerta Márquez (from 1913 to 1914) severely damaged US-German relations.

In August 1914 World War I broke out in Europe. The resumption of unrestricted submarine warfare by Germany (previously halted to avoid giving the United States a reason to enter the war) and the German offer of an alliance with Mexico caused a total deterioration of relations between the United States and the German Empire. In 1917 President Woodrow Wilson (in office 1913–1921) declared war on Germany.

THE UNITED STATES, THE WEIMAR REPUBLIC, AND NAZI GERMANY

After the end of World War I in 1918 the United States withdrew from Europe in terms of political influence but not in terms of economic activities. In Germany the Weimar Republic introduced a democratic republican system to replace the imperial government. The Wilson administration sought an arrangement whereby Germany would be able to absorb American exports and investments. As the 1919 Treaty of Versailles, the formal diplomatic end of the war, did not meet with the approval of the US Senate, the separate peace treaty of 1921 between the United States and Germany and the conclusion of a bilateral trade agreement in 1923 became central to postwar relations.

The question of German reparations was a central subject of postwar international disputes during the 1920s. The United States insisted that only a Germany with a sound economy would be able to pay for the damage it had wrought and therefore tried to have Germany's payments reduced. But the American mediation efforts at the same time served to pave the way for America's own economic and commercial expansion. Until 1931 Germany received almost $2.5 billion in loans from the United States. In addition there were portfolio and direct investments from American firms and individuals in Germany, with the Ford Motor Company opening a European production plant at Cologne in 1925. The stock market crash of 1929 led to a depression in both countries. The National Socialist Party (Nazi Party) was on the rise, and by 1930 the Weimar Republic's politics of peaceful reform came to an end.

President Franklin Delano Roosevelt (in office 1933–1945) was confronted with Nazi Germany's attempts to achieve hegemony over Europe. No wonder that Washington terminated the Reciprocal Trade Agreement Act in October 1934. The Hitler regime's flagrant violations of civil rights and the deadly attacks on Jews in November 1938 (known as Kristallnacht) forced the United States to recall its ambassador from Berlin. Washington clearly showed its disapproval of the Third Reich's subsequent aggressive actions, not least its occupation of parts of Czechoslovakia, but diplomatic relations between the two countries were not yet broken off. Nazi Germany ignored Roosevelt's appeals for peace, and the Second World War began in September 1939. The Japanese attack on the US naval base at Pearl Harbor, Hawai'i, on December 7, 1941, induced Nazi Germany to declare war on the as yet neutral United States.

THE UNITED STATES AND GERMANY DURING THE COLD WAR

Following Germany's surrender to the Allies in 1945, the four countries of the Grand Alliance—The United States, the Soviet Union, Great Britain, and France—divided Germany into four occupation zones with the common aim of eliminating all Nazi influence, introducing democratic institutions, and prosecuting former Nazi leaders for war crimes. A deep distrust characterized the relations between the Western democracies and the Soviet Union because of Soviet policies in Eastern Europe, Greece, and Iran.

As early as 1947 the American Joint Chiefs of Staff began to recognize the security of Western Europe as integral to the security of the United States. But without West Germany a true forward strategy against the Soviet Union, which had control over the eastern part of Germany, seemed impossible to establish. The economic revival of West Germany and the end of the politics of demilitarization were therefore to be of primary importance from the standpoint of US security.

In June 1948 the United States led the efforts to limit the effects of the Soviet blockade of West Berlin with a well-organized airlift lasting 323 days. During the Berlin blockade the population of the Western zones of occupation developed a kind of boundless trust in their main protector and embraced the American way of life; fascination with American music, literature, art, and movies was not limited to the younger generation. Perceiving the threat of the Soviet Union as the enemy on the horizon, the United States ended their traditional policy of steering clear of permanent alliances. In 1949 the United States became a founding member of the North Atlantic Treaty Organization (NATO), and sought to include the Federal Republic of Germany (West Germany), established in the same year, as an armed member. The Korean War and developments in the German Democratic Republic (East Germany), established as a communist regime by the Soviet Union in 1949, made it easier for West German citizens to embrace rearming as a NATO member; the country joined NATO in May 1955, and the Bundeswehr, the German Armed Forces, soon became an important pillar in the transatlantic security system.

In August 1961 the East German regime, with Soviet consent, built a wall between East and West Berlin. Soon a deadly fenced and mined border divided the two parts of Germany. Most Germans in West Berlin and West Germany reacted enthusiastically when President John F. Kennedy (in office 1961–1963), in his speech against the backdrop of the Berlin Wall in 1963, uttered his unforgettable statement of solidarity, "Ich bin ein Berliner" (I am a citizen of Berlin).

But soon West German political opinions began to diverge over the question of the future development of Western policy towards the Communist bloc in general and East Germany in particular. At first Washington disapproved of West Germany's steps towards a German and European policy of détente, termed the "new eastern policy," but the West German government tried diligently to combine its interests with America's security interests. In retrospect West Germany's ratification of treaties with the Soviet Union, Poland, and East Germany may be considered as contributing to the US-Soviet Strategic Arms Limitation Talks (SALT) and Antiballistic Missile Treaty in the 1970s.

The winds of change blew stronger in the late 1980s. In a speech in Berlin in 1987, President Ronald Reagan (in office 1981–1989) called on Soviet leader Mikhail Gorbachev (in office 1985–1991) to "tear down this wall." When the fall of the Berlin Wall occurred two years later, and with the politics of openness instituted by Gorbachev in 1990, Chancellor Helmut Kohl (in office 1982–1998) saw a realistic window of opportunity for unification. President George H. W. Bush (in office 1989–1993), who strongly supported the unification of the two German states, made sure that a united Germany would remain a reliable member of NATO. About 60,000

US military personnel stationed in Germany continued to protect the common security interests of both countries.

THE UNITED STATES AND GERMANY SINCE UNIFICATION

In the post–Cold War era, relations between the reunified Germany and the United States continued to be very close. Both nations faced new challenges. After the September 11, 2001, terrorist attacks on New York and Washington both countries united in global counterterrorism efforts, with Germany part of the NATO alliance supporting the US invasion of Afghanistan. Besides a trustworthy partner in international relations, the United States became Germany's third-largest supplier of goods of all kinds and its principal trading partner outside the European Union. It has been estimated that almost six thousand companies in both countries depend on the relationship.

In 2013, during the administration of President Barack Obama (in office 2009–) a leaker revealed that the US National Security Agency (NSA) was engaging in bulk collection of metadata. President Obama visited Germany's chancellor Angela Merkel (in office 2005–) in Berlin, and their meeting calmed the German public's concerns. However, the rumor then spread that even Merkel's cell phone had been tapped by American agencies, and the German government asked the CIA station chief in Berlin to leave the country.

In all relations there are ups and downs. In 2014 German foreign minister Walter Steinmeier met with US secretary of state John Kerry in Vienna and noted that the German-US ties are important and necessary for both nations. Berlin and Washington continue to work on improving this enduring relationship.

SEE ALSO *Central Intelligence Agency (CIA); Cold War; Eisenhower, Dwight D.; Internationalism; Interventionism; Isolationism; Judaism; Marshall Plan; Roosevelt, Franklin D.; Strategic Defense Initiative (Star Wars); Truman, Harry S.; United Nations; Wilson, Woodrow; World War I; World War II*

BIBLIOGRAPHY

De Grazia, Victoria. *Irresistible Empire: America's Advance through Twentieth-Century Europe.* Cambridge, MA: Belknap Press of Harvard University Press, 2005.

Gatzke, Hans W. *Germany and the United States: A "Special Relationship"?* Cambridge, MA: Harvard University Press, 1980.

Hodge, Carl C. and Cathal J. Nolan, eds. *Shepherd of Democracy? America and Germany in the Twentieth Century.* Westport, CT: Greenwood, 1992.

Jonas, Manfred. *The United States and Germany: A Diplomatic History.* Ithaca, NY: Cornell University Press, 1984.

Junker, Detlef, et al. eds. *The United States and Germany in the Era of the Cold War, 1945–1990: A Handbook.* 2 vols. New York: Cambridge University Press, 2004.

Nolan, Mary. *The Transatlantic Century: Europe and America, 1890–2010.* Cambridge: Cambridge University Press, 2012.

Pommerin, Reiner, ed. *The American Impact on Postwar Germany.* Providence, RI, and Oxford, UK: Berghahn Books, 1995.

Pommerin, Reiner, ed. *Culture in the Federal Republic of Germany, 1945–1995.* Oxford, UK, and Washington, DC: Berg Publishers, 1996.

Szabo, Stephen F. *Parting Ways: The Crisis in German-American Relations.* Washington, DC: Brookings Institution Press, 2004.

Reiner Pommerin
Professor of Modern and Contemporary History
University of Dresden, Germany

GLOBAL SOUTH

The Global South is a broad concept that denotes a geographical place, an imagined space, and an analytical construct. In the context of the history of the Americas, the Global South, sometimes referred to as the *hemispheric South*, includes the southern part of the United States, the Caribbean, Mexico, Central America, and South America. The boundaries of this area are fluid in nature and can reference any area south of the northern industrialized hemisphere. The Global South is thought to share a set of common characteristics: tropical climates and diseases, a history of racial slavery, one-crop or plantation agriculture, and rural poverty. It is a site for a transnational movement of capital, labor, and goods and considered to be the antipode of modern capitalism.

The idea of the Global South reflects the way in which the discipline of American studies, originally rooted in a study of New England, has begun to reconsider "America" from a transnational perspective, embracing the connections between seemingly disparate countries. Some scholars in the field known as *new southern studies* have used the framework of postcolonialism to challenge regional boundaries and reimagine the US South as both colonizer and colonized, center and periphery, foreign and American, backward and progressive. In fact, one of the ironies of the South noted by C. Vann Woodward (1993) is the region's perceived commonalities with other countries and cultures around the world and its shared experience with conquest, military occupation, and rehabilitation in the wake of destruction. Thus the Global South offers a corrective to the longstanding belief in southern exceptionalism. In jettisoning the North-South binary framework in the fields of southern history and literature it becomes apparent that the belief in US southern distinctiveness (i.e., backwardness) was part of a commonplace discourse about distinctive southern areas in the transnational world.

The Global South also can signify an even wider geographical area including Southeast Asia, Africa, and Latin America or what is sometimes problematically referred to as the *Third World*. This iteration of the Global South can be traced back to the 1970s, when observers tried to answer why certain countries struggled with the difficulties of economic development. The presumption that large infusions of capital would lead to modernity was complicated by the existence of the Global South. Critics of this process see the exploitation and subordination of indigenous peoples in this geographic area as the inevitable effect of imperialism, capitalism, or what scholars currently refer to as *neoliberalism*. The transnational reach of capitalism, ensuing class inequalities, exploitation of resources, and racial and gendered marginalization is characteristic of the Global South. In addition, studies of the Global South often address the way in which the subaltern (those who are subjugated) identify themselves as such and resist the encroachment of this hegemonic process. Subaltern studies involves examining how those who are marginalized exercise their agency, construct identities, and both adopt and refashion the traditions of those who are in power in the Global South.

SEE ALSO *Africa; Asia; South America; Third World*

BIBLIOGRAPHY

Smith, Jon, and Deborah Cohn, eds. *Look Away! The U.S. South in New World Studies*. Durham, NC: Duke University Press, 2004.

Woodward, C. Vann. "The Irony of Southern History." In *The Burden of Southern History*, 187–212. 3rd ed. Baton Rouge: Louisiana University Press, 1993.

Ziolkowski, Jan M., guest ed. Special issue, "Globalization and the Future of Comparative Literature." *The Global South* 1, 1–2 (2007).

Natalie J. Ring
Associate Professor of History
University of Texas at Dallas

GLOBAL WARMING

Former vice president Al Gore, notified that he had won the 2007 Nobel Peace Prize for his work on climate change, referred to global warming as a "true planetary emergency." "The climate crisis," he continued, "is not a political issue, it is a moral and spiritual challenge to all humanity" (Gibbs 2007). By the end of the first decade of the twenty-first century, global warming had become the key environmental issue across the globe. Despite Gore's words, the topic has become one of the most debated and political in the United States.

THE PROCESS OF GLOBAL WARMING

Global warming, often referred to as *climate change*, stems from the complicated relationship between the sun and the earth's atmosphere, water, and plant life. When the earth initially formed, its atmosphere was mostly carbon dioxide. Plants emerged, taking in carbon dioxide and releasing oxygen. The carbon dioxide absorbed by the plants then decomposed and eventually formed coal and oil deposits. Plants essentially remove carbon dioxide from the atmosphere and store it underground.

The earth's atmosphere, now made up almost exclusively of nitrogen and oxygen, contains only trace amounts of other substances. Some of these substances, primarily water vapor, carbon dioxide, and methane, are known as *greenhouse gases*, and play an important role in the global ecology. Sunlight passes through the atmosphere to the earth, warming the ground during the day. At night, the energy flows back up into the atmosphere, where it either escapes or is directed back down by greenhouse gases. This process, known as the *greenhouse effect*, is generally seen as positive: greenhouse gases keep the temperature of most of the earth's water above freezing. If too little greenhouse gas existed, more ice would form, causing more of the sun's light to be reflected back into space, lowering the overall temperature of the planet.

Humans have long used plant matter in its various forms as an energy source. Large-scale farming and urbanization, with concurrent deforestation and the burning of wood, certainly affected the environment prior to the nineteenth century. During the 1800s, however, the scope and magnitude of this change shifted. The Industrial Revolution brought with it mechanization that required more energy than wood yielded. Beginning in Europe and shifting to the United States and the world, people began using coal and oil deposits in increasing amounts. Burning these fossil fuels released large amounts of stored carbon dioxide back into the atmosphere, particularly after World War II (1939–1945). Huge levels of deforestation, particularly in the Amazon rainforest, also eliminated natural carbon sinks, exacerbating the problem.

With more greenhouse gases in the atmosphere, the planet retains more heat from the sun, a process known as *global warming*. Ice melts and therefore reflects less heat. Since global warming does not necessarily mean an absence of cold weather, scientists have adopted the term *climate change* as well. Overall, a delicate balance exists between the sun's energy, the amount of liquid and frozen

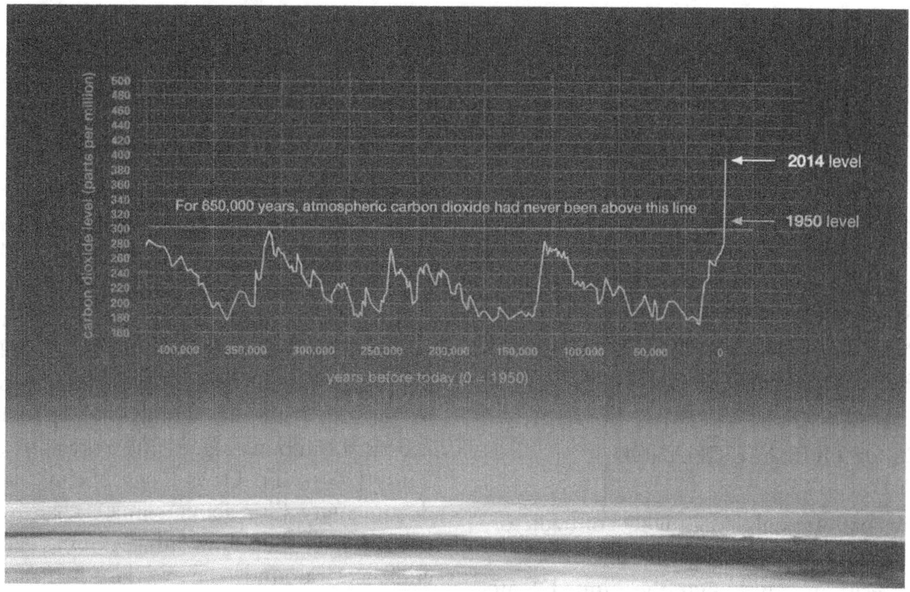

Rising levels of atmospheric carbon dioxide. *The burning of fossil fuels has released tremendous amounts of stored carbon dioxide back into the atmosphere, particularly since World War II. Deforestation, especially in the Amazon rainforest, has also eliminated natural carbon sinks, exacerbating the problem. With more greenhouse gases, the planet retains more heat from the sun, a process known as global warming.* NASA

water, the quantity of plants, and the makeup of the atmosphere. This balance plays a pivotal role in the habitability and geography of the planet.

Scientific data reveal several trends. According to the National Aeronautics and Space Administration (NASA) and National Oceanic and Atmospheric Administration (NOAA), the amount of carbon dioxide in mid-2015 hit 400.57 parts per million, the highest level in fifty-five years of measurement. The average global temperature has risen 1.4 degrees Fahrenheit (0.8 degrees Celsius) since 1880. Not only is the amount of land ice dropping by 2.58 billion metric tons per year, but the amount of Arctic ice measured each September is dropping by 13.3 percent per decade. Compounding these issues, the natural means of reducing carbon dioxide is also experiencing a dramatic change: the earth's forest cover has declined by 1.5 million square kilometers (about 580,000 square miles) in the period between 2000 and 2012. Faced with such evidence, the vast majority of scientists agree that not only is global warming occurring, but that humans have played a significant role in causing it.

WORLDWIDE EFFORTS TO ADDRESS GLOBAL WARMING

Although the earth's climate has always been in flux, the concept of global warming and confusion surrounding that term are quite recent. Climate scientists began describing global warming in articles and books in the 1970s. By the late 1980s, the international community had begun to examine the issue more closely. In June 1992, the United Nations Conference on Environment and Development, known as the Earth Summit, convened in Rio de Janeiro, Brazil, with the participation of 172 governments and 2,400 representatives from nongovernmental organizations worldwide. The summit's focus was wide-ranging, with participants discussing the possible impacts of global warming, such as water scarcity, as well as causes and possible solutions, including new production methods, alternative sources of energy, and alternative modes of transportation. The conference also recognized the primacy of basic rights and health for all humans. Member countries, including the United States, signed agreements at the Earth Summit committing to a reduction of carbon-dioxide emissions.

Five years after the Earth Summit, global leaders drafted the Kyoto Protocol, which committed parties to setting targets for the reduction of greenhouse gases. Targets varied by country and depended on levels of production and on economic factors. In addition, countries could trade emissions amounts on the open market. The Kyoto Protocol exempted developing nations, including China, Brazil, and India, from the requirements of the protocol on the grounds that developed nations are more responsible for current global-warming problems. The protocol also established a fund to help developing countries gain access to green technology as they industrialized. Eventually signed by the

European Community and thirty-seven other nations, the Kyoto Protocol took eight years to ratify, and proved a limited success. In the protocol's first commitment period (2008–2012), participating countries' greenhouse gas emissions dropped by more than 22 percent from 1990 levels, well over the 5-percent target. Global emissions, however, rose 65 percent over the same period, mostly as a result of activity in the United States and China. Scholars have argued over the efficacy of the Kyoto Protocol: although it failed to reduce greenhouse gases overall, it did provide an important first step in international cooperation on the issue of global warming.

THE POLITICS OF CLIMATE CHANGE IN THE UNITED STATES

The United States has often played a highly contradictory role in the globalization of environmental issues, in particular global warming. Although the United States signed the 1992 Earth Summit agreements, change did not occur within the country. Bill Clinton, who became president in 1993, campaigned for higher fuel efficiency in American cars, but quickly acquiesced to the automobile industry's demand for delays in favor of more research. In addition, the United States never ratified the Kyoto Protocol. Certainly the United States has been a key producer of greenhouse gases. In 1990, the United States and the developed nations accounted for two-thirds of all global emissions. According to the US Environmental Protection Agency (EPA), the United States has regularly emitted between 5,000 and 6,000 million metric tons of carbon dioxide per year since 1990.

Despite these numbers, Americans have proven reluctant to take a leadership role in cutting greenhouse gas emissions. In response to Kyoto, for example, the US Senate passed the Byrd-Hagel Resolution by a vote of ninety-five to zero, expressing its disapproval of any treaty that failed to require all nations, including developing nations, to reduce emissions. Much of the opposition stemmed from an overall political shift to the right in the United States beginning with the Ronald Reagan administration (1981–1989). Republicans have proved unwilling to accept limits on business and industry, and often actively campaigned against environmental regulations. Opposition to "big government" and "excessive regulation" led to a strengthened anti-environmental movement in the 1990s. Supporters of the wise-use movement, for example, used antifederal rhetoric to stress individual and property rights in an attempt to open up federal land for grazing, logging, and other business interests. This political turn intensified with the election of George W. Bush to the presidency in 2000. Bush owed much to coal interests, and worked during his presidency to open new coal plants in many areas. Reluctance to reduce dependence on fossil fuels has led to ever-more drastic methods of extracting oil, including deep-sea drilling and hydraulic fracturing.

THE ACTIVISM OF AL GORE

After losing the 2000 presidential election to Bush, Al Gore began his work on climate change in earnest, becoming the person most associated with the cause in the early twenty-first century. While serving as Clinton's vice president, Gore had supported the Kyoto Protocol, education programs on climate change, and various NASA monitoring programs. After the 2000 election, Gore's commitment to the cause and his number of speaking engagements increased, culminating in the release of *An Inconvenient Truth* (2006, dir. Davis Guggenheim), an award-winning documentary film about climate change focusing on an educational slide-show that Gore had presented to audiences around the world. *An Inconvenient Truth* recommended ways that individuals could help ameliorate climate change, including increasing their recycling efforts, changing their driving habits, planting trees, and adjusting thermostats, among other things.

Even with a relatively conservative agenda, Gore attracted critics. Both pro- and anti-environmentalists lambasted his use of private planes, his multiple homes, and even his nonvegetarian diet. For his part, Gore participated in carbon-offset programs, donating money when he traveled by air, for example. Although he did later stress the need to change to cleaner energy, Gore avoided direct attacks on capitalism or business. He clung to technological fixes as solutions to climate change, promoting the Virgin Earth Challenge beginning in 2007, which offered $25 million to whomever produced technology to remove carbon dioxide from the atmosphere. For his efforts "to build up and disseminate greater knowledge about man-made climate change," Gore, along with the Intergovernmental Panel on Climate Change, won the 2007 Nobel Peace Prize.

CLIMATE CHANGE DENIAL

Scientists generally agree on the concept of climate change, as well as the human role in it. However, individual studies differ on the rate of change, the levels that create problems, and the possible consequences. In the wake of absolute scientific consensus, dissent from "climate change deniers" has grown louder. Rather than see these disagreements among scientists as the scientific process at work, politicians and some of the general public claim that global warming needs further study before governments adopt policies to deal with it.

Climate change deniers oppose the idea of global warming from several angles. Failing to distinguish between weather and climate change, they frequently cite continued cold temperatures as evidence that the earth is not warming. In addition, to refute the idea of human causation, they look to historical trends, pointing out that temperature change has happened over the earth's history and that current trends are just part of a natural occurrence. Climate change deniers also tend to draw on earlier anti-environmental rhetoric, whereby environmental legislation is seen as an undue burden on business and industry. In addition, American climate change deniers often resent globalization as a blow to American prestige.

Climate change deniers work to promote scientists who stand against the mainstream views of global warming. One of the most prominent of these has been Wei-Hock "Willie" Soon of the Harvard-Smithsonian Center for Astrophysics, who supports the idea that climate change is not caused by human activity. Soon has become a leading authority for climate deniers, even after revelations that he receives funding from sources with vested interests against emission reductions: ExxonMobil, the American Petroleum Institute, and the Koch Charitable Foundation. Republican senator James Inhofe from Oklahoma, who has served as chair of the Senate Committee on Environment and Public Works, relies on Soon in his assertions that the entire concept of global warming is a hoax.

In another attack on consensus views, climate change deniers touted "climategate" as evidence of a widespread conspiracy in which climate change scientists had manipulated and falsified data. In 2009, hackers stole a large number of e-mails from the Climate Research Unit in the United Kingdom and published them online. The impact on public opinion proved to be short-lived, as a closer inspection of the documents by various organizations revealed the claims of a conspiracy to be a misrepresentation (Henig 2009).

Climate change deniers have taken further steps to avoid global warming as a topic. In 2015, Florida governor Rick Scott, a Republican, reportedly banned the use of the words *climate change* and *global warming* in any official communication from the state's environmental protection agency. The governor denied the charges leveled by the Florida Center for Investigative Journalism (Korten 2015), although several employees confirmed the story. Wisconsin followed suit more explicitly. Shortly after the Florida story broke, a public land trust in the state voted to block its employees from working on any climate change issue on trust time.

AWARENESS AND ACTIVISM

Despite efforts by deniers to discredit or ignore the topic, climate change will remain a central political issue for the next generation: younger Americans, in particular, see it as pivotally important. In an Ipsos poll conducted in early 2015, 94 percent of American eighth graders indicated that they believed that global warming is real, and 85 percent believed that humans caused it. This concern among children extends beyond the United States. In a poll of Canadian children aged eight to eleven, 39 percent listed climate change as the most important environmental problem. Children also showed an awareness of the meanings of the terms *global warming* and *climate change*.

Some young people are beginning to do more than just express opinions. Kids vs. Global Warming, an organization founded by then-teenager Alec Loorz, who became inspired to act after watching *An Inconvenient Truth* at age twelve, filed a lawsuit against the federal government in the summer of 2014 for not dealing adequately with the problem of global warming. The organization works to spread awareness of the problems of climate change, and, through Loorz's website (www.imatteryouth.org), seeks to empower young people who want their voices heard and respected by adults. Under the slogan "Our Climate, Our Future, Our Revolution," iMatter asserts that "the voice of the generation most impacted by the climate crisis must be heard" and recognizes young people who are taking steps against global warming. In 2013, Loorz wrote a "Declaration of Independence from Fossil Fuels," which was presented to Senator Barbara Boxer, a leading member of the Senate Committee on Environment and Public Works. Interestingly, the group also takes a dig at how adults, including Gore, have urged children to act: the site stresses that the solution to global warming is "going to take a whole lot more than riding our bikes and changing lightbulbs. We need to look at the core of the problem."

Candidates in the 2016 presidential campaign continued to focus on the issue. Republican candidate Jeb Bush described himself as a "skeptic" on climate change. On the other hand, Democrat Hillary Clinton committed to "tackling climate change" if elected. Republican desires to ignore or push aside the problems presented by climate change are not reflected in the general public's views. In an Ipsos/Reuters poll conducted in February 2015, two-thirds of the American public indicated that they believed that world leaders must act on the issue of climate change.

Climate change has become the primary environmental topic of the early twenty-first century. Although the international community has begun to take steps to resolve the problem of greenhouse gas emissions, the United States and other major emitters must join in efforts for the problem to be addressed effectively. Another Earth Summit in Paris in late 2015 held promise for the implementation of additional measures.

SEE ALSO *Bush, George W.; Clinton, William Jefferson; Earth Day; Gore, Albert, Jr.; National Aeronautics and Space Administration (NASA); National Oceanic and Atmospheric Administration (NOAA); Ozone Depletion; Silent Spring (Rachel Carson, 1962)*

BIBLIOGRAPHY

Gibbs, Walter. "Gore and UN Panel Are Awarded Nobel Peace Prize." *New York Times*, October 12, 2007. http://www.nytimes.com/2007/10/12/world/europe/12iht-nobel.3.7870475.html?pagewanted=all&_r=0

Henig, Jess. "Climategate: Hacked E-Mails Show Climate Scientists in a Bad Light but Don't Change Scientific Consensus on Global Warming." FactCheck.org, December 10, 2009. http://www.factcheck.org/2009/12/climategate/

iMatter: Kids vs Global Warming. http://www.imatteryouth.org/

Intergovernmental Panel on Climate Change. http://www.ipcc.com

Ipsos Public Affairs. "Nine in Ten 8th Graders Agree That Climate Change Is Real and Human Activity Significantly Contributes to Climate Change." IPSOS press release, March 13, 2015. http://www.ipsos-na.com/news-polls/pressrelease.aspx?id=6792

Ipsos/Reuters Poll: Climate Change. February 26, 2015. http://www.ipsos-na.com/news-polls/pressrelease.aspx?id=6778

Korten, Tristram. "In Florida, Officials Ban Term 'Climate Change.'" Florida Center for Investigative Reporting. March 8, 2015. http://fcir.org/2015/03/08/in-florida-officials-ban-term-climate-change/

NASA, Jet Propulsion Laboratory, Earth Science Communications Team. "Global Climate Change: Vital Signs of the Planet." http://climate.nasa.gov

United Nations. "UN and Climate Change." http://www.un.org/climatechange

HISTORY AND SCIENCE

Christianson, Gale E. *Greenhouse: The 200-Year Story of Global Warming*. New York: Walker, 1999.

Global Climate Change. The Reference Shelf. Ipswich, MA: Wilson, 2013.

Howe, Joshua P. *Behind the Curve: Science and the Politics of Global Warming*. Seattle: University of Washington Press, 2014.

McKibben, Bill, ed. *The Global Warming Reader*. New York: OR Books, 2011.

Orestes, Naomi, and Erik M. Conway. *Merchants of Doubt: How a Handful of Scientists Obscured the Truth on Issues from Tobacco Smoke to Global Warming*. New York: Bloomsbury Press, 2010.

Ruddiman, William F. *Plows, Plagues, and Petroleum: How Humans Took Control of Climate*. Princeton, NJ: Princeton University Press, 2005.

THE DENIER POINT OF VIEW

Inhofe, James. *The Greatest Hoax: How the Global Warming Conspiracy Threatens Your Future*. Washington, DC: WND, 2012.

Plimer, Ian. *Heaven and Earth: Global Warming, the Missing Science*. Lanham, MD: Taylor, 2009.

Elizabeth D. Blum
Professor, Department of History
Troy University

GLOBALIZATION

Globalization is the process of unifying markets (and the cultural behavior) on a worldwide scale through expansionist ideologies, the perfection of industrial capitalism, and the modernization of production, transport, and communication wrought by technology. The term was coined in 1983 by Theodore Levitt (1925–2006), a marketing professor at Harvard Business School, and became a buzzword in the early 1990s after the Cold War ended. During this period, advances in technology created an increasingly unified global marketplace for labor and capital, which has equalized the prices of both around the world. Such integration has been occurring for centuries, but until the late nineteenth century and the advent of Anglo-American economic power, true globalization linked localities and regions everywhere in ways that harmonized people, states, and outlooks. The American version of post–Cold War globalization featured a dynamic neoliberal pursuit of free trade and open investments overseas, expanded circulation of money, an insistence that capitalism fostered democracy, and the tightened bonds of culture and business practices. Globalization represented an ideology pushed and perpetuated by American exceptionalism, itself promoted by the conservative turn in US politics that privileged free enterprise, open markets, and high technology as ideal forces in the world economy, just as they were critical to the ascendance of the United States.

THE IMPACT OF DEREGULATION AND FINANCIALIZATION

The processes of globalization acquired momentum beginning in the late 1970s. New communications and transport technology played a role, but the wave of deregulation spearheaded by the United States and the United Kingdom led to economic liberalization and launched the era of modern globalization. The regulatory structures put in place over decades by Labor governments in the United Kingdom and by the New Deal in the United States began to wane. The regime of fixed exchange rates ended, and flexible rates gave greater power to transnational investors. Meanwhile, an era of *financialization* took root, in which financial instruments became increasingly important to the way that other goods and services were produced and consumed, allowing financiers to influence and profit from sectors in which they had not been deeply involved before. Capital markets were, in the last instance, transnational. Thus, even a local bank lending against the value of a house down the street was ultimately connected to global institutions, and financialization meant that more and more spheres of everyday activity could potentially influence, and be influenced by, credit conditions thousands of miles away.

In the United States, once-stable industries, such as automobiles, steel, and machine tools, lost market shares to new entrants, at first often manufacturers from Japan. In other sectors, US firms took advantage of the decentralized markets that opened at home and abroad. Deindustrialization swept the country beginning in the 1970s, and the more open climate for international business of the 1980s created winners and losers alike, reshuffling the fortunes of various sectors in all countries that were part of this process. Like other surges in global integration, this one conferred advantages on those people best informed about the wider world, and upon those people and firms whose assets were most mobile, and who were best able to seek the highest returns wherever they might be had.

THE NEW WASHINGTON CONSENSUS

The world of ideas fomented this political push for market liberalism, providing intellectual support. Nationalism, though critical to foreign policy and domestic politics, gave way somewhat to a more global view of money, in some respects a return to laissez-faire doctrines formalized in the nineteenth century, now championed by economists such as Milton Friedman (1912–2006). In Davos, Switzerland, business leaders met starting in 1982, and soon expanded their networks to bring together world leaders to discuss public policy issues in an annual World Economic Forum. In the United States, business lobbying accelerated against unions, taxes, and regulations and in favor of more free enterprise. What had once been a "Washington Consensus" of an activist and expansive role for government evolved into a consensus in favor of neoclassical economics and an attack on Keynesianism. Entrepreneurship, competition, free trade, and labor competition were the cardinal features of the era. President Ronald Reagan (1911–2004) extolled these principles and, when he could, enacted them by privatizing government services and liberalizing trade.

As Reagan left office in 1989, he bequeathed to his successors major changes in the economy, politics, and culture that reflected the rising era of globalization. New institutions accompanied the freer exchanges of goods, capital, and culture that quickened and enlarged state and transnational contacts. Among these were the North American Free Trade Agreement (NAFTA) and the World Trade Organization (WTO) of the mid 1990s, both of which liberalized commerce, integrated business practices and methods, and stressed a rules-based economic system. The administration of President Bill Clinton even made globalization its foreign policy mantra, as it perceived the potential of prosperity by harmonizing world economic behavior, customs, development, and democracy. America stood at the helm, in this view of the situation, guiding all who would embrace it to a new Washington Consensus of universalist and integrative market-based globalization.

But while the benefits were many, and the process seemingly inevitable due to new technologies abetted by a free-market ideology, the costs were also significant and debates raged over the desirability of globalization. At the center of the argument in the United States was the issue of how far the government should go toward promoting market-based capitalism throughout the world. Business was generally in favor, but the labor movement, many academics, environmentalists, and several members of Clinton's own Democratic Party—who favored traditional big government policies—were not. A rebounding American economy in the mid-1990s persuaded people across the political spectrum that globalization had advantages, however, and with the advent of widespread use of the Internet—with 304 million users worldwide by 2000—it even had a certain cachet.

DRIVERS OF GLOBALIZATION

Globalization, rather than outright Americanization, quickened among the world's cosmopolitan elites, as well as the masses. For the upper reaches of populations, convergence was clear in business and finance, government, academia, media, and sports, but the middle class and the poor joined the process of globalization as well. They communicated by fax, cell phone, and e-mail, then through such social media networks as Twitter and Facebook. By 2000, one million conversations occurred simultaneously through satellite; by 2010, that technology allowed 4.6 billion of the world's nearly 7 billion people to talk and do business through cell phones.

The traditional drivers of globalization also accelerated. In transportation, ship tonnage rose sixfold from the mid-1950s, but air freight grew even faster (albeit from a much smaller base), and costs plummeted. Another element of globalization, migration, also exploded. By 2000, two million people a day crossed a border somewhere in the world. Corporations also drove the process. Some 7,000 transnational companies existed in 1970; thirty years later, there were 63,000 parent firms with nearly 700,000 foreign affiliates, with a substantial number of intercompany arrangements. Branding worldwide led to tremendous expansion in profits. Marlboro cigarettes, Nike shoes, and a host of other companies gained global market shares.

The integration of equity and bond markets, or financial globalization, was another hallmark of the post-1990 surge in globalization. The middle and upper classes invested savings overseas at ever greater rates, with US-based global mutual funds climbing from $16 billion in 1986 to $321 billion by 1997. The velocity of foreign exchange was staggering; in 1973, the average daily turnover in the global exchange market was $15 billion, but by 1998, some $1.5 trillion passed through the markets every day, and about $5 trillion in 2013. Thanks to electronic trading, billions of dollars could be invested into markets in a flash, and just as quickly removed.

ECONOMIC VOLATILITY

When home prices in the United States began to fall in 2006, a rash of home-mortgage defaults, especially among borrowers with subprime loans, ensued and triggered a massive number of foreclosures across the country. Loans and securities backed by subprime mortgages lost their value, straining the banking and insurance systems in the United States, and then worldwide. A global credit crunch followed. Major risk-taking players in investment markets—Bear Stearns, American International Group (AIG), Lehman Brothers, Merrill Lynch, and Citigroup—went out of business or were acquired by competitors for a fraction of their previous value. In the United Kingdom and Ireland, the state acquired large shares of formerly private banks to keep them solvent. As central banks scrambled to pump liquidity into frozen money markets, the International Monetary Fund (IMF) warned that the housing slump in the United States, Spain, and elsewhere would not only hurt the North; developing nations would also suffer from slackening demand.

The world economy eventually stabilized, due to massive intervention by governments, but recovery was spotty, incomplete, and slow—providing fodder for a renewed round of critiques of globalization. Clearly, the rapidity and scope of economic integration had led to great volatility that prompted repeated crises in the world economy. Before the crash of 2008, international markets had been instrumental in a run on the Mexican peso in 1995, the 1997–1998 Asian financial contagion, and the dot.com bubble burst of 2001. Developing and poor countries played vocal parts in the new round of criticism, as the United States, multinational corporations, and private investors had encouraged them to deregulate their capital markets and open their economies to foreign investment. This made them susceptible to outside pressures from institutions, nations, and world economic fluctuations. Changes in one country could affect entire regions, as in 1997 when the Thai baht plummeted in value, setting off a currency "flu" that sickened other

An employee working in a Walmart store, Beijing, China, 2014. *In the 1990s the world's biggest retailer, Walmart, like many other corporations, came under fire for its low pay and lack of insurance benefits, with critics contending that globalization has given rise to poor working conditions around the world.* ZHANG PENG/LIGHTROCKET/GETTY IMAGES

nations. Those favoring the Washington Consensus of liberalization and globalization, however, blamed such crises on the host countries' corrupt practices, inefficiencies, and lack of oversight. Optimists argued that not only did globalization help these emerging countries but it was an irrevocable phenomenon that could not be halted. And why should it, since it brought such great rewards?

BACKLASH

Critics of globalization countered with additional concerns over labor, environment, and national sovereignty. The world's biggest retailer, Walmart, came under fire for its low pay and lack of insurance benefits, as did many other corporations. Globalization, critics contended, gave rise to sweatshop conditions around the world as capitalist firms competed to find the cheapest labor anywhere. In the environmental arena, globalization came under attack for promoting a "race to the bottom" among countries seeking foreign investment, each trying to outdo the others in rolling back environmental protections in the competition to woo firms. To many critics, the international organizations and agreements dedicated to liberalizing trade, such as the WTO and NAFTA, elevated the principle of deregulation at the expense of adequate labor or environmental standards. A backlash against the power of bureaucrats in the WTO and IMF arose, as concerns about the role of government oversight called into question the power of a handful of unelected individuals immune to democratic pressures. Opponents of globalization also pointed to the growing power of transnational corporations and financiers to destabilize nations and markets and undermine democratically achieved labor and environmental regulations.

The protest movement against globalization exploded at the turn of the millennium. Antiglobalization forces first took to the streets of the United States in 1999, when the WTO was meeting in Seattle to plan a new round of trade negotiations. Demonstrations followed over the next several years at gatherings of the United Nations, the IMF and World Bank, the Davos World Economic Forum, the Summit of the Americas, and the Group of Seven industrial powers' meetings. In the period from 2008 to 2012, economic depression, national protests under the banner of the Occupy Wall Street movement, and other protests in Europe were shaped in part by a critique of a global capitalist system that was skewed against the masses but had been very lucrative for cooperative authoritarian leaders like those the protestors were trying to oust.

LONG-TERM TRENDS

Since the more modern era of globalization, beginning in the nineteenth century, the process has emerged, waned, and flourished, largely in response to the behavior of governments and the uneven march of technology. But the long-term trend is now clear: the world has become more unified, and people from prime ministers to peasants have learned to take into account global conditions when making their decisions. Globalization is now among the defining trends in world history, and will likely remain so in the future.

SEE ALSO *Clinton, William Jefferson; Deindustrialization; Exceptionalism; Group of Five and its Successors (G5, G7, G8, G20); Marlboro; McDonald's; Neoliberalism; North American Free Trade Agreement (NAFTA); World Bank; World Trade Organization*

BIBLIOGRAPHY

Eckes, Alfred E., Jr., and Thomas W. Zeiler. *Globalization and the American Century*. Cambridge: Cambridge University Press, 2003.

Friedman, Thomas. *The Lexus and the Olive Tree*. Rev. ed. New York: Farrar, Straus, Giroux, 2000.

Lechner, Frank J., and John Boli, eds. *The Globalization Reader*. 5th ed. Malden, MA: Wiley, 2015.

Levitt, Theodore. "The Globalization of Markets." *Harvard Business Review* 61, 3 (1983): 92–102.

Stiglitz, Joseph E. *Globalization and Its Discontents*. New York: Norton, 2002.

Thomas W. Zeiler
Professor of History
University of Colorado Boulder

GODZILLA

Godzilla, a giant, irradiated, reptilian monster created by the Japanese studio Tōhō in 1954, is an internationally recognized movie icon. The subject of thirty features often described as the world's longest-running film franchise, Godzilla has become a lasting symbol in the global imagination of Japan, the "monster on the loose" movie genre, and popular fears of nuclear weaponry.

Godzilla was inspired by Hollywood "creature features," including *King Kong* (1933) and *The Beast from 20,000 Fathoms* (1953), but was very much a product of Japan in the 1950s and the anxieties generated by the Cold War. The original film in the series, known as *Gojira* (1954) in Japanese, drew on raw memories of the 1945 atomic bombings of Hiroshima and Nagasaki and Japan's defeat in World War II. The movie was also directly inspired by the Lucky Dragon Incident of March 1, 1954, in which a Japanese fishing boat was accidentally exposed to radiation from the

Castle Bravo test of an American hydrogen bomb on Bikini Atoll in the Marshall Islands. The Tōhō producer Tomoyuki Tanaka (1910–1997) originally developed the idea of a science fiction movie featuring a surviving dinosaur, awakened, irradiated, and mutated by US atomic testing in the South Pacific, that attacks Tokyo. In *Gojira* the monster (famously portrayed by a human actor in a bulky rubber suit walking through miniature sets) is finally vanquished by a new super-weapon developed by a Japanese scientist.

Gojira was intended as a serious film with a somber political message, drawing on pacifist sentiments in Japan and warning audiences of the potentially catastrophic consequences of nuclear warfare. When, however, the film was released in the United States in 1956 as *Godzilla, King of the Monsters!*, Hollywood distributors edited out sections of the Japanese original that could be considered critical of America or American nuclear testing. US moviegoers were well acquainted with rampaging cinematic monsters at the time, as Hollywood studios had produced a stream of movies like *Them!* (1954) and *Beginning of the End* (1957) that played on widespread fears of the Communist menace and nuclear radiation during the Cold War. Films featuring giant creatures from Japan (including Godzilla, the silkmoth Mothra, and the turtle Gamera) would become common from the late 1950s at American drive-in theaters, on Saturday double-features in small-town movie palaces, and on late-night television.

The popularity of the original Godzilla film encouraged Tōhō to produce sequels, beginning with *Godzilla Raids Again* (1955). Over time, the tone and look of the movies changed considerably, reflecting shifts in audience demographics and interests: in the 1960s and 1970s, Godzilla features increasingly became formulaic, lighthearted action films aimed at young viewers. Although the solemnity of *Gojira* was lost as the series progressed, several central themes (including tensions with the United States and ambivalence over rapid advances in science and technology) continued to characterize the franchise. Tōhō released twenty-eight Godzilla movies between 1954 and 2004. In 1998 and 2014 Hollywood studios attempted to reboot the series with blockbuster films heavy on special effects.

SEE ALSO *Bikini Atoll; Cold War; Hollywood; Nuclear Weapons*

BIBLIOGRAPHY

Napier, Susan J. "Panic Sites: The Japanese Imagination of Disaster from *Godzilla* to *Akira*." *Journal of Japanese Studies* 19, 2 (1993): 327–351.

Noriega, Chon. "Godzilla and the Japanese Nightmare: When 'Them!' Is U.S." *Cinema Journal* 27, 1 (1987): 63–77.

Tsutsui, William M. *Godzilla on My Mind: Fifty Years of the King of Monsters*. New York: Palgrave Macmillan, 2004.

William M. Tsutsui
President and Professor of History
Hendrix College

GOMPERS, SAMUEL

SEE *AFL-CIO: Labor's Foreign Policy.*

GOOD NEIGHBOR POLICY

In his inaugural address of March 4, 1933, President Franklin Delano Roosevelt declared that his global policy would be that of "the good neighbor—the neighbor who resolutely respects himself and, because he does so, respects the rights of others." The term came to summarize his administration's approach to the nations of Latin America, marked by increased economic and political cooperation and a commitment to nonintervention and noninterference in the internal affairs of other countries. "Good neighbor" was first used in such a context by Roosevelt's predecessor, Herbert Hoover (1874–1964), who desired an end to the domineering "big stick" diplomacy (deriving from "speak softly and carry a big stick," a saying admired by President Theodore Roosevelt) that marked the first decades of the twentieth century. It was under Roosevelt, though, that a recognizable policy emerged, with nonintervention its keystone.

The practical results of the new approach were apparent in Roosevelt's refusal to intervene in Cuba during political turmoil there in 1933, the withdrawal of US Marines from Haiti the following year, and the signing of eleven reciprocal trade agreements that reduced tariffs with various Latin American nations. A less admirable consequence of noninterference was the concurrent tolerance, and in some cases embrace, of repressive dictatorial regimes such as that of Rafael Trujillo, who ruled the Dominican Republic from 1930 to 1961 (Roorda 1998). Nonetheless, Roosevelt's public renunciation of the right of hemispheric intervention was largely welcomed, and the Good Neighbor policy ensured his lasting popularity throughout the Americas (Loveman 2010).

The motivations for the Good Neighbor policy were both domestic and global. Seeking ways to combat the Great Depression, the policy was an international extension of Roosevelt's New Deal program of reforms to stimulate economic recovery, ensuring access to cheap raw materials while providing potential markets for finished goods and ending expensive military occupations. For the nations of Latin America, their economies also devastated by the global depression and resulting collapse in raw material prices, the Good Neighbor policy promised a resumption in the trade that had been severely restricted by European and North American economic nationalism.

International political developments, particularly the global instability caused by the increasingly expansionist actions of Germany, Italy, and Japan, also reinforced the United States' commitment to closer hemispheric ties. Although a physical attack on the Americas was thought unlikely, policy makers in Washington became increasingly concerned about the ideological threat of fascism, particularly in Argentina and Brazil, with their large populations of German immigrants (Langley 2010). The desire for hemispheric unity in response to an increasingly unstable and threatening global situation was reflected in a series of agreements signed in 1936 and 1938 and culminating in the Act of Havana in 1940, declaring solidarity, reaffirming nonintervention pledges, and promising immediate consultations if any nation was threatened by war. The value of the Good Neighbor policy was apparent once the United States entered World War II, with almost all the nations of Latin America contributing substantially to the war effort.

As the closest southern neighbor of the United States, Mexico served as an inspiration for and a continual test of the Good Neighbor policy. During Mexico's bloody revolutionary period, roughly 1910 to 1920, President Woodrow Wilson had twice dispatched United States military forces over the border, evoking bitter memories of the conflicts of the previous century. Mexico's hostility to its northern neighbor was reflected in government boycotts of American goods in 1927 and subsequent "buy at home" campaigns aimed at combating what was seen as US economic imperialism (Moreno 2003).

Of greater consequence, land reform programs begun by President Lázaro Cárdenas (1895–1970) in 1934 redistributed property owned by foreign investors, straining relations with Washington and challenging Roosevelt's vision of a cooperative hemisphere. The greatest test of Good Neighbor diplomacy followed with the nationalization of Mexico's oil industry in 1938. Countries such as the United Kingdom severed relations and imposed sanctions, but the reaction from Washington was more restrained. Although some called for tough measures, the position of Ambassador to Mexico Josephus Daniels (1862–1948), that Pan-American solidarity could "save democracy [and] oil ought not to smear it," won out (Gellman 1979). Fearing that reprisals might push Mexico into closer economic relations with Germany and keen to maintain Pan-American unity, the Roosevelt administration pressured reluctant oil companies into settling the dispute (Koppes 1982). The extensive economic and military cooperation between the United States and Mexico during World War II would prove the value of Good Neighbor diplomacy and the wisdom of resolving the oil dispute amicably (Moreno 2003).

SEE ALSO *Mexico; Roosevelt, Franklin D.*

BIBLIOGRAPHY

Gellman, Irwin F. *Good Neighbor Diplomacy: United States Policies in Latin America, 1933–1945.* Baltimore: Johns Hopkins University Press, 1979.

Koppes, Clayton R. "The Good Neighbor Policy and the Nationalization of Mexican Oil: A Reinterpretation." *Journal of American History* 69, 1 (1982): 62–81.

Langley, Lester D. *America and the Americas: The United States in the Western Hemisphere.* 2nd ed. Athens: University of Georgia Press, 2010.

Loveman, Brian. *No Higher Law: American Foreign Policy and the Western Hemisphere since 1776.* Chapel Hill: University of North Carolina Press, 2010.

Moreno, Julio. *Yankee Don't Go Home!: Mexican Nationalism, American Business Culture, and the Shaping of Modern Mexico, 1920–1950.* Chapel Hill: University of North Carolina Press, 2003.

Roorda, Eric Paul. *The Dictator Next Door: The Good Neighbor Policy and the Trujillo Regime in the Dominican Republic, 1930–1945.* Durham, NC: Duke University Press, 1998.

Thomas Tunstall Allcock
Lecturer in American History
University of Manchester

GORE, ALBERT, JR.

1948–

Albert Arnold "Al" Gore Jr. is an American politician and environmental advocate who represented the state of Tennessee in the US House of Representatives from 1977 to 1985 and in the US Senate from 1985 to 1993. Gore served as the vice president of the United States from 1993 to 2001 under President Bill Clinton (b. 1946).

The second son of US representative and later senator Albert Gore Sr. (1907–1998) and attorney Pauline (LaFon) Gore (1912–2004), Al Gore grew up primarily in Washington, DC, splitting time between the capitol's "embassy row" and the prestigious St. Albans School and the family farm in Carthage, Tennessee. He graduated with a degree in government from Harvard University in 1969, and, despite his and his father's antiwar positions, he enlisted in the US Army in 1970, serving with the Twentieth Engineering Brigade in Vietnam in 1971. After an honorable discharge, Gore returned to Tennessee to enroll at Vanderbilt University, first on a scholarship in the divinity school and later at Vanderbilt Law School. He also worked as an investigative reporter for *The Tennessean*, focusing on municipal corruption in Nashville (Turque 2000).

Gore left law school in 1976 to run for the seat in the US House of Representatives once held by his father. During his tenure in Congress, Gore earned a reputation as a clear-thinking, well-informed Democratic moderate particularly concerned with issues of science, energy, and national security. Part of a group of young congressmen known as "Atari Democrats" who were passionate about technological and environmental issues, Gore championed climate change research and high-speed communications infrastructure on the House and Senate floor throughout the 1980s (*Mother Jones* 1983; Dionne 1989). He participated in hearings on global climate change as early as 1980, and through his place on the Energy and Commerce Committee and the Committee on Science and Technology, he used the issue to attack Ronald Reagan's (1911–2004) energy and environmental policies in a series of hearings between 1981 and 1984, focusing especially on the relationship between the "greenhouse effect" and America's energy portfolio (Howe 2014, 128–130). In 1986, he introduced the Supercomputer Network Study Act, and later he crafted the High Performance Computing Act of 1991, which led to the establishment of a national information infrastructure, or "information superhighway," upon which the modern Internet is based. Gore also came out in support of arms control, introducing the "Gore Plan" in 1982, which was intended to reduce the likelihood of a nuclear first strike by eliminating multiple-warhead ballistic devices from the world arsenal, and supporting other arms reductions efforts well into his vice presidency (Zelnick 1999).

Former vice president Al Gore speaking at a session of the World Economic Forum in Davos, Switzerland, January, 2015. *After losing a close and controversial presidential election to George W. Bush in 2000, Gore focused his efforts more squarely on environmental advocacy. In 2007, he was awarded the Nobel Peace Prize, an honor he shared jointly with the Intergovernmental Panel on Climate Change.* FABRICE COFFRINI/AFP/GETTY IMAGES

After an unsuccessful run for the Democratic presidential nomination in 1988, Gore accepted the nomination as Clinton's running mate in the 1992 presidential election. Not a contender in the primaries, Gore was selected primarily for his foreign policy experience, which Clinton lacked, and for his continuing and increasingly popular work on environmental issues, including global warming, toxic wastes, and the emerging field of sustainable development. His popular 1992 book, *Earth in the Balance*, enumerated a set of pressing human and environmental concerns that had become increasingly relevant to both domestic politics and American foreign relations. As vice president, Gore would take the lead in turning the commitments made by the George H. W. Bush (b. 1924) administration at the 1992 United Nations Conference on Environment and Development into politically acceptable action on global environmental problems. Most importantly, Gore worked with the American negotiating team led by Stuart Eizenstat (b. 1943) to convince European nations to accept emissions trading and the clean development mechanism as components of the 1997 Kyoto Protocol to the 1992 United Nations Framework Convention on Climate Change (Howe 2014, 192). Despite his success abroad, however, Gore met stiff resistance in the Senate in the form of the unanimous Byrd-Hagel Resolution against any protocol that involved targets and timetables for emissions reductions and failed to include specific developing-world commitments. The Kyoto Protocol was never introduced to the Senate for ratification.

After losing a close and controversial presidential election to George W. Bush (b. 1946) in 2000, Gore focused his efforts more squarely on environmental advocacy, and in 2006 he released a documentary on global warming directed by Davis Guggenheim (b. 1963) called *An Inconvenient Truth*. Based on an educational slide-show that Gore had delivered to audiences around the world, the film performed exceptionally well at the box office, significantly raising mainstream awareness of climate change both in the United States and abroad (Garofoli 2006). In 2007, Gore's efforts to popularize global warming earned him the Nobel Peace Prize, which he was awarded jointly with the Intergovernmental Panel on Climate Change (Grandin 2008).

SEE ALSO *Bush, George W.; Clinton, William Jefferson; Global Warming; Internet*

BIBLIOGRAPHY

Dionne, E. J. "Greening of Democrats: An 80s Mix of Idealism and Shrewd Politics." *New York Times*, June 14, 1989.

Garofoli, Joe. "Gore Movie Reaching the Red States, Too." *The San Francisco Chronicle*, July 8, 2006.

Gore, Albert, Jr. *Earth in the Balance: Ecology and the Human Spirit*. Boston: Houghton Mifflin, 1992.

Grandin, Karl, ed. *Les Prix Nobel: The Nobel Prizes 2007*. Stockholm: Nobel Foundation, 2008.

Guggenheim, Davis, dir. *An Inconvenient Truth*. Hollywood, CA: Paramount Pictures, 2006.

Howe, Joshua P. *Behind the Curve: Science and the Politics of Global Warming*. Seattle: University of Washington Press, 2014.

"The Swift Demise of the Atari Democrat." *Mother Jones* 8, 5 (June 1983): 9.

Turque, Bill. *Inventing Al Gore*. Boston: Houghton Mifflin, 2000.

Zelnick, Robert. *Gore: A Political Life*. Washington, DC: Regnery, 1999.

Joshua P. Howe
Assistant Professor of History and Environmental Studies
Reed College

GRAHAM, WILLIAM (BILLY) FRANKLIN, JR.

1918–

Billy Graham came to national prominence during an eight-week evangelistic campaign in Los Angeles during the fall of 1949. He stood as America's most famous evangelist for the following six decades. Over the course of his career, Graham preached to over 200 million people in ninety-nine countries; more than three million people registered "commitments for Christ" at his crusades (Wacker 2014, 21). He had personal relationships with twelve US presidents, forging close friendships with Lyndon Johnson, Richard Nixon, Ronald Reagan, and George H. W. Bush. Among twentieth-century American Christian leaders, only Martin Luther King Jr. surpassed Graham in influence.

Reared on a modest farm near Charlotte, North Carolina, Graham dedicated his life to Jesus at a 1934 revival. His education took him to three evangelical schools: Bob Jones College, Florida Bible Institute, and Wheaton College. At Wheaton he earned a degree in anthropology and met his wife, Ruth Bell, daughter of the Presbyterian missionary L. Nelson Bell, who worked with Graham to launch the evangelical Christian periodical *Christianity Today* in 1956. After graduating, Graham served as a pastor in the Chicago suburbs and as president of Northwestern Schools, a Minneapolis college and seminary. But Graham's skills and inclination pointed him toward full-time evangelism. After resigning from Northwestern in 1952, Graham spent the remainder of his career focused on full-time evangelism, annually leading an average of six to eight "crusades," each lasting

Billy Graham preaching in Trafalgar Square, London, 1954. *America's most famous evangelist for six decades, Graham became a figure of international prominence, preaching to over 200 million people in ninety-nine countries over the course of his career.* **FRED RAMAGE/HULTON ARCHIVE/GETTY IMAGES**

several days. Crusades featured daily services in which crowds numbering in the thousands would hear hymns, testimonials from Christian celebrities, and a sermon from Graham. At the end of each sermon, Graham invited attendees to "make a decision for Christ." Hundreds responded, coming forward to meet with counselors at the front of the stadium. By the 1970s the biggest crusades were happening abroad.

Political issues frequently appeared in Graham's sermons and interviews. He first won attention as a fervent anticommunist who, like many evangelical Christians in the early years of the Cold War, believed the world was rapidly nearing its end. The newspaper publisher William Randolph Hearst (1863–1951) approved of Graham's anticommunism and instructed his editors to cover Graham's 1949 Los Angeles crusade. Graham traveled to Korea and Vietnam during American wars, preaching to American troops and voicing pro-war positions. Graham's public support for his good friend Richard Nixon persisted long after most Americans had soured on both Nixon and the Vietnam War; in the wake of Watergate and Nixon's resignation, Graham's views moderated. He expressed vocal support for nuclear disarmament in the late 1970s and traveled to Moscow as part of a Soviet-sponsored peace conference in 1982. During that trip Graham expressed measured appreciation for religious freedom in the Soviet Union. Anti-Soviet American conservatives criticized Graham for those remarks. Although Graham later gave context to his comments, saying he knew that the Soviets had staged his visit carefully, he abandoned the fervent anticommunism of his earlier years. Graham conducted several crusades in Soviet-bloc countries during the 1980s and returned to the USSR in 1984.

As a white southern evangelist, Graham's views on race also won wide attention. Although he occasionally allowed local organizers to set up segregated seating at his earliest campaigns, Graham did not preach to segregated audiences after 1953. He invited Martin Luther King Jr. to pray at the 1957 New York crusade, and in sermons and magazine articles he lambasted the segregation of American churches. Graham also refused to preach to segregated audiences in apartheid-era South Africa. During his 1973 South Africa crusade, Graham spoke to 100,000 people in the first major mixed-race gathering in the nation's history. He identified racial prejudice as one of the United States' foremost sins.

Yet Graham balked at the growing radicalism of the civil rights movement during the 1960s. He never wavered in his belief that preaching the gospel meant focusing on individual conversion. For Christians more inclined to view sin as a structural problem, Graham's evangelical faith proved insufficient in the struggle for racial equality. During the 1970s and 1980s, Graham made his strongest statements against American racial injustice abroad, in South Africa and the Soviet Union. Simultaneously, Graham also called for a moratorium on capital punishment in the United States, given the racial prejudice of the American justice system. By the 1990s he advocated for racial intermarriage. Graham disappointed critics who rightly charged that the evangelist could have done more to combat racial injustice, but he just as often challenged white supporters who did not share his belief in the urgency of the problem.

Graham's longevity and mostly unblemished legacy testify to his personal integrity, his reliance on an expert evangelistic team, and the resonance of his views with a vast swath of the American public throughout the second half of the twentieth century. During those years he gently nudged white evangelicals to embrace nuclear disarmament and responsibility for racial injustice. Though Graham's core message about human sin and the need for Jesus never changed, he slowly transformed from an un-self-conscious hell-and-brimstone preacher to a more thoughtful and worldly elder statesman.

SEE ALSO *Missionary Diplomacy; Religions*

BIBLIOGRAPHY

Graham, Billy. *Just As I Am: The Autobiography of Billy Graham.* Rev. ed. New York: HarperOne, 2007.

Martin, William. *A Prophet with Honor: The Billy Graham Story.* New York: Morrow, 1991.

Miller, Steven P. *Billy Graham and the Rise of the Republican South.* Philadelphia: University of Pennsylvania Press, 2009.

Wacker, Grant. *America's Pastor: Billy Graham and the Shaping of a Nation.* Cambridge, MA: Belknap Press of Harvard University Press, 2014.

Seth Dowland
Assistant Professor of Religion
Pacific Lutheran University

GRAND TOUR

Beginning in the seventeenth century, aristocratic families in England sent their most promising sons on multiyear tours of the European Continent. They would expose themselves to its art, music, and cuisine, meet powerful and influential people, discreetly engage in inappropriate activities, and in other ways "finish" the education they had begun at Oxford or Cambridge. This undeniably aristocratic practice was known as the *Grand Tour.* In the nineteenth century, Americans established a Grand Tour tradition of their own, but it was problematic from the start. The trouble was that a Grand Tour seemed aristocratic and thereby un-American to many of the women and men who had the means to undertake such an experience.

AN ARISTOCRATIC TOUR WITH ANTI-AMERICAN CONNOTATIONS

Why was the Grand Tour a problematic enterprise for Americans? On the one hand, the vast majority of white Americans traced their ancestry to Europe. They self-identified as Europeans, consumed its culture, and sought the validation of cultural authorities from the Old World. The author James Fenimore Cooper (1789–1851) hearkened to those ties when a character in his novel *Home as Found* (1838) called American grand tourists "Hajjis," those taking "the pilgrimage to Paris, instead of Mecca; and the pilgrim must be an American, instead of a Mohommedan" (1871, 45). On the other hand, post-Revolutionary Americans sought to define a distinct national identity that rejected much of the European past—hereditary monarchy, aristocracy, militarism, and Roman Catholicism, to begin with.

From the beginnings of American leisure travel to Europe in the late eighteenth century, would-be grand tourists had to resolve this powerful tension in American culture between staking a claim to full participation in Western civilization and charting a new path as Americans and republicans for whom the traditions and rituals of a Grand Tour had, supposedly, little relevance. In 1788, Thomas Jefferson (1743–1826) drafted his "Hints to Americans Travelling in Europe," in which he first urged newly independent Americans to stay home, learn about each other, and avoid the corruptions of the Old World. Conceding that many people would ignore that advice, Jefferson urged them to turn European travel into a learning experience that would enhance their commitment to republicanism. Throughout much of the nineteenth century, American travelers to Europe struggled to reconcile the appeal of a European tour with its anti-American connotations.

In the late nineteenth century, as a more confident United States emerged whole from the travails of the

Civil War (1861–1865), European travel seemed to present less of a dilemma. Flush with Gilded Age cash, Americans could go abroad unafraid that they would be infected by Old World contagions. Nevertheless, as the novels of Henry James (1843–1916) remind us, those fears never completely receded into the background. Those reservations withdrew even more during the "American Century," when post-Revolutionary fears of infection by Old World luxury and dissipation seemed hardly relevant to a hegemonic United States facing the very real threat of Soviet Russia. Yet even today—as fascination with Princess Diana (1961–1997) and the royal princes William and Harry reminds us—Americans struggle to deny that the Old World is somehow better, more genuine, than the New, and that there is something special about Europeans with a title in front of their names.

THE LURE OF EUROPE FOR AMERICAN TRAVELERS

Europe has long been the favored destination for American travelers. In the nineteenth century, 90 percent or more of Americans who traveled abroad went to the Old World. More recently, that number has fluctuated between 45 and 55 percent. For most of American history, the expense of European travel has limited it to the well-to-do. Overseas travel was also, until the late nineteenth century, uncomfortable, unpredictable, and dangerous. Early steamships, introduced in the 1840s, offered the cachet of novelty but had little else to recommend them. They were cramped, dirty, noisy, and prone to breakdowns—hardly the palaces on the water that emerged during the golden age of steam travel at the end of the century. Nevertheless, American travel overseas rose at an annual rate of about 5 percent beginning in the 1820s—rising even faster before the Civil War (6.7 percent) than after (4.3 percent). The frequency, means, and demographic profile of American travel to Europe has changed considerably since the nineteenth century. Before the Civil War, women constituted only 10 to 20 percent of overseas travelers. By World War I (1914–1918), women represented 40 percent of Americans visiting Europe, and in the post-1950 period, that figure has exceeded 50 percent.

Before transatlantic airplane travel, Americans could only reach Europe by sea. As late as 1940, over 90 percent of Americans going to Europe did so on a ship. That fact alone held down the numbers of Americans able to visit the Old World, since passenger fares (as opposed to freight costs) remained inelastic throughout this period. By 1950, only 51 percent of travelers arrived by ship, and that figure declined rapidly thereafter; 8.6 percent of American travelers crossed the Atlantic by sea in 1970. Tourist-class tickets (about $300), introduced in the early 1950s, followed soon after by economy-class tickets, finally made travel affordable for the upper-middle class. That decade also saw the introduction of jet airplane service across the Atlantic. Those developments ended the steamship era and opened up European travel to people of middling means.

Between 1950 to 1970, the number of Americans abroad rose 700 percent—an annual increase of nearly 11 percent. Lower fares explain much of the rise, but the consistent increase in American leisure travel to Europe cannot be explained by a single cause. Population increase, the rise in personal incomes, improvements in the speed and comfort of travel, the development of a tourist industry, including guidebooks and package tours, all spurred what more than one historian has called the American "invasion" of Europe.

Relatively few Americans could afford the conventional British Grand Tour of several leisurely years lived abroad. Americans' forays into Europe tended to be quicker and more superficial than that which a well-connected British aristocrat could enjoy. Also, Americans felt compelled to make Great Britain an essential (if not the only) part of their European experience. Almost every American grand tourist visited England, and many toured Scotland as well, with fewer moving on to Ireland. A conventional Grand Tour would take the traveler through France, with the ultimate destination being Italy. Until the twentieth century, most Americans did not get that far, if only because of the difficult, unpredictable travel conditions. The spread of rail links across the Continent in the latter half of the nineteenth century eased this task considerably, opening up a much wider portion of the European Continent to curious American travelers. Still, early Americans visited Paris, if at all possible, because of that city's reputation as the most civilized in the world. If there are common threads in the Grand Tour tradition in American history, they are the impulse to sustain contact with civilization and the grudging realization that Americans see Europe—not the United States—as its font.

SEE ALSO *Atlantic Ocean; Europe; Expatriate Artists; Foreign Performing Artists; Steamship*

BIBLIOGRAPHY

Cooper, James Fenimore. *Home as Found.* New York: Hurd and Houghton, 1871. First published 1838.

Dulles, Foster Rhea. *Americans Abroad: Two Centuries of European Travel.* Ann Arbor: University of Michigan Press, 1964.

Dupont, Brandon, Alka Gandhi, and Thomas J. Weiss. "The American Invasion of Europe: The Long Term Rise in Overseas Travel, 1820–2000." National Bureau of Economic

Research (NBER) Working Paper 13977. 2008. http://www.nber.org/papers/w13977

Fox, Stephen R. *Transatlantic: Samuel Cunard, Isambard Brunel, and the Great Atlantic Steamships.* New York: HarperCollins, 2003.

Kilbride, Daniel. *Being American in Europe, 1750–1860.* Baltimore, MD: Johns Hopkins University Press, 2013.

Levenstein, Harvey. *Seductive Journey: American Tourists in France from Jefferson to the Jazz Age.* Chicago: University of Chicago Press, 1998.

Mackintosh, Will B. "Ticketed Through: The Commodification of Travel in the Nineteenth Century." *Journal of the Early Republic* 32 (Spring 2012): 61–89.

Mulvey, Christopher. *Transatlantic Manners: Social Patterns in Nineteenth-Century Anglo-American Travel Literature.* Cambridge, UK, and New York: Cambridge University Press, 1990.

Stowe, William W. *Going Abroad: European Travel in Nineteenth-Century American Culture.* Princeton, NJ: Princeton University Press, 1994.

Vance, William L. *America's Rome*, Vol. 1: *Classical Rome*; Vol. 2: *Catholic and Contemporary Rome.* New Haven, CT: Yale University Press, 1989.

Withey, Lynne. *Grand Tours and Cook's Tours: A History of Leisure Travel, 1750 to 1915.* New York: Morrow, 1997.

Daniel Kilbride
Professor of History
John Carroll University

GREAT DEPRESSION

The United States emerged from World War I (1914–1918) as the world's greatest creditor, a role for which it was ill prepared because of the structure of its monetary institutions and its protectionist policies. While other nations had been forced to abandon the gold standard, the United States had remained on it throughout the war. Because the gold standard had provided stability to the prewar world, there was a general tendency to rejoin it as soon as possible. The Federal Reserve System (the Fed) tried to help other countries to reach this goal.

The Fed had been established shortly before the war. A bank panic of 1907 had prompted discussions about the need for a strong lender of last resort. The Fed not only performed this role, but it also took upon itself the task of preserving national price stability. This forced it to deviate from the rules of the gold standard, which demanded a free flow of gold. Such a free flow would lead to increased prices in the country receiving gold and decreased prices in the country losing gold. The market mechanism was supposed to restore the equilibrium. Gold would flow back to the country that now offered goods at lower prices.

This mechanism to restore equilibrium applied to trade but not to the relations between creditor and debtor. After the war, as the Allies had to serve their war debts, the United States experienced a great inflow of gold, but the Fed sterilized it so as to preserve price stability (Eichengreen 1992). Moreover, the United States, shielded by protectionism, did not offer much scope for its debtors to earn the money they owed by exporting goods to America. The Fed thus faced a dilemma, which it tried to resolve by using its gold as a backing for large amounts of federal loans to European countries. But the interest due on these loans would then augment the flow of gold to the United States, leading to further deflation in Europe.

The Roaring Twenties, or Golden Twenties as they were known in Europe, were a "defaultless decade," and Americans were eager to invest in foreign countries. Whereas earlier European borrowers had come to America to ask for loans, toward the end of the 1920s American agents peddled sizable loans on visits to Europe. The total flow of funds amounted to $1.2 to $1.5 billion annually from 1924 to 1928; bonds formed the lion's share, and stocks amounted to an average of $10 million annually, but increased to $41 million in 1928. In 1929 this flow was reduced, but by 1930 the annual debt service on American loans abroad amounted to $900 million (Mintz 1951). This was much more than the British had derived from their capital export before the war.

The United States was deeply involved in European economic affairs. The Dawes Plan of 1924 and the 1929 Young Plan for the restructuring of German reparations were a testimony to this involvement. The Allies needed these reparations in order to pay their war debts to the United States. This the Americans knew very well, but officially they did not recognize any connection between the two and insisted on the full payment of those war debts. If the United States had canceled those debts, history may have taken a different turn. By canceling the debts, the US could have pressed the Allies to give up the demand for reparations, relieving Germany of a burden that determined its politics and contributed to the rise of the Nazi Party.

THE EFFECTS OF AGRICULTURAL AND INDUSTRIAL OVERPRODUCTION

The devastation of European agriculture proved to be a boon for American farmers who extended their cultivation and could sell their produce at good prices. The major crop was wheat, production of which increased by leaps and bounds. By 1925 the annual European wheat production (excluding Russia) once more reached the prewar level of about 35 million tons. At that time the

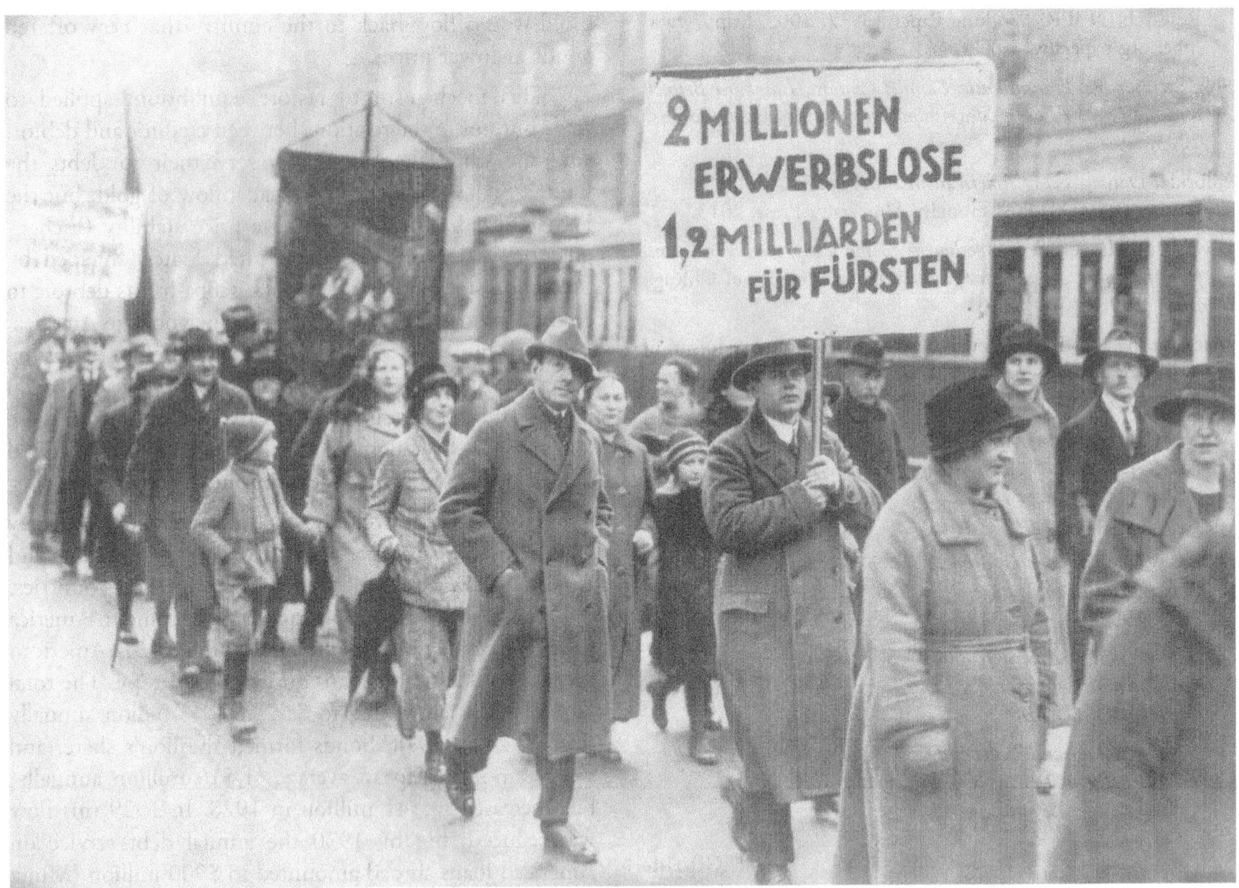

Demonstration by the unemployed, Berlin, Germany, circa 1930 (the banner says "2 million unemployed, 1.2 billion for princes"). *The United States emerged from World War I as the world's greatest creditor. To pay their war debts to the United States, the Allies needed German reparations, which placed a burden on the German economy.* HULTON ARCHIVE/GETTY IMAGES

annual production of the four great wheat exporters, the United States, Canada, Argentina, and Australia, was 40 million tons, of which they exported 19 million. By 1928 they produced 54 million tons, of which they exported 23 million.

Wheat prices started falling, but a more precipitous fall was imminent. Farmers could postpone the day of reckoning by means of credit for which they could offer stored wheat as collateral. This was possible as long as the Fed followed a policy of easy money, which also affected the stock market. When the Fed raised the interest rate in order to check the exuberance of the stock market, the action was not very successful because speculators did not mind paying higher interest rates as long as they could expect even higher returns from the stock market. The rise in interest rates did have a negative effect on farm credits. The ratchet, which had so far supported the wheat price level, broke and an avalanche of wheat inundated the world market. Other commodities such as cotton were soon affected in the same way. Even rice prices tumbled, though rice was mostly consumed in the Asian countries producing it and was traded in the world market only to a limited extent. The world trade in commodities lost about half of its value but remained more or less at the same level in terms of volume (Rothermund 1996). The peasants at the periphery of the world market suffered most at that time as they were heavily indebted and burdened with taxes (Rothermund 2002).

This was also a time of industrial overproduction (of automobiles, electric goods, and other goods) in the United States. Mass production had come to stay, but it was not yet matched by a growth of mass consumption. In the 1920s about a quarter of the US population were still farmers, many of them without any supply of electricity. Moreover, though industrial production of new goods has impressive results, the subsequent phase, which is characterized by an increase of productivity, may lead to a reduction of employment as fewer workers are needed to do the job. This in turn affects the purchasing power of the people required for supporting mass consumption. The production of automobiles may serve as an example of the rapid expansion and sudden decline of a major

American industry. In 1919, 1.9 million automobiles were manufactured in the United States; in 1929 that number increased to 4.5 million, but by 1932 production receded to 1.1 million. This was in keeping with the general rise and fall of the American economy. Between 1919 and 1929 manufacturing output increased by 38 percent, though employment slightly declined because of increases in productivity. By 1933 this output had declined by 50 percent, and there was large-scale unemployment. The Depression hit farmers even more severely, with their average income dwindling from $945 in 1929 to $304 in 1932 (Fearon 2004).

While the stock market was still booming, the tendencies of both agricultural and industrial overproduction were signaling an impending disaster. The investment in shares of all kinds of companies exceeded real investment in the means of production by a ratio of 27 to 1. Many of the companies attracting speculators were holding companies that did not produce anything but only controlled other companies. This house of cards was bound to collapse.

THE STOCK MARKET CRASH AND DEBT-DEFLATION TRAP

There are great debates among those who believe in a direct link between the crash of 1929 and the onset of the Great Depression and others who argue that this crash was merely incidental and not among the causes of the Great Depression. Those in the latter camp point out that the American stock market crash of 1987 was far more severe than that of 1929 but did not lead to a depression. However, the contexts of the two crashes were very different. The 1987 crash started in Hong Kong and only then spread to New York, where it was enhanced by the new device of electronic program trading. The market soon recovered whereas in 1929 it did not, as the earlier crash was followed by the failure of banks and a general credit crunch.

The hallmark of the Great Depression was a severe deflation that could have been corrected by the Fed if it had adopted a policy of easy money. Benjamin Strong, who had served as the governor of the Reserve Bank of New York from 1914 till his death in 1928, had long determined the monetary policy of the Fed and had actually predicted the coming depression shortly before his death. It remains a moot question whether he would have been able to fight it. His colleagues at the Fed were conservative bankers. The instrument they employed was the discounting of good commercial bills, which in those days were scarce. Raising the interest rate in order to prevent the outflow of gold was the only measure they understood. It was an irony of fate that they sat on a pile of hoarded gold and were still concerned with stopping its outflow.

During the early 1930s, as the Depression persisted, prices kept declining by about 8 percent annually. Prices in the world market also remained at a low level. In 1933 America's most brilliant economist, Irving Fisher (1867–1947), came up with his debt-deflation theory, which explained the persistence of the Depression. He argued that the attempts of debtors to clear their debts actually landed them in a trap. The more debts were repaid, the more the remaining debts appreciated. Fisher likened this process to the capsizing of a ship. It first tilts toward a tipping point, and once it reaches this point it turns upside down with increasing speed. At the time of the stock market crash Fisher had still been optimistic. He had then lost his own considerable fortune. This also ruined his professional reputation as an economist, and people were no longer prepared to listen to him when he announced his new theory. It came to be appreciated only by later generations and has attracted renewed attention. The economist Ben Bernanke, prior to his two terms as Fed chairman (2006–2014), showed that in a period of debt deflation the costs of financial intermediation rise (Bernanke 2000). This contributes to the persistence of a depression. The causes and consequences of the Great Depression remain a challenge to economists, and research continues.

THE ROOSEVELT REVOLUTION

President Herbert Hoover (1929–1933) had failed in his attempts to fight the Great Depression. A technocrat who had worked in government during World War I and had served as commerce secretary after the war, he was conservative in his economic policy, and his feeble measures after the onset of the Depression were in vain. His most notable action was the signing of the Smoot-Hawley Tariff Act of June 1930—another example of American protectionist legislation—which aimed to shield American farmers against imports, particularly from Canada. In the context of the international spread of the Depression, this act was a signal for the worldwide triumph of protectionism. Hoover also introduced a one-year moratorium on war debts and reparations in June 1931. He was mainly concerned with German debts to American creditors, but he could not prevent the collapse of the German banking system soon after the moratorium expired. In August 1931 the British abandoned the gold standard. The announcement of this decision was drafted by the staff of J. P. Morgan, the American banker who was the greatest creditor of the Bank of England (Rothermund 1996). This was a harbinger of Franklin D. Roosevelt's abandoning of the gold standard two years later.

Roosevelt routed Hoover in the elections of 1932 and immediately started his "revolution," as it was called by his supporters. In the first months of his administration he got more laws passed than had any other president before him; some of the acts were later declared unconstitutional by the Supreme Court, but his New Deal galvanized the nation. In the congressional elections of 1934 Roosevelt was rewarded with solid majorities in the House of Representatives and the Senate. More than the new government programs created by the spate of legislation, Roosevelt's decision to abandon the gold standard in April 1933 and to devalue the dollar by about 40 percent helped him to overcome the Depression. Whereas the British abandonment of the gold standard in 1931 was due to dwindling gold reserves, the United States was not at all short of gold. Roosevelt's devaluation was simply meant to reflate the American economy and raise farm prices, the farmers being his main constituency. Roosevelt, who was mainly interested in domestic reconstruction, refused to attend the World Economic Conference in London in July 1933. The French had infuriated him by insisting on the maintenance of the gold standard. Although he had earlier agreed to broker an interim stabilization agreement, he sent a provocative message admonishing the Europeans to put their own house in order.

SEE ALSO *Americanization; Dollar Diplomacy; Empire, US; Exceptionalism; Exports, Exportation; General Allotment Act (Dawes Severalty Act, 1877); Internationalism; Interventionism; Isolationism; Morgan, J. P.; Rockefeller Foundation; World War I; World War II*

BIBLIOGRAPHY

Bernanke, Ben S. *Essays on the Great Depression.* Princeton, NJ: Princeton University Press, 2000.

Eichengreen, Barry. *Golden Fetters: The Gold Standard and the Great Depression, 1919–1939.* New York: Oxford University Press, 1992.

Fearon, Peter. "Economy, American." In *Encyclopedia of the Great Depression,* Vol. 1, edited by Robert S. McElvaine. New York: Macmillan Reference USA, 2004.

Mintz, Ilse. *Deterioration in the Quality of Foreign Bonds Issued in the United States, 1920–1930.* New York: National Bureau of Economic Research, 1951; repr., New York: Arno Press, 1978.

Rothermund, Dietmar. *The Global Impact of the Great Depression, 1929–1939.* London and New York: Routledge, 1996.

Rothermund, Dietmar. "Currencies, Taxes and Credit: Asian Peasants in the Great Depression, 1930–1939." In *The Interwar Depression in an International Context,* edited by Harold James, 15–34. Munich: Oldenbourg, 2002.

Dietmar Rothermund
Emeritus Professor
University of Heidelberg

GREAT FAMINE

The history of Ireland's Great Famine (1845–1849), and of the prolonged reluctance on both sides of the Atlantic to confront its impact, is rooted in the deteriorating socioeconomic conditions in Ireland from the mid-1700s onward. Mounting pressures exerted by expanding population levels prompted widespread subdivision of landholdings and escalating dependence on potato cultivation among tenant-farmers and cottiers. Frequent food shortages and rising political tensions following the 1801 Act of Union amalgamating Ireland and Great Britain elicited dire Malthusian forecasts of population exceeding supply by the 1830s, and an expanding stream of Catholics joined Ulster-Scots compatriots in transatlantic migration. Subsequent exploration of the Famine's impact, the legacy of emigration, and the relationship of the global diaspora with the ancestral home—as well as the potential return to pre-Famine population densities by the mid-twenty-first century—continues to inform Irish national self-reflection on a sustained history of outward movement. At the sesquicentennial of the Famine in the 1990s, formal commemoration efforts had to contend with questions of why public remembrance of Ireland's Great Famine had required a century and a half to materialize.

Between 1845 and 1849 a succession of potato-crop failures caused by an invasive blight led to widespread starvation and disease, and Ireland experienced a combined loss of one-quarter of its population of eight million through death and emigration. British government-sponsored assistance programs administered according to laissez-faire ideologies favored by the Whig Party, and relief measures organized by benevolent landlords and charitable agencies, notably the Quakers, failed to alleviate this unprecedented calamity in Ireland's modern history. The prosperous classes evaded the worst effects, but impoverished smallholders in the north, west, and south of the country proved particularly vulnerable. Visiting travel writers and publications such as *The Illustrated London News* and *The Boston Pilot* exposed terrible scenes of death and disease to English and American audiences.

By the year branded Black '47, North American port cities witnessed the Famine's impact at first hand. Of the 2.1 million emigrants who left Ireland between 1845 and 1855, 95 percent exchanged dreadful "coffin" ship conditions for teeming slums in Boston, New York, Philadelphia, Quebec, and other eastern havens. Over 70 percent of Great Hunger escapees crossed the Atlantic to the United States, and 28 percent sought refuge in Canada. Hundreds of thousands of Irish also fled to English and Scottish urban sanctuaries, with a further thirty thousand emigrating to Australia.

Confronting established strains of nativist antipathy to Catholics and Anglo-Saxon–based preconceptions about the Irish, survivors settled in cities where tenements and shantytowns offered rudimentary shelter and the promise of escape from their indigent state. The Irish, widely regarded as brutish Catholics who were wholly unprepared for American citizenship and popularly suspected of subscription to papal authority, navigated a harsh landscape of survival. Images of "Paddy" and "Bridget" featured recurrently in the pages of the humor magazine *Punch* and other contemporary publications. However, midcentury demand for manual labor in construction, law enforcement, service, and manufacturing offered a crucial lifeline to the Famine Irish. Nativist anti-Irish sentiment was evident in the Know-Nothing and other native-born American political currents of the 1850s, but prominence within Tammany Hall, New York City's Democratic Party political machine, and expanding Catholic parishes soon institutionalized these church and party affiliations as cornerstones of ethnic Irish settlement.

Several contending factors shaped immigrant Irish culture in the decades following the Famine. One was the significant Irish involvement in the Union Army during the Civil War, with a concurrent decline in nativist tensions. Another was the persistence within immigrant enclaves of the sense of exile as well as charges of British culpability for the Famine's force. The rhetoric of proscribed radical nationalist groups such as the Fenians and Clan na Gael, in their ongoing struggle for Ireland's freedom, kept the Famine's name alive in years when it was otherwise marginalized. For ethnic Irish struggling to overcome powerful sociocultural and economic barriers, invoking the calamitous episode that prompted the massive transatlantic migration risked the perpetuation of negative associations with destitution and incompatibility with American citizenship standards. By the early 1900s Irish immigrants were experiencing rising levels of prosperity and prolific engagement in urban politics. As a result, the Famine was effectively decoupled from what had become an increasingly acceptable ethnic experience.

It was not until decades later, aided by the passage of time and the election of President John F. Kennedy in 1960, that Irish Americans confronted a century-long silence. The commemorations associated with the mid-1990s sesquicentennial thus marked a turning point, as an ethnic heritage that had survived in private channels of remembrance and isolated strains of cultural memory ascended within a 36-million-strong ethnic community. The commemorative impulse that is still in process today reflects not only the long-term impact of the Famine and the transformative role this episode had within Irish American culture, but the maturation of an ethnic group indissolubly bound to the memory of its past.

SEE ALSO *Fenian Brotherhood; Know-Nothings; Nativism*

BIBLIOGRAPHY

Crawford, E. Margaret, ed. *The Hungry Stream: Essays on Emigration and Famine.* Belfast: Centre for Emigration Studies, 1997.

Daly, Mary E. *The Famine in Ireland.* Dublin: Dundalgan Press, 1986.

Donnelly, James S., Jr. *The Great Irish Potato Famine.* Thrupp, Stroud, Gloucestershire, UK: Sutton, 2001.

Gray, Peter. *The Irish Famine.* London: Thames and Hudson, and New York: Harry N. Abrams, 1995.

Gribben, Arthur, ed. *The Great Famine and the Irish Diaspora in America.* Amherst: University of Massachusetts Press, 1999.

Kelly, Mary C. *Ireland's Great Famine in Irish-American History: Enshrining a Fateful Memory.* Lanham, MD: Rowman & Littlefield, 2014.

Kinealy, Christine. *This Great Calamity: The Irish Famine, 1845–52.* Dublin: Gill and Macmillan, 1994.

Morash, Christopher. *Writing the Irish Famine.* Oxford, UK, and New York: Oxford University Press, 1995.

O'Gráda, Cormac. *Ireland's Great Famine: Interdisciplinary Perspectives.* Dublin: University College Dublin Press, 2006.

O'Sullivan, Patrick, ed. *The Meaning of the Famine.* Vol. 6 of *The Irish World Wide: History, Heritage, Identity.* London and New York: Leicester University Press, 1997.

Quinn, Peter. *Looking for Jimmy: A Search for Irish America.* Woodstock, NY: Overlook Press, 2007.

Woodham Smith, Cecil. *The Great Hunger: Ireland 1845–1849.* London: Hamish Hamilton, and New York: Harper and Row, 1962.

Mary C. Kelly
Professor of History
Franklin Pierce University

GREEK REVOLUTION

In 1821 Greek revolutionaries rebelled against their Ottoman Turk rulers, leading to a decade-long conflict that captured the interest of Europeans and Americans alike. Americans came to understand the Greek Revolution (1821–1832) through the lens of philhellenism, a transatlantic movement, and their own revolution. Believing in a strong cultural and intellectual link between the United States, ancient Greece, and democratic Athens, Americans saw Greece as the source of American democracy and American values. In their charitable support for Greece, Americans portrayed the Greek struggle for independence as a climactic battle between Western freedom and Oriental despotism. The popular movement to support the Greeks involved American missionaries, diplomats, merchants, and reformers. In the aftermath of the Barbary Wars (1801–1805, 1815–1816), however, the United States government and some

American merchants sought to establish a commercial agreement with the Ottoman Empire. Thus began a debate over to what extent Americans should support the Greek Revolution.

The first news of the Greek Revolution arrived in the United States in May 1821. At first, support for the Greeks was merely literary and sentimental in focus. Americans followed newspaper reports of the exploits of the English poet Lord Byron (1788–1824) as a soldier in the Greek army. American authors romanticized the Greek cause with poems published in newspapers, magazines, and pamphlets, praising the modern Greeks for rebelling against the Turks. More substantive support of the Greek cause began in 1822, when constituents demanded that Congress officially recognize Greek independence and provide assistance for the war effort. Some members of Congress embraced the cause while others pointed out that the Ottoman Empire could be a valuable commercial ally in the Mediterranean. After Daniel Webster of Massachusetts gave a stirring speech in the House of Representatives favoring the Greeks in December 1822, support for Greek aid rose to a fever pitch. President James Monroe, however, in his State of the Union address outlining what would become known as the Monroe Doctrine, declined to aid Greece.

Undiscouraged, Americans who favored the Greeks began to organize aid societies at the grass-roots level. A variety of local organizations, including community and religious groups with both male and female members, printed pamphlets to spread interest in the Greek Revolution. The larger Greek aid societies in cities such as New York, Boston, and Philadelphia served as collection centers for smaller organizations throughout the country. Important philhellenic leaders such as the politician Edward Everett (1794–1865) of Boston and the publisher Mathew Carey (1760–1839) of Philadelphia propelled their aid societies to national and international fame. Women also played an important role in the movement as they often led the organization of charitable gatherings. In many cases, women's participation in the Greek cause surpassed that of men. Owing both to male and female leadership, public interest in the Greek Revolution remained consistent for the duration of the war.

Greek enthusiasts held fundraising events—lectures, balls, toasts, and parades—around patriotic holidays, including Washington's Birthday and the Fourth of July, declaring that the Greeks were "brother patriots in distress." In some cases, attendees to charitable balls were even asked to dress in the garments of their great-grandfathers and great-grandmothers in order to draw a connection between the revolutionary generation and their support for Greece. Carey and other Greek supporters referred in print to the trials endured by patriots of the American Revolution, arguing that the Greeks endured far greater oppression under the Turks. This rhetoric generated consistent donations of money and supplies. By the end of the Greek Revolution, Americans had donated tens of thousands of dollars to local Greek aid societies.

Greek aid societies eventually joined forces with American missionaries. The interests of the American Board of Commissioners for Foreign Missions in having a presence in Greece evolved from merely evangelizing to also providing American education. The missionary spirit of spreading American ideals through education as well as religion fed the desire to assist Greece and its citizens as a developing independent nation. At first, the American Board distributed thousands of printed materials through their representatives and offered education to a handful of Greek refugees. Missionaries recruited a number of promising young Greek boys whose families were devastated by the Greek Revolution for an education in New England. Many of these students were even given the opportunity to pursue advanced degrees.

Over the next several years, Greek aid societies and missionaries embraced the idea of fundraising and recruiting teachers for the purpose of opening schools in Greece. Emma Willard (1787–1870), founder of the Troy Female Seminary in Troy, New York, led the way for organizing the development of Greek schools, working with both missionaries and philhellenes. One Greek refugee who supported these efforts wrote: "the strong and refined arm of American philanthropy fed, clothed and educated many an infant descendant of those god-like fathers of the Grecian race" (Castanis 1851, 212). The first of these American schools was established in Athens in 1829.

The Greek Revolution revealed diverging views of how to guarantee and spread American Revolutionary ideals. Supporters of a commercial treaty with the Ottoman Empire claimed that American aid for Greece threatened one of the chief goals of the American Revolution: the cultivation of free trade. American negotiators were faced with a difficult task when forced to explain to Turkish authorities why so many Americans supported Greek independence. American diplomats negotiating the treaty with the Ottoman Empire recommended that in order to pacify Turkish concerns over American allegiances, American philhellenes should redirect their support from military aid to civilian aid with items such as food and clothing. This shift in charitable focus led in part to the increased interest in building schools in Greece. After many years of negotiation, the Ottoman Empire agreed to a commercial treaty with the United States in 1830, allowing members of both sides of the debate access to Greece and the eastern Mediterranean.

SEE ALSO *1848 Revolutions; Kossuth, Louis*

BIBLIOGRAPHY

Allison, Robert. *The Crescent Obscured: The United States and the Muslim World, 1776–1815*. New York: Oxford University Press, 1995.

Castanis, Christophoros Plato. *The Greek Exile; or, A Narrative of the Captivity and Escape of Christophorus Plato Castanis, During the Massacre on the Island of Scio, by the Turks, Together with Various Adventures in Greece and America*. Philadelphia: Lippincott, Grambo, 1851.

Egan, Jim. *Oriental Shadows: The Presence of the East in Early American Literature*. Columbus: Ohio State University Press, 2011.

Field, James A., Jr. *America and the Mediterranean World, 1776–1882*. Princeton, NJ: Princeton University Press, 1969.

Finnie, David H. *Pioneers East: The Early American Experience in the Middle East*. Cambridge, MA: Harvard University Press, 1967.

Kelley, Mary. *Learning to Stand & Speak: Women, Education, and Public Life in America's Republic*. Chapel Hill: University of North Carolina Press, 2006.

Lambert, Frank. *The Barbary Wars: American Independence in the Atlantic World*. New York: Hill and Wang, 2005.

Larrabee, Stephen Addison. *Hellas Observed: The American Experience of Greece, 1775–1865*. New York: New York University Press, 1957.

Marr, Timothy. *The Cultural Roots of American Islamicism*. Cambridge and New York: Cambridge University Press, 2006.

Repousis, Angelo. "'The Cause of the Greeks': Philadelphia and the Greek War for Independence, 1821–1828." *Pennsylvania Magazine of History and Biography* 123, 4 (1999): 333–363.

Repousis, Angelo. "'The Trojan Women': Emma Hart Willard and the Troy Society for the Advancement of Female Education in Greece." *Journal of the Early Republic* 24, 3 (2004): 445–476.

Richard, Carl J. *The Golden Age of the Classics in America: Greece, Rome, and the Antebellum United States*. Cambridge, MA: Harvard University Press, 2009.

St. Clair, William. *That Greece Might Still Be Free: The Philhellenes in the War of Independence*. Rev. ed. Cambridge, MA: Open Book, 2008.

Winterer, Caroline. *The Mirror of Antiquity: American Women and the Classical Tradition, 1750–1900*. Cornell University Press, 2009.

Maureen Connors Santelli

Assistant Professor

Northern Virginia Community College

GREEN REVOLUTION

In the 1960s, *Green Revolution* became the term used to identify the breeding of high-yielding plant varieties (HYVs), particularly wheat and rice, by agricultural scientists to help alleviate the problem of hunger in developing nations. In 1944, Norman Borlaug (1914–2009), an employee of the Rockefeller Foundation, led a team of agricultural scientists at the Cooperative Mexican Agricultural Program who were working to improve Mexico's wheat production. Borlaug's team bred early maturing, semidwarf, high-yielding wheat varieties that could support heavy heads of grain if irrigated and fertilized. Borlaug's work in Mexico and later his influence on similar research in India and Pakistan gained food security for these nations—first Mexico by 1956, then Pakistan in 1968 and Indian in 1972.

In 1960, the Rockefeller and Ford Foundations helped create the International Rice Research Institute (IRRI) in the Philippines. At the IRRI, agricultural scientists experimented with hybrid rice varieties that also produced high yields with irrigation and large applications of fertilizer. By the mid-1980s, many East Asian nations had become self-sufficient in rice production.

In general, the Green Revolution resulted from the "package" application of hybrid seeds, fertilizers, and irrigation to produce bountiful harvests so that small-scale farmers could meet subsistence needs in food-deficit nations. The success of Green Revolution agricultural technology, however, depended on state assistance in the form of subsidized fertilizer, grain price supports to ensure profits, and government grain purchases to create market demand and encourage production, as well as marketing assistance, credit, roads and other infrastructure, and applied agricultural instruction to educate farmers about the use of Green Revolution technologies.

The Green Revolution became a success in South and East Asia not only because governments wanted to ensure food security for their people, but also because agricultural policy was driven by nationalism, the Cold War communist threat, and fear of Malthusian famine. The principal beneficiaries of the Green Revolution were countries considered vital to the Cold War strategy of Western nations. The World Bank and the International Monetary Fund also provided assistance for Green Revolution agricultural development to ensure economic stability in developing nations during the late twentieth century.

Agricultural and social scientists, as well as environmentalists, have debated the merits of the Green Revolution. Some have criticized it because HYVs require large and expensive applications of fertilizer, water, and pesticides, which can damage the environment. Critics charged that Green Revolution agricultural practices depleted water supplies, contributed to soil salinity, and caused soil exhaustion from multiple cropping, which, in turn, required the use of more fertilizer with each succeeding crop. Many hybrid varieties also attracted insects that became immune to pesticides. Other critics charged that large-scale, wealthy landowners consolidated small farms or plots that they had rented to subsistence farmers, forced the farmers from the land, and used Green Revolution technologies to produce grain surpluses for profit rather than for distribution to the underfed and malnourished.

By the early 1980s, most farmers in developing nations did not plant HYVs because they often proved unsuitable for local environments, and farmers could not afford to purchase hybrid seeds and fertilizer or invest in irrigation systems. In addition, some governments preferred to accept donations of cheap grain from other nations and nongovernmental agencies to feed urban populations whose political loyalty they wanted to maintain, rather than invest in costly and time-consuming agricultural science that would help subsistence farmers feed their families and provide a sustainable surplus for others in rural and urban areas.

During the late twentieth century, research to develop new seed varieties by genetic manipulation in laboratories rather than in experimental fields began a new phase of the Green Revolution. Genetically modified crops varieties, however, also caused criticism from consumers over potential health hazards from eating foods made from genetically modified organisms (GMOs). In addition, the extension of the Green Revolution to sub-Saharan Africa became problematic because of environmental limitations, native food preferences, lack of political support, cultural differences that determined land-use patterns, civil war, and terrorist activities.

By the early twenty-first century, agricultural scientists involved in the Green Revolution continued to argue that their only responsibility to society involved producing high-yielding grain crops to feed hungry people. Social scientists and environmentalists responded that the Green Revolution had created social problems relating to employment, women, land reform, rural poverty, and governmental aid, among others. Although the Green Revolution had alleviated hunger in some developing nations, it had not eliminated the possibility of severe food shortages based on population increases. Food security for poor farm families and urban populations in developing nations remained a problem. Borlaug and other Green Revolution scientists, however, always contended that more food was better than less food, and that if Green Revolution technologies damaged the environment, new technologies would be discovered to solve those problems.

SEE ALSO *Borlaug, Norman; Department of Agriculture, US; Ford Foundation; Rockefeller Foundation; United States Agency for International Development (USAID)*

BIBLIOGRAPHY

Cullather, Nick. *The Hungry World: America's Cold War Battle Against Poverty in Asia.* Cambridge, MA: Harvard University Press, 2010.

Djurfeldt, Göran, Hans Holmén, Magnus Jirström, and Rolf Larsson, eds. *The African Food Crisis: Lessons from the Asian Green Revolution.* Wallingford, UK: CABI, 2005.

Perkins, John H. *Geopolitics and the Green Revolution: Wheat, Genes, and the Cold War.* New York: Oxford University Press, 1997.

Pilcher, Jeffrey M. *Food in World History.* New York: Routledge, 2006.

Sen, Bandhudas. *The Green Revolution in India: A Perspective.* New York: Wiley, 1974.

R. Douglas Hurt
Professor and Department Head
Department of History, Purdue University

GREENPEACE

Greenpeace is a global environmental organization headquartered in Amsterdam and with branches in almost fifty countries. It is best known for its often-spectacular direct action protests, such as unfurling banners on dizzyingly high smokestacks or harassing whalers from small inflatable boats, although it also employs more conventional methods, such as lobbying. Greenpeace campaigns focus on numerous environmental problems around the world, many of which are locally or regionally specific. However, the issues with which it is most associated—and which have occupied it over much of its forty-five-year history—include nuclear weapons, whaling, industrial pollution, toxic chemicals, and forest preservation.

Greenpeace began life in Vancouver, Canada, in 1971, when a group of older, mostly American peaceniks joined forces with Canadian countercultural activists to protest against US nuclear testing in Alaska. Inspired by a 1958 Quaker voyage, in which activists attempted to sail a yacht into the Eniwetok test zone in the mid-Pacific, the Vancouver protesters—several of whom were also Quakers—chartered an old halibut seiner and tried to sail it into the H-bomb test zone in the Aleutians. The group called itself the Don't Make a Wave Committee—a reference to the widespread fear that the explosion might cause a tidal wave to crash onto the Canadian shore—and named their boat the *Greenpeace*, a compound word expressing their hope that the campaign would unite the peace movement with the nascent environmental movement. Despite considerable effort, the boat never made it all the way to the test zone. Nevertheless, those involved with the campaign felt that their movement—which combined the Quaker notion of "bearing witness," nonviolent direct action, and a carefully planned media strategy—could be the lead apostle in a new and potentially powerful form of activism. Thus, in early 1972, the Don't Make a Wave Committee became the Greenpeace Foundation.

From the beginning, there was an element of both synergy and tension between the early members of Greenpeace. Two of the key founders, Irving Stowe (1915–1974) and Jim Bohlen (1926–2010), were middle-aged Quakers from the United States. Many of their fellow activists, on the other hand, were a generation younger and adhered to the ideals and practices of the counterculture of the 1960s. While united in their opposition to nuclear weapons and environmental despoliation, these two factions frequently clashed on tactical and philosophical grounds. Stowe and Bohlen, for example, hoped that Greenpeace could help change the world by applying political pressure to governments. In contrast, Bob Hunter (1941–2005), a Vancouver journalist and the leading countercultural member of the group, felt that the only way to save the planet was to complete the consciousness revolution begun by the 1960s counterculture.

These competing visions did not preclude various members from cooperating with one another. From 1972 onward, Greenpeace set its sights on French nuclear testing in the South Pacific. By 1974, however, Hunter felt that the antinuclear protests had peaked and it was time for a change of direction. Against the will of many of the older Quakers, he pushed Greenpeace in the direction of deep ecology and animal rights. For the next several years, the organization primarily devoted itself to protesting whaling in the Pacific and seal hunting in eastern Canada. Regardless of their relative importance, these campaigns attracted far more attention and donations than the antinuclear protests, and Greenpeace began to grow rapidly. Throughout the late 1970s, Greenpeace groups sprang up throughout Canada, the United States, New Zealand, Australia, and Western Europe. This rapid growth led to a power struggle, particularly between the founders in Vancouver and the newer groups in the United States.

The result of this protracted and complicated struggle was the birth of Greenpeace International in 1980. Led by David McTaggart (1932–2001), a hardheaded Canadian businessman who had captained the Greenpeace voyages against French nuclear testing in the early 1970s, Greenpeace International became an efficient, well-run global nongovernmental organization (NGO). Membership and donations rose dramatically, enabling the organization to purchase new ships and other expensive equipment and to hire an array of full-time professional staff. Ample funding led to a variety of new campaigns throughout the world, including protests against chemical manufacturers and the decimation of forests in Canada and the Amazon, and campaigns against the fossil fuel industry.

Greenpeace has promoted an ecological sensibility throughout the world. Its activism against industries and governments is a way of "stinging" them with this sensibility, thereby causing pain in the form of negative publicity and widespread opprobrium (Wapner 1996). The 1986 whaling moratorium and the 2010 European ban on trade in illegal timber are among the organization's most high-profile successes. Beyond these, however, Greenpeace has also helped change policy and practice in numerous areas (Greenpeace International). At the same time, the organization has also endured significant backlashes. In 1985, for example, French agents blew up a Greenpeace ship, the *Rainbow Warrior*, in Auckland Harbour, killing a Greenpeace photographer, while in 2013, Russian coast guard agents arrested a group of activists that had boarded an Arctic oil platform. The activists initially faced ten-year prison sentences, but were later given amnesty.

SEE ALSO *Earth Day; Global Warming; Nongovernmental Organizations (NGOs); Silent Spring (Rachel Carson, 1962)*

BIBLIOGRAPHY

DeLuca, Kevin M. *Image Politics: The New Rhetoric of Environmental Activism.* New York: Guilford Press, 1999.

Greenpeace International. "Greenpeace: 43 Years of Inspiring Action." http://www.greenpeace.org/international/en/about/victories/

Hunter, Robert. *Warriors of the Rainbow: A Chronicle of the Greenpeace Movement.* New York: Holt, Rinehart, and Winston, 1979.

McTaggart, David, with Helen Slinger. *Shadow Warrior: The Autobiography of Greenpeace International Founder David McTaggart.* London: Orion, 2002.

Wapner, Paul. *Environmental Activism and World Civic Politics.* Albany: State University of New York Press, 1996.

Weyler, Rex. *Greenpeace: How a Group of Ecologists, Journalists, and Visionaries Changed the World.* Vancouver, BC: Raincoast, 2004.

Zelko, Frank S. *Make It a Green Peace! The Rise of Countercultural Environmentalism.* New York: Oxford University Press, 2013.

Frank Zelko
Associate Professor, History and Environmental Studies
University of Vermont

GROUP OF FIVE AND ITS SUCCESSORS (G5, G7, G8, G20)

On March 25, 1973, in a time of monetary disorder, US treasury secretary George Shultz (b. 1920) invited his German, French, and British counterparts to meet privately in the library of the White House. They all preferred their lively exchanges in this "Library Group" to the formal talks with the International Monetary Fund (IMF); the French and German finance ministers—Valéry Giscard d'Estaing (b. 1926) and Helmut Schmidt (b. 1920)—were particularly impressed. The participants continued meeting in secret and invited Japan, thus creating the Group of Five, or G5.

BIRTH OF THE G7 SUMMIT

In 1974, Giscard became president of France and Schmidt became federal German chancellor. They proposed a summit in the spirit of the Library Group to resolve monetary differences and discuss a response to economic problems provoked by rising oil prices. President Gerald Ford (1913–2006), advised by Schultz, decided to participate. The leaders of the G5 countries, plus Italy, held their first summit at Rambouillet near Paris in November 1975. The summit participants successfully agreed on a new monetary regime for the IMF, based on a US-French proposal, which has endured to this day.

Thereafter, the summits were organized annually, with Canada and the European Community (later the European Union or EU) joining the original members. The aim was to use the authority of heads of government to resolve intractable problems and provide collective management of the world economy. President Jimmy Carter (b. 1924) made great use of the summit to develop cooperative economic strategies. The group agreed to adopt trade liberalization through the General Agreement on Tariffs and Trade (GATT); Germany and Japan stimulated growth in return for American discipline over oil imports; and measures were taken to limit energy use in response to a second surge of oil prices.

During the 1980s, President Ronald Reagan (1911–2004) used the summit to advance foreign policy objectives. Reagan hosted the 1983 summit, which reached important agreements on missile defense, and he ensured that later summits produced a common response to terrorism. During this period, economic issues were returned to the G5 finance ministers. The strong dollar was widening the US external deficit and increasing protectionist pressures. In 1985, US treasury secretary James Baker (b. 1930) held a meeting of the G5 at the Plaza Hotel in New York to decide on measures to bring down the dollar. These measures were announced in the G5's first ever public statement and worked very well. But after the G5's cover was blown, Italy and Canada, as summit members, demanded the opportunity to take part. The 1986 summit in Tokyo created a new G7 finance ministers group, which met openly. Thereafter, the G5 became redundant and only the G7 finance ministers met. Accordingly, the summit became known as the G7.

THE G7 SUMMIT BECOMES G8

As the Soviet empire crumbled, the G7 leaders launched in 1989 a coordinated program to help East European countries escape from communism. The next year's summit, hosted by President George H. W. Bush (b. 1924), began a similar transition for Russia, a longer and harder task. The Russian leader Boris Yeltsin (1931–2007) became a regular guest at the summits, taking part in political debates. President Bill Clinton (b. 1946), the host in 1997, called it "the summit of the eight," and the following year the G7 was formally converted to the G8. Russia was permitted to join for political reasons, to balance the admission of East European countries to NATO. The finance ministers remained the G7.

After the Asian financial crisis of 1997 to 1999, the G7 finance ministers designed "new international financial architecture" to prevent a recurrence. This move was endorsed by the G7 leaders and accepted by the IMF and World Bank. It included a new G20 finance ministers grouping of "systemically important countries," proposed by US treasury secretary Robert Rubin (b. 1938) and his deputy Larry Summers (b. 1954). The G20 recognized, for the first time, the importance of emerging economies. Alongside the G8 countries and the European Union, it included Argentina, Australia, Brazil, China, India, Indonesia, Mexico, Saudi Arabia, South Africa, South Korea, and Turkey.

RISE OF THE G20

The G8 summit addressed both political and economic issues in the early 2000s. On American initiative, the group agreed on measures to combat terrorism and the spread of weapons of mass destruction. It also worked with African leaders to generate stronger growth, better governance, and greater security in that continent. The G8 attempted outreach to major emerging countries, like Brazil, China, and India, but could not agree on a consistent approach and thus alienated them.

The G7 finance ministers also favored their own network, rather than sharing power with the G20. Yet when the global financial crisis struck in 2008, followed by a deep recession, the G7 economies were the worst hit. Emerging countries survived much better and needed to be involved in any international response. President George W. Bush (b. 1946), therefore, called the first G20 summit in Washington that November. Two more G20 summits followed in 2009, in London and Pittsburgh, flanking a G8 summit in L'Aquila, Italy. President Barack Obama (b. 1961), who was not impressed by the G8, declared from the chair at Pittsburgh that henceforth the G20 would be "the premier forum for our international economic cooperation."

The G20 mounted an effective response to the financial and economic crisis. The emerging powers took part on equal terms, with leaders and finance ministers closely integrated. The G20 endorsed economic stimulus programs to check the recession, and launched reforms to improve financial regulation worldwide. The group also mobilized substantial resources for the IMF and reformed the fund's decision-making process to reflect the rise of emerging countries. Yet once the crisis was past, the momentum slackened. A program to coordinate economic policy that was adopted at Pittsburgh made only slow progress up to 2014, because the large emerging powers did not feel they had full ownership of the process. This situation may not change until China hosts the G20 summit in 2016.

The G8 was eclipsed for a time, but Obama decided that it was useful for politically charged topics outside the purely economic agenda of the G20, and he hosted a summit at Camp David in 2012. The next year's summit, chaired by the United Kingdom, demonstrated that the G8 could contribute to progress on economic issues, such as tax avoidance, that complemented the G20's work without conflicting with it.

In 2014, the other leaders refused to attend a G8 summit hosted by Russia after its annexation of Crimea and met as the G7 in Brussels, Belgium, instead. If Russia's absence persists, the summit should become economically more cohesive, though less influential politically. Meanwhile, the G7 finance ministers still trace their roots to the original G5.

SEE ALSO *International Monetary Fund; World Bank; World Trade Organization*

BIBLIOGRAPHY

Bayne, Nicholas. *Staying Together: The G8 Summit Confronts the 21st Century.* Aldershot, UK: Ashgate, 2005.

Hajnal, Peter I. *The G8 System and the G20: Evolution, Role, and Documentation.* Aldershot, UK: Ashgate, 2007.

Kirton, John J. *G20 Governance for a Globalized World.* Farnham, UK: Ashgate, 2013.

Putnam, Robert D., and Nicholas Bayne. *Hanging Together: Cooperation and Conflict in the Seven-Power Summits.* Cambridge, MA: Harvard University Press, 1987.

Nicholas Bayne
Fellow, International Trade Policy Unit
London School of Economics and Political Science

GUANTÁNAMO BAY

Guantánamo Bay is a wide and deep harbor at the southeastern tip of Cuba that opens into the Caribbean Sea. It provides easy access to the Windward Passage between the Caribbean and Atlantic oceans as well as to any of the other islands in the Caribbean or to the Panama Canal. During the Spanish-American War, on June 10, 1898, a US marine detachment led by Colonel Robert Huntington took possession of Guantánamo Bay following a successful amphibious assault. Guantánamo then became a US coaling and ship-repair facility.

On December 10, 1903, a large US naval base was installed at Guantánamo. Guantánamo Naval Station, often called Gitmo, occupies an area of approximately 45 square miles of land and water. The bilateral treaty that provides the diplomatic and legal basis for this military facility contains unique language that President Theodore Roosevelt dictated and Cuban president Tomás Estrada Palma accepted. It enabled the United States to lease Guantánamo for an open-ended period and left unresolved the issue of the applicability of US law and constitutional freedoms to Guantánamo. On May 29, 1934, President Franklin D. Roosevelt authored a new lease that restated the basic terms in the 1903 treaty. It remains in force.

Since Cuba became independent of Spain in 1898, Cuban nationalists have generally viewed Guantánamo as an unwanted, permanent military installation on their soil. During the US military occupation of Cuba, which lasted until 1902, the White House insisted that Cuban legislators incorporate the so-called Platt Amendment into their constitution as a precondition for the withdrawal of US troops from Cuba. The amendment specified that, "to maintain the independence of Cuba…the Government of Cuba will sell or lease to the United States lands necessary for coaling or naval stations." President Franklin Roosevelt abrogated much of the Platt Amendment, but at the same time he renewed the Guantánamo lease.

Following the onset of World War II, in October 1940 the distinguished Cuban nationalist and statesman Cosme de la Torriente (1872–1956) wrote in *Foreign Affairs* that, "if the United States government should ever decide to abandon the Guantánamo station, Cuba might have to ask the United States to stay." Guantánamo subsequently proved its strategic value as the hub of an interlocking convoy system that shielded such strategic goods as oil, bauxite, rubber, sugar, and coffee from attacks by German U-boats. These attacks caused havoc in Caribbean waters and the Florida Straits throughout 1942 and much of 1943, until German Admiral Karl Dönitz ended his destructive campaign.

Since 1959 the Cuban government has consistently and repeatedly protested the US presence on Cuban soil as illegal because it was imposed on Cuba by force. Shortly after January 2002, when the first planeload of suspected international terrorists arrived from Afghanistan at the Guantánamo Bay naval station, "Guantánamo" became an international watchword for detention, national security, torture, and the debate over America's war on terror. Clashing views over Guantánamo have divided US society and led to new tensions between the United States and its allies. Although President Barack Obama, at the outset of his first term in 2009, signed an executive order aimed at closing Guantánamo, his administration subsequently upheld the position that some detainees—deemed too dangerous to be transferred—could be held at Guantánamo's Camp Delta indefinitely. As of mid-2015, 122 prisoners remained incarcerated under the designation "enemy combatants."

SEE ALSO *Bay of Pigs; Castro, Fidel; Cuba; Cuban Missile Crisis; Imperialism; Spanish-American War; War on Terror*

BIBLIOGRAPHY

Cuban Ministry of Foreign Affairs. *Guantanamo, Yankee Naval Base of Crimes and Provocations.* Havana, 1970. Translation by U.S. Joint Publications Research Service, Arlington, VA, 1977. http://www.dtic.mil/cgi-bin/GetTRDoc?Location=U2&doc=GetTRDoc.pdf&AD=ADA373599

Schwab, Stephen Irving Max. *Guantánamo, USA: The Untold History of America's Cuban Outpost.* Lawrence: University Press of Kansas, 2009.

Strauss, Michael J. *The Leasing of Guantanamo Bay.* Westport, CT: Praeger, 2009.

Torriente y Peraza, Cosme de la. "Cuba, America, and the War." *Foreign Affairs* 19, 1 (1940): 145–155. https://www.foreignaffairs.com/articles/cuba/1940-10-01/cuba-america-and-war

Stephen Irving Max Schwab
Adjunct Assistant Professor of History
University of Alabama

GUATEMALA

As World War II (1939–1945) came to an end, Guatemala was in the midst of its first experience with democracy following the end of the thirteen-year dictatorship of General Jorge Ubico (1878–1946), from 1931 to 1944. The Democratic Spring (1944–1954) that followed the Ubico regime was an attempt at a capitalist revolution designed to break the feudal relations that defined the country's agro-export economy. Both nationalist and democratic, the government sought to integrate all Guatemalans, including the Maya, into a new, modern capitalist economy. When Jacobo Arbenz (1913–1971) was elected in 1952, he instituted a national land reform program expropriating fallow land from large landholders, including the United Fruit Company. While landless and land-poor peasants greeted this redistribution of land with much enthusiasm, the United Fruit Company, Guatemalan elites, and the US government called it communism. Ultimately, through the prism of the Cold War and the economic interests of key advisers, the administration of President Dwight Eisenhower (1890–1969) justified the 1954 CIA-orchestrated overthrow of the democratically elected government of Arbenz. For the next three decades this military coup d'état set the stage for US support of military dictatorships in Guatemala, which saw twelve different generals and military juntas leading the Guatemalan government (sometimes through fraudulent elections and sometimes through coups) until the 1985 election of civilian president Vinicio Cerezo (b. 1942).

The 1960s saw the growth of the Guatemalan guerrilla movement, which had begun with a small group of disgruntled army officers who attempted a coup against the corrupt and unpopular government of General Miguel Ydígoras Fuentes (1895–1982) in November 1960. This failed coup led to the development of an armed insurgency. In 1966, the US-trained Guatemalan army began a series of coordinated attacks in urban and rural areas, including mass disappearances of urban activists critical of the regime and indiscriminant bombing of villages believed to support guerrilla operations in Zacapa and Izabal. From 1966 to 1968 thousands of civilians were killed or disappeared during this first counterinsurgency campaign. Counterinsurgency violence and surveillance practices established in these campaigns would be used by the army to attack the guerrillas and control the civilian population for the next thirty years.

In 1978 the Guatemalan army garnered international attention when it opened fire on a group of unarmed K'ekchi' Maya peasants protesting for land and killed dozens of men, women, and children in what became known as the Panzós massacre. That same year, the Guatemalan army also began a selective campaign of political disappearance and assassination in Guatemala City and other urban and rural centers. In tandem, it accelerated construction of military bases throughout rural Guatemala. Prior to 1979, the army had divided the country into nine military zones, each with a large army base in its center. By 1982, the army had designated each of the twenty-two departments as a military zone accompanied by multiple army bases in municipalities and army garrisons in villages throughout the country. Forced recruitment into the Guatemalan army ensured the requisite number of troops for this extension of the military infrastructure. In 1982 troops were increased from twenty-seven thousand to thirty-six thousand. This expanded army presence was accompanied by an acceleration of army violence, from selective urban and rural assassinations and disappearances to extreme urban repression and multiple village massacres, which ultimately led to genocide including the killing of two hundred thousand civilians and army massacres in 626 Maya villages. This armed conflict continued, with varying degrees of intensity, until December 29, 1996, when the government and the URNG (Union Revolucionaria Nacional de Guatemala, or Guatemala National Revolutionary Union) guerrillas signed the Guatemalan Peace Accords. At the time of the signing of the accords, the URNG had twenty-five hundred official combatants and the army had some sixty thousand soldiers and more than 270,000 civil patrollers under army command. Following the release of the 1999 Guatemalan truth commission report issued by the Commission for Historical Clarification, President Bill Clinton (b. 1946) apologized to the people of Guatemala for the US role supporting brutal regimes.

SEE ALSO *Banana Republics; Central Intelligence Agency (CIA); Covert Wars; United Fruit Company*

BIBLIOGRAPHY

Comisión para el esclarecimiento histórico (Commission for Historical Clarification; CEH). *Guatemala: Memoria del Silencio.* 12 vols. Guatemala City: CEH, 1999.

Cullather, Nick. *Secret History: The CIA's Classified Account of Its Operations in Guatemala, 1952–1954.* Stanford, CA: Stanford University Press, 1999.

Handy, Jim. *Gift of the Devil: A History of Guatemala.* Boston: South End Press, 1998.

Levenson-Estrada, Deborah. *Trade Unionists against Terror: Guatemala City 1954–1985.* Chapel Hill: University of North Carolina Press, 1994.

Sanford, Victoria. *Buried Secrets: Truth and Human Rights in Guatemala.* New York: Palgrave Macmillan, 2003.

Sanford, Victoria. "Why Truth Still Matters: Impunity and Justice in Contemporary Guatemala." In *Comparative Peace Processes in Latin America,* edited by Cynthia Aronson, 351–372. Stanford, CA: Stanford University Press and Woodrow Wilson International Center for Scholars, 2012.

Victoria Sanford
Professor and Chair, Department of Anthropology
Director, Center for Human Rights and Peace Studies
Lehman College, City University of New York

GULF OF TONKIN RESOLUTION

The Gulf of Tonkin Resolution, passed by a joint session of Congress on August 7, 1964, granted President Lyndon B. Johnson (LBJ) the authority "to take all necessary measures to repel any armed attack against the forces of the United States and to prevent further aggression" in Vietnam. The measure supplanted a declaration of war and gave LBJ a blank check to escalate America's military involvement in Vietnam without further congressional authorization. There was almost no debate over the resolution and only two votes against it.

Two alleged torpedo attacks in the Gulf of Tonkin, off the coast of North Vietnam, provided the pretext for Johnson to introduce this resolution. A National Security Agency study, declassified in 2005, confirms that an engagement between the North Vietnamese navy and the USS *Maddux* did occur on August 2, 1964. However, it concludes that the alleged attack against the USS *Turner Joy* on August 4 never took place. The report states, "In truth, Hanoi's navy was engaged in nothing that night but the salvage of the two boats damaged on August 2." Scanty evidence regarding these events did little to deter LBJ from launching limited retaliatory attacks against North Vietnamese naval bases and introducing a congressional authorization on the use of force. On the contrary, Johnson's administration, having already determined that something must be done to bolster the embattled Republic of Vietnam, had been waiting for an opportune moment to step up the pressure on North Vietnam. The Gulf of Tonkin Resolution was based on an authorization that his administration had drawn up and tabled months earlier.

Johnson was motivated in part by domestic political concerns. As he fought a tough reelection campaign against the hawkish Republican candidate, Barry Goldwater (1909–1998), the political and military situation in South Vietnam was deteriorating steadily. His opportunistic show of strength following the Tonkin Gulf incident essentially removed Vietnam as a campaign issue by undercutting Goldwater's insistence that the president lacked the fortitude to stand up to Communist aggression. At the same time, LBJ was able to satisfy his dovish constituents with promises that he would not send American troops halfway around the world to fight Vietnam's battles.

As Johnson campaigned for reelection, Hanoi significantly increased its support for the southern insurgency, forcing Johnson to decide between escalation and withdrawal. Despite significant international and domestic support for an American military withdrawal, LBJ's administration saw escalation as the only viable response to the rapid deterioration of South Vietnamese stability. To pull out of Vietnam would have meant going against a long policy history, based on the domino theory, of defending South Vietnam against Communist infiltration. Most of Johnson's key policy advisors had been personally involved with creating that policy and were reluctant to change course. The president was concerned that a withdrawal from Vietnam might undermine the credibility of the United States around the world. Furthermore, he feared that domestic political backlash against the abandonment of South Vietnam could imperil his domestic political programs, harm the Democratic Party, and sully his own political legacy.

In early 1965 Johnson's administration took advantage of the latitude granted by the Gulf of Tonkin Resolution to escalate the protracted US involvement in Vietnam to full-scale war. Washington's two-pronged strategy to avoid the collapse of the South Vietnamese government combined air strikes with the introduction of America's first dedicated ground troops. By mid-1966 the number of US ground forces in Vietnam increased to about 350,000, and the number would grow steadily to its peak of nearly 500,000 in 1967.

In 1971, as public opposition to the war mounted during the presidency of Richard M. Nixon, Congress voted to repeal the Gulf of Tonkin Resolution in an effort to restore limits to presidential power and to reclaim the congressional authority to declare war. The 1973 War Powers Resolution, passed over Nixon's veto, went even farther to require the president to consult with Congress regarding decisions to send US forces into hostilities or imminent hostilities.

SEE ALSO *Agent Orange; Cold War; Domino Theory; Ho Chi Minh; Johnson, Lyndon Baines; McNamara, Robert S.; Nguyễn Ngọc Loan executing Nguyễn Văn Lém (Eddie Adams, 1968); Phan Thị Kim Phúc (Nick Ut, 1972); Vietnam War*

BIBLIOGRAPHY

Logevall, Fredrik. *Choosing War: The Lost Chance for Peace and the Escalation of War in Vietnam.* Berkeley: University of California Press, 1999.

Logevall, Fredrik. *The Origins of the Vietnam War.* New York: Routledge, 2001.

Moïse, Edwin E. *Tonkin Gulf and the Escalation of the Vietnam War.* Chapel Hill: University of North Carolina Press, 1996.

Prados, John. *Vietnam: The History of an Unwinnable War, 1945–1975.* Lawrence: University Press of Kansas, 2009.

Jessica M. Chapman
Associate Professor of History
Williams College

H

HAGUE CONFERENCES (1899, 1907)

The Hague Conferences, convened in the Netherlands at the turn of the twentieth century, responded to the escalating international arms race and set important precedents establishing international organizations and regulating the laws of war.

THE FIRST HAGUE CONFERENCE (1899)

In August 1898, Czar Nicholas II of Russia (1868–1918), concerned by military and naval construction, particularly on the part of Germany and Great Britain, issued a call for a conference of major nations to address the rapid buildup of armaments. The meeting, convened on May 18, 1899, at the summer palace of the Dutch royal family, gathered representatives from twenty-six nations, mostly from Europe. Representing the United States were Andrew D. White (1832–1918), the US ambassador to Germany; Seth Low (1850–1916), president of Columbia University; Stanford Newel (1839–1907), US minister to the Netherlands; Captain Alfred Thayer Mahan (1840–1914) for the US Navy; and representing the US Army, Captain William R. Crozier (1855–1942).

Discussions at The Hague focused on three main topics: disarmament, the laws of war, and arbitration. On July 28, 1899, participants adopted a series of conventions. While they could reach no agreement on the reduction of arms or limitation of defense budgets, participants issued a collective statement that arms control was "extremely desirable for the increase of the material and moral welfare of mankind" (Scott 1915, 28). Delegates agreed to bar the use of "inhumane weapons," such as asphyxiating gases, exploding bullets, or weapons released from balloons. Other conventions, drawing heavily from the so-called Lieber Code developed in 1863 by political theorist Francis Lieber (c. 1798–1872) during the US Civil War (1861–1865) and the 1864 Geneva Convention, clarified the laws of war, including the status of soldiers and civilians, the treatment of prisoners and the wounded, and the declaration and cessation of hostilities. Finally, the nations adopted a Convention for the Pacific Settlement of International Disputes, which established protocols for mediation at the Permanent Court of Arbitration (PCA), established in 1900 and known as the Hague Tribunal. The United States ratified the Hague Conventions in 1900 but declined to endorse their provisions on inhumane weapons, including gas warfare. The United States later participated in the PCA but sent only a handful of minor disputes there for settlement.

For the United States, the conference offered the opportunity to act on the world stage among the European great powers. Like the diplomats of other states, the Americans were reluctant to compromise on matters deemed to impede on national sovereignty. Doubtful from the outset that the conference would achieve any binding limitation on arms, the United States nevertheless believed participation at The Hague would yield influence in the international arena. For the thousands of Americans active in the newly resurgent peace movement, however, the Hague Conference offered hope of halting the arms race and establishing arbitration as the primary means for the resolution of international conflict. To the peace activists and international law advocates who increasingly pressed for arbitration—most notably in forums such as the Lake Mohonk Conferences on International Arbitration that met annually from 1895 to 1916—the establishment of the PCA and the delegates' publicly stated affirmations of arbitration represented groundbreaking accomplishments. Advocates of international organization were likewise pleased by the issuance of statements in which the convention spoke as an organization distinct from the sovereign nation-states that participated, as well as by the delegates' call for a future meeting.

THE SECOND HAGUE CONFERENCE (1907)

In September 1905, just after the conclusion of the Russo-Japanese War, Czar Nicholas II—at the urging of President Theodore Roosevelt (1858–1919)—called a second Hague Conference. More than two hundred delegates from forty-four nations convened from June 15 to October 18, 1907, to revisit and extend topics taken up eight years earlier. Roosevelt's leadership reflected the expanded US role in the world following the Spanish-American War (1898), the Boxer Rebellion (1900), and the US-brokered Treaty of Portsmouth ending the Russo-Japanese War (1904–1905). The US delegation, headed by Joseph H. Choate (1832–1917), a former ambassador to Great Britain, included retired Civil War general Horace Porter (1837–1921); Uriah M. Rose (1834–1913), an Arkansas judge; US minister to the Netherlands David Jayne Hill (1850–1932); Admiral Charles S. Sperry (1847–1911); and General George B. Davis (1847–1914).

International arms buildups were so advanced by 1907 that few believed any new agreements would emerge on that subject, and in fact arms control was never seriously addressed by the conference. Delegates voted to support compulsory arbitration in principle, but despite the advocacy of many, they were unable to agree on means to make arbitration mandatory. They did adopt the Drago-Porter Convention requiring arbitration of debt-related international conflicts, a provision meant to protect Latin American and Caribbean states from US and European interventions. Participating nations affirmed many of the 1899 conference's provisions regarding the laws of warfare and extended them in matters of naval warfare and the rights and obligations of neutral nations in wartime.

The United States ratified the 1907 Hague Convention in April 1908, but once again refused to endorse its provisions on chemical weapons and cited the Monroe Doctrine (1823) to claim exemption from the Drago-Porter Convention. Roosevelt pursued the conference for domestic political reasons, reflecting the increased visibility and organization of internationalist and peace movements in the United States, such as the American Peace Society and the Inter-Parliamentary Union, both active supporters of the Hague Conferences. Activists were disappointed by the conference's meager results, but believed that stated commitments to arbitration and international organization were important beginnings on which the peace movement could expand, and were heartened by the announcement of regular meetings, with the next gathering scheduled for 1915.

ASSESSMENT AND LEGACY

In retrospect, the Hague Conferences have been deemed failures because they were unable to stop the rapid buildup of arms among the great powers, or—despite the August 1913 dedication of an elaborate Hague Peace Palace funded by Andrew Carnegie (1835–1919)—prevent the outbreak of World War I (1914–1918). In that sense, the military treaties that formed the Triple Alliance between Germany, Austria-Hungary, and Italy after 1882, and other treaties that established the Triple Entente between France, Russia, and Britain by 1907, turned out to have a far more immediate impact on world events. Due to war, the 1915 Hague conference was cancelled, although leading figures in the women's movement—including Jane Addams (1860–1935) and others active in the Women's Peace Party—nevertheless met there in hopes of pressing the warring powers to settle the conflict through negotiation.

Despite their limits, the Hague Conferences marked a turning point in the establishment of permanent international institutions. Delegates also laid down laws and customs for war on land that remain in force today. American participation in the Hague Conferences—and discussions publicized by peace organizations—contributed to a growing global awareness among ordinary Americans. The Hague also provided important precedents for later twentieth-century institutions. The Permanent Court of Arbitration, the first standing body for the resolution of international conflicts, was replaced by the Permanent Court of International Justice in 1921 and then by the International Court of Justice, created after the founding of the United Nations in 1945.

SEE ALSO *Britain; Carnegie Endowment for International Peace; Federal Council of Churches; Roosevelt, Franklin D.; Self-Determination; Tariff; United Nations; Wilson, Woodrow; World Trade Organization; World War I*

BIBLIOGRAPHY

Davis, Calvin DeArmond. *The United States and the First Hague Peace Conference.* Ithaca, NY: Cornell University Press, 1962.

Davis, Calvin DeArmond. *The United States and the Second Hague Peace Conference: American Diplomacy and International*

Organization, 1899–1914. Durham, NC: Duke University Press, 1976.

Kuehl, Warren F. *Seeking World Order: The United States and International Organization to 1920.* Nashville, TN: Vanderbilt University Press, 1969.

Scott, James Brown, ed. *The Hague Conventions and Declarations of 1899 and 1907.* New York: Oxford University Press, 1915.

Christopher Capozzola
Associate Professor of History
Massachusetts Institute of Technology

HAITI

Since the revolutionary era, the United States has influenced Haiti by participating first in its partial ostracism, then over a century later by intervening militarily, including as recently as 2004. Haiti has influenced the United States by evoking its race-based desires and fears. Race and religion especially have marked US-Haitian relations.

EIGHTEENTH- AND NINETEENTH-CENTURY US RELATIONS WITH HAITI

US warnings about negative Haitian spillovers began after Haiti became, from 1790 to 1804, the first and only nation in the Americas born of a successful slave rebellion. President Thomas Jefferson's (1743–1826) administration remained neutral because Jefferson did not want to help France keep its empire. But he and other slave owners were horrified by the brutal race war in Haiti and feared that US slaves would follow their example.

Before and after the revolution, the French restricted Haitian trade, but US merchants largely ignored the laws. Politically, however, the United States towed the French line and refused to extend diplomatic relations to Haiti. President James Monroe (1758–1831) also did not include Haiti in his doctrine of protecting Latin American nations against European interventions.

The United States waited until June 5, 1862, to recognize Haiti. Southerners argued in favor of withholding recognition for racial reasons, and officials resented hosting black diplomats. But abolitionist senator Charles Sumner (1811–1874) convinced President Abraham Lincoln (1809–1865) that recognizing Haiti would hold European powers at bay as Spain was reclaiming the Dominican Republic. Haitian ports soon provided bases to be used against the Confederacy.

For some African Americans, Haiti held unique promise. Missionaries spoke not only of a homeland safe from white supremacy but also of an obligation: "Every colored man should feel bound to sustain the national existence of Hayti," said one Episcopal deacon (Dubois 2012, 154). Haiti was one of the few posts for African American diplomats, including Frederick Douglass (1817/8–1895). Haitian leader Fabre Geffrard (1806–1878) offered travel costs and credit to any African American who settled in his land. In the early 1860s, more than two thousand Americans migrated.

US OCCUPATION: 1915–1934

Until 1915, elite education and religion in Haiti remained almost entirely French. Germans often married Haitians to get around the prohibition against foreigners buying land. And the country remained atomized, its politics unstable and violent. Washington long worried that European gunboats might land, and the outbreak of World War I in 1914 added fears of Germany taking Haiti's Môle Saint-Nicolas and blocking passage to the newly opened Panama Canal. The US State Department, concerned also about the treasury, sent marines and Wall Street bankers to take half the Haitian National Bank and the entire national railway.

In July 1915, US Marines and Navy bluejackets occupied Haiti when a mob broke into the French legation, dragged out President Jean Vilbrun Guillaume Sam (1859–1915), and tore him to pieces. As President Woodrow Wilson (1856–1924) put it, the occupation's goal was to "put an end to revolution." One marine added that "these people are no more fitted to govern themselves than a tribe of apes," to which his solution was "a white man's government" (McPherson 2014, 33, 31).

Codifying the occupation was the Haitian-American Convention of September 1915, which allowed US "treaty officials" to veto Haitian decisions. In 1918, a rewritten constitution reversed the prohibition against foreigners owning land, and US citizens bought up 43,000 acres. Marines also built hundreds of miles of roads, numerous hospitals and schools, and a national constabulary called the Gendarmerie.

Partly because of their enforcement of the *corvée* or forced-labor law, marines faced two waves of violent resistance—a short-lived one by *caco* followers of Haiti's generals in 1915 and a longer one in 1918 to 1920 by 15,000 *cacos* led by Charlemagne Péralte (1886–1919). In the second *caco* war, 1,861 Haitians died versus thirteen US soldiers.

Vodou, the syncretic African-based religion of most Haitians, had been officially banned for decades, but Haitian elites allowed it to survive and even joined in its dances and ceremonies. US occupiers, primed by books and movies that demonized Haiti as a land of cannibals and zombies, tried in vain to enforce the ban.

African Americans continued to have a more hopeful approach. W. E. B. Du Bois (1868–1963) and James Weldon Johnson (1871–1938) were among the most persistent critics of the occupation. Haiti inspired many during the Harlem Renaissance of the 1920s and 1930s, including Langston Hughes (1902–1967) and Zora Neale Hurston (1891–1960), who both visited the island. Unfortunately, much of the mixed-race Haitian elite wanted nothing to do with African Americans or their recommendations for technical training.

After mounting protests by Haitians and their transnational network of allies, the nineteen-year US occupation ended in 1934.

THE DUVALIER AND ARISTIDE ERAS

The era of the Duvalier dictators, Papa Doc (1957–1971) and his son Baby Doc (1971–1986), was marked by internal repression by the Tonton Macoutes, but the strongmen ensured Cold War collaboration. Many well-educated Haitians moved to Canada, France, or New York and Florida.

The mixed desires to stabilize democracy and avoid waves of poor immigrants to US shores accounted for the last two US interventions in Haiti. In the first, the Bill Clinton administration restored to power Jean-Bertrand Aristide, a Catholic priest who had overwhelmingly won the presidential election in 1990 but was ousted by a military junta in 1991. In fall 1994, the junta left Haiti rather than face a US force, and US and Caribbean soldiers patrolled Haiti.

A decade later, Aristide's rule had been weakened by a united opposition of sweatshop owners, armed guerrillas who opposed the disbanding of the army, and international financiers who choked off credit. These accused Aristide of fraudulent elections and of allying with street thugs. In February 2004, when fears of Haitian "boat people" became real, the George W. Bush administration convinced Aristide to flee aboard a US plane. This intervention was even more multinational, backed by the United Nations' Resolution 1529 and its Multinational Interim Force made up of US, French, Chilean, and Canadian soldiers.

The UN force eventually became the UN Stabilization Mission in Haiti, known as MINUSTAH. It remained in a politically unstable Haiti through the 2010 earthquake that devastated Port-au-Prince. The US military sent massive amounts of aid, and hundreds of aid organizations settled in the country. Bill Clinton, as UN special envoy, coordinated much of the fundraising and reconstruction.

SEE ALSO *Dollar Diplomacy; Empire, US; Exceptionalism; Gender; Interventionism; Missionary Diplomacy; Monroe Doctrine (1823); Open Door Policy*

BIBLIOGRAPHY

Dubois, Laurent. *Haiti: The Aftershocks of History*. New York: Metropolitan, 2012.

Heinl, Robert Debs, Jr., and Nancy Gordon Heinl. *Written in Blood: The Story of the Haitian People, 1492–1971*. Boston: Houghton Mifflin, 1978.

Largey, Michael D. *Vodou Nation: Haitian Art Music and Cultural Nationalism*. Chicago: University of Chicago Press, 2006.

McPherson, Alan. *The Invaded: How Latin Americans and Their Allies Fought and Ended U.S. Occupations*. New York: Oxford University Press, 2014.

Plummer, Brenda Gayle. *Haiti and the United States: The Psychological Moment*. Athens: University of Georgia Press, 1992.

Renda, Mary A. *Taking Haiti: Military Occupation and the Culture of U.S. Imperialism, 1915–1940*. Chapel Hill: University of North Carolina Press, 2001.

Alan McPherson
Professor of International and Area Studies
University of Oklahoma

HAITIAN REVOLUTION

In August 1791, enslaved people in the northern plains of Saint-Domingue, France's most valuable colony, lit the cane fields on fire and rebelled against the brutal slave system. News of these events quickly reached the shores of the new United States of America. Throughout the Haitian Revolution, at least twenty thousand black, white, and mixed-race refugees disembarked on American shores. Newspapers published their stories, as well as other official proclamations and policies from Saint-Domingue, as Americans sought to find an explanation for the Haitian Revolution that did not implicate their own slave system. While some in the United States supported the Haitian Revolution, none wanted to see the same scenes replay in their cities and on their plantations. The Haitian Revolution, most Americans argued, came about because of the specific kind of slavery practiced in French Saint-Domingue.

THE AMERICAN REACTION

The Haitian Revolution sparked debate about the nature of American republicanism and forced Americans to be self-reflexive. The result was diverse articulations of American nationalism. Many whites sought to create distance between their own political project while nonwhites hoped that Dominguan and Haitian politics might create a more inclusive version of American citizenship and identity. Few Americans acknowledged the parallels between their own revolution and the events unfolding in Saint-Domingue. However, the arrival of thousands of French refugees from Saint-Domingue contributed to a broader discussion about migration and citizenship in the new United States.

Most Americans did not recognize the capacity for political thought or action among the enslaved population. Rather, they saw the rebellion as a form of disease, one that they hoped to prevent from spreading onto American soil. As a preventative measure, they were extremely wary of nonwhite migrants from Saint-Domingue. Some of these black and mixed-race migrants had come to the United States willingly, either on their own or with their masters or former masters, while others had been forced against their will to leave the colony.

Despite their precautions against the spread of the revolution, white Americans found—or thought they found—evidence of "French" initiative in rebellions or plans for rebellion among the enslaved population of the United States, the most famous being Gabriel's Rebellion in 1800 in Richmond, Virginia. By attributing these events to outside agitators, white Americans were able to maintain the front that their slave system was benevolent. Although black and mixed-race residents were inspired by the actions and ideologies of the Haitian Revolution, for the most part this resulted in individual rather than collective action. For example, enslaved individuals resisted their legal status by running away and suing for their freedom.

DOMINGUAN REFUGEES IN THE UNITED STATES

Refugees from the Haitian Revolution began arriving in the United States almost immediately after the first uprising in 1791. The US government aided French colonists' efforts to suppress the rebellion by extending them credit in order to purchase military supplies. Support waned, however, when white French colonists fled the colony; many in the United States saw this as cowardice and accused them of shirking their responsibilities in Saint-Domingue. Americans also blamed Dominguan colonists for the uprising and refused to acknowledge the political ideologies of the enslaved rebels. The Dominguan refugee population was composed of both royalists and republicans, but all of them claimed rights as citizens of the French republic in order to participate in the governance of the colony and most were sure to emphasize the natural connection between Dominguan republicans and the United States. Not all Americans were convinced.

After the battle of Cap Français in 1793 and the declaration of emancipation in Saint-Domingue, thousands of French refugees arrived in the United States. News of the violence in the colony encouraged a renewal of support for French refugees. Ideas of republican philanthropy inspired Americans to organize sizeable relief campaigns to aid French refugees in American port cities. Americans, however, continued to criticize Dominguan colonists, especially after war broke out between France and Britain and the British occupied the south and west of Saint-Domingue (1793–1798). This led Americans to accuse colonists of loyalty to the British Crown.

The perceived political uncertainty of these migrants in the United States meant that the American government, just like the French government, could not settle on a uniform policy to deal with them and therefore they were subject to temporary and halfway measures. The relationship between the United States and the refugees, as well as with the colony itself, became increasingly complicated as the relationship between the United States and France deteriorated into violence. The Quasi War (1798–1800), two years of naval skirmishes with the French, mostly in the Caribbean, was a period of very high anti-French sentiment, which opened the door for an alliance between the United States and the colonial government in Saint-Domingue, under the leadership of the former slave Toussaint Louverture (1743–1803).

THE US RELATIONSHIP WITH SAINT-DOMINGUE

The United States had enjoyed a close relationship with Saint-Domingue since American independence because of trade agreements signed in the 1780s. This relationship strengthened after 1793 when France opened trade with Saint-Domingue and American merchants were quick to take advantage of the new opportunities available. After US-French relations soured and the federal government prohibited trade with the French Empire in 1798, Louverture petitioned to have Saint-Domingue exempted from the embargo. American merchants supported the increasing independence of Louverture's government, including a special trade relationship. When the 1798 Non-Intercourse Act came up for renewal in 1799, the US government included an amendment known as "Toussaint's clause," which allowed American merchants to trade with the parts of the French Empire that were not participants in the war, despite a renewal of the embargo on trade.

This was a moment in which the American government prioritized economic advancement over racism. In doing so, the United States helped Saint-Domingue achieve greater autonomy from the French metropole. Independence in Saint-Domingue was not yet on the table, but the US government knew that its actions might encourage a move toward sovereignty under Louverture's leadership; nevertheless, Americans were wary and unsure of the benefits and pitfalls of this possibility. Later in 1799, the United States entered into an agreement with Jamaica and Saint-Domingue (under

Louverture) in order to secure additional commercial benefits and protection for American merchants in Saint-Domingue.

The end of the Quasi War in 1800, however, meant that the US government could no longer explicitly allow its merchants to trade with the ports occupied by Louverture's government, because this would foster the independence of the island—a fact that was becoming more and more appealing to the United States in light of the potential acquisition of the territory of Louisiana from Napoléon Bonaparte (1769–1821).

INDEPENDENCE AND OFFICIAL RECOGNITION

Bonaparte, recently established as first consul of France, resented what he perceived as a challenge to his authority, and he sent an army to disarm, kill, and deport the colonial leadership of Louverture's government. It is likely that Bonaparte also instructed his brother-in-law, General Victor Emmanuel Leclerc (1772–1802), to reinstitute slavery in the colony. At the very least, rumors began to spread in the colony that this was the case. Leclerc's arrival in Saint-Domingue reignited the smoldering revolution and transformed the war into a war for independence. While Louverture had struggled for greater colonial autonomy, the revolution had not pursued political independence under his leadership. The French army's arrival changed this. It was only when it became clear to the former slaves in the colony that their legal freedom could not be assured under French authority that they began the fight for independence. President Thomas Jefferson (1743–1826) was reluctant to aid Leclerc's forces because of concern over the territory of Louisiana, recently reacquired by the French. The Leclerc expedition did not achieve the quick victory that Bonaparte had hoped and the war dragged on. By the beginning of 1803, it was clear that a French victory was unlikely. The failure to regain control of Saint-Domingue contributed significantly to the sale of Louisiana to the United States in 1803.

After two years of violent warfare between the French forces and the "brigands"—as they were called, now under the direction of Jean-Jacques Dessalines (c. 1758–1806)—the French evacuated the western side of the island. On January 1, 1804, Dessalines and his leading generals announced the independence of the island to the population of Saint-Domingue and to the world at large—the country was to be called "Hayti."

The US government did not immediately act on this news, and merchants continued to trade with the ports that they had previously been frequenting. Haiti's ambiguous status, however, posed problems both within the United States and between American officials and French representatives in the country. French officials were relentless in their efforts to convince the US government to prohibit the trade.

Finally, in February 1806, the US government completely prohibited all trade with Haiti. In so doing, Jefferson and the US Congress overlooked their obligations under the law of nations in order to appease the French, to gain an upper hand in securing the Floridas, and to help assuage the fears of southern slaveholders. The prohibition continued until 1810, at which point American merchants were again free to trade with Haiti. In 1813, the United States appointed commercial agents to Cap Haïtien and Port-au-Prince, despite continuing to withhold official diplomatic recognition.

In 1808, Bonaparte's troops invaded Spain and ousted King Ferdinand VII (1784–1833). The Cuban government remained loyal to Ferdinand and expelled all Frenchmen from the colony. Their number was significant, since Cuba had been a primary destination for people of all colors fleeing the revolution. In 1809, about ten thousand people who had been declared French by the Cuban government arrived in New Orleans. These refugees again posed many of the same problems as the earlier migrants; however, the 1808 American prohibition on the importation of foreign slaves was at the heart of the discussion about this new wave of migration. The governor of Louisiana, however, petitioned the federal government for an exemption on the penalties that would be meted out to any ship captains who broke the ban and imported slaves. This substantial migration nearly doubled the population of New Orleans.

The United States was the last nation of the Atlantic world to extend official diplomatic recognition to Haiti. Along with the prohibition on trade between Haiti and the United States from 1806 to 1810, the American policy allowed the British to become Haiti's primary trade partner. Nonetheless, Haitian leaders continued to try to secure official recognition by the United States throughout the nearly six decades of diplomatic nonrecognition. For example, President Jean-Pierre Boyer (1776–1850) undertook an aggressive campaign in the mid-1820s to encourage and support the migration of free people of color from the United States to Haiti. Boyer hoped that the emigration plans would encourage diplomatic recognition by the United States. While thousands of black and mixed-race Americans migrated to Haiti in the mid-1820s, the program did not succeed in achieving Boyer's goal. Most of the emigrants returned home, because their experiences in Haiti did not meet their expectations. Finally, in 1862, in the midst of the American Civil War, the United States extended diplomatic recognition to Haiti. Without any southern representatives in Congress, President Abraham Lincoln (1809–1865) successfully proposed sending diplomatic representatives to Haiti and Liberia.

The complex relationship between the United States and Saint-Domingue and Haiti reflected the changing interplay of economic, ideological, and political ambitions in the late eighteenth- and early nineteenth-century Atlantic world. The actions of American citizens and of the American government both at home and abroad shaped the course of events during the Haitian Revolution. At the same time, events in Saint-Domingue and Haiti challenged American citizens to reconceptualize their own self-identity in the context of the Age of Revolution.

SEE ALSO *Antislavery; Caribbean; French Revolution; Toussaint Louverture*

BIBLIOGRAPHY

Brown, Gordon. *Toussaint's Clause: The Founding Fathers and the Haitian Revolution.* Jackson: University of Mississippi Press, 2005.

Gaffield, Julia. *Haitian Connections in the Atlantic World: Recognition after Revolution.* Chapel Hill: University of North Carolina Press, 2015.

Johnson, Ronald Angelo. *Diplomacy in Black and White: John Adams, Toussaint Louverture, and Their Atlantic World Alliance.* Athens: University of Georgia Press, 2014.

Kaisary, Philip. *The Haitian Revolution in the Literary Imagination: Radical Horizons, Conservative Constraints.* Charlottesville: University of Virginia Press, 2014.

Logan, Rayford Whittingham. *The Diplomatic Relations of the United States with Haiti, 1776–1891.* Chapel Hill: University of North Carolina Press, 1941.

Matthewson, Tim. *A Proslavery Foreign Policy: Haitian-American Relations during the Early Republic.* Westport, CT: Praeger, 2003.

Scott, Rebecca, and Jean Hébrard. *Freedom Papers: An Atlantic Odyssey in the Age of Emancipation.* Cambridge, MA: Harvard University Press, 2012.

White, Ashli. *Encountering Revolution: Haiti and the Making of the Early Republic.* Baltimore, MD: Johns Hopkins University Press, 2010.

Julia Gaffield
Assistant Professor
Georgia State University

HARLEM RENAISSANCE/ NEW NEGRO MOVEMENT

The New Negro Movement, popularly known as the Harlem Renaissance, was an unprecedented outburst of African American cultural productivity that peaked in the 1920s and was an integral part of American and transatlantic modernism. The black intellectuals who were the driving force behind it viewed the realm of culture and artistic expression as the foundation for a reinvented black identity and community, and consequently as a path to political equality.

The Harlem Renaissance, far from being limited to the neighborhood that is part of its popular name, must be understood beyond the local or even national perspective. Internationally, one of the most important factors that helped bring about the movement was World War I (1914–1918). The outbreak of war and the resulting demand for workers—to replace those who had enlisted and to fill manufacturing jobs related to military production, especially with the war having the effect of reducing immigration from Europe—gave an additional stimulus to the Great Migration of southern African Americans to the North and thus contributed to the rise of black urban communities and cultural milieus. The black press, *The Crisis* in particular, devoted considerable attention to the war effort, and some leaders advocated black military service as a way to achieve racial emancipation. Eventually, 200,000 black soldiers were sent to France, and many earned high military honors. The triumphant homecoming parade of the 369th Infantry Regiment, popularly known as the Harlem Hellfighters, fostered a sense of pride and a militant stance that characterized what black socialist magazines later identified as the "New Negro." Thus the symbolic significance of the Great War differed markedly for black intellectuals and artists than for the writers of the so-called Lost Generation, such as Ernest Hemingway and F. Scott Fitzgerald. In a 1919 editorial in *The Crisis*, W. E. B. Du Bois (1868–1963) attempted to channel the military service of black soldiers into the struggle for equality at home, writing, "*We return from fighting. We return fighting*" (14).

Alain Locke (1885–1954), a writer, teacher, and literary theorist who became known as the "father" of the Harlem Renaissance, was the editor of *The New Negro*, a 1925 anthology of black and white writers. Locke compared the postwar position of African Americans to the contemporaneous national awakenings in Europe. He referred to "New Poland" and "New Czechoslovakia" as models for African American community, and other black critics pointed to "New Ireland," the prewar Irish literary renaissance. The writer and civil rights activist James Weldon Johnson (1871–1938), for example, claimed that the use of the vernacular tradition by the Irish playwright J. M. Synge (1871–1909) should serve as an inspiration for black poets. In the European awakenings, the New Negro intellectuals found an exemplar of the aesthetic search for artistic expression melded with the political struggle for emancipation. These national movements for cultural independence also recognized folk tradition as the source of modern art, which was analogous to the interest in black vernacular culture among New Negro artists.

Many members of the New Negro community traveled extensively or became expatriates, factors that lent the movement a transnational character. Among the older generation, many intellectuals were educated in Europe. Du Bois studied in Berlin and frequently traveled to England and France as a leader of the Pan-African movement. Locke studied for four years in Oxford, where he was a member of the Cosmopolitan Club. From Oxford he moved to Berlin, where he took an interest in contemporary youth and gay liberation organizations, whose ideas shaped his vision of the New Negro. Most of the younger artists—Langston Hughes (1902–1967), Jean Toomer (1894–1967), Gwendolyn Bennett (1902–1981), Jessie Fauset (1882–1961), Countee Cullen (1903–1946), and Nella Larsen (1891–1964)—also traveled widely in the 1920s and 1930s, and many studied in Europe or joined American expatriate communities. Transatlantic travels were even more instrumental in the careers of popular entertainers closely related to the New Negro group. The dancer and singer Josephine Baker (1906–1975) and the singer Paul Robeson (1898–1976) became more famous in London and Paris than in the United States.

TRAVELERS AND EXPATRIATES

Both black and white American modernist expatriates sought artistic inspiration as well as an escape from American preoccupation with fears of spreading communism (the Red Scare of the late teens and early twenties), the race riots of the Red Summer (1919), and the Scopes trial (1925), concerning the teaching of evolution in the schools. For African Americans, Europe additionally was a place where racial discrimination had been less oppressive and interracial relations less policed than in America. Many New Negro writers, including Larsen, Fauset, Bennett, Hughes, and Claude McKay (1889–1948), explored this difference and set their works in the European context.

Among the European destinations of African Americans, Paris was especially significant because it fostered the connection with black people from the French colonies. The presence of New Negro artists in the city greatly affected the Francophone Négritude movement, which opposed French colonial rule and its politics of forced assimilation. Several Harlem Renaissance writers, such as Hughes and Walter White (1893–1955), published their works in *Revue du Monde Noir*, a magazine of the movement. The single most important African American text that played a role in the Négritude movement, however, was McKay's *Banjo* (1929), which was immediately translated into French. The novel, set on the docks of Marseilles, depicts the black community of sailors and jazz musicians, celebrating the cultural energy of the African diaspora as an antidote to the sterility of Western civilization. McKay was celebrated as the father of Négritude aesthetics. In contrast, the work received somewhat less attention from American readers and literary critics.

Whereas many African Americans joined the expatriate community in Europe, Hughes and Zora Neale Hurston (1891–1960) also traveled to the Caribbean, and both wrote about their experiences. The Caribbean influence on the New Negro movement was even more powerfully exerted, however, by the wave of immigration from the West Indies in the 1920s. Two leading writers of the renaissance, McKay and Eric Walrond (1898–1966), came from Jamaica and from Guyana by way of Barbados, respectively, and their writings offer a fresh perspective on American race relations. Both eventually left New York to live in London. Before moving to Europe, however, Walrond worked with another famous Caribbean immigrant, the father of the Back to Africa movement, Marcus Garvey (1887–1940). Although Garvey's black nationalism was at odds with the New Negro platform, the pageantry of his Universal Negro Improvement Association (UNIA) deeply affected the Harlem milieu of the 1920s. Intellectuals from the Caribbean tended to be more militant and socialist in their outlooks, and thus, apart from contributing to the demographic diversity of the black community in the United States, they radicalized the politics and aesthetics of the New Negro.

MODERNISM AND POLITICS

New Negro writers and artists were at the nexus of transnational migrations that profoundly influenced modernist aesthetics, but the movement had a complex relationship to modernist experimentation. Avant-garde innovations frequently took the form of primitivism, fueled by contemporary interest in non-Western cultures. European fascination with Africa in particular was eagerly taken up by many black artists and intellectuals. Locke, in one of his *New Negro* essays, listed a catalog of French and German modernists who were inspired by African art, and he advocated an analogous synthesis of primitivism and innovation in black literature and art. African themes and inspirations were visible in numerous literary works (e.g., Toomer's *Cane*, Hughes's "Danse Africaine," Richard Bruce Nugent's [1906–1987] "Sahdji," Cullen's "Heritage") and in works of visual art (Nugent, Aaron Douglas [1898–1979], Lois Mailou Jones [1905–1998], Meta Warrick Fuller [1877–1968]). Yet identification with "primitive" African cultures, especially in more popular and sensational forms and in texts set in contemporary America rather than imaginary Africa, bred anxiety among many black critics, who saw such images as a perpetuation of stereotypes that pandered to white fantasies. Thus African American explorations of non-Western idioms were rippled with the tension between modernist innovation, which used those idioms as a source of cultural renewal, and primitivism, which stigmatized the black community as savage and exotic.

Although the initial optimism of the movement was already questioned by the younger generation in the mid-twenties, and its progressive politics were generally regarded as misguided after the Great Depression and the Harlem riot of 1935, the Harlem Renaissance still constitutes one of the most momentous events in American cultural history. Contrary to the idea that the movement depended on fads and fleeting tastes and inevitably ended with the cessation of white sponsorship, many artists continued their activity in the 1930s within the Federal Writers' Project, part of the Works Progress Administration. In the 1960s, the rise of black studies in academia brought new audiences to the works of the New Negro movement. In the 1970s and 1980s, particularly with the publication of Alice Walker's *In Search of Our Mothers' Gardens* (1983), much attention was paid to the women writers of the movement and to the movement's masculinist politics. Later scholars have examined same-sex themes in the works of Nugent, McKay, Cullen, Locke, Hughes, and Wallace Thurman (1902–1934). These themes were also represented and explored in two films, Isaac Julien's *Looking for Langston* (1989) and Rodney Evans's *Brother to Brother* (2004).

SEE ALSO *Ali, Muhammad; Black Power Movement; Great Depression; King, Martin Luther, Jr.; Lost Generation; Malcolm X; Universal Negro Improvement Association (UNIA); World War I*

BIBLIOGRAPHY

Du Bois, W. E. B. "Returning Soldiers." *The Crisis* 18 (May 1919): 13–14.

Edwards, Brent Hayes. *The Practice of Diaspora: Literature, Translation, and the Rise of Black Internationalism.* Cambridge, MA: Harvard University Press, 2003.

Fabre, Michel. *From Harlem to Paris: Black American Writers in France, 1840–1980.* Urbana: University of Illinois Press, 1991.

Gilroy, Paul. *The Black Atlantic: Modernity and Double Consciousness.* Cambridge, MA: Harvard University Press, 1994.

Hutchinson, George. *The Harlem Renaissance in Black and White.* Cambridge, MA: Belknap Press of Harvard University Press, 1995.

Johnson, James Weldon, ed. *The Book of American Negro Poetry.* New York: Harcourt, Brace, 1922.

Lemke, Sieglinde. *Primitivist Modernism: Black Culture and the Origins of Transatlantic Modernism.* Oxford and New York: Oxford University Press, 1998.

Locke, Alain, ed. *The New Negro: An Interpretation.* New York: Albert and Charles Boni, 1925.

North, Michael. *The Dialect of Modernism: Race, Language, and Twentieth-Century Literature.* New York: Oxford University Press, 1994.

Schwarz, A. B. Christa. *Gay Voices of the Harlem Renaissance.* Bloomington: Indiana University Press, 2003.

Stovall, Tyler Edward. *Paris Noir: African Americans in the City of Light.* Boston: Houghton Mifflin, 1996.

Anna Pochmara
Assistant Professor, Institute of English Studies
University of Warsaw

HAWAI'I

Hawai'i's contact with Europe and the Americas is relatively short when compared with the rest of the Pacific. Western cultural and economic imperialism in Hawai'i began when James Cook (1728–1779) arrived on January 8, 1778. A captain in the British navy, Cook engaged in three expeditions to the Pacific, where he gained fame as an explorer, navigator, and cartographer. Early British explorers like Cook and his compatriot George Vancouver (1757–1798) sought to discover, name, and classify all that inhabited the Pacific. Cook and his crew were the first Europeans to encounter Native Hawaiians and their islands, which he named the Sandwich Islands. While Cook gained recognition for this discovery, his 1779 death at the hands of Hawaiians at Kealakekua Bay fueled his celebrity.

THE ISLANDS' ROLE IN EARLY GLOBAL TRADE

By the mid-1780s, Hawai'i became a regular stopping point for Europeans, Americans, Russians, and other foreigners involved in a global trade that included Europe, New England, the eastern Pacific from Alaska to Tierra del Fuego, the Sandwich Islands, and Canton, China. Western traders and sailors hunted marine mammals, such as sea otters and fur seals—and later whales—which they eventually sold to wealthy customers. Hawai'i proved to be the perfect place to obtain fresh food and water on the way to China from the American coast, and trade continued to increase during the first half of the nineteenth century.

By the 1790s, a small number of foreign merchants and deserters had created an expatriate community in the Sandwich Islands. There they competed with Hawaiians to provision the foreign ships from the American coast. They also vied with each other to sell Western manufactured goods, such as weapons, alcohol, silk, furniture, and even sailing ships to Kamehameha I (d. 1819) and the Hawaiian chiefs, known as *ali'i.* The chiefs were aided in their trade relations with the outsiders by

OBOOKIAH

Obookiah is the anglicized pronunciation of the name of Henry 'Ōpūkaha'ia (c. 1787–1818), the first Hawaiian immigrant to rise to nationwide prominence in the United States. His remarkable life and early death led to the founding of the Foreign Mission School at Cornwall, Connecticut, and over forty years of intense mission activity in Hawai'i.

'Ōpūkaha'ia was born in the Ka'ū district of Hawai'i Island during the wars of conquest of Kamehameha the Great (d. 1819). His parents were executed during Nāmakehā's rebellion against Kamehameha's rule (c. 1798). After serving several years as a priest of the god Lono in *heiau* (temples) near Kealakekua, he and future missionary Thomas Hopu (or Hopoo, b. 1795) gained passage to New England, where a probably apocryphal tradition described 'Ōpūkaha'ia as weeping at the steps of Yale College for the reason "that nobody give me learning" (*An Account of Five Youths* 1816, 9).

Henry, as he came to be known, lived with a series of prominent Congregationalist ministers under whose tutelage he soon showed himself a promising scholar and a powerful advocate of devotion to Christ and the conversion of those who lived where "the words of the Savior never yet had been" (Demos 2014, 27). Following his baptism and admission to church membership, he frequently expressed his hope to return to Hawai'i to proclaim the gospel, calling upon his fellow Christians, who lived in a "gospel land," to abandon their complacency and renew their devotion.

A popular speaker, 'Ōpūkaha'ia left a powerful impression throughout New England. As a dark-skinned convert born in a "heathen" land, he was a living contradiction to the widespread stereotype that such "heathens" were not like whites and that they could not be saved, much less civilized or educated. His fervor and personal charisma often left his audience ashamed of such comfortable assumptions and led to much soul-searching and a new dedication to foreign missions.

Although 'Ōpūkaha'ia's words had stirred many New Englanders to the cause of foreign missions, especially the beginnings of the Sandwich Islands Mission, it was his death, termed by some a martyrdom, that caught the attention of the evangelical world. Stricken with typhus in January 1818, he faced his end with dignity, patience, and courage. His passing in February was deemed a cause of rejoicing rather than tragedy because, as some who attended his funeral had noted, it showed that "he came here to teach Christians how to die" (Caldwell 1818, 53). Following his death, his story became even more widely known through *The Memoirs of Obookiah,* prepared by his friend and one-time tutor, Edwin Dwight. It was a best seller in America and elsewhere and was soon translated into the language of Hawai'i, where 'Ōpūkaha'ia remains, even today, a well-known figure.

The year following his death (1819) saw the departure for Hawai'i of the first missionaries under the auspices of the American Board of Commissioners for Foreign Missions (ABCFM), an endeavor that soon resulted in the adoption of 'Ōpūkaha'ia's faith throughout the Hawaiian Kingdom. This was the beginning of Hawai'i's intimate relationship with the United States, a connection that eventually resulted in the annexation of the kingdom by the American government (1898), a union opposed by nearly every native-born Hawaiian citizen (Silva 2004).

BIBLIOGRAPHY

Anonymous. *An Account of Five Youths from the Sandwich Islands Now Receiving an Education in This Country.* New York: J. Seymour, 1816.

Caldwell, John Edwards, ed. "Death of Obookiah: Extract of Letter from a Lady in Connecticut to Her Friend in Boston, Dated February 21st." *The Christian Herld* 5, 2 (April 1818): 53–54.

Demos, John. *The Heathen School: A Story of Hope and Betrayal in the Age of the Early Republic.* New York: Vintage Books, 2014.

Dwight, Edwin W. *Memoirs of Henry Obookiah: A Native of Owhyhee and a Member of the Foreign Mission School Who Died at Cornwall, Conn., Feb. 17, 1818, Aged 26 Years.* New Haven, CT: Religious Intelligencer, 1818.

Dwight, Edwin W. *Ka Moolelo o Heneri Opukahaia, ua hanau ma Hawaii M.H. 1787 a make ma Amerika, Feberuari 17, 1818. Oia ka Hua Mua o Hawaii nei.* New York: American Tract Society, 1867. [*The Story of Henry 'Ōpūkaha'ia, Born in Hawai'i in 1787, Died in America, February 17, 1818. The First Fruits of Hawai'i.*] This is a Hawaiian translation and adaptation of Dwight's *Memoirs of Henry Obookiah,* including corrections and with new information collected at Kealakekua, Hawai'i by Rev. J. W. Papaula.

Silva, Noenoe K. *Aloha Betrayed: Native Hawaiian Resistance to American Colonialism.* Durham, NC: Duke University Press, 2004.

Jeffrey Lyon
Department of Religion
University of Hawai'i at Mānoa

two British sailors—Isaac Davis (c. 1758–1810) and John Young (c. 1742–1835)—who eventually were made *ali'i* by Kamehameha. These men helped Kamehameha unite the islands under his authority by 1810. Later, in 1815, the Russian American Company signed a "treaty" with the high chief Kaumuali'i (c. 1778–1824) of Kaua'i, and they eventually built three small forts on the island. Prior to 1820, the British remained the most powerful group of foreigners in the islands.

THE ARRIVAL OF AMERICAN MISSIONARIES

In 1820, American missionaries—sponsored by the Massachusetts-based American Board of Commissioners for Foreign Missions—landed in the Sandwich Islands. Influenced by the Second Great Awakening, they sought to convert the world, including Native Hawaiians, to their brand of evangelical Christianity. Although initially reluctant to allow them residence, eventually Liholiho (c. 1797–1824)—Kamehameha's son and successor—gave the missionaries permission to stay. Less than a year before their arrival, Liholiho and two female high chiefs had been instrumental in overturning the taboo system that had structured all aspects of Hawaiian life for generations. Now, the American missionaries stepped into this void, which led to conflict with the resident foreign community and other Hawaiians for decades to come.

The arrival of the American mission offered the Hawaiian chiefs and commoners a second competing vision of Western "civilization." The European and American merchants who lived in or visited the islands presented the Hawaiians with a hedonistic lifestyle; when not involved in trade, they spent most of their time drinking, gambling, and sleeping with the Hawaiians. As an alternative, the American evangelists proposed a religious life that avoided almost all pleasures and focused instead on church and prayer meetings and the adoption of American material culture, especially clothing. If this was all that the missionaries offered, they might not have been so successful. However, from the start they also gave the gift of learning, eventually organizing schools across the islands and teaching both the chiefs and commoners to read and write in Hawaiian. Liholiho's coruler, the Queen Regent Ka'ahumanu (c. 1768–1832), quickly understood the value of education in advancing her position in the world and her power within the Sandwich Islands. By the end of the 1820s, Ka'ahumanu and a significant number of high chiefs converted to Christianity and urged the commoners to do the same.

The conversion of Ka'ahumanu and her chiefly allies to Christianity caused conflict with the *ali'i* who did not convert, as well as with the resident foreign community. The foreign merchants and sailors wanted to continue their hedonistic lifestyle, and Liholiho and a number of chiefs joined them, as they had similar sentiments. At the same time, the missionaries and their chiefly allies endeavored to introduce laws based on the Ten Commandments. In the 1820s and 1830s, conflicts over religion and trade led the British, American, and French navies to come to the islands to settle disputes between the *ali'i* and the resident foreigners. In 1839, a French frigate under the command of Captain Cyrille P. T. Laplace (1793–1875) threatened to fire on the community of Honolulu unless the chiefs paid a bond of $20,000, permitted the import of French wines, and tolerated religious freedom for Catholics. The Hawaiians gave in to this gunboat diplomacy because they were incapable of repelling the French ship.

THE CONSTITUTION OF 1840

The dispute with the French, as well as with foreigners from Britain and the United States, threatened the sovereignty of the chiefs. By 1840, they felt compelled to change their government in order to stave off foreign imperialists. With the help of former members of the American mission and a few other foreigners, Kamehameha III (1813–1854) promulgated a constitution for the Hawaiian kingdom. Establishing a constitutional monarchy, it divided the government into executive, legislative, and judicial branches. In 1848, Kamehameha III agreed to the Great Māhele, legislation that divided Hawaiian lands into thirds, one each for the crown, chiefs, and commoners. Eventually foreigners bought or leased the majority of the land meant for the commoners. By the end of the century, commoners owned less than 1 percent of the land.

The constitution of 1840 was meant to confirm the power of the chiefs and stave off Western attacks on Hawaiian sovereignty. Instead, because the *ali'i* relied on foreign advisors to explain this new Western-style government, the chiefs found themselves increasingly cut out of the government. As foreign men gained prominence in the government, many of the same men grew economically powerful as they passed legislation that promoted the growth of sugar plantations. This legislation benefitted the growing Caucasian population while cutting Hawaiian commoners off from their traditional access to land and resources. At the same time, it created an underclass of Asian plantation workers, as sugar planters searched continuously for cheap sources of labor.

OVERTHROW OF THE MONARCHY AND US ANNEXATION

On June 30, 1887, a group of Americans calling themselves the Hawaiian League forced King Kalākaua (1836–1891) to replace his cabinet of ministers with a cabinet made up of league members. In previous months, the Hawaiian League had bought a large cache of arms from San Francisco. Soon, they threatened to assassinate Kalākaua unless he agreed to sign a new constitution. Known as the Bayonet Constitution, this new document stripped the Hawaiian monarchy of much of its power, putting it instead in the hands of Americans, Europeans, and a minority of the Hawaiian elite in the cabinet and legislature. It also changed the voting requirements, allowing foreign residents who had not been naturalized to vote. Additionally, it denied Asians the right to vote and established strict property requirements for Caucasian and Hawaiian men. These requirements excluded the majority of Hawaiian commoners from voting.

When Queen Lili'uokalani (1838–1917) came to the throne in 1891, she sought to promulgate a new constitution, returning power to the monarchy and voting rights to the majority of poor Hawaiians and Asians. American and European businessmen already felt anxious about the end of the 1875 Reciprocity Treaty that allowed them to sell sugar freely to the United States. Now, this anxiety, combined with the queen's intended new constitution, caused them to form a Committee of Safety to overthrow the queen and seek annexation to the United States. On January 16, 1893, 162 American marines and sailors from the USS *Boston* came ashore, ostensibly to protect the peace. The next day, the Committee of Safety forced Lili'uokalani, who feared the bloodshed of her people, to step down from the throne. In a statement, the queen gave temporary control of the government to the United States rather than the provisional government of American and European businessmen. Although the investigator sent by the United States ruled in the *Blount*

Ceremony marking the annexation of the Hawaiian islands as a US territory, Honolulu, August 1898. *Revolutionaries hoping for annexation by the United States after the abdication of the queen had to wait until President William McKinley, who favored the plan, succeeded the anti-imperialist Grover Cleveland.* PAN PACIFIC PRESS/HISTORICAL/CORBIS

Report that the overthrow of the Hawaiian monarchy was illegal and that the queen should be returned to the throne, the provisional government refused to comply. Instead, they proclaimed the Republic of Hawaii on July 4, 1894, and missionary son Sanford B. Dole (1844–1926) served as its first president. After counterinsurgents endeavored to restore the monarchy in 1895, Lili'uokalani was arrested, and she lived under house arrest until her pardon in 1896. It was during this period that the queen officially abdicated the throne.

While the revolutionaries hoped for immediate annexation to the United States, it took longer than they expected. The American president, Grover Cleveland (1837–1908), was an anti-imperialist who did not favor annexation. It was not until William McKinley (1843–1901) became president in 1897 that Hawai'i became an American territory. On July 4, 1898, Congress passed the Newlands Resolution, making Hawai'i part of the United States. Embroiled in the Spanish-American War, both McKinley and Congress understood the strategic importance of Hawai'i. Both Congress and Caucasians in Hawai'i worried about having a territory with a governing body elected by a nonwhite majority. Nonetheless, in 1900 Congress passed the Hawaiian Organic Act. This act established a popularly elected bicameral legislature and a territorial governor appointed by the president of the United States, as well as a supreme court. Once again, Hawaiian men could vote in local elections.

WORLD WAR II AND STATEHOOD

Until World War II, Hawai'i remained marginal to the United States. In the first decades of the twentieth century, the United States built up military bases in the territory and fortified the entire coastline of O'ahu with gun batteries. At the same time, entrepreneurs began to develop Hawai'i's tourist industry, and sugar and pineapple production boomed. Hawai'i's status as a sleepy backwater changed with the Japanese attack on Pearl Harbor on December 7, 1941. On that day, the Japanese killed or wounded 3,581 Americans and devastated the United States' Pacific battle fleet. At the same time, the Japanese brought the Hawaiian Islands to the center of American popular consciousness. Hawai'i may have been far away, but the Japanese attack occurred on American territory and American people.

After the attack on Pearl Harbor, the territorial governor, Joseph B. Poindexter (1869–1951), declared martial law, suspended habeas corpus, created the Hawaii Territorial Guard to protect the islands, and gave control of the government to Commanding General Walter Short (1880–1949) of the US Army. Within forty-eight hours of the attack, several hundred male leaders of the Japanese community were arrested. Eventually, nearly two thousand Japanese and Japanese Americans in Hawai'i were sent to internment camps on the mainland of the United States. This amounted to less than 1 percent of the Japanese inhabitants of the islands. Some of these same men later served in the 442nd Regiment Combat Team that gained fame and honor while fighting in Europe. Hawai'i also hosted hundreds of thousands of servicemen during the war. After the war, these same men remembered their time in the islands fondly, which benefitted Hawai'i's growing postwar tourist industry.

On August 21, 1959, Hawai'i became the fiftieth state. Some people in Hawai'i had been lobbying for statehood since the beginning of the century. However, many Native Hawaiians objected to statehood because they desired Hawaiian independence, while members of both houses of Congress objected to admitting a state that had so many nonwhite voters. Undoubtedly, the islands' importance to the Pacific War in World War II and the positive views of so many servicemen helped the movement for statehood gain support on the US mainland. With the approval of Congress and President Dwight D. Eisenhower's (1890–1969) signature, Hawai'i joined the Union.

SEE ALSO *Foreign Mission Movement; Foreign Mission School (Cornwall, CT); Pacific Islands; Pacific Ocean*

BIBLIOGRAPHY

Bingham, Hiram. *A Residence of Twenty-One Years in the Sandwich Islands, or, The Civil, Religious, and Political History of Those Islands.* New York: Praeger, 1969. First published 1847.

Daws, Gavan. *Shoal of Time: A History of the Hawaiian Islands.* Honolulu: University of Hawai'i Press, 1968.

Grimshaw, Patricia. *Paths of Duty: American Missionary Wives in Nineteenth-Century Hawaii.* Honolulu: University of Hawai'i Press, 1989.

Igler, David. *The Great Ocean: Pacific Worlds from Captain Cook to the Gold Rush.* New York: Oxford University Press, 2013.

Kame'eleihiwa, Lilikalā. *Native Land and Foreign Desires: Pehea Lā E Pono Ai? How Shall We Live in Harmony?* Honolulu: University of Hawai'i Press, 1992.

Kirch, Patrick. *A Shark Going Inland Is My Chief: The Island Civilization of Ancient Hawai'i.* Berkeley: University of California Press, 2012.

Love, Eric T. L. *Race over Empire: Racism and U.S. Imperialism, 1865–1900.* Chapel Hill: University of North Carolina Press, 2004.

MacLennan, Carol A. *Sovereign Sugar: Industry and Environment in Hawai'i.* Honolulu: University of Hawai'i Press, 2014.

Sahlins, Marshall. *Islands of History.* Chicago: University of Chicago Press, 1985.

Sahlins, Marshall. *Anahulu: The Anthropology of History in the Kingdom of Hawaii*, Vol. 1: *Historical Ethnography*. Chicago: University of Chicago Press, 1992.

Thigpen, Jennifer. *Island Queens and Mission Wives: How Gender and Empire Remade Hawai'i's Pacific World*. Chapel Hill: University of North Carolina Press, 2014.

Jennifer Fish Kashay
Associate Professor of History
Colorado State University

HAYMARKET BOMBING

In Chicago in May 1886, during the general strike for an eight-hour workday, a group of anarchists held a protest meeting in Haymarket Square. As nearly two hundred police officers surrounded protesters and ordered the crowd to disperse, someone threw a bomb toward the police officers. Five officers were immediately killed. Ordering further dispersal, police shot indiscriminately into the crowd, and some protesters shot back. Two more police officers and at least three civilians were killed. Within the year, seven Chicago labor leaders, both directly and indirectly involved in the general strike and anarchist meetings, were sentenced to death for inciting violence and treason within the state of Illinois. One was sentenced to fifteen years in prison. The bombing was the culmination of trans-Atlantic socialist and anarchist discussions on strategies for securing tangible change for working people. Its effect was to further provoke anti-immigrant, and particularly antisocialist, sentiment in the United States.

At the time of the bombing, Chicago's working class was home to a number of different strands of socialist thinking. Through much of the 1870s, the Socialist Labor Party had contained both English-language and foreign-language sections, of which particular chapters convened and voted on their own. By far the largest percentage of foreign-born immigrants in Chicago were German-speaking; many of these immigrants operated groceries or gymnasiums or published newspapers with editorial staff drawn directly from Germany. One historian describes Chicago during that period as the "fifth largest German city in the world" (Messer-Kruse 2012, 44). During the early 1870s, a majority of members of both the English-language and German-language sections supported socialist candidates for all levels of office and the democratic electoral process. Yet although the diasporic German peoples were initially hopeful that the election of socialists to local and national levels in both Germany and the United States would have the gradual effect of creating a social-democratic republic, they lost hope in this strategy in both places throughout the 1870s and 1880s. According to the revolutionary socialist theory of the German political philosopher Karl Marx (1818–1883), revolution depended on the maturity of capitalism and the "self-consciousness" of the working classes, but many immigrant radicals, particularly those from less industrialized areas of the world—including Russia, Italy, and Spain—were discouraged by what they saw as impractical preconditions.

To add to the discontent with this perceived gradualism, in the 1870s German socialists, both in Germany and the United States, became frustrated with the suppression of elected socialists, which German chancellor Otto von Bismarck (1815–1898) achieved through parliamentary-approved legislation. The moment gave rise to activists like the Russian anarchist Mikhail Bakunin (1814–1876), who articulated a clear alternative to the internationally connected workingmen's organization, led from the top, that Marx envisioned. Bakunin wrote of a widely held "socialist instinct" among the poor that hastened imminent revolt. In his estimation, the mass of working people, "because of its social position…is more truly socialist than all the scientific and bourgeois socialists combined" (Messer-Kruse 2012, 33). Bakunin sought the creation of small, secret cells that could expose the hypocrisy of the existing order with sudden eruptions of incendiary violence.

By 1881, this subset of socialists began to meet internationally. At the London Congress of the International Working People's Association (IWPA), European American anarchists affirmed the principles of their "Black International." Edward Nathan-Ganz, a naturalized American citizen whose origins are unclear but who claimed Budapest as his birthplace, represented the United States at the Congress and published his reflections widely. He called for a secret anarchist school where workers could learn chemistry for weapons production. A few months later, American anarchists organized a Chicago Congress, at which two of the future leaders of the Haymarket bombing, August Spies (1855–1887) and Albert Parsons (1848–1887), were in attendance. Spies and Parsons returned to the German section of the SLP with a new confidence in completely rejecting electoral politics and legislative gradualism. Other American anarchist writers, such as Johann Most (1846–1906), published numerous articles on the value of dynamite, both literally and philosophically, in sparking change. In their 1883 Pittsburgh Congress, "revolutionary socialists," as they called themselves, vowed to "attack jointly and with force our common enemy, the capitalists" and urged workers to arm themselves (Messer-Kruse 2012, 95).

International anarchist networks were no secret. By advertising their ideas, they made themselves a target for legislators and civic leaders who were suspicious of socialists, especially southern and eastern European immigrants, as a threat to American institutions. Both the Catholic church and American Protestant churches widely denounced socialism as a threat to Christianity in the 1890s and beyond. Remaining members of the Socialist Labor Party worked harder to defend socialism as a legitimate set of principles, but they fought a losing battle even as they distanced themselves from radicals. In the public mind, the Haymarket bombing created associations between socialism and violence, nihilism, immigration, and iconoclasm, and contributed directly to the conservative political administrations of the 1890s.

SEE ALSO *1848 Revolutions; Nativism*

BIBLIOGRAPHY

Green, James. *Death in the Haymarket: A Story of Chicago, the First Labor Movement, and the Bombing that Divided Gilded Age America.* New York: Pantheon, 2006.

Marcantonio, Vito. "Labor's Martyrs: Haymarket 1887, Sacco and Vanzetti 1927." New York: Workers Library, 1937.

Messer-Kruse, Timothy. *The Haymarket Conspiracy: Transatlantic Anarchist Networks.* Urbana: University of Illinois Press, 2012.

Janine Giordano Drake
Assistant Professor of History
University of Great Falls

HEARST, WILLIAM RANDOLPH

SEE *Yellow Journalism.*

HEMINGWAY, ERNEST

SEE *Lost Generation.*

HERITAGE FOUNDATION

SEE *Think Tanks.*

HERZEL, THEODOR

SEE *Zionism.*

HINDUISM

"Hinduism" emerged through a process of encounter, influence, and exchange between Britain and India that began in the colonial period of the eighteenth century. Richard King, a historian of Asian religions, has argued that it is an anachronism to project "Hinduism" back into the precolonial history of India: "before the unification begun under imperial rule and consolidated by the Independence of 1947, it makes no sense to talk of an Indian 'nation,' nor of a religion called 'Hinduism' that might be taken to represent the belief system of the Hindu people" (1999, 107). The "Hinduism" found around the world today emerged from the colonial period as an agonistic category constructed by conflict, coercion, and collusion between Europeans and South Asians.

Hinduism, then, is a "bringing together of beliefs, rites, and practices consciously selected from the past" (Thapar 1989, 56). These selections range from Sanskrit sacred texts, myths that include a pantheon of gods, and monotheistic sects to ritual temple worship, meditation, yoga, medicine, and ordering of the society. Individuals who identify as Hindu might worship at a temple to a god or goddess. They might think about how the idea of *dharma*, or cosmic duty, shapes their lives. They might practice meditation or yoga. They might study the Bhagavad Gita, a text in which the god Krishna teaches his friend Arujuna about *dharma.* They might believe in reincarnation and *karma*, or the law of cosmic action. They might attend a lecture at the Vedanta Society. They might believe in God or they might believe in gods. Like all religious identities, the label Hindu carries little weight. The real question is, what kind of Hindu?

The fraught history of the term Hinduism has major implications for understanding the relationship between Hinduism and America. The history of that relationship hinges on the emergence of Hinduism as a term in American culture. American awareness of Hinduism increased in the late nineteenth century, most notably with Swami Vivekananda's speech titled "Hinduism" at the 1893 World's Parliament of Religion in Chicago. Thus there is a period of American encounters with religion in India before "Hinduism" and a period afterward, when Americans began to use the term Hinduism to describe the religion of India. Before Americans used that term, they used "Hindoo religion," "the religion of the Hindoos," "Brahmanism," and "heathenism" to describe religion in India. These shifts in terms and spellings are not insignificant. They each mark a different construction of religion in India by different Americans.

NINETEENTH-CENTURY REPRESENTATIONS

The earliest American encounters with religion in India came through trade. In the late eighteenth century, New England merchants began a lucrative trade with India and China. In 1807 imports from India to America tallied over $4 million (Bhagat 1970, 138). A group of these mariners in Salem, Massachusetts, founded the East India

Marine Society (EIMS) to support voyages and merchants that went beyond the Cape of Good Hope and into Asian waters. These mariners brought back a variety of objects from India including painted clay statues of Rama and Sita, the divine couple from the Sanskrit epic the Ramayana, and a stone hand broken from a granite statue inside the cave temple of Elephanta near present-day Mumbai. They kept all of these items in their "cabinet of curiosities" in the Marine Society Hall of Salem. They did not describe these items as Hindu or as part of "Hinduism" but rather as representing a more general exotic "Orient." In an 1821 publication by the EIMS, the description of two clay statues of the god and goddess Rama and Sita read simply, "a group of idols worshipped in Bengal." For these merchants, India was a land of idols, not Hinduism.

The majority of Americans who encountered India in the nineteenth century did so through print, not trade, with America, Great Britain, and India forming an Anglophone triangle that spread a variety of representations of Indian culture and religion. As Americans learned more about India, they began to construct representations of what they called "Hindoo religion" or "the religion of the Hindoos." For example, Hannah Adams (1755–1831), in her 1817 *Dictionary of All Religions and Religious Denominations: Jewish, Heathen, Mahometan, Christian, Ancient, and Modern*, included an entry on "Hindoos" in which she attempted to dispassionately describe the beliefs of the "Hindoo system." Like the theologian Joseph Priestley (1733–1804), who in 1799 published *A Comparison of the Institutions of Moses with Those of the Hindoos and Other Ancient Nations*, Adams relied on British sources that she found in American libraries and bookshops. There was a divide in Adams's description between a pure theological religion of ancient India and a polluted popular religion of contemporary India. For example, she described the ancient Sanskrit texts, the belief in reincarnation, and the belief in a "Supreme Being" and the gods Vishnu, Shiva, and Brahma. These were the "originally pure" aspects of ancient Hindoo religion, according to Adams. But she also described contemporary religious practices in India as "oblations most costly, and sacrifices the most sanguinary" and *sati*, or widow immolation, "a voluntary sacrifice of too singular and shocking a nature to pass unnoticed" (Adams 1992, 110–111). Thus for Adams, Hindoo religion began as a pure system of religion in ancient times that had declined to a religion of idolatry and shocking ritual.

The divide between positive representations of ancient Hindoo religion based on Sanskrit texts and negative representations of contemporary Hindoo religion based on popular practices persisted throughout the nineteenth century. When the American Board of Commissioners for Foreign Missions (ABCFM) sent the first American missionaries to India in 1812, these missionaries sent back reports that characterized Hindoo religion as one of bloody rituals, erotic imagery, and noise. In their reports, missionaries described animal sacrifices, *sati*, "lewd dancing" at festivals, and the worship of "idols." Such representations grew in popularity as more Americans traveled to India and more British reports from India reached the United States. By the mid-nineteenth century, the image of the "Hindoo fakir," or holy man, spread out on a bed of nails or engaged in some form of "superstitious" self-torture became widespread in American print culture.

While these images of contemporary ritual and practice circulated, another set of representations imagined India as a land of religious wisdom and contemplation. This began in the 1820s when religious liberal Unitarians encountered the Vedanta philosophy of Rammohun Roy (c. 1772–1833), an Indian religious and social reformer. Roy believed the ancient Vedic Sanskrit texts taught the existence of a united monotheistic Godhead. He was also critical of contemporary religious practice involving "idols." Unitarians in New England lauded Roy as a "Unitarian Hindoo," and some even called him a Christian. Following Roy, other religious liberals took an interest in Sanskrit texts such as the Vedas, Laws of Manu, and Bhagavad Gita. The Transcendentalist writers Ralph Waldo Emerson (1803–1882) and Henry David Thoreau (1817–1862) praised the contemplation and mysticism of the Hindoos as a needed balance to American materialism and activity. Eventually, liberal writers ranging from Lydia Maria Child (1802–1880) to James Freeman Clarke (1810–1888) described "Brahmanism" as the ancient religion of India drawn from the Sanskrit texts. Similarly, the founders of the Theosophical Society, Madame Helena Blavatsky (1831–1891) and Henry Steel Olcott (1832–1907), believed India to be the home of the ancient "wisdom religion." For these religious liberals, ancient Hindoo wisdom and mysticism could save America from the materialism and activity of the Industrial Revolution.

When Swami Vivekananda (1863–1902) arrived in Chicago in 1893 to represent "Hinduism," the term for what was now considered a world religion, at the World's Parliament of Religions he had to navigate between the positive image of ancient India and the negative view of contemporary India. Like Rammohun Roy before him, Vivekananda taught a Vedanta form of Hinduism and argued that the Sanskrit texts taught that Hinduism was a religion of a Supreme Being, universal in its scope, tolerant of religious difference, and consistent with current trends in science. For Christian critics that pointed to *sati*, Vivekananda responded by pointing to Christian witch burning. As Americans began to think of Asian religions in terms of "world religions" such as

Buddhism, Daoism, Confucianism, and Hinduism, Vivekananda codified the vision of what "Hinduism" would be in the American imagination.

TWENTIETH-CENTURY REPRESENTATIONS AND IMMIGRATION

Yet the negative representations of contemporary Hinduism as heathenism or idolatry continued into the twentieth century and took on a new racial dimension. When Punjabi Sikhs immigrated to the West Coast in the early twentieth century, they were quickly labeled "Hindoos" by white laborers competing for the same jobs. This led to the US Supreme Court case of *United States v. Bhagat Singh Thind* (261 U.S. 204 [1923]), in which the Court ruled that a "Hindoo" like Thind (who was actually Sikh) could not become a naturalized citizen because he was not "white" and could not be assimilated into white American culture. Then, in 1924, the government passed the Immigration Act of 1924 (the Johnson-Reed Act) effectively banning immigration to the United States from Asia, including India.

Despite the immigration exclusion of 1924, a few Indian Hindus and Americans interested in Hinduism managed to find an audience in the United States. In 1920 Swami Yogananda (1893–1952) brought his form of yoga, called Kriya Yoga, to the United States, began lecturing around the country in 1923, founded the Self-Realization Fellowship in 1925, and lived in the United States until his death. Meanwhile, Jiddu Krishnamurti (1895–1986), an Indian who grew up among the Theosophical Society, taught "mindless awareness" and meditation beginning in the 1930s. Beginning in 1903, the Anglo-American William Walter Atkinson published a series of books on yoga under the pseudonym Yogi Ramacharka. The popularity of yoga and Vedanta in America during the early twentieth century is signaled in the title of Wendell Thomas's 1930 book *Hinduism Invades America*. This popularity continued into the 1950s and 1960s as Vedic philosophy and yogic practice filtered into the American counterculture.

In 1965 the US Congress reformed immigration law and allowed immigrants from South Asia into the United States. These immigrants were mostly skilled technical or medical workers who would contribute to the United States' technological growth during the Cold War. But they brought their Hinduism with them, introducing into the United States a new variety of Hindu practices, beliefs, traditions, and stories.

Vasudha Narayanan (2012) has proposed a five-fold taxonomy to account for the variety of post-1965 Hinduism in America: First, "domestic/informal groups" meet to sing devotional songs, recite prayers, or share devotion to the same Indian guru or teacher. These groups are most common in the South Asia diaspora community. Second, "global organizations" have branches in the United States such as Vedanta centers, the International Society for Krishna Conciousness (ISKCON), and the Brahma Kumaris. Third, temples either organized by a local community or built by international temple-building societies function as both religious and cultural centers in America. Fourth, many immigrant Hindus and second-generation Hindu Americans turn to online communities. Finally, "quasi-religious-cultural groups" blend religious content with performances of dance or music.

TWENTY-FIRST CENTURY

While all of these forms of Hinduism continue to grow among immigrants and their children, nonimmigrant Americans continue to turn to Hinduism for religious practices, texts, and beliefs. Yoga and meditation have become cultural mainstays in America, and, like religious liberals before them, "spiritual but not religious" Americans continue to look to India for ancient wisdom and spirituality. This interest in Hinduism by non-Hindus has prompted reactions from the Indian American community, such as the Hindu American Foundation's (HAF) "Take Back Yoga" campaign to educate Americans about yoga as an ancient practice "rooted in Hindu thought." From the early representations of "Hindoo religion" to the HAF campaign, what counts as "Hinduism" in America has been an ongoing contest over representation.

SEE ALSO *India; Vivekananda, Swami; World's Parliament of Religions (1893)*

BIBLIOGRAPHY

Adams, Hannah. *A Dictionary of All Religions and Religious Denominations: Jewish, Heathen, Mahometan, Christian, Ancient and Modern.* (1817.) Edited by Thomas A. Tweed. 4th ed. Atlanta: Scholars Press, 1992.

Altman, Michael Jordan. "Imagining Hindus: India and Religion in Nineteenth-Century America." PhD diss., Emory University, 2013.

Bhagat, G. *Americans in India, 1784–1860.* New York: New York University Press, 1970.

Coward, Harold G., John R. Hinnells, and Raymond Brady Williams, eds. *The South Asian Religious Diaspora in Britain, Canada, and the United States.* Albany: State University of New York Press, 2000.

Doniger, Wendy. "Hindus in America 1900–." In *The Hindus: An Alternative History*, 636–653. New York: Penguin, 2009.

Forsthoefel, Thomas A., and Cynthia Ann Humes, eds. *Gurus in America.* Albany: State University of New York Press, 2005.

Goldberg, Philip. *American Veda?: From Emerson and the Beatles to Yoga and Meditation.* New York: Harmony Books, 2010.

Jackson, Carl T. *Vedanta for the West: The Ramakrishna Movement in the United States.* Bloomington: Indiana University Press, 1994.

King, Richard. *Orientalism and Religion: Postcolonial Theory, India and "the Mystic East."* London and New York: Routledge, 1999.

Lindgren, James M. "'That Every Mariner May Possess the History of the World': A Cabinet for the East India Marine Society of Salem." *New England Quarterly* 68, 2 (1995): 179–205.

Mann, Gurinder Singh, Paul David Numrich, and Raymond Brady Williams. *Buddhists, Hindus, and Sikhs in America: A Short History.* New York: Oxford University Press, 2008.

Masuzawa, Tomoko. *The Invention of World Religions.* Chicago: University of Chicago Press, 2005.

Narayanan, Vasudha. "Creating the South Indian 'Hindu' Experience in the United States." In *The Life of Hinduism,* edited by John Stratton Hawley and Vasudha Narayanan, 231–248. Berkeley: University of California Press, 2006.

Narayanan, Vasudha. "Hinduism in America." In *Cambridge History of Religions in America,* Vol. 3: *1945 to the Present,* edited by Stephen J. Stein, 331–356. New York: Cambridge University Press, 2012.

Seager, Richard Hughes. *The World's Parliament of Religions: The East/West Encounter, Chicago, 1893.* Bloomington: Indiana University Press, 1995.

Syman, Stefanie. *The Subtle Body: The Story of Yoga in America.* New York: Farrar, Straus and Giroux, 2010.

Thapar, Romila. "Syndicated Hinduism." In *Hinduism Reconsidered,* edited by Herman Kulke and Günther-Dietz Sontheimer, 54–81. New Delhi: Manohar, 1989.

Tweed, Thomas A., and Stephen Prothero, eds. *Asian Religions in America: A Documentary History.* New York: Oxford University Press, 1999.

Versluis, Arthur. *American Transcendentalism and Asian Religions.* New York: Oxford University Press, 1993.

Waghorne, Joanne Punzo. "Beyond Pluralism: Global Gurus and the Third Stream of American Religiosity." In *Gods in America: Religious Pluralism in the United States,* edited by Charles Lloyd Cohen and Ronald L. Numbers, 228–248. New York: Oxford University Press, 2013.

Williams, Raymond Brady. *Religions of Immigrants from India and Pakistan: New Threads in the American Tapestry.* Cambridge and New York: Cambridge University Press, 1988.

Williamson, Lola. *Transcendent in America: Hindu-Inspired Meditation Movements as New Religion.* New York: New York University Press, 2010.

Michael J. Altman
Assistant Professor of Religious Studies
University of Alabama

HIROHITO, EMPEROR (1901–1989)

SEE *Japan.*

HIROSHIMA

SEE *Manhattan Project; World War II.*

HISS, ALGER

SEE *Spies and Espionage.*

HO CHI MINH
1890–1969

Ho Chi Minh was the first president of the Democratic Republic of Vietnam, a former colony of France that declared its independence on September 2, 1945. For Ho, this was the culmination of years of organizing and a World War II partnership with the US Office of Strategic Services (OSS), the precursor of the Central Intelligence Agency (CIA). They were planning joint action against the Japanese occupation forces in Indochina when the War in the Pacific ended with a Japanese surrender on August 14.

The son of a mandarin scholar from a poor province in central Vietnam, Ho left school early and in 1911 traveled to Europe and America in a quest for knowledge and connections to help his people gain their freedom. Disappointed by his failure to win concessions from France at the post–World War I Paris Peace Conference (1919), Ho moved on to Moscow to request help from the Communist International. With meager Russian aid, he traveled to southern China, where he trained Vietnamese émigrés to become revolutionaries. French repression prevented Ho from returning home for many years, but he did build a small nucleus of supporters that returned to Vietnam to organize anti-French uprisings and a communist party.

Ho's 1945 independence declaration, using language from the US Declaration of Independence, stated Vietnam's right to become a free nation. Ho emphasized that the French had forfeited any claims to Vietnam by surrendering their power to Japan. The Vietnamese remember this period as the "August Revolution," when towns throughout Vietnam took power from the Japanese. But it was only the start of Ho Chi Minh's long struggle for independence.

Although the OSS supported Vietnamese independence, Washington opted to support the return of French power to Indochina. By March 1946, Ho Chi Minh's government was forced to negotiate an agreement that permitted the French to return for a period of five years. This led to fruitless negotiations over the status and territory of Vietnam, which deteriorated into outright war in December 1946. Ho became president of a government in resistance, which only returned to power in Hanoi after nine years of fighting. The 1954 peace settlement at Geneva, however, divided Vietnam at the seventeenth parallel, with Ho's communist government being forced to wait for full reunification until nationwide elections could be held in 1956. These were never held, as the United States entered the struggle to preserve a noncommunist South Vietnam. Vietnam was fighting a costly war against US power when Ho Chi Minh died in 1969. Full independence came with Hanoi's 1975 victory, thirty years after Ho Chi Minh's initial declaration.

The United States was perplexed by Ho Chi Minh's mixture of communism and nationalism. The once dominant belief that he was a Stalinist communist who cloaked his true ideas with nationalist rhetoric is rejected by many historians. Those sympathetic to Ho see his reliance on communist allies in the USSR and China as his only option in the face of French and, later, US opposition. He was a pragmatist who believed in social justice, but most evidence shows that he was not attached to extreme communist dogmas of class struggle. His byword was *solidarity*, although he failed to keep all Vietnamese nationalists in his coalition of patriots. The creation of "Ho Chi Minh Thought" in the 1990s was an expedient that the government adopted to hold Vietnam together as the communist world was disintegrating. In his lifetime, Ho never claimed to be a theorist.

SEE ALSO *Cold War; Decolonization; Vietnam War*

BIBLIOGRAPHY

Brocheux, Pierre. *Ho Chi Minh*. Paris: Presses de Sciences Po, 2000.

Duiker, William. *Ho Chi Minh: A Life*. New York: Hyperion, 2000.

Quinn-Judge, Sophie. *Ho Chi Minh: The Missing Years*. Berkeley: University of California Press, 2002.

Quinn-Judge, Sophie. "Ho Chi Minh and the Making of his Image." In *The Birth of a Party State: Vietnam since 1945*, edited by Christopher E. Goscha and Benoit de Treglode, 159–171. Paris: Les Indes Savantes, 2004. Bilingual book.

Sophie Quinn-Judge
Associate Professor of History and Associate Director of the Center for Vietnamese Philosophy, Culture, and Society
Temple University

HOLLYWOOD

Most people around the world come into contact with the United States through Hollywood movies. In the early twenty-first century, the companies associated with Hollywood own between 40 and 90 percent of the movies shown in most parts of the world (Miller et al. 2005). Hollywood's revenue from outside the United States is more than double that of its domestic market. Over the course of little more than a century, Hollywood has earned admiration and notoriety, become famous and feared, as it has attained both economic and cultural dominance throughout most of the world. Yet what this means is not always apparent. Hollywood is not only one thing or place. *Hollywood* is a floating term, a historical and transnational signifier derived from the name of a place in southern California and designating the entertainment business oligopoly based there. *Hollywood* has also come to refer to a distinct style of storytelling, a particular national cinema, and a highly visible form of cultural hegemony.

THE RISE OF THE FILM INDUSTRY IN LOS ANGELES

Hollywood began as a place that can still be found in Los Angeles below the 45-foot (13.75-meter) tall, bright white capital letters spelling out HOLLYWOOD on the edge of the Santa Monica Mountains. Yet to suggest that this place under the sign is Hollywood, while accurate, would be misleading and incomplete. There are at least three neighborhoods and twenty-three townships across the United States called Hollywood (Bean 2008). When the sign in California was erected in 1923, it was to sell real estate, and it read "HOLLYWOODLAND." This most famous Hollywood had already been named, apparently in the 1880s, although there are competing legends as to who named it and why. A hilly agricultural area just northwest of downtown Los Angeles, it was incorporated in 1903 but had merged with Los Angeles by 1910. By then, movies were already being made in the area. Southern California offered much that appealed to the burgeoning film industry: it was warm and sunny, with "320 days for good photography" (Bowser 1990); a variety of shooting locations were within hours of each other (beaches, mountains, deserts, forests, cities, farms); land was available and cheap; the labor pool was growing; and, not incidentally, Los Angeles was well known as "the nation's leading open-shop, nonunion city" (Sklar 1994).

Filmmaking in Los Angeles is thought to have begun in 1907 on a temporary (winter) basis. Soon, multiple film companies were arriving and spreading across southern California. By 1912, the Nestor Company had purchased property on the corner of Gower Street and Sunset Boulevard and was building the first studio actually located in Hollywood (Bowser 1990). When Universal City opened in the nearby San Fernando Valley in 1915, it was clear that Los Angeles would displace New York as the prime location for US filmmaking. The geographic distance between Los Angeles and New York, where most corporate headquarters remained, fostered an illusory sense of independence from the strictly financial concerns of the business side of the art of filmmaking. The clustering of talent, skilled labor, facilities, and resources in one sunny location, meanwhile, fostered a mutually agreeable entanglement between the film industry and Los Angeles as each grew up and grew enormous together. Although the name *Hollywood* did not come into popular use as a metonym for the American film industry for another decade, the entire Los Angeles area was already becoming "Hollywood." Hollywood movies would soon become the first dominant American cultural export (Koszarski 1994).

THE AMERICANIZATION OF CINEMA

Hollywood's dominance, however, was not an inevitable development. During the time US firms were migrating to California, the majority of films viewed by US filmgoers were imported (the French film industry was the world's leader). A Progressive Era campaign to "Americanize" the cinema in the United States (Abel 2006) was followed by World War I (1914–1918) and its decimation of European film industries. The business of filmmaking in the United States consolidated into an efficient, modern industry in California in the 1920s, with both domestic and international markets ripe for new product. As the domestic market grew, and as working-class immigrant audiences were increasingly supplanted by middle-class viewers, the domestic audience could be relied upon to recoup a film's production costs. This allowed filmmaking companies to tailor export prices to local markets around the world, consistently undercutting local productions with high-quality American films.

American movie exports were already becoming economically important for the industry by 1914. The federal government soon proved willing to assist with international trade. President Woodrow Wilson (1856–1924) asserted what would essentially become US policy guiding Hollywood foreign circulation: "The film has come to rank as a very high medium for the dissemination of public intelligence and since it speaks a universal language it lends itself importantly to the presentation of America's plans and purposes" (Puttnam and Watson 2000, 76). By 1926, Hollywood films represented nearly three-fourths of the European box office (Epstein 2005).

THE EVOLUTION OF HOLLYWOOD STUDIOS AND THE GROWTH OF THEIR INTERNATIONAL MARKET

Over the course of the 1920s, a vertically integrated Hollywood studio system emerged in which a single company controlled all aspects of film production and distribution and dominated domestic exhibition as well. Although ostensibly competing for talent, market share, and intellectual property, the eight "major" studios colluded in a number of ways. The domestic market was divvyed up and prioritized through a system of zoning and clearance. Theaters not outright owned by a studio were forced to block book (rent multiple films rather than one at a time) and blind bid (rent films sight unseen), thus ensuring a regularized domestic market for Hollywood films. Although these practices were industry standards by the 1930s, the US Supreme Court found them, along with vertical integration, to be in violation of antitrust legislation in 1949, and such practices were discontinued domestically. Although some foreign-made films were available and a number of smaller companies (sometimes collectively known as Poverty Row) made hundreds of movies each year, by the 1930s and 1940s, the eight major Hollywood studios accounted for 90 percent of American film production and 60 percent of all world film production (Maltby 1995).

With the domestic market nearly saturated, Hollywood found the export market frustratingly unpredictable. After the postwar peak, nations around the world began imposing censorship, import quotas, repatriation restrictions on money, and heavy import taxes on imported films. The studio system oligopoly responded through organized cooperation, forming a series of trade organizations and lobbying the federal government. Federal government assistance, starting with the Foreign Film Service, formed in Washington, DC, as a division of the Committee on Public Information in 1917, helped to open European, South American, and East Asian markets during and following World War I. Characterizing market penetration as a gateway to broader American trade, Hollywood united behind the slogan "trade follows film" (Puttnam and Watson 2000).

When many of the world's film industries were again decimated following World War II (1939–1945), the Office of War Information joined with Hollywood in 1945 to form the Motion Picture Export Association (MPEA), a government-supported industry trade cartel facilitating the opening of foreign markets to American films (Schatz 1997). The goals of the film industry and the government were so closely aligned in the 1940s that the MPEA was often called the "little State Department." So effective was this organization in facilitating Hollywood overseas distribution (and even exhibition) that the box office share of Hollywood films in Europe and Japan grew from about 30 percent in 1950 to 90 percent by 1990 (Miller et al. 2005). Hollywood export companies like United International Pictures (UIP) resumed practices such as block booking, blind bidding, and output deals that are illegal domestically. In 1994, the MPEA changed

Film stars such as Humphrey Bogart and Lauren Bacall (on the first step) on their way back to California after protesting a congressional probe of alleged Communism in Hollywood, October 1947. *Over the course of little more than a century, Hollywood has earned admiration and notoriety, become famous and feared, as it has attained both economic and cultural dominance around most of the world.* BETTMANN/CORBIS

its name to the Motion Picture Association (MPA) to signal a new emphasis on global protection of Hollywood intellectual property. In the early twenty-first century, the MPA has been involved in enforcing intellectual property laws in more than eighty countries. Washington has continued to rely on Hollywood as a key resource for "soft power" in world diplomacy, through which American ideology can be economically and efficiently distributed overseas in the guise of entertainment.

The eight major studios, meanwhile, have faced further consolidation, reorganization, and new ownership since the 1960s. Those that remained by 2015 were subsidiaries of the six media industry conglomerates that constitute Hollywood. Rather than making, distributing, and exhibiting movies as they did with the studio system model, in 2015 Hollywood studios functioned as global distribution and publicity companies, organizing productions and trading in intellectual property. The studios subcontracted and outsourced the actual production (even financing) of most movies. Frequently this involved finding cheaper, less regulated labor outside the United States. It also involved seeking out tax and other fiscal incentives. If a production did not completely "run away" outside the United States, at least some part of it, from animation to digital effects to costume sewing, was likely to involve international labor. As of 2015, Hollywood facilitated the production and subsequent distribution of movies and profited from the licensing of intellectual property (Miller et al. 2005; Bettig 2008).

THE HOLLYWOOD STYLE OF STORYTELLING AND A UNIQUE NATIONAL CINEMA

What has remained remarkably consistent in all this time is the product for which Hollywood is known: a distinctive style of visual storytelling almost instantly recognizable around the world as a Hollywood film. Hollywood films are known for looking expensive and having "high production values," but also for valuing wealth, beauty, and youth. They combine spectacle and melodrama with verisimilitude and continuity and usually have a happy ending. The Hollywood film developed as a particular combination of narrative and formal style, cleverly combining nineteenth-century bourgeois realism and stage melodrama. As the product of a studio system that sought to regularize the mass serial production of narrative, certain recurring features of style in Hollywood films have surely become part of their appeal.

Hollywood films typically feature an individual protagonist who is goal-oriented and comes into conflict with the goals of other characters, each recognizable through a set of consistent character traits. A psychologically (rather than socially or naturally) motivated chain of clear cause and effect leads to the ultimate (usually happy) resolution of conflict. Typically, the narrative includes an intertwined second story involving heterosexual romance. These stories are told with techniques of camera work, lighting, acting style, and "continuity" editing designed to efface their own presence, allowing the viewer to inhabit the world of the story, invisibly occupying an ideal space in which to ascertain the next important development. This approach produces a kind of formal narrative transparency that has been described as "excessively obvious cinema" (Bordwell, Staiger, and Thompson 1985, 3–11). These qualities help explain Hollywood's apparently universal appeal. The transparency of Hollywood films allows "audiences to project indigenous values, beliefs, rites, and rituals into imported media," so that films can be imagined as always having locally identifiable qualities, wherever and by whomever they are encountered (Olson 1999, 5).

While the international appeal of Hollywood films cannot be denied, this very structure carries with it a recognizably American ideology. Hollywood films are energetic and efficient, simply presuming universality as they focus on goal-oriented individualism, economic success and consumerism, and superficial optimism. Such qualities are recognizably American to audiences outside the United States, where they are encountered as culturally distinct and different (Maltby 2004). The openness of Hollywood films to a variety of cultural readings makes them an unusual kind of national cinema. Film industries in many countries are supported by quotas on movie imports and receive direct government funding. They are often also required to produce national identity through their films and abide by rules concerning depictions of their country. Hollywood has no such responsibility. Hollywood instead lobbies for laws and international agreements related to intellectual property licensing and piracy enforcement, access to trade markets and local partnerships, and financial repatriation of profits. Hollywood, moreover, has never been coterminous with American cinema. The United States has always produced a diverse and varied body of film beyond Hollywood, including documentaries, experimental cinema, independent narrative and art films, and cinemas of diasporic and minority cultures (Martin 1995).

Hollywood's interplay with the rest of world may best be characterized through the idea of entanglement (Govil 2015). Hollywood may circulate as a kind of national cinema, but Hollywood's filmmakers see their work as universal. Hollywood has developed the world's most widely imitated film style, which is designed to efface itself. National cinemas around the world define themselves (their style, narrative, and intent) in opposition to Hollywood. Hollywood, meanwhile, has a long, promiscuous history of investing in, coproducing with, and regularly appropriating from national cinemas around the world. Hollywood has taken styles, ideas, locations, and especially talent (writers, directors, actors) from other countries, yet has retained a consistency in overall style, structure, and process. For all the legal, cultural, and nationalistic resistance to Hollywood, millions of people around the world rush to see the next Hollywood blockbuster. All of this, as well, must be collected under the sign of "Hollywood."

SEE ALSO *Disney; The Quiet American (Graham Greene, 1955); Television*

BIBLIOGRAPHY

Abel, Richard. *Americanizing the Movies and "Movie-Mad" Audiences, 1910–1914.* Berkeley: University of California Press, 2006.

Bean, Jennifer M. "The Imagination of Early Hollywood: Movieland and the Magic Cities, 1914–1916." In *Early Cinema and the "National,"* edited by Richard Abel, Giorgio Bertellini, and Rob King, 332–342. New Barnet, UK: Libbey, 2008.

Bettig, Ronald V. "Hollywood and Intellectual Property." In *The Contemporary Hollywood Film Industry*, edited by Paul McDonald and Janet Wasko, 195–206. Oxford, UK: Blackwell, 2008.

Bordwell, David, Janet Staiger, and Kristin Thompson. *The Classical Hollywood Cinema: Film Style and Mode of Production to 1960.* New York: Columbia University Press, 1985.

Bowser, Eileen. *The Transformation of Cinema, 1907–1915.* Berkeley: University of California Press, 1990.

Epstein, Edward Jay. *The Big Picture: The New Logic of Money and Power in Hollywood.* New York: Random House, 2005.

Govil, Nitin. *Orienting Hollywood: A Century of Film Culture between Los Angeles and Bombay.* New York: New York University Press, 2015.

Koszarski, Richard. *An Evening's Entertainment: The Age of the Silent Feature Picture, 1915–1928.* Berkeley: University of California Press, 1994.

Maltby, Richard. *Hollywood Cinema.* Cambridge, MA: Blackwell, 1995. 2nd ed., 2003.

Maltby, Richard. "Introduction: 'The Americanization of the World'" In *Hollywood Abroad: Audiences and Cultural Exchange*, edited by Melvyn Stokes and Richard Maltby, 1–20. London: BFI, 2004.

Martin, Michael T., ed. *Cinemas of the Black Diaspora: Diversity, Dependence, and Oppositionality.* Detroit, MI: Wayne State University Press, 1995.

Miller, Toby, Nitin Govil, John McMurria, Richard Maxwell, and Ting Wang. *Global Hollywood 2.* London: BFI, 2005.

Olson, Scott Robert. *Hollywood Planet: Global Media and the Competitive Advantage of Transparency.* Mahwah, NJ: Erlbaum, 1999.

Puttnam, David, and Neil Watson. *Movies and Money.* New York: Vintage, 2000. First published 1997.

Schatz, Thomas. *Boom and Bust: American Cinema in the 1940s.* Berkeley: University of California Press, 1997.

Sklar, Robert. *Movie-Made America: A Cultural History of American Movies.* Rev. ed. New York: Vintage, 1994.

Shawn Shimpach
Associate Professor, Department of Communication and Interdepartmental Program in Film Studies
University of Massachusetts, Amherst

HOLOCAUST

From 1933 to 1945 Germany was ruled by the totalitarian fascist regime of the Nazi party under Adolf Hitler. During the Nazi era Jews and other groups faced persecution, violence, and death. This article uses the term *Holocaust* to refer to the slaughter of six million Jews throughout Europe (and to a lesser extent in North Africa) between 1933 and 1945, and in particular as a result of the Final Solution, a deliberate, systematic plan carried out by this regime between 1941 and 1945. Though the term Holocaust views events across Europe and over several years as a collective whole, it is also important to note that these events unfolded quite differently in various regions, and local sociopolitical factors heavily influenced persecution of Jews and other groups. This article focuses on American responses to the Holocaust after 1945, including the meaning of the Holocaust for Jews and non-Jews and debate over whether or not Jewish suffering during that time period was unique.

In the wake of the Holocaust, approximately 100,000 Jews immigrated to the United States, in addition to just over 300,000 non-Jewish displaced persons. Many survivors went to Israel, either for ideological reasons or because they had not received permission to enter other countries, including the United States. However, the significance of the Holocaust has greatly exceeded the numerical expansion of the American population by its refugees and survivors. The Holocaust has increasingly been a major question for and expression of Jewish identity in America. In the 2013 Pew Research Poll "A Portrait of Jewish Americans," 73 percent of those polled listed "remembering the Holocaust" as essential to being Jewish, making it the most common response. Furthermore, many non-Jews have insisted on connecting the event to American history and values.

Prior to and during World War II, Jewish and non-Jewish Americans tended to see Jews as one group among many victims. Disabled people, perceived enemies of the state, homosexuals, and religious, ethnic, and national groups including Sinti and Roma, Poles, and Jehovah's Witnesses were all persecuted during this period. Americans learned of the persecution of Jews in Germany, Austria, and other countries, but news of the forcing of Jews into ghettos, the *Einsatzgrüppen* (mobile killing squads) in Eastern Europe, and the death camps emerged only gradually. Reports during and immediately following the war of the camps, such as Chełmno, Majdanek, Bełzek, Sobibór, Treblinka, and Auschwitz-Birkenau, referenced their specific history, location, and inhabitants. A shift toward conceptualizing the "Holocaust" as a larger event took place as Americans began to see a relationship between various camps and events. This generalization made it possible to interpret the Holocaust as a single event in collective memory. The opening of the United States Holocaust Memorial Museum in 1993 on the National Mall in Washington, DC, represented the culmination of the centralization of the Holocaust in American consciousness. The museum locates the Holocaust within the American landscape and is part of a long process of questioning the meaning and implications of the Holocaust in American communities, religion and philosophy, media, education, and politics.

EARLY RESPONSES

Prior to the emergence in 1960 of a public narrative about the Holocaust, Jewish Americans struggled to understand the events in Western and Eastern Europe of the Nazi era. There were no models for memorializing destruction on this scale, no clear way to integrate the knowledge of what happened into Jewish consciousness. Jewish Americans experimented with language and forms of remembrance. The word "Holocaust" appeared in English-language memorials, from museum exhibits to scholarship, in the 1940s and 1950s, though it was not the only term used. "Holocaust" is the Greek translation of the Hebrew term *'olah*, from the Hebrew root meaning "to go up" and referring (in some contexts) to a burnt sacrifice to God. In Jewish antiquity, it was believed that when humans made a sacrifice or *'olah*, the smoke rose and the odor pleased God. The use of "Holocaust" for the death of six million Jews is thus problematic for some because it implies a sacrifice that pleases God.

Jewish Americans used terms in English, Yiddish, and Hebrew, from Hitler *tsaytn* ("Hitler times") to variations of *khurbn* (destruction), which is also used to describe the destruction of the First and Second Temples in Jerusalem in antiquity. Some used names of camps to stand in for the entire time period, especially "Dachau" during the early postwar years, though "Auschwitz" would become more frequently used in the late twentieth century. In such cases, the use of a single camp as a symbol can obscure the diversity of events and methods of killing. In the American press, journalists used terms such as "the six million," "the catastrophe," "Hitler holocaust," and "victims of Nazi persecutions." Jewish Americans spoke of "survivors," "the remnant," "the saving remnant," and "displaced persons." In Israel and among some Jewish Americans, the term used to refer to the deaths of the six million was and remains the *Shoah*, a Hebrew word meaning a total calamity.

Many attempts by Jewish Americans to create memorials, such as days of remembrance or public installations, failed due to bureaucratic and political obstacles as well as lack of funding. Memorials in the United States arose in different political and cultural contexts from those in Europe, where the sites of destruction were located. The State of Israel created Yad Vashem as its official memorial to the Holocaust, while seeking to overturn Jewish suffering as the foundation for a national narrative. Americans had to decide how to integrate narratives of the Holocaust not only into American history but also American landscapes. Jewish Americans were influenced by European and Israeli narratives, and participated in them by sending money abroad to support refugees as well as memorials. Jews in America faced the question of how much to allow the

State of Israel to control the narrative of Jewish history, including but not limited to the Holocaust. The Yad Vashem institution sought to prevent Jewish Americans from creating any memorials in the United States, but Jewish Americans went ahead with local and international projects such as erecting monuments, participating in rituals such as burials of Torah scrolls, and writing and publishing books, especially *yizker bikher*, memorial books that commemorated Jewish life in towns throughout Europe.

Jewish Americans also considered several possibilities for designating a single day of remembrance. Some advocated the ninth of the Hebrew month of Av, the traditional day of mourning for the destruction of the First and Second Temples; ultimately the Synagogue Council of America rejected this day as much for practical reasons (it fell during the summer, when many are traveling) as any theological ones. In 1951 the Israeli Knesset approved the twenty-seventh of Nisan as Yom Ha-Shoah U'Mered HaGetaot (the Day of Catastrophe and Ghetto Rebellion). This date linked Jewish resistance—in particular the Warsaw Ghetto Uprising—to remembrance. American observance of what came to be known more succinctly as Yom Ha-Shoah demonstrates the simultaneous but sometimes conflicting Jewish American goals of remembering the suffering of Jews in Europe and participating in contemporary Jewish life, especially establishing connections with the State of Israel. Jewish Americans also integrated remembrance of the six million into their observance of Passover.

COMMUNAL MEMORY, MEDIA, AND POLITICS

The collective Holocaust consciousness that developed in Jewish American communal memory was influenced by the publication of key works of Jewish literature; the trial in Jerusalem of one of the main Nazi perpetrators, Adolf Eichmann; Jewish theological and philosophical responses; and images in television and other media.

Key Works of Literature. Two texts in particular have been foundational: *The Diary of Anne Frank* and Elie Wiesel's *Night*. Published in Dutch in 1947, the diary was published in English translation in 1952. It was subsequently adapted for theater and film in the United States. Because of the very nature of the diary, written while in hiding and ending before Anne's deportation to Auschwitz, it provided a view of Jewish persecution under Nazism within a narrow frame. Thus the Holocaust became the context for Frank's diary, with the reader knowing the outcome not only of Anne's life but of so many others, more than its central theme. The book, theater performances, and film emphasized the diary's value to liberal ideals and postwar optimism.

In *Night*, published in English translation in the United States in 1960, Wiesel, an Auschwitz survivor, writes explicitly of Jewish suffering in the death camps. He recalls life in Hungary, deportation to and daily life in Auschwitz, and the loss of his family, ultimately including his father shortly before the liberation of Auschwitz. *Night* emerged within the context of numerous Yiddish-language memoirs of towns destroyed throughout Europe that recalled vibrant Jewish life. By reading the memoirs of individual survivors, Jews in the immediate postwar period began to confront the events of the Holocaust. Many other individual survivors also drafted memoirs in a variety of languages.

The Eichmann Trial and the Six-Day War. Many Jewish Americans did not connect the Holocaust and Zionism during the early 1940s or even immediately after the war ended. Given the ongoing suffering in European displaced persons camps, many Jewish Americans came to view mass immigration to Israel as the best option for the remnants of European Jewry. However, an ideological and nearly theological understanding of the State of Israel as a kind of redemption for the Holocaust did not become widespread until the 1960s.

The Eichmann trial, which took place from April to August 1961 in the Jerusalem District Court, pushed Jewish suffering into a new position in public memory, calling attention to the death of six million Jews as a unique event that must be conceptualized separately from other events during the Second World War. The trial, through which the American public had its first encounter with modern Hebrew, projected an image of national power and Israeli identity, though not even all Israeli citizens or Jews called to testify in the trial could speak or understand Hebrew. Greater numbers of Jewish Americans began to see Israel as responsible for the future of Jewish life, particularly after the 1967 Six-Day War. The perceived unlikely victory of Israel against attack by Arab armies forged a new sense of Israel's strength and righteousness.

Jewish Theology and Philosophy. Religious, theological, and philosophical responses to the Holocaust in North America have responded to the uniqueness of the Holocaust as an event in Jewish and world history and the implications of the Holocaust for a covenantal conception of God. Theodicy, the question of how a good and just God could permit suffering and evil, is a long-standing theme in Jewish and other religious-philosophical works; but for post-Holocaust thinkers, the Holocaust created a particular problem because it elevated these questions to a new level of urgency in the face of such widespread horror. A range of American and

European Jewish theologico-philosophical responses, from ultra-Orthodox to Reform to "secular philosophy," have produced ongoing and overlapping conversations.

For those using biblical or traditional Jewish sources, certain themes recur: the *Akedah* or "binding of Isaac" in Genesis 22, the book of Job (for examples, see especially the work of Martin Buber and Robert Gordis), the "suffering servant" in Isaiah (Abraham Joshua Heschel, Eliezer Berkovits), *hester panim* or "God hiding God's Face" in Deuteronomy 31 and Micah 3 (Buber, Joseph Soloveitchik, Zvi Kolitz, Berkovits), *mipnei hateinu* or "on account of our sins" (Joel Teitelbaum, Isaac Hutner), or a theologico-philosophical commitment to free will (Berkovits, Arthur Cohen). More radical responses have also been produced, including arguments that Auschwitz represents a new revelation (Emil Fackenheim); that Jews are now in a new covenantal age (Irving "Yitzchak" Greenberg); that God must be redefined in theological and gendered terms (Hans Jonas, Cohen, Melissa Raphael); that there is no God or no covenant with God, though this does not invalidate Jewish peoplehood (Richard Rubenstein); that traditional theology has been rendered indefensible, but the Holocaust imposes new ethical demands (Emmanuel Levinas, Amos Funkenstein); and that the Holocaust is simply a mystery that cannot be explained (Wiesel, Andre Schwarzbart, Nellie Sachs). Non-Jews, most especially Christians, have also contended with the implications of the Holocaust for theology and religious practice. The Holocaust renders problematic Christian claims of supersessionism, that the new covenant in Christ invalidated the Jewish covenant with God, which some scholars have implicated in the complacency of bystanders, and indeed in the participation of perpetrators, in the execution of so many Jews.

Media. Visual media have played an important role in Americans' conception of the Holocaust. Of the thousands of images taken by photojournalists and soldiers during the liberation of the death camps, a handful of photos emerged as symbols of the horror. In American television and film, the Holocaust has become a central moral paradigm.

That the Holocaust seeped into American culture beyond specifically Jewish stories underscores the shared interest among Jews and non-Jews in memorializing and understanding its implications. In the middle of the twentieth century, photojournalism and television were still new media that had yet to earn their place as "serious" forms of culture. By consolidating a moral discourse around the Holocaust, photojournalism, television, and film, each able to convey visual information that words could not, each gained a certain status vis-à-vis the Holocaust.

DIFFUSION IN AMERICAN CULTURE

Conceptualizing the Holocaust in America underlines two themes: the victimhood of Jews, and the ability of good to triumph over evil (in particular the ability of American liberalism to save these victims). But if what many take to be the lesson of Anne Frank's diary is really true, that at heart all humanity is really good, others have been prompted to ask if the Holocaust would then not have happened in the first place. Americans have wrestled repeatedly with these questions, highlighting how deeply responses to the Holocaust in the United States have been embedded in and contributed to American culture.

Since the last quarter of the twentieth century, survivor testimony, film and television, and the construction of monuments in national American settings have continued to diffuse the Holocaust into Jewish and non-Jewish consciousness. The placing of Holocaust monuments and museums in the United States can be viewed as "arbitrary," in that they are not created on sites of destruction. Holocaust memorials are also created in complex contemporary contexts and Holocaust memory is in tension with many ongoing political questions. For example, President Jimmy Carter's proposal of a national memorial to the Jewish Holocaust in Washington, DC, followed his sale of fighter planes to Saudi Arabia, and President Bill Clinton's dedication of the United States Holocaust Memorial Museum took place even as he chose not to intervene in the Rwandan genocide. Americans have viewed events from Bosnia to Rwanda to Sudan through the lens of the Holocaust, though it has not always been clear to what ends. If monuments in Washington, New York, Boston, San Francisco, Miami, and many other American cities have connected the Holocaust to American consciousness—albeit in multiple, complex, sometimes unclear or contradictory ways—these museums have also helped each local city legitimize its own significance.

If American monuments tend to centralize lessons of pluralism, this emphasis is not an inevitable lesson of the Holocaust. German memorials address the role of Germans as perpetrators of crimes against Jews, yet also ask how the Jews' suffering fits into broader national narratives of suffering under Nazism and Communism. Monuments in Poland triangulate the suffering of Jews under fascism, the role of Polish nationalism, and persecutions under Soviet communism. Early monuments in Poland subsumed Jewish deaths under Polish and Communist rubrics, but more recent monuments—influenced heavily by Israeli Jews—have insisted on Jewish particularity, resistance, and even Zionism. In Israel the theme of victimhood and weakness is far less emphasized than that of heroism and strength. Israel's image of itself as central to all Jewish identity rests both on the calamity of the Final Solution and on the creation of a self-defending modern Jewish nation-state.

The Jewish interest in educating people about the Holocaust is sometimes in tension with those who question to what extent the Holocaust was unique, pointing to the suffering of other groups. As with many subjects, there is the question of who controls the narrative and who determines what meanings are to be drawn from it. Jews as well as non-Jews will continue to debate the relationship of group identity to a historical record of atrocity.

SEE ALSO *Armenian Genocide; Ethnic Cleansing; Genocide; Human Rights; Israel; Judaism; Roosevelt, Franklin D.; United Nations; Universal Declaration of Human Rights; World War II*

BIBLIOGRAPHY

Arendt, Hannah. Excerpts from *Eichmann in Jerusalem.* In *The Portable Hannah Arendt*, edited by Peter Baehr. New York: Penguin, 2000.

Braiterman, Zachary. *(God) After Auschwitz: Tradition and Change in Post-Holocaust Jewish Thought.* Princeton, NJ: Princeton University Press, 1998.

Cole, Tim. *Selling the Holocaust: From Auschwitz to Schindler—How History Is Bought, Packaged, and Sold.* New York: Routledge, 1999.

Diner, Hasia R. *We Remember with Reverence and Love: American Jews and the Myth of Silence after the Holocaust, 1945–1962.* New York: New York University Press, 2009.

Eckardt, A. Roy. "Christians and Jews: Along a Theological Frontier." *Encounters* 40 (Spring 1979): 89–127.

Fackenheim, Emil L. *God's Presence in History: Jewish Affirmations and Philosophical Reflections.* New York: New York University Press, 1970.

Fackenheim, Emil L. *To Mend the World: Foundations of Post-Holocaust Jewish Thought.* Reprint, Bloomington: Indiana University Press, 1994.

Gubkin, Liora. *You Shall Tell Your Children: Holocaust Memory in American Passover Ritual.* New Brunswick, NJ: Rutgers University Press, 2007.

Haggith, Toby, and Joanna Newman, eds. *Holocaust and the Moving Image: Representations in Film and Television since 1933.* London and New York: Wallflower Press, 2005.

Katz, Steven T. *Historicism, the Holocaust, and Zionism: Critical Studies in Modern Jewish Thought and History.* New York: New York University Press, 1992.

Katz, Steven T., Shlomo Biderman, and Gershon Greenberg, eds. *Wrestling with God: Jewish Theological Responses during the Holocaust.* Oxford and New York: Oxford University Press, 2007.

Kaufman, Menahem. *An Ambiguous Partnership: Non-Zionists and Zionists in America, 1939–1948.* Translated by Ira Robinson. Jerusalem: Magnes Press, and Detroit, MI: Wayne State University Press, 1991.

Levkov, Ilya, ed. *Bitburg and Beyond: Encounters in American, German, and Jewish History.* New York: Shapolsky, 1987.

Linenthal, Edward T. *Preserving Memory: The Struggle to Create America's Holocaust Museum.* New York: Viking, 1995.

Magid, Shaul. "The American Jewish Holocaust 'Myth' and 'Negative Judaism': Jacob Neusner's Contribution to American Judaism." In *A Legacy of Learning: Essays in Honor of Jacob Neusner.* Edited by Alan J. Avery-Peck, Bruce Chilton, William Scott Green, and Gary G. Porton. Leiden, the Netherlands, and Boston: Brill, 2014.

Morgan, Michael L. *Beyond Auschwitz: Post-Holocaust Jewish Thought in America.* Oxford and New York: Oxford University Press, 2001.

Neusner, Jacob. *Stranger at Home: "The Holocaust," Zionism, and American Judaism.* Chicago: University of Chicago Press, 1981.

Novick, Peter. *The Holocaust in American Life.* Boston: Houghton Mifflin, 1999.

Pew Research Center. "A Portrait of Jewish Americans." Survey of United States Jews. February 20–June 13, 2013.

Rittner, Carol, and John K. Roth, eds. *"Good News" after Auschwitz?: Christian Faith within a Post-Holocaust World.* Macon, GA: Mercer University Press, 2001.

Rosenfeld, Alvin H. *A Double Dying: Reflections on Holocaust Literature.* Bloomington: Indiana University Press, 1980.

Rubenstein, Richard L. *After Auschwitz: Radical Theology and Contemporary Judaism.* Indianapolis, IN: Bobbs-Merrill, 1966.

Rubenstein, Richard. *After Auschwitz: History, Theology, and Contemporary Judaism.* 2nd ed. Baltimore: Johns Hopkins University Press, 1992.

Seidman, Naomi. "The Holocaust in Every Tongue." In *Faithful Renderings: Jewish-Christian Difference and the Politics of Translation.* Chicago: The University of Chicago Press, 2006.

Shandler, Jeffrey. *While America Watches: Televising the Holocaust.* New York: Oxford University Press, 1999.

Wiesel, Elie. *Night.* 1st ed. of new translation, by Marion Wiesel. New York: Hill and Wang, 2006.

Young, James E. *The Texture of Memory: Holocaust Memorials and Meaning.* New Haven, CT: Yale University Press, 1993.

Zelizer, Barbie. *Remembering to Forget: Holocaust Memory through the Camera's Eye.* Chicago: University of Chicago Press, 1998.

Jessica Carr
Assistant Professor in Religious Studies
Lafayette College

HOLY LAND

Many Americans use the term "Holy Land" to refer to the area where they believe most biblical events occurred, including the life of Jesus—roughly, the land between the Jordan River and the Mediterranean Sea. They have also used synonyms such as Palestine, Zion, Canaan, and the Promised Land. This historical conception would today fall across political borders and include areas of Lebanon, Syria, and Jordan, though the majority of it lies within Israel and the Palestinian territories.

In the nineteenth century, many American tourists combined anti-Catholic and anti-Muslim sentiments with hopes that Protestant influence could foster a restoration of Jews to the Holy Land and thereby fulfill biblical prophecy. In the twentieth century this mainstream view splintered: liberal Protestants moved away from restorationism after developing concerns for the native population, while many evangelicals believed they were seeing biblical prophecy fulfilled in the state of Israel's founding in 1948.

One of the main goals of the American Board of Commissioners for Foreign Missions (ABCFM), formed in 1810, was Jewish restoration. The ABCFM announced a mission to Palestine in 1818 staffed by Pliny Fisk and Levi Parsons, who believed himself the first American missionary to enter Jerusalem. Missionary organizations found Jews unreceptive, while Ottoman law protected Muslims from evangelization. Missionaries thus focused on converting native Christians away from Catholic and Orthodox traditions, and also opened schools.

American Protestants who toured the Holy Land had been imagining it their entire lives and often associated it with studying the Bible at home with family. Their writings about the Holy Land shared common themes. For example, most expressed disappointment that the physical place was not grand but rather seemed drab and barren. This trope had religious significance because they believed God had desolated the land to punish Jewish disbelief. Many expressed a desire to see the land

Jerusalem, as seen from the northern wall, 1897. Stereoscope by Jesse Hurlbut. *American Protestants who toured the Holy Land in the nineteenth century often expressed disappointment that the physical place was not grand as they had imagined. Many expressed a desire to see the region improved through Western intervention.* PRINT COLLECTOR/HULTON ARCHIVE/GETTY IMAGES

improved through Western intervention. Israeli leaders have argued that the Zionist pioneers accomplished the redemption of the land for which those writers pined.

Another strong theme was the inferiority of the Holy Land's non-Protestant forms of Christianity. Many rejected traditional Christian sites, notably the Church of the Holy Sepulchre in Jerusalem, using anti-Catholic rhetoric. They focused approvingly on natural sites, such as the Sea of Galilee. They also turned increasingly to archaeological sites, which could represent an imagined glorious biblical period rather than the land in its fallen state.

Most American Protestant travelers believed the Bible's events really happened, and they left the Holy Land even more convinced. Their travel writing became a primary venue for repudiating the claims of higher critics whose work called the Bible's historical accuracy into question. The biblical scholar Edward Robinson (1794–1863), who explored the Holy Land in 1838 with the conviction that scientifically studying the land could silence higher critics, published his results in the three-volume *Biblical Researches in Palestine* (1841). William McClure Thomson (1806–1894) wanted to evangelize in the Holy Land but ended up in nearby Beirut working with Maronite Christians. He traveled often to Jerusalem and the Galilee, and after decades in the region published the widely read *The Land and the Book* (1859), in which he argued that the land constituted a fifth Gospel for illuminating Jesus's message. Thomson ridiculed higher critics for spending years in libraries when he could look around and come up with explanations he thought were better than theirs.

Members of the church led by Henry Ward Beecher (1813–1887) planned an organized tourist excursion to Europe and the Holy Land in the late 1860s aboard the ship *Quaker City*. Beecher himself stayed behind, and thus the most famous passenger was a young Mark Twain, who wrote *The Innocents Abroad* (1869) about the trip. Herman Melville's visit to the Holy Land provided the inspiration for *Clarel* (1876), the longest poem in American literature, which critiqued Americans' mania for Jewish restoration. He based the character Nathan on the true story of Warder Cresson, the first American consul to Jerusalem. Cresson, a Quaker who converted to Judaism after studying restorationist ideas, started an agricultural settlement in Palestine and was buried on the Mount of Olives.

Holy Land models were built in the United States to benefit Americans who did not travel there. The Methodist bishop John Heyl Vincent (1832–1920) visited Palestine in 1863, and in 1874 he cofounded the Chautauqua Institution, which became known for providing popular adult education. One of its first endeavors was a scale model of the Holy Land, known as Palestine Park, on the shores of Chautauqua Lake. The St. Louis World's Fair of 1904 included a Jerusalem Exhibit that was noteworthy for reproducing Ottoman Jerusalem, including the Dome of the Rock, rather than ancient Jerusalem. Holy Land reproductions in America continued in the twentieth century with the Great Passion Play in Eureka Springs, Arkansas, and the Holy Land Experience theme park in Orlando, Florida.

Biblical archaeologists built on Robinson's explorations by excavating for biblical evidence. Melvin Grove Kyle's *Explorations at Sodom* (1927), meant to popularize the results of an expedition, read like a classic Holy Land narrative in which an American made incredible biblical connections simply through keen observation. Kyle's expedition colleague William Foxwell Albright (1891–1971) became vaunted as the "father of biblical archaeology." Albright, who despised higher criticism, argued that all discoveries corroborated the biblical record. Some of Albright's biggest detractors were continental biblical scholars like Martin Noth (1902–1968), who criticized biblical archaeologists' tendency to find what they were looking for. In the ecumenical climate after World War II, Albright notably formed alliances with Catholics and Jews who shared his commitment to the Bible as a historical document at a time when liberal Protestants were moving away from such readings.

In the twentieth century many Protestants with long-term exposure to the region opposed Zionism out of concern for the native population and opposition to ethnic nationalism. Christina Jones wrote that when she and her husband, Willard, arrived in 1922 to run the Quaker school in Ramallah, they replaced their Sunday-school version of the Holy Land with knowledge of and love for the native population. After refusing to leave during the hostilities of 1948, in 1952 the Joneses headed the Near East Christian Council on refugee work and spent many years speaking publicly in the United States about Palestinian refugees.

Today the United States is seen internationally as the bastion of Christian Zionism, a term that refers to evangelical Protestants' religiously based support for Israel. Many Christian Zionists subscribe to premillennial dispensationalist beliefs, including the idea that Jews must be ingathered to Israel to trigger end-times events. Many evangelicals saw Israel's founding in 1948, and its takeover of territories with biblical significance in the Six-Day War (1967), as evidence that biblical prophecy was being fulfilled. Dispensationalist ideas had been formulated and popularized in the late nineteenth century, as in W. E. Blackstone's *Jesus is Coming* (1878). Hal Lindsey's *The Late, Great Planet Earth* (1970) recast dispensationalist arguments in light of the Six-Day War. In 1998 Tim

LaHaye and Jerry B. Jenkins started publishing the *Left Behind* series, which fictionalizes premillennial dispensationalism and takes place largely in America and the Holy Land. Today Christian Zionist ministers, for example John Hagee, lead large American tours to the Holy Land that present support for Israel and adherence to the Christian faith as synonymous.

SEE ALSO *Balfour Declaration (1917); Catholicism; Islam; Israel; Judaism; Middle East; Palestine; Protestantism; United Nations; World War I; World War II; Zionism*

BIBLIOGRAPHY

Long, Burke O. *Imagining the Holy Land: Maps, Models, and Fantasy Travels.* Bloomington: Indiana University Press, 2003.

Rogers, Stephanie Stidham. *Inventing the Holy Land: American Protestant Pilgrimage to Palestine, 1865–1941.* Lanham, MD: Lexington Books, 2011.

Vogel, Lester I. *To See a Promised Land: Americans and the Holy Land in the Nineteenth Century.* University Park: Pennsylvania State University Press, 1993.

Brooke Sherrard
Instructor
Louisiana State University

HOOVER-STIMSON DOCTRINE

SEE *Manchuria.*

HOUSTON, SAM

SEE *Texas Republic.*

HOW THE OTHER HALF LIVES (JACOB RIIS, 1890)

How the Other Half Lives, Studies among the Tenements of New York, "with illustrations chiefly from photographs taken by the author," by Jacob August Riis (1849–1914) was published by Scribner's in New York in 1890. Its forty-three illustrations included seventeen then-novel halftone photographic prints. Immediately and enduringly popular, the first edition was reprinted several times, soon followed by a British edition. Scribner's kept *How the Other Half Lives* in print until 1947; as of 2015 it has appeared in at least seventy-nine editions in English from numerous publishers.

Riis had spent a decade as a New York police reporter when he wrote *How the Other Half Lives,* his downtown headquarters and official connections affording close observation of crowded, unsanitary tenement conditions and reformers' efforts to improve them. He saw as well the initial wave of the country's so-called new immigrants in the 1880s, most of whom entered at New York City. The often young and unskilled new arrivals, primarily Catholics, Orthodox Christians, and Jews from southern and eastern Europe and Russia, settled in city tenements hoping for nearby industrial production work. The new immigration, totaling twenty million by 1920, doubled the US population and drastically changed its demographics.

Riis himself, decidedly "old" immigration, had arrived in New York from Denmark in 1870, his northern European origin and Protestant faith both typical of most pre-1880 immigrants and familiar to Americans. Although he spent some years wandering and penniless, his autobiography conveys his ambition for middle-class respectability and disdain for the workers' solidarity that drove unionization and labor protest throughout the Gilded Age. It was not difficult for him to frame his subject as "the other half."

The invention of flash powder in 1887 inspired Riis to embark on a series of nighttime photographic expeditions that would provide many of the images for his popular illustrated lectures, for several illustrated newspaper and magazine articles published in 1888, and for *How the Other Half Lives.* Some flash-lit photographs reveal crowded tenement rooms and unkempt hallways, startled occupants of cheap lodging houses, sodden drinkers, crowded sweatshops, and whole families toiling at piecework. Others, clearly posed, replicate subjects familiar from the era's illustrated magazines—newsboys, angelic children, Chinese opium smokers. The lifelike drama of scenes nearby yet normally obscure thrilled Riis's middle-class lecture audiences. Now held at the Museum of the City of New York and frequently reproduced, Riis's images are a primary reason for contemporary interest in *How the Other Half Lives* and in Riis, spurring American and European photojournalists to "revisit" the other half and scholars to debate their place in photographic history.

In *How the Other Half Lives,* the handful of imperfect halftones and illustrators' line-drawn copies could not replicate the lectures' photographic impact. Rather, the book's text—Riis's narrative "studies among the tenements"—conveys the drama in his message. Seemingly modeled on Charles Dickens's *American Notes* (1842), many chapters read as guided tours, proceeding through dense street crowds vivid against looming tenement backdrops, up dark stairs to airless rooms, down dismal alleys, and past the lighted doorways of grimy saloons. A stream of anecdotes recounts Riis's

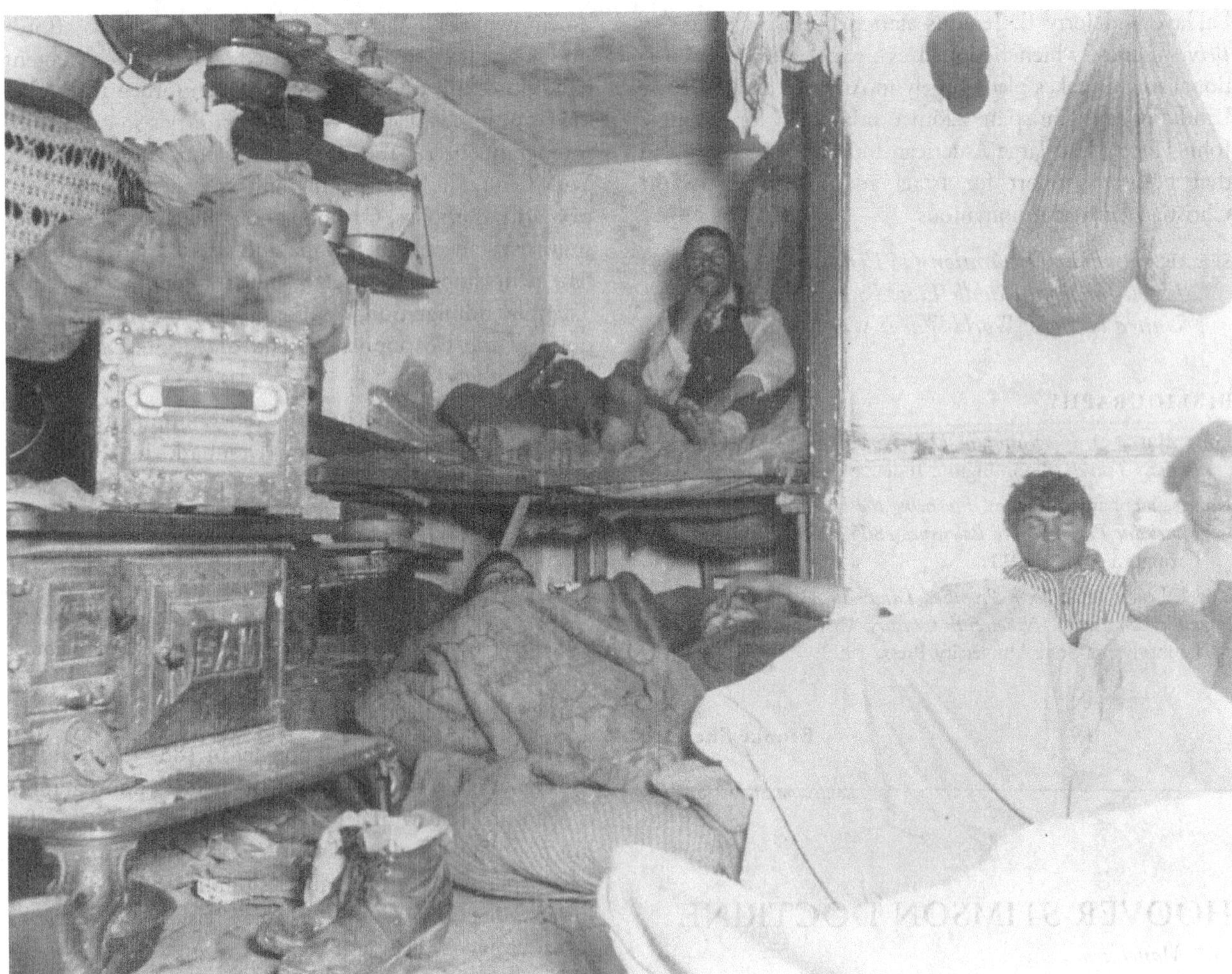

"Five Cents a Spot," from* How the Other Half Lives *(1890), text, illustrations, and photographs by Jacob Riis. *Riis, a former police reporter, embarked on a series of photographic expeditions, some of them revealing crowded tenement rooms and unkempt hallways, startled occupants of cheap lodging houses, sodden drinkers, crowded sweatshops, and toiling families. The lifelike drama of scenes nearby yet normally obscure thrilled Riis's middle-class lecture audiences. (The Jacob A. Riis Collection at the Museum of the City of New York houses this and other Riis images.)* JACOB A. RIIS/ARCHIVE PHOTOS/GETTY IMAGES

personal encounters among the tenements, many stories becoming a means to assign each ethnic group an essential, distinctly un-American, character. Despite his evident sympathy for the tolls of grinding poverty and squalid surroundings, Riis's unabashed resort to racial stereotypes jarringly reminds the reader of his place among *this* half.

Inextricable from its descriptions and anecdotes is the book's delineation of "the tenement house problem" and its proposal for reform. Emphasizing that three fourths of New York's population lived in tenements, Riis spelled out the dangers posed to city and nation by their proliferation at the hands of profit-hungry speculators. *How the Other Half Lives* offers a "Christian" solution: Tenement ownership must be a form of philanthropy taken up by charitable American landlords who would cap their profits at 5 percent.

Despite their limitations, the photographs in *How the Other Half Lives* distinguish the book as a seminal example of the documentary photo-text form that would flourish in twentieth-century America and to a lesser extent abroad. Although Riis did not take all the photographs he showed, he ranks as a visionary photojournalist who anticipated the vast possibilities of photographic storytelling. In form and content, the book resembles contemporary English and American reformist tracts and exposés and the crime-obsessed city-mystery genre spurred by the photographic police surveillance initiated by Alphonse Bertillon (1853–1914) in France. The success of *How the Other Half Lives* made Riis a public figure in the United States; he went on to publish more than a dozen books on American and Danish subjects, eventually leaving newspaper work to write and lecture full-time.

SEE ALSO *Addams, Jane; Immigration and Naturalization Service; Immigration Quotas; Nativism; Settlement House Movement; Transatlantic Reform*

BIBLIOGRAPHY

Hales, Peter. *Silver Cities: The Photography of American Urbanization, 1839–1915.* Philadelphia, PA: Temple University Press, 1984.

Riis, Jacob A. *How the Other Half Lives: Studies among the Tenements of New York.* Edited and introduced by David Leviatin. Boston: Bedford/St. Martin's, 1996.

Riis, Jacob A. *How the Other Half Lives: Authoritative Text, Contexts, Criticism.* Edited by Hasia R. Diner. New York: Norton, 2009.

Stange, Maren. *Symbols of Ideal Life: Social Documentary Photography in America, 1890–1950.* New York: Cambridge University Press, 1989.

Stein, Sally. "Making Connections with the Camera: Photography and Social Mobility in the Career of Jacob Riis." *Afterimage* 10, 10 (May 1983): 9–16.

Maren Stange
Professor of American Studies
Faculty of Humanities and Social Sciences
The Cooper Union, New York

HUGHES, LANGSTON

SEE *Harlem Renaissance/New Negro Movement.*

HUMAN RIGHTS

Human rights constitute one of the most important ideas of twentieth-century politics. The emergence and spread of human rights norms, arguably since 1941 and especially since the 1970s, has reshaped US foreign relations and reframed the way that politicians, diplomats, and ordinary citizens understand the goals of US foreign policy and the nation's role in the world.

Scholars of the United States and human rights face a number of important challenges, among them defining what precisely human rights are and deciding where and when to begin their inquiries. Much recent work has searched for precursors to contemporary activism in nineteenth- and early-twentieth-century abolitionist, suffrage, labor, and humanitarian movements, although these earlier movements had neither the movement infrastructure nor the grounding in international law of their post–World War II successors.

THE UNITED STATES AND THE EMERGENCE OF GLOBAL HUMAN RIGHTS

This state of affairs began to change in 1941, when US president Franklin Roosevelt (1882–1945) and British prime minister Winston Churchill (1874–1965) described Allied war aims in the Atlantic Charter. The charter, Roosevelt's Four Freedoms speech, and other wartime declarations advanced a distinctive conception of human rights, shaped by transatlantic activism and dialogue and grounded in social-democratic visions of economic and social rights.

Four years later, however, with the war drawing to a close and Washington engaged in planning for a postwar order, concerns with human rights took a backseat to the emerging rivalry with the Soviet Union and the promotion of US economic and security interests. The United States dominated the 1945 San Francisco Conference, which created the United Nations, and US-based nongovernmental organizations (NGOs) represented the bulk of the more than one hundred groups permitted to attend. But US and other Western officials blocked inclusion of human rights from the Charter of the United Nations, and in the three-year debate leading to the promulgation of the 1948 Universal Declaration of Human Rights (UDHR), US officials expressed increasing ambivalence about the global project of human rights.

The 1948 UDHR did bear the stamp of US influence, especially that of former First Lady and US representative to the United Nations Eleanor Roosevelt. But US, Soviet, and British efforts crippled the UDHR at its inception by blocking efforts by smaller countries to include enforcement mechanisms, splitting the human rights covenants in two to ensure the separation of civil and political from economic and social rights, inserting the "domestic jurisdiction" clause elevating state sovereignty over universal rights, and beating back proposals enabling individuals or groups to petition the new Human Rights Commission.

This opposition to a strong UN human rights system had many roots. Southern determination to preserve white supremacy helped to drive conservative opposition. Soviet advocacy of economic and social rights, meanwhile, provided a rationale for opposing collective conceptions of rights in the name of anticommunism. Finally, the federal courts and both major US political parties considered international human rights, especially economic and social rights, as a threat to US sovereignty.

THE EISENHOWER YEARS AND THE 1960s

With these considerations in mind, the Eisenhower administration distanced itself from the UDHR and announced that it would not be bound by human rights obligations in its domestic or foreign policy. By this point the deepening Cold War had politicized discussion of human rights to a degree that made it virtually impossible to forge any meaningful domestic consensus.

For the next two decades human rights remained on the margins of US foreign policy. Domestic activists and NGOs continued to advocate for human rights and press for government action regarding South Africa, Brazil, Biafra, and other places, bridging the gap between humanitarianism and human rights activism and setting important precedents for later organizing. But without a legislative framework to plug into, institutional points of entry to the executive branch, or a favorable domestic political environment, such efforts did not penetrate deeply into the public consciousness or decisively affect policy.

The United States was thus largely absent from debates leading to passage in 1966 of the International Covenant on Economic, Social and Cultural Rights. Washington remained vulnerable to charges that it failed to acknowledge decolonization as a human right, voting against or abstaining on the landmark 1960 UN Declaration on Decolonization and other symbolic measures from which anticolonial forces drew moral and political legitimacy. Soviet officials often sided with anticolonial movements and the newly independent Afro-Asian states in debates at the United Nations, and critiqued racism in the United States, emboldening human rights opponents in Congress. US officials, for their part, sought to avoid scrutiny of domestic abuses and shield undemocratic allies. They also wielded human rights as a club against Soviet political and religious repression and the occupation of Eastern Europe, virtually from the moment of the UN Human Rights Committee's creation and especially during the 1980s.

AMNESTY INTERNATIONAL AND 1970s ACTIVISM

Nearly a quarter century after the signing of the UDHR, human rights finally emerged as a significant US foreign policy issue, part of a wider global embrace of human rights politics and activism in the 1970s. This human rights surge had many roots: the institutionalization of human rights at the United Nations; opposition to the Vietnam War; disillusionment with Cold War politics more generally; popular resistance to military takeovers in Brazil, Chile, Greece, and the Philippines; President Jimmy Carter's (b. 1926) measured embrace of human rights; the fading of civil rights as a Cold War headache; and technological shifts facilitating more transnational forms of NGO activism.

Amnesty International, arguably the most important human rights organization of the 1970s, embodied many of these trends, which shaped activism in the United States and globally through its grassroots model of letter writing in support of political prisoners; its efforts to research, gather, and disseminate information on abuses; and its utilization of sophisticated media campaigns to "name and shame" rights-abusing governments. The Ford Foundation's decision in the early 1970s to fund legal aid and human rights NGOs led many to become both more professionalized and more dependent upon philanthropic support for their operations.

Activists and NGOs in the 1970s increasingly directed their attention at states and the foreign support that enabled or facilitated abuses. The US government became a target of campaigners because of its outsized role in providing economic and military aid to abusive regimes, its influence in multilateral forums, and the relative openness of its political system. Successive US administrations adjusted uneasily to the public attention on the US record on human rights. One key point of entry was Congress. Congressional human rights supporters held hearings on abuses in Latin America and Asia; pushed through section 502(b) of the Foreign Assistance Act, which conditioned US foreign aid on human rights grounds; required the State Department to submit annual human rights reports to Congress; created a new State Department bureau for human rights and humanitarian affairs; and, through the Jackson-Vanik amendment of 1974, conditioned Soviet trade preferences on its emigration practices.

Collectively these measures created crucial forums for gathering information about and publicizing human rights abuses, provided legislative targets around which activists could mobilize, and, arguably, changed the culture of the State Department by embedding a concern for human rights into its daily routines. In many countries the US embassy and the officers charged with compiling the annual human rights report became key sites for local activists to convey information and seek protection.

These changes, driven by law, shifts in the broader political culture, and the proliferation of human rights NGOs in the United States and around the world, faced strong resistance from bureaucracies defending turf, Cold War–fighting congressional representatives, executive branch officials hostile to human rights politics, and repressive regimes themselves. Presidents Richard Nixon (1913–1994) and Gerald Ford (1913–2006) and Secretary of State Henry Kissinger (b. 1923) generally disparaged human rights and sent clear signals to repressive anticommunist regimes, such as the Argentinian junta that took over in 1976, that they would not be pressured on such grounds, regardless of congressional intent.

Nixon and Ford, however, also pursued détente with the USSR, which helped lead to the signing of the Helsinki Final Act in August 1975 and the emergence of the so-called Helsinki human rights network. By the 1980s

AMNESTY INTERNATIONAL

Established in 1961 in London, Amnesty International (AI) is the largest and arguably the first nongovernmental organization to promote human rights across the globe. At first a modest organization whose members clustered in Western Europe, AI originally targeted what it called "prisoners of conscience" (POC)—men and women detained for their beliefs who had not advocated violence. AI spotlighted the plight of these prisoners through letter-writing campaigns to pressure governments to release them. In so doing, AI projected political impartiality in an effort to transcend the binary division of the Cold War: in forming groups that "adopted" POCs, its members penned letters of support in equal measure to countries in the West, the East, and the global South. As AI improved its research and monitoring techniques in the 1970s, its mandate and tactics, as well as its grassroots reach, expanded. It launched campaigns against torture, the death penalty, due process rights, and "disappearances"; in the 1990s and after, it turned its attention to bolstering women's rights, humanitarian law, and social, economic, and cultural rights as enumerated in a host of United Nations human rights treaties. Structurally, its affiliates joined local groups, which were attached to a national body (e.g., AI-Germany), which in turn reported to AI's international secretariat in London and coordinated efforts at international forums. However, AI was not without controversy. Famously, its prohibition on the adoption of prisoners who endorsed violence ruled out antiapartheid activist Nelson Mandela (1918–2013) as a POC. Critics accused AI for its predominately Western origins and membership, and more generally for diagnosing symptoms of rights abuses rather than addressing root causes and the larger structural conditions under which rights abuses took place.

AI is currently the most prominent human rights organization in the United States, claiming some 250,000 members in Amnesty International-United States (AI-USA). And yet it made little imprint on the landscape of American social movements until the 1973 end of the Vietnam War, after which the number of AI-USA groups skyrocketed from 6 in 1970, to 202 by 1980, to 413 by 1990. AI-USA quickly amassed a sizable donor base through the expansion of direct-mail fund-raising in the 1970s; by the 1980s, AI-USA was AI's largest and most influential donor nation. In 1976 AI-USA established an office in Washington, DC, a move that evinced a growing lobby for human rights that began to pressure the US government to more fully embrace human rights principles in its foreign policy. Its relationship to US policy makers was, at times, fraught: AI frequently accused the US State Department of soft-pedaling human rights abuses in countries deemed strategically important to US interests, especially under President Ronald Reagan. More recently, AI has criticized the United States for violations of international law in the nation's global "war on terrorism," notably for redefining torture as "enhanced interrogation" and for indefinitely detaining so-called enemy combatants at Guantánamo Bay and black sites (secret prisons).

BIBLIOGRAPHY

Clark, Ann Marie. *Diplomacy of Conscience: Amnesty International and Changing Human Rights Norms.* Princeton, NJ: Princeton University Press, 2001.

Hopgood, Stephen. *Keepers of the Flame: Understanding Amnesty International.* Ithaca, NY: Cornell University Press, 2006.

Keys, Barbara J. *Reclaiming American Virtue: The Human Rights Revolution of the 1970s.* Cambridge, MA: Harvard University Press, 2014.

Patrick William Kelly
A. W. Mellon Postdoctoral Fellow in the Humanities and Humanistic Sciences
University of Wisconsin–Madison

support for the "Helsinki network" was a moral touchstone of US policy toward the Soviet Union, vividly illustrating the power of human rights norms and the nonstate forces promoting them to reshape US foreign policy.

THE MODERN HUMAN RIGHTS MOVEMENT

In many ways, however, the modern human rights movement began with the election of Jimmy Carter (b. 1924) in 1976. His use of the term "embedded it for the first time in popular consciousness and ordinary language" (Moyn 2010, 155). More than simply employing the rhetoric of human rights, Carter strengthened the bureaucratic capacity of the State Department to promote them by upgrading the assistant secretary of state for human rights to cabinet status and appointing capable and determined officials to staff the bureau for human rights and humanitarian affairs. From 1977 to 1979 the administration, often prodded by Congress, curtailed or suspended economic or military assistance to a number of Latin American states and pariah states such as Rhodesia, although to debatable effect.

Carter's human rights policies provoked strong opposition. Critics of Carter on the right, such as Jeanne Kirkpatrick (1926–2006), accused him of abandoning longtime allies such as Anastasio Somoza (1925–1980) in Nicaragua and Mohammad Reza Shah Pahlavi (1918–1980) of Iran. Moreover, the human rights diplomacy directed at the Soviet bloc had genuine consequences, hindering efforts to negotiate the second Strategic Arms Limitation Treaty (SALT II). In East and Southeast Asia more traditional geopolitical concerns ruled the roost, and the Carter White House sought closer ties with Suharto's (1921–2008) Indonesia, muted human rights concerns to renegotiate military base agreements with Ferdinand Marcos (1917–1989) in the Philippines, maintained close ties to South Korea's military-led government, and backed Pol Pot's (1925–1998) Khmer Rouge after Vietnam invaded Cambodia in 1979, putting an end to the Khmer Rouge genocide.

The administration of President Ronald Reagan (1911–2004) promptly repudiated its predecessor's emphasis on human rights, at least outside of Eastern Europe, and declared that terrorism would be the primary concern of US foreign policy. The signals sent by US officials that anticommunist governments would receive strong support in their battles against leftist guerrillas or liberation movements emboldened repressive regimes in Africa and Central America to embark on programs of state terrorism against their own populations. But the administration also faced a well-organized Central America solidarity movement seeking to pressure Congress to cut off US military assistance to El Salvador and end the Contra war against Nicaragua.

Like the antiapartheid movement, Central America solidarity activists represented a broad swath of American civic life—from churches to labor unions to sectarian organizations—mobilizing a mix of religious, political, labor, and human rights discourses, and illustrating how the latter were becoming a vernacular language of social justice. Other activists, including well-established Jewish organizations, finally pressured Reagan into signing the Genocide Convention Implementation Act in 1987, one among many shifts that the reduction of Cold War tensions and foreign policy disasters such as the Iran-Contra scandal in the president's second term seemed to enable.

For many American officials, the collapse of communist regimes at the end of the 1980s heralded the triumph of a Western conception of human rights rooted in civil and political liberty. Yet the 1990s witnessed contradictory dynamics. International human rights law expanded to include gender, sexuality, disability, immigration, public health, worker rights, and other concerns. At the same time the post–Cold War era produced spasms of genocidal violence in Eastern Europe and Rwanda; drift by the United States and some European nations toward armed humanitarian intervention; and growing acceptance of international and transitional justice.

During this period the United States signed or ratified international human rights conventions on civil and political rights, racial discrimination, children's rights, and torture. But the US government continued to maintain close ties to authoritarian regimes, subordinated human rights to the expansion of trade with growing powers such as China, and actively blocked the international community from intervening to stop the genocide in Rwanda, with little public outcry. Following the terrorist attacks of September 11, 2001, and the 2003 invasion of Iraq, the United States seemed to roll back the clock to an earlier era, actively disavowing international human rights law and embracing torture, extrajudicial assassination, and other human rights crimes in the name of counterterrorism. The willingness of a plurality of the American public to support the open abuse of human rights as a wartime expedient raises profound questions about the thin purchase of such ideas in a country still ambivalent about its relation to international law, more than sixty years after passage of the UDHR. These dynamics suggest that human rights will continue to play a contested role in US foreign relations in the decades to come.

SEE ALSO *Armenian Genocide; Contemporary Genocides and US Policy; Ethnic Cleansing; Genocide; Holocaust; United Nations; Universal Declaration of Human Rights*

BIBLIOGRAPHY

Borgwardt, Elizabeth. *A New Deal for the World: America's Vision for Human Rights.* Cambridge, MA: Harvard University Press, 2007.

Keys, Barbara J. *Reclaiming American Virtue: The Human Rights Revolution of the 1970s.* Cambridge, MA: Harvard University Press, 2014.

Moyn, Samuel. *The Last Utopia: Human Rights in History.* Cambridge, MA: Harvard University Press, 2010.

Schmidli, William Michael. *The Fate of Freedom Elsewhere: Human Rights and U.S. Cold War Policy toward Argentina.* Ithaca, NY: Cornell University Press, 2013.

Soohoo, Cynthia, Catherine Albisa, and Martha F. Davis. *Bringing Human Rights Home: A History of Human Rights in the United States* (abridged edition). Philadelphia: University of Pennsylvania Press, 2009.

Bradley Simpson
Associate Professor of History and Asian Studies
University of Connecticut

I

IMMIGRATION

In the nineteenth century, immigrants and immigrant labor became vital to both the nation's continued westward expansion and the expansion of the nation's industrial economy, so immigration remained largely unrestricted until the end of the century. Between the American Revolution and the Civil War, the United States saw waves of migration from Ireland, Germany, and China. The potato famine and resulting changes in inheritance laws spurred the migration of millions of Irish, while Germans sought economic opportunity and hoped to avoid military drafts and ongoing war. Chinese migrants sought an escape from economic changes in China and an opportunity to earn money. All three immigrant groups relied on published accounts from travelers and personal connections with previous migrants to gain a sense of the opportunities available to them in the United States. Gottfried Duden (1789–1856), a German lawyer who traveled to Missouri to purchase land, published one of the earliest and most influential of these accounts in Germany in 1829. His book about conditions in Missouri, *Report on a Journey to the Western States of North America,* portrayed Missouri as a land of fertile soil and new opportunities, and these descriptions, along with nearly 150 other published accounts in Germany in the early 1800s, caused tens of thousands of Germans to immigrate to the United States.

Irish immigrants, particularly the young, single women who would staff the homes of middle- and upper-class northern families, entered American popular culture as "Bridgets." News reports, articles in magazines such as *Harper's Bazaar,* and American silent films stereotyped Irish domestic workers as both "man crazy" and, as one historian wrote, "terrible cooks, poor house cleaners, temperamental if not violent, and awkward in handling the family's precious china and crockery" (Diner 1983, 86). Many of the zealous reformers of the mid-nineteenth century aimed their efforts about temperance, the proper observance of the Sabbath, and public school reform at the Irish and their children, whom they blamed for the crime and corruption of the American city. American Catholics, including laypeople and members of religious orders, organized charitable groups to help impoverished Irish Catholics and protect them from the proselytizing of Protestant reformers, and Catholic parishes established parochial schools to educate the children of immigrants.

Migrants from Europe, along with native-born Americans, flooded the American West following the passage of the Homestead Act of 1862, which offered 160 acres of "free" Western land to settlers who lived on and maintained the homestead for five years. Immigrants who planned to claim land under the Homestead Act also had to sign documents declaring their intent to become citizens after the same period. The United States publicized this act extensively throughout Western Europe, boasting of the high wages available to American workers and to free land now available in the United States. American officials saw the Homestead Act as an opportunity to displace indigenous populations and settle sparsely populated Western land with white, Christian immigrants who planned to settle permanently and become American citizens.

EARLY EFFORTS AT REGULATION

Immigration was one of the first areas of American policy that fell clearly under the mandate of the federal government. In the years following the Civil War, Congress supplanted local and state regulations regarding immigration with federal restrictions and established a complex bureaucracy that screened potential migrants to the United States. The Page Law, passed in 1875, banned the immigration of women for the purposes of prostitution, and further required Chinese women to prove that they were not immigrating at the behest of men who operated brothels for the largely male Chinese population. The Chinese Exclusion Act, signed into law in 1882, banned migration from China entirely and marked the beginning of an era of increasing immigration restriction based on race or national origin. These laws often reflected American beliefs about the inferiority of Asians and other nonwhite racial groups. Migrants from modern-day Lebanon, who began to arrive in the United States in the late nineteenth century, were by 1915 successfully able to convince American courts that they were white and therefore eligible for citizenship. Asians, including Bhagat Singh Thind (1892–1967), an immigrant from India who unsuccessfully challenged his exclusion from citizenship based on the scientific classification of Indians as "Caucasian," continued to be excluded (*United States v. Bhagat Singh Thind*, 261 U.S. 204 (1923), 573).

Further immigration restrictions passed in 1882 barred entry to the United States to persons deemed "idiots" or "lunatics," people with contagious diseases, and those considered likely to become a public charge. Additional legislation in 1891 added people convicted of crimes of moral turpitude, and also began to allow for the deportation of immigrants who were convicted of certain crimes or who became a public charge. These pieces of legislation reflected a growing belief among many Americans in the nineteenth century that immigrants, particularly those of a non–Western European background, depressed American wages and brought perversion and moral degeneracy to America's shores. Federal immigration agents, reflecting these beliefs, used the vague public-charge element of immigration policy to exclude not only people with no visible means of support in the United States but also people with disabilities, mental illnesses, diseases such as epilepsy or tuberculosis, and people deemed sexually deviant. Immigration policy gave these agents a great deal of power in determining the eligibility of individuals who entered the United States as immigrants. Laws regarding deportation gave government officials the ability to exclude immigrants for any number of reasons, often years after their migration. In 1919, in the wake of the Bolshevik Revolution and the resulting Red scare in the United States, government officials used regulations on deportation to permanently remove nearly a thousand immigrant radicals, including noted anarchist Emma Goldman (1869–1940), from the United States.

WORLD WAR I AND THE POSTWAR ERA

Proponents of immigration restriction in the United States formed some of the first modern lobbying organizations to influence the outcome of immigration-related legislation in the 1890s. The Immigration Restriction League (IRL), the first of these organizations, was formed in 1894 and would ally with Progressive Era eugenicists, organized labor, and others to work for the passage of a literacy requirement for all immigrants to the United States. The IRL lobbied Congress for over twenty years before literacy requirements became part of the 1917 Immigration Act, which also further restricted immigration from Asia. Restrictionists would finally achieve the passage of the Johnson-Reed Act in 1924, which barred immigrants from Asia and Africa entirely and prioritized immigrants from Western Europe, whom supporters of restriction considered better able to assimilate to American society.

The Johnson-Reed Act, as well as the Great Depression of the 1930s, significantly reduced the number of immigrants arriving in the United States. Moreover, an isolationist tendency in foreign policy, which an overwhelming majority of Americans supported throughout the 1920s, kept the United States relatively distant from some of the developments in migration policy during this era. Refugees, including stateless people who lost citizenship in any nation in the wake of post–World War I boundary shifts in Europe, became an important element of the work of the League of Nations. The US government did not participate in the League, nor did it accept the Nansen passport, a League of Nations–developed document named after Fridtjof Nansen (1861–1930), the high commissioner on refugees, which gave legal identities to stateless persons. These passports allowed stateless persons to legally immigrate and gain the rights and legal protections that came with twentieth-century citizenship. However, American charitable organizations, both religious and secular, played an active role collecting funds for the League of Nations and their programs to assist refugees after World War I.

During the same era, as a result of immigration restriction and the debates over the loyalty of American immigrants during World War I, immigrants and their allies introduced the notion of cultural pluralism to the American discourse about ethnicity and identity. Louis Adamic (1898–1951), a writer and immigrant from Slovenia, was one of the best-known proponents of multiculturalism in the 1930s and 1940s. He and other immigrants argued that they could both Americanize and maintain elements of their native cultures. Adamic argued that the theory of Americanization harmed the children of immigrants, who felt ashamed of their heritage and inferior to native-born Americans. He and other supporters of multiculturalism formed the Common Council for American Unity in 1939, and Adamic began to gather and publish information about a variety of ethnic and racial groups in the hopes of educating second-generation immigrants about their heritage and their ethnic community in the United States. He documented the contributions of immigrants to every aspect of American life and protested the exclusion of the experiences of immigrants and racial minorities from popular culture, including magazines and films.

WORLD WAR II AND BEYOND

As conditions in Germany worsened through the 1930s, both Jewish victims of Nazi racial policy and political opponents of the new government requested the right to emigrate as refugees. American Jews mobilized to educate the public about the plight of Jewish refugees in Europe and urged Congress to permit refugees to enter the United States outside of the quota system. In 1938, representatives from the United States and thirty-one other nations met in France in an attempt to settle the refugee crisis in Germany. Only one nation, the Dominican Republic, agreed to increase the number of refugees it would accept. However, the delegates also created the Intergovernmental Committee on Refugees, a body that, by the end of World War II, counted members from thirty-six nations and adopted a program to aid refugees from throughout Europe who had been displaced during World War II. This organization joined a variety of intergovernmental groups, such as the United Nations Relief and Rehabilitation Administration (UNRRA), international social service agencies representing Jewish, Catholic, and Lutheran refugees, and other military and governmental bodies to assist refugees and displaced persons living in Germany after World War II.

During and after World War II, Americans' ideas about immigrants and immigration restrictions changed drastically. In the wake of Nazi racial purity policies, the ideas of Adamic and other proponents of cultural pluralism became widely accepted. Religious and ethnic organizations in the United States organized to assist refugees and others impacted by the war, and they began massive publicity campaigns to educate Americans about the plight of war refugees. These groups spurred millions of ordinary Americans to contact lawmakers about immigration-related issues. Members of Congress began to make exceptions to the national quota system for displaced persons, foreign students, and military spouses, including women from Asia who were otherwise racially ineligible for immigration.

During the war, more than 120,000 American GIs would overcome bureaucratic obstacles and the opposition of the US military to marry women in Western Europe, Australia, Africa, and Asia. In 1945, Congress passed Public Law 271, commonly known as the "War Brides Act," which excluded the spouses of American soldiers from quota restrictions. Americans, who were initially suspicious of the motives of foreign women who married American troops and opposed to their admission to the United States, would after the war come to welcome the women, seeing them as symbols of the strength of the postwar family and confirmation of the role of America as a world leader after the war. In early 1946, daily newspapers throughout the nation reported on the arrival of foreign women and their emotional reunions with their husbands. They published stories about women who marveled at the easy availability of food, clothing, and household items that had been rationed for years in Europe, reassuring Americans who were concerned about the nation's economic future and the status of traditional gender roles after the war.

Americans also took an active role in the resettlement of millions of refugees who flooded displaced persons camps throughout Germany. Religious bodies, ethnic groups, and proponents of cultural pluralism began to organize charitable and lobbying efforts to assist refugees with their physical needs and to press American lawmakers to allow immigration outside the quota system to refugees in Europe. The Citizens Committee on Displaced Persons lobbied Congress to admit at least 100,000 displaced persons annually, arguing that skilled, professionally trained refugees would have a positive impact on the American economy. As the Cold War began to take shape, American policymakers became interested in a program of resettlement that would portray displaced persons as escapees from communism and the United States as a nation that would allow them a new start. The Displaced Persons Act of 1948 and the Refugee Relief Act of 1953 authorized the migration of over 400,000 refugees to the United States.

Government and military officials enlisted the assistance of charity and social service agencies that worked with refugees in the 1920s and 1930s in recruiting American sponsors who would find housing and work for displaced persons and matching them with displaced persons in Europe who awaited resettlement. This sponsorship program allowed refugees to demonstrate their ability to support themselves after arrival in the United States, a key element of the public-charge clause in immigration policy. Religious and secular groups began the process of raising money and recruiting sponsors, while their counterparts in Europe screened refugees for their suitability for immigration to the United States, helped them navigate the complicated immigration bureaucracy, and matched them with available sponsors.

CHANGING ATTITUDES ABOUT IMMIGRATION

In 1952, Congress passed a number of revisions to the Johnson-Reed Act, which highlighted the importance of immigration policy to America's status in the world. Supporters of a more liberal policy and an end to the quota system noted the status of the United States among the nations whose quotas remained small, while those who favored a continuation of national origin quotas feared that communists would use a more liberal immigration policy to infiltrate the United States. President Harry S. Truman (1884–1972) vetoed this act, citing the continued discrimination against Eastern European immigrants, but Congress successfully overrode his veto. These revisions to immigration law ended racial restrictions to immigration, which also eased tensions between the United States and many Asian nations. However, the law allotted only a tiny number of quota immigrants to Asia, and it counted any Asian immigrant, regardless of that immigrant's original citizenship, under the "Asian" quota. The law established a system of preferences for visa applications, including family reunification—a key element of the War Brides Act—and a preference for migrants with special skills or professions that officials deemed useful to the American economy.

In the wake of this legislation, which was roundly criticized within liberal circles and among organizations that had been active in resettling refugees, in 1953 Truman authorized the President's Commission on Immigration and Naturalization, including representatives from Jewish, Catholic, and Lutheran agencies, academics, and legal experts, to take testimony on immigration policy in the United States and to recommend changes. The commission reflected changing American attitudes about immigration and about their nation's role in the world, arguing that immigration caused "a continuous flow of creative abilities and ideas that have enriched our nation" (President's Commission 1953, xiv). A wide variety of American institutions, including the General Federation of Women's Clubs, the National Council of Churches, and the Federation of Atomic Scientists, complained about the impact of America's immigration laws on the nation's foreign-policy aims and on the activities of their organizations. The commission's report criticized the nation's current laws for harming America's standing in the world and linked America's postwar crusade against communism with the need for a more liberal immigration policy.

The arrival of refugees fleeing Cuba after Fidel Castro (b. 1926) seized power in 1959 would further associate refugee resettlement with the nation's Cold War aims. American officials hoped the departure of large numbers of Cubans for the United States would embarrass communist leaders and destabilize Cuban society. Americans and their allies began rumors in Cuba that children would be sent to the Soviet Union for indoctrination or would be drafted into the military, which led tens of thousands of Cubans to send their children to the United States to join extended families, enter boarding schools, or enter the foster care system, in a program called Operation Peter Pan. Castro offered Cubans two more opportunities to migrate to the United States, first between 1965 and 1973, when Americans operated twice-daily "Freedom Flights" that brought refugees to Miami, and again in 1980, when more than 125,000 Cubans came to the United States as part of the Mariel boatlift. The United States would continue to admit refugees from communism throughout the twentieth century, including overseeing the resettlement of refugees from Vietnam in the 1970s.

In 1965, President Lyndon Baines Johnson (1908–1973) signed into law the Hart-Celler Act, which serves as the basis of modern immigration law in the United States. Supporters argued that this legislation, which ended the national-origin quota system, would not significantly change traditional patterns of immigration to the United States. Instead, they saw it as a law that would reflect the nation's commitment to equal treatment and would halt a form of immigration restriction that harmed the nation's standing overseas. This legislation still reflected the belief of most Americans, including most proponents of a more liberal immigration policy, that numerical restriction remained a necessary element of American immigration policy. Regardless of the intentions of the bill's supporters, the act has, in fact, caused monumental change in immigration to the United States. Not only did the number of immigrants arriving in the United States increase after 1965, but immigration also became centered in Latin America, Africa, and Asia rather than Western Europe. Studies of recent migration also indicate that family reunification is an important element of recent migration, with many immigrants eventually sponsoring the migration of at least one immediate family member.

SEE ALSO *Americanization; Empire, US; Exceptionalism; Immigration and Naturalization Service; Immigration Quotas; Nativism; Passport*

BIBLIOGRAPHY

Abrams, Kerry. "The Hidden Dimensions of Nineteenth Century Immigration Law." *Vanderbilt Law Review* 62, 5 (October 2009): 1354–1418.

Baynton, Douglas. "Defectives in the Land: Disability and American Immigration Policy, 1882–1924." *Journal of American Ethnic History* 24, 3 (Spring 2005): 31–44.

Canaday, Margot. *The Straight State: Sexuality and Citizenship in Twentieth-Century America.* Princeton, NJ: Princeton University Press, 2011.

Decker, Robert Julio. "Citizenship and Its Duties: The Immigration Restriction League as a Progressive Movement." *Immigrants and Minorities: Historical Studies in Ethnicity, Migration, and Diaspora* 32, 2 (January 2014): 162–182.

Diner, Hasia. *Erin's Daughters in America: Irish Immigrant Women in the Nineteenth Century.* Baltimore, MD: Johns Hopkins University Press, 1983.

Flynn, Peter. "How Bridget Was Framed: The Irish Domestic in Early American Cinema, 1895–1917." *Cinema Journal* 50, 2 (Winter 2011): 1–20.

García, María Cristina. *Havana USA: Cuban Exiles and Cuban Americans in South Florida, 1959–1994.* Berkeley: University of California Press, 1996.

Gatrell, Peter. *Free World?: The Campaign to Save the World's Refugees, 1956–1963.* Cambridge: Cambridge University Press, 2011.

Gualtieri, Sarah. "Becoming White: Race, Religion, and the Founding of Syrian/Lebanese Ethnicity in the United States." *Journal of American Ethnic History* 20, 4 (Summer 2001): 29–58.

Hester, Torrie. "'Protection, Not Punishment': Legislative and Judicial Formation of US Deportation Policy, 1882–1904." *Journal of Ethnic History* 30, 1 (Fall 2010): 11–36.

"Intergovernmental Committee on Refugees." *International Organization* 1, 1 (February 1947): 144–145.

Jasso, Guillermina, and Mark R. Rosenzweig. "Family Reunification and the Immigration Multiplier: US Immigration Law, Origin-Country Conditions, and the Reproduction of Immigrants." *Demography* 25, 3 (Autumn 1991): 291–311.

Kamphoefner, Walter. "Immigrant Epistolary and Epistemology: On the Motivators and Mentality of Nineteenth-Century German Immigrants." *Journal of American Ethnic History* 28, 3 (Spring 2009): 34–54.

Kaplan, Marion A. *Dominican Haven: The Jewish Refugee Settlement in Sosúa, 1940–1945.* New York: Museum of Jewish Heritage, 2008.

Kaprelian-Churchill, Isabel. "Rejecting 'Misfits': Canada and the Nansen Passport." *International Migration Review* 28, 2 (Summer 1994): 281–306.

Lo, Shauna. "Chinese Women Entering New England: Chinese Exclusion Act Case Files, Boston, 1911–1925." *New England Quarterly* 81, 3 (September 2008): 383–409.

Loescher, Gil, and John A. Scanlan. *Calculated Kindness: Refugees and America's Half-Open Door, 1945–Present.* New York: Free Press, 1998.

Meyer, Gerald. "The Cultural Pluralist Response to Americanization: Horace Kallen, Randolph Bourne, Louis Adamic, and Leonard Covello." *Socialism and Democracy* 22, 3 (November 2008): 19–51.

Ngai, Mae M. *Impossible Subjects: Illegal Aliens and the Making of Modern America.* Princeton, NJ: Princeton University Press, 2005.

President's Commission on Immigration and Naturalization. *Whom Shall We Welcome?: Report of the President's Commission on Immigration and Naturalization.* Washington, DC: US Government Printing Office, 1953.

"*United States v. Bhagat Singh Thind.*" *American Journal of International Law* 17, 3 (July 1923): 572–578.

Urban, Andrew. "Irish Domestic Servants: 'Biddy' and Rebellion in the American Home, 1850–1900." *Gender & History* 21, 2 (August 2009): 263–286.

Virden, Jenel. *Good-bye, Piccadilly: British War Brides in America.* Urbana: University of Illinois Press, 1996.

Anna Amundson
Visiting Assistant Professor, Department of History
Florida State University

IMMIGRATION AND NATIONALITY ACT OF 1965

The Immigration and Nationality Act of 1965 proved a radical reform of US immigration policy that changed the nation's ethnic and racial composition. It eliminated the long-debated national origins quotas, codified a system of preferences developed in part based on Cold War foreign policy concerns, and ended anti-Asian immigration discrimination. At the same time, however, it also created a new cap on migration within the Western Hemisphere that complicated long-standing patterns of seasonal migration. As a result, the impact of the act proved profound for both the domestic and international relations of the United States.

Calls to alter fundamental aspects of existing US immigration law grew after the Second World War and persisted even through the hard-fought passage of the Immigration and Nationality Act of 1952 over the veto of President Harry Truman (1884–1972). Thereafter, two camps warred in the immigration debate. Restrictionists emphasized the national security imperative, and they preferred to maintain the national origins quotas created in the 1920s and manage them within a tightly controlled annual limit on immigration visas. Liberals by and large did not question the need for an annual ceiling but argued that existing policies undermined American foreign policy goals. They sought instead to eliminate the nationality-based limits in place for the Eastern Hemisphere in favor of a more equitable preference system that placed applicants in line for visas based on their skills, family reunification needs, or refugee status.

By the early 1960s, politicians across the political spectrum were arguing in favor of a revised law. Support for national origins quotas had waned considerably, but voices calling for a cap on immigration from the Western Hemisphere joined the mix. Historically, the quota system did not apply to the Americas, although a number of different provisions governed the movement of immigrants and seasonal labor migrants. After the passage of the 1964 Civil Rights Act with its antidiscrimination measures, the last defense of national origins died out. The Johnson administration's new immigration proposal was designed to codify existing immigration practices, although to secure passage of the bill the administration accepted an amendment advocated by some Republicans, southern Democrats, and labor leaders capping Western Hemisphere immigration at 120,000 visas per year.

In its final form, the Immigration and Nationality Act of 1965 granted the Eastern Hemisphere an annual quota of 170,000 visas, with no more than 20,000 to come from any one country. Visas would be issued based on a series of preferences, with four of the seven focusing on family reunification (particularly allowing the adult children and siblings of American citizens or permanent residents to enter), accounting for almost three quarters of the total available visas. Preferences three and six granted entry to individuals with skill sets, occupations, knowledge, or education of value to or needed by the United States; these took up another 20 percent of the available slots. The act reserved the final preference and only 6 percent of the remaining visas for refugees, defined as people fleeing communism or the Middle East. Adding the new cap for the Western Hemisphere, the act assumed a total of 290,000 new immigrants each year.

Although not intended to be revolutionary at the time of its passage, the act profoundly changed the composition of future immigration to the United States. Importantly, this was the first time since the Chinese Exclusion Act in 1882 that East Asian migrants had equal access to immigration: Even the 1952 act, which theoretically ended Asian exclusion, maintained sharp quota limits on non-Europeans. The postwar entry of increasing numbers of Asian immigrants as nonquota immigrants, war brides, and refugees led to a rapidly growing population as Asian Americans took advantage of new family reunification provisions. When combined with the return of economic prosperity in Western Europe, decolonization, and improved transportation networks, the 1965 act created opportunities for new sources of immigration and led to a diversification of the foreign-born population. By a decade after its passage, three quarters of new immigrants annually came from the developing world.

Soon after passage, problems emerged with the act that threatened US relations with its allies and neighbors. The new restrictions on the Western Hemisphere created immediate difficulties for Canada and, in the longer term, for Mexico, necessitating a series of additional measures to attempt to regularize and control steady migration, particularly over the southern US border. Refugee provisions built into the 1965 act also proved unequal to the challenges the United States faced with the end of the Vietnam War and the Cold War, revealing once again the difficulties of making immigration policy align with foreign policy.

SEE ALSO *Chinese Exclusion Act (1882); Immigration; Immigration and Naturalization Service; Immigration Quotas; Immigration Restriction League; Nativism*

BIBLIOGRAPHY

Schrag, Peter. *Not Fit for Our Society: Immigration and Nativism in America.* Berkeley: University of California Press, 2010.

Teitelbaum, Michael S., and Myron Weiner, eds. *Threatened Peoples, Threatened Borders: World Migration and U.S. Policy.* New York: Norton, 1995.

Zolberg, Aristide R. *A Nation by Design: Immigration Policy in the Fashioning of America.* Cambridge, MA: Harvard University Press, 2006.

Meredith Oyen
Assistant Professor
University of Maryland, Baltimore County

IMMIGRATION AND NATURALIZATION SERVICE

The Immigration and Naturalization Service (INS) was a US agency from 1933 to 2003 that was housed initially in the Department of Labor and later in the Department of Justice and tasked with enforcing immigration laws and providing immigrant services such as naturalization. INS antecedents can be traced to at least the Civil War, and although the agency was disbanded in March 2003 as part of a government restructuring after the September 11, 2001, terrorist attacks, its functions continue to be carried out by agencies within the Department of Homeland Security. During its seven decades of operations, INS activities were often dictated by global events that affected the contours of international migration and US foreign policy objectives. It was the first agency many foreigners interacted with when coming to America, so its activities shaped US culture and perceptions abroad.

EARLY AMERICAN IMMIGRATION REGULATION

The Constitution stipulates little regarding immigration regulation, and the task was left primarily to the states for America's first hundred years as a country. Congress formed a short-lived federal precursor organization of the INS in 1864 when it created a commissioner of immigration within the State Department to facilitate immigration to northern states to assist with the Civil War. The agency, however, was disbanded four years later and the states resumed primary regulation of immigration until the US Supreme Court ruling in *Henderson v. Mayor of the City of New York* (1875) stipulated that the federal government had exclusive regulation over immigration. As large numbers of foreigners from new sending countries increasingly arrived in America in the late nineteenth century, Congress began to assert this right by passing laws restricting entrance to specified groups of people. Among these laws were the Chinese Exclusion Act and the

Immigration Act of 1882, which barred foreigners from a specified country and those deemed poor, insane, or unable to take care of themselves.

INS FORMATION AND ACTIVITIES THROUGH WWII

The federal government developed bureaucratic machinery to enforce its immigration laws in 1891 by creating the Office of the Superintendent of Immigration, which was established under the Department of the Treasury, and with more than twenty inspection stations a foundation of the future INS immigration enforcement function was built. Congress next passed the Act of March 2, 1895, which elevated the Office of Immigration to the Bureau of Immigration and renamed the agency leader's title from superintendent to commissioner-general of immigration. The federal government continued to enhance control over immigration with the Act of February 14, 1903, which transferred the Bureau of Immigration from the Treasury Department to the newly created Department of Commerce and Labor because extant immigration laws were often purportedly designed to protect US workers. Congress again broadened federal control over immigration with the Basic Naturalization Act of 1906, and the Bureau of Immigration was expanded into the Bureau of Immigration and Naturalization to oversee this legislation. But this organizational arrangement was short-lived because the Department of Commerce and Labor splintered into separate cabinet departments in 1913. With this reorganization the Bureau of Immigration and Naturalization also divided into distinct bureaus within the Department of Labor.

With this bureaucratic configuration in place, the federal government changed its immigration policy stance and ended the "open-door" era with the 1921 and 1924 Quota Acts, which significantly restricted immigration to the United States from the Eastern Hemisphere and resulted in a mere fraction of foreigners coming to America compared to previous decades. The INS was formed in this policy milieu on June 10, 1933, when Executive Order 6166 brought back together the Bureau of Immigration and Bureau of Naturalization under one agency within the Department of Labor. The quota legislation and the Great Depression resulted in limited immigration to the United States and few foreigners requiring services in the 1930s, so the INS focused on preventing unauthorized entry into the country, deporting immigrants believed criminal or subversive, and working with other agencies to take legal action against those breaking immigration laws. The geopolitical environment shifted by the end of the decade, and the Second World War (1939–1945) prompted the June 1940 passage of the President's Reorganization Plan No. V, which moved the INS to the Department of Justice and refocused the agency on the national security imperatives of the era. During the war period, the INS was tasked with helping to carry out the Alien Registration Program and fingerprinting immigrants, operating internment camps for immigrants from enemy nations such as Japan, enhancing border patrols to secure US territory, conducting background checks on immigrant defense workers, and administering a program to import temporary foreign agricultural laborers to assist with farming while soldiers were fighting abroad.

INS: POST–WORLD WAR II ACTIVITIES AND 2003 DISSOLUTION

With total immigration numbers to the United States low after World War II because of the restrictive quota policies, the INS focused on implementing American refugee laws to assist with the war fallout, administering the Bracero program and the temporary importation of Mexican agricultural workers, enforcing immigration laws, and assisting with reforming immigration policy. This last effort culminated in the Immigration and Nationality Act of 1965, which ended the quota laws and more equitably and widely opened the American immigration system to foreigners, resulting in more immigrants arriving from Asia and Central and South America than Europe.

As in previous decades, INS activities were shaped by global events in the 1970s and 1980s, and the agency was charged with responding to new travel technologies facilitating international travel and a societal concern over unauthorized immigration. For example, the Immigration Reform and Control Act (IRCA) of 1986 tasked the INS with enforcing sanctions against American employers who hired undocumented immigrants, deporting unauthorized immigrants discovered to be working illegally, and administering a legalization program that gave many undocumented immigrants in the country at the time a path to citizenship.

By the late 1990s, after nearly three quarters of a century of growth, the INS had expanded to over thirty thousand employees (from less than ten thousand workers in the 1970s), and it carried out numerous functions, including regulating the permanent and temporary entry of foreigners, inspecting immigrants at ports of entry and patrolling borders, administering naturalization and asylum for refugees, and detaining and removing immigrants who were violating laws. The September 11, 2001, events and the fact that the terrorists legally entered the country led to a reconstitution of US immigration procedures toward tighter immigrant screening, enhanced border security, and a stronger approach to deporting criminal aliens. President George W. Bush (b. 1946) sought to carry out these objectives and prevent another 9/11 by forming the Department of Homeland Security (DHS), which included a bureaucratic reshuffling that dissolved the INS in March 2003 and redistributed its previous functions among three new agencies within the DHS: Customs and Border Patrol (CBP), Immigration and Customs Enforcement (ICE), and US Citizenship and Immigration Services (USCIS). Although the INS no longer exists in name, its bureaucratic duties continue to be carried out today by these new agencies.

INS FUNCTIONS, STRUCTURE, AND LEGACY, 1933–2003

While the foci of INS operations varied from 1933 to 2003 based on global events and migration patterns, the agency's broad functions remained constant and consisted of immigrant enforcement and service tasks. The INS enforcement operations included screening travelers arriving in the United States, fielding agents to monitor border areas, checking US employment places for undocumented workers, identifying and prosecuting alien smuggling operators, detaining suspected alien criminals and undocumented immigrants for proceedings to determine their status, and deporting those found in violation of laws. The INS immigrant service functions included assisting and processing immigrants, travelers, and temporary workers wanting to come to the United States, training government employees to administer immigration laws, conducting legal proceedings for immigrants challenging decisions about their status, and providing naturalization services or the granting of citizenship status to legal immigrants. The agency carried out its duties through an organization that by its final years was housed in the Department of Justice and consisted of four primary divisions: field operations, management, policy and planning, and programs. The agency, led by a presidentially appointed and Senate-approved federal commissioner overseen by the attorney general, had offices throughout the United States and foreign countries. Due to its global reach it often worked with the Department of State and the United Nations.

Through its existence the INS interacted with over thirty million immigrants, so its activities virtually spanned the globe and had a large impact on US culture and foreign relations. The agency constituted a pseudo-diplomatic body in the sense that its actions toward immigrants could improve or injure perceptions of America in the international community. As the first US bureaucracy with which many immigrants interacted, it had a lasting effect on their impressions of the country. And the large numbers of foreign nationals who came into contact with the INS, as well as the agency's dual mandate to provide immigrant services and enforce immigrant laws, guaranteed that over its long history, the INS was alternatively seen as America's welcoming greeter or its stern gatekeeper. But however its activities were perceived, the INS played a central role in immigrant lives and immigration debates throughout the twentieth century, so its actions will remain engrained in the American ethos.

SEE ALSO *Alien Contract Labor Law/Foran Act (1885); Americanization; Angel Island; Chinese Exclusion Act (1882); Department of Homeland Security; Department of State; Ellis Island; Immigration; Immigration and Nationality Act of 1965; Immigration Quotas; Indian Citizenship Act (1924); Nativism; Race; Whiteness*

BIBLIOGRAPHY

Calavita, Kitty. *Inside the State: The Bracero Program, Immigration, and the I.N.S.* New York: Routledge, 1992.

Code of Federal Regulations, 8: Aliens and Nationality. Washington, DC: Office of the Federal Register, 2007.

Dixon, Edward H., and Mark A. Galan. *The Immigration and Naturalization Service (Know Your Government).* New York: Chelsea House, 1990.

Gabaccia, Donna R. *Foreign Relations: American Immigration in Global Perspective.* Princeton, NJ: Princeton University Press, 2012.

Magaña, Lisa. *Straddling the Border: Immigration Policy and the INS.* Austin: University of Texas Press, 2003.

Masanz, Sharon D. *History of the Immigration and Naturalization Service: A Report.* Washington, DC: Government Printing Office, 1980.

Morris, Milton D. *Immigration—The Beleaguered Bureaucracy.* Washington, DC: Brookings Institution, 1985.

Smith, Marian L. "An Overview of INS History." In *A Historical Guide to the U.S. Government,* edited by George T. Kurian, 305–308. New York: Oxford University Press, 1998.

Smith, Marian L. "The Immigration and Naturalization Service (INS) at the U.S.-Canadian-Border, 1893–1993: An Overview of Issues and Topics." *Michigan Historical Review* 26, 2 (Fall 2000): 127–147.

Totten, Robbie J. "National Security and U.S. Immigration Policy, 1776–1790." *Journal of Interdisciplinary History* 39, 1 (Summer 2008): 37–64.

Totten, Robbie J. "Security and Immigration Policy: An Analytical Framework for Reform." In *Undecided Nation: Political Gridlock and the Immigration Crisis,* edited by Tony Payan and Erika de la Garza, 253–270. New York: Springer International, 2014.

UCSIS History Office and Library, *Overview of INS History.* http://www.uscis.gov/sites/default/files/USCIS/History%20and%20Genealogy/Our%20History/INS%20History/INSHistory.pdf

Robbie J. Totten
Chair and Assistant Professor, Political Science Department
American Jewish University

IMMIGRATION QUOTAS

The United States is a nation of immigrants, and yet it has at times attempted to restrict the number of newcomers it received. Throughout the twentieth century, the federal government used quotas to shape the composition of its immigrant population. These quotas set limits according to country of origin, and as such, reflect racial politics and diplomatic strategy.

INCREASINGLY EXCLUSIONARY IMMIGRATION LAWS

The year 1921 marked the establishment of the nation's first quantitative immigration-quota law, but immigration laws had their origin in the first decades after the Revolutionary War (1775–1783). The United States first attempted to limit immigration in 1798 with the passage of the Naturalization and Alien Acts, which targeted Irish and French immigrants. These acts made citizenship more difficult for foreigners and allowed for the expulsion of aliens the government deemed dangerous (Tichenor 2002, 2). Records for immigration are incomplete for the early national period; numbers were not first officially counted until 1820, when a new law required that the master or captain of a ship from abroad deliver a manifest of all passengers at ports of arrival (Eckerson 1966, 5). Immigration levels were fairly low until the 1830s, when British, Irish, and German immigrants began coming to the United States in larger numbers. Despite relative openness for the first half of the nineteenth century, many native-born Anglo Americans began to resent job competition from Irish and German Catholic immigrants. This nativist sentiment generated animosity toward newcomers.

Greater awareness of public health issues, too, sparked concerns about immigrants bringing contagious diseases to the United States. These fears led to the creation of quarantine stations and the construction of Swinburne Island and Hoffman Island in New York Bay as places to send foreign passengers deemed unwell. Their use increased as New York's Ellis Island became a major hub for immigrant arrivals.

Growing concern with the effects of immigration on the United States culminated in restrictive legislation in the closing decades of the nineteenth century. The Page Act of 1875 prohibited the immigration of "undesirables," namely, Asian convicts and prostitutes. In 1882, the Chinese Exclusion Act became the first law implemented to prevent a specific ethnic group from immigrating to the United States. This act marked the beginning of explicitly race- and nationality-based discrimination in immigration policy. It was not repealed until 1943, causing many Chinese emigrants to be detained at the Angel Island Immigration Station in San Francisco Bay for years.

In 1891, the Bureau of Immigration was established to federally administer all immigration laws, which were becoming increasingly exclusionary. In the first decades of the twentieth century, the number of immigrants arriving in the United States exceeded one million annually, and many Americans grew weary of accepting so many newcomers (Eckerson 1966, 5). Additionally, the study of eugenics entered into political debates. This pseudoscience purported to prescribe methods for bettering the human race and encouraged policy makers to conceptualize the purification of America's population.

The US Congress's Joint Immigration Commission, formed in 1907 and chaired by Senator William P. Dillingham (1843–1923), warned of the negative consequences of immigration from southern and eastern Europe and proposed a literacy test to restrict the eligibility of many foreigners for entrance. President William Howard Taft (1857–1930) vetoed the bill in 1911, but six years later it passed. Although the literacy test was ultimately a discriminatory policy, some congressmen had intended it to end discrimination against Asians, by applying it equally to all immigrants (Ly and Weil 2010, 47–48). Other acts were passed to exclude beggars and anarchists, as well as people with diseases and disabilities. Sometimes the United States cooperated with foreign governments in its exclusion, as it did in 1907 with the "Gentlemen's Agreement with Japan," in which the Japanese government secretly agreed to prevent the emigration of Japanese laborers (Eckerson 1966, 10).

Following World War I (1914–1918), Warren G. Harding (1865–1923) won the presidential election on an "America First" platform, ushering in a period of fervent nationalism and doubts about immigrants' patriotism (Tichenor 2002, 143). This nationalism was reflected in the Emergency Immigration Act of 1921, which for the first time established a quota system for US immigration. Support for the quota system ranged from staunch restriction based on specific countries to more equitable immigration policies. Missionary Sidney Lewis Gulick (1860–1945), for example, lobbied actively against the racist policies of Dillingham and the Immigration Restriction League, and sought a balance between permissive admittance rules and stricter citizenship qualifications (Ly and Weil 2010, 54). The ultimate 1921 law, backed by Congressman Albert Johnson (1869–1957), chairman of the House Committee on Immigration and Naturalization, contained a national-origins formula, which mandated that a total of 3 percent of the number of US residents from any given country living in the United States at the time of the 1910 census be allowed to enter the United States (Eckerson 1966, 6). This legislation was intended to be temporary, but quotas remained a prominent feature in US immigration management until the 1960s. Congressman Johnson worked with the Immigration Committee to craft a more discriminatory immigration bill, which became law in 1924, despite some opposition from Bureau of Immigration head William Walter Husband (1871–1942) and others. Informed by eugenics, the quotas for the 1924 National Origins Act privileged immigrants from northern and western Europe, who received 84 percent of the immigrant slots (Stewart 1924, 276–277). Another law in 1929 firmly established the national-origins quota system by capping immigrant admissions at 153,714 and once again reserving the majority of slots for favored European groups (Tichenor 2002, 146).

THE IMPACT OF THE GREAT DEPRESSION AND WORLD WAR II

The international crises of the 1930s and 1940s forced American policy makers to modify immigration regulations. Economic hardship during the Great Depression (1929–1939) made many Americans wary of increasing immigrant quotas, even as the rise of fascism and Nazism in Europe forced many European Jews to seek asylum in the United States. Quota immigration dipped in the early 1930s, but reached a peak of 62,402 in 1939 as the depression began to lift (Eckerson 1966, 9).

During World War II (1939–1945), lawmakers viewed immigration as a national security issue, while at the same time seeking solutions for the labor shortages created by the war. In 1943, the US government launched the bracero program by signing bilateral agreements with Mexico, Honduras, Barbados, and Jamaica that allowed for the admittance of temporary laborers. Between 1930 and 1965, almost two million immigrants born in Canada and Mexico entered the United States, many of them Mexican braceros. The bracero program ended in 1964, but Mexican immigration continued, much of it illegal (Eckerson 1966, 11).

Following World War II, Cold War relations with the Soviet Union shaped immigration policy, as the United States worked to stamp out communism at home and abroad. While a 1948 law permitted immigration beyond quota limits for persons displaced by the war, the Immigration and Nationality Act of 1952 reaffirmed the national-origins quota system, and extended provisions of the Internal Security Act of 1950 by creating new stipulations for exclusion and deportations based on political activities and ideologies. At the same time, however, the US government passed a series of refugee acts throughout the 1950s and 1960s to provide asylum to refugees fleeing communist regimes (Tichenor 2002, 4). This would continue during the Vietnam War (1954–1975), as the United States welcomed refugees from Indochina and sought to establish its reputation as a moral bulwark against communism.

THE COLD WAR AND CIVIL RIGHTS ERA

The post–World War II years were also a time of civil rights reforms, which prompted many policy makers to advocate more equitable immigration policies. In 1963, President John F. Kennedy (1917–1963), a proponent of open immigration, introduced a bill that would eliminate prejudiced quotas. His bill expired before it became law, but two years later the Hart-Cellar Act abolished the national-origins quota system (Kennedy 1966, 138).

For the remainder of the twentieth century, the United States received between one and two million immigrants almost every year. Its quota system no longer discriminated by nationality; instead, immigrants were admitted in the order in which they filed for visas. New preference categories were based on family relationships and job skills. While emigration from Western Europe had once comprised roughly three-quarters of quota immigration, the end of overt discrimination led to an increase in immigration from Asia, Africa, and the Middle East (Eckerson 1966, 4). Despite higher immigration caps in the 1980s and 1990s, illegal immigration, especially from Mexico and Central America, persisted. The Immigration Reform and Control Act of 1986 gave amnesty to some illegal immigrants while also imposing penalties on employers who hired them. The Illegal Immigration Reform and Individual Responsibility Act of 1996 marked a return to more restrictive immigration policies by strengthening border enforcement and making deportation easier.

THE TWENTY-FIRST CENTURY

In the first decades of the twenty-first century, policy makers continued to debate how best to manage immigration to the United States. Mexico, China, and India were the biggest sender countries, but in order to prevent domination by any individual immigrant group, US legislation mandated that no group of immigrants from a single country was allowed to exceed 7 percent of the total number of immigrants to the United States in a single year (American Immigration Council 2014). As the century progresses, it seems likely that US immigration policy will continue to oscillate between restriction and openness, and quotas will ebb and flow, but the United States will remain an immigration nation.

SEE ALSO *Alien Contract Labor Law/Foran Act (1885); Angel Island; Chinese Exclusion Act (1882); Ellis Island; Nativism*

BIBLIOGRAPHY

American Immigration Council. "How the United States Immigration System Works: A Fact Sheet." March 1, 2014. http://www.immigrationpolicy.org/just-facts/how-united-states-immigration-system-works-fact-sheet

Eckerson, Helen F. "Immigration and National Origins." Special issue, "The New Immigration." *Annals of the American Academy of Political and Social Science* 367 (1966): 4–14.

Jacoby, Tamar. "Immigration Nation." *Foreign Affairs* 85, 6 (2006): 50–65.

Kennedy, Edward M. "The Immigration Act of 1965." Special issue, "The New Immigration." *Annals of the American Academy of Political and Social Science* 367 (1966): 137–149.

Ly, Son-Thierry, and Patrick Weil. "The Antiracist Origin of the Quota System." Special issue, "Migration Politics." *Social Research* 77, 1 (2010): 45–78.

Rubin, Ernest. "Immigration and Population Trends in the United States, 1900–1940." *American Journal of Economics and Sociology* 6, 3 (1947): 345–362.

Stewart, Ethelbert. "The New Immigration Quotas, Former Quotas, and Immigration Intakes." *Monthly Labor Review* 19, 2 (1924): 1–11.

Tichenor, David. *Dividing Lines: The Politics of Immigration Control in America.* Princeton, NJ: Princeton University Press, 2002.

Yang, Philip Q. "The Demand for Immigration to the United States." *Population and Environment* 19, 4 (1998): 357–383.

Lindsay Schakenbach Regele
Assistant Professor
Miami University

IMMIGRATION RESTRICTION LEAGUE

The Immigration Restriction League (IRL) was founded in Boston by three Harvard alumni in 1894. Despite being a small organization operated by few executives, it quickly became the most important anti-immigration lobby group in the United States. Prominent members of the New England social and academic elite supported the league as vice presidents and by providing funding. To achieve its goal of a significant numerical limitation of the so-called new immigration from southern and eastern Europe, the IRL operated similarly to other Progressive Era reform movements: It investigated immigration and its effects with scientific methods, created awareness of the perceived problem by publishing pamphlets and statistics, participated in public debates, and cooperated with newspapers. While the league initially relied on personal connections to politicians, it professionalized its activities after the turn of the century and employed lobbyists in Washington, building a bipartisan anti-immigration coalition of patriotic societies, unions, farmers' associations, and legislators.

The league's beliefs combined older strains of nativism with contemporary scientific racism. Through academic networks, the idea that European populations could be distinguished into different races crossed the Atlantic and reverberated in American anthropology and the social sciences. The IRL could thus claim that in contrast to the putatively superior races of northwestern Europe, new immigrants did not meet the standards of whiteness, as indicated by higher rates of criminality, mental illness, and pauperism. Since these characteristics corresponded with illiteracy, the league argued, a literacy test would bar "undesirable" immigrants effectively and impartially—simultaneously achieving the IRL's goal of excluding new immigrants disproportionately. Bills requiring male immigrants and unaccompanied women to be able to read in their own language were introduced by the league's political allies but repeatedly failed to pass Congress or override presidential vetoes.

In public debates about urban living conditions, the IRL regularly engaged with other Progressive Era associations. Reformers active in the settlement and Americanization movements and those advocating municipal reforms based on European models relied on approaches that would empower immigrant communities, ameliorate living conditions, or motivate political representatives to engage with the social effects of industrialization and urbanization. In contrast to this civic conception of American citizenship characterized by participation, the league redefined these social issues in racial terms, claiming that immigrants lacked the Anglo-Saxons' proclivity for self-government as well as their higher social and moral standards. Connecting this argument to the idea of race suicide, the IRL claimed that Anglo-Saxon birthrates were decreasing because of adverse social conditions caused by immigration and would eventually change the American population's racial composition fundamentally if immigration were not restricted.

IRL executives also used this argument to appeal to the American Federation of Labor (AFL) and other unions by suggesting that supposedly docile and frugal new immigrants undercut American wage levels, drawing on prejudices against Asian immigrants that were shared in the Anglophone world. After the first literacy test bill had been vetoed by President Grover Cleveland (1837–1908) in 1897, Natal, Australia, and New Zealand used it as a model to exclude racialized immigrant groups. These countries enacted laws that required immigrants to pass a dictation test in a language determined by immigration officers, often testing non-Europeans in languages they were not conversant with to exclude them. The IRL, in turn, could then praise these settler colonies as models for successfully protecting "free white labor" from immigrant competition. The IRL also argued that these countries efficiently excluded immigrants classified as disabled, suffering from mental illness, or "likely to become a public charge" and lobbied for the strict application of existing American regulations against such individual "deficiencies."

After the turn of the century, the IRL increasingly engaged with psychiatrists and eugenicists. Since new research by American and European scientists seemed to suggest that hereditary factors were more important than the environment in determining behavior, both communities could be convinced that the domestic policies they advocated, such as forced sterilization, would be ineffective if "inferior" immigrants kept arriving. When wartime anxieties about immigrants' loyalty and concerns about the postwar economy added to the support of the coalition the IRL had built, the Immigration Act of 1917, which included a literacy test, was passed over President Woodrow Wilson's (1856–1924) veto. This restrictive policy was mirrored in the Anglophone world: in Australia, the dictation test was increasingly applied to Europeans deemed racially, politically, or socially undesirable. Canada, on the other hand, adopted a wide range of measures after 1919 to limit immigration from eastern Europe and Asia significantly. When the American literacy test proved to be less effective than the IRL had expected, the league cooperated with eugenic organizations to lobby aggressively for immigration quotas in the 1920s. After these had been established, the league's activities slowly dwindled.

SEE ALSO *American Protective Association; Chinese Exclusion Act (1882); Immigration; Immigration and Nationality Act of 1965; Immigration Quotas; Know-Nothings; Nativism; "The New Colossus" (Emma Lazarus, 1883); Whiteness*

BIBLIOGRAPHY

Cannato, Vincent J. *American Passage: The History of Ellis Island.* New York: HarperCollins, 2009.

Higham, John. *Strangers in the Land: Patterns of American Nativism, 1860–1925.* New Brunswick, NJ: Rutgers University Press, 2008.

Lake, Marilyn, and Henry Reynolds. *Drawing the Global Colour Line: White Men's Countries and the International Challenge of Racial Equality.* Carlton, Victoria, Australia: Melbourne University, 2008.

Solomon, Barbara Miller. *Ancestors and Immigrants: A Changing New England Tradition.* Boston: Northeastern University Press, 1989.

Robert Julio Decker
Lecturer in North American History
University of Bristol

IMPERIALISM

Since the founding of the Republic, imperialism has played a central role in America's interaction with the world. It has influenced national responses to global affairs, defined foreign relations with many regions of the world, and shaped perceptions abroad of US intentions and abilities.

Because the label *imperialism* has often been used for political or propagandistic purposes, its scholarly application to interpretations of American history is still controversial. Stripped of its polemical dimension, however, the term *imperialism* describes all attitudes, strategies, abilities, and activities designed to create and maintain formal or informal empire.

American imperialism was driven by three mutually reinforcing attitudes and concerns: the quest for security, the pursuit of prosperity, and the desire for national greatness. Over the last two and a half centuries these driving forces, while never undisputed, proved remarkably durable and sufficiently flexible to accommodate transformations within the United States and the world around it.

THE FIRST PHASE: SETTLER IMPERIALISM

During the first phase of imperialism, the United States steadily expanded across the continent and ventured into Asia, the Pacific Ocean, and the Caribbean basin. Security against the potential threat of the British, French, Spanish, and Russian empires in North America was a paramount concern for the militarily weak young Republic.

This concern provided an important impetus for America's own imperialism. President James Monroe's (1758–1831) famous 1823 warning against European colonial adventures in the New World was as much an expression of insecurity as it was a pronouncement of hemispheric imperial ambition. The old imperialist siren song of expansion now received an American transposition that claimed not only exception to the machinations of Old World great power politics but reinterpreted imperialism as a defensive reflex against the potentialities of European imperial incursions in North America. Empire-building was thus conceptually translated into an anticolonial measure for national survival.

While critics claimed that a republican polity could not expand by conquest and expect a successful reproduction of its constitutional system, supporters of imperial expansion, such as Monroe, Benjamin Franklin (1706–1790), Alexander Hamilton (1755–1804), James Madison (1751–1836), Thomas Jefferson (1743–1826), and John Quincy Adams (1767–1848), argued in one way or another that extensive territory and republic were not only compatible but a safeguard against national decline.

While independence had created the basis for a departure from British imperialism, Americans have also been acculturated to imperialist worldviews that framed their understanding of a wide range of issues, from international affairs to race and ethnicity. Paradoxically then, while Americans had freed themselves from empire, they would go on to replicate many of its imperialist political, economic, military, and cultural practices.

At the heart of American settler imperialism was the successive acquisition and conquest of vast transcontinental spaces populated by a multitude of Native American cultures. In part, such acquisitions were negotiated with other empires, such as the Louisiana Purchase from France in 1803 and the purchase of Alaska from Russia in 1867. Further land transfers were negotiated with indigenous cultures that were increasingly marginalized by the aggressive imperialist dynamic of the settler empire. This form of imperialism targeted Native Americans with forced resettlements, prolonged asymmetrical colonial warfare, and internal colonization. By the end of the nineteenth century, indigenous cultures were militarily defeated, confined to a reservation system, and exposed to intrusive cultural assimilation programs designed to eradicate indigenous cultural identities.

Settler imperialism also expanded into the southwestern borderlands and culminated in the Mexican-American War (1846–1948). In the Treaty of Guadalupe Hidalgo (1848), the victorious United States annexed roughly 500,000 square miles (1,295,000 square kilometers) of territory (today's states of California, New Mexico, Arizona, Utah, and parts of Colorado and Wyoming). The complete annexation of Mexico would have been possible but was rejected on racial grounds as opponents feared the eventual inclusion of a large Hispanic population as detrimental to the body politic.

Imperialist racism played a contradictory role during this period of American expansion. Although notions of Anglo-Saxonist racial superiority interlaced much of the discourse of "manifest destiny," contributed to the violent marginalization of Native Americans, and established imperialist race and labor regimes in the US South and Southwest, racism also prevented or delayed the acquisition of some further territory, such as Mexico in the 1840s, the Dominican Republic in the 1860s, and Hawai'i in the early 1890s.

While concepts of racial superiority could have an inhibiting effect on expansion, the nation's impressive economic and demographic growth acted as a dynamo of American imperialism. The quest for prosperity in the form of land and resources fueled the ever expanding settler empire. At the same time, it also provided an important driving force for noncolonial, informal imperialism beyond the North American continent. It complemented punitive military expeditions, missionary reform, and educational modernization in the Caribbean basin, the Pacific Ocean, and the Asian mainland. By the late nineteenth century, however, this informal imperialism provided a rationale for formal empire, which in turn fostered further informal imperialism in adjacent areas.

Alongside the largely uncoordinated activities of businessmen, adventurers, missionaries, and explorers, some Americans also developed broader imperialist grand strategies. In the 1850s and 1860s, William H. Seward (1801–1872), secretary of state under Presidents Abraham Lincoln (1809–1865) and Andrew Johnson (1808–1875), not only negotiated the purchase of Alaska in 1867 but also advocated territorial expansion, access to global markets, the acquisition of Hawai'i and islands in the Caribbean, and the construction of an interoceanic canal in Central America. Seward promoted the idea of imperial gravity by which Mexico, Canada, and the Caribbean basin would ultimately become part of the United States. A further concept was developed toward the end of the nineteenth century by naval officer Alfred Thayer Mahan (1840–1914), who advocated for a strong navy, a canal in Central America, access to international markets, and the annexation of Hawai'i and other Pacific or Caribbean islands.

Seward and Mahan provided American imperialism with intellectual depth, connected continental and overseas imperialism in a grand strategy, and offered contemporaries a coherent panorama of foreign policy options for their rising empire. Both contributed to the expanding imperialist imaginary, which received further stimulus after victory in the Spanish-American War of 1898. The subsequent Peace of Paris transferred the Philippines, Guam, Cuba, and Puerto Rico to US control. The United States also annexed Hawai'i and later added Wake Island (1899), parts of Samoa (1900), the Panama Canal Zone (1904), and the Virgin Islands (1917) to its colonial empire.

THE SECOND PHASE: OVERSEAS IMPERIALISM

The second phase of imperialism was driven by strategic considerations, the desire for commercial opportunities, concern about the impact of the closed frontier (1890) on national identity and social stability, a gendered understanding of imperialism as a rejuvenating exercise in character-building, and the desire for national aggrandizement. The shift from continental settler imperialism to overseas imperialism sparked one of the most profound foreign policy debates in US history. Prominent imperialists, such as Theodore Roosevelt (1858–1919), Albert Beveridge (1862–1927), Henry Cabot Lodge (1850–1924), Alfred Thayer Mahan, and Brooks Adams (1848–1927), interpreted the acquisition of colonies as a logical extension of America's settler imperialism and a desirable step for the country's rise to great-power status.

Anti-imperialists, such as Carl Schurz (1829–1906), Edward Atkinson (1827–1905), Andrew Carnegie (1835–1919), Mark Twain (1835–1910), and Jane Addams (1860–1935), objected and described formal imperialism as a violation of America's political and constitutional core values with potentially destructive consequences for the American polity itself.

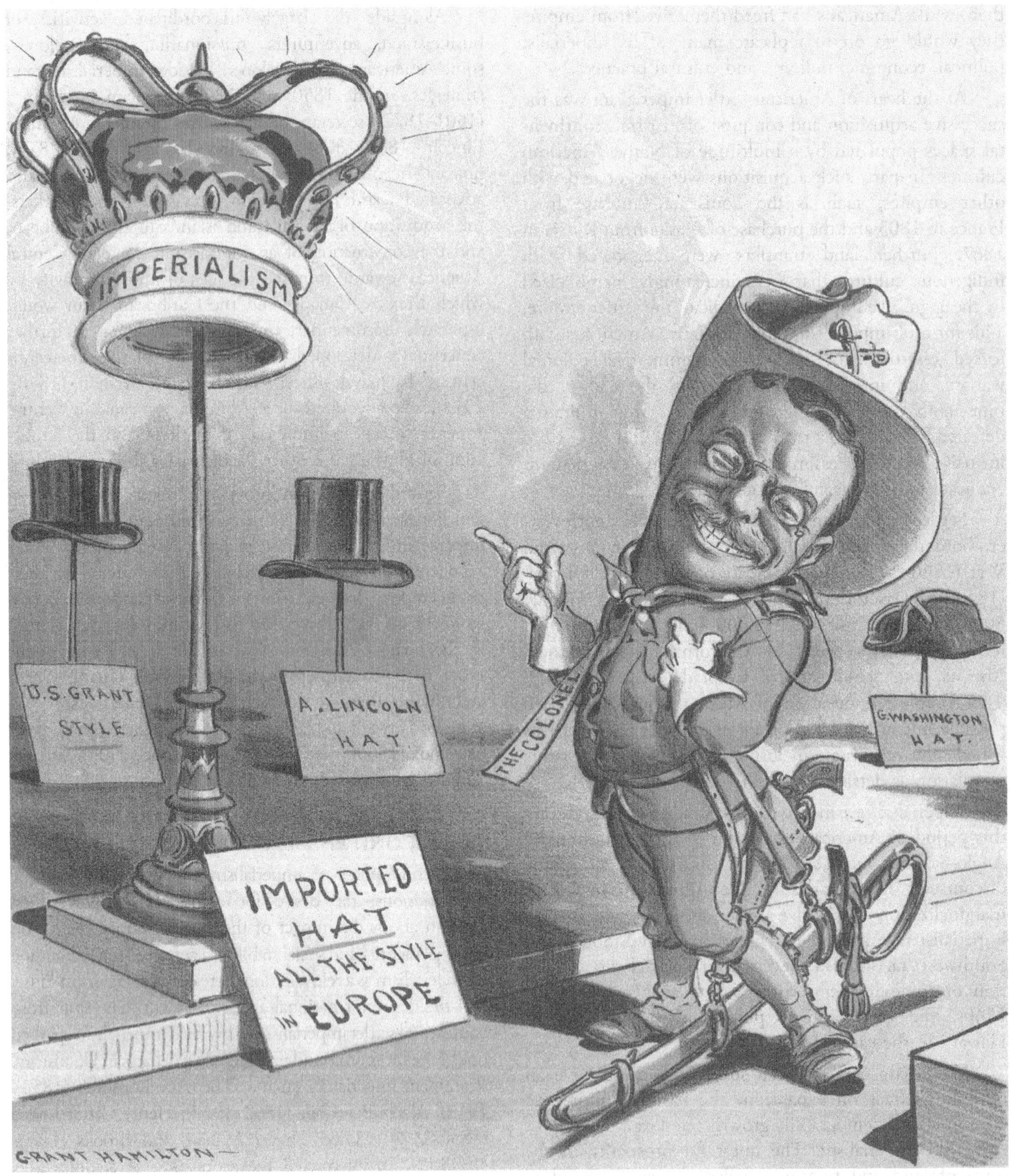

Satirical cartoon of President Theodore Roosevelt, shown admiring his favorite among a display of presidential hats. *In the early twentieth century, prominent imperialists such as Theodore Roosevelt viewed the acquisition of colonies as a logical extension of America's settler imperialism and a desirable step for the country's rise to great-power status.* UNIVERSAL HISTORY ARCHIVE/UIG/GETTY IMAGES

The debate over the merits and pitfalls of formal imperialism received widespread national and international attention, in particular as the optimistic assessments of empire-enthusiasts were severely tested in America's largest colony, the Philippines, where the United States fought one of the bloodiest and most costly colonial wars between 1899 and 1913. In the end, however, it was the imperialists who carried the day as empire became a widely accepted and rarely contested way of life.

While empires were powerful competitors, they also cooperated in multiple and often surprising ways. The US colonial empire was deeply embedded in interimperial circuits and transnational exchanges. Interimperial knowledge transfers from European empires and Japan informed American imperialism on a wide range of issues from governance to social engineering and environmental management.

At the same time, Americans also reexamined their own national history of expansion for guidance as imperial experiences, habits, and repertoires had been deeply woven into the fabric and mental reference frames of nineteenth-century American society. This habitual imperialism had manifested itself in policy choices, military experience, technological developments, cultural trends, consumer preferences, and racial outlooks. When American colonizers arrived in the nation's new tropical empire they carried with them not only the flag but also the intellectual and cultural baggage of a century of imperialism.

Although overseas imperialism produced an equally impressive residue of cultural and mental habits of empire, Americans assumed an increasingly ambivalent position toward the benefits of formal imperialism. Whereas Theodore Roosevelt's administration and the progressive imperialists had been optimistic about the ordering and civilizing influence of colonial empires, Woodrow Wilson's (1856–1924) liberal democratic internationalism diagnosed an inherently destructive dynamic in the imperial rivalries of the great powers. This climatic change, however, did not translate into the dissolution of America's colonial empire, self-determination in the European imperial possessions, or an end to the nation's habitual informal imperialism in Latin America.

In Latin America, the United States followed the established pattern of informal empire and regularly utilized the huge power differential between the nation and its southern neighbors to secure political control and advance economic and cultural dominance. Washington frequently intervened to contain unrest, protect investments, or collect debts.

"Gunboat diplomacy" complemented "dollar diplomacy" and became an instrument of policing the "American Mediterranean" as interventions targeted such nations as Mexico, Cuba, the Dominican Republic, and Haiti, and American Marines became a common sight in many countries of the Caribbean basin. In several cases, the short-term application of naval force turned into long-term military occupations, as in Haiti (1915–1943) and Nicaragua (1912–1933).

In the global arena, American power resulted first and foremost from the nation's dominant position in the international economic order. Although institutional internationalism and, in particular, League of Nations membership did not materialize as an option for the United States in the interwar years, liberal-democratic internationalism permeated all aspects of American foreign relations. Commercial internationalism became a core component of the conceptualization of America's relations with the world.

The weakness of the Old World and the strength of the American economy catapulted the United States to center stage in the world economy. Washington pressed for open access to international trade, negotiated debt-settlements, laid the foundations for international trade institutions, and intensified US trade relations with every corner of the globe. Of equal importance and driven by America's rise to economic primacy was the nation's effort to secure control over global information links. Finally, the interwar years also witnessed the massive expansion of the export of popular culture. The rise of Hollywood's movie industry was symptomatic for the global appeal of American popular culture. Such primacy was viewed critically and interpreted by many Europeans and Latin Americans as cultural imperialism.

Confronted with authoritarian power contenders in Europe and Asia, an international system dominated by the increasing regression of many nations (including the United States) to strict economic nationalism and forceful imperialist responses to the challenges of modernity, the United States intervened for a second time within a generation following the Japanese attack on Pearl Harbor in 1941. Unlike after World War I (1914–1918), victory in 1945 completed the power shift from the Pax Britannica to global America as the United States was determined to apply economic, military, political, and cultural power in a framework of institutional internationalism to secure a worldwide liberal-democratic internationalist order.

CRITICISM OF AMERICAN IMPERIALISM

Since the end of World War II (1939–1945) critics of US foreign relations at home and abroad have repeatedly described the United States as an imperialist power. Such critiques rest on the observation that Washington has used its preponderant economic might after 1945 to define the contours of a global capitalist order that deepened the power differentials between the world's industrial core and its neocolonial peripheries. Closely related is the charge that the global spread of the icons of the "American way of life" that accompanied the dynamic of the US economy constituted cultural imperialism designed to replace local or regional identities with American dominance.

Furthermore, critics charge that the anti-imperial and anticolonial stance of the United States during the Cold War was largely rhetorical. As the European powers were no longer able to uphold their colonial regimes, Washington frequently intervened to control or delay the process of decolonization, most prominently in Southeast Asia.

Finally, claims of American imperialism during the Cold War and beyond are also based on the observation that US administrations supported antidemocratic regimes, and utilized overt and covert interventions to reorganize nations and governments along American strategic parameters. The arrogance of power inherent in Washington's heavy-handed quest for allegiance is often held responsible for the erosion of the nation's credibility in many world regions.

The persistence of such imperial hubris, exemplified more recently by extraordinary renditions, the Guantánamo Bay detention camp, the Abu Ghraib prisoner abuse and torture, and attempts by the National Security Agency (NSA) at global surveillance, underlines how a long history of imperialist habits has left its mark on the practice and perception of America's role in world affairs.

SEE ALSO *Anti-imperialism; Empire, US; Internationalism; Isolationism; League of Nations; Paris Peace Conference (1919); Realism (International Relations); Roosevelt, Theodore; Spanish-American War; Twain, Mark; Wilson, Woodrow; World War I*

BIBLIOGRAPHY

Adas, Michael. *Dominance by Design: Technological Imperatives and America's Civilizing Mission.* Cambridge, MA: Belknap Press of Harvard University Press, 2006.

Bender, Thomas. *A Nation among Nations: America's Place in World History.* New York: Hill and Wang, 2006.

Drinnon, Richard. *Facing West: The Metaphysics of Indian-Hating and Empire-Building.* Norman: University of Oklahoma Press, 1997.

Go, Julian. *American Empire and the Politics of Meaning: Elite Political Cultures in the Philippines and Puerto Rico during U.S. Colonialism.* Durham, NC: Duke University Press, 2008.

Go, Julian. *Patterns of Empire: The British and American Empires, 1688 to the Present.* Cambridge: Cambridge University Press, 2011.

Go, Julian, and Anne L. Foster, eds. *The American Colonial State in the Philippines: Global Perspectives.* Durham, NC: Duke University Press, 2003.

Greenberg, Amy S. *Manifest Manhood and the Antebellum American Empire.* Cambridge: Cambridge University Press, 2005.

Hendrickson, David C. *Union, Nation, or Empire: The American Debate over International Relations, 1789–1941.* Lawrence: University Press of Kansas, 2009.

Hilfrich, Fabian. *Debating American Exceptionalism: Empire and Democracy in the Wake of the Spanish-American War.* New York: Palgrave Macmillan, 2012.

Hixson, Walter L. *The Myth of American Diplomacy: National Identity and U.S. Foreign Policy.* New Haven, CT: Yale University Press, 2008.

Hixson, Walter L. *American Settler Colonialism: A History.* New York: Palgrave Macmillan, 2013.

Hoganson, Kristin L. *Fighting for American Manhood: How Gender Politics Provoked the Spanish-American and Philippine-American Wars.* New Haven, CT: Yale University Press, 1998.

Hoganson, Kristin L. *Consumers' Imperium: The Global Production of American Domesticity, 1865–1920.* Chapel Hill: University of North Carolina Press, 2007.

Hunt, Michael. *Ideology and U.S. Foreign Policy.* New Haven, CT: Yale University Press, 1987.

Hunt, Michael. *The American Ascendancy: How the United States Gained and Wielded Global Dominance.* Chapel Hill: University of North Carolina Press, 2007.

Immerman, Richard H. *Empire for Liberty: A History of American Imperialism from Benjamin Franklin to Paul Wolfowitz.* Princeton, NJ: Princeton University Press, 2010.

Jacobson, Matthew Frye. *Barbarian Virtues: The United States Encounters Foreign Peoples at Home and Abroad, 1876–1917.* New York: Hill and Wang, 2000.

Kagan, Robert. *Dangerous Nation.* New York: Knopf, 2006.

Kramer, Paul A. *The Blood of Government: Race, Empire, the United States, and the Philippines.* Chapel Hill: University of North Carolina Press, 2006.

Kramer, Paul A. "Power and Connection: Imperial Histories of the United States in the World." *American Historical Review* 116, 5 (2011): 1348–1391.

LaFeber, Walter. *The Cambridge History of American Foreign Relations,* Vol. 2: *The American Search for Opportunity, 1865–1913.* Cambridge: Cambridge University Press, 1993.

Love, Eric T. *Race over Empire: Racism and U.S. Imperialism, 1865–1900.* Chapel Hill: University of North Carolina Press, 2004.

Mayers, David. *Dissenting Voices in America's Rise to Power.* Cambridge: Cambridge University Press, 2007.

Meinig, D. W. *The Shaping of America: A Geographical Perspective on 500 Years of History,* Vol. 2: *Continental America, 1800–1867.* New Haven, CT: Yale University Press, 1993.

Meinig, D. W. *The Shaping of America: A Geographical Perspective on 500 Years of History,* Vol. 3: *Transcontinental America, 1850–1915.* New Haven, CT: Yale University Press, 1998.

Ninkovich, Frank. *The United States and Imperialism.* Malden, MA: Blackwell, 2001.

Nugent, Walter. *Habits of Empire: A History of American Expansion.* New York: Knopf, 2008.

Paolino, Ernest N. *The Foundations of the American Empire: William Henry Seward and U.S. Foreign Policy.* Ithaca, NY: Cornell University Press, 1973.

Perkins, Bradford. *The Cambridge History of American Foreign Relations,* Vol. 1: *The Creation of a Republican Empire, 1776–1865.* Cambridge: Cambridge University Press, 1993.

Rosenberg, Emily S. *Spreading the American Dream: American Economic and Cultural Diplomacy, 1890–1945.* New York: Hill and Wang, 1982.

Rydell, Robert W. *All the World's a Fair: Visions of Empire at American International Expositions, 1876–1916.* Chicago: University of Chicago Press, 1984.

Sexton, Jay. *The Monroe Doctrine: Empire and Nation in Nineteenth-Century America.* New York: Hill and Wang, 2011.

Stephanson, Anders. *Manifest Destiny: American Expansion and the Empire of Right.* New York: Hill and Wang, 1995.

Tyrell, Ian. *Transnational Nation: United States History in Global Perspective since 1789.* Houndsmills, Basingstoke, UK: Palgrave MacMillan, 2007.

Tyrell, Ian. *Reforming the World: The Creation of America's Moral Empire.* Princeton, NJ: Princeton University Press, 2010.

Weeks, William Earl. *Building the Continental Empire: American Expansion from the Revolution to the Civil War.* Chicago: Ivan R. Dee, 1996.

Frank Schumacher
Associate Professor of History
University of Western Ontario

IMPRESSMENT

Impressment was the practice of forcefully recruiting individuals into the armed services and is associated with compelling American citizens into the British navy during the early Republic. The British began to impress seamen as early as the seventeenth century, but it only became a regular feature of recruitment in the eighteenth century. The British government considered the practice essential to man an expanding navy that was necessary to defend the island nation from invasion during the wars for empire with France. Many people in Great Britain, however, questioned impressment and saw it as a violation of English liberty. Indeed, pressing triggered riots in England in the eighteenth century and led to court cases that upheld the legality of the practice, but which insisted that a warrant be issued to the impress officer and that only seamen were liable to this form of recruitment.

Colonial Americans also opposed impressment with riots and believed that a law passed in 1708, popularly referred to as the Sixth of Anne, left them immune to the press gang. Impressment contributed to the growing discontent during the colonial American resistance movement of the 1760s and 1770s, and Thomas Jefferson (1743–1826) included a reference to the forced recruitment of Americans in the navy in the Declaration of Independence. During the Revolutionary War, the British pressed some American sailors captured at sea, while imprisoning others. Because the demand for mariners was so high during the War for Independence, even the small Continental navy pressed some seamen into service. In the years immediately after the Treaty of Paris of 1783, the issue was relatively unimportant, since the British navy decommissioned many ships and did not need as many men. American diplomats, however, protested the occasional forced recruitment of men by the British and hoped to settle the matter in the early 1790s.

The Anglo-French Wars from 1793 to 1815 changed the situation. The British navy expanded, draining its own merchant ships of much of their manpower. Simultaneously, the US merchant marine grew dramatically as America became the greatest neutral trader in the world. That booming merchant marine needed more skilled seamen to sail its ships. Although plenty of young Americans pursued their fortunes in the 1790s by going to sea, the British navy provided a reservoir of skilled mariners who eagerly sought the better pay and working conditions on American ships. The only way for these British seamen to gain a berth in the American merchant marine was by first deserting British service. Recognizing that crews on American merchant ships often included His Majesty's subjects, British naval officers began to search those ships in British ports and on the high seas. In 1794, John Jay (1745–1829) sought an agreement on the issue during the negotiations that led to a commercial treaty (the Jay Treaty). Indeed, it was during these negotiations that Jay probably introduced the officious sounding word *impressment.* Jay failed in his effort to include a provision against impressment in the treaty. In turn, Republicans popularized the term *impressment* in their attacks on the treaty.

The controversy over impressment centered on definitions of subjecthood and citizenship. Most Americans claimed that citizenship could be either a birthright or a voluntary act. Thus an individual who emigrated to the United States after independence could become a naturalized citizen after a set number of years. The British Crown insisted that once a subject of the king, always a subject of the king (except for those who had already resided in the United States before 1783). The British, however, allowed for naturalization themselves while denying it to the United States.

In an effort to clarify American citizenship for sailors, and offer some protection for seamen, Congress passed a bipartisan seamen's protection act in 1796. This measure set up special agents in the West Indies and Great Britain who would assist in identifying Americans improperly impressed in the British navy, and also provided for special documents, called *protections,* which were statements of citizenship issued by government officials in the United States. Both measures had limited success. The agents managed to get several thousand sailors released from the British navy between 1796 and the outbreak of the War of 1812. Although the British never claimed the

IMPRESSMENT OF BOSTONIANS BY KNOWLES.

Impressment of American sailors in Boston by the British navy before the War of 1812. Hand-colored woodcut of a nineteenth-century illustration. *Between the 1790s and the War of 1812 the British impressed at least ten thousand seamen from American ships. Impressment was a major diplomatic problem in the lead-up to the conflict, with President James Madison calling it one of the two key reasons for declaring war.* NORTH WIND PICTURE ARCHIVES/ALAMY

right to impress American citizens, they took at least ten thousand seamen from American ships, asserting that they were British subjects. British officers also often rejected protections because the documents were easily forged and were sold illicitly.

Impressment became a more acute problem after 1803 when the British need for sailors increased. In 1806, President Thomas Jefferson's cabinet decided not to push for a settlement of the issue; they determined that the American merchant marine gained skilled seamen deserting from British service while losing mainly less skilled Americans taken through impressment. Despite this calculation, most Republican politicians continued to trumpet the issue and used it to tar both the British government and the Federalist Party.

This political use of impressment within the United States became even easier after the British navy fired upon the USS *Chesapeake* and took four known deserters from the ship in 1807. Impressment continued as a major diplomatic problem, and a political tool of the Republicans, in the lead-up to the War of 1812. In June 1812, President James Madison (1751–1836) identified impressment as one of the two key reasons for declaring war. When word arrived that summer that the British had relented on neutral rights (the other reason), impressment remained as the sole rationale for continuing the conflict. However important the issue was in explaining the war, the final peace treaty included no provision concerning impressment. Yet, without ever making it official policy, thereafter Great Britain all but ended the practice of taking men from American ships.

SEE ALSO *Britain; Jay Treaty (1795); Neutrality Act of 1794; Passport; War of 1812*

BIBLIOGRAPHY

Brunsman, Denver. *The Evil Necessity: British Naval Impressment in the Eighteenth-Century Atlantic World.* Charlottesville: University of Virginia Press, 2013.

Gilje, Paul A. *Free Trade and Sailors' Rights in the War of 1812.* New York: Cambridge University Press, 2013.

Rogers, Nicholas. *The Press Gang: Naval Impressment and Its Opponents in Georgian Britain.* London: Continuum, 2007.

Selement, George. "Impressment and the American Merchant Marine, 1782–1812." *Mariner's Mirror* 59, 4 (1973): 409–418.

Paul A. Gilje
George Lynn Cross Research Professor
Department of History, University of Oklahoma

INDIA

Both India and the United States began at the margins of the British Empire. As the historian P. J. Marshall has noted, "in the 1760s and 1770s, while an empire in America was disintegrating, an empire was being consolidated in eastern India" (2005, 53). Yet connections between America and the Indian subcontinent date back to an even earlier period. In New England in 1721, the Puritan minister Cotton Mather (1663–1728) published *India Christiana*, in which he imagined a connection between India and America. Missionary work among "heathens" in India and America was part of a larger project of European Christian expansion, with the two lands marking the edges of Christendom.

After the American Revolution, more substantial connections emerged between colonial India and the young United States. New England merchants began trading in Asian ports in the late eighteenth century. By 1791, 92 percent of US revenues came from impost and tonnage duties (Bean 2001). Cargo came into American ports from India, China, and throughout the Pacific. In 1806 Jacob Crowninshield (1770–1808), a US congressman and shipper from Salem, Massachusetts, described the India trade from his hometown to then Secretary of State James Madison: "We send from 30 to 50 ships annually to Calcutta... It is estimated that we have imported in some years at least three millions of dollars worth of goods from Calcutta" (Reinoehl 1959). The India trade bolstered the economy of the young United States.

In addition to goods and money, New England ships brought back cultural artifacts from their trips to Bombay and Calcutta. In 1799 the mariners of Salem founded the East India Marine Society (EIMS) for sailors who had traveled past the Cape of Good Hope. The society established a "cabinet of curiosities" full of Indian artifacts. The collection included drawings of Indian scenes, statues of Indian gods and goddesses, and even a "hubble-bubble" glass pipe. The cabinet grew into a museum full of "Oriental" pieces. The EIMS collection is still housed at the Peabody-Essex Museum in Salem.

The same boats that carried goods and mariners also carried missionaries. In 1813 the British ended a ban on missionary activity in their Indian colonies. The American Board of Commissioners for Foreign Missions (ABCFM) was the first of many organizations to send missionaries to India. Throughout the nineteenth century American missionaries sent home accounts of "idolatry" and "heathenism" among the "Hindoos." Beginning in the 1820s a different representation of religion in India emerged among American religious liberals. Unitarian Christians in New England encountered a philosophical and monotheistic image of Indian religion in the philosophical works of the Indian reformer Rammohun Roy (c. 1772–1883). The Transcendentalists, such as Ralph Waldo Emerson (1803–1882) and Henry David Thoreau (1817–1862), read Sanskrit Indian texts such as the Laws of Manu and the Bhagavad Gita. By the time of the Civil War, there were two competing images of religion in India: mystical and meditative monism or dark and idolatrous heathenism. Swami Vivekananda (1863–1902), a Hindu reformer, did his best to navigate these two representations when he arrived in Chicago at the World's Parliament of Religions in 1893.

While images of the "Hindoo" circulated in American culture, the first immigrants from India began to arrive in the United States in the early twentieth century. Punjabi men began to immigrate to the West Coast of the United States in the first decade of the twentieth century. Initially, these migrants took jobs working for the railroads and lumber companies; but they soon turned to agricultural labor, and many eventually owned farmland in Southern California. The Punjabi immigrants were for the most part Sikhs, and in 1912 they built the first Sikh *gurdwara*, or temple, in America in Stockton, California. This first wave of Indian immigration also brought anti-imperialist political activists to the United States. For example, the Ghadar Party, formed in 1913, advocated for a revolution in India that would end British rule and even organized two thousand men who returned to India as revolutionaries after the outbreak of World War I (1914–1918).

Beginning with the 1913 Alien Land Law in California, a series of exclusionary laws aimed at ending South Asian immigrant land ownership gained momentum after the war. Confusion over whether Indians counted as "white" according to naturalization laws meant that some courts allowed Indian immigrants to become naturalized citizens while others did not. The Supreme Court settled the confusion in *United States v. Bhagat Sigh Thind* (261 U.S. 204 [1923]) by excluding Indians from citizenship. Justice George Sutherland ruled that "'free white persons' are words of common speech," and the term so used "does not include the body of people to whom the appellee belongs" (261 U.S. at 215). Following the decision, the US State Department sought to denaturalize many previously naturalized Indian American citizens. In 1924 the National Origins Act put an effective end to Indian immigration to the United States.

In 1927 the journalist Katherine Mayo, in her best-selling book *Mother India*, asked, "But what does the average American actually know about India? That Mr. Gandhi lives there; also tigers." She described Indians as typified by "inertia, helplessness, lack of initiative and originality, lack of staying power and sustained loyalties, sterility of enthusiasm, weakness of life-vigor" (1927, 16). Mayo's racist and demeaning image of India held sway for decades, as the book went through twenty-seven editions by the mid-1950s (Rotter 2000). America stationed troops in India during World War II; a few even snake-danced through New Delhi during Christmas of 1943. Also that year many Americans took notice of Mohandas Gandhi's fast in protest of the British government. But even after India's independence in 1947, little changed between India and the United States until the Cold War.

In the 1960s, in need of educated professionals to jumpstart the American position in the Space Race and defend against the Soviet threat, the United States looked east for engineers, doctors, and scientists. Congress passed the Immigration and Nationality Act of 1965, which reopened immigration from India and the rest of Asia while prioritizing highly skilled, professionally trained immigrants. From 1966 to 1977, 83 percent of the immigrants from India entered under the category of professional or technical workers (Prashad 2000). These post-1965 immigrants built diaspora communities in the United States that include religious societies, temples, *gurdwaras*, and civic groups. Furthermore, the Indian diaspora in America has been vocal in politics back in India through groups such as the Vishwa Hindu Parishad of America (VHPA). Following the September 11, 2001, terrorist attacks and the war on terror, America has depended on India as an ally in South Asia.

SEE ALSO *Cold War; Empire, US; Exceptionalism; Interventionism; Strategic Defense Initiative (Star Wars)*

BIBLIOGRAPHY

Bean, Susan S. *Yankee India: American Commercial and Cultural Encounters with India in the Age of Sail, 1784-1860.* Salem, MA: Peabody Essex Museum, 2001.

Jensen, Joan M. *Passage from India: Asian Indian Immigrants in North America.* New Haven, CT: Yale University Press, 1988.

Kurien, Prema A. *A Place at the Multicultural Table: The Development of an American Hinduism.* New Brunswick, NJ: Rutgers University Press, 2007.

Marshall, P. J. *The Making and Unmaking of Empires: Britain, India, and America, c. 1750–1783.* Oxford and New York: Oxford University Press, 2005.

Mayo, Katherine. *Mother India.* New York: Harcourt, Brace, 1927.

Narayanan, Vasudha. "Hinduism in America." In *Cambridge History of Religions in America*, Vol. 3: *1945 to the Present*, edited by Stephen J. Stein, 331–356. New York: Cambridge University Press, 2012.

Prashad, Vijay. *The Karma of Brown Folk.* Minneapolis: University of Minnesota Press, 2000.

Reinoehl, John H. "Some Remarks on the American Trade: Jacob Crowninshield to James Madison 1806." *William and Mary Quarterly*, Third Series, 16, 1 (1959): 83–118.

Rotter, Andrew Jon. *Comrades at Odds: The United States and India, 1947–1964.* Ithaca, NY: Cornell University Press, 2000.

Shukla, Sandhya Rajendra. *India Abroad: Diasporic Cultures of Postwar America and England.* Princeton, NJ: Princeton University Press, 2003.

Slate, Nico. *Colored Cosmopolitanism: The Shared Struggle for Freedom in the United States and India.* Cambridge, MA: Harvard University Press, 2012.

Whitehill, Walter Muir. *The East India Marine Society and the Peabody Museum of Salem: A Sesquicentennial History.* Salem, MA: Peabody Museum, 1949.

Michael J. Altman
Assistant Professor of Religious Studies
University of Alabama

INDIAN CITIZENSHIP ACT (1924)

The Indian Citizenship Act (ICA) of 1924 unilaterally conferred US citizenship upon all indigenous people residing within the boundaries of the United States. The ICA made 125,000 indigenous people into legal US citizens. There were approximately 300,000 indigenous people in the United States at the time, and the majority were already US citizens. Two general features of the ICA are important to understand. The first is its place in the historical and political context of the United States as a settler colonial state and society. The second is the response of indigenous people to US settler colonial practices and policies, including the ICA, and the commitment of many indigenous people to maintain citizenship within their own nations.

THE ICA IN THE CONTEXT OF US SETTLER COLONIAL RULE

The key text of the ICA states: "That all non-citizen Indians born within the territorial limits of the United States be, and they are hereby, declared to be citizens of the United States: *Provided*, That the granting of such citizenship shall not in any manner impair or otherwise affect the right of any Indian to tribal or other property." In one sense, this phrasing seems to respect the citizenship of indigenous people in their own nations. However, in the wider context of US settler colonial rule and US Indian policy, the presumptions and implications of the ICA are more troubling. To speak of the United States as a settler colonial state and society is to mark it as a nation and government built upon the colonization of and settlement upon indigenous lands, often violently dispossessed. Into a wider context, the founding and development of the United States occurred through the globally familiar practices of colonialism, violent territorial acquisition, and active settlement on dispossessed territory.

The post–Civil War era of American settler colonial governance witnessed the effort to further consolidate settler colonial rule by the continued appropriation of indigenous lands and the aggressive effort to eliminate indigenous people *qua* indigenous people. In many ways, the phrase "kill the Indian, save the man" defined the aims of US Indian policy during this period. This phrase is an 1887 quote attributed to Colonel Richard Henry Pratt (1840–1924), who in 1879 founded the Carlisle Indian School in Pennsylvania, where many indigenous children were forcibly taken and then compelled to assume new names and adopt American settler modes of language and dress.

The ICA was passed in 1924 during the period of US Indian policy that is often termed the Allotment Era, beginning with the General Allotment (Dawes Severalty) Act in 1887 and ending with the Indian Reorganization Act of 1934. During these decades, the US federal government sought to force the breakup of indigenous nations and tribes by dispersing indigenous landholdings into individually apportioned private-property holdings. The US government further sought to assimilate indigenous people into the American political society by enforced schooling, but often resorted to killing them through such massacres as that at Wounded Knee in 1890. Unilaterally conferred US citizenship was another assimilatory policy reflective of the wider policy aims of US settler colonial rule during this period.

The ICA was the result of two decades of work by "Friends of the Indian" organizations (comprised of nonindigenous Americans) and federal legislators to address specific concerns. One concern was that indigenous people were not assimilating—or, in the popular terminology of the time, "civilizing"—quickly enough through the allotment process, which was supposed to turn indigenous people into individualized American property holders who had earned US citizenship. A second concern was that, as non-US citizens, indigenous people were more vulnerable to exploitation, especially as it concerned efforts of the American settler population to acquire allotted indigenous land, sometimes through manipulative methods.

THE RESPONSE OF INDIGENOUS PEOPLE

There was no single unified response by indigenous people to the ICA. Rather, the prospect and then conferral of US citizenship was met with responses that covered the spectrum from eager acceptance to outright rejection. Carlos Montezuma (c. 1866–1923) of the Yavapai Nation was a strong advocate of US citizenship for indigenous people, a view largely based on the fact that indigenous men had been drafted into the US military during World War I (1914–1918) whether they were US citizens or not. Service in the US military provided a pathway to earned US citizenship for indigenous people. However, to Montezuma, the fact that the US government deemed indigenous people eligible to be drafted in the first place meant that they were already worthy of the status and rights of US citizenship, regardless of whether or not as individuals they served in the military. Montezuma argued that a major roadblock to indigenous people gaining more rights within the United States was the paternalistic practices and views of the Bureau of Indian Affairs, which "tells the country we are competent to be soldiers, but are not competent to be citizens" (Montezuma 1917). In this way, Montezuma's concerns corresponded with those of progressive legislators in the Congress who viewed the conferral of US citizenship as a way to reduce the power of US state institutions over indigenous people. Charles Eastman (1858–1939) of the Santee Sioux Nation also advocated US citizenship, seeing incorporation into the United States as a positive development, on the whole, as long as indigenous people did not have to completely surrender their relationship to their community and culture. However, Eastman did not want such citizenship to be imposed upon indigenous people.

While Montezuma and Eastman offer evidence that some indigenous people were open to US citizenship, other indigenous leaders, such as Clinton Rickard (1882–1971) of the Tuscarora Nation, stood firmly against the acceptance of US citizenship and rejected its unilateral conferral. Rickard's view reflected the position of the Haudenosaunee people (often known as the Iroquois Confederacy, comprised of the Cayuga, Mohawk, Oneida, Onondaga, Seneca, and Tuscarora Nations) that they were citizens of their own indigenous nations and not of the settler colonial nation and state. In this sense, the conferral of US citizenship through the ICA was another act of colonial imposition upon indigenous national sovereignty, an effort to further subsume indigenous political communities into the US settler colonial body.

To this day, Haudenosaunee territory spans the boundaries of the United States and Canada, and the active assertion of indigenous national citizenship in defiance of US or Canadian citizenship represents an important articulation of indigenous national sovereignty. In this light, the passage of the ICA in 1924 with the purpose of making indigenous people US citizens continues to be a contested and unsettled matter. Indigenous resistance to US citizenship is thus another mode through which many indigenous people refuse the idea that US settler colonial rule is itself a settled matter.

SEE ALSO *Americanization; Borderlands; Cherokee Nation v. Georgia (1831); Civilization Fund; General Allotment Act (Dawes Severalty Act, 1877); Indian Removal Act (1830)*

BIBLIOGRAPHY

Indian Citizenship Act. June 2, 1924. In *United States Statutes at Large*, Vol. 43: *1923–1925*, 253. Washington, DC: 1925.

Montezuma, Carlos. "Drafting Indians and Justice." *Wassaja* 2, 7 (October 1917). Reprinted in *Talking Back to Civilization: Indian Voices from the Progressive Era*, edited by Frederick E. Hoxie, 126. Boston and New York: Bedford/St. Martins, 2001.

Kevin Bruyneel
Professor of Politics
Babson College

INDIAN OCEAN

American involvement in the Indian Ocean (IO) stretches from colonial America to the present. Activities have included trade, immigration, tourism, and military involvement. Traditionally, the IO sphere encompasses the area of ocean that stretches from the eastern coast of South Africa to the western coasts of China and Australia, and from Southeast Asia down to a point above Antarctica. Although Indian Ocean World (IOW) studies tend to be restricted to networks circulating solely within these boundaries, understanding the constructed nature of these boundaries is imperative. Traditional IOW scholarship tends not to discuss extensively its relationship to transatlantic trade and migration circuits, viewing them as outside the scope of the field. This is partially due to the periodization of the field, which views the importance of the IOW as a tangible network as diminishing in the mid-nineteenth century, giving way to a global system. However, even in its early history, the IO is not isolated from the Atlantic or the Pacific Oceans, and interconnections exist between them. America's involvement in the Indian Ocean expanded over time, corresponding to the country's transition from a peripheral ex-British colony to its post–Second World War position as the center of a new world order.

EARLY CONTACTS

Early American involvement in the IO is tied to its relations with the French and British during the American Revolution and to America's involvement in the slave trade. Until the beginning of the Cold War, American involvement in the area was concentrated in Mauritius and Réunion. When Antoine Raymond Joseph de Bruni d'Entrecasteaux (1737–1793), a French explorer known for his travels in the Pacific, was appointed the governor of Isle de France (Mauritius) in 1771, he urged France to reduce foreign trade barriers in an effort to develop the island into a main trading station between Europe and Asia. After the American Revolutionary War ended in 1783, American involvement in the IO reflected its convergence with French commercial and political interests. By 1786 American traders were using Isle de France as a port on their way to Canton, China. This network coincided with Isle de France's efforts to develop commercial contacts with Eastern and Far Eastern seaports, in the hopes that foreign trade would make the colony more self-sufficient and less of a burden on the French metropolitan for its needs. Through this network, American neutral carriers became a key customer of the island. American involvement with Isle de France intensified after the outbreak of the French Revolution in 1789, during which the center of French government in the Indian Ocean transferred from Pondicherry to Isle de France. After this point, Isle de France could not rely as heavily on France for support and instead turned to foreign trade and privateering for additional support. American neutral carriers were to bring them news about their other possessions in the Indian Ocean, the rest of the world, and in France. British cruisers often targeted these American neutral carrier ships. After Britain's 1810 invasion and conquest of Isle de France and the Anglo-American War of 1812–1815, America's commercial relationship with the Mascarene Islands were at best sporadic from 1850 to 1870 and almost ceased after the opening of the Suez Canal in 1869.

Transatlantic and IO slave-trading networks were not isolated, as supplies of slaves from the IO networks often fed transatlantic flows of slaves to the Caribbean. However, Indian Ocean slave-trading networks did not provide any significant portion of slaves sent to the United States. This is largely because it was more cost effective to transport slaves from West Africa because of the shorter distance, which ensured fewer casualties in transport. The trading networks that intersected IO networks and transatlantic networks destined for the United States mainly consisted of other commodities, such as coffee and cotton, and luxury items such as ivory, cloves, and brandy.

TWENTIETH-CENTURY DEVELOPMENTS AND THE COLD WAR

In the late nineteenth century to the early twentieth century, American involvement in the IO was not particularly active. Although migrants from areas surrounding the IO did make their way to the United States during this period, they often crossed the Pacific Ocean and settled the western coast of the United States. These migrants were largely Indian or Chinese indentured laborers who worked in mining and railway construction. Other migrants from these areas included Chinese merchants and Indian agricultural workers from Punjab who also made their way to the United States. Thus, similar to Atlantic Ocean circuits, Pacific Ocean circuits of trade and migration also intersected with IO circuits.

The Cold War marked the beginning of intensified American involvement in the IO. This period, characterized by an American-centric world order, is one in which the Indian Ocean became an important geopolitical sphere of containment policy. Involvement included the establishment of military bases, support for anticolonial movements, aid to newly independent nation-states, and involvement in proxy wars in areas bordering the IO. From the 1950s to the 1970s, American encouragement for decolonization was a component of containment policy, which viewed the granting of independence and the establishment of solidarity with the new nations as a superior alternative to anticolonial nationalists turning to Soviet support.

The establishment of military bases and engagement in proxy wars such as the Vietnam War were two direct forms of containment policy in the IO. The establishment of military presences on the island of Diego Garcia in the Seychelles and in Pakistan are prominent examples. In the case of Pakistan, an air station was established in exchange for aid and military assistance. In the 1950s, the United States asked to lease the Peshawar Airport to be used in surveillance flights over the Soviet Union. In 1956, the government of the United Kingdom proclaimed that Diego Garcia was to be included in a new separate colony, known as the British Indian Ocean Territory (BIOT), and administered in Seychelles as a precondition for Mauritian independence. From 1965 until 1971, the UK government forcibly removed the over fifteen hundred residents of Diego Garcia to Mauritius. In 1971, an American military base was established, which followed a 1966 agreement with the UK that leased the island to the United States for fifty years. American and British officials were able to justify the expulsion of island residents by invoking national security, with the specific threat to national security ranging over time from decolonization, to the need to balance Soviet assets in the region and establish a forward operating base in the Near East, to the global war on terror.

Finally, contemporary American involvement in the IO resembles Cold War patterns. After the outbreak of the war on terror, the United States continued to see the IO as a pluralistic geopolitical region, but one in which terrorism containment initiatives were necessary for the maintenance of an American-centric world order. As traditional IO scholarship suggests, the significance of focusing on American involvement in the IO sphere diminishes as that sphere ceases to be an isolated arena of analysis.

SEE ALSO *Africa; Asia; China; Foreign Mission Movement*

BIBLIOGRAPHY

Alpers, Edward A. *The Indian Ocean in World History.* Oxford: Oxford University Press, 2014.

Hofmeyr, Isabel. "The Black Atlantic Meets the Indian Ocean: Forging New Paradigms of Transnationalism for the Global South–Literary and Cultural Perspectives." *Social Dynamics* 33, 2 (2007): 3–32.

Hooper, Jane, and David Eltis. "The Indian Ocean in Transatlantic Slavery." *Slavery and Abolition* 34, 3 (2013): 353–375.

Houbert, Jean. "The Indian Ocean Creole Islands: Geo-Politics and Decolonisation." *Journal of Modern African Studies* 30, 3 (September 1992): 465–484.

Jackson, Ashley. *War and Empire in Mauritius and the Indian Ocean.* New York: Palgrave, 2001.

Kaplan, Robert D. *Monsoon: The Indian Ocean and the Future of American Power.* New York: Random House, 2011.

Madeley, John. *Diego Garcia: A Contrast to the Falklands.* Rev. ed. London: Minority Rights Group, 1985.

Mancham, James R. *War on America: Seen from the Indian Ocean.* St. Paul, MN: Paragon House, 2002.

Ostheimer, John M., ed. *The Politics of the Western Indian Ocean Islands.* New York: Praeger, 1975.

Sand, Peter H. *United States and Britain in Diego Garcia: The Future of a Controversial Base.* New York: Palgrave Macmillan, 2009.

Scarr, Deryck. *Slaving and Slavery in the Indian Ocean.* New York: St. Martin's Press, 1998.

Toussaint, Auguste. *Early American Trade with Mauritius.* Port Louis, Mauritius: Esclapon, 1954.

Heena Mistry
PhD Candidate, Department of History
Queen's University

INDIAN REMOVAL ACT (1830)

The Indian Removal Act became law on May 28, 1830, after surviving bitter debates in Congress and the Senate and massive national opposition. It was the first legislative recommendation sent to Congress by President Andrew Jackson (1767–1845) and by far the most controversial and damaging administrative measure of his term (1829–1837). The act provided the president with the authority to appropriate vacant western lands in order to relocate Indian tribes that were willing to relinquish their homes east of the Mississippi River. Each tribe was to receive a patent guaranteeing new lands "in perpetuity" in the "Indian Territory" (which later became Oklahoma) in exchange for millions of acres coveted by white settlers and state governments, especially in the Southeast. Besides negotiated (and often fraudulent) removal or "land transfer" treaties, the act also led to the forced and brutal expulsion of tens of thousands of Indian peoples from their homelands and the deaths of thousands more. The significance of the Indian Removal Act lay in the unprecedented political opposition and multiple antiremoval campaigns it generated among both whites and Indians, the moral questions and constitutional debates it raised, and the devastating forced exodus its violent and chaotic implementation resulted in for many Native American tribes in the first half of the nineteenth century.

ORIGINS OF THE ACT

The Indian Removal Act of 1830 was the outcome of several decades of inconsistent federal Indian policy and of the unremitting pressures of American settlers on Indian lands. Following the Treaty of Paris in 1783, the new US government was unable to enforce its initial "defeated nations" approach against resisting Indian tribes, reverting instead to a modified version of the treaty system initiated during the colonial period. First talks of removing Indians west of the Mississippi were introduced by Thomas Jefferson (1743–1826), but the policy coexisted with a program to promote tenets of "civilization" among tribes, including farming, Western gender roles, literacy, entrepreneurial attitudes, and Christianity, all with a view to potential future civil incorporation to the nation. Only tribes that proved incapable or unwilling to adjust to white civilization would, in this scenario, be removed from the violent and corrupting pressures of frontier settlements. The "civilization policy," Jacksonian Democrats and removal advocates argued in the late 1820s and 1830s, had proven a failure and thus made relocation the only viable, benevolent, and paternalistic option to "save the Indians" from extinction. By then, however, southeastern tribes had in fact integrated many aspects of Western culture, religion, and economics into their societies while also retaining indigenous cultural traits. Among these "civilized tribes" (Choctaws, Chickasaws, Muskogee [Creeks], and Seminoles) stood most prominently the Cherokees, successful, Christian, slaveholding planters who published a bilingual newspaper and controlled vast and fertile territories in northwestern Georgia (where gold was discovered in 1829), southwestern North Carolina, and parts of Tennessee and Alabama. What had "failed" was in reality the scheme that, upon embracing individualistic and commercial values, Indians would willingly sell their land surplus. Instead, through the removal crisis, the Cherokees and other tribes adroitly manipulated Western institutions, rhetoric, and legal structures to retain their lands and resist white pressures. While it impacted many Indian nations throughout the eastern United States (including the Potawatomi Indians of southwestern Michigan and northern Indiana and bands of Shawnee, Ottawa, and Sauk Indians), the clash between the state of Georgia and the Cherokee Nation (c. 1820–1838) came to define and embody the terms and outcomes of the Removal Act controversy.

THE REMOVAL DEBATES

The core of the removal debates centered on sovereignty and jurisdiction, both in terms of the constitutional balance of power between state and federal authority and the muddled status of indigenous peoples within the United States. Georgia clamored for the federal government to uphold the Compact of 1802, which had promised to extinguish Indian land titles in exchange for the state surrendering to the United States its western colonial charter claims. Southern states also unilaterally extended jurisdiction over Indian peoples after about 1820, on the grounds that their status was akin to an unacceptable *imperium in imperio*. Principal Chief John Ross (1790–1866), in 1836, during the series of crises leading to the ultimate removal of his people, responded to Georgia's interloping by stating that "the Cherokees are a distinct people, sovereign to some extent, have a separate political existence as a society, or body politic, and a capability of being contracted with in [sic] a national capacity, [as] stands admitted by the uniform practice of the United States from 1785" (Conser 1978, 197). While unwilling to unambiguously declare all federal Indian treaties to date unconstitutional, Jackson argued that they could not trump states' rights; the federal government could thus not act to protect Indians against the states, leaving natives no choice but to leave or submit.

The Cherokees had been strengthening their national government since the early 1800s in an effort to retain control over their lands and better respond to white encroachments. First, in 1817, the Principles of Government and National Council replaced the looser traditional associations of Towns; Towns were Cherokee settlements and the surrounding lands that functioned as self-governing polities ruled through consensus and were connected through matrilineal clans. In 1827, the Cherokees then moved to pass a new constitution that provided more power to their chief, lessened the role of women in governance, and grounded their claim to sovereignty in their ancestral right to the land. The Cherokees took the sovereignty debate to court and won, twice. In *Cherokee Nation v. Georgia* (1831), Chief Justice John Marshall (1755–1835) confirmed the status of Indian nations as separate states but not quite foreign nations. Instead, he defined them as "domestic dependent nations," not completely independent from the federal authority but nevertheless impervious to state law. In a subsequent case, *Worcester v. Georgia* (1832), Marshall confirmed that the Cherokees had historically enjoyed government-to-government relations as sovereign states and that only the federal government had supreme authority in conducting negotiations with Indian nations. The ruling held that states had no criminal jurisdiction in Indian country. Jackson infamously overlooked the decisions and proceeded to enforce eviction as a military operation of ethnic cleansing. Five hundred thousand dollars were set aside by Congress for the implementation of the act, which included a provision for the government to provide for the tribes through their first year in their new western territory. Overall lack of sufficient planning and oversight led to unspeakable suffering and high death tolls for Indians during the actual removal process. During the Trail of Tears an estimated four thousand Cherokees perished from starvation, abuse, encampment conditions, and exposure.

EFFECTS OF THE REMOVAL POLICY

The Removal Act drove a profound wedge into the fabric of Cherokee society. Elias Boudinot (born Gallegina Uwati, 1802–1839) and John Ridge (born Skah-tle-loh-skee, c. 1802–1839) were two of the signers of the fraudulent Treaty of New Echota (1835), which ceded all Cherokee lands east of the Mississippi for $5 million. It was ratified by the Senate in 1836 despite strong opposition from the majority of the Cherokee Nation and Chief Ross, who had not attended the proceedings. Members of the planter elite, educated in a Connecticut boarding school, and both married to white women, Boudinot and Ridge had faced white racism firsthand and had become convinced that nothing positive would come from Indians and whites continuing to cohabit. They saw relocation as their people's last and best alternative. They paid with their lives for what other Cherokees saw as betrayal and were assassinated along with another member of the treaty party once in Oklahoma.

The Indian Removal Act stirred a variety of opposition movements that crystallized crucial issues faced by the United States in the first half of the century and had far-reaching repercussions, especially for the antislavery and women's rights movements. John Ross led the National (Cherokee) Party in a nonviolent opposition campaign, involving intense lobbying in Washington, sophisticated public relations outreach, and ambitious legal battles. White missionaries, such as Jeremiah Evarts (1781–1831), prominent northern female activists like the "benevolent ladies of Hartford," led by Catharine Beecher (1800–1878) and Lydia Sigourney (1791–1865), and political opponents (Whig) to Jacksonian Democrats, such as Senator Theodore Frelinghuysen (1787–1862), also voiced their outrage, to no avail. The Removal Act provided a tragic precedent that guided US Indian policy until the start of the allotment era in the 1880s.

SEE ALSO *Cherokee Nation v. Georgia (1831); Foreign Mission School (Cornwall, CT); General Allotment Act (Dawes Severalty Act, 1877); Reservation; Worcester v. Georgia (1832)*

BIBLIOGRAPHY

Conser, Walter, Jr. "John Ross and the Cherokee Resistance Campaign, 1833–1838." *Journal of Southern History* 44, 2 (May 1978): 197 (cites *Ross et al. to US Congress*, June 21, 1836, *House Document no. 286,* 24th Cong., 1st sess. p. 3).

Davis, Ethan. "An Administrative Trail of Tears: Indian Removal." *American Journal of Legal History* 50, 1 (January 2008–2010): 49–100.

Hershberger, Mary. "Mobilizing Women, Anticipating Abolition: The Struggle against Indian Removal in the 1830s." *Journal of American History* 86, 1 (June 1999): 15–40.

McLoughlin, William G. *Cherokee Renascence in the New Republic.* Princeton, NJ: Princeton University Press, 1986.

Miles, Tiya. "'Circular Reasoning': Recentering Cherokee Women in the Antiremoval Campaigns." *American Quarterly* 61, 2 (June 2009): 221–243.

Oberg, Michael Leroy. *Native America: A History.* Malden, MA: Wiley-Blackwell, 2010.

Perdue, Theda, and Michael D. Green. *The Cherokee Nation and the Trail of Tears.* New York: Penguin, 2007.

Prucha, Francis Paul, ed. *Documents of United States Indian Policy.* 3rd ed. Lincoln: University of Nebraska Press, 2000.

Remini, Robert V. *The Legacy of Andrew Jackson: Essays on Democracy, Indian Removal, and Slavery.* Baton Rouge: Louisiana State University Press, 1988.

Remini, Robert V. *Andrew Jackson and His Indian Wars.* New York: Viking, 2001.

Shown Harjo, Susan, ed. *Nation to Nation: Treaties between the United States and American Indian Nations.* Washington, DC: Smithsonian Institution, 2014.

Céline Carayon
Assistant Professor of History
Salisbury University

INDUSTRIALIZATION

The United States was the second nation in the world, following Great Britain, to undergo large-scale industrialization. From the beginning of the nineteenth century to the middle of the twentieth, the United States transformed from a postcolonial agricultural nation to a global industrial superpower. Throughout the nation's history, manufacturing has had a profound impact on labor, immigration, and international policies. Indeed, it has shaped the United States' engagement with the rest of the world.

THE TRANSITION TO MECHANIZED PRODUCTION

Although the transition from an agrarian economy to one based on mechanized production was not fully apparent until the latter part of the nineteenth century, the process was already under way at the time of the Revolution. During the war American emissaries acted as covert labor recruiting agents to lure skilled workers from abroad, and the Continental Congress encouraged the manufacture of weapons. State governments, meanwhile, worked to subsidize the manufacture of certain war materials, as well as manufactures generally, by means of bounties and immunities (Matson and Onuf 1990). Following the war, policy makers debated the virtues and vices of domestic manufacturing initiatives. Some feared that the United States would inherit the poverty and social dislocation associated with British industrial cities; others believed manufacturing was necessary for economic independence (McCoy 1980). In 1791 the Society to Establish Useful Manufacture, which produced textiles, founded Paterson, New Jersey, the nation's first planned industrial city. The company was funded by federal bonds but struggled to become profitable. In general, the United States lacked the technology and mechanical skills necessary for industrialization. Additionally, though it boasted a robust agricultural output and a thriving shipping industry and trade, its markets were glutted with British manufactures (Thompson 2009).

Those in favor of industry recognized that immigration was important (Ben-Atar 2004). Under the Naturalization Act of 1790, the nation opened its arms to free white immigrants of "good character," while manufacturing advocates traveled overseas to encourage British artisans and mechanics to emigrate and state governments subsidized immigration and imported technology (Lovett 1952). The man often heralded as the "Father of the American Industrial Revolution," Samuel Slater (1768–1835), was a British immigrant. Slater helped build textile factories in Rhode Island using British textile technology, including water frames, which were water-powered machines for spinning thread or yarn from wool or cotton fibers. These machines were some of the major technologies of the early Industrial Revolution, along with the power loom, which Massachusetts merchant Francis Cabot Lowell (1775–1817) copied from English models (Rosenberg 2011) and implemented in eastern Massachusetts. The factory system Lowell established using these mechanized machines for weaving cloth was the first in which every stage of processing raw cotton into finished cloth could be performed in one building (Appleton 1858).

Before the introduction of the steam engine, most early factories were powered by water. The steam engine allowed manufacturing to spread to areas not located at a water source and also dramatically improved transportation. The first steamboats began operating in the early 1800s, and the first steam locomotive appeared in 1830 (Johnson 2013). Commercial railroads began replacing the canals that had been built in the 1810s and 1820s. New technologies and modes of transport helped generate sustained industrial growth by the middle of the nineteenth century. New England cemented its position as home to one-industry factory towns, supplying the nation with textiles, shoes, guns, and clocks, while New York, Philadelphia, and New Jersey perfected the urban industrial model of small shops that produced highly specialized goods. Delaware emerged as the capital of gunpowder production, while Pennsylvania became known for its iron industry. In the South, slave labor and knowledge sustained the factory production of sugar and other commodities (Licht 1995).

In the 1850s United States manufacturers showcased their wares and inventions at the international Crystal Palace Exhibition in London and became known for their "American System of Manufactures," which was the method of interchangeability and mechanization used in the American tool, arms, and clock industries (Hoke 1990). They also began exporting arms all over the world, and textiles to Latin America and Africa.

Following the Civil War (1861–1865) industrialization increased dramatically, hastened by the construction of intercontinental railroads. Railroads became big businesses in the 1860s, helped by federal land grants and corporate charters, tax breaks, foreign capital, and immigrant laborers (North 1961). Railroads increased connections among industries, consumers, and markets and led to the development of industry in new areas (Cootner 1963). While Philadelphia and New York City remained the preeminent manufacturing sectors, Chicago became a major center of industrial grain and meat production, and Illinois in general developed a thriving steel industry (Licht 1995; Cronon 2009). Steel became one of the biggest industries in the United States, fueled by demand from railroad construction. Federal incorporation laws made it easy for the steel industry, along with other industries such as oil and communications, to form monopolies in the last decades of the nineteenth century (Licht 1995).

LABOR UNREST

With the rise of big industry came increased labor unrest. Workers had organized strikes and unions since the start of industrialization, but in the latter part of the nineteenth century the scope and scale of unions and organized protest movements dramatically increased. The earliest organized working movements emerged among native-born skilled craftsmen in cities like New York, but as the composition of the manufacturing labor force changed, so too did worker movements (Wilentz 1984). In the 1830s women textile workers in Lowell, Massachusetts, led one of the first female strikes, and in general workers began organizing according to working-class subcultures, which were largely based on skill level, religion, ethnicity, or gender (Licht, 1995).

In the late 1840s immigration increased dramatically as a result of social revolutions in Europe and industrial job opportunities in the United States (North 1961). The first waves of immigrants were largely from Western Europe; around the turn of the twentieth century, the United States began receiving larger numbers of immigrants from eastern and southern Europe. The United States also received many immigrants from Canada; by the end of the century the number of Canadians born in the United States was equal to 22 percent of Canada's population (Ramirez 2009). Immigration fueled the expansion of industry, which in turn increased labor strife.

In the 1870s an economic depression in Europe spread to the United States, and company owners cut wages in response. The Great Railroad Strike of 1877 marked the start of major conflict between labor and capital that would persist through the first decades of the twentieth century (Licht 1995). Although national unions formed to fight for better working conditions, these organizations often excluded immigrants, women, and racial minorities until the twentieth century (Bucki 1995). Progressive Era reforms in the early twentieth century curbed some of the power of industrial corporations and instituted welfare programs to ease the labor and living conditions of the more than seven million people who had moved from rural to urban America for industrial work in the last three decades of the nineteenth century. And in 1935 the National Labor Relations Act gave federal protection to the gains unions had made earlier in the century by legislating workers' rights to union membership and fair working conditions (Maier, Smith, Keyssar, and Kevles 2006).

THE WORLD WARS AND THE GREAT DEPRESSION

The world wars brought new opportunities and challenges. The United States became a major supplier of finished manufactured goods to the Allied powers during World War I (1914–1918) (Fordham 2007). Productivity increased as a result of wartime demand and the implementation of scientific labor management practices. Following the war, the assembly line, pioneered by automobile manufacturer Henry Ford, became a hallmark of American industry and was adopted in Europe as well. During the Depression, US policy makers debated whether protective measures or international openness was the best solution for a depressed industrial economy. Tariffs had been a contentious political issue since the beginning of the nineteenth century, and the Smoot-Hawley Tariff of 1930 was especially controversial, sparking boycotts and tariff retaliation from foreign governments.

The United States changed course with the institution of reciprocal trade agreements, but these did little compared to World War II (1939–1945) in pulling the United States out of the Depression. Influenced by European thinkers and socialist policies, the US government mobilized all of society's resources as it engaged in wartime industrial planning (Hughes 2004). Women and minorities found new job opportunities in industrial production, as government orders expanded not only the shipbuilding, aircraft, and munitions industries but also consumer industries (Maier, Smith, Keyssar, and Kevles 2006).

Following World War II the manufacture of cars and household products increased, interstate highways made possible the movement of goods by freight truck, and industrial production and research centers shifted to newly developed suburban areas. Innovations in the container ship led to the rise of intermodal transport and greatly facilitated the sale of partially manufactured goods all over the globe. After decades of domestic industrial expansion, however, industrial production began to shift overseas. Beginning in the 1970s, US corporations took advantage of the lower labor and factory costs in other countries. The United States began to specialize in services and high-tech industries, such as biotechnology and information technology, rather than heavy manufacturing. Faced with increased imports, major US industries such as steel, automobile, and electronics declined throughout the last decades of the twentieth century. As a result, many manufacturing jobs were eliminated and once-thriving industrial cities fell into urban decay (Maier, Smith, Keyssar, and Kevles 2006).

In the first decades of the twenty-first century, rising labor and production costs in developing countries and lower energy costs at home began to shift some manufacturing back to the United States. As the nation stands poised to reindustrialize, it will continue to struggle with issues of immigration, fair labor practices, and protective trade policies. Since the building of the first American factories over two centuries ago, industry has been inseparable from the nation's policies and relationships both at home and abroad.

SEE ALSO *Airplanes; Americanization; Automobiles; Cold War; Exceptionalism; Exports, Exportation; Internationalism; Isolationism; Military-Industrial Complex; Trains; Weaponry; World War I; World War II; World's Fairs*

BIBLIOGRAPHY

Appleton, Nathan. *Introduction of the Power Loom, and Origin of Lowell.* Lowell, MA: B. H. Penhallow, 1858.

Ben-Atar, Doron S. *Trade Secrets: Intellectual Piracy and the Origins of American Industrial Power.* New Haven, CT: Yale University Press, 2004.

Bucki, Cecelia F. "Workers and Politics in the Immigrant City in the Early Twentieth-Century United States." *International Labor and Working-Class History* 48, *Workers and Citizenship in Europe and North America* (Fall 1995): 28–48.

Cootner, Paul H. "The Role of the Railroads in United States Economic Growth." *Journal of Economic History* 23, 4 (1963): 477–521.

Cronon, William. *Nature's Metropolis: Chicago and the Great West.* New York: Norton, 2009.

Fordham, Benjamin O. "Revisionism Reconsidered: Exports and American Intervention in World War I." *International Organization* 61, 2 (2007): 277–310.

Hindle, Brooke, and Steven Lubar. *Engines of Change: The American Industrial Revolution, 1790–1860.* Washington, DC: Smithsonian Institution Press, 1986.

Hoke, Donald R. *Ingenious Yankees: The Rise of the American System of Manufactures in the Private Sector.* New York: Columbia University Press, 1990.

Hughes, Thomas P. *American Genesis: A Century of Invention and Technological Enthusiasm, 1870–1970.* Chicago: University of Chicago Press, 2004.

Johnson, Walter. *River of Dark Dreams: Slavery and Empire in the Cotton Kingdom.* Cambridge, MA: Belknap Press of Harvard University Press, 2013.

Licht, Walter. *Industrializing America: The Nineteenth Century.* Baltimore: Johns Hopkins University Press, 1995.

Lovett, Robert W. "The Beverly Cotton Manufactory: Or Some New Light on an Early Cotton Mill." *Bulletin of the Business Historical Society* 26, 4 (1952): 218–242.

Maier, Pauline, Merritt Roe Smith, Alexander Keyssar, and Daniel J. Kevles. *Inventing America: A History of the United States,* Vol. 2: *From 1865.* 2nd ed. New York: Norton, 2006.

Matson, Cathy D., and Peter S. Onuf. *A Union of Interests: Political and Economic Thought in Revolutionary America.* Lawrence: University Press of Kansas, 1990.

McCoy, Drew R. *The Elusive Republic: Political Economy in Jeffersonian America.* Chapel Hill: University of North Carolina Press, 1980.

North, Douglass Cecil. *The Economic Growth of the United States, 1790–1860.* Englewood Cliffs, NJ: Prentice-Hall, 1961.

Ramirez, Bruno. "Emigration from Canada to the United States in the Nineteenth and Twentieth Centuries." *OAH Magazine of History* 23, 4 (2009): 31–34.

Rees, Jonathan. *Industrialization and the Transformation of American Life: A Brief Introduction.* Armonk, NY, and London: M. E. Sharpe, 2013.

Rosen, William. *The Most Powerful Idea in the World: A Story of Steam, Industry, and Invention.* Chicago: University of Chicago Press, 2012.

Rosenberg, Nathan. *Technology and American Economic Growth.* New York: Harper and Row, 1972.

Thomson, Ross. *Structures of Change in the Mechanical Age: Technological Innovation in the United States, 1790–1865.* Baltimore: Johns Hopkins University Press, 2009.

Tucker, Barbara M. *Samuel Slater and the Origins of the American Textile Industry, 1790–1860.* Ithaca, NY: Cornell University Press, 1984.

Wilentz, Sean. *Chants Democratic: New York City and the Rise of the American Working Class, 1788–1850.* London and New York: Oxford University Press, 1984.

Lindsay Schakenbach Regele
Assistant Professor
Miami University

THE INFLUENCE OF SEA POWER UPON HISTORY (ALFRED THAYER MAHAN, 1890)

Captain Alfred Thayer Mahan (1840–1914) was the author of the 428-page book titled *The Influence of Sea Power upon History, 1660–1783.* It was published by Little, Brown and Company in Boston, Massachusetts, in early May 1890 and has never been out of print since that time. Translated into French (1894–1896), Russian (1895), German (1896), Japanese (1897), Swedish (1899–1900), Spanish (1900), and Chinese (1997), the volume has had an enormous impact on naval strategic thinking around the world. It laid the foundation for the modern study of naval history and influenced the conduct of naval strategy in the first and second world wars.

This book was the first in a series of four volumes that Mahan devoted to the theme of sea power, a term that he deliberately coined to draw attention to his abstract concept of maritime power. Little, Brown published all his book-length works, including the three subsequent volumes in this series: *The Influence of Sea Power upon the French Revolution and Empire* (1892); *The Life of Nelson: The Embodiment of the Sea Power of Great Britain* (1897); and *Sea Power in the War of 1812* (1905). These, along with Mahan's other writings, brought the term *sea power* into wide currency through historical examinations of naval strategy and naval command.

The work had its origins in an invitation to Mahan, dated July 22, 1884, from Rear Admiral Stephen B. Luce (1827–1917), to take up the position of lecturer in naval history and tactics at the nascent US Naval War College in Newport, Rhode Island, an institution that would be formally established several months later. At that time, Mahan was commanding the USS *Wachusett* on the Pacific coast of South America. He began his general reading to prepare for his new assignment in the library of the Phoenix Club in Lima, Peru. On completing his sea assignment, the Navy Department ordered Mahan to his home in New York City. Mahan met Luce at Newport on October 20, 1885, at which time Luce gave him a year's research leave at his home, where he had easy access to sources at the New York Public Library. Luce directed him to consider the interrelationships of naval and military tactics, strategy, diplomacy, and national power.

Luce, who had been influenced by British naval historian Sir John Knox Laughton (1830–1915) and his 1874 article "The Scientific Study of Naval History," gave Mahan an assignment that was dramatically different from all previous major studies of naval history, which had focused on tactical engagements between ships. Although Mahan completed the research for his lecture series in September 1886, he initially resisted publication, thinking that officers would no longer come to the college courses if the lectures were published. In 1889, retired naval lieutenant William McCarty Little (1845–1915) became Mahan's initial conduit to the publisher Little, Brown. Luce, Laughton, and Theodore Roosevelt (1858–1919) wrote the first book reviews, all published anonymously. An unidentified author reviewed it for *The New York Times*.

In 1887, Admiral Luce invited Roosevelt to lecture at the Naval War College on the War of 1812, thereby creating the first personal connection between Roosevelt and Mahan when that lecture took place at Newport in September 1888. Thus began what one historian has aptly called an "ambiguous relationship," based initially on a shared interest in naval history and later, from 1897 to 1898, on a mutual interest in strategic planning. While Mahan thought of himself as a scholar and thinker, Roosevelt saw his value as a writer and polemicist. Although there were differences in viewpoint between the two men, they were both advocates of a large navy with modern battleships as something necessary to a major nation. Both also agreed with social Darwinist ideas, the need for overseas naval stations, and the annexation of Hawai'i. In addition, both were concerned about the rising power of Germany and Japan.

Mahan had chosen to examine the naval wars between 1660 and 1815, not only because they were the most recent major naval wars but because he also found them suggestive of historical parallels with his own time. Mahan's arguments were deeply nuanced in historical circumstances, but others used his name and work to promote them as a much more rigid and doctrinaire interpretation about decisive fleet battles. To American readers, Mahan's works complemented Frederick Jackson Turner's 1893 essay on "The Significance of the Frontier in American History" by suggesting the means for the country to follow the closing of the frontier. Mahan's argument that historically navies existed to protect maritime trade and colonies resonated with leading American politicians, including Roosevelt and Henry Cabot Lodge (1850–1924), who saw historical lessons for American naval power and overseas expansion. For British readers, Mahan's work explained and confirmed their faith in the Royal Navy as central to their dominant world power, while in Germany, Japan, and other countries, Mahan's work was used to confirm a perceived need to build major battleship navies that could fight a future, climacteric fleet battle.

SEE ALSO *Navy, US; Roosevelt, Theodore; Wilson, Woodrow; World War I*

BIBLIOGRAPHY

Ferreiro, Larrie D. "Mahan and the 'English Club' of Lima, Peru: The Genesis of *The Influence of Sea Power Upon History.*" *Journal of Military History* 72, 3 (2008): 901–906.

Hattendorf, John B., ed. *The Influence of History on Mahan: The Proceedings of a Conference Marking the Centenary of Alfred Thayer Mahan's* The Influence of Sea Power upon History, 1660–1783. Newport, RI: Naval War College Press, 1991.

Hattendorf, John B., and Lynn C. Hattendorf, comps. *A Bibliography of the Works of Alfred Thayer Mahan.* Newport, RI: Naval War College Press, 1986.

Hattendorf, John B., B. Mitchell Simpson III, and John R. Wadleigh. *Sailors and Scholars: The History of the Naval War College, 1884–2014.* 2nd ed. Chaps. 2–3. Newport, RI: Naval War College Press, 2015.

Lambert, Andrew, ed. *Letters and Papers of Professor Sir John Knox Laughton, 1830–1915.* Publications of the Navy Records Society, 143. Aldershot, UK: Ashgate for the Navy Records Society, 2002.

Laughton, John Knox. "The Scientific Study of Naval History." *Journal of the Royal United Services Institution* 18 (1874): 508–527.

Laughton, John Knox. "Captain Mahan on Maritime Power." *Edinburgh Review* 352 (October 1890): 420–453.

Luce, Stephen B. "The Influence of Sea Power upon History." *The Critic* 17, 343 (1890): 41–42.

"New Publications: Sea Power in History." *New York Times*, April 19, 1891, 19, cols. 2–4.

Roosevelt, Theodore. "The Influence of Sea Power upon History." *Atlantic Monthly* 66, 396 (1890): 563–567.

Seager, Robert, II, and Doris D. Maquire, eds. *Letters and Papers of Alfred Thayer Mahan.* 3 vols. Annapolis, MD: Naval Institute Press, 1975.

Sumida, Jon Tetsuro. *Inventing Grand Strategy and Teaching Command: The Classic Works of Alfred Thayer Mahan Reconsidered.* Baltimore, MD: Johns Hopkins University Press; Washington, DC: Woodrow Wilson Center Press, 1997.

Turk, Richard W. *The Ambiguous Relationship: Theodore Roosevelt and Alfred Thayer Mahan.* Westport, CT: Greenwood Press, 1987.

John B. Hattendorf
Ernest J. King Professor of Maritime History
US Naval War College

INSULAR POSSESSIONS

In 1789, when George Washington (1732–1799) was inaugurated as the first president under the new Constitution, the United States consisted of eleven states—North Carolina and Rhode Island had not yet ratified the Constitution—stretching from what is now Maine (then Massachusetts) in the north to the southern border of Georgia. The western boundary was provided by the eastern bank of the Mississippi River. By the turn of the twentieth century, the United States had not only reached to the Pacific coast, but had also extended well into the Pacific Ocean with both Hawai'i and Guam (not to mention the Aleutian Islands that were part of the purchase of Alaska from Russia in 1867), and southward into the Caribbean Sea. Puerto Rico was one of the spoils of victory in the Spanish-American War (1898), as were the Philippine Islands and Guam. The addition of these "insular possessions" are important moments in the history of American expansionism, one of the central themes (and realities) of nineteenth-century American history.

THE CHALLENGE OF EXPANSIONISM TO REPUBLICAN GOVERNMENT

American expansionism challenged at least one notion of what the Framers' generation defined as "republican government": Could such a government be maintained over an extended territory consisting of an ever-larger population? Political philosophers such as Montesquieu (1689–1755) and David Hume (1711–1776) doubted that it could. A central theme of *The Federalist* (1787–1788) was that they were, in effect, wrong, and that an "extended republic" was altogether possible. Indeed, expansion was, according most famously to *Federalist* No. 10, conducive to protecting liberty. However, *Federalist* No. 2, by John Jay (1745–1829), emphasized, plausibly or not, the status of the American people as truly "united": "a people descended from the same ancestors, speaking the same language, professing the same religion, attached to the same principles of government, very similar in their manners and customs." American expansion demolished any credence that might be given to such a notion. Consider only Louisiana, a French-speaking Catholic territory whose white citizens were nonetheless absorbed into the United States by 1812, just as the Mexican War (1846–1848) brought into the territorial Union many Spanish-speakers (and Catholics). Even more strikingly, both the Louisiana Purchase (1803) and the Mexican War brought under American control literally hundreds of American Indian tribes, the members of which had a decidedly uncertain status with regard to membership in the American community.

These questions about the character of the American community, both implicit and explicit, inevitably came to the fore with the addition of the new insular possessions to the American empire. Previous expansions had taken place under the assumption that the newly added territories would, sooner or later, become admitted to the Union as full states. To be sure, admission was sometimes delayed, awaiting enough settlement by English-speaking whites to swamp existing (and indigenous) populations and assure that political control would be in presumptively proper hands. What is distinctive about the insular territories gained from Spain, however, is that there was never any such assumption about entry into the Union after a suitable time.

The Spanish-American War and the absorption of the new territories were hardly uncontroversial. Imperialism was an important issue during the 1900 presidential campaign. The Democratic candidate, William Jennings Bryan (1860–1925), like such luminaries as Mark Twain (1835–1910) and William James (1842–1910), was bitterly critical of what were described as attempts by the United States to emulate European countries by creating empires whose inhabitants would simply be ruled by the national government, with little or no regard for the rights of local inhabitants. (An insurrection by Philippine nationalists would be put down with great brutality.) Bryan lost, of course, and the architects of the "splendid little war" with Spain triumphed. Theodore Roosevelt (1858–1919), the self-proclaimed "hero of San Juan Hill," would become president after McKinley's assassination.

THE *INSULAR CASES*

Shortly thereafter, the constitutionality of this new political reality was tested before the US Supreme Court in a group of cases collectively known as the *Insular Cases.* As a popular question of the time asked, "Did the Constitution follow the flag?" Did traditional constitutional norms automatically apply wherever the American flag identified a given territory as being under American control? Or did Congress have the power under the Constitution to rule the inhabitants of the newly acquired territories without recognizing a variety of rights?

The issue presented in the most important of the *Insular Cases*, *Downes v. Bidwell* (1901), was whether Puerto Rico should be conceptualized as "within" the United States for purposes of a constitutional clause that prohibited Congress from allowing divergent tariffs in different ports within the United States. (That is, Congress could not pass tariff laws that preferred Boston to Philadelphia, or New York to Charleston; all had to be treated equally.) Did the "uniformity clause" apply to San Juan, Puerto Rico (or to any of the other newly acquired territories)? The Court said no. The reason offered by several of the justices, in an analysis that later became adopted by the entire Court, was that Puerto Rico had not been "incorporated" into the Union by Congress. As "unincorporated territories," Puerto Rico and the other newly acquired territories were subject to more-or-less plenary control by Congress and the national government.

The dissenters, who rejected the ostensible distinction between "incorporated" and "unincorporated" territories, paid attention to the 1857 *Dred Scott* case, widely regarded as the worst case in American constitutional history because of its declaration that descendants of black slaves could never become citizens within the American political community. But the paradox of Chief Justice Brooke Roger Taney's (1777–1864) opinion in that case was its insistence that Congress held the territories in trust for all citizens; it was consequently unconstitutional for Congress, as in the Missouri Compromise (1820), to prevent American citizens from taking their lawfully owned slaves with them into the territories added to the Union by the Louisiana Purchase or the Mexican War. What this meant, in effect, is that the Constitution most definitely *did* follow the flag. For Taney and the majority, the Constitution was, in effect, a proslavery Constitution. Slavery was obviously no longer a central issue in 1901, but *Dred Scott* could still be powerfully cited by dissenters like Justice John Marshall Harlan (1833–1911) in behalf of the proposition that constitutional rights indeed accompanied the flag, which included, in this case, Puerto Rico and the other new insular territories.

Justice Harlan noted that one of the relevant Supreme Court opinions referred to the degree to which the new territories were inhabited by "alien races, differing from the bulk of the American people in religion, customs, laws, methods of taxation, and modes of thought." This, in effect, justified the deprivation to them of traditional constitutional norms. "We decline," the Court proclaimed, "to hold that there is anything in the Constitution to forbid such action." Justice Harlan begged to disagree. "Whether a particular race will or will not assimilate with our people, and whether they can or cannot with safety to our institutions be brought within the operation of the Constitution, is a matter to be thought of when it is proposed to acquire their territory by treaty." What he laconically described as a "mistake in the acquisition of territory, although such acquisition seemed at the time to be necessary, cannot be made the ground for violating the Constitution or refusing to give full effect to its provisions." What this means, at least according to Justice Harlan, is that there is not one set of norms for those regarded as genuine Americans and another set for "alien races" who, by being defined as inhabitants of "unincorporated territories," can be denied the benefits of most of those norms. (Even the majority agreed that certain "fundamental norms" would apply in the "unincorporated" as well as "incorporated" territories, but these did not extend, for example, to any rights of self-government or, as the Court later determined, the right to enjoy trial by jury.)

CONTINUING QUESTIONS

Of course, the Philippines has been an independent country since 1946. Puerto Ricans were granted US citizenship by Congress in 1917 as a result of the Jones Act, but they continue to be deprived of any voting membership in Congress or the ability to help choose the president of the United States. Although historically most of the Puerto Rican public was almost equally divided between a preference for statehood and maintenance of the current "commonwealth" status (with the remainder supporting independence), a referendum in November 2012 for the first time suggested that a majority of Puerto Ricans in fact supported statehood. Thus, 54 percent of the electorate rejected the "commonwealth" status; CNN reported that, "voting on a second proposition, 61% chose statehood as the alternative, compared with 33% for the semi-autonomous 'sovereign free association' and 6% for outright independence" (Castillo 2012). It remains an open political question whether Congress would in fact be willing to admit what is sometimes called the world's largest remaining territory into full membership in the Union. Would Congress, for example, object to the fact that Spanish is by far the dominant language in Puerto Rico, not to mention that a new state would be entitled to approximately seven seats in the House of Representatives, in addition to two senators (and, therefore, nine electoral votes in choosing the president)?

The *Insular Cases* continue to be important with regard to other territorial possessions of the United States. Just as persons born in Puerto Rico have automatically become US citizens since 1917, other statutes have extended similar rights of citizenship to those born in Guam and the US Virgin Islands (bought from Denmark in 1917). But this is not true of persons born in American Samoa.

There is also the question of the status of the Guantánamo Bay naval base that the United States holds in an ostensibly perpetual lease from Cuba (though the current Cuban government does not recognize the validity of the lease and refuses to cash the annual rental checks given it by the United States). The George W. Bush administration chose to send many detainees captured as part of its "global war on terror" to Guantánamo because of the administration's belief that Guantánamo was sufficiently "outside" the United States to be free from the imposition of a variety of constitutional norms that would clearly have applied had, for example, the detainees been sent to prisons on the mainland. The Supreme Court, without mentioning the *Insular Cases*, nevertheless treated Guantánamo as sufficiently under American control to require the accompaniment of habeas corpus rights, a stinging defeat for the administration (*Rasul v. Bush*, 542 U.S. 466 [2004]).

SEE ALSO *Caribbean; Spanish-American War*

BIBLIOGRAPHY

Burnett, Christina Duffy, and Burke Marshall, eds. *Foreign in a Domestic Sense: Puerto Rico, American Expansion, and the Constitution*. Durham, NC: Duke University Press, 2001.

Castillo, Mariano. "Puerto Ricans Favor Statehood for First Time." CNN, November 8, 2012. http://www.cnn.com/2012/11/07/politics/election-puerto-rico/

Downes v. Bidwell, 182 U.S. 244 (1901)

Jay, John. *Federalist* No. 2: "Concerning Dangers from Foreign Force and Influence." 1787. http://thomas.loc.gov/home/histdox/fed_02.html

Raustiala, Kal. *Does the Constitution Follow the Flag? The Evolution of Territoriality in American Law*. New York: Oxford University Press, 2009.

Sparrow, Bartholomew H. *The Insular Cases and the Emergence of American Empire*. Lawrence: University Press of Kansas, 2006.

Sanford Levinson
W. St. John Garwood and W. St. John Garwood Jr. Centennial Chair in Law, University of Texas Law School
Professor of Government, University of Texas at Austin

INTERCONTINENTAL BALLISTIC MISSILES

Intercontinental ballistic missiles (ICBMs) fly mainly above the atmosphere to targets at a distance of 5,000 miles or more. Following the creation in 1952 of the thermonuclear or hydrogen bomb, the US Air Force was chosen over the US Army to build US long-range strategic missiles, and it began developing ICBMs in 1954. The Soviet Union also began developing its own ICBM that year. Both Cold War superpowers began ICBM test flights in 1957, and their first operational ICBMs went on station in 1959. Since that time, ICBMs have formed one leg of America's "triad" of nuclear deterrence, along with nuclear weapons carried on bomber aircraft, and submarine-launched ballistic missiles (SLBMs).

America's first ICBMs, Atlas and Titan I and II, were liquid-fueled rockets that had limitations as weapons because their fuel was extremely difficult to handle. They were soon replaced by solid-fuel ICBMs, starting with Minuteman in 1962, which were smaller, easier to handle, and could remain ready for launch around the clock for long periods of time. Early liquid-fueled American and Russian ICBMs were well suited to be space-launch vehicles, and the Soviet R-7 ICBM launched the first artificial satellite of the Earth, Sputnik, in 1957. ICBMs were used to launch most early satellites and space probes, along with the first humans into orbit. The R-7 was designed to carry a far heavier bomb than Atlas and Titan, and this allowed the Soviet Union to take an early lead in the space race between the two superpowers into the 1960s. But the R-7's size limited its utility as an ICBM because it required massive launch pads that precluded the use of silos to protect it from a first-strike attack by the other side. All American land-based ICBMs could be deployed in silos.

Although the Soviet Union was thought to have the lead in ICBMs in the late 1950s, it quickly became known that the United States in fact held the clear lead through the 1960s until the Soviets deployed large numbers of new ICBMs late in the decade. The US Navy began deploying its first SLBM, Polaris, in 1961, and later replaced it with Poseidon and then Trident I and II missiles. In the 1970s both the United States and Soviet Union began equipping their ICBMs and SLBMs with multiple independent reentry vehicles (MIRVs), and soon both sides agreed to limit the numbers of missiles and MIRVs. The large numbers of missiles and warheads possessed by the two superpowers underlay the concept of mutually assured destruction (MAD).

Under agreements reached at the end of the Cold War, both the United States and Russia sharply reduced the numbers of ICBMs. Since the retirement of the MX Peacekeeper ICBM, the US land-based force has consisted of Minuteman III missiles. China, India, Israel, the United Kingdom, and France have ICBMs or SLBMs, and there are concerns that other countries such as Iran and North Korea are developing ICBMs. The United States developed systems designed to defend against ICBMs; these systems, especially the program called the Strategic Defense

Initiative begun by President Ronald Reagan in 1983, have prompted debates over efficacy and cost.

SEE ALSO *Air Force, US; Department of Defense, US; Deterrence; Mutual Assured Destruction (MAD); Nuclear Weapons; Strategic Defense Initiative (Star Wars)*

BIBLIOGRAPHY

Baucom, Donald R. *The Origins of SDI, 1944–1983.* Lawrence: University Press of Kansas, 1992.

Gainor, Christopher. "The Atlas and the Air Force: Reassessing the Beginnings of America's First Intercontinental Ballistic Missile." *Technology and Culture* 54, 2 (2013): 346–370.

Heefner, Gretchen. *The Missile Next Door: The Minuteman in the American Heartland.* Cambridge, MA: Harvard University Press, 2012.

Sheehan, Neil. *A Fiery Peace in a Cold War: Bernard Schriever and the Ultimate Weapon.* New York: Random House, 2009.

Christopher Gainor
Historian
Foresight Science and Technology

INTERNATIONAL BUSINESS MACHINES CORPORATION (IBM)

The origins of the International Business Machines Corporation, known as IBM, date back to the manual processing of the 1880 United States population census, which took seven years to complete. The predicted ten-year processing for the 1890 census prompted a contest within the US Census Bureau for a more efficient method of tabulating census data. The statistician Herman Hollerith, the son of German immigrants living in Buffalo, New York, won this contest. He developed a mechanical tabulator based on punched cards to rapidly calculate statistics from millions of data pieces. In 1896 Hollerith formed the Tabulating Machine Company in Washington, DC, which merged with the International Time Recording Company and the Computing Scale Company in 1911 to form the Computing-Tabulating-Recording Company (CTR), based in New York City. In the following years CTR evolved into a highly successful international holding company based around punch-card tabulating machines. In 1924 the company was renamed International Business Machines.

IBM continued its business success during the Depression era by constantly increasing the capacity of its punch-card technology and by winning major government contracts to maintain employment records. Earlier than many of its competitors, IBM established a division to lead research, development, and engineering efforts for the entire IBM product line. With the United States' entry into World War II (1939–1945), IBM actively supported the government's war efforts by funding and supporting, among other technologies, the development of the Harvard Mark I computer, an electromechanical calculator that could perform large computations automatically.

In 1943 IBM introduced the first truly electronic computer by substituting vacuum tubes for electric relays, which dramatically increased information processing speeds and reliability. Recognizing the market potential of computer technology, during the early 1950s IBM pioneered the development and mass production of a range of intermediate- and large-sized computers to handle accounting, scientific computations, and other commercial applications. By the late 1950s IBM's fully transistorized computers were being used by the US Air Force in its early warning systems for missiles and by NASA for the control of space flights.

During the Cold War IBM was also intricately involved in the development of the Semi-Automatic Ground Environment (SAGE) early warning system. Between 1958 and 1984, SAGE became the technological backbone for the North American Aerospace Defense Command (NORAD). SAGE offered real-time information processing of approaching enemy aircraft, which it received from radar stations across the country connected by telephone lines. It then automatically generated transmissions of relevant information to the pilots of intercepting fighter aircraft.

The introduction of IBM's System/360 in 1964 represented the next radical shift for the global computer industry. IBM replaced the predominant "one size fits all" product philosophy with a diversified product family that ranged from mini- to supercomputers, which all shared the same software. As their computation needs evolved, customers could easily upgrade to larger systems without wasting time and money for new software. The System/360 would prove essential in the successful Apollo project to transport human beings to the moon and back. In 1969 IBM introduced the Customer Information Control System (CISC), a transaction processing system designed for online and batch processing that is still widely used by banks and insurance companies around the world. Two years later IBM presented the floppy disk, which became the industry standard for storing personal computer data until the early 1990s.

IBM was also at the forefront of the personal computer (PC) revolution, which gained momentum during the late 1970s through companies such as Commodore, Atari, and Apple. The IBM PC was introduced in 1981 and mainly intended for personal home users and small businesses. It was vastly successful and quickly became the worldwide industry standard, mainly because of its open architecture, which allowed other manufacturers to develop and offer IBM-compatible peripheral components and software without the need to purchase additional licenses. The IBM PC made computers affordable for the ordinary user, leading to a dramatically growing global consumer market for PCs.

In hindsight, IBM's open architecture approach proved a strategic mistake because it enabled its competitors to offer cheap clones of the IBM PC as well as a wide range of IBM-compatible peripheral devices. The outsourcing of computer chip production to Intel and software development to Microsoft, as well as IBM's underestimation of the Internet's impact on technological and market evolution, endangered its long-term viability. Multibillion-dollar losses during the late 1980s and early 1990s finally forced the company onto a path of radical restructuring and strategic reorientation. IBM abandoned its consumer PC business and began focusing on large mainframe computer systems, integrated information technology (IT) services, and on-demand e-business solutions (cloud computing) for corporate business clients.

SEE ALSO *Air Force, US; Department of Defense, US; Internet*

BIBLIOGRAPHY

Chposky, James, and Ted Leonsis. *Blue Magic: The People, Power and Politics Behind the IBM Personal Computer.* New York: Facts on File, 1988.

Fisher, Franklin M., James W. McKie, and Richard B. Mancke. *IBM and the U.S. Data Processing Industry: An Economic History.* New York: Praeger, 1983.

Lev-Ram, Michal. "IBM CEO Ginni Rometty Gets Past the Big Blues." September 18, 2014. http://fortune.com/2014/09/18/ginni-rometty-ibm/

Pugh, Emerson W. *Building IBM: Shaping an Industry and Its Technology.* Cambridge, MA: MIT Press, 1996.

Stefan Fritsch
Assistant Professor of International Relations and Comparative Government
Bowling Green State University

INTERNATIONAL CONFERENCE ON HUMAN RIGHTS, 1968

SEE *Human rights.*

INTERNATIONAL LABOR ORGANIZATION

The United States played a surprisingly important role in the creation of the International Labor Organization (ILO) at the Versailles Peace Conference in 1919, despite its failure to join the organization until 1934. After the United States became a member of the ILO, US representatives helped to move the organization in new directions and would also be at the center of many organizational controversies. Although the United States ratified relatively few ILO conventions by comparison with other industrialized countries, debates over these conventions helped to crystallize cultural and political divisions within American society and to shape the United States' relations with other countries.

ROOTS OF THE ILO

The roots of the ILO lie in World War I (1914–1918). Only shortly after many belligerent labor movements in Europe pledged to loyally support their governments in 1914, they also took steps to revive the international labor movement and demanded a role for labor at any future peace conference and in any future international organizations. When the United States entered the war in 1917, the leader of the American Federation of Labor (AFL), Samuel Gompers (1850–1924), joined in the chorus of those demanding a role for labor at Versailles. Yet President Woodrow Wilson (1856–1924), despite the close partnership that developed between the AFL and the US government during the war, was initially reluctant to include labor in the peace negotiations or to make workers' rights and an international labor body a component of the peace treaty.

Upon arriving in Paris, however, Wilson joined other plenipotentiaries in creating a Commission on International Labor Legislation to consider how the future League of Nations might address labor issues. Doubtless the spread of Bolshevism and class unrest across the globe influenced the decision of world leaders to grant this voice to labor during the peace negotiations. Yet many European labor movements boycotted the peace conference when the plenipotentiaries refused to allow German labor delegates to attend. This development provided an opening for Gompers, who travelled to Paris despite the European labor boycott and was appointed to chair the Commission on International Labor Legislation. Many other countries, in the absence of trade union representatives, appointed social policy experts to serve on the commission.

Despite his position as chair, Gompers often found himself on the defensive within the commission. From the beginning, he had doubts about the efficacy of an international labor organization attached to the League of Nations and instead focused on the inclusion of a labor bill of rights directly in the Versailles Treaty. Yet European delegates felt that a labor charter would be meaningless without an organization to enforce these rights. Fresh from their wartime experiences with economic collaboration, European delegates supported a tripartite structure for the future international labor organization, with two government, one business, and one labor representative for each national delegation that attended yearly conventions. Although not an opponent of tripartism, Gompers insisted that government, like business and labor, should be allowed only one representative within national delegations. He argued that working people would have no faith in an organization in which they were a "minority of one in four." The commission, however, supported the 2-1-1 ratio over Gompers's objections—a membership schematic that has persisted to the present day (McKillen 2013, 192–193).

On two other issues, however, Gompers proved more successful. He prevented Italian and French delegates from making the ILO into a "super-parliament" whose decisions on international labor standards would automatically have the force of international law. Instead, Gompers worked with American historian James Shotwell (1874–1965) to develop provisions whereby conventions passed by the ILO would have the force of law within nations only if they were ratified by national legislatures or other appropriate bodies in a manner comparable to treaties. Gompers argued that democratic nations like the United States would otherwise be reluctant to join the ILO because it would undermine their own constitutionally determined procedures for legislating labor issues. Gompers also successfully championed the inclusion of a labor bill of rights—albeit one much different from that initially envisioned by the AFL—within the Versailles Treaty itself.

Upon returning to the United States, both Wilson and Gompers became vigorous advocates for US membership in the ILO. In particular, Wilson used the labor bill of rights and the proposed ILO to try to win support for the Versailles Peace Treaty during his whistle-stop tour in the fall of 1919. The president badly miscalculated, however, for the proposed ILO soon became a political liability that incited wide-ranging opposition from both the political right and the left. Conservative Republicans wondered whether the ILO would try to interfere in decisions that were best left to US employers and employees and also worried openly that nonwhite nations within the ILO might try to use their newfound power to undermine the racial division of labor within the United States. At the opposite end of the spectrum, left-leaning groups dismissed the ILO as a mirage that would encourage worker complacency without empowering them. The African American socialist paper *The Messenger*, for example, criticized the ILO as "a bit of capitalist deception which is about as valuable to labor as the belief of a hungry man that a brick is a sausage"(McKillen 2013, 195, 224).

Widespread public opposition in turn paved the way for the US Senate to pass a motion that made the exclusion of the labor provisions one of the fourteen reservations to the treaty. When the Senate voted down the treaty both with and without reservations, it also preempted US membership in the ILO. The United States remained outside the organization throughout the 1920s.

US MEMBERSHIP AND INFLUENCE

The onset of the Great Depression, however, inspired a new interest in international labor standards within the United States. The Franklin D. Roosevelt (1882–1945) administration became increasingly interested in ILO proposals for reducing unemployment and maintaining wage levels during times of economic downturn. Also important in lobbying on behalf of the ILO were a network of women social welfare advocates and the American Association for Labor Legislation. More surprising was the interest of some employers and Republican politicians in international labor standards as a way to save ailing industries. Among these was New Hampshire Republican governor John Winant (1889–1947), who would later become director-general of the ILO. Winant initially sought to save his state's troubled textile industry by creating a regional pact with other northeastern state governments that committed them to maintaining wages and prices. Yet the pact proved ineffectual because of competition from southern states. Winant subsequently cooperated with some of Roosevelt's New Deal policies and began to travel in circles that emphasized US membership in the ILO as a way to overcome diverse state standards. Supporters of ILO membership in the United States argued that because ILO conventions would be passed as treaties by the Senate, they would override problematic state legislation in a way that Roosevelt's National Recovery Administration could not (Lorenz 2001, 75–103).

Increased popular support for the ILO in turn paved the way for Congress to endorse US membership in the organization. Upon joining the ILO in 1934, the Roosevelt administration was invited to recommend an American for a leadership position. It suggested John Winant, who served for a short time as an assistant director before accepting a position on Roosevelt's Social Security Board. Winant returned to the ILO in 1937. Soon thereafter, due to intense lobbying by the Roosevelt administration, Winant was elected director-general of the ILO, despite his inexperience and the opposition of some European appointees. During his two-year term as director, Winant oversaw the wartime relocation of the ILO's governing office from Geneva to Montreal, signaling a shift in the "centre of gravity" within the organization away from Europe (Hughes and Haworth 2010, 293–311).

EXPANDING MISSION

Initially, the shift seemed to reinvigorate the organization, and US secretary of labor Frances Perkins (1880–1965) and other Roosevelt appointees strove to broaden the ILO's functions to include possible postwar reconstruction. These efforts, however, faltered as some worried that the ILO's tripartite structure would provide inadequate scaffolding for such work. Instead, new organizations, such as the United Nations Relief and Rehabilitation Administration, emerged to deal with these issues. At an important meeting in Philadelphia, the ILO chose another path, expanding its social justice mission by emphasizing in a declaration that it was committed to guaranteeing economic security and equal opportunity to all human beings regardless of race, creed, or sex. At the San Francisco summit that created the United Nations in 1945, the Soviet Union questioned the ILO's right to exist and become a part of the UN network of organizations, but by 1946 the ILO secured status as a UN specialized agency, thereby ensuring its future survival (Goethem 2010, 313–340).

From 1948 to 1970, David Morse (1907–1990), an American, served as director-general of the ILO, guiding it through both the East-West divide of the Cold War and the North-South divide that followed in the wake of postwar decolonization. A liberal internationalist who, in the words of Daniel Roger Maul, sought to "offer a New Deal with a decidedly anti-communist slant to the world," Morse nonetheless chose to support Soviet reentry into the ILO in 1954. This policy in turn proved controversial among both business and labor groups in the United States, who accused Morse of being soft on communism. Morse also welcomed newly emerging or previously unrepresented nations in Asia, Latin America, and Africa into the ILO, increasing its size from 55 countries in 1947 to 121 in 1970. As membership changed, the ILO shifted more of its budget from the monitoring and implementation of labor standards in industrialized countries to technical and developmental assistance programs for poorer nations (Maul 2010, 371, 379–387).

OPPOSITION IN THE UNITED STATES

US employer groups dissatisfied with the ILO launched campaigns to force US withdrawal from the organization beginning in the 1950s. With the United States now enjoying unprecedented prosperity, they objected to international labor standards as an unfair and unnecessary infringement on the free market. In contrast to Winant, they also viewed the process of convention ratification as undemocratic and opposed even widely accepted conventions on maternity leave and the universal right to health insurance as socialistic. Yet while business groups prevented the United States from ratifying many conventions during the early Cold War, they failed in their efforts to force the United States to withdraw from the organization.

A more formidable threat to US membership in the ILO came from the American Federation of Labor–Congress of Industrial Organizations (AFL-CIO). From the perspective of AFL-CIO president George Meany (1894–1980), Soviet and Eastern bloc government control of union and employer representatives within their delegations undermined the integrity of the ILO's tripartite membership structure and prevented human rights questions within these areas from being addressed. Meany became particularly concerned when the Soviet Union sought more leadership positions within the ILO in the 1960s. In 1970, shortly after Morse's successor, C. Wilfred Jenks (1909–1973), appointed Pavel Astapenko of the Soviet Union as one of the ILO's assistant directors, Meany successfully lobbied Congress to have the US appropriations for ILO membership rescinded. The appropriations constituted about one-quarter of the ILO's budget. In the meantime, the US government also grew increasingly concerned with the political positions taken by the ILO. In 1977, the United States withdrew from the organization, but returned in 1981 after the ILO condemned Russian treatment of labor dissidents and took up the cause of Lech Wałesa and the Solidarity Union in Poland (Lorenz 2001, 189–227).

REKINDLED US INTEREST

In the years since the end of the Cold War, interest in the ILO in the United States has been rekindled by a variety of labor, consumer, and human rights activists seeking to counteract the influence of institutions like the World Trade Organization and World Bank in an increasingly globalized economy. Yet whether the United States can play an important role in using the ILO to protect workers' rights in the future seems dependent upon Americans' willingness to overcome the sense of American exceptionalism and distrust of international organizations that has hindered US participation in the ILO in the past.

SEE ALSO *AFL-CIO: Labor's Foreign Policy; Industrialization; League of Nations; Paris Peace Conference (1919); World War I*

BIBLIOGRAPHY

Cobble, Dorothy Sue. "A Higher Standard of Life for the World: U.S. Labor Women's Reform Internationalism and the Legacies of 1919." *Journal of American History* 100, 4 (2014): 1052–1085.

Cox, Robert W. "ILO: Limited Monarchy." In *The Anatomy of Influence: Decision Making in International Organization*, edited by Robert W. Cox, Harold K. Jacobson, and G. Curzon, 102–138. New Haven, CT: Yale University Press, 1973.

Galenson, Walter. *The International Labor Organization: An American View.* Madison: University of Wisconsin Press, 1981.

Hughes, Stephen, and Nigel Haworth. "A Shift in the Centre of Gravity: The ILO under Harold Butler and John G. Winant." In *ILO Histories: Essays on the International Labour Organization and Its Impact on the World during the Twentieth Century*, edited by Jasmien Van Daele et al., 293–311. Bern, Switzerland: Peter Lang, 2010.

Lorenz, Edward C. *Defining Global Justice: The History of U.S. International Labor Standards Policy.* Notre Dame, IN: University of Notre Dame, 2001.

Maul, Daniel Roger. "The Morse Years: The ILO 1948–1970." In *ILO Histories: Essays on the International Labour Organization and Its Impact on the World during the Twentieth Century*, edited by Jasmien Van Daele et al., 365–400. Bern, Switzerland: Peter Lang, 2010.

McKillen, Elizabeth. *Making the World Safe for Workers: Labor, the Left, and Wilsonian Internationalism.* Urbana: University of Illinois Press, 2013.

Shotwell, James T. *The Origins of the International Labor Organization.* 2 vols. New York: Columbia University Press, 1934.

Van Daele, Jasmien, Magaly Rodríguez García, Geert Van Goethem, and Marcel van der Linden, eds. *ILO Histories: Essays on the International Labour Organization and Its Impact on the World during the Twentieth Century.* Bern, Switzerland: Peter Lang, 2010.

Van Goethem, Geert. "Phelan's War: The International Labour Organization in Limbo (1941–1948)." In *ILO Histories: Essays on the International Labour Organization and Its Impact on the World during the Twentieth Century*, edited by Jasmien Van Daele et al., 313–340. Bern, Switzerland: Peter Lang, 2010.

Elizabeth McKillen
Professor of History
University of Maine

INTERNATIONAL MONETARY FUND

The International Monetary Fund (IMF, or the Fund) is a supranational institution designed to facilitate global monetary stability by regulating currency exchange rates and providing loans to alleviate balance-of-payments deficits among member countries. It was created at the July 1944 United Nations Monetary and Financial Conference held in Bretton Woods, New Hampshire, where delegates from forty-four allied countries gathered to resuscitate the global capitalist system after the breakdown of the international economy during the Great Depression of the 1930s.

At the Bretton Woods conference the two central architects of the new order, Harry Dexter White of the United States and John Maynard Keynes of Great Britain, agreed that management of the global economy necessitated the creation of new institutions capable of preventing the beggar-thy-neighbor approach countries took during the early years of the Depression—that is, a policy by which a nation seeks to improve its own economy at the expense of its neighbors by employing protectionist policy instruments. Although Keynes wanted a single clearing union tasked with both ensuring stability in balance of payments (a method of tracking a nation's international economic transactions) and providing loans for reconstruction and development, White argued that the two functions should be separated, with the International Bank for Reconstruction and Development (IBRD or World Bank) taking responsibility for reconstruction and development lending and the IMF for balance-of-payments assistance. Additionally, the IMF was tasked with managing currency exchange rates. The United States enjoyed a preponderance of economic power, helping to ensure that White's plan was accepted.

Until 1971 the IMF provided those two basic functions. First, under the Bretton Woods system, the US Treasury agreed to purchase gold at the rate of $35 per ounce from other central banks, thus linking the value of the dollar to gold. Other countries in turn pegged the value of their currencies to the dollar. The dollar functioned as the global reserve currency. Revaluation of a member country's currency relative to the dollar required IMF approval.

Second, the IMF served as an emergency lender to countries facing balance-of-payments difficulties. In such cases a team of IMF economists visited and reported on political and economic conditions in the distressed country. The team subsequently recommended a series of policy reforms—usually aimed at increasing tax collection and decreasing expenses, especially expenses derived from state-owned industries and social welfare programs. Emergency lending from the IMF and other institutions—including private Wall Street banks and agencies of the US government—was generally conditioned upon the government's agreement to implement the IMF team's reforms.

Completion of these tasks advanced US foreign policy objectives. US officials sought a stable global economic environment based on the principles of market capitalism; the IMF embraced the same mission. Moreover, because the US balance of payments was in surplus following World War II, the Fund's US architects ensured that the IMF would be able to compel deficit countries to adjust their policies to move toward balance, but would not have the same ability to influence the policy of countries in surplus. The Fund's lending programs ensured that existing loans would not go into default—a benefit for lenders, which generally included American banks.

President Richard Nixon's August 1971 decision to suspend the exchange of gold for dollars at $35 per ounce ended the Bretton Woods system and altered the global monetary landscape. A floating exchange rate system emerged by default, rendering the IMF's responsibility to manage rates moot. However, the Fund continued its role as balance-of-payments stabilization lender and supervisor of market fealty. Indeed, beginning during the 1980s and continuing throughout the 1990s and 2000s, the IMF's role as the supervisor of global capitalism became even more prominent. Under the Washington Consensus, a set of economic reform policies developed by Washington, DC–based institutions, the IMF conditioned lending—most often to countries in the Global South—upon even more economically orthodox policy reforms. As a result, the IMF emerged as the target of antiglobalization protesters' frustration, both in the United States and Europe, and especially throughout the Global South, where austerity had a negative impact on the working class and the poor.

Since the onset of the global recession in 2007–2008 there have been indications that the IMF's approach is changing. Rather than endorse austerity, for example, the Fund has instead argued that significant spending cuts and tax increases are likely to inhibit economic recovery, and it has endorsed the use of capital controls in crisis circumstances. IMF officials also called for fiscal stimulus to head off the economic crisis. During the era of the Washington Consensus, the IMF staunchly rejected any hint of a Keynesian approach; during the 2010s the Fund has often emerged as Keynesianism's most powerful institutional proponent on the global stage.

Just as the IMF's earlier approach was consistent with the policies of the Ronald Reagan, George H. W. Bush, Bill Clinton, and George W. Bush administrations, its shift since 2008 has largely been aligned with the Barack Obama administration's preferences. Obama endorsed stimulus at home and abroad in response to the financial crisis, and his administration has shared the IMF's reevaluation of its deregulatory agenda.

SEE ALSO *Bretton Woods; Keynesian Economics; World Bank*

BIBLIOGRAPHY

Eckes, Alfred E., Jr. *A Search for Solvency: Bretton Woods and the International Monetary System, 1941–1971.* Austin: University of Texas Press, 1975.

Eichengreen, Barry. *Exorbitant Privilege: The Rise and Fall of the Dollar and the Future of the International Monetary System.* Oxford and New York: Oxford University Press, 2011.

Kedar, Claudia. *The International Monetary Fund and Latin America: The Argentine Puzzle in Context.* Philadelphia: Temple University Press, 2013.

Dustin Walcher
Associate Professor and Chair
Department of History & Political Science
Southern Oregon University

INTERNATIONAL WOMEN'S YEAR (IWY), 1975

In mid-June 1975, thousands of people converged on Mexico City for the first-ever United Nations International Women's Year (IWY) conference—delegates for the official, intergovernmental conference of UN member states; reporters representing everything from major newspapers and wire services to local feminist newsletters; and participants in an unofficial tribune of nongovernmental organizations (NGOs). Billed by organizers and journalists alike as the "greatest consciousness-raising event in history," the conference marked a pivotal moment for both the United Nations and transnational feminism.

IWY started as an idea proposed by the Women's International Democratic Federation (WIDF), an NGO started in Paris in 1945 and headquartered in East Berlin that had long been the target of State Department sanctions and Cold War rivalries. At the 1972 meeting of the UN's Commission on the Status of Women, WIDF convinced two representatives to propose 1975 as a year to assess the commission's progress toward its goals of improving women's rights and opportunities. As the IWY proposal wended its way through the UN system, it acquired three themes—equality, development, and peace—and an icon of a dove with the Greek symbol for woman in its body and the mathematical symbol for equality in its tail feathers. In the UN's geopolitical schema, *equality* stressed the liberal, Western commitment to political rights and professional and educational opportunities; *development* responded to the Third World's call for transformed economic and trade policies, as well as programs that promoted industrialization; and *peace* became a catchall for the socialist and communist countries' calls for disarmament, antiracism, and anticolonialism. As soon as the United Nations passed a resolution dubbing 1975 as IWY, the WIDF began preparations for a World Congress of Women to draw activists and NGO advocates to East Berlin in October of that year.

When the US State Department realized that the major IWY event would take place "behind the Iron Curtain," the US delegation to the Commission on the Status of Women proposed an alternative IWY conference that would take place in the Third World. Warsaw Pact countries objected to its expense and countered with a proposal for more sustained, decentered activities rather than a single conference. In the end, the General Assembly approved the conference proposal but allocated no budget; the IWY conference would be paid for by contributions to a voluntary fund that accepted donations from governments, NGOs, and individuals. Planning for IWY took place amid cresting waves of decolonization that added dozens of new member states to the United Nations, radically changing the dynamics within its General Assembly as an alliance of newly decolonized nations, oil-producing countries, and the regions then dubbed the Third World banded together into a Non-Aligned Movement to challenge the dyadic Cold War opposition between the capitalist West and the communist East.

By the time the hastily planned and woefully underfunded conference got underway in mid-June 1975, it would be preceded by an experts' seminar on women and development, as well as a journalists' "encounter," and the NGO tribune would run parallel to the government conference 5 kilometers (3.1 miles) to the south—events planned predominantly by small groups of New York–based organizers. Initially imagined as a three-day preconference of established NGOs that enjoyed UN consultative status, the NGO tribune had mushroomed into an open forum that anyone could attend, becoming, as the *New York Times* described it, "the scene of much shouting, scheming, plotting, and general hell-raising" (June 29, 1975, 2). The US feminist Betty Friedan (1921–2006) sparked protests when she led a group that claimed to represent the tribune to the government conference, despite organizers' insistence that no one was authorized to represent the tribune. Claims for lesbian rights precipitated another set of protests by those who saw them as a US-generated distraction from more pressing concerns of class struggle and global inequalities.

The official government conference, despite its composition of instructed delegations following predictable scripts, witnessed its own share of shouting and scheming as conflicts erupted over Zionism and apartheid. In both venues, participants argued about whether incorporating women into the labor market would emancipate them or merely add to their burdens. As development schemes increasingly stressed the importance of making women more "productive," participants disagreed about who might take up the uncommodified labor obligations conventionally performed by women. The IWY conference and attendant activities—such as workshops, research projects, and legislative campaigns—generated three more UN conferences: Copenhagen (1980), Nairobi (1985), and Beijing (1995). More importantly, it fostered countless transnational networks of women and nongovernmental organizations (NGOs) working on a wide variety of issues.

SEE ALSO *The Feminine Mystique (Betty Friedan, 1963); Feminism, Women's Rights; Gender; New Woman; Paul, Alice Stokes; Roosevelt, Eleanor; Rosie the Riveter; Suffrage; Wollstonecraft, Mary*

BIBLIOGRAPHY

Klemesrud, J. "Scrappy, Unofficial Women's Parley Sets Pace," *New York Times*, June 29, 1975, 2.

Olcott, Jocelyn. "Cold War Conflicts and Cheap Cabaret: Performing Politics at the 1975 United Nations International Women's Year Conference in Mexico City." *Gender and History* 22, 3 (2010): 733–754.

Pietilä, Hilkka, and Jeanne Vickers. *Making Women Matter: The Role of the United Nations.* Updated and expanded ed. London and Atlantic Highlands, NJ: Zed, 1994.

United Nations, Centre for Economic and Social Information. *Meeting in Mexico: The Story of the World Conference of the International Women's Year (Mexico City, 19 June–2 July 1975).* New York: United Nations, 1975.

Zinsser, Judith P. "From Mexico to Copenhagen to Nairobi: The United Nations Decade for Women, 1975–1985." *Journal of World History* 13, 1 (2002): 139–168.

Jocelyn Olcott
Associate Professor of History
Duke University

INTERNATIONALISM

The concept of internationalism in American foreign relations is not easy to define, and the word has held a number of different meanings that have varied over time. Because very little has been done to work out a specific definition, its meaning is frequently assumed and modifiers often added—cultural internationalism, economic internationalism, labor internationalism, and liberal internationalism. Nevertheless, most considerations of internationalism are underpinned by at least one of two strands of thought: one that sees internationalism as the opposite of isolationism, the other as the opposite of nationalism.

When viewed as the opposite of isolationism, internationalism is the willingness of the United States to engage in great-power politics beyond its borders, usually with military force. The struggle between the concepts of internationalism and isolationism, though occurring since the nation's origins, was especially prevalent in the first half of the twentieth century. This relatively geographic understanding of internationalism often conflates internationalism with interventionism, and it lies at the heart of a version of national history in which internationalism triumphed over isolationism during and immediately after World War II.

When seen as the opposite of nationalism, internationalism is less about whether the United States is engaged in world affairs and more about the nature of that engagement. This internationalist history focuses on how the United States has promoted international cooperation on political, economic, and cultural levels in an attempt to secure a more just and peaceful world. It does so by emphasising multilateralism, arbitration, and the American role in creating international organizations, most notably the League of Nations and the United Nations.

EIGHTEENTH AND NINETEENTH CENTURIES

Despite the nation's origins in interaction with Europe, in the early years of the republic the United States sought to avoid internationalism in both of the above forms. George Washington's Farewell Address (1796) famously stated that the United States should "steer clear of permanent alliances with any portion of the foreign world," while Jefferson's First Inaugural Address (1801) called for friendship with all nations but no "entangling alliances" (McDougall 1997, 46, 49). This worldview—frequently described as one of isolationism—continued through the nineteenth century, building on statements such as those by Secretary of State John Quincy Adams, in 1821, that America "goes not abroad in search of monsters to destroy" and the Monroe Doctrine of 1823 (McDougall 1997, 36). Washington and his successors knew it would be impossible to completely isolate the nation from the rest of the world, and the United States expanded its economic interests as the century progressed. Yet the nation largely avoided being drawn into European great-power rivalries until the end of the century, at which point, as a result of a combination of political, economic, and cultural interests, the nation began its rapid rise to great-power status.

A significant step forward in terms of international involvement came in 1898 with the Spanish-American War. Through its victory in this conflict, which pitted the United States against a European imperial power in both the Western Hemisphere and Asia, the nation achieved great-power status. And with the acquisition of the Philippines, Guam, and Puerto Rico, it acquired its own empire. In addition to this expanded international activity, the United States during this era increasingly engaged in multilateral international cooperation. The Hague Conventions of 1899 and 1907 created treaties to develop international laws on the conduct of war and provide a forum for international arbitration. A sign of American internationalism in every sense was the successful role of President Theodore Roosevelt in the mediation of the Russo-Japanese War in 1905.

EARLY TWENTIETH CENTURY

Much of the internationalist movement of this period was driven by private individuals and organizations. Between 1910 and 1915 a number of internationalist organizations took shape, including the World Peace Foundation, the Carnegie Endowment for International Peace, the World's Court League, and the League to Enforce Peace, which worked in different ways toward the same aims: the promotion of peace and an end to all war. Despite their differences, their work reflected the belief that multilateral machinery such as a court of arbitration or an international organization would be sufficient to ensure peace, and that having signed on to such bodies, nations would always be bound to go along with their decisions.

World War I (1914–1918) and its aftermath limited what had been a growing sense of American internationalism at the start of the twentieth century. After failed attempts to remain neutral in the conflict, the United States entered the war in 1917. President Woodrow Wilson, as part of his peace proposals, proposed a League of Nations to ensure that another such war could not occur. By becoming engaged in great-power rivalries in Europe, the nation briefly appeared to be moving far beyond the advice of its Founding Fathers. Not only was the United States considering being part of a permanent alliance, but that alliance was a distinctly American idea. However, as a result of growing disillusionment with the war and the peace process that followed, unilateral tendencies surfaced in Congress, most notably in response to the proposed League's Article 10, which appeared to hand over national sovereign powers to the new international League. Congress subsequently rejected American entry into the League, a move that critics of the decision saw as a retreat into isolationism.

Of course, the nation did not fall into total isolation; instead it returned to a position similar to that of 1914, with a reluctance to commit to international involvements outside the Western Hemisphere paired with a suspicion of multilateral obligations. While the United States led the Washington Naval Conferences of 1921–1922 and played a key role in the 1928 Kellogg-Briand Pact, both of these actions sought to avoid war, and though the former had binding commitments they were largely in America's favor. As international aggression resurfaced in the 1930s, the popular desire of the American public was to stay out of both European and Asian conflicts, and efforts toward US membership in the Permanent Court of International Justice (or World Court) failed.

WORLD WAR II AND THE COLD WAR

The Second World War (1939–1945), however, appeared to mark the triumph of American internationalism in every sense. The Japanese attack on Pearl Harbor on December 7, 1941, brought the nation into the war and ended two years of heated debate regarding the nation's place in the world. The United States subsequently declared war on Germany, committing the nation to military engagement in Europe, Asia, and Africa. As the war progressed, there was a growing sense that the nation's rejection of its international obligations in 1920 had been a mistake, and that the same mistake could not be allowed to happen again. In the final year of the war the United States led the way in creating a number of international treaties and commitments, firming up the international economic system with the Bretton Woods agreements of 1944 that created the International Monetary Fund and the World Bank. More notably, the United Nations was founded as a new multilateral organization to ensure future peace and security. By the end of the war, the United States was determined not to retreat from its new international role, and it appeared that the machinery to ensure a peaceful postwar world was in place.

Yet just as internationalism appeared triumphant, the nature of that internationalism was called into question. During the era of the Cold War with the Soviet Union, most American leaders considered themselves internationalists. And there was no question that America's global commitments grew as the nation dedicated itself to containing international communism. Increased activity overseas included the use of force in wars in Korea and Vietnam and covert action in locations such as Iran, Guatemala, and Chile. Collective security alliances were expanded, notably the North Atlantic Treaty Organization (NATO). Internationalism became increasingly synonymous with American leadership of the free world, as it appeared that the United States was searching overseas for communist monsters to destroy.

This internationalism bore relatively little resemblance to the multilateral internationalism of the first half of the century. It focused on national defense and the national interest rather than international law and peace and justice. Part of the problem was that universal multilateralism was not a universal solution to great-power problems. The veto power in the UN Security Council meant that the organization failed to live up to expectations with respect to peace and security. Instead, the United States chose to work through more willing and selective multilateral groupings such as NATO, as well as creating other less effective and less convincing groupings such as the Southeast Asia Treaty Organization. An exception was the Korean War, which was fought under a UN flag, but this was only due to a Soviet boycott of the Security Council.

The Cold War record of American internationalism was at best mixed. The United States engaged in arms limitation talks with the Soviet Union to control the number of nuclear weapons, as in the Strategic Arms Limitation Talks (SALT) of the 1970s, but with limited success in terms of arms reduction. The United States also pressed the Soviet Union on the growing importance of human rights, though here (as had been the case with earlier drives to international law and organization) the main impetus came from nongovernmental organizations. Reflecting a growing sense of unilateralism in the 1980s, the United States withdrew from the United Nations Educational, Scientific, and Cultural Organization (UNESCO) in 1984 out of frustration with its policies. And though the United States had joined the International Court of Justice in 1946, it withdrew its acceptance of the Court's jurisdiction in 1984 following a contentious case brought against it by Nicaragua. All of this led Thomas Hughes, then the head of the Carnegie Endowment for International Peace, to decry the "twilight of internationalism" (1985–1986, 47).

THE POST–COLD WAR WORLD

The collapse of the Soviet Union in 1991 and the consequent end of the Cold War briefly provided a ray of hope for American internationalists, as cooperation with post-Soviet Russia offered new possibilities for a revitalized UN. The Gulf War of 1990–1991 presented the prospect of genuine multilateral cooperation; the UN Security Council passed Resolution 678, and a diverse array of nations subsequently liberated Kuwait from invading Iraqi forces. However, as the 1990s progressed, hopes for a genuinely resurgent multilateralism in a more peaceful world were dashed. The United States' frustration with UN peacekeeping failures in Bosnia and Somalia led to official limits on US peacekeeping efforts elsewhere. More broadly, with the end of the Cold War there was a growing popular and Congressional reaction against internationalism, and an increased feeling that the United States no longer needed to play a wider global role in any sense.

Following the terrorist attacks of September 11, 2001, the conviction arose among members of government and the public that once again US international military involvement was necessary. Yet the internationalism of the George W. Bush administration (2001–2009) was largely unilateral, and though the UN authorized military action in Afghanistan against the Taliban and al-Qaeda, the United States did not seek a broad coalition of support. It did seek one for its invasion of Iraq but achieved only a "coalition of the willing," as it was unable to obtain wider international agreement on the need to depose Saddam Hussein. The Bush administration's negative attitude toward the 1972 Anti-Ballistic Missile Treaty, the Kyoto

Protocol on climate change, and the International Criminal Court were further indications of unilateralism.

The administration of Barack Obama (2009–) attempted to regain the international goodwill lost during the Bush years. Yet, like most presidents since 1945, Obama struggled with the tension between broad global leadership and narrower national interests. Considerations of how American internationalism should be defined are ongoing, particularly through debates over the concept of liberal internationalism, the role of—and the nation's place in—international organizations, and the nature of democracy promotion. Although the United States has firmly moved beyond the relative isolation of the nineteenth century, debates over the exact extent and nature of America's world role show little sign of ending.

SEE ALSO *Isolationism; League of Nations; Paris Peace Conference (1919); Realism (International Relations); Roosevelt, Theodore; Spanish-American War; Wilson, Woodrow; World War I*

BIBLIOGRAPHY

Herman, Sondra R. *Eleven Against War: Studies in American Internationalist Thought, 1898–1921.* Stanford, CA: Hoover Institution Press, 1969.

Hoopes, Townsend, and Douglas Brinkley. *FDR and the Creation of the U.N.* New Haven, CT: Yale University Press, 1997.

Hughes, Thomas L. "The Twilight of Internationalism." *Foreign Policy* 61 (Winter 1985–1986): 25–48.

Josephson, Harold. *James T. Shotwell and the Rise of Internationalism in America.* Rutherford, NJ: Fairleigh Dickinson University Press, 1975.

Knock, Thomas J. *To End All Wars: Woodrow Wilson and the Quest for a New World Order.* Princeton, NJ: Princeton University Press, 1995.

Kuehl, Warren F. *Seeking World Order: The United States and International Organization to 1920.* Nashville, TN: Vanderbilt University Press, 1969.

Luck, Edward C. *Mixed Messages: American Politics and International Organization, 1919–1999.* Washington, DC: Brookings Institution Press, 1999.

McDougall, Walter A. *Promised Land, Crusader State: The American Encounter with the World since 1776.* Boston: Houghton Mifflin, 1997.

Ninkovich, Frank *Global Dawn: The Cultural Foundation of American Internationalism, 1865–1890.* Cambridge, MA: Harvard University Press, 2009.

Ostrower, Gary B. *The United Nations and the United States.* New York: Twayne, 1998.

Andrew Johnstone
Senior Lecturer in American History
University of Leicester

INTERNET

In the first half of the twentieth century, as telephone technology became commercial, the telecommunications company AT&T was formed to create and deploy universal, long-distance telephone service across the United States. Bell Labs, the research arm of AT&T, discovered and published fundamental scientific principles that form the basis of digital communication, which would later be used in the Internet. In addition, Bell Labs invented the transistor, a key component that enables low-cost digital computer and communication technologies.

During the 1950s and 1960s, several US corporations—International Business Machines (IBM), Burroughs, Univac, National Cash Register (NCR), Control Data Corporation (CDC), General Electric (GE), Radio Corporation of America (RCA), and Honeywell—led in the development of commercial computers. The early computers were characterized as "stand-alone" because each computer operated by itself. It quickly became apparent that restricting a computer to a single room was inefficient, and companies began exploring ways to have input/output (I/O) devices, such as printers, remote from the computers.

In the 1960s, researchers considered a fundamental challenge: how to create computer networks that would allow computers to communicate. The AT&T engineers who pioneered the long-distance telephone network had chosen a circuit-switched paradigm that reserved a pair of wires for each phone call. When a user dialed a call, the phone system chose wires between the calling and called telephones, and reserved the wires for the duration of the call. Researchers exploring computer networks took an alternative approach that is known as packet switching. The basic concept of packet switching was discovered independently by Paul Baran at the Rand Corporation in the United States and Donald Davies at the National Physical Laboratory (NPL) in the United Kingdom.

PACKET SWITCHING EXPERIMENTS AND THE ARPANET

During the 1960s the United States was the center of networking research, and many experiments were conducted. At Xerox Corporation's Palo Alto Research Center, David Boggs and Robert Metcalf invented a packet-switching technology called Ethernet that is still widely used.

One of the largest computer network experiments, and perhaps the most significant, from this time was funded by the Advanced Research Projects Agency (ARPA). ARPA, which later changed its name to the Defense Advanced Research Projects Agency (DARPA), is a research arm of the US Department of Defense that studies a wide range of topics of interest to the US military. To carry out research, ARPA issues grants and contracts to researchers in US universities, government research labs, and US corporations. In the 1960s each research group needed a computer that cost millions of dollars. ARPA launched a major project to build an experimental computer network with the goal of allowing researchers to share expensive computers. Called ARPANET, the network was the first large-scale network to use packet switching. Geographically, ARPANET spanned the continental United States, reaching from the Massachusetts Institute of Technology (MIT) in Cambridge, Massachusetts, to Stanford University in Palo Alto, California. ARPANET included many university and ARPA contractor sites throughout the country, and was later extended to include a site in Norway that ARPA used to detect seismic activity resulting from nuclear tests in the Soviet Union.

THE INTERNET

By the early 1970s it had become apparent that no single network technology would satisfy all needs. Some designs, such as Ethernet, were relatively inexpensive but could connect computers only over a short distance (within a single office building). Other designs, such as ARPANET, spanned long distances but were extremely expensive. Researchers wondered how a computer network could be devised that combined the advantages of low cost for short connections with the ability to span long distances when needed.

In 1973 two researchers working at ARPA, Vinton Cerf and Robert Kahn, solved the problem. Instead of trying to devise a single technology, Cerf and Kahn proposed interconnecting multiple types of networks and then using software to make the resulting system appear to operate like a giant global network. We use the term *Internet* to describe the system Cerf and Kahn envisioned. Because it consists of interconnected networks, the Internet is characterized as a network of networks. The Internet approach allows designers to choose a network technology that is best for each situation. For example, a low-cost Ethernet can be used to connect all the computers in an office building, and a more expensive long-distance technology can be used to interconnect buildings.

INTERNET COMMUNICATION PROTOCOLS

The interconnection of networks is straightforward: special-purpose computer systems called routers are used, an approach that has its origins in the ARPANET. A router does not run conventional software but instead only handles packet forwarding. Each packet contains a specification of the computer to which the packet is destined. When the packet arrives at a router, software in the router examines the destination in the packet, chooses a shortest path to the destination, and sends the packet along the path.

Although the basic idea of interconnecting networks is straightforward, many technical problems needed to be solved before it could become practical. Routers needed a way to learn the shortest path to each destination. An application on a sending computer needed a way to identify the destination computer. Because packet switching networks experience congestion analogous to highway congestion during rush hour, sophisticated mechanisms were needed to detect congestion, find alternative paths, and avoid overloading a congested link. ARPA funded researchers who solved the technical problems and made the Internet approach viable and practical. We use the term *communication protocols* to characterize the solutions; the basic communication protocols used in the Internet resulted from ARPA funding.

CONTRIBUTIONS BY THE NATIONAL SCIENCE FOUNDATION

During the 1980s the US National Science Foundation (NSF) made several important contributions to the Internet. Early in the decade NSF funded the Computer Science NETwork (CSNET) project, with the purpose of connecting all university computer science departments to the Internet.

The CSNET project expanded the fledgling Internet in two ways. First, it moved beyond the group of researchers who developed the technology to include the first large set of users, some of whom knew nothing about computer networking. Second, it introduced new types of networks. ARPA worked jointly with NSF to support the expansion. In 1983 ARPA separated the ARPANET into two parts: MILNET, which was used by the US military, and the civilian ARPANET. Because the ARPANET became the major cross-country network to which many universities attached, the term *backbone network* was used to describe its role.

Following the success of CSNET, NSF expanded the Internet further by including other university science departments (e.g., physics, biology, and chemistry). By 1986, so many packets were being sent over the ARPANET backbone that NSF began planning an upgrade with more than twenty-five times as much capacity. In 1987, with contributions from three US companies, IBM, Merit, and MCI, NSF switched to a new Internet backbone called NSFNET. Over the decade following its introduction, the NSFNET backbone was enhanced two more times.

ISPS, INTERNET APPLICATIONS, AND THE WORLD WIDE WEB

Although the NSFNET backbone allowed Internet traffic to grow substantially, the most important contribution NSF made was in the organization of the Internet. ARPA had used a two-level hierarchy with a single large backbone (ARPANET) connecting all Internet sites. To handle a much larger Internet, NSF created a three-level hierarchy with a set of regional networks in the middle. Instead of connecting individual sites (universities and companies), the NSFNET backbone connected regional networks, and each site attached to one of those regional networks. For example, one regional network connected sites in the state of New York. The concept of a three-level hierarchy was important because regional networks evolved into Internet Service Providers (ISPs), or companies that run a regional network, provide connections to customers, and forward traffic to a backbone. To accommodate the new organization, NSF funded the development of additional communication protocols, including the routing protocols used in the global Internet.

Unlike the telephone system, the Internet is designed to provide only a packet delivery service; all applications associated with the Internet (e.g., e-mail, the World Wide Web, Internet search, social networking, and video streaming) run on computers that connect to the Internet. In fact, the Internet was in place before most modern applications were created. For example, by 1988 programmers had created various Internet services, including file upload and download, and a hypertext system called Gopher. Between 1989 and 1991 a researcher at Cern in Switzerland combined many of the previous applications into a single hypertext system, and the World Wide Web was born. The Internet did not need to change to accommodate the Web. The idea of separating applications from the Internet has made innovation both easy and inexpensive.

THE TRANSFORMATION OF COMMUNICATION

In the 1970s use of the ARPANET was restricted to researchers who were funded by ARPA or military personnel who needed access. In the 1980s NSF and ARPA took steps toward an open and commercial Internet by relaxing restrictions. Initially, use was opened to all US science faculty, and then all university faculty and students were permitted to use the Internet. NSF led the transition to an international Internet by helping to fund connections to universities in foreign countries. Eventually, the Internet transitioned to a global, commercial communication system that connects individuals, organizations, and companies around the world.

The Internet has transformed global communication in two fundamental ways. First, because it provides low-cost communication over long distances, the Internet allows communities of interest to form that span multiple countries. Second, because it has merged the telephone paradigm of communication between pairs of individuals with the broadcast paradigm in which a media company disseminates content to a wide audience, the Internet has democratized communication and provided individuals with the opportunity to create content that can be viewed by an arbitrarily large audience. The unlimited production of information by individuals makes censorship and control difficult.

The Internet's impact on society has been both rapid and substantial. Facilities for activities such as online shopping, online social networks, and online airline bookings are now used daily by those who have Internet access. Of course, any societal transformation as significant as the Internet has some drawbacks. Local shops may find it difficult to compete with online stores, and travel agents may find it difficult to compete with online travel services. More important, the Internet has introduced a digital divide between individuals who have access to Internet services and those who lack access and thus cannot participate.

SEE ALSO *Department of Defense, US; Globalization*

BIBLIOGRAPHY

Baran, P. "On Distributed Communications Networks." *IEEE Transactions on Communication Systems* 12, 1 (1964): 1–9.

Cerf, Vinton G., and Robert E. Kahn. "A Protocol for Packet Network Interconnection." *IEEE Transactions on Communication Technology* COM-22, 5 (May 1974): 627–641. http://www.cs.princeton.edu/courses/archive/fall06/cos561/papers/cerf74.pdf

Comer, Douglas. "The Computer Science Research Network CSNET: A History and Status Report." *Communications of the ACM* 26, 10 (October 1983): 747–753.

Davies, D. W., K. A. Bartlett, R. A. Scantlebury, and P. T. Wilkinson. "A Digital Communications Network for Computers Giving Rapid Response at Remote Terminals." *Proceedings of the First ACM Symposium on Operating System Principles* (October 1967): 2.1–2.17.

Douglas E. Comer
Distinguished Professor of Computer Science
Purdue University

INTERNMENT CAMPS

Commonly known by such euphemisms as "relocation" and "internment," the removal and incarceration of 120,000 West Coast Japanese Americans during World War II (1939–1945) is marked by a debate about terminology that illuminates the international dimensions of American history. To use the more apt phrase, "concentration camps," when speaking of the Japanese American experience points toward the Holocaust. While

Nazi Germany was systematically detaining, enslaving, and annihilating six million Jews and other targeted groups, the United States—citing national security and the belief that hearing boards could not determine the loyalties of individual Japanese Americans—ignored the constitutional right of due process and expelled all citizens and residents of Japanese descent from California and the western portions of Oregon, Washington, and Arizona. Placed in temporary "assembly centers" that were often the cattle stalls at county fairgrounds, Japanese Americans ultimately found themselves in ten "relocation centers" run by the civilian War Relocation Authority (WRA) in California, Idaho, Wyoming, Colorado, Utah, Arizona, and Arkansas.

TERMINOLOGY

These camps are popularly, if inaccurately, called *internment camps*. Internment is a process regulated under national and international law for the treatment of enemy nationals in a time of war. While the United States interned approximately eight thousand Japanese nationals and several thousand German and Italian nationals in actual internment camps during World War II, two-thirds of the individuals held in the WRA camps were American citizens, making problematic their designation as "internment camps." Today, scholars and activists tend to use more descriptively accurate terms like *incarceration*, *concentration*, and *detention* for the camps that held the bulk of the West Coast Japanese American population between 1942 and 1945. These terms highlight America's participation in global patterns of racially motivated denial of civil liberties and undemocratic long-term detention of targeted civilian groups.

A GLOBAL PATTERN OF MASS DETENTION AND RELOCATION

The forced exile and incarceration of West Coast Japanese Americans reflected a hemispheric policy of removing Japanese citizens and residents from their homes during World War II. Canada ejected twenty thousand residents of Japanese descent from its Pacific Coast and placed them in isolated inland areas. Mexico forced its Japanese residents in Baja California to inland areas during the war, while placing economic and political restrictions on all residents of Japanese descent. Twelve Latin American countries collaborated with the United States by incarcerating Japanese, Italian, and German enemy aliens. Several of the countries sent to the United States three thousand enemy alien diplomats and civilians, including families with children, to be used by the United States in prisoner exchanges with Axis nations. Eighty percent of these deportees came from Peru, and seventy percent of them were ethnic Japanese.

The United States charged these Latin Americans with unlawful entry into the country upon arrival and housed them in internment camps run by the Immigration and Naturalization Service (INS) under the auspices of the Justice Department. The INS held to national and international conventions about the treatment of prisoners of war, making conditions in these camps generally better than in the WRA camps. Between early 1942 and September 1943, the United States brokered prisoner exchanges with the help of the Swiss and Spanish governments, using prisoners at INS camps as trading chips for American diplomats and civilians imprisoned in Japan and Japanese-held territories. After the war, Peru refused to repatriate the Peruvian Japanese internees, and the United States refused to offer them citizenship for another decade. Australia, New Zealand, and French-held New Caledonia were the first countries to incarcerate their Japanese populations. This widespread practice of exiling, deporting, and imprisoning residents and citizens of Japanese ancestry muted the likelihood that other nations would condemn the United States' practice.

On February 19, 1942, three months after Japan attacked Pearl Harbor and the United States entered World War II, President Franklin D. Roosevelt signed Executive Order 9066 in response to growing anti-Japanese racism, wartime hysteria, and political maneuvering on the West Coast. The order, drafted by the military, gave the secretary of war the right to create military zones in the United States and its territories from which it could exclude any persons or groups. Although the order did not specify any particular population, the crafters of the order intended it to remove the Japanese American population from the West Coast.

OPPOSITION AND ACQUIESCENCE

As the United States marched to war, Japanese American groups, such as the Japanese American Citizens League (JACL) and the New York City–based Japanese American Committee for Democracy, defended the patriotism of Japanese Americans. In order to show Japanese American support for the war effort, such organizations promoted blood drives and the sale of war bonds in Japanese American communities. The JACL ultimately encouraged Nisei (second-generation Japanese Americans) and Issei (first-generation Japanese Americans, who were legally denied citizenship) to support mass exclusion from the West Coast and incarceration in prison camps as a means to prove their patriotism. Acquiescence to incarceration became the ultimate sacrifice that they hoped would demonstrate their loyalty to the United States. As scholars have pointed out, military service in the highly decorated 442nd unit went further in convincing the American public of Japanese American patriotism.

Japanese Americans arriving at the Manzanar internment camp, Owens Valley, California, March 21, 1942. *Three months after Japan attacked Pearl Harbor, President Franklin D. Roosevelt, ignoring the constitutional right of due process, signed an Executive Order whose purpose was to remove the Japanese American population from the West Coast and place them in "relocation centers."* ELIOT ELISOFON/THE LIFE PICTURE COLLECTION/GETTY IMAGES

Although the majority of Japanese Americans cooperated with government orders and entered the camps, many found ways to resist overweening attempts to regulate and order their lives in the camps. Individuals practiced work-stoppage and strikes to protest poor working conditions and unjust wages in the camps. Others refused to answer the poorly worded loyalty questionnaires designed to funnel the incarcerated into military service or resettlement opportunities in the Midwest, arguing that the government should not demand their service until it returned their civil rights. Their refusal landed twelve thousand men, women, and children in a segregation camp aimed at "repatriating" them to Japan after the war.

Few individuals or organizations initially emerged to combat the rising tide of anti-Japanese hysteria and racist propaganda on the West Coast. As Galen Merriam Fisher (1873–1955), a former missionary and one of the founders of the Northern California Committee for Fair Play for Citizens and Aliens of Japanese Ancestry, suggested, few "thinking Americans" believed their government capable of denying the civil liberties of an entire group of citizens and residents based solely on race. Most did not care or were unaware. The Committee for Fair Play, the pacifist and Quaker-based American Friends Service Committee (AFSC), West Coast chapters of the American Civil Liberties Union (ACLU), and individuals motivated by religious and political values did act on behalf of Japanese Americans during the war. They protested government decisions, ran public-relations campaigns, helped Japanese Americans leaving the camps to resettle in midwestern locales, and aided several thousand Nisei in their efforts to attend colleges outside the exclusion zone. These organizations joined many

Japanese Americans in viewing the incarceration process as a stain on American democracy.

Critics of the incarceration camps repeatedly raised the concern that the United States' summary abrogation of Japanese American civil liberties and mass detention played into enemy hands. They questioned how the United States could claim to be fighting for democracy while it imprisoned 120,000 innocent citizens and residents without due process. Their fear that the Japanese military would use the incarceration of Japanese Americans as propaganda and as an excuse to hurt American POWs had a foundation in reality, as Japan did try to rally its allies in the Greater East Asia Co-Prosperity Sphere with images of American racism toward its nonwhite populations. US treatment of Japanese Americans threatened American claims of exceptionalism.

The final years of the war saw more vocal opposition to the mass expulsion and incarceration of Japanese Americans. Some individuals compared the experience to Nazi treatment of groups that did not conform to Adolf Hitler's Aryan ideal. Activists linked the denial of Japanese American civil rights and due process to other democratic failures in the United States. The nullification of the constitutional rights of Japanese Americans threatened the fragile freedom of other oppressed groups like African Americans and Chinese Americans. By the end of the war, organizations like the ACLU and the National Association for the Advancement of Colored People (NAACP) were using the internment and legal cases that grew out of it to support greater civil rights for all Americans.

POSTWAR REASSESSMENT

The incarceration camps disappeared from public conversation in the postwar period. Most Japanese Americans engaged in rebuilding their lives and businesses; national attention on the courageous exploits of Japanese American soldiers averted attention to confinement and doubts about loyalty. In the late 1960s, buoyed by the civil rights and other "rights" movements, third-generation Japanese Americans (Sansei) led a redress movement that encouraged a reexamination of incarceration. Memoirs, historical works, and the reopening and overturning of the cases of Gordon Hirabayashi, Fred Korematsu, and Minoru Yasui educated an ignorant public about the history of the camps and ignited political interest. President Ronald Reagan signed the 1988 Civil Rights Act that provided an apology and $20,000 to each survivor. Internment camps like Manzanar Relocation Center in California, designated a national historic site by Congress in 1992, draw international visitors interested in this part of American history. In the post-9/11 era, politicians and pundits have compared American policy toward terrorists and minority groups to the World War II internment of Japanese Americans.

SEE ALSO *Buddhism; Japan; Roosevelt, Franklin D.; Shinto; World War II*

BIBLIOGRAPHY

Connell, Thomas. *America's Japanese Hostages: The World War II Plan for a Japanese Free Latin America.* Westport, CT: Praeger, 2002.

Daniels, Roger. "Words Do Matter: A Note on Inappropriate Terminology and the Incarceration of the Japanese Americans." In *Nikkei in the Pacific Northwest: Japanese Americans and Japanese Canadians in the Twentieth Century*, edited by Louis Fiset and Gail Nomura, 183–207. Seattle: University of Washington Press, 2005.

Garcia, Jerry. *Looking Like the Enemy: Japanese Mexicans, the Mexican State, and U.S. Hegemony, 1897–1945.* Tucson: University of Arizona Press, 2014.

Hayashi, Brian Masaru. *Democratizing the Enemy: The Japanese American Internment.* Princeton, NJ: Princeton University Press, 2004.

Robinson, Greg. *A Tragedy of Democracy: Japanese Confinement in North America.* New York: Columbia University Press, 2009.

US Commission on Wartime Relocation and Internment of Civilians. *Personal Justice Denied: Report of the Commission on Wartime Relocation and Internment of Civilians.* Washington, DC: GPO, 1983.

Beth Shalom Hessel
Executive Director
Presbyterian Historical Society, Philadelphia

INTERVENTIONISM

Interventionism is the interference by a state in another state's affairs. The act of intervention can be both overt and covert, with the key difference being that the former requires some form of justification by the intervening power, while the latter involves a hidden hand and thus, in theory, no trace to the sponsor. Covert intervention has obvious appeal but carries greater political risks in the event of exposure. Traditionally, interventionism has been pursued by individual states, but the rise of multinational organizations during the twentieth century, such as the United Nations (UN) and the North Atlantic Treaty Organization (NATO), has resulted in multistate mobilizations to intervene in foreign affairs. Yet that is not to suggest the onset of an age of international community or global consensus given that, more often than not, the push to intervene is led by the most powerful states. Interventionism was closely associated with the United States during its rise to superpower status during the long twentieth century.

TERMINOLOGY AND TYPES OF INTERVENTION

There are numerous types of intervention, including those predicated on deterrence, prevention, punishment, peacekeeping, waging war, nation building, interdiction, and humanitarianism. The means to interfere are similarly diverse, beginning with "softer" political, economic, cultural, and psychological forms. The more common methods entail "harder" military interventions involving ground troops, air and sea power, special operations forces, and a vast array of hardware, as well as covert intervention involving intelligence tradecraft comprising espionage, surveillance, and clandestine action. The manner and method of intervention demands a broad national security infrastructure and significant financial and technical capabilities, which means interventionism is often the preserve of major powers. This is why, amid the contemporary concerns regarding rogue states, chemical and nuclear weapons, and terrorism, the United States remains preoccupied by Chinese and Russian geopolitical strength long after the end of the Cold War.

That the term *intervention* carries the suffix *-ism* hints at how it has become a distinctive practice that occurs with a degree of regularity. The appeal of the term lies in it being less aggressive and historically loaded than other labels, such as *invasion*. The latter, signifying a full-blown assault on the national sovereignty of another state, sits uncomfortably with the American historical narrative of a nation that broke free from the Old World. In the words of Thomas Paine, the United States would "begin the world over" (*Common Sense*, 1776), leaving behind wars of occupation and invasions that were the hallmark of imperial European powers. *Intervention*, with its less antagonistic connotations, sits more comfortably in rationalizing American-style involvement abroad.

The US role in world affairs increased exponentially over the course of the twentieth century, leading some to question whether intervention is synonymous with war. That it should be considered as distinct is not a point of lexical gymnastics but is of practical relevance to understanding how the United States has intervened. On only five occasions has the United States declared war, with the two world wars the only examples from the twentieth century. Since war must be formally declared by the US Congress, intervention has tremendous appeal to the executive branch. Presidents undoubtedly dominate in the realm of foreign affairs, although circumventing the legislative branch is only possible through interventions, rather than wars, abroad. On only a handful of occasions has Congress raised major objections to executive-led interventionism, which indicates a general bipartisanship regarding the importance for America to be active in world affairs.

UNILATERAL AND MULTILATERAL INTERVENTIONISM

The debate about US interventionism largely revolves around the issue of unilateral or multilateral action, rather than an internationalism versus isolationism dichotomy. George Herring, in his 2008 survey of US foreign relations, noted that "the enduring idea of an isolationist America is a myth often conveniently used to safeguard the nation's self-image of its innocence," with the United States "an active and influential player in world affairs" since 1776 (Herring 2008, 1). The historic aversion to the concept of interfering abroad is rooted in concerns that the young republic avoid what George Washington termed "entangling alliances" and maintain the ability to act unilaterally. It was imperative not to be dragged into foreign—primarily European—wars. The essential message in Washington's Farewell Address of 1796, echoed in Thomas Jefferson's inaugural address of 1801, resonated long beyond the eighteenth and nineteenth centuries.

Indeed, the key plank of isolationist thought in the twentieth century was to stay clear of binding political and military alliances and commitments to collective security. The objective was to maintain American unilateralism in foreign affairs. Opposition to US involvement in conflicts outside the Western Hemisphere met a stern test with the outbreak of World War I (1914–1918). Woodrow Wilson eventually led the United States into battle in 1917, but to ease concerns about binding military alliances, the United States entered the war as an "associate power" fighting under its own, separate command, rather than under the Allies. Wilson's vision of a world institution of like-minded nations was promoted forcefully at the Paris Peace Conference (1919) but would be scuppered by the "irreconcilables" in Congress in the name of upholding America's unilateral tradition. The so-called isolationism of the 1930s was a period in which the United States was involved in world affairs, primarily led by business and corporate interests, but avoided any entangling alliances. It was paramount to maintain a free hand to intervene as and when US interests dictated.

While the conclusion of the Great War marked the end of Wilson's vision of a liberal international order, albeit one in which the United States would provide essential leadership, wartime fighting revealed the benefits of multilateral intervention against aggressors. Moreover, it offered crucial lessons for organizing the peace the next time the United States went to war. Like Wilson, Franklin Delano Roosevelt had also declared that he would not send American troops to fight in Europe when the world was plunged into war in 1939. But after the realities of Fascist aggression were made apparent by the Japanese attack on Pearl Harbor in December 1941 and Germany's subsequent declaration of war on the United States, the debate was moot. That the United States had to intervene was self-evident and, in light of the overwhelming economic and military supremacy it enjoyed by the end of fighting, so was the notion that it had to play a central role in the postwar order. The creation of the United Nations (1945) and NATO (1949) was a radical departure from the American tradition of nonbinding alliances. Nonetheless it was not the end of unilateral interventions.

INTERVENTIONISM IN THE LONG TWENTIETH CENTURY

The United States had intervened abroad during the nineteenth century, most notably in the Barbary Wars (1801–1805, 1815), the Mexican-American War (1846–1848), and the Second Opium War (1856–1860). Yet systematic and sustained interventionism began with war with Spain in 1898. A remarkably one-sided US victory led to the acquisition of territories in Cuba, Puerto Rico, Guam, and—following the Philippine-American War (1899–1902)—occupation of the Philippines. The Spanish-American War had been launched as a humanitarian fight on behalf of Cuba but turned into the beginnings of an American empire. Indeed, Cuba became a site of repeated US interventions during the century, as well as a semipermanent naval base at Guantánamo Bay.

The Western Hemisphere would be subject to repeated American interventions. Theodore Roosevelt's Corollary to the 1823 Monroe Doctrine justified US intervention in Latin America in cases where "chronic wrongdoing" or "incompetence" threatened to destabilize the region. Roosevelt supported the efforts of Panamanian revolutionaries to gain independence from Colombia, recognizing the new state of Panama as the location for an isthmus canal. The Roosevelt Corollary made the United States a unilateral police force in the hemisphere and featured interventions in Panama, Santo Domingo, and Cuba during Roosevelt's time in the White House.

Roosevelt's successor also dispatched troops to the region on multiple occasions. The United States intervened in Cuba, Panama, Honduras, Dominican Republic, Haiti, Nicaragua, and Mexico during Woodrow Wilson's presidency. Indeed, Wilson's interventions in Central America exceeded those of Roosevelt, a leader more commonly associated with wielding a "Big Stick." Another Roosevelt, Franklin, provided an intermission to US interventionism through his "Good Neighbor" policy. Unilateral interventionism nonetheless returned with force in the aftermath of World War II (1939–1945). The most prominent overt and covert cases have included Guatemala (1954, 1966), Panama (1958, 1989), Cuba (1961), the Dominican Republic (1965), Chile (1973), Nicaragua and El Salvador (1980s), Grenada (1983), Haiti (1994, 2004), and Venezuela (2002).

Americans also overcame reservations about deeper involvement in European affairs in the twentieth century. The United States joined a multinational Allied expedition force in 1918 during the Russian Civil War (1917–1922) and supported the anti-Bolshevik White movement in the aftermath of World War I. American intervention remained in the minds of Soviet leaders as tensions between the two nations increased over the following decades. World War II brought about a marriage of convenience with Moscow, although US-Soviet relations quickly descended into a Cold War marked by wars short of hot, military war. Setting aside any residual objections to involvement in European affairs and collective security arrangements, the United States intervened in the continent to bolster the Western sphere by backing anticommunist forces in France (1947) and Italy (1948) and helping to create West Germany (1948–1949). The economic reconstruction of Europe through the Marshall Plan (1948)—and the associated political and cultural influences it entailed—buttressed the military commitment with NATO.

American interventions sought to consolidate Western Europe, while schemes were launched in the Eastern sphere to undermine communist regimes. Yet the latter were primarily small-scale, covert CIA efforts in Hungary, Yugoslavia, Albania, Ukraine, Poland, Romania, and Czechoslovakia (1947–1951) that posed no real threat to Soviet domination over the region. Liberation would never be fully embraced as a state policy but would be pursued by a number of state-sponsored groups—nominally private entities—like the National Committee for a Free Europe, Radio Free Europe, and the Congress for Cultural Freedom. Nongovernmental organizations like the American Federation of Labor and Congress of Industrial Organizations (AFL-CIO) also allied with the CIA as covert interventions were pursued by a "state-private network."

The rise of American globalism meant interventions also took place throughout the Global South, in Asia, the Middle East, and Africa. Alongside the great powers, the United States helped put down the anti-imperialist Boxer Rebellion in China (1899–1901). At the same time, the United States pressed an "Open Door" policy for free trade with China, hinting at one of the tensions in American interventionism during the century: reconciling anti-imperialist rhetoric with imperialistic actions. World War II brought renewed attention to the Pacific as the United States played the pivotal role in defeating Japan and shaping the country's subsequent reconstruction. Cold War conflicts in Asia would, however, prove problematic. The Korean War (1950–1953) was sanctioned by the United Nations in 1950, but the United States dominated the UN-led South Korean war effort. The 1953 armistice may have brought an end to fighting, but the stalemate continues to cast a long shadow over the peninsula.

A deeper quagmire awaited in Vietnam as US interventionism confronted an insurmountable challenge in the form of communist-inspired nationalism. From low-scale covert assistance to the French in the aftermath of World War II to full-scale American involvement in 1965, US power faced the limits of what interventionism could accomplish. Vietnam embodied the ugly, unacceptable face of US interventionism. The conflict provoked unprecedented national soul-searching and endless debates about the supposed lessons that the defeat offered. Interventions after Vietnam would be open to greater public and congressional scrutiny.

The wave of decolonization triggered by the collapse of European colonialism brought fresh opportunities and challenges for the United States. On the one hand, the new nations had, like the United States, broken the shackles of European domination and sought to modernize; on the other hand, the United States had aligned with European colonialists and, for some in the Global South, Americans were regarded as the new imperialists. Several nationalists and members of the nonaligned movement caused consternation in Washington as nations pursued independent modernization plans and rejected the bipolar Cold War framework. US interventions in Africa and the Middle East increased toward the latter part of the twentieth century and continued into the next, a trajectory that showed how issues—from nationalism, natural resources (e.g., oil), and regional conflicts (e.g., Israeli-Palestine)—were more pressing than the Cold War. Overt invasions and covert plots have included Iran (1953, 1985–1987), Lebanon (1958), Iraq (1960, 1990, 2003), the Congo (1964), Afghanistan (1979, 2002), and Libya (1986, 2011).

During the 1990s, humanitarian concerns emerged as a key rationale for multinational interventions in Bosnia and Kosovo. Yet the notion that individual states' interests ebbed as those of the international community flowed was jolted in the United States by the terrorist attacks on September 11, 2001. The subsequent wars in Afghanistan and Iraq marked, notwithstanding the formal coalitions assembled by the George W. Bush administration, the forceful return of unilateral interventionism. The Taliban and Saddam Hussein regimes were quickly swept aside by overwhelming American military power, but the broader struggle against terrorism proved less straightforward. US interventionism was confronting a diffuse and elusive threat. The means and methods of intervention have evolved since the war with Spain in 1898 to fighting religious extremism in the early twenty-first century, but intervention has still involved troops on the ground. One recent development that promises to change the face of intervention—for the United States and the world—is the ability to fight remotely using unmanned, weaponized drones.

IDEOLOGY AND LEADERSHIP

The nature of US interventionism has been subject to vigorous debate inside the United States. Such discussions have often revealed the key battle line concerning America's role in the world: whether the country should stand apart and lead by example or be an active participant in international affairs. The most prominent US interventions and attempts to shape the world have triggered intense domestic debates, from anti-imperialists in the late nineteenth century, to the anti–Vietnam War movement in the 1960s and 1970s, to opposition to the Iraq War in the early twenty-first century. Debating US interventions can be said to be a mirror for how Americans view themselves.

Yet such discussions have generally not prevented interventions. Protecting US national interests, upholding values and traditions, and ensuring a stable world order are often sufficient to rationalize interventionism. From Theodore Roosevelt's belief in a civilizing mission in the Western Hemisphere, to Madeleine Albright's assertion of an "indispensable nation," to George W. Bush's declaration to create a world order favorable to freedom, elite policy makers have led the drive to assert American leadership in the international arena. American interventions have had immediate ramifications for the places in question but have also produced longer-term consequences. International hostility toward the United States is closely correlated to the locales where US interventions have taken place. Interventions have, however, also shaped the United States and Americans. Debates about the limits and arrogance of US power have tapped into broader questions about American values and the purpose of shaping the world in an American image.

SEE ALSO *Global South; Internationalism; Isolationism; League of Nations; Paris Peace Conference (1919); Realism (International Relations); Roosevelt, Theodore; Spanish-American War; Wilson, Woodrow; World War I*

BIBLIOGRAPHY

Cooper, John Milton, Jr. *Breaking the Heart of the World: Woodrow Wilson and the Fight for the League of Nations.* New York: Cambridge University Press, 2001.

Grow, Michael. *U.S. Presidents and Latin American Interventions: Pursuing Regime Change in the Cold War.* Lawrence: University Press of Kentucky, 2008.

Haass, Richard N. *Intervention: The Use of American Military Force in the Post–Cold War World.* Rev. ed. Washington DC: Carnegie Endowment for International Peace, 1999.

Herring, George C. *From Colony to Superpower: U.S. Foreign Relations since 1776.* New York: Oxford University Press, 2008.

Hunt, Michael H. *Ideology and U.S. Foreign Policy.* New ed. New Haven, CT: Yale University Press, 2009. First published 1987.

Nichols, Christopher McKnight. *Promise and Peril: America at the Dawn of a Global Age.* Cambridge MA: Harvard University Press, 2011.

Nye, Joseph S. *Bound to Lead: The Changing Nature of American Power.* New York: Basic, 1990.

Westad, Odd Arne. *The Global Cold War: Third World Interventions and the Making of Our Times.* Cambridge: Cambridge University Press, 2005.

Kaeten Mistry
Lecturer in American History
University of East Anglia

IRAN

For almost four decades, the United States and the Islamic Republic of Iran have been locked in an antagonistic relationship neither side seems able to escape. Each government has developed a narrative about the other laced with grievances and characterized by deep mutual mistrust. While many Iranians blame a pattern of American interference in the country's internal affairs dating back at least to the early 1950s, US officials have viewed Iran's hostile policies since the 1979 Iranian Revolution as the main source of all subsequent difficulties.

EARLY CONTACTS

The earliest American presence in Iran consisted primarily of Christian missionaries who began arriving in the early 1800s. The first formal diplomatic contacts date to 1850. The two governments finally established full relations on June 11, 1883.

Over the next several decades, a handful of Americans achieved some prominence in Iran. Howard Baskerville (1885–1909), for example, was a young teacher who gave his life in support of the Constitutional Revolution that began in 1905. Morgan Schuster (1877–1960) was a senior adviser to the Qajar regime on financial policy from 1911 to 1912, while Arthur Millspaugh (1883–1955) played a similar role from 1922 to 1927. However, sustained American interest in Persia/Iran did not develop until World War II (1939–1945), when the Franklin D. Roosevelt (1882–1945) administration sent several thousand troops to help train Iran's military and facilitate a vital supply line to the Red Army.

FROM HEROES TO VILLAINS

After the war, the United States enjoyed a brief period of unalloyed admiration in Iran when President Harry Truman (1884–1972) helped mount an international campaign to force the Soviet Union to withdraw its forces from the northern province of Azerbaijan, which all the allies had pledged to do within six months of the end of hostilities. Although most of the success for prevailing on Moscow belongs to the Iranians themselves—aided by Soviet missteps—Washington's demonstrated respect for the country's sovereignty earned widespread appreciation in Iran.

The complex nature of American objectives came under intense scrutiny less than a decade later in 1953 when a coup ousted Prime Minister Mohammad Mosaddeq (1882–1967), the prime mover behind the nationalization of Iran's oil industry in 1951. President Truman balked at insistent British lobbying to overthrow Mosaddeq, but the incoming Dwight Eisenhower (1890–1969) administration proved more amenable to the idea. The United States and Britain were the principal architects of the operation, which took place in mid-August 1953. The plan initially failed, but its organizers regrouped and on August 19 crushed Mosaddeq's supporters. A number of Iranian agents, military officers, government officials, bazaar merchants, and mullahs (most of whom were undoubtedly unaware of the US and British roles) were critical to the outcome.

GENDARME OF THE GULF

The coup's success brought back to power Shah Mohammad Reza Pahlavi (1919–1980), who had briefly fled the country. He remained in power with US backing for the next twenty-five years. While some observers have theorized that protecting commercial oil interests was Washington's ultimate objective, contemporaneous records show that the overriding concern, exaggerated though it may have been, was to avert a Soviet or communist takeover of the country. Petroleum was indeed a vital asset, but as a strategic resource in the Cold War, not primarily as a commercial prize.

For the remaining Eisenhower years, the United States provided substantial military and economic aid to solidify the shah's position. The two countries consolidated their bond in other ways—for example, establishing the infamous secret police organization SAVAK, and expanding commercial and cultural ties.

Subsequent administrations shared the vision of the global communist menace and of Iran as a key ally in the Cold War. However, President John F. Kennedy (1917–1963) and his advisers also pressed the monarchy to institute systematic reforms, an approach that did not sit well with the shah. Nevertheless, the shah took a number of steps, including launching the White Revolution in January 1963, which yielded some positive results in such areas as land redistribution. Paradoxically, in combination with rapidly expanding oil revenues, the reforms also generated sizable economic dislocations, as well as public opposition, notably among the Shiite clergy. In 1964, the authorities arrested a prominent cleric and vocal critic of the shah named Ayatollah Ruhollah Khomeini (1902–1989) and forced him into exile. The move prompted major demonstrations, which were quickly quelled but were a foretaste of unrest to come.

President Lyndon B. Johnson (1908–1973) instituted a substantial drop in aid to Iran, reflecting a reduced focus on most world events other than the Vietnam War and the Arab-Israeli crisis. President Richard M. Nixon (1913–1994) retained Johnson's overarching global priorities but with vastly different implications for Iran policy. Sharing similar strategic perspectives, Nixon and the shah had a common interest in seeing Iran emerge as a major regional power. Such a development would simultaneously create a buffer against a potential Soviet advance toward the Persian Gulf and elevate the international standing of Iran's ruler. Nixon consequently granted the shah—now referred to by critics as the "Gendarme of the Gulf"—virtually unfettered access to the Pentagon's high-tech arsenal, something previous presidents had refused to do.

REVOLUTION

The shah's growing independence from the United States allowed him to assert his influence in a variety of ways—for example, by curtailing American intelligence gathering in the country. US analysts were thus largely unable to anticipate growing anti-shah sentiments, which eventually erupted into violent protests. On New Year's Eve 1977, President Jimmy Carter (b. 1924) famously toasted Iran as an "island of stability in one of the more troubled areas of the world" thanks to the "great leadership of the Shah." One year later, in January 1979, Mohammad Reza Pahlavi fled the country for a second time, and the exiled Ayatollah Khomeini returned to an enormous popular welcome.

Iran's Revolutionary Guards prepare to burn an American flag after recapturing territory from Iraq during the Iran-Iraq War, February 1986. *Washington supported Iraq in the long war between Saddam Hussein's Iraq and Ayatollah Khomeini's Iran, which the State Department identified as a state sponsor of terrorism and whose expansionist behavior it sought to contain.* **KAVEH KAZEMI/HULTON ARCHIVE/GETTY IMAGES**

The revolution threw US policy into disarray. President Carter attempted to reach out to the interim government, but after he allowed the shah to seek medical treatment in New York, an Iranian hardline group responded by seizing the US Embassy in Tehran on November 4 and taking its staff hostage. The ensuing crisis lasted 444 days, resulting in a rupture in official relations, a failed hostage rescue attempt, and the start of decades of US sanctions.

The crisis was compounded a few weeks later, on December 25, by the Soviet invasion of Afghanistan. President Carter promulgated the Carter Doctrine in January 1980, declaring that the United States would treat an attack on the Persian Gulf as an "assault on the vital interests of the United States" and respond with military force, if necessary.

The loss of influence in Iran, the main strategic prize in the Gulf region, contributed to Carter's defeat in the presidential election of 1980. The new president, Ronald Reagan (1911–2004), entered office pledging to reassert American global primacy and to confront the new scourge of international terrorism. However, his administration failed to reach a consensus on policy toward Iran. On the one hand, the State Department identified the Islamic Republic as a state sponsor of terrorism and attempted to contain its expansionist behavior. On the other hand, from 1985 to 1986, Reagan authorized a series of secret arms deals with Tehran—then entangled in a war with Iraq—which provided the Islamic Republic with sophisticated missiles in return for help in freeing American hostages being held by Hezbollah in Lebanon. Among other negative effects, such as undermining the administration's declared counterterrorism policy, the Iran-Contra affair also created confusion in Tehran about US intentions. Washington's support for Iraq's Saddam Hussein (1937–2006) during the war intensified Tehran's ill will toward the United States.

AFTER KHOMEINI

Reagan's successor, George H. W. Bush (b. 1924), initially hoped for improved ties with the Islamic Republic. His inaugural address incorporated the phrase "goodwill begets goodwill" as a signal to Tehran. The recent end of the Iran-Iraq War seemed to present an opportunity, but Khomeini's death in June 1989 complicated the political scene inside Iran. Meanwhile, patterns of Iranian conduct, from Khomeini's fatwa against author Salman Rushdie in February 1989 to the killing of opposition figures, notably Shapour Bakhtiar in 1991, put off US officials, whose attention was also diverted by momentous political developments, such as the revolutions in Eastern Europe in 1989, Iraq's invasion of Kuwait the following year, and the Middle East peace process.

THE REFORM PERIOD

President Bill Clinton (b. 1946) took office initially disinclined to focus on Iran. Like other presidents before him, he held that many of Tehran's policies—spreading its revolutionary ideology, supporting groups such as Hamas and Hezbollah, and undermining the Arab-Israeli peace process—were antithetical to American interests. In mid-1993, the administration announced the policy of "dual containment," which treated both Iran and Iraq as undesirable regimes that needed to be held in check. In late 1996, Clinton signed the Iran and Libya Sanctions Act, describing Tehran explicitly as a terrorist supporter. With the surprise 1997 election of reform-oriented President Mohammad Khatami (b. 1943), however, the president's attitude changed. He quickly authorized a series of public gestures and concrete economic measures to express his backing for the concept of a "dialogue among civilizations."

A lingering obstacle to US cooperation was the June 1996 Khobar Towers bombing in Saudi Arabia, which US intelligence blamed on Iran. Unwilling to punish Khatami for actions possibly approved by his predecessors, Clinton continued to press for an improvement in ties, including attempting to communicate directly with Tehran's leaders, as well as ending selected sanctions and acknowledging the United States' role in the 1953 coup. By 1999, renewed suppression of political opponents by Iranian hardliners helped persuade US officials that Khatami would be unable to realize his aspirations for a rapprochement.

SEPTEMBER 11 AND ITS AFTERMATH

When George W. Bush (b. 1946) assumed office in early 2001, his administration, like others before it, had no clear consensus on whether to seek modifications in Iranian behavior or a change in regime. However, the September 11 attacks created a wholly unexpected climate for potential collaboration. For a brief period, both sides pursued a common interest in defeating the Taliban and al-Qaeda in Afghanistan and Saddam Hussein in Iraq. Iranian and American officials on the ground cooperated fruitfully, particularly during the process of establishing a new government in Afghanistan.

Two episodes at the start of 2002 disrupted these developments. In early January, Israel seized the *Karine A*, a vessel reported by official Israeli sources to be carrying weapons provided by Iran to the Palestinian Authority. A few weeks later, President Bush in his State of the Union address defined Iran as part of an "Axis of Evil," along with Iraq and North Korea. He deplored Tehran's role as an exporter of terror and its pursuit of weapons of mass destruction. The speech brought sharp denunciations from Tehran but criticisms from other quarters, too, including Iranians sympathetic to opening their country more to the outside world.

The persistent mistrust of both governments repeatedly hindered prospects for closer ties. In May 2003, for example, two months after the US occupation of Iraq, the State Department received a fax, later confirmed by Iranian officials to have originated from their government. The document outlined a possible "grand bargain" with Washington, but the Bush administration disregarded it, claiming later its authenticity had been in doubt.

For most of Bush's presidency, suspicions about an undeclared nuclear weapons program dominated policy debates on Iran. When Mahmoud Ahmadinejad (b. 1956) replaced Khatami as president in 2005, he rejected earlier steps aiming at good faith negotiations with the West, instead ordering a resumption of nuclear activity that further raised US concerns. Meanwhile, the Bush administration faced questions about its hard line after a 2007 intelligence community assessment that Iran had stopped pursuing a nuclear weapon in 2003. Bush himself confronted pressures from some senior advisers, as well as Israeli leaders, to eliminate the Iranian nuclear threat through military strikes.

THE OBAMA PRESIDENCY

Barack Obama's (b. 1961) accession to the White House in early 2009 promised new directions in Middle East policy. In March, he sent a video message to the Iranian people on Nowruz, Iran's traditional new year, saying he was "committed to diplomacy that addresses the full range of issues before us." In June, he delivered a landmark speech in Cairo pledging to approach the Islamic Republic "without preconditions on the basis of mutual respect." Eight days later, when Ahmadinejad won a controversial reelection bid, sparking massive protests and a brutal crackdown, Obama chose to continue to pursue a dialogue with the regime, including reportedly writing his second letter to Supreme Leader Ali Khamenei (b. 1939) seeking "better cooperation" between the two countries.

A principal focus of Obama's approach has been Iran's nuclear program. In 2009, the United States actively supported a plan to fuel the Tehran Research Reactor—a high priority for Iran—through a fuel exchange involving Russia and France. Tehran at first agreed but then backed away. The following year, Brazil and Turkey brokered a similar agreement, apparently with Obama's personal encouragement, but in the end the United States balked, arguing later that the terms were no longer acceptable. Instead, Washington joined a new, more robust UN sanctions regime against the Islamic Republic.

In 2013, the election of President Hassan Rouhani (b. 1948), a more pragmatic figure with close ties to the Supreme Leader, paved the way for a major breakthrough in nuclear talks. In November of that year, the P5+1 (the United States, the United Kingdom, France, Russia, China, and Germany) reached an interim agreement with Iran designed to lead to a comprehensive accord. The deal called for Iran to halt its nuclear program, reduce its uranium stockpiles, agree to more frequent international inspections, and take additional steps in return for a partial lifting of sanctions and access to certain frozen assets. The two sides extended the interim deadline twice, setting their sights on a final political pact by the end of March 2015 with a set of complex technical annexes by June 30. It would take two more extensions of talks, punctuated by the eleventh-hour insertion of provisions for eventually lifting embargoes against Iran on conventional weapons and ballistic missiles, before the sides finally reached an accord, announced on July 14, 2015. Hailed by the negotiating parties and condemned by detractors—primarily in the United States, Iran and Israel—the agreement's fate remained to be decided as of the publication of this volume.

After many years of common ignorance followed by a period of growing interdependence during the Pahlavi era, the postrevolution phase of US interactions with Iran has featured both a succession of hostile encounters and a string of missed opportunities to reduce tensions. Notwithstanding the remarkable breakthrough represented by the July 14 nuclear agreement, that pattern appears likely to hold until the perception of shared interests in other areas of the relationship can overcome the effects of decades of mutual mistrust.

SEE ALSO *Americanization; Cold War; Empire, US; Exceptionalism; Internationalism; Interventionism; Iran Hostage Crisis; Iran-Contra Scandal; Islam; Secularization; World War II*

BIBLIOGRAPHY

Alvandi, Roham. *Nixon, Kissinger, and the Shah: The United States and Iran in the Cold War*. New York: Oxford University Press, 2014.

Bill, James A. *The Eagle and the Lion: The Tragedy of American-Iranian Relations*. New Haven, CT: Yale University Press, 1988.

Blight, James G., Janet M. Lang, Hussein Banai, Malcolm Byrne, and John Tirman. *Becoming Enemies: U.S.-Iran Relations and the Iran-Iraq War, 1979–1988*. Lanham, MD: Rowman & Littlefield, 2012.

Carter, Jimmy. "Tehran, Iran Toasts of the President and the Shah at a State Dinner." December 31, 1977. *American Presidency Project*, edited by Gerhard Peters and John T. Woolley. http://www.presidency.ucsb.edu/ws/?pid=7080

Gasiorowski, Mark J. *U.S. Foreign Policy and the Shah: Building a Client State in Iran*. Ithaca, NY: Cornell University Press, 1991.

Gasiorowski, Mark J., and Malcolm Byrne, eds. *Mohammad Mosaddeq and the 1953 Coup in Iran.* Syracuse, NY: Syracuse University Press, 2004.

Goode, James F. *The United States and Iran, 1946–51: The Diplomacy of Neglect.* New York: Macmillan, 1989.

Kuniholm, Bruce R. *The Origins of the Cold War in the Near East: Great Power Conflict and Diplomacy in Iran, Turkey, and Greece.* Princeton, NJ: Princeton University Press, 1980.

Obama, Barack. "Remarks by the President in Celebration of Nowruz." March 20, 2009. https://www.whitehouse.gov/the_press_office/VIDEOTAPED-REMARKS-BY-THE-PRESIDENT-IN-CELEBRATION-OF-NOWRUZ/

Obama, Barack. "Remarks by President on a New Beginning." June 4, 2009. Cairo University, Egypt. https://www.whitehouse.gov/the_press_office/Remarks-by-the-President-at-Cairo-University-6-04-09

Parsi, Trita. *A Single Role of the Dice: Obama's Diplomacy with Iran.* New Haven, CT: Yale University Press, 2012.

Slavin, Barbara. *Bitter Friends, Bosom Enemies: Iran, the U.S., and the Twisted Path to Confrontation.* New York: St. Martin's Press, 2007.

Malcolm Byrne
Director of Research
The National Security Archive at The George Washington University

IRAN HOSTAGE CRISIS

The Iran hostage crisis was a watershed in the relationship between the United States and the Islamic Republic of Iran. It began on November 4, 1979, when a group called the "Students Following the Line of the Imam" took possession of the US embassy in Tehran. The students, who were supporters of Ayatollah Ruhollah Khomeini (1902–1989), took sixty-six Americans hostage, fifty-two of whom were held in captivity for 444 days. The hostage crisis strengthened the hardliners in Iran, torpedoed Jimmy Carter's (b. 1924) presidency, and damaged the official US-Iran relationship.

BACKGROUND TO THE CRISIS

International developments helped to precipitate the hostage crisis. The hostage-takers, like many Iranians, resented the US government for providing military aid and economic support to Shah Mohammad Reza Pahlavi (1919–1980), an authoritarian monarch who ruled Iran for four decades. The Iranian Revolution brought an end to the Pahlavi monarchy on January 16, 1979, Khomeini returned to the country after fifteen years in exile on February 1, and the final holdouts from the old regime were defeated on February 11. Yet the revolutionaries feared that the United States might intervene, as the Central Intelligence Agency (CIA) had in the 1953 coup against Prime Minister Mohammad Mosaddeq (1882–1967), to thwart the revolution, reinstate the ailing shah, and protect America's strategic and economic interests in the Persian Gulf region. Their fears seemed to materialize when, on October 22, 1979, the Carter administration admitted the shah into the United States for cancer treatment. Adding to the atmosphere of suspicion was the meeting between US National Security Adviser Zbigniew Brzezinski (b. 1928) and a group of moderate Iranian officials at a celebration in Algiers, Algeria, on November 1. The hostage-takers, who called the US embassy a "nest of spies," determined that the best way to prevent American interference in Iran's internal affairs was to occupy the embassy and take its personnel hostage.

Domestic politics also motivated the hostage-takers and their supporters. With the shah gone, various factions fought for control of the Iranian state. Those factions included but were not limited to religious hardliners, moderate Islamists, secular liberals, Marxist-Leninists, and several guerrilla groups. The most important domestic issue in the summer and fall of 1979 was the drafting of a new constitution, which would define what it meant for Iran to be an Islamic Republic. Mehdi Bazargan (1908–1995), the liberal prime minister of the Provisional Government and the cofounder of the Liberation Movement of Iran, put forward a draft that was informed by Islamic principles but did not grant as much power to the *ulama* (Islamic scholars) as the one that the hardliners offered. In the end, the hardliners won the debate, and Khomeini's concept of the "mandate of the jurist" made him the supreme leader of Iran with the final say on all domestic and foreign affairs. The onset of the hostage crisis one month prior to the national referendum strengthened the hardliners and rallied a majority of Iranian voters behind the constitution. The Iranian people voted to approve the constitution in December 1979.

THE US RESPONSE AND NEGOTIATIONS

The Carter administration attempted to secure the hostages' release on multiple occasions. An initial diplomatic effort in November 1979 broke down and resulted in the United States placing the first of many rounds of sanctions on Iran. By early April 1980, after working through back channels, the administration thought that a deal was in the offing. But when Iran's Revolutionary Council failed to come to a unanimous conclusion on whether to transfer the hostages from the embassy to official custody, Khomeini ignored the advice of the moderates in his government, including President Abolhassan Banisadr (b. 1933), and opted against the hostages' release. The failure of diplomacy, which was the preferred course of Secretary of State Cyrus Vance (1917–2002), strengthened the hand of Brzezinski, who called for a military option. On April 25, the Carter administration attempted to free the hostages through a military intervention known as Operation Eagle Claw. The intervention was a failure, ending with the deaths of eight Americans who were part of the rescue mission. Vance resigned from his post, and the summer began with no prospects on the horizon.

Negotiations resumed in fall 1980. In September, Carter administration officials began to communicate with a relative of Khomeini's in West Germany. While progress was made in these talks, Iraq's invasion of Iran on September 22 forced the Iranian leadership to divert its attention to defending the homeland against foreign aggression. By the middle of October, a new channel opened up between Washington and Tehran via Algerian officials. During the final stages of the negotiations, the sticking point was the shah's personal fortune, which the Iranians wanted returned from American banks. This issue, which was not negotiable from the American point of view, scuttled the possibility of a deal before the one-year anniversary of the hostage-taking. November 4 was also a presidential election day in the United States. Deputy Secretary of State Warren Christopher (1925–2011), the lead American negotiator, eventually brokered a deal in Algiers that included a US pledge of nonintervention and a promise to unfreeze approximately four billion dollars of Iranian assets in return for the hostages' safe passage out of Tehran. All of the hostages made it home safely after the Iranians released them moments after Ronald Reagan (1911–2004) took the oath of office on January 20, 1981.

CONSEQUENCES FOR US–IRAN RELATIONS AND DOMESTIC POLITICS

The hostage crisis had profound consequences for American and Iranian domestic politics, as well as for US-Iran relations. Carter's inability to secure the hostages' release in a timely manner made the president appear weak and ineffective, which contributed to Reagan's electoral victory in 1980. In Iran, the hostage crisis enabled Khomeini to consolidate his power, launch a "cultural revolution," and ensure that the conservative Islamic Republican Party dominated Iranian politics. While the political discourse in both countries turned to the right, the official binational relationship sank to new lows. The United States severed relations with the Islamic Republic in April 1980, ushering in a period of tension and discord between the two governments far removed from the decades of cooperation that preceded the hostage crisis.

SEE ALSO *Carter, James Earl, Jr.; Central Intelligence Agency (CIA); Iran; Middle East; Mossadegh, Mohammad; Organization of the Petroleum Exporting Countries (OPEC); Reagan, Ronald Wilson*

BIBLIOGRAPHY

Bowden, Mark. *Guests of the Ayatollah: The First Battle in America's War with Militant Islam.* New York: Grove Press, 2006.

Farber, David. *Taken Hostage: The Iran Hostage Crisis and America's First Encounter with Radical Islam.* Princeton, NJ: Princeton University Press, 2005.

House Committee on Foreign Affairs. *The Iran Hostage Crisis: A Chronology of Daily Developments.* 97th Cong., 1st sess. A report prepared for the Committee on Foreign Affairs, US House of Representatives, by the Foreign Affairs and National Defense Division, Congressional Research Service, Library of Congress. Washington, DC: GPO 1981.

Kreisberg, Paul H., ed. *American Hostages in Iran: The Conduct of a Crisis.* New Haven, CT: Yale University Press, 1985.

Moses, Russell Leigh. *Freeing the Hostages: Reexamining U.S.-Iranian Negotiations and Soviet Policy, 1979–1981.* Pittsburgh: University of Pittsburgh Press, 1996.

Sick, Gary. *All Fall Down: America's Tragic Encounter with Iran.* New York: Random House, 1986.

Matthew Shannon
Department of History
Emory and Henry College

IRAN-CONTRA SCANDAL

The Iran-Contra affair was a political scandal in the 1980s that grew out of two separate covert operations that implicated a number of White House officials, including President Ronald Reagan (1911–2004), in potentially illegal acts. Unlike most political scandals, Iran-Contra was not primarily about financial corruption or self-interested electoral gain, but was rooted in differing conceptions of the use of power in the foreign policy arena.

THE IRAN ARMS-FOR-HOSTAGES OPERATION

The Iran side of the affair featured secret negotiations between the Reagan administration and the Islamic Republic of Iran during 1985 and 1986. The United States aimed to obtain the freedom of American hostages being held in Lebanon by Iran's client, Hezbollah, while Iran sought US missiles for its war with Iraq. Since the 1979 Iranian revolution and Iran's seizure of the US embassy, Washington and Tehran had been bitter adversaries. Furthermore, Iran was on the State Department's list of state sponsors of terrorism, and Reagan had made the fight against terrorism a core principle of his foreign policy.

In July 1985, Israeli prime minister Shimon Peres (b. 1923) dispatched an envoy to inform the US national security adviser that Israel was prepared to help

Washington regain a measure of political access to Iran by facilitating an opening to so-called moderates in the Iranian regime who were said to be amenable to improving ties with the United States. The envoy suggested that each side begin by providing a sign of good intentions: arms from the United States and a commitment by Iran to help release the American hostages in Lebanon.

The national security adviser, Robert C. McFarlane (b. 1937), apprised Reagan, who was deeply sympathetic to the hostages' plight and who soon gave his approval. McFarlane, in turn, obtained the acquiescence of Secretary of State George P. Shultz (b. 1920) and Defense Secretary Caspar W. Weinberger (1917–2006), both of whom consistently opposed the plan in principle.

Over the next fifteen months, 2,004 TOW antitank missiles and various spare parts were delivered to Iran. At first, Israel served as the go-between, taking US-made weapons from its stocks, but after a botched shipment of HAWK antiaircraft missiles in November 1985, the United States took direct control. Three American hostages were freed, but three more were captured during the same period. Throughout, the operation was characterized by broken promises, miscommunications, and logistical mishaps. Still, all sides persisted. Even when McFarlane's secret mission to Tehran in May 1986 failed, the president chose to continue.

THE NICARAGUAN CONTRA OPERATION

The Iran operation was also notable for what became known as the "diversion"—the redirection of profits from the arms sales to support US-backed rebels fighting the Marxist-oriented Sandinista regime in Nicaragua. One of Reagan's top objectives in foreign policy was to roll back international communism, especially in Central America. Since overthrowing a long-time US ally in 1979, the Sandinistas had increasingly relied on the USSR and Cuba, which Reagan considered a menace to US security. However, he was never able to persuade the American public to agree on the gravity of the threat. Therefore, with the encouragement of CIA director William J. Casey (1913–1987), the president authorized a covert program beginning in 1981 that was ostensibly intended to interdict arms flowing to leftists in the region but in reality aimed increasingly at regime change in Nicaragua through a broad program of support for the rebels, known as the Contras.

The Contra operation soon drew the attention of Congress, which had been kept in the dark about its true objectives. Congress passed a series of restrictive measures, but the Reagan team repeatedly found ways to evade the constraints. After revelations that the United States had been involved in mining Nicaraguan harbors in 1984, Congress in October of that year passed—and Reagan signed—the so-called Boland Amendment (in fact one in a series of amendments under that title), which prohibited US military or intelligence support for the rebels.

Rather than comply, Reagan charged McFarlane with keeping the rebels together "body and soul" until Congress resumed official funding. McFarlane turned to a Marine lieutenant colonel assigned to the National Security Council staff named Oliver L. North (b. 1943) to carry out the president's wishes. North, who also played a key role in the Iran arms deals, later credited the CIA director with providing regular guidance regarding both operations, including how to keep them concealed from Congress.

For the next two years, working with a small network of private individuals and front companies (collectively dubbed the Enterprise) along with a handful of CIA and military officials in the field, North engaged in a variety of legally dubious activities: soliciting wealthy private donors, procuring weapons, and providing battlefield and political advice to the rebels.

At the same time, senior US officials, including the president, engaged in soliciting various forms of support for the Contras from foreign governments. Saudi Arabia donated $32 million, Taiwan $2 million, and more than a dozen others were approached for assistance, typically without adherence to strict legal requirements provided by the US attorney general.

EXPOSURE AND INVESTIGATION

On October 5, 1986, the covert arms-supply operation was exposed when a Sandinista soldier shot down one of the Enterprise's cargo planes over the Nicaraguan jungle. The administration denied a connection to the plane. After the disclosure of the Iran operation one month later, the White House was similarly evasive, but on November 25, 1986, the president announced that both stories were not only essentially true but had been connected through the diversion of Iran arms profits to the Contras. He denied any personal knowledge of the diversion.

For the next several years, a mix of media, congressional, and legal investigations ensued. Congress held televised hearings during the summer of 1987 and the courts appointed an independent counsel, Lawrence Walsh (1912–2014), to look into legal violations. Walsh obtained fourteen guilty verdicts or pleas and Congress produced a sharply critical report of widespread administration deception and wrongdoing. Public indignation was high yet tempered by the slow trickling out of the full story and the popularity of key players like Reagan and North, as well as the nature of their intentions and the complexity of the issues. President Reagan's approval ratings plummeted, but world events, such as the collapse of the USSR and Reagan's own subsequent actions, helped to restore his standing by the end of his presidency.

SEE ALSO *Freedom Fighters; Iran; Middle East; Reagan, Ronald Wilson*

BIBLIOGRAPHY

Byrne, Malcolm. *Iran-Contra: Reagan's Scandal and the Unchecked Abuse of Presidential Power.* Lawrence: University Press of Kansas, 2014.

Draper, Theodore. *A Very Thin Line: The Iran-Contra Affairs.* New York: Hill and Wang, 1991.

Kornbluh, Peter, and Malcolm Byrne, eds. *The Iran-Contra Scandal: The Declassified History.* New York: New Press, 1993.

US Senate Select Committee on Secret Military Assistance to Iran and the Nicaraguan Opposition, and House Select Committee to Investigate Covert Arms Transactions with Iran. *Iran-Contra Investigation: Joint Hearings.* Vols. 100-1–100-11. 100th Congress, 1st Sess., 1987. Senate Report 100-216.

Walsh, Lawrence E. *Final Report of the Independent Counsel for Iran/Contra Matters.* US Court of Appeals for the District of Columbia Circuit, August 4, 1993. Vol. 1: *Investigations and Prosecutions*; Vol. 2: *Indictments, Plea Agreements, Interim Reports to the Congress, and Administrative Matters*; and Vol. 3: *Comments and Materials Submitted by Individuals and Their Attorneys Responding to Volume I of the Final Report.* Washington, DC: GPO, 1993.

Walsh, Lawrence E. *Firewall: The Iran-Contra Conspiracy and Cover-Up.* New York: Norton, 1997.

Malcolm Byrne
Director of Research
The National Security Archive at The George Washington University

IRAQ

US-Iraq relations have been characterized primarily by their instability. Iraq's many changes, from monarchy, to republic, then brutal dictatorship and deeply troubled democracy, hindered the development of a common basis for relations. As a result, some combination of internal Iraqi and global events were usually necessary to compel temporary interest. This pattern continued until the US invasion in 2003, which bound the United States and Iraq together for the foreseeable future.

NINETEENTH CENTURY

Throughout the nineteenth century, American missionaries travelled to "Mesopotamia," then a holding of the Ottoman Empire. Missionaries' appeals were rife with Orientalist imagery, depicting the region as exotic and mysterious. Despite such misrepresentations, local Christian sects, such as the Chaldeans and Nestorians, often provided mission groups with an entrée to the area. These efforts left a substantial legacy, and into the mid-twentieth century, Jesuit-run Baghdad College remained one of Iraq's best schools, educating many of Iraq's elites (Hahn 2012, 17–19).

TWENTIETH CENTURY

The modern state of Iraq began in 1920 as a League of Nations mandate. The Ottoman Empire sided with the Central Powers in World War I (1914–1918), only to lose badly to Entente armies allied with local forces. The ensuing peace established the modern state of Turkey as the empire's successor, with the remaining provinces divided up and administered at the behest of the League of Nations. Three such provinces were combined into a single entity, known as Iraq, under British authority and with Baghdad as its capital. The British selected King Faisal I (1885–1933) to provide a veneer of sovereignty, though his powers were sharply circumscribed. The primary interest of the British administration was oil. The nation-states of Europe needed secure access to the commodity to power their navies and fuel their increasingly mechanized armies (Dawisha 2009, 12–17).

Though gripped by an isolationist mood, the United States continued to look out for US commercial interests abroad. Consistent with the long-standing policy maintaining an "open door" for US investment and goods in foreign markets, US officials repeatedly protested the treatment of American oil companies and geologists operating in the region. These complaints eased when, in 1928, a consortium of US firms joined with British, French, and Dutch firms in the Turkish Petroleum Company, renamed the Iraq Petroleum Company (IPC) a year later (Yergin 2011, 185–189).

Their oil interests secure, US officials pursued their interests in Iraq primarily through the British, even after Iraq gained independence in 1932. During World War II (1939–1945), Secretary of State Cordell Hull (1871–1955) resisted openly endorsing British control, but when a former prime minister with fascist sympathies attempted to overthrow the government, the United States backed the British to the hilt. A British army invaded and restored the government, and the United States endorsed this outcome by stationing several thousand soldiers there for the remainder of the war (O'Sullivan 2012, 38–43).

After 1945, support for the British became subordinate to containing communism. Access to oil remained essential for both national security and domestic economics. Middle Eastern oil underpinned the nascent Western European recovery, which was itself considered essential to stemming communist infiltration. Limiting Soviet influence in the region required developing better relations, but rising anti-British and nationalist sentiment made this difficult. Complicating the US position were the inroads the Soviet Union made with the Kurds, a rebellious minority group located in Iraq's mountainous north, and recurrent political and labor unrest in the capital (Hahn 2012, 24–25).

Though events such as the creation of Israel in 1947 continued to disrupt the relationship, the US government alternately tried to ply the Iraqi government with guns and butter. The Harry S. Truman administration (1945–1953) prodded the IPC to greatly increase government royalty payments, significantly boosting the government's coffers, though success in this regard did not change the Iraqis' ambivalent outlook. Where butter failed, the Dwight D. Eisenhower administration (1953–1961) tried guns instead, significantly expanding security cooperation, and transferring millions of dollars of defense articles. The Eisenhower administration also tried to unite the "Northern Tier" of Middle Eastern countries into an anti-Soviet, NATO-like arrangement. These efforts came to fruition with the 1955 Baghdad Pact, joining Britain, Turkey, Iraq, Iran, and Pakistan together in a single collective security agreement, though Eisenhower refused to join for fear of antagonizing the regional powers left out of the agreement (Hahn 2012, 27–29).

Fostering closer ties with the United States could do little if it undermined the government in the eyes of its people. Arab nationalists harshly criticized the Baghdad Pact for abdicating to Western influence. In 1958, a conspiracy of hundreds of Iraqi military officers with nationalist leanings overthrew the monarchy and established a nominal republic (Abdullah 2003, 152–153). Though similar unrest in Lebanon and Jordan that year prompted Eisenhower to intervene, Iraq's size and the scope of its domestic problems outweighed the potential benefits. Searching for influence by shoring up the Iraqi government had failed.

Political instability continued to roil Iraq, making it difficult to forge lasting relationships. US officials mainly sought to keep Soviet influence to a minimum, while preventing Iraq from going to war with its neighbors. In 1961, Prime Minister Abd al-Karim Qasim (1914–1963) threatened the small, oil-rich state of Kuwait, but a combination of US pressure and British reoccupation of Kuwait halted such efforts. In retaliation, Qasim loosened restrictions on Communist Party activity (Hahn 2012, 46–48).

Backing down over Kuwait and now perceived to be coddling communists, Qasim was overthrown in 1963. During the Arab-Israeli War of 1967, the Iraqi government suspended relations with the United States. In 1968, before relations could be restored, the military-dominated government was overthrown, now by the Baath Party. The Baathists adhered to a Pan-Arabist, socialist platform, though they quickly became better known for their ruthless, repressive governance (Abdullah 2003, 164–166). The ensuing purges left virtually no power centers from which to challenge their authority.

Iraq garnered little attention from the United States in the 1970s. The Baathist government nationalized the IPC in 1971, and increasingly partnered with the Soviet Union for investment and technical assistance in the oil industry. The partnership was rocky, however, and the Richard Nixon administration (1969–1974) believed that the Baathists' repressive ways would result in their ouster (Hahn 2012, 55).

In 1979, Vice President Saddam Hussein (1937–2006), one of the most ruthless and powerful figures in the Iraqi government, forced the resignation of the elderly president. Another wave of purges followed. In the same year, popular unrest deposed the shah of Iran, paving the way for the creation of the Islamic Republic under Ayatollah Khomeini (1902–1989). Secularist Iraq began to more closely resemble an ally of convenience against emergent Islamic fundamentalism.

Baathist Iraq dreamed of ruling over all Arabs, of which Iran had many, while Iran dreamed of dominion over all Shiites, which constituted most of Iraq. The threat each posed to the other was clear. In 1980, Hussein invaded Iran to "liberate" Arab populations in the country's southwest. The war seesawed before settling into a costly war of attrition, claiming over one million lives (Hahn 2012, 70–72).

The US position trended closer to Iraq as Iran repelled the initial attack and made inroads into Iraq. Iraq's brutality, its active nuclear weapons program, and its periodic use of chemical weapons gave US officials pause. But all were preferable to an Iranian victory (Duelfer 2009, 35–36). In 1985, Iran began attacking Iraqi oil tankers traversing the Persian Gulf. Faced with the prospect of a local conflict harming the world economy, President Ronald Reagan ordered US naval forces to the Persian Gulf to protect the tankers, which now carried the flag of neutral countries. When the war ended with a draw in 1988, the US-Iraqi relationship was closer than ever before (Hahn 2012, 79–82).

THE PERSIAN GULF WARS

Hussein next turned his attention and substantial military to Kuwait. In 1990, Hussein threatened war with Kuwait over border disputes regarding oil extraction. The George H. W. Bush administration (1989–1993) tried to discourage this course of action, but Hussein assumed that he risked only a strong, but temporary, rebuke. Hussein invaded and easily conquered Kuwait.

Foreign policy elites were familiar with Hussein from the previous decade, but the invasion of Kuwait vaulted

Iraq and its leader into widespread public consciousness for the first time. Tales of the regime's violence and cruelty flooded the airwaves. Cruelty notwithstanding, the Bush administration saw Hussein's actions as a threat to the emerging post–Cold War order. Allowing the unprovoked attack and annexation of one state by another set a dangerous precedent. Furthermore, the administration worried that Hussein's ambitions would not end with Kuwait, but that the economic and political power gained from Kuwait's massive oil wealth would only make him strong enough to threaten the rest of the region, particularly Saudi Arabia and Israel (Hahn 2012, 94–95).

Capitalizing on these concerns, Bush constructed a thirty-four-nation coalition, with United Nations backing, to oust Iraq from Kuwait. Even after victory seemed assured, Bush remained focused on prudent avoidance of risks. Thus once the Iraqi army was driven into full retreat, Bush opted against deposing Hussein by force. Such an act would exceed the UN mandate, shatter the coalition, and saddle the United States with managing Iraq's reconstruction (Hahn 2012, 106).

The postwar situation proved messy, with a series of halfway measures backed by the United Nations and NATO. These measures included: "no-fly zones" over most of northern and southern Iraq, to protect Kurdish and Shiite populations; intrusive inspections to confirm that Iraq abandoned its nuclear, chemical, and biological weapons programs (also known as weapons of mass destruction, or WMDs); and a brutal suite of economic sanctions.

Throughout the 1990s, Hussein reveled in the image of one who could rebel against the will of the United States and survive. In 1992, Hussein was still in power, but Bush lost his bid for reelection. The sanctions-and-inspections regime allowed Hussein to demonstrate his noncompliance with few consequences. Iraqi forces routinely shot at NATO planes enforcing the no-fly zones, and interfered with weapons inspectors, expelling them completely in 1997. President Bill Clinton ordered a round of bombing in response, but Hussein survived by simply waiting it out. Getting tough on Hussein was a bipartisan endeavor, with both houses of Congress adopting a formal policy of "regime change" in 1998. As President George W. Bush took office in 2001, a band of foreign-policy hawks and anti-Hussein hardliners known as *neoconservatives* found positions throughout the administration. Their ranks included Vice President Richard Cheney (b. 1941), Deputy Secretary of Defense Paul Wolfowitz (b. 1943), and Undersecretary of Defense Douglas Feith (b. 1953) (Hahn 2012, 129–131).

The terrorist attacks of September 11, 2001, forced a reassessment of Iraq. Administration thinkers came to believe that the costs of inaction in the face of threats to national security increasingly outweighed the costs of acting preemptively to stop them. One nightmare scenario stood out: nonstate actors acquiring WMD and using them against the United States. Despite being ideologically incompatible with al-Qaeda, Hussein's status as an international scofflaw, potentially in possession of WMD, made him too much of a threat to tolerate (Duelfer 2009, 205).

The George W. Bush administration (2000–2008) assembled a case for invasion, relying on an ambiguous UN mandate, WMD intelligence that later proved to be incorrect, and rhetorical comparisons to al-Qaeda in lieu of actual operational connections. A modest international coalition composed primarily of US and British forces invaded Iraq in March 2003, declaring victory in May, with all essential state functions falling to the US military (Hahn 2012, 144–146, 160).

US OCCUPATION AND RECONSTRUCTION

The United States wrongly expected a speedy transition to a new government. Instead, a protracted insurgency developed, with al-Qaeda-led foreign fighters, militant ex-Baathists, and Shiite militias all pitted against one another and against the occupation forces. American casualties began to mount. Previously peaceful communities uprooted and reconfigured themselves to segregate and protect groups that once coexisted. From Americans' perspective, Iraq became the land of civilian car-bombings, roadside bombs, and a seemingly ineffectual US military (Hahn 2012, 179–181). The lack of an "exit strategy" nearly cost Bush reelection in 2004, and in 2006 led to devastating electoral losses for the Republican Party.

Violence reached a bloody crescendo in 2006 and 2007 when US forces, under General David Petraeus (b. 1952), implemented a new counterinsurgency strategy intended to reduce violence and create time for the Iraqi government and security forces to grow and prove themselves. In an unexpected turn of events, Sunni tribesmen in Iraq's western provinces revolted against al-Qaeda at the same time, allowing a "surge" of military personnel to focus on Baghdad (Ricks 2009, 27–31, 66–67).

The new strategy worked. A popularly elected government took form in 2006, with Nouri al-Maliki (b. 1950), a Shiite, becoming prime minister. Violence rapidly declined in 2008 as well. When President Barack Obama took office in 2009, his primary contribution to Iraq policy was sticking to the existing timeline for withdrawal. The military wished to maintain a reserve force, but Iraqi haggling over its legal status scuttled the agreement. Absent such an accord, the last US forces left the country in December 2011. American forces suffered more than four thousand deaths, with over thirty thousand wounded. War-related Iraqi deaths exceeded one hundred thousand (Hahn 2012, 193–194).

All was still not well in Iraq. Al-Maliki increasingly used his internal security forces as a sectarian tool to protect Shiites and harass Sunnis. When these tactics caused a surge in support for secular, nonsectarian parties, al-Maliki refused to step aside or meaningfully include them in his coalition. Disaffected Sunnis proved fertile ground for expansion of the Islamic State in the Levant (ISIL), an extremist group born of the Syrian civil war. Having recovered some leverage, the Obama administration refused to commit significant forces to fighting ISIL's spread until the polarizing prime minister stepped aside. Though initially resistant, al-Maliki eventually relented. Three years after leaving Iraq in 2011, US forces returned for a mission of unknown duration.

SEE ALSO *Afghanistan; Britain; Cold War; Empire, US; Exceptionalism; Internationalism; Interventionism; Iran; Orientalism; September 11, 2001; War on Terror*

BIBLIOGRAPHY

Abdullah, Thabit A. J. *A Short History of Iraq.* London: Pearson, 2003. 2nd ed., 2010.

Arango, Tim. "Maliki Agrees to Relinquish Power in Iraq." *New York Times*, August 14, 2014.

Dawisha, Adeed. *Iraq: A Political History from Independence to Occupation.* Princeton, NJ: Princeton University Press, 2009.

Duelfer, Charles. *Hide and Seek: The Search for Truth in Iraq.* New York: Public Affairs, 2009.

Hahn, Peter L. *Missions Accomplished? The United States and Iraq since World War I.* Oxford: Oxford University Press, 2012.

Khedery, Ali. "Why We Stuck with Maliki—and Lost Iraq." *Washington Post*, July 3, 2014.

O'Sullivan, Christopher D. *FDR and the End of Empire: The Origins of American Power in the Middle East.* New York: Palgrave Macmillan, 2012.

Ricks, Thomas E. *The Gamble: General David Petraeus and the American Military Adventure in Iraq.* New York: Penguin, 2009.

Woodward, Bob. *The War Within: A Secret White House History, 2006–2008.* New York: Simon and Schuster, 2008.

Yergin, Daniel. *The Prize: The Epic Quest for Oil, Money, and Power.* New York: Simon and Schuster, 2011. First published 1991.

Matthew J. Ambrose
Independent Scholar

IRON CURTAIN

On March 5, 1946, Winston Churchill (1874–1965) took the podium in the gymnasium of Westminster College in Fulton, Missouri, to speak on world affairs. In his speech, "The Sinews of Peace," the former prime minister of the United Kingdom graphically portrayed the dangerous spread of Soviet control over Eastern and Central Europe as creating an "Iron Curtain." "From Stettin in the Baltic to Trieste in the Adriatic, an iron curtain has descended across the Continent." The curtain divided Europe into two spheres of culture. Those behind the Iron Curtain, in "the Soviet sphere," were subjected to a police state, while those on the Western side of the curtain were being challenged by "Communist fifth columns" that were endangering "Christian civilization." This state of affairs did not represent the goals for which Britain and the United States had fought or the "essentials of permanent peace." Churchill called for a "fraternal association of English-speaking peoples" to ensure the future peace of the world and to deny the Soviets "the indefinite expansion of their power and doctrines."

It was not the first time the term *Iron Curtain* had been used to define territories occupied by the Soviet Union and the horrors facing those caught behind it. In 1944 and 1945, German propaganda minister Joseph Goebbels (1897–1945) employed the term and forecast "mass slaughter" for those behind the curtain if Germany surrendered. In early May 1945, Churchill used the term in a telegram to President Harry S. Truman (1884–1972), and again in August in a speech to the British House of Commons. In both cases, he used the image of an iron curtain to delineate areas under Soviet control and suggest that a "tragedy on a prodigious scale" could be taking place behind it. Yet, despite these earlier usages, it was the Fulton speech that generated worldwide controversy and made *Iron Curtain* an iconic term associated with the Cold War and those regions under Soviet/Communist control.

The Fulton speech is remembered because it came at a critical time as the United States, the United Kingdom, and the Soviet Union were reassessing their relationships. Its importance was heightened by the presence of President Truman on the platform, which gave the content of the speech political credence. Almost immediately, the speech became a topic for discussion across the globe, making the phrase and concept of the Iron Curtain into an iconic Cold War household term.

The response was exactly what Churchill wanted. Before the speech, he told an audience at the American embassy in Havana, Cuba, that it was his "fate to issue 'clarion calls'" about the dangers he foresaw. The Anglo-American world, he said, needed to work together to preserve the world "from chaos" created by the "Soviet Communist menace" (Norweb 1946). Following the speech, Churchill informed British prime minister Clement Attlee (1883–1967) that he thought the

Winston Churchill, with President Harry Truman, before a notable address at Westminster College in Fulton, Missouri, March 5, 1946. *In the "Sinews of Peace" address, Churchill, the former UK prime minister, graphically portrayed the dangerous spread of Soviet control over Eastern and Central Europe as creating an "Iron Curtain," a term that became widely used throughout the Cold War period.* POPPERFOTO/GETTY IMAGES

speech was a success and that Truman appeared "equally pleased before and after" the speech. Within months of Churchill's speech, the term *Iron Curtain* had become cemented as an expression used in the West to describe the line separating the communist world and the free world.

SEE ALSO *Cold War*

BIBLIOGRAPHY

Churchill, Winston. "The Sinews of Peace." The Iron Curtain speech. Westminster College, Fulton, MO, March 5, 1946. https://www.nationalchurchillmuseum.org/sinews-of-peace-iron-curtain-speech.html

Harbutt, Fraser J. *The Iron Curtain: Churchill, America, and the Origins of the Cold War.* New York: Oxford University Press, 1986.

Norweb, Raymond Henry. "R. Henry Norweb to President Harry S. Truman, February 7, 1946." State Department File: 711.41/2-746. National Archives II, College Park, MD.

Ward, Jeremy K. "Winston Churchill and the 'Iron Curtain' Speech." *The History Teacher* 1, 2 (1968): 5–13, 57–63.

James L. Gormly
Professor of History
Washington and Jefferson College

ISLAM

Islam is the world's second-largest and fastest-growing religion, with approximately 1.5 billion followers, including five to six million who live in the United States. Over

80 percent of American Muslims are US citizens; more than a third are African American; and over seventy-seven countries are represented among Muslim American immigrant groups, with significant representation from South Asia, Arab nations, and Africa. Since the nation's founding, American Muslims have contributed to American culture and history in numerous ways. At the same time, they have been shaped by broader political, cultural, and social trends. Like followers of other American religions, US Muslims observe their religion to varying degrees, and observance cannot be adequately captured in such measures as mosque attendance or membership.

The Arabic term *Muslim* designates a person who submits to God. As a global religion, Islam is characterized by diverse practices and beliefs, variously held by Muslims in a range of social, cultural, and political circumstances. At the same time, Islam is ideally understood to transcend the particularities of its adherents, who constitute the *umma*, or the universal community of Muslims. Generally, Muslims embrace the conviction encapsulated in the *shahada*, or declaration of faith: there is no God but Allah, and Muhammad is the messenger of God. This statement affirms monotheism and revelatory prophecy through the line of biblical prophets, culminating in the Qur'an, the final revelation of the Prophet Muhammad ibn Abdallah (c. 570–632). *Hadith*, or the words and deeds of Muhammad, serve as the other scriptural source.

In addition to these texts, Muslims have produced vast textual and artistic traditions. Key rituals include five daily prayers (*salat*), fasting during the month of Ramadan, charity (*zakat*), and the pilgrimage to Mecca (*hajj*). About 90 percent of the global Muslim population identifies as Sunni, while the remaining 10 percent identify as Shiite. Historically, these two groups have differed on the basis of religious leadership and aspects of ritual practice, as well as interpretative and legal approaches to foundational sources.

COLONIAL AND ANTEBELLUM AMERICA

America's encounter with Islam began with the fifteenth- and sixteenth-century efforts of European powers to undermine Muslim dominance in global trade networks through exploration. African Muslims often disrupted prevailing racial and religious categories. They were portrayed as neither wholly African nor Muslim and as potential converts to Christianity. European traders and settlers attempted to rely on African Muslims to advance missionary and commercial aims in Africa, with the hope, largely unsuccessful, of converting Muslims themselves to Christianity. In the antebellum period, several thousand West African Muslims were forcibly brought as slaves. Some were literate and educated, and had participated in transnational networks linking them to other parts of the Muslim world, mainly through Sufi brotherhoods. Through oral history and the limited number of available documents, scholars have begun to reconstruct a dynamic and complex set of beliefs and practices that drew from a range of religious traditions, including Islam, other African religions, and Christianity. Slaves' religious lives were deeply affected by economic and social conditions, leading many to convert to Christianity (GhaneaBassiri 2010, 92–93).

Muslims also figured in early American imaginings about religion and citizenship. Records of deliberations on the US Constitution show how delegates used Muslims as a category in their heated debates surrounding the religious test clause. Delegates referred to Muslims as "Mohammadens" or "Mahotans," an erroneous designation aligning Islam with the worship of or devotion to the Prophet Muhammad. In these debates, as in many American conceptions of Islam, participants understood Islam as a conceptual category through which to grapple with the boundaries and limits of democracy, citizenship, and freedom, rather than considering Muslims as an enduring American religious community (Spellberg 2014).

INDUSTRIALIZATION, NATIONALISM, AND IMMIGRATION

In the post–Civil War era, the United States' rapid industrialization, technological advancements, urbanization, and early imperial projects brought increasing diversity to burgeoning cities, as well as material goods and knowledge of various cultures and faiths, including Islam. European and American colonial ventures also facilitated new cultural and religious contacts. The late nineteenth and early twentieth centuries also saw an increased awareness among white Americans of "other" religions. For many spiritual seekers of the time, Islam was one among many "Eastern" or "Oriental" religions that potentially espoused universal truths that aligned with liberal Protestantism. Muhammad Alexander Russell Webb (1846–1916), a Protestant convert to Islam, the spokesperson for the faith at the 1893 World's Parliament of Religions in Chicago, argued that Islam was compatible with Victorian ideals of reason, progress, and universal brotherhood. At the same time, other academic and popular works portrayed Islam and Muslim societies as sites of corruption, decadence, and sexual intrigue.

By the 1920s, about sixty thousand Muslims had immigrated to the United States, from various parts of the globe. The largest group, identified as Syrians from Levant in the Ottoman Empire, were largely men in search of better economic prospects. Many of these immigrants became familiar with the United States through Protestant missionaries, who established a network of schools in the region during the nineteenth century. In general, these missions failed to produce many converts. Other immigrants arrived during this period from the Balkans, northern India, and Yemen. Faced with discrimination and challenges to achieving full citizenship, these immigrants frequently downplayed their Muslim identity in favor of claiming white ethnicity, which enabled them to fit into the period's recognized hierarchies of religion and race.

Following the abolition of the Ottoman Empire in 1922, American Muslims fostered international networks in the wake of nationalist movements that swept across former Ottoman territories. These organizations promoted forms of belonging within America while also maintaining ties to immigrant homelands. Social service groups, nationalist parties, and ethnic-based organizations brought Muslims together, but at the same time downplayed religion in favor of ethnicity and nationality as the primary form of identity (GhaneaBassiri 2010, 144–164).

The early twentieth century also brought new Islamic movements that appealed to African American communities. One important group was the Ahmadiyya, a South Asian missionary organization founded by Ghulam Ahmad (1835–1908). The Ahmadi leader Muhammad Sadiq (1872–1957) brought to the United States a message of equality among believers across all races. He emphasized the role of Islam in Africa and the idea that Arabic was originally spoken by black people. The Ahmadiyya was one of the first, but by no means the only, transnational Muslim organization to reach out specifically to African Americans in their missionizing efforts.

Narratives of alternative origins also figured prominently in the Nation of Islam, founded in 1930 by Wallace Fard. Instead of positing African origins, Fard's successor, Elijah Muhammad (1897–1975), articulated an origins myth that stressed the Asiatic roots of African Americans. During the 1950s and 1960s, the Nation of Islam espoused a vision for black salvation through the fulfillment of selfhood and the global restoration of black redemption that transcended both connections with Africa and national borders. Its members adopted middle-class practices, displaying values of thrift, modesty, and healthy eating as markers of black Muslim piety. Among the diverse groups active during the civil rights movement, the Nation of Islam advocated for a distinct religious and political program of racial justice and a forceful critique of structural racism in the United States (Curtis 2014, 146–156).

RACE, ETHNICITY, AND INSTITUTIONALIZATION DURING THE COLD WAR

The transnational geographies of the Nation of Islam and other African American Muslim communities also saw important shifts during the mid-twentieth century. Before Malcolm X's (1925–1965) famous pilgrimage to Mecca in 1964, the Nation of Islam minister had cultivated transnational connections with Sunni Muslims, including within such groups as the Muslim World League, an Islamist organization committed to challenging socialist and secular Arab influence, as well as with Islamic revivalists and Muslim scholars in Africa and Asia. As his break with Elijah Muhammad become more pronounced, Malcolm X articulated his goals in terms of global human rights and racial justice. In his last speeches, Malcolm advanced a Pan-Africanist vision and stressed the connections between economic and racial inequality in the United States and anticolonial movements throughout the world.

Elijah Muhammad's son and successor, Warith Deen Mohammed (1933–2008), increasingly sought to bring the Nation of Islam into the Sunni *umma* while also reinvigorating Islamic identity with an affirmation of black ethnicity. This shift was marked by the application of Bilalian to black communities. In the Islamic tradition, Bilal was the first *muezzin*, the person who performs the call to prayer. He was also an emancipated black slave and one of the first converts to Islam. By the 1980s, W. D. Mohammed had embraced America as a site of national belonging for black Sunni Muslims, rather than a place of alienation and exclusion.

With the passage of the Hart-Cellar Act in 1964, large numbers of Muslim students and professionals immigrated to the United States. Their presence ushered in new institution-building efforts that built upon the growth of Islamic institutions established in black communities. Many founders of national Muslim organizations, such as the Islamic Society of North America and the Muslim Students Association, were influenced by what is known as the *global Islamic revival*. These activists emphasized Islam as the most important form of identity. They sought to transcend ethnic and national difference among America's increasingly diverse Muslim population, and worked to promote visible forms of devotion. The 1960s and 1970s saw the growth of mosques across the United States, representing a wide range of ethnic and religious orientations, including major mosques founded by Shi'i communities. Some mosques received funding or have maintained ties to revivalist and Islamist organizations, such as the Tabligh-i Jamaat or Saudi-funded groups. However, most mosques grew out of local communities seeking a place of worship and community. As a result, American mosques reflect the diverse ethnic, racial, theological, socioeconomic, and legal perspectives of their congregants, and serve a wide variety of religious, social, and recreational purposes.

Other American Muslims became more involved in American politics, directing their energies toward lobbying efforts, particularly to combat discrimination and to address the Arab-Israeli conflict. Within academia, the influential Palestinian-American scholar Ismail al-Faruqi (1921–1986) called for the Islamization of knowledge, seeking to invigorate academic inquiry with resources and vocabulary taken from Islamic sources.

The United States' military, economic, religious, and political activities increased considerably in the Middle East after the Second World War (1939–1945). Support for Israel and oil interests led to further US involvement and, at times, escalating tensions with Muslim-majority nations. In the United States, these varied involvements collided to produce a wealth of cultural representations of the "Middle East," Arabs, and Muslims. Popular culture and film tended to conflate Islam with Arab identity and to ignore the lives and experiences of Arab Americans, instead depicting Muslims as members of a foreign and potentially antagonistic group. At the same time, such institutions as the Islamic Center in Washington, DC, represented Cold War assertions of America's role as a protector of all religious faiths and as a global beacon of religious tolerance and diversity, including for Islam.

The 1979 Iranian Revolution constituted a turning point in both expressions of global Muslim identity and American perceptions of Muslims and Islam, especially the association of Islam with violence, particularly terrorism. For American Muslims, as with Muslims globally, the Iranian Revolution further consolidated the importance of Muslim identity and helped to spark increasing religious observance among both Sunni and Shi'i Muslims, including visible signs of Islamic identity, such as the *hijab* or headscarf.

The war in Afghanistan during the 1980s also had significant effects for the political activities of American Muslims. In order to combat Soviet and communist influence, the United States worked with Pan-Islamic and Islamist missionary organizations through its alliance with Saudi Arabia. During the 1980s, American Muslims with varying political and religious ideologies also began to participate more fully in American politics, using the political process as a means to advance the interests of Muslims and to improve their communities, which they saw as an enduring presence in the United States and as making important contributions to American society writ large.

CONTEMPORARY TRANSNATIONAL CONNECTIONS

Through the late twentieth and early twenty-first centuries, American Muslims continued to cultivate transnational affiliations, often through networks of scholars. Shi'i mosques and organizations are often connected to religious authorities and institutions abroad. Many important contemporary Muslim leaders studied with renowned scholars abroad in regions usually associated with Islam, such as the Arabian Peninsula, as well as in other regions that are of importance to Islam but marginal in popular American representations. A prime example is Hamza Yusuf (b. 1960), the dynamic, enormously influential speaker and creator of Zaytuna College in Berkeley, California, who converted to Islam as a young adult. Yusuf cultivated his authority, in part, through his studies with North and West African scholars, especially in Mauritania. He has been instrumental in reviving what he calls "traditional" Islamic education rooted in premodern scholarship to provide contemporary Muslims with exemplary models and a repository of transformative knowledge (Grewal 2013, 305–313).

American Muslims also participate in Sufi orders (known as *tariqas*), which are among the oldest transnational organizations in Islam. Sufism refers to the mystical practices that have historically formed the basis of Islamic piety. One of the most important is the Bawa Muhaiyaddeen Fellowship, which includes Muslim and non-Muslim members, and connects its followers to communities in Sri Lanka and elsewhere. Orders such as the Naqshbandiyya, an influential organization across multiple continents, has established significant institutions in Europe and North America. Finally, the Maryamiyya Order, which blends Sufism and perennialist philosophy, has been enormously influential among prominent scholars of religious studies, including Huston Smith (b. 1919), an expert on comparative religion, and Seyyed Hossein Nasr (b. 1933), a prominent Iranian intellectual (GhaneaBassiri 2010). The Hizmet movement, led by the influential and controversial Turkish figure Fethullah Gülen (b. 1941), has created schools, interfaith institutes, and travel programs for American students under the auspices of the Niagara Foundation.

POST-9/11 CULTURE AND POLITICS

The post-9/11 era resulted in increasing public attention to, and law enforcement surveillance of, Muslim communities, especially those with international connections. The global war on terror and ongoing military campaigns against Islamic militants have reinforced the conflation of Islam and terrorism and erroneous conceptions that Islam is uniquely oppressive. American Muslims have been questioned over their loyalties to the American state, echoing historical scrutiny leveled against Catholics and other religious minorities. In 2010, the planned building of a Muslim community center and mosque, known as Cordoba House, in Lower Manhattan met with intense opposition and bitter debates about the status of Islam in American society, even though the project was led by Feisal Abdul Rauf (b. 1948), an outspoken proponent of interfaith dialogue and author of *What's Right with Islam Is What's Right with America* (2004). The conflict revealed ongoing public suspicion about Islam and Muslims and the persistence of racialized tropes that represent Islam as a foreign religion incompatible with American democracy. Organizations such as the Council on American-Islamic Relations (CAIR) and Karamah (Muslim Women Lawyers for Human Rights) work at the national and international level to address discrimination and prejudice through legal advocacy and lobbying efforts. Racialized representations of Muslims are far from exclusive to the United States, but rather travel through the global circulation of labor and affect Muslim immigrants of varying racial and national backgrounds. Negotiating hierarchies of race, class, and gender figures prominently into how recent immigrants from West Africa, as well as South Asia, navigate their position in American society and construct ties to their homelands (Abdallah 2010, 13; Curtis 2014, 156–166).

The period since 9/11 has also been one of intense institution-building activity among American Muslims, leading to the creation of diverse institutions designed to meet a host of religious, social, and cultural needs of families and local communities, from educational institutions to social service agencies to international relief organizations. American Muslim women have been at the forefront of these initiatives, demonstrating the varied gendered roles among Muslims, and their ongoing negotiation in public and private spaces.

Often lost in the political scrutiny are the contributions Muslims have made to American society in the areas of social justice, culture, sports, and politics. This includes Muslim musicians, such as hip-hop musician Lupe Fiasco (b. 1982); athletes, such as Muhammad Ali (b. 1942) and Kareem Abdul-Jabbar (b. 1947); and many other artists, comedians, journalists, academics, community activists, and professionals negotiating what it means to be an American Muslim, alongside a whole range of other identities, in the early twenty-first century.

SEE ALSO *Afghanistan; Clash of Civilizations (Samuel Huntington); Iran; Iraq; Moorish Science Temple; Nation of Islam; Orientalism; Ottoman Empire; Said, Edward*

BIBLIOGRAPHY

Abdallah, Zain. *Black Mecca: The African Muslims of Harlem.* New York: Oxford University Press, 2010.

Curtis, Edward, IV. *The Call of Bilal: Islam in the African Diaspora.* Chapel Hill: University of North Carolina Press, 2014.

GhaneaBassiri, Kambiz. *A History of Islam in America: From the New World to the New World Order.* New York: Cambridge University Press, 2010.

Grewal, Zareena. *Islam Is a Foreign Country: American Muslims and the Global Crisis of Authority.* New York: New York University Press, 2013.

Hammer, Juliane, and Omid Safi, eds. *The Cambridge Companion to American Islam.* New York: Cambridge University Press, 2013.

Mamdani, Mahmood. *Good Muslim, Bad Muslim: America, the Cold War, and the Roots of Terror.* New York: Doubleday, 2004.

Marr, Timothy. *The Cultural Roots of American Islamicism.* New York: Cambridge University Press, 2006.

McAlister, Melani. *Epic Encounters: Culture, Media, and U.S. Interests in the Middle East since 1945.* Berkeley: University of California Press, 2005.

Spellberg, Denise. *Thomas Jefferson's Qur'an: Islam and the Founders.* New York: Vintage, 2014.

Justine Howe
Assistant Professor
Case Western Reserve University

ISOLATIONISM

Isolationism as a historic attitude in the United States has traditionally been defined as a refusal to participate in wars outside the Western hemisphere, particularly in Europe, along with opposition to binding military alliances and to participation in organizations of collective security. Above all, the isolationist desires to maintain US autonomy and to ensure that the country's freedom of action remains unhindered by the activities of allies. Isolationists differ from pacifists—those who refuse to sanction any conflict, would renounce any war, and withhold backing for any conflict—in that isolationists often favor unilateral military action, or what some call the doctrine of the "free hand." Indeed, some isolationists are stridently nationalistic, and they may endorse military preparations, sanction certain forms of imperialism, or engage in outright war, especially in Latin America or in the Pacific. Most isolationists do not seek literally to "isolate" the United States from the world's culture or commerce.

John Milton Cooper Jr. accurately writes that the word *isolationism* "remains loaded with emotional connotations that present barriers to any analysis" (1969, 1). Proponents of the isolationist position usually reject the label, finding it derogatory. They have long preferred such terms as *neutralist, nationalist, noninterventionist, anti-interventionist, hemispherist,* and *continentalist*—the last term favored by historian Charles A. Beard.

A LONG-STANDING TRADITION

By the above definition, American policy was isolationist until the twentieth century. From 1787, when the US

Constitution was written, through the early twentieth century, the nation pursued an isolationist foreign policy. The stance was articulated in such documents as Thomas Paine's *Common Sense* (1776), which warned that continental ties to Britain tend "directly to involve this continent in European wars"; John Adams's *Model Treaty* (1776), envisioning a purely commercial treaty with France, a proposal the French rejected; George Washington's Farewell Address (1796), advising his countrymen to "steer clear of permanent Alliances"; Thomas Jefferson's First Inaugural Address (1801), in which he sought "peace, commerce and honest friendship with all nations, entangling alliances with none"; and James Monroe's annual message of 1823, in which the fifth president proclaimed the Monroe Doctrine, which announced that the United States should avoid European conflicts.

Of course, a nation may pursue an isolationist foreign policy while involving itself extensively in political and military matters outside its borders. In 1918, the United States fought Britain; in 1846, Mexico; and in 1898, Spain. All such engagements were unilateral decisions by the United States and hence did not violate the classic isolationism espoused in the eighteenth century. During the nineteenth century, the United States encouraged the revolts of Latin American nations against Spain, vied with Britain to control the Oregon Territory, and sympathized with the European revolutions of 1830 and 1848. The United States entered into only one agreement involving joint action with another power, the Clayton-Bulwer Treaty of 1850 with Britain, which limited US action in building a canal across Nicaragua. Toward the end of the century, the United States possessed its own colonies and played a decisive role in reshaping a new military balance in the world. Yet just three months before the outbreak of World War I in 1914, President Woodrow Wilson insisted that the United States should not form alliances with foreign powers. Even in 1917, when the United States entered World War I, it did so as an "associated power" and not as a full-scale partner of the Allies, so as to avoid any obligations that might come from a binding military alliance.

When World War I broke out, isolationists sought to restrict US financial and commercial ties to the Allies, who dominated the seas. The isolationist ranks included socialists, reformers, German and Irish Americans, such manufacturers as Henry Ford, such publishers as William Randolph Hearst, and a number of legislators, often from the Midwest, such as Senators Robert M. La Follette and George W. Norris. Many sought, without success, an impartial arms embargo. They often opposed loans to belligerents and "preparedness" measures, such as the bolstering of the armed forces. They also objected to American citizens traveling on belligerent ships and to President Woodrow Wilson's strident notes to Germany concerning submarine sinkings. When, in February 1917, the United States broke diplomatic relations with Germany, a small group of senators (whom Wilson called "a little group of willful men") filibustered against an armed ship bill, forcing the president to act unilaterally. The president's call on April 2 for war against Germany met with opposing votes from six senators and fifty representatives.

THE INTERWAR PERIOD, 1918–1939

Only when President Wilson sought American entry into the League of Nations did isolationism face its first real challenge and emerge as a distinctive political position. The United States displayed its determination to remain aloof from coercive international bodies when, in 1919 and 1920, the US Senate twice turned down entrance into the League of Nations. Whether the opponents were "irreconcilables" (e.g., Senators William E. Borah and Hiram Johnson), or "strong reservationists" (e.g., Senator Henry Cabot Lodge and former secretary of state and senator Elihu Root), all opposed Article X of the League of Nations Covenant, which pledged members to respect "the territorial integrity and existing political independence" of League members.

The war experience and Wilson's subsequent postwar settlement caused some isolationists to stress America's role as a champion of weak states. Such "peace progressives," as Robert David Johnson (1995) has called them, included Senators Borah, Johnson, La Follette, Norris, John Blaine, Henrik Shipstead, and Burton K. Wheeler. Such figures opposed oil diplomacy in Mexico and US occupation of Nicaragua and Haiti, while favoring radical disarmament, the peace movement, and economic assistance to Germany. By the 1930s, their isolationism had taken a more nationalistic tone, as they sought, above all, insulation from great power conflicts.

Only in the 1930s, when President Franklin D. Roosevelt sought discretionary power to aid victims of aggression, was the general isolationist consensus threatened. In 1934, Congress forbade private loans to defaulting nations and, a year later, Congress voted down membership in the World Court. From 1934 to 1936, Senator Gerald P. Nye chaired the Special Senate Committee Investigating the Munitions Industry (the Nye Committee), which probed the close ties between the United States and Allied military on the one side and arms manufacturers and financiers on the other. The committee focused especially on the industrialist Pierre du Pont and banker J. P. Morgan and the enormous profits they made during World War I. The hearings led to further legislative efforts to avoid the pitfalls by which the United States entered World War I.

From 1935 to 1937, Congress passed a series of bills called the Neutrality Acts. Included was legislation imposing an arms embargo on belligerents once the president declared war. The legislation also prohibited loans and credit to belligerents, and banned Americans from traveling on ships belonging to belligerents. The 1937 law forbade the arming of all merchant ships trading with belligerents and gave the president discretionary authority to sell nonembargoed goods on a "cash-and-carry basis," by which belligerents pay for shipments at the time of purchase and transport all goods in their own vessels.

Even here, however, isolationists were divided. Historian Manfred Jonas (1966) notes that a "belligerent" element—represented by Senators Johnson and Borah and Representative Hamilton Fish—stressed international law and an absolute right to trade. Conversely, a more "timid" group—exemplified by Senators Nye and Arthur Vandenberg—were willing to forego at least some element of foreign commerce.

In January 1938, the House, by a vote of 209 to 188, turned down a constitutional amendment introduced by Representative Louis Ludlow that would have restricted Congress's power to declare war to cases of actual or imminent invasion of the United States or its territories or attack by a non-American nation on a state in the Western Hemisphere. In any other case, Congress would allow voters to choose, by means of a national referendum, whether they wished to go to war.

THE DEBATE OVER WORLD WAR II, 1939–1941

Once Adolf Hitler invaded Poland on September 1, 1939, isolationists fought Roosevelt's interventionist policies without success. In November 1939, Congress voted for military aid to Britain and France on a cash-and-carry basis, thereby repealing the arms embargo. In September 1940, Congress approved military conscription. A year later, Congress approved an extension to the terms of army draftees. In November 1941, Congress repealed cash-and-carry by authorizing the arming of American merchant vessels and by permitting them to carry cargoes to belligerent ports. Acting on his own authority, Roosevelt occupied Greenland (April 1941) and Iceland (July 1941), froze Japanese assets (July 1941), issued a set of war aims with Britain called the Atlantic Charter (August 1941), extended aid to the Soviet Union (October 1941), and entered into an undeclared naval war with Germany (fall 1941). Isolationism was over well before the attack on Pearl Harbor.

The more militant isolationists, who leaned toward an uninvolved stance in World War II, included Senators Nye, Wheeler, Bennett Champ Clark, and Arthur W. Vandenberg, as well as Representative Hamilton Fish, aviator Charles Lindbergh, publishers Hearst and Robert R. McCormick, and elitist theorist Lawrence Dennis. More moderate isolationists favored cash-and-carry and sought to aid Britain without risking war. Such figures included former president Herbert Hoover, business executive and former general Robert E. Wood, and former governor of Kansas Alfred M. Landon.

A number of groups battled against intervention, including the quasi-pacifist National Council for the Prevention of War and the short-lived No Foreign War Committee. In September 1940, the country's major isolationist organization, the America First Committee (AFC), was formed as a clearinghouse for research, lectures, and radio broadcasts. The AFC was founded by Yale law student R. Douglas Stuart, chaired by General Wood, and included in its ranks such figures as Lindbergh, diplomat William R. Castle, former New Dealer and general Hugh Johnson, and advertising executive Chester Bowles. Lindbergh, Nye, Wheeler, financial writer John T. Flynn, Socialist leader Norman Thomas, and Congressman Hamilton Fish addressed huge AFC rallies. At its peak, the AFC had 450 chapters, a membership of 850,000, and an income of $370,000 donated by 25,000 contributors. Although it was unable to defeat any of Roosevelt's legislative proposals, it pushed the president to be more circumspect on such matters as extending draftees' terms and convoying British vessels. Although the president's legislative policies were always supported in the polls, the AFC stressed that nearly 80 percent of the American people, expressing themselves in the same polls, opposed a declaration of war on the Axis powers.

Several leading isolationists endorsed conscription for hemispheric defense, but many more saw little need for a mass army. In isolationist eyes, a new American Expeditionary Force would simply prolong the struggle overseas and cost more than a million US lives. Although most isolationists coupled their foreign policy sentiments with condemnations of Germany and Nazism, they often sought negotiation between England and Germany, fearing above all Soviet domination of Europe. They claimed that Hitler's blitzkrieg tactics had shown that mass armies were obsolete; hence, they called for small, highly mobile volunteer forces. Many feared direct confrontation with Japan, claiming that Japan's actions in China and Southeast Asia were purely Asian matters.

Isolationists differed as to the efficacy of large naval fleets, while strongly stressing air power, which, they claimed, was the most cost-effective way of defending the United States. They argued that while no foreign power was able to conduct continuous bombardment of the nation, the United States could easily pick off any attacking planes. Moreover, a strong air arm was not dependent on untrained conscripts.

Classic isolationism ended on December 7, 1941, with the Japanese attack on Pearl Harbor. After the attack, the AFC promptly disbanded.

THE COLD WAR AND AFTER

During the Cold War, isolationists, though still strong in the Midwest and Great Plains states, met with continual failure. In 1945, the United States became a charter member of the United Nations, occupying a seat on its powerful Security Council. In 1948, the United States launched a massive aid program, the Marshall Plan, and a year later the country entered its first binding military alliance in 171 years, the North Atlantic Treaty Organization (NATO).

With the outbreak in 1950 of the Korean War, which the United States fought under UN auspices, many still opposed collective security but reversed their traditional stance to back the "victory" strategy of General Douglas MacArthur. During the "Great Debate" of 1950 to 1951, financier Joseph P. Kennedy found commitments to Berlin and Korea unwise, while Herbert Hoover claimed that the Americas were still "surrounded by a great moat." The 1948 and 1952 presidential bids of isolationist-leaning Senator Robert A. Taft failed. Such World War I "revisionist" historians as Beard, Charles Callan Tansill, and Harry Elmer Barnes indicted the Roosevelt administration, asserting again that the isolationist position had been the correct one and even at times finding an administration conspiracy behind the Pearl Harbor attack. This time their works did not gain scholarly acceptance. In 1953 and 1954, Senator John W. Bricker proposed a constitutional amendment limiting presidential power, but it was opposed by President Dwight D. Eisenhower and was defeated in the Senate. As a military alternative to NATO, victory over the Soviet Union through air power was espoused by General Bonner Fellers but lacked widespread support.

Furthermore, the "new isolationists," as they were called, were divided. Historian Ted Galen Carpenter (1980) separates them into three categories: (1) *doctrinaire* isolationists, who maintained an absolutist position (e.g., elitist theorist Lawrence Dennis, Senator William Langer); (2) *pragmatic* isolationists, who would modify such institutions as the United Nations and NATO (e.g., Taft, Senator Kenneth Wherry); and (3) *marginal* isolationists, who accepted political commitments but not military alliances (e.g., Hoover, Senator Bricker).

Many Americans opposed participation in the Vietnam War (1965–1975), the Gulf War (1990–1991), the Iraq War (2003–2011), and the Afghan War (2001–2014), and in general called for a curbing of US commitments. Few, however, could be called generic isolationists, though at times they were accused of being such. They did not in principle repudiate overseas military assistance, economic sanctions, membership in collective security organizations, or even the use of combat forces in certain conditions. Since the 1980s, several "neo-isolationist" political scientists (e.g., Earl Ravenel, Andrew J. Bacevich) and historians (e.g., William Appleman Williams, Ted Galen Carpenter) have warned against American messianism and military efforts to impose Western-style democracy upon Third World nations. They describe their position as favoring interest-based policies, strategic disengagement, strategic independence, and national strategy. Remnants of classic isolationism are found in such entities as the Cato Institute, the paleoconservative and libertarian movements, the writings of journalist Pat Buchanan, the editorial staff of *Chronicles* magazine, and the presidential bids of industrialist Ross Perot and Congressman Ron Paul.

SEE ALSO *Internationalism; League of Nations; Paris Peace Conference (1919); Realism (International Relations); Roosevelt, Theodore; Spanish-American War; Wilson, Woodrow; World War I*

BIBLIOGRAPHY

Carpenter, Ted Galen. "The Dissenters: American Isolationists and Foreign Policy, 1945–1954." PhD diss., University of Texas, 1980.

Cole, Wayne S. *Roosevelt and the Isolationists, 1932–45*. Lincoln: University of Nebraska Press, 1983.

Cooper, John Milton, Jr. *The Vanity of Power: American Isolationism and the First World War, 1914–1917*. Westport, CT: Greenwood, 1969.

Doenecke, Justus D. *Not to the Swift: The Old Isolationists in the Cold War Era*. Lewisburg, PA: Bucknell University Press, 1979.

Doenecke, Justus D. *Storm on the Horizon: The Challenge to American Intervention, 1939–1941*. Lanham, MD: Rowman and Littlefield, 2000.

Johnson, Robert David. *The Peace Progressives and American Foreign Relations*. Cambridge, MA: Harvard University Press, 1995.

Jonas, Manfred. *Isolationism in America, 1935–1941*. Ithaca, NY: Cornell University Press, 1966.

Nichols, Christopher McKnight. *Promise and Peril: America at the Dawn of a Global Age*. Cambridge, MA: Harvard University Press, 2011.

Justus D. Doenecke
Emeritus Professor of History
New College of Florida

ISRAEL

Throughout its history, Israel has been linked with the United States in a complex, multifaceted, and sometimes tendentious "special relationship," a relationship that is said to be "irreducible" to any one factor.

The modern history of Israel may be dated from Jewish immigration to Palestine (the Jewish people's biblical "promised land") in the second half of the nineteenth century and the founding of the World Zionist Organization in 1897. The Balfour Declaration (1917) expressed the support of the British government for the establishment of a Jewish national home in Palestine. Jewish immigration and nation-building grew throughout much of the British Mandate (1922–1948), frequently eliciting violent Arab reaction.

The November 1947 United Nations plan to partition Palestine into a Jewish and an Arab state was accepted by the Zionists but denounced by the Arabs, who prepared for war to secure all of Palestine for an Arab state. Between November 1947 and May 1948, the Arabs in Palestine waged a campaign of terror against Jewish communities throughout the country. Civil war ensued as small militant Zionist factions launched violent reprisals against the Arabs and symbols of the British Mandate. Hagana, the Zionist movement's defense force, supported the militant groups in response to escalating Arab violence.

On May 14, 1948, the Jewish state proclaimed its independence. Moments later, the Arab League declared war and five Arab armies invaded, initiating a long and bitter war in which some seven hundred thousand Arabs fled or were expelled from Palestine. Armistice agreements were signed in spring 1949 between Israel and Egypt, Syria, Jordan, and Lebanon. Negotiations for peace treaties were to follow but did not.

After Israel declared its independence, the United States was the first state to grant recognition. Washington withheld arms to all combatants in Israel's War of Independence (1948–1949), but financial aid from the United States (public and private) was vital in facilitating Israel's absorption and resettlement of waves of immigrants and the creation of a modern economy.

In Israel's early decades, the two states developed a diplomatic-political relationship based on the need to maintain the survival and security of Israel while seeking a resolution of the Arab-Israeli conflict. But while they agreed on the general concept, the two sides often differed on the precise means of achieving the desired result.

This dynamic—concurrence on broad principles with disagreement over specific policies or issues—has always characterized the United States' involvement in Israel's history. Vice President Joseph Biden in December 2014 noted that the two countries are able "to speak honestly," and cannot avoid the "normal disagreements that occur between friends."

The US-Israel bilateral relationship grew after the Six-Day War (1967), when a congruence of mutual interests prevailed on many core concerns. The Richard Nixon administration's massive weapons airlift during the Yom Kippur War (1973) initiated very significant levels of US economic and military assistance. There was congruence of interest between Israel's Menachem Begin and President Jimmy Carter at Camp David in 1978, but there was significant tension over Palestinian autonomy.

Israel was viewed by President Ronald Reagan as a strategic asset against Soviet incursion in the Middle East and was designated a "major non-NATO ally." Significant tension existed between Israel's Yitzhak Shamir and President George H. W. Bush over Jewish settlement activity in disputed territories occupied by Israel since the Six-Day War. Yet they cooperated when Iraqi Scud missiles struck Israel during the Persian Gulf War (January–February 1991), as well as at the Madrid Middle East Peace Conference in October 1991.

Yitzhak Rabin and President Bill Clinton shared a close friendship and an understanding of Israel's strategic challenges. Strains in the bilateral relationship reemerged under Benjamin Netanyahu's right-wing Likud government, especially over the pace of Palestinian negotiations. Nevertheless, Israel and the United States in October 1998 concluded an important memorandum of understanding on strategic cooperation concerning weapons of mass destruction and long-range missiles. Positive relations resumed between Clinton and the Labor Party's Ehud Barak. With Barak's concurrence, Clinton expended considerable energy in unsuccessful efforts to broker Israeli-Syrian talks and permanent Israeli-Palestinian peace at Camp David in July 2000.

Despite occasional differences over the al-Aksa intifada that began in September 2000, Ariel Sharon and President George W. Bush concurred on post-9/11 strategic challenges. They also came to agree on Sharon's strategy of unilaterally separating Israelis from their Palestinian Arab neighbors. Bush was the first US president to formally speak about a two-state solution involving Israel and an independent Palestinian state, a state with "new leaders, leaders not compromised by terror" (Bush 2002). Sharon received from Bush letters of understanding concerning two diplomatic issues of core concern to Israel: the "right of return" of Palestinian refugees to Israel, and Jewish settlements in disputed territories occupied by Israel since the Six-Day War. Sharon's successor, Ehud Olmert, pledged at the Annapolis Conference in November 2007 to fulfil Bush's vision of a two-state solution for the Israeli-Palestinian conflict.

Significant tension existed between President Barack Obama and Benjamin Netanyahu (elected again as prime minister in 2009), whose personalities and ideologies clashed. Substantively, there were disagreements over Palestinian diplomacy, as well as tension concerning Iran's nuclear weapons program. Netanyahu disagreed with Obama over the efficacy of sanctions and left on the table the threat of Israeli unilateral military action against Iran should diplomacy and deterrence fail.

Despite these differences, there remained a concurrence between the two governments concerning the broad objective of an Israeli-Palestinian two-state agreement, as well as America's support for Israel's security and survival against all regional adversaries. This was manifested in significant US military assistance and separate additional support for Israel's combat-proven antiballistic missile defense system (elements jointly produced with US contractors).

There also were presidential reassurances. Speaking alongside Netanyahu in March 2012, President Obama encapsulated the special relationship that has bound the two countries throughout Israel's history when he announced, "My personal commitment—a commitment that is consistent with the history of other occupants of this Oval Office … to the security of Israel is rock solid … the United States will always have Israel's back when it comes to Israel's security."

SEE ALSO *American Israel Public Affairs Committee (AIPAC); Arab-Israeli Conflict; Camp David Accords (1978)*

BIBLIOGRAPHY

Biden, Joseph. "Remarks by Vice President Joe Biden to the 2014 Saban Forum." December 7, 2014. http://www.whitehouse.gov/the-press-office/2014/12/07/remarks-vice-president-joe-biden-2014-saban-forum

Bush, George W. "President Bush Calls for New Palestinian Leadership." June 24, 2002. http://georgewbush-whitehouse.archives.gov/news/releases/2002/06/20020624-3.html

Gilboa, Eytan. "US-Israel Mixed Messages on Iran." BESA Center Perspectives Paper No. 181. 2012. http://besacenter.org/perspectives-papers/mixed-messages-the-us-israel-dispute-over-iran/

Gilboa, Eytan, and Efraim Inbar, eds. *US-Israeli Relations in a New Era: Issues and Challenges after 9/11.* New York: Routledge, 2009.

Obama, Barack. "Remarks by President Obama and Prime Minister Netanyahu of Israel." March 5, 2012. http://www.whitehouse.gov/the-press-office/2012/03/05/remarks-president-obama-and-prime-minister-netanyahu-israel

Reich, Bernard. *Securing the Covenant: United States-Israel Relations after the Cold War.* Westport, CT: Greenwood, 1995.

Reich, Bernard, and Shannon Powers. "The United States and Israel: The Nature of a Special Relationship." In *The Middle East and the United States: History, Politics, and Ideologies*, edited by David W. Lesch and Mark L. Haas, 220–243. 5th ed. Boulder, CO: Westview Press, 2012.

Zanotti, Jim. *Israel: Background and U.S. Relations.* Congressional Research Service, Report for Congress. July 14, 2014.

David H. Goldberg
Middle East Scholar
Toronto, Ontario, Canada

ITALY

The complex cultural, economic, human, and political-ideological ties that mark contemporary US-Italian relations developed slowly across two centuries. Culture and limited trade were the primary links between the two peoples prior to the 1880s. Large-scale migration beginning in the 1880s, followed by US-sponsored financial stabilization programs in the early twentieth century, expanded the relationship. Prior to the 1940s, religion played a controversial role in the diplomatic and political relationship. Thereafter, World War II and the Cold War built structures that have supported a long-term partnership.

US-ITALIAN RELATIONS FROM THE COLONIAL ERA TO WORLD WAR I

The American relationship with Italy predates the Revolution. Trade between the American colonies and the Mediterranean states, including those in Italy, grew markedly during the eighteenth century. American elites felt the cultural pull of Italy, and American artists and writers began to take up residence in large numbers in the late eighteenth century, a trend that continued throughout the nineteenth century (Amfitheatrof 1980). Shortly after the War of 1812, the United States stationed a naval force in the Mediterranean to protect its expanding commerce. The Italian states were frequent ports of call for both US warships and merchant vessels (Field 1969; Lambert 2005). Interest in the American Revolution (1775–1783) was widespread among Italian elites (Venturi 1989). One of Italy's reforming monarchs, Pietro Leopoldo of Tuscany (r. 1764–1790), utilized American models in a never-realized project for a Tuscan constitution. Virginia neighbors Filippo Mazzei (1730–1816) and Thomas Jefferson (1743–1826) developed business plans while sharing Enlightenment culture. Mazzei acted as Virginia's secret representative in Europe, purchasing arms to defeat the British and lobbying Pietro Leopoldo to invest in his new homeland (Marchione 1994).

The ideological impact of the American Revolution lessened in the wake of the French Revolution. Italy's rulers returned to power after Napoléon Bonaparte's defeat in 1815, imposing a restrictive political order. The Catholic Church, Italy's most influential cultural institution, vigorously condemned the ideas that formed the basis of American politics: constitutionalism, republicanism, tolerance, and representative government. The domestic liberal-nationalist opponents of the Restoration largely found inspiration in France's revolution. With the exception of Giuseppe Garibaldi (1807–1882) and Carlo Cattaneo (1801–1869), few Italian democrats found American democracy attractive (Lovett 1982; Riall

2007). The Italian states suppressed Protestant missionary activity because it mixed religious and political messages that challenged their hold on the masses. Ironically, papal Rome offered a tolerant, avant-garde setting in which American artists and writers flourished (Hawthorne [1860] 2012). Wealthy Americans also frequented Italy's major artistic and cultural centers.

During the fifty-five years that separated Italy's unification (1859–1860) from its entry into World War I in 1915, the diplomatic relationship between the United States and the kingdom of Italy became more complex. The Italian state encouraged and facilitated the passage of millions of Italians to the United States to hold down its population growth and lessen social unrest (Tomasi and Engel 1970). The cash remittances a growing Italian emigrant community sent home became a critical element in Italy's balance of trade. The United States and Italy clashed over xenophobic treatment of these migrants. During and after World War I, US loans first supported the Italian war effort, and, in the later 1920s, they facilitated postwar economic and political stabilization under Fascism. Direct American investment in Italy faced formal and informal trade barriers. However, alone among the European powers, Italy paid off its World War I debts (Migone 2015).

RELIGION, MIGRATION, AND THE RISE OF MUSSOLINI

Under Benito Mussolini (1883–1945), Italy ramped up its profit-making tourist industry. American elites, while normally contemptuous of Italian immigrants, were delighted to spend heavily in Grand Tour cultural enrichment. The American passion for ancient Rome and Renaissance Italy often complemented a lack of interest in the achievements and problems of modern Italy. Mussolini aggressively promoted Italian culture and claimed to be Italy's great modernizer. American elites responded enthusiastically to a regime that restrained migration and disciplined Italians' "natural" tendency to "anarchy." They ignored Fascist violence, its authoritarian character, and Mussolini's utilization of the Italian American community to influence US foreign policy. The US government supported the Mussolini myth. Republican administrations provided financial assistance in order to fold Italy into their postwar European stabilization programs (Diggins 1972).

Religion and migration remained major disruptive factors in the relationship. Throughout the nineteenth and early twentieth centuries, the identification of the American Republic with Protestantism was strong (Wood 2015). Fearing that the Holy See would manipulate expanding Catholic migration to subvert democracy, and ignoring the American Catholic Church's enthusiastic promotion of assimilation, US Protestants tended to focus on the condemnation of American values contained in the *Syllabus of Errors*, issued by Pope Pius IX (1792–1878) in 1864 and reiterated by Pius X (1835–1914) in the early twentieth century.

The Great Depression (1929–1939) undercut US influence with Mussolini by ending American financing of European stabilization. In the mid-1930s, Italy invaded Ethiopia, allied with Nazi Germany, embraced economic autarchy, and rejected US efforts to promote economic recovery through expanded trade.

INCREASING US INVOLVEMENT IN ITALIAN AFFAIRS DURING WORLD WAR II

World War II (1939–1945) led to a dramatic turn in the Italian-American relationship. During the period of US neutrality (1939–1941), the Franklin Roosevelt (1882–1945) administration, failing to win Italian cooperation for its peacemaking efforts, initiated economic warfare against Italy and suppressed Fascist activities among Italian Americans. Japan's December 1941 attack at Pearl Harbor, and Italy's immediate declaration of war on the United States, led to major, unexpected, American involvement in Italy's internal affairs. Winston Churchill (1874–1965) successfully nudged the United States into participation in a Mediterranean military campaign that led to the 1943 landings on Sicily and the Italian peninsula. Initially, the British dominated Italian affairs, but Washington assumed major responsibility for the political and economic reconstruction of Italy as a bankrupt and manpower-strapped British Empire's power faded between 1944 and 1945 (Ellwood 1977).

The reasons for greater US involvement were both domestic and diplomatic. Roosevelt believed that the "Italian vote" was critical to his winning a fourth term as president. In 1942, he pledged that Italy would enjoy the right to determine its postwar government and would be treated differently than a defeated Germany and Japan. He then removed restrictions on Italian aliens residing in the United States. As the 1943 invasion progressed, Roosevelt initiated aid programs for Italy, while including American Italians in these operations and in the occupation regime (Hersey 1944; Malaparte 2013; Burns 2004).

The Catholic vote was another element in Roosevelt's planning. Beginning in 1939, the president built bridges to the Vatican, sending a "personal envoy," Myron Taylor (1874–1959), to Rome (Di Nolfo 1980). Pope Pius XII (1876–1958) turned to the American Church to extract more economic assistance from the US government and to focus Americans on the threat of the Italian Communist Party (Partito Comunista Italiano, or PCI). As the 1944 presidential election approached, Roosevelt rolled out a

"New Deal for Italy" that included increased economic assistance and expanded authority for the Italian government, and the United States replaced Britain as Italy's primary foreign reference. The Catholic Church and the Italian American community successfully mobilized voters for Roosevelt (Miller 1986).

COUNTERING ITALIAN COMMUNISM DURING THE COLD WAR

The Cold War led to an expansion in US involvement in Italy. Americans found competent interlocutors among Italian center parties, above all the Christian Democrats, and forged a short-lived but effective alliance with the Holy See that insured the basic precondition for a successful aid program: its management by a stable and representative government.

The Cold War in Europe was as much about countering national communist movements as it was about the Soviet threat. The size and ambitions of the PCI worried Italy's center, center right, and reformist left, who suspected that the PCI was playing a "double game" aimed at creating a Soviet-style workers' state. Washington's nightmare was a communist victory in a democratic election. The PCI enjoyed enormous prestige and support as a result of its role in the wartime resistance. The party also enjoyed heavy Soviet financing and possessed a battle-tested paramilitary capability. Italian economic recovery was frustratingly slow, providing the left with a wedge issue. To block a communist-led government "short of war," the United States deployed its economic, diplomatic, and psychological tools in support of the center parties in Italy's April 1948 elections (Mistry 2014).

The center's election victory did not resolve the Italian problem. During the next three decades, American policy involved supporting the center parties, inducing defections from the left, and integrating Italy into emerging European economic and defense structures. Italy's 1948 constitution mirrored Italian and European experiences, emphasizing the role of the central government in group interests and public welfare. Successive governments accepted a large communist sphere, a sort of state within the state, at the local level and in unionized sectors of the economy as part of the price for internal peace. This *compromesso all'italiana* (compromise Italian-style) worked to the benefit of all, including the United States (Rizas 2012).

Italy's economy recovered, and by the mid-1950s the country was in the midst of a long-term boom. Overcoming the turbulence that marked the late 1960s and early 1970s, Italy became a prosperous society struggling to free itself from the dominance of its political parties and the Catholic Church (Del Pero 2001; Nuti 1999). In the 1990s, party dominance collapsed, and the Bill Clinton administration drew the curtain on the Cold War, accepting the former communists' membership in Italy's government.

BUILDING DURABLE US-ITALIAN TIES

Durable institutional ties between Italy and the United States emerged in the postwar period. Military cooperation, information sharing, joint training exercises, and staff education programs instilled confidence and common value sets. NATO, a political-military project, guaranteed the stability of democratic regimes against internal threats and created mechanisms for continuous state-to-state exchanges on a range of political, economic, and military issues, including intelligence sharing. Since the 1980s, Italy has sent its military into operations in Lebanon, the Balkans, Iraq, and Africa, frequently in partnership with the United States (Miller 1992).

While Americans and Europeans face barriers to direct investment in Italy, Italian companies, such as Fiat and the smaller producers of food, wines, textiles, shoes, and other luxury goods, as well as advanced aeronautics, have prospered in the US market. Applying monopoly practices, Luxottica has conquered the US and world eyewear sector. Americans' fascination with Italy's art, culture, cuisine, and fashion continues, as does Italians' interest in US cultural production. Italy ranks right behind France as the favorite destination of American travelers. American tourism and reciprocal Italian visits are a source of economic development for both countries and reinforce existing cultural ties between the two nations (Miller 2002).

The United States used its power with persistence to construct a new international system. Italy joined multinational initiatives like the United Nations, the Marshall Plan, the World Bank and International Monetary Fund (IMF), the Commission on Security and Cooperation in Europe (CSCE), the Organization for Security and Co-operation in Europe (OSCE), the World Trade Organization (WTO), the Group of Seven (Eight) and Group of Twenty, and the Organization for Economic Cooperation and Development (OECD). Italy rejected much of its own historical past, abandoning the use of force, accepting the loss of its small and costly colonial empire, playing an important role in the first stages of European integration, aligning with the other major democracies, and attempting to play an active role in international affairs (Ortona 1984–1989).

Italians continue to migrate in small numbers and usually integrate into US society without the mediation of the Italian American community. From sports to courts, from literature to the sciences, in politics and diplomacy, Italian Americans made major contribution to the United States while they entered a new environment characterized less by ethnic identity than economic status (Puzo 2004).

The close US-Vatican alliance of the 1940s and 1950s gave way as the Catholic Church moved away from its identity as a European-centered and Eurocentric religion. On issues of social justice, the Holy See aligned more with the economically developing states. Pope John Paul II's (1978–2005) challenge to the Soviet empire and the establishment of formal diplomatic relations between the United States and the Holy See in 1983 masked a restructuring of the American hierarchy that brought the US Catholic Church into line with the pope's traditionlist agenda (Reese 1996).

The US-Italian relationship has endured in spite of intergovernmental clashes over sovereignty and murky intelligence "scandals." Experience taught American policy makers that the legitimacy of democratic Italy's government rested on the exercise of its sovereignty. Italian groups critical of Italy's American connection have failed to offer a realistic alternative for a middle-size power that needs to guarantee its security and advance its interests through participation in a solid system of international organizations (Galli della Loggia 2003).

SEE ALSO *Americanization; Catholicism; Immigration; Protestantism; Roosevelt, Franklin D.; United Nations; Whiteness; World War I; World War II*

BIBLIOGRAPHY

Amfitheatrof, Eric. *The Enchanted Ground: Americans in Italy, 1760–1980.* Boston: Little Brown, 1980.

Burns, John Horne. *The Gallery.* New York: New York Review of Books, 2004. First published 1947.

Del Pero, Mario. *L'alleato scomodo: Gli USA e la DC negli anni del centrismo (1948–1955).* Rome: Carocci, 2001.

Diggins, John P. *Mussolini and Fascism: The View from America.* Princeton, NJ: Princeton University Press, 1972.

Di Nolfo, Ennio. *Vaticano e Stati uniti, 1939–1952.* Milan, Italy: Feltrinelli, 1980.

Ellwood, David W. *L'alleato nemico: La politica dell'occupazione anglo-americana in Italia, 1943–1946.* Milan, Italy: Feltrinelli, 1977.

Field, James A., Jr. *America and the Mediterranean World, 1776–1882.* Princeton, NJ: Princeton University Press, 1969.

Galli della Loggia, Ernesto. *La morte della patria: La crisi dell'idea di nazione tra Resistenza, antifascismo e Repubblica.* Bari, Italy: Laterza, 2003.

Hawthorne, Nathaniel. *The Marble Faun.* Cambridge, MA : Belknap Press of Harvard University Press, 2012. First published 1860.

Hersey, John. *A Bell for Adano.* New York: Knopf, 1944.

Lambert, Frank. *The Barbary Wars: American Independence in the Atlantic World.* New York: Hill and Wang, 2005.

Lovett, Clara M. *The Democratic Movement in Italy,* 1830–1876. Cambridge, MA: Harvard University Press, 1982.

Malaparte, Curzio. *The Skin.* Translated by David Moore. New York: New York Review of Books, 2013. First published 1949 in Italian.

Marchione, Margherita. *Philip Mazzei: World Citizen (Jefferson's "Zealous Whig").* Lanham, MD: University Press of America, 1994.

Migone, Gian Giacomo. *The United States and Fascist Italy: The Rise of American Finance in Europe.* Translated by Molly Tambor. New York: Cambridge University Press, 2015.

Miller, James Edward. *The United States and Italy, 1940–1950.* Chapel Hill: University of North Carolina Press, 1986.

Miller, James Edward. *La politica estera di una media potenza.* Bari, Italy: Laicata, 1992.

Miller, James Edward. *Politics in a Museum: Governing Postwar Florence.* Westport, CT: Praeger, 2002.

Mistry, Kaetan. *The United States, Italy, and the Origins of Cold War: Waging Political Warfare, 1945–1950.* New York: Cambridge University Press, 2014.

Nuti, Leopoldo. *Gli Stati uniti e l'apertura a sinistra.* Bari, Italy: Laterza, 1999.

Ortona, Egidio. *Anni d'America.* 3 vols. Bologna, Italy: Mulino, 1984–1989.

Outram, Dorinda. *The Enlightenment.* 3rd ed. New York: Cambridge University Press, 2013.

Puzo, Mario. *The Fortunate Pilgrim.* New York: Random House, 2004. First published 1964.

Reese, Thomas J. *Inside the Vatican: The Politics and Organization of the Catholic Church.* Cambridge, MA: Harvard University Press, 1996.

Riall, Lucy. *Garibaldi: Invention of a Hero.* New Haven, CT: Yale University Press, 2007.

Rizas, Sotiras. *The Rise of the Left in Southern Europe: Anglo-American Responses.* London: Pickering and Chatto, 2012.

Tomasi, Silvano M., and Madeline H. Engel, eds. *The Italian Experience in the United States.* New York: Center for Migration Studies, 1970.

Venturi, Franco. *The End of the Old Regime, 1768–1776: The First Crisis.* Translated by R. Burr Litchfield. Princeton, NJ: Princeton University Press, 1989.

Wood, Gordon. "A Different Story of What Shaped America." *New York Review of Books,* July 9, 2015, 27–29.

James Edward Miller
Independent Scholar
Washington, DC

J

JACKSON, ANDREW

1767–1845

Andrew Jackson offered Americans in the 1830s a wide-ranging vision of continental and global expansion. His support for the policy of Indian removal resulted in the Indian Removal Act of 1830, which relocated almost fifty thousand southern Indians to lands west of the Mississippi River. Native American affairs were the purview of the War Department, and during the James Monroe (1758–1831) administration, John C. Calhoun (1782–1850) developed the concept of trading eastern for western lands. The Indians negotiated various treaties through the 1820s, but because moving to Arkansas, Oklahoma, and Kansas remained voluntary, only a small number chose to comply. The agricultural boom of the era, however, prompted white settlers to threaten Indian lands, and violence loomed large.

The 1830 legislation left the tribes without the assistance or protection of the federal government and under the control of the various states. With the reality of removal facing them, some Indians resisted. The Cherokee sought relief in the US Supreme Court, where they won support in 1832 as "dependent nations" free from state law. The Seminoles skirmished with US troops in the scrub pine of Florida in the Second Seminole War (1835–1842). In the Midwest, the Fox and Sac Indians also fought back, resulting in a crushing defeat in the Black Hawk War (1832) on the Illinois-Iowa border. All opposition proved futile. Ultimately, the army assembled the tribes and escorted them by boat and on foot across the Mississippi River. Most of the eastern Indians were removed by 1840, often accompanied by tragedy. The most memorable incident, during the Martin Van Buren (1782–1862) presidency, remains the legendary Cherokee "Trail of Tears" in 1838, with the loss of four thousand lives. "Old Hickory" (as Jackson was called), who often emerges as the primary villain in the process, championed removal following his campaign against the Creek Indians of Alabama during the War of 1812 and after his invasion of Florida during the First Seminole War of 1818. As president, he and a Democratic Congress enforced a long-standing policy. The responsibility for the fate of the eastern Indians should be shared with several other administrations and, significantly, white Americans who coveted Native American lands at any cost.

Jackson aggressively steered his foreign policy. He pursued the annexation of Texas and parts of California as key elements of domestic expansion. In 1829, he boldly instructed his minister to Mexico to offer $5 million for Texas. He also sought to add valuable farmland, provide security for the southwest border and the Gulf of Mexico, and supplement territory for Indian removal. A perfect storm of divisive Mexican politics, a bungling American diplomat in Anthony Butler (1787–1849), and the brewing revolt among Anglo settlers in Texas doomed the purchase. A similar fate befell California, as the Mexicans rejected an offer of $500,000 for San Francisco Bay, an acquisition that would have benefited both Far Eastern merchants and the fishing industry.

These territorial failures did not discourage Jackson from dispatching emissaries worldwide to negotiate commercial treaties to enhance the profits of American farms and factories. Diplomats signed agreements with old European powers such as Great Britain, Russia, and Turkey, as well as with the emerging nations of Mexico,

LYNCOYA

White adoption of Indian children was not unheard of in the early Republic, but a case involving Andrew Jackson remains noteworthy. "Old Hickory" (as Jackson was called) was unapologetic in his views that Native Americans were not equal to whites. He had dealt with them since his boyhood in the Carolinas, however, and developed a paternalistic respect for them and their culture. Even so, Jackson's adoption of an Indian infant seems remarkable, given his legendary reputation as a bold and brutal military chieftain in his contests with the Creeks of Alabama (1813–1814) and the Seminoles of Florida in 1818.

Jackson's complex relationship with Native Americans is most revealing in his dispatch of three Indian boys to the Hermitage, the Jackson home in Nashville, Tennessee, c. 1813. The general and his wife, Rachel (1767–1828), were childless, and Jackson sent home a boy named Theodore, who sadly died in early 1814. Jackson also dispatched Charley to Nashville, intended for his young ward, Andrew Jackson Donelson (1799–1871). Charley reached the Hermitage in March and stayed with Rachel and their adopted son Andrew Jr. (1808–1865) until Lyncoya (c. 1812–1828) arrived. Lyncoya was an infant brought to Jackson on the bloody battlefield at Tallushatchee in Alabama in November 1813. His mother had been killed, he had no relatives, and none of the Creek women would care for him, so Jackson had him sent back to the Hermitage. No doubt the rejected orphan stirred painful memories. The general saw the possibility of divine intervention and confided to Rachel, "When I reflect that he as to his relations is so much like myself, I feel an unusual sympathy" (Cheathem 2013, 80).

Lyncoya's upbringing has been the subject of some controversy. The general instructed that he be educated and welcomed as a member of the family. Jackson provided the child with private tutors and enrollment at Cumberland College in Tennessee. West Point seemed ideal, but Jackson's appeal for Lyncoya's admittance during the administration of recent foe John Quincy Adams (1767–1848) was denied. At home, Andrew Jr. claimed that his mother thought highly of Lyncoya and treated him very well. Even so, he had difficulty adjusting to plantation life and attempted to run away several times to the Creek Nation. Jackson referred to him as "a lost sheep without a shepherd" (Cheathem 2013, 80) and was saddened that he chose to spend time with the slaves. By 1827, Lyncoya had decided to become a saddler and was apprenticing in Nashville when he contracted a winter cold so severe that he took a leave and sought the healing powers of the Hermitage. Rachel nursed him with diet and medicine, but Lyncoya grew steadily weaker and died on June 1, 1828, likely of tuberculosis, several months before his seventeenth birthday.

His death devastated Rachel, who never recovered and expired herself six months later. Gauging Jackson's affections for Lyncoya is more difficult. There is mention of him as "a favorite son" (Remini 1981, 194), and during Old Hickory's frequent absences from Nashville, he often inquired about and encouraged the child. "Tell Lyncoya I expect him to be a good boy" (Brands 2005, 381), he admonished Rachel. Jackson makes no mention of Lyncoya's passing, however, in his letters.

BIBLIOGRAPHY

Brands, H. W. *Andrew Jackson: His Life and Times.* New York: Doubleday, 2005.

Cheathem, Mark R. *Andrew Jackson: Southerner.* Baton Rouge: Louisiana State University Press, 2013.

Remini, Robert V. *Andrew Jackson and the Course of American Empire, 1767–1821.* New York: Harper & Row, 1977.

Remini, Robert V. *Andrew Jackson and the Course of American Freedom, 1822–1832.* New York: Harper & Row, 1981.

John M. Belohlavek
Professor of History
University of South Florida

Chile, Venezuela, and Peru-Bolivia in Latin America. Imaginative and resourceful, Jackson sent New England sea captain Edmund Roberts (1784–1836) on a secret mission (1832–1834) to explore possible agreements in Asia. Americans had engaged in the China trade since the 1780s, but Jackson had wider ambitions. Roberts reinforced those notions when he returned with treaties signed by officials in Siam and Muscat on the Red Sea. An enthused Roberts sailed on a second mission in 1835 with the intent of opening ties with Cochin China (Vietnam) and Japan, but he died of cholera in China in June 1836 before he could complete his new assignment. Jackson also joined the Senate in promoting a trans-isthmian route across Central America. The mission of Charles Biddle

(1788–1836) to Colombia in 1835 produced a treaty, but one that reflected the self-interest of the agent's company, and it was rejected by the president.

Jackson asserted American nationalism by sending the frigate *Potomac* to punish the Sumatran "pirates" who attacked a US pepper trader in 1831. More broadly, he demanded and received funds from Spain, Naples, Portugal, and Denmark for claims resulting from damages done to American shipping during the Napoleonic Wars. When the French delayed payment of an agreed-upon $4.6 million, a tense situation resulted, bringing about saber rattling and tough talk before calmer heads prevailed.

In sum, Jackson successfully removed the Indians, expanded trade, garnered respect for the flag, and obtained payment of outstanding debts, but at a cost to the Native Americans and his own reputation.

SEE ALSO *Cherokee Nation v. Georgia (1831); Indian Removal Act (1830); War of 1812*

BIBLIOGRAPHY

Belohlavek, John M. *"Let the Eagle Soar!": The Foreign Policy of Andrew Jackson.* Lincoln: University of Nebraska Press, 1985.

Brands, H. W. *Andrew Jackson: His Life and Times.* New York: Doubleday, 2005.

Cheathem, Mark R. *Andrew Jackson: Southerner.* Baton Rouge: Louisiana State University Press, 2013.

Heidler, David S., and Jeanne T. Heidler. *Indian Removal.* New York: Norton, 2007.

Meacham, John. *American Lion: Andrew Jackson in the White House.* New York: Random House, 2008.

Remini, Robert V. *Andrew Jackson and the Course of American Empire, 1767–1821.* New York: Harper & Row, 1977.

Remini, Robert V. *Andrew Jackson and the Course of American Freedom, 1822–1832.* New York: Harper & Row, 1981.

Satz, Ronald N. *American Indian Policy in the Jacksonian Era.* Lincoln: University of Nebraska Press, 1975.

Van Every, Dale. *The Disinherited: The Lost Birthright of American Indian.* New York: William Morrow, 1966.

John M. Belohlavek
Professor of History
University of South Florida

JACKSON, MICHAEL
1958–2009

Born in the gritty midwestern steel town of Gary, Indiana, at the cusp of the civil rights movement, Michael Jackson became one of the most influential artists of the twentieth century and among the most recognizable figures in the world. Following his death in 2009 at the age of fifty, vigils were held from Los Angeles to Tokyo, Moscow to Rio de Janeiro. His memorial was watched by an estimated one billion people, more viewers than tuned in to observe the funeral of former US president Ronald Reagan.

THE JACKSON 5 YEARS

Jackson first rose to fame as the talented young lead singer of the Jackson 5, a musical group made up of Jackson and his four older brothers, Jackie, Jermaine, Tito, and Marlon. Marketed by Motown Records, America's premier black label, as "crossover" pop with a dose of funk and soul, the group became the first act in American history to have their first four singles—"I Want You Back," "ABC," "The Love You Save," and "I'll Be There"—reach number one on the Billboard Hot 100. Adorned in their trademark flower-power outfits and halo afros, the Jackson 5 made breakthrough appearances on *The Ed Sullivan Show*, *The Tonight Show Starring Johnny Carson*, and *American Bandstand*. They were also featured in their own Saturday morning cartoon series on ABC. By 1972, the Jackson brothers were playing sold-out concerts throughout Europe, including a Royal Variety Performance attended by Queen Elizabeth of England. By the mid-1970s, Jacksonmania had spread to Africa, South America, Japan, Australia, the Philippines, and the West Indies, as the group sold over fifty million records and racked up seventeen Top 40 hits.

EARLY SOLO CAREER

It was Jackson's career as a solo artist, however, that saw him become an international icon. During filming of the musical *The Wiz* (1978) in the late 1970s, Jackson teamed up with legendary producer Quincy Jones, who had previously worked with such talents as Frank Sinatra, Count Basie, Duke Ellington, and Ray Charles. Jackson and Jones assembled an A-Team of musicians and songwriters that included Stevie Wonder, Paul McCartney, and Rod Temperton, and began recording. The resulting effort, *Off the Wall* (1979), became the best-selling album to date by an African American artist. It also produced four Top Ten hits, a record at the time for a solo album.

The breakthrough success of *Off the Wall* was followed by the phenomenon of *Thriller* (1982). Arriving at the beginning of the Reagan era in the midst of a deep recession, *Thriller* changed the way music was consumed, heard, and seen, helping resurrect the music industry in the process. *Thriller*'s release fortuitously coincided with the emergence of the Sony Walkman, the compact disc (CD), cable television (including MTV), the era of the blockbuster in Hollywood cinema, and globalization, all forces that helped propel it to unprecedented heights. But it was Jackson's unique genre-blending music, innovative short films, and intriguing persona that took advantage of these forces. By early 1984, *Thriller* had spent a record thirty-seven weeks at number one, produced a record seven Top Ten hits, and become the best-selling album in rock 'n' roll history, both in the United States and globally.

CULTURAL IMPACT, INTERNATIONAL POPULARITY, AND CHARITABLE WORK

Thriller helped break down numerous racial, cultural, and national barriers. In the United States, *Thriller*'s singles and videos challenged and ultimately changed racially exclusionary programming on radio and MTV. In apartheid-ridden South Africa, it was the country's best-selling album of 1983. In the Soviet Union, meanwhile, at the height of the Cold War, Jackson's album was secretly swapped by young people in the form of bootleg cassettes. Jackson would later become the first major American artist to appear in commercials and perform in Russia following the fall of the Soviet Union. Jackson also became the first American pop star to appear on television in China in the 1980s.

In the wake of *Thriller*, all of Jackson's subsequent albums sold far more internationally than they did in the United States. His post-*Thriller* career also saw a heightened social consciousness and political activism. In 1985, the humanitarian anthem "We Are the World," cowritten by Jackson and Lionel Richie, became the fastest-selling single in history and the vehicle driving the charity effort USA for Africa. Featuring such artists as Stevie Wonder, Diana Ross, Bob Dylan, and Bruce Springsteen, "We Are the World" raised an estimated $60 million for famine relief in Ethiopia, Tanzania, and the Sudan.

In 1992, Jackson created the Heal the World Foundation, named after his 1991 anthem, "Heal the World." The foundation opened offices around the world, dedicating money and resources to address famine, poverty, disease, and war relief, among other causes.

Musicians Stevie Wonder, Aretha Franklin, Michael Jackson, and Diana Ross (front, left to right), celebrating the inauguration of President Bill Clinton, Washington, DC, January 1993. *In the 1980s Jackson's career began to reflect a heightened social consciousness and political activism. He performed the song "Gone Too Soon," which he had released on World AIDS Day, at President Bill Clinton's inaugural gala to garner support and funding for AIDS research.* CYNTHIA JOHNSON/LIAISON/HULTON ARCHIVE/GETTY IMAGES

The following year, Jackson released the single "Gone Too Soon" on World AIDS Day; he also performed the song at President Bill Clinton's inaugural gala to garner support and funding for AIDS research. In 1995, Jackson's *HIStory* album included two of his most significant global protest songs: "They Don't Care about Us," a salvo against racism and oppression (two short films were created for the song by American director Spike Lee, one of which was filmed in an impoverished favela in Rio de Janeiro, Brazil), and "Earth Song," an apocalyptic blues-operatic plea against social and environmental destruction that reached number one in fifteen countries.

In his final decades, media attention focused far less on Jackson's creative work, and more on scandal and controversy, including his physical appearance, childlike behavior, sexuality, and other perceived eccentricities. In 1993 and again in 2003, Jackson became the subject of international headlines when allegations surfaced of child molestation. After an exhaustive trial covered by more than two thousand reporters from at least thirty-five countries, Jackson was acquitted of all charges in 2005.

Jackson has been named the most charitable pop star in history by Guinness World Records, giving an estimated $500 million dollars to humanitarian organizations throughout his life. Since his death in 2009, he has consistently topped lists of top-earning deceased global icons. In spite of the controversy and scandals that plagued his final years, Jackson remains a beloved figure across the world who transcended borders of race, class, and nation.

SEE ALSO *Dylan, Bob; Presley, Elvis Aaron; Rock 'n' Roll; USA for Africa ("We are the World")*

BIBLIOGRAPHY

George, Nelson. *Thriller: The Musical Life of Michael Jackson.* New York: Da Capo Press, 2010.

Martin, Sylvia J. "The Roots and Routes of Michael Jackson's Global Identity." *Society* 49, 3 (2012): 284–290.

Stevens, Hampton. "Michael Jackson's Unparalleled Influence." *Atlantic*, June 24, 2010.

Vogel, Joseph. *Man in the Music: The Creative Life and Work of Michael Jackson.* New York: Sterling, 2011.

Joseph Vogel
Instructor
University of Rochester

JAPAN

The United States and Japan have had one of the closest and most complicated bilateral relationships in the world. The two nations first encountered one another in the mid-nineteenth century, and, following an era of imperialist competition, fought fiercely in the Asia-Pacific arena of World War II. In the postwar era, the two countries forged a close alliance that was unprecedented, to a degree that Mike Mansfield, the then–US Ambassador to Japan, declared in 1989 that it was the "most important bilateral relationship in the world." However, with changing international and regional environments in the post–Cold War era, the US-Japanese relationship has been changing.

Roughly speaking, the history of US-Japanese relations can be divided into four phases: (1) the formative years following the two nations' first encounter in the second half of the nineteenth century; (2) imperialist rivalry and clashes in the first half of the twentieth century; (3) US occupation of Japan and the tightening of the Cold War alliance in the second half of the twentieth century; and (4) diversification and redefinition of the relationship in the post–Cold War era.

THE FORMATIVE YEARS

The formative years of US-Japanese relations should be understood in terms of the broader historical contexts of the first half of the nineteenth century: the extension of European colonialism in East Asia, and westward movement and expansionism in the United States. Britain's Opium War with China (1839–1842) provided a timely opportunity to bring an American presence to East Asia. After the war, US delegations secured most-favored-nation status, which gave Americans the commercial and legal privileges Britain had obtained, and this set the stage for US commercial expansion in the region. This was also the era of "manifest destiny." With victory in the Mexican-American War (1846–1848), the United States obtained vast territories in the American Southwest and West, leading many Americans to look even further westward, beyond the Pacific.

Against this backdrop, President Millard Fillmore (1800–1874) sent a special mission to Japan. Although Japan had maintained extensive commercial relations with Holland and China, a series of visits by Commodore Matthew C. Perry (1794–1858) in 1853 and 1854 "opened" Japan for Americans. In the first visit, Perry's warships sailed into Uraga Bay near Edo (Tokyo), where he handed Japanese officials President Fillmore's letter, which outlined US demands for securing trade agreements, setting up coaling stations for US ships, and obtaining assurances for the safe treatment of shipwrecked American sailors. This first visit, however, was more ritualistic than substantial because Japanese officials were reluctant to engage in communications.

Perry's second visit was more productive. This time, acutely aware of the outcome of the Opium War, the

Japanese were more receptive, accepting the Treaty of Kanagawa (1854), in which Japan agreed to assist shipwrecked Americans, but continuing to avoid broad commercial relations. Eventually, in 1858, Townsend Harris (1804–1878), the first resident American diplomat to Japan, concluded a genuine commercial treaty. Thus the foundation for the relationship between the two countries was set before the outbreak of civil wars in both countries in the 1860s.

Beyond this official relationship, many private citizens contributed to broadening American-Japanese relations. For example, a number of Americans, such as William Elliot Griffis (1843–1928), William Smith Clark (1826–1886), and Leroy Lansing Janes (1838–1909), lived in Japan in the 1870s and taught science, agriculture, and Western thought and Christianity at local schools. Likewise, many Japanese, including Nakahama Manjiro (1827–1898), Niijima Jo (1843–1890), and Tsuda Umeko (1864–1929), studied in the United States and became educators in Japan. Niijima and Tsuda established new American-style schools, predecessors of the present Doshisha University and Tsuda College, respectively. In addition to these direct interactions, increasing communications deepened cultural understandings, which can be observed, for instance, in the beginning of a "Japonism" movement among American and European artists, as well as the rise of "American fever" in Meiji Japan. Such cultural interactions, in turn, provided chances to reconsider traditional worldviews in each society. According to Joseph Henning (2000), such interactions with Japan challenged conventional American assumptions about previously unquestioned hierarchies concerning race, religion, and civilization.

IMPERIALIST RIVALRY AND THE US-JAPANESE WAR

In the first half of the twentieth century, the two countries' relationship became tense, leading eventually to a war that cost millions of lives. Interestingly, Washington and Tokyo generally maintained a friendly, or at least cooperative, relationship during most of this period. President Theodore Roosevelt (1858–1919), for instance, took the trouble to mediate the Russo-Japanese War (1904–1905), resulting in the Portsmouth Treaty (1905). At the same time, Secretary of War William H. Taft (1857–1930) and Prime Minister Katsura Taro (1848–1913) agreed in a memorandum on Japan's influence in Korea and the US influence in the Philippines. A similar agreement in 1908 between Elihu Root (1845–1937), US secretary of state, and Takahira Kogoro (1854–1926), the Japanese ambassador to the United States, recognized Japan's dominance in Korea and Manchuria and US interests in Hawai'i and the Philippines.

Even after the clash over China in the 1910s, Washington and Tokyo maintained cooperative attitudes through the 1917 Lansing-Ishii agreement, under which Japan pledged dedication to America's Open Door policy, while the United States acknowledged Japan's special interest in China. This cooperative relationship reached its zenith at the Washington Disarmament Conference (1921–1922), which resulted in a number of key treaties aimed at maintaining peace in Asia.

Yet, US-Japanese relations began to deteriorate during this period. Administrators in both countries agonized less over diplomacy than domestic politics and social problems at home—namely, racism and anti-Asian immigrant feelings in the United States and anti-American sentiments in Japan. One of the earliest events that contributed to the deterioration of the two countries' relations was the San Francisco School Board's decision in 1906 to expel Japanese and Korean students from all public schools in the district, which stirred up a storm of indignation in Japan. Similar reactions were provoked by the Alien Land Law in California (1913), which prohibited Japanese from owning land, and the 1924 Immigration Act, which effectively prohibited Asian immigration to the United States. In all of these cases, anti-Japanese feelings in the United States and anti-American sentiments in Japan developed rapidly, leading to the broad circulation of war-scare literature in both countries.

In the 1930s, US-Japanese relations worsened rapidly. The Great Depression that began in 1929 hit the Japanese economy hard. The crisis was especially severe for Japanese farmers, whose products, such as silk and rice, suddenly lost their export markets after high tariffs were imposed by panicking governments across the world. It was during this period that Manchuria, a region in northeast China, came to be seen as Japan's "lifeline." After signing imperialistic agreements with Russia and the United States following the Russo-Japanese War, Japan had been expanding its dominance, particularly in the southern part of Manchuria, and had been relying on Manchuria for food, raw materials, and trade.

Although the Japanese government had been maintaining a moderate and cooperative policy toward the West, a group of ambitious officers in the Kwantung Army in Manchuria had their own plan. They saw this moment of crisis during the Depression as an opportunity to secure Japan's political and economic position in Manchuria; thus, in September 1931, they blew up tracks on the Japanese-owned Manchurian railway near Mukden (Shenyang) and announced that it was the work of Chinese military forces. Japan used this incident as a pretext to attack Chinese army forces, separating Manchuria from China and founding the puppet state of Manchukuo in March 1932. When the United States issued the so-called Stimson Doctrine (1932) of nonrecognition, and when the League of Nations similarly took a stance of nonrecognition, Japan harden its attitude and walked out of the league.

Nonetheless, it is misleading to view the two countries as from this moment plunged headlong into war. In fact, most Americans, including President Herbert Hoover (1874–1964), saw no vital US interests in Manchuria. Even with the outbreak of the Sino-Japanese War in July 1937 and the notorious Nanjing massacre in December of that year, Washington's official policy remained ambivalent. It was not until 1940 to 1941, when Japan expanded its war into French Indochina and simultaneously attacked Kota Bharu in British Malaya and Pearl Harbor in Hawai'i, that Washington reacted decisively. In its first six months, the war unfolded with swift, dramatic victories for the Japanese, who occupied an area from the Philippines to Singapore and Burma and to the islands of the Central and South Pacific. The turning of the tide came quickly, however, in mid-1942 in a naval battle near the Midway Islands, followed by a series of US victories, culminating in the dropping of two atomic bombs, on Hiroshima and Nagasaki, and the surrender of Japan in August 1945.

US OCCUPATION AND THE TIGHTENING OF THE COLD WAR ALLIANCE

After the war, the United States occupied Japan from 1945 to 1952. Americans, under the control of the Supreme Commander of Allied Powers (SCAP), General Douglas MacArthur (1880–1964), had two main purposes in the occupation of Japan: demilitarization and democratization. Firstly, the SCAP dissolved the Japanese army and navy, purged two hundred thousand men considered responsible for the war from public offices, and held trials in which six thousand military men were tried, with nine hundred executed.

Secondly, the SCAP sought to reform Japan's society and economy through democratization. The background for this reform was American officials' belief that Japanese militarism stemmed from the illnesses of traditional Japanese society, such as monopoly, tyranny, and poverty. Thus, to construct a peaceful nation, Japan had to do more than disband its military. In this sprit, the SCAP conducted a rapid series of reform projects, including securing political and civil rights, emancipating women, promoting labor activism, and implementing land reform. Many of these programs, however, were checked or canceled as the Cold War climate spread in East Asia in the late 1940s and early 1950s. Eventually, the Chinese Revolution in 1949 and the Korean War that began in 1950 convinced Washington to conclude a peace treaty with Japan and make it an ally against communism. In September 1951, the San Francisco Peace Treaty was signed, followed by the US-Japan Security Treaty.

From the 1950s through the 1980s, the United States and Japan maintained a close alliance. Yet, while it is often considered a peaceful and harmonious partnership, US-Japanese relations in this period were full of negotiations, conflicts, and even violent clashes. In the 1950s, for example, when Japan's economy and society recovered from the devastation of the war, Japanese demands for an equal relationship increased. In particular, many Japanese resented the continued presence of US military forces in their territory. These protests, combined with opposition to the Security Treaty, reached their zenith in 1960 when the pact came up for renewal. Thousands of Japanese took to the streets and protested the US-Japanese alliance. Although the treaty itself was renewed, Prime Minister Kishi Nobusuke (1896–1987) was forced to resign. Deeply concerned about the situation, President Dwight Eisenhower (1890–1969) attempted to bolster conservative elements in Japanese politics by secretly funding the ruling Liberal Democratic Party.

The background for the United States' support for Japan during this period was the increase in US involvement in Asia, notably in Vietnam. Japan was the first non-Western nation to "succeed" in modernizing itself, and thus it served as a model for modernization and development projects in other Asian countries. Put simply, Japan became a public relations weapon in Cold War battles against communism. Therefore, throughout the 1960s, the John F. Kennedy (1917–1963) and Lyndon B. Johnson (1908–1973) administrations attached great importance to Japan, emphasizing an equal partnership between the two countries. In fact, Washington was more receptive to Japan's demands during the peak of the Cold War and the Vietnam War than at any other time. One of the most contentious issues at that time was the return of Okinawa and the Bonin Islands to Japanese control. Washington was keenly aware of the volatile nature of the Okinawa issue and feared that it could lead to the fall of the pro-American government of Prime Minister Sato Eisaku (1901–1975). Thus the Bonin Islands and Okinawa were returned to Japan in 1968 and 1972, respectively.

Another volatile issue involved the "economic war" between the United States and Japan in the 1970s and 1980s. By the time Richard Nixon (1913–1994) took office in 1969, the US trade deficit with Japan was growing, and it continued to grow in subsequent decades. The primary focus in terms of trade was on textiles in the 1970s and electrical and automotive products in the 1980s. In both cases, the Japanese offered better products at lower prices, which caused a slowdown of the US economy and a rise in unemployment. Some Americans blamed Japan, with interest groups and lobbyists pressuring Congress to pass high tariffs to protect American goods. The Japanese government tried to stem such moves by voluntarily setting limits on key exports. With frustrations mounting by the mid-1980s, commentators in both countries began using extreme, aggressive, and even racist rhetoric. Such economic conflicts continued into the early 1990s.

REDEFINITION OF THE US-JAPANESE RELATIONSHIP IN THE POST–COLD WAR ERA

Since the mid-1990s, the nature of US-Japanese relations has changed radically. After all, the close bilateral relationship between the two countries was primarily a product of the Cold War. During most of that period, Japan was the only industrialized and democratized nation in Asia, and, thus, was valuable as a model for modernization in the non-Western world. By the end of the Cold War, however, Japan was no longer the only such nation. Moreover, with the end of the Cold War, Japan's geopolitical significance changed, even though the seeds of regional conflict remain in East Asia.

Furthermore, in September 1995, American servicemen's kidnapping and rape of a twelve-year-old Japanese girl in Okinawa raised concerns about the meaning of the US-Japanese security alliance. Protests against the presence of the US military in Japan swelled rapidly throughout the country. In order to contain the situation, President Bill Clinton and Prime Minister Hashimoto Ryutaro (1937–2006) agreed in 1995 to reduce the size of US bases in Okinawa, including a plan to relocate Marine Corps Air Station Futenma, even though, as of 2015, this plan had not been implemented.

In the early twenty-first century, the US-Japanese relationship was once again in the limelight due to Prime Minister Koizumi Junichiro's support for President George W. Bush during the Iraq War. Yet with fundamental changes in international and regional environments, including the end of the Cold War, the decline of the Japanese economy, and the rising Chinese economy, the US-Japanese relationship has undergone a change. Observing recent developments, Jeremi Suri forecast in 2014 that the special bilateral partnership would become a "looser regional relationship with neighboring countries involved," and that relations in upcoming decades would be "more distant and multilateral," with "more independence, more compromise" (Suri 2014).

In the social and cultural arenas, however, there have been much closer interactions between Americans and Japanese since the mid-twentieth century, as manifested in the popularity of Japanese anime, manga, and novels in America, as well as the popularity of baseball and Hollywood films in Japan. To borrow Andrew McKevitt's words, American and Japanese grassroots fans of these products of popular culture have engaged in the processes of cultural globalization and created "local, non-elite communities that envisioned a world of cultural interconnectedness" (2010, 894).

SEE ALSO *Internment Camps; League of Nations; Manhattan Project; Paris Peace Conference (1919); Roosevelt, Eleanor; Roosevelt, Franklin D.; Self-Determination; Shinto; Treaty of Versailles; United Nations; Universal Declaration of Human Rights; Wilson, Woodrow; World War I; World War II*

BIBLIOGRAPHY

Auslin, Michael R. *Negotiating with Imperialism: The Unequal Treaties and the Culture of Japanese Diplomacy, 1858–1872.* Cambridge, MA: Harvard University Press, 2004.

Auslin, Michael. *Pacific Cosmopolitans: A Cultural History of U.S.-Japan Relations.* Cambridge, MA: Harvard University Press, 2011.

Dickinson, Frederick R. *World War I and the Triumph of a New Japan, 1919–1930.* New York: Cambridge University Press, 2013.

Dower, John W. *War without Mercy: Race and Power in the Pacific War.* New York: Pantheon, 1986.

Dower, John W. *Embracing Defeat: Japan in the Wake of World War II.* New York: Norton, 2000.

Funabashi, Yoichi. *Alliance Adrift.* New York: Council on Foreign Relations, 1999.

Guthrie-Shimizu, Sayuri. *Transpacific Field of Dreams: How Baseball Linked the United States and Japan in Peace and War.* Chapel Hill: University of North Carolina Press, 2012.

Havens, Thomas R. H. *Fire Across the Sea: The Vietnam War and Japan, 1965–1975.* Princeton, NJ: Princeton University Press, 1987.

Henning, Joseph M. *Outposts of Civilization: Race, Religion, and the Formative Years of American-Japanese Relations.* New York: New York University Press, 2000.

Hirobe, Izumi. *Japanese Pride, American Prejudice: Modifying the Exclusion Clause of the 1924 Immigration Act.* Stanford, CA: Stanford University Press, 2001.

Iriye, Akira. *Across the Pacific: An Inner History of American–East Asian Relations.* New York: Harcourt, Brace, Jovanovich, 1967.

Iriye, Akira. *Pacific Estrangement: Japanese and American Expansion, 1887–1911.* Cambridge, MA: Harvard University Press, 1972.

Kawamura, Noriko. *Turbulence in the Pacific: Japanese-U.S. Relations during World War I.* Westport, CT: Praeger, 2000.

Kitamura, Hiroshi. *Screening Enlightenment: Hollywood and the Cultural Reconstruction of Defeated Japan.* Ithaca, NY: Cornell University Press, 2010.

Koikari, Mire. *Pedagogy of Democracy: Feminism and the Cold War in the U.S. Occupation of Japan.* Philadelphia: Temple University Press, 2008.

Koshiro, Yukiko. *Trans-Pacific Racisms and the U.S. Occupation of Japan*. New York: Columbia University Press, 1999.

Kovner, Sarah. *Occupying Power: Sex Workers and Servicemen in Postwar Japan*. Stanford, CA: Stanford University Press, 2012.

LaFeber, Walter. *The Clash: A History of U.S.-Japan Relations*. New York: Norton, 1997.

Masuda, Hajimu. "Rumors of War: Immigration Disputes and the Social Construction of American-Japanese Relations, 1905–1913." *Diplomatic History* 33, 1 (2009): 1–37.

Masuda, Hajimu. "Fear of World War III: Social Politics of Japan's Rearmament and Peace Movements, 1950–3." *Journal of Contemporary History* 47, 3 (2012): 551–571.

McKevitt, Andrew C. "'You Are Not Alone!': Anime and the Globalizing of America." *Diplomatic History* 34, 5 (2010): 893–921.

Miller, Jennifer M. "Fractured Alliance: Anti-Base Protests and Postwar U.S.-Japanese Relations." *Diplomatic History* 38, 5 (2014): 953–986.

Sasaki-Uemura, Wesley. *Organizing the Spontaneous: Citizen Protest in Postwar Japan*. Honolulu: University of Hawai'i Press, 2001.

Schaller, Michael. *The American Occupation of Japan: The Origins of the Cold War in Asia*. New York: Oxford University Press, 1985.

Schaller, Michael. *Altered States: The United States and Japan since the Occupation*. New York: Oxford University Press, 1997.

Shibusawa, Naoko. *America's Geisha Ally: Reimagining the Japanese Enemy*. Cambridge, MA: Harvard University Press, 2006.

Spector, Ronald. *Eagle against the Sun: The American War with Japan*. New York: Vintage, 1985.

Suri, Jeremi. "On This Pearl Harbor Anniversary, Our Relationship with Japan Is Changing Again." *Houston Chronicle*, December 6, 2014.

Thorne, Christopher G. *The Issue of War: States, Societies, and the Far Eastern Conflict of 1941–1945*. New York: Oxford University Press, 1985.

Masuda Hajimu
Department of History
National University of Singapore

JAY, JOHN
1745–1829

John Jay is often remembered for his contribution to the new American nation's legal and constitutional order, as an author of the *Federalist Papers* (1787–1788), and as first chief justice of the US Supreme Court. He should, however, also be remembered as one of the most active and significant of the new American republic's foreign diplomats. He proved instrumental in establishing the newly independent nation's place in relation to European powers throughout his career, serving both in foreign policy posts in the United States and as a diplomat in Europe.

FOREIGN AFFAIRS

Elected to the Continental Congress from his home state of New York, Jay soon took an active role in its business. In 1778, Congress elected Jay its president. In this role, Jay dealt with foreign affairs, especially relations with allied France. To gain further support, Congress sent Jay in 1779 as the nation's first minister to Spain (and third ambassador to Europe, after Benjamin Franklin [1706–1790] and John Adams [1735–1826]), with the instruction to procure a Spanish alliance and gain much-needed funds. Despite his best efforts, Jay had little success in Spain, as the Spanish Court was uninterested in an American alliance and was too financially strapped itself to provide much beyond what Jay needed to avoid financial embarrassment. After the Battle of Yorktown (1781), Congress sent Jay to Paris to work with Franklin and Adams on the peace treaty with Great Britain. Here, Jay shouldered a great deal of the negotiating responsibility. He and Adams agreed in pursuing a diplomatic strategy meant to secure American national interest without deferring to the French foreign minister, the Comte de Vergennes (1717–1787). They thus established a separate peace with Great Britain, which gained the United States recognition of independence and territory to the Mississippi River.

Returning to the United States after both sides had confirmed the peace treaty, Jay was quickly returned to Congress. Congress soon elected him to be secretary of foreign affairs, the only executive position in the Confederation government and the one charged with dealing with foreign powers. In this role, Jay witnessed the weakness of the American government, especially as it related to other nations. Because Congress did not have the power to tax, it could not repay foreign debts; because Congress did not have power over the states, the states were violating terms of the peace treaty, mistreating both Loyalists and Indian tribes. For these reasons, Jay was much concerned to promote a new form of government through the 1787 Constitution. His experience of national weakness in relating to foreign powers had demonstrated to him the need for an energetic, efficient national government to deal with international affairs. During this time, Jay also carried on negotiations with Don Diego de Gardoqui (1735–1798), a Spanish diplomat. Spain controlled New Orleans at the time, and Jay considered—though did not implement—a plan to prohibit American navigation on the southern Mississippi for twenty-five years in exchange for a Spanish trade treaty. Still, as word of the negotiation spread, Jay's actions planted suspicion among

Portrait of John Jay. *One of the most active and significant of the new American republic's foreign diplomats, Jay served both in foreign policy posts in the United States and in Europe and was instrumental in establishing the nation's place in relation to European powers.* © EVERETT HISTORICAL/ SHUTTERSTOCK.COM

southerners, who wondered if the national government had their best interests at heart.

SUPREME COURT

With the establishment of the new Constitution, President George Washington (1732–1799) appointed Jay as the first chief justice of the Supreme Court. Even in this role, Jay remained engaged with foreign policy questions. In Court rulings such as *Glass v. Sloop Betsey* (1794), he strengthened the administration's stance of neutrality. In his grand jury charges, he often lectured on the citizens' responsibility to support the national government against foreign influences. His opposition to foreign influence was most apparent in his hostility toward Citizen Edmond-Charles Genêt (1763–1834), the Jacobin ambassador to the United States. In pursuing France's interest in its recently begun war with Great Britain, Genêt hoped to prod the United States from its stance of neutrality, and he threatened to appeal over President Washington's head to the people to achieve his goals. Jay, along with Federalist Rufus King (1755–1827), worked to stop Genêt's mission and negate his influence.

JAY TREATY

Because Jay's knowledge and skill in international affairs were well recognized, he was a logical choice for Washington to select when the need came for a special envoy to Great Britain in 1794. Britain, due to its war with France, had begun to stop American ships to impress sailors and seize cargo bound for France. Additionally, other disputed issues remained from the end of the American Revolution, including British troops still on American soil in the Northwest Territory and the lack of trade opportunities in the Caribbean. As hostilities grew, war became a very real possibility, and Washington sent Jay to London to avert it. Although Jay was negotiating from a position of weakness vis á vis Great Britain, he obtained a treaty, the Jay Treaty, which scholars have subsequently concluded was the best possible. It did not end impressment, but it did remove British troops from American territory and opened up several Caribbean ports for American trade. Although the treaty provoked a strong reaction from Democratic-Republicans, Jay was confident in the peace he had secured—which would last until 1812.

Returning to New York, Jay learned he had been elected the state's governor. Even this position involved him in foreign affairs, as he had to prepare the state's coastal defenses during the Quasi-War with France from 1797 to 1798. He retired from public life in 1801 but continued to pay close attention to foreign affairs.

ASSESSMENT

Throughout his time in diplomatic service, Jay found himself representing a young, weak republic contending with much more powerful European states. Accurate assessments of the situation and shrewd maneuvering characterized Jay's diplomacy. He practiced a realistic, rather than an ideological, diplomacy. Both his cultural and religious sensibilities predisposed him to friendliness with Great Britain, especially after American independence was recognized and the French Revolution grew more violent. Even so, he was guided throughout by the primacy of his search for American national interest. The result of his diplomatic activity was to keep America out of unnecessary foreign conflicts and strengthen the fledgling nation's economic and strategic position, so that it could defend itself against European powers and pursue its republican nation-building in peace.

SEE ALSO *Adams, John; American Revolution; Franklin, Benjamin; Jay Treaty (1795); Jefferson, Thomas; Washington, George*

BIBLIOGRAPHY

Den Hartog, Jonathan. *Patriotism and Piety: Federalist Politics and Religious Struggle in the New American Nation.* Charlottesville: University of Virginia Press, 2015.

Monaghan, Frank. *John Jay: Defender of Liberty against Kings and Peoples.* New York: Bobbs-Merrill, 1935.

Morris, Richard. *The Peacemakers: The Great Powers and American Independence.* New York: Harper and Row, 1965.

Stahr, Walter. *John Jay: Founding Father.* New York: Hambledon and London, 2005.

Jonathan Den Hartog
Associate Professor of History
University of Northwestern–St. Paul, Minnesota

JAY TREATY (1795)

The Jay Treaty was a treaty signed between the United States and the United Kingdom, negotiated by the American John Jay (1745–1829) in 1794 and ratified by the US Senate the following year. The treaty improved Anglo-American relations, strengthened the nation's stance of neutrality, and allowed the new nation further time to establish itself without going to war against a European power. It simultaneously sparked intense partisan activity domestically, helping to define the emerging two-party system of Federalists and Democratic-Republicans.

The conflict with Britain developed both from unresolved long-term issues dating to the American Revolution and from more immediate problems arising from Britain's recently declared war with France. The greatest issue remaining from the Revolution was the presence of British troops still stationed on American soil, in the Northwest Territory. From these forts, the British were able to supply Indian tribes who were attacking American settlers on the frontier. Additionally, the countries continued to dispute payments due on both sides, with the British demanding American repayment of property seized from Loyalists and the Americans demanding reimbursement for slaves freed or carried off by the retreating British. Then, with the outbreak of the Anglo-French conflict in 1793, Britain decided to enforce its naval dominance. They seized American ships sailing for French ports (even though the Americans were flying a neutral flag) and began to impress American sailors. With such growing tensions, President George Washington (1732–1799) decided in 1794 to send Jay, the chief justice of the US Supreme Court, as his minister plenipotentiary to negotiate a treaty that would resolve these issues.

Arriving in Britain later in 1794, Jay immediately set to work to craft a treaty of mutual benefit. In this, he primarily worked with British foreign secretary William Grenville (1759–1834). Jay was able to convince the British that America did not want war and that a mutually advantageous treaty would head off conflict. The result was the "Jay Treaty," completed by the end of the year. The treaty guaranteed withdrawal of British troops from frontier posts. It also opened a few British West Indies ports to American shipping. In regard to seized American shipping, it agreed to a joint commission to reimburse wrongly seized shipping, although it did not end the practice of seizing ships trading with France. It did not remove British taxes on American goods, although it encouraged the importation of British goods into America. It also tacitly accepted continued British impressment of American sailors. Since Britain and France were at war, the treaty could be interpreted as a repudiation of the Franco-American alliance of 1778, although Jay did not believe it did so. Jay was clearly bargaining from a position of weakness, but the treaty was likely the best he could have negotiated. Jay expressed his contentment with the result as he sent it back to America.

Arriving in the United States, the treaty received a stormy welcome. The Jay Treaty was the first significant treaty to arise under the new Constitution, and Americans disagreed on how it should be handled. Washington thought senatorial "advice and consent" might only mean asking the Senate's opinion of ratification. Once submitted to the Senate, though, the treaty met much opposition from Democratic-Republicans, especially those from the South. The treaty was ratified by a single vote (twenty to ten). The next year, the Democratic-Republicans attempted to forestall its implementation by denying it funding in the House of Representatives, an endeavor that also failed. As these political processes were going on, Democratic-Republicans launched a popular campaign of opposition, channeled through their newspaper operatives. In this campaign, Jay was vilified as a slave to England, which continued the oppression for which Americans had fought the revolution. Meanwhile, the French were celebrated, and the treaty was denounced for standing in the way of Americans supporting the French Revolution.

In an early moment where international affairs shaped American domestic politics, then, the Jay Treaty debate helped polarize American politics and draw distinctions between the Federalists, who supported President Washington's stance of neutrality, and the Democratic-Republicans, who retained hostility to Great Britain and favored more support for France and its revolution. Despite the popular protest, the treaty was approved and did guarantee for Americans a greater range of options for relating to other Atlantic powers. It strengthened the policy of neutrality favored by both President Washington and his successor John Adams (1735–1826). It bought the United States greater time to grow, expand its foreign commerce, and develop its national identity and capacities, preserving peace until the outbreak of the War of 1812.

SEE ALSO *Adams, John; Jay, John; XYZ Affair*

BIBLIOGRAPHY

Bemis, Samuel Flagg. *Jay's Treaty: A Study in Commerce and Diplomacy*. Rev. ed. New Haven, CT: Yale University Press, 1962.

Combs, Jerald. *The Jay Treaty: Political Battleground of the Founding Fathers*. Berkeley: University of California Press, 1970.

Den Hartog, Jonathan. *Patriotism and Piety: Federalist Politics and Religious Struggle in the New American Nation*. Charlottesville: University of Virginia Press, 2015.

Estes, Todd. *The Jay Treaty Debate, Public Opinion, and the Evolution of Early American Political Culture*. Amherst: University of Massachusetts Press, 2006.

Jonathan Den Hartog
Associate Professor of History
University of Northwestern–St. Paul, Minnesota

JAZZ

When America's segregated regiments landed in France during World War I (1914–1918), so did jazz. The leader of the all-black, two-thousand-soldier Fifteenth New York Regiment's marching band, Lieutenant James Reese Europe (1881–1919), was a famous bandleader before America entered the war. Army officials—all white—soon saw that playing ragtime music, which was popular at home, would boost American morale and win French friends to whom the music was new. Though the music played by official bands was not jazz, with no room for improvisation, it was filled with jazzlike riffs and rhythms that impressed British, French, and Italian bandmasters and audiences alike.

THE POPULARIZATION OF AMERICAN JAZZ IN EUROPE

Private jazz tours and performances flourished in Europe during the interwar period. This was especially true in France, with influential American jazz artists, including Sidney Bechet (1897–1959) and Josephine Baker (1906–1975), moving to Paris during the 1920s. When Duke Ellington (1899–1974) and his orchestra traveled to Europe in March 1939, they were more popular there than at home. Adoring crowds greeted them in Le Havre, Brussels, Antwerp, The Hague, Utrecht, Amsterdam, Copenhagen, Stockholm, and Paris. Germany, however, already barred jazz and black foreigners. When Ellington's train was delayed in Hamburg, Nazi troops prevented the men from getting off even to stretch their legs.

When America returned to the battlefields during World War II (1939–1945), so again did jazz, this time primarily in the form of swing. With many male musicians drafted, all-women bands toured the United States to help sell war bonds and, by October 1942, *Down Beat* ran a regular column called *Killed in Action*. Benny Goodman (1909–1986) and many others volunteered for the USO and produced special recordings, known as "V Discs," for those stationed overseas. Artie Shaw (1910–2004) led a navy band that toured the South Pacific, performing for troops desperate for a taste of home and even enduring seventeen attacks by Japanese planes.

In Germany—where even the word *jazz* was outlawed—jazz became a powerful symbol of resistance. In Nazi-occupied Paris, musicians gave famous American jazz songs new French titles so they could continue playing them. Jazz proved so popular that in 1942 German propaganda minister Joseph Goebbels (1897–1945), who called jazz subhuman, decided to co-opt it, ordering the organization of a radio swing band that reworded familiar American songs with new, antisemitic lyrics. Young German fans, however, continued defying the Gestapo, secretly listening to forbidden records and Allied radio. It was not until the Cold War, though, that the US government used jazz—not ragtime or swing—as a diplomatic tool.

JAZZ DIPLOMACY DURING THE COLD WAR

The US government transmitted a powerful, political message about racial equality in America by supporting the broadcast and live performance of jazz music overseas. Beginning in 1956, the State Department declared that it would use jazz as a tool to combat communism. That year, it sent international superstar Dizzy Gillespie (1917–1993) abroad as a "goodwill ambassador," an honorific title denoting a figure sent to promote the ideals of one nation in another. The State Department also began broadcasting Willis Conover's (1920–1996) jazz program overseas on the Voice of America (VOA). The *New York Times* described jazz, which was rooted in black American culture, as America's "secret sonic weapon" during the Cold War (Belair 1955, 1). As historian Penny von Eschen put it, jazz "suddenly became America's music," and black

A 1958* New Yorker *Cartoon by Mischa Richter. *The original caption reads: "This is a diplomatic mission of the utmost delicacy. The question is, who's the best man for it—John Foster Dulles or Satchmo?" The debate at the table—who would be the best man for a delicate mission of diplomacy, the secretary of state or jazz musician Louis Armstrong?—highlights the influence and power of jazz as an American export during the Cold War period.* LIBRARY OF CONGRESS, PRINTS AND PHOTOGRAPHS DIVISION.

American jazz musicians became "critical to the music's potential as a Cold War weapon" (2004, 3).

The heyday of so-called jazz diplomacy coincided with the American civil rights movement, the decolonization of Africa and Asia, and, of course, the cultural and political rivalry between the United States and the Soviet Union. Jazz diplomacy began as soon as Washington began exporting jazz, and it lasted through the late 1960s. The export of national culture by governments in an effort to win allies and ease differences was central to the Cold War efforts.

President Dwight Eisenhower (1890–1969) was particularly attuned to the psychological aspects of the conflict, and under his leadership Washington's attention to cultural diplomacy grew. The perception that American culture was predominantly materialistic during its post–World War II economic boom led even America's allies in Europe to eschew American culture as inferior. This perception grew increasingly problematic as Moscow championed its own cultural diplomacy, selling its national intellectual ideas, technology, art, and literature overseas in order to influence and attract other peoples. In the mid-1950s, the US government increased its support for cultural activities abroad, including radio programs, libraries, concerts, and plays that highlighted American achievements. Initial efforts, however, were much like those of Moscow and the European capitals, including overseas productions of ballets and symphonies.

THE REAL AMBASSADORS

From 1961 to 1962, jazz pianist and composer Dave Brubeck (1920–2012) and his wife Iola (1923–2014), a lyricist, wrote the satirical musical *The Real Ambassadors* in collaboration with Louis Armstrong (1901–1971), who starred as a fictionalized version of himself as an American goodwill ambassador in the fictional African nation of Talgalla. The authors drew on their real-life experiences traveling abroad on behalf of the US State Department. Though tasked with demonstrating the positive and unique aspects of American culture to foreign audiences, Brubeck, Armstrong, their bands, and others like them were private American citizens sent to perform on behalf of the US government.

The Real Ambassadors focused on the ambivalent relationship between official State Department representatives and these private performers, and the question of who truly represented America. The fictional Armstrong's ideas are shown to deviate from those of the US government over the course of the show. He is warned by the government before his departure for Africa, "When you travel in a far-off land / Remember, you're more than just a band./You represent the USA / So watch what you think and do and say" (Von Eschen 2004a, 83). When he arrives in Talgalla, he is mistaken for the US ambassador. Confusion ensues when the actual ambassador arrives days later. Although Armstrong clarifies that he is not the ambassador, he challenges the authority of the US government, singing "I'm the real Ambassador! / It is evident I wasn't sent by the government to take your place / All I do is play the blues and meet the people face to face" (Von Eschen 2004a, 88).

The show highlighted the divisive issue of racial discrimination. The juxtaposition of sharp words and sentiment with simple melodies mirrored the irony of the US government sending black musicians overseas to demonstrate American democracy and equality at a time when Jim Crow policies remained thoroughly entrenched. As was the case in real life, the fictional Armstrong did not always heed what the government wanted him to represent. For instance, Armstrong had publicly denounced Dwight Eisenhower's initial refusal to intervene in the 1957 school-desegregation crisis in Little Rock, Arkansas, stating "the way they are treating my people in the South, the Government can go to hell." Following Eisenhower's intervention in Arkansas, which Armstrong thought was "just wonderful," Armstrong declared that he would rather play in the Soviet Union than in the state where Governor Orval Faubus "might hear a couple of notes—and he don't deserve that" (Von Eschen 2004a, 63–64).

The show also satirized American actions in developing nations. Talgalla is described as "the newest of new African

Unlike other expressions of culture, jazz, popularized by American troops and through privately financed performances during and after the two world wars, was recognized around the world as uniquely American. Many jazz proponents asserted that it stimulated freedom, which the American government touted as a defining factor of American identity. Just as Americans "agree in advance on the laws and customs we abide by," Willis Conover explained, "Americans were then free, as in jazz, to do whatever they wished within those constraints" (Crist 2009, 162).

Government-sponsored jazz performances often coincided with American geopolitical interests, and American cultural and political propaganda efforts often merged. Washington sent Dizzy Gillespie to Greece in 1956 following riots outside the US Information Service in Athens in protest of American support for the country's right-wing dictator. When Gillespie arrived, he was met with cheering crowds, and Greek students hoisted him onto their shoulders while chanting his name. The US-government-supported tours of the Dave Brubeck Quartet and the Duke Ellington Orchestra in Iraq in 1958 and 1963, respectively, occurred in the middle of coups.

Around the world, many people who rejected American policies celebrated jazz, jazz performers, and those who brought jazz to them. This imbued the art form with great potential power. A poignant 1958 *New Yorker* cartoon showed officials sitting around a table, with the caption, "This is a diplomatic mission of the utmost delicacy. The question is, who's the best man for it—John Foster Dulles or Satchmo?"

IMPLICIT RACISM IN AMERICAN CULTURAL DIPLOMACY

Though Henry Luce (1898–1967) flagged jazz as a potent element of American culture and called for its use in American foreign policy in his famed 1941 essay

nations," which had been "unknown and unrecognized as a nation until the two great superpowers simultaneously discovered its existence" (Von Eschen 2004a, 84). Armstrong performed in Africa years before the US government sponsored him to do so. One black American government employee, attending one of Armstrong's concerts in Ghana in 1956—the year before that country became the first African nation to decolonize—remarked that over fifty thousand people reacted "as though a King had returned home from abroad" (Higgin 2014, 235). The effusive Ghanaian response prompted George V. Allen, named the director of the US Information Agency the following year, to remark that Armstrong was "a more important American than I will ever be" (Higgin 2014, 235). When Ghana received its independence, the State Department, which had been planning to send Armstrong to the Soviet Union before he spoke out against the government's response to the Little Rock crisis, deemed Armstrong too expensive to send there, sending another, more affordable jazz performer, Wilbur de Paris, instead. The State Department did not send Armstrong to Africa until 1960, coinciding not only with the Year of Africa, in which seventeen nations decolonized, but also the crisis in the Congo. The US government did not send "the Real Ambassador" to Africa until, as the musical's narrator noted, the superpowers "discovered" it.

By the 1960s, many more-militant civil rights activists eschewed Armstrong as an Uncle Tom who served the US government, overlooking his objections to the government's lack of action on civil rights. *The Real Ambassadors* repositioned Armstrong as an activist by demonstrating that though he served as a goodwill ambassador, he did not follow the government's wishes to "Never face a problem, always circumvent. / Stay away from issues. / Be discreet—when controversy enters, you retreat" (Van Eschen 2004a, 83).

A 1961 studio recording of *The Real Ambassador* and a performance of the show in concert form at the Monterrey Jazz Festival in September 1962 garnered critical acclaim. Plans for a Broadway production of the politically controversial show never came to fruition.

BIBLIOGRAPHY

Franzius, Andrea. "Soul Call: Music, Race, and the Creation of American Cultural Policy, 1920–1966." PhD thesis, Duke University, 2006.

Higgin, Hannah. "Disseminating American Ideals in Africa, 1949–1969." PhD thesis, University of Cambridge, 2014.

Monson, Ingrid. *Freedom Sounds: Civil Rights Call Out to Jazz and Africa.* Oxford: Oxford University Press, 2007.

Von Eschen, Penny. *Satchmo Blows Up the World: Jazz Ambassadors Play the Cold War.* Cambridge, MA: Harvard University Press, 2004a.

Von Eschen, Penny. "*The Real Ambassadors.*" In *Uptown Conversation: The New Jazz Studies,* edited by Robert G. O'Meally, Brent Hayes Edwards, and Farah Jasmine Griffin. New York: Columbia University Press, 2004b.

Hannah Nicole Higgin
History Faculty
Blair Academy

"The American Century," Washington was slow to heed his message. Facing charges of racism from the Soviet bloc, developing nations, and its allies alike, the US government sent black Americans overseas as goodwill ambassadors before it deployed jazz as a diplomatic tool. This was in large part because jazz remained controversial in the upper echelons of American society.

The US government began broadcasting jazz overseas at a time when black Americans still fought for equal rights and the domestic media still routinely associated jazz with drugs and crime. The decision to send black jazz trumpeter Dizzy Gillespie, who grew up impoverished in segregated South Carolina, took the idea that Americans valued people of all colors one step further than the previous deployment of black performers had. Not only did Washington value nonwhite Americans who excelled at nonracialized tasks, including classical music and athletics, but by officially supporting the dissemination of jazz, the US government attempted to demonstrate that it also valued nonwhite American culture. Support for jazz performances by both black and white performers was meant to signify the US government's support for racial equality, and demonstrate to foreigners that America represented the bastion of democratic culture.

These ideals, however, were not necessarily expressed at home. Highlighting the implicit racism in Washington's policies, the government paid white performers much more than their black counterparts. For instance, Dave Brubeck (1920–2012), who felt his tour for the State Department was a financial sacrifice, was paid significantly more than Dizzy Gillespie. Brubeck and his team of four received $4,000 a week, whereas Gillespie and his team of twenty made $2,500 a week two years earlier. Even so, the chairman of the House Appropriations Committee wielded the amount paid to Gillespie as a pretext for dramatically curtailing the US Information

Agency's budget request, highlighting the lingering controversy over sending black Americans overseas as cultural ambassadors.

Despite the increased "cultural prestige" of jazz beginning in the mid-1950s, many Americans still felt it was not a particularly highbrow form of art even into the next decade. Though "where they have appeared before the right audiences"—a slight against audience sophistication, itself a racially tinged sentiment—jazz performers were "enthusiastically received," a 1962 State Department report noted. Still, jazz was "certainly no substitute for the great symphonies" (Higgin 2014, 233). Many of the US government's representatives on the ground overseas agreed.

THE ENDURING INTERNATIONAL APPEAL OF JAZZ

The tremendous positive response garnered by overseas jazz performances countered these notions, however. Dizzy Gillespie, Benny Goodman, Louis Armstrong, Duke Ellington, Sidney Bechet, Muddy Waters, Gerry Mulligan, and Dave Brubeck, among many others, all toured under US government auspices. When Armstrong performed in the Soviet bloc in 1965, he was able to cross into East Germany without his papers, which was unheard of. Upon seeing the famed black American, one of the border guards proclaimed "Satchmo! ... This is Satchmo!" In 1969, President Richard Nixon (1913–1994) awarded Duke Ellington the Medal of Freedom for carrying, in Nixon's words, "the message of freedom to all the nations of the world through music, through understanding, understanding that reaches over all national boundaries and over all boundaries of prejudice and over all boundaries of language."

Although the VOA's Willis Conover was not widely known in the United States, he was lauded overseas for his program, which lasted for forty years. A survey in Poland in the 1950s showed that Conover was the "best-known living American," and many credited the popularity of jazz among young Russians to Conover's broadcasts. The cultural attaché at the American embassy in Moscow noted that young Russians learned English from Conover, even adopting his accent when they spoke. Russian fans celebrated Conover's lasting legacy in 2001, marking the fifth anniversary of his death with a three-day jazz festival. Clearly, jazz diplomacy spoke volumes.

In 1987, the US Congress declared jazz a national treasure in order to rectify the fact that its country of origin had never before "properly recognized nor accorded" jazz an "institutional status commensurate with its value and importance." Congress adopted a formal resolution stating that jazz introduced the world to "a uniquely American musical synthesis and culture." Jazz continues to serve, as the resolution put it, as "a true international language adopted by musicians around the world as a music best able to express contemporary realities from a personal perspective" (Walser 1999, 332–333).

SEE ALSO *Rock 'n' Roll*

BIBLIOGRAPHY

Belair, Felix, Jr. "United States Has Secret Sonic Weapon—Jazz." *New York Times*, November 6, 1955, 1.

Crist, Stephen A. "Jazz as Democracy? Dave Brubeck and Cold War Politics." *Journal of Musicology* 26, 2 (2009): 133–174.

Cull, Nicholas J. *The Cold War and the United States Information Agency: American Propaganda and Public Diplomacy, 1945–1989.* Cambridge: Cambridge University Press, 2008.

Davenport, Lisa E. *Jazz Diplomacy: Promoting America in the Cold War Era.* Jackson: University Press of Mississippi, 2009.

Dizard, Wilson P., Jr. *Inventing Public Diplomacy: The Story of the U.S. Information Agency.* Boulder, CO: Lynne Rienner, 2004.

Franzius, Andrea. "Soul Call: Music, Race, and the Creation of American Cultural Policy, 1920–1966." PhD thesis, Duke University, 2006.

Higgin, Hannah. "Disseminating American Ideals in Africa, 1949–1969." PhD thesis, University of Cambridge, 2014.

Monson, Ingrid. *Freedom Sounds: Civil Rights Call Out to Jazz and Africa.* Oxford: Oxford University Press, 2007.

Nixon, Richard. "Remarks on Presenting the Presidential Medal of Freedom to Duke Ellington." April 29, 1969. *American Presidency Project*, edited by Gerhard Peters and John T. Woolley. http://www.presidency.ucsb.edu/ws/?pid=2026

Osgood, Kenneth. *Total Cold War: Eisenhower's Secret Propaganda Battle at Home and Abroad.* Lawrence: University Press of Kansas, 2006.

Sorensen, Thomas C. *The Word War: The Story of American Propaganda.* New York: Harper and Row, 1968.

Von Eschen, Penny. *Satchmo Blows Up the World: Jazz Ambassadors Play the Cold War.* Cambridge, MA: Harvard University Press, 2004.

Walser, Robert, ed. *Keeping Time: Readings in Jazz.* Oxford: Oxford University Press, 1999. 2nd ed., 2014.

Ward, Geoffrey C., and Ken Burns. *Jazz: A History of America's Music.* New York: Knopf, 2000.

Hannah Nicole Higgin
History Faculty
Blair Academy

THE JAZZ SINGER

Almost a century after its much-ballyhooed premiere on stage and screen, *The Jazz Singer* by American author Samson Raphaelson (1894–1983) remains the paradigmatic presentation of the powerful conflicts, both internal and external, that children of immigrants face in their efforts to acculturate to life in America. The fictional 1920s tale of a synagogue cantor on New York's Lower East Side who must make an agonizing choice between the religious demands of his own community and his aspiration to become a blackface star on Broadway retains its popularity to this very day.

Based on Raphaelson's short story "The Day of Atonement," which appeared in *Everybody's Magazine* in 1922, the stage version opened on Broadway in the same year, starring the Jewish actor George Jessel (1898–1981) as the main character, Jakie Rabinowitz. When it was turned into a film in 1927, *The Jazz Singer* was one of the first movies of its era to include spoken dialogue and singing in some of its scenes, most of which were silent. Now starring Jewish actor Al Jolson (1886–1950), the film helped to make Jolie, as he was known, into one of the most beloved entertainers in America. The film was remade twice, in 1952 and in 1980; it was also reformulated as a radio version in 1936 and 1947, and as a television version in 1959.

The Jazz Singer centers on a lower-class Jewish family on the Lower East Side, the immigrant Jewish neighborhood of the time. The father-son relationship is torn asunder by the son's dramatic rebellion against his father's insistence that he continue the generations-long family tradition of serving as cantor in their synagogue. At the same time, *The Jazz Singer* raises a fundamental question, which remains unanswered to this day, about the precarious status of African Americans and the ongoing—often invidious—distinctions made in American society between those who immigrated to America of their own free will and those who were dragged here in chains. *The Jazz Singer* manages simultaneously to forge a connection between two alien "races" (Jewish and black) and to suggest that Jews have trumped African Americans in their wider acceptance and success in America.

In so doing, *The Jazz Singer*, as the influential critic Michael Rogin (1996) noted, suggests that Jews and other ethnic minorities joined the dominant white group in America by belittling African Americans through blackface performances. Indeed, *The Jazz Singer* is situated at the emotional, economical, and racial fault line between Europe and America. Its context is ultimately as much a European one as an American one, since the action plays out against the values and milieu of an Old World that has been imported into the New World in a particularly unstable, incomplete, and problematic way.

The Jazz Singer film does not appear to have gained much of a following overseas. Indeed, an anonymous critic for the *Times of London* complained about the crude use of sound sequences and wrote nothing about the actual themes of the film. Nevertheless, when the American actress Judy Garland (1922–1969), whose use of drugs and alcohol had derailed her career, made an acclaimed comeback on stage in London in 1951, she performed some of Jolson's signature songs, although without the blackface. The connection with *The Jazz Singer* was clear—an iconic non-Jewish, white actress reinvigorated her own career by adopting the persona of a famous Jewish entertainer performing songs about African American life, in a way that appealed to foreign audiences as much as to domestic ones. (Garland reprised her performance of Jolson's iconic number "Swanee" in the 1954 Warner Brothers film *A Star is Born.*) Jolson had made his own celebrated debut in the United Kingdom in 1942 by entertaining the American troops stationed in Dublin, Limerick, Belfast, Glasgow, and London.

In its global context, *The Jazz Singer* remains a dramatic and cinematic touchstone of a period in American history when an unprecedented influx of foreign immigrants was remaking the very soul and substance of American culture. Anxieties about the loss of white Protestant hegemony were rampant, leading to the cessation, through federal legislation, of almost all immigration from both southern and eastern Europe in the early to mid-1920s. These immigrants, conservationist Madison Grant (1865–1937) complained in his best-selling white supremacist book *The Passing of the Great Race* (1916)—which Adolf Hitler reportedly called his "Bible"—took on the language, clothing, and names of native-born Americans and even made "conquests" of non-Jewish women. Jakie Rabinowitz, who eschews the Yiddish language in favor of speaking English, dons fashionable American attire, adopts "Jack Robin" as his stage name, and romances a blonde non-Jewish chorus girl, could be seen as an exact case in point.

And yet, the very struggle that Jakie undergoes in trying to figure out where his true loyalties lie speaks to the enduring appeal of *The Jazz Singer*, which continues to resonate with immigrants who teeter between fealty to their national or ethnic heritage and attraction to the American tendency toward reinvention of one's identity.

SEE ALSO *Hollywood; Immigration; Judaism; Minstrelsy; Whiteness*

BIBLIOGRAPHY

Alexander, Michael. *Jazz Age Jews.* Princeton, NJ: Princeton University Press, 2001.

Grant, Madison. *The Passing of the Great Race; or, The Racial Basis of European History.* New York: Scribner's, 1916.

Merwin, Ted. *In Their Own Image: New York Jews in Jazz Age Popular Culture.* New Brunswick, NJ: Rutgers University Press, 2006.

"Piccadilly Theatre." *Times of London*, September 28, 1928, 12.

Rogin, Michael. *Blackface, White Noise: Jewish Immigrants in the Hollywood Melting Pot.* Berkeley: University of California Press, 1996.

Ted Merwin
Associate Professor of Religion & Judaic Studies
Director of the Milton B. Asbell Center for Jewish Life
Dickinson College, Carlisle, PA

JEFFERSON, THOMAS
1743–1826

As a diplomat and statesman, Thomas Jefferson profoundly influenced American foreign relations during the early Republic. Well-versed in Enlightenment ideas, Jefferson held an idealist vision for the future relations of the United States but embraced a realist foreign policy to achieve American goals. Throughout his life, Jefferson's actions regarding foreign affairs were grounded upon the belief that the United States was an agrarian republic with a growing population that required free trade with European markets and access to western lands in order to thrive.

JEFFERSON'S PUSH FOR INDEPENDENCE

At the outset of the American Revolution (1775–1783), Jefferson played a key role in the push for independence. In his first major work, *A Summary View of the Rights of British America* (1774), Jefferson argued that the British Parliament had no legislative authority over the American colonies. Additionally, Britain's Navigation Acts limited the ability of Americans to acquire wealth through freely engaging in commerce with foreign countries. At the meeting of the Second Continental Congress, Jefferson was among the delegates who favored independence from Great Britain and penned a draft of the Declaration of Independence (1776). In addition to its famous statements in favor of inalienable rights, the declaration enumerated a number of American grievances against King George III (1738–1820), including "cutting off our Trade with all parts of the world."

After the Revolutionary War, Jefferson authored *Notes on the State of Virginia* in response to a French diplomat's request for information regarding the individual states. The *Notes* were a wide-ranging compendium of Jefferson's philosophy, as well as statements of fact that spanned the state's natural history, geography, and political economy. At the core of Jefferson's views in the *Notes* was the belief that republics were inherently transitory, and as such, they required a virtuous citizenry to achieve political stability. In an agrarian republic predominated by citizen farmers, international commerce based upon free trade and protected by a limited naval presence abroad would guarantee Americans wealth, manufactured goods, and political liberty, all while preventing the development of the corrupting institutions and influences associated with Great Britain.

DIPLOMATIC ROLE IN THE EARLY REPUBLIC

In 1784, Congress appointed Jefferson to Europe in order to negotiate commercial treaties premised upon John Adams's (1735–1826) Model Treaty (1776). In his later position of minister to France (1785–1789), Jefferson sought to end the mercantilist policies of the *ancien régime* and was successful in allowing the free importation of American whale oil and tobacco into French markets. As a witness of attempts to reform the French monarchy in the late 1780s, Jefferson increasingly believed in the importance of the example set by the American Revolution for the spread of liberty around the world. In this vein, during American debates over the ratification of the US Constitution, Jefferson urged his contemporaries to adjoin a statement of liberties in the form of a bill of rights. During the meeting of the Estates-General in 1789, which ushered in the French Revolution, Jefferson assisted the Marquis de Lafayette (1757–1834) in drafting the Declaration of the Rights of Man and of the Citizen. This charter was introduced to the French National Assembly just three days before Parisian crowds stormed the Bastille and confronted Louis XVI (1754–1793) at Versailles.

At the end of 1789, Jefferson returned to America, where George Washington (1732–1799) soon appointed him to head the State Department (1790–1793) due to his diplomatic experience in Europe. As a member of Washington's cabinet, Jefferson helped shape an American foreign policy that would exploit international circumstances to ensure the political and economic independence of the Republic. The 1790 Nootka Sound crisis, for example, found Jefferson advocating neutrality in a possible Spanish-British war due to the leverage that neutrality would give in negotiating American access to the Mississippi River with the Spanish. Access to the Gulf of Mexico via the Mississippi was key for the western development of the country. On the other hand, Jefferson's adversary in the cabinet, Treasury Secretary Alexander Hamilton (1755–1804), generally favored increasing American political ties to its largest trading partner, Great Britain, and during the Nootka crisis encouraged Washington to allow the British to travel through American territory in order to attack Spanish possessions.

At the outbreak of the French revolutionary wars in 1792 and 1793, Jefferson believed that the interests of the United States and France were aligned, but that the

United States should avoid getting involved in a European war. During Citizen Edmond Genet's (1763–1834) mission to America in 1793, following the execution of Louis XVI, Jefferson was at first optimistic at the arrival of the French Republic's envoy. However, Genet's insistence that he be allowed to outfit French privateers in American ports in order to attack British shipping earned him the ire of Washington's entire cabinet and his dismissal.

Following Jefferson's retirement at the end of the year, the 1794 Jay Treaty polarized American politics into competing camps. Federalists supported the treaty and closer relations with Britain, while Democratic-Republicans opposed the treaty and supported closer relations with France. The rapprochement between Britain and America led the French Directory to authorize the seizure of American vessels trading with enemy ports, and propelled the United States into a "Quasi-War" (1798–1800) with France. As Adams's vice president (1797–1801) and the head of the opposition party during the Quasi-War, Jefferson opposed Federalist policies that were designed to prosecute an undeclared war and abridge civil liberties.

JEFFERSON'S PRESIDENCY

The election of 1800 ushered in a period where, as president (1801–1809), Jefferson was able to pursue his dual goals of ensuring American freedom to trade abroad and secure access to western lands. Following a declaration of war by Tripoli in 1801, Jefferson sent the US Navy to the Mediterranean to protect American merchants and blockade hostile ports. Jefferson also authorized negotiations that would cede the port of New Orleans from France to the United States. When Napoléon Bonaparte (1769–1821) authorized the sale of the entire Louisiana Territory in 1803, Jefferson quickly accepted the purchase despite misgivings about its potential unconstitutionality. The Louisiana Purchase effectively doubled the size of the United States and offered a way to ensure that American farmers would be able to exploit the agricultural resources of the Mississippi River Valley. By acquiring new territory, the Louisiana Purchase also provided a means for Jefferson (and future US presidents) to both entice and coerce Native Americans to give up their lands east of the Mississippi for lands west of it. While Indian removal would not take place for another thirty years, the Louisiana Purchase made the transfer of lands a real feature of American diplomacy with native tribes in the ensuing decades.

At the tail end of Jefferson's presidency, the *Chesapeake* affair nearly plunged the United States into war. During the summer of 1807, a British warship attacked an American frigate in order to reclaim sailors who had deserted the Royal Navy and were serving onboard the American vessel. In addition to both British and French restrictions on American trade and the resulting seizures of merchant ships, there were numerous calls for war in 1807. Jefferson and his allies in Congress, however, proposed an embargo on all exports in order to compel the European powers to allow American shipping without restriction and force the British to renounce the policy of impressment. Jefferson's Embargo Act, in effect from December 1807 until he left office in March 1809, was premised upon the belief that international markets required American agriculture more than Americans needed foreign manufactured goods. While seemingly incompatible with a free-trade philosophy, the Jeffersonian export embargo was designed to achieve just such a reality through economic coercion in the short term. Although the embargo failed to convince either Britain or France to loosen their trading restrictions, it demonstrated Jefferson's commitment to usher in an era where an expansive agricultural republic would have free access to foreign ports.

SEE ALSO *Adams, John; Declaration of Independence; Embargo Act (1807); Franklin, Benjamin; French Revolution; Jay, John; Jay Treaty (1795); Louisiana Purchase; Washington, George*

BIBLIOGRAPHY

Cogliano, Francis D. *Emperor of Liberty: Thomas Jefferson's Foreign Policy*. New Haven, CT: Yale University Press, 2014.

Kaplan, Lawrence S. *Jefferson and France: An Essay on Politics and Political Ideas*. New Haven, CT: Yale University Press, 1967.

Lambert, Frank. *The Barbary Wars: American Independence in the Atlantic World*. New York: Hill and Wang, 2005.

Onuf, Peter S. *Jefferson's Empire: The Language of American Nationhood*. Charlottesville: University Press of Virginia, 2000.

Spivak, Burton. *Jefferson's English Crisis: Commerce, Embargo, and the Republican Revolution*. Charlottesville: University Press of Virginia, 1979.

Tucker, Robert W., and David C. Hendrickson. *Empire of Liberty: The Statecraft of Thomas Jefferson*. New York: Oxford University Press, 1990.

Wallace, Anthony F. C. *Jefferson and the Indians: The Tragic Fate of the First Americans*. Cambridge, MA: Belknap Press of Harvard University Press, 1999.

Andrew J. B. Fagal
The Papers of Thomas Jefferson
Princeton University

JEWISH WELFARE BOARD

Although a soldier's assertion of a racial, ethnic, queer, or other minority identity seemed for most of human history to threaten the uniformity upon which discipline in the armed services depends, it is now widely accepted in the United States that military personnel do not lose their individual identities as soon as they don their uniforms. The National Jewish Welfare Board (JWB) deserves a large part of the credit for this change. Founded in 1917, just after the United States' entry in the First World War (1914–1918), the JWB became one of the largest and most influential Jewish organizations in America, enhancing Jewish life both at home and abroad and serving as a model to other groups, such as the Salvation Army and the National Catholic Community Service.

SUPPORT FOR JEWISH SOLDIERS DURING WORLD WARS I AND II

An extension of the Council of Young Men's Hebrew and Kindred Associations (CYMHKA) and the Jewish Community Centers (JCCs), which had arisen in 1913 to promote the cultural, social, and educational needs of American Jews, the JWB focused initially on providing chaplains, prayer books, ritual items, kosher food, entertainment, and cultural activities for Jewish soldiers serving abroad. The organization's "Star of David Men" were specially trained chaplains and laypeople sent overseas to lead Sabbath and holiday services and to minister to the wounded.

After the First World War, the JWB turned its attention to caring for injured soldiers in the Veterans Administration (VA) hospitals, maintaining services to military bases and naval stations, and building up the network of JCCs, Young Men's Hebrew Associations (YMHAs), Young Women's Hebrew Associations (YWHAs), and other civilian Jewish groups throughout the nation. The JWB also rapidly swung into action with the beginning of the Second World War (1939–1945), sending hundreds of chaplains to the West Indies, India, Burma, China, North Africa, the Pacific Islands, Europe, and the Middle East.

Providing kosher food to soldiers, including food for the celebration of Jewish holidays, was a particular priority of the JWB: by 1946, the JWB, working with the United Service Organization for National Defense (USO), had furnished 900,000 packages of matzo (unleavened bread for the celebration of Passover), 30,000 gallons of wine, 50,000 cans of kosher meat, and 50,000 pounds of salami—this last item in line with the familiar slogan in New York delicatessens that urged the parents of Jewish soldiers to "Send a Salami to Your Boy in the Army." At the same time, JCCs ran blood drives, sold war bonds, and collected clothing and books to ship overseas. JWB chaplains were especially active in Europe, Australia, India, and China, where they renovated spaces for religious services, kosher kitchens, and snack bars. They were among the first American military personnel to enter the concentration camps and rescue the survivors of the Holocaust.

POSTWAR MISSION TO STRENGTHEN JEWISH IDENTITY

Following the Second World War, the JWB used the expertise that it gained in wartime to assist the JCCs in their mission of strengthening Jewish identity at home. At a time when new JCCs were opening at a rapid pace—between 1945 and 1969, a total of 120 new JCCs were constructed—the JWB helped them to manage their employees, improve their training programs, budget their income and expenses, negotiate for supplies, provide health insurance and retirement plans, sponsor athletic competitions (often in tandem with Jewish athletes in Israel, South America, and other parts of the world), develop both day and overnight camps, and meet the needs of a growing clientele of both young families and senior citizens. In addition to organizing international conferences on the social, cultural, and recreational needs of world Jewry, they also promoted the establishment of JCC and YMHA-type centers in France, Italy, Spain, and other countries. With the founding of the State of Israel in 1948, the Jewish homeland became a priority. The JWB and JCCs took special responsibility for the Jerusalem Y, which opened in 1950, and the board pioneered an exchange program for American and Israeli social workers.

The rise of the civil rights movement provided new opportunities for the JCCs to reach out to African Americans and to combat rising anti-Semitism in the African American community. By sponsoring educational, social, and recreational programs in urban neighborhoods, the JCCs attempted to expand their services beyond the Jewish community to serve African Americans, Puerto Ricans, and other disadvantaged minorities. Attention turned back to Israel in 1967 with the advent of the Six-Day War, which prompted an unprecedented outpouring of support from American Jews, with the JWB and JCCs playing a leading role in fund-raising and sending supplies to help the Jewish state to achieve victory. In the 1970s, the movement to free Soviet Jews from oppression became a new priority, with JWB/JCC-sponsored demonstrations and resettlement efforts—including the provision of housing, employment, health care, and legal representation—throughout the country.

New domestic challenges to the American Jewish community arose in the 1980s, with a rise in the rate of intermarriage and a disinclination of many Jews to join synagogues or to become otherwise involved in Jewish life. The JWB redoubled its efforts to further Jewish identity by expanding its educational and cultural programming, with a special focus on the increasing population of Jewish elderly. At the same time, the JWB connected American

Jewish athletes, musicians, and other artists with their counterparts in Canada, South America, and Israel. The JWB also encouraged young American Jews to study, work, or do volunteer work in Israel (including assisting on Israeli military bases), with the hope that more American Jews would make *aliyah* (move permanently to Israel). By 1979, there were also ninety-one community centers in Israel, thanks in large part to the efforts of the JWB.

In 1990, the JWB took on a new name: the Jewish Community Centers of North America (JCC Association or JCCA). The JCCA continued its focus on promoting American Jews' relationship to Israel by offering summer programs in Israel for American teenagers and working with the newly established Birthright organization to send college students on intensive ten-day trips to Israel. The JCCA also sponsored an increasing number of international competitions for Jewish athletes through the Maccabi program. In addition, the JCCA helped to build thirty-eight JCCs in the former Soviet Union.

At the beginning of the twenty-first century, the JCCA adopted new technological means of training its Jewish communal professionals and educators. It collaborated with the National Foundation of Jewish Culture, which was in existence from 1960 to 2014 to sponsor cutting-edge arts events. And, in 2011, it worked with its JWB Chaplains Council to establish a memorial in Arlington National Cemetery for all rabbis who perished while on active duty. The JCCA thus continues to honor its century-old roots as an organization formed to serve the needs of Jews in the military and to inspire greater commitment to the Jewish heritage among civilians and soldiers alike.

SEE ALSO *Carnegie Endowment for International Peace; Catholicism; Cold War; Federal Council of Churches; Hague Conferences (1899, 1907); Internationalism; Judaism; Knights of Columbus; Protestantism; Religions; Roosevelt, Franklin D.; Secularization; Wilson, Woodrow; World War I; World War II; World's YWCA/YMCA*

BIBLIOGRAPHY

American Jewish Historical Society. Guide to the Records of the National Jewish Welfare Board, Undated, 1889–1995. Center for Jewish History, New York and Boston. http://digifindingaids.cjh.org/?pID=186993

Cooperman, Jessica. "The Jewish Welfare Board and Religious Pluralism in the American Military of World War I." *American Jewish History* 98, 4 (2014): 237–261.

Ted Merwin
Associate Professor of Religion and Judaic Studies
Director of the Milton B. Asbell Center for Jewish Life
Dickinson College, Carlisle, Pennsylvania

JOHN CARLOS AND TOMMIE SMITH, MEXICO CITY OLYMPICS (JOHN DOMINIS, 1968)

On the evening of October 16, 1968, Tommie Smith (b. 1944), John Carlos (b. 1945), and Peter Norman (1942–2006) took to the medal stage in Olympic Stadium in Mexico City. Americans Smith and Carlos finished first and third in the 200-hundred meter sprint, securing the gold and bronze medals for the United States. As the two black students from San Jose State College stepped forward to revel in the spoils of their victory, they wore black socks with no shoes in a nod to black poverty and a

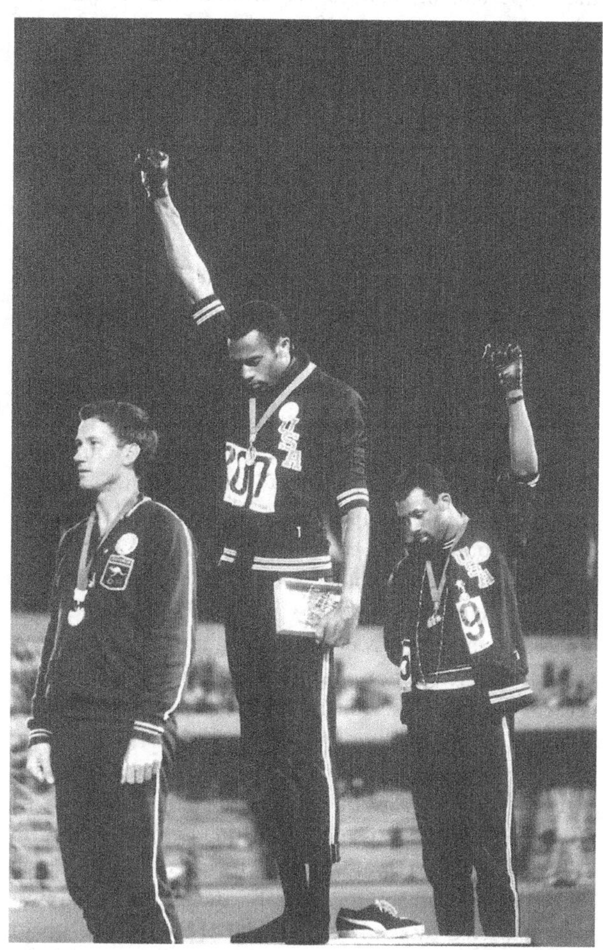

American athletes Tommie Smith and John Carlos offer the black power salute, Summer Olympics, Mexico City, 1968. Smith (center) wears black socks with no shoes in a nod to black poverty, and a single black glove as a representation of black strength and unity. *John Dominis, a* LIFE *magazine photographer, captured what has become an indelible and iconic image of the 1960s. The black power salute became synonymous with militancy and civil unrest and ignited a firestorm of debate about race relations.* JOHN DOMINIS/TIME & LIFE PICTURES/ GETTY IMAGES

single black glove as a representation of black strength and unity. During the national anthem, each man raised a gloved, clenched fist to the sky and bowed his head. John Dominis (1921–2013), a photographer with *Life* magazine, was on the scene and captured what has become one of the more indelible and iconic images of that era. This simple and peaceful gesture became synonymous with militancy and civil unrest and ignited a firestorm of debate about race relations in the late 1960s. In an interview with *Smithsonian* magazine, Dominis said of the gold medal ceremony, "I didn't think it was a big news event. I was expecting a normal ceremony. I hardly noticed what was happening when I was shooting" (Davis 2008, 12). Dominis's photo was picked up by the Associated Press and appeared in newspapers around the world; the subsequent commentary from the press was one of disdain and anger. Associated Press sportswriter Will Grimsley (1914–2002) described the protest as a "Nazi-like" salute (Peterson 2009, 106–107). *New York Times* columnist and 1956 Pulitzer Prize winner Arthur Daley (1905–1974) called the protest "disgraceful, insulting, and embarrassing" (Peterson 2009, 111). The disdain in the American sports press, according to then *Oakland Tribune* sports reporter Blaine Newnham, was the perceived violation of the sanctity of the Olympics and the inference of politics in the sports world (Peterson 2009, 114–115).

The view abroad was far more forgiving, especially in the pages of the *London Times,* as sportswriter Neil Allen seemingly understood the political and social significance of the protest, writing that the two medalists made "racial [and] political capital out of the most treasured moments of their sporting careers" (Peterson 2009, 114). The difference in reaction could have easily been chalked up to context. In the late 1960s, some blacks in the United States saw the progress of the civil rights movement as an illusion and felt action was necessary. The issue of race, certainly with its incendiary connotations in the United States, was nonexistent abroad. Smith and Carlos were members of the Olympic Project for Human Rights (OPHR), whose mission was to liberate blacks in the United States by using the international platform provided by sports. While it is clear that the two men filled the purpose of the OPHR, the protest itself was misinterpreted by many in the United States. The image showed blacks in a silent, peaceful demonstration with the intent of bringing attention to the substandard social conditions blacks faced in the United States. Instead, because of the positions of power Smith and Carlos held and the image of the gloved closed fist, their gesture is often viewed, incorrectly, as a nod to the black power movement, militancy, and violence rather than as a civil rights protest. Smith long refuted the misinterpretation, calling the protest a statement on human rights. In the twenty-first century, Dominis's image and the protest by Smith and Carlos are viewed in a more progressive and courageous light and have paved the way for the use of athletics as a means of political and ideological commentary.

SEE ALSO *Black Power Movement; Olympics*

BIBLIOGRAPHY

Berger, Martin A. *Seeing through Race: A Reinterpretation of Civil Rights Photography.* Berkeley: University of California Press, 2011.

Davis, David. "Taking a Stand." *Smithsonian* 39, 5 (August 2008): 12–14.

Edwards, Harry. *The Revolt of the Black Athlete.* New York: Free Press, 1970.

Henderson, Simon. *Sidelined: How American Sports Challenged the Black Freedom Struggle.* Lexington: University Press of Kentucky, 2013.

Peterson, Jason. "A 'Race' for Equality: Print Media Coverage of the 1968 Olympic Protest by Tommie Smith and John Carlos." *American Journalism* 26, 2 (Spring 2009): 99–121.

Smith, Tommie, and David Steele. *Silent Gesture: The Autobiography of Tommie Smith.* Philadelphia, PA: Temple University Press, 2007.

Jason Peterson
Assistant Professor of Communication
Charleston Southern University

JOHNSON, LYNDON BAINES
1908–1973

Lyndon B. Johnson, the thirty-fourth president of the United States, hoped that his most important legacy would be the Great Society, an ambitious program of social reform and civil rights measures. By the end of his presidency, however, Johnson's decisions to commit more than five hundred thousand US troops to the war in Southeast Asia undermined his domestic achievements.

THE GREAT SOCIETY

When he became president on November 22, 1963, following the assassination of John F. Kennedy, Johnson was eager to prove the effectiveness of his leadership. Unlike Kennedy, who considered the Cold War his most important challenge as president, Johnson gave highest priority to domestic reform. He emphasized to White House aides that he was a "Roosevelt New Dealer" (Dallek 1998, 61). His service as director of the National Youth Administration in his home state of Texas and as a Democratic member of the House of Representatives during Franklin D. Roosevelt's presidency convinced him that government should play a major role in providing opportunities for economic and social improvement and preparing people to take advantage of them through education and job-training programs. As president, Johnson was determined to "out-Roosevelt" Roosevelt, that is, to establish a record in domestic reform that exceeded the achievements of the New Deal (Patterson 2012, 50).

For Johnson, the Great Society was both a set of programs and a vision of America's future. As he explained in a commencement address at the University of Michigan in May 1964, the Great Society would provide "abundance and liberty for all" while elevating the quality of life. The work of creating such a society would never be complete; instead it would be "a challenge constantly renewed." Johnson believed that an essential first step toward the Great Society was eradicating poverty. In his first State of the Union address, he announced a new "War on Poverty" and persuaded Congress to provide $1 billion for job-training and community-action programs. Eliminating racial injustice was also fundamental to the Great Society, and Johnson won a major victory when Congress approved the Civil Rights Act of 1964, a revision of a bill Kennedy had sent to Capitol Hill a year earlier. This landmark legislation banned racial discrimination in public accommodations and in employment.

Following Johnson's landslide victory in the presidential election of 1964, Congress approved a flood of Great Society legislation. Among the most important measures were Medicare and Medicaid, the Voting Rights Act, federal aid to elementary, secondary, and higher education, the Model Cities program, and establishment of the National Endowments for the Arts and the Humanities. Huge Democratic majorities in the Senate and House allowed Johnson to achieve such phenomenal success. Also essential was Johnson's remarkable skill at guiding legislation through Congress, which he had developed as Senate majority leader during the 1950s, as well as his legendary techniques of persuasion, which were known as "the treatment." Johnson may not have outdone Roosevelt, but the Great Society ranks with the New Deal as one of the two most important programs of liberal reform in the twentieth century.

ESCALATION IN VIETNAM

In foreign affairs as in domestic policy, Johnson tried early in his presidency to win public and congressional support by declaring that he was following Kennedy's policies. In his first major address after Kennedy's assassination, Johnson proclaimed, "let us continue." He hoped to capitalize on sympathy for the fallen president, while at the same time proving that he had the skill and strength to turn Kennedy's proposals into legislative achievements, such as the Civil Rights Act of 1964, or to fulfill his predecessor's commitments abroad, such as preserving the independence of South Vietnam. Johnson relied on the counsel of the same advisors who had shaped Kennedy's national security policy—Secretary of State Dean Rusk (1909–1994), Secretary of Defense Robert McNamara (1916–2009), and National Security Advisor McGeorge Bundy (1919–1996). Like Kennedy, Johnson increased US military and economic assistance to South Vietnam. He also raised the number of US military advisors from 16,300 at the time of Kennedy's death to 23,500 a year later. Like Kennedy, who believed in the domino theory, Johnson thought that failure in Vietnam would have adverse effects on US international credibility and the security of the "free world."

While Johnson made many public statements about continuing the US commitment to South Vietnam, he privately expressed anxieties about growing US military involvement in Southeast Asia. In a telephone conversation with Bundy, for example, he described South Vietnam as a troubling dilemma. "I don't think it's worth fighting for and I don't think that we can get out. It's just the biggest damned mess that I ever saw" (Beschloss 1997, 370). Despite such concerns, Johnson took strong action following clashes between US and North Vietnamese naval forces in the Gulf of Tonkin in August 1964. Congress provided the broad new authority he requested to protect US forces in Southeast Asia under the Gulf of Tonkin Resolution, and Johnson ordered retaliatory air strikes on North Vietnamese targets. This crisis worked to Johnson's political advantage as it neutralized criticism from his opponent in the presidential election, Senator Barry Goldwater (1909–1998), who called for military action to win in Vietnam and attain victory in the Cold War. Johnson's short-term success came at a high cost, as it eventually became known that administration officials had failed to disclose information that the second of the two alleged North Vietnamese attacks in the Tonkin Gulf had never occurred. The president's handling of this crisis was an early example of what became known as the *credibility gap*, the disparity between what Johnson said about Vietnam and what actually happened.

Even though he pledged during the fall election campaign that he would not send American combat forces to Southeast Asia, Johnson made critical decisions during winter of 1964 to 1965 that transformed the Vietnam conflict into a major US war. The chronic weakness and corruption of the Saigon government in the face of growing enemy strength and effectiveness accounted for Johnson's decisions. In February 1965, the president authorized continuous bombing of North Vietnamese targets, a campaign that became known as Rolling Thunder. US Marines then went ashore at Danang the following month to protect US air bases, although their

President Lyndon B. Johnson visiting American troops in Vietnam, 1966. *Johnson feared that a defeat in Vietnam would destroy his presidency along with his Great Society domestic reforms. Privately, he worried about a long, costly, indecisive war; publicly, he insisted that the war required neither hard choices nor sacrifices.* INTERIM ARCHIVES/ARCHIVE PHOTOS/GETTY IMAGES

mission quickly expanded to include search-and-destroy operations. On July 28, Johnson announced a major troop increase, although he did not disclose that his decisions would bring the number of US military personnel in Vietnam to 175,000 by the end of the year. He also insisted that there had been no change in the mission of US forces, even though they were taking over the main burden of fighting.

THE COSTS OF WAR

Johnson tried to divert attention from his escalation in Vietnam because of his concern about the Great Society. He later described the competing relationship between "that bitch of a war" and "the woman I really loved—the Great Society" (Kearns 1976, 251). He feared that a defeat in Vietnam would destroy his presidency, along with his ambitious plans for domestic reform. A major increase in the US war effort, however, would create doubts about whether the country could also afford costly social programs. Johnson hoped to minimize these difficulties by concealing the costs and risks of the expanding war. He never disclosed that the Joint Chiefs of Staff had warned that success in Vietnam would require a half million troops and several years of fighting. Nor did he reveal the fears he expressed in private that the enemy would match any escalation and the result would be a deadlier and indecisive war. Instead, Johnson insisted that the Vietnam War required neither hard choices nor sacrifices. As he declared in his State of the Union Address in 1966, "This Nation is mighty enough … to pursue our goals in the rest of the world while still building a Great Society here at home."

The realities of war overwhelmed such optimism. Johnson soon privately conceded that the Vietnam War had become too costly to expand the Great Society. Even maintaining the budgets of some programs at current levels proved difficult as US troop strength rose to 385,300 by the end of 1966 and 485,600 a year later. Federal budget deficits increased, and inflation started to climb. Conservative critics of the Great Society used the rising expenses of war as justification to call for cuts in programs they had never supported. Liberals rebuked the president for prosecuting a controversial war that drained funds from vital social welfare efforts. Martin Luther King Jr. (1929–1968), for example, charged that "the promises of the Great Society have been shot down on the battlefield of Vietnam" (Hill 1967).

Despite such criticisms, programs like the War on Poverty continued to provide valuable social services and helped lower the poverty rate from 19.5 percent in 1963 to 12.8 percent in 1968 (Pach 2006, xiv). But when the Kerner Commission issued a report in early 1968 about the frightening wave of recent urban violence and advocated substantial increases in housing, job-training, and education programs to improve living standards in inner cities, Johnson dismissed the recommendations as unrealistic.

Johnson's presidency became a casualty of the Vietnam War. Protests by antiwar groups, such as Students for a Democratic Society, became larger and more frequent as Johnson committed more troops to Vietnam. Conservative critics also attacked Johnson for not using sufficient military force to win the war. Assailed by both hawks and doves, Johnson lost mainstream support for a war that became increasingly costly in lives and resources. By August 1967, polls showed that less than one-third of the American people approved of the president's Vietnam policies. During the Tet Offensive in early 1968, popular support for Johnson's handling of the war sank even lower, leading to his announcement on March 31 that he would not seek another term as president.

OTHER INTERNATIONAL AND COLD WAR ISSUES

Vietnam overshadowed Johnson's policies concerning other international and Cold War issues. When rioting occurred in the Canal Zone in January 1964, Johnson worked to restore order and, at the end of the year, agreed to negotiations with Panama for a new treaty governing the canal. The president showed less restraint in dealing with disturbances in the Dominican Republic in April 1965. Johnson feared communist threats, worried about "another Cuba," and dispatched more than twenty thousand US troops to quell the violence. Elections occurred a year later, but many Latin Americans protested Yankee interventionism.

Johnson also worked toward improved relations with the Soviet Union. He met Premier Alexei Kosygin (1904–1980) in Glassboro, New Jersey, in June 1967, signed the Nuclear Nonproliferation Treaty in July 1968, and expected to visit Moscow in October 1968 to establish plans for further arms-control negotiations. The Soviet invasion of Czechoslovakia in August, however, forced Johnson to cancel the Moscow summit.

LEGACY

In March 1965, when he addressed a joint session of Congress and called for the passage of voting rights legislation that would insure that African Americans would no longer be denied their constitutional right to exercise the franchise, Johnson revealed how he hoped his presidency would be remembered. "I do not want to be the President who built empires, or sought grandeur, or extended dominion," he asserted. "I want to be the President who educated young children to the wonders of their world … who helped to feed the hungry … who helped the poor to find their own way and who protected the right of every citizen to vote in every election." Johnson made this statement only days after he sent the first US combat troops to Vietnam. He was the president who advanced civil rights, improved health care, and aided the poor. He was also the president who committed the United States to one of its longest and most controversial wars.

SEE ALSO *Bundy, McGeorge; Cold War; Gulf of Tonkin Resolution; Kennedy, John Fitzgerald; Kennedy, Robert; McNamara, Robert S.; New Left; Student Nonviolent Coordinating Committee (SNCC); Students for a Democratic Society (SDS); United States Agency for International Development (USAID); Vietnam War*

BIBLIOGRAPHY

Beschloss, Michael R., ed. *Taking Charge: The Johnson White House Tapes, 1963–1964.* New York: Simon and Schuster, 1997.

Dallek, Robert. *Flawed Giant: Lyndon Johnson and His Times, 1961–1973.* New York: Oxford University Press, 1998.

Hill, Gladwin. "Dr. King Advocates Quitting Vietnam." *New York Times*, February 26, 1967, 1.

Johnson, Lyndon B. "Remarks at the University of Michigan." May 22, 1964. American Presidency Project, edited by John T. Woolley and Gerhard Peters. http://www.presidency.ucsb.edu/ws/index.php?pid=26262&st=&st1=

Johnson, Lyndon B. "Special Message to Congress: The American Promise." March 15, 1965. American Presidency Project, edited by John T. Woolley and Gerhard Peters. http://www.presidency.ucsb.edu/ws/index.php?pid=26805&st=&st1=

Johnson, Lyndon B. "Annual Message to the Congress on the State of the Union." January 12, 1966. American Presidency Project, edited by John T. Woolley and Gerhard Peters. http://www.presidency.ucsb.edu/ws/index.php?pid=28015&st=&st1=

Kearns (Goodwin), Doris. *Lyndon Johnson and the American Dream.* New York: Harper and Row, 1976.

Pach, Chester J. *The Johnson Years.* New York: Facts on File, 2006.

Patterson, James T. *The Eve of Destruction: How 1965 Transformed America.* New York: Basic Books, 2012.

Chester J. Pach
Associate Professor, Department of History
Ohio University

JOINT CHIEFS OF STAFF

The Joint Chiefs of Staff (JCS) serve as the US president's chief military advisors. The JCS consists of the heads of the four major services—US Army, US Air Force, US Navy, and US Marine Corps—and the National Guard. They advise the president, the secretary of defense, and the National Security Council on everything related to the nation's defense and security. Indeed, the heads of major operational commands report to the secretary of defense and the president of the United States directly, not to or through the JCS.

ORIGIN

The chiefs as a group do not oversee the operations of the US armed forces abroad. Theater commanders, for example, in Iraq and Afghanistan reported to the head of Central Command, who reports in turn to the secretary of defense and the president, bypassing, at least formally, the JCS. Until the Second World War (1939–1945), there was no central advisory body in the military. Theater commanders had a great degree of independence, even as communications technology advanced enough to make central control a possibility. To be sure, the telegraph that followed the US Railway Administration in the Civil War (1861–1865) allowed President Abraham Lincoln (1809–1865) to keep in touch with his commanders, but Ulysses S. Grant (1822–1885), for example, did pretty much as he wanted. And even after Grant assumed control over all Union armies, the navy acted on its own. It was difficult to arrange for joint military action with the army and navy, a situation that worsened during the Spanish-American War (1898) and the invasion of Cuba, as well as during the various occupations in the Caribbean. During the First World War (1914–1918), John Pershing (1860–1948) insisted on operational independence for the American Expeditionary Force. But the move to total war required a greater degree of coordination and prioritizing of resources. A decade before the First World War, President Theodore Roosevelt (1858–1919) tried: the current JCS is a successor to the Joint Army and Navy Board, established by Roosevelt in 1903 to foster cooperation between the services. It was initially of little importance, and outsiders described it as "a planning and deliberative body rather than a center of executive authority" (JCS, "Origin of Joint Concepts").

In 1919, based on experiences during the First World War, the two service secretaries agreed to strengthen the somewhat moribund Joint Board, and assigned it the task of developing plans for mobilization for a next war. Membership consisted of the chiefs, their principal deputies, and the chief planning officers for both services. But the Joint Board had no authority to implement its recommendations, plans, or decisions. The need for better coordination became apparent with the onset of the Second World War, and the first meeting of the reorganized and renamed Joint Chiefs of Staff took place in 1942.

WORLD WAR II AND AFTER

The situation changed during the Second World War at the Arcadia Conference (December 1941–January 1942), when President Franklin Roosevelt (1882–1945) and British prime minister Winston Churchill (1874–1965) formed the Combined Chiefs of Staff to coordinate actions across the globe. The British had tried to bring their service chiefs together as far back as 1924, but it took the Second World War for Admiral William Leahy (1875–1959) to try the same in the United States. As a consequence, he was named chief of staff to the commander in chief of the army and navy. Still, Army general George C. Marshall (1880–1959) acted as superior to Dwight Eisenhower (1890–1969) in the European theater of operations and, to the extent that Douglas MacArthur (1880–1964) would acknowledge anyone's authority, Marshall did the same with MacArthur in the Southwest Pacific theater of operations.

In 1947, President Harry Truman (1884–1972) signed the National Security Act, which changed the Joint Chiefs' functioning. The act created the Department of Defense; separated the US Army and the Army Air Corps, which was renamed the US Air Force; and established the Director of Central Intelligence as a follow-up of a sort to the wartime Office of Strategic Services. The act made clear that the chiefs, who were equal in stature to one another, served as advisors to the civilian leadership and not as superiors to theater commanders. Nonetheless, that practice continued, which resulted in an amendment to the act in 1953 specifically forbidding such contact with field commanders. In this era, the commandant of the Marine Corps gained equal status as a member of the Joint Chiefs.

In the aftermath of the Korean War (1950–1953) and the Vietnam War (1954–1975), the Joint Chiefs received much criticism. Douglas MacArthur exercised nearly independent authority over combat operations in Korea, assumed that the other services would give in to his demands, and by crossing the thirty-eighth parallel and driving to the Chinese (and Soviet) border(s), he brought the United States and the new People's Republic of China into a conflict that was not overcome until Richard Nixon's famous trip to China in 1972. During the Vietnam War, General Earle Wheeler (1908–1975), the chairman of the JCS, offered little useful advice either to President Lyndon Johnson (1908–1973) or to the Vietnam ground commander, William Westmoreland (1914–2005), about the prosecution of the war. Vietnam represented, among other things, a failure of leadership, and the Joint Chiefs were at the center of the failure.

The Goldwater-Nichols Act (1986) changed the JCS once again. While each of the chiefs could offer advice directly to the president if requested, the legislation elevated the chairman to act as the person assigned to represent the views of the other four service chiefs to the civilian authorities. Previously, the four chiefs sought consensus, and thus advice offered to the president might have pleased none of the chiefs. The reform required the chairman to provide advice directly to the military's civilian masters. A subsequent amendment, passed in 1992, created the position of vice chair, increasing the number of chiefs to six—the chair, vice chair, and the chiefs of staff of each of the four services. The National Defense Reauthorization Act of 2012 added the chief of staff of the National Guard Bureau to the Joint Chiefs, making the number of chiefs seven.

SEE ALSO *Central Intelligence Agency (CIA); Department of Defense, US; Department of Homeland Security; Department of State; National Security Agency (NSA); National Security Council (NSC)*

BIBLIOGRAPHY

History of the Joint Chiefs of Staff. 11 vols. Various authors. Washington, DC: Office of Joint History, Office of the Chairman of the JCS, 1996–2015.

Joint Chiefs of Staff (JCS). *Organizational Development of the Joint Chiefs of Staff, 1942–1987.* Washington, DC: Joint Secretariat, JCS, 1988.

Joint Chiefs of Staff (JCS). "Origin of Joint Concepts." http://www.jcs.mil/About/OriginofJointConcepts.aspx

McMaster, H. R. *Dereliction of Duty: Lyndon Johnson, Robert McNamara, the Joint Chiefs of Staff, and the Lies That Led to Vietnam.* New York: Harper Collins, 1997.

Millett, Allan R. *The Reorganization of the Joint Chiefs of Staff: A Critical Analysis.* Washington, DC: Pergamon-Brassey's, 1986.

Penny, Mark. *The Inside Story of the Forty-Year Battle between the Joint Chiefs of Staff and America's Civilian Leaders.* New York: Houghton Mifflin, 1989.

Stoler, Mark A. *Allies and Adversaries: The Joint Chiefs of Staff, the Grand Alliance, and U.S. Strategy in World War II.* Chapel Hill: University of North Carolina Press, 2000.

Charles M. Dobbs
Professor Emeritus
Iowa State University

JONES-SHAFROTH ACT (1917)

SEE *Puerto Rico.*

JUDAISM

Performances of Judaism and conceptions of Jewish identity in America have negotiated the importance of *halakha* (Jewish law), other Jewish practices, and the novelty of both American disestablishment and the country's unique relationship between religion and civic society. Traditional Judaism has included the importance of the Hebrew Bible and its interpretations. The Hebrew Bible is commonly known as the *Tanakh*, an acronym referring to *Torah* (teachings), *Nevi'im* (prophets), and *Ketuvim* (writings). These texts are shared with the Christian Old Testament and include many stories and figures in common with the Islamic Qur'an. Jews have also produced and considered authoritative many interpretations and commentaries on the Bible, especially the Talmud, compiled from the first to sixth centuries CE, which includes halakha, as well as many nonbinding stories and interpretations called *aggadah*. However, the dynamic practices of Judaism have not been limited to these texts, and many practices emerged that were not necessarily rooted in these texts.

THE DIVERSITY OF AMERICAN JUDAISM

Jews came to America from many different regions with unique local cultures and practices. Once in America, Jews participated in diverse and complex social, cultural, and political processes. There has not been a centralized Jewish body that could regulate Jewish community or observance, so local communities and individual Jews have been free to negotiate their own understandings of heritage, halakha, and change. Identification with Judaism has thus occurred in tension with more amorphous understandings and practices of peoplehood and culture. However, the idea that Jews have something in common persists and continues to shape what many different Jewish individuals and groups have argued Judaism is or should be.

A 2013 Pew survey, "A Portrait of Jewish Americans," demonstrates the diversity of Jews' understandings of Judaism and Jewishness today. While many Americans may think of Judaism as a "religion," religion as a category may not fully capture or resonate with all the complexities of Jewish life. Among adults who identify as "Jewish" in some way, 78 percent understand themselves as "Jewish by religion," while 22 percent identify as "Jews of no religion." Alternatively, 62 percent of adult Jews said "being Jewish is mainly a matter of ancestry/culture," 15 percent said "religion," and 23 percent said "religion and ancestry/culture." Because of the importance of peoplehood and culture, many have considered themselves secular or ethnic Jews. Such Jews may participate in a range of practices, such as Holocaust remembrance, use of the Yiddish language, adherence to Zionism, Jewish foodways, or the practice of social justice, without affirming halakha or belief in God.

COMMUNITIES AND PRACTICES

The earliest Jewish community in America was established in 1654 in New Amsterdam (renamed New York City a decade later). These were Sephardic Jews who migrated from Brazil from a community of Dutch Jews previously hailing from Amsterdam. Today, 4 to 7 percent of Jews in America are not of Germanic or Eastern European Ashkenazi descent. These other Jews include mainly Sephardi, Mizraḥi, and Romaniote Jews. While these three groups are often lumped together as Sephardi, they are culturally and historically distinct and self-identify as such. *Sephardic* technically refers to Spanish- and Portuguese-speaking Jews of Western Europe and Ladino-speaking Jews of the Ottoman Empire. *Mizraḥi* refers to Arabic-speaking Jews native to the Middle East and West Asia. *Romaniote* refers to Greek-speaking Jews native to the former Byzantine Empire.

Although the history of Jews and Judaism in the United States cannot be explained solely through a rigid periodization linked to immigration waves, immigration from various regions influenced the observance of Judaism in colonial America and the United States and its various cultural iterations. Sephardim characterized the earliest Jewish immigrants to the American colonies, but beginning in the early nineteenth century, greater numbers of Ashkenazi Jews, mostly from Germany, began to immigrate and form substantial communities.

Reform Judaism began in the United States in the 1820s in Charleston, South Carolina. Reform Jews in America turned away from some practices of halakha that they perceived to be anachronistic. They did not see how such practices were useful in their American lives, but they preserved their own understandings of Jewish traditions. For example, covenant remained central to the identity of Jewish Americans, as illustrated by the permanence of circumcision in Jewish observance. Though many Jews did not observe *kashrut* (halakhic dietary restrictions), they refrained from eating pork and observed special rules for holy days.

Rabbis such as Isaac Mayer Wise (1819–1900), David Einhorn (1809–1879), and Kaufmann Kohler (1843–1926) led the late-nineteenth-century institutionalization of Reform Judaism in America. Although they supported the changes that Jewish laypeople in America were already instituting in their lives, they maintained many aspects of Jewish tradition, such as in marriage, Sabbath observance, and language. Classical Reform Judaism rejected hopes for a messiah that would restore Jewish territorial rights in the land of Palestine/Israel. This position was a response to the nascent Zionist movement. Since the early twentieth century, however, many Reform Jews have embraced some form of attachment to Israel as a national center for Jews. Reform Jews have tended to see halakha and Jewish texts, such as the Talmud, as important ties to Jewish heritage but products of Jewish history. As such, Reform Jews do not consider either to be authoritative when in conflict with their modern ethical, social, and political values.

Various Jewish movements labeled *Orthodoxy* solidified in response to Reform Judaism in America and globally. Not all Jews agreed with Reform's widespread abrogation of halakha and Talmudic authority, although this did not necessarily mean they opposed change. At the same time, beginning in the late nineteenth century, large numbers of Eastern European Ashkenazi Jews immigrated to the United States, numerically displacing Jews of German heritage.

The tensions that arose over these various forms of Jewish identity caused Jews from different ethnic, national, and religious communities to struggle with what might count as acceptable forms of Jewish life. Some German Jews advocated what became known as an Orthodox position toward halakha and the authority of Talmud, and an even greater percentage of Eastern European Jews supported Orthodox Judaism, even if they were not always fully observant of halakha. Jews who became known as *ultra-Orthodox* or *Haredi* (literally, "[one who] trembles" before God; see Isaiah 66:2) rejected many cultural developments that they feared would dilute Judaism. Yiddish has remained the lingua franca for many Haredim, and they have opposed changes to Jewish dress (that is, dress rooted in premodern Eastern Europe), synagogue architecture, gender norms, and many other aspects of life that could appear to be influenced by American or Christian culture. The Holocaust decimated many Eastern European Jewish communities, including Hasidim ("pious ones," referring to the pietistic practices of kabbalah that developed in Eastern Europe) and Mitnagdim ("opponents," who advocated textual study in learning centers known as Yeshivas over many Hasidic practices), but some survivors relocated to the United States, Israel, and other countries and attempted to continue living according to their heritage.

Since the late twentieth century, an increasing number of Jews called *ba'alei teshuvah* (returners) not raised in Orthodox homes have been attracted to Orthodox life. The rabbi Zalman Schachter-Shalomi (1924–2014) led a movement known as Jewish Renewal, which combines Hasidism with egalitarianism toward women and a willingness to experiment with halakha. Other *Havurah* ("fellowship" in Hebrew, referring to small groups of Jews who come together for study or to hold Shabbat and holiday services) movements demonstrated new Jewish American interests in embracing halakha and Jewish tradition without participating in Orthodoxy. Thus Orthodox Judaism is not monolithic; it represents a spectrum from "modern" to "ultra" Orthodox, influenced by many dynamics globally and in America.

The Conservative movement emerged at the turn of the twentieth century in the United States as an approach that sought to embrace Reform Jews' instinct for change and yet also maintain a sense of Talmudic and halakhic authority. Solomon Schechter (1847–1915), the institutional leader of Conservative Judaism, argued that just as the rabbis had interpreted Torah to suit their needs, so could contemporary Jews. Thus, Talmud and halakha remained important, but Schechter placed interpretive authority in the Jewish community as a whole.

Mordecai Kaplan (1881–1983), a rabbi trained at the Conservative movement's Jewish Theological Seminary in New York and associated with Modern Orthodoxy in his early rabbinic career, led the Reconstructionist movement. Although Kaplan's Reconstructionist movement never gained large numbers of Jews in America, it has been influential well beyond its denominational boundary. Influenced by Zionism, Kaplan saw Judaism as a complete culture. Through Jewish Community Centers, the many Jewish communities who adapted the idea sought to create a space that filled all needs of Jews, social and recreational. By making the Jewish center the location of Jewish social life, Jews found a way to participate in American activities, such as bowling, attending movies, and swimming, without forfeiting their Jewish identity.

Kabbalah, often called Jewish mysticism, has been an important practice within many Jewish movements, but some practitioners, beginning in the late 1960s, also created a separate movement that draws both Jews and non-Jews. Philip Berg (1927–2013), an American rabbi influenced by Buddhism, Hinduism, Native American religion, and New Age movements, created the Research Centre of Kabbalah in 1970, with an academy in Jerusalem and a publishing house in New York. In the 1990s, Los Angeles became the main headquarters of the Kabbalah Centre, which emphasizes the special role of Jews in understanding and disseminating the knowledge contained in traditional texts. The Kabbalah Centre also opens up the kabbalistic tradition (though not all of Judaism) to non-Jews. At the Kabbalah Centre, Jews and non-Jews can practice kabbalistic techniques, such as contemplating the letters of traditional texts (called *scanning* at the Kabbalah Centre), meditating on divine names, and wearing red strings and purifying oneself with kabbalah water. The directors of the Kabbalah Centre consider these techniques available to non-Jews because they are not halakhic commandments.

According to the 2013 Pew Survey, 35 percent of Jewish Americans associate with the Reform movement, making it the largest denomination. The next largest group, 30 percent of Jewish Americans, identifies with no denomination, while 18 percent associate with Conservative Judaism, 10 percent with Orthodox Judaism, and 6 percent with "other." Denominational boundaries remain fluid, continually shifting in their ideologies and philosophies, as well as their constituencies. About half of those who say they were raised Orthodox or Reform have remained within their denomination, while only about a third of those raised Conservative have remained within the Conservative movement. Jewish Americans switch denominations for many reasons, ranging from philosophical and theological commitments, to political and social questions, to practical issues, such as proximity to congregations.

GENDER AND JUDAISM IN THE UNITED STATES

In social interaction, religious worship and community, and education, women found their ways into Jewishness and Judaism. Men and women worked out anxieties in America by renegotiating women's roles in Judaism. After the Civil War (1861–1865), mass-market capitalism expanded in the United States. This economic development coincided with increased immigration of Eastern European Ashkenazi Jews. Jewish immigrants consumed American material goods as a means of acculturating and adapting Judaism to American circumstances. American household goods, fashions, and foods cultivated a sense of belonging, even for those who struggled to learn English or to achieve full middle-class status in the first years after immigration. Because women were associated with the home, women had control over family consumption. This power was embodied in the *baleboste*, a Yiddish word for a woman who runs the house. Gendered stereotypes have played an important role in the dynamic relationship among Jewish Americans and with broader American society. Jews and others have used such stereotypes as the "Jewish mother" and the "Jewish American princess" to critique and control the image of Jews in American culture.

The United States has seen large numbers of women attending synagogues compared to men, a broader sociological phenomenon in the United States. Despite the large presence of women in Jewish American congregations, their rights have been slow to develop, generally changing in step with American society as a whole. Although Orthodox Jews have not tended to consider halakhic gender norms as standing in opposition to women's rights, Conservative and Reform Jews have challenged some aspects of halakhic gender regulations. Prior to the nineteenth century, the practice of halakha required a *meḥitza* or division between men and women in synagogues. Christian congregations also separated genders until the eighteenth century, when a movement toward family seating began. Adapting to these norms expressing the importance of family was thus part of the process of acculturation for Jewish Americans who chose mixed seating. In 1851, Anshe Emeth in Albany, New York, led by Rabbi Isaac Mayer Wise, became the first synagogue in world to have mixed seating after the emerging congregation acquired a former Baptist church building.

In Western European and American cultures, women were often blamed for the loss of Jewish identity. Some claimed that because women were responsible for the domestic sphere, they were also responsible, as mothers, for inculcating Jewish values and practices in children, both boys and girls. However, in traditional Ashkenazi Jewish communities, men, not women, were in charge of training boys to be Jews, and Jewish education for girls had not been emphasized. Thus a blanket responsibility for children and Jewish identity marked a shift in gender roles, while simultaneously facilitating adaptation to American culture and ideas of family. Once "religion" had been placed under the umbrella of the "domestic sphere," conventionally associated with women, women were able to form activist groups and other organizations, such as Ladies Hebrew Benevolent Societies, the National Council of Jewish Women, the Jewish Women's Religious Congress, Hadassah, and many others. By forming these groups, women followed the scripts of prevailing gender norms while simultaneously pushing against those norms as they created places for themselves in Jewish communal space.

In addition to the significance of women's participation in organizational life, the twentieth and twenty-first centuries have seen ongoing ritual experimentation that negotiated girls and women's roles. Bat mitzvahs and confirmation ceremonies that included girls marked major innovations in Judaism and gender performance. In the early twentieth century, bar mitzvahs had fallen out of practice, and bat mitzvahs were not automatically accepted, even by the Reform tradition. Popular rather than rabbinic practice influenced greater observance of both.

In 1972, Sally Priesand (b. 1946) became the first woman to be ordained as a rabbi in the Reform movement. Reconstructionist (since 1974) and Conservative Judaism (since 1985) also began ordaining women, and a small number of Orthodox women have been ordained (since 2013), though often as *maharat* (*manhiga hilkhatit rukhanit toranit*, or a female leader of Jewish law, spirituality, and Torah).

RACE, ETHNICITY, AND NATION: DISCRIMINATION AND INCLUSION

The history of Jews' characterization of Jewish peoplehood has been complicated and dynamic. In colonial America, Jews understood themselves more readily as a nation than as a race, at a time when *nation* described an ethnic group born abroad as opposed to a group tied to the modern sense of nation-state. But after American independence, Americans came to see themselves as a single nation, and Jews shifted away from the language of *nation* toward that of *religious community*. However, the desire to maintain a sense of group identity in the face of widespread Americanization after the 1870s led to greater use of the term *race* among Jews. For some, *race* seemed to allow a distinct sense of group identity without creating concerns over dual allegiance. Jews thus began to use the dominant American discourse, but they defined themselves. They maintained a tension between wanting to fit into American culture by being white and wanting to see themselves as one race among many in the United States, operating outside of easy black/white dichotomies. Non-Jewish Americans similarly maintained this complex tension through the end of the nineteenth century, bolstering Jews' sense of their ability to maintain distinctiveness through the discourse of race.

Some Americans have articulated economic and social anxiety through antisemitism, although never with the same cultural and structural power in the United States as in Europe. Historian Ira Katznelson has argued that while Jewishness has sometimes been understood to be a marker of difference, it has nevertheless largely been "one way to be an American, whereas in Europe to be a Jew frequently meant not to be a European" (1995, 168). Perhaps the greatest legal measures of discrimination against Jews in the United States were not those restricting the rights of Jews within the nation, but those preventing further immigration. The 1921 Emergency Quota Act and 1924 Johnson-Reed Act all but curtailed the possibility for Jewish immigration to the United States, although the legislation did not explicitly name Jews as targets and restricted against many other immigrant groups as well. Jews have also experienced social discrimination, exclusion, and occasional threats and violence. While the specter of antisemitism has complicated Jews' sense of security in America, antisemitism has never been as strong in the United States as in other global communities.

Jewish life in the United States has influenced American concepts of integration for many religious and ethnic groups. While many early Americans expected full assimilation to white Anglo-Saxon norms, Jewish playwright Israel Zangwill (1864–1926) helped popularize a notion of the "melting pot," the idea that each immigrant group's best characteristics would influence American culture, the more negative characteristics would fall away, and Americans would ultimately build a single culture from the many "ingredients" of each incoming ethnic group.

In response, Jewish American philosopher Horace Kallen (1882–1974) argued for "cultural pluralism" in the

United States. Kallen and others who took up his vision saw pluralism as a corrective to assimilation and the melting pot. Kallen argued that democracy was "anti-assimilationist" and that all Americans had a right to associate with distinct cultural groups so long as they shared certain overarching American values of democracy. This respect not only for individual but for group rights undergirded Kallen's vision of Zionism, which he considered to be the future of Judaism. Kallen saw Zionism as an alternative to Orthodoxy, which he considered outdated, and to Reform Judaism, which he argued discarded too much of Jewish heritage. Louis Brandeis (1856–1941), a Jewish lawyer who became a justice on the US Supreme Court in 1916, shared Kallen's ideas of cultural pluralism and Zionism, arguing that Zionism would allow Jewish Americans to be better Jews and better Americans.

Within this context, Zionist Americans negotiated their images of themselves and the Holy Land. The construction of American Zionism also racialized Jewish Americans as acculturated white Americans, yet still marked them as distinctive as Jews. This racial discourse was coupled with optimistic language of progress, though that very language belied the insecurities felt by Jewish Americans in interwar America, paralleling the insecurities of many Americans during this period of social change. But Zionists believed their positive image in the United States would be best achieved by promoting the distinctive qualities of Jews and by highlighting their good standing and contributions.

Antisemitic discrimination and violence against Jews in Europe, from social exclusion to pogroms in Eastern Europe to the Holocaust, have influenced Jewish life in America in many ways. Many Jews who experienced these tragedies fled to America, bringing memories of home, family left behind, and their social experiences in Europe. Legal restrictions on immigration limited what Jewish Americans could do for their European counterparts after the 1920s, though some Jewish Americans supported various programs to assist European Jews as antisemitism and Nazism intensified. Since the postwar years, Jewish Americans have commemorated the deaths of six million Jews in the Holocaust. The Holocaust entered mainstream American discourse increasingly after the 1960s, and memory of the Holocaust has shaped Jewish communal identity, as well as American national discourse on suffering and genocide.

Though Jews have never constituted more than 2 to 3 percent of the population of the country as a whole, they have often lived in neighborhoods where a majority or a significant number of residents were Jewish. This tendency can be compared to living arrangements among many other American groups. However, American Jews have never lived in totally insular neighborhoods, and Jews have lived among many other ethno-religious groups throughout the United States. In the mid-twentieth century, suburbanization restructured Jewish experiences, as it did for many Americans. The ability of Jews to move into many suburban neighborhoods alongside white non-Jews during the mid-twentieth century facilitated a greater sense of Jews as white and greater Jewish integration into the American middle class, although not all Jews achieved or desired that status.

Jews have addressed race, identity, and belonging in media and politics. For example, the performance by Jewish singer and actor Al Jolson (1886–1950) in the 1927 film *The Jazz Singer* earned widespread popularity. Jolson performed in blackface, which allowed him to participate in American culture and yet marked Jewish difference through race. However, this performance—possible in an American environment in which antisemitism was less virulent than in Europe—reified blackness as a marker of outsider difference, not to mention many racist stereotypes in the United States. Jolson epitomized a trend in popular culture of Jews blurring and re-forming color boundaries that continued throughout the twentieth and twenty-first centuries.

In addition to their activities in media and culture, many white Jews participated in the civil rights movement, especially as lawyers and activists. Because many Jewish rights in the United States were gained via the legal system, American Jews were invested in the use of the legal system to gain acceptance in America. They believed this approach could help blacks as well, and that blacks and Jews could band together to reform the American legal system for the benefit of minorities. However, by the late 1950s to 1960s, many black Americans had lost faith in the country's legal system, which was an ongoing source of tension in black-Jewish relations.

While many assume that "Jews" are white, or at least discrete from black Americans, the reality has been much more complex. There are, for example, multiple groups of "black Jews," in addition to broader questions about whether Ashkenazi and Sephardic Jews are white, black, or neither. Shared narratives about Exodus and redemption have been important for many African American Christians. However, some African Americans have gone beyond a figurative identification with the Christian Old Testament to see blacks as the true Israel or ancient Hebrews. Major movements have included the Church of the Living God, the Pillar Ground of Truth for All Nations (founded in 1886); the Church of God and Saints of Christ (1899); the Commandment Keepers (1919); and the African Hebrew Israelites of Jerusalem (1966). These movements creatively combined elements of black Christianity, Judaism (sometimes including identification with Beta Israel, or Ethiopian Jews), black nationalism, and civil rights while producing new practices. Additionally, many black Jews, who often come to Judaism through conversion or intermarriage, have practiced some form of halakhic Judaism.

Jewish intermarriage rates in the nineteenth century were around 7 percent in the United States. About 44 percent of Jewish Americans today are intermarried, and a majority of those married since 1995 have a non-Jewish spouse. Although some Jews lament their belief that intermarriage will inevitably lead to the weakening of the Jewish community and Judaism, many Jewish Americans embrace their identities as half or partial Jews. Some Jews welcome new combinations of Jewish and other identities. Intermarriage between religious and ethnic groups is increasingly common in the United States; thus whether it is embraced or rejected, intermarriage will be a component of twenty-first-century Jewish life.

SEE ALSO *Arab-Israeli Conflict; Balfour Declaration (1917); Holocaust; Israel; The Jazz Singer; Jewish Welfare Board; Melting Pot; Protestant-Catholic-Jew (Will Herberg, 1955); World War II; Zionism*

BIBLIOGRAPHY

Alexander, Michael. *Jazz Age Jews.* Princeton, NJ: Princeton University Press, 2001.

Benor, Sarah Bunin. *Becoming Frum: How Newcomers Learn the Language and Culture of Orthodox Judaism.* New Brunswick, NJ: Rutgers University Press, 2012.

Ben-Ur, Aviva. *Sephardic Jews in America: A Diasporic History.* New York: New York University Press, 2009.

Diner, Hasia. *In the Almost Promised Land: American Jews and Blacks, 1915–1935.* Baltimore, MD: Johns Hopkins University Press, 1977.

Diner, Hasia. *A Time for Gathering: The Second Migration, 1820–1880.* Baltimore, MD: Johns Hopkins University Press, 1992.

Dinnerstein, Leonard. *Uneasy at Home: Antisemitism and the American Jewish Experience.* New York: Columbia University Press, 1987.

Faber, Eli. *A Time for Planting: The First Migration, 1654–1820.* Baltimore, MD: Johns Hopkins University Press, 1992.

Feingold, Henry L. *A Time for Searching: Entering the Mainstream, 1920–1945.* Baltimore, MD: Johns Hopkins University Press, 1992.

Goldstein, Eric. *The Price of Whiteness: Jews, Race, and American Identity.* Princeton, NJ: Princeton University Press, 2006.

Gurock, Jeffrey. *Orthodox Jews in America.* Bloomington: Indiana University Press, 2009.

Heilman, Samuel. *Sliding to the Right: The Contest for the Future of American Jewish Orthodoxy.* Berkeley: University of California Press, 2006.

Heinze, Andrew. *Adapting to Abundance: Jewish Immigrants, Mass Consumption, and the Search for American Identity.* New York: Columbia University Press, 1990.

Hertzberg, Arthur. *The Zionist Idea: A Historical Analysis and Reader.* Philadelphia: Jewish Publication Society, 1997.

Hyman, Paula. *Gender and Assimilation in Modern Jewish History: The Roles and Presentations of Women.* Seattle: University of Washington Press, 1995.

Joselit, Jenna Weissman. *The Wonders of America: Reinventing Jewish Culture, 1880–1950.* New York: Hill and Wang, 1994.

Katznelson, Ira. "Between Separation and Disappearance: Jews on the Margins of American Liberalism." In *Paths of Emancipation: Jews, States, and Citizenship*, edited by Pierre Birnbaum and Ira Katznelson, chap. 6. Princeton, NJ: Princeton University Press, 1995.

Magid, Shaul. *American Post-Judaism: Identity and Renewal in a Postethnic Society.* Bloomington: Indiana University Press, 2013.

Mendes-Flohr, Paul, and Jehuda Reinharz, eds. *The Jew in the Modern World: A Documentary History.* 3rd ed. New York: Oxford University Press, 2010.

Meyer, Michael. *Response to Modernity: A History of the Reform Movement in Judaism.* Detroit, MI: Wayne State University Press, 1995.

Moore, Deborah Dash. *At Home in America: Second Generation New York Jews.* New York: Columbia University Press, 1981.

Myers, Jody. *Kabbalah and the Spiritual Quest: The Kabbalah Centre in America.* Westport, CT: Praeger, 2007.

Pew Research Center. "A Portrait of Jewish Americans." Survey, October 1, 2013. http://www.pewforum.org/2013/10/01/jewish-american-beliefs-attitudes-culture-survey/

Prell, Riv-Ellen. *Prayer and Community: The Havurah in American Judaism.* Detroit, MI: Wayne State University Press, 1989.

Prell, Riv-Ellen. *Fighting to Become Americans: Assimilation and the Trouble between Jewish Women and Jewish Men.* Boston: Beacon Press, 1999.

Raboteau, Albert. "African Americans, Exodus, and the American Israel." In *Religion and American Culture: A Reader*, edited by David G. Hackett, 73–86. New York: Routledge, 1995.

Sarna, Jonathan. "The Debate over Mixed Seating in the American Synagogue." In *Religion and American Culture: A Reader*, edited by David Hackett, 272–290. New York: Routledge, 1995.

Sarna, Jonathan. *American Judaism: A History.* New Haven, CT: Yale University Press, 2004.

Satlow, Michael. *Creating Judaism: History, Tradition, and Practice.* New York: Columbia University Press, 2006.

Wenger, Beth. *History Lessons: The Creation of American Jewish Heritage.* Princeton, NJ: Princeton University Press, 2010.

Jessica Carr
Assistant Professor in Religious Studies
Lafayette College

K

KELLOGG-BRIAND PACT

In the summer of 1928, the great powers promised to renounce war as an instrument of national policy. Their representatives signed an agreement that became known as the Pact of Paris, or the Kellogg-Briand Pact in honor of its creators, US secretary of state Frank B. Kellogg (1856–1937) and French foreign minister Aristide Briand (1862–1932). Newspaper editorials, radio speeches, and public gatherings around the world celebrated the pact as a sign of progress and international cooperation. Despite these celebrations, it quickly became clear that the pact contained critical flaws. It lacked clear definitions to identify aggressors or justify a defensive war, and it contained no enforcement mechanism to punish violators. As an instrument of US foreign policy, the pact quickly failed. Its creation and early use, however, illustrate the constrained foreign policy goals of the interwar Republican administrations and the rise and fall of peace activists' ideological and political power in the United States.

A PROPOSAL TO PROMOTE PEACE AND GLOBAL STABILITY

Kellogg proposed a multilateral agreement to outlaw war in part to avoid an entangling alliance with France. Briand sought to mitigate French security fears by building a system of bilateral nonaggression treaties with other powers. In April 1927, he announced a proposal for a treaty outlawing war between France and the United States. Kellogg and President Calvin Coolidge (1872–1933) feared that signing such an agreement would create a de facto alliance obligating the United States to defend France. Coolidge and Kellogg preferred to continue the "involvement without commitment" pattern of foreign relations begun by President Warren Harding (1865–1923). Harding had promised a "return to normalcy" after years of President Woodrow Wilson's (1856–1924) increases in US commitments abroad. Foreign policy priorities during the Harding and Coolidge administrations shifted toward indirect promotion of US commercial interests and backed away from Wilson's attempts to lead a new global diplomatic order. Secretaries of State Charles Evans Hughes (1862–1948) and Kellogg hoped to create international agreements that would promote global stability without creating new economic or military obligations.

At first, Kellogg refused to respond to Briand's offer. Pressure from peace activists, however, soon brought him to consider reworking the bilateral treaty between France and the United States into a multilateral instrument consistent with the administration's vision for America's global role.

THE ROLE OF PEACE ACTIVISTS

Peace activists laid the groundwork for a treaty outlawing war and directly shaped its creation. During the 1920s, the peace movement in the United States had substantial public support and political clout. Activists organized themselves in a dizzying range of organizations and causes. Radical organizations, including the National Council for Prevention of War and the Women's International League for Peace and Freedom, hoped for political shifts from militarism and nationalism toward social justice and pacifism. Reaching out to other radical activists in Europe and Asia, they mobilized global public opinion for peace.

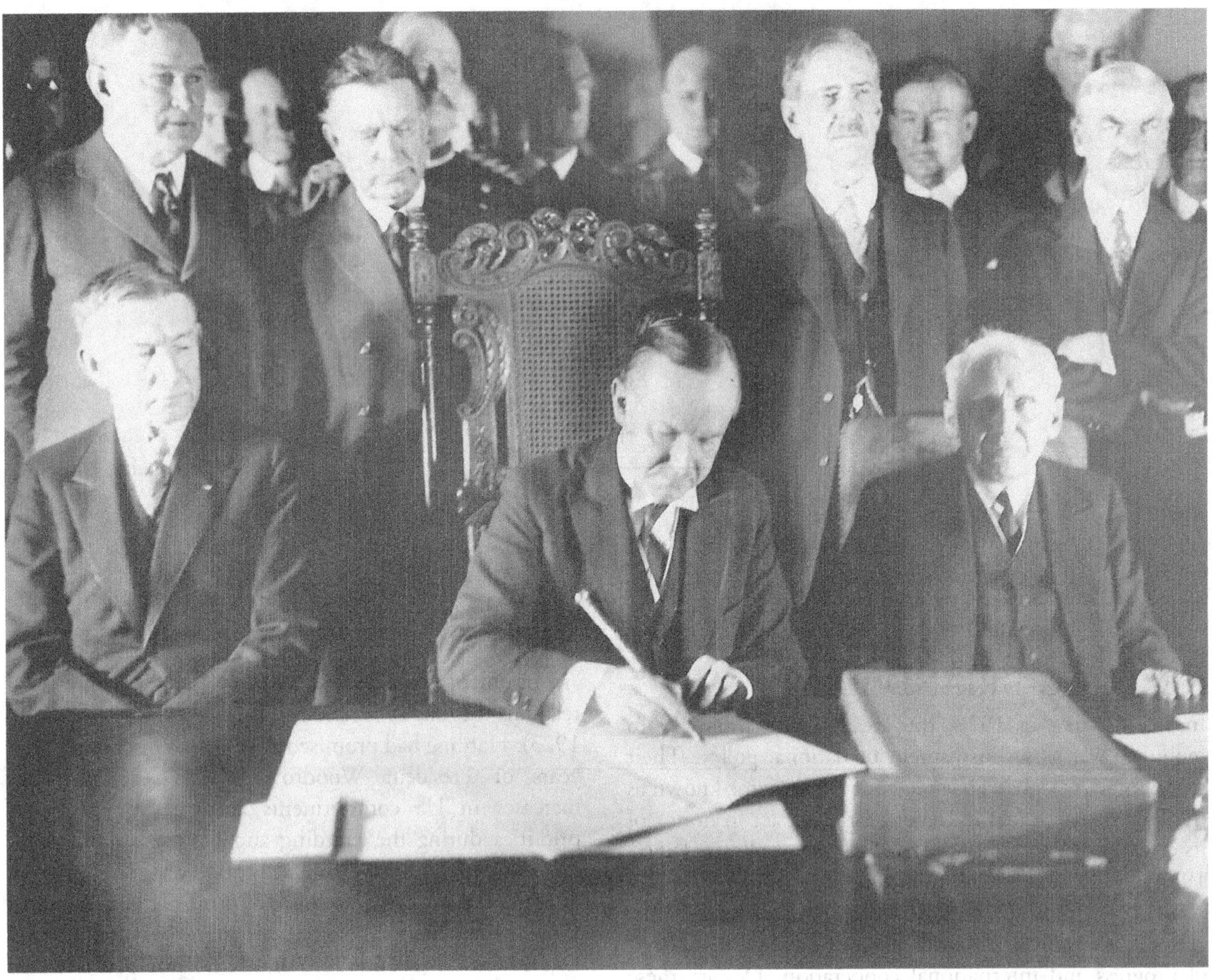

President Calvin Coolidge signing the Kellogg-Briand Pact, 1928. At left, Vice President Charles G. Dawes; Secretary of State Frank B. Kellogg is seated at right. *By the late 1930s, events had transformed the pact from a grand means to prevent war, as its authors had intended, to a procedural precedent in international law. The main legacy of the Kellogg-Briand Pact was in influencing legal standards on the use of military force and on crimes against peace.* DIZ MUENCHEN GMBH, SUEDDEUTSCHE ZEITUNG PHOTO/ALAMY

Other activists prioritized cooperation with the League of Nations and other international organizations. Nicholas Murray Butler (1862–1947), president of Columbia University and of the Carnegie Endowment for International Peace, numbered among the well-connected conservative or establishment-oriented peace activists. They hoped to push the United States toward a larger global role to preserve peace while also safeguarding its national autonomy and security. Many in this wing of the peace movement hoped that legal agreements and treaties could reduce global conflict. Although these various strains of peace activism coexisted uneasily, they collaborated to influence policy through public opinion and ties to policy makers.

Peace was popular. Support for peace and global stability helped spur the State Department to convene the 1921–1922 Washington naval conference to limit arms. Legal agreements for disarmament, arbitration, and consultation among nations fit peace activists' goals and State Department priorities. Activists used international ties to pressure diplomats at home and abroad toward their goals. Butler and two other conservative activists, James Shotwell (1874–1965) and Salmon Levinson (1865–1941), claimed that they had used their influence to persuade Briand to offer the United States a treaty outlawing war. Shotwell and Butler had discussed their peace goals with Briand while traveling in Europe, and Levinson led a group advocating the outlawry of war. It is unlikely, however, that their ideas directly inspired Briand's offer. All three used newspaper editorials and personal connections to pressure Kellogg toward accepting. Other peace activists joined to mobilize public opinion.

Kellogg outflanked Briand and appeased domestic peace activists by revising the bilateral treaty into a pact for all nations of the world. While unhappy, Briand appreciated the public relations benefit such an agreement would bring. Kellogg deliberately kept the proposal short and simple. The policy section had only two main provisions: the signatories renounced war as an instrument of national policy, and they would resolve disputes only by "pacific means." Kellogg knew that adding precise definitions and specific means for enforcement would make other great powers shy away and anger the Republican-dominated US Senate. Mobilized public opinion would be sufficient to enforce the treaty, Kellogg claimed.

WIDESPREAD GLOBAL SUPPORT

The new proposal garnered widespread public support in the United States and around the world. Kellogg and delegates from fifteen other nations signed the treaty on August 27, 1928, using a massive golden pen donated by the mayor of Le Havre, France. Forty-seven other nations would ratify the treaty over the next few years, making nearly every nation in the world a signatory. The US Senate ratified the treaty by an eighty-five-to-one margin. Nevertheless, like many of the signatories, the Senate added a "reservation" clarifying that the United States retained the right to self-defense and was not automatically obligated to intervene if an aggressor violated the pact. The pact's lack of specificity and nations' reservations quickly hamstrung any chance for effective enforcement.

IMPACT AND LEGACY

Although peace activists in the United States and abroad realized the pact was flawed, they used it creatively during the 1930s to bolster their fights for international cooperation, disarmament, and a halt to outbreaks of war. With poster campaigns, rallies, and school curricula, activists educated the public about the pact and its obligations. The League of Nations Association and other groups in the United States argued that signing the pact meant the United States should join the League and the World Court and participate more directly in international organizations. Other groups, particularly radical activists, mobilized an international signature campaign connecting the treaty to disarmament. This movement climaxed when women from around the world delivered hundreds of thousands of petitions to the 1932 Disarmament Conference, urging the gathered diplomats to live up to the spirit of the Kellogg-Briand Pact. Activists in the United States also urged the State Department to invoke the pact and intervene to stop conflicts in Manchuria and Ethiopia.

Neither League of Nations members nor Kellogg's successors as secretary of state found the pact effective in responding to the 1931 Manchurian crisis and the 1935 Italo-Ethiopian War. Japan and Italy had both signed the agreement. Without clear guidelines to punish violators or force nations to take action, however, the pact only added to the League and the United States' uncertainty and lack of desire to act. Secretary of State Henry L. Stimson (1867–1950) made reference to it when negotiating with Japan, but to little avail. By the late 1930s, events had transformed the pact from a grand means to prevent war to a procedural precedent in international law. Its most significant legacy was in influencing legal standards on the use of military force and on crimes against peace, including at the 1945–1946 Nuremberg Tribunal of Nazi war criminals.

SEE ALSO *France; League of Nations; Paris Peace Conference (1919); Treaty of Versailles; United Nations; World War I; World War II*

BIBLIOGRAPHY

Chatfield, Charles, ed. *Peace Movements in America.* New York: Schocken, 1974.

DeBoe, David Cornelius. "Secretary Stimson and the Kellogg-Briand Pact." In *Essays in American Foreign Policy,* edited by David C. DeBoe, Margaret F. Morris, and Sandra L. Myers, 31–53. Arlington: University of Texas Press, 1974.

Ferrell, Robert H. *Peace in Their Time: The Origins of the Kellogg-Briand Pact.* New Haven, CT: Yale University Press, 1952.

Ferrell, Robert H. *Frank B. Kellogg; Henry L. Stimson.* New York: Cooper Square, 1963.

Foster, Carrie A. *The Women and the Warriors: The U.S. Section of the Women's International League for Peace and Freedom, 1941–1946.* Syracuse, NY: Syracuse University Press, 2004.

Josephson, Harold. *James T. Shotwell and the Rise of Internationalism in America.* Cranbury, NJ: Associated University Press, 1975.

Kellogg-Briand Pact. 1928. http://avalon.law.yale.edu/20th_century/kbpact.asp

Kneeshaw, Stephen J. *In Pursuit of Peace: The American Reaction to the Kellogg-Briand Pact, 1928–1929.* New York: Garland, 1991.

Limberg, Michael. "'In Relation to the Pact': Radical Pacifists and the Kellogg-Briand Pact, 1928–1939." *Peace and Change* 39, 3 (2014): 395–420.

Roscher, Bernhardt. "The Renunciation of War as an Instrument of National Policy." *Journal of the History of International Law* 4, 2 (2002): 293–309.

Michael Limberg
PhD Candidate
University of Connecticut

KENNAN, GEORGE F.

1904–2005

George Frost Kennan enjoyed a varied career during his long life. Born and raised in a Presbyterian household in

Milwaukee, he attended a stern preparatory school, St. John's Military Academy in Delafield, Wisconsin. From there he matriculated at Princeton University, from which he was graduated in 1925. After passing the State Department's requisite written and oral exams, Kennan obtained appointment as a Foreign Service officer in 1926. At one time or another, in subsequent years he assumed the role of diplomat, policy maker, scholar, and establishment dissenter.

In his capacity as diplomat, Kennan belonged to a small cadre of highly trained Soviet experts. He was among a handful of young Foreign Service officers who accompanied Ambassador William C. Bullitt (1891–1967) to Moscow in December 1933, soon after Soviet-US relations were normalized. During the critical years of 1944 to 1946, Kennan served at the embassy in Moscow as the principal advisor to Ambassador W. Averell Harriman (1891–1986). While in that position, Kennan sent his "long telegram" to the State Department on February 22, 1946. Intended by him to arouse Washington to the challenges posed by Soviet power to the West, the telegram impressed Washington officialdom and helped give shape and purpose to evolving American foreign policy, later captured in the term *containment.*

Kennan himself twice held ambassadorships—briefly in 1952 to the Soviet Union, then from 1961 to 1963 to the Yugoslavia of Josip Broz Tito (1892–1980). Neither of these ambassadorships was successful, the first being particularly discouraging. Kennan was declared persona non grata in September 1952 by the Soviet government after delivering himself in public of impolitic remarks, likening his life in the USSR to what he experienced while posted in Nazi Germany from 1939 to 1941. In the 1960s, anticommunist fundamentalists in Congress who failed to appreciate the independent line that Tito was pursuing—away from Moscow dictate—and the concomitant advantages to the West undermined Kennan's mission to Belgrade.

A leading architect of America's early Cold War strategy, Kennan—and his reputation—remains closely linked to the administration of President Harry S. Truman (1884–1972) and its foreign policy. While director of the State Department's Policy Planning Staff (PPS) from 1947 to 1949, Kennan helped devise the Marshall Plan, one of the more creative and effective of Washington's Cold War projects. He was also a forceful proponent of the political-economic revival of postwar Japan. During his tenure as PPS director, Kennan published, under the pseudonym X, his "Sources of Soviet Conduct" in the July 1947 issue of *Foreign Affairs.* This article, along with the "long telegram," was destined to become a seminal document of the Cold War era. The most oft-quoted phrase from the X-article has been for many years an object of scholarly scrutiny: "Soviet pressure against the free institutions of the Western world is something that can be contained by the adroit and vigilant application of counter-force at a series of constantly shifting geographical and political points, corresponding to the shifts and maneuvers of Soviet policy" (Kennan 1951, 120). The preponderance of evidence, traceable to diverse sources contemporaneous with the X-article, indicates that Kennan's conception of containment was anchored in economic-political methods and only secondarily in military ones, notwithstanding the ambiguous language of the *Foreign Affairs* piece. He tried during his PPS tenure to emphasize the primacy of diplomacy and believed that the Cold War could be successfully waged by measures short of outright warfare.

From the early 1950s onward, Kennan was connected to the Institute for Advanced Study in Princeton, New Jersey. He devoted most of his time there to historical research centered on the deep origins of World War I, international relations, and Soviet politics. Additionally, he composed two volumes of memoirs, maintained a voluminous diary (whose earliest entries dated to childhood), and delivered high-profile lectures on pressing public questions.

Long unhappy with the main thrust of US foreign policy, Kennan's dissenting voice was most clearly heard in the 1960s, when in public forums he denounced America's Indochina war. Later, most notably in the 1980s, as the Soviet-US rivalry intensified, he warned in stirring language against the dangers posed by the nuclear arms race. In 1981, he famously advised—on the occasion of accepting the Albert Einstein Peace Prize—that the two superpowers should reduce by 50 percent their stockpiles of nuclear weapons. A year later, he exclaimed against what he saw as a version of blasphemy inherent in US strategic doctrine and the amassing of weapons of mass destruction:

> The readiness to use nuclear weapons against other human beings—against people whom we do not know, whom we have never seen, and whose guilt or innocence it is not for us to establish—and, in doing so, to place in jeopardy the natural structure upon which all civilization rests, as though the safety and the perceived interests of our generation are more important than everything that has ever taken place or could take place in civilization: this is nothing less than a presumption … an indignity—an indignity of monstrous dimension—offered to God! (Mayers 1988, 314)

SEE ALSO *Cold War; Truman Doctrine*

BIBLIOGRAPHY

Gaddis, John Lewis. *George F. Kennan: An American Life.* New York: Penguin, 2011.

Kennan, George F. *American Diplomacy, 1900–1950*. Chicago: University of Chicago Press, 1951.

Kennan, George F. *Memoirs: 1925–1950*. Boston: Little, Brown, 1967.

Kennan, George F. *Memoirs: 1950–1963*. Boston: Little, Brown, 1972.

Kennan, George F. *Sketches from a Life*. New York: Pantheon, 1989.

Kennan, George F. *Around the Cragged Hill: A Personal and Political Philosophy*. New York: Norton, 1993.

Kennan, George F. *At a Century's Ending: Reflections, 1982–1995*. New York: Norton, 1996.

Kennan, George F. *The Kennan Diaries*. Edited by Frank Costigliola. New York: Norton, 2014.

Mayers, David. *George Kennan and the Dilemmas of U.S. Foreign Policy*. New York: Oxford University Press, 1988.

David Mayers
Professor, History Department, Political Science Department
Boston University

KENNEDY, JOHN FITZGERALD
1917–1963

John F. Kennedy, the thirty-fifth president of the United States, was born on May 29, 1917, in Brookline, Massachusetts. He attended Choate School, spent a year at Princeton College, and then went to Harvard College, from which he graduated in 1940. While John was still in college, his father, Joseph Kennedy (1888–1969), was appointed ambassador to Great Britain, and John Kennedy spent several vacations and part of a school year in England and on the continent. Out of these experiences came a senior thesis, which recounted and condemned England's prewar policy of appeasement. Published as *Why England Slept*, it became a best seller in 1940.

CONGRESSIONAL CAREER

After a brief attendance at Stanford Business School in 1941, Kennedy enlisted in the US Navy. He served as the commander of a torpedo boat (PT 109), which was sunk in a 1943 South Pacific engagement; this event was heavily publicized in Kennedy's subsequent political career. Upon his discharge from the service, Kennedy worked for a few months as a journalist before he plunged into a campaign for the US Congress in Massachusetts's Eleventh District. He was elected in 1946 with little difficulty from the predominantly Irish-Italian district. His tenure in the lower chamber was a conventional one, although he created a small furor in 1949 when he attacked President Harry S. Truman (1884–1972) and the State Department for what he considered the unnecessary loss of mainland China to the communists.

In 1952, Kennedy ran for the US Senate against the popular incumbent senator from Massachusetts, Republican Henry Cabot Lodge (1902–1985). Despite Republican Dwight D. Eisenhower's (1890–1969) easy win in the state, Kennedy demonstrated remarkable popularity by defeating Lodge by approximately seventy thousand votes. As a senator, Kennedy's first few years in office were marked by pivotal personal and political events that shaped his future career. In September 1953, he married Jacqueline Lee Bouvier (1929–1994), a beautiful, cultured woman of twenty-four, who would later gain an immense following as the first lady. In October of the next year, Kennedy underwent a long, difficult back operation.

During the months when he was convalescing from his back operation, Kennedy wrote *Profiles in Courage*, a study of fidelity to political principle exhibited by seven American politicians over a 150-year period. The book, published in early 1956, was a best seller and gave Kennedy important national exposure.

CAMPAIGN FOR THE PRESIDENCY

By the time Kennedy officially announced his candidacy for the presidency in January 1960, he held a slight edge in the opinion polls over his chief rivals, including Senator Lyndon Johnson (1908–1973), a Democrat from Texas, who became his running mate. In the general election campaign, neither Kennedy nor his Republican opponent, Vice President Richard M. Nixon (1913–1994), could find an issue that sharply divided them. Both thought, however, that foreign policy was the overriding issue in the election. Both favored a strong defense and vigorous diplomacy to ensure continued American leadership of the West. Although Kennedy took a somewhat less aggressive stance than did his rival on the need to defend Nationalist China's island outposts, the Democratic candidate criticized the Republicans for not taking stronger action against Cuba, and he warned of an ominous, but later disproven, "missile gap" between the United States and the USSR.

Many political observers thought the turning point in the campaign came on September 26 during the first of four televised debates between the two candidates. Kennedy, who had sought the debate, proved confident and vigorous, while his opponent, still recovering from a two-week hospital stay, appeared hesitant and weary. Neither candidate "won" the debate, but Kennedy's cool, relaxed style proved attractive to many viewers.

In the election, a record turnout gave Kennedy the victory by a mere 113,057-vote margin—the smallest of the twentieth century. He carried fewer states than Nixon

President John F. Kennedy welcoming the Diplomatic Corps at the Quai d'Orsay, Paris, May 31, 1961. *Upon being elected, Kennedy planned to conduct American diplomacy himself rather than delegate authority to his secretary of state, viewing foreign affairs as his most important responsibility and most difficult challenge.* ROGER VIOLLET COLLECTION/GETTY IMAGES

but defeated his opponent in the Electoral College vote, 303 to 219.

THE PRESIDENCY

The new president assembled a cabinet that reflected his own sense of political realism and the worldview of liberal internationalism. Amid some controversy, Kennedy appointed his brother Robert Kennedy (1925–1968) as attorney general. He unhesitatingly reappointed conservatives Allen Dulles (1893–1969) and J. Edgar Hoover (1895–1972) to lead the Central Intelligence Agency (CIA) and Federal Bureau of Investigation (FBI), respectively. Finally, Kennedy gave individuals closely associated with the Republican Eastern Establishment the posts he thought most vital. Moderate Republicans Robert S. McNamara (1916–2009) and C. Douglas Dillon (1909–2003) were appointed to head the Departments of Defense and the Treasury, respectively. Kennedy chose the rather colorless head of the Rockefeller Foundation, Dean Rusk (1909–1994), as secretary of state. The new president planned to conduct American diplomacy himself and saw in Rusk a man who would administer the State Department without threatening White House dominance in international affairs.

Foreign Affairs. Kennedy considered the conduct of foreign affairs his most important responsibility and his most difficult challenge. In an inaugural address devoted almost exclusively to world affairs, he pledged the nation "to pay any price, bear any burden, meet any hardship, support any friend, oppose any foe, to assure the survival and success of liberty." Kennedy thought the Cold War was at its "hour of maximum danger," and he called for sacrifice and commitment by all citizens. In what became the most memorable line in a speech that many historians then considered the best since Abraham Lincoln's,

Kennedy proclaimed, "Ask not what your country can do for you—ask what you can do for your country."

With his most influential foreign policy advisers, General Maxwell Taylor (1901–1987), McGeorge Bundy (1919–1996), and Robert McNamara—"the best and the brightest," as the journalist David Halberstam (1934–2007) would later call them—the president sought a new and more effective strategy for countering the communist military and political threat. These New Frontiersmen held their fiscally conservative and ideologically rigid predecessors responsible for a dangerous overreliance on the nuclear deterrent. Kennedy's foreign policy strategists sought a more "flexible" response to the communists, one that would counter the enemy regardless of the form its offensive took: local brushfire insurgencies, ideological warfare, or diplomatic maneuver.

The Peace Corps, Food for Peace, the Alliance for Progress, and economic aid for underdeveloped nations and for the dissident communist regimes of Yugoslavia and Poland were programs inaugurated or increased by the administration as part of its more flexible strategy in the Cold War. At the same time, Kennedy favored an expanded military establishment possessing sufficient conventional, nuclear, and counterinsurgency forces to effectively oppose any level of communist aggression.

During his first year in office, Kennedy faced a difficult series of diplomatic and military pressures and reverses. He accepted the neutralization of Laos in early 1961 as the most advantageous solution to a troublesome local situation. In April, the president suffered a personal humiliation when a CIA-planned exile invasion of Cuba was routed at the Bay of Pigs. Later in the spring, the Soviets stepped up their pressure on West Berlin and demanded that the West recognize as permanent the postwar division of Germany. When Kennedy met with Nikita Khrushchev (1894–1971) in Vienna in June, the new president appeared shaken by the Russian leader's intransigence and believed he had failed to make a strong impression on the premier.

While Kennedy could do little to rectify the American situation in Laos or Cuba, he was determined to demonstrate US firmness in Berlin and Vietnam. In July, the president reaffirmed the American will to defend West Berlin by ordering 250,000 reservists to active duty and asking Congress for another increase in the military budget. At the same time, he outlined a sweeping civil defense program designed to show the Russians America's willingness to risk nuclear war over the German city. The USSR responded to the crisis by building the Berlin Wall in August and letting the issue of a German settlement die by the end of the year. Nor did Kennedy ever consider a political settlement for Vietnam. After coming under fire for agreeing to do so in Laos, he was even more determined to avoid it. The number of American troops in South Vietnam under Kennedy increased steadily, reaching some 16,500 before the end of 1963.

Cuban Missile Crisis. Kennedy confronted his most serious Cold War crisis in October 1962, when American intelligence discovered that the Soviets had begun to install offensive missiles in Cuba. Working closely with his brother Robert, Kennedy rejected the views of his advisers, who favored an immediate air strike, but he also opposed an extended period of negotiations or a public trade-off of Soviet missiles in Cuba for American rockets in Italy or Turkey. Instead, Kennedy and a special committee of the National Security Council, which met each day to "manage" the crisis, decided to impose a "quarantine" of the island, a measure that went into effect on October 24. On October 28, the Soviets turned back from the potential naval confrontation and agreed to remove their Cuban missiles. We were "eyeball to eyeball," said Dean Rusk, "They blinked first." (quoted in Graebner, Burns, and Siracusa 2010, 270).

When Khrushchev later suggested that negotiations be reopened regarding a long-deferred nuclear test ban treaty, Kennedy quickly assented. Disagreement over on-site inspection of underground nuclear tests stalled the talks, but in a speech delivered at American University on June 10, 1963, Kennedy announced that he was sending Averell Harriman (1891–1986) to Moscow to negotiate a more limited test ban agreement excluding the controversial underground tests. In July, a limited nuclear test ban agreement was initialed in Moscow and, with surprisingly little domestic opposition, ratified by the Senate in September. It was Kennedy's most enduring achievement in foreign affairs.

Death of a President. On November 22, 1963, while riding through downtown Dallas in a motorcade, President Kennedy was shot and killed by a lone assassin, later identified as Lee Harvey Oswald. Within thirty minutes of the shooting, seventy-five million Americans had heard the news; by late afternoon ninety million Americans, or 99.8 percent of the adult population, had heard of the president's death. The global community was also in mourning, with the news of the assassination dominating the media of every major capital in the world. The assassination of John F. Kennedy had been the greatest simultaneous experience in the history of the modern world to that time.

SEE ALSO *Bay of Pigs; Castro, Fidel; Cold War; Cuba; Cuban Missile Crisis; Johnson, Lyndon Baines; Kennedy, Robert; Laos; McNamara, Robert S.; Nuclear Weapons; Peace Corps; United States Agency for International Development (USAID); Vietnam War*

BIBLIOGRAPHY

Dallek, Robert. *An Unfinished Life: John F. Kennedy, 1917–1965.* New York: Little, Brown, 2003.

Graebner, Norman A., Richard Dean Burns, and Joseph M. Siracusa. *America and the Cold War, 1941–1991: A Realist Interpretation.* Santa Barbara, CA: Praeger, 2010.

Kennedy, John F. Inaugural Address. January 20, 1961. http://www.jfklibrary.org/Asset-Viewer/BqXIEM9F4024ntFl7SVAjA.aspx

Naftali, Timothy, Philip Zelikow, and Ernest May, eds. *The Presidential Recordings: John F. Kennedy.* 3 vols. New York: Norton, 2001. http://millercenter.org/presidentialrecordings/kennedy/jfk-norton-volumes

Schlesinger, Arthur M., Jr. *A Thousand Days: John F. Kennedy in the White House.* Boston: Houghton Mifflin, 1965.

Sorensen, Theodore C. *Kennedy.* New York: Harper and Row, 1965.

Joseph Siracusa
Professor of Human Security and International Diplomacy
Royal Melbourne Institute of Technology University

KENNEDY, ROBERT
1925–1968

Robert Francis Kennedy, the younger brother of President John Fitzgerald Kennedy (1917–1963), played a vital role in many momentous events of the 1950s and 1960s. In 1952, at the age of twenty-six, Robert managed then-representative John F. Kennedy's campaign for the US Senate in Massachusetts. His efforts helped his brother win against the incumbent republican senator, Henry Cabot Lodge (1902–1985). Out of this Senate campaign was born the extraordinary political partnership of John and Robert Kennedy.

EARLY CAREER IN GOVERNMENT

Upon graduating from Harvard and then the University of Virginia Law School, Robert Kennedy began his career in government as a young lawyer on the staff of the US Senate's Permanent Investigations Subcommittee, chaired by Wisconsin senator (and Kennedy family friend) Joseph McCarthy (1908–1957). In the intense Cold War environment that existed between the United States and the Soviet Union in the early 1950s, Senator McCarthy abused the committee's investigative powers for partisan gain. Robert Kennedy quickly soured on McCarthy's tactics and resigned his post.

In 1955, the Democrats held a Senate majority and Arkansas senator John McClellan (1896–1977) appointed Robert Kennedy to be the lead counsel for the subcommittee that McCarthy had exploited. At the age of twenty-nine, Kennedy oversaw a staff of forty and rapidly earned a reputation as a dogged investigator. Two years later, when Senator McClellan chaired a new committee, the Senate Select Committee on Improper Activities in the Labor and Management Field (known as the "Rackets Committee"), he asked Kennedy to be its chief counsel. (Senator John F. Kennedy also served on the committee.) The Rackets Committee investigated corruption in some of the nation's biggest labor unions, including the Teamsters Union under the leadership of James Hoffa. The committee's televised hearings for the first time gave John and Robert Kennedy a high degree of national notoriety.

ATTORNEY GENERAL AND ADVISOR IN THE JOHN F. KENNEDY ADMINISTRATION

In 1960, Robert Kennedy managed his brother's campaign for president of the United States. The election, where John F. Kennedy narrowly defeated Vice President Richard Nixon (1913–1994), was one of the closest in American history. President Kennedy became the nation's youngest president ever to be elected and its first Catholic. He appointed Robert to be his attorney general. He joined Secretary of Defense Robert McNamara (1916–2009) and Secretary of State Dean Rusk (1909–1994) in a cabinet that prided itself on its energy and spirit.

At the age of thirty-five, Robert Kennedy oversaw the Department of Justice with over thirty-one thousand employees and a $400 million budget. He was the second-youngest attorney general in US history (the youngest in 140 years) and the first brother of a president ever to hold the position.

In April 1961, following the disastrous CIA-led Bay of Pigs invasion of Cuba, Robert was thrust close to the center of decision making in the White House. His brother came to rely on his loyalty and political advice. Robert became President Kennedy's most trusted adviser on all matters foreign and domestic. The goal of the US-led attack on Cuba was to overthrow the government of Fidel Castro, who had come to power in a revolution on the island in January 1959.

In October 1962, Robert Kennedy played a key role as his brother's secret emissary to Soviet officials in peacefully resolving the Cuban missile crisis, which, if mishandled, could have led to nuclear war between the United States and Soviet Union. Following the peaceful resolution of the missile crisis, President Kennedy successfully negotiated the first-ever treaty with the Soviet Union that put limits on the testing of nuclear weapons: the Atmospheric Test Ban Treaty of 1963.

As attorney general, Robert cracked down on organized crime, and enforced federal court orders banning racial segregation in the South. Robert Kennedy crafted the federal response to the often-violent racial clashes surrounding the Freedom Rides, the enrollment of the first African American students at the University of Mississippi and the University of Alabama, and the May 1963 confrontations in Birmingham, Alabama, that pitted Police Commissioner Eugene "Bull" Connor (1897–1973) against nonviolent protesters led by Dr. Martin Luther King Jr. (1929–1968).

THE US SENATE AND CAMPAIGN FOR THE PRESIDENCY

On November 22, 1963, when President Kennedy was assassinated in Dallas, Texas, Robert's life was forever altered. Up to that point, the driving force of his life had been to serve his brother's political career. In 1964, Robert began to carve out a political path in his own right when he succeeded in winning a US Senate seat from New York.

As senator, Robert Kennedy soon found himself disagreeing with many of the policies of the Democratic administration of President Lyndon Baines Johnson (1908–1973). Kennedy believed many of Johnson's "Great Society" domestic programs were being mismanaged, but he most pointedly criticized the president's escalation of the Vietnam War. By the election year 1968, Kennedy could not in good conscience support Johnson's Vietnam policies and therefore could not endorse his reelection. A growing wing of the Democratic Party that opposed the Vietnam War urged Kennedy to run for president in 1968.

On March 12, 1968, in Delano, California, Senator Kennedy met with Cesar Chavez (1927–1993), the head of the United Farm Workers union, to break a twenty-five-day protest fast in the name of nonviolence. Four days later, Kennedy announced that he was running in the remaining Democratic primaries to challenge President Johnson for the party's nomination. Johnson, however, decided that he would not seek the Democratic nomination.

On the night of April 4, 1968, while campaigning in Indianapolis, Kennedy expressed his feelings extemporaneously upon being told that the Reverend Martin Luther King Jr. had been shot and killed earlier that evening. Kennedy was scheduled to speak in an African American neighborhood, where he announced to those assembled that Dr. King had died. In his remarks, he quoted the ancient Greek poet Aeschylus, and for the first time in a public address he spoke about his brother's assassination.

Robert Kennedy's path to the presidency in 1968 opened up as he won primaries in Indiana, Nebraska, South Dakota, and California (he had lost in Oregon). He was close to achieving his goal of winning enough Democratic delegates to block Vice President Hubert Humphrey (1911–1978) from winning the party's nomination on the first ballot at the Democratic National Convention in Chicago.

On June 5, 1968, after winning the California primary and delivering his victory speech at the Ambassador Hotel in Los Angeles, an assailant shot Senator Kennedy in the head with a $30 Iver-Johnson .22-caliber pistol. He died twenty-five hours later. At the time of his death, Kennedy controlled about seven hundred Democratic delegates at the Chicago convention, and with the help of Chicago Mayor Richard J. Daley (1902–1976), whose core constituency mirrored Kennedy's own, he had a real chance of winning the nomination and perhaps beating the Republican nominee, Richard Nixon, in the general election.

SEE ALSO *Bay of Pigs; Castro, Fidel; Cold War; Cuba; Cuban Missile Crisis; Johnson, Lyndon Baines; Kennedy, John Fitzgerald; McNamara, Robert S.; Nuclear Weapons; Vietnam War*

BIBLIOGRAPHY

Evan, Thomas. *Robert Kennedy: His Life*. New York: Simon and Schuster, 2000.

Hilty, James W. *Robert Kennedy: Brother Protector*. Philadelphia: Temple University Press, 1997.

Newfield, Jack. *Robert Kennedy: A Memoir*. New York: Dutton, 1969.

Palermo, Joseph A. *In His Own Right: The Political Odyssey of Senator Robert F. Kennedy*. New York: Columbia University Press, 2001.

Palermo, Joseph A. *Robert F. Kennedy and the Death of American Idealism*. New York: Pearson Longman, 2008.

Schlesinger, Arthur M., Jr. *Robert Kennedy and His Times*. Boston: Houghton Mifflin, 1978.

Talbot, David. *Brothers: The Hidden History of the Kennedy Years*. New York: Free Press, 2007.

Joseph A. Palermo
Professor of History
California State University, Sacramento

KEYNESIAN ECONOMICS

John Maynard Keynes (1883–1946) was born in the Victorian era, but his work in economics was deeply influential in the modern era, especially with regard to unemployment and macroeconomic policies. His work in economics is fascinating but often misunderstood. While most economists think of him as neoclassical—the school of economic thought solidified by one of Keynes's predecessors at Cambridge University, Alfred Marshall (1842–1924)—Keynes preferred to think of himself as a classical economist. Today, many critics try to brand him with the label "socialist," but he very much considered himself a conservative, a philosophy that is reflected in his career and writings.

THE POST–WORLD WAR I PERIOD AND THE GREAT DEPRESSION

Like so many thinkers of his time, Keynes was deeply affected by World War I (1914–1918) and the obvious shortcomings of the Treaty of Versailles. His analysis of Versailles correctly predicted an economic disaster for Germany. Despite a successful academic career and a reputation for scholarly engagement and genius, Keynes's first truly influential work was not published until 1936, a mere ten years before his passing. His *General Theory* contradicted much of the neoclassical school on macroeconomic policies.

In the United States and around the world, the key economic issue of the 1930s was the Great Depression, which resulted in unemployment and incredible economic recession. Until Keynes's *General Theory,* most influential economists argued that government should spend less during a recession because increased savings would lead to investment and, eventually, income and employment gains. Many others argued that economics was an academic inquiry only and should never be used as a policy guide. Employment gains from government inaction never came, and as governments stood idly by, the recession deepened. Indeed, many commentators today forget that Franklin Roosevelt's (1882–1945) entire first term preceded Keynes's *General Theory,* and so the first hundred days of the New Deal were not directly influenced by Keynes. Keynes and Roosevelt did meet and exchange correspondence, and while they expressed mutual admiration in public, privately Roosevelt was unimpressed by Keynes' apparently overly statistical presentation and the President came away still preferring a balanced budget approach. Despite enlarging the New Deal in his second one hundred days, Roosevelt did not pull the United States out of the Great Depression during the 1930s. While many economists argued that this proved government spending cannot work to fix a recession, Keynes argued that Roosevelt had not spent enough. In fact, Keynes insisted that full-employment deficit spending should be the norm during downward turns in the business cycle—in other words, governments should fix recessions by spending enough to achieve full employment, no matter the size of the deficit. Only the immense spending of World War II (1939–1945) pulled the United States out of its decade-long recession.

BRETTON WOODS AND THE POST–WORLD WAR II PERIOD

After World War II, Keynes was much more influential in European and American economic policies. This was by his design; he spent a great deal of time and effort from 1944 to 1946 building, influencing, and politically negotiating the outcomes of the 1944 Bretton Woods agreements. He worked so hard on these projects that he exhausted himself, which may have contributed to his untimely passing in 1946. In the immediate aftermath of the war there were many political and financial difficulties, especially between the United States and Great Britain. Keynes took it upon himself to speak directly with American congressional representatives and British members of Parliament in order to secure all the important facets of the Bretton Woods agreements. He found this distasteful but important—left to their own devices, politicians might ignore economists or seek out only those with whom they already agreed.

The result of the Bretton Woods agreements was the creation of the International Monetary Fund (IMF), the World Bank, and the General Agreement on Tariffs and Trade (GATT). The policies and financial weight of these institutions dominated the economics of the Cold War era, often working in conjunction with political policies such as the Truman Doctrine and the containment of the Soviet Union. While GATT represented Keynes's appreciation for the principles of free trade (namely, lowering barriers to trade, such as tariffs), membership and participation were voluntary, and thus gains in trade from GATT were achieved only incrementally. Still, it was a vast improvement from the retaliatory trade practices of the 1930s. The IMF and the World Bank grew and changed over time; by the 1960s their goals had been so thoroughly expanded and revised that they would have been unrecognizable to Keynes had he lived that long. Originally envisioned as postwar rebuilding and development tools, they became instruments by which the United States and Europe dominated the international economy of the Cold War with policies that stabilized some nations while destabilizing others.

In the wake of Keynes's Bretton Woods system, the global economy achieved incredible growth during a period known as Pax Americana (1945–1973). Despite that success, which in the United States came during and after the heavy, Keynesian-style spending of World War II and the Truman (1945–1953) and Eisenhower (1953–1961) administrations, Keynesian economics came under fire. Milton Friedman (1912–2006), creator of the Chicago School, ushered in a new era of economic thought that reverted backward to the old pre–New Deal ideas of limited government fiscal action, instead focusing on monetarism and using the Federal Reserve to manipulate the financial economy. His ideas eventually became known as neoliberal economics. On the one hand, Friedman's approach was in tune with the changing circumstances of the late 1960s and 1970s. The American economy was changing from an industrial to a postindustrial economy, with services and financial sectors growing as manufacturing fell. Thus, neoliberalism's emphasis on the financial economy was appropriate. On the other hand, in order to establish a new model for managing the economy, Friedman and others had to engage in special pleading to demonstrate somehow that Keynes had been wrong even though his predictions were accurate and his policies fruitful.

There is no singular idea of Keynesian economics. Keynes's writings and ideas are complicated, and he often argued with himself as vehemently as he argued with others. Keynes thought himself to be conservative because he was weary of capitalism and its many claims of efficiency that might undo traditional practices or ways of life. Nonetheless, he recognized that economic policy very much affects people and their livelihoods, and he sought a set of principles that would stabilize the macroeconomics of a nation against the whims of the roller-coaster nature of the business cycle, which had tended toward cycles of boom and bust since the Industrial Revolution. In seeking full employment he thought he was guarding society from the flaws in capitalism while using its strengths to keep society stable, employed, and therefore content. Despite his critiques of capitalism, Keynes defended it as the best system available. To him, the system was a large, unwieldy machine that should be controlled by policy in order to achieve better outcomes. The neoliberals who continue to criticize him see capitalism as far less flawed. They argue that the machine should run on its own with fewer controls, an idea they often summarize as laissez-faire economics.

SEE ALSO *Bretton Woods; Economics; Friedman, Milton; International Monetary Fund; Neoliberalism*

BIBLIOGRAPHY

Bowles, Samuel, Richard Edwards, and Frank Roosevelt. *Understanding Capitalism: Competition, Command, and Change.* New York: Oxford University Press, 2005.

Brue, Stanley L., and Randy R. Grant. *The Evolution of Economic Thought.* Mason, OH: Thomson/South-Western, 2007.

Chang, Ha-joon. *Bad Samaritans: The Myth of Free Trade and the Secret History of Capitalism.* New York: Bloomsbury Press, 2008.

Heilbroner, Robert. *The Worldly Philosophers: The Lives, Times, and Ideas of the Great Economic Thinkers.* 7th ed. New York: Touchstone, 1999.

Keynes, John Maynard. *The General Theory of Employment, Interest and Money.* New York: Harcourt, Brace, 1936.

Krugman, Paul, and Robin Wells. *Economics: Second Edition in Modules.* New York: Worth, 2012.

Reynolds, David. *One World Divisible: A Global History since 1945.* New York: Norton, 2000.

Peter A. McCord
Professor of History
State University of New York, Fredonia

KING, MARTIN LUTHER, JR.

1929–1968

Baptist minister and civil and human rights activist Martin Luther King Jr. helped lead the movement that ended legal segregation and secured voting rights for African Americans in the 1950s and 1960s, fought for an end to war and global poverty, and criticized colonialism and imperialism around the world. King embraced the philosophy of nonviolence and advocated for nonviolent resistance as the most effective way for oppressed people around the world to secure their freedom.

LEADER IN THE US CIVIL RIGHTS MOVEMENT

Born in Atlanta, Georgia, in 1929, King entered Morehouse College at age fifteen and had earned a bachelor of divinity degree from Crozer Theological Seminary and a PhD in systematic theology from Boston University by the time he was twenty-six. In 1954, he became the pastor of the Dexter Avenue Baptist Church in Montgomery,

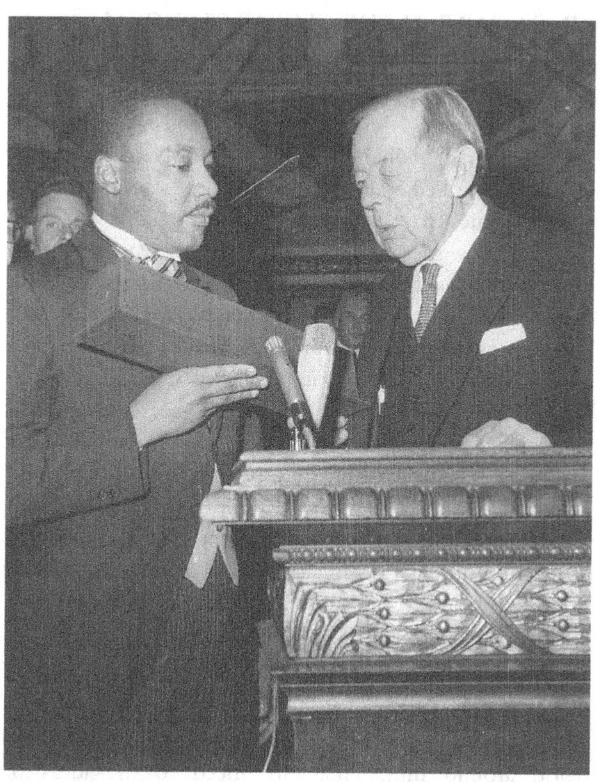

Martin Luther King Jr. receiving the Nobel Peace Prize gold medal from the chairman of the Nobel Committee, Oslo, Norway, December 10, 1964. *King embraced the philosophy of nonviolence and advocated for nonviolent resistance as the most effective way for oppressed people to secure their freedom. His life and work were transformative in the United States and internationally.* AP IMAGES

Alabama. When blacks in Montgomery launched a boycott of the segregated buses there in 1955, King became the public leader of the movement and through his work on the boycott came to embrace nonviolent civil disobedience as a powerful tool in the fight against racial oppression.

In 1957, King helped found the Southern Christian Leadership Conference (SCLC), a group of ministers that aimed to coordinate the struggle against segregation in the South. As president of the SCLC, King organized and led nonviolent demonstrations in Birmingham and in Selma, Alabama, that helped secure the passage of the 1964 Civil Rights Act and the 1965 Voting Rights Act. He called on America to live up to its democratic ideals in his "I Have a Dream Speech," delivered at the March on Washington in 1963. From 1965 until his assassination in 1968, King organized demonstrations against discriminatory housing in northern cities, and fought for worker's rights and for public policies to end poverty. He also became a vocal critic of the US war in Vietnam and was active in the antiwar movement. In 1964, King won the Nobel Peace Prize.

KING'S PART IN THE GLOBAL STRUGGLE AGAINST IMPERIALISM AND OPPRESSION

Although known primarily as a leader of the southern civil rights movement, King always understood his activism as part of a larger global struggle. Very early in his public career, he linked the fight against segregation in the United States to the struggle against colonialism and imperialism worldwide, a global vision that he developed more fully over the course of his life. For King, the black freedom struggle in the United States was "part of [an] overall movement in the world in which oppressed people are revolting against … imperialism and colonialism" (Cone 1987, 456). He described segregation and colonialism as aspects of an old world order that were being swept away by nonwhite people around the world who had become determined to end their own exploitation. King also described racism in the United States as a form of internal colonialism that marginalized and exploited black Americans like European imperialism exploited people living in Africa and Asia.

King's understanding of the struggle in the United States as part of a broader global fight against imperialism and oppression was shaped by events going on in the world around him. First introduced to the ideas of Mahatma Gandhi (1869–1948) as a student at Crozer Theological Seminary, King came to see Gandhi's use of nonviolent civil disobedience to free India from the yoke of British imperialism as a model for African Americans struggling against legal segregation in the United States. He described Gandhi as the "guiding light" of the Montgomery bus boycott's "technique of non-violent social change" (King 2012, 100). In 1959, King spent a month traveling through India in order to study the philosophy and use of nonviolence more deeply.

The many African nations that achieved political independence from European colonial powers in the 1950s and 1960s also inspired King. When Ghana—formerly the British colony of the Gold Coast—became the first sub-Saharan African nation to achieve its independence in 1957, King attended the celebrations there. King saw the wave of independence movements that swept the African continent—thirty-one more African countries would gain their freedom from European imperialist powers before King's death in 1968—as evidence that the era of colonialism, segregation, and discrimination was passing away. King warned US policy makers that if they did not embrace black civil rights at home, they risked losing the allegiance of these newly independent nations to the Soviet Union and its ideology of communism. America, he warned, could not imagine itself isolated from the world but had to recognize the ways in which its policies and practices had global implications.

King's activism extended beyond America's borders. A vocal critic of the apartheid regime in South Africa, King helped raise awareness of the evils of apartheid—which he described as worse than racism in the United States since blacks there were denied even the right of nonviolent protest—and he called on the United States and the United Kingdom to isolate the white South African regime by imposing economic sanctions. In 1957, King sponsored a worldwide Declaration of Conscience that protested apartheid. In 1962, he helped found the American Negro Leadership Conference on Africa, and that same year he cosponsored an Appeal for Action against Apartheid with Albert Luthuli (1898–1967), a leader of the black South African resistance movement. King warned that world powers must act to end apartheid before conditions there erupted in violence and an armed rebellion, and he told black Americans that they must "find the resources to aid [their] suffering brothers in his ancestral homeland" (King 2012, 42–43). As a result of his outspoken criticism, the South African government refused to grant King a visa to visit the country, and they declared him a "subversive."

King also criticized American foreign policy, especially the Vietnam War, famously describing the US government as the "biggest purveyor of violence in the world today" in his 1967 speech at New York's Riverside Church (King 2012, 167). He called on his country to accept its moral responsibilities as a great power to serve the needs of the oppressed around the world.

To King, racism, war, and economic inequality were interrelated evils that had to be addressed and transformed if the world hoped to survive. The struggle of American blacks for equality within the United States would be meaningless, he argued, unless it was linked to a broader fight against poverty and war worldwide. "Equality with whites will not solve the problems of either whites or Negroes if it means equality in a world society stricken by poverty and in a universe doomed to extinction by war," he wrote in 1967 (King 2012, xiv). People of the world had one large world house, King insisted, and they had to learn to live together equitably and with respect.

INTERNATIONAL LEGACY

King's life and work not only helped transform race relations in the United States, but they also inspired people around the world in their own struggle against poverty and oppression. Today King's birthday is celebrated not just in the United States, but in more than one hundred countries around the globe. There are public monuments to him and streets named after King in places as wide-ranging as Zambia, South Africa, India, and France, illustrating the truth of his father's claim that "He did not belong to us, he belonged to the world" (Cone 1987, 455). Today King remains a powerful symbol of an approach to global relations that privileges people over things, favors nonviolence over violence, and insists on humankind's common humanity and shared destiny.

SEE ALSO *Cold War: Race and the Cold War; Human Rights; Malcolm X*

BIBLIOGRAPHY

Cone, James H. "Martin Luther King, Jr., and the Third World." *Journal of American History* 74, 2 (1987): 455–467.

Gaines, Kevin. "The Civil Rights Movement in a World Perspective." *OAH Magazine of History* 21, 1 (2007): 57–64.

King, Martin Luther, Jr. *"In a Single Garment of Destiny": A Global Vision of Justice*. Edited by Lewis V. Baldwin. Boston: Beacon Press, 2012.

Richardson, Henry J., III. "Dr. Martin Luther King, Jr., as an International Human Rights Leader." *Villanova Law Review* 52 (2007): 471–485.

Renee Romano
Professor of History, Africana Studies and Comparative American Studies
Oberlin College

KISSINGER, HENRY
1923–

Henry Kissinger, one of most famous and controversial American diplomats of the twentieth century, was born in Fürth, Germany, on May 27, 1923, into a middle-class Jewish family. The Kissingers emigrated to the United States in August 1938 after the Nazis came to power. When Kissinger was drafted into the US Army in 1943, his German background and high intelligence led him to be selected to serve in the Army's Counterintelligence Corps. After the war, he worked for the American occupation government of Germany.

Kissinger returned to the United States in 1947 and entered Harvard University, where over the next twenty years he would forge a successful career as an academician and public intellectual. His doctoral dissertation examined diplomacy and peacemaking at the 1815 Congress of Vienna. Kissinger emphasized in particular the role of British Foreign Secretary Viscount Castlereagh and the Austrian Prince von Metternich, praising their achievement of restoring an international order after the revolutionary destructiveness of the Napoleonic Wars. To Kissinger, the Congress of Vienna negotiated a peace based on the balance of power between Europe's most powerful countries, a settlement which endured almost a century until the outbreak of World War I. Throughout his career, Kissinger embraced the realpolitik or realist diplomacy similar to that of the diplomats at the Congress of Vienna, a diplomacy which required the threat of military force and relegated ideological and moral principles to secondary positions in the pursuit of stability.

Kissinger's *Nuclear Weapons and Foreign Policy*, published in 1957, criticized the Dwight Eisenhower (1890–1969) administration's reliance on a strategy of "massive retaliation" and accepted the possibility of limited nuclear war. The book became a surprise best seller and vaulted Kissinger into the forefront of "defense intellectuals." Though associated with the liberal Republican Nelson Rockefeller (1908–1979), Kissinger became a part-time adviser to both Presidents John Kennedy (1917–1963) and Lyndon Johnson (1908–1973) during the 1960s, even making several trips to Paris as an intermediary in the hope of beginning peace talks to end the Vietnam War.

In 1969, Richard Nixon (1913–1994) appointed Kissinger as his national security adviser. Nixon appreciated Kissinger's foreign policy realism, and wanted him to centralize foreign-policy making in the National Security Council, excluding the State Department and other parts of the bureaucracy. Convinced that his political success required both this centralization and a high degree of secrecy, Nixon hoped to use Kissinger's brilliance to implement a set of dramatic changes in foreign policy, including ending the war in Vietnam, establishing détente with the Soviet Union, and opening a new relationship with China.

Kissinger quickly became Nixon's closest foreign policy adviser. With Nixon's approval, Kissinger established a "backchannel" relationship with Soviet ambassador Anatoly Dobrynin (1919–2010) and conducted secret negotiations with the North Vietnamese in Paris. A breakthrough occurred in early 1971, when Chinese leaders indicated a willingness to receive an American envoy for talks, and Kissinger traveled secretly to Beijing. Using "triangular diplomacy," Nixon and Kissinger successfully pushed the Soviets toward a summit and a Strategic Arms Limitation Treaty (SALT I), and gradually isolated Hanoi, ultimately leading to the Paris Peace Agreements, which ended American involvement in the Vietnam War. These foreign policy successes contributed to Nixon's reelection but also to Kissinger's fame as a master diplomat.

When the Watergate scandal undermined Nixon's authority, the president appointed the popular Kissinger as secretary of state. He became the first immigrant and the first Jew to hold that office. During the Yom Kippur War in October 1973, Kissinger arranged the ceasefire between Israel and Egypt, but not before putting American forces on a worldwide alert to deter what he perceived as possible Soviet unilateral moves into the region. Kissinger then engaged in "shuttle diplomacy," arranging disengagement agreements between Israel and Egypt and Syria. The strong bond with Egypt which Kissinger forged for the United States, combined with the expulsion of the Soviets from their position in Cairo, became a cornerstone of American Middle Eastern policy for the next four decades.

Kissinger was at the height of his popularity and international fame when Nixon resigned in August 1974 and Gerald Ford (1913–2006) became president. Ford admired Kissinger, who remained the president's chief foreign affairs adviser. But the collapse of South Vietnam in April 1975, the increasing unpopularity of détente in the wake of Soviet persecution of dissidents and Soviet Jews, and congressional investigations into the Nixon administration's involvement in the overthrow of Chilean president Salvador Allende (1908–1973) began to tarnish Kissinger's foreign policy achievements. Attacked from both the Left and the Right, Kissinger's realpolitik approach, with its emphasis on the limits of American power and its disdain for ideology and human rights in foreign policy, was rejected by the electorate in the 1976 election, which brought Jimmy Carter to power.

Kissinger remained an active commentator on foreign affairs after he left office, although he would never again hold a significant government position. After writing the first two volumes of his memoirs, he established an international business consulting firm, Kissinger Associates. At the 1980 Republican convention, he tried to convince Ronald Reagan (1911–2004) to select Ford as his vice presidential running mate, with Kissinger as a likely secretary of state. Although that gambit failed, Kissinger became a frequent guest at the Reagan White House, and advised the administration on a number of issues, especially concerning the Middle East. In 1983, Kissinger headed Reagan's Commission on Central America, which recommended policies for dealing with potential communist subversion in the region. Kissinger was also an informal adviser to Republican presidents George H. W. Bush and George W. Bush. Many of Kissinger's friends and protégés, including Alexander Haig (1924–2010), Brent Scowcroft (b. 1925), Lawrence Eagleburger (1930–2011), and Paul Bremer (b. 1941), played significant roles in American foreign policy. Although controversial, Kissinger became an icon and a symbol of American foreign policy. He was cited for his authority by both John McCain (b. 1936) and Barack Obama (b. 1961) in their first presidential debate in 2008.

SEE ALSO *Arab-Israeli Conflict; Détente; Ford, Gerald R.; Nixon, Richard Milhous; Organization of the Petroleum Exporting Countries (OPEC); Vietnam War*

BIBLIOGRAPHY

Dallek, Robert. *Nixon and Kissinger: Partners in Power.* New York: Harper Collins, 2007.

Del Pero, Mario. *The Eccentric Realist: Henry Kissinger and the Shaping of American Foreign Policy.* Ithaca, NY: Cornell University Press, 2010.

Hanhimäki, Jussi. *The Flawed Architect: Henry Kissinger and American Foreign Policy.* New York: Oxford University Press, 2004.

Hersh, Seymour M. *The Price of Power: Kissinger in the Nixon White House.* New York: Summit, 1983.

Hitchens, Christopher. *The Trial of Henry Kissinger.* London: Verso, 2001.

Isaacson, Walter. *Kissinger: A Biography.* New York: Simon and Schuster, 1992.

Suri, Jeremi. *Henry Kissinger and the American Century.* Cambridge, MA: Harvard University Press, 2007.

Thomas A. Schwartz
Professor of History and Political Science
Vanderbilt University

KITCHEN DEBATE

The Kitchen Debate took place in July 1959 between Soviet premier Nikita Khrushchev (1894–1971) and US vice president Richard Nixon (1913–1994). The stage for this Cold War battle of words was the American Exhibition in Moscow, the first unfettered opportunity to present the "American way of life" in Moscow's

Vice President Richard Nixon points at Soviet premier Nikita Khrushchev, Moscow, 1959. *Emblematic of Cold War conflicts, the Kitchen Debate was a famous battle of words between Khrushchev and Nixon that began in the kitchen of a model suburban home at the American Exhibition in Moscow and resumed in a television studio.* HULTON ARCHIVE/ARCHIVE PHOTOS/GETTY IMAGES

Sokolniki Park. The Soviet half of the 1958 bilateral agreement setting up this exchange was an exhibition installed in the New York Coliseum in June 1959. The famous exchange between Khrushchev and Nixon began in the kitchen of a model suburban home on exhibit grounds in Moscow and resumed in a television studio. A portion of the recording survives.

Nixon prepared for his meeting with Khrushchev as though for a boxing match. His strength lay in the consumer goods that flooded the exhibition. He hoped to back the premier into a product-lined corner. Khrushchev, knowing that he would be confronted in this American space, warily kept on the move, until he paused amid kitchen and laundry appliances. Nixon engaged him by praising the virtues of the consumer society; Khrushchev spoke of social equality.

The Kitchen Debate has been seen as emblematic of Cold War conflicts reverberating through the contesting cultures. Kitchens had already become the seat of ideological statements by both sides. The United States had promoted an American kitchen in Europe through the post–World War II Marshall Plan and through Western European design competitions. The Soviet Union had begun to redesign apartments to accommodate more items of convenience, particularly for Soviet women. The venues for the debate favored Nixon: first a product-rich kitchen, followed by a recording studio set up with color cameras recording to videotape, then a new technology. Khrushchev played to the camera; Nixon spoke through the lens to American voters who would see this production, in the hope of solidifying his position as candidate for the 1960 presidential election. Both knew what the camera and the immediacy of television meant.

Scholars, particularly those based in the United States, have interpreted the Kitchen Debate as a harbinger of eventual American victory in the Cold War, in which the USSR would succumb to an inundation of consumer goods that would be increasingly demanded by Soviet citizens, particularly women. This was the "Nylon War" that sociologist David Riesman (1909–2002) had predicted in a 1951 essay. Indeed, the American Exhibition was crammed full of such goods. After the perceived loss in the battle of the pavilions at the Brussels World's Fair in 1958, US designers sharpened their message and aimed directly at the notebooks that they knew visitors would carry with them. Others have questioned this interpretation. They point to the increasing availability of consumer goods in the USSR and to the perceived Soviet technological superiority during this post-*Sputnik* period. One point of view highlights convergence—advances in technology make ideologically different cultures increasingly similar. The other treats the American and the Soviet sides as debating different, but at that time viable, forms of modernism.

SEE ALSO *Cold War; Nixon, Richard Milhous*

BIBLIOGRAPHY

Castillo, Greg. *Cold War on the Home Front: The Soft Power of Midcentury Design.* Minneapolis: University of Minnesota Press, 2010.

De Grazia, Victoria. *Irresistible Empire: America's Advance through Twentieth-Century Europe.* Cambridge, MA: Belknap Press of Harvard University Press, 2005.

Haddow, Robert H. *Pavilions of Plenty: Exhibiting American Culture Abroad in the 1950s.* Washington, DC: Smithsonian Institution Press, 1997.

Hixson, Walter. *Parting the Curtain: Propaganda, Culture, and the Cold War, 1945–1961.* New York: St. Martin's Press, 1997.

Marling, Karal Ann. *As Seen on TV: The Visual Culture of Everyday Life in the 1950s.* Cambridge, MA: Harvard University Press, 1994.

Masey, Jack, and Conway Lloyd Morgan. *Cold War Confrontations: US Exhibitions and Their Role in the Cultural Cold War.* Baden, Switzerland: Lars Müller, 2008.

Nixon, Richard. *Six Crises*. Garden City, NY: Doubleday, 1962.

Oldenziel, Ruth, and Karin Zachmann, eds. *Cold War Kitchen: Americanization, Technology, and European Users*. Cambridge, MA: MIT Press, 2009.

Reid, Susan. "The Khrushchev Kitchen: Domesticating the Scientific-Technological Revolution." *Journal of Contemporary History* 40, 2 (2005): 289–316.

Reid, Susan. "Who Will Beat Whom? Soviet Popular Reception of the American National Exhibition in Moscow, 1959." *Kritika: Explorations in Russian and Eurasian History* 9, 4 (2008): 855–904.

Richmond, Yale. *Cultural Exchange and the Cold War: Raising the Iron Curtain*. University Park: Pennsylvania State University Press, 2003.

Riesman, David. "The Nylon War." In *Abundance for What? and Other Essays*. Garden City, NY: Doubleday, 1964.

Salisbury, Harrison. *A Journey for Our Times: A Memoir*. New York: Harper and Row, 1983.

Eric J. Sandeen

Professor of American Studies, University of Wyoming

Founding Director, Wyoming Institute for Humanities Research

KNIGHTS OF COLUMBUS

Founded in the late nineteenth century, the Knights of Columbus is a Roman Catholic fraternal order that was started to offer insurance benefits to a small group of Catholic men. In the decades since the founding, the order has grown to include a larger membership dedicated to the cause of combatting anti-Catholicism and demonstrating American patriotism.

FOUNDING AND INITIAL GROWTH

Coming together under the direction Fr. Michael McGivney (1852–1890) in Waterbury, Connecticut, in 1882, the founders of the Knights of Columbus (KC) could never have envisioned that their order would grow to include a membership of hundreds of thousands, with a reach beyond the borders of the United States. Offering camaraderie and mutual assistance through sick and death benefits, the order was born in an era when fraternal organizations blossomed. While not officially sponsored by the Catholic Church, McGivney's men emphasized that a vigorous Catholicism was compatible with American ideals. Initially chartered by men of Irish descent, later members hailed from many different nationalities. The order quickly spread from its New England roots, and by 1905 there were councils in every state in the United States, as well as in Mexico, Canada, and the Philippines.

By selecting Christopher Columbus as the order's namesake, the men sought to locate Catholics in the nation's origins. In their inductions and degree ceremonies, the KC performed rituals that spoke to their dedication to one another, to their Catholicism, and to America. In 1899, the order added a Fourth Degree that focused on patriotic Catholic citizenship.

While mutual benefit and charity were central missions of the order, the KC worked to counteract anti-Catholic sentiments. In the 1890s, the KC countered bursts of anti-Catholicism fomented by the American Protective Association and exacerbated by the economic hardships of that decade. Despite the KC's response, anti-Catholicism continued to swell in the early decades of the twentieth century, stoked by articles in *The Menace* and *Watson's Magazine* arguing that the KC were part of a papal conspiracy to thwart progressive and populist reform.

In its early years, the order undertook a number of national initiatives that emphasized the contributions of Catholics to the United States. First, the KC raised funds to create a chair of American history at the Catholic University of America in Washington, DC. By 1914, the KC had raised half a million dollars for the university from their more than three hundred thousand members. During this period, the KC also lobbied the US Congress to authorize and help fund the Columbus Memorial in Washington, DC. This work was accompanied by a vigorous promotion for the celebration of Columbus Day.

WORLD WAR I

The needs created by World War I (1914–1918) provided the KC with a way to clearly demonstrate their loyalty and patriotism by serving the members of the armed forces. Joining the YMCA and the Red Cross, the KC provided recreational facilities and support services for soldiers at home and abroad. The planning and execution of this work required the order to iron out its relationship with the newly established National Catholic War Council, which represented the interests of individual Catholic dioceses and their bishops. Once these territorial issues were settled, the KC went on to become an important presence for soldiers, staffing recreational centers with volunteer "secretaries" and chaplains at training camps and overseas at major ports and regimental headquarters near the front.

With the war's close in 1918, the KC turned their attention to reconstruction efforts. Clubs were opened in Germany, London, and Rome, while they continued their work in France. In the United States, the KC provided employment services to returning soldiers and established broad educational programs that helped those returning men to readjust to civilian life.

The return to normalcy brought another surge of anti-Catholicism. The KC responded by creating the Historical Commission, which produced a monograph series on the contributions of different racial groups. These texts aimed to counterbalance Anglo-centric American history narratives, and offered a stark contrast to the xenophobic messages from the Ku Klux Klan and other organizations that viewed Catholics as dangerous and disloyal.

THE MEXICAN REVOLUTION

Combatting anti-Catholic sentiment at home was important, but the KC viewed the climate for Catholics in Mexico as dire. The first Mexican KC councils were established by 1905 and grew steadily for the next three decades. Communist revolutionary tumult resulted in waves of anti-Catholicism that created a hostile climate for the practice of the faith in Mexico. A major portion of the Mexican Catholic hierarchy fled to the United States to escape the hostilities. In 1923, the administration of President Álvaro Obregón (1880–1928) expelled the Vatican's apostolic delegate from Mexico for violating the constitutional ban on public worship. Then, in 1926, the Plutarco Elías Calles (1877–1945) administration expelled hundreds of priests, closed schools, and required clergy to register with the government. The Mexican Catholic hierarchy resisted this pressure by declaring that the Church in Mexico would stop performing all public religious ceremonies.

In response, the KC launched an aggressive lobbying effort to push the US government to end its silence on the anticlericalism and persecution in Mexico and to refuse to recognize the Calles regime. At the same time, the order undertook an extensive public campaign of education about the situation in Mexico, which was bolstered by statements of support from the Catholic hierarchy. The KC in Mexico offered strong support for the Calles opposition, while the US government and representatives of the National Catholic Welfare Conference (NCWC) tried to negotiate a diplomatic solution.

In 1929, these negotiations resulted in a tenuous truce that calmed the situation temporarily, but by the middle of the 1930s, anticlericalism was again at a crisis point. The KC Supreme Board turned to the Franklin D. Roosevelt (1882–1945) administration and sympathetic members of Congress, calling for a Senate investigation. Roosevelt opposed the idea of an investigation. As a result, the KC expressed very pointed and public disappointment with the president. The KC also found themselves at odds with the diplomatic agenda of the NCWC and the US bishops. But, by the close of the decade, the Mexican government began to demonstrate more openness to the Catholic Church, calming the discord.

THE GREAT DEPRESSION, WORLD WAR II, THE COLD WAR, AND MODERN AMERICA

While the KC struggled with the situation in Mexico, the United States and then the world plunged into an economic depression. Although the KC undertook charitable work, their structures were not equipped to offer a significant intervention in the face of the devastation wrought by the Great Depression. Furthermore, with the rising threat of world war, the KC found themselves just one among many Catholic organizations prepared to offer support to the war effort. As a result, Supreme Knight Francis Matthews (1887–1952) deferred to the direction of the bishops' newly formed National Catholic Community Service. This arrangement made it possible to coordinate Catholic war work, but required Matthews to yield a degree of autonomy that was not acceptable to many other KC leaders.

At the war's end, the KC turned their attention to promulgating a strong message of anticommunism. Joining the prevailing mood of alarm about the infiltration of communism at home, the KC undertook an advertising campaign, "The Knights of Columbus Crusade for the Preservation and Promotion of American Ideals." This fusion of religious dedication and nationalist patriotism reached its high point when the order campaigned successfully to have the phrase "under God" added to the Pledge of Allegiance in 1954.

By the time John F. Kennedy (1917–1963), a Catholic, was elected president in 1960, the KC found themselves on shifting ground. In Rome, the Catholic Church underwent a profound introspective process at the Second Vatican Council (1962–1965), which resulted in changes in worship practices and relationships with non-Catholics. At the same time, the 1960s brought a shift in family dynamics and reproductive politics. The KC responded to these upheavals by strengthening their relationship with the Catholic hierarchy, working on education campaigns, and strongly supporting the Catholic Church's stance on reproductive issues.

SEE ALSO *AFL-CIO: Labor's Foreign Policy; Industrialization; League of Nations; Paris Peace Conference (1919); World War I*

BIBLIOGRAPHY

Hatcher, Anthony. "Adding God: Religious and Secular Press Framing in Response to the Insertion of 'Under God' in the Pledge of Allegiance." *Journal of Media and Religion* 7, 3 (2008): 170–189.

Kauffman, Christopher J. *Faith and Fraternalism: The History of the Knights of Columbus, 1882–1982*. New York: Harper and Row, 1982.

Kauffman, Christopher J. *Patriotism and Fraternalism in the Knights of Columbus: A History of the Fourth Degree*. New York: Crossroad, 2001.

Kendall, Adam G. "The Whitewash Committee of 1914: The Knights of Columbus, Freemasonry, and Anti-Catholicism in California." *European Journal of American Culture* 33, 1 (2014): 49–60.

Koehlinger, Amy. "'Let Us Live for Those Who Love Us': Faith, Family, and the Contours of Manhood among the Knights of Columbus in Late Nineteenth-Century Connecticut." *Journal of Social History* 38, 2 (2004): 455–469.

Nordstrom, Justin. "A War of Words: Childhood and Masculinity in American Anti-Catholicism, 1911–1919." *U.S. Catholic Historian* 20, 1 (2002): 57–81.

Powers, Richard Gid. "American Catholics and Catholic Americans: The Rise and Fall of Catholic Anticommunism." *U.S. Catholic Historian* 22, 4 (2004): 17–35.

Redinger, Matthew. "'To Arouse and Inform': The Knights of Columbus and United States-Mexican Relations, 1924–1937." *Catholic Historical Review* 88, 3 (2002): 489–518.

Rowland, Thomas J. "Irish-American Catholics and the Quest for Respectability in the Coming of the Great War, 1900–1917." *Journal of American Ethnic History* 15, 2 (1996): 3–31.

Schlereth, Thomas J. "Columbia, Columbus, and Columbianism." *Journal of American History* 79, 3 (1992): 937–968.

Slawson, Douglas J. "The National Catholic Welfare Conference and the Mexican Church-State Conflict of the Mid-1930's: A Case of Déjà Vu." *Catholic Historical Review* 80, 1 (1994): 58–96.

Sharon M. Leon
Associate Professor, Departments of History and Art History
George Mason University

KNOW-NOTHINGS

The Know-Nothings were a nativist organization that railed against the impact of mass immigration, as well as the growing strength of the Catholic Church. In the decade before the American Civil War (1861–1865), the Know-Nothings emerged as the second political party in the northern states before their eclipse by the newly formed Republican Party.

ORIGINS

The Know-Nothings were formally known as the Order of the Star Spangled Banner (OSSB), an organization founded in New York City in 1850 by Charles B. Allen. From 1852, members of another nativist group, the Order of United Americans (OUA), infiltrated the OSSB, installing the New York merchant James W. Barker as president, and setting the stage for the movement's spectacular electoral success.

The origin of the term *Know-Nothings* remains obscure. It is commonly thought that it derived from an instruction to all members to feign ignorance when questioned about their activities. However, the first public use of the term, a series of hostile articles published in 1853 in the *New York Tribune*, made no reference to this (Anbinder 1992). Though intended to be pejorative, members subsequently embraced the name.

ANTI-CATHOLIC AND ANTI-IMMIGRANT PROGRAM

The rise of the Know-Nothings was due to several factors, including popular disenchantment with the two-party system and the turmoil produced by slavery extension. A principal reason, however, was widespread unease with the political and social impact of mass immigration. The period from 1845 to 1854 witnessed an unprecedented surge, with some 2,900,000 migrants arriving in the United States. Many were poor and Catholic, fleeing the potato famine in Ireland and the political repression that followed the failed uprisings in the German states in 1848. Know-Nothing activists blamed these newcomers for a raft of problems blighting the nation's cities, from crime to poverty and disease, and they accused European governments of deliberately offloading their unwanted populations onto American shores. Immigrants were further resented for unsettling traditional social customs, such as the Sunday Sabbath. In cities such as Philadelphia and New York, the usual calm and tranquility of the day was disrupted by the music and festivities of what quickly became known as the Continental Sabbath.

The Know-Nothings concentrated their attack on what they perceived as the growing political power of the Catholic Church. Controlling an army of uneducated and submissive Catholic voters, and aiming for political as well as spiritual domination, Rome was preparing, the Know-Nothings warned, to seize control of the pillars of the American Republic. Aided by unscrupulous politicians, the church hierarchy was accused of trading votes in exchange for political favors. One such favor was state funding of its parochial schools, a demand that nativists interpreted as an attempt to undermine one of the founding institutions of American citizenship, the common school system. Fundamentally, the Know-Nothings rejected Catholicism as incompatible with the spirit of American democracy. Bound to a slavish obedience to priest and bishop, the Catholic voter lacked the independence and judgment that were needed to exercise the ballot in a responsible manner. Protestantism, in contrast, by encouraging individuals to read and to interpret the Bible, and by elevating conscience over obedience, was perfectly adapted to a republican democracy.

Though advocating measures to bar certain types of immigrants, particularly criminals and paupers, the Know-Nothings never called for blanket quotas or caps. Their focus instead was on reforming naturalization laws. The first demand was to lengthen the period of residency required for citizenship from five to twenty-one years. At the end of this period, Know-Nothings reasoned, immigrants would have imbibed the spirit and principles of American republicanism, and would then be able to exercise their political rights in an independent and responsible manner. To further guarantee the purity of the electoral system, Know-Nothings proposed banning the foreign-born from all municipal, state, and national political offices. The Know-Nothings were also strident advocates of the separation of church and state, a principle that they understood as the best defense against the political aspirations of Rome.

SUCCESS AND OPPOSITION

This program attracted intense opposition. Democratic Party leaders denounced the Know-Nothings as conspirators animated by religious bigotry. Elements of the rival Republican Party were also lukewarm. Abraham Lincoln wrote that if the Know-Nothings were to take control, the Declaration of Independence would need to be amended to read that all men were created equal except "foreigners and Catholics." Yet in the 1853–1855 period, the Know-Nothings achieved a series of stunning electoral victories, electing eight governors, more than one hundred congressmen, and mayors in Boston, Philadelphia, and Chicago, as well as thousands of local officials. In Massachusetts, Connecticut, Rhode Island, and New Hampshire, Know-Nothings controlled the state executive and legislative branches, and they enjoyed a majority in the lower house in Pennsylvania. In Massachusetts, the Know-Nothing legislature abolished Irish militia companies, banned the teaching of foreign languages, stopped state courts from naturalizing the foreign-born, and established a joint legislative committee, the so-called Nunnery Committee, to investigate charges of abuse in Catholic convents. More than thirteen hundred foreign-born paupers were deported. Taking aim at the Continental Sabbath, Pennsylvania lawmakers passed the "Jug Law," which banned the sale of liquor on the Sunday Sabbath.

Buoyed by this success, activists looked with confidence to the national election of 1856, nominating former President Millard Fillmore as the candidate of what was now termed the American Party. However, the movement was unable to build a durable national political machine. Partly this was a result of ineptitude on the part of its legislators. In Massachusetts, the members of the Nunnery Committee were accused of fraud and of boorish behavior. More fundamentally, the party could not escape the slavery issue. At the 1856 Baltimore convention, northern delegates walked out rather than accept a proposal to support slavery where it already existed. Though achieving 21 percent of the popular vote, Fillmore carried only the state of Maryland, and the Know-Nothings never again became a political force.

Though short-lived, the Know-Nothing movement showed the depth of anti-immigrant and anti-Catholic sentiment in nineteenth-century America. Many of its arguments would be taken up by later nativist groups, from the American Protective Association in the 1890s to the Ku Klux Klan of the 1920s.

SEE ALSO *Nativism*

BIBLIOGRAPHY

Anbinder, Tyler. *Nativism and Slavery: The Northern Know-Nothings and the Politics of the 1850s.* New York: Oxford University Press, 1992.

Billington, Ray Allen. *The Protestant Crusade.* New York: Macmillan, 1938.

Knobel, Dale T. *Paddy and the Republic: Ethnicity and Nationality in Antebellum America.* Middletown, CT: Wesleyan University Press, 1986.

Timothy Verhoeven
Senior Lecturer
School of Philosophical, Historical, and International Studies
Monash University, Australia

KNOX, HENRY

SEE *Civilization Fund.*

KOREAN WAR

North Korea attacked South Korea on June 25, 1950, igniting the Korean War. Five days later, President Harry S. Truman committed US ground troops to prevent Communist conquest of the peninsula. However, US involvement in Korea immediately after World War II helped create the circumstances that led to the conventional phase of a civil war with origins dating from Japan's annexation of Korea in 1910. By early 1945, President Franklin D. Roosevelt had secured Allied support for a postwar trusteeship to achieve Korea's independence. When Truman became president upon the death of Roosevelt that April, Soviet expansion in Eastern Europe had begun to alarm US leaders. An atomic attack on Japan, Truman expected, would preempt Soviet entry into the Pacific war and allow for unilateral US control over Korea. Instead, on August 8, Soviet premier Joseph Stalin declared war on Japan and sent the Red Army into Korea. Stalin's acceptance of Truman's last-minute proposal to divide Korea into American and Soviet occupation zones averted Communist control over the entire peninsula.

US forces arrived in southern Korea on September 8, 1945, and were unable to maintain order. Koreans wanted immediate independence. Ignorant of Korea's history or culture, American occupation officials relied for advice on wealthy landlords and businessmen who could speak English, although many were former Japanese collaborators. Simultaneously, the Soviets spurned US requests to coordinate occupation policies and allow free movement across the 38th parallel. Worsening Soviet-American relations in Europe meant that neither side would permit reunification except on terms denying its adversary control over Korea. This became clear when Soviet-American negotiators failed to agree on a representative group of Koreans to serve in a provisional government early in 1946. Meanwhile, political and economic deterioration escalated in southern Korea. Seeking an answer to its dilemma, the United States turned to the United Nations, which passed a resolution late in 1947 providing for supervised national elections. The Truman administration knew Moscow would not cooperate, but by then its policy sought to create a separate South Korea able to defend itself.

In May 1948 the United Nations supervised undemocratic elections in the south alone, resulting in the formation of the Republic of Korea (ROK) in August. In September the Soviet Union sponsored the creation of the Democratic People's Republic of Korea (DPRK). There were now two Koreas, each bent on reuniting the nation regardless of cost. Moscow withdrew its forces from North Korea in December 1948, while the United States delayed leaving until June 1949 because of violent opposition to the new ROK government. That summer, ROK and DPRK units clashed in military battles at the 38th parallel. Meanwhile, the United States was providing economic and military aid to build a self-reliant South Korea. By June 1950 the US policy of qualified containment showed signs of success, as President Syngman Rhee's government had ended spiraling inflation. The ROK army's virtual elimination of guerrilla activities prompted the Truman administration to consider increasing military aid, but because of Rhee's public talk about invading the north, the United States decided not to provide tanks, heavy artillery, or warplanes.

Throughout 1949 Stalin rejected the persistent requests of DPRK premier Kim Il Sung for approval to invade the ROK because he did not want to ignite a war with the United States. In April 1950, however, Kim persuaded him that a mass uprising against Rhee's regime guaranteed a quick and easy victory. Stalin's delivery of new arms and equipment allowed the Korean People's Army (KPA) to launch a powerful military offensive to conquer South Korea. Truman's first action was to refer the matter to the UN Security Council in hopes that the ROK military, with indirect US help, could repel the invasion. On June 25 a UN Security Council resolution called on North Korea to cease firing and withdraw, but the KPA continued its advance. Two days later the Security Council asked UN members to provide support to defend the ROK. On June 30 Truman reluctantly sent ground troops after General Douglas MacArthur, US occupation commander in Japan, advised that without US intervention the Communists would conquer South Korea.

Of the defenders under MacArthur's command, 90 percent were South Korean and American, with the rest of the forces from fifteen UN member nations. The United States provided weapons, equipment, and logistical support. At first, US forces suffered a string of defeats, as the KPA occupied most of South Korea. Early in August UN forces stopped the KPA and established the Pusan Perimeter in the peninsula's southeast corner. Despite the desperate situation, MacArthur devised plans for a counteroffensive in coordination with an amphibious landing behind enemy lines at the port of Inchon, twenty miles west of Seoul. The Joint Chiefs of Staff delayed approval because of narrow access, high tides, and seawalls, but the September 15 operation was a spectacular success. It allowed the US Eighth Army to break out and advance north to unite with the X Corps, liberating Seoul two weeks later and sending the KPA scurrying back into North Korea. Anticipating this turn of events, Truman already had approved a plan to cross the 38th parallel and reunify Korea. Invading North Korea was a serious blunder that transformed a three-month war into a conflict lasting three years.

On October 2 the Chinese foreign minister Zhou Enlai warned the Indian ambassador to the People's Republic of China (PRC), who had emerged as an informal liaison between Beijing and Washington, that the PRC would intervene if US forces crossed the 38th parallel, but the Truman administration thought he was bluffing. On October 7 the UN offensive began after the United Nations authorized action to "ensure conditions of stability throughout Korea." On October 19 the Chinese People's Volunteers Force (CPVF) crossed the Yalu River. Even after the first battle between UN and CPVF troops a week later, MacArthur was supremely confident. On November 6 the Chinese attacked advancing UN forces and quickly withdrew. After hesitating, Truman approved air strikes on the Korean side of the Yalu bridges. MacArthur, ignoring China's final warning, launched his "Home by Christmas Offensive" on November 24. The next day, a massive CPVF counterattack sent UN forces into a chaotic retreat. Truman immediately decided to pursue a cease-fire. Opposing this course of action, MacArthur submitted a "Plan for Victory" that called for a naval blockade of China's coast, air attacks on Manchuria, deploying Nationalist Chinese forces in Korea, and staging assaults on mainland China from Taiwan.

In early 1951 Lieutenant General Matthew B. Ridgway, the new US Eighth Army commander, halted the Communist advance southward. Soon, UN

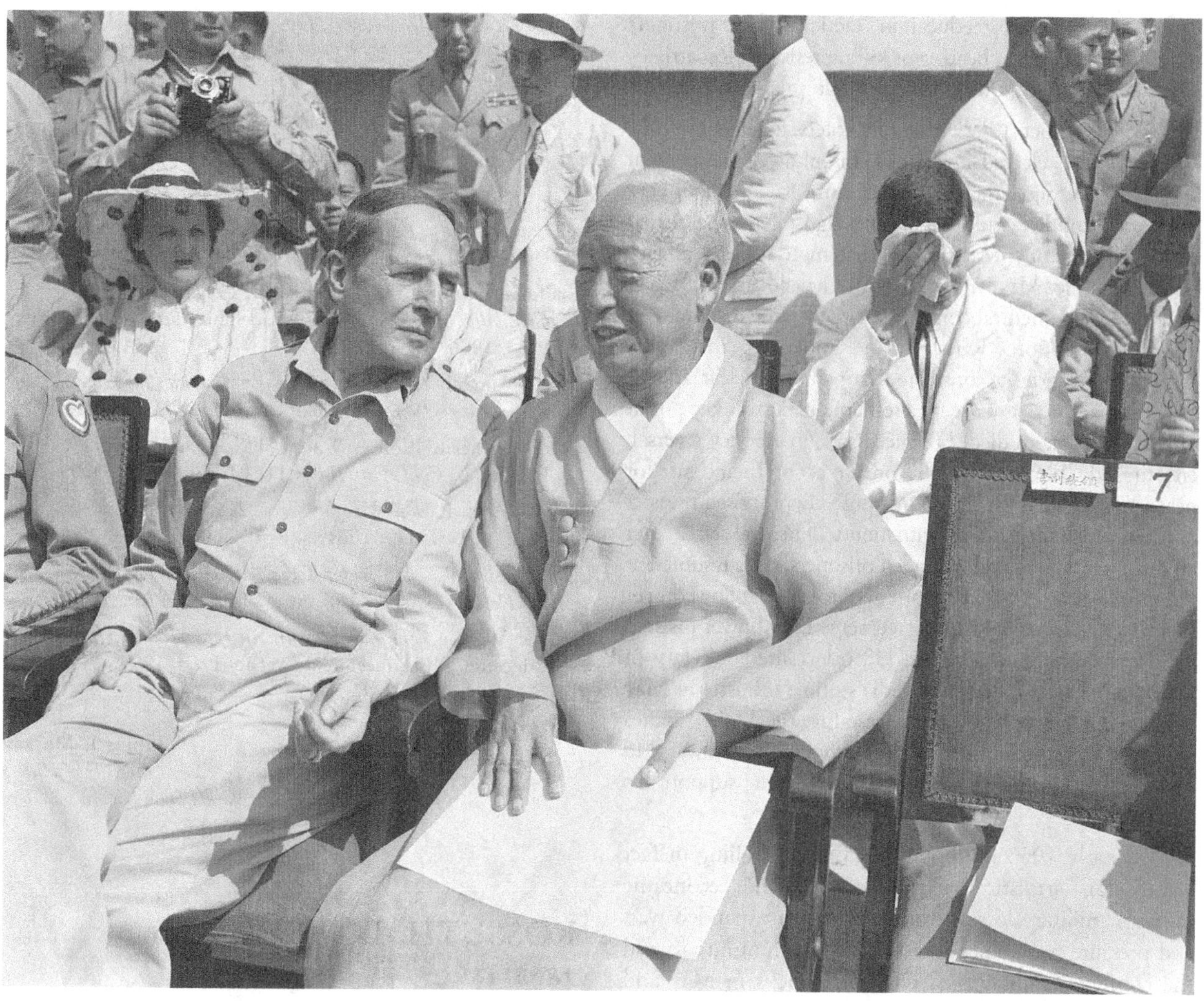

General Douglas MacArthur with South Korean president Syngman Rhee during ceremonies proclaiming Korea a republic, 1948. *In August 1948 the Republic of Korea (ROK) was formed in the south, and in September the Soviet Union sponsored the creation of the Democratic People's Republic of Korea (DPRK) in the north. The two Koreas were each bent on reuniting the nation regardless of cost.* **BETTMANN/CORBIS**

counterattacks restored the front north of the 38th parallel. In March, MacArthur, frustrated with Washington's refusal to escalate the war, issued a demand for the enemy's immediate surrender. This sabotaged a planned cease-fire initiative, ultimately resulting in Truman's relieving him of command on April 11. Then two major Communist offensives to force UN troops off the peninsula ended in May with the CPVF and KPA suffering huge losses. A UN counteroffensive restoring the front north of the parallel persuaded China and North Korea to join the United States in seeking a cease-fire. The belligerents agreed to open truce negotiations on July 10 at Kaesong. The Communists engaged in antics at the outset to humiliate their adversary, fouling the negotiating atmosphere. But the UN delegation created the first major roadblock when it proposed a demilitarized zone almost entirely in North Korea.

Beginning in late October, after the talks moved to Panmunjom, there was rapid progress toward resolving almost all issues. A deadlock then emerged over repatriation of prisoners of war (POWs). Truman ordered the UN delegation to assume an inflexible stance against returning Communist prisoners to China and North Korea against their will, while the Communists demanded return of all the POWs as the Geneva Convention required. Truman certainly believed in the moral rightness of his position but was not unaware of the propaganda value of Communist prisoners defecting to the "free world." However, a vast majority of North Korean POWs were actually South Koreans who had either joined voluntarily or were impressed into the KPA. Thousands of Chinese prisoners were Nationalist soldiers trapped in China at the end of China's civil war who now had the chance to escape to Taiwan. Also, Chinese Nationalist guards at UN POW camps used terrorist "reeducation" tactics to force prisoners to refuse repatriation, beating or killing resisters. Repatriates were tattooed with anti-Communist slogans.

In November 1952 American voters angered by "Mr. Truman's war" elected Dwight D. Eisenhower president in large part because they expected him to end the very unpopular conflict. Fulfilling a campaign pledge, he visited Korea in December, concluding that more ground attacks would be futile. Meanwhile, the UN General Assembly had proposed that a neutral commission resolve the dispute over POW repatriation. Rather than embracing this plan, Eisenhower seriously considered launching nuclear attacks on China to force it to accept a settlement. At this key point, on March 5, Stalin died. His successors, in a policy reversal, encouraged China and North Korea to act on their desire for peace. On March 30 Zhou Enlai publicly proposed transfer of those POWs rejecting repatriation to a neutral state. After an exchange of sick and wounded prisoners, talks resumed at Panmunjom on April 26. Sharp disagreement followed over the final details of the truce agreement. Eisenhower insisted later that China had accepted US terms after Secretary of State John Foster Dulles told India's prime minister in May that, absent progress toward a cease-fire, the United States would end existing limitations on its conduct of the war. No documentary evidence has as yet surfaced to support his contention.

By early 1953 both Washington and Beijing in fact wanted an armistice, having tired of the economic burdens, military losses, worries about an expanded war, and pressure from allies and the world community to end the conflict. China staged powerful attacks in May and June against ROK defensive positions to win concessions on the final terms of an armistice. Before the Korean War ended on July 27, the United States had vastly increased defense spending, strengthened the Atlantic Alliance militarily, and lobbied to rearm West Germany. In Asia the conflict saved Jiang Jieshi's regime on Taiwan and made the ROK a long-term US client. Sino-American relations were embittered for two decades, especially after Washington persuaded the United Nations to brand China an aggressor in Korea. The war helped Mao Zedong's regime fortify control at home and elevate its image abroad. To meet this challenge US leaders, acting on what they saw as Korea's main lesson, used military means with disastrous results in Vietnam.

SEE ALSO *Cold War; Dulles, John Foster; Eisenhower, Dwight D.; MacArthur, Douglas; Truman, Harry S.*

BIBLIOGRAPHY

Casey, Steven. *Selling the Korean War: Propaganda, Politics, and Public Opinion in the United States, 1950–1953.* New York: Oxford University Press, 2008.

Cumings, Bruce. *The Origins of the Korean War.* Vol. 1: *Liberation and the Emergence of Separate Regimes, 1945–1947.* Princeton, NJ: Princeton University Press, 1981.

Cumings, Bruce. *The Origins of the Korean War.* Vol. 2: *The Roaring of the Cataract, 1947–1950.* Princeton, NJ: Princeton University Press, 1990.

Foot, Rosemary. *A Substitute for Victory: The Politics of Peacemaking at the Korean Armistice Talks.* Ithaca, NY: Cornell University Press, 1990.

Kaufman, Burton I. *The Korean War: Challenges in Crisis, Credibility, and Command.* Philadelphia: Temple University Press, 1986.

Matray, James I. *The Reluctant Crusade: American Foreign Policy in Korea, 1941–1950.* Honolulu: University of Hawaii Press, 1985.

Matray, James I. "Korea's War at Sixty: A Survey of the Literature." *Cold War History* 11, 1 (February 2011): 99–129.

Millett, Allen R. *The War for Korea, 1945–1950: A House Burning.* Lawrence: University of Kansas Press, 2005.

Millett, Allen R. *The War for Korea, 1950–1951: They Came from the North.* Lawrence: University of Kansas Press, 2010.

Stueck, William. *The Korean War: An International History.* Princeton, NJ: Princeton University Press, 1995.

James I. Matray
Professor of History
California State University, Chico

KOSSUTH, LOUIS

1802–1894

The most controversial foreigner to visit the United States during the nineteenth century, the Hungarian Lajos "Louis" Kossuth arrived in the United States as a celebrated fallen revolutionary, seeking support for Hungary's independence movement from the Habsburg Empire. Although he did not gain official US support, his celebrity provoked debate about America's role in the world and prompted both antislavery and, especially during the Civil War, pro-secession groups to see Hungary's cause as inspiration for their own.

A journalist and nationalist member of the Hungarian parliament who learned English while in prison, Kossuth was inspired by the 1848 French revolution to demand establishment of a Hungarian republic. As president of the de facto Hungarian nation he met the US chargé d'affaires to Austria, William Stiles (1808–1865). Reflecting how conservative Americans would interpret Kossuth, Stiles, a Georgia slave owner, later denounced the Hungarian struggle for its radical assertion of "human rights," not, to Stiles, the more practical "right of local self-government" asserted by the *American* War of Independence (Roberts 2009, 129).

The Hungarian uprising showed potential for victory through early 1849, but when Russian troops intervened, the Hungarians surrendered. The Habsburgs executed many Hungarian leaders, treatment that not only gained Hungary sympathy but also became part of American political rhetoric: abolitionists condemned the Fugitive Slave Law of 1850 by labeling slave-catchers acting under its authority "Haynaus," for the Hungarians' nemesis, Austrian General Julius Jacob von Haynau (1786–1853), and their victims "Kossuths." Kossuth took refuge in the Ottoman Empire, which, by providing him asylum, grew in Americans' esteem.

Animated by the pro-interventionist wing of the Democratic Party, known as Young Americans, Congress authorized the transport of Kossuth to the United States. The *USS Mississippi* delivered the Hungarian and his retinue to New York City on December 5, 1851. Archbishop John Hughes (1797–1864) denounced Kossuth for his attack on the Catholic Church's opposition to the 1848 revolutions, but 100,000 New Yorkers turned out to hail Kossuth as a second George Washington. Kossuth then departed New York for Washington, DC, where as the official guest of the US government he addressed Congress and received toasts from presidential contenders Daniel Webster (1782–1852) and Stephen Douglas (1813–1861), who tried to exploit Kossuth's appeal. Webster even publicly denounced Austria, calling it but "a patch on the earth's surface," triggering a temporary suspension of US–Austrian relations (Shewmaker 1976, 308). But Kossuth was politely denounced by Senator Henry Clay (1777–1852) and President Millard Fillmore (1800–1874), who feared that intervention to rescue Hungary would entangle Americans in European war.

Kossuth left Washington for New England and then the Old Northwest, where crowds swelled to hear his speeches on behalf of universal democracy. After visiting the battleground and old North Bridge in Concord, Massachusetts, he was introduced at the town hall by the essayist Ralph Waldo Emerson (1803–1882), who declared, "We think that the graves of our heroes around us throb to-day to a footstep that sounded like their own" (Kossuth 1852, 22). Kossuth's style of coat, hat, and beard became the rage, and Americans took up dancing the polka and mazurka for their radical East European flair. Similar to their expressions of sympathy for other revolutionaries, including Alphonse de Lamartine (1790–1869) of France and Giuseppe Garibaldi (1807–1882) of Italy, several American towns and counties renamed themselves "Kossuth." Some notable northerners criticized Kossuth. Francis Bowen (1811–1890), the editor of the *North American Review*, exposed the Hungarians' persecution of Serb and Croat minorities. The abolitionist William Lloyd Garrison (1805–1879), upon learning that Kossuth would not condemn slavery, reversed his support and called the Hungarian a fraud. But in general northerners embraced Kossuth, either as a legatee of the American Revolution or as merely a fascinating spectacle. He raised perhaps two million dollars and received weapons from private citizens and state arsenals, though these made little difference in Hungary's fate.

Kossuth's reception in the South was more tempered, although he emphasized that Hungary's cause was what would soon be known as a "state's right." Secessionists in 1860 would appeal for European intervention by comparing the Confederacy to Hungary. But outside New Orleans, where immigrants, as they did in the North, greeted him warmly, southern leaders discouraged attention to Kossuth's liberal internationalism. Future Confederate general Robert E. Lee (1807–1870) declared that the United States "are [*sic*] not called on to engage in the quixotic scheme of righting European wrongs. Nor would it advance the principle of self-government by destroying the only nation where it exists" (Roberts 2009, 163). Disappointed, Kossuth stirred controversy when he told German Americans to vote for the Young American Franklin Pierce for the presidency. He left the United States for England on July 14, 1852, spending the rest of his life hoping that a Hungarian republic would emerge and summon him home.

Late in Kossuth's visit Senator William Seward (1801–1872) called for an official warning to Russia to relent in its suppression of Hungarian freedom. Seward urged US opposition to "acts of national injustice, oppression, and usurpation, whenever or wherever they may occur" (Roberts 2009, 161). Reflecting Kossuth's longer-term impact, Seward's resolution foretold of future interventions on behalf of human rights. Commemorating this, the American Hungarian Federation gave a bust of Kossuth to Congress, which placed it in the Capitol on March 15, 1990.

SEE ALSO *1848 Revolutions*

BIBLIOGRAPHY

Curti, Merle. "Austria and the United States, 1848–1852: A Study in Diplomatic Relations." *Smith College Studies in History* 11 (1926): 137–206.

Roberts, Timothy. *Distant Revolutions: 1848 and the Challenge to American Exceptionalism.* Charlottesville: University of Virginia Press, 2009.

Roberts, Timothy. "Lajos Kossuth and the Permeable American Orient of the Mid-Nineteenth Century." *Diplomatic History*, advance access, December 1, 2014. doi:10.1093/dh/dhu070

Shewmaker, Kenneth. "Daniel Webster and the Politics of Foreign Policy, 1850–1852." *Journal of American History* 63, 2 (1976): 303–315.

Timothy M. Roberts
Associate Professor, Department of History
Western Illinois University

L

LAFAYETTE, MARQUIS DE

1757–1834

The Marquis de Lafayette was a French military and political leader whose actions in America and Europe contributed to America's national independence and the emergence of early American nationalism. Born to the privileges of the French nobility, Lafayette began the conventional military career of eighteenth-century French aristocrats. Early accounts of the American Revolution (1775–1783) attracted his attention, however, and America's first diplomatic agent in Paris offered him a military position if he could cross the Atlantic—which he did (without French authorization) by purchasing his own ship.

Arriving in Pennsylvania in 1777, he received an honorary commission as a major general in the Continental Army. American political leaders believed his noble family connections might help establish a strategic French alliance, but he unexpectedly transformed this honorary commission into a substantive military role as he became a loyal friend of George Washington (1732–1799), suffered wounds at the Battle of Brandywine (1777), joined the inner circle of Continental officers, and quickly learned new military strategies and political ideas.

Washington came to view Lafayette as a kind of surrogate son whom he trusted in cross-cultural mediations with French government ministers and French commanders of the forces that joined the war after the French-American alliance was signed in 1778. Lafayette also conducted a highly successful military campaign in Virginia during the spring and summer of 1781, which isolated Britain's southern army and created the strategic opportunity for Washington to lead the main American-French forces to a decisive victory at Yorktown.

Lafayette thus facilitated the alliance that opened a military-political pathway to American nationhood, but he made even greater contributions to early American nationalism by repeatedly affirming that the American Revolution promoted universal natural rights and advanced the international cause of human freedom. He provided much-desired European confirmations for the already emerging American belief that the new nation would be the most exceptional in all of human history.

By the time the French Revolution began in 1789, Lafayette had also become a symbol of American political values in France. He therefore asserted his symbolic American identity when he proposed that the new French National Assembly should adopt a Declaration of the Rights of Man and Citizen, accepted the Assembly's appointment to become the first commander of the French National Guard, and dropped his noble title. Evoking the political significance of citizen soldiers he had known in America and viewing himself as a French successor to the citizen-commander George Washington, Lafayette sought to push the French Revolution toward a constitutional monarchy that would defend the individual rights and social order that he associated with the American Republic.

When more radical French revolutionaries forced Lafayette to flee for his life and then violently repressed the opposition to their new republic, Americans used the European hostility for Lafayette to confirm their belief that they had completed the only successful modern revolution and constituted the only truly free nation.

Although Lafayette eventually returned to France after seven years in foreign monarchical prisons and exile, he retained his symbolic significance in the United States as the steadfast European who sacrificed his own interests to defend American conceptions of freedom and representative government.

His most important later contributions to American national identity developed during his famous final visit to the United States in 1824 and 1825. Invited by President James Monroe (1758–1831) and the US Congress, Lafayette made a triumphal tour of all twenty-four states and spoke to large crowds in every major city from New England to New Orleans. He was celebrated as both the special friend of George Washington and the greatest European friend of all Americans, and he enthusiastically reciprocated the praise by constantly reaffirming the main themes of American nationalism.

He stressed everywhere that America's Revolution was the most successful, virtuous revolution in modern history, that America's constitutional, republican government had established the freest political system in the world, and that the new nation's rapid economic growth proved the superiority of American institutions. Although he criticized slavery and warned against sectional conflicts, he was honored in the North and South alike as the European who best understood what Americans believed about themselves. He was the only distinguished foreigner who could still refer to his own experiences when he told Americans that they had created the free nation for which the Continental Army had fought at Yorktown.

Lafayette therefore became the most influential European in early American history through his valuable service to the American Revolution and through his even more valuable contributions to the enduring nationalist belief in American exceptionalism. His cross-cultural mediations and symbolic roles also show how American national identity has always been shaped by transnational interactions with people and events in other modern societies.

SEE ALSO *American Revolution; France; French Revolution; Washington, George*

BIBLIOGRAPHY

Auricchio, Laura. *The Marquis: Lafayette Reconsidered.* New York: Knopf, 2014.

Gaines, James R. *For Liberty and Glory: Washington, Lafayette, and their Revolutions.* New York: Norton, 2007.

Idzerda, Stanley J., Anne C. Loveland, and Marc H. Miller. *Lafayette, Hero of Two Worlds: The Art and Pageantry of His Farewell Tour of America, 1824–1825.* New York: Queens Museum, 1989.

Kramer, Lloyd. *Lafayette in Two Worlds: Public Cultures and Personal Identities in an Age of Revolutions.* Chapel Hill: University of North Carolina Press, 1996.

Lloyd Kramer
Professor of History
University of North Carolina, Chapel Hill

LANSING, ROBERT

SEE *Self-Determination.*

LAOS

By early 1961, the political crisis in Laos had become a serious threat to the John F. Kennedy (1917–1963) administration's credibility in the Southeast Asian Treaty Organization (SEATO). A coalition of Prince Souvanna Phouma's (1901–1984) neutralist forces and the Communist Pathet Lao guerrillas, supported by the USSR, threatened to overwhelm the unpromising US-backed regime of Prince Boun Oum (1911–1981). During the presidential transition, Dwight Eisenhower (1890–1969) argued that Laos was the real key to the future of Southeast Asia. Once in possession of Laos, the Communists, he warned, would bring extreme pressure on Thailand, Cambodia, and South Vietnam.

The National Intelligence Estimate of March 28, 1961, warned that Laos posed an inescapable challenge to the United States as well. "The governments of [Southeast Asia]," ran the report, "tend to regard the Laotian crisis as a symbolic test of intentions, wills and strengths between the major powers of the West and the Communist Bloc.... In short, the loss of Laos would severely damage the US position and its influence in Thailand and South Vietnam" (US Department of State 1988, Doc. 22).

Kennedy responded to the worsening situation in Laos by advising Moscow, Beijing, and Hanoi via television that the United States would not tolerate a Communist conquest of that country. Still, landlocked Laos, despite the heavy official American commitment to its political independence, was not a matter of major public or congressional concern. This afforded the president room to maneuver. In April, Kennedy followed the British and Soviet lead in calling a fourteen-nation conference in Geneva to resolve the Laotian question. For the troubled Asian allies, the Geneva Conference was not promising. Washington and London had committed their countries to the establishment of a "neutral and independent" Laos, but SEATO's Asian members rejected Laotian neutrality as a desirable goal, convinced that Asian neutrals always leaned strongly toward the USSR. Vice President Lyndon Johnson (1908–1973), in his Southeast Asian report of May 23, advised the administration that Geneva's failure to protect Southeast Asia would render SEATO meaningless and compel the United States to search for a new approach to regional security. Kennedy, determined to avoid US military involvement in Laos, had no choice but to entrust Southeast Asia's future to the Geneva negotiations.

For its part, because of its own lack of genuine preparation and cohesion, SEATO's perpetuation demanded the avoidance of direct involvement in Laos. Equally important, whereas such action would only elicit token participation from Asian allies, it risked the open opposition of its European members, especially Britain and France.

In early October 1961, after weeks of wrangling, the Geneva Conference agreed to neutralize Laos and instructed Souvanna Phouma to form a coalition government that would include representatives of the right, center, and left in Laotian politics. By the spring of 1963, the Pathet Lao had deserted the government, driving the center toward the right and subjecting the country to a renewal of the Laotian civil war. Thereafter, the Pathet Lao, with North Vietnamese help, solidified their control over much of the country, especially its eastern fringes.

Kennedy escaped a military confrontation in Laos; he would not do so in Vietnam. For nearly a decade beginning in 1964, Laos was subjected to heavy US bombing as part of the wider war in Indochina. Following the change of regimes in Vietnam and Cambodia in 1975, a Communist government also came to power in Laos, aligning itself with Vietnam and the Soviet bloc. US-Laos relations deteriorated after 1975 as diplomatic relations were downgraded. After the collapse of the Soviet Union in 1991, Laos sought to improve relations with Washington, culminating with the restoration of full diplomatic relations in 1992. In July 2012, Secretary of State Hillary Clinton visited Laos. This marked the first visit by a US secretary of state since 1955.

SEE ALSO *Cold War; Kennedy, John Fitzgerald; Rusk, Dean; Vietnam War*

BIBLIOGRAPHY

Adams, Nina S., and Alfred W. McCoy, eds. *Laos: War and Revolution.* New York: Harper and Row, 1970.

Castle, Timothy N. *At War in the Shadow of Vietnam: U.S. Military Aid to the Royal Lao Government, 1955–1975.* New York: Columbia University Press, 1993.

Stevenson, Charles A. *The End of Nowhere: American Policy toward Laos since 1954.* Boston: Beacon Press, 1972.

US Department of State. National Intelligence Estimate, March 28, 1961: "Outlook in Mainland Southeast Asia." In *Foreign Relations of the United States, 1961–1963,* Vol. 1: *Vietnam, 1961,* Doc. 22. Washington, DC: GPO, 1988. https://history.state.gov/historicaldocuments/frus1961-63v01/d22

Joseph Siracusa
Professor of Human Security and International Diplomacy
Royal Melbourne Institute of Technology University

LAW, THOMAS
1756–1834

Born in Cambridge, England, in 1756, Thomas Law was the sixth son of Mary Christian and Edmund Law, bishop of Carlisle. Over the course of his life, he would move from Great Britain to British India to the United States, promoting an ideal of Enlightenment imperialism that he wished to implement across the globe. In 1773, Law journeyed to India as a clerk, or "writer," in the service of the East India Company. By the 1780s, he had worked his way up through the ranks, becoming a revenue collector, judge, and district ruler in the northern province of Bihar. Like many other East India "nabobs," Law made a small fortune in the process. Unlike many of his colleagues, Law was also something of an intellectual, a person who desired not only to obtain personal wealth but to deploy Enlightenment principles of political philosophy and moral economy in order to advance society and improve civilization. These ideals underlay his long career, extending from British India to the early American Republic.

An inveterate reformer, Law implemented a number of important economic and religious reforms in India. Most significantly, in an effort to root out corruption and fraud, he dramatically altered the system of land tenure and taxation among the natives of his district. Abolishing the customary system of landholding, he created a new class of private-property owners (*zamindars*) who would essentially act as landlords and tax collectors, governing the peasants (*ryots*) who farmed the land. He also altered the method of calculating the land tax, establishing a taxation rate that would be fixed in perpetuity. This change was intended to benefit both the Indian natives and his employer, the East India Company. Impressed with Law's experiments, Charles Marquis Cornwallis (1738–1805), the governor-general of India, incorporated key elements of Law's plan into his "permanent settlement," adopted in 1793 for all of northern India.

In 1791, with his health in decline, Law returned to Britain, accompanied by his three Eurasian sons, born of a Hindu *bibi* or concubine. In London, Law soon grew disillusioned with the politics of the East India Company and of a British nation on the verge of war with France. Seeking a fresh start, he turned away from Britain's empire in the East and looked toward its former empire in the West.

In 1794, Law along with his mixed-race children emigrated to the young United States. Flush with capital, Law began heavily investing in land, especially in the new national capital at Washington, DC. In 1796 he married Eliza Parke Custis (1776–1831), who introduced him into the highest echelons of American society and also cheerfully accepted Law's mixed-race sons into the family. Although the couple separated in 1804 and divorced in 1811, they shared custody of their own daughter, Eliza Law (Rogers) (1797–1822).

Over time, Thomas Law established himself as a key player in the social and political life of early Washington, DC. In order to promote trade, he built an India wharf, constructed a sugar-refining operation, and secured funds to build a canal cutting through the city. In order to generate more liquid capital for investments, he devised and promoted a comprehensive plan for creating a national paper currency. After the burning of the capital during the War of 1812, he, along with other business leaders, successfully persuaded Congress to keep the seat of government in Washington. Yet he was not simply an entrepreneur. As an Enlightenment thinker, he firmly believed in the relationship between economic development and cultural refinement and proceeded to establish the city's first theater, dancing society, agricultural society, and the Columbian Institute for the Promotion of Arts and Sciences, a learned society that was the predecessor of the Smithsonian Institution. He frequently published works of poetry, moral philosophy, and political economy. Law also prided himself on his scientific inventions and progressive farming techniques.

Although often teetering on the verge of bankruptcy, Law managed to be one of the most crucial behind-the-scenes players in early Washington, DC. During the first decades of the nineteenth century, he turned his attention to the two most serious social problems impeding the country's growth into a great empire: slavery and Native Americans. Applying the lessons of Enlightenment social engineering that he had tested in India, Law created elaborate plans for devolving private property to American Indians and encouraging their assimilation into American society. In order to ameliorate the condition of slaves, Law produced a comprehensive plan that called for immediate, compensated abolition, followed by a term of indentured servitude for former slaves. Once freed, former slaves would be colonized outside the boundaries of the United States. Sensitive to the controversial nature of his plans, Law did not publish his ideas or introduce them into Congress. Nonetheless, he circulated his proposals widely among the nation's political elite and tirelessly advocated their adoption.

By the time of his death in 1834, Law had earned the respect of some of the nation's most important political figures from all parties, including Thomas Jefferson (1743–1826), John Quincy Adams (1767–1848), John C. Calhoun (1782–1850), and Henry Clay (1777–1852). His actions left a permanent imprint on British India and the nation's capital, where he created institutions and policies that promoted his Enlightenment beliefs in economic improvement, social harmony, and political justice. His vision of empire provided a concrete link between Britain's empire in India and the rising territorial empire of the early United States.

SEE ALSO *Empire, US*

BIBLIOGRAPHY

Clark, Allen C. *Greenleaf and Law in the Federal* City. Washington, DC: Roberts, 1901.

Clark, Anna C., and Aaron Windel. "The Early Roots of Liberal Imperialism: 'The Science of a Legislator' in Eighteenth-Century India." *Journal of Colonialism and Colonial History* 14, 2 (2013).

Guha, Ranajit. *A Rule of Property for Bengal: An Essay on the Idea of Permanent Settlement.* Durham, NC: Duke University Press, 1996. First published 1963 by Mouton.

Lynch, James B., Jr. *The Custis Chronicles: The Virginia Generation.* Camden, ME: Picton Press, 1997.

Zagarri, Rosemarie. "The Significance of the 'Global Turn' for the Early American Republic: Globalization in the Age of Nation-Building." *Journal of the Early Republic* 31, 1 (2011): 1–37.

Rosemarie Zagarri
University Professor and Professor of History
George Mason University

LEAGUE OF NATIONS

Before World War I (1914–1918), there was considerable enthusiasm in the United States among political commentators and members of the political elite for the creation of an international organization that would provide a venue to resolve conflicts or at least ameliorate warfare between states.

THE EMERGENCE OF THE LEAGUE OF NATIONS AFTER WORLD WAR I

The conflagration that devastated Europe from 1914 to 1918 provided the impetus for the creation of an international diplomatic forum where conflicts could be mediated without actually going to war. The organization that emerged from these deliberations was the League of Nations, founded in 1919. The immediate inspiration for the name of the organization has been credited to French

The Melting Pot, by cartoonist David Low for* The Bulletin *(Sydney, Australia), January 1919. *The League of Nations was conceived as an international peace-keeping organization. The ideal was the sacrifice of national self-interest for the furtherance of brotherhood and peace.* ASSOCIATED NEWSPAPERS LTD/SOLO SYNDICATION

author and statesman Léon Bourgeois (1851–1925), who set out its basic characteristics in his book *Pour la société des nations,* most likely first published at some point between 1909 and 1910.

Although the proposed League of Nations drew wide support both before and after the war, the actual shape and formal establishment of the League flowed in significant measure from the efforts of US president Woodrow Wilson (1856–1924). The United States did not enter the war until April 1917, but its pivotal role in facilitating Germany's defeat put it in a strong position to influence the 1919 Treaty of Versailles. Wilson was instrumental in the inclusion of wording in the final version of the treaty that paved the way for the creation of the League of Nations.

Wilson's diplomacy and public statements in the lead-up to the Treaty of Versailles were reinforced by comments from former US president William Howard Taft (1857–1930). Like Wilson, Taft drew attention to the need for a high-level political forum that would provide a means for both the great powers and smaller states to sort out their differences and ensure that there would be no repetition of the "Great War." Although numerous Americans and Europeans agreed that the cataclysm of the war made such a forum necessary, it is often assumed that if Wilson had not pushed as hard as he did for the League of Nations, it may not have been established. Wilson also had enough influence and political capital in Europe to ensure that his concerns would remain on the agenda of the peace conference.

Even before the United States formally entered the war, Wilson had commented, both formally and informally, that a League of Nations should be part of the peace settlement. His most important statement on this theme was expressed in a speech to the US Congress on January 8, 1918, in which Wilson set out his bold vision for a League of Nations and described the central role the United States should play in this project. At the center of his call to Congress to support such a league was the "Fourteen Points," which concerned the agenda once the war ended and laid the groundwork for what would become the League of Nations.

FUNDAMENTAL PROBLEMS

Despite Wilson's enthusiasm and the support inside and outside the United States, the League of Nations was built on two organizational and operational contradictions that, especially in hindsight, ensured its demise by the late 1930s. One fundamental problem was lack of support in the US Senate, which failed to ratify the Treaty of Versailles, ensuring that the United States would play no part in the League of Nations, let alone serve in a leadership role. This disconnect between the US government's words and actions was evident to many European observers. The second fundamental problem centered on the issues of colonialism and imperialism, and the racism that was integral to the international stature of the major colonial powers, whose view was that whatever shape the League of Nations took, it would have to have clear geographical, ethnic, or "racial" limits (embodied in the colonial and imperial interests of Britain and France, in particular), but also the Netherlands, Belgium, Portugal, and Spain, which still had colonial holdings after World War I). To put it another way, the League of Nations held out the promise of the end of colonialism even as its key members continued to operate as colonial powers inside and outside of the League of Nations.

The colonial question, or more accurately the tepid manner in which it was addressed, weakened the League of Nations from the outset. The absence of the United States from the League did not magnify US inability to deal with colonialism and racism, because the United States was itself expanding its empire prior to the war. Despite the US government's public criticism of colonialism, it behaved in a "neocolonial" fashion in the Americas, especially the Caribbean, and had taken formal colonial control of the Philippines from Spain between 1898 and 1902.

The first indication that the postwar settlement was going to have serious implications for colonialism, imperialism, and racism occurred at the end of 1917. The Russian Revolution of November 1917 brought an end to the Romanov Empire and its participation in World War I. Among other things, Vladimir Lenin (1870–1924) and the Bolsheviks permitted Russia's former enemies to take control of territory in the west that had previously fallen under Romanov control. More significantly, they reorganized the rest of the Russian Empire to create the Union of Soviet Socialist Republics and spoke increasingly in support of anticolonial nationalism around the world. Such public declarations concerned Britain and France, as well as other colonial powers, as to what sort of world order would follow World War I.

This issue became more urgent when it became clear that the Russian Empire was not going to be the only imperial polity to collapse as the war ravaged large parts of Europe. At the same time, the colonial powers were bringing troops from their colonies in Africa and Asia to reinforce the war effort in Europe. At this juncture, the United States and key European leaders began to draft early versions of the document that would eventually emerge as the Covenant of the League of Nations. They made certain that the final document would not contain provisions that called for the recognition of anticolonial nationalists and their desire to end colonialism. Nor would the Covenant establish a framework for nascent sovereign nation-states.

It was widely assumed by 1918 that the demise of the Romanov Empire was going to be followed by the end of the Austro-Hungarian and Ottoman empires, culminating with the collapse of imperial Germany. It was also expected that the territorial legacy and widespread nationalism that had emerged within the borders of these former empires would be among the main concerns of the League of Nations. At the same time, it was also hoped that the League would provide constraints on the number of new nation-states, as well as where they would come into being. The League quickly recognized erstwhile colonies as nation-states in some instances, particularly in Europe.

The League also created a category known as a *mandate*, which put a newly minted Iraq, as well as Transjordan and Palestine, under the control of Britain. France, meanwhile, took over the mandates of Syria and Lebanon. In the Middle East, the imperial powers were supposed to work toward turning profoundly contrived nations into sovereign nation-states that would take on full membership in the League of Nations. In Africa and Asia meanwhile, German colonies simply defaulted to Britain or France, allowing for the expansion of their imperial power in these regions.

THE DEATH OF THE LEAGUE OF NATIONS

Within the League of Nations itself, racist ideas about the inability of non-Europeans to preside over independent nation-states were prevalent. Although a Mandate Commission was set up, it was taken for granted that colonial subjects beyond Europe and the United States were racially or culturally inferior and not yet ready to govern themselves. Even so, the mandates in the Middle East were expected to make a relatively quick transition to national independence.

Iraq was formally admitted to the United Nations as a sovereign nation-state in 1930. In other parts of the world, it was taken for granted that a long process of civilizing colonial subjects was needed before they would be ready for national independence. The fact was never addressed that key members of the League of Nations—Britain and France in particular, both of which held seats on the Mandate Commission—presided over major colonial empires in Asia and Africa that they had no intention of relinquishing.

The Japanese stood apart from this debate insofar as they were in the process of turning Japan into an imperial power at the same time that the Japanese leadership articulated a racist civilizing mission toward the rest of Asia. In fact, Japan eventually resigned from the League of Nations after the League called into question the legitimacy of Japan's conquest and occupation of Manchuria in the early 1930s. The profound limits of the League of Nations were obvious for all to see in the Manchurian crisis.

The League moved slowly in response to a request from the Chinese government to address Japan's invasion of Manchuria in 1931. None of the great powers could be expected to oppose an act of imperialism when they themselves were imperial states with colonies around the globe. The League did produce a report critical of the Japanese invasion of Manchuria. Japan ignored the report and formally resigned its membership.

The League of Nation's numerous shortcomings ensured that it never played the role in international affairs that its early promoters had hoped it would. The lack of cooperation and collective action between nation-states that had encouraged political leaders to call for a League of Nations in the first place was the very thing that undermined the League once it was created. The League of Nations was dissolved in 1946. However, World War II led to the reinvention of the League of Nations in the United Nations, which built on the earlier organization under strong US leadership.

Compared to the United Nations, it was beyond the League of Nations' capacity to deal with any international issue that involved one or more of the great powers. The United States' relationship with the League was hobbled by the failure of Washington to even join the organization and by the way the United States was increasingly coming to perceive itself as the great power in the Americas generally and Latin America more specifically. The United States expanded its influence in the region via a series of military interventions and withdrawals once a suitable government had been established that was receptive to US-based companies and to Washington's heavy-handed diplomacy. Not only was the United States not a member of the very organization that President Wilson had helped bring into being, it behaved in a quasi-imperial fashion in the Americas, weakening the League's efforts in the Western Hemisphere to act as the guarantor of last resort for the sovereignty of its members.

SEE ALSO *Internationalism; Interventionism; Isolationism; Paris Peace Conference (1919); Roosevelt, Eleanor; Roosevelt, Franklin D.; Roosevelt, Theodore; Taft, William Howard; Treaty of Versailles; United Nations; Universal Declaration of Human Rights; Wilson, Woodrow; World War II*

BIBLIOGRAPHY

Fromkin, David. *A Peace to End All Peace: The Fall of the Ottoman Empire and the Creation of the Modern Middle East.* New York: Holt, 2009. First published 1989.

Jarboe, Andrew Tait, and Richard S. Fogarty, eds. *Empires in World War I: Shifting Frontiers and Imperial Dynamics in a Global Conflict.* London: Tauris, 2014.

Knock, Thomas J. *To End All Wars: Woodrow Wilson and the Quest for a New World Order.* New York: Oxford University Press, 1992.

MacMillan, Margaret. *The War That Ended Peace: The Road to 1914.* New York: Random House, 2013.

Mazower, Mark. *No Enchanted Palace: The End of Empire and the Ideological Origins of the United Nations.* Princeton, NJ: Princeton University Press, 2009.

Mazower, Mark. *Governing the World: The History of an Idea.* New York: Penguin Press, 2012.

Reynolds, David. *The Long Shadow: The Legacies of the Great War in the Twentieth Century.* New York: Norton, 2014.

Rogan, Eugene. *The Fall of the Ottomans: The Great War in the Middle East.* New York: Basic Books, 2015.

Thorne, Christopher. *The Limits of Foreign Policy: The West, the League, and the Far Eastern Crisis of 1931–1933.* London: Hamilton, 1972.

Tuchman, Barbara. *The Guns of August.* New York: Random House, 1962.

Walters, F. P. *A History of the League of Nations.* London: Oxford University Press, 1952.

Wawro, Geoffrey. *A Mad Catastrophe: The Outbreak of World War I and the Collapse of the Habsburg Empire.* New York: Basic Books, 2014.

Mark T. Berger
Adjunct Professor, Department of Defense Analysis
Naval Postgraduate School

LEND-LEASE ACT (1941)

The Lend-Lease Act, officially titled "An Act to Further Promote the Defense of the United States" (Public Law 77–11), was signed into law on March 11, 1941, by President Franklin D. Roosevelt (1882–1945). The act provided Roosevelt with executive power to "sell, transfer title to, exchange, lease, lend, or otherwise dispose of, to any such government any defense article" that the president believed would be used in the defense of the United States and its allies fighting against Nazi Germany, Fascist Italy, and Japan. The Lend-Lease program ran from March 1941 through September 1945 and totaled more than $50.1 billion (roughly $650 billion in 2014 monies) in material support for the war. This accounted for 17 percent of the total US war expenditure.

The Lend-Lease program was critical in defeating the Axis powers in World War II.

BACKGROUND

In order to keep the United States from becoming too entangled in international conflicts, Congress passed a series of Neutrality Acts from 1935 to 1939. Roosevelt was eager to provide assistance to Western democracies, but was initially working against US political and public opinion. On September 5, 1939, the United States formally proclaimed its neutral stance in the European conflicts. Over time, this neutrality began to diminish, especially after 1939 when Nazi Germany achieved victories in Czechoslovakia and Poland and, in 1940, when the Nazis invaded France, Belgium, Luxembourg, Denmark, Norway, and the Netherlands. During this time, the United States established its first-ever peacetime draft and increased the defense budget from $2 billion to $10 billion.

With Great Britain fully engaged in war, Prime Minister Winston Churchill (1874–1965) actively sought US support to prolong its resistance to Nazi Germany. In 1940, Roosevelt opened negotiations with Churchill to secure leases to British-held naval bases and airfields across the Caribbean and the Canada Atlantic coast. In September 1940, these negotiations developed into the "Destroyers for Bases" agreement, by which the United States agreed to transfer fifty surplus American destroyers to the British and Canadian Royal Navies. In return, the United States would obtain ninety-nine-year rent-free leases at military installations in Bermuda and Newfoundland. This helped Great Britain redeploy military assets and was key in the 1940 Battle of Britain.

On December 8, 1940, with finances dwindling, Churchill sent Roosevelt a letter outlining Great Britain's critical need for wartime support. On December 17, Roosevelt gave a sympathy-provoking speech, which included the parable of a neighbor who asks to borrow a garden hose to put out the fire burning his own house. The neighbor with the hose (an analogy to the United States) does not ask for the original cost of the hose but allows the neighbor to borrow the hose, extinguish the fire, and then return it. The allegorical story was used by Roosevelt to sway American citizens who were not comfortable with going to war but would give to others for the sake of security.

Roosevelt was advocating that the United States become an "arsenal of democracy," but his ability to act was limited by the cash-and-carry provision of the Neutrality Acts. Under this provision, Great Britain had to pay up front for war materials. Working within the Neutrality Acts, Roosevelt designated a large amount of US military equipment as "surplus" and approved its delivery to Great Britain in 1940. Great Britain made cash payments of $4.5 billion in 1940, but by 1941, the British had nearly exhausted their financial resources.

In an effort to help alleviate Great Britain's war-related material and financial difficulties, Roosevelt developed the Lend-Lease program. Although it helped, it also placed considerable demands on Great Britain. Namely, it required Great Britain to conduct an audit of all British assets, exhaust the British gold reserves, and sell British-owned American companies, which included Courtaulds, Shell, and Lever. These demands were partly to appease US critics opposed to helping wealthy countries like Great Britain. Additionally, Great Britain and France had both defaulted on their World War I debts. The Lend-Lease program also allowed the British to repair their warships at US ports and construct training camps for their military.

DETAILS OF THE LEND-LEASE ACT

In the beginning, the most vocal opponents to the Lend-Lease bill were isolationist Republicans who feared its passage would result in the United States going to war. Over time, US public opinion increasingly began to view isolationists as appeasing and even sympathizing with the Nazis. The US House of Representatives passed the Lend-Lease bill on February 9, 1941. In March, the Senate also passed it. Both votes were along party lines, with Democrats, Roosevelt's party, voting overwhelmingly in favor.

After passage, the administration of the Lend-Lease program fell under the direction of Edward R. Stettinius (1900–1949) and his Office of Lend-Lease Administration. He held the post until September 1943. After this, the Office of Lend-Lease was combined into the Foreign Economic Administration (FEA) under the direction of Leo Crowley (1889–1972). By October 1941, approximately $1 billion in Lend-Lease support was delivered to Great Britain. The Lend-Lease program was extended to China in April 1941, the USSR in October 1941, and an additional forty-one countries were deemed eligible over the next few years, with six countries electing to not participate. By 1945, Great Britain had received $31.4 billion, the Soviet Union $11.3 billion, France $3.2 billion, China $1.6 billion, and the remaining forty countries $2.6 billion.

REPAYMENT

For most nations, the Lend-Lease repayment began right after the war. The United States did not anticipate repayment from the Soviet Union. Collectively, the total repayment for the program was $7.8 billion, with $6.8 billion from Great Britain. A significant portion of the repayment came in the form of rent on air and naval bases and transfers of technology, food, and raw materials from Great Britain and France to the United States. The transfers started as early as September 1940 during the Battle of Britain, when the British Technical and Scientific Mission (the Tizard Mission) traveled to the United States in order to continue work on military resources. A significant resource brought to the United States was the electron-resonance magnetron, which was essential to the development of radar and long-range navigation. The Tizard Mission worked on various defense weaponry technologies, including antitank and antisubmarine technologies, the gyro gunsight, and plastic explosives. Under the Lend-Lease Act, the British were to share technology advancements discovered after the war. These equipment transfers included the military ambulance Austin K2/Y, the photo-reconnaissance aircraft de Havilland DH.98 Mosquito, and various aircraft engines.

Under the Lend-Lease Act, unused equipment was to be returned, but Great Britain opted to keep the Lend-Lease equipment after the war. An agreement was reached where the nonreturned equipment would be sold to Great Britain at a 90-percent discount and packaged into an £1.075 billion in 50 annual payments, with a five-year, interest-free, grace-period loan called the Anglo-American Loan. Great Britain's repayment of the loan was completed in 2006. Almost all nations had cleared their Lend-Lease obligations to the United States by the later part of the 1960s, with the exception of the USSR. After the war, the United States requested $1.3 billion from the USSR, which counteroffered with $170 million. The amount due was disputed by the USSR, and in 1972 the United States agreed to a payment of roughly half the amount, or $772 million. Due to the Cold War hostilities, the USSR did not make good on its obligation until 1990, when the Soviet Union collapsed.

SEE ALSO *Cash and Carry; Roosevelt, Franklin D.; Tariff; World War II*

BIBLIOGRAPHY

Dallek, Robert. *Franklin D. Roosevelt and American Foreign Policy, 1932–1945.* New York: Oxford University Press, 1979.

Dobson, Alan P. *US Wartime Aid to Britain, 1940–1946.* New York: St. Martin's Press, 1986.

Kimball, Warren F. *The Most Unsordid Act: Lend-Lease, 1939–1941.* Baltimore, MD: Johns Hopkins University Press, 1969.

Kimball, Warren F. *Forged in War: Roosevelt, Churchill, and the Second World War.* New York: Morrow, 1997.

US House of Representatives. Lend Lease Bill, HR 77A-D13. Record Group 233, National Archives, January 10, 1941.

Andrew Hund
Assistant Professor of Sociology
The United Arab Emirates University (UAEU)

LEVI STRAUSS & CO.

Levi Strauss & Co. has a long international tradition. It was founded in 1853 by Bavarian immigrant Levi Strauss (1829–1902) and today is a global corporation with three geographic divisions. Originally a wholesale store that sold a variety of domestic and international dry goods, Levi Strauss & Co. now produces and markets blue jeans and other apparel all over the world. Since the second half of the twentieth century, the Levi's brand has become a symbol of America's casual fashion culture.

ORIGINS AND EARLY SUCCESS

In the late 1840s, Levi Strauss immigrated to New York with his mother and sister and began working at his brothers' wholesaling store. Several years later, Strauss moved out to California, where gold-mining opportunities made the new state a destination for people from all over the world. San Francisco, in particular, was booming, and Strauss opened a store there on California Street (Downey 2007, 9). Strauss sold cloth to storekeepers throughout the West; one of these customers helped launch Strauss's business to international fame. Jacob Davis (1831–1908), a Latvian Jewish immigrant who worked in Reno, Nevada, as a tailor, wrote to Strauss about a technique he had developed for fastening pocket openings on his customers' pants, using Strauss's cloth. The two men applied for a patent from the US Patent Office in 1873 and, within two years, received one in Great Britain as well (Great Britain Patent Office 1876). Davis moved to San Francisco, where he partnered with Strauss and headed their first manufacturing venture, making riveted waist overalls out of blue denim and brown cotton duck (Downey 2007, 15).

The business continued to grow, and Strauss applied for its incorporation in 1890. During this decade, the company also made its first pair of Levi's 501 Jeans, which became popular among workers. It would be almost another half century, however, before jeans reached a more mainstream audience. In the 1930s, western dude ranches were common vacation destinations for Americans living on the East Coast, prompting Levi Strauss & Co. to launch a new cowboy-inspired line of western wear. The company continued to innovate, introducing Lady Levi's in 1934, adding the red tab in 1936, and covering the back pocket rivets on jeans in 1937. Product changes continued during World War II (1939–1945), when the US government declared jeans an essential piece of apparel worn by those engaged in defense work and mandated certain changes to their design (Downey 2007, 59).

GLOBAL EXPANSION

After the war, Levi Strauss & Co. became a full-fledged global corporation and brand, expanding distribution to the entire United States and overseas (Downey 2007, 59). In 1959, the company showcased its wares at the American Fashion Industries exhibit in Moscow and started exporting to Europe. Six years later, it created an international division to expand sales in Europe and Asia. During the 1960s and 1970s, Levi Strauss & Co. opened factories in twenty-three countries (Levi Strauss & Co. 2015). Sales were bolstered by the firm's association with American youth culture, casual fashion, and rock 'n' roll. Advertisements featured popular rock bands and celebrated American experiences and individuality. Rather than tailor marketing to local cultures, the company adhered to its original branding. The strategy worked. Consumers overseas eagerly purchased the company's new denim fashions, and Levi's jeans became an international emblem of postindustrial culture (Cray 1978).

Levi's remained popular throughout the twentieth century, and Levi Strauss & Co. earned the status of the world's leading producer of jeans. When jeans sales dipped in the 1980s, the company launched Dockers khakis, which entered the European market the following decade. Declining sales around the turn of the twenty-first century eventually reversed course, and by 2007 the company was profitable again and positioned itself to move into outdoor goods.

BUSINESS ETHICS

Throughout its existence, Levi Strauss & Co. has received attention for both its strong business ethics and its workplace degradations. During the last decades of the nineteenth century, founder Levi Strauss engaged in philanthropic activities in San Francisco, where he donated money to orphanages and relief societies and provided funds for scholarships at University of California, Berkeley. The company established the first code of conduct for apparel manufacturers and opened one of the first racially integrated factories in the South in the 1960s (Levi Strauss & Co. 2015). Under CEO Robert D. Haas (b. 1942), who started his tenure at Levi Strauss & Co. in 1984, the firm carried out an "Aspiration Statement," a value-based philosophy crafted by top management to promote workplace diversity and ethical management. This plan doubled the percentage of minority managers and raised the percentage of women in management ranks to over 50 percent (Schwerin 1998, 103–104). The company employs workers in sixty countries, who, although not unionized, are reportedly treated well.

Despite its commitment to "conscious capitalism," the company's guiding philosophy bumped up against the economic realities of globalization in the 1990s. Cheaper products from overseas and low-wage plants in Asia and the Caribbean made it difficult for the company to produce goods profitably in the United States. Levi Strauss & Co. began closing US factories and subcontracting labor outside national borders, prompting the former employees of a closed San Antonio plant to form a major activist group to protest the outsourcing of their jobs to Costa Rica. Battling accusations that it subjected its foreign workers to sweatshop conditions, Levi Strauss & Co. has worked to restore its reputation as an ethical business (Thigpen 2011). As it entered the twenty-first century, the company dedicated itself to environmental sustainability and community-building both domestically and internationally (Levi Strauss & Co. 2015). It joined the Better Cotton Initiative, which was launched in 2005 by a group of commodity experts, in order to promote sustainable cotton production. Initiatives such as this revealed the Company's twenty-first century mission to remedy its 100-plus-year dependence on low-wage agriculture, which had begun in the American South and then continued in Asia, Africa, and Latin America (Levi Strauss & Co. 2015).

THE LEVI'S TRADITION

Its long history as an American producer ended in 2003 when the company closed its last US factory, but Levi Strauss & Co. remains an iconic American brand. While its products are manufactured outside the United States, its advertisements and products are distinctly American in their promotion of rock music, individuality, and informality. The company's headquarters remain in San Francisco, where they operate as a working design studio and a public exhibit for Levi's products and traditions (Liebhold 2011). Indeed, tradition and originality continue to serve as the company's hallmarks as Levi's are sold in the United States and all over the world.

SEE ALSO *Globalization; Rock 'n' Roll*

BIBLIOGRAPHY

Cray, Ed. *Levi's: The Shrink to Fit Business That Stretched to Cover the World.* Boston: Houghton Mifflin, 1978.

Downey, Lynn. *Levi Strauss & Co.* Mount Pleasant, SC: Arcadia, 2007.

Great Britain Patent Office. *The Commissioners of Patents' Journal, 1875.* London: Office of the Commissioners of Patents, 1876.

Levi Strauss & Co. "Heritage Timeline." 2015. http://www.levistrauss.com/our-story/#heritage-timeline

Liebhold, Peter. "Levi Strauss & Co. Corporate and Americas Division Headquarters." *Public Historian* 33, 1 (2011): 83–86.

Schwerin, David. *Conscious Capitalism: Principles for Prosperity.* Oxford, UK: Butterworth Heinemann, 1998.

Thigpen, Peter. "Can We Find Another Half a Cheer? A Response to James O'Toole and David Vogel's 'Two and a Half Cheers for Conscious Capitalism.'" *California Management Review* 53, 3 (2011): 118–123.

Lindsay Schakenbach Regele
Assistant Professor
Miami University

LIBERIA

African American settlers founded the modern state of Liberia in 1822. The settlers who arrived first were free and formerly enslaved African Americans, predominately from the Upper South states of Virginia and Maryland. Individual state colonization societies, like those in Pennsylvania, Virginia, Maryland, New York, and Indiana, were responsible for raising funds and finding potential emigrants. This localized approach meant that there was not a systematic method for soliciting interest in emigration among either the free black community or slave owners who might be interested in manumitting. Emigrants thus had a variety of backgrounds and experiences in the United States before they reached Liberia. This affected their choice of occupation, their social standing, their relationship with the United States, and their access to capital on arrival in the new settlement.

Until its independence in 1847, Liberia was governed by the American Colonization Society (ACS). The ACS acted as an independent, nongovernmental organization, but it was also linked to US government policy through government contracts, the Navy's West African anti–slave trade squadron, and personal connections. Because of the ACS's quasi-governmental remit, as well as the uncertain position of African Americans—both free and enslaved—in the United States in the period before the Civil War (1861–1865), and the sometimes tense relationship between African American settlers and the Bassa, Dey, Gola, Vai, Grebo, Kpelle, and Kru, whom they had come to live among in Liberia, the relationship between America and Liberia has historically been unusually close and full of controversy.

AMERICO-LIBERIANS' RELATIONSHIP WITH INDIGENOUS LIBERIANS

Both the colony and the Republic of Liberia had a complicated relationship with the Liberians they displaced with their arrival. There was some confusion over the rights actually conferred by the original land-purchase agreement, which had been forced from the Dey leader, King Peter, at Cape Mesurado at gunpoint, and the earliest settlers soon found themselves in the first of many armed conflicts with surrounding populations. A perception among the American settlers that they were more "civilized" and therefore had a right to settle and cultivate the land led to repeated armed battles with indigenous Liberians who did not want to cede their land or change their culture.

Missionary organizations, the ACS, and many settlers saw their "return" to Africa as a means of "civilizing" and Christianizing African peoples. Settlers from southern states especially noted that moving to Liberia allowed them to preach—something they had been prevented from doing in the United States. In the nineteenth and twentieth centuries, African American missionaries and settlers carried out most of the missionary work in Liberia, as independent missionaries as well as for such groups as the Richmond African Baptist Missionary Society, the American Missionary Crusade, the American Board of Commissioners for Foreign Missions, the Southern Baptist Convention, and the Carver Foreign Missions organization. Most missionary organizations in the nineteenth century sought to "civilize" and Christianize, either in tandem or with civilization preceding conversion. Despite the success of mission work (the current population of Liberia is roughly 50 percent Christian), most indigenous Liberians were not seen as "civilized" enough to participate in civic life, a situation that persisted well into the twentieth century.

INDEPENDENCE AND LEADERSHIP

In an attempt to strengthen the settlements in the face of both indigenous fighting and trading competition from British and Sierra Leonean traders, Liberians proposed a new constitution in 1838 uniting the settlements and appointing one governor—the white ACS agent, Thomas Buchanan (1808–1841)—for all the territories. Maryland-in-Liberia, at the southeastern-most point of the modern state, did not join the new confederation, and continued to operate its own government until 1857. Joseph Jenkins Roberts (1809–1876), the first black governor of Liberia, succeeded Buchanan after his death in 1841. Roberts, an emigrant from Virginia who had made a name in trade, went on to become the first president of the independent Republic of Liberia in 1847.

The republic gained independence as a result of waning interest in colonization in the United States and disputes with Britain and Sierra Leone over the sovereign position of the colony. Liberia's government was repeatedly challenged by British and Sierra Leonean traders over its ability to control coastal trade within territory claimed by Liberia. With no recourse to official US diplomatic channels—the government politely asked Britain to respect Liberian territory, but refused to officially claim the colony or support it in any more formal way—Liberia's leaders asked the ACS to allow them to become independent. Because of the politics of race relations in the United States, however, America did not officially recognize Liberia until 1862.

The first ten presidents of Liberia, and twelve of the first fourteen, were born in the United States. The True Whig Party dominated politics from the 1870s until 1980. Indigenous Liberians were precluded from citizenship until 1904, and prevented from voting until 1946 (a property-based franchise) and 1963. Despite some features of the republic's society that allowed for the assimilation of indigenous Liberians, and some hybrid cultural traits that acknowledged the African surroundings, the Americo-Liberians often felt pressure on the world stage to emphasize their "civilization" in contrast with indigenous Liberians. The new country wanted to be taken seriously as an international trading power—most notably to keep the French, British, and Sierra Leonean traders from undermining their sovereignty and their trading rights.

LIBERIA'S POST-INDEPENDENCE RELATIONSHIP WITH THE UNITED STATES

After independence, trading links that had been established with the United States by the earliest settlers became increasingly important in making an argument for a continued relationship between the two countries. British dominance in West Africa from the 1850s cast Liberia into a new role as America's commercial and strategic "foothold" in Africa. The African commodities that became increasingly important in the late nineteenth century—especially palm oil, rubber, cotton, sugar, and coffee—were all grown in Liberia. With commodity prices rising in the 1860s, the Liberian government, under the leadership of President Edward Roye (1815–1872), took a loan from several British banks to build the nation's infrastructure. When commodity prices crashed in the 1870s, Liberia's finances were damaged to such an extent that only repeated American diplomatic intervention and the occasional appearance of the US Navy off Liberia's coast through the period of the "scramble for Africa" (1880–1914) kept the country from succumbing to British annexation.

After serving as a base for allied troops in World War I (1914–1918), territorial annexation by European powers was no longer a concern. The United States still needed Liberia, however. In 1926, the American Firestone Rubber Company negotiated a deal with the Liberian government that would grant it a one-million-acre lease for ninety-nine years for six cents per acre. The Liberian government took the deal because Firestone also provided a $5 million loan to cover the nation's outstanding debts. This deal effectively handed over the country's finances to the rubber industry and to Firestone in particular. It also made Liberia even more strategically important for the United States as its only supply of non-European rubber.

Liberia retained this strategic role after World War II (1939–1945), when it was an important ally in the Cold War and in America's soft-power diplomacy during decolonization. The Peace Corps and American missionary associations joined some long-standing back-to-Africa groups in sending people to Liberia. Scholarships, business interests, and increasingly close diplomatic links kept Liberians coming to America. However, with the independence of African states from imperial rule in the 1950s and 1960s, conservative, procapitalist Liberia no longer attracted as much interest from American back-to-Africa or Pan-Africanist movements, which saw their ideas enacted by socialist regimes elsewhere in the continent.

INSTABILITY AND CIVIL WAR

Despite some concessions to democracy in the 1960s and 1970s, and the beginnings of a more inclusive Liberian state, William Tolbert (1913–1980)—the twentieth Americo-Liberian president—was assassinated in 1980 by Samuel Doe (1951–1990), a member of the Krahn ethnic group and a soldier in the Liberian army. This ended the rule of the Americo-Liberians and also began a long period of instability and civil war.

The continuation of the Cold War throughout the 1980s meant that US policy effectively remained unchanged for a decade after Doe's ascent to power. At the end of the Cold War, however, the United States stopped funding Doe's regime, and civil war, financial collapse, and the reign of Charles Taylor (b. 1948) destroyed much of the country's infrastructure, including its education and healthcare systems. Taylor, who led the National Patriotic Front of Liberia into the country through Côte d'Ivoire to overthrow Doe in 1989, was half Americo-Liberian, attended university in the United States, initially had the backing of numerous Americo-Liberians who had fled to the United States in 1980, and, it transpired at his trial for war crimes at the Hague, had at some point worked for US intelligence agencies.

After Taylor was finally removed from power in 2003, Liberian-US relations remained strong, with a significant Liberian expatriate community lobbying for support of the country in the United States, and the first female president of Liberia, Ellen Johnson Sirleaf (b. 1938), having lived a significant portion of her life in the United States. Aid and commodity exports continued to dominate economic relations between the countries into the twenty-first century. Despite the end of exclusive Americo-Liberian rule in 1980, the descendants of the nineteenth-century American settlers still largely dominate the government, economy, and institutions.

SEE ALSO *Africa; American Colonization Society; Back-to-Africa Movement; Colonization Movement; Foreign Mission Movement*

BIBLIOGRAPHY

Akpan, M. B. "Black Imperialism: Americo-Liberian Rule over the African Peoples of Liberia, 1841–1964." *Canadian Journal of African Studies/Revue Canadienne des Etudes Africaines* 7, 2 (1973): 217–236.

Beyan, Amos J. *The American Colonization Society and the Creation of the Liberian State: A Historical Perspective, 1822–1900.* Lanham, MD: University Press of America, 1991.

Burin, Eric. *Slavery and the Peculiar Solution: A History of the American Colonization Society.* Gainesville: University Press of Florida, 2005.

Burrowes, Carl Patrick. "Black Christian Republicanism: A Southern Ideology in Early Liberia, 1822–1847." *Journal of Negro History* 86, 1 (2001): 30–44.

Dunn, Elwood D., Amos J. Beyan, and Carl Patrick Burrowes. *Historical Dictionary of Liberia.* 2nd ed. Lanham, MD: Scarecrow Press, 2001.

Ellis, Stephen. *Mask of Anarchy: The Destruction of Liberia and the Religious Dimension of an African Civil War.* New York: New York University Press, 1999.

Everill, Bronwen. "'Destiny Seems to Point Me to That Country': Early Nineteenth-Century African American Migration, Emigration, and Expansion." *Journal of Global History* 7, 1 (2012): 53–77.

Everill, Bronwen. *Abolition and Empire in Sierra Leone and Liberia.* New York: Palgrave Macmillan, 2013.

Gardner, Leigh. "The Rise and Fall of Sterling in Liberia, 1847–1943." *Economic History Review* 67, 4 (2014): 1089–1112.

Harris, David. "From 'Warlord' to 'Democratic' President: How Charles Taylor Won the 1997 Liberian Elections." *Journal of Modern African Studies* 37, 3 (1999): 431–455.

Holsoe, Svend E. "A Study of Relations between Settlers and Indigenous Peoples in Western Liberia, 1821–1847." *African Historical Studies* 4, 2 (1971): 331–362.

Howard, Lawrence. "American Involvement in Africa South of the Sahara, 1800–1860." PhD diss., Harvard University, 1956.

Jalloh, Alusine, and Toyin Falola, eds. *The United States and West Africa: Interactions and Relations.* Rochester, NY: University of Rochester Press, 2008.

Lindsay, Lisa. "Boundaries of Slavery in Mid-Nineteenth-Century Liberia." In *Borderlands in World History, 1700–1914*, edited by Paul Readman, Cynthia Radding, and Chad Bryant, 258–276. New York: Palgrave Macmillan, 2014.

Mills, Brandon. "'The United States of Africa': Liberian Independence and the Contested Meaning of a Black Republic." *Journal of the Early Republic* 34, 1 (2014): 79–107.

Mouser, Bruce L. "The Baltimore-Pongo Connection: African Entrepreneurism, Colonial Expansionism, or African Opportunism?" *International Journal of African Historical Studies* 33, 2 (2000): 313–333.

Mower, J. H. "The Republic of Liberia." *Journal of Negro History* 32, 3 (1947): 265–306.

Rosenberg, Emily S. "The Invisible Protectorate: The United States, Liberia, and the Evolution of Neocolonialism, 1909–40." *Diplomatic History* 9, 3 (1985): 191–214.

Sanneh, Lamin. *Abolitionists Abroad: American Blacks and the Making of Modern West Africa.* Cambridge, MA: Harvard University Press, 1999.

Sirleaf, Ellen Johnson. *This Child Will Be Great: Memoir of a Remarkable Life by Africa's First Woman President.* New York: Harper, 2009.

Temperly, Howard. "African-American Aspirations and the Settlement of Liberia." *Slavery and Abolition* 21, 2 (2000): 67–92.

Tyler-McGraw, Marie. *An African Republic: Black and White Virginians in the Making of Liberia.* Chapel Hill: University of North Carolina Press, 2007.

West, Richard. *Back to Africa: A History of Sierra Leone and Liberia.* London: Cape, 1970.

Bronwen Everill
Department of History
King's College London

LIFE (MAGAZINE)

LIFE magazine debuted in 1936 as the first American picture newsmagazine, and, following *Time* and *Fortune*, the third publication in Henry Luce's (1898–1967) publishing empire, Time Inc. Relying on the simple eloquence of photography, the degree to which American culture had become increasingly visually oriented, and the immense appeal of a true general interest magazine, with its mixture of news, sports, celebrity, essays, and a focus on the "American way of life," *LIFE* magazine was an immediate, enormous success. A quarter of a million newsstand copies sold out on the first day, and within three months the magazine sold at the rate of a million copies per week. *LIFE* reached the height of its popularity in the 1940s and 1950s, peaking at a subscription rate of 5.8 million and an estimated readership of 20 million. *LIFE* is widely considered the quintessential American magazine of the mid-twentieth century.

PIONEERING PHOTOJOURNALISM

Before television began to provide widespread visual coverage of the news, *LIFE* served as the nation's primary vehicle to visually represent, and define, the news. The magazine's first issue, in November of 1936, featured a cover image of the Works Progress Administration's Fort Peck Dam, by famed photographer Margaret Bourke-White (1904–1971). The photo drew attention to the Great Depression, which was ongoing, as well as to the immense power of a nation that could launch monumental projects even during a time of crisis. The inside cover featured a photograph of a doctor holding a baby in a hospital delivery room, framed by the caption, "Life Begins." From the start, the magazine was linked, purposefully and indelibly, to the momentous and the everyday, to stories large and small, to the role of the family in the United States and the role of the United States in the world.

LIFE developed a formula for photojournalism that would be widely imitated. For each main news or feature story, a half- or full-page photo would introduce a topic, which would be explained in further detail in accompanying text. A series of photographs of varied sizes, accompanied by captions, would follow, and a final full-page photograph would culminate the presentation. Other, smaller pieces would follow, each relying on the visual to tell its story. Because of the high production cost of delivering so many photographs, on expensive, slick stock paper, it was a few years before *LIFE* made money for its parent company. Publisher Luce, whose wife Clare Boothe Luce (1903–1987) had originally convinced him of the viability of this kind of project, decided to ride things out by having *Time* and *Fortune* subsidize the new magazine. By 1939, *LIFE* had begun to make money, and from there its fortunes improved exponentially.

A CELEBRATION OF AMERICAN LIFE

From the start, *LIFE* magazine interpreted the news, provided low-cost entertainment, and fostered a sense of national identity. It also provided a great many everyday life features, focusing on food, architecture, entertainment, child rearing, home decorating, nutrition, exercise, even furniture making, celebrating the range of what might fit in the category of the "American way of life." Luce's determination to pay tribute to small-town life, everyday acts of patriotism, advances in technology, and the triumph of American-style democracy in other parts of the world, resulted in features and articles that furthered

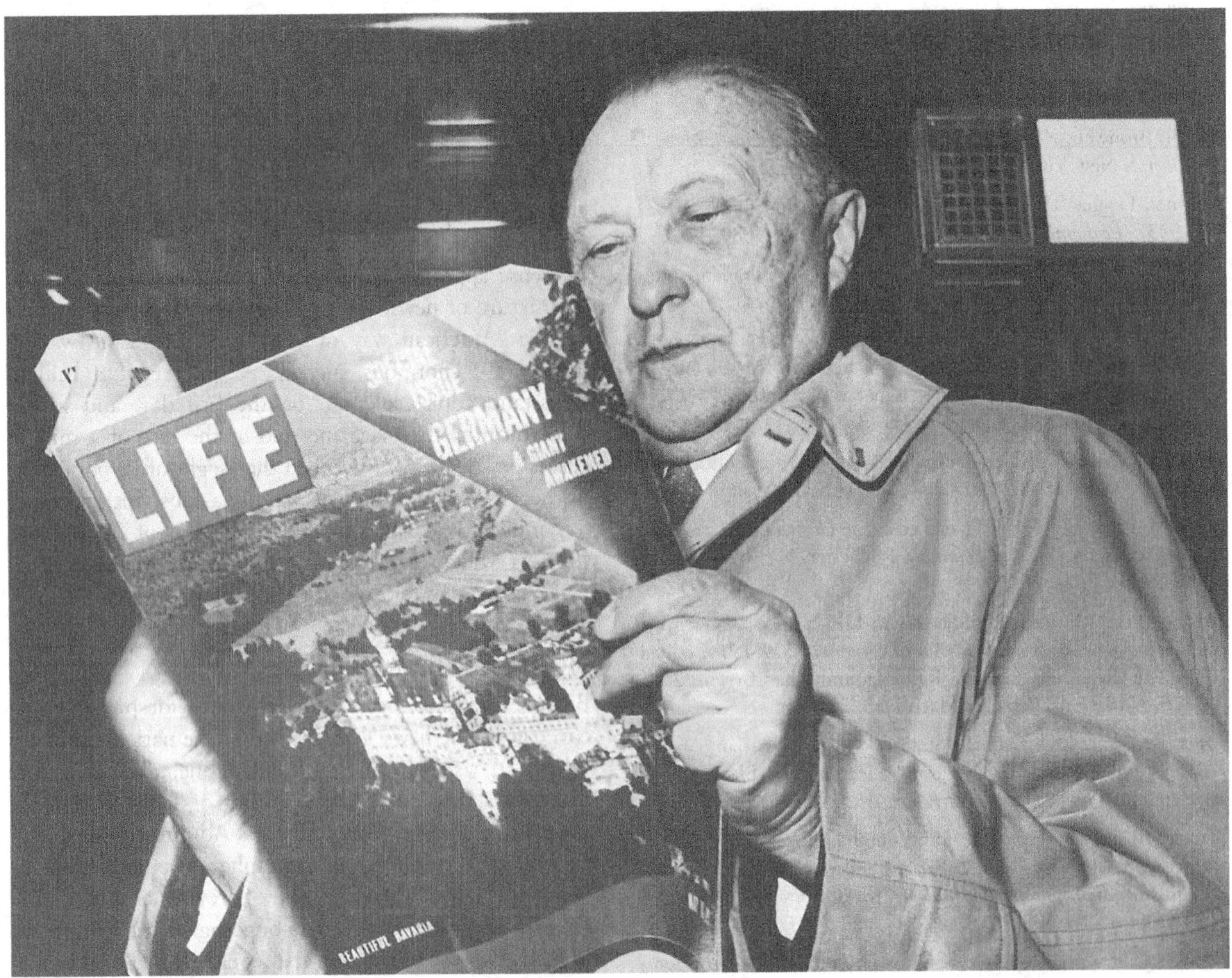

German chancellor Konrad Adenauer reads a* LIFE *special edition on Germany, 1954. LIFE, *widely considered the quintessential American magazine of the mid-twentieth century, also had an international flavor, presenting its readers with cultural, religious, political, and military aspects of life outside the United States.* AP IMAGES

the notion of the newsmagazine as an instrument of the national purpose.

Like many magazine publishers and editors of the nineteenth and twentieth centuries, Luce strove to valorize what he considered traditional American values at the same time that he helped move his readership into the modern age. *LIFE* continually engaged its readers in a visual conversation about the nation, one that promoted patriotism and celebrated the possibilities of individualism. Because photographs seem to tell an unadulterated story, the magazine, particularly in the postwar period, when many among its readership favored a return to "normalcy," convincingly promoted the idea that the nation was marked most prominently by middle-class affluence, contentment in domestic life, and a clear enactment of supremacy on the global stage. By forging what seemed a personal connection to its readers, *LIFE*'s editors used images to bring the nation together and to tell a story that would appeal, as Luce claimed, to the secretary of defense as well as the taxi driver (Wainwright 1986, 416).

LIFE'S INTERNATIONAL FOCUS

As much as *LIFE* is known for its celebration of the domestic side of American life, the magazine had an international focus from the start. The Japanese invasion of China, the Spanish Civil War, and the growing threat posed by Adolf Hitler provided dramatic opportunities for photojournalists and garnered some early exclusives, including photographs of Chinese Communist leaders Mao Zedong and Zhou Enlai and photographs taken from the roof of the US embassy in Moscow during the Nazi invasion of the Soviet Union. Between November 1936 and October 1938, cover photos featured individual American, Japanese, German, Chinese, Czech, and Hungarian soldiers in uniform, suggesting the imminence of war. Providing an interview with Hitler in June of 1941, and other shorter features in the months preceding the attack on Pearl Harbor, publisher Luce hoped to disabuse Americans of the idea that isolationism would prevail. Once the United States became involved in the war, *LIFE* provided extensive coverage, pairing serious reporting on military missions with lighter pieces about soldiers' lives and ways to keep morale high on the home front.

LIFE magazine attempted to interest its readers in the cultural and religious as well as political and military aspects of life outside the United States. Essays on topics like "the national purpose" and "the worlds' great religions" provided opportunities for readers to place their own experiences in larger contexts. *LIFE* carried memoirs of world leaders, including Sir Winston Churchill, Harry S. Truman, and the Duke of Windsor, and features on many others, including Gamal Abdel Nasser, Nikita Krushchev, Fidel Castro, and Alexander Solzhenitsyn. The magazine introduced its readers to independence movements in Africa, the role of the United States in the United Nations, Americans in prisons abroad, feminism in Europe, and, in a return to serious war coverage, the Vietnam War. This time, *LIFE*'s war coverage garnered the prestigious National Magazine Award, but competition from television and from the rise of special interest and special audience magazines proved too much for the general interest magazine. *LIFE* ceased publication for the first time in 1969, and was reintroduced in various print formats until its final demise in 2007.

SEE ALSO *Earthrise (Bill Anders, 1968); Luce, Henry; Vietnam War; V-J Day in Times Square (Alfred Eisenstaedt, 1945); World War I; World War II*

BIBLIOGRAPHY

Elson, Robert T. *Time Inc.: The Intimate History of a Publishing Empire*, Vol. 1: *1923–1941*. New York: Atheneum, 1968.

Elson, Robert T. *Time Inc.: The Intimate History of a Publishing Empire*, Vol. 2: *1941–1960*. New York: Atheneum, 1973.

Kozol, Wendy. LIFE*'s America: Family and Nation in Postwar Photojournalism*. Philadelphia: Temple University Press, 1994.

Sumner, David E. *The Magazine Century: American Magazines since 1900*. New York: Peter Lang, 2010.

Wainwright, Loudon. *The Great American Magazine: An Inside History of* LIFE. New York: Knopf, 1986.

Jennifer Scanlon
William R. Kenan Jr. Professor of Gender and Women's Studies
Bowdoin College

LIMITED TEST BAN TREATY

The spread of radioactive fallout resulting from atmospheric nuclear tests aroused global public protests in the 1950s. Albert Schweitzer (1875–1965), Linus Pauling (1901–1994), and a number of peace groups urged President Dwight Eisenhower (1890–1969) to find a way to halt the testing. Since the Soviets were also testing, the Eisenhower administration insisted that continued US testing was vital to maintaining the security of the free world. When a 1957 Gallup Poll revealed that 63 percent of the American people favored a nuclear test ban, as opposed to 20 percent three years earlier, the president initiated the tripartite (US-British-Soviet) test ban negotiations. Eisenhower turned to technical experts to develop a verification system; however, as they kept searching for more and more refinements to reduce the already low, generally acceptable, error rate, it became

President John F. Kennedy prepares to sign the Limited Test Ban Treaty as cabinet members and senators look on, 1963. *The Limited Test Ban Treaty, an arms accord between the United States and the Soviet Union, banned signatories from testing new nuclear devices in the atmosphere, space, territorial waters, or at sea, while permitting underground tests.* HULTON-DEUTSCH COLLECTION/ CORBIS

impossible to be absolutely certain that no cheating was going on. Consequently, the negotiation of a comprehensive test ban was abandoned in 1963 for a limited test ban agreement.

In the end, Eisenhower's efforts resulted only in obtaining an informal test moratorium, but John F. Kennedy (1917–1963) came to the presidency committed to obtaining a comprehensive ban on tests. His sobering encounter with Nikita Khrushchev (1894–1971) at Vienna in 1961 and the subsequent Berlin crisis, however, derailed his plans. The October 1962 Cuban missile crisis, paradoxically, brought Kennedy and Khrushchev closer together. In the immediate aftermath of the missile crisis, Kennedy sought better relations with the Soviet Union by demonstrating a willingness to resume negotiations on arms control and other tension-reducing measures. In a letter dated October 27, 1962, Khrushchev called for negotiations on a nuclear test ban treaty; thereafter, Kennedy assigned the issue top priority. Initial negotiations quickly snagged on the question of on-site verification. Finally, on May 30, 1963, Kennedy, joined by British prime minister Harold Macmillan (1894–1986), suggested a conference in Moscow to resolve the conflict.

Kennedy selected veteran diplomat W. Averell Harriman (1891–1986) to represent the United States at the Moscow test ban negotiations. The Joint Chiefs had long opposed a comprehensive test ban without guaranteed verification and on-site inspection, but they were agreeable to a limited test ban that permitted underground testing. On July 2, Khrushchev offered such a partial treaty, eliminating the problem of inspection by barring tests in the atmosphere, outer space, and under water but allowing underground tests. On July 25, Harriman, Lord Hailsham (1907–2001) representing Britain, and Andrey Gromyko (1909–1989) of the Soviet Union initialed a partial test ban treaty.

In the US Senate, the treaty, formally signed in August, faced strong opposition from the right, but public opinion mobilized behind the president sufficiently to assure a favorable vote of eighty-one to nineteen allowing ratification. This gain in East-West relations sponsored other improvements. In January, NATO announced the removal of the Jupiter missiles from Turkey. In June, Kennedy and Khrushchev established a direct communications "hot line" between Washington and Moscow; later, there would be one connecting London with Moscow. Also, the United States and the USSR agreed to support a UN resolution barring weapons of mass destruction from outer space, as well as a nonproliferation nuclear weapons treaty that would be developed into treaties under President Lyndon Johnson (1908–1973).

SEE ALSO *Cold War; Nuclear Weapons*

BIBLIOGRAPHY

Burns, Richard Dean, and Joseph M. Siracusa. *A Global History of the Nuclear Arms Race: Weapons, Strategy, and Politics.* 2 vols. Santa Barbara, CA: Praeger, 2013.

Divine, Robert A. *Blowing on the Wind: The Nuclear Test Ban Debate, 1954–1960.* New York: Oxford University Press, 1978.

Siracusa, Joseph M. *Nuclear Weapons: A Very Short Introduction.* Oxford: Oxford University Press, 2008.

Joseph Siracusa

Professor of Human Security and International Diplomacy

Royal Melbourne Institute of Technology University

LINCOLN, ABRAHAM

1809–1865

During Abraham Lincoln's only visit to a diplomat's residence during the American Civil War—shortly before his first inauguration in March 1861—he mentioned to Dr. Rudolf Schleiden (1815–1895), minister of the Republic of Bremen, the often cited words: "I don't know anything about diplomacy. I will be very apt to make blunders." Indeed, Lincoln never had traveled overseas, and except for a short glimpse of Canada when he visited Niagara Falls had never left the United States.

LINCOLN'S EARLY VIEWS

However, long before he became president, Abraham Lincoln had developed a keen sense of the unique role the United States played in the world. Lincoln's vision for the exceptional position of the United States on the world stage as a democratic example is intimately intertwined with his foreign policy during the Civil War. In his speeches during this conflict he often emphasized the significance of its outcome for the world. For example, in his message to Congress on July 4, 1861, Lincoln wrote: "On the side of the Union, it is a struggle for maintaining in the world, that form, and substance of government, whose leading object is, to elevate the condition of men—to lift artificial weights from all shoulders—to clear the paths of laudable pursuit for all—to afford all, an unfettered start, and a fair chance, in the race of life" (Basler 1953, Vol. 4, 438).

Although Lincoln had never traveled abroad, foreign countries were part of his mental map. Lincoln's knowledge about historical, political, cultural, and legal conditions in Europe was gained by his great appetite for literature and his voracious reading of newspapers. As a young congressman in Washington, DC, he witnessed how the revolutionary events in Europe were broadly discussed. His opposition to the Mexican-American War had acquainted him with Mexico. Through his intimate acquaintance with German Americans in Illinois, especially exiled leaders of the revolution of 1848–1849, who had become important ethnic leaders within the then nascent Republican Party, Lincoln learned about common transatlantic ideological bonds.

LINCOLN'S VIEWS AS PRESIDENT

When Lincoln arrived in Washington in February 1861, one of the first meetings he had was with his former rival in the presidential campaign, Senator William H. Seward (1801–1872), soon to be secretary of state. Lincoln told Seward in a straightforward manner that he intended to "leave [to him] almost entirely" the handling of foreign affairs (Seward 1891, 511). And indeed Lincoln left the pragmatic day-to-day diplomatic business to Seward, discussing with him only the relevant matters of key foreign policy issues.

In general, the primary focus of Lincoln's foreign policy was to prevent recognition of the Confederacy on the part of the European powers, especially Britain and France. In order to hit the central economic nerve of the Confederacy—its cotton exports to Europe—Lincoln proclaimed a naval blockade of the Confederacy on April 19, 1861, a decision that had far-reaching foreign policy consequences. From the beginning of the war, Lincoln had considered the armed secession of the Southern states as a "war of rebellion," and he did everything he could to avoid granting the Confederates the status of a belligerent power. However, according to international law the blockade was an official act of war against another sovereign entity. Hence, it was only logical that foreign governments began to recognize the Confederacy as a belligerent power. Great Britain granted belligerent status to the Confederacy and proclaimed neutrality on May 13,

1861, Spain on June 17, and Brazil on August 1. Other foreign governments followed. These acts challenged Lincoln's interpretation of the South's secession as a national insurrection. As a political pragmatist, however, Lincoln recognized the constraints defined by international law and hence chose a middle way: On the whole he treated the Confederacy as a nonlegal entity, but when he needed to, he accepted the demands of international law, for example, in regards to the naval blockade and, importantly, in the exchange of prisoners of war between North and South.

But Lincoln became concerned that this recognition of belligerency could lead ultimately to recognition of the Confederacy, and hence he considered the European declarations of neutrality and the recognition of belligerency as an interference in the domestic affairs of the United States. Indeed they had severe consequences for the subsequent course of the war: The Confederacy had thereby gained the right, for example, to apply for loans or to purchase arms from neutral nations that were now allowed to build warships and sell them to the Confederacy. It has been estimated that because of the British supplies and weaponry transported by blockade runners, the Confederacy was able to sustain the war one to two years longer than it would have without this support.

Seward had reacted angrily to the European declarations and drafted a bellicose memorandum with an unequivocal message: Should Great Britain not accept the Union naval blockade and continue to further negotiate with "rebellious" Confederate envoys, or even to recognize the Confederacy, this would be tantamount to a declaration of war against the Union. As with previous proposals by Seward, Lincoln was adamantly opposed to a war with a foreign power in order to distract from internal national dissent. But he wanted to check his assessment and therefore consulted with one of the most knowledgeable experts on Great Britain, Senator Charles Sumner (1811–1874) of Massachusetts, chairman of the Senate Committee on Foreign Relations. Sumner advised Lincoln not to forward the memorandum to the British under any circumstances, as this would in fact mean war with England. Lincoln confirmed his assessment, deleted some provocative passages, and asked Seward to transmit the memorandum to the American ambassador in London, Francis Adams (1807–1886), with a specific constraint: Its content should be regarded as a guideline to the Union's foreign policy and should be communicated orally at a suitable opportunity. Nevertheless, Adams was to point out that should Great Britain recognize the Confederacy, the Union would respond with a declaration of war against England. As the next few weeks demonstrated, this determination had its intended effects in England, where further considerations of the recognition of the Confederacy were postponed, an attitude subsequently shared by the French government. Given his positive experience in cooperation with Sumner, Lincoln used his expertise as a kind of corrective to Seward's foreign policy ideas and made Sumner his "second secretary of state" and trusted adviser. Seward accepted Sumner's function, and this trio proved to be an effective foreign policy team.

THE *TRENT* AFFAIR

In November and December 1861, the "*Trent* Affair" caused excitement at home and in Great Britain and brought the two nations to the brink of war. The incident took place on November 8, 1861, when the USS *San Jacinto,* under the command of Captain Charles Wilkes (1798–1877), intercepted the British ship RMS *Trent* and seized, as contraband of war, two Confederate diplomats who were bound for Britain and France to seek diplomatic recognition for the Confederacy and to lobby for financial and military support. This public pressure caused significant problems for Lincoln's foreign policy, since Wilkes had violated international law with his interdiction of a neutral ship. Although Lincoln first supported Wilkes's decision, he came to realize that this incident could severely endanger Anglo-American relations, lead to recognition of the Confederacy, and even cause an armed conflict with Great Britain, especially since the British government not only demanded the immediate release of the prisoners but also asked for an official apology from Lincoln. In order to support their demands, the British government ordered troops to the Canadian-American border and a ban on British exports to the Union, including important chemicals for the Union's war industries.

The following weeks demonstrated Lincoln's strong qualities of crisis management, and an efficiently orchestrated team play demonstrated Lincoln's subtle strategic thinking based on responsible and rational thinking. Lincoln listened carefully to the advice of his cabinet members, especially Seward, and finally concluded that his policy of "one war at a time" was the prime guiding principle of his foreign policy and had to be followed at all costs in order to win the war at home. For a while Lincoln considered the option of referring the case to international arbitration, but he realized that this plan would not be accepted by the British government. Hence, on Christmas Day 1861, Lincoln finally gave the order to release the two Confederate envoys, citing international law. However, he did not offer an official apology to the British government, which, greatly relieved, renounced the demand for an apology and considered the release of the envoys as a sufficient face-saving gesture to end the crisis.

The *Trent* crisis had made it clear to Lincoln that it was important to promulgate Northern propaganda abroad, especially to mold pro-Union public opinion in Great Britain. In other words, Lincoln used a soft power approach in foreign policy. Again, he listened carefully to what friends and experts told him about the mood in Europe concerning the Union's war efforts. Since Sumner was very well connected with British liberal reformers, he could provide Lincoln with substantial information concerning public opinion in England.

FURTHER DIPLOMATIC EFFORTS

To demonstrate to the conservative governments in Europe that he firmly believed in transatlantic republican bonds, in the summer of 1861 Lincoln invited Italian national hero General Giuseppe Garibaldi (1807–1882) to receive a major-general's commission in the Union army. Although Garibaldi declined, it was a symbolic gesture that was important for Lincoln.

The military events of the Civil War were intimately connected to the diplomatic front, and hence in the summer of 1862 Confederate victories seemed to raise the possibility of British and French intervention as peace mediators. However, with the Union victory at Antietam in September 1862 and Lincoln's preliminary Emancipation Proclamation of September 22, the British withdrew their plans to support the Confederacy. Lincoln's decision to transform the war into a fight against slavery made it impossible for Great Britain especially to call for intervention on the side of the Confederacy. After the final Emancipation Proclamation of January 1, 1863, Lincoln intensified his public diplomacy approach by selecting personalities who would be able to mold public opinion in Great Britain, such as the famous abolitionist and clergyman Henry Ward Beecher (1813–1887), brother of Harriet Beecher Stowe (1811–1896), the author of *Uncle Tom's Cabin*. Lincoln was quite aware that public opinion in Great Britain was far from monolithic, commenting in February 1863 that "there were three parties in England: an aristocratic party, which cannot be sorry to see the Republic break up; a class allied to the South through trade relations; and a third, larger, or if not larger, of more import, which sympathizes warmly with the cause of the North" (Fehrenbacher and Fehrenbacher 1996, 308). Lincoln was firmly convinced that the Emancipation Proclamation "had helped us decidedly in our foreign relations" (Fehrenbacher and Fehrenbacher 1996, 182).

Another diplomatic front opened up when Napoleon III took advantage of the war in the United States and launched an invasion of the Republic of Mexico in 1862 and later established a puppet regime, the Second Mexican Empire, with Maximilian I (1832–1867) as emperor. This French intervention severely challenged the Monroe Doctrine, but despite this provocation and demands for support from the Mexican republican government under Benito Juárez (1806–1872), Lincoln subtly chose a middle way between the rhetoric of moral and diplomatic support and a more decisive message to the conservative European governments (provided by Seward) that financial support to the Juárez government was likely to be implemented soon. Lincoln, however, who never diplomatically recognized Maximilian's empire, made it very clear to his cabinet that financial and military support for Mexico was out of the question, since the dangers of a war with France were too high. "One war at a time" remained his principle.

The greatest loyalty to the Union cause during the Civil War was shown by Russia. Russia became the most pivotal force that deterred British-French attempts to interfere in the Civil War on the side of the Confederacy, since those nations were not certain how Russia would react in case of intervention. Lincoln was quite aware that the Russian tsar, Alexander II (1818–1881), supported the idea of a centralized government and a unified nation because of his own problems at home with secessionist movements. He was also aware that Russia was interested in limiting the power of Great Britain. But Lincoln also realized that Russia, "where despotism can be taken pure, and without the base alloy of hypocracy [sic], was too important to be alienated" ("Lincoln to Joshua F. Speed, August 24, 1855," cited in Basler 1953, Vol. 2, 323).

In the fall of 1862 Lincoln sent a very personal letter to the tsar in which he directly asked him about his stance toward intervention. The tsar made it clear in his reply that Russia would firmly support the Union in its quest for one "indivisible nation." Lincoln was very moved by this reply and considered it the most loyal response from any government. By sending over parts of his fleet to New York and San Francisco in the fall of 1863, the tsar underlined his attitude of loyalty and evidently heightened the morale of the Union and delighted Lincoln, who even sent his wife, Mary, to New York to greet the Russians. Prussia took a similar loyal stance during the war, even threatening Great Britain and France in case they intervened on the Confederate side.

Lincoln had no expertise in foreign policy before he entered the White House, but he became a swift learner in foreign policy, capable of understanding the dialectics of the military fronts and the international challenges and exercising the essential qualities of a diplomat: rational thinking combined with patience and honesty, no overestimation of one's own capabilities, and absence of hubris. His main goal was to prevent the Civil War from becoming an international conflict in which the Confederacy would have been supported by European powers. Lincoln's vision for the role of the United States on the world stage was founded on his deep conviction that his nation under providence would offer the world hope for liberty and democratic governments in the future. This vision was not connected to power and expansion but rather to Lincoln's firm belief that the American example would spread around the world.

SEE ALSO *The Civil War; Confederate States of America; Seward, William H.*

BIBLIOGRAPHY

Basler, Roy P., ed. *The Collected Works of Abraham Lincoln.* 9 vols. New Brunswick, NJ: Rutgers University Press, 1953.

Beran, Michael Knox. *Forge of Empires, 1861–1871: Three Revolutionary Statesmen and the World They Made.* New York: Free Press, 2007.

Carwardine, Richard, and Jay Sexton, eds. *The Global Lincoln.* New York: Oxford University Press, 2011.

Doyle, Don. *The Cause of All Nations: An International History of the American Civil War.* New York: Basic Books, 2015.

Fehrenbacher, Don E., and Virginia Fehrenbacher, eds. *Recollected Words of Abraham Lincoln.* Stanford, CA: Stanford University Press, 1996.

Ferris, Norman B. "Lincoln and Seward in Civil War Diplomacy: Their Relationship at the Outset Reexamined." *Journal of the Abraham Lincoln Association* 12, 1 (1991): 21–42.

Jones, Howard. *Blue and Gray Diplomacy: A History of Union and Confederate Foreign Relations.* Chapel Hill: University of North Carolina Press, 2010.

Mahin, Dean B. *One War at a Time: The International Dimensions of the American Civil War.* Washington, DC: Brassey's, 1999.

Monaghan, Jay. *Abraham Lincoln Deals with Foreign Affairs: A Diplomat in Carpet Slippers.* New York: Bobbs-Merrill, 1945.

Peraino, Kevin. *Lincoln in the World: The Making of a Statesman and the Dawn of American Power.* New York: Crown, 2013.

Seward, Frederick W. *Seward at Washington, as Senator and Secretary of State: A Memoir of his Life, with Selections from his Letters, 1846-1861.* New York: Derby and Miller, 1891.

Jörg Nagler
Professor of North American History
Friedrich-Schiller-Universität, Historisches Institut

LIPPMANN, WALTER

1889–1974

Walter Lippmann, journalist, philosopher, advisor to presidents, and occasional shadow diplomat, made annual study trips abroad, where he met with world leaders and influential thinkers. Most famously, when relations between the United States and the Soviet Union were especially chilly in 1958, Russia invited Lippmann to Moscow to meet with Nikita Khrushchev (1894–1971).

ROLE IN WORLD WAR I AND THE POSTWAR PEACE

By the time he was twenty-five, Lippmann had published three books and had become one of the founding editors of *The New Republic* magazine. World War I (1914–1918) dramatically altered his interests and career trajectory. In 1915, he published his first book on international relations, *The Stakes of Diplomacy.* In 1917, President Woodrow Wilson (1856–1924) appointed Lippmann to the Inquiry: a quasi-secret group of scholars that was charged with developing a plan for the postwar world. The youngest member, Lippmann was put in charge of recruiting the scholars and served as the group's secretary during its formative stages. The Inquiry contributed to redrawing the borders of postwar Europe and drafted Wilson's *Fourteen Points.* It provided a model and vision for the subsequent creation of the US Council on Foreign Relations.

In 1918, Lippmann was commissioned a captain in army intelligence and was sent to England to participate in the meetings of the Inter-Allied Propaganda Board. Wilson's chief advisor, Colonel Edward House (1858–1938), asked Lippmann to assess the effectiveness of US propaganda abroad; based upon what Lippmann learned from his British and French counterparts, he strongly criticized the naïveté of the US Committee on Public Information's (CPI) propaganda activities in Europe. Wilson rejected Lippmann's criticism and reaffirmed his support of the CPI. Lippmann was then assigned to an army propaganda unit in France, where he wrote leaflets urging enemy soldiers to surrender and interviewed recently captured prisoners of war. He found that while enemy combatants professed a willingness to die for their country, few could explain the causes of the war or Germany's war aims. This insight would inform Lippmann's 1922 sociological classic, *Public Opinion.*

Lippmann accompanied House to Versailles, but came away from the peace negotiations deeply disillusioned with President Wilson's performance, and concluded that the harsh terms imposed on Germany by the Allies created conditions that would lead to future hostilities. Lippmann originally favored the League of Nations, but after the war he joined *The New Republic* editors in opposing ratification of the peace treaty, a decision he later regretted.

TEST OF DISINTERESTED JOURNALISM

In 1920, during the height of the US domestic Red scare, Lippmann and journalist Charles Merz (1888–1952) published a study of newspaper coverage of the Russian Revolution using the *New York Times* as the test case. They demonstrated that the paper systematically misrepresented the facts of events in Russia, concluding that internal and external censorships resulted in distortion of coverage in ways that represented America's hopes for an Allied victory in Europe and for the defeat of communism rather than factually reporting the conflict. If America's greatest newspaper failed the test of disinterested reporting so badly, then, they argued, lesser papers did much worse. "A Test of the News," along with Lippmann's *Liberty and the News* (1920), contributed to extensive reforms in journalism.

LIPPMANN'S REALIST APPROACH TO INTERNATIONAL AFFAIRS

Disillusioned by the carnage in Europe, America never joined the League of Nations, and generally embraced an isolationist stance after World War I, but Lippmann always advocated diplomatic engagement. He is considered a "realist" in international affairs in contrast to Wilsonian idealists, who advocate spreading American values and institutions globally. Lippmann maintained that the United States and other nation-states should act in their own strategic self-interest, but he opposed imperialism. Unlike the realpolitik of Henry Kissinger (b. 1923), Lippmann's realism has a moral dimension similar to the approaches of theologian Reinhold Niebuhr (1892–1971) and political scientist Han Morgenthau (1904–1980).

Undertaking a secret mission to Cuba in 1928 with the ambassador to Mexico, Dwight Morrow (1873–1931), Lippmann played an active role in helping to broker a diplomatic compromise involving the United States, Mexico, and the Catholic Church, which avoided an armed US intervention in Mexico.

In 1937, Lippmann published *The Good Society*, a book that still fuels controversy. Responding to the rise of totalitarianism, Lippmann explored threats to the future of liberal democracy. The next year, French philosopher Louis Rougier (1889–1982) organized the Colloque Walter Lippmann, a conference of prominent European intellectuals in Paris to honor the book. Lippmann attended the Paris colloquium, which culminated in the French government making him a knight of the Legion of Honor.

After the war, Austrian economist Friedrich Hayek (1899–1992) used the 1938 meeting as precedent and inspiration for creating the Mont Pelerin Society. Originally composed of a pluralistic group of intellectuals, the society was later dominated by free-market fundamentalists and is frequently viewed as the incubator of neoliberalism. Conservatives have tried to claim Lippmann, but he never joined the Mont Pelerin Society, rejected laissez-faire ideologies, and generally endorsed Keynesian economics.

Lippmann supported the US war effort during World War II (1939–1945), including the internment of Japanese Americans, and he is faulted for not speaking out against the death camps. He is generally credited with naming "the Cold War," although he never claimed originality in coining the term. He was highly critical of the Truman Doctrine and of diplomat George Kennan's (1904–2005) "containment" policy, favoring instead ongoing diplomatic engagement with the Soviet Union. Lippmann was against sending US troops to Korea in the 1950s. He opposed the Vietnam War and actively campaigned against it; his antiwar activities led President Lyndon B. Johnson (1908–1973), whom Lippmann had once supported, to denounce the journalist repeatedly, including in his farewell address. Lippmann lost influence within the foreign policy establishment in his later years; however, there has recently been a renewal of interest in his coherent strategic approach to foreign policy in response to America's polarized domestic politics and its postmillennial wars in the Middle East.

Lippmann's column, *Today and Tomorrow*, which was routinely monitored by the offices of world leaders, ran from 1931 to 1967 and was syndicated in more than 250 newspapers in the United States and abroad, with an estimated readership of eight million. Lippmann published his final column in *Newsweek* in 1971. He carried on a vast correspondence with domestic and international political figures and officials, as well as leading intellectuals. Their views often influenced the editorial stances he developed in his columns, which, in turn, influenced public opinion at home and abroad. No American journalist has exercised more international influence than Walter Lippmann.

SEE ALSO *Cold War; Vietnam War*

BIBLIOGRAPHY

Blum, D. Steven. *Walter Lippmann: Cosmopolitanism in the Century of Total War.* Ithaca, NY: Cornell University Press, 1984.

Burgin, Angus. *The Great Persuasion: Reinventing Free Markets since the Depression.* Cambridge, MA: Harvard University Press, 2012.

Goodwin, Craufurd D. *Walter Lippmann: Public Economist.* Cambridge, MA: Harvard University Press, 2014.

Jansen, Sue Curry. *Walter Lippmann: A Critical Introduction to Media and Communication Theory.* New York: Peter Lang, 2012.

Lippmann, Walter. *U.S. Foreign Policy: Shield of the Republic.* Boston: Little, Brown, 1942.

Porter, Patrick. "Beyond the American Century: Walter Lippmann and American Grand Strategy, 1943–1950." *Diplomacy and Statecraft* 22, 4 (2011): 557–577.

Riccio, Barry D. *Walter Lippmann: Odyssey of a Liberal.* New Brunswick, NJ: Transaction, 1994.

Steel, Ronald. *Walter Lippmann and the American Century.* Boston: Little, Brown, 1980.

Walter Lippmann Papers. Manuscripts and Archives (MS 326). Yale University Library, New Haven, CT.

Sue Curry Jansen
Professor, Media & Communication
Muhlenberg College

LIVINGSTON, ROBERT

SEE *Department of Foreign Affairs.*

LODGE, HENRY CABOT
1850–1924

Henry Cabot Lodge was a US senator from Massachusetts from 1893 until his death in 1924. The Republican served as chair of the Senate Foreign Relations Committee (1919–1924) and as the first recognized Senate majority leader (1920–1924). Lodge, an ardent internationalist and close friend of Theodore Roosevelt (1858–1919), is best known for his opposition to and subsequent defeat of the Treaty of Versailles (1919) as negotiated by President Woodrow Wilson (1856–1924).

CAREER AS AN INTERNATIONALIST AND IMPERIALIST

Throughout his career in the Senate and as a leader of the Republican Party, Lodge was known as an internationalist and supporter of an expanding American role in the world. Like Roosevelt, Lodge favored American intervention in Cuba in support of its revolt against Spanish rule. In addition to supporting the declaration of war against Spain, Lodge called early on for the acquisition and annexation of the Spanish colony of the Philippines. As the Senate's leading supporter of American imperialism, Lodge played a major role in the ratification of the Treaty of Paris (1899), which brought the United States control of Guam, Puerto Rico, and the Philippines, as well as Cuban independence and the payment of $20 million to Spain. Also like Roosevelt, Lodge subscribed to the naval theories of Admiral Alfred T. Mahan (1840–1914), which called for a large American navy to protect America's overseas possessions and to project American power globally. Lodge was a strong supporter of Roosevelt's calls for increased naval appropriations.

Lodge was also an early advocate for restrictions on immigration. Despite his conviction that once a person became a citizen it did not matter whether he or she was native born, Lodge became a spokesman for the Immigration Restriction League and a member of the Dillingham Commission, which recommended legislation placing restrictions on certain categories of immigrants.

Like many imperialists, Lodge supported American intervention in World War I (1914–1918) on the side of the Allies. To relieve pressure from imperialists like Lodge and Roosevelt, Wilson called for increasing naval appropriations and doubling the size of the army, although he justified these actions as necessary to defend American neutrality. After the German resumption of unrestricted submarine warfare on January 31, 1917, Wilson broke diplomatic relations with Germany. On April 4, Wilson sought and Congress approved a declaration of war. Although Lodge supported the president's call for war, the two men's dislike for each other grew.

Throughout the war, Lodge criticized the administration for its overt idealism, specifically criticizing Wilson's Fourteen Points as unrealistic and a sign of weakness. Like the French, Lodge believed Germany should be punished by hobbling the German economy, a move that would prevent the Germans from rebuilding militarily and perpetrating future aggression. During the midterm elections in 1918, Wilson broke tradition and campaigned for a continued Democratic majority in Congress in order to demonstrate national unity behind his policies. Many Americans were alienated by this politicizing of the war, and many progressives had opposed entry in the first place. Subsequently, the Republicans gained control of both houses of Congress, and Lodge was elevated to the chair of the Foreign Relations Committee. In that position, he played a major role in the ratification process of any peace treaty.

OPPOSITION TO THE TREATY OF VERSAILLES

Wilson, spurning the advice of the State Department, decided to exclude the Republicans and all senators from the negotiating team that accompanied him to Versailles. Lodge and the Republicans made it clear that the Senate was not a rubber-stamp body and would closely scrutinize any treaty the president negotiated. Wilson believed the Republicans were bluffing, both because the Senate had never rejected a peace treaty and because most of the Republicans, especially Lodge, were internationalists who would agree that the United States should play a major role in global affairs. Nevertheless, Lodge opposed the Treaty of Versailles.

For Lodge, the most significant problem with the treaty was the Covenant of the League of Nations, the international organization that Wilson hoped would prevent future aggression through collective security. In particular, Lodge opposed Article X of the covenant, which allowed the League of Nations Council to call on member nations to defend the political and territorial integrity of fellow members faced with aggression. Wilson considered Article X the heart of the League of Nations, a moral commitment on the part of members to each other's security. Lodge considered it a violation of American sovereignty and the US Constitution.

Lodge and his allies in the Senate became known as the "reservationists" after they proposed fourteen reservations or amendments to the treaty. Lodge and the reservationists argued that the Treaty of Versailles and the Covenant of the League of Nations violated the Constitution by usurping congressional control over the declaration of war, violated American sovereignty by turning over control of American foreign policy to the League of Nations, and violated the Monroe Doctrine by allowing Latin American nations to charge the United States with aggression. The proposed reservations would address these concerns by explicitly stating that the League of Nations Council could not override the Constitution, that American sovereignty and control over US foreign policy would be respected, and that the Monroe Doctrine would be recognized as international law.

On November 15, 1919, Lodge called the treaty, including the reservations, to a vote. The Senate voted fifty-five to thirty-nine in favor, short of a two-thirds majority. The Senate then voted on the unamended treaty, and it too fell short, fifty-three to thirty-eight. The Senate once again voted on the Lodge version of the treaty on March 19, 1920. Once again, the treaty fell seven votes short of a two-thirds majority. With this rejection of the Treaty of Versailles, the United States never joined the League of Nations. Whether the Americans' nonparticipation made a difference in the League's operation is a matter of debate; what is certain is that Lodge's opposition to Wilson's draft of the treaty is consistently blamed for the failure of America to become a member.

CONTRIBUTIONS TO THE WASHINGTON CONFERENCE

President Warren Harding (1865–1923) appointed Lodge to the American delegation to the Washington Conference on Naval Disarmament (November 12, 1921–February 6, 1922). Lodge contributed to the negotiations and subsequent ratification of the three treaties the conference produced. These treaties included an agreement to a ten-year holiday on capital ship production and a cap on the tonnage of such ships; limitations on the building of fortifications in the Pacific; respect for China's territorial and political integrity; and acceptance of the Open Door policy for trade in China.

LEGACY

Despite his contributions to the Washington Conference, Lodge's global reputation matched his historical one: he is primarily remembered for engineering the Senate's rejection of the Treaty of Versailles. Despite his internationalist behaviors and support for American participation in the war, most Europeans blamed Lodge for the failure of the League of Nations to prevent the aggression that culminated in World War II (1939–1945). Lodge's name has become synonymous with isolationism and an unwillingness on the part of the United States to play a leadership role in world affairs during the 1930s, a stark contrast to Lodge's actual beliefs. Finally, this perception of Lodge has served as a historical contrast to the perception of Wilson as the visionary internationalist who sought to promote collective security.

SEE ALSO *Dollar Diplomacy; Isolationism; League of Nations; Missionary Diplomacy; Panama Canal; Paris Peace Conference (1919); Philippines; Preparedness; Roosevelt, Theodore; Senate Foreign Relations Committee; Spanish-American War; Taft, William Howard; Wilson, Woodrow; World War I*

BIBLIOGRAPHY

Ambrosius, Lloyd E. *Wilsonianism: Woodrow Wilson and His Legacy in American Foreign Relations.* New York: Palgrave Macmillan, 2002.

Garraty, John A. *Henry Cabot Lodge: A Biography.* New York: Knopf, 1953.

Widenor, William. *Henry Cabot Lodge and the Search for an American Foreign Policy.* Berkeley: University of California Press, 1980.

Zimmerman, Warren. *First Great Triumph: How Five Americans Made Their Country a World Power.* New York: Farrar, Strauss, and Giroux, 2002.

Richard M. Filipink
Associate Professor
Western Illinois University

LOST GENERATION

The lost generation was a group of mostly male, white, American writers who attained prominence in the 1920s, including E. E. Cummings (1894–1962), John Dos Passos (1896–1970), Ernest Hemingway (1899–1961), and F. Scott Fitzgerald (1896–1940). These writers expressed disillusionment with, and alienation from, mainstream American civilization and art. This disillusionment was fueled by their experiences in World War I (1914–1918), during which many had served as volunteer ambulance drivers in France and Italy, including Hemingway, Cummings, Dos Passos, Malcolm Cowley (1898–1989), William Slater Brown (1896–1997), Dashiell Hammett (1894–1961), and Harry Crosby (1898–

1929). Subsequently, many chose self-imposed exile in Europe, especially in Paris, and immersed themselves in modern European literature by writers such as Fyodor Dostoevsky (1821–1881), Ivan Turgenev (1818–1883), Gustave Flaubert (1821–1880), Joseph Conrad (1857–1924), James Joyce (1882–1941), and Marcel Proust (1871–1922).

Although no single literary style united the group, the prose writers generally rejected the naturalism of the previous generation to develop formally innovative and often bitterly ironic narratives. Poets such as Cummings devised irreverent and typographically unorthodox verse that often questioned American conventions of sexuality and patriotism. This group was an influential subset of American modernism, and did much to shape its stylistic and thematic preoccupations, often through international little magazines such as *Broom*, *transition*, *The Little Review*, and *S_4N*. The term is also sometimes used more broadly to include American writers who rejected American moral and artistic norms in the 1920s and 1930s but did not share the biographical profile of this core group, writers including Hart Crane (1899–1932), William Faulkner (1897–1962), Thomas Wolfe (1900–1938), T. S. Eliot (1888–1965), Ezra Pound (1885–1972), and Thornton Wilder (1897–1975).

The phrase "lost generation" had been pioneered in Germany in 1912 by the expressionist painter Franz Pfemfert (1879–1954) in the magazine *Die Aktion*. It later gained widespread use across Europe to designate the generation of men decimated by World War I, but by the 1930s it was largely associated with this specifically American group. This was, in part, due to the influence of several memoirs self-mythologizing the group's geographical, aesthetic, political, and spiritual "exile" from America during the 1920s, memoirs including Cummings's *The Enormous Room* (1922), Cowley's *Exile's Return* (1934, rev. 1951), Robert McAlmon's (1896–1956) *Being Geniuses Together* (1938, rev. 1968 with Kay Boyle), and the essays collected in Fitzgerald's *The Crack-Up and Other Essays* (1945). The most influential of all, Hemingway's *A Moveable Feast*, appeared posthumously in 1964; this tied the origin of the term to Gertrude Stein (1874–1946), who had characterized "all of you young people who served in the war" as "a lost generation" who "have no respect for anything. You drink yourselves to death" (Hemingway 1964, 26). Hemingway had earlier popularized the phrase by using it as one of his twinned epigraphs to *The Sun Also Rises* (1926; the other was from Ecclesiastes)—a novel following a group of disenchanted and dissipated young Americans in Paris and Pamplona that became the definitive text of the movement, and which was originally titled *The Lost Generation*.

The group was closely associated with artistic Paris in the 1920s; the strength of the dollar against the franc in the 1920s allowed many young American artists to live there cheaply. Many later spent significant time on the French Riviera, where a circle of artists and writers centered on the American expatriate painter Gerald Murphy (1888–1964) and his wife Sara (1883–1975).

Cowley, who became the definitive chronicler of the lost generation, linked it to five distinguishing characteristics: first, a birthdate of around 1900; second, a shared educational background, including college, which served to "destroy whatever roots we had in the soil ... making us homeless citizens of the world" (Crowley 1951, 27). Third was a "spectatorial attitude" of disengagement toward the politics and the patriotisms of World War I cultivated by the volunteer ambulance drivers; however, they also experienced a physical danger that "revivified the subjects that had seemed forbidden because they were soiled by many hands and robbed of meaning: danger made it possible to write once more about love, adventure, death" (Crowley 1951, 42). Fourth was a "war in bohemia," that is, the war of bohemians, often based in Greenwich Village or Paris, against middle-class norms of morality, economics, and art; and fifth was the condition of exile, often in Europe, which functioned as an extension of the "psychic alienation" (from family and mainstream society) they had already felt. Many of the group, including Hemingway, Cummings, Dos Passos, Cowley, and Matthew Josephson (1899–1976) would extend their alienation from mainstream American political, aesthetic, and moral conventions into an engagement with the international communist movement, an interest that peaked in the 1930s.

SEE ALSO *Transatlantic Reform; World War I*

BIBLIOGRAPHY

Cowley, Malcolm. *Exile's Return: A Literary Odyssey of the 1920s.* New York: Viking, 1951.

Cowley, Malcolm. *A Second Flowering: Works and Days of the Lost Generation.* New York: Viking, 1973.

Dolan, Marc. "The (Hi)story of Their Lives: Mythic Autobiography and 'The Lost Generation.'" *Journal of American Studies* 27, 1 (1993): 35–56.

Hemingway, Ernest. *A Moveable Feast.* New York: Scribner's, 1964.

Monk, Craig. *Writing the Lost Generation: Expatriate Autobiography and American Modernism.* Iowa City: University of Iowa Press, 2008.

Soto, Michael. *The Modernist Nation: Generation, Renaissance, and Twentieth-Century American Literature.* Tuscaloosa: University of Alabama Press, 2007.

Mark Whalan

Robert D. and Eve E. Horn Professor of English

University of Oregon

LOUISIANA PURCHASE

The Louisiana Purchase was a transformative event in US foreign relations and domestic policy. Signed and ratified in 1803, the treaty constituted an agreement between the United States and France that doubled the national domain of the United States in exchange for $15 million. In the years that followed, Americans came to celebrate the Louisiana Purchase as one of the greatest events in the young nation's history. At the time it was ratified, however, Americans were more ambivalent, greeting news of the Purchase with a combination of delight, relief, frustration, and fear.

DEVELOPMENTS LEADING TO THE TREATY

The Louisiana Purchase emerged as the result of overlapping developments on both sides of the Atlantic. In the United States securing unrestricted passage and trade down the length of the Mississippi River had been one of the principal foreign policy goals of the young republic. Meanwhile the territory west of the Mississippi had been the subject of the intense imperial rivalries of eighteenth-century Europe. France founded Louisiana in the early eighteenth century, only to cede the ill-defined colony to Spain in 1763. In 1800 Spain restored Louisiana to France through a secret treaty in which France would own Louisiana but Spain would continue to execute daily governance.

News of this secret agreement (often called the retrocession) coincided with Thomas Jefferson's victory in the presidential election of 1800. Americans immediately began discussing the situation as the "Mississippi crisis." Americans decried what they saw as European duplicity. When Spanish officials in New Orleans imposed new restrictions on American trade, some Americans demanded a military response while others feared the outcome of a war with Spain. Nobody was more worried about trade restrictions then western settlers, and their increasingly heated demands for a resolution led some Americans to fear that even if the Mississippi crisis did not lead to war, it might lead to disunion.

The Jefferson administration immediately situated the Mississippi crisis at the center of its foreign policy. Throughout the negotiations that followed, American policy makers were clear in the extent of their territorial aspirations. President Jefferson and Secretary of State James Madison instructed American diplomats in both Paris and Madrid that the United States should acquire only New Orleans and "the Floridas" (a term used to describe the Gulf Coast and the Florida peninsula). American policy makers sought to consolidate federal sovereignty east of the Mississippi rather than extend American claims west of the Mississippi. The reasons were simple. Many federal policy makers believed the United States lacked the capacity to govern any additional land. While some Americans like Jefferson imagined a United States that extended into the far West, even for Jefferson such territorial expansion was an event best left for the future.

As the Americans learned, the Europeans would not budge because they had no reason to do so, and the United States lacked any leverage to alter this state of affairs. When the situation changed, it did so for reasons that had little to do with American goals or American statecraft. For over a decade the French government had sought to quell the rising racial revolt on the island colony of Saint Domingue. The revolt began in the early 1790s as free people of color demanded full citizenship and local self-government within a reformed French empire. The movement later exploded into a broad-based slave revolt. By the spring of 1803 the French leadership had concluded it could no longer preserve white rule in Saint Domingue. Without this colony, which had generated enormous profits from vast sugar plantations, there was no reason for France to keep Louisiana, which had served as a base to protect and supply the island. Meanwhile, Napoléon Bonaparte (1769–1821) was preparing to renew hostilities with Great Britain after a brief two-year peace and needed an infusion of new funds to mobilize for war. The French eventually abandoned Saint Domingue, and the victorious slaves and free people of color declared the independence of Haiti in 1804.

THE FRENCH PROPOSAL

It was under these circumstances that French negotiators proposed a treaty with the United States through which France would cede all its territory on the North American mainland. The boundaries of the Louisiana Purchase were phrased in the vaguest language possible, but it was immediately apparent that the agreement would double the size of the United States. In exchange the United States agreed to pay $11.5 million and forgive $3.5 million in outstanding French debts. The treaty also mandated that the white residents of Louisiana would become US citizens with minimal delay, and the United States would be obligated to preserve existing treaties with Indians.

When news reached the United States, Americans celebrated the fact that the Louisiana Purchase guaranteed American control of the Mississippi River, and that it had done so without the war that many had feared. But Americans lamented the fact that the Purchase failed to deliver the Floridas. They worried about the price tag, which the United States managed to pay only by creating an elaborate debt system financed by British and Dutch banks. American policy makers had no desire to respect existing Indian treaties, a requirement of the treaty.

Finally, critics in the United States claimed that the white population of Louisiana would be inherently disloyal, was unprepared for citizenship, and lacked the capacity for representative self-government.

Americans also soon learned that rather than resolving American diplomatic concerns the Louisiana Purchase only created new ones. Looking across the Atlantic, the United States found itself in an intractable dispute over the boundaries of Louisiana. Looking to the West, the United States found itself negotiating with numerous, unfamiliar Indians. Indeed, the United States might claim Louisiana, but Indians remained the real governing authority in much of the North American West.

ESTABLISHING AUTHORITY IN THE WEST

It was in response to this state of affairs that the United States engaged in a series of lengthy, expensive, and challenging projects designed to establish federal authority in the West. In the short term, the Jefferson administration commissioned a series of expeditions to survey the West and establish initial diplomatic ties with Indians. The most famous of these ventures was the Lewis and Clark Expedition of 1804–1806 (often called the Corps of Discovery), but it was only one of several expeditions that sought to map out the Louisiana Purchase.

While American explorers traversed the West, American negotiators in Europe sought to define boundaries with Spanish Mexico and British Canada. It took the end of the Napoleonic Wars, the collapse of the Spanish empire, and a thaw in long-standing British-American tensions for these negotiations to bear fruit. By 1821 the United States had finally secured a series of treaties that established the boundaries that now appear in the textbook maps of the Louisiana Purchase. These boundaries encompassed over 800,000 square miles, extending from the Mississippi River to the Rocky Mountains, from the Gulf of Mexico to the present US-Canadian border.

Meanwhile, white Americans found that their objectives with Indians took far longer to achieve. The federal government pursued a strategy designed to make Indians accept federal sovereignty. The federal government also sought to coerce Indians into moving from the lands coveted by the white settlers who descended on the West in the decades following the Louisiana Purchase. Indians rejected this policy through negotiation and warfare, preserving their own power in much of the West. In the end it took the army created by the Civil War, under the leadership of Civil War veterans like William Tecumseh Sherman (1820–1891) and Philip Sheridan (1831–1888), to finally crush the last pockets of Indian independence. It was only in the 1870s that the United States truly governed all the territory it had acquired through the Louisiana Purchase. And though white Americans sought to treat Indians as a "domestic" issue, throughout much of the nineteenth century Indians in the North American West constituted a diplomatic force no less powerful than the Europeans.

Finally, in the wake of the Louisiana Purchase the federal government struggled to build a system of domestic governance that could meet the nation's new boundaries. Extending a system that had first developed east of the Mississippi, the United States established a series of territories, each of which was under direct federal supervision. Only when a territory demonstrated that it had reached a viable population threshold and had established institutions of self-government would Congress consider converting the territory into a state. This process of new state creation was truly revolutionary in its time, constituting a dramatic break from the old system of empire and colony that had ruled much of North America.

Long before 1803, determining the fate of the Mississippi Valley had shaped the American relationship with the larger world. And long after it was signed, the Louisiana Purchase continued to shape the nation's destiny. By the end of the nineteenth century, however, most Americans had forgotten the uncertainty that greeted the Louisiana Purchase or the struggles that came in its wake. Instead, Americans chose to celebrate the Purchase as a model of American statecraft and a testament to the virtues of an expanding democracy.

SEE ALSO *Haitian Revolution; Jefferson, Thomas*

BIBLIOGRAPHY

Aron, Stephen. *American Confluence: The Missouri Frontier from Borderland to Border State*. Bloomington: Indiana University Press, 2006.

Kastor, Peter J. *The Nation's Crucible: The Louisiana Purchase and the Creation of America*. New Haven, CT: Yale University Press, 2004.

Kukla, John. *A Wilderness So Immense: The Louisiana Purchase and the Destiny of America*. New York: Knopf, 2003.

Peter J. Kastor
Professor of History and American Culture Studies
Washington University in St. Louis

LOYALISTS

Loyalists, comprising perhaps 30 percent of the entire population of the American colonies, were those who opposed American independence and therefore worked to keep the colonies as part of the British empire. Overt Loyalists, who openly affiliated with the Loyalist cause by serving in Loyalist militias, signing public declarations of support for the British, and otherwise risking Patriot retaliation, numbered perhaps 20 percent of the total white population. These American Loyalists were part of an even larger group—the majority of American colonists who were disaffected and did not support the Revolution. Only one-third of Americans actively supported the Patriot cause. The rest were active Loyalists, pacifists, and people who merely wanted to avoid any involvement at all.

Because Loyalists were motivated by a wide variety of concerns it is impossible to paint a picture of an "average" Loyalist. Some were motivated by ethnic discrimination or by past political fights. Minority populations often trusted the British as their traditional protector against the untrammeled power of colonial elites. A minority of Loyalists, but a vocal and influential one, was ideologically committed to a vision of a cosmopolitan yet strong society and government epitomized by the British empire that they believed was fairer and more protective of freedom than what the American Patriots could possibly promise. Many were also conservative by temperament and warned repeatedly about the ill-considered decision to bring the chaos of civil war to society.

The majority of white Loyalists stayed in the United States after the Revolution, where they found that initially hostile state governments and victorious Patriots chose to warm to them as time passed. During the war itself state governments sought to control Loyalists, forcing them to take loyalty oaths and then banishing prominent individuals when they refused. Yet after the war even Loyalists who initially had their property confiscated were often able to reclaim it after the passage of a few years. The children and grandchildren of Loyalists went on to reach the economic and social status that their families had before the Revolution. Native American Loyalists—Native American groups that allied with the British during the war—stayed in the new United States as well. They had often chosen the British cause out of the belief that the Americans, whom they called the "long knives," were less respectful of Native American autonomy. After the Revolution they would sadly be proved correct.

THE LOYALISTS WHO LEFT

The minority of Loyalists who did leave the United States after the Revolution overwhelmingly went to Canada; others went to Jamaica, elsewhere in the Caribbean, and Great Britain. Even this minority comprised 60,000 white people as well as at least 15,000 people of African descent. They were followed by another wave of "late Loyalists" who moved to upper Canada between the Revolution and the War of 1812, responding to offers of free land. There is some evidence to suggest that Loyalists who ended up emigrating were more likely to be ethnic, racial, or religious minorities. These Loyalists faced a true Atlantic diaspora, and they drew the empire tighter as they hopped from location to location throughout the Atlantic world trying to better their lot. The British did try to recompense Loyalists for their losses from the Revolution, but generally even those Loyalists who received a formal payout from the Loyalist Claims Commission received only about 40 percent of their losses. The Loyalists who accepted land grants in Canada may have felt economically cheated, but they helped the British establish their power in that land. Bitter Loyalists also shaped Canadian politics and culture for generations, encouraging loyalty to the Crown and anger toward the United States.

The Loyalists who left the new United States also brought with them a commitment to local self-rule through democratic assemblies as a bulwark of English liberty. Across the empire they clashed with colonial governors and the British imperial administration as they pressed for greater autonomy and rights—sounding very much like the American Patriots during the American Revolution. In fact, the vocal Loyalists quickly became a thorn in the side of the British governing authorities. The diverse origins and beliefs of the Loyalist émigrés also helped teach the British governing authorities that they ran an empire of many ethnicities and faiths. In addition, the Loyalist diaspora also had stabilizing properties. Loyalist immigration into previously tenuous colonies such as East Florida, Grenada, and St. John's Bay in Canada helped swell the population, allowing Great Britain to solidify its hold on these lands. And the connections Loyalists brought with them on their peregrinations across the empire, from kinship to mercantile relationships kept fresh through epistolary conversations, helped solidify the empire and smooth out cultural differences from place to place.

BLACK LOYALISTS

African and African American slaves overwhelmingly chose the British cause as they identified the British, not Americans, as their liberators. The last royal governor of Virginia, in a desperate move to retain his authority over the rebellious colony, offered freedom to male slaves who fled to British lines and fought for the British. Dunmore's Proclamation (1775), as it became known, was not actually backed by the British government, which was worried about appearing to support emancipation in America at the same time that its Caribbean colonies were enormously profitable on the backs of hundreds of thousands of slaves. Yet the proclamation encouraged American slaves to consider the American Revolution a war for freedom, and to see the British as the real emancipators.

Everywhere British soldiers went, but especially in the American South, both male and female slaves of all ages fled to their lines seeking freedom. Perhaps 20 percent of the enslaved southern population ultimately sought refuge from slavery in British-controlled garrison cities such as Charleston. Some three thousand of these black Loyalists accepted British offers to resettle them in Canada, and other unfortunate ex-slaves found themselves sold back into slavery in the Caribbean. White Loyalists and British soldiers profited from their ability to take slave property with them as they left the United States. In Jamaica newly arrived slaves found limited food supplies and frequent hurricanes, which led to more than fifteen thousand deaths among the enslaved population. Slaves brought to other parts of the Caribbean found themselves subject to a work regime that was even more dangerous and oppressive than what they had faced in the American South.

Black Loyalists in Canada found that resettled white Loyalists opposed even routine land grants to black settlers. Faced with such open racial hostility, some twelve hundred black Loyalists left Canada and joined the British black resettlement project in Sierra Leone. A few black Loyalists even found themselves involuntary colonists in the penal colony of Australia. Loyalists were very much a people of the world.

SEE ALSO *American Revolution; Canada; Simcoe, John Graves; War of 1812*

BIBLIOGRAPHY

Calhoon, Robert M., Timothy M. Barnes, and George A. Rawlyck, eds. *Loyalists and Community in North America.* Westport, CT: Greenwood Press, 1994.

Chopra, Ruma. *Unnatural Rebellion: Loyalists in New York City during the Revolution.* Charlottesville: University of Virginia Press, 2011.

Frey, Sylvia. *Water from the Rock: Black Resistance in a Revolutionary Age.* Princeton, NJ: Princeton University Press, 1991.

Jasanoff, Maya. *Liberty's Exiles: American Loyalists in the Revolutionary World.* New York: Knopf, 2011.

Mason, Keith. "The American Loyalist Diaspora and the Reconfiguration of the British Atlantic World." In *Empire and Nation: The American Revolution in the Atlantic World,* edited by Eliga H. Gould and Peter S. Onuf, 239–259. Baltimore: Johns Hopkins University Press, 2005.

Piecuch, Jim. *Three Peoples, One King: Loyalists, Indians, and Slaves in the Revolutionary South, 1775–1782.* Columbia: University of South Carolina Press, 2008.

Pybus, Cassandra. *Epic Journeys of Freedom: Runaway Slaves of the American Revolution and Their Global Quest for Liberty.* Boston: Beacon Press, 2006.

Smith, Paul H. "The American Loyalists: Notes on Their Organization and Numerical Strength." *William and Mary Quarterly* 3rd. ser., 25, 2 (1968): 259–277.

Rebecca Brannon
Assistant Professor
James Madison University

LUCE, HENRY
1898–1967

Henry Robinson Luce was a leading twentieth-century news publisher and an outspoken advocate for an active US foreign policy.

Born in Penglai, China, Luce grew up in a family of American Presbyterian missionaries. After graduating from Yale University in 1920, he and classmate Briton Hadden (1898–1929) developed a plan to launch a weekly magazine that aggregated and interpreted news headlines for busy readers. *Time,* first published in March 1923, quickly became one of the most widely read publications in the world. In 1930, Luce went on to found *Fortune,* a business magazine. He launched the illustrated weekly *Life* in 1936. Beginning in 1932, Time Inc. also distributed *The March of Time,* a radio and film news production. In 1923, Luce married Lila Ross Hotz (1899–1999); they divorced in 1935, and a year later, he married Clare Boothe Brokaw (1903–1987). He had two children.

Luce became deeply engaged with foreign affairs as war loomed in Asia and Europe in the late 1930s, and he used his publications to advocate his views. He pressed for American aid to China after the Japanese invasion in 1937, spearheading United China Relief, a fundraising organization. Luce argued for greater US military preparedness in the event of war with Germany, and endorsed President Franklin D. Roosevelt's (1882–1945) Lend-Lease program. Luce, a lifelong Republican, devoted much of his energy to attacking anti-interventionists within his own party. In 1940, in part to preempt the nomination of a less internationally oriented Republican candidate, he convinced prominent attorney Wendell L. Willkie (1892–1944) to challenge Roosevelt for the White House, but Roosevelt's popularity and Willkie's inability to distinguish himself clearly from his Democratic opponent led to defeat.

Soon thereafter, Luce offered readers of *Life*'s February 17, 1941, issue a distillation of his views on US foreign policy. In "The American Century," Luce argued that World War II (1939–1945) had transformed America's place in the world, despite the fact that the United States had not yet entered the war. Whether Americans liked it or not, active US engagement with world affairs was both a national responsibility and an opportunity for global leadership. Both applauded and criticized by readers, the essay conveyed Luce's ideological commitments and revealed his perceptive understanding of the power of American media and consumer culture in the international arena.

After World War II, Luce's international attention focused on anticommunism, especially in Asia. Despite his superficial knowledge of the region, and limited travel there since his childhood, Luce exercised a substantial influence on US public opinion about Asia and policy toward the region. Luce, a longtime friend of Chinese Nationalist leader Jiang Jieshi (Chiang Kai-shek, 1887–1875), urged readers of *Time* and *Life* to support the Jiang regime, even as it became increasingly clear that Mao Zedong (1893–1976) and his communist armies were sure to triumph in the Chinese civil war. The "loss" of China, widely attributed in Luce's publications to the weaknesses of American liberals, became a contentious issue in US foreign policy debates after 1949. Luce supported US and United Nations efforts in the Korean War (1950–1953) and urged UN forces to confront Chinese communists directly. Luce and his publications backed General Douglas MacArthur (1880–1964) after President Harry Truman (1884–1972) dismissed him in April 1951. Luce's anticommunist efforts coincided with the crusade of Senator Joseph McCarthy (1908–1957); in practice, Luce kept his distance from the polarizing Wisconsin politician.

Luce enthusiastically supported the 1952 presidential campaign of Dwight D. Eisenhower (1890–1969), whose victory marked a decisive defeat for the isolationist wing of the Republican Party and its leader, Ohio senator Robert A. Taft (1889–1953). At no point were Luce's ideas more closely connected to those of the White House than during the Eisenhower years. Secretary of State John Foster Dulles (1888–1959), a longtime Luce ally, convinced Eisenhower to appoint Clare Boothe Luce as US ambassador to Italy in 1953. Henry Luce was an early and vocal advocate of US aid for the republic of South Vietnam and its premier, Ngo Dinh Diem (1901–1963). Despite protests, Luce continued to support the US war in Vietnam until his death in 1967.

Henry Luce transformed American news journalism, and, as one of the most influential private citizens in twentieth-century US politics, Luce wielded an outsized influence over US foreign policy both in Washington and in ordinary American households. His foreign policy views both reflected and shaped the confidence and the anxiety of the United States in the world in the Cold War era.

SEE ALSO *"The American Century" (Henry Luce, 1941); LIFE (magazine)*

BIBLIOGRAPHY

Brinkley, Alan. *The Publisher: Henry Luce and His American Century.* New York: Knopf, 2010.

Herzstein, Robert E. *Henry R. Luce: A Political Portrait of the Man Who Created the American Century.* New York: Scribner's, 1994.

Jessup, John K., ed. *The Ideas of Henry Luce.* New York: Atheneum, 1969.

Christopher Capozzola
Associate Professor of History
Massachusetts Institute of Technology

LYNCHING

Lynching, a term that is American in origin, refers to extralegal mob violence committed in the name of social order and with community sanction. During the Jim Crow era in the United States, it became primarily a racial form of terror that reinforced white supremacy. The more than five thousand lynchings, many of them public, that were perpetrated against African Americans and other minorities in this period garnered considerable international attention. That attention served as a powerful tool for activists who hoped that global shame would motivate US political leaders to protect African American lives.

SHAME THROUGH INTERNATIONAL EXPOSURE

Ida B. Wells (1862–1931) was one of the first activists to use this tactic when she famously traveled to Great Britain in 1893 and 1894 and exposed the brutality of lynching to sympathetic audiences in public meetings and speeches. British interest in American mob violence, though, predated Wells's tours, as news of lynchings had traveled across the Atlantic since the 1830s. Most British commentators in the nineteenth century accepted that such violence was necessary as a means of social control in frontier societies like America, but believed it was unacceptable for British civilized society. Wells's campaign, however, convinced many in Britain that lynching was an indefensible instrument of white supremacy. Yet by conceiving of this barbarism in terms of extralegal violence and contrasting it to what they considered to be their civilized social norms, British citizens could overlook their use of state violence to exert racial control over colonial subjects in Africa and India (Silkey 2013).

Subsequent activists followed Wells's lead by using international exposure to bring embarrassment to a nation that, especially during World War I (1914–1918), saw itself as a force of justice and democracy in the world. Although the US government indicted other nations for their disregard for civil rights, they argued, the United States had denied African Americans full citizenship and failed to protect them from mob violence. When President Woodrow Wilson (1856–1924) attacked German barbarism to rally support for the war, the National Association for the Advancement of Colored People (NAACP) lobbied him, unsuccessfully, to denounce lynching in order to boost US credibility abroad. Throughout the 1920s, activists continued to stress that the brutality of American lynch mobs surpassed offenses committed by America's enemies. This approach required that activists tactically define lynching as a uniquely American phenomenon, one that stood out as a conspicuously shameful practice in the world, while downplaying atrocities that occurred in other countries (Waldrep 2011). Such strategies only intensified as the efforts of the NAACP to lobby Congress to pass federal antilynching legislation heated up in the 1930s. After Claude Neal was lynched in 1934 in Florida, for instance, the NAACP sent its report of the lynching to 144 newspapers in forty countries (Wood 2009, 203).

CONDEMNATION OF LYNCHING BY AMERICA'S ANTAGONISTS

Antagonists of the United States were, in turn, quick to publicize lynching accounts and condemn American racism, in part to deflect attention away from their own abuses. During the interwar period, Soviet authorities theorized that racial violence was the inevitable byproduct of a ruthless, capitalist society. In contrast, they promoted the Soviet Union as an enlightened nation where such barbarism would never happen (Roman 2013). Similarly, throughout the 1930s, newspapers in Nazi Germany regularly published lynching reports as evidence of US hypocrisy. The Nazi press was sympathetic to the US racial caste system, but outraged by US condemnation of their racial practices. These accounts also served to substantiate Nazi belief in the superiority of what they saw as their orderly police state (Wood 2009, 203–204; Apel 2004, 55–57).

Japan, too, used American lynchings to further its political goals on the international stage in the first half of the twentieth century. Although Japanese culture had its own traditions of vigilantism, it drew attention to US lynchings and race riots to expose the pretense of US claims to democracy. At the Paris Peace Conference in 1919, Japan unsuccessfully proposed a "racial equality clause" as part of the covenant of the newly formed League of Nations, a proposal that would have undermined racial segregation in the United States. By condemning US lynching in Paris, Japan ironically intended to bolster its imperialistic designs by representing itself as the only nonwhite world power. Its rhetorical attacks on US lynching intensified when the US Congress passed the Immigration Act of 1924, which excluded all Asiatic peoples from American borders, a particular insult to Japanese citizens, who saw themselves as superior to other Asians. The murder of two Japanese immigrants and the attempted lynching of two others in California that same year was further fodder for Japanese denunciations of American racial violence. These denunciations escalated in the 1930s as the US government increasingly criticized Japanese expansion in East Asia. During the war, the Japanese government launched a propaganda campaign that emphasized racial atrocities in the United States in order to cultivate African American sympathy for Japan and undermine the solidarity of African Americans with the United States (Sakashita 2013).

LYNCHING OF MEXICANS IN THE AMERICAN SOUTHWEST

These kinds of condemnations only indirectly aided the cause of black antilynching activists, but for Mexicans in the United States, international pressure had a direct effect on the decline of lynching. Hundreds of Mexican nationals in the Southwest had been subject to acts of mob violence perpetrated by Anglo-Americans since the Mexican War in 1848. The Mexican government regularly launched investigations of these lynchings and issued complaints, in vain, to state governments or the US State Department. By the late nineteenth century, though, these protests began to have an effect as the United States sought stronger diplomatic relations with Mexico. This was particularly so in the 1920s, when the State Department exerted pressure on Mexican authorities to protect the safety of US citizens within their borders. In turn, it heeded Mexican calls to protect their citizens in the Southwest by compelling state governments to prevent lynchings or prosecute them after the fact (Carrigan and Webb 2013).

EFFORTS TO END RACIST VIOLENCE IN THE POST–WORLD WAR II ERA

The lynching of African Americans persisted longer, but lynching had become a national embarrassment by the 1940s. Civil rights groups after World War II (1939–1945) used both the Cold War and the formation of the United Nations to press the US government to address ongoing racial injustice, including violence. In 1946, the National Negro Congress presented the United Nations with a petition asking the organization to address racial oppression in the United States. This action created tensions between civil rights activists and anticommunist liberals, who saw it as an attack on US credibility against the Soviet Union, which had amped up its condemnation of American racism in the wake of World War II (Berg 2007).

In 1951, the Civil Rights Congress presented a document titled *We Charge Genocide* to the United Nations. It accused the US government of genocide according to the UN Genocide Convention for its complicity in lynching and other forms of racial brutality. The document was widely denounced in the United States, including by the NAACP, and the United Nations ignored it. Nevertheless, this kind of pressure, amidst Cold War tensions, led President Harry Truman (1884–1972) to support federal antilynching legislation and make concerted efforts to expand civil rights for African Americans. Racist violence did not disappear by any means after World War II, but its prevalence did decline over time, and perpetrators no longer received unqualified sanction. The reasons for this decline are complex, but international censure undoubtedly played a significant role.

SEE ALSO *League of Nations; National Association for the Advancement of Colored People (NAACP); Paris Peace Conference (1919); United Nations; Wells-Barnett, Ida B.; Whiteness*

BIBLIOGRAPHY

Apel, Dora. *Imagery of Lynching: Black Men, White Women, and the Mob.* New Brunswick, NJ: Rutgers University Press, 2004.

Berg, Manfred. "Black Civil Rights and Liberal Anti-Communism: The NAACP in the Early Cold War." *Journal of American History* 94, 1 (2007): 75–96.

Carrigan, William D., and Clive Webb. *Forgotten Dead: Mob Violence against Mexicans in the United States, 1848–1928.* New York: Oxford University Press, 2013.

Roman, Meredith L. "U.S. Lynch Law and the Fate of the Soviet Union: The Soviet Uses of American Racial Violence." In *Swift to Wrath: Lynching in Global Historical Perspective*, edited by William D. Carrigan and Christopher Waldrep, 215–236. Charlottesville: University of Virginia Press, 2013.

Sakashita, Fumiko. "Lynching across the Pacific: Japanese Views and African American Responses in the Wartime Antilynching Campaign." In *Swift to Wrath: Lynching in Global Historical Perspective*, edited by William D. Carrigan and Christopher Waldrep, 181–214. Charlottesville: University of Virginia Press, 2013.

Silkey, Sarah L. "British Public Debates and the 'Americanization' of Lynching." In *Swift to Wrath: Lynching in Global Historical Perspective*, edited by William D. Carrigan and Christopher Waldrep, 160–180. Charlottesville: University of Virginia Press, 2013.

Waldrep, Christopher. "Lynching 'Exceptionalism': The NAACP, Woodrow Wilson, and Keeping Lynching American." In *Globalizing Lynching History: Vigilantism and Extralegal Punishment from an International Perspective*, edited by Manfred Berg and Simon Wendt, 35–52. New York: Palgrave Macmillan, 2011.

Wood, Amy Louise. *Lynching and Spectacle: Witnessing Racial Violence in America, 1890–1940.* Chapel Hill: University of North Carolina Press, 2009.

Amy Louise Wood
Associate Professor of History
Illinois State University